Management Accounting

Third Edition

Will Seal, Ray H. Garrison, Eric W. Noreen

The McGraw-Hill Companies

London Boston Burr Ridge, IL Dubuque, IA Madison, WI New York San Francisco St. Louis Bangkok Bogotá Caracas Kuala Lumpur Lisbon Madrid Mexico City Milan Montreal New Delhi Santiago Seoul Singapore Sydney Taipei Toronto

Management Accounting, Third Edition
Will Seal, Ray H. Garrison, Eric W. Noreen
ISBN-13 978-0-07-712164-8
ISBN-10 0-07-712164-3

Published by McGraw-Hill Education
Shoppenhangers Road
Maidenhead
Berkshire
SL6 2QL
Telephone: 44 (0) 1628 502 500
Fax: 44 (0) 1628 770 224
Website: www.mcgraw-hill.co.uk

British Library Cataloguing in Publication Data
A catalogue record for this book is available from the British Library

Library of Congress Cataloging in Publication Data
The Library of Congress data for this book has been applied for from the Library of Congress

Acquisitions Editor: Natalie Jacobs/Mark Kavanagh
Development Editor: Karen Harlow
Marketing Manager: Vanessa Boddington
Head of Production: Beverley Shields

Text Design by Jonathan Coleclough
Cover design by Fielding Design
Printed and bound in Spain by Grafo, S.A.

ISBN-13 978-0-07-712164-8
ISBN-10 0-07-712164-3

This book is dedicated to my family

Will Seal

Brief table of contents

Detailed table of contents

Preface

This text offers a comprehensive and balanced introduction to management accounting theory and practice. The text combines a solid grounding in technical material with a fresh look at emerging issues relevant to accounting practice. The new edition builds on the success of the 2nd edition, producing a book specifically aimed at students in the UK and Europe. It is a clear and accessible book promoting practice as a method of learning through numerical examples, vignettes, graded end-of-chapter exercises, problems and cases. The text has been updated to include new research and developments in the discipline and also to reflect market feedback.

The main changes and developments to this edition are:

- Generally, the material on the *service sector* content has been increased as well as more material on specific topics such as *environmental management accounting, revenue management, lean production, sales/ production mix* and *value-based management.*
- Although there is new material, the book is more compact with the removal of three chapters. Much of the key material from these chapters has been relocated in the book. The division of the book into four parts is an innovation for this edition.

Each chapter has been fully updated to reflect the latest development in management accounting, and notable chapter changes include:

- **Chapter 1** – additional coverage on emerging issues, highlighting the increasing importance of services, managing for value, the sustainability agenda and corporate governance.
- **Chapter 2** – coverage of the difference and similarities between costs in services and manufacturing activities. Material on service costing is also developed in Chapters 3 and 5 where appropriate.
- **Chapter 10** – this chapter has been edited to focus more on the practice of capital budgeting. Key techniques of decision making under uncertainty have been taken from old Chapter 11 and put in appendices in Chapter 10. (Please note that as the old Chapter 11 has now been removed subsequent chapter numbers have changed.)
- **Chapter 13** – new material on sales mix, production mix and yield variances.
- **Chapter 15** – new material on revenue management with special reference to hotels and airlines.
- **Chapter 16** – revised to integrate profit planning, value-based management and strategy management accounting.
- **Chapter 17** – updated coverage which includes more new material on environmental management accounting.
- **Chapter 18** – this chapter now includes old Chapters 18 and 19 in a single chapter with the themes of business process management and the lean enterprise.
- **Chapter 19** – this chapter now has a more strategic cost management perspective and is more integrated with previous chapters. This is now the last chapter.

Superior pedagogy

The book includes a full suite of pedagogical learning tools designed to make teaching and learning stimulating and efficient, all presented in a visually impressive format. In each chapter you will find: **Learning Objectives**, **Key Terms**, **Summaries**, **Questions**, **Exercises**, **Problems** and **Cases**, and a selection from **Management Accounting in Action** vignettes, worked Examples, **Focus on Current Practice** vignettes, **Group Exercises** and **Internet Exercises**. At the back of the book you will find a full **Bibliography** to make reading around the subject easy and a **Glossary** for quick reference.

Comprehensive coverage

With complete coverage of core technical material and emerging issues, this text perfectly balances the need to combine practical understanding with deeper explanations of how management accounting remains relevant and compelling in an ever-changing world.

Accessible style

Written in a style that makes learning interesting and understanding easy, *Management Accounting* takes a highly refreshing approach to its subject ensuring its popularity with lecturers and students alike.

Acknowledgements

Our thanks go to the following reviewers for their comments at various stages in the text's development:

Emad Awadallah, University of Hertfordshire
Alan Benson, University of Hull
Steve Dungworth, De Montfort University
John Fletcher, Middlesex University
Dimitrios Gounopoulos, University of Surrey
Mohammad Hudaib, University of Essex
William Jackson, Heriot-Watt University
Roland Kaye, University of East Anglia
Cathy Knowles, Oxford Brookes University
Carsten Kyhnauv, University of Southern Denmark
Mehran Noghabai, Linköping University
Hanno Roberts, BI Oslo
Teerooven Soobaroyen, Aberystwyth University
Anthony Stevenson, Bedfordshire University
Greg Stoner, University of Glasgow
Chretien Straetmans, Hogeschool Zuyd
Petar Sudar, University of Westminster
Sander Van Triest, University of Amsterdam

We would also like to extend our thanks to McGraw-Hill Education New York and William Lanen, Shannon Anderson and Michael Maher for granting permission to reproduce the material in Appendices 13A and B.

Every effort has been made to trace and acknowledge ownership of copyright and to clear permission for material reproduced in this book. The publishers will be pleased to make suitable arrangements to clear permission with any copyright holders whom it has not been possible to contact.

Guided tour

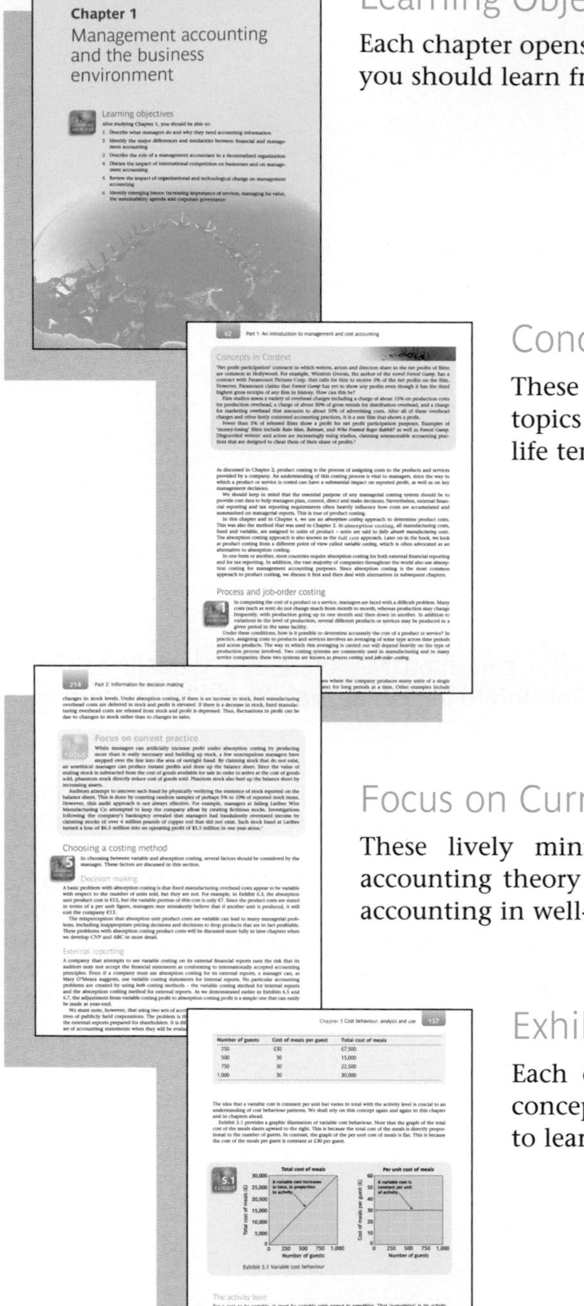

Learning Objectives

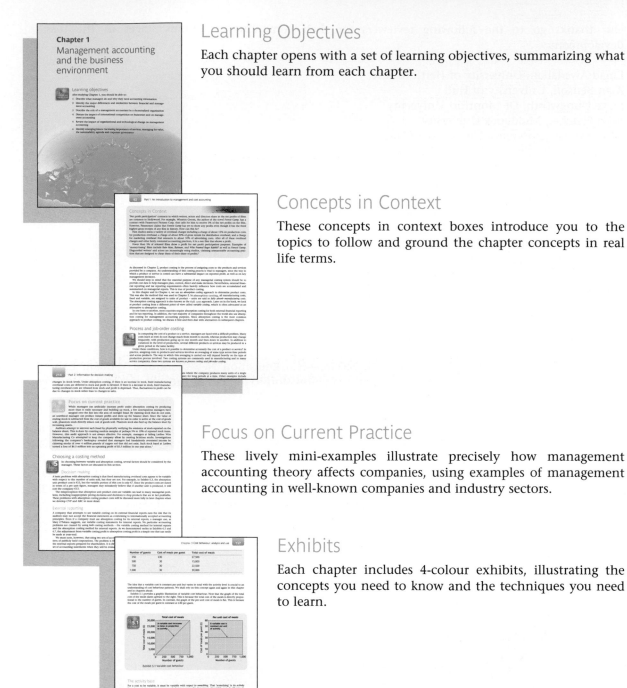

Each chapter opens with a set of learning objectives, summarizing what you should learn from each chapter.

Concepts in Context

These concepts in context boxes introduce you to the topics to follow and ground the chapter concepts in real life terms.

Focus on Current Practice

These lively mini-examples illustrate precisely how management accounting theory affects companies, using examples of management accounting in well-known companies and industry sectors.

Exhibits

Each chapter includes 4-colour exhibits, illustrating the concepts you need to know and the techniques you need to learn.

Management Accounting in Action

These dialogues follow different management accounting issues through chapters to demonstrate them in practice in the real world.

Key Terms

These are highlighted throughout the chapter, and definitions provided in a glossary at the back of the book.

Summary

This briefly reviews and reinforces the main topics you will have covered in each chapter to ensure you have acquired a solid understanding of the key topics.

End of Chapter Assessment Material

Each chapter has a wealth of assessment material designed to make learning and self-testing easy and fun. You will find the following features in most chapters:

- Review problems
- Review solutions
- Questions
- Group Exercises
- Exercises
- Problems
- Cases

Technology to enhance learning and teaching

Visit **www.mcgraw-hill.co.uk/textbooks/seal** today

Online Learning Centre (OLC)

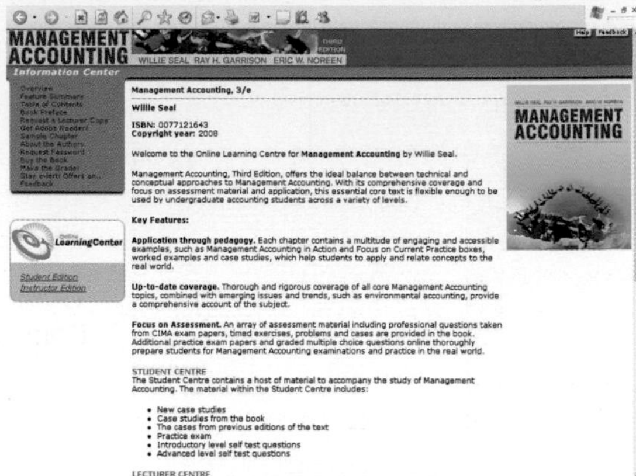

After completing each chapter, log on to the supporting Online Learning Centre website. Take advantage of the study tools offered to reinforce the material you have read in the text, and to develop your knowledge of management accounting in a fun and effective way.

Resources for students include:

- *Self Test Questions – Introductory*
- *Self Test Questions – Advanced*
- *Practice Exam Questions*
- *Case Studies*

Also available for lecturers:

- *PowerPoint slides*
- *Solutions to Exercises*
- *Lecturer Manual*
- *Case Study Solutions*
- *Group Exercises*
- *Artwork from book*
- *Test bank*

Test bank available in McGraw-Hill EZ Test Online

A test bank of hundreds of questions is available to lecturers adopting this book for their module. A range of questions is provided for each chapter including multiple choice, true or false, and short answer or essay questions. The questions are identified by type, difficulty, and topic to help you to select questions that best suit your needs and are accessible through an easy-to-use online testing tool, **McGraw-Hill EZ Test Online**.

McGraw-Hill EZ Test Online is accessible to busy academics virtually anywhere – in their office, at home or while travelling – and eliminates the need for software installation. Lecturers can choose from question banks associated with their adopted textbook or easily create their own questions. They also have access to hundreds of banks and thousands of questions created for other McGraw-Hill titles. Multiple versions of tests can be saved for delivery on paper or online through WebCT, Blackboard and other course management systems. When created and delivered though EZ Test Online, students' tests can be immediately marked, saving lecturers time and providing prompt results to students.

To register for this FREE resource, visit www.eztestonline.com

Custom Publishing Solutions: Let us help make our *content* your *solution*

At McGraw-Hill Education our aim is to help lecturers to find the most suitable content for their needs delivered to their students in the most appropriate way. Our **custom publishing solutions** offer the ideal combination of content delivered in the way which best suits lecturer and students.

Our custom publishing programme offers lecturers the opportunity to select just the chapters or sections of material they wish to deliver to their students from a database called Primis at www.primisonline.com.

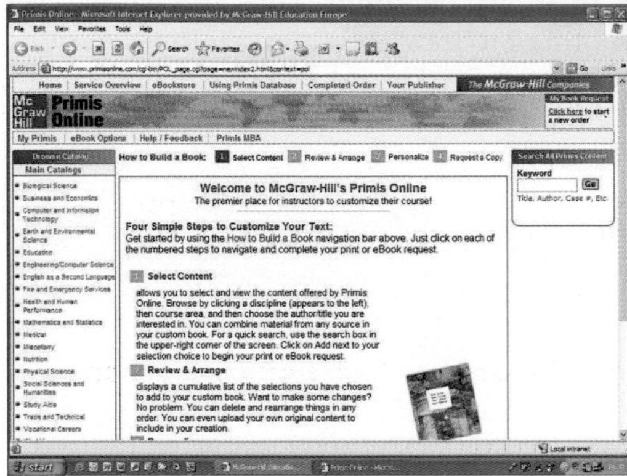

Primis contains over two million pages of content from:

- textbooks
- professional books
- case books – Harvard Articles, Insead, Ivey, Darden, Thunderbird and BusinessWeek
- Taking Sides – debate materials

Across the following imprints:

- McGraw-Hill Education
- Open University Press
- Harvard Business School Press
- US and European material

There is also the option to include additional material authored by lecturers in the custom product – this does not necessarily have to be in English.

We will take care of everything from start to finish in the process of developing and delivering a custom product to ensure that lecturers and students receive exactly the material needed in the most suitable way.

With a Custom Publishing Solution, students enjoy the best selection of material deemed to be the most suitable for learning everything they need for their courses – something of real value to support their learning. Teachers are able to use exactly the material they want, in the way they want, to support their teaching on the course.

Please contact your local McGraw-Hill representative with any questions or alternatively contact Warren Eels e: warren_eels@mcgraw-hill.com.

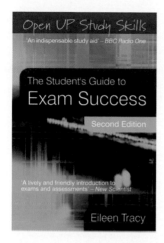

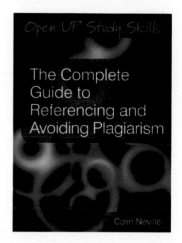

Part I

An introduction to management and cost accounting: cost terms, systems design and cost behaviour

Chapter 1
Management accounting and the business environment

Learning objectives

After studying Chapter 1, you should be able to:

1 Describe what managers do and why they need accounting information

2 Identify the major differences and similarities between financial and management accounting

3 Describe the role of a management accountant in a decentralized organization

4 Discuss the impact of international competition on businesses and on management accounting

5 Review the impact of organizational and technological change on management accounting

6 Identify emerging issues: increasing importance of services, managing for value, the sustainability agenda and corporate governance

Concepts in Context

We will see in this chapter how management accounting practices have had to respond to changes in the business environment. For example, airlines such as easyJet have developed a business model enabled by new technology and deregulation in the airline industry. According to the company website, easyJet keeps costs low by eliminating the unnecessary costs and 'frills' which characterize 'traditional' airlines. This is done in a number of ways: 1. Use of the internet to reduce distribution costs; 2. Maximizing the utilization of the substantial assets thus reducing unit cost; 3. Ticketless travel which helps to reduce significantly the cost of issuing, distributing, processing and reconciling millions of tickets each year; 4. No free lunch – eliminating free catering on-board reduces cost and unnecessary bureaucracy and management; 5. Efficient use of airports – easyJet flies to main destination airports throughout Europe, but gains efficiencies through rapid turnaround times, and progressive landing charges agreements with the airports; 6. Paperless operations – the management and administration of the company is undertaken entirely on IT systems which can be accessed through secure servers from anywhere in the world enabling huge flexibility in the running of the airline.[1]

Management accounting is concerned with providing information to managers – that is, people inside an organization who direct and control its operations. In contrast, **financial accounting** is concerned with providing information to shareholders, creditors and others who are outside an organization. Management accounting provides the essential data with which organizations are actually run. Financial accounting provides the scorecard by which a company's past performance is judged.

Because it is manager oriented, any study of management accounting must be preceded by some understanding of what managers do, the information managers need, and the general business environment. Accordingly, the purpose of this chapter is briefly to examine these subjects.

The work of management and the need for management accounting information

Every organization – large and small – has managers. Someone must be responsible for making plans, organizing resources, directing personnel and controlling operations. In this chapter, we will use a particular organization – a music business, Good Vibrations Ltd – to illustrate the work of management. What we have to say about the management of Good Vibrations Ltd, however, is very general and can be applied to virtually any organization. Managers at Good Vibrations Ltd, like managers everywhere, carry out three major activities – **planning, directing and motivating** and **controlling**. Planning involves selecting a course of action and specifying how the action will be implemented. Directing and motivating involves mobilizing people to carry out plans and run routine operations. Controlling involves ensuring that the plan is actually carried out and is appropriately modified as circumstances change. Management accounting information plays a vital role in these basic management activities – but most particularly in the planning and control functions.

Planning

The first step in planning is to identify alternatives and then to select from among the alternatives the one that does the best job of furthering the organization's objectives. The basic objective of Good Vibrations Ltd is to earn profits for the owners of the company by providing superior service at competitive prices in as many markets as possible. To further this objective, every year top management carefully considers a range of options, or alternatives, for expanding into new geographic markets. This year management is considering opening new stores in Shanghai, Helsinki and Milan.

When making this and other choices, management must balance the opportunities against the demands made on the company's resources. Management knows from bitter experience that opening a store in a major new market is a big step that cannot be taken lightly. It requires enormous amounts of time and energy from the company's most experienced, talented and busy professionals. When the company attempted to open stores in both Beijing and Paris in the same year, resources were stretched too thinly. The result was that neither store opened on schedule, and operations in the rest of the company suffered. Therefore, entering new markets is planned very, very carefully.

Among other data, top management looks at the sales volumes, profit margins and costs of the company's established stores in similar markets. These data, supplied by the management accountant, are combined with projected sales volume data at the proposed new locations to estimate the profits that would be generated by the new stores. In general, virtually all important alternatives considered by management in the planning process have some effect on revenues or costs, and management accounting data are essential in estimating those effects.

After considering all of the alternatives, Good Vibrations Ltd's top management decided to open a store in the burgeoning Shanghai market in the third quarter of the year, but to defer opening any other new stores to another year. As soon as this decision was made, detailed plans were drawn up for all parts of the company that would be involved in the Shanghai opening. For example, the Personnel Department's travel budget was increased, since it would be providing extensive on-site training to the new personnel hired in Shanghai.

As in the Personnel Department example, the plans of management are often expressed formally in **budgets**, and the term budgeting is applied generally to describe this part of the planning process. Typically, budgets are prepared annually and represent management's plans in specific, quantitative terms. In addition to a travel budget, the Personnel Department will be given goals in terms of new hires, courses taught, and detailed breakdowns of expected expenses. Similarly, the manager of each store will be given a target for sales volume, profit, expenses, pilferage losses and employee training. These data will be collected, analysed, and summarized for management use in the form of budgets prepared by management accountants.

Directing and motivating

In addition to planning for the future, managers must oversee day-to-day activities and keep the organization functioning smoothly. This requires the ability to motivate and effectively direct people. Managers assign tasks to employees, arbitrate disputes, answer questions, solve on-the-spot problems, and make many small decisions that affect customers and employees. In effect, directing is that part of the managers' work that deals with the routine and the here and now. Management accounting data, such as daily sales reports, are often used in this type of day-to-day decision making.

Controlling

In carrying out the **control** function, managers seek to ensure that the plan is being followed. **Feedback**, which signals whether operations are on track, is the key to effective control. In sophisticated organizations this feedback is provided by detailed reports of various types. One of these reports, which compares budgeted to actual results, is called a **performance report**. Performance reports suggest where operations are not proceeding as planned and where some parts of the organization may require additional attention. For example, before the opening of the new Shanghai store in the third quarter of the year, the store's manager will be given sales volume, profit and expense targets for the fourth quarter of the year. As the fourth quarter progresses, periodic reports will be made in which the actual sales volume, profit and expenses are compared to the targets. If the actual results fall below the targets, top management is alerted that the Shanghai store requires more attention. Experienced personnel can be flown in to help the new manager, or top management may come to the conclusion that plans will have to be revised. As we shall see in following chapters, providing this kind of feedback to managers is one of the central purposes of management accounting.

The end results of managers' activities

As a customer enters one of the Good Vibrations stores, the results of management's planning, directing and motivating, and control activities will be evident in the many details that make the difference between a pleasant and an irritating shopping experience. The store will be clean, fashionably decorated and logically laid out. Featured artists' videos will be displayed on TV monitors throughout the store, and the background rock music will be loud enough to send older patrons scurrying for the classical music section. Popular CDs will be in stock, and the latest hits will be available for private listening on earphones. Specific titles will be easy to find. Regional music, such as CantoPop in Hong Kong, will be prominently featured. Checkout staff will be alert, friendly and efficient. In short, what the customer experiences does not simply happen; it is the result of the efforts of managers who must visualize and fit together the processes that are needed to get the job done.

The planning and control cycle

The work of management can be summarized in a model such as the one shown in Exhibit 1.1. The model, which depicts the **planning and control cycle**, illustrates the smooth flow of management activities from planning through directing and motivating, controlling, and then back to planning again. All of these activities involve decision making, so it is depicted as the hub around which the other activities revolve.

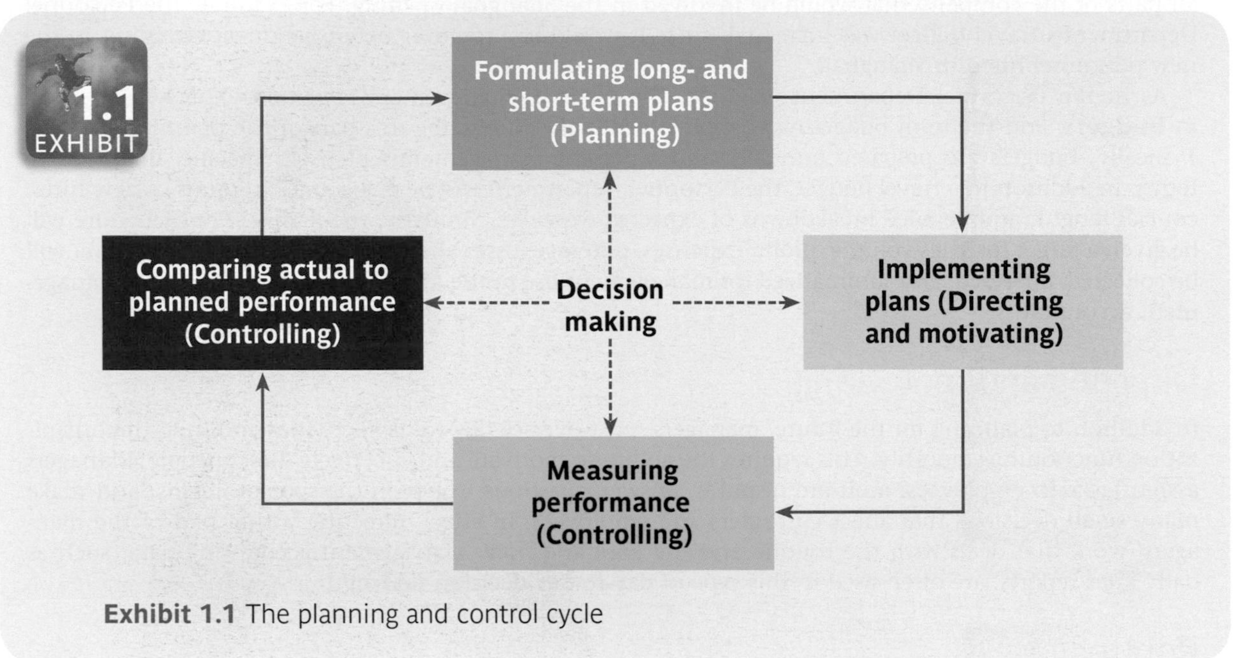

Exhibit 1.1 The planning and control cycle

Comparison of financial and management accounting

Financial accounting reports are prepared for the use of external parties such as shareholders and creditors, whereas management accounting reports are prepared for managers inside the organization. This contrast in basic orientation results in a number of major differences between financial and management accounting, even though both financial and management accounting rely on the same underlying financial data. These differences are summarized in Exhibit 1.2.

As shown in Exhibit 1.2, in addition to the difference in who the reports are prepared for, financial and management accounting also differ in their emphasis between the past and the future, in the type of data provided to users and in several other ways. These differences are discussed in the following paragraphs.

Emphasis on the future

Since planning is such an important part of the manager's job, management accounting has a strong future orientation. In contrast, financial accounting primarily provides summaries of past financial transactions. These summaries may be useful in planning, but only to a point. The difficulty with summaries of the past is that the future is not simply a projection of what has happened in the past. Changes are constantly taking place in economic conditions, customer needs and desires, competitive conditions and so on. All of these changes demand that the manager's planning be based in large part on estimates of what will happen rather than on summaries of what has already happened.

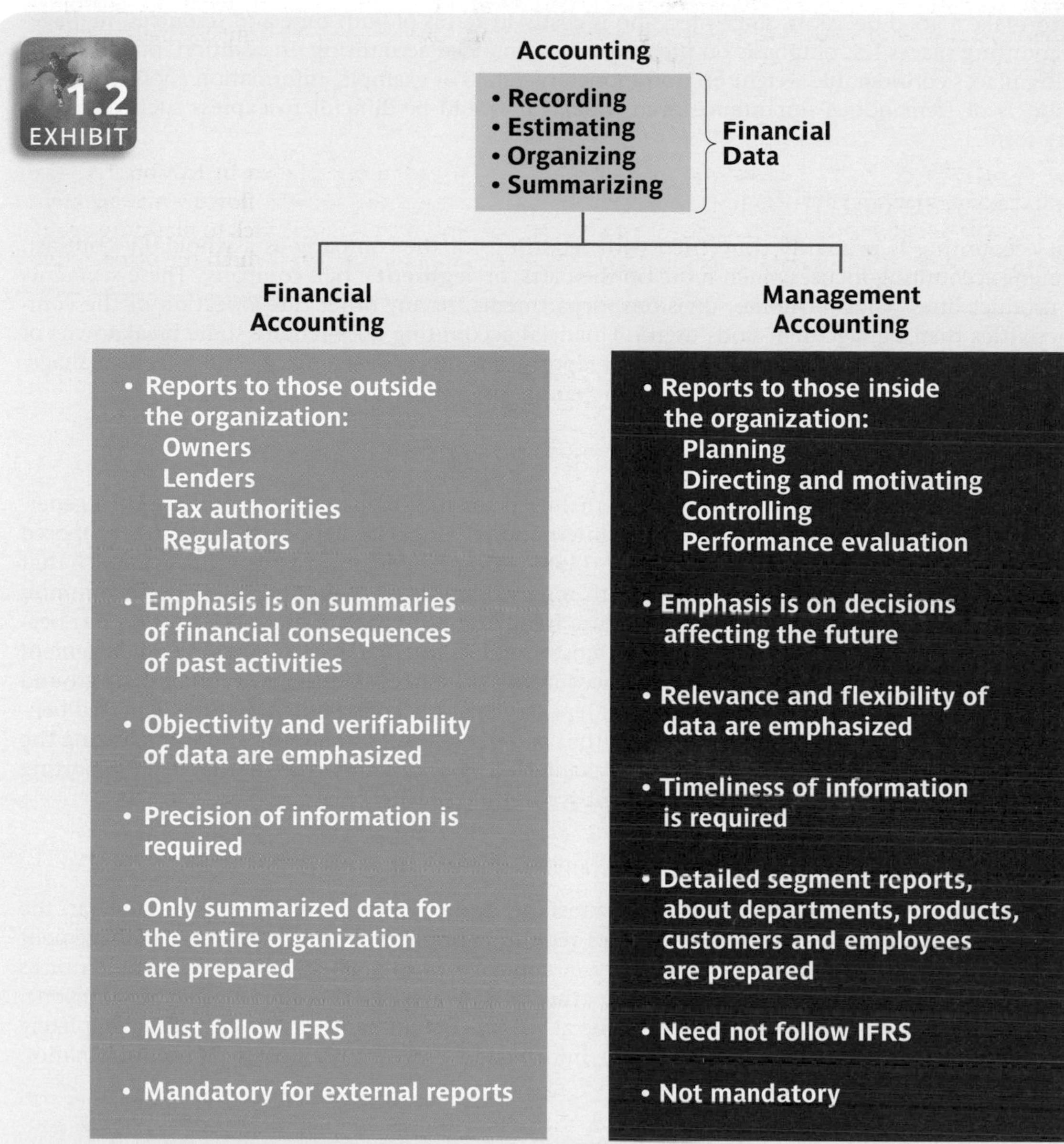

Exhibit 1.2 Comparison of financial and management accounting

Relevance and flexibility of data

Financial accounting data are expected to be objective and verifiable. However, for internal uses the manager wants information that is relevant even if it is not completely objective or verifiable. By relevant, we mean appropriate for the problem at hand. For example, it is difficult to verify estimated sales volumes for a proposed new store at Good Vibrations Ltd, but this is exactly the type of information that is most useful to managers in their decision making. The management accounting information system should be flexible enough to provide whatever data are relevant for a particular decision.

Less emphasis on precision

Timeliness is often more important than precision to managers. If a decision must be made, a manager would much rather have a good estimate now than wait a week for a more precise answer. A decision involving tens of millions of pounds does not have to be based on estimates that are precise down to the penny, or even to the pound. Estimates that are accurate to the nearest million pounds may be precise enough to make a good decision. Since precision is costly in terms of both time and resources, management accounting places less emphasis on precision than financial accounting. In addition, management accounting places considerable weight on non-monetary data. For example, information about customer satisfaction is of tremendous importance even though it would be difficult to express such data in a monetary form.

Segments of an organization

Financial accounting is primarily concerned with reporting for the company as a whole. By contrast, management accounting focuses much more on the parts, or **segments**, of a company. These segments may be product lines, sales territories, divisions, departments, or any other categorization of the company's activities that management finds useful. Financial accounting does require some breakdowns of revenues and costs by major segments in external reports, but this is a secondary emphasis. In management accounting, segment reporting is the primary emphasis.

International Financial Reporting Standards (IFRS)

Financial accounting statements prepared for external users must be prepared in accordance with generally accepted accounting principles such as the International Financial Reporting Standards proposed by the International Accounting Standards Board (IASB). External users must have some assurance that the reports have been prepared in accordance with some common set of ground rules. These common ground rules enhance comparability and help reduce fraud and misrepresentation, but they do not necessarily lead to the type of reports that would be most useful in internal decision making. Management accounting is not bound by generally accepted accounting principles. Managers set their own ground rules concerning the content and form of internal reports. The only constraint is that the expected benefits from using the information should outweigh the costs of collecting, analysing and summarizing the data. Nevertheless, as we shall see in subsequent chapters, it is undeniably true that financial reporting requirements have heavily influenced management accounting practice.

Management accounting – not mandatory

Financial accounting is mandatory; that is, it must be done. Various outside parties such as the Stock Exchange regulators and the tax authorities require periodic financial statements. Management accounting, on the other hand, is not mandatory. A company is completely free to do as much or as little as it wishes. There are no regulatory bodies or other outside agencies that specify what is to be done, or, for that matter, whether anything is to be done at all. Since management accounting is completely optional, the important question is always, 'Is the information useful?' rather than, 'Is the information required?'

Basic organizational structure

Since organizations are made up of people, management must accomplish its objectives by working through people. Managing directors of companies like Good Vibrations Ltd could not possibly execute all of their company's strategies alone; they must rely on other people. This is done by creating an organizational structure that permits **decentralization** of management responsibilities.

Decentralization

Decentralization is the delegation of decision-making authority throughout an organization by providing managers at various operating levels with the authority to make decisions relating to their area of responsibility. Some organizations are more decentralized than others. Because of Good Vibrations Ltd's geographic dispersion and the peculiarities of local markets, the company is highly decentralized.

Good Vibrations Ltd's managing director sets the broad strategy for the company and makes major strategic decisions such as opening stores in new markets, but much of the remaining decision-making authority is delegated to managers on various levels throughout the organization. These levels are as follows: the company has a number of retail stores, each of which has a store manager as well as a separate manager for each section such as international rock and classical/jazz. In addition, the company has support departments such as a central Purchasing Department and a Personnel Department. The organizational structure of the company is depicted in Exhibit 1.3.

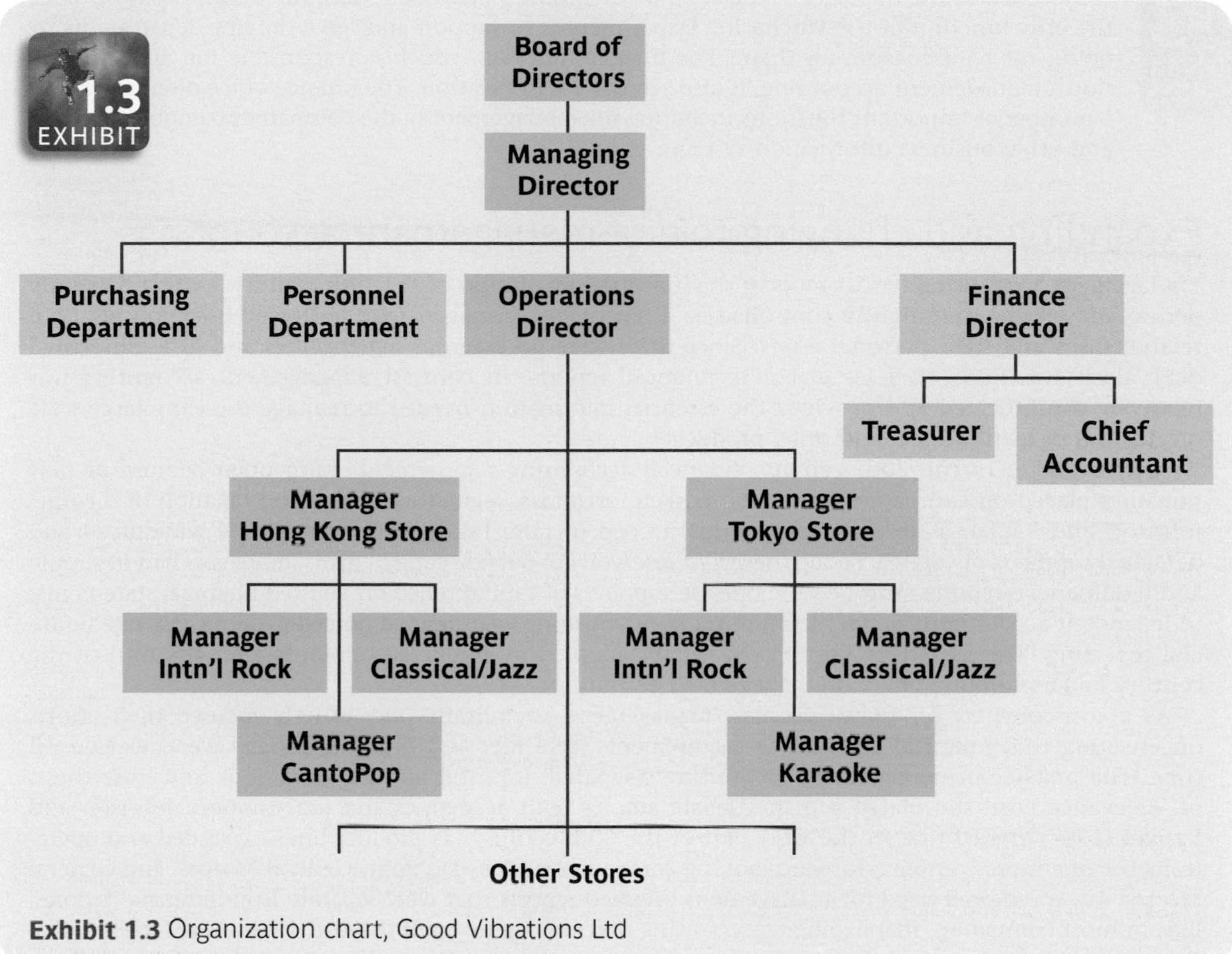

Exhibit 1.3 Organization chart, Good Vibrations Ltd

The arrangement of boxes shown in Exhibit 1.3 is called an **organization chart**. The purpose of an organization chart is to show how responsibility has been divided among managers and to show formal lines of reporting and communication, or chain of command. Each box depicts an area of management responsibility, and the lines between the boxes show the lines of formal authority between managers. The chart tells us, for example, that the store managers are responsible to the operations manager. In turn, the latter is responsible to the company managing director who, in turn, is responsible to the board of directors. Following the lines of authority and communication on the organization chart, we can see that the manager of the Hong Kong store would ordinarily report to the operations director rather than directly to the managing director of the company.

Informal relationships and channels of communication often develop outside the formal reporting relationships on the organization chart as a result of personal contacts between managers. The informal structure does not appear on the organization chart, but it is often vital to effective operations.

Line and staff relationships

An organization chart also depicts **line** and **staff** positions in an organization. A person in a line position is directly involved in achieving the basic objectives of the organization. A person in a staff position, by contrast, is only indirectly involved in achieving those basic objectives. Staff positions support or provide assistance to line positions or other parts of the organization, but they do not have direct authority over line positions. Refer again to the organization chart in Exhibit 1.3. Since the basic objective of Good Vibrations Ltd is to sell recorded music at a profit, those managers whose areas of responsibility are directly related to the sales effort occupy line positions. These positions, which are shown in green in the exhibit, include the managers of the various music departments in each store, the store managers, the operations manager and members of top management.

By contrast, the manager of the central Purchasing Department occupies a staff position, since the only function of the Purchasing Department is to support and serve the line departments by doing their purchasing for them. The finance function, which is responsible for the organization's management accounting, is also seen as a staff position. The finance office often combines a number of important functions including the management of the company's computer services and other business information systems.

Expanding and changing role of management accounting

Management accounting has its roots in the industrial revolution of the 19th century. During this early period, most firms were tightly controlled by a few owner–managers who borrowed based on personal relationships and their personal assets. Since there were no external shareholders and little unsecured debt, there was little need for elaborate financial reports. In contrast, management accounting was relatively sophisticated and provided the essential information needed to manage the early large-scale production of textiles, steel and other products.[2]

After the turn of the 20th century, financial accounting requirements burgeoned because of new pressures placed on companies by capital markets, creditors, regulatory bodies and taxation of income. Johnson and Kaplan state that 'many firms needed to raise funds from increasingly widespread and detached suppliers of capital. To tap these vast reservoirs of outside capital, firms' managers had to supply audited financial reports. And because outside suppliers of capital relied on audited financial statements, independent accountants had a keen interest in establishing well-defined procedures for corporate financial reporting. The inventory costing procedures adopted by public accountants after the turn of the century had a profound effect on management accounting.'[3]

As a consequence, for many decades, management accountants increasingly focused their efforts on ensuring that financial accounting requirements were met and financial reports were released on time. The practice of management accounting stagnated. Johnson and Kaplan's book and their thesis of 'Relevance Lost' stimulated a major debate among both academics and practitioners. Johnson and Kaplan (1987) argued that in the early part of the 20th century, as product lines expanded and operations became more complex, forward-looking companies such as Du Pont, General Motors, and General Electric saw a renewed need for management oriented reports that were separate from financial reports. But, in most companies, management accounting practices up through the mid-1980s were largely indistinguishable from practices that were common prior to the First World War. In recent years, however, new economic forces have led to many important innovations in management accounting. These new practices will be discussed in detail later, and especially in Chapters 16–19. These chapters have been written to compare approaches that accept physical and organizational limitations and optimize subject to given **constraints** with more recent approaches that are based on management practices aimed at shifting constraints. These chapters reflect the way that management accounting practices have evolved since the publication of the 'Relevance Lost' thesis.

Another development that has affected what might be judged to be relevant information is the realization that companies' demand for management information is affected by their strategies. Corporate strategy recognizes that managers may *choose* the industries that they operate in. As we shall see in Chapter 16, management accounting information, known as **strategic management accounting**, may be collected in order to help them make these choices.

International diversity in management accounting traditions

Management accounting is sometimes presented as a universal tool kit. Yet this image of the subject hides the different traditions in different countries. For example, although we might expect to find basic economic calculations on costs and revenues to be of interest to managers in any system of competitive capitalism, these calculations may be the province of different professional groupings (such as engineers or business economists) in different countries. Although the professional organization of auditors is very widespread throughout the world, the professional organization of management accounting is far less prevalent. The variation in professional organization does not mean that management accounting techniques cannot be applied in different countries but rather that the occupations that control them differ in different countries for all sorts of complex historical[4] and institutional reasons.[5] Indeed, many European countries have problems with the term 'management accounting' because the professions are organized differently and have different rankings in terms of status and technical expertise.[6]

Different traditions mean that historical debates such as the 'Relevance Lost thesis' may have resonance in the US or the UK but not necessarily in Germany or Japan. Indeed, many critics of US (and, by extension, UK) management accounting techniques were partly informed by a historical analysis of the US experience and partly by a perceived competitive weakness compared to the economic successes of Japan in the 1970s and 80s. There is some evidence that management accounting practices are tending to converge under some of the influences such as globalization and new technology, which will be discussed below.[7]

Globalization and international competition

4 LEARNING OBJECTIVE

Over the last few decades, competition has become worldwide in many industries. This has been caused by reductions in tariffs, quotas and other barriers to free trade; improvements in global transportation systems; and increasing sophistication in international markets. These factors work together to reduce the costs of conducting international trade and make it possible for foreign companies to compete on a more equal footing with local firms. As well as continuing expansion of the European Union (EU), competition from rapidly growing countries such as China and India have led to global economic restructuring with new locations for the outsourcing of manufacturing (China) and services (India) by Western and Japanese multinational companies.

Reductions in trade barriers have made it easier for agile and aggressive companies to expand outside of their home markets. As a result, very few firms can afford to be complacent. A company may be very successful today in its local market relative to its local competitors, but tomorrow the competition may come from halfway around the globe. As a matter of survival, even firms that are presently doing very well in their home markets must become world-class competitors. On the bright side, the freer international movement of goods and services presents tremendous export opportunities for those companies that can transform themselves into world-class competitors. And, from the standpoint of consumers, heightened competition promises an even greater variety of goods, at higher quality and lower prices.

What are the implications for management accounting of increased global competition? It would be very difficult for a firm to become world-class if it plans, directs and controls its operations and makes decisions using a second-class management accounting system. An excellent management accounting system will not by itself guarantee success, but a poor management accounting system can stymie the best efforts of people in an organization to make the firm truly competitive.

Throughout this text we will highlight the differences between obsolete management accounting systems that get in the way of success and well-designed management accounting systems that can enhance a firm's performance. It is noteworthy that elements of well-designed management accounting systems have originated in many countries. More and more, management accounting has become a discipline that is worldwide in scope.[8]

Changes in the business environment and management accounting

New business processes and technologies

5 LEARNING OBJECTIVE

The last two decades have been a period of tremendous ferment and change in the business environment. Competition in many industries has become worldwide in scope, and the pace of innovation in products and services has accelerated. This has been good news for consumers, since intensified competition has generally led to lower prices, higher quality and more choices. However, the last two decades have been a period of wrenching change for many businesses and their employees. Many managers have learned that cherished ways of doing business do not work any more and that major changes must be made in how organizations are managed and in how work gets done. These changes are so great that some observers view them as a second industrial revolution.

This revolution is having a profound effect on the practice of management accounting – as we will see throughout the rest of the text. First, however, it is necessary to have an appreciation of the ways in which organizations are transforming themselves to become more competitive. Since the early 1980s, many companies have gone through several waves of improvement programmes, starting with **just-in-time (JIT)** and passing on to **total quality management (TQM)**, process re-engineering, and various other management programmes – including in some companies the **theory of constraints (TOC)**. When properly implemented, these improvement programmes can enhance quality, reduce cost, increase output, eliminate delays in responding to customers and ultimately increase profits. They have not, however, always been wisely implemented, and there is considerable controversy concerning the ultimate value of each of these programmes. Nevertheless, the current business environment cannot be properly understood without an appreciation of what each of these approaches attempts to accomplish.

These management approaches have implications for management accounting. In particular, they open up the possibility of managing areas like quality, stock and constraints rather than optimizing a given situation. For example, the traditional optimizing approach for stock management, the economic order quantity (EOQ), has to be placed alongside approaches such as JIT that try to eliminate stock. Later in the book, we contrast a number of optimizing models with more contemporary, active management approaches.

Another significant change that we analyse in later chapters is the influence of new technology, especially in computers and telecommunications. These technologies have not just resulted in the automation of existing manual management accounting systems but have enabled the restructuring of whole industries and economies. Even if some of the hype surrounding the internet has died down a little since the heady days of the late 1990s, the internet has, and is, changing the way business is done. New forms of competition, organization and technologies have implications for management accounting. Some of the more traditional merits of management accounting (such as the idea that businesses plan to make profits!) may have reasserted themselves after the collapse of the 'dotcom' bubble, but the longer lasting changes in **business process** require a response from management accounting if the subject is to remain relevant.

One sector that has changed dramatically in recent years is the airline business, particularly with the success in both Europe and North America of the 'no-frills' airlines such as easyJet, Ryanair, Southwest Airlines. The low-cost airline illustrates many of the features of the combined impact of new organizational forms, business processes, new technology and new personnel approaches.

The low-cost airline example illustrates a combination of new thinking about air travel combined with well-known principles of standardization. The use of new technologies such as databases is combined with older technologies such as the telephone – the essence is the integration of a number of previously separated activities such as booking, ticketing and payment processing.

Enterprise resource planning systems

Some technological changes have not just affected the environment of management accounting but have had a direct impact on the collection and dissemination of management information.[9] The increasing use of sophisticated real time information systems known as **enterprise resource planning (ERP)** provided by companies such as SAP, Oracle, J.D. Edwards and Baan, has changed the nature of management accounting work and the role of the finance function.[10] One of the emerging implications for the management accountant is that there is more emphasis on business support rather than routine information gathering. Furthermore, not only is there a greater dispersion of finance personnel into process areas, but accounting information itself has become more dispersed throughout the organization as it becomes more accessible to non-accounting personnel. We will explore the impact of ERP in more detail in Chapter 18.

Deregulation and privatization

It is also worth noting that the increased competition in the airline industry was not possible until the deregulation effects of 'open skies' policies. Deregulation and privatization of former state-owned monopolies had a significant impact in Europe especially in the UK, which pioneered these policies. The changes in ownership and increased competition has not only affected the huge public utilities that were privatized, such as British Telecom or British Rail, they also had a knock-on effect on the companies that supplied these giants. As we can see with the example of the telecom industry (see Chapter 16), the changes in the industry have led to a boom and bust cycle that has shaken confidence in the business models that were introduced to respond to the new competition.

After financial scandals at Enron and other companies, one area where the trend has been towards tighter, rather than lighter, regulation is **corporate governance**. Any companies listed in North America are subject to the Sarbanes–Oxley Act (2002), while UK companies are expected to comply with the Combined Code (2006) on corporate governance. Although it is too early to be certain, the recent problems faced by Western banks especially in the US and the UK may lead to new banking regulations in the UK as well. We will review the implications of corporate governance in the next section and, in more detail, in Chapter 17.

The increased importance of service sector management

Management accounting has expanded its influence from its traditional base in manufacturing to service sectors, which themselves have become increasing sources of employment and income in many economies. Many traditional management accounting approaches to issues such as costing were developed with manufacturing industry in mind. In comparison with traditional manufacturing, where the product is easy to see and touch, products in service industries are less tangible. A bank may offer a number of different 'products' such as types of account or loans which are defined by dimensions such as accessibility or repayment terms, secured or unsecured and so on. Services cannot be stored in inventory so that managers in banks and other service industries may be less interested in *product* cost but, rather, which *customers* are profitable and which customers are not. Service industries provide new challenges and opportunities for management accounting information, particularly as competitive success is especially dependent on intangible assets such as employee expertise and customer relations.

Not only are service activities becoming more important relative to manufacturing but they are increasingly subject to reorganization in both public and private sectors.[11] In particular, we have seen the emergence of **shared service centres** where the support services of an entire corporation are concentrated in a single geographical location. Other companies have gone a stage further by sub-contracting them to independent companies in a practice known as **outsourcing**.[12]

Management accounting's spread into the public sector is driven by government demands for new measures of performance and new delivery systems. Although its precise form and motivation varies in different countries, this phenomenon, often referred to as the 'New Public Management',[13] may be seen as a global movement.[14] These developments are not without controversy, especially where there is an attempt to apply, in the not-for-profit, public sector organizations, the same management philosophies and techniques that were originally developed for private, profit-making organizations.

Managing for value

Traditionally, accountants were portrayed as 'bean-counters' or 'corporate policemen' with an emphasis on past performance and organizational control. While these functions are still part of an accountant's role, the trend recently has been to emphasize the creation and management of value. Pressures from corporate raiders and new sources of capital, such as private equity, mean that managers have to be increasingly aware of shareholder value. As will be explored in Chapters 14, 16 and 17, there are challenges both to *measure* shareholder value and to discover how to *create* it through the adoption and implementation of corporate strategies. Managers are also aware of the importance of *customer value* and its relationship to shareholder value. Managing for value has to balance the possible gains to short-run profitability arising from cost-cutting exercises to possible long-run damage to shareholder value as costs may be cut at the expense of customer satisfaction. For the management accountant the challenge is not just to devise appropriate financial and non-financial metrics to measure value but to try and understand cause-and-effect relationships.[15]

Managing for environmental sustainability

Whilst concern about the environment has been around for some decades, the threat of rapid human-induced climate change has raised the profile of a whole range of environmental sustainability issues. Even managers focusing on shareholder value may be concerned about the environment for three main reasons. First, there is a compliance motive – companies may find that they are forced through regulation and green taxes to manage environmental resources more carefully. Second, eco-efficiency not only may save the planet but reduce the business costs. Finally, there may be strategic reasons – companies may have customers who demand green business policies and who are increasingly suspicious of 'environmental window dressing' through environmental reporting. **Environmental management accounting** is not just about reporting but collecting and analysing *physical* information on flows of energy, water and other materials as well as *monetary* information on environmental costs and benefits in order to make environmentally sensitive decisions.[16]

Corporate governance, professional and business ethics

A thorough analysis of what makes a profession goes beyond the scope of this book. Technical competence is one part of being professional. Another important aspect is the adherence to a code of ethics. For example, the Chartered Institute of Management Accountants, which is the largest body specifically for management accountants in the UK, have themselves pointed out that being a professional means having responsibilities beyond the narrow pursuit of profit at any cost. In common with other accountancy bodies, they have a code of practice and mechanisms for monitoring and enforcing professional ethics.

If ethical standards were not generally adhered to, there would be undesirable consequences for everyone. Essentially, abandoning ethical standards would lead to a lower standard of living with lower-quality goods and services, less to choose from, and higher prices. In short, following ethical rules is not just a matter of being 'nice'; it is absolutely essential for the smooth functioning of an advanced market economy. For example, one of the short-term consequences of the Enron scandal[17] is that investors have become suspicious about the reliability of reported accounting numbers. Other problems have arisen in other parts of the financial services industry in the UK, where managers offered unsustainable guaranteed returns or incentivized the sales personnel so that they gave faulty investment or pensions advice. Unfortunately, the single-minded emphasis placed on short-term profits in some companies may make it seem as if the only way to get ahead is to act unethically. When top managers say, in effect, that they will only be satisfied with bottom-line results and will accept no excuses, they are asking for trouble.

Recent high-profile scandals show that accountants are often placed in difficult ethical positions. Other issues such as transfer pricing practice in multinational companies (which we look at in Chapter 15) and the 'laundering' of illegally obtained money provide particularly pressing challenges to the integrity of all finance professionals.

Although we argued earlier in this chapter that management accounting is mainly concerned with internal reporting, management accountants cannot totally avoid taking responsibility for the integrity of the basic financial data that forms the basis of both financial and management reports (see Exhibit 1.2). Indeed, as we shall learn in the next three chapters, the classification and computation of cost can have a significant impact on reported profit. In Chapter 17 we will look in more detail at the relationships between corporate strategy, risk management and corporate governance.

Some implications for the roles of management accountants: a first look

The changes in the business environment discussed above have potentially left management accountants with a multitude of roles. The roles may depend on the size of the organization, its line of business and a whole range of issues discussed above and in subsequent chapters. But the role played by the management accountant may also depend on their location in the large corporation. For example, in Exhibit 1.4, we can see that in head office, issues of corporate governance and strategy may be a major concern. In the so-called back office area, the focus will be on more operational matters associated with business processes, organizational structure and information technology. In the front office, the management accountant may be operating outside the designated finance function in multi-functional teams with more direct contact with customers, suppliers and helping to manage frontline processes. In order to fulfil these multiple roles, management accountants need to master a diversity of techniques, concepts and practices which will be elaborated the following chapters.[18]

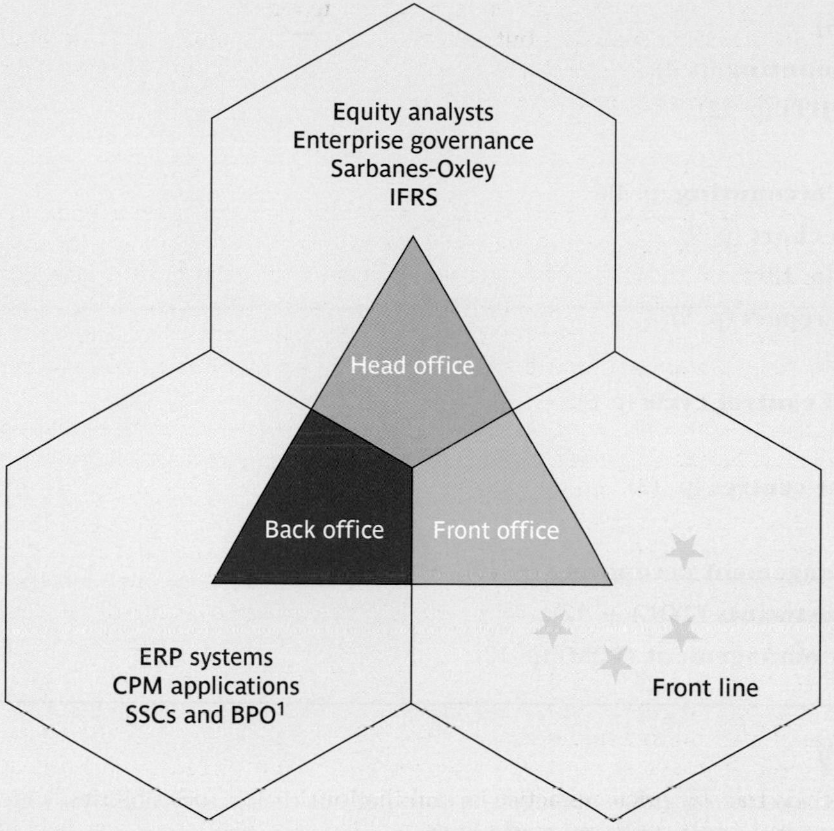

[1]Enterprise resource planning (ERP), corporate performance management (CPM), shared service centres (SSCs) and business process outsourcing (BPO).

Exhibit 1.4 The diverse roles of management accountants within large corporations

(reproduced with permission from *Improving decision making in organizations* (2007) CIMA technical report, p. 5)

Key terms for review

At the end of each chapter, a list of key terms for review is given. These terms are highlighted in colour. Full definitions can be found in the glossary at the end of the book. Carefully study each term to be sure you understand its meaning, since these terms are used repeatedly in the chapters that follow. The list for Chapter 1 follows.

Budget (p. 5).

Business process (p. 12).

Constraints (p. 10).

Control (p. 5).

Controlling (p. 4).

Corporate governance (p. 13)

Decentralization (p. 8).

Directing and motivating (p. 4).

Enterprise resource planning (ERP) (p. 12).

Environmental management accounting (p. 14).
Feedback (p. 5).
Financial accounting (p. 4).
Just-in-time (JIT) (p. 12).
Line (p. 9).
Management accounting (p. 4).
Organization chart (p. 9).
Outsourcing (p. 13)
Performance report (p. 5).
Planning (p. 4).
Planning and control cycle (p. 6).
Segments (p. 8).
Shared service centres (p. 13).
Staff (p. 9).
Strategic management accounting (p. 10).
Theory of constraints (TOC) (p. 12).
Total quality management (TQM) (p. 12).

Summary

- Management accounting assists managers in carrying out their responsibilities, which include planning, directing and motivating, and controlling.
- Since management accounting is geared to the needs of the manager rather than to the needs of outsiders, it differs substantially from financial accounting. Management accounting is oriented more towards the future, places less emphasis on precision, emphasizes segments of an organization (rather than the organization as a whole), is not governed by generally accepted accounting principles, and is not mandatory.
- Most organizations are decentralized to some degree. The organization chart depicts who works for whom in the organization and which units perform staff functions rather than line functions. Accountants perform a staff function – they support and provide assistance to others inside the organization.
- The business environment in recent years has been characterized by increasing competition and a relentless drive for continuous improvement. Several approaches have been developed to assist organizations in meeting these challenges, including just-in-time (JIT), total quality management (TQM), and the theory of constraints (TOC). Organizations have also restructured with outsourcing and relocation of company activities. Reformed public sectors are increasingly applying management accounting techniques.
- Ethical standards serve a very important practical function in an advanced market economy. Without widespread adherence to ethical standards, the economy would slow down dramatically. Ethics are the lubrication that keep a market economy functioning smoothly.

Questions

1–1 What is the basic difference in orientation between financial and management accounting?

1–2 What are the three major activities of a manager?

1–3 Describe the four steps in the planning and control cycle.

1–4 What function does feedback play in the work of the manager?

1–5 Distinguish between line and staff positions in an organization.

1–6 What are the major differences between financial and management accounting?

1–7 Briefly describe the impact of new technology, globalization and deregulation on the practice of management accounting.

1–8 Suggest three ways in which management accounting in services may differ from its practice in manufacturing industry.

1–9 Suggest three reasons why value seeking companies should care about the environment.

1–10 Why is adherence to ethical standards important for the smooth functioning of an advanced market economy?

Exercises

E1–1 Time allowed: 10 minutes

Listed below are a number of terms that relate to organizations, the work of management and the role of management accounting:

Budgets	Chief Accountant	Decentralization
Directing and motivating	Feedback	Financial accounting
Line	Management accounting	Non-monetary data
Performance report	Planning	Precision
Staff		

Choose the term or terms above that most appropriately complete the following statements:

1 A position on the organization chart that is directly related to achieving the basic objectives of an organization is called a ________ position.

2 When ________, managers oversee day-to-day activities and keep the organization functioning smoothly.

3 The plans of management are expressed formally in ________.

4 ________ consists of identifying alternatives, selecting from among the alternatives the one that is best for the organization, and specifying what actions will be taken to implement the chosen alternative.

5 A ________ position provides service or assistance to other parts of the organization and does not directly achieve the basic objectives of the organization.

6 The delegation of decision-making authority throughout an organization by allowing managers at various operating levels to make key decisions relating to their area of responsibility is called ________.

7 Management accounting places less emphasis on ________ and more emphasis on ________ than financial accounting.

8 ________ is concerned with providing information for the use of those who are inside the organization, whereas ________ is concerned with providing information for the use of those who are outside the organization.

9 The accounting and other reports coming to management that are used in controlling the organization are called ________.

10 The manager in charge of the accounting department is generally known as the ________.

11 A detailed report to management comparing budgeted data against actual data for a specific time period is called a ________.

PROBLEMS

Problems

P1–2 Preparing an organization chart Time allowed: 30 minutes

Upton University is a large private university located in the Midlands. The university is headed by a vice-chancellor who has five pro-vice chancellors reporting to him. These pro-vice chancellors are responsible for, respectively, auxiliary services, admissions and records, academics, financial services (controller), and physical plant.

In addition, the university has managers over several areas who report to these pro-vice chancellors. These include managers over central purchasing, the university press, and the university bookstore, all of whom report to the pro-vice chancellor for auxiliary services; managers over computer services and over accounting and finance, who report to the pro-vice chancellor for financial services; and managers over grounds and custodial services and over plant and maintenance, who report to the pro-vice chancellor for physical plant.

The university has four colleges – business, humanities, fine arts, and engineering and quantitative methods – and a law school. Each of these units has a dean who is responsible to the academic pro-vice chancellor. Each college has several departments.

Required

1 Prepare an organization chart for Upton University.

2 Which of the positions on your chart would be line positions? Why would they be line positions? Which would be staff positions? Why?

3 Which of the positions on your chart would have need for accounting information? Explain.

P1–3 Ethics and the manager

Richmond plc operates a chain of department stores. The first store began operations in 1965, and the company has steadily grown to its present size of 44 stores. Two years ago, the board of directors of Richmond approved a large-scale remodelling of its stores to attract a more upmarket clientele. Before finalizing these plans, two stores were remodelled as a test. Linda Potter, assistant controller, was asked to oversee the financial reporting for these test stores, and she and other management personnel were offered bonuses based on the sales growth and profitability of these stores. While completing the financial reports, Potter discovered a sizeable stock of outdated goods that should have been discounted for sale or returned to the manufacturer. She discussed the situation with her management colleagues; the consensus was to ignore reporting this stock as obsolete, since reporting it would diminish the financial results and their bonuses.

Required

1 Would it be ethical for Potter *not* to report the stock as obsolete?

2 Would it be easy for Potter to take the ethical action in this situation?

P1–4 Ethics

Suppose all garages routinely followed the practice of attempting to sell customers unnecessary parts and services by recommending unnecessary or expensive repairs.

Required

1 How would this unethical behaviour affect customers?

2 How might customers attempt to protect themselves against this unethical behaviour?

3 How would this unethical behaviour probably affect profits and employment in the garage industry?

Group exercise

GE1-5 Ethics on the job

Ethical standards are very important in business, but they are not always followed. If you have ever held a job – even a summer job – describe the ethical climate in the organization where you worked. Did employees work a full day or did they arrive late and leave early? Did employees honestly report the hours they worked? Did employees use their employer's resources for their own purposes? Did managers set a good example? Did the organization have a code of ethics and were employees made aware of its existence? If the ethical climate in the organization you worked for was poor, what problems, if any, did it create?

Internet exercise

IE1-6

Access the website of the *Association for Accountancy and Business Affairs* (www.visar.csustan.edu/aaba/home.htm), click on one of the issues and follow the links to newspaper cuttings and other sources.

Cases

C1-7 Deregulation, new technology and the reorganization of the finance function Time allowed: 40 minutes

Megacorp plc is a large international utilities company. The company's business environment has changed rapidly in recent years as a result of the various phases of privatization, deregulation, and the resultant industry restructuring. During the past two years, a shared service centre (SSC) has been established in South Yorkshire, consolidating processes that were formerly dealt with in individual business units (such as power generating stations) in many separate locations. The manager in charge of the finance function explained some of the issues as follows:

'We actually run ourselves on process lines – "Purchase-to-Pay" or "Procurement-to-Pay", and "Order-to-Cash". The Sales Ledger is consolidated nationally but the rest is all done locally – we run software systems that these days allow you to have both remote sites and central operations and there is still visibility and transparency across the organization. The same applies to the nominal ledger and other accounting. We do all the statutory accounts centrally now and the main database, the main nominal ledger, is based on a server in this building. But, of course, the data can be accessed anywhere. The accounts are still "owned" by the local Finance Director, Finance Controller and finance teams out in each one of the local business units. The finance people in the local business units need to "own" the statutory accounts even though they don't prepare them these days. If they don't "own" the accounts, then they are signing something without understanding what's there.'

Required

Discuss how the organization and culture of the finance function in Megacorp has been affected by new information technology, the deregulation of power generation and the more recent post-Enron concerns with financial probity.

You might find it helpful to refer to CIMA (2001b) and May (2002).

Endnotes

1 Adapted from the easyJet company website, 24 March 2005.

2 Chandler (1977).

3 Johnson and Kaplan (1987), pp. 129–30.

4 Again see Johnson and Kaplan (1987). See also Loft (1995); Ezzamel, Hoskin and Macve (1990).

5 See, for example, Armstrong (1985) and Armstrong (1987).

6 Bhimani (1996).

7 Granlund and Lukka (1998b).

8 See Granlund and Lukka (1998b).

9 See Scapens, Ezzamel, Burns and Baldvinsdottir (2003).

10 See May (2002).

11 See, for example, Bain and Taylor (2000).

12 Hayward (2002); CIMA (2001a).

13 Hood (1995).

14 Olson, Guthrie and Humphrey (1998).

15 For a historical view on value based management see Ittner and Larker (2001). For a very recent attempt to analyse the cost of customer satisfaction see Cugini, Caru and Zerbini (2007).

16 See IFAC (2005).

17 See, for example, Gordon (2002).

18 See Burns and Baldvinsdottir (2007).

Chapter 2

An introduction to cost terms, concepts and classifications

Learning objectives

After studying Chapter 2, you should be able to:

1 Identify each of the three basic cost elements involved in the manufacture of a product

2 Distinguish between product costs and period costs and give examples of each

3 Prepare a schedule of cost of goods manufactured in good form

4 Explain the flow of direct materials cost, direct labour cost, and manufacturing overhead cost

5 Begin to appreciate the differences between costing for manufacturing and for services

6 Identify and give examples of variable costs and fixed costs

7 Define and give examples of direct and indirect costs

8 Define cost classifications used in making decisions: differential costs, opportunity costs and sunk costs

Concepts in Context

This chapter introduces issues concerned with the classification of costs. These issues may be controversial. For example, the BBC has been accused of concealing the true costs of its individual channels by reporting the cost of items such as news gathering, marketing and publicity under separate headings instead of allocating them as overheads to each channel. It was alleged that the corporation wished to reduce the apparent costs both of expanding into digital broadcasting and the budget of BBC 1, the channel that competes with the main commercial broadcasters. The BBC responded by claiming that the new format reflected the corporation's internal reporting system and that the new format was 'more transparent'.[1]

As explained in Chapter 1, the work of management focuses on planning, which includes setting objectives and outlining how to attain these objectives; and control, which includes the steps to take to ensure that objectives are realized. To carry out these planning and control responsibilities, managers need information about the organization. From an accounting point of view, this information often relates to the costs of the organization.

In management accounting, the term 'cost' is used in many different ways. This is because there are many types of costs, and these costs are classified differently according to the immediate needs of management. For example, managers may want cost data to prepare external financial reports, to prepare planning budgets, or to make decisions. Each different use of cost data demands a different classification and definition of costs. For example, the preparation of external financial reports requires the use of historical cost data, whereas decision making may require current cost data.

In this chapter, we discuss many of the possible uses of cost data and how costs are defined and classified for each use. Our first task is to explain how costs are classified for the purpose of preparing external financial reports – particularly in manufacturing companies. To set the stage for this discussion, we begin the chapter by defining some terms commonly used in manufacturing.

General cost classifications

Costs are associated with all types of organizations – business, non-business, manufacturing, retail and service. Generally, the kinds of costs incurred and the way in which these costs are classified depends on the type of organization involved. Management accounting is as applicable to one type of organization as to another. For this reason, we will consider in our discussion the cost characteristics of a variety of organizations – manufacturing, merchandising and service.

Our initial focus in this chapter is on manufacturing companies, since their basic activities include most of the activities found in other types of business organizations. Manufacturing companies are involved in acquiring raw materials, producing finished goods, marketing, distributing, billing and almost every other business activity. Therefore, an understanding of costs in a manufacturing company can be very helpful in understanding costs in other types of organizations.

Yet, as we argued in the previous chapter, service activities are becoming increasingly important in many advanced economies so that we also need to develop cost concepts that apply to non-manufacturing organizations. For example, these cost concepts apply to fast-food outlets such as McDonald's, Pizza Hut and Burger King; TV companies such as the BBC; consulting firms such as Price Waterhouse Coopers and McKinsey; and your local hospital. The exact terms used in these industries may not be the same as those used in manufacturing, but the same basic concepts apply. With some slight modifications, which will be discussed later in this chapter, these basic concepts also apply to merchandising companies such as Tesco, Sainsbury's, Next and Gap, that resell finished goods acquired from manufacturers and other sources. With that in mind, let us begin our discussion of manufacturing costs.

Manufacturing costs

Most manufacturing companies divide manufacturing costs into three broad categories: **direct materials**, **direct labour**, and **manufacturing overhead**. A discussion of each of these categories follows.

Direct materials

The materials that go into the final product are called **raw materials**. This term is somewhat misleading, since it seems to imply unprocessed natural resources like wood pulp or iron ore. Actually, raw materials refer to any materials that are used in the final product; and the finished product of one company can become the raw materials of another company. For example, the plastics produced by Du Pont are a raw material used by Compaq Computer in its personal computers.

Direct materials are those materials that become an integral part of the finished product and that can be physically and conveniently traced to it. This would include, for example, the seats Airbus purchases from subcontractors to install in its commercial aircraft. Also included is the tiny electric motor Panasonic uses in its CD players to make the CD spin.

Sometimes it isn't worth the effort to trace the costs of relatively insignificant materials to the end products. Such minor items would include the solder used to make electrical connections in a Sony TV. Materials such as solder and glue are called **indirect materials** and are included as part of manufacturing overhead, which is discussed later in this section.

Direct labour

The term direct labour is reserved for those labour costs that can easily (i.e., physically and conveniently) be traced to individual units of product. Direct labour is sometimes called *touch labour*, since direct labour workers typically touch the product while it is being made. The labour costs of assembly-line workers, for example, would be direct labour costs, as would the labour costs of carpenters, bricklayers and machine operators.

Labour costs that cannot be physically traced to the creation of products, or that can be traced only at great cost and inconvenience, are termed **indirect labour** and treated as part of manufacturing overhead, along with indirect materials. Indirect labour includes the labour costs of caretakers, supervisors, materials handlers and night security guards. Although the efforts of these workers are essential to production, it would either be impractical or impossible accurately to trace their costs to specific units of product. Hence, such labour costs are treated as indirect labour.

In some industries, major shifts are taking place in the structure of labour costs. Sophisticated automated equipment, run and maintained by skilled indirect workers, is increasingly replacing direct labour. In a few companies, direct labour has become such a minor element of cost that it has disappeared altogether as a separate cost category. More is said in later chapters about this trend and about the impact it is having on cost systems. However, the vast majority of manufacturing and service companies throughout the world continue to recognize direct labour as a separate cost category.

Manufacturing overhead

Manufacturing overhead, the third element of manufacturing cost, includes all costs of manufacturing except direct materials and direct labour. Manufacturing overhead includes items such as indirect materials; indirect labour; maintenance and repairs on production equipment; and heat and light, property taxes, depreciation and insurance on manufacturing facilities. A company also incurs costs for heat and light, property taxes, insurance, depreciation and so forth, associated with its selling and administrative functions, but these costs are not included as part of manufacturing overhead. Only those costs associated with *operating the factory* are included in the manufacturing overhead category.

Various names are used for manufacturing overhead, such as *indirect manufacturing cost, factory overhead*, and *factory burden*. All of these terms are synonymous with manufacturing overhead.

Manufacturing overhead combined with direct labour is called **conversion cost**. This term stems from the fact that direct labour costs and overhead costs are incurred in the conversion of materials into finished products. Direct labour combined with direct materials is called **prime cost**.

Non-manufacturing costs

Generally, non-manufacturing costs are subclassified into two categories:

1 Marketing or selling costs

2 Administrative costs

Marketing or selling costs include all costs necessary to secure customer orders and get the finished product or service into the hands of the customer. These costs are often called *order-getting* and *order-filling* *costs*. Examples of marketing costs include advertising, shipping, sales travel, sales commissions, sales salaries and costs of finished goods warehouses.

Administrative costs include all executive, organizational and clerical costs associated with the *general management* of an organization rather than with manufacturing, marketing or selling. Examples of administrative costs include executive compensation, general accounting, secretarial, public relations and similar costs involved in the overall general administration of the organization *as a whole*.

Product costs versus period costs

2 LEARNING OBJECTIVE

In addition to the distinction between manufacturing and non-manufacturing costs, there are other ways to look at costs. For instance, they can also be classified as either **product costs** or **period costs**. To understand the difference between product costs and period costs, we must first refresh our understanding of the matching principle from financial accounting.

Generally, costs are recognized as expenses on the *profit and loss account* (sometimes alternatively known as the *income statement*) in the period that benefits from the cost. For example, if a company pays for liability insurance in advance for two years, the entire amount is not considered an expense of the year in which the payment is made. Instead, half of the cost would be recognized as an expense each year. This is because both years – not just the first – benefit from the insurance payment. The unexpensed portion of the insurance payment is carried on the balance sheet as an asset called prepaid insurance. You should be familiar with this type of *accrual* from your financial accounting course.

The *matching principle* is based on the accrual concept and states that *costs incurred to generate a particular revenue should be recognized as expenses in the same period that the revenue is recognized.* This means that if a cost is incurred to acquire or make something that will eventually be sold, then the cost should be recognized as an expense only when the sale takes place – that is, when the benefit occurs. Such costs are called *product costs*.

Product costs

For financial accounting purposes, product costs include all the costs that are involved in acquiring or making a product. In the case of manufactured goods, these costs consist of direct materials, direct labour and manufacturing overhead. Product costs are viewed as 'attaching' to units of product as the goods are purchased or manufactured, and they remain attached as the goods go into stock awaiting sale. So, initially, product costs are assigned to a stock account on the balance sheet. When the goods are sold, the costs are released from stock as expenses (typically called cost of goods sold) and matched against sales revenue. Since product costs are initially assigned to stocks, they are also known as *stock-related costs*.

We want to emphasize that product costs are not necessarily treated as expenses in the period in which they are incurred. Rather, as explained above, they are treated as expenses in the period in which the related products *are sold*. This means that a product cost such as direct materials or direct labour might be incurred during one period but not treated as an expense until a following period when the completed product is sold.

Period costs

Period costs are all the costs that are not included in product costs. These costs are expensed on the profit and loss account in the period in which they are incurred, using the usual rules of accrual accounting you have already learned in financial accounting. Period costs are not included as part of the cost of either purchased or manufactured goods. Sales commissions and office rent are good examples of the kind of costs we are talking about. Neither commissions nor office rent are included as part of the cost of purchased or manufactured goods. Rather, both items are treated as expenses on the profit and loss account in the period in which they are incurred. Thus, they are said to be period costs.

As suggested above, *all selling and administrative expenses are considered to be period costs*. Therefore, advertising, executive salaries, sales commissions, public relations, and other non-manufacturing costs discussed earlier would all be period costs. They will appear on the profit and loss account as expenses in the period in which they are incurred.

Exhibit 2.1 contains a summary of the cost terms that we have introduced so far.

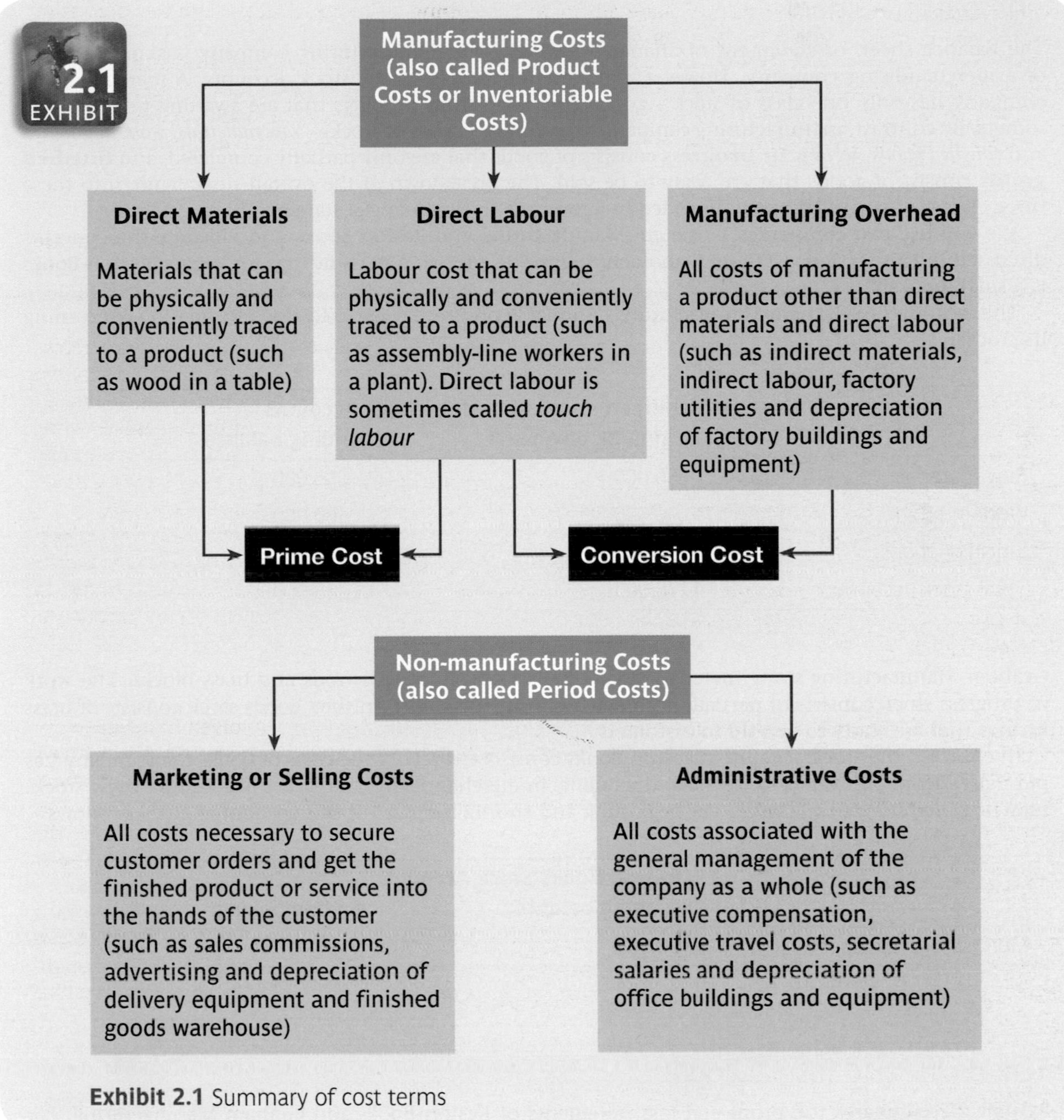

Exhibit 2.1 Summary of cost terms

Cost classifications on financial statements

In introductory financial accounting, you learn that firms prepare periodic financial reports for creditors, shareholders and others to show the financial condition of the firm and the firm's earnings performance over some specified interval. The reports you study were probably those of merchandising companies, such as retail shops, which simply purchase goods from suppliers for resale to customers.

The financial statements prepared by a *manufacturing* company are more complex than the statements prepared by a merchandising company. Manufacturing companies are more complex organizations than merchandising companies because the manufacturing company must produce its goods as well as market them. The production process gives rise to many costs that do not exist in a merchandising company, and somehow these costs must be accounted for on the manufacturing company's financial statements. In this section, we focus our attention on how this accounting is carried out in the balance sheet and profit and loss account.

The balance sheet

The balance sheet, or statement of financial position, of a manufacturing company is similar to that of a merchandising company. However, there are differences in the stock accounts. A merchandising company has only one class of stock – goods purchased from suppliers that are awaiting resale to customers. By contrast, manufacturing companies have three classes of stocks – *raw materials, work in progress* and *finished goods*. **Work in progress** consists of goods that are only partially completed, and **finished goods** consist of goods that are ready to be sold. The breakdown of the overall stock figure into these three classes of stocks is usually provided in a footnote to the financial statements.

We will use two companies – Graham Manufacturing and Reston Books – to illustrate the concepts discussed in this section. Graham Manufacturing makes precision brass fittings for yachts. Reston Books is a small bookshop.

The footnotes to Graham Manufacturing's Annual Report reveal the following information concerning its stocks:

Graham Manufacturing Corporation Stock Accounts		
	Beginning balance	**Ending balance**
Raw materials	£60,000	£50,000
Work in progress	90,000	60,000
Finished goods	125,000	175,000
Total stock accounts	£275,000	£285,000

Graham Manufacturing's raw materials stock consists largely of brass rods and brass blocks. The work in progress stock consists of partially completed brass fittings. The finished goods stock consists of brass fittings that are ready to be sold to customers.

In contrast, the stock account at Reston Books consists entirely of the costs of books the company has purchased from publishers for resale to the public. In merchandising companies like Reston, these stocks may be called *merchandise stock*. The beginning and ending balances in this account appear as follows:

Reston Books Stock Account		
	Beginning balance	**Ending balance**
Merchandise stock	£100,000	£150,000

The profit and loss account

Exhibit 2.2 compares the profit and loss statements of Reston Books and Graham Manufacturing. For purposes of illustration, these statements contain more detail about cost of goods sold than you will generally find in published financial statements.

At first glance, the profit and loss statements of merchandising and manufacturing firms like Reston Books and Graham Manufacturing are very similar. The only apparent difference is in the labels of some of the entries that go into the computation of the cost of goods sold figure. In the exhibit, the computation of cost of goods sold relies on the following basic equation for stock accounts:

Basic equation for stock accounts

Beginning balance + Additions to stock = Ending balance + Withdrawals from stock

The logic underlying this equation, which applies to any stock account, is illustrated in Exhibit 2.3. During a period, there are additions to the stock account through purchases or other means. The sum of the additions to the account and the beginning balance represents the total amount of stock that is avail-

2.2 EXHIBIT

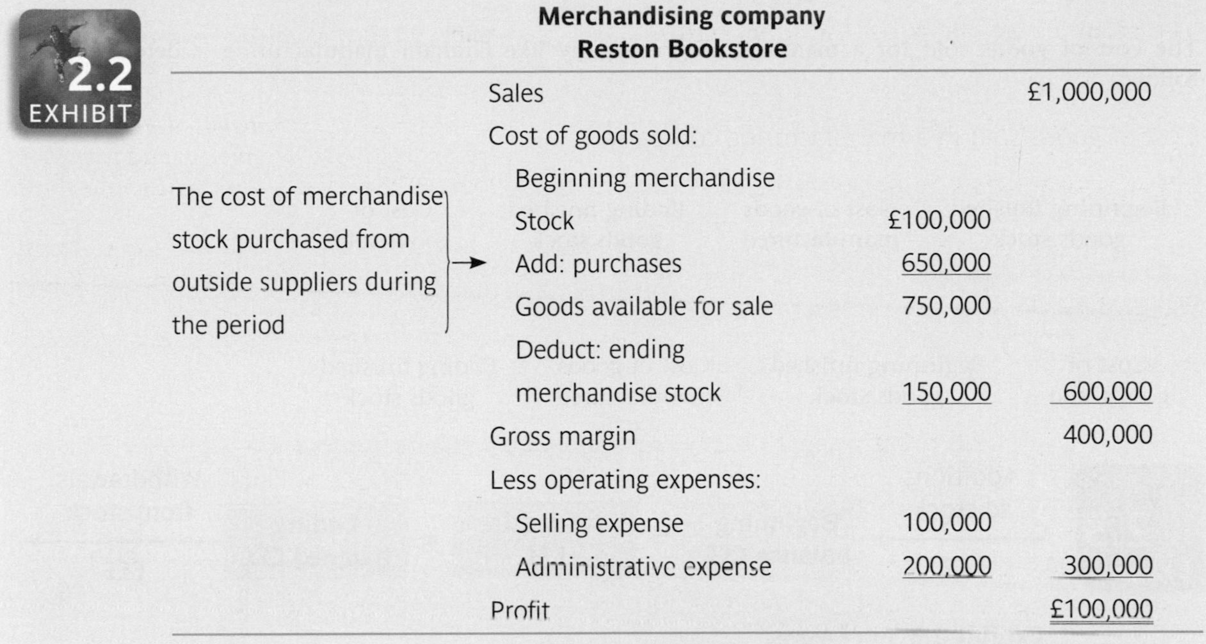

Merchandising company
Reston Bookstore

	Sales		£1,000,000
	Cost of goods sold:		
	Beginning merchandise		
The cost of merchandise stock purchased from outside suppliers during the period →	Stock	£100,000	
	Add: purchases	650,000	
	Goods available for sale	750,000	
	Deduct: ending merchandise stock	150,000	600,000
	Gross margin		400,000
	Less operating expenses:		
	Selling expense	100,000	
	Administrative expense	200,000	300,000
	Profit		£100,000

Manufacturing company
Graham Manufacturing

	Sales		£1,500,000
	Cost of goods sold:		
The manufacturing costs associated with the goods that were finished during the period. (see Exhibits 2.4 and 2.5 for details) →	Beginning finished goods stock	£125,000	
	Add: cost of goods Manufactured	850,000	
	Goods available for sale	975,000	
	Deduct: ending finished goods stock	175,000	800,000
	Gross margin		700,000
	Less operating expenses:		
	Selling expense	250,000	
	Administrative expense	300,000	550,000
	Profit		£150,000

Exhibit 2.2 Comparative profit and loss statements: merchandising and manufacturing companies

able for use during the period. At the end of the period, all of the stock that was available must either be in ending stock or have been withdrawn from the stock account.

These concepts are applied to determine the cost of goods sold for a merchandising company like Reston Books as follows:

Cost of goods sold in a merchandising company

Beginning merchandise stock + Purchases = Ending merchandise stock + Cost of goods sold

or

Cost of goods sold = Beginning merchandise stock + Purchases − Ending merchandise stock

The cost of goods sold for a manufacturing company like Graham manufacturing is determined as follows:

Cost of goods sold in a manufacturing company

Beginning finished goods stock + Cost of goods manufactured = Ending finished goods stock + Cost of goods sold

or

Cost of goods sold = Beginning finished goods stock + Cost of goods manufactured − Ending finished goods stock

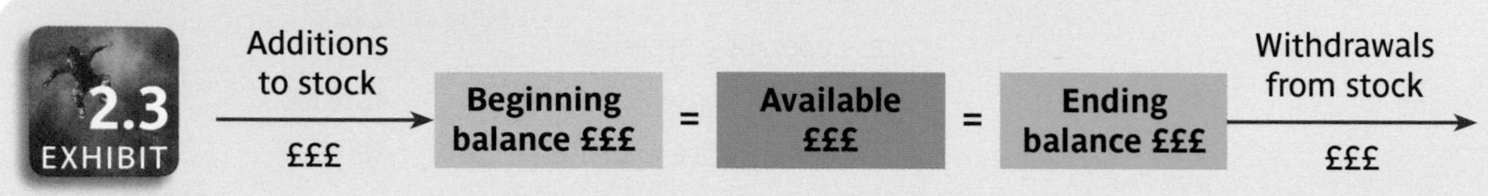

Exhibit 2.3 Stock flows

To determine the cost of goods sold in a merchandising company like Reston Books, we need only to know the beginning and ending balances in the Merchandise Stock account and the purchases. Total purchases can be easily determined in a merchandising company by simply adding together all purchases from suppliers.

To determine the cost of goods sold in a manufacturing company like Graham Manufacturing, we need to know *the cost of goods manufactured* and the beginning and ending balances in the Finished Goods stock account. The **cost of goods manufactured** consists of the manufacturing costs associated with goods that were *finished* during the period. The cost of goods manufactured figure for Graham Manufacturing is derived in Exhibit 2.4, which contains a *schedule of cost of goods manufactured.*

Schedule of cost of goods manufactured

At first glance, the **schedule of cost of goods manufactured** in Exhibit 2.4 appears complex and perhaps even intimidating. However, it is all quite logical. Notice that the schedule of cost of goods manufactured contains the three elements of product costs that we discussed earlier – direct materials, direct labour and manufacturing overhead. The total of these three cost elements is *not* the cost of goods manufactured, however. The reason is that some of the materials, labour and overhead costs incurred during the period relate to goods that are not yet completed. The costs that relate to goods that are not yet completed are shown in the work in progress stock figures at the bottom of the schedule. Note that the beginning work in progress stock must be added to the manufacturing costs of the period, and the ending work in progress stock must be deducted, to arrive at the cost of goods manufactured.

The logic underlying the schedule of cost of goods manufactured and the computation of cost of goods sold is laid out in a different format in Exhibit 2.5. To compute the cost of goods sold, go to the top of the exhibit and work your way down using the following steps:

1 Compute the raw materials used in production in the top section of the exhibit.

2 Insert the total raw materials used in production (£410,000) into the second section of the exhibit, and compute the total manufacturing cost.

3 Insert the total manufacturing cost (£820,000) into the third section of the exhibit and compute the cost of goods manufactured.

4 Insert the cost of goods manufactured (£850,000) into the bottom section of the exhibit, and compute the cost of goods sold.

Direct materials:			
Beginning raw materials stock*	£60,000		
Add: Purchases of raw materials	400,000		
Raw materials available for use	460,000		← Direct Materials
Deduct: Ending raw materials stock	50,000		
Raw materials used in production			
		£410,000	
Direct labour		60,000	← Direct Labour
Manfacturing overhead:			
Insurance, factory	6,000		
Indirect labour	100,000		
Machine rental	50,000		
Utilities, factory	75,000		← Manufacturing Overhead
Supplies	21,000		
Depreciation, factory	90,000		
Property taxes, factory	8,000		
Total overhead costs		350,000	
Total manufacturing costs:		820,000	
Add: Beginning work in progress stock		90,000	
		910,000	← Cost of goods Manfactured
Deduct: Ending work in progress stock		60,000	
Cost of goods manufactured (see Exhibit 2.2)		£850,000	

Exhibit 2.4 Schedule of cost of goods manufactured

*We assume in this example that the Raw Materials stock account contains only direct materials and that indirect materials are carried in a separate Supplies account. In Chapter 3, we discuss the procedure to be followed if *both* direct and indirect materials are carried in a single account.

Product costs – a closer look

4 LEARNING OBJECTIVE

Earlier in the chapter, we defined product costs as consisting of those costs that are involved in either the purchase or the manufacture of goods. For manufactured goods, we stated that these costs consist of direct materials, direct labour and manufacturing overhead. To understand product costs more fully, it will be helpful at this point to look briefly at the flow of costs in a manufacturing company. By doing so, we will be able to see how product costs move through the various accounts and affect the balance sheet and the profit and loss account in the course of producing and selling products.

Exhibit 2.6 illustrates the flow of costs in a manufacturing company. Raw materials purchases are recorded in the Raw Materials stock account. When raw materials are used in production, their costs are

	Computation of raw materials used in production	
	Beginning raw materials stock	£60,000
+	Purchases of raw materials	400,000
−	Ending raw materials stock	50,000
=	Raw materials used in production	£410,000
	Computation of total manufacturing cost	
	Raw materials used in production	£410,000
+	Direct labour	60,000
+	Total manufacturing overhead costs	350,000
=	Total manufacturing cost	£820,000
	Computation of cost of goods manufactured	
	Beginning work in progress stock	£90,000
+	Total manufacturing cost	820,000
−	Ending work in progress stock	60,000
=	Cost of goods manufactured	£850,000
	Computation of cost of goods sold	
	Beginning finished goods stock	£125,000
+	Cost of goods manufactured	850,000
−	Ending finished goods stock	175,000
=	Cost of goods sold	£800,000

Exhibit 2.5 An alternative approach to computation of cost of goods sold

transferred to the Work in Progress stock account as *direct materials*. Notice that *direct labour* cost and *manufacturing overhead* cost are added directly to Work in Progress. Work in Progress can be viewed most simply as an assembly line where workers are stationed and where products slowly take shape as they move from one end of the assembly line to the other. The direct materials, direct labour and manufacturing overhead costs added to Work in Progress in Exhibit 2.6 are the costs needed to complete these products as they move along this assembly line.

Notice from the exhibit that as goods are completed, their cost is transferred from Work in Progress into Finished Goods. Here the goods await sale to a customer. As goods are sold, their cost is then transferred from Finished Goods into Cost of Goods Sold. It is at this point that the various material, labour and overhead costs that are required to make the product are finally treated as expenses.

Stock-related costs

As stated earlier, product costs are often called stock-related (or inventoriable[2]) costs. The reason is that these costs go directly into stock accounts as they are incurred (first into Work in Progress and then into Finished Goods), rather than going into expense accounts. Thus, they are termed **stock-related costs**. *This is a key concept in management accounting, since such costs can end up on the balance sheet as assets if goods are only partially completed or are unsold at the end of a period.* To illustrate this point, refer again to the data in Exhibit 2.6. At the end of the period, the materials, labour and overhead costs that are associated with the units in the Work in Progress and Finished Goods stock accounts will appear on the balance sheet as part of the company's assets. As explained earlier, these costs will not become expenses until later when the goods are completed and sold.

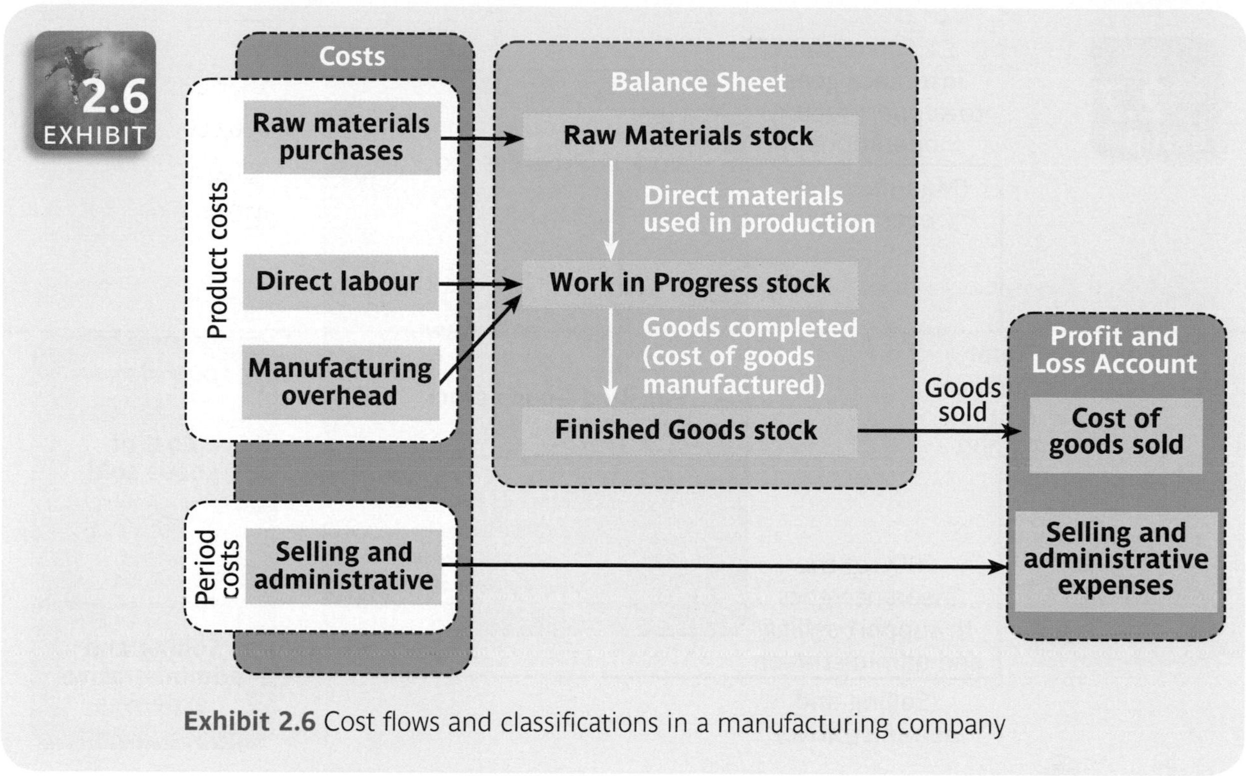

Exhibit 2.6 Cost flows and classifications in a manufacturing company

As shown in Exhibit 2.6, selling and administrative expenses are not involved in the manufacture of a product. For this reason, they are not treated as product costs but rather as period costs that go directly into expense accounts as they are incurred.

An example of cost flows

To provide a numerical example of cost flows in a manufacturing company, assume that a company's annual insurance cost is £2,000. Three-quarters of this amount (£1,500) applies to factory operations, and one-quarter (£500) applies to selling and administrative activities. Therefore, £1,500 of the £2,000 insurance cost would be a product (stock-related) cost and would be added to the cost of the goods produced during the year. This concept is illustrated in Exhibit 2.7, where £1,500 of insurance cost is added into Work in Progress. As shown in the exhibit, this portion of the year's insurance cost will not become an expense until the goods that are produced during the year are sold – which may not happen until the following year or even later. Until the goods are sold, the £1,500 will remain as part of the asset, stock (either as part of Work in Progress or as part of Finished Goods), along with the other costs of producing the goods.

By contrast, the £500 of insurance cost that applies to the company's selling and administrative activities will go into an expense account immediately as a charge against the period's revenue.

Thus far, we have been mainly concerned with classifications of manufacturing costs for the purpose of determining stock valuations on the balance sheet and cost of goods sold on the profit and loss account of external financial reports. There are, however, many other purposes for which costs are used, and each purpose requires a different classification of costs. We will consider several different purposes for cost classifications in the remaining sections of this chapter. These purposes and the corresponding cost classifications are summarized in Exhibit 2.8. To maintain focus, we suggest that you refer back to this exhibit frequently as you progress through the rest of this chapter.

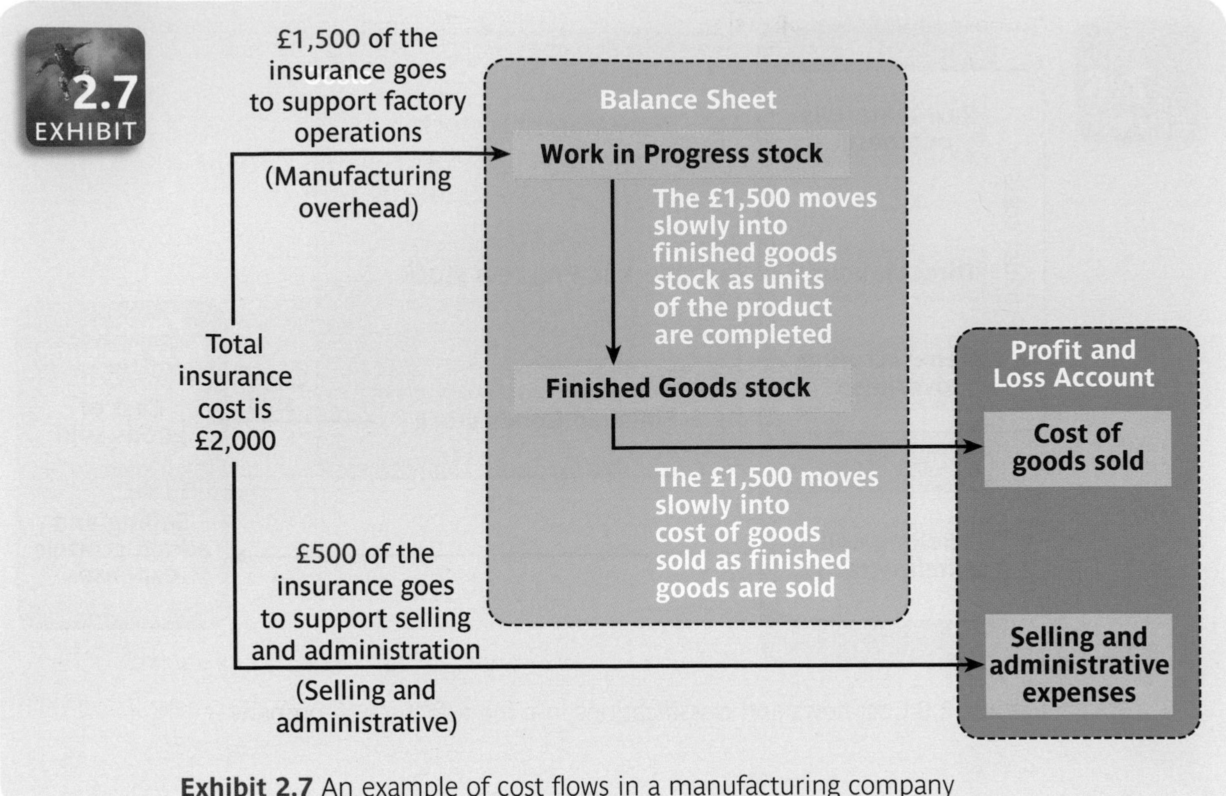

Exhibit 2.7 An example of cost flows in a manufacturing company

Costing in service organizations: a first look

Although many basic cost concepts and classifications can equally be applied to manufacturing and service operations, there are some important general differences between manufacturing and service businesses. An influential study on services[3] suggested that the main differences between services and manufacturing are that:

- Services cannot be stored as inventory – thus in many service businesses (with the obvious exception of merchandising), there is very little interest in *inventory valuation* with its attendant balance sheet/profit and loss account issues discussed above;
- Service outputs are often specially customized for a client – service outputs are often *heterogeneous* rather than *homogenous* with many intangible characteristics which make it hard to define output;
- In services, the customer is usually present in the delivery process – there is a *simultaneity* of service production and consumption with the consequence that 'services cannot be counted, measured, inspected, tested or verified in advance of sale'.[4]

Historically, these differences have had an effect on how costing has developed in service organizations. For example, in many service organizations such as banks, the main cost object was the *department* rather than the *product*.[5] We will also see in later chapters how service organizations raise special issues of *cost behaviour*, *pricing* and *management control*.

Cost classifications for predicting cost behaviour

Quite frequently, it is necessary to predict how a certain cost will behave in response to a change in activity. For example, a manager may want to estimate the impact that a 5% increase in long-distance calls would have on the company's total electricity bill or on the total wages the company pays its long-distance operators. **Cost behaviour** means how a cost will react or respond to changes in the level of business activity. As the activity level rises and falls, a par-

Purpose of cost classification	Cost classifications
Preparing external financial statements	■ Product costs (inventoriable) ■ Direct materials ■ Direct labour ■ Manufacturing overheads ■ Period costs (expensed) ■ Non-manufacturing costs ■ Marketing or selling costs ■ Administrative costs
Predicting cost behaviour in response to changes in activity	■ Variable cost (proportional to activity) ■ Fixed cost (constant in total)
Assigning costs to cost objects such as departments or products	■ Direct cost (can easily be traced) ■ Indirect cost (cannot easily be traced; must be allocated)
Making decisions	■ Differential cost (differs between alternatives) ■ Sunk cost (past cost not affected by a decision) ■ Opportunity cost (forgone benefit)

Exhibit 2.8 Summary of cost classifications

ticular cost may rise and fall as well – or it may remain constant. For planning purposes, a manager must be able to anticipate which of these will happen; and if a cost can be expected to change, the manager must know by how much it will change. To help make such distinctions, costs are often categorized as variable or fixed.

Variable cost

A **variable cost** is a cost that varies, in total, in direct proportion to changes in the level of activity. The activity can be expressed in many ways, such as units produced, units sold, miles driven, beds occupied, lines of print, hours worked, and so forth. A good example of a variable cost is direct materials. The cost of direct materials used during a period will vary, in total, in direct proportion to the number of units that are produced. To illustrate this idea, consider the example of a car factory. Each car requires one battery. As the output of cars increases and decreases, the number of batteries used will increase and decrease proportionately. If car production goes up 10%, then the number of batteries used will also go up 10%. The concept of a variable cost is shown in graphic form in Exhibit 2.9.

It is important to note that when we speak of a cost as being variable, we mean the *total* cost rises and falls as the activity level rises and falls. This idea is presented below, assuming that a battery costs £24:

Number of cars produced	Cost per battery	Total variable cost – batteries
1	£24	£24
500	24	12,000
1,000	24	24,000

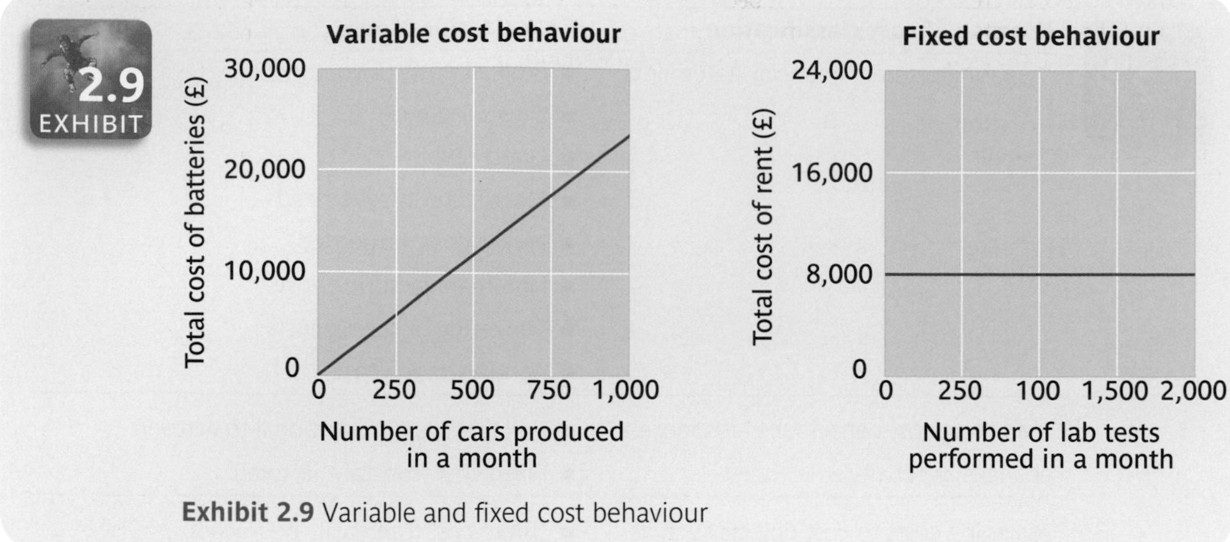

Exhibit 2.9 Variable and fixed cost behaviour

One interesting aspect of variable cost behaviour is that a variable cost is constant if expressed on a *per unit* basis. Observe from the tabulation above that the per unit cost of batteries remains constant at £24 even though the total amount of cost involved increases and decreases with activity.

There are many examples of costs that are variable with respect to the products and services provided by a company. In a manufacturing company, variable costs include items such as direct materials and some elements of manufacturing overhead such as lubricants, shipping costs and sales commissions. For the present we will also assume that direct labour is a variable cost, although as we shall see later, direct labour may act more like a fixed cost in many situations. In a merchandising company, variable costs include items such as cost of goods sold, commissions to salespersons and billing costs. In a hospital, the variable costs of providing health care services to patients would include the costs of the supplies, drugs, meals and, perhaps, nursing services.

The activity causing changes in a variable cost need not be how much output is produced or sold. For example, the wages paid to employees at a video outlet will depend on the number of hours the shop is open and not strictly on the number of videos rented. In this case, we would say that wage costs are variable with respect to the hours of operation. Nevertheless, when we say that a cost is variable, we ordinarily mean it is variable with respect to the volume of revenue-generating output – in other words, how many units are produced and sold, how many videos are rented, how many patients are treated and so on.

Fixed cost

A **fixed cost** is a cost that remains constant, in total, regardless of changes in the level of activity. Unlike variable costs, fixed costs are not affected by changes in activity. Consequently, as the activity level rises and falls, the fixed costs remain constant in total amount unless influenced by some outside force, such as price changes. Rent is a good example of a fixed cost. Suppose a hospital rents a machine for £8,000 per month that tests blood samples for the presence of leukaemia cells. The £8,000 monthly rental cost will be sustained regardless of the number of tests that may be performed during the month. The concept of a fixed cost is shown in graphic form in Exhibit 2.9.

Very few costs are completely fixed. Most will change if there is a large enough change in activity. For example, suppose that the capacity of the leukaemia diagnostic machine at the hospital is 2,000 tests per month. If the clinic wishes to perform more than 2,000 tests in a month, it would be necessary to rent an additional machine, which would cause a jump in the fixed costs. When we say a cost is fixed, we mean it is fixed within some *relevant range*. The **relevant range** is the range of activity within which the assumptions about variable and fixed costs are valid. For example, the assumption that the rent for diagnostic machines is £8,000 per month is valid within the relevant range of 0 to 2,000 tests per month.

Fixed costs can create difficulties if it becomes necessary to express the costs on a per unit basis. This is because if fixed costs are expressed on a per unit basis, they will react inversely with changes in activity. In the hospital, for example, the average cost per test will fall as the number of tests performed increases. This is because the £8,000 rental cost will be spread over more tests. Conversely, as the number of tests performed in the clinic declines, the average cost per test will rise as the £8,000 rental cost is spread over fewer tests. This concept is illustrated in the table below:

Monthly rental cost	Number of tests performed	Average cost per test
£8,000	10	£800
8,000	500	16
8,000	2,000	4

Note that if the hospital performs only ten tests each month, the rental cost of the equipment will average £800 per test. But if 2,000 tests are performed each month, the average cost will drop to only £4 per test. More will be said later about the problems created for both the accountant and the manager by this variation in unit costs.

Examples of fixed costs include straight-line depreciation, insurance, property taxes, rent, supervisory salaries, administrative salaries and advertising.

A summary of both variable and fixed cost behaviour is presented in Exhibit 2.10.

2.10 EXHIBIT

	Behaviour of the cost (within the relevant range)	
Cost	**In total**	**Per unit**
Variable cost	Total variable cost increases and decreases in proportion to changes in the activity level	Variable costs remain constant per unit
Fixed cost	Total fixed cost is not affected by changes in the activity level within the relevant range	Fixed costs decrease per unit as the activity level rises and increases per unit as the activity level falls

Exhibit 2.10 Summary of variable and fixed cost behaviour

Cost classifications for assigning costs to cost objects

Costs are assigned to objects for a variety of purposes including pricing, profitability studies and control of spending. A **cost object** is anything for which cost data are desired – including products, product lines, customers, jobs and organizational subunits. For purposes of assigning costs to cost objects, costs are classified as either *direct* or *indirect*.

Direct cost

A **direct cost** is a cost that can be easily and conveniently traced to the particular cost object under consideration. The concept of direct cost extends beyond just direct materials and direct labour. For example, if Reebok is assigning costs to its various regional and national sales offices, then the salary of the sales manager in its Tokyo office would be a direct cost of that office.

Indirect cost

An **indirect cost** is a cost that cannot easily and conveniently be traced to the particular cost object under consideration. For example, a soup factory may produce dozens of varieties of canned soups. The factory manager's salary would be an indirect cost of a particular variety such as chicken noodle soup. The reason is that the factory manager's salary is not caused by any one variety of soup but rather is incurred as a consequence of running the entire factory. *To be traced to a cost object such as a particular product, the cost must be caused by the cost object.* The factory manager's salary is called a *common cost* of producing the various products of the factory. A **common cost** is a cost that is common to a number of costing objects but cannot be traced to them individually. A common cost is a particular type of indirect cost.

A particular cost may be direct or indirect, depending on the cost object. While the soup factory manager's salary is an *indirect* cost of manufacturing chicken noodle soup, it is a *direct* cost of the manufacturing division. In the first case, the cost object is the chicken noodle soup product. In the second case, the cost object is the entire manufacturing division.

Cost classifications for decision making

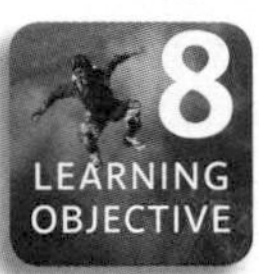

Costs are an important feature of many business decisions. In making decisions, it is essential to have a firm grasp of the concepts *differential cost*, *opportunity cost* and *sunk cost*. These are extremely important principles in management accounting that we will return to cover in more detail in Chapter 9.

Differential cost and revenue

Decisions involve choosing between alternatives. In business decisions, each alternative will have certain costs and benefits that must be compared to the costs and benefits of the other available alternatives. A difference in costs between any two alternatives is known as a **differential cost**. A difference in revenues between any two alternatives is known as **differential revenue**.

A differential cost is also known as an **incremental cost**, although technically an incremental cost should refer only to an increase in cost from one alternative to another; decreases in cost should be referred to as *decremental costs*. Differential cost is a broader term, encompassing both cost increases (incremental costs) and cost decreases (decremental costs) between alternatives.

The accountant's differential cost concept can be compared to the economist's marginal cost concept. In speaking of changes in cost and revenue, the economist employs the terms *marginal cost* and *marginal revenue*. The revenue that can be obtained from selling one more unit of product is called marginal revenue, and the cost involved in producing one more unit of product is called marginal cost. The economist's marginal concept is basically the same as the accountant's differential concept applied to a single unit of output.

Differential costs can be either fixed or variable. To illustrate, assume that Nature Way Cosmetics is thinking about changing its marketing method from distribution through retailers to distribution by door-to-door direct sale. Present costs and revenues are compared to projected costs and revenues in the table on page 37, which indicates that the differential revenue is £100,000 and the differential costs total £85,000, leaving a positive differential profit of £15,000 under the proposed marketing plan.

The decision of whether Nature Way Cosmetics should stay with the present retail distribution or switch to door-to-door direct selling could be made on the basis of the profits of the two alternatives. As we see in the above analysis, the profit under the present distribution method is £160,000, whereas the profit under door-to-door direct selling is estimated to be £175,000. Therefore, the door-to-door direct distribution method is preferred, since it would result in £15,000 higher profit. Note that we would have arrived at exactly the same conclusion by simply focusing on the differential revenues, differential costs and differential profit, which also show a £15,000 advantage for the direct selling method.

In general, only the differences between alternatives are relevant in decisions. Those items that are the same under all alternatives and that are not affected by the decision can be ignored. For example, in the Nature Way Cosmetics example above, the 'Other expenses' category, which is £60,000 under both alternatives, can be ignored, since it has no effect on the decision. If it were removed from the calculations, the door-to-door direct selling method would still be preferred by £15,000.

	Retailer distribution (present)	Direct sale distribution (proposed)	Differential costs and revenues
Revenues (V)	£700,000	£800,000	£100,000
Cost of goods sold (V)	350,000	400,000	50,000
Advertising (F)	80,000	45,000	(35,000)
Commissions (V)	0	40,000	40,000
Warehouse depreciation (F)	50,000	80,000	30,000
Other expenses (F)	60,000	60,000	0
Total	540,000	625,000	85,000
Profit	£160,000	£175,000	£15,000

V = Variable; F = Fixed

Opportunity cost

Opportunity cost is the potential benefit that is given up when one alternative is selected over another. To illustrate this important concept, consider the following examples:

Example 1

Vicki has a part-time job that pays her £100 per week while attending college. She would like to spend a week at the beach during spring break, and her employer has agreed to give her the time off, but without pay. The £100 in lost wages would be an opportunity cost of taking the week off to be at the beach.

Example 2

Suppose that Tesco is considering investing a large sum of money in land that may be a site for a future store. Rather than invest the funds in land, the company could invest the funds in high-grade securities. If the land is acquired, the opportunity cost will be the investment income that could have been realized if the securities had been purchased instead.

Example 3

Steve is employed with a company that pays him a salary of £20,000 per year. He is thinking about leaving the company and going to university. Since going to university would require that he give up his £20,000 salary, the forgone salary would be an opportunity cost of seeking further education.

Opportunity cost is not usually entered in the accounting records of an organization, but it is a cost that must be explicitly considered in every decision a manager makes. Virtually every alternative has some opportunity cost attached to it. In example 3 above, for instance, if Steve decides to stay at his job, there still is an opportunity cost involved: it is the greater income that could be realized in future years as a result of returning to university.

Sunk cost

A **sunk cost** is a cost *that has already been incurred* and that cannot be changed by any decision made now or in the future. Since sunk costs cannot be changed by any decision, they are not differential costs. Therefore, they can and should be ignored when making a decision.

To illustrate a sunk cost, assume that a company paid £50,000 several years ago for a special-purpose machine. The machine was used to make a product that is now obsolete and is no longer being sold. Even though in hindsight the purchase of the machine may have been unwise, no amount of regret can undo that decision. And it would be folly to continue making the obsolete product in a misguided attempt to 'recover' the original cost of the machine. In short, the £50,000 originally paid for the machine has already been incurred and cannot be a differential cost in any future decisions. For this reason, such costs are said to be sunk and should be ignored in decisions.

Summary

- In this chapter, we have looked at some of the ways in which managers classify costs. How the costs will be used – for preparing external reports, predicting cost behaviour, assigning costs to cost objects, or decision making – will dictate how the costs will be classified.
- For purposes of valuing stocks and determining expenses for the balance sheet and profit and loss account, costs are classified as either product costs or period costs. Product costs are assigned to stocks and are considered assets until the products are sold. At the point of sale, product costs become cost of goods sold on the profit and loss account. In contrast, following the usual accrual practices, period costs are taken directly to the profit and loss account as expenses in the period in which they are incurred.
- In a merchandising company, product cost is whatever the company paid for its merchandise. For external financial reports in a manufacturing company, product costs consist of all manufacturing costs. In both kinds of companies, selling and administrative costs are considered to be period costs and are expensed as incurred.
- For purposes of predicting cost behaviour – how costs will react to changes in activity – managers commonly classify costs into two categories – variable and fixed. Variable costs, in total, are strictly proportional to activity. Thus, the variable cost per unit is constant. Fixed costs, in total, remain at the same level for changes in activity that occur within the relevant range. Thus, the average fixed cost per unit decreases as the number of units increases.
- For purposes of assigning costs to cost objects such as products or departments, costs are classified as direct or indirect. Direct costs can conveniently be traced to the cost objects. Indirect costs cannot conveniently be traced to cost objects.
- For purposes of making decisions, the concepts of differential costs and revenue, opportunity cost and sunk cost are of vital importance. Differential cost and revenue are the cost and revenue items that differ between alternatives. Opportunity cost is the benefit that is forgone when one alternative is selected over another. Sunk cost is a cost that occurred in the past and cannot be altered. Differential cost and opportunity cost should be considered carefully in decisions. Sunk cost is always irrelevant in decisions and should be ignored.
- These various cost classifications are *different* ways of looking at costs. A particular cost, such as the cost of cheese in a cheese burger, could be a manufacturing cost, a product cost, a variable cost, a direct cost, and a differential cost – all at the same time.
- Looking ahead to Chapters 3 to 9, we will take a more detailed look at the different aspects of cost introduced in this chapter. In Chapter 11, when we introduce the concept of standard cost, we will show how costs may be used for organizational control purposes.

Key terms for review

Administrative costs (p. 24).

Common cost (p. 36).

Conversion cost (p. 23).

Cost behaviour (p. 32).

Cost object (p. 35).

Cost of goods manufactured (p. 28).

Differential cost (p. 36).

Differential revenue (p. 36).

Direct cost (p. 35).

Direct labour (p. 22).

Direct materials (p. 22).

Finished goods (p. 26).

Fixed cost (p. 34).
Incremental cost (p. 36).
Indirect cost (p. 36).
Indirect labour (p. 23).
Indirect materials (p. 23).
Manufacturing overhead (p. 22).
Marketing or selling costs (p. 23).
Opportunity cost (p. 37).
Period costs (p. 24).
Prime cost (p. 23).
Product costs (p. 24).
Raw materials (p. 23).
Relevant range (p. 35).
Schedule of cost of goods manufactured (p. 28).
Stock-related costs (p. 30).
Sunk cost (p. 37).
Variable cost (p. 33).
Work in progress (p. 26).

Further reading

For an interesting perspective on the historical development of cost and management accounting, refer to Johnson (1987) and Johnson and Kaplan (1987).

Most accounting systems have major shortcomings when it comes to providing management with high-quality information. For one of the early and still one of the best overviews of the limitations of accounting systems in today's competitive environment, see Kaplan (1984); see also Böer and Jeter (1993).

Review problems

Many new cost terms have been introduced in this chapter. It will take you some time to learn what each term means and how properly to classify costs in an organization. To assist in this learning process, consider the following examples:

Review problem 1: cost terms

Porter Company manufactures furniture, including tables. Selected costs associated with the manufacture of the tables and the general operation of the company are given below:

1 The tables are made of wood that cost £100 per table
2 The tables are assembled by workers, at a wage cost of £40 per table
3 Workers assembling the tables are supervised by a factory supervisor who is paid £25,000 per year
4 Electrical costs are £2 per machine-hour. Four machine-hours are required to produce a table
5 The depreciation cost of the machines used to make the tables totals £10,000 per year
6 The salary of the managing director of Porter Company is £100,000 per year
7 Porter Company spends £250,000 per year to advertise its products
8 Salespersons are paid a commission of £30 for each table sold
9 Instead of producing the tables, Porter Company could rent its factory space out at a rental income of £50,000 per year

In the following tabulation, these costs are classified according to various cost terms used in the chapter. *Carefully study the classification of each cost.* If you do not understand why a particular cost is classified the way it is, reread the section of the chapter discussing the particular cost term. The terms *variable cost* and *fixed cost* refer to how costs behave with respect to the number of tables produced in a year.

Solution to review problem 1: cost terms

				Product cost			To units of product			
	Variable cost	**Fixed cost**	**Period (selling and administrative) cost**	**Direct materials**	**Direct labour**	**Manufacturing overhead**	**Direct**	**Indirect**	**Sunk cost**	**Opportunity cost**
1. Wood used in a table (£100 per table)	X			X			X			
2. Labour cost to assemble a table (£40 per table)	X				X		X			
3. Salary of the factory supervisor (£25,000 per year)		X				X		X		
4. Cost of electricity to produce tables (£2 per machine-hour)	X					X		X		
5. Depreciation of machines used to produce tables (£10,000 per year)		X				X		X	X*	
6. Salary of the managing director (£100,000 per year)		X	X							
7. Advertising expense (£250,000 per year)		X	X							
8. Commissions paid to salespersons (£30 per table sold)	X		X							
9. Rental income forgone on factory space										X†

*This is a sunk cost, since the outlay for the equipment was made in a previous period.

†This is an opportunity cost, since it represents the potential benefit that is lost or sacrificed as a result of using the factory space to produce tables. Opportunity cost is a special category of cost that is not ordinarily recorded in an organization's accounting books. To avoid possible confusion with other costs, we will not attempt to classify this cost in any other way except as an opportunity cost.

Review problem 2: schedule of cost of goods manufactured and profit and loss account

The following information has been taken from the accounting records of Klear-Seal Company for last year:

Selling expenses	£140,000
Raw materials stock, 1 January	90,000
Raw materials stock, 31 December	60,000
Utilities, factory	36,000
Direct labour cost	150,000
Depreciation, factory	162,000
Purchases of raw materials	750,000
Sales	2,500,000
Insurance, factory	40,000
Supplies, factory	15,000
Administrative expenses	270,000
Indirect labour	300,000
Maintenance, factory	87,000
Work in progress stock, 1 January	180,000
Work in progress stock, 31 December	100,000
Finished goods stock, 1 January	260,000
Finished goods stock, 31 December	210,000

Management wants to organize these data into a better format so that financial statements can be prepared for the year.

Required

1 Prepare a schedule of cost of goods manufactured as in Exhibit 2.4.

2 Compute the cost of goods sold.

3 Using data as needed from 1 and 2 above, prepare a profit and loss account.

Solution to review problem 2: schedule of cost of goods manufactured and profit and loss account

1

Klear-Seal Company
Schedule of cost of goods manufactured
For the year ended 31 December

Direct materials:		
Raw materials stock, 1 January	£90,000	
Add: Purchases of raw materials	750,000	
Raw materials available for use	840,000	
Deduct: Raw materials stock, 31 December	60,000	
Raw materials used in production		£780,000
Direct labour		150,000
Manufacturing overhead:		
Utilities, factory	36,000	
Depreciation, factory	162,000	
Insurance, factory	40,000	
Supplies, factory	15,000	
Indirect labour	300,000	
Maintenance, factory	87,000	
Total overhead costs		640,000
Total manufacturing costs		1,570,000
Add: Work in progress stock, 1 January		180,000
		1,750,000
Deduct: Work in progress stock, 31 December		100,000
Cost of goods manufactured		£1,650,000

2 The cost of goods sold would be computed as follows:

Finished goods stock,1 January	£260,000
Add: Cost of goods manufactured	1,650,000
Goods available for sale	1,910,000
Deduct: Finished goods stock, 31 December	210,000
Cost of goods sold	£1,700,000

3

Klear-Seal Company
Profit and loss account
For the year ended 31 December

Sales		£2,500,000
Less cost of goods sold (above)		1,700,000
Gross margin		800,000
Less selling and administrative expenses:		
Selling expenses	£140,000	
Administrative expenses	270,000	
Total expenses		410,000
Profit		£390,000

Questions

2–1 What are the three major elements of product costs in a manufacturing company?

2–2 Distinguish between the following: (a) direct materials, (b) indirect materials, (c) direct labour, (d) indirect labour, and (e) manufacturing overhead.

2–3 Explain the difference between a product cost and a period cost.

2–4 Describe how the profit and loss account of a manufacturing company differs from the profit and loss account of a merchandising company.

2–5 Of what value is the schedule of cost of goods manufactured? How does it tie into the profit and loss account?

2–6 Describe how the stock accounts of a manufacturing company differ from the stock account of a merchandising company.

2–7 Why are product costs sometimes called stock-related costs? Describe the flow of such costs in a manufacturing company from the point of incurrence until they finally become expenses on the profit and loss account.

2–8 Is it possible for costs such as salaries or depreciation to end up as assets on the balance sheet? Explain.

2–9 What is meant by the term 'cost behaviour'?

2–10 'A variable cost is a cost that varies per unit of product, whereas a fixed cost is constant per unit of product.' Do you agree? Explain.

2–11 How do fixed costs create difficulties in costing units of product?

2–12 Why is manufacturing overhead considered an indirect cost of a unit of product?

2–13 Define the following terms: differential cost, opportunity cost, and sunk cost.

2–14 Only variable costs can be differential costs. Do you agree? Explain.

Exercises

E2–1 Time allowed: 15 minutes

The following are a number of cost terms introduced in the chapter:

Variable cost	Product cost
Fixed cost	Sunk cost
Prime cost	Conversion cost
Opportunity cost	Period cost

Choose the term or terms above that most appropriately describe the cost identified in each of the following situations. A cost term can be used more than once.

1 Lake Company produces a bag that is very popular with college students. The cloth going into the manufacture of the bag would be called direct materials and classified as a _______ cost. In terms of cost behaviour, the cloth could also be described as a _______ cost.

2 The direct labour cost required to produce the bags, combined with the manufacturing overhead cost involved, would be known as _______ cost.

3 The company could have taken the funds that it has invested in production equipment and invested them in interest-bearing securities instead. The interest forgone on the securities would be called _______ cost.

4 Taken together, the direct materials cost and the direct labour cost required to produce bags would be called _______ cost.

5 The company used to produce a smaller bag that was not very popular. Some three hundred of these smaller bags are stored in one of the company's warehouses. The amount invested in these bags would be called a _______ cost.

6 The bags are sold through agents who are paid a commission on each bag sold. These commissions would be classified by Lake Company as a _______ cost. In terms of cost behaviour, commissions would be classified as a _______ cost.

7 Depreciation on the equipment used to produce the bags would be classified by Lake Company as a _______ cost. However, depreciation on any equipment used by the company in selling and administrative activities would be classified as _______ cost. In terms of cost behaviour, depreciation would probably be classified as a _______ cost.

8 A _______ cost is also known as a stock-related cost, since such costs go into the Work in Progress stock account and then into the Finished Goods stock account before appearing on the profit and loss account as part of cost of goods sold.

9 The salary of Lake Company's managing director would be classified as a _______ cost, since the salary will appear on the profit and loss account as an expense in the time period in which it is incurred.

10 Costs can often be classified in several ways. For example, Lake Company pays £5,000 rent each month on its factory building. The rent would be part of manufacturing overhead. In terms of cost behaviour, it would be classified as a _______ cost. The rent can also be classified as a _______ cost and as part of _______ cost.

E2–2 Time allowed: 10 minutes

A product cost is also known as a stock-related cost. Classify the following costs as either product (stock-related) costs or period (non-stock-related) costs in a manufacturing company:

1 Depreciation on salespersons' cars

2 Rent on equipment used in the factory

3 Lubricants used for maintenance of machines

4 Salaries of finished goods warehouse personnel

5 Soap and paper towels used by factory workers at the end of a shift

6 Factory supervisors' salaries

7 Heat, water and power consumed in the factory

8 Materials used in boxing units of finished product for shipment overseas (units are not normally boxed)

9 Advertising outlays

10 Workers' compensation insurance on factory employees

11 Depreciation on chairs and tables in the factory lunchroom

12 The salary of the switchboard operator for the company

13 Depreciation on a Lear Jet used by the company's executives

14 Rent on rooms at a West Country resort for holding of the annual sales conference

15 Attractively designed box for packaging breakfast cereal.

E2–3 Time allowed: 15 minutes

The Devon Motor Company produces cars. During April, the company purchased 8,000 batteries at a cost of £10 per battery. Devon withdrew 7,600 batteries from the storeroom during the month. Of these, 100 were used to replace batteries in cars being used by the company's travelling sales staff. The remaining 7,500 batteries withdrawn from the storeroom were placed in cars being produced by the company. Of the cars in production during April, 90% were completed and transferred from work in progress to finished goods. Of the cars completed during the month, 30% were unsold on 30 April.

There were no stocks of any type on 1 April.

Required

1 Determine the cost of batteries that would appear in each of the following accounts on 30 April:

(a) Raw Materials

(b) Work in Progress

(c) Finished Goods

(d) Cost of Goods Sold

(e) Selling Expense.

2 Specify whether each of the above accounts would appear on the balance sheet or on the profit and loss account at 30 April.

E2–4 Time allowed: 10 minutes

Below are a number of costs that are incurred in a variety of organizations:

1 X-ray film used in the radiology lab at Queens Medical Centre in Nottingham

2 The costs of advertising a Madonna rock concert in London

3 Depreciation on the Planet Hollywood restaurant building in Hong Kong

4 The electrical costs of running a roller coaster at Blackpool

5 Property taxes on a local cinema

6 Commissions paid to salespersons at McGraw-Hill

7 Property insurance on a Coca-Cola bottling plant

8 The costs of synthetic materials used to make Nike running shoes

9 The costs of shipping Panasonic televisions to retail shops

10 The cost of leasing an ultra-scan diagnostic machine at St Thomas's hospital in London.

Required

Classify each cost as being variable or fixed with respect to the number of units of product or services sold by the organization. Set out your answers as follows.

Cost Item	Cost behaviour	
	Variable	Fixed

Place an X in the appropriate column for each cost to indicate whether the cost involved would be variable or fixed with respect to the number of units of products or services sold by the organization.

E2–5 Time allowed: 20 minutes
The following cost and stock data are taken from the accounting records of Mason Company for the year just completed:

Costs incurred:		
Direct labour cost		£70,000
Purchases of raw materials		118,000
Indirect labour		30,000
Maintenance, factory equipment		6,000
Advertising expense		90,000
Insurance, factory equipment		800
Sales salaries		50,000
Rent, factory facilities		20,000
Supplies		4,200
Depreciation, office equipment		3,000
Depreciation, factory equipment		19,000

	Beginning of the Year	End of the Year
Stocks:		
Raw materials	£7,000	£15,000
Work in progress	10,000	5,000
Finished goods	20,000	35,000

Required

1 Prepare a schedule of cost of goods manufactured in good form

2 Prepare the cost of goods sold section of Mason Company's profit and loss account for the year.

E2–6 Time allowed: 15 minutes
Below are listed various costs that are found in organizations:

1 Hamburger buns in a McDonald's outlet
2 Advertising by a dental office
3 Apples processed and canned by Del Monte Corporation
4 Shipping canned apples from a Del Monte plant to customers

5 Insurance on a Bausch & Lomb factory producing contact lenses
6 Insurance on IBM's corporate headquarters
7 Salary of a supervisor overseeing production of circuit boards at Hewlett-Packard
8 Commissions paid to *Encyclopedia Britannica* salespersons
9 Depreciation of factory lunchroom facilities at an ICI plant
10 Steering wheels installed in BMWs.

Required

Classify each cost as being either variable or fixed with respect to the number of units sold. Also classify each cost as either a selling and administrative cost or a product cost. Prepare your answer sheet as shown below.

Cost item	Cost behaviour		Selling and administrative cost	Product cost
	Variable	Fixed cost		

Place an X in the appropriate columns to show the proper classification of each cost.

Problems

PROBLEMS

P2–7 Cost identification Time allowed: 30 minutes

Wollongong Group Ltd of New South Wales, Australia, acquired its factory building about ten years ago. For several years the company has rented out a small annex attached to the rear of the building. The company has received a rental income of £30,000 per year on this space. The renter's lease will expire soon and, rather than renewing the lease, the company has decided to use the space itself to manufacture a new product.

Direct materials cost for the new product will total £80 per unit. To have a place to sell finished units of product, the company will rent a small warehouse nearby. The rental cost will be £500 per month. In addition, the company must rent equipment for use in producing the new product; the rental cost will be £4,000 per month. Workers will be hired to manufacture the new product, with direct labour cost amounting to £60 per unit. The space in the annex will continue to be depreciated on a straight-line basis, as in prior years. This depreciation is £8,000 per year.

Advertising costs for the new product will total £50,000 per year. A supervisor will be hired to oversee production; her salary will be £1,500 per month. Electricity for operating machines will be £1.20 per unit. Costs of shipping the new product to customers will be £9 per unit.

To provide funds to purchase materials, meet payrolls and so forth, the company will have to liquidate some temporary investments. These investments are presently yielding a return of about £3,000 per year.

Required

Prepare an answer sheet with the following column headings:

Name of the cost	Variable cost	Fixed cost	Product cost			Period (selling and administrative) cost	Opportunity cost	Sunk cost
			Direct materials	Direct labour	Manufacturing overhead			

List the different costs associated with the new product decision down the extreme left column (under Name of the cost). Then place an X under each heading that helps to describe the type of cost involved. There may be Xs under several column headings for a single cost (for example, a cost may be a fixed cost, a period cost and a sunk cost; you would place an X under each of these column headings opposite the cost).

P2–8 Supply missing production and cost data Time allowed: 30 minutes

Supply the missing data in the following cases. Each case is independent of the others.

	Case			
	1	2	3	4
Direct materials	£4,500	£6,000	£5,000	£3,000
Direct labour	?	3,000	7,000	4,000
Manufacturing overhead	5,000	4,000	?	9,000
Total manufacturing costs	18,500	?	£20,000	?
Beginning work in progress stock	2,500	?	3,000	?
Ending work in progress stock	?	1,000	4,000	3,000
Cost of goods manufactured	£18,000	£14,000	£?	£?
Sales	£30,000	£21,000	£36,000	£40,000
Beginning finished goods stock	1,000	2,500	?	2,000
Cost of goods manufactured	?	?	?	17,500
Goods available for sale	?	?	?	?
Ending finished goods stock	?	1,500	4,000	3,500
Cost of goods sold	17,000	?	18,500	?
Gross margin	13,000	?	17,500	?
Operating expenses	?	3,500	?	?
Profit	£4,000	£ ?	£5,000	£9,000

P2–9 Cost classification Time allowed: 20 minutes

Various costs associated with the operation of a factory are given below:

1 Electricity used in operating machines

2 Rent on a factory building
3 Cloth used in drapery production
4 Production superintendent's salary
5 Cost of labourers assembling a product
6 Depreciation of air purification equipment used in furniture production
7 Caretaker salaries
8 Peaches used in canning fruit
9 Lubricants needed for machines
10 Sugar used in soft-drink production
11 Property taxes on the factory
12 Cost of workers painting a product
13 Depreciation on cafeteria equipment
14 Insurance on a building used in producing TV sets
15 Picture tubes used in TV sets.

Required

Classify each cost as being either variable or fixed with respect to the number of units produced and sold. Also indicate whether each cost would typically be treated as a direct cost or an indirect cost with respect to units of product. Prepare your answer sheet as shown below:

	Cost behaviour		To units of product	
Cost Item	**Variable**	**Fixed**	**Direct**	**Indirect**
Example: Factory insurance		X		X

P2–10 Cost identification Time allowed: 40 minutes

The Dorilane Company specializes in producing a set of wooden patio furniture consisting of a table and four chairs. The set enjoys great popularity, and the company has ample orders to keep production going at its full capacity of 2,000 sets per year. Annual cost data at full capacity follow:

To units of product	Product cost
Factory labour, direct	£118,000
Advertising	50,000
Factory supervision	40,000
Property taxes, factory building	3,500
Sales commissions	80,000
Insurance, factory	2,500
Depreciation, office equipment	4,000
Lease cost, factory equipment	12,000
Indirect materials, factory	6,000
Depreciation, factory building	10,000
General office supplies (billing)	3,000
General office salaries	60,000
Direct materials used (wood, bolts, etc.)	94,000
Utilities, factory	20,000

Required

1 Prepare an answer sheet with the column headings shown below. Enter each cost item on your answer sheet, placing the pound amount under the appropriate headings. As examples, this has been done already for the first two items in the list above. Note that each cost item is classified in two ways: first, as variable or fixed, with respect to the number of units produced and sold; and second, as a selling and administrative cost or a product cost. (If the item is a product cost, it should be classified as being either direct or indirect as shown.)

	Cost behaviour		Selling or administrative cost	Product cost	
Cost item	**Variable**	**Fixed**		**Direct**	**Indirect***
Factory labour, direct	£118,000			£118,000	
Advertising		£50,000	£50,000		

* To units of product.

2 Total the pound amounts in each of the columns in 1 above. Compute the cost to produce one patio set.

3 Assume that production drops to only 1,000 sets annually. Would you expect the cost per set to increase, decrease, or remain unchanged? Explain. No computations are necessary.

4 Refer to the original data. The managing director's brother-in-law has considered making himself a patio set and has priced the necessary materials at a building supply shop. The brother-in-law has asked the managing director if he could purchase a patio set from the Dorilane Company 'at cost', and the managing director agreed to let him do so.

(a) Would you expect any disagreement between the two men over the price the brother-in-law should pay? Explain. What price does the managing director probably have in mind? The brother-in-law?

(b) Since the company is operating at full capacity, what cost term used in the chapter might be justification for the managing director to charge the full, regular price to the brother-in-law and still be selling 'at cost'?

P2–11 Cost classification Time allowed: 25 minutes

Listed below are a number of costs typically found in organizations.

1 Property taxes, factory
2 Boxes used for packaging detergent
3 Salespersons' commissions
4 Supervisor's salary, factory
5 Depreciation, executive cars
6 Workers assembling computers
7 Packing supplies for shipments
8 Insurance, finished goods warehouses
9 Lubricants for machines
10 Advertising costs
11 'Chips' used in producing calculators
12 Shipping costs on merchandise sold
13 Magazine subscriptions, factory lunchroom

14 Thread in a garment factory
15 Billing costs
16 Executive life insurance
17 Ink used in textbook production
18 Fringe benefits, assembly-line workers
19 Yarn used in sweater production
20 Receptionist, executive offices.

Required

Prepare an answer sheet with column headings as shown below. For each cost item, indicate whether it would be variable or fixed with respect to the number of units produced and sold; and then whether it would be a selling cost, an administrative cost, or a manufacturing cost. If it is a manufacturing cost, indicate whether it would typically be treated as a direct cost or an indirect cost with respect to units of product. Three sample answers are provided for illustration.

				Manufacturing (product) cost	
Cost Item	**Variable or fixed**	**Selling cost**	**Administrative cost**	**Direct**	**Indirect**
Direct labour	V			X	
Executive salaries	F		X		
Factory rent	F				X

P2–12 Cost identification Time allowed: 20 minutes

Tracy Beckham began dabbling in pottery several years ago as a hobby. Her work is quite creative, and it has been so popular with friends and others that she has decided to quit her job with an aerospace firm and manufacture pottery full time. The salary from Tracy's aerospace job is £2,500 per month.

Tracy will rent a small building near her home to use as a place for manufacturing the pottery. The rent will be £500 per month. She estimates that the cost of clay and glaze will be £2 for each finished piece of pottery. She will hire workers to produce the pottery at a labour rate of £8 per pot. To sell her pots, Tracy feels that she must advertise heavily in the local area. An advertising agency states that it will handle all advertising for a fee of £600 per month. Tracy's brother will sell the pots; he will be paid a commission of £4 for each pot sold. Equipment needed to manufacture the pots will be rented at a cost of £300 per month.

Tracy has already paid some start-up fees associated with her business. These fees amounted to £500. A small room has been located in a tourist area that Tracy will use as a sales office. The rent will be £250 per month. A phone installed in the room for taking orders will cost £40 per month. In addition, a recording device will be attached to the phone for taking after-hours messages.

Tracy has some money in savings that is earning interest of £1,200 per year. These savings will be withdrawn and used to get the business going. For the time being, Tracy does not intend to draw any salary from the new company.

Required

1 Prepare an answer sheet with the following column headings:

Name of the cost	Variable cost	Fixed cost	Product cost: Direct materials	Direct labour	Manufacturing overhead	Period (selling and administrative) cost	Opportunity cost	Sunk cost

List the different costs associated with the new company down the extreme left column (under Name of cost). Then place an X under each heading that helps to describe the type of cost involved. There may be Xs under several column headings for a single cost. (That is, a cost may be a fixed cost, a period cost, and a sunk cost; you would place an X under each of these column headings opposite the cost.)

Under the Variable cost column, list only those costs that would be variable with respect to the number of units of pottery that are produced and sold.

2 All the costs you have listed above, except one, would be differential costs between the alternatives of Tracy producing pottery or staying with the aerospace firm. Which cost is not differential? Explain.

P2–13 Schedule of cost of goods manufactured; cost behaviour Time allowed: 50 minutes
Various cost and sales data for Meriwell Company for the just completed year follow:

Finished goods stock, beginning	£20,000
Finished goods stock, ending	40,000
Depreciation, factory	27,000
Administrative expenses	110,000
Utilities, factory	8,000
Maintenance, factory	40,000
Supplies, factory	11,000
Insurance, factory	4,000
Purchases of raw materials	125,000
Raw materials stock, beginning	9,000
Raw materials stock, ending	6,000
Direct labour	70,000
Indirect labour	15,000
Work in progress stock, beginning	17,000
Work in progress stock, ending	30,000
Sales	500,000
Selling expenses	80,000

Required

1 Prepare a schedule of cost of goods manufactured.

2 Prepare a profit and loss account.

3 Assume that the company produced the equivalent of 10,000 units of product during the year just completed. What was the unit cost for direct materials? What was the unit cost for factory depreciation?

4 Assume that the company expects to produce 15,000 units of product during the coming year. What per unit cost and what total cost would you expect the company to incur for direct materials at this level of activity? For factory depreciation? (In preparing your answer, assume that direct materials is a variable cost and that depreciation is a fixed cost; also assume that depreciation is computed on a straight-line basis.)

5 As the manager responsible for production costs, explain to the managing director any difference in unit costs between Questions 3 and 4 above.

P2–14 Preparing manufacturing statements Time allowed: 50 minutes
Swift Company was organized on 1 March of the current year. After five months of start-up losses, management had expected to earn a profit during August, the most recent month. Management was disappointed, however, when the profit and loss account for August also showed a loss. August's profit and loss account follows.

Swift Company
Profit and loss account
For the month ended 31 August

Sales		£450,000
Less operating expenses:		
Indirect labour cost	£12,000	
Utilities	15,000	
Direct labour cost	70,000	
Depreciation, factory equipment	21,000	
Raw materials purchased	165,000	
Depreciation, sales equipment	18,000	
Insurance	4,000	
Rent on facilities	50,000	
Selling and administrative salaries	32,000	
Advertising	75,000	462,000
Net loss		£(12,000)

After seeing the £12,000 loss for August, Swift's managing director stated, 'I was sure we'd be profitable within six months, but our six months are up and this loss for August is even worse than July's. I think it's time to start looking for someone to buy out the company's assets – if we don't, within a few months there won't be any assets to sell. By the way, I don't see any reason to look for a new manager. We'll just limp along with Sam for the time being.'

The company's management accountant resigned a month ago. Sam, a new assistant in the management accounting office, prepared the profit and loss account above. Sam has had little experience in manufacturing operations. Additional information about the company is as follows:

(a) Some 60% of the utilities cost and 75% of the insurance apply to factory operations. The remaining amounts apply to selling and administrative activities.

(b) Stock balances at the beginning and end of August were:

	1 August	31 August
Raw materials	£8,000	£13,000
Work in progress	16,000	21,000
Finished goods	40,000	60,000

(c) Only 80% of the rent on facilities applies to factory operations; the remainder applies to selling and administrative activities.

The managing director has asked you to check over the profit and loss account and make a recommendation as to whether the company should look for a buyer for its assets.

Required

1 As one step in gathering data for a recommendation to the managing director, prepare a schedule of cost of goods manufactured in good form for August.

2 As a second step, prepare a new profit and loss account for August.

3 Based on your statements prepared in Questions 1 and 2 above, would you recommend that the company look for a buyer?

P2–15 Schedule of cost of goods manufactured; cost behaviour Time allowed: 40 minutes
Selected account balances for the year ended 31 December are provided below for Superior Company:

Selling and administrative salaries	£110,000
Insurance, factory	8,000
Utilities, factory	45,000
Purchases of raw materials	290,000
Indirect labour	60,000
Direct labour	?
Advertising expense	80,000
Cleaning supplies, factory	7,000
Sales commissions	50,000
Rent, factory building	120,000
Maintenance, factory	30,000

Stock balances at the beginning and end of the year were as follows:

	Beginning of the year	End of the year
Raw materials	£40,000	£10,000
Work in progress	?	35,000
Finished goods	50,000	?

The total manufacturing costs for the year were £683,000; the goods available for sale totalled £740,000; and the cost of goods sold totalled £660,000.

Required

1 Prepare a schedule of cost of goods manufactured in good form and the cost of goods sold section of the company's profit and loss account for the year.

2 Assume that the pound amounts given above are for the equivalent of 40,000 units produced during the year. Compute the unit cost for direct materials used and the unit cost for rent on the factory building.

3 Assume that in the following year the company expects to produce 50,000 units. What per unit and total cost would you expect to be incurred for direct materials? For rent on the factory building? (In preparing your answer, you may assume that direct materials is a variable cost and that rent is a fixed cost.)

4 As the manager in charge of production costs, explain to the managing director the reason for any difference in unit costs between Question 2 and Question 3 above.

P2–16 Classification of salary cost Time allowed: 15 minutes

You have just been hired by Ogden Company to fill a new position that was created in response to rapid growth in sales. It is your responsibility to co-ordinate shipments of finished goods from the factory to distribution warehouses located in various parts of the country so that goods will be available as orders are received from customers.

The company is unsure how to classify your annual salary in its cost records. The company's cost analyst says that your salary should be classified as a manufacturing (product) cost; the controller says that it should be classified as a selling expense; and the managing director says that it does not matter which way your salary cost is classified.

Required

1 Which viewpoint is correct? Why?

2 From the point of view of the reported net income for the year, is the managing director correct in his statement that it does not matter which way your salary cost is classified? Explain.

P2–17 Ethics and the manager Time allowed: 25 minutes

M.K. Gallant is managing director of Kranbrack Corporation, a company whose shares are traded on a national exchange. In a meeting with investment analysts at the beginning of the year, Gallant had predicted that the company's earnings would grow by 20% this year. Unfortunately, sales have been less than expected, and Gallant concluded within two weeks of the end of the fiscal year that it would be impossible ultimately to report an increase in earnings as large as predicted unless some drastic action was taken. Accordingly, Gallant has ordered that wherever possible, expenditures should be postponed to the new year – including cancelling or postponing orders with suppliers, delaying planned maintenance and training, and cutting back on end-of-year advertising and travel. Additionally, Gallant ordered the company's management accountant carefully to scrutinize all costs that are currently classified as period costs and reclassify as many as possible as product costs. The company is expected to have substantial stocks of work in progress and finished goods at the end of the year.

Required

1 Why would reclassifying period costs as product costs increase this period's reported earnings?

2 Do you believe Gallant's actions are ethical? Why or why not?

P2–18 Cost behaviour; manufacturing statement; unit costs Time allowed: 40 minutes

Visic Company, a manufacturing firm, produces a single product. The following information has been taken from the company's production, sales, and cost records for the just completed year.

Production in units	29,000
Sales in units	?
Ending finished goods stock in units	?
Sales in pounds	£1,300,000
Costs:	
Advertising	105,000
Entertainment and travel	40,000
Direct labour	90,000
Indirect labour	85,000
Raw materials purchased	480,000
Building rent (production uses 80% of the space administrative and sales offices use the rest)	40,000
Utilities, factory	108,000
Royalty paid for use of production patent, £1.50 per unit produced	?
Maintenance, factory	9,000
Rent for special production equipment, per year	£7,000
plus £0.30 per unit produced	?
Selling and administrative salaries	210,000
Other factory overhead costs	6,800
Other selling and administrative expenses	17,000

	Beginning of year	End of year
Stocks:		
Raw materials	£20,000	£30,000
Work in progress	50,000	40,000
Finished goods	0	?

The finished goods stock is being carried at the average unit production cost for the year. The selling price of the product is £50 per unit.

Required

1 Prepare a schedule of goods manufactured for the year.

2 Compute the following:

(a) The number of units in the finished goods stock at the end of the year

(b) The cost of the units in the finished goods stock at the end of the year.

3 Prepare a profit and loss account for the year.

Cases

C2–19 Missing data; statements; stock computation Time allowed: 50 minutes

'I was sure that when our battery hit the market it would be an instant success,' said Roger Strong, founder and managing director of Solar Technology Ltd. 'But just look at the gusher of red ink for the first quarter. It's obvious that we're better scientists than we are businesspeople.' The data to which Roger was referring is as follows:

Solar Technology Ltd
Profit and loss account
For the quarter ended 31 March

Sales (32,000 batteries)		£960,000
Less operating expenses:		
Selling and administrative salaries	£110,000	
Advertising	90,000	
Maintenance, production	43,000	
Indirect labour cost	120,000	
Cleaning supplies, production	7,000	
Purchases of raw materials	360,000	
Rental cost, facilities	75,000	
Insurance, production	8,000	
Depreciation, office equipment	27,000	
Utilities	80,000	
Depreciation, production equipment	100,000	
Direct labour cost	70,000	
Travel, sales persons	40,000	
Total operating expenses		1,130,000
Net loss		£(170,000)

'At this rate we'll be out of business within a year,' said Annika Smith, the company's accountant. 'But I've double-checked these figures, so I know they're right.' Solar Technology was organized at the beginning of the current year to produce and market a revolutionary new solar battery. The company's accounting system was set up by Margie Wallace, an experienced accountant who recently left the company to do independent consulting work. The statement above was prepared by Smith, her assistant.

'We may not last a year if the insurance company doesn't pay the £226,000 it owes us for the 8,000 batteries lost in the warehouse fire last week,' said Roger. 'The loss adjuster says our claim is inflated, but he's just trying to pressure us into a lower figure. We have the data to back up our claim, and it will stand up in any court.'

On 3 April, just after the end of the first quarter, the company's finished goods storage area was swept by fire and all 8,000 unsold batteries were destroyed. (These batteries were part of the 40,000 units completed during the first quarter.) The company's insurance policy states that the company will be reimbursed for the 'cost' of any finished batteries destroyed or stolen. Smith has determined this cost as follows:

$$\frac{\text{Total costs for the quarter, £1,130,000}}{\text{Batteries produced during the quarter, 40,000}} = \text{£28.25 per unit}$$

8,000 batteries × £28.25 – £226,000

The following additional information is available on the company's activities during the quarter ended 31 March:

	Beginning of the quarter	End of the quarter
Raw materials	0	£10,000
Work in progress	0	50,000
Finished goods	0	?

(a) Stocks at the beginning and end of the quarter were as follows:

(b) Of the rental cost, 80% are for facilities and 90% of the utilities cost relate to manufacturing operations. The remaining amounts relate to selling and administrative activities.

Required

1 What conceptual errors, if any, were made in preparing the profit and loss account above?

2 Prepare a schedule of cost of goods manufactured for the first quarter.

3 Prepare a corrected profit and loss account for the first quarter. Your statement should show in detail how the cost of goods sold is computed.

4 Do you agree that the insurance company owes Solar Technology £226,000? Explain your answer.

C2–20 Stock computations from incomplete data Time allowed: 60 minutes

Hector Wastrel, a careless employee, left some combustible materials near an open flame in Salter Company's plant. The resulting explosion and fire destroyed the entire plant and administrative offices. Justin Quick, the company's controller, and Constance Trueheart, the operations manager, were able to save only a few bits of information as they escaped from the roaring blaze. Once they had reached safety, they began to assess the damage.

'What a disaster,' cried Justin. 'And the worst part is that we have no records to use in filing an insurance claim.'

'I know,' replied Constance. 'I was in the plant when the explosion occurred, and I managed to grab this brief summary sheet that contains information on one or two of our costs. It says that our direct labour cost this year has totalled £180,000 and that we have purchased £290,000 in raw materials. But I'm afraid that doesn't help much; the rest of our records are just ashes.'

'Well, not completely,' said Justin. 'I was working on the year-to-date profit and loss account when the explosion knocked me out of my chair. I instinctively held onto the page I was working on, and from what I can make out our sales to date this year have totalled £1,200,000 and our gross margin rate has been 40% of sales. Also, I can see that our goods available for sale to customers has totalled £810,000 at cost.'

'Maybe we're not so badly off after all,' exclaimed Constance. 'My sheet says that prime cost has totalled £410,000 so far this year and that manufacturing overhead is 70% of conversion cost. Now if we just had some information on our beginning stocks.'

'Hey, look at this,' cried Justin. 'It's a copy of last year's annual report, and it shows what our stocks were when this year started. Let's see, raw materials was £18,000, work in progress was £65,000, and finished goods was £45,000. 'Super,' yelled Constance. 'I think we can make this work.'

To file an insurance claim, the company must determine the amount of cost in its stocks as of the date of the fire. You may assume that all materials used in production during the year were direct materials.

Required

Determine the amount of cost in the Raw Materials, Work in Progress, and Finished Goods stock accounts as of the date of the fire. (*Hint*: One way to proceed would be to reconstruct the various schedules and statements that would have been affected by the company's stock accounts during the period.)

Endnotes

1 *Financial Management*, September 2003, p. 4.

2 In many countries, such as the US, 'stock' is known as 'inventory'. With globalization of capital markets and accounting, terms such as *stock* and *inventory* are increasingly used interchangeably. Other examples of interchangeable terms are *profit* (UK) = *net income* (US), *debtors* (UK) = *accounts receivable* (US) and *creditors* (UK) = *accounts payable* (US), *work in progress* (UK) = *work in process* (US).

3 Fitzgerald, Johnston, Brignall, Silvestro and Voss (1991).

4 Brignall, Fitzgerald, Johnston and Silvestro (1991, p. 228).

5 See Soin, Seal and Cullen (2002).

Chapter 3
Systems design: job-order costing

Learning objectives

After studying Chapter 3, you should be able to:

1. Distinguish between process costing and job-order costing
2. Identify the documents used in a job-order costing system
3. Compute predetermined overhead rates
4. Prepare journal entries to record costs in a job-order costing system
5. Apply overhead cost to Work in Progress using a predetermined overhead rate
6. Prepare T-accounts to show the flow of costs in a job-order costing system
7. Compute underapplied or overapplied overhead cost and prepare the journal entry to close the balance in Manufacturing Overhead to the appropriate accounts
8. Explain the implications of basing the predetermined overhead rate on activity at capacity rather than on estimated activity for the period
9. (Appendix 3A) Analyse the allocation of service department costs

Concepts in Context

'Net profit participation' contracts in which writers, actors and directors share in the net profits of films are common in Hollywood. For example, Winston Groom, the author of the novel *Forrest Gump,* has a contract with Paramount Pictures Corp. that calls for him to receive 3% of the net profits on the film. However, Paramount claims that *Forrest Gump* has yet to show any profits even though it has the third highest gross receipts of any film in history. How can this be?

Film studios assess a variety of overhead charges including a charge of about 15% on production costs for production overhead, a charge of about 30% of gross rentals for distribution overhead, and a charge for marketing overhead that amounts to about 10% of advertising costs. After all of these overhead charges and other hotly contested accounting practices, it is a rare film that shows a profit.

Fewer than 5% of released films show a profit for net profit participation purposes. Examples of 'money-losing' films include *Rain Man, Batman,* and *Who Framed Roger Rabbit?* as well as *Forrest Gump.* Disgruntled writers[1] and actors are increasingly suing studios, claiming unreasonable accounting practices that are designed to cheat them of their share of profits.[2]

As discussed in Chapter 2, product costing is the process of assigning costs to the products and services provided by a company. An understanding of this costing process is vital to managers, since the way in which a product or service is costed can have a substantial impact on reported profit, as well as on key management decisions.

We should keep in mind that the essential purpose of any managerial costing system should be to provide cost data to help managers plan, control, direct and make decisions. Nevertheless, external financial reporting and tax reporting requirements often heavily influence how costs are accumulated and summarized on managerial reports. This is true of product costing.

In this chapter and in Chapter 4, we use an *absorption costing* approach to determine product costs. This was also the method that was used in Chapter 2. In **absorption costing**, all manufacturing costs, fixed and variable, are assigned to units of product – units are said to *fully absorb manufacturing costs.* The absorption costing approach is also known as the **full cost** approach. Later on in the book, we look at product costing from a different point of view called *variable costing,* which is often advocated as an alternative to absorption costing.

In one form or another, most countries require absorption costing for both external financial reporting and for tax reporting. In addition, the vast majority of companies throughout the world also use absorption costing for management accounting purposes. Since absorption costing is the most common approach to product costing, we discuss it first and then deal with alternatives in subsequent chapters.

Process and job-order costing

In computing the cost of a product or a service, managers are faced with a difficult problem. Many costs (such as rent) do not change much from month to month, whereas production may change frequently, with production going up in one month and then down in another. In addition to variations in the level of production, several different products or services may be produced in a given period in the same facility.

Under these conditions, how is it possible to determine accurately the cost of a product or service? In practice, assigning costs to products and services involves an averaging of some type across time periods and across products. The way in which this averaging is carried out will depend heavily on the type of production process involved. Two costing systems are commonly used in manufacturing and in many service companies; these two systems are known as *process costing* and *job-order costing.*

Process costing

A **process costing system** is used in situations where the company produces many units of a single product (such as frozen orange juice concentrate) for long periods at a time. Other examples include producing paper, refining aluminium ingots, mixing and bottling beverages, and producing industrial chemicals. All of these industries are characterized by an essentially homogeneous product that flows evenly through the production process on a continuous basis.

The basic approach in process costing is to accumulate costs in a particular operation or department for an entire period (month, quarter, year) and then to divide this total by the number of units produced during the period. The basic formula for process costing is as follows:

$$\text{Unit cost (per litre, kilo, bottle)} = \frac{\text{total manufacturing cost}}{\text{Total units produced (litres, kilos, bottles)}}$$

Since one unit of product (litre, kilo, bottle) is indistinguishable from any other unit of product, each unit is assigned the same average cost as any other unit produced during the period. This costing technique results in a broad, average unit cost figure that applies to homogeneous units flowing in a continuous stream out of the production process.

Job-order costing

A **job-order costing system** is used in situations where many *different* products are produced each period. For example, a Levi Strauss clothing factory would typically make many different types of denim jackets for both men and women during a month. A particular order might consist of 1,000 men's denim jackets, style number A312, medium size. This order of 1,000 jackets is called a *batch* or a *job*. In a job-order costing system, costs are traced and allocated to jobs and then the costs of the job are divided by the number of units in the job to arrive at an average cost per unit.

Other examples of situations where job-order costing would be used include large-scale construction projects, commercial aircraft, greeting cards and airline meals. All of these examples are characterized by diverse outputs. Each construction project is unique and different from every other – the company may be constructing simultaneously a dam in Zaire and a bridge in Indonesia. Likewise, each airline orders a different type of meal from its catering supplier.

Job-order costing is also used extensively in service industries. Hospitals, law firms, TV studios, accounting firms, advertising agencies and repair shops, for example, all use a variation of job-order costing to accumulate costs for accounting and billing purposes. Although the detailed example of job-order costing provided in the following section deals with a manufacturing firm, the same basic concepts and procedures are used by many service organizations.

The record-keeping and cost assignment problems are more complex when a company sells many different products and services than when it has only a single product. Since the products are different, the costs are typically different. Consequently, cost records must be maintained for each distinct product or job. For example, a lawyer in a large criminal law practice would ordinarily keep separate records of the costs of advising and defending each of her clients. And the Levi Strauss factory mentioned above would keep separate track of the costs of filling orders for particular styles, sizes and colours of jeans. Thus, a job-order costing system requires more effort than a process-costing system.

In this chapter, we focus on the design of a job-order costing system. In the following chapter, we focus on process costing and also look more closely at the similarities and differences between the two costing methods.

Job-order costing – an overview

To introduce job-order costing, we will follow a specific job as it progresses through the manufacturing process. This job consists of two experimental couplings that Yost Precision Machining has agreed to produce for Loops Unlimited, a manufacturer of roller coasters. The couplings connect the cars on the roller coaster and are a critical component in the performance and safety of the ride. Before we begin our discussion, recall from Chapter 2 that companies generally classify manufacturing costs into three broad categories: (1) direct materials, (2) direct labour, and (3) manufacturing overhead. As we study the operation of a job-order costing system, we will see how each of these three types of costs is recorded and accumulated.

Management accounting in action: the issue

Yost Precision Machining is a small company in Birmingham that specializes in fabricating precision metal parts that are used in a variety of applications ranging from deep-sea exploration vehicles to the inertial triggers in car air bags. The company's top managers gather every day at 8:00 a.m. in the company's conference room for the daily planning meeting. Attending the meeting this morning are: Jean Yost, the company's managing director; David Fowler, the marketing manager; Debbie Turner, the production manager; and Marcus White, the company finance director. The managing director opened the meeting:

Jean: The production schedule indicates we'll be starting job 2B47 today. Isn't that the special order for experimental couplings, David?

David: That's right, Jean. That's the order from Loops Unlimited for two couplings for their new roller coaster ride for Magic Mountain.

Debbie: Why only two couplings? Don't they need a coupling for every car?

David: That's right. But this is a completely new roller coaster. The cars will go faster and will be subjected to more twists, turns, drops and loops than on any other existing roller coaster. To hold up under these stresses, Loops Unlimited's engineers had to redesign the cars and couplings completely. They want to test the design thoroughly before proceeding to large-scale production. So they want us to make just two of these new couplings for testing purposes. If the design works, then we'll have the inside track on the order to supply couplings for the whole ride.

Jean: We agreed to take on this initial order at our cost just to get our foot in the door. Marcus, will there be any problem documenting our cost so we can get paid?

Marcus: No problem. The contract with Loops stipulates that they will pay us an amount equal to our cost of goods sold. With our job-order costing system, I can tell you that number on the day the job is completed.

Jean: Good. Is there anything else we should discuss about this job at this time? No? Well then let's move on to the next item of business.

Measuring direct materials cost

Yost Precision Machining will require two M46 Housings and four G7 Connectors to make the two experimental couplings for Loops Unlimited. If this were a standard product, there would be a bill of materials for the product. A **bill of materials** is a document that lists the type and quantity of each item of materials needed to complete a unit of product. In this case, there is no established bill of materials, so Yost's production staff determined the materials requirements from the blueprints submitted by the customer. Each coupling requires two connectors and one housing, so to make two couplings, four connectors and two housings are required.

When an agreement has been reached with the customer concerning the quantities, prices and shipment date for the order, a *production order* is issued. The Production Department then prepares a *materials requisition form* similar to the form in Exhibit 3.1. The **materials requisition form** is a detailed source document that (1) specifies the type and quantity of materials to be drawn from the storeroom, and (2) identifies the job to which the costs of the materials are to be charged. It serves as a means for controlling the flow of materials into production and also for making entries in the accounting records.

The Yost Precision Machining materials requisition form in Exhibit 3.1 shows that the company's Milling Department has requisitioned two M46 Housings and four G7 Connectors for job 2B47. This completed form is presented to the storeroom, who then issue the necessary raw materials. The storeroom is not allowed to release materials without such a form, bearing an authorized signature.

Job cost sheet

After being notified that the production order has been issued, the Accounting Department prepares a *job cost sheet* similar to the one presented in Exhibit 3.2. A **job cost sheet** is a form prepared for each separate job that records the materials, labour and overhead costs charged to the job.

3.1 EXHIBIT

Materials Requisition Number 14873 Date March 2
Job Number to be Charged 2B47
Department Milling

Description	Quantity	Unit Cost	Total Cost
M46 Housing	2	£124	£248
G7 Connector	4	103	412
			£660

Authorized Signature *Bill White*

Exhibit 3.1 Materials requisition form

After direct materials are issued, the Accounting Department records their costs directly on the job cost sheet. Note from Exhibit 3.2, for example, that the £660 cost for direct materials shown earlier on the materials requisition form has been charged to job 2B47 on its job cost sheet. The requisition number 14873 is also recorded on the job cost sheet to make it easier to identify the source document for the direct materials charge.

In addition to serving as a means for charging costs to jobs, the job cost sheet also serves as a key part of a firm's accounting records. The job cost sheets form a subsidiary ledger to the Work in Progress account. They are detailed records for the jobs in process that add up to the balance in Work in Progress.

Measuring direct labour cost

Direct labour cost is handled in much the same way as direct materials cost. Direct labour consists of labour charges that are easily traced to a particular job. Labour charges that cannot easily be traced directly to any job are treated as part of manufacturing overhead. As discussed in Chapter 2, this latter category of labour costs is termed *indirect labour* and includes tasks such as maintenance, supervision and clean up.

Workers use *time tickets* to record the time they spend on each job and task. A completed **time ticket** is an hour-by-hour summary of the employee's activities throughout the day. An example of an employee time ticket is shown in Exhibit 3.3.

When working on a specific job, the employee enters the job number on the time ticket and notes the amount of time spent on that job. When not assigned to a particular job, the employee records the nature of the indirect labour task (such as clean up and maintenance) and the amount of time spent on the task.

At the end of the day, the time tickets are gathered and the Accounting Department enters the direct labour-hours and costs on individual job cost sheets. (See Exhibit 3.2 for an example of how direct labour costs are entered on the job cost sheet.) The daily time tickets are source documents that are used as the basis for labour cost entries into the accounting records.

JOB COST SHEET

Job Number 2B47 — Date Initiated March 2

Date Completed

Department Milling — Units Completed

Item Special order coupling

For Stock

Direct Materials		Direct Labour			Manufacturing Overhead		
Req. No.	Amount	Ticket	Hours	Amount	Hours	Rate	Amount
14873	£660	843	5	£45			

Cost Summary		Units Shipped		
		Date	Number	Balance
Direct Materials	£			
Direct Labour	£			
Manufacturing Overhead	£			
Total Cost	£			
Unit Cost	£			

Exhibit 3.2 Job cost sheet

The system we have just described is a manual method for recording and posting labour costs. Many companies now rely on computerized systems and no longer record labour time by hand on sheets of paper. One computerized approach uses bar codes to enter the basic data into the computer. Each employee and each job has a unique bar code. When an employee begins work on a job, he or she scans three bar codes using a handheld device much like the bar code readers at a supermarket check-out. The first bar code indicates that a job is being started; the second is the unique bar code on his or her identity badge; and the third is the unique bar code of the job itself. This information is fed automatically via an electronic network to a computer that notes the time and then records all of the data. When the employee completes the task, he or she scans a bar code indicating that the task is complete, the bar code on his or her identity badge, and the bar code attached to the job. This information is relayed to the computer that again notes the time, and a time ticket is automatically prepared. Since all of the source data is already in computer files, the labour costs can be automatically posted to job cost sheets (or their electronic equivalents). Computers, coupled with technology such as bar codes, can eliminate much of the drudgery involved in routine bookkeeping activities while at the same time increasing timeliness and accuracy.

3.3 EXHIBIT

Time Ticket No. 843 Date March 3

Employee Mary Holden Station 4

Started	Ended	Time Completed	Rate	Amount	Job Number
7:00	12:00	5.0	£9	£45	2B47
12:30	2.30	2.0	9	18	2B50
2:30	3:30	1.0	9	9	Maintenance
Totals		8.0		£72	

Supervisor *Bill White*

Exhibit 3.3 Employee time ticket

3 LEARNING OBJECTIVE

Application of manufacturing overhead

Manufacturing overhead must be included with direct materials and direct labour on the job cost sheet since manufacturing overhead is also a product cost. However, assigning manufacturing overhead to units of product can be a difficult task. There are three reasons for this.

1 Manufacturing overhead is an indirect cost. This means that it is either impossible or difficult to trace these costs to a particular product or job.

2 Manufacturing overhead consists of many different items ranging from the grease used in machines to the annual salary of the production manager.

3 Even though output may fluctuate due to seasonal or other factors, manufacturing overhead costs tend to remain relatively constant due to the presence of fixed costs.

Given these problems, about the only way to assign overhead costs to products is to use an allocation process. This allocation of overhead costs is accomplished by selecting an *allocation base* that is common to all of the company's products and services. An **allocation base** is a measure such as direct labour-hours (DLH) or machine-hours (MH) that is used to assign overhead costs to products and services.

The most widely used allocation bases are direct labour-hours and direct labour cost, with machine-hours and even units of product (where a company has only a single product) also used to some extent.

The allocation base is used to compute the **predetermined overhead rate** in the following formula:

$$\text{Predetermined overhead rate} = \frac{\text{Estimated total manufacturing overhead cost}}{\text{Estimated total units in the allocation base}}$$

Note that the predetermined overhead rate is based on *estimated* rather than actual figures. This is because the *predetermined* overhead rate is computed *before* the period begins and is used to apply overhead cost to jobs throughout the period. The process of assigning overhead cost to jobs is called **overhead application**. The formula for determining the amount of overhead cost to apply to a particular job is:

Overhead applied to a particular job = Predetermined overhead rate × Amount of allocation base incurred by the job

So, for example, if the predetermined overhead rate is £8 per direct labour-hour, then £8 of overhead cost is *applied* to a job for each direct labour-hour incurred by the job. When the allocation base is direct labour-hours, the formula becomes:

Overhead applied to a particular job = Predetermined overhead rate × Actual direct labour-hours charged to the job

Using the predetermined overhead rate

To illustrate the steps involved in computing and using a predetermined overhead rate, let's return to Yost Precision Machining. The company has estimated its total manufacturing overhead costs to be £320,000 for the year and its total direct labour-hours to be 40,000. Its predetermined overhead rate for the year would be £8 per direct labour-hour, as shown below:

$$\text{Predetermined overhead rate} = \frac{\text{Estimated total manufacturing overhead cost}}{\text{Estimated total units in the allocation base}}$$

$$\frac{\pounds 320{,}000}{40{,}000 \text{ direct labour-hours}} = \pounds 8 \text{ per direct labour-hour}$$

The job cost sheet in Exhibit 3.4 indicates that 27 direct labour-hours were charged to job 2B47. Therefore, a total of £216 of overhead cost would be applied to the job:

Overhead applied to job 2B47 = Predetermined overhead rate × Actual direct labour-hours charged to job 2B47

£8/DLH × 27 direct labour-hours = £216 of overhead applied to job 2B47

This amount of overhead has been entered on the job-cost sheet in Exhibit 3.4. Note that this is *not* the actual amount of overhead caused by the job. There is no attempt to trace actual overhead costs to jobs – if that could be done, the costs would be direct costs, not overhead. The overhead assigned to the job is simply a share of the total overhead that was estimated at the beginning of the year. When a company applies overhead cost to jobs as we have done – that is, by multiplying actual activity by the predetermined overhead rate – it is called a **normal cost system**.

The overhead may be applied as direct labour-hours are charged to jobs, or all of the overhead can be applied at once when the job is completed. The choice is up to the company. If a job is not completed at year-end, however, overhead should be applied to value the work in progress stock.

The need for a predetermined rate

Instead of using a predetermined rate, a company could wait until the end of the accounting period to compute an actual overhead rate based on the *actual* total manufacturing costs and the *actual* total units in the allocation base for the period. However, managers cite several reasons for using predetermined overhead rates instead of actual overhead rates:

1. Before the end of the accounting period, managers would like to know the accounting system's valuation of completed jobs. Suppose, for example, that Yost Precision Machining waits until the end of the year to compute its overhead rate. Then there would be no way for managers to know the cost of goods sold for job 2B47 until the close of the year, even though the job was completed and shipped to the customer in March. The seriousness of this problem can be reduced to some extent by computing the actual overhead more frequently, but that immediately leads to another problem as discussed below.
2. If actual overhead rates are computed frequently, seasonal factors in overhead costs or in the allocation base can produce fluctuations in the overhead rates. Managers generally feel that such fluctuations in overhead rates serve no useful purpose and are misleading.
3. The use of a predetermined overhead rate simplifies record keeping. To determine the overhead cost to apply to a job, the accounting staff at Yost Precision Machining simply multiplies the direct labour-hours recorded for the job by the predetermined overhead rate of £8 per direct labour-hour.

JOB COST SHEET

Job Number 2B47 | Date Initiated March 2

Date Completed

Department Milling | Units Completed 2

Item *Special order coupling*

For Stock

Direct Materials		Direct Labour			Manufacturing Overhead		
Req. No.	Amount	Ticket	Hours	Amount	Hours	Rate	Amount
14873	£ 660	843	5	£ 45	27	£8/DLH	£216
14875	506	846	8	60			
14912	238	850	4	21			
	£1,404	851	10	54			
			27	£180			

Cost Summary		Units Shipped		
		Date	Number	Balance
Direct Materials	£1,404	March 8	—	2
Direct Labour	£ 180			
Manufacturing Overhead	£ 216			
Total Cost	£1,800			
Unit Cost	£ 900*			

*£1,800 ÷ 2 units = £900 per unit.

Exhibit 3.4 A completed job cost sheet

For these reasons, most companies use predetermined overhead rates rather than actual overhead rates in their cost accounting systems.

Choice of an allocation base for overhead cost

An allocation base should be used that is a *cost driver* of overhead cost. A **cost driver** is a factor, such as machine-hours, beds occupied, computer time, or flight-hours, that causes overhead costs. If a base is used to compute overhead rates that does not 'drive' overhead costs, then the result will be inaccurate overhead rates and distorted product costs. For example, if direct labour-hours is used to allocate overhead, but in reality overhead has little to do with direct labour-hours, then products with high direct labour-hour requirements will shoulder an unrealistic burden of overhead and will be over-costed.

Most companies use direct labour-hours or direct labour cost as the allocation base for manufacturing overhead. However, as discussed in earlier chapters, major shifts are taking place in the structure of costs in many industries. In the past, direct labour accounted for up to 60% of the cost of many products, with overhead cost making up only a portion of the remainder. This situation has been changing – for two reasons.

First, sophisticated automated equipment has taken over functions that used to be performed by direct labour workers. Since the costs of acquiring and maintaining such equipment are classified as overhead, this increases overhead while decreasing direct labour. Second, products are themselves becoming more sophisticated and complex and change more frequently. This increases the need for highly skilled indirect workers such as engineers. As a result of these two trends, direct labour is becoming less of a factor and overhead is becoming more of a factor in the cost of products in many industries.

In companies where direct labour and overhead costs have been moving in opposite directions, it would be difficult to argue that direct labour 'drives' overhead costs. Accordingly, in recent years, managers in some companies have used *activity-based costing* principles to redesign their cost accounting systems. Activity-based costing is a costing technique that is designed to reflect more accurately the demands that products, customers and other cost objects make on overhead resources. The activity-based approach is discussed in more detail in Chapter 8.

We hasten to add that although direct labour may not be an appropriate allocation basis in some industries, in others it continues to be a significant driver of manufacturing overhead.[3] The key point is that the allocation base used by the company should really drive, or cause, overhead costs, and direct labour is not always an appropriate allocation base.

Computation of unit costs

With the application of Yost Precision Machining's £216 manufacturing overhead to the job cost sheet in Exhibit 3.4, the job cost sheet is almost complete. There are two final steps. First, the totals for direct materials, direct labour and manufacturing overhead are transferred to the Cost Summary section of the job cost sheet and added together to obtain the total cost for the job. Then the total cost (£1,800) is divided by the number of units (2) to obtain the unit cost (£900). As indicated earlier, *this unit cost is an average cost and should not be interpreted as the cost that would actually be incurred if another unit were produced*. Much of the actual overhead would not change at all if another unit were produced, so the incremental cost of an additional unit is something less than the average unit cost of £900.

The completed job cost sheet is now ready to be transferred to the Finished Goods stock account, where it will serve as the basis for valuing unsold units in ending stock and determining cost of goods sold.

Summary of document flows

The sequence of events discussed above is summarized in Exhibit 3.5. A careful study of the flow of documents in this exhibit will provide a good overview of the overall operation of a job-order costing system.

Management accounting in action: the wrap-up

In the 8:00 a.m. daily planning meeting on 9 March, Jean Yost, the managing director of Yost Precision Machining, once again drew attention to job 2B47, the experimental couplings:

Jean: I see job 2B47 is completed. Let's get those couplings shipped immediately to Loops Unlimited so they can get their testing program under way. Marcus, how much are we going to bill Loops for those two units?

Marcus: Just a second, let me check the job cost sheet for that job. Here it is. We agreed to sell the experimental units at cost, so we will be charging Loops Unlimited just £900 a unit.

Jean: Fine. Let's hope the couplings work out and we make some money on the big order later.

4 LEARNING OBJECTIVE

Job-order costing – the flow of costs

We are now ready to take a more detailed look at the flow of costs through the company's formal accounting system. To illustrate, we shall consider a single month's activity for Rand Company, a producer of gold and silver commemorative medallions. Rand Company has two jobs in process during April, the first month of its fiscal year.

Job A, a special minting of 1,000 gold medallions commemorating the invention of motion pictures, was started during March and had £30,000 in manufacturing costs already accumulated on 1 April.

Job B, an order for 10,000 silver medallions commemorating the fall of the Berlin Wall, was started in April.

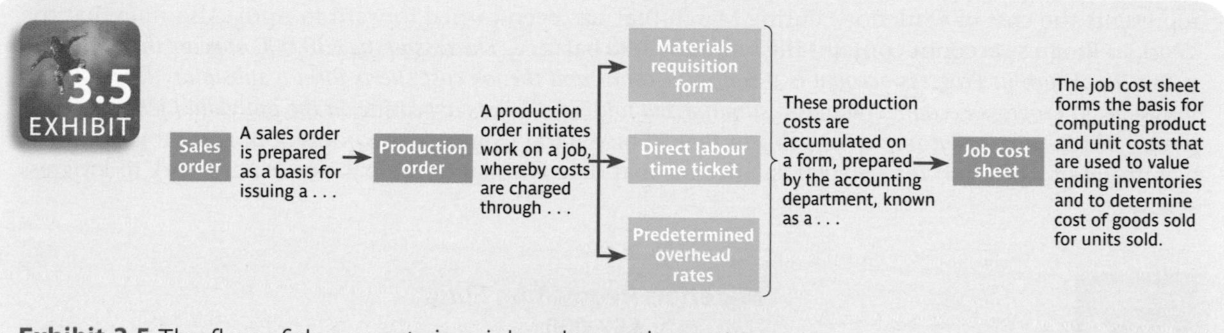

Exhibit 3.5 The flow of documents in a job-order costing system

The purchase and issue of materials

On 1 April, Rand Company had £7,000 in raw materials on hand. During the month, the company purchased an additional £60,000 in raw materials. The purchase is recorded in journal entry (1) below:

	(1)	
Raw materials	£60,000	
Creditors		£60,000

As explained in Chapter 2, Raw materials is an asset account. Thus, when raw materials are purchased, they are initially recorded as an asset – not as an expense.

Issue of direct and indirect materials

During April, £52,000 in raw materials were requisitioned from the storeroom for use in production. Entry (2) records the issue of the materials to the production departments.

	(2)	
Work in progress	£50,000	
Manufacturing overhead	2,000	
Raw materials		£52,000

The materials charged to Work in Progress represent direct materials for specific jobs. As these materials are entered into the Work in Progress account, they are also recorded on the appropriate job cost sheets. This point is illustrated in Exhibit 3.6, where £28,000 of the £50,000 in direct materials is charged to job A's cost sheet and the remaining £22,000 is charged to job B's cost sheet. (In this example, all data are presented in summary form and the job cost sheet is abbreviated.)

The £2,000 charged to Manufacturing Overhead in entry (2) represents indirect materials used in production during April. Observe that the Manufacturing Overhead account is separate from the Work in Progress account. The purpose of the Manufacturing Overhead account is to accumulate all manufacturing overhead costs as they are incurred during a period.

Before leaving Exhibit 3.6 we need to point out one additional thing. Notice from the exhibit that the job cost sheet for job A contains a beginning balance of £30,000. We stated earlier that this balance represents the cost of work done during March that has been carried forward to April. Also note that the Work in Progress account contains the same £30,000 balance. *The reason the £30,000 appears in both places is that the Work in Progress account is a control account and the job cost sheets form a subsidiary ledger. Thus, the Work in Progress account contains a summarized total of all costs appearing on the individual job cost sheets for all jobs in progress at any given point in time.* (Since Rand Company had only job A in progress at the beginning of April, job A's £30,000 balance on that date is equal to the balance in the Work in Progress account.)

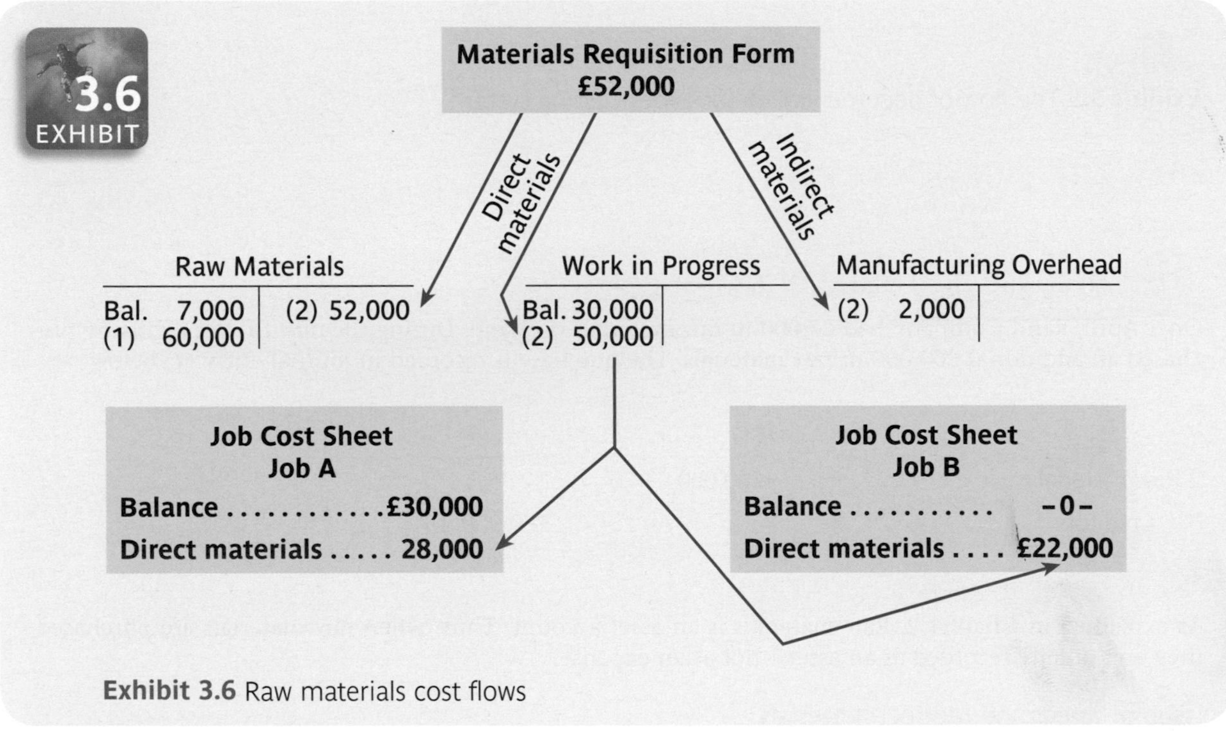

Exhibit 3.6 Raw materials cost flows

Issue of direct materials only

Sometimes the materials drawn from the Raw Materials stock account are all direct materials. In this case, the entry to record the issue of the materials into production would be as follows:

Work in progress	XXX	
Raw materials		XXX

Labour cost

As work is performed in various departments of Rand Company from day to day, employee time tickets are filled out by workers, collected and forwarded to the Accounting Department. In the Accounting

Department, the tickets are costed according to the various employee wage rates, and the resulting costs are classified as either direct or indirect labour. This costing and classification for April resulted in the following summary entry:

	(3)	
Work in progress	60,000	
Manufacturing overhead	15,000	
Salaries and wages payable		75,000

Only direct labour is added to the Work in Progress account. For Rand Company, this amounted to £60,000 for April.

At the same time that direct labour costs are added to Work in Progress, they are also added to the individual job cost sheets, as shown in Exhibit 3.7. During April, £40,000 of direct labour cost was charged to job A and the remaining £20,000 was charged to job B.

The labour costs charged to Manufacturing Overhead represent the indirect labour costs of the period, such as supervision, janitorial work and maintenance.

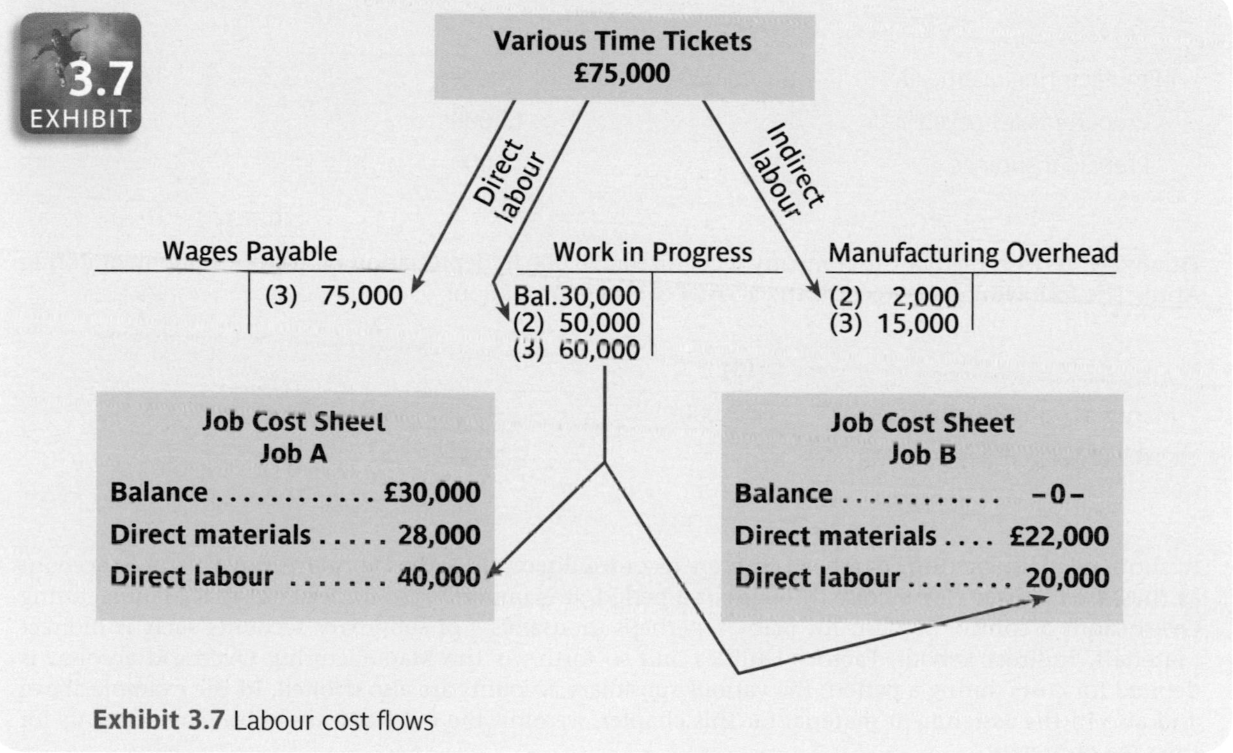

Exhibit 3.7 Labour cost flows

Manufacturing overhead costs

Recall that all costs of operating the factory other than direct materials and direct labour are classified as manufacturing overhead costs. These costs are entered directly into the Manufacturing Overhead account as they are incurred. To illustrate, assume that Rand Company incurred the following general factory costs during April:

Utilities (heat, water, and power)	£21,000
Rent on factory equipment	16,000
Miscellaneous factory costs	3,000
Total	£40,000

The following entry records the incurrence of these costs:

	(4)	
Manufacturing overhead	40,000	
Creditors		40,000

In addition, let us assume that during April, Rand Company recognized £13,000 in accrued property taxes and that £7,000 in prepaid insurance expired on factory buildings and equipment. The following entry records these items:

	(5)	
Manufacturing overhead	20,000	
Property taxes payable		13,000
Prepaid insurance		7,000

Finally, let us assume that the company recognized £18,000 in depreciation on factory equipment during April. The following entry records the accrual of this depreciation:

	(6)	
Manufacturing overhead	18,000	
Accumulated depreciation		18,000

In short, *all* manufacturing overhead costs are recorded directly into the Manufacturing Overhead account as they are incurred day by day throughout a period. It is important to understand that Manufacturing Overhead is a control account for many – perhaps thousands – of subsidiary accounts such as Indirect Materials, Indirect Labour, Factory Utilities and so forth. As the Manufacturing Overhead account is debited for costs during a period, the various subsidiary accounts are also debited. In the example above and also in the assignment material for this chapter, we omit the entries to the subsidiary accounts for the sake of brevity.

The application of manufacturing overhead

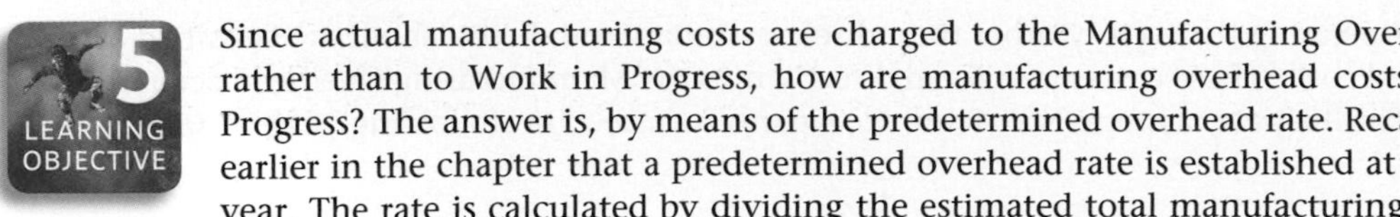

Since actual manufacturing costs are charged to the Manufacturing Overhead control account rather than to Work in Progress, how are manufacturing overhead costs assigned to Work in Progress? The answer is, by means of the predetermined overhead rate. Recall from our discussion earlier in the chapter that a predetermined overhead rate is established at the beginning of each year. The rate is calculated by dividing the estimated total manufacturing overhead cost for the year by the estimated total units in the allocation base (measured in machine-hours, direct labour-hours, or some other base). The predetermined overhead rate is then used to apply overhead costs to jobs. For example, if direct labour-hours is the allocation base, overhead cost is applied to each job by multiplying the number of direct labour-hours charged to the job by the predetermined overhead rate.

To illustrate, assume that Rand Company has used machine-hours in computing its predetermined overhead rate and that this rate is £6 per machine-hour. Also assume that during April, 10,000 machine-hours were worked on job A and 5,000 machine-hours were worked on job B (a total of 15,000 machine-hours). Thus, £90,000 in overhead cost (15,000 machine-hours × £6 = £90,000) would be applied to Work in Progress. The following entry records the application of Manufacturing Overhead to Work in Progress:

	(7)	
Work in progress	90,000	
Manufacturing overhead		90,000

The flow of costs through the Manufacturing Overhead account is shown in Exhibit 3.8.

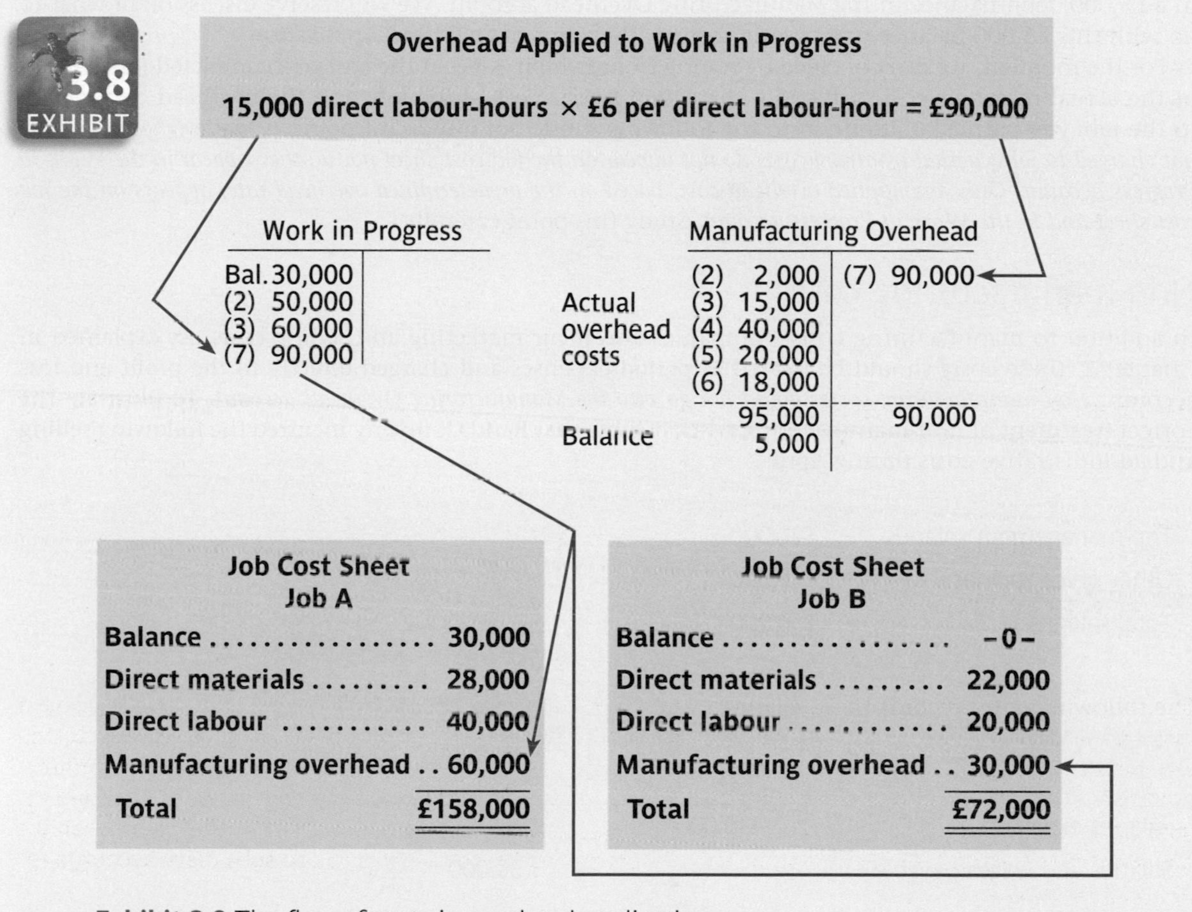

Exhibit 3.8 The flow of costs in overhead application

The 'actual overhead costs' in the Manufacturing Overhead account in Exhibit 3.8 are the costs that were added to the account in entries (2)–(6). Observe that the incurrence of these actual overhead costs entries (2)–(6) and the application of overhead to Work in Progress [entry (7)] represent two separate and entirely distinct processes.

The concept of a clearing account

The Manufacturing Overhead account operates as a clearing account. As we have noted, actual factory overhead costs are debited to the accounts as they are incurred day by day throughout the year. At certain intervals during the year, usually when a job is completed, overhead cost is released from the

Manufacturing Overhead account and is applied to the Work in Progress account by means of the predetermined overhead rate. This sequence of events is illustrated below:

Manufacturing overhead (a clearing account)	
Actual overhead costs are charged to the account as these costs are incurred day by day throughout the period →	→ Overhead is applied to Work in Progress using the predetermined overhead rate

As we emphasized earlier, the predetermined overhead rate is based entirely on estimates of what overhead costs are *expected* to be, and it is established before the year begins. As a result, the overhead cost applied during a year will almost certainly turn out to be more or less than the overhead cost that is actually incurred. For example, notice from Exhibit 3.8 that Rand Company's actual overhead costs for the period are £5,000 greater than the overhead cost that has been applied to Work in Progress, resulting in a £5,000 debit balance in the Manufacturing Overhead account. We will reserve discussion of what to do with this £5,000 balance until a later section, Problems of Overhead Application.

For the moment, we can conclude by noting from Exhibit 3.8 that the cost of a completed job consists of the actual materials cost of the job, the actual labour cost of the job, and the overhead cost *applied* to the job. Pay particular attention to the following subtle but important point: *actual overhead costs are not charged to jobs; actual overhead costs do not appear on the job cost sheet nor do they appear in the Work in Progress account. Only the applied overhead cost, based on the predetermined overhead rate, appears on the job cost sheet and in the Work in Progress account.* Study this point carefully.

Non-manufacturing costs

In addition to manufacturing costs, companies also incur marketing and selling costs. As explained in Chapter 2, these costs should be treated as period expenses and charged directly to the profit and loss account. *Non-manufacturing costs should not go into the Manufacturing Overhead account.* To illustrate the correct treatment of non-manufacturing costs, assume that Rand Company incurred the following selling and administrative costs during April:

Top-management salaries	£21,000
Other office salaries	9,000
Total salaries	£30,000

The following entry records these salaries:

	(8)	
Salaries expense	30,000	
Salaries and wages payable		30,000

Assume that depreciation on office equipment during April was £7,000. The entry is as follows:

	(9)	
Depreciation expense	7,000	
Accumulated depreciation		7,000

Pay particular attention to the difference between this entry and entry (6) where we recorded depreciation on factory equipment. In journal entry (6), depreciation on factory equipment was debited to

Manufacturing Overhead and is therefore a product cost. In journal entry (9) above, depreciation on office equipment was debited to Depreciation Expense. Depreciation on office equipment is considered to be a period expense rather than a product cost.

Finally, assume that advertising was £42,000 and that other selling and administrative expenses in April totalled £8,000. The following entry records these items:

	(10)	
Advertising expense	42,000	
Other selling and administrative expense	8,000	
Creditors		50,000

Since the amounts in entries (8) to (10) all go directly into expense accounts, they will have no effect on the costing of Rand Company's production for April. The same will be true of any other selling and administrative expenses incurred during April, including sales commissions, depreciation on sales equipment, rent on office facilities, insurance on office facilities and related costs.

Cost of goods manufactured

When a job has been completed, the finished output is transferred from the production departments to the finished goods warehouse. By this time, the accounting department will have charged the job with direct materials and direct labour cost, and manufacturing overhead will have been applied using the predetermined rate. A transfer of these costs must be made within the costing system that parallels the physical transfer of the goods to the finished goods warehouse. The costs of the completed job are transferred out of the Work in Progress account and into the Finished Goods account. The sum of all amounts transferred between these two accounts represents the cost of goods manufactured for the period. (This point was illustrated earlier in Exhibit 2.6 in Chapter 2.)

In the case of Rand Company, let us assume that job A was completed during April. The following entry transfers the cost of job A from Work in Progress to Finished Goods.

	(11)	
Finished goods	158,000	
Work in progress		158,000

The £158,000 represents the completed cost of job A, as shown on the job cost sheet in Exhibit 3.8. Since job A was the only job completed during April, the £158,000 also represents the cost of goods manufactured for the month.

Job B was not completed by the end of the month, so its cost will remain in the Work in Progress account and carry over to the next month. If a balance sheet is prepared at the end of April, the cost accumulated thus far on job B will appear as 'Work in progress stock' in the assets section.

Cost of goods sold

As units in finished goods are shipped to fill customers' orders, the unit cost appearing on the job cost sheets is used as a basis for transferring the cost of the items sold from the Finished Goods account into the Cost of Goods Sold account. If a complete job is shipped, as in the case where a job has been done to a customer's specifications, then it is a simple matter to transfer the entire cost appearing on the job cost sheet into the Cost of Goods Sold account. In most cases, however, only a portion of the units involved in a particular job will be immediately sold. In these situations, the unit cost must be used to determine how much product cost should be removed from Finished Goods and charged to Cost of Goods Sold.

For Rand Company, we will assume 750 of the 1,000 gold medallions in job A were shipped to customers by the end of the month for total sales revenue of £225,000. Since 1,000 units were produced and the total cost of the job from the job cost sheet was £158,000, the unit product cost was £158. The following journal entries would record the sale (all sales are on account):

	(12)	
Debtors	225,000	
Sales		225,000
	(13)	
Cost of goods sold	118,500	
Finished goods		118,500
(£158 per unit × 750 units = £118,500)		

With entry (13), the flow of costs through our job-order costing system is completed.

Summary of cost flows

6 LEARNING OBJECTIVE

To pull the entire Rand Company example together, journal entries (1) to (13) are summarized in Exhibit 3.9. The flow of costs through the accounts is presented in T-account form in Exhibit 3.10.

Exhibit 3.11 presents a schedule of cost of goods manufactured and a schedule of cost of goods sold for Rand Company. Note particularly from Exhibit 3.11 that the manufacturing overhead cost on the schedule of cost of goods manufactured is the overhead applied to jobs during the month – not the actual manufacturing overhead costs incurred. The reason for this can be traced back to journal entry (7) and the T-account for Work in Progress that appears in Exhibit 3.10. Under a normal costing system as illustrated in this chapter, applied – not actual – overhead costs are applied to jobs and thus to Work in Progress stock. Note also the cost of goods manufactured for the month (£158,000) agrees with the amount transferred from Work in Progress to Finished Goods for the month as recorded earlier in entry (11). Also note that this £158,000 figure is used in computing the cost of goods sold for the month.

A profit and loss account for April is presented in Exhibit 3.12. Observe that the cost of goods sold figure on this statement (£123,500) is carried down from Exhibit 3.11.

Problems of overhead application

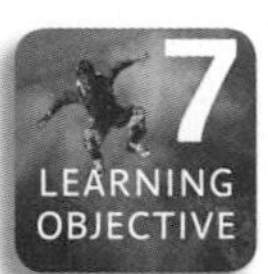

We need to consider two complications relating to overhead application. These are (1) the computation of underapplied and overapplied overhead and (2) the disposition of any balance remaining in the Manufacturing Overhead account at the end of a period.

Underapplied and overapplied overhead

Since the predetermined overhead rate is established before a period begins and is based entirely on estimated data, there generally will be a difference between the amount of overhead cost applied to Work in Progress and the amount of overhead cost actually incurred during a period. In the case of Rand Company, for example, the predetermined overhead rate of £6 per hour resulted in £90,000 of overhead cost being applied to Work in Progress, whereas actual overhead costs for April proved to be £95,000 (see Exhibit 3.8). The difference between the overhead cost applied to Work in Progress and the actual overhead costs of a period is termed either **underapplied** or **overapplied overhead**. For Rand Company, overhead was underapplied because the applied cost (£90,000) was £5,000 less than the actual cost (£95,000). If the tables had been reversed and the company had applied £95,000 in overhead cost to Work in Progress while incurring actual overhead costs of only £90,000, then the overhead would have been overapplied.

What is the cause of underapplied or overapplied overhead? The causes can be complex. Nevertheless, the basic problem is that the method of applying overhead to jobs using a predetermined overhead

	Debit	Credit
(1)		
Raw materials	60,000	
Creditors		60,000
(2)		
Work in progress	50,000	
Manufacturing overhead	2,000	
Raw materials		52,000
(3)		
Work in progress	60,000	
Manufacturing overhead	15,000	
Salaries and wages payable		75,000
(4)		
Manufacturing overhead	40,000	
Creditors		40,000
(5)		
Manufacturing overhead	20,000	
Property taxes payable		13,000
Prepaid insurance		7,000
(6)		
Manufacturing overhead	18,000	
Accumulated depreciation		18,000
(7)		
Work in progress	90,000	
Manufacturing overhead		90,000
(8)		
Salaries expense	30,000	
Salaries and wages payable		30,000
(9)		
Depreciation expense	7,000	
Accumulated depreciation		7,000
(10)		
Advertising expense	42,000	
Other selling and administrative expense	8,000	
Creditors		50,000
(11)		
Finished goods	158,000	
Work in progress		158,000
(12)		
Debtors	225,000	
Sales		225,000
(13)		
Cost of goods sold	118,500	
Finished goods		118,500

Exhibit 3.9 Summary of Rand Company journal entries

Debtors

	Debit		Credit
	XX*		
(12)	225,000		

Creditors

	Debit		Credit
			XX
		(1)	60,000
		(4)	40,000
		(10)	50,000

Capital Stock

	Debit		Credit
			XX

Prepaid Insurance

	Debit		Credit
	XX		
		(5)	7,000

Retained Earnings

	Debit		Credit
			XX

Raw Materials

	Debit		Credit
Bal.	7,000	(2)	52,000
(1)	60,000		
Bal.	15,000		

Salaries and Wages Payable

	Debit		Credit
			XX
		(3)	75,000
		(8)	30,000

Sales

	Debit		Credit
		(12)	225,000

Work in Progress

	Debit		Credit
Bal.	30,000	(11)	158,000
(2)	50,000		
(3)	60,000		
(7)	90,000		
Bal.	72,000		

Property Taxes Payable

	Debit		Credit
			XX
		(5)	13,000

Cost of Goods Sold

	Debit		Credit
(13)	118,500		

Salaries Expense

	Debit		Credit
(8)	30,000		

Finished Goods

	Debit		Credit
Bal.	10,000	(13)	118,500
(11)	158,000		
Bal.	49,500		

Depreciation Expense

	Debit		Credit
(9)	7,000		

Advertising Expense

	Debit		Credit
(10)	42,000		

Accumulated Depreciation

	Debit		Credit
			XX
		(6)	18,000
		(9)	7,000

Other Selling and Administrative Expense

	Debit		Credit
(10)	8,000		

Manufacturing Overhead

	Debit		Credit
(2)	2,000	(7)	90,000
(3)	15,000		
(4)	40,000		
(5)	20,000		
(6)	18,000		
Bal.	5,000		

Explanation of entries:

1 Raw materials purchased
2 Direct and indirect materials issued into production
3 Direct and indirect factory labour cost incurred
4 Utilities and other factory costs incurred
5 Property taxes and insurance incurred on the factory
6 Depreciation recorded on factory assets
7 Overhead cost applied to Work in Progress
8 Administrative salaries expense incurred
9 Depreciation recorded on office equipment
10 Advertising and other expense incurred
11 Cost of goods manufactured transferred into finished goods
12 Sale of job A recorded
13 Cost of goods sold recorded for job A

*XX = Normal balance in the account (for example, Debtors normally carries a debit balance)

Exhibit 3.10 Summary of cost flows – Rand Company

Cost of goods manufactured		
Direct materials		
Raw materials stock, beginning	£7,000	
Add: Purchases of raw materials	60,000	
Total raw materials available	67,000	
Deduct: Raw materials stock, ending	15,000	
Raw materials used in production	52,000	
Less indirect materials included in manufacturing overhead	2,000	£50,000
Direct labour		60,000
Manufacturing overhead applied to work in progress		90,000
Total manufacturing costs		200,000
Add: Beginning work in progress stock		30,0000
		230,000
Deduct: Ending work in progress stock		72,000
Cost of goods manufactured		£158,000
Cost of goods sold		
Finished goods stock, beginning		£10,000
Add: Cost of goods manufactured		158,000
Goods available for sale		168,000
Deduct: Finished goods stock, ending		49,500
Unadjusted cost of goods sold		118,500
Add: Underapplied overhead		5,000
Adjusted cost of goods sold		£123,500

*Note that the underapplied overhead is added to cost of goods sold. If overhead were overapplied, it would be deducted from costs of goods sold.

Exhibit 3.11 Schedules of cost of goods manufactured and cost of goods sold

rate assumes that actual overhead costs will be proportional to the actual amount of the allocation base incurred during the period. If, for example, the predetermined overhead rate is £6 per machine-hour, then it is assumed that actual overhead costs incurred will be £6 for every machine-hour that is actually worked. There are at least two reasons why this may not be true. First, much of the overhead often consists of fixed costs. Since these costs are fixed, they do not grow as the number of machine-hours incurred increases. Second, spending on overhead items may or may not be under control. If individuals who are responsible for overhead costs do a good job, those costs should be less than were expected at the beginning of the period. If they do a poor job, those costs will be more than expected. As we indicated above, however, a fuller explanation of the causes of underapplied and overapplied overhead will have to wait for later chapters.

To illustrate what can happen, suppose that two companies – Turbo Crafters and Black & Howell – have prepared the following estimated data for the coming year:

Rand Company Profit and Loss Account For the month ending 30 April		
Sales		£225,000
Less cost of goods sold (118,500 + £5,000)		123,500
Gross margin		101,500
Less selling and administrative expenses:		
Salaries expense	£30,000	
Depreciation expense	7,000	
Advertising expense	42,000	
Other expense	8,000	87,000
Profit		£14,500

Exhibit 3.12 Profit and loss account

	Company	
	Turbo Crafters	**Black & Howell**
Predetermined overhead rate based on	Machine-hours	Direct materials cost
Estimated manufacturing overhead	£300,000 (a)	£120,000 (a)
Estimated machine-hours	75,000 (b)	–
Estimated direct materials cost	–	£80,000 (b)
Predetermined overhead rate, (a)/(b)	£4 per machine-hour	150% of direct materials cost

Now assume that because of unexpected changes in overhead spending and changes in demand for the companies' products, the *actual* overhead cost and the *actual* activity recorded during the year in each company are as follows:

	Company	
	Turbo Crafters	**Black & Howell**
Actual manufacturing overhead costs	£290,000	£130,000
Actual machine-hours	68,000	–
Actual direct material costs	–	£90,000

For each company, note that the actual data for both cost and activity differ from the estimates used in computing the predetermined overhead rate. This results in underapplied and overapplied overhead as follows:

	Company	
	Turbo Crafters	**Black & Howell**
Actual manufacturing overhead costs	£290,000	£130,000
Manufacturing overhead cost applied to Work in Progress during the year:		
68,000 actual machine-hours × £4	£272,000	
£90,000 actual direct materials cost × 150%		£135,000
Underapplied (overapplied) overhead	£18,000	£(5,000)

For Turbo Crafters, notice that the amount of overhead cost that has been applied to Work in Progress (£272,000) is less than the actual overhead cost for the year (£290,000). Therefore, overhead is underapplied. Also notice that the original estimate of overhead in Turbo Crafters (£300,000) is not directly involved in this computation. Its impact is felt only through the £4 predetermined overhead rate that is used.

For Black & Howell, the amount of overhead cost that has been applied to Work in Progress (£135,000) is greater than the actual overhead cost for the year (£130,000), and so overhead is overapplied.

A summary of the concepts discussed above is presented in Exhibit 3.13.

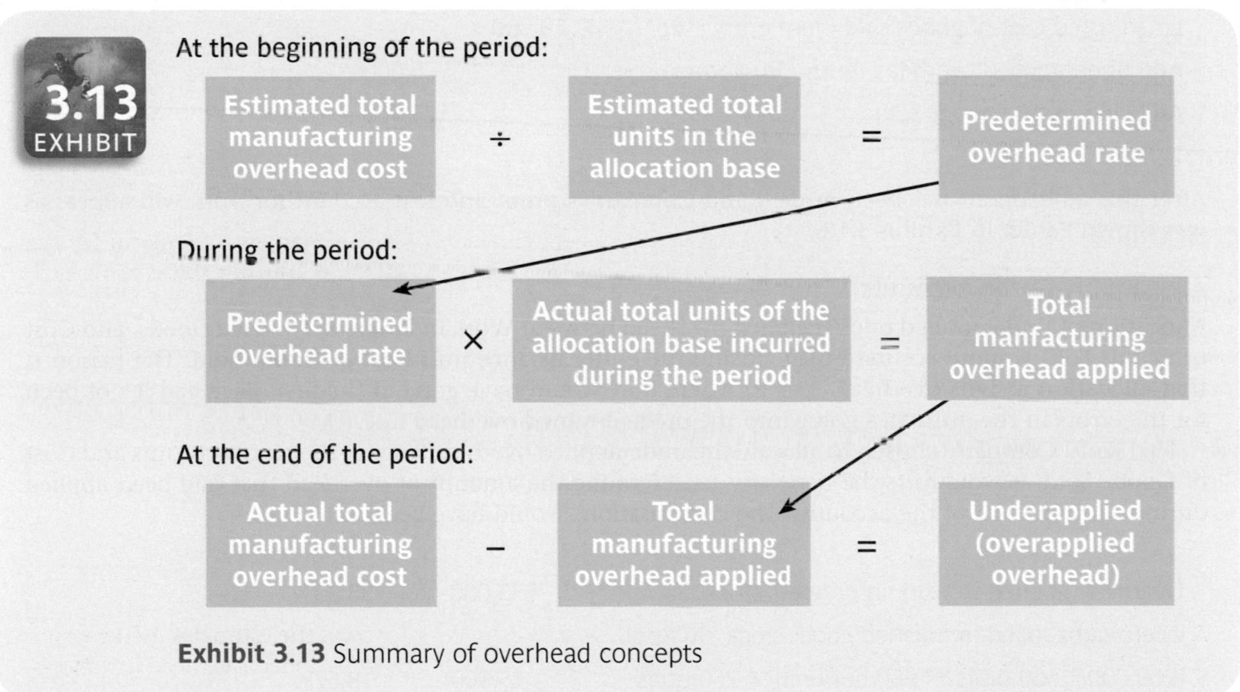

Exhibit 3.13 Summary of overhead concepts

Disposition of underapplied or overapplied overhead balances

What disposition should be made of any underapplied or overapplied balance remaining in the Manufacturing Overhead account at the end of a period? Generally, any balance in the account is treated in one of two ways:

1 Closed out to Cost of Goods Sold.

2 Allocated between Work in Progress, Finished Goods, and Cost of Goods Sold in proportion to the overhead applied during the current period in the ending balances of these accounts.

The second method, which allocates the underapplied or overapplied overhead among ending stock and Cost of Goods Sold, is equivalent to using an 'actual' overhead rate and is for that reason considered by many to be more accurate than the first method. Consequently, if the amount of underapplied or overapplied overhead is material, many accountants would insist that the second method be used. In problem assignments we will always indicate which method you are to use for disposing of underapplied or overapplied overhead.

Closed out to cost of goods sold

As mentioned above, closing out the balance in Manufacturing Overhead to Cost of Goods Sold is simpler than the allocation method. Returning to the example of the Rand Company, the entry to close the £5,000 of underapplied overhead to Cost of Goods Sold would be as follows:

	(14)	
Cost of goods sold	5,000	
Manufacturing overhead		5,000

Note that since there is a debit balance in the Manufacturing Overhead account, Manufacturing Overhead must be credited to close out the account. This has the effect of increasing Cost of Goods Sold for April to £123,500:

Unadjusted cost of goods sold (from entry (13))	£118,500	
Add underapplied overhead (entry (14) above)		5,000
Adjusted cost of goods sold		£123,500

After this adjustment has been made, Rand Company's profit and loss account for April will appear as was shown earlier in Exhibit 3.12.

Allocated between accounts

Allocation of underapplied or overapplied overhead between Work in Progress, Finished Goods, and Cost of Goods Sold is more accurate than closing the entire balance into Cost of Goods Sold. The reason is that allocation assigns overhead costs to where they would have gone in the first place had it not been for the errors in the estimates going into the predetermined overhead rate.

Had Rand Company chosen to allocate the underapplied overhead among the stock accounts and Cost of Goods Sold, it would first be necessary to determine the amount of overhead that had been applied during April in each of the accounts. The computations would have been as follows:

Overhead applied in work in progress stock, 30 April	£30,000	33.33%
Overhead applied in finished goods stock, 30 April		
(£60,000/1,000 units = £60 per unit) × 250 units	15,000	16.67%
Overhead applied in cost of goods sold, April		
(£60,000/1,000 units = £60 per unit) × 750 units	45,000	50.00%
Total overhead applied	£90,000	100.00%

Based on the above percentages, the underapplied overhead (i.e., the debit balance in Manufacturing Overhead) would be allocated as in the following journal entry:

Work in progress (33.33% × £5,000)	1,666.50	
Finished goods (16.67% × £5,000)	833.50	
Cost of goods sold (50.00% × £5,000)	2,500.00	
Manufacturing Overhead		5,000.00

Note that the first step in the allocation was to determine the amount of overhead applied in each of the accounts. For Finished Goods, for example, the total amount of overhead applied to job A, £60,000, was divided by the total number of units in job A, 1,000 units, to arrive at the average overhead applied of £60 per unit. Since there were still 250 units from job A in ending finished goods stock, the amount of overhead applied in the Finished Goods Stock account was £60 per unit multiplied by 250 units or £15,000 in total.

If overhead had been overapplied, the entry above would have been just the reverse, since a credit balance would have existed in the Manufacturing Overhead account.

A general model of product cost flows

The flow of costs in a product costing system is presented in the form of a T-account model in Exhibit 3.14. This model applies as much to a process costing system as it does to a job-order costing system. Examination of this model can be very helpful in gaining a perspective as to how costs enter a system, flow through it, and finally end up as Cost of Goods Sold on the profit and loss account.

Multiple predetermined overhead rates

Our discussion in this chapter has assumed that there is a single predetermined overhead rate for an entire factory called a **plantwide overhead rate**. This is, in fact, a common practice – particularly in smaller companies. In larger companies, multiple predetermined overhead rates are often used. In a **multiple predetermined overhead rate** system there is usually a different overhead rate for each production department. Such a system, while more complex, is considered to be more accurate, since it can reflect differences across departments in how overhead costs are incurred.

For example, overhead might be allocated based on direct labour-hours in departments that are relatively labour intensive and based on machine-hours in departments that are relatively machine intensive. When multiple predetermined overhead rates are used, overhead is applied in each department according to its own overhead rate as a job proceeds through the department.

Job-order costing in service companies

We stated earlier in the chapter that job-order costing is also used in service organizations such as law firms, film studios, hospitals and repair shops, as well as in manufacturing companies. In a law firm, for example, each client represents a 'job', and the costs of that job are accumulated day by day on a job cost sheet as the client's case is handled by the firm. Legal forms and similar inputs represent the direct materials for the job; the time expended by lawyers represents the direct labour; and the costs of secretaries, clerks, rent, depreciation, and so forth, represent the overhead. An example of a job costing approach for a legal firm is shown in Exhibit 3.15.

In a film studio each film produced by the studio is a 'job', and costs for direct materials (costumes, props, film, etc.) and direct labour (actors, directors and extras) are accounted for and charged to each film's job cost sheet. A share of the studio's overhead costs, such as utilities, depreciation of equipment, salaries of maintenance workers, and so forth, is also charged to each film. However, there is considerable controversy about the methods used by some studios to distribute overhead costs among films, and these controversies sometimes result in lawsuits.

In total, the reader should be aware that job-order costing is a versatile and widely used costing method, and may be encountered in virtually any organization where there are diverse products or services.

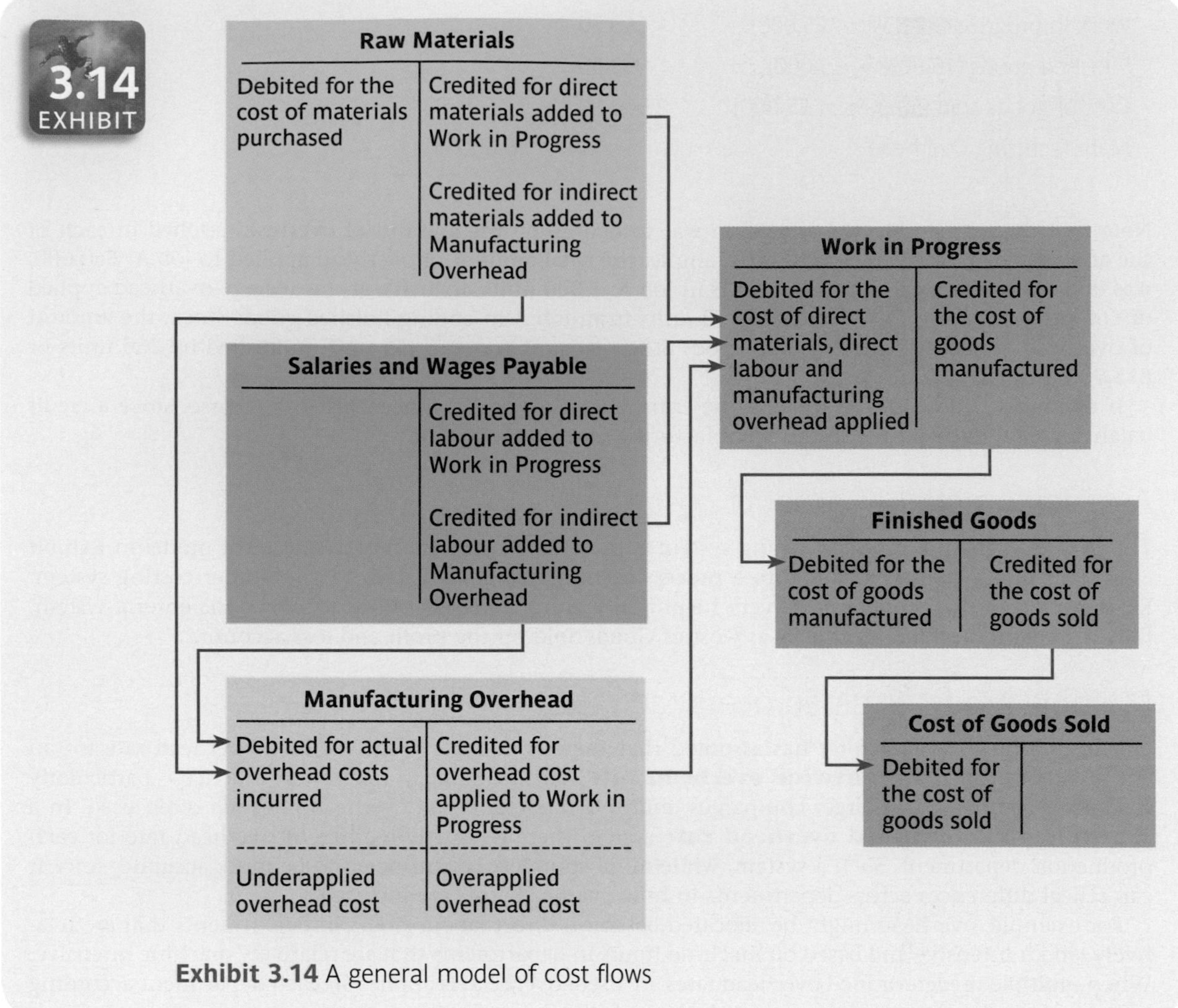

Exhibit 3.14 A general model of cost flows

The predetermined overhead rate and capacity

8 LEARNING OBJECTIVE

Companies typically base their predetermined overhead rates on the estimated, or budgeted, amount of the allocation base for the upcoming period. This is the method that is used in the chapter, but it is a practice that has recently come under severe criticism.[4] An example will be very helpful in understanding why. Prahad Corporation manufactures music CDs for local recording studios. The company has a CD duplicating machine that is capable of producing a new CD every 10 seconds from a master CD. The company leases the CD duplicating machine for £3,600,000 per year, and this is the company's only manufacturing overhead. With allowances for setups and maintenance, the machine is theoretically capable of producing up to 900,000 CDs per year. However, due to weak retail sales of CDs, the company's commercial customers are unlikely to order more than 600,000 CDs next year. The company uses machine time as the allocation base for applying manufacturing overhead. These data are summarized as follows:

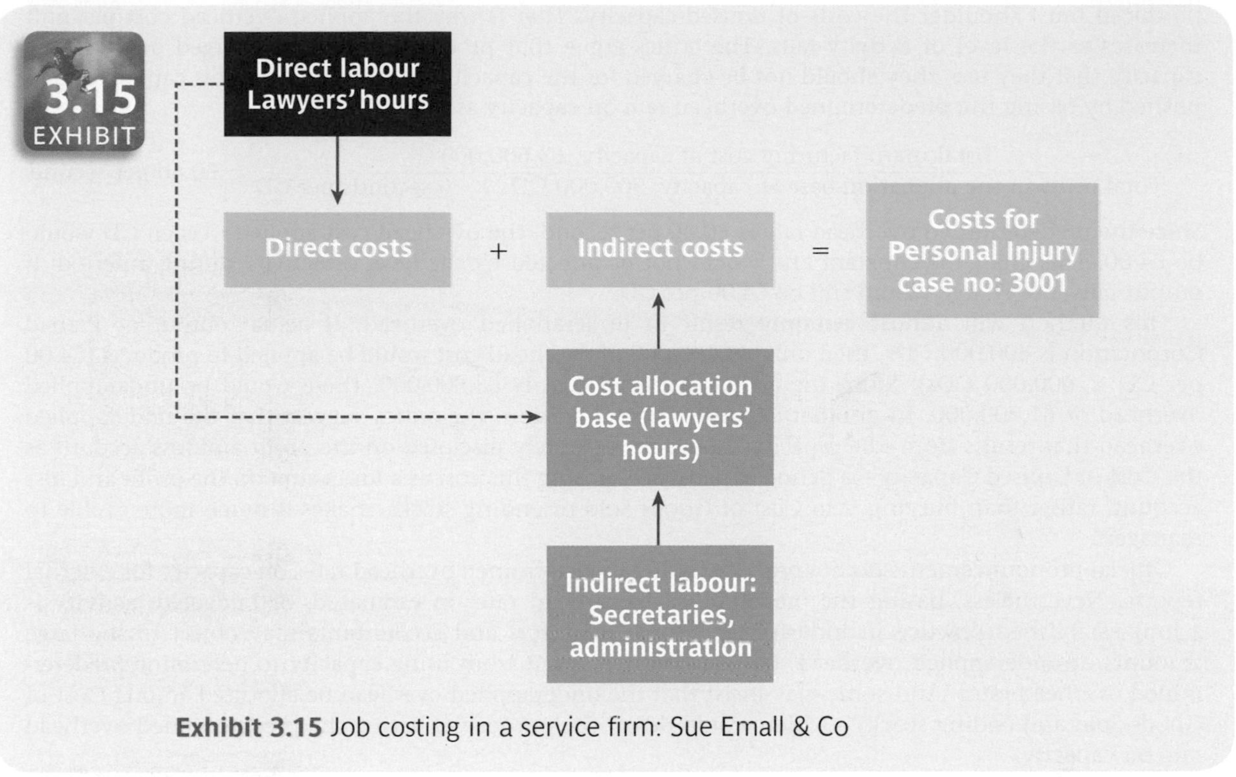

Exhibit 3.15 Job costing in a service firm: Sue Emall & Co

Prahad Corporation data	
Total manufacturing overhead cost	£3,600,000 per year
Allocation base: machine time per CD	10 seconds
Capacity	900,000 CDs per year
Budgeted output for next year	600,000 CDs

If Prahad follows common practice and computes its predetermined overhead rate using estimated, or budgeted, figures, then its predetermined overhead rate for next year would be £0.60 per second of machine time computed as follows:

$$\frac{\text{Estimated total manufacturing overhead cost, £3,600,000}}{\text{Estimated total units in the allocation base, 600,000 CDs} \times \text{10 seconds per CD}} = \text{£0.60 per second}$$

Since each CD requires 10 seconds of machine time, each CD will be charged for £6.00 of overhead cost.

Critics point out that there are two problems with this procedure. First, if predetermined overhead rates are based on budgeted activity, then the unit product costs will fluctuate depending on the budgeted level of activity for the period. For example, if the budgeted output for the year was only 450,000 CDs, the predetermined overhead rate would be £0.80 per second of machine time or £8.00 per CD rather than £6.00 per CD. In general, if budgeted output falls, the overhead cost per unit will increase; it will appear that the CDs cost more to make. Managers may then be tempted to increase prices at the worst possible time – just as demand is falling.

Second, critics point out that under the traditional approach, products are charged for resources that they do not use. When the fixed costs of capacity are spread over estimated activity, the units that are produced must shoulder the costs of unused capacity. That is why the applied overhead cost per unit increases as the level of activity falls. The critics argue that products should be charged only for the capacity that they use; they should not be charged for the capacity they do not use. This can be accomplished by basing the predetermined overhead rate on capacity as follows:

$$\frac{\text{Total manufacturing cost at capacity, £3,600,000}}{\text{Total units in the allocation base at capacity, 900,000 CDs} \times \text{10 seconds per CD}} = \text{£0.40 per second}$$

Since the predetermined overhead rate is £0.40 per second, the overhead cost applied to each CD would be £4.00. This charge is constant and would not be affected by the level of activity during a period. If output falls, the charge would still be £4.00 per CD.

This method will almost certainly result in underapplied overhead. If actual output at Prahad Corporation is 600,000 CDs, then only £2,400,000 of overhead cost would be applied to products (£4.00 per CD × 600,000 CDs). Since the actual overhead cost is £3,600,000, there would be underapplied overhead of £1,200,000. In another departure from tradition, the critics suggest that the underapplied overhead that results from idle capacity should be separately disclosed on the profit and loss account as the Cost of Unused Capacity – a period expense. Disclosing this cost as a lump sum on the profit and loss account, rather than burying it in Cost of Goods Sold or ending stocks, makes it much more visible to managers.

Official pronouncements do not prohibit basing predetermined overhead rates on capacity for external reports. Nevertheless, basing the predetermined overhead rate on estimated, or budgeted, activity is a long-established practice in industry, and some managers and accountants may object to the large amounts of underapplied overhead that would often result from using capacity to determine predetermined overhead rates. And some may insist that the underapplied overhead be allocated among Cost of Goods Sold and ending stocks – which would defeat the purpose of basing the predetermined overhead rate on capacity.

Summary

- Job-order costing and process costing are widely used to track costs. Job-order costing is used in situations where the organization offers many different products or services, such as in furniture manufacturing, hospitals, accounting and legal firms. Process costing is used where units of product are homogeneous, such as in flour milling or cement production.
- Materials requisition forms and labour time tickets are used to assign direct materials and direct labour costs to jobs in a job-costing system.
- Manufacturing overhead costs are assigned to jobs through use of a predetermined overhead rate. The predetermined overhead rate is determined before the period begins by dividing the estimated total manufacturing cost for the period by the estimated total allocation base for the period.
- The most frequently used allocation bases are direct labour-hours and machine-hours. Overhead is applied to jobs by multiplying the predetermined overhead rate by the actual amount of the allocation base used by the job.
- Since the predetermined overhead rate is based on estimates, the actual overhead cost incurred during a period may be more or less than the amount of overhead cost applied to production. Such a difference is referred to as underapplied or overapplied overhead.
- The underapplied or overapplied overhead for a period can be either (1) closed out to Cost of Goods Sold or (2) allocated between Work in Progress, Finished Goods, and Cost of Goods Sold.
- When overhead is underapplied, manufacturing overhead costs have been understated and therefore stocks and/or expenses must be adjusted upwards. When overhead is overapplied, manufacturing overhead costs have been overstated and therefore stocks and/or expenses must be adjusted downwards.

Key terms for review

Absorption costing (p. 62).

Allocation base (p. 67).

Bill of materials (p. 64).
Cost driver (p. 69).
Full cost (p. 62).
Job cost sheet (p. 64).
Job-order costing system (p. 63).
Materials requisition form (p. 64).
Multiple predetermined overhead rate (p. 85).
Normal cost system (p. 68).
Overapplied overhead (p. 78).
Overhead application (p. 67).
Plantwide overhead rate (p. 85).
Predetermined overhead rate (p. 67).
Process costing system (p. 62).
Time ticket (p. 65).
Underapplied overhead (p. 78).

Review problem: job-order costing

Hogle Company is a manufacturing firm that uses job-order costing. On 1 January, the beginning of its fiscal year, the company's stock balances were as follows:

Raw materials	£20,000
Work in progress	15,000
Finished goods	30,000

The company applies overhead cost to jobs on the basis of machine-hours worked. For the current year, the company estimated that it would work 75,000 machine-hours and incur £450,000 in manufacturing overhead cost. The following transactions were recorded for the year:

(a) Raw materials were purchased on account, £410,000.
(b) Raw materials were requisitioned for use in production, £380,000 (£360,000 direct materials and £20,000 indirect materials).
(c) The following costs were incurred for employee services: direct labour, £75,000; indirect labour, £110,000; sales commissions, £90,000; and administrative salaries, £200,000.
(d) Sales travel costs were incurred, £17,000.
(e) Utility costs were incurred in the factory, £43,000.
(f) Advertising costs were incurred, £180,000.
(g) Depreciation was recorded for the year, £350,000 (80% relates to factory operations, and 20 per cent relates to selling and administrative activities).
(h) Insurance expired during the year, £10,000 (70% relates to factory operations, and the remaining 30% relates to selling and administrative activities).
(i) Manufacturing overhead was applied to production. Due to greater than expected demand for its products, the company worked 80,000 machine-hours during the year.
(j) Goods costing £900,000 to manufacture according to their job cost sheets were completed during the year.
(k) Goods were sold on account to customers during the year at a total selling price of £1,500,000. The goods cost £870,000 to manufacture according to their job cost sheets.

Required

1 Prepare journal entries to record the preceding transactions.

2 Post the entries in (1) above to T-accounts (don't forget to enter the opening balances in the stock accounts).

3 Is Manufacturing Overhead underapplied or overapplied for the year? Prepare a journal entry to close any balance in the Manufacturing Overhead account to Cost of Goods Sold. Do not allocate the balance between ending stock and Cost of Goods Sold.

4 Prepare a profit and loss account for the year.

Solution to review problem: job-order costing

1	**(a)** Raw materials	410,000	
	Creditors		410,000
	(b) Work in progress	360,000	
	Manufacturing overhead	20,000	
	Raw materials		380,000

(c)	Work in progress	75,000	
	Manufacturing overhead	110,000	
	Sales commissions expense	90,000	
	Administrative salaries expense	200,000	
	Salaries and wages payable		475,000
(d)	Sales travel expense	17,000	
	Creditors		17,000
(e)	Manufacturing overhead	43,000	
	Creditors		43,000
(f)	Advertising expense	180,000	
	Creditors		180,000
(g)	Manufacturing overhead	280,000	
	Depreciation expense	70,000	
	Accumulated depreciation		350,000
(h)	Manufacturing overhead	7,000	
	Insurance expense	3,000	
	Prepaid insurance		10,000

(i) The predetermined overhead rate for the year would be computed as follows:

$$\frac{\text{Estimated manufacturing overhead, £450,000}}{\text{Estimated machine – hours, 75,000}} = \text{£6 per hour}$$

Based on the 80,000 machine-hours actually worked during the year, the company would have applied £480,000 in overhead cost to production: 80,000 machine-hours × £6 = £480,000.The following entry records this application of overhead cost:

	Work in progress	480,000	
	Manufacturing overhead		480,000
(j)	Finished goods	900,000	
	Work in progress		900,000
(k)	Debtors	1,500,000	
	Sales		1,500,000
	Cost of goods sold	870,000	
	Finished goods		870,000

2

Debtors

(k) 1,500,000	

Manufacturing overhead

(b)	20,000	**(i)**	480,000
(c)	119,000		
(e)	43,000		
(g)	280,000		
(h)	7,000		
	460,000		480,000
		Bal.	20,000

Sales

	(k) 1,500,000

Cost of goods sold

(k) 870,000	

Prepaid Insurance

	Dr		Cr
(h)	10,000		

Accumulated Depreciation

	Dr		Cr
(g)	350,000		

Commissions Expense

	Dr		Cr
(c)	90,000		

Administrative Salary Expense

	Dr		Cr
(c)	200,000		

Raw Materials

	Dr		Cr
Bal.	20,000	(b)	380,000
(a)	410,000		
Bal.	50,000		

Creditors

	Dr		Cr
		(a)	410,000
		(d)	17,000
		(e)	43,000
		(f)	180,000

Sales Travel Expense

	Dr		Cr
(k)	1,500,000		

Advertising Expense

	Dr		Cr
(f)	180,000		

Work in Progress

	Dr		Cr
Bal.	15,000	(j)	900,000
(b)	360,000		
(c)	75,000		
(i)	480,000		
Bal.	30,000		

Salaries and Wages Payable

	Dr		Cr
		(c)	475,000

Depreciation Expense

	Dr		Cr
(g)	70,000		

Finished Goods

	Dr		Cr
Bal.	30,000	(k)	870,000
(j)	900,000		
Bal.	60,000		

Insurance Expense

	Dr		Cr
(h)	3,000		

3 Manufacturing overhead is overapplied for the year. The entry to close it out to Cost of goods sold is as follows:

	Dr	Cr
Manufacturing overhead	20,000	
Cost of goods sold		20,000

4

Hogle Company
Profit and loss account
For the year ended 31 December

Sales		£1,500,000
Less cost of goods sold (£870,000 – £20,000)		850,000
Gross margin		650,000
Less selling and administrative expenses:		
Commissions expense	£90,000	
Administrative salaries expense	200,000	
Sales travel expense	17,000	
Advertising expense	180,000	
Depreciation expense	70,000	
Insurance expense	3,000	560,000
Profit		£90,000

Appendix 3A: Service department costing

Departments within an organization can be divided into two broad classes: (1) operating departments and (2) service departments. **Operating departments** include those departments or units where the central purposes of the organization are carried out. Examples of such departments or units would include the Surgery Department in hospitals and producing departments such as Milling, Assembly, and Painting in manufacturing companies.

Service departments, by contrast, do not engage directly in operating activities. Rather, they provide services or assistance to the operating departments. Examples of service departments include Cafeteria, Internal Auditing, Personnel, Cost Accounting, and Purchasing. Although service departments do not engage directly in the operating activities of an organization, the costs that they incur are generally viewed as being part of the cost of the final product or service, the same as are materials, labour and overhead in a manufacturing company or medications in a hospital. As we shall see in Chapter 19, one emerging trend is for companies to either outsource service activities and/or concentrate them in a shared service centre.

Chapter 1 stated that most organizations have one or more service departments that provide services for the entire organization. The major question we consider here is: How much of a service department's cost is to be allocated to each of the units that it serves? This is an important question, since the amount of service department cost allocated to a particular unit can have a significant impact on the computed cost of the goods or services that the unit is providing and can affect an operating unit's performance evaluation.

Allocations using the direct and step methods

Allocating service department costs begins with selecting the proper allocation base – the first topic in this section. After completing this discussion, we will move on to consider how to account for services that service departments provide to each other.

Selecting allocation bases

Many companies use a two-stage costing process. In the first stage, costs are assigned to the operating departments; in the second stage, costs are assigned from the operating departments to products and services. We focused on the second stage of this allocation process in the main part of this chapter. Costs are usually assigned from a service department to other departments using an allocation base, which is some measure of activity. The costs being allocated should be 'driven' by the allocation base. Ideally, the total cost of the service department should be proportional to the size of the allocation base. Managers also often argue that the allocation base should reflect as accurately as possible the benefits that the various departments receive from the services that are being provided. For example, most managers would argue that the square feet of building space occupied by each operating department should be used as the allocation base for janitorial services since both the benefits and costs of janitorial services tend to be proportional to the amount of space occupied by a department. Examples of allocation bases for some service departments are listed in Exhibit 3A.1. A given service department's costs may be allocated using more than one base. For example, data processing costs may be allocated on the basis of CPU minutes for mainframe computers and on the basis of the number of personal computers used in each operating department.

Although the previous paragraph explains how to select an allocation base, another critical factor should not be overlooked. The allocations should be clear and straightforward and easily understood by the managers to whom the costs are being allocated.

Interdepartmental services

Many service departments provide services for each other, as well as for operating departments. The Cafeteria Department, for example, provides food for all employees, including those assigned to other service departments. In turn, the Cafeteria Department may receive services from other service departments, such as from Custodial Services or from Personnel. Services provided between service departments are known as **interdepartmental or reciprocal services**.

Service Department	Bases (cost drivers) Involved
Laundry	Kilos of laundry
Airport Ground Services	Number of flights
Cafeteria	Number of employees; number of meals
Medical Facilities	Cases handled; number of employees; hours worked
Materials Handling	Hours of service; volume handled
Data Processing	CPU minutes; lines printed; disk storage used; number of personal computers
Custodial Services (buildings and grounds)	Square metres occupied
Cost Accounting	Labour-hours; clients or patients serviced
Power	KWh used; capacity of machines
Human Resources	Number of employees; employee turnover; training hours
Receiving, Shipping, and Stores	Units handled; number of requisitions; space occupied
Factory Administration	Total labour-hours
Maintenance	Machine-hours

Exhibit 3A.1 Examples of bases used in allocating service department costs

	Service Department		Operating Department		
	Hospital Administration	Custodial Services	Laboratory	Daily Patient Care	Total
Departmental costs before allocation	£360,000	£90,000	£261,000	£689,000	£1,400,000
Allocation:					
Hospital Administration costs (18⁄48, 30⁄48)*	(360,000)		135,000	225,000	
Custodial Services costs (5⁄50, 45⁄50)†		(90,000)	9,000	81,000	
Total costs after allocation	£ -0-	£ -0-	£405,000	£995,000	£1,400,000

*Based on the employee-hours in the two operating departments, which are 18,000 hours + 30,000 hours = 48,000 hours.

†Based on the space occupied by the two operating departments, which is 5,000 square metres +45,000 square metres = 50,000 square metres.

Exhibit 3A.2 Direct method of allocation

Three approaches are used to allocate the costs of service departments to other departments. These are known as the *direct method*, the *step method*, and the *reciprocal method*. All three methods are discussed in the following paragraphs.

Direct method

The **direct method** is the simplest of the three cost allocation methods. It ignores the services provided by a service department to other service departments and allocates all costs directly to operating departments. Even if a service department (such as personnel) provides a large amount of service to another service department (such as the cafeteria), no allocations are made between the two departments. Rather, all costs are allocated directly to the operating departments. Hence the term direct method.

To provide an example of the direct method, assume that Mountain View Hospital has two service departments and two operating departments as shown below:

	Service department		Operating department		
	Hospital Administration	Custodial Services	Laboratory	Daily Patient Care	Total
Departmental costs before allocation	£360,000	£90,000	£261,000	£689,000	£1,400,000
Employee hours	12,000	6,000	18,000	30,000	66,000
Space occupied (square metres)	10,000	200	5,000	45,000	60,200

In the allocations that follow, Hospital Administration costs will be allocated on the basis of employee-hours and Custodial Services costs will be allocated on the basis of square metres occupied.

The direct method of allocating the hospital's service department costs to the operating departments is shown in Exhibit 3A.2. Several things should be carefully noted in this exhibit. First, even though there are employee-hours in both the Hospital Administration Department itself and in the Custodial Services Department, these employee-hours are ignored when allocating service department costs using the direct method. *Under the direct method, any of the allocation base attributable to the service departments themselves is ignored; only the amount of the allocation base attributable to the operating departments is used in the allocation.* Note that the same rule is used when allocating the costs of the Custodial Services Department. Even though the Hospital Administration and Custodial Services departments occupy some space, this is ignored when the Custodial Services costs are allocated. Finally, note that after all allocations have been completed, all of the departmental costs are contained in the two operating departments. These costs will form the basis for preparing overhead rates for purposes of costing products and services produced in the operating departments.

Although the direct method is simple, it is less accurate than the other methods since it ignores interdepartmental services. This can lead to distorted product and service costs. Even so, many organizations use the direct method because of its simplicity.

Step method

Unlike the direct method, the **step method** provides for allocation of a service department's costs to other service departments, as well as to operating departments. The step method is sequential. The sequence typically begins with the department that provides the greatest amount of service to other service departments. After its costs have been allocated, the process continues, step by step, ending with the department that provides the least amount of services to other service departments. This step procedure is illustrated in graphic form in Exhibit 3A.3, assuming that the Hospital Administration costs are allocated first at Mountain View Hospital.

Exhibit 3A.4 uses the allocations of the Mountain View Hospital to show the details of the step method. Note the following three key points about these allocations. First, under the Allocation heading

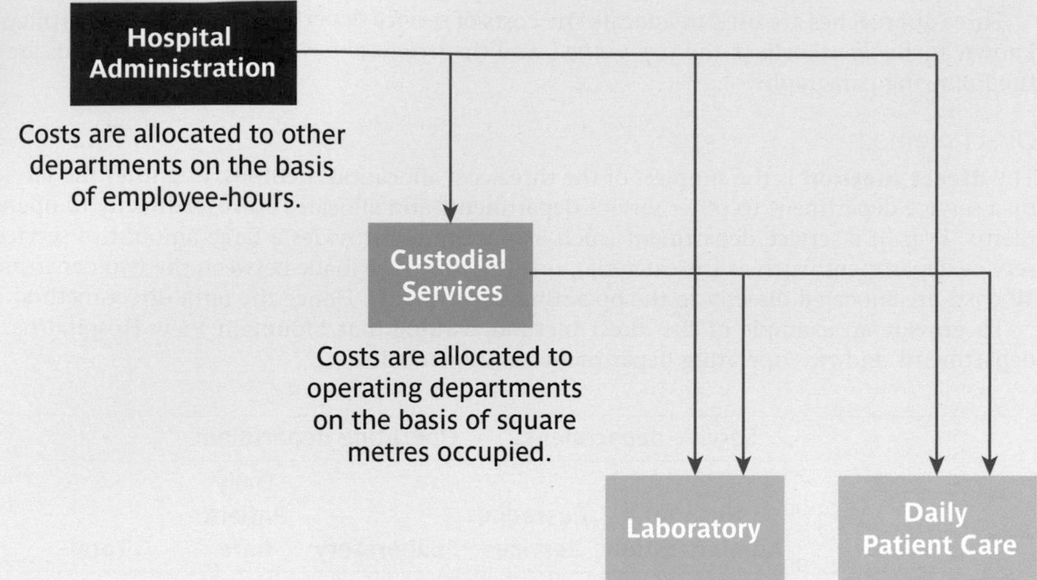

Exhibit 3A.3 Graphic illustration – step method

in Exhibit 3A.4, you see two allocations, or steps. In the step method, the first step allocates the costs of Hospital Administration to another service department (Custodial Services) as well as to the operating departments. The allocation base for Hospital Administration costs now includes the employee-hours for Custodial Services as well as for the operating departments. However, the allocation base still excludes the employee-hours for Hospital Administration itself. *In both the direct and step methods, any amount of the allocation base attributable to the service department whose cost is being allocated is always ignored.* Second, looking again at Exhibit 3A.4, note that in the second step under the Allocation heading, the cost of Custodial Services is allocated to the two operating departments, and none of the cost is allocated to Hospital Administration even though Hospital Administration occupies space in the building. *In the step method, any amount of the allocation base that is attributable to a service department whose cost has already been allocated is ignored.* After a service department's costs have been allocated, costs of other service departments are not reallocated back to it. Third, note that the cost of Custodial Services allocated to other departments in the second step (£130,000) in Exhibit 3A.4 includes the costs of Hospital Administration that were allocated to Custodial Services in the first step in Exhibit 3A.4.

Reciprocal method

The **reciprocal method** gives full recognition to interdepartmental services. Under the step method discussed above only partial recognition of interdepartmental services is possible, since the step method always allocates costs forward – never backward. The reciprocal method, by contrast, allocates service department costs in *both* directions. Thus, since Custodial Services in the prior example provides service for Hospital Administration, part of Custodial Services' costs will be allocated *back* to Hospital Administration if the reciprocal method is used. At the same time, part of Hospital Administration's costs will be allocated forward to Custodial Services. This type of reciprocal allocation requires the use of simultaneous linear equations. These equations can be complex and will not be illustrated here. Examples of the reciprocal method can be found in more advanced cost accounting texts.

The reciprocal method is rarely used in practice for two reasons. First, the computations are relatively complex. Although the complexity issue could be overcome by use of computers, there is no evidence that computers have made the reciprocal method more popular. Second, the step method usually provides results that are a reasonable approximation of the results that the reciprocal method would provide. Thus, companies have little motivation to use the more complex reciprocal method.

	Service Department		Operating Department		
	Hospital Administration	Custodial Services	Laboratory	Daily Patient Care	Total
Departmental costs before allocation	£360,000	£90,000	£261,000	£689,000	£1,400,000
Allocation:					
Hospital Administration costs (6/54, 18/54, 30/54)*	(360,000)	40,000	120,000	200,000	
Custodial Services costs (5/50, 45/50)†		(130,000)	13,000	117,000	
Total costs after allocation	£ -0-	£ -0-	£394,000	£1,006,000	£1,400,000

*Based on the employee-hours in Custodial Services and the two operating departments, which are 6,000 hours + 18,000 hours + 30,000 hours = 54,000 hours.

†As in Exhibit 3A.2, this allocation is based on the space occupied by the two operating departments.

Exhibit 3A.4 Step method of allocation

Revenue producing departments

It is important to note that even though most service departments are cost centres and therefore generate no revenues, a few service departments, such as the cafeteria, may charge for the services they perform. If a service department generates revenues, these revenues should be offset against the department's costs, and only the net amount of cost remaining after this offset should be allocated to other departments within the organization. In this manner, the other departments will not be required to bear costs for which the service department has already been reimbursed.

Effect of allocations on operating departments

Once allocations have been completed, what do the operating departments do with the allocated service department costs? The allocations are typically included in performance evaluations of the operating departments and also included in determining their profitability.

In addition, if the operating departments are responsible for developing overhead rates for costing of products or services, then the allocated costs are combined with the other costs of the operating departments, and the total is used as a basis for rate computations. This rate development process is illustrated in Exhibit 3A.5.

Some cautions in allocating service department costs

Pitfalls in allocating fixed costs

Rather than allocate fixed costs in predetermined lump-sum amounts, some firms allocate them by use of a *variable* allocation base that fluctuates from period to period. This practice can distort decisions and create serious inequities between departments. The inequities will arise from the fact that the fixed costs allocated to one department will be heavily influenced by what happens in *other* departments or segments of the organization.

To illustrate, assume that Kolby Products has a car service centre that provides maintenance work on the fleet of cars used in the company's two sales territories. The car service centre costs are all fixed.

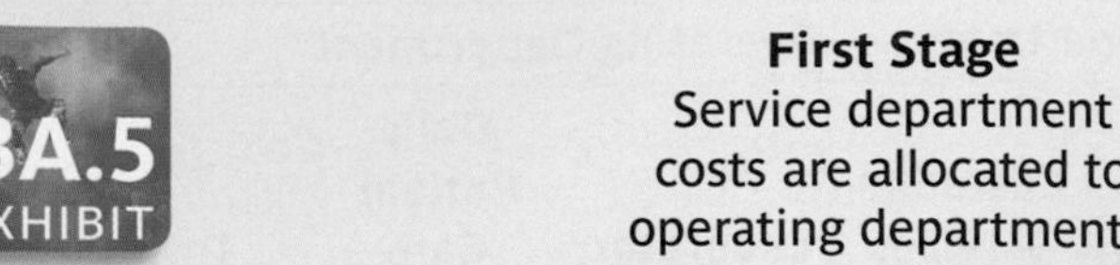

First Stage
Service department costs are allocated to operating departments.
Second Stage
Operating department overhead costs, plus allocated service department costs, are applied to products and services by means of departmental overhead rates.

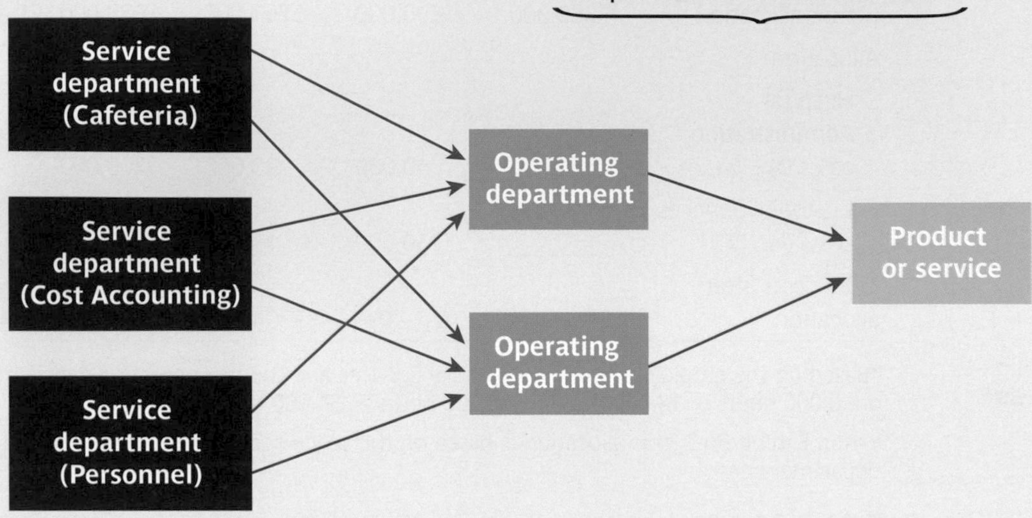

Exhibit 3A.5 Effect of allocation on products and services

Contrary to good practice, the company allocates these fixed costs to the sales territories on the basis of actual miles driven (a variable base). Selected cost data for the last two years follow:

	Year 1	Year 2
Car service centre costs (all fixed)	£120,000 (a)	£120,000 (a)
Western sales territory (miles driven)	1,500,000	1,500,000
Eastern sales territory (miles driven)	1,500,000	900,000
Total miles driven	3,000,000 (b)	2,400,000 (b)
Allocation rate per mile, (a)/(b)	£0.04	£0.05

Notice that the Western sales territory maintained an activity level of 1,500,000 miles driven in both years. On the other hand, the Eastern sales territory allowed its activity to drop off from 1,500,000 miles in Year 1 to only 900,000 miles in Year 2. The car service centre costs that would have been allocated to the two sales territories over the two-year span using actual miles driven as the allocation base are as follows:

Year 1:	
Western sales territory: 1,500,000 miles at £0.04	£60,000
Eastern sales territory: 1,500,000 miles at £0.04	60,000
Total cost allocated	£120,000
Year 2:	
Western sales territory: 1,500,000 miles at £0.05	£75,000
Eastern sales territory: 900,000 miles at £0.05	45,000
Total cost allocated	£120,000

In Year 1, the two sales territories share the service department costs equally. In Year 2, however, the bulk of the service department costs are allocated to the Western sales territory. This is not because of any increase in activity in the Western sales territory; rather, it is because of the decrease in activity in the Eastern sales territory. Even though the Western sales territory maintained the same level of activity in both years, the use of a variable allocation base has caused it to be penalized with a heavier cost allocation in Year 2 because of what has happened in another part of the company.

This kind of inequity is almost inevitable when a variable allocation base is used to allocate fixed costs. The manager of the Western sales territory undoubtedly will be upset about the inequity forced on his territory, but he will feel powerless to do anything about it. The result will be a loss of confidence in the system and considerable ill feeling.

Beware of sales as an allocation base

Over the years, sales have been a favourite allocation base for service department costs. One reason is that a sales base is simple, straightforward, and easy to work with. Another reason is that people tend to view sales as a measure of well-being, or 'ability to pay', and, hence, as a measure of how readily costs can be absorbed from other parts of the organization.

Unfortunately, sales are often a very poor allocation base, for the reason that sales vary from period to period, whereas the costs being allocated are often largely fixed in nature. As discussed earlier, if a variable base is used to allocate fixed costs, inequities can result between departments, since the costs being allocated to one department will depend in large part on what happens in *other* departments. For example, a let-up in sales effort in one department will shift allocated costs off that department and onto other, more productive departments. In effect, the departments putting forth the best sales efforts are penalized in the form of higher allocations, simply because of inefficiencies elsewhere that are beyond their control. The result is often bitterness and resentment on the part of the managers of the better departments.

Consider the following situation encountered by one of the authors:

A large men's clothing store has one service department and three sales departments – Suits, Shoes and Accessories. The Service Department's costs total £60,000 per period and are allocated to the three sales departments according to sales. A recent period showed the following allocation:

	Department			
	Suits	Shoes	Accessories	Total
Sales by department	£260,000	£40,000	£100,000	£400,000
Percentage of total sales	65%	10%	25%	100%
Allocation of service department costs, based on percentage of total sales	£39,000	£6,000	£15,000	£60,000

In a following period, the manager of the Suits Department launched a very successful programme to expand sales by £100,000 in his department. Sales in the other two departments remained unchanged. Total service department costs also remained unchanged, but the allocation of these costs changed substantially, as shown below:

	Department			
	Suits	Shoes	Accessories	Total
Sales by department	£360,000	£40,000	£100,000	£500,000
Percentage of total sales	72%	8%	20%	100%
Allocation of service department costs, based on percentage of total sales	£43,200	£4,800	£12,000	£60,000
Increase (or decrease) from prior allocation	4,200	(1,200)	(3,000)	–

The manager of the Suits Department complained that as a result of his successful effort to expand sales in his department, he was being forced to carry a larger share of the service department costs. On the other hand, the managers of the departments that showed no improvement in sales were relieved of a portion of the costs that they had been carrying. Yet there had been no change in the amount of services provided for any department.

The manager of the Suits Department viewed the increased service department cost allocation to his department as a penalty for his outstanding performance, and he wondered whether his efforts had really been worth while after all in the eyes of top management.

Sales should be used as an allocation base only in those cases where there is a direct causal relationship between sales and the service department costs being allocated. In those situations where service department costs are fixed, they should be allocated according to the three guidelines discussed earlier.

Should all costs be allocated?

As a general rule, any service department costs that are incurred as a result of specific services provided to operating departments should be allocated back to these departments and used to compute overhead rates and to measure performance and profitability. The only time when this general rule is not followed is in those situations where, in the view of the management, allocation would result in an undesirable behavioural response from people in the operating departments. This is particularly a problem when, in violation of the principles stated earlier, fixed costs are allocated to operating units on the basis of their actual usage of a service. For example, in periods when departments are under pressure to cut costs, they may be reluctant to use the services of systems design analysts and internal consultants because of the charges that would be involved.

To avoid discouraging use of a service that is beneficial to the entire organization, some firms do not charge for the service at all. These managers feel that by making such services a free commodity, departments will be more inclined to take full advantage of their benefits.

Other firms take a somewhat different approach. They agree that charging according to usage may discourage utilization of such services as systems design, but they argue that such services should not be free. Instead of providing free services, these firms take what is sometimes called a **retainer fee approach**. Each department is charged a flat amount each year, regardless of how much or how little of the service it utilizes. If a department knows it is going to be charged a certain amount for systems design services, *regardless of usage*, then it is more likely to use the service. We will discuss these issues further in Chapter 19 in the section on shared service centres.

Key terms for review (Appendix 3A)

Direct method (p. 95).

Interdepartmental services or reciprocal services (p. 93).

Operating departments (p. 93).

Reciprocal method (p. 96).

Retainer fee approach (p. 101).

Service departments (p. 93).

Step method (p. 95).

Questions

3–1 Why are actual overhead costs not traced to jobs as are direct materials and direct labour costs?

3–2 When would job-order costing be used in preference to process costing?

3–3 What is the purpose of the job cost sheet in a job-order costing system?

3–4 What is a predetermined overhead rate, and how is it computed?

3–5 Explain how a sales order, a production order, a materials requisition form and a labour time ticket are involved in producing and costing products.

3–6 Explain why some production costs must be assigned to products through an allocation process. Name several such costs. Would such costs be classified as direct or as indirect costs?

3–7 Why do firms use predetermined overhead rates rather than actual manufacturing overhead costs in applying overhead to jobs?

3–8 What factors should be considered in selecting a base to be used in computing the predetermined overhead rate?

3–9 If a company fully allocates all of its overhead costs to jobs, does this guarantee that a profit will be earned for the period?

3–10 What account is credited when overhead cost is applied to Work in Progress? Would you expect the amount applied for a period to equal the actual overhead costs of the period? Why or why not?

3–11 What is underapplied overhead? Overapplied overhead? What disposition is made of these amounts at period end?

3–12 Enumerate two reasons why overhead might be underapplied in a given year.

3–13 What adjustment is made for underapplied overhead on the schedule of cost of goods sold? What adjustment is made for overapplied overhead?

3–14 Sigma Company applies overhead cost to jobs on the basis of direct labour cost. Job A, which was started and completed during the current period, shows charges of £5,000 for direct materials, £8,000 for direct labour, and £6,000 for overhead on its job cost sheet. Job B, which is still in process at year-end, shows charges of £2,500 for direct materials and £4,000 for direct labour. Should any overhead cost be added to job B at year-end? Explain.

3–15 A company assigns overhead cost to completed jobs on the basis of 125% of direct labour cost. The job cost sheet for job 313 shows that £10,000 in direct materials has been used on the job and that £12,000 in direct labour cost has been incurred. If 1,000 units were produced in job 313, what is the cost per unit?

3–16 What is a plantwide overhead rate? Why are multiple overhead rates, rather than a plantwide rate, used in some companies?

3–17 What happens to overhead rates based on direct labour when automated equipment replaces direct labour?

3–18 What is the difference between a service department and an operating department? Give several examples of service departments.

3–19 How are service department costs assigned to products and services?

3-20 What are interdepartmental service costs? How are such costs allocated to other departments under the step method?

3-21 How are service department costs allocated to other departments under the direct method?

Exercises

E3–1 Time allowed: 10 minutes

Which method of determining product costs, job-order costing or process costing, would be more appropriate in each of the following situations?

(a) A glue factory

(b) A textbook publisher such as McGraw-Hill

(c) An Esso oil refinery

(d) A facility that makes frozen orange juice

(e) A paper mill

(f) A custom home builder

(g) A garage that customizes vans

(h) A manufacturer of speciality chemicals

(i) A car repair garage

(j) A tyre manufacturing plant

(k) An advertising agency

(l) A law firm.

E3–2 Time allowed: 20 minutes

Kingsport Containers Ltd, of the Bahamas, experiences wide variation in demand for the 200-litre steel drums it fabricates. The leakproof, rustproof steel drums have a variety of uses from storing liquids and bulk materials to serving as makeshift musical instruments. The drums are made to order and are painted according to the customer's specifications – often in bright patterns and designs. The company is well known for the artwork that appears on its drums. Unit costs are computed on a quarterly basis by dividing each quarter's manufacturing costs (materials, labour and overhead) by the quarter's production in units. The company's estimated costs, by quarter, for the coming year follow:

	Quarter			
	First	Second	Third	Fourth
Direct materials	£240,000	£120,000	£60,000	£180,000
Direct labour	128,000	64,000	32,000	96,000
Manufacturing overhead	300,000	220,000	180,000	260,000
Total manufacturing costs	£668,000	£404,000	£272,000	£536,000
Number of units to be produced	80,000	40,000	20,000	60,000
Estimated cost per unit	£8.35	£10.10	£13.60	£8.93

Management finds the variation in unit costs to be confusing and difficult to work with. It has been suggested that the problem lies with manufacturing overhead, since it is the largest element of cost. Accordingly, you have been asked to find a more appropriate way of assigning manufacturing overhead cost to units of product. After some analysis, you have determined that the company's overhead costs are mostly fixed and therefore show little sensitivity to changes in the level of production.

Required

1 The company uses a job-order costing system. How would you recommend that manufacturing overhead cost be assigned to production? Be specific and show computations.

2 Recompute the company's unit costs in accordance with your recommendations in Question 1 above.

E3–3 Time allowed: 20 minutes

The Polaris Company uses a job-order costing system. The following data relate to October, the first month of the company's fiscal year.

(a) Raw materials purchased on account, £210,000.

(b) Raw materials issued to production, £190,000 (£178,000 direct materials and £12,000 indirect materials).

(c) Direct labour cost incurred, £90,000; indirect labour cost incurred, £110,000.

(d) Depreciation recorded on factory equipment, £40,000.

(e) Other manufacturing overhead costs incurred during October, £70,000 (credit Creditors).

(f) The company applies manufacturing overhead cost to production on the basis of £8 per machine-hour. There were 30,000 machine-hours recorded for October.

(g) Production orders costing £520,000 according to their job cost sheets were completed during October and transferred to Finished Goods.

(h) Production orders that had cost £480,000 to complete according to their job cost sheets were shipped to customers during the month. These goods were sold at 25% above cost. The goods were sold on account.

Required

1 Prepare journal entries to record the information given above.

2 Prepare T-accounts for Manufacturing Overhead and Work in Progress. Post the relevant information above to each account. Compute the ending balance in each account, assuming that Work in Progress has a beginning balance of £42,000.

E3–4 Time allowed: 15 minutes

The following cost data relate to the manufacturing activities of Chang Company during the just completed year:

Manufacturing overhead costs incurred:	
Indirect materials	£15,000
Indirect labour	130,000
Property taxes, factory	8,000
Utilities, factory	70,000
Depreciation, factory	240,000
Insurance, factory	10,000
Total actual costs incurred	£473,000
Other costs incurred:	
Purchases of raw materials (both direct and indirect)	£400,000
Direct labour cost	60,000
Stocks:	
Raw materials, beginning	20,000
Raw materials, ending	30,000
Work in progress, beginning	40,000
Work in progress, ending	70,000

The company uses a predetermined overhead rate to apply overhead cost to production. The rate for the year was £25 per machine-hour. A total of 19,400 machine-hours was recorded for the year.

Required

1 Compute the amount of underapplied or overapplied overhead cost for the year.

2 Prepare a schedule of cost of goods manufactured for the year.

E3–5 Time allowed: 15 minutes

The following information is taken from the accounts of Latta Company. The entries in the T-accounts are summaries of the transactions that affected those accounts during the year.

Manufacturing overhead

(a)	460,000	(b)	390,000
Bal.	70,000		

Work in progress

Bal.	5,000	(c)	710,000
	260,000		
	85,000		
(b)	390,000		
Bal.	40,000		

Finished goods

Bal.	50,000	(d)	640,000
(c)	710,000		
Bal.	120,000		

Cost of goods sold

(d)	640,000		

The overhead that had been applied to Work in Progress during the year is distributed among the ending balances in the accounts as follows:

Work in progress, ending	£19,500
Finished goods, ending	58,500
Cost of goods sold	312,000
Overhead applied	£390,000

For example, of the £40,000 ending balance in Work in Progress, £19,500 was overhead that had been applied during the year.

Required

1 Identify reasons for entries (a) to (d).

2 Assume that the company closes any balance in the Manufacturing Overhead account directly to Cost of Goods Sold. Prepare the necessary journal entry.

3 Assume instead that the company allocates any balance in the Manufacturing Overhead account to the other accounts in proportion to the overhead applied in their ending balances. Prepare the necessary journal entry, with supporting computations.

E3–6 Time allowed: 15 minutes
Estimated cost and operating data for three companies for the upcoming year follow:

	Company		
	X	**Y**	**Z**
Direct labour-hours	80,000	45,000	60,000
Machine-hours	30,000	70,000	21,000
Direct materials cost	£400,000	£290,000	£300,000
Manufacturing overhead cost	536,000	315,000	480,000

Predetermined overhead rates are computed using the following bases in the three companies:

Company	Overhead rate based on:
X	Direct labour-hours
Y	Machine-hours
Z	Direct materials cost

Required

1 Compute the predetermined overhead rate to be used in each company during the upcoming year.

2 Assume that Company X works on three jobs during the upcoming year. Direct labour-hours recorded by job are: job 418, 12,000 hours; job 419, 36,000 hours; job 420, 30,000 hours. How much overhead cost will the company apply to Work in Progress for the year? If actual overhead costs total £530,000 for the year, will overhead be underapplied or overapplied? By how much?

E3–7 Time allowed: 15 minutes
White Company has two departments, Cutting and Finishing. The company uses a job-order costing system and computes a predetermined overhead rate in each department. The Cutting Department bases

its rate on machine-hours, and the Finishing Department bases its rate on direct labour cost. At the beginning of the year, the company made the following estimates:

	Department	
	Cutting	Finishing
Direct labour-hours	6,000	30,000
Machine-hours	48,000	5,000
Manufacturing overhead cost	£360,000	£486,000
Direct labour cost	50,000	270,000

Required

1 Compute the predetermined overhead rate to be used in each department.

2 Assume that the overhead rates that you computed in Question 1 above are in effect. The job cost sheet for job 203, which was started and completed during the year, showed the following:

	Department	
	Cutting	Finishing
Direct labour-hours	6	20
Machine-hours	80	4
Materials requisitioned	£500	£310
Direct labour cost	70	150

Compute the total overhead cost applied to job 203.

Would you expect substantially different amounts of overhead cost to be assigned to some jobs if the company used a plantwide overhead rate based on direct labour cost, rather than using departmental rates? Explain. No computations are necessary.

E3–8 Time allowed: 25 minutes

The Ferre Publishing Company has three service departments and two operating departments. Selected data from a recent period on the five departments follow:

The company allocates service department costs by the step method in the following order: A (number of employees), B (space occupied), and C (hours of press time). The company makes no distinction between variable and fixed service department costs.

	Service department			Operating department		
	A	B	C	1	2	Total
Overhead costs	£140,000	£105,000	£48,000	£275,000	£430,000	£998,000
Number of employees	60	35	140	315	210	760
Square feet of space occupied	15,000	10,000	20,000	40,000	100,000	185,000
Hours of press time	–	–	–	30,000	60,000	90,000

Required

Using the step method, allocate the service department costs to the operating departments.

E3–9 Time allowed: 25 minutes
Refer to the data for the Ferre Publishing Company in E8–1. Assume that the company allocates service department costs by the direct method, rather than by the step method.

Required

Assuming that the company uses the direct method, how much overhead cost would be allocated to each operating department?

Problems

P3–10 Straightforward journal entries; partial T-accounts; profit and loss account Time allowed: 35 minutes

Gold Nest Company of Guandong, China, is a family-owned enterprise that makes birdcages for the South China market. A popular pastime among older Chinese men is to take their pet birds on daily excursions to teahouses and public parks where they meet with other bird owners to talk and play mahjong. A great deal of attention is lavished on these birds, and the birdcages are often elaborately constructed from exotic woods and contain porcelain feeding bowls and silver roosts. Gold Nest Company makes a broad range of birdcages that it sells through an extensive network of street vendors who receive commissions on their sales. The Chinese currency is the renminbi, which is denoted by Rmb. All of the company's transactions with customers, employees and suppliers are conducted in cash; there is no credit.

The company uses a job-order costing system in which overhead is applied to jobs on the basis of direct labour cost. At the beginning of the year, it was estimated that the total direct labour cost for the year would be Rmb200,000 and the total manufacturing overhead cost would be Rmb330,000. At the beginning of the year, the stock balances were as follows:

During the year, the following transactions were completed:

Raw materials	Rmb25,000
Work in progress	10,000
Finished goods	40,000

(a) Raw materials purchased for cash, Rmb275,000.

(b) Raw materials requisitioned for use in production, Rmb280,000 (materials costing Rmb220,000 were charged directly to jobs; the remaining materials were indirect).

(c) Costs for employee services were incurred as follows:

Direct labour	Rmb180,000
Indirect labour	72,000
Sales commissions	63,000
Administrative salaries	90,000

(d) Rent for the year was Rmb18,000 (Rmb13,000 of this amount related to factory operations, and the remainder related to selling and administrative activities).

(e) Utility costs incurred in the factory, Rmb57,000.

(f) Advertising costs incurred, Rmb140,000.

(g) Depreciation recorded on equipment, Rmb100,000. (Rmb88,000 of this amount was on equipment used in factory operations; the remaining Rmb12,000 was on equipment used in selling and administrative activities.)

(h) Manufacturing overhead cost was applied to jobs, Rmb.—?—

(i) Goods that cost Rmb675,000 to manufacture according to their job cost sheets were completed during the year.

(j) Sales for the year totalled Rmb1,250,000. The total cost to manufacture these goods according to their job cost sheets was Rmb700,000.

Required

1 Prepare journal entries to record the transactions for the year.

2 Prepare T-accounts for inventories, Manufacturing Overhead, and Cost of Goods Sold. Post relevant data from your journal entries to these T-accounts (don't forget to enter the beginning balances in your stock accounts). Compute an ending balance in each account.

3 Is Manufacturing Overhead underapplied or overapplied for the year? Prepare a journal entry to close any balance in the Manufacturing Overhead account to Cost of Goods Sold.

4 Prepare a profit and loss account for the year. (Do not prepare a schedule of cost of goods manufactured; all of the information needed for the profit and loss account is available in the journal entries and T-accounts you have prepared.)

P3–11 Disposition of underapplied or overapplied overhead Time allowed: 25 minutes
Bieler & Cie of Altdorf, Switzerland, makes furniture using the latest automated technology. The company uses a job-order costing system and applies manufacturing overhead cost to products on the basis of machine-hours. The following estimates were used in preparing the predetermined overhead rate at the beginning of the year:

Machine-hours	75,000
Manufacturing overhead cost	Sfr900,000

The currency in Switzerland is the Swiss franc, which is denoted by Sfr.

During the year, a glut of furniture on the market resulted in cutting back production and a buildup of furniture in the company's warehouse. The company's cost records revealed the following actual cost and operating data for the year:

Machine-hours	60,000
Manufacturing overhead cost	Sfr850,000
Stocks at year-end:	
Raw materials	30,000
Work in progress (includes overhead applied of 36,000)	100,000
Finished goods (includes overhead applied of 180,000)	500,000
Cost of goods sold (includes overhead applied of 504,000)	1,400,000

Required

1 Compute the company's predetermined overhead rate.

2 Compute the underapplied or overapplied overhead.

3 Assume that the company closes any underapplied or overapplied overhead directly to Cost of Goods Sold. Prepare the appropriate journal entry.

4 Assume that the company allocates any underapplied or overapplied overhead to Work in Progress, Finished Goods, and Cost of Goods Sold on the basis of the amount of overhead applied in each account. Prepare the journal entry to show the allocation for the year.

5 How much higher or lower will profit be if the underapplied or overapplied overhead is allocated rather than closed directly to Cost of Goods Sold?

P3–12 T-account analysis of cost flows Time allowed: 35 minutes
Selected ledger accounts of Moore Company are given below for the just completed year:

Raw Materials

Bal. 1/1	15,000	Credits	?
Debits	120,000		
Bal. 12/31	25,000		

Manufacturing Overhead

Debits	230,000	Credits	?

Work in progress

Bal. 1/1	20,000	Credits	470,000
Direct materials	90,000		
Direct labour	150,000		
Overhead	240,000		
Bal. 12/31	?		

Factory Wages Payable

Debits	185,000	Bal. 1/1	9,000
		Credits	180,000
		Bal. 12/31	4,000

Finished Goods

Bal. 1/1	40,000	Credits	?
Debits	?		
Bal. 12/31	60,000		

Cost of Goods Sold

Debits	?		

Required

1 What was the cost of raw materials put into production during the year?

2 How much of the materials in Question 1 above consisted of indirect materials?

3 How much of the factory labour cost for the year consisted of indirect labour?

4 What was the cost of goods manufactured for the year?

5 What was the cost of goods sold for the year (before considering underapplied or overapplied overhead)?

6 If overhead is applied to production on the basis of direct labour cost, what rate was in effect during the year?

7 Was manufacturing overhead underapplied or overapplied? By how much?

8 Compute the ending balance in the Work in Progress stock account. Assume that this balance consists entirely of goods started during the year. If £8,000 of this balance is direct labour cost, how much of it is direct materials cost? Manufacturing overhead cost?

P3–13 Job cost sheets; overhead rates; journal entries Time allowed: 60 minutes
AOZT Volzhskije Motory of St Petersburg, Russia, makes marine motors for vessels ranging in size from harbour tugs to open-water icebreakers. (The Russian currency is the rouble, which is denoted by RUR. All currency amounts below are in thousands of RUR.)

The company uses a job-order costing system. Only three jobs – 208, 209, and 210 – were worked on during May and June. Job 208 was completed on 20 June; the other two jobs were uncompleted on 30 June. Job cost sheets on the three jobs are as follows:

Job cost sheet

	Job 208	Job 209	Job 210
May costs incurred:*			
Direct materials	RUR9,500	RUR5,100	RUR–
Direct labour	8,000	3,000	–
Manufacturing overhead	11,200	4,200	–
June costs incurred:			
Direct materials	–	6,000	7,200
Direct labour	4,000	7,500	8,500
Manufacturing overhead	?	?	?

*Jobs 208 and 209 were started during May.

The following additional information is available:

(a) Manufacturing overhead is applied to jobs on the basis of direct labour cost.

(b) Balances in the stock accounts at 31 May were:

Raw materials	RUR30,000
Work in progress	?
Finished goods	50,000

Required

1 Prepare T-accounts for Raw Materials, Work in Progress, Finished Goods, and Manufacturing Overhead. Enter the 31 May balances given above; in the case of Work in Progress, compute the 31 May balance and enter it into the Work in Progress T-account.

2 Prepare journal entries for *June* as follows:

(a) Prepare an entry to record the issue of materials into production and post the entry to appropriate T-accounts. (In the case of direct materials, it is not necessary to make a separate entry for each job.) Indirect materials used during June totalled RUR3,600.

(b) Prepare an entry to record the incurrence of labour cost and post the entry to appropriate T-accounts. (In the case of direct labour cost, it is not necessary to make a separate entry for each job.) Indirect labour cost totalled RUR7,000 for June.

(c) Prepare an entry to record the incurrence of RUR19,400 in various actual manufacturing overhead costs for June (credit Creditors). Post this entry to the appropriate T-accounts.

3 What apparent predetermined overhead rate does the company use to assign overhead cost to jobs? Using this rate, prepare a journal entry to record the application of overhead cost to jobs for June (it is not necessary to make a separate entry for each job). Post this entry to appropriate T-accounts.

4 As stated earlier, Job 208 was completed during June. Prepare a journal entry to show the transfer of this Job off of the production line and into the finished goods warehouse. Post the entry to appropriate T-accounts.

5 Determine the balance at 30 June in the Work in Progress stock account. How much of this balance consists of costs charged to Job 209? To Job 210?

P3–14 Journal entries; T-accounts; statements; pricing Time allowed: 120 minutes
Froya Fabrikker A/S of Bergen, Norway, is a small company that manufactures specialty heavy equipment for use in North Sea oil fields. (The Norwegian currency is the krone, which is denoted by Nkr.) The

company uses a job-order costing system and applies manufacturing overhead cost to jobs on the basis of direct labour-hours. At the beginning of the year, the following estimates were made for the purpose of computing the predetermined overhead rate: manufacturing overhead cost, Nkr360,000; and direct labour-hours, 900.

The following transactions took place during the year (all purchases and services were acquired on account):

(a) Raw materials were purchased for use in production, Nkr200,000.

(b) Raw materials were requisitioned for use in production (all direct materials), Nkr185,000.

(c) Utility bills were incurred, Nkr70,000 (90% related to factory operations, and the remainder related to selling and administrative activities).

(d) Salary and wage costs were incurred:

Direct labour (975 hours)	Nkr230,000
Indirect labour	90,000
Selling and administrative salaries	110,000

(e) Maintenance costs were incurred in the factory, Nkr54,000.

(f) Advertising costs were incurred, Nkr136,000.

(g) Depreciation was recorded for the year, Nkr95,000 (80% related to factory equipment, and the remainder related to selling and administrative equipment).

(h) Rental cost incurred on buildings, Nkr120,000 (85% related to factory operations, and the remainder related to selling and administrative facilities).

(i) Manufacturing overhead cost was applied to jobs, Nkr.—?—

(j) Cost of goods manufactured for the year, Nkr770,000.

(k) Sales for the year (all on account) totalled Nkr1,200,000. These goods cost Nkr800,000 to manufacture according to their job cost sheets.

(l) The balances in the stock accounts at the beginning of the year were:

Raw materials	Nkr30,000
Work in progress	21,000
Finished goods	60,000

Required

1 Prepare journal entries to record the preceding data.

2 Post your entries to T-accounts. (Don't forget to enter the beginning stock balances above.) Determine the ending balances in the stock accounts and in the Manufacturing Overhead account.

3 Prepare a schedule of cost of goods manufactured.

4 Prepare a journal entry to close any balance in the Manufacturing Overhead account to Cost of Goods Sold. Prepare a schedule of cost of goods sold.

5 Prepare a profit and loss account for the year.

6 Job 412 was one of the many jobs started and completed during the year. The job required Nkr8,000 in direct materials and 39 hours of direct labour time at a total direct labour cost of Nkr9,200. The job contained only four units. If the company bills at a price 60% above the unit cost on the job cost sheet, what price per unit would have been charged to the customer?

P3–15 Job and service costing Time allowed: 35 minutes

A company has been carrying out work on a number of building contracts (including Contract ABC) over the six month period ended 31 May 1999. The following information is available:

	All contracts (including ABC)	Contract ABC
Number of contracts worked on in the six months to 31.5.99	10	–
Value	£76.2m	£6.4m
Duration (average 13 months)	8–22 months	11 months
Contract months	53*	6
Direct labour costs in the period	£9.762m	£1.017m
Raw material costs in the period	£10.817m	£1.456m
Distance from base (average)	16 kilometres	23 kilometres
Value of work certified at 31.5.99	–	£5.180m

*Contract months for 'All Contracts' are the sum contract during the six month period.

Contract ABC commenced on 1 September 1998. As at 30 November 1998 cumulative costs on the contract, held in work-in-progress, totalled £1.063m (including overheads).

The company confidently predicts that further costs after 31 May 1999 to complete Contract ABC on time (including overheads) will not exceed £0.937m. Overheads incurred over the six month period to 31 May 1999, which are to be apportioned to individual contracts, are:

	£m
Stores operations	1.56
Contract general management	1.22
Transport	1.37
General administration	4.25
The bases of apportionment are:	
Stores operations	– contract value × contract months
Contract general management	– direct labour costs
Transport	– distance from base × contract months
General administration	– contract months

Required

1

(a) Apportion overheads to Contract ABC for the six month period to 31 May 1999 (to the nearest £000 for each overhead item). *(6 marks)*

(b) Determine the expected profit/loss on Contract ABC, and the amount of profit/loss on the contract that you recommend be included in the accounts of the company for the six month period to 31 May 1999. *(7 marks)*

2 The company is introducing a service costing system into its stores operations department. Outline the key factors to consider when introducing the service costing system. *(7 marks)*

(Total 20 marks)

ACCA Management Information, June 1999

P3–16 Cost Allocation: Step Method versus Direct Method Time allowed: 40 minutes
The Sendai Co. Ltd. of Japan has budgeted costs in its various departments as follows for the coming year:

Factory administration	¥270,000,000
Custodial services	68,760,000
Personnel	28,840,000
Maintenance	45,200,000
Machining – overhead	376,300,000
Assembly – overhead	175,900,000
Total cost	¥965,000,000

The Japanese currency is the yen, denoted by ¥. The company allocates service department costs to other departments in the order listed below.

Department	Number of employees	Total labour-hours	Square feet of space occupied	Direct labour-hours	Machine-hours
Factory administration	12	–	5,000	–	–
Custodial services	4	3,000	2,000	–	–
Personnel	5	5,000	3,000	–	–
Maintenance	25	22,000	10,000	–	–
Machining	40	30,000	70,000	20,000	70,000
Assembly	60	90,000	20,000	80,000	10,000
	146	150,000	110,000	100,000	80,000

Machining and Assembly are operating departments, the other departments all act in a service capacity. The company does not make a distinction between fixed and variable service department costs. Factory Administration is allocated on the basis of labour-hours; Custodial Services on the basis of square feet occupied; Personnel on the basis of number of employees; and Maintenance on the basis of machine-hours.

Required

1 Allocate service department costs to departments using the step method. Then compute predetermined overhead rates in the operating departments using a machine-hours basis in Machining and a direct labour-hours basis in Assembly.

2 Repeat (1) above, this time using the direct method. Again compute predetermined overhead rates in Machining and Assembly.

3 Assume that the company doesn't want to bother with allocating service department costs but simply wants to compute a single plantwide overhead rate based on total overhead costs (both service department and operating department) divided by total direct labour-hours. Compute the overhead rate.

4 Suppose a job requires machine and labour time as follows:

	Machine-hours	Direct labour-hours
Machining department	190	25
Assembly department	10	75
Total hours	200	100

Using the overhead rates computed in (1), (2), and (3) above, compute the amount of overhead cost that would be assigned to the job if the overhead rates were developed using the step method, the direct method and the plantwide method.

Cases

C3–17 Critical thinking; interpretation of manufacturing overhead rates Time allowed: 40 minutes

Kelvin Aerospace plc manufactures parts such as rudder hinges for the aerospace industry. The company uses a job-order costing system with a plantwide predetermined overhead rate based on direct labour-hours. On 16 December 2005, the company's finance director made a preliminary estimate of the predetermined overhead rate for the year 2006. The new rate was based on the estimated total manufacturing overhead cost of £3,402,000 and the estimated 63,000 total direct labour-hours for 2006:

$$\text{Predetermined overhead rate} = \frac{£3{,}402{,}000}{63{,}000 \text{ hours}} = £54 \text{ per direct labour-hour}$$

This new predetermined overhead rate was communicated to top managers in a meeting on 19 December. The rate did not cause any comment because it was within a few pennies of the overhead rate that had been used during 2005. One of the subjects discussed at the meeting was a proposal by the production manager to purchase an automated milling machine built by Sunghi Industries. The managing director of Kelvin Aerospace, Harry Arcany, agreed to meet with the sales representative from Sunghi Industries to discuss the proposal.

On the day following the meeting, Mr Arcany met with Jasmine Chang, Sunghi Industries' sales representative. The following discussion took place:

Arcany: Wally, our production manager, asked me to meet you since he is interested in installing an automated milling machine. Frankly, I'm sceptical. You're going to have to show me this isn't just another expensive toy for Wally's people to play with.

Chang: This is a great machine with direct bottom-line benefits. The automated milling machine has three major advantages. First, it is much faster than the manual methods you are using. It can process about twice as many parts per hour as your present milling machines. Second, it is much more flexible. There are some up-front programming costs, but once those have been incurred, almost no setup is required to run a standard operation. You just punch in the code for the standard operation, load the machine's hopper with raw material, and the machine does the rest.

Arcany: What about cost? Having twice the capacity in the milling machine area won't do us much good. That centre is idle much of the time anyway.

Chang: I was getting there. The third advantage of the automated milling machine is lower cost. Wally and I looked over your present operations, and we estimated that the automated equipment would eliminate the need for about 6,000 direct labour-hours a year. What is your direct labour cost per hour?

Arcany: The wage rate in the milling area averages about £32 per hour. Fringe benefits raise that figure to about £41 per hour.

Chang: Don't forget your overhead.

Arcany: Next year the overhead rate will be £54 per hour.

Chang: So including fringe benefits and overhead, the cost per direct labour-hour is about £95.

Arcany: That's right.

Chang: Since you can save 6,000 direct labour-hours per year, the cost savings would amount to about £570,000 a year. And our 60-month lease plan would require payments of only £348,000 per year.

Arcany: That sounds like a no-brainer. When could you install the equipment?

Shortly after this meeting, Mr Arcany informed the company's finance director of the decision to lease the new equipment, which would be installed over the Christmas holiday period. The finance director realized that this decision would require a recomputation of the predetermined overhead rate for the year 2006 since the decision would affect both the manufacturing overhead and the direct labour-hours for the year. After talking with both the production manager and the sales representative from Sunghi Industries, the finance director discovered that in addition to the annual lease cost of £348,000, the new machine would also require a skilled technician/programmer who would have to be hired at a cost of £50,000 per year to maintain and program the equipment. Both of these costs would be included in factory overhead. There would be no other changes in total manufacturing overhead cost, which is almost entirely fixed. The finance director assumed that the new machine would result in a reduction of 6,000 direct labour-hours for the year from the levels that initially had been planned.

When the revised predetermined overhead rate for the year 2006 was circulated among the company's top managers, there was considerable dismay.

Required

1. Recompute the predetermined rate assuming that the new machine will be installed. Explain why the new predetermined overhead rate is higher (or lower) than the rate that was originally estimated for the year 2006.
2. What effect (if any) would this new rate have on the cost of jobs that do not use the new automated milling machine?
3. Why would managers be concerned about the new overhead rate?
4. After seeing the new predetermined overhead rate, the production manager admitted that he probably wouldn't be able to eliminate all of the 6,000 direct labour-hours. He had been hoping to accomplish the reduction by not replacing workers who retired or quit, but that had not been possible. As a result, the real labour savings would be only about 2,000 hours – one worker. In the light of this additional information, evaluate the original decision to acquire the automated milling machine from Sunghi Industries.

C3–18 Ethics predetermined overhead rate and capacity Time allowed: 90 minutes

Pat Miranda, the new controller of Vault Hard Drives plc, has just returned from a seminar on the choice of the activity level in the predetermined overhead rate. Even though the subject did not sound exciting at first, she found that there were some important ideas presented that should get a hearing at her company. After returning from the seminar, she arranged a meeting with the production manager J. Stevens and the assistant production manager Marvin Washington.

Pat: I ran across an idea that I wanted to check out with both of you. It's about the way we compute predetermined overhead rates.

J.: We're all ears.

Pat: We compute the predetermined overhead rate by dividing the estimated total factory overhead for the coming year by the estimated total units produced for the coming year.

Marvin: We've been doing that as long as I've been with the company.

J.: And it has been done that way at every other company I've worked at, except at most places they divide by direct labour-hours.

Pat: We use units because it is simpler and we basically make one product with minor variations. But, there's another way to do it. Instead of dividing the estimated total factory overhead by the estimated total units produced for the coming year, we could divide by the total units produced at capacity.

Marvin: Oh, the Sales Department will love that. It will drop the costs on all the products. They'll go wild over their cutting prices.

Pat: That *is* a worry, but I wanted to talk to both of you first before going over to Sales.

J.: Aren't you always going to have a lot of underapplied overhead?

Pat: That's correct, but let me show you how we would handle it. Here's an example based on our budget for next year.

Budgeted (estimated) production	160,000 units
Budgeted sales	160,000 units
Capacity	200,000 units
Selling price	£60 per unit
Variable manufacturing cost	£15 per unit
Total manufacturing overhead cost (all fixed)	£4,000,000
Administrative and selling expenses (all fixed)	£2,700,000
Beginning inventories	–0–

Traditional approach to computation of the predetermined overhead rate

$$\frac{\text{Estimated total manufacturing overhead cost, £4,000,000}}{\text{Estimated total units produced, 160,000}} = \text{£25 per unit}$$

Budgeted Profit Statement

Revenue (160,000 units × £60)		£9,600,000
Cost of goods sold:		
Variable manufacturing (160,000 units × £15)	£2,400,000	
Manufacturing overhead applied (160,000 units × £25)	4,000,000	6,400,000
Gross margin		3,200,000
Administration and selling expenses		2,700,000
Profit		£ 500,000

New approach to computation of the predetermined overhead rate using capacity in the denominator

$$\frac{\text{Estimated total manufacturing overhead cost, £4,000,000}}{\text{Total units at capacity, 200,000}} = \text{£20 per unit}$$

Budgeted Profit Statement

Revenue (160,000 units × £60)		£9,600,000
Cost of goods sold:		
Variable manufacturing (160,000 units × £15)	£2,400,000	
Manufacturing overhead applied (160,000 units × £20)	3,200,000	5,600,000
Gross margin		4,000,000
Cost of unused capacity [(200,000 units – 160,000 units) × £20]		800,000
Administrative and selling expenses		2,700,000
Profit		£ 500,000

J.: Whoa!! I don't think I like the look of that 'Cost of unused capacity'. If that thing shows up on the profit statement, someone from headquarters is likely to come down here looking for some people to lay off.

Marvin: I'm worried about something else too. What happens when sales are not up to expectations? Can we pull the 'hat trick'?

Pat: I'm sorry, I don't understand.

J.: Marvin's talking about something that happens fairly regularly. When sales are down and profits look like they are going to be lower than the CEO told the owners they were going to be, the CEO comes down here and asks us to deliver some more profits.

Marvin: And we pull them out of our hat.

J.: Yeah, we just increase production until we get the profits we want.

Pat: I still don't understand. You mean you increase sales?

J.: No, we increase production. We're the production managers, not the sales managers.

Pat: I get it. Since you have produced more, the sales force have more units they can sell.

J.: No, the marketing people don't do a thing. We just build inventories and that does the trick.

Required

In all of the questions below, assume that the predetermined overhead rate under the traditional method is £25 per unit and under the new method it is £20 per unit. Also assume that under the traditional method any underapplied or overapplied overhead is taken directly to the income statement as an adjustment to Cost of Goods Sold.

1. Suppose actual production is 160,000 units. Compute the profits that would be realized under the traditional and new methods if actual sales are 150,000 units and everything else turns out as expected.
2. How many units would have to be produced under each of the methods in order to realize the budgeted profit of £500,000 if actual sales are 150,000 units and everything else turns out as expected?
3. What effect does the new method based on capacity have on the volatility of profit?
4. Will the 'hat trick' be easier or harder to perform if the new method based on capacity is used?
5. Do you think the 'hat trick' is ethical?

Further reading

One of the drawbacks of traditional cost accounting systems is their inability to provide different information for different purposes without undergoing an extensive special study. Kaplan identifies the major functions of accounting systems and outlines a number of the major characteristics or demands of different functions addressed by cost data. See Kaplan (1988).

Part of the reason for overhead costs rising is that companies are investing in new manufacturing technology. Modern computer-integrated manufacturing systems and other highly automated manufacturing systems have different cost structures and, therefore, different product costing requirements than conventional manufacturing systems. Dhavale (1989) develops a model for flexible manufacturing systems.

Endnotes

1. As this edition is under preparation, writers in Hollywood are on strike!
2. Engel and Ikawa (1997).
3. Foster and Gupta (1990). In the UK, survey data have suggested that 68–73% of manufacturing companies used direct labour as an allocation base – see Drury and Tayles (1994).
4. McNair (1994).

Chapter 4

Systems design: process costing

Learning objectives

After studying Chapter 4, you should be able to:

1. Prepare journal entries to record the flow of materials, labour and overhead through a process costing system
2. Compute the equivalent units of production for a period by the weighted-average method
3. Prepare a quantity schedule for a period by the weighted-average method
4. Compute the costs per equivalent unit for a period by the weighted-average method
5. Prepare a cost reconciliation for a period by the weighted-average method
6. (Appendix 4A) Compute the equivalent units of production for a period by the FIFO method
7. (Appendix 4A) Prepare a quantity schedule for a period by the FIFO method
8. (Appendix 4A) Compute the costs per equivalent unit for a period by the FIFO method
9. (Appendix 4A) Prepare a cost reconciliation for a period by the FIFO method

Concepts in Context

Using an old family recipe, Emma started a company that produced a special sort of old style lemonade. At first the company struggled, but as sales increased, the company expanded rapidly. Emma soon realized that to expand any further, it would be necessary to borrow money. The investment in additional equipment was too large for her to finance out of the company's current cash flows.

Emma was disappointed to find that few banks were willing to make a loan to such a small company, but she finally found a bank that would consider her loan application. However, Emma was informed that she would have to supply up-to-date financial statements with her loan application.

Emma had never bothered with financial statements before – she felt that as long as the balance in the company's cheque book kept increasing, the company was doing fine. She was puzzled how she was going to determine the value of the lemonade in the work in progress and finished goods stocks. The valuation of the lemonade would affect both the cost of goods sold and the inventory balances of her company. Emma thought of perhaps using job-order costing, but her company produces only one product. Raw ingredients were continually being mixed to make more lemonade, and more bottled lemonade was always coming off the end of the bottling line. Emma didn't see how she could use a job-order costing system since the job never really ended. Perhaps there was another way to account for the costs of producing the lemonade.

As explained in the preceding chapter, there are two basic costing systems in use: job-order costing and process costing. A job-order costing system is used in situations where many different jobs or products are worked on each period. Examples of industries that would typically use job-order costing include furniture manufacture, special-order printing, shipbuilding and many types of service organizations.

By contrast, **process costing** is most commonly used in industries that produce essentially homogeneous (i.e., uniform) products on a continuous basis, such as bricks, cornflakes or paper. Process costing is particularly used in industries that convert basic raw materials into homogeneous products, such as aluminium ingots, paper manufacturing, flour milling, petroleum and lubricating oils and breakfast cereals. In addition, process costing is often employed in companies that use a form of process costing in their assembly operations, such as Panasonic (video monitors), Compaq (personal computers), Toyota (cars), and Sony (CD players). A form of process costing may also be used in utilities that produce gas, water and electricity. As suggested by the length of this list, process costing is in very wide use.

Our purpose in this chapter is to extend the discussion of product costing to include a process costing system.

Comparison of job-order and process costing

In some ways process costing is very similar to job-order costing, and in some ways it is very different. In this section, we focus on these similarities and differences in order to provide a foundation for the detailed discussion of process costing that follows.

Similarities between job-order and process costing

It is important to recognize that much of what was learned in the preceding chapter about costing and about cost flows applies equally well to process costing in this chapter. That is, we are not throwing out all that we have learned about costing and starting from scratch with a whole new system. The similarities that exist between job-order and process costing can be summarized as follows:

1. The same basic purposes exist in both systems, which are to assign material, labour and overhead cost to products and to provide a mechanism for computing unit costs.
2. Both systems maintain and use the same basic manufacturing accounts, including Manufacturing Overhead, Raw Materials, Work in Progress, and Finished Goods.
3. The flow of costs through the manufacturing accounts is basically the same in both systems.

As can be seen from this comparison, much of the knowledge that we have already acquired about costing is applicable to a process costing system. Our task now is simply to refine and extend this knowledge to process costing.

Differences between job-order and process costing

The differences between job-order and process costing arise from two factors. The first is that the flow of units in a process costing system is more or less continuous, and the second is that these units are indistinguishable from one another. Under process costing, it makes no sense to try to identify materials, labour and overhead costs with a particular order from a customer (as we did with job-order costing), since each order is just one of many that are filled from a continuous flow of virtually identical units from the production line. Under process costing, we accumulate costs *by department*, rather than by order, and assign these costs equally to all units that pass through the department during a period.

A further difference between the two costing systems is that the job cost sheet has no use in process costing, since the focal point of that method is on departments. Instead of using job cost sheets, a document known as a **production report** is prepared for each department in which work is done on products. The production report serves several functions. It provides a summary of the number of units moving through a department during a period, and it also provides a computation of unit costs. In addition, it shows what costs were charged to the department and what disposition was made of these costs. The department production report is the key document in a process costing system.

The major differences between job-order and process costing are summarized in Exhibit 4.1.

Job-order costing	Process costing
1. Many different jobs are worked on during each period, with each job having different production requirements.	1. A single product is produced either on a continuous basis or for long periods of time. All units of product are identical.
2. Costs are accumulated by individual job.	2. Costs are accumulated by department.
3. The *job cost sheet* is the key document controlling the accumulation of costs by a job.	3. The *department production report* is accumulation and disposition of costs by a department.
4. Unit costs are computed *by job* on the job cost sheet.	4. Unit costs are computed *by department* on the department production report.

Exhibit 4.1 Differences between job-order and process costing

A perspective of process cost flows

Before presenting a detailed example of process costing, it will be helpful to see how manufacturing costs flow through a process costing system.

Processing departments

A **processing department** is any location in an organization where work is performed on a product and where materials, labour or overhead costs are added to the product. For example, a potato crisp factory might have three processing departments – one for preparing potatoes, one for cooking, and one for inspecting and packaging. A brick factory might have two processing departments – one for mixing and moulding clay into brick form and one for firing the moulded brick. A company can have as many or as few processing departments as are needed to complete a product or service. Some products and services may go through several processing departments, while others may go through only one or two. Regardless of the number of departments involved, all processing departments have two essential features. First, the activity performed in the processing department must be performed uniformly on all of the units passing through it. Second, the output of the processing department must be homogeneous.

The processing departments involved in making a product such as bricks would probably be organized in a sequential pattern. By *sequential* processing, we mean that units flow in sequence from one department to another. An example of processing departments arranged in a sequential pattern is given in Exhibit 4.2, which illustrates a potato chip processing plant.

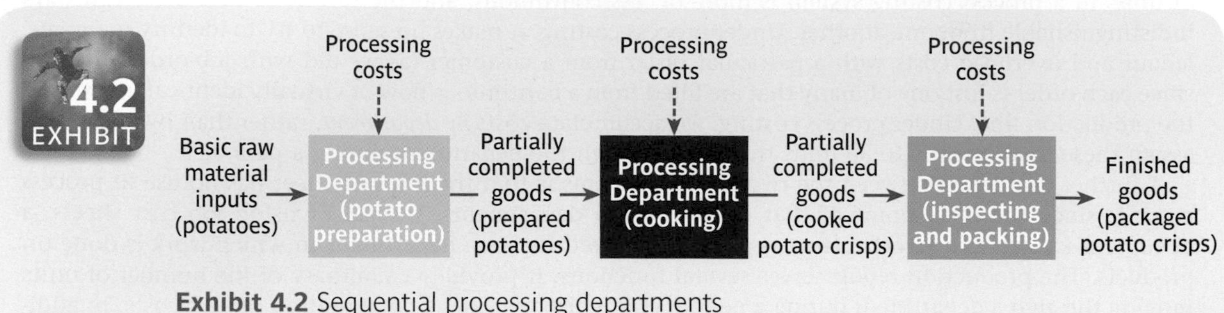

Exhibit 4.2 Sequential processing departments

A different type of processing pattern, known as *parallel processing*, is required to make some products. Parallel processing is used in those situations where, after a certain point, some units may go through different processing departments than others. For example, Exxon and Shell Oil in their petroleum refining operations input crude oil into one processing department and then use the refined output for further processing into several end products. Each end product may undergo several steps of further processing after the initial refining, some of which may be shared with other end products and some of which may not.

An example of parallel processing is provided in Exhibit 4.3, which shows the process flows in a Coca-Cola™ bottling plant. In the first processing department, raw materials are mixed to make the basic concentrate. This concentrate can be used to make bottled Coke or it may be sold to restaurants and bars for use in soda fountains. Under the first option, the concentrate is sent on to the bottling department where it is mixed with carbonated water and then injected into sterile bottles and capped. In the final processing department, the bottles are inspected, labels are applied, and the bottles are packed in cartons. If the concentrate is to be sold for use in soda fountains, it is injected into large sterile metal cylinders, inspected and packaged for shipping. This is just an example of one way in which parallel processing can be set up. The number of possible variations in parallel processing is virtually limitless.

The flow of materials, labour and overhead costs

Cost accumulation is simpler in a process costing system than in a job-order costing system. In a process costing system, instead of having to trace costs to hundreds of different jobs, costs are traced to only a few processing departments.

A T-account model of materials, labour and overhead cost flows in a process costing system is given in Exhibit 4.4. Several key points should be noted from this exhibit. First, note that a separate Work in Progress account is maintained for *each processing department*. In contrast, in a job-order costing system there may be only a single Work in Progress account for the entire company. Second, note that the completed production of the first processing department (Department A in the exhibit) is transferred into the Work in Progress account of the second processing department (Department B), where it undergoes further work. After this further work, the completed units are then transferred into Finished Goods. (In Exhibit 4.4, we show only two processing departments, but there can be many such departments in a company.)

Finally, note that materials, labour and overhead costs can be added in any processing department – not just the first. Costs in Department B's Work in Progress account would therefore consist of the materials, labour and overhead costs entered directly into the account plus the costs attached to partially completed units transferred in from Department A (called **transferred-in costs**).

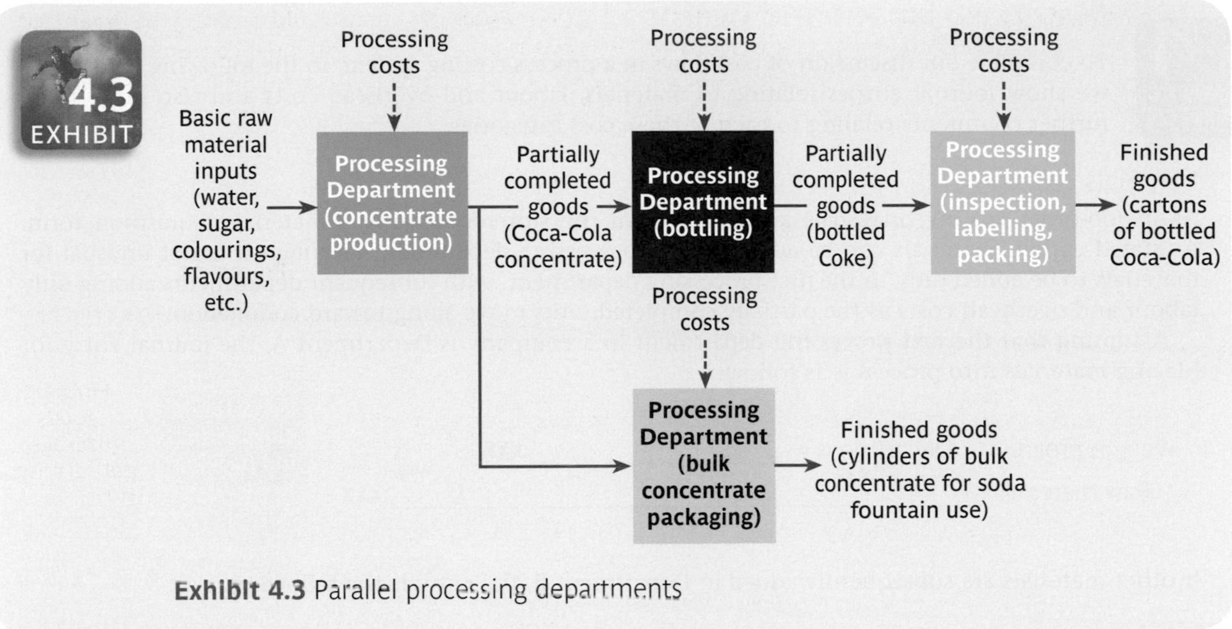

Exhibit 4.3 Parallel processing departments

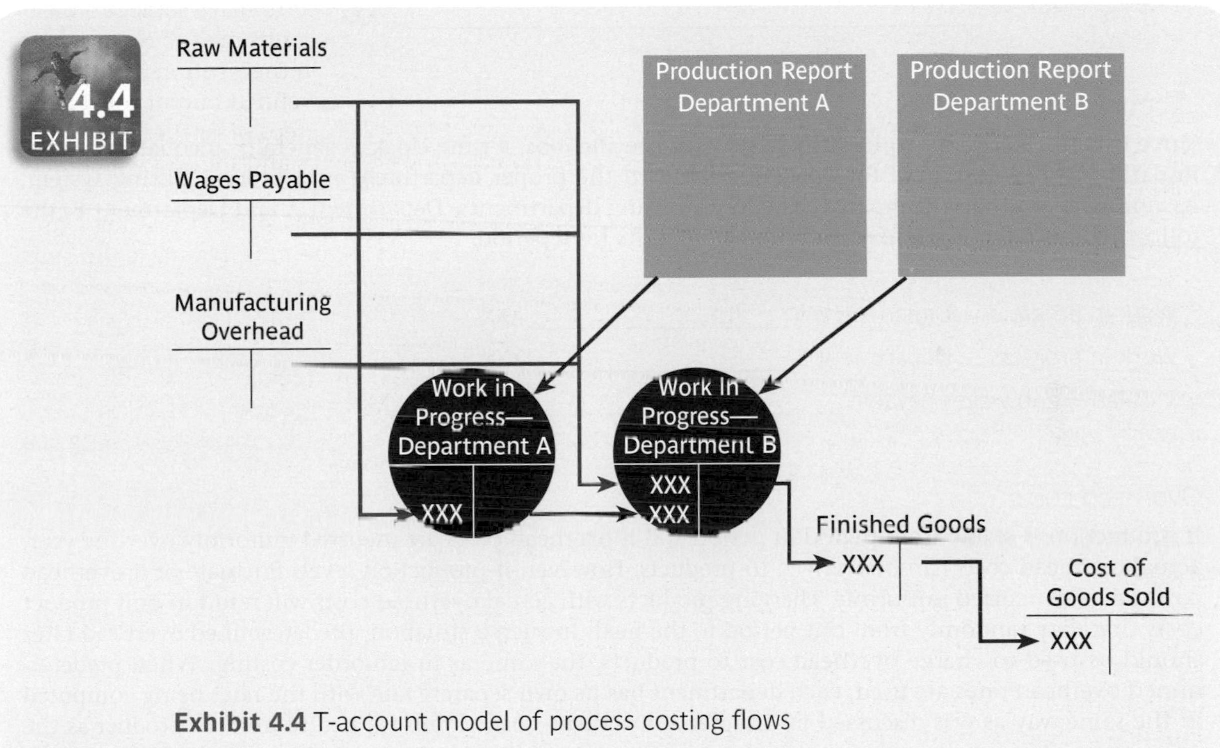

Exhibit 4.4 T-account model of process costing flows

Materials, labour and overhead cost entries

To complete our discussion of cost flows in a process costing system, in the following paragraphs we show journal entries relating to materials, labour and overhead costs and also make brief, further comments relating to each of these cost categories.

Materials costs

As in job-order costing, materials are drawn from the storeroom using a materials requisition form. As stated earlier, materials can be added in any processing department, although it is not unusual for materials to be added only in the first processing department, with subsequent departments adding only labour and overhead costs as the partially completed units move along toward completion.

Assuming that the first processing department in a company is Department A, the journal entry for placing materials into process is as follows:

Work in progress – Department A	XXX	
Raw materials		XXX

If other materials are subsequently added in Department B, the entry is the following:

Work in progress – Department B	XXX	
Raw materials		XXX

Labour costs

Since it is not necessary to identify costs with specific jobs, a time clock is generally adequate for accumulating labour costs and for allocating them to the proper department in a process costing system. Assuming again that a company has two processing departments, Department A and Department B, the following journal entry will record the labour costs for a period:

Work in progress – Department A	XXX	
Work in progress – Department B	XXX	
Salaries and wages payable		XXX

Overhead costs

If production is stable from period to period and if overhead costs are incurred uniformly over the year, actual overhead costs can be charged to products. However, if production levels fluctuate or if overhead costs are not incurred uniformly, charging products with actual overhead costs will result in unit product costs that vary randomly from one period to the next. In such a situation, predetermined overhead rates should be used to charge overhead cost to products, the same as in job-order costing. When predetermined overhead rates are used, each department has its own separate rate with the rates being computed in the same way as was discussed in Chapter 3. Overhead cost is then applied to units of product as the units move through the various departments. Since predetermined overhead rates are widely used in process costing, we will assume their use throughout the remainder of this chapter.

If a company has two processing departments, Department A and Department B, the following journal entry is used to apply overhead cost to products:

Work in progress – Department A	XXX	
Work in progress – Department B	XXX	
Manufacturing overhead		XXX

Completing the cost flows

Once processing has been completed in a department, the units are transferred to the next department for further processing, as illustrated earlier in the T-accounts in Exhibit 4.4. The following journal entry is used to transfer the costs of partially completed units from Department A to Department B:

Work in progress – Department B	XXX	
Work in progress – Department A		XXX

After processing has been completed in Department B, the costs of the completed units are then transferred to the Finished Goods stock account:

Finished Goods	XXX	
Work in progress – Department B		XXX

Finally, when a customer's order is filled and units are sold, the cost of the units is transferred to Cost of Goods Sold:

Cost of goods sold	XXX	
Finished goods		XXX

To summarize, we stated earlier that the cost flows between accounts are basically the same in a process costing system as they are in a job-order costing system. The only noticeable difference at this point is that in a process costing system there is a separate Work in Progress account for each department.

Management accounting in action: the issue

Sabine Poitiers, president of Allez Skis, was worried about the future of the company. After a rocky start, the company had come out with a completely redesigned ski called The Ultimate. It was made of exotic materials and featured flashy graphics. Exhibit 1.5 illustrates how this ski is manufactured. The ski was a runaway best seller – particularly among younger skiers – and had provided the company with much-needed cash for two years. However, last year a dismal snowfall in the Alps had depressed sales, and Allez was once again short of cash. Sabine was worried that another bad ski season would force Allez into bankruptcy.

Just before starting production of next year's model of The Ultimate, Sabine called Henri Simeon, the company finance director, into her office to discuss the reports she would need in the coming year.

Sabine: Henri, I am going to need more frequent cost information this year. I really have to stay on top of things.

Henri: What do you have in mind?

Sabine: I'd like reports at least once a month that detail our production costs for each department and for each pair of skis.

Henri: That shouldn't be much of a problem. We already compile almost all of the necessary data for the annual report. The only complication is our work in progress stock. This hasn't been a problem in our annual reports, since our fiscal year ends at a time when we have finished producing skis for the last model year and haven't yet started producing for the new model year. Consequently, there isn't any work in progress stock to value for the annual report. But that won't be true for monthly reports.

Sabine: I'm not sure why that is a problem, Henri. But I'm sure you can work out how to solve it.

Henri: You can count on me.

4.5
EXHIBIT

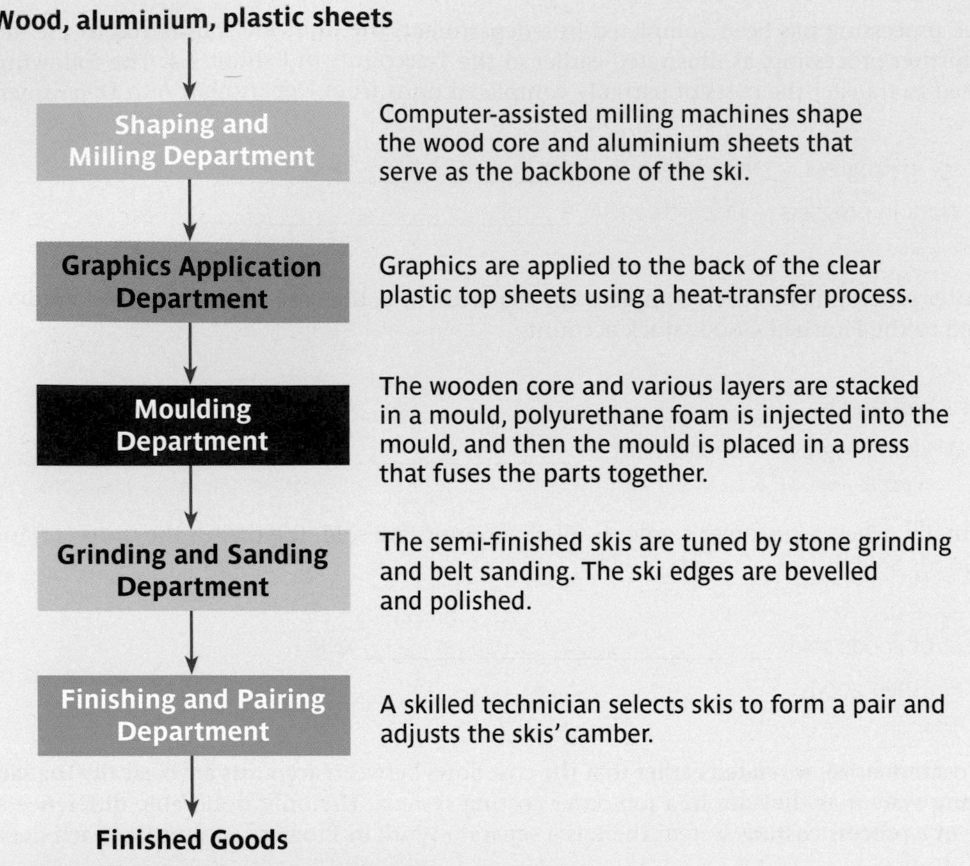
Wood, aluminium, plastic sheets
Shaping and Milling Department
Computer-assisted milling machines shape the wood core and aluminium sheets that serve as the backbone of the ski.
Graphics Application Department
Graphics are applied to the back of the clear plastic top sheets using a heat-transfer process.
Moulding Department
The wooden core and various layers are stacked in a mould, polyurethane foam is injected into the mould, and then the mould is placed in a press that fuses the parts together.
Grinding and Sanding Department
The semi-finished skis are tuned by stone grinding and belt sanding. The ski edges are bevelled and polished.
Finishing and Pairing Department
A skilled technician selects skis to form a pair and adjusts the skis' camber.
Finished Goods

Exhibit 4.5 The production process at Allez Skis

Adapted from Bill Gout, Jesse James Doquilo, and Studio MD, 'Capped Crusaders', *Skiing*, October 1993, pp. 138–44.

Equivalent units of production

Henri, the finance director of Allez Skis, was concerned with the following problem: After materials, labour and overhead costs have been accumulated in a department, the department's output must be determined so that unit costs can be computed. The difficulty is that a department usually has some partially completed units in its ending stock. It does not seem reasonable to count these partially completed units as equivalent to fully completed units when counting the department's output. Therefore, Henri will mathematically convert those partially completed units into an *equivalent* number of fully completed units. In process costing, this is done using the following formula:

$$\text{Equivalent units} = \text{Number of partially completed units} \times \text{Percentage completion}$$

As the formula states, **equivalent units** is defined to be the product of the number of partially completed units and the percentage completion of those units. The equivalent units is the number of complete units that could have been obtained from the materials and effort that went into the partially complete units.

For example, suppose the Moulding Department at Allez has 500 units in its ending work in progress stock that are 60% complete. These 500 partially complete units are equivalent to 300 fully complete units (500 × 60% = 300). Therefore, the ending work in progress stock would be said to contain 300 equivalent units. These equivalent units would be added to any fully completed units to determine the period's output for the department – called the *equivalent units of production*.

There are two different ways of computing the equivalent units of production for a period. In this chapter, we discuss the **weighted-average method**. In Appendix 4A, the **FIFO method** is discussed. The FIFO method of process costing is a method in which equivalent units and unit costs relate only to work done during the current period. In contrast, the weighted-average method blends together units and costs from the current period with units and costs from the prior period. In the weighted-average method, the **equivalent units of production** for a department are the number of units transferred to the next department (or to finished goods) plus the equivalent units in the department's ending work in progress stock.

Weighted-average method

Under the weighted-average method, a department's equivalent units are computed as described above:

Weighted-Average Method (a separate calculation is made for each cost category in each processing department)

Equivalent units of production = Units transferred to the next department or to finished goods + Equivalent units in ending work in progress stock

We do not have to make an equivalent units calculation for units transferred to the next department, since we can assume that they would not have been transferred unless they were 100% complete with respect to the work performed in the transferring department.

Consider the Shaping and Milling Department at Allez. This department uses computerized milling machines to shape precisely the wooden core and metal sheets that will be used to form the backbone of the ski. The following activity took place in the department in May, several months into the production of the new model of The Ultimate ski:

		Percentage completed	
	Units	Materials	Conversion
Work in progress, 1 May	200	50	30
Units started in production during May	5,000		
Units completed during May and transferred to the next department	4,800	100*	100*
Work in progress, 31 May	400	40	25

*It is always assumed that units transferred out of a department are 100% complete with respect to the processing done in that department.

Note the use of the term 'conversion' in the table. Conversion cost, as defined in Chapter 2, is direct labour cost plus manufacturing overhead cost. In process costing, conversion cost is often – but not always – treated as a single element of product cost.

Also note that the 1 May beginning work in progress was 50% complete with respect to materials costs and 30% complete with respect to conversion costs. This means that 50% of the materials costs required to complete the units had already been incurred. Likewise, 30% of the conversion costs required to complete the units had already been incurred.

Since Allez's work in progress stock are at different stages of completion in terms of the amounts of materials cost and conversion cost that have been added, two equivalent unit figures must be computed. The equivalent units computations are given in Exhibit 4.6.

	Materials	Conversion
Units transferred to the next department	4,800	4,800
Work in progress, 31 May:		
400 units × 40%	160	
400 units × 25%	—	100
Equivalent units of production	4,960	4,900

Exhibit 4.6 Equivalent units of production: weighted-average method

Note from the computation in Exhibit 4.6 that units in the beginning work in progress stock are ignored. The weighted-average method is concerned only with the fact that there are 4,900 equivalent units for conversion cost in ending stock and in units transferred to the next department – the method is not concerned with the additional fact that some of this work was accomplished in prior periods. This is a key point in the weighted-average method that is easy to overlook.

The weighted-average method blends together the work that was accomplished in prior periods with the work that was accomplished in the current period. In the FIFO method, the units and costs of prior periods are cleanly separated from the units and costs of the current period. Some managers believe the FIFO method is more accurate for this reason. However, the FIFO method is more complex than the weighted-average method and for that reason is covered in Appendix 4A.

A visual perspective of the computation of equivalent units of production is provided in Exhibit 4.7. The data are for conversion costs in the Shaping and Milling Department of Allez Skis. Study this exhibit carefully before going on.

Production report – weighted-average method

The production report developed in this section contains the information requested by the managing director of Allez Skis. The purpose of the production report is to summarize for management all of the activity that takes place in a department's Work in Progress account for a period. This activity includes the units and costs that flow through the Work in Progress account. As illustrated in Exhibit 4.8, a separate production report is prepared for each department.

Earlier, when we outlined the differences between job-order costing and process costing, we stated that the production report takes the place of a job cost sheet in a process costing system. The production report is a key management document and is vital to the proper operation of the system. The production report has three separate (though highly interrelated) parts:

1 A quantity schedule, which shows the flow of units through the department and a computation of equivalent units.

2 A computation of costs per equivalent unit.

3 A reconciliation of all cost flows into and out of the department during the period.

We will use the following data for the May operations of the Shaping and Milling Department of Allez Skis to illustrate the production report. Keep in mind that this report is only one of the five reports that would be prepared for the company since the company has five processing departments.

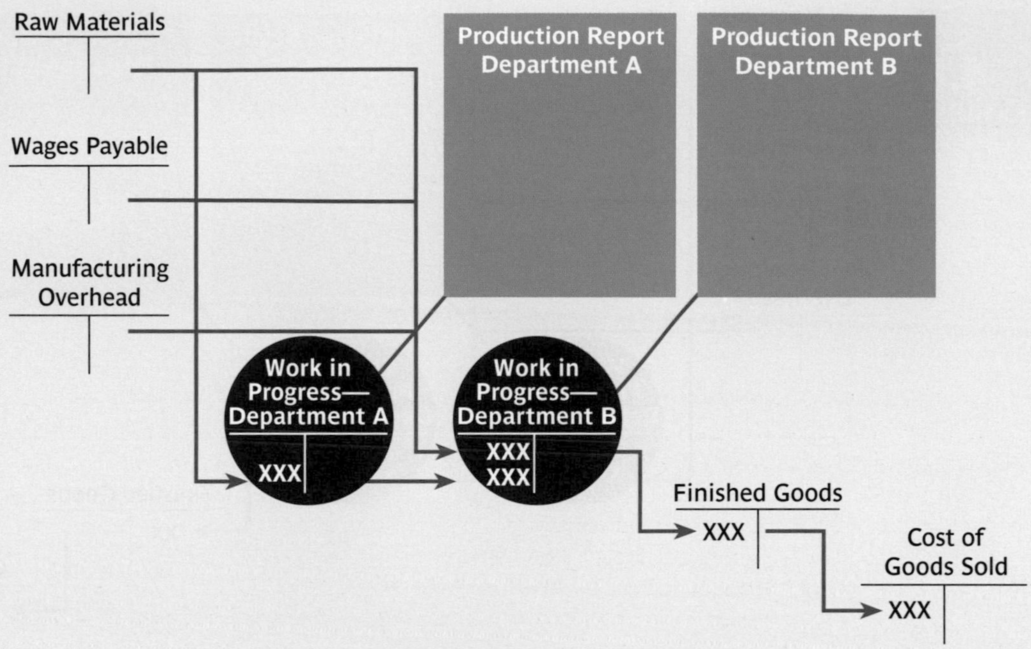

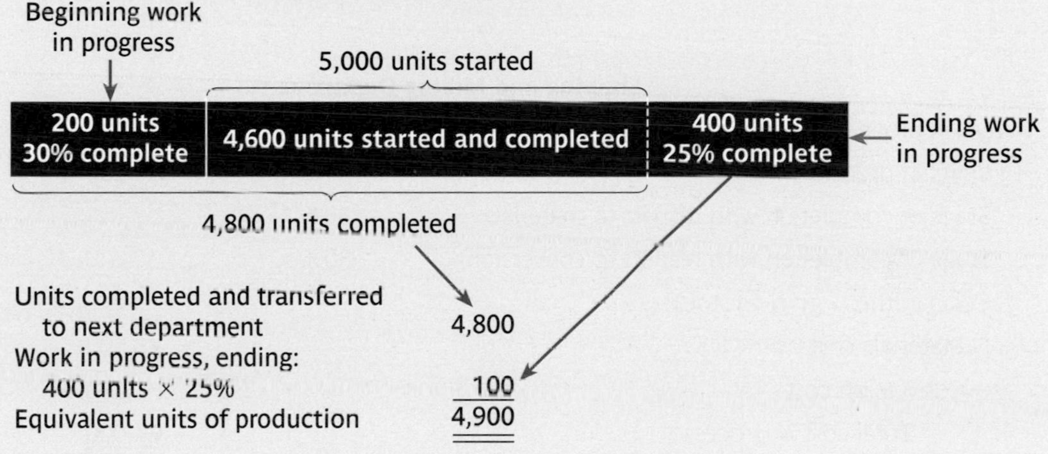

Units completed and transferred to next department	4,800
Work in progress, ending: 400 units × 25%	100
Equivalent units of production	4,900

Exhibit 4.7 Visual perspective of equivalent units of production

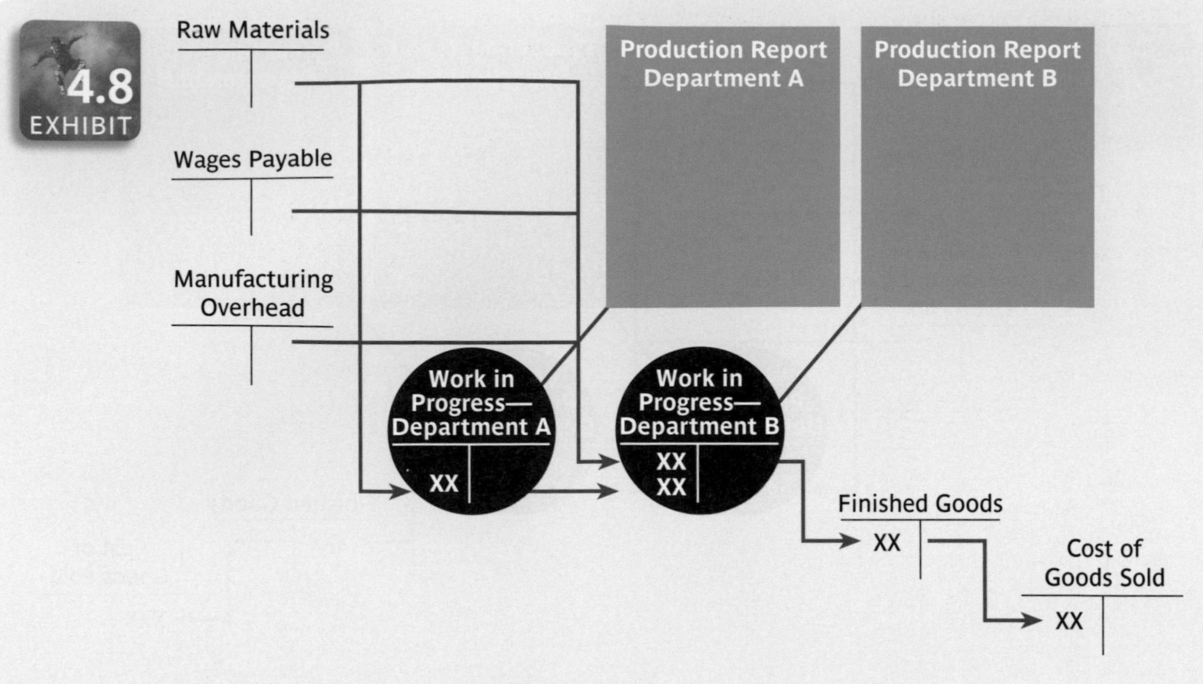

Exhibit 4.8 The position of the production report in the flow of costs

Shaping and Milling Department

Work in progress, beginning:		
Units in process		200
Stage of completion with respect to materials	50%	
Stage of completion with respect to conversion	30%	
Costs in the beginning stock:		
Materials cost		€3,000
Conversion cost		1,000
Total cost in process		€4,000
Units started into production during May		5,000
Units completed and transferred out		4,800
Costs added to production during May:		
Materials cost		€74,000
Conversion cost		70,000
Total cost added in the department		€144,000
Work in progress, ending:		
Units in process		400
Stage of completion with respect to materials	40%	
Stage of completion with respect to conversion	25%	

In this section, we show how a production report is prepared when the weighted average method is used to compute equivalent units and unit costs. The preparation of a production report under the FIFO method is illustrated in Appendix 4A at the end of this chapter.

Step 1: prepare a quantity schedule and compute the equivalent units

The first part of a production report consists of a **quantity schedule**, which shows the flow of units through a department and a computation of equivalent units. To illustrate, a quantity schedule combined with a computation of equivalent units is given below for the Shaping and Milling Department of Allez Skis.

Quantity schedule			
Units to be accounted for:			
Work in progress, 1 May (50% materials; 30% conversion added last month)	200		
Started into production	5,000		
Total units	5,200		
		Equivalent units	
		Materials	**Conversion**
Units accounted for as follows:			
Transferred to the next department	4,800	4,800	4,800
Work in progress, 31 May (40% materials; 25% conversion added this month)	400	160*	100†
Total units and equivalent units of production	5,200	4,960	4,900

*40% × 400 units = 160 equivalent units.

†25% × 400 units = 100 equivalent units.

The quantity schedule permits the manager to see at a glance how many units moved through the department during the period as well as to see the stage of completion of any in-process units. In addition to providing this information, the quantity schedule serves as an essential guide in preparing and tying together the remaining parts of a production report.

Step 2: compute costs per equivalent unit

As stated earlier, the weighted-average method blends together the work that was accomplished in the prior period with the work that was accomplished in the current period. That is why it is called the weighted-average method; it averages together units and costs from both the prior and current periods by adding the cost in the beginning work in progress stock to the current period costs. These computations are shown below for the Shaping and Milling Department for May:

Shaping and Milling Department

	Total cost	Materials	Conversion	Whole unit
Cost to be accounted for:				
Work in progress, 1 May	€4,000	€3,000	€1,000	
Cost added in the Shaping and Milling Department	144,000	74,000	70,000	
Total cost (a)	€148,000	€77,000	€71,000	
Equivalent units of production (Step 1 above) (b)		4,960	4,900	
Cost per EU, (a) / (b)		€15.524 +	€14.490	= €30.014

The cost per equivalent unit (EU) that we have computed for the Shaping and Milling Department will be used to apply cost to units that are transferred to the next department, graphics application, and will also be used to compute the cost in the ending work in progress stock. For example, each unit transferred out of the Shaping and Milling Department to the Graphics Application Department will carry with it a cost of €30.014. Since the costs are passed on from department to department, the unit cost of the last department, Finishing and Pairing, will represent the final unit cost of a completed unit of product.

Step 3: prepare a cost reconciliation

The purpose of a **cost reconciliation** is to show how the costs that have been charged to a department during a period are accounted for. Typically, the costs charged to a department will consist of the following:

1 Cost in the beginning work in progress stock.

2 Materials, labour, and overhead costs added during the period.

3 Cost (if any) transferred in from the preceding department.

In a production report, these costs are generally titled 'Cost to be accounted for'. They are accounted for in a production report by computing the following amounts:

1 Cost transferred out to the next department (or to Finished Goods).

2 Cost remaining in the ending work in progress stock.

In short, when a cost reconciliation is prepared, the 'Cost to be accounted for' from step 2 is reconciled with the sum of the cost transferred out during the period plus the cost in the ending work in progress stock. This concept is shown graphically in Exhibit 4.9. Study this exhibit carefully before going on to the cost reconciliation below for the Shaping and Milling Department.

Example of a cost reconciliation

To prepare a cost reconciliation, *follow the quantity schedule line for line and show the cost associated with each group of units*. This is done in Exhibit 4.10, where we present a completed production report for the Shaping and Milling Department.

The quantity schedule in the exhibit shows that 200 units were in process on 1 May and that an additional 5,000 units were started into production during the month. Looking at the 'Cost to be accounted for' in the middle part of the exhibit, notice that the units in process on 1 May had €4,000 in cost attached to them and that the Shaping and Milling Department added another €144,000 in cost to production during the month. Thus, the department has €148,000 (€4,000 + €144,000) in cost to be accounted for.

This cost is accounted for in two ways. As shown on the quantity schedule, 4,800 units were transferred to the Graphics Application Department, the next department in the production process. Another 400 units were still in process in the Shaping and Milling Department at the end of the month. Thus, part of the €148,000 'Cost to be accounted for' goes with the 4,800 units to the Graphics Application Department, and part of it remains with the 400 units in the ending work in progress stock in the Shaping and Milling Department.

Each of the 4,800 units transferred to the Graphics Application Department is assigned €30.014 in cost, for a total €144,067. The 400 units still in process at the end of the month are assigned costs according to their stage of completion. To determine the stage of completion, we refer to the equivalent units computation and bring the equivalent units figures down to the cost reconciliation part of the report. We then assign costs to these units, using the cost per equivalent unit figures already computed.

After cost has been assigned to the ending work in progress stock, the total cost that we have accounted for (€148,000) agrees with the amount that we had to account for (€148,000). Thus, the cost reconciliation is complete.

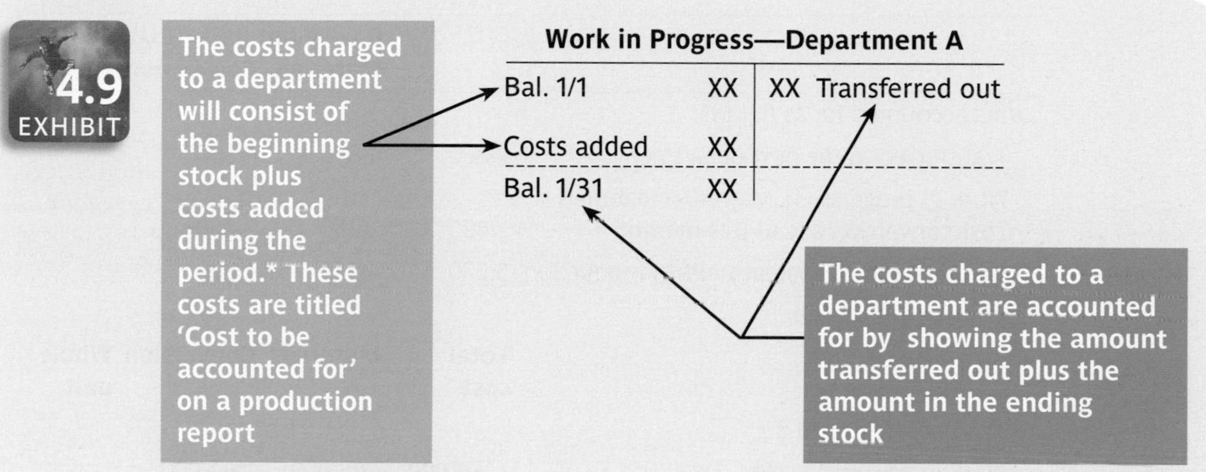

4.9
EXHIBIT
The costs charged to a department will consist of the beginning stock plus costs added during the period.* These costs are titled 'Cost to be accounted for' on a production report
Work in Progress—Department A
Bal. 1/1 XX
XX Transferred out
Costs added XX
Bal. 1/31 XX
The costs charged to a department are accounted for by showing the amount transferred out plus the amount in the ending stock

*Departments that follow Department A will need to show the amount of cost transferred in from preceding departments.

Exhibit 4.9 Graphic illustration of the cost reconciliation part of a production report

Allez Skis Shaping and Milling Department Production Report (weighted-average method)

Quantity schedule and equivalent units

	Quantity schedule		
Units to be accounted for			
Work in progress, 1 May (50% materials; 30% conversion added last month)	200		
Started into production	5,000		
Total units	5,200		
		Equivalent units (EU)	
		Materials	**Conversion**
Units accounted for as follows:			
Transferred to the next department	4,800	4,800	4,800
Work in progress, 31 May (40% materials 25% conversion added this month)	400	160*	100†
Total units and equivalent units of production	5,200	4,960	4,900

Costs per equivalent unit

	Total cost	**Materials**	**Conversion**	**Whole unit**
Cost to be accounted for:				
Work in progress, 1 May	**€4,000**	€3,000	€1,000	
Cost added in the Shaping and Milling Department	**144,000**	74,000	70,000	
Total cost (a)	**€148,000**	€77,000	€71,000	
Equivalent units of production (above) (b)		4,960	4,900	
Cost per EU, (a) ÷ (b)		€15.524 +	€14.490 =	€30.014

Cost reconciliation

	Total cost	**Equivalent units (above)**	
		Materials	**Conversion**
Cost accounted for as follows:			
Transferred to next department **4,800** units × **€30.014** each	**€144,067**	4,800	4,800
Work in progress, 31 May:			
Materials, at €15.524 per EU	2,484	160	
Conversion, at €14.490 per EU	1,449		100
Total work in progress, 31 May	3,933		
Total cost	€148,000		

*40% × 400 units = 160 equivalent units.

†25% × 400 units = 100 equivalent units.

EU = Equivalent unit.

Exhibit 4.10 Production report – weighted-average method

Management accounting in action: the wrap-up

Henri: Here's an example of the kind of report I can put together for you every month. This particular report is for the Shaping and Milling Department. It follows a fairly standard format for industries like ours and is called a production report. I hope this is what you have in mind.

Sabine: The quantity schedule makes sense to me. I can see we had a total of 5,200 units to account for in the department, and 4,800 of those were transferred to the next department while 400 were still in process at the end of the month. What are these 'equivalent units'?

Henri: That's the problem I mentioned earlier. While there are 400 units still in process, they are far from complete. When we compute the unit costs, it wouldn't make sense to count them as whole units.

Sabine: I suppose not. I see what you are driving at. Since those 400 units are only 25% complete with respect to our conversion costs, they should only be counted as 100 units when we compute the unit costs for conversion.

Henri: That's right. Is the rest of the report clear?

Sabine: Yes, it does seem pretty clear, although I want to work the numbers through on my own to make sure I thoroughly understand the report.

Henri: Does this report give you the information you wanted?

Sabine: Yes, it does. I can tell how many units are in process, how complete they are, what happened to them, and their costs. While I know the unit costs are averages and are heavily influenced by our volume, they still can give me some idea of how well we are doing on the cost side. Thanks, Henri.

A comment about rounding errors

If you use a calculator or computer spreadsheet and do not round off the costs per equivalent unit, there shouldn't be any discrepancy between the 'Cost to be accounted for' and the 'Cost accounted for' in the cost reconciliation. However, if you round off the costs per equivalent unit, the two figures will not always exactly agree. For the report in Exhibit 4.10, the two figures do agree, but this will not always happen. In all of the homework assignments and other materials, we follow two rules: (1) all the costs per equivalent unit are rounded off to three decimal places as in Exhibit 4.10, and (2) any adjustment needed to reconcile the 'Cost accounted for' with the 'Cost to be accounted for' is made to the cost 'transferred' amount rather than to the ending stock.

Operation costing

The costing systems discussed in Chapters 3 and 4 represent the two ends of a continuum. On one end we have job-order costing, which is used by companies that produce many different items – generally to customers' specifications. On the other end we have process costing, which is used by companies that produce basically homogeneous products in large quantities. Between these two extremes there are many hybrid systems that include characteristics of both job-order and process costing. One of these hybrids is called **operation costing**.

Operation costing is used in situations where products have some common characteristics and also some individual characteristics. Shoes, for example, have common characteristics in that all styles involve cutting and sewing that can be done on a repetitive basis, using the same equipment and following the same basic procedures. Shoes also have individual characteristics – some are made of expensive leathers and others may be made using inexpensive synthetic materials. In a situation like this, where products have some common characteristics but also must be handled individually to some extent, operation costing may be used to determine product costs.

As mentioned above, operation costing is a hybrid system that employs aspects of both job-order and process costing. Products are typically handled in batches when operation costing is in use, with each batch charged for its own specific materials. In this sense, operation costing is similar to job-order costing. However, labour and overhead costs are accumulated by operation or by department, and these costs are assigned to units as in process costing. If shoes are being produced, for example, each shoe is charged the same per unit conversion cost, regardless of the style involved, but it is charged with its specific materials cost. Thus, the company is able to distinguish between styles in terms of materials, but it is able to employ the simplicity of a process costing system for labour and overhead costs.

Examples of other products for which operation costing may be used include electronic equipment (such as semiconductors), textiles, clothing and jewellery (such as rings, bracelets, and medallions). Products of this type are typically produced in batches, but they can vary considerably from model to model or from style to style in terms of the cost of raw materials. Therefore, an operation costing system is well suited for providing cost data.

Summary

- Process costing is used in situations where homogeneous products or services are produced on a continuous basis. Costs flow through the manufacturing accounts in basically the same way in both job-order and process costing systems. A process costing system differs from a job-order system primarily in that costs are accumulated by department (rather than by job) and the department production report replaces the job cost sheet.
- To compute unit costs in a department, the department's output in terms of equivalent units must be determined. In the weighted-average method, the equivalent units for a period are the sum of the units transferred out of the department during the period and the equivalent units in ending work in progress stock at the end of the period.
- The activity in a department is summarized on a production report. There are three separate (though highly interrelated) parts to a production report. The first part is a quantity schedule, which includes a computation of equivalent units and shows the flow of units through a department during a period. The second part consists of a computation of costs per equivalent unit, with unit costs being provided individually for materials, labour and overhead as well as in total for the period. The third part consists of a cost reconciliation, which summarizes all cost flows through a department for a period.

Key terms for review

Cost reconciliation (p. 132).

Equivalent units (p. 126).

Equivalent units of production (p. 127).

FIFO method (p. 127).

Operation costing (p. 135).

Process costing (p. 120).

Processing department (p. 121).

Production report (p. 121).

Quantity schedule (p. 131).

Transferred-in cost (p. 122).

Weighted-average method (p. 127).

Appendix 4A: FIFO method

The FIFO method of process costing differs from the weighted-average method in two basic ways: (1) the computation of equivalent units, and (2) the way in which costs of beginning stock are treated in the cost reconciliation report. The FIFO method is generally considered more accurate than the weighted-average method, but it is more complex.[1] The complexity is not a problem for computers, but the FIFO method is a little more difficult to understand and to learn than the weighted average method.

Equivalent units – FIFO method

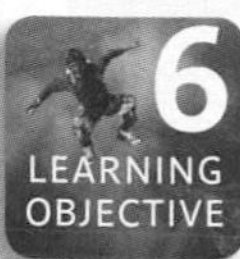

The computation of equivalent units under the FIFO method differs from the computation under the weighted-average method in two ways.

First, the 'units transferred out' figure is divided into two parts. One part consists of the units from the beginning stock that were completed and transferred out, and the other part consists of the units that were both *started* and *completed* during the current period.

Second, full consideration is given to the amount of work expended during the current period on units in the *beginning* work in progress stock as well as on units in the ending stock. Thus, under the FIFO method, it is necessary to convert both stock to an equivalent units basis. For the beginning stock, the equivalent units represent the work done to *complete* the units; for the ending stock, the equivalent units represent the work done to bring the units to a stage of partial completion at the end of the period (the same as with the weighted-average method).

The formula for computing the equivalent units of production under the FIFO method is more complex than under the weighted-average method:

FIFO Method

[a separate calculation is made for each cost category in each processing department]

Equivalent units of production = Equivalent units to complete beginning stock*
+ Units started and completed during the period
+ Equivalent units in ending work in progress stock

*Equivalent units to complete beginning stock = Units in beginning stock × (100 − Percentage completion of beginning stock)

Or, the equivalent units of production can also be determined as follows:

Equivalent units of production = Units transferred out
+ Equivalent units in ending work in progress stock
− Equivalent units in beginning stock

To illustrate the FIFO method, refer again to the data for the Shaping and Milling Department at Allez Skis. The department completed and transferred 4,800 units to the next department, the Graphics Application Department, during May. Since 200 of these units came from the beginning stock, the Shaping and Milling Department must have started and completed 4,600 units during May. The 200 units in the beginning stock were 50% complete with respect to materials and only 30% complete with respect to conversion costs when the month started. Thus, to complete these units the department must have added another 50% of materials costs and another 70% of conversion costs (100% − 30% = 70%). Following this line of reasoning, the equivalent units for the department for May would be computed as shown in Exhibit 4A.1.

Comparison of equivalent units of production under the weighted-average and FIFO methods

Stop at this point and compare the data in Exhibit 4A.1 with the data in Exhibit 4.6 in the chapter, which shows the computation of equivalent units under the weighted-average method. Also refer to Exhibit 4A.2, which provides a visual comparison of the two methods.

	Materials	Conversion
Work in progress,1 May:		
200 units × (100% − 50%)*	100	
200 units × (100% − 30%)*		140
Units started and completed in May	4,600†	4,600†
Work in progress,31 May:		
400 units × 40%	160	
400 units × 25%		100
Equivalent units of production	4,860	4,840

*This is the work needed to complete the units in beginning stock.

†4,800 units transferred out to the next FIFO method assumes that the units in beginning stock are finished first.

Exhibit 4A.1 Equivalent units of production: FIFO method

The essential difference between the two methods is that the weighted-average method blends work and costs from the prior period with work and costs in the current period, whereas the FIFO method cleanly separates the two periods. To see this more clearly, consider the following comparison of the two calculations of equivalent units:

	Materials	Conversion
Equivalent units – weighted-average method	4,960	4,900
Less equivalent units in beginning stock:		
200 units × 50%	100	
200 units × 30%		60
Equivalent units of production – FIFO method	4,860	4,840

From the above, it is evident that the FIFO method removes the equivalent units that were already in beginning stock from the equivalent units as defined using the weighted-average method. Thus, the FIFO method isolates the equivalent units due to work performed during the current period. The weighted-average method blends together the equivalent units already in beginning stock with the equivalent units due to work performed in the current period.

Production report – FIFO method

The steps followed in preparing a production report under the FIFO method are the same as those discussed earlier for the weighted-average method. However, since the FIFO method makes a distinction between units in the beginning stock and units started during the year, the cost reconciliation portion of the report is more complex under the FIFO method than it is under the weighted-average method. To illustrate the FIFO method, we will again use the data for Allez Skis on page 131.

Step 1: Prepare a quantity schedule and compute the equivalent units

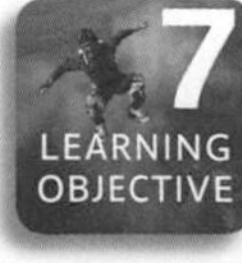

There is only one difference between a quantity schedule prepared under the FIFO method and one prepared under the weighted-average method. This difference relates to units transferred out. As explained earlier in our discussion of equivalent units, the FIFO method divides units transferred out into two parts. One part consists of the units in the beginning stock and the other

ALLEZ SKIS
Shaping and Milling Department
Conversion Costs

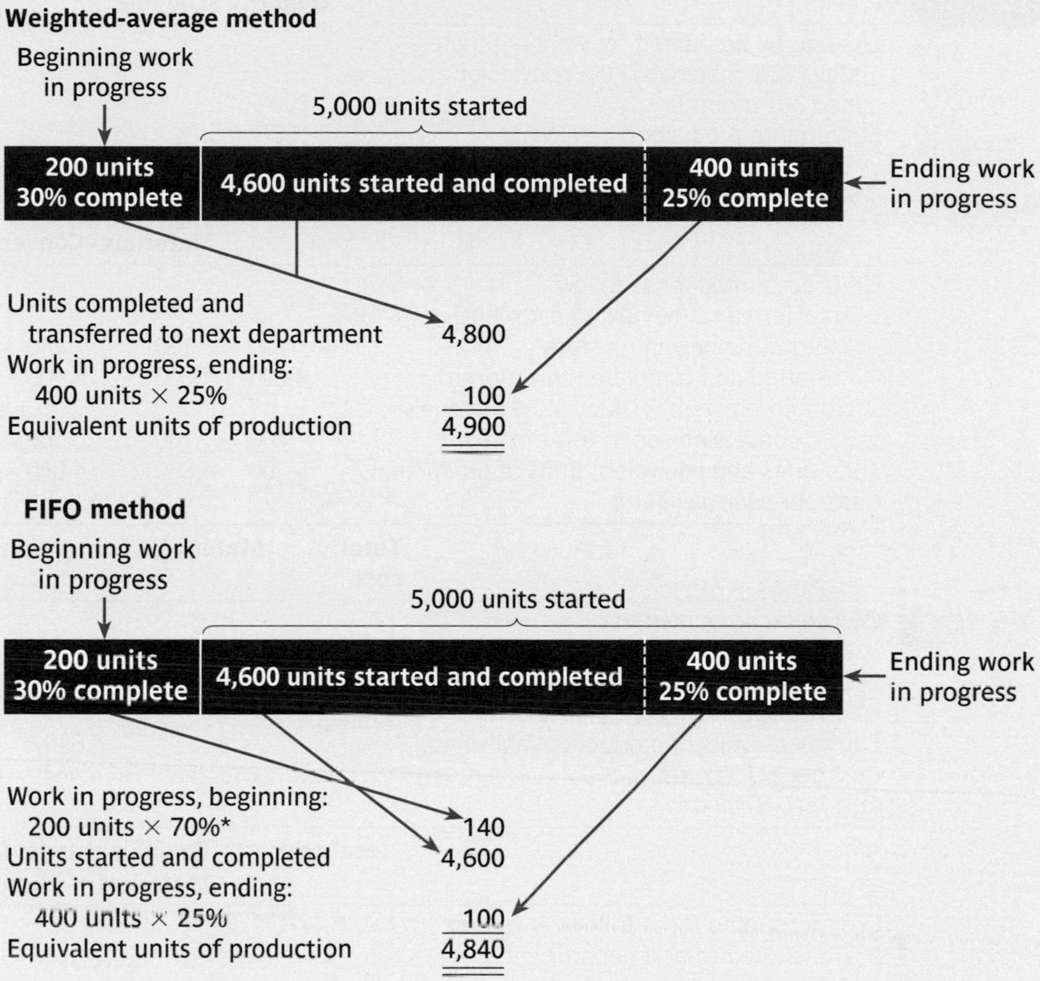

Weighted-average method

Beginning work in progress → 200 units 30% complete | 4,600 units started and completed | 400 units 25% complete ← Ending work in progress

(5,000 units started = 4,600 units started and completed + 400 units 25% complete)

Units completed and transferred to next department	4,800
Work in progress, ending:	
400 units × 25%	100
Equivalent units of production	4,900

FIFO method

Beginning work in progress → 200 units 30% complete | 4,600 units started and completed | 400 units 25% complete ← Ending work in progress

(5,000 units started = 4,600 units started and completed + 400 units 25% complete)

Work in progress, beginning:	
200 units × 70%*	140
Units started and completed	4,600
Work in progress, ending:	
400 units × 25%	100
Equivalent units of production	4,840

*100% − 30% = 70%. This 70% represents the work needed to complete the units in beginning stock.

Exhibit 4A.2 Visual perspective of equivalent units of production

part consists of the units started and completed during the current period. A quantity schedule showing this format for units transferred out is presented in Exhibit 4A.3, along with a computation of equivalent units for the month.

We explained earlier that in computing equivalent units under the FIFO method, we must first show the amount of work required *to complete* the units in the beginning stock. We then show the number of units started and completed during the period, and finally we show the amount of work completed on the units still in process at the end of the period. Carefully trace through these computations in Exhibit 4A.3.

Allez Skis Shaping and Milling Department Production Report (FIFO method)

Quantity schedule and equivalent units

	Quantity schedule		
Units to be accounted for work in progress, 1 May (50% materials; 30% conversion added last month)	200		
Started into production	5,000		
Total units	5,200		
		Equivalent Units (EU)	
		Materials	**Conversion**
Units accounted for as follows:			
Transferred to the next department:			
From the beginning stock*	200	100	140
Started and completed this month†	4,600	4,600	4,600
Work in progress, 31 May (40% materials; 25% conversion added this month)‡	400	160	100
Total units and equivalent units of production	5,200	4,860	4,840

Costs per equivalent unit

	Total cost	**Materials**	**Conversion**	**Whole unit**
Cost to be accounted for:				
Work in progress,1 May	€4,000			
Cost added in the department (a)	144,000	74,000	£70,000	
Total cost	€148,000			
Equivalent units of production (above) (b)		4,860	4,840	
Cost per EU, (a) ÷ (b)		€15.226 +	€14.463 =	€29.869

Cost reconciliation

	Total cost	**Equivalent units (above)**	
		Materials	**Conversion**
Cost accounted for as follows:			
Transferred to next department:			
From the beginning stock:			
Cost in the beginning stock	€4,000		
Cost to complete these units:			
Materials, at €15.226 per EU	1,523	100*	
Conversion, at €14.463 per EU	2,025		140*
Total cost	7,548		
Units started and completed this month, at €29.689 per unit	136,570	4,600†	4,600†
Total cost transferred	144,118		
Work in progress, 31 May:			
Materials, at €15.226 per EU	2,436	160‡	
Conversion, at €14.463 per EU	1,446		100‡
Total work in progress, 31 May	3,882		
Total cost	148,000		

*Materials 200 × (100% − 50%) = 100 equivalent units. Conversion 200 × (100% − 30%) = 140 equivalent units

†5000 units started − 400 units in ending stock = 4,600 units started completed.

‡Materials: 400 × (40%) = 160 equivalent units. Conversion: 400 × (25%) = 100 equivalent units.

EU = Equivalent Units.

Exhibit 4A.3 Production report – FIFO method

Step 2: Compute the costs per equivalent unit

In computing unit costs under the FIFO method, we use only those costs that were incurred during the current period, and we ignore any costs in the beginning work in progress stock. Under the FIFO method, unit costs relate only to work done during the current period.

The costs per equivalent unit (EU) computed in Exhibit 4A.3 are used to cost units of product transferred to the next department; in addition, they are used to show the cost attached to partially completed units in the ending work in progress stock.

Step 3: Prepare a cost reconciliation

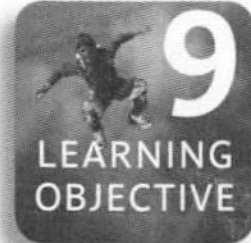

The purpose of cost reconciliation is to show how the costs charged to a department during a period are accounted for. With the FIFO method, two cost elements are associated with the units in the beginning work in progress stock. The first element is the cost carried over from the prior period. The second element is the cost needed *to complete* these units. For the Shaping and Milling Department, €4,000 in cost was carried over from last month. In the cost reconciliation in Exhibit 4A.3, we add to this figure the €1,523 in materials cost and €2,025 in conversion cost needed to complete these units. Note from the exhibit that these materials and conversion cost figures are computed by multiplying the costs per equivalent unit for materials and conversion by the equivalent units of work needed *to complete* the items that were in the beginning stock. (The equivalent units figures used in this computation are brought down from the 'Equivalent units' portion of the production report.)

For units started and completed during the month, we simply multiply the number of units started and completed by the total cost per unit to determine the amount transferred out. This would be €136,570 (4,600 units × €29.689 = €136,570) for the department.

Finally, the amount of cost attached to the ending work in progress stock is computed by multiplying the cost per equivalent unit figures for the month by the equivalent units for materials and conversion costs in the ending stock. Once again, the equivalent units needed for this computation are brought down from the 'Equivalent units' portion of the production report.

Exhibit 4A.4 summarizes the major similarities and differences between production reports prepared under the weighted-average and FIFO methods.

A comparison of costing methods

In most situations, the weighted-average and FIFO methods will produce very similar unit costs. If there never is any ending stock, as in an ideal JIT environment, the two methods will produce identical results. The reason for this is that without any ending stock, no costs can be carried forward into the next period and the weighted-average method will base the unit costs on just the current period's costs – just as in the FIFO method. If there is ending stock, either erratic input prices or erratic production levels would also be required to generate much of a difference in unit costs under the two methods. This is because the weighted-average method will blend the unit costs from the prior period with the unit costs of the current period. Unless these unit costs differ greatly, the blending will not make much difference.

Nevertheless, from the standpoint of cost control, the FIFO method is superior to the weighted-average method. Current performance should be measured in relation to costs of the current period only, and the weighted-average method mixes costs of the current period with costs of the prior period. Thus, under the weighted-average method, the manager's apparent performance is influenced by what happened in the prior period. This problem does not arise under the FIFO method, since it makes a clear distinction between costs of prior periods and costs incurred during the current period. For the same reason, the FIFO method also provides more up-to-date cost data for decision-making purposes.

Some managers prefer the weighted-average method because they feel that the weighted-average method is simpler to apply than the FIFO method. Although this was true in the past when much accounting work was done by hand, computers can handle the additional calculations with ease once they have been appropriately programmed.

Weighted-average method	FIFO method
Quantity schedule and equivalent units	
1. The quantity schedule includes all units transferred out in a single figure.	1. The quantity schedule divides the units transferred out into two parts. One part consists of units in the beginning stock, and the other part consists of units started and completed during the current period.
2. In computing equivalent units, the units in the beginning stock are treated as if they were started and completed during the current period.	2. Only work needed to *complete* units in the beginning stock is included in the computation of equivalent units. Units started and completed during the current period are shown as a separate figure.
Total and unit costs	
1. The 'Cost to be accounted for' part of the report is the same for both methods.	1. The 'Cost to be accounted for' part of the report is the same for both of methods.
2. Costs in the beginning stock are added in with costs of the current period in computations of costs per equivalent unit.	2. Only costs of the current period are included in computations of costs per equivalent unit.
Cost reconciliation	
1. All units transferred out are treated the same, regardless of whether they were part of the beginning stock or started and completed during the period.	1. Units transferred out are divided into two groups: (a) units in the beginning stock, and (b) units started and completed during the period.
2. Units in the ending stock have cost applied to them in the same way under both methods.	2. Units in the ending stock have cost applied to them in the same way under both methods.

Exhibit 4A.4 Comparison of production report content

Review problem: process cost flows and reports

Luxguard Home Paint Company produces exterior latex paint, which it sells in one litre containers. The company has two processing departments – Base Fab and Finishing. White paint, which is used as a base for all the company's paints, is mixed from raw ingredients in the Base Fab Department. Pigments are added to the basic white paint, the pigmented paint is squirted under pressure into one-litre containers, and the containers are labelled and packed for shipping in the Finishing Department. Information relating to the company's operations for April is as follows:

(a) Raw materials were issued for use in production: Base Fab Department, £851,000; and Finishing Department, £629,000.

(b) Direct labour costs were incurred: Base Fab Department, £330,000; and Finishing Department, £270,000.

(c) Manufacturing overhead cost was applied: Base Fab Department, £665,000; and Finishing Department, £405,000.

(d) Basic white paint was transferred from the Base Fab Department to the Finishing Department, £1,850,000.

(e) Paint that had been prepared for shipping was transferred from the Finishing Department to Finished Goods, £3,200,000.

Required

1 Prepare journal entries to record items (a) to (e) above.

2 Post the journal entries from Question 1 above to T-accounts. The balance in the Base Fab Department's Work in Progress account on 1 April was £150,000; the balance in the Finishing Department's Work in Progress account was £70,000. After posting entries to the T-accounts, find the ending balance in each department's Work in Progress account.

3 Prepare a production report for the Base Fab Department for April. The following additional information is available regarding production in the Base Fab Department during April:

Production data:	
Units (litres) in process, 1 April: 100% complete as to materials, 60% complete as to labour and overhead	30,000
Units (litres) started into production during April	420,000
Units (litres) completed and transferred to the Finishing Department	370,000
Units (litres) in process, 30 April: 50% complete as to materials, 25% complete as to labour and overhead	80,000
Cost data:	
Work in progress stock, 1 April:	
Materials	£92,000
Labour	21,000
Overhead	37,000
Total cost	£150,000
Cost added during April:	
Materials	£851,000
Labour	330,000
Overhead	665,000

Solution to review problem: process cost flows and reports

1 (a)	Work in Progress – Base Fab Department	851,000	
	Work in Progress – Finishing Department	629,000	
	Raw Materials		1,480,000
(b)	Work in Progress – Base Fab Department	330,000	
	Work in Progress – Finishing Department	270,000	
	Salaries and Wages Payable		600,000
(c)	Work in Progress – Base Fab Department	665,000	
	Work in Progress – Finishing Department	405,000	
	Manufacturing Overhead		1,070,000
(d)	Work in Progress – Finishing Department		1,850,000
	Work in Progress – Base Fab Department		1,850,000
(e)	Finished Goods	3,200,000	
	Work in Progress – Finishing Department		3,200,000

2

Raw materials

Bal.	XXX	(a)	1,480,000

Salaries and wages payable

		(b)	600,000

Work in progress – Base Fab department

Bal.	150,000	(d)	1,850,000
(a)	851,000		
(b)	330,000		
(c)	665,000		
Bal.	146,000		

Manufacturing overhead

(Various actual cost)		(c)	1,070,000

Work in progress – Finishing department

Bal.	70,000	(e)	3,200,000
(a)	629,000		
(b)	270,000		
(c)	405,000		
(d)	1,850,000		
Bal.	24,000		

Finished goods

Bal.	XXX		
(e)	3,200,000		

Luxguard Home Paint Company
Production report – Base Fab department
For the month ended 30 April

Quantity Schedule and Equivalent Units

	Quantity schedule			
Units (litres) to be accounted for:				
Work in progress, 1 April (all materials, 60% labour and overhead added last month)	30,000			
Started into production	420,000			
Total units	450,000			
		Equivalent Units (EU)		
		Material	**Labour**	**Overhead**
Units (litres) accounted for as follows:				
Transferred to Finishing Department	370,000	370,000	370,000	70,000
Work in progress, 30 April (50% materials, 25% labour and overhead added this month)	80,000	40,000*	20,000*	20,000*
Total units and equivalent units of production	450,000	410,000	390,000	390,000

Costs per Equivalent Unit

	Total cost	Materials	Labour	Overhead	Whole unit
Cost to be accounted for:					
Work in progress, 1 April	£150,000	£92,000	£21,000	£37,000	
Cost added by the Finishing Department	1,846,000	851,000	330,000	665,000	
Total cost, a	£1,996,000	£943,000	£351,000	£702,000	
Equivalent units of production (b)	–	410,000	390,000	390,000	
Cost per EU, a /b	–	£2.30 +	0.90 +	£1.80 =	£5.00

Cost Reconciliation

	Total cost	**Equivalent Units (above)**		
		Materials	**Labour**	**Overhead**
Cost accounted for as follows:				
Transferred to Finishing Department:				
370,000 units × £5.00 each	£1,850,000	370,000	370,000	370,000
Work in progress, 30 April:				
Materials, at £2.30 per EU	92,000	40,000		
Labour, at £0.90 per EU	18,000		20,000	
Overhead, at £1.80 per EU	36,000			20,000
Total work in progress	146,000			
Total cost	£1,996,000			

*Materials: 80,000 units × 50% = 40,000 equivalent units; labour and overhead: 80,000 units × 25% = 20,000 equivalent units. EU = Equivalent Unit.

Questions

4–1 Under what conditions would it be appropriate to use a process costing system?

4–2 What similarities exist between job-order and process costing?

4–3 Costs are accumulated by job in a job-order costing system; how are costs accumulated in a process costing system?

4–4 What two essential features characterize any processing department in a process costing system?

4–5 Distinguish between departments arranged in a sequential pattern and departments arranged in a parallel pattern.

4–6 Why is cost accumulation easier under a process costing system than it is under a job-order costing system?

4–7 How many Work in Progress accounts are maintained in a company using process costing?

4–8 Assume that a company has two processing departments, Mixing and Firing. Prepare a journal entry to show a transfer of partially completed units from the Mixing Department to the Firing Department.

4–9 Assume again that a company has two processing departments, Mixing and Firing. Explain what costs might be added to the Firing Department's Work in Progress account during a period.

4–10 What is meant by the term equivalent units of production when the weighted-average method is used?

4–11 What is a quantity schedule, and what purpose does it serve?

4–12 Under process costing, it is often suggested that a product is like a rolling snowball as it moves from department to department. Why is this an apt comparison?

4–13 Watkins Trophies Ltd produces thousands of medallions made of bronze, silver and gold. The medallions are identical except for the materials used in their manufacture. What costing system would you advise the company to use?

4–14 Give examples of companies that might use operation costing.

4–15 (Appendix 4A) How does the computation of equivalent units under the FIFO method differ from the computation of equivalent units under the weighted-average method?

4–16 (Appendix 4A) On the cost reconciliation part of the production report, the weighted-average method treats all units transferred out in the same way. How does this differ from the FIFO method of handling units transferred out?

4–17 (Appendix 4A) From the standpoint of cost control, why is the FIFO method superior to the weighted-average method?

Exercises

E4–1 Time allowed: 10 minutes

Chocolaterie de Geneve, SA, is located in a French-speaking canton in Switzerland. The company makes chocolate truffles that are sold in popular embossed tins. The company has two processing departments – Cooking and Moulding. In the Cooking Department, the raw ingredients for the truffles are mixed and then cooked in special candy-making vats. In the Moulding Department, the melted chocolate and other ingredients from the Cooking Department are carefully poured into moulds and decorative flourishes are applied by hand. After cooling, the truffles are packed for sale. The company uses a process costing system. The following T-accounts show the flow of costs through the two departments in April (all amounts are in Swiss francs):

Work in progress – cooking

Bal. 1 April	8,000	Transferred out	160,000
Direct materials	42,000		
Direct labour	50,000		
Overhead	75,000		

Work in progress – moulding

Bal. 1 April	4,000	Transferred out	240,000
Transferred in	160,000		
Direct labour	36,000		
Overhead	45,000		

Required

Prepare journal entries showing the flow of costs through the two processing departments during April.

E4–2 Time allowed: 10 minutes

Clonex Labs uses a process costing system. The following data are available for one department for October:

		Percentage completed	
	Units	**Materials**	**Conversion**
Work in progress, 1 October	30,000	65	30
Work in progress, 31 October	15,000	80	40

The department started 175,000 units into production during the month and transferred 190,000 completed units to the next department.

Required

Compute the equivalent units of production for October assuming that the company uses the weighted-average method of accounting for units and costs.

E4–3 Time allowed: 10 minutes

(Appendix 4A) Refer to the data for Clonex Labs in E4–2.

Required

Compute the equivalent units of production for October assuming that the company uses the FIFO method of accounting for units and costs.

E4–4 Time allowed: 15 minutes

Finlay Fisheries processes salmon for various distributors. Two departments are involved – Department 1 and Department 2. Data relating to kilos of salmon processed in Department 1 during July are presented below:

	Kilos of salmon	**Percentage completed***
Work in progress, 1 July	20,000	30
Started into processing during July	380,000	–
Work in progress, 31 July	25,000	60

*Labour and overhead only.

All materials are added at the beginning of processing in Department 1. Labour and overhead (conversion) costs are incurred uniformly throughout processing.

Required

Prepare a quantity schedule and a computation of equivalent units for July for Department 1 assuming that the company uses the weighted-average method of accounting for units.

E4–5 Time allowed: 10 minutes

(Appendix 4A) Refer to the data for Finlay Fisheries in E4–4.

Required

Prepare a quantity schedule and a computation of equivalent units for July for Department 1 assuming that the company uses the FIFO method of accounting for units.

E4–6 Time allowed: 10 minutes

Hielta Oy, a Finnish company, processes wood pulp for various manufacturers of paper products. Data relating to tons of pulp processed during June are provided below:

		Percentage completed	
	Tons of pulp	Materials	Labour and overhead
Work in progress, 1 June	20,000	90	80
Work in progress, 30 June	30,000	60	40
Started into processing during June	190,000	–	–

Required

1 Compute the number of tons of pulp completed and transferred out during June.

2 Prepare a quantity schedule for June assuming that the company uses the weighted-average method.

E4–7 Time allowed: 10 minutes

(Appendix 4A) Refer to the data for Hielta Oy in E4–6.

Required

1 Compute the number of tons of pulp completed and transferred out during June.

2 Prepare a quantity schedule for June assuming that the company uses the FIFO method.

E4–8 Time allowed: 20 minutes

Pureform manufactures a product that passes through two departments. Data for a recent month for the first department follow:

	Units	Materials	Labour	Overhead
Work in progress, beginning	5,000	£4,500	£1,250	£1,875
Units started in process	45,000			
Units transferred out	42,000			
Work in progress, ending	8,000			
Cost added during the month	–	52,800	21,500	32,250

The beginning work in progress stock was 80% complete as to materials and 60% complete as to processing. The ending work in progress stock was 75% complete as to materials and 50% complete as to processing.

Required

1 Assume that the company uses the weighted-average method of accounting for units and costs. Prepare a quantity schedule and a computation of equivalent units for the month.

2 Determine the costs per equivalent unit for the month.

E4–9 Time allowed: 20 minutes
(Appendix 4A) Refer to the data for Pureform in E4–8.

Required

1 Assume that the company uses the FIFO method of accounting for units and costs. Prepare a quantity schedule and a computation of equivalent units for the month.

2 Determine the costs per equivalent unit for the month.

E4–10 Time allowed: 20 minutes
Helox Ltd manufactures a product that passes through two production processes. A quantity schedule for a recent month for the first process follows:

Quantity schedule

Units to be accounted for:			
Work in progress, 1 May (all materials, 40% conversion cost added last month)	5,000		
Started into production	180,000		
Total units	185,000		
		Equivalent units	
	Total cost	**Materials**	**Conversion**
Units accounted for as follows:			
Transferred to the next process	175,000	?	?
Work in progress, 31 May (all materials, 30% conversion cost added this month)	10,000	?	?
Total units	185,000	?	?

Costs in the beginning work in progress stock of the first processing department were: materials, £1,200; and conversion cost, £3,800. Costs added during the month were: materials, £54,000; and conversion cost, £352,000.

Required

1 Assume that the company uses the weighted-average method of accounting for units and costs. Determine the equivalent units for the month for the first process.

2 Compute the costs per equivalent unit for the month for the first process.

E4–11 Time allowed: 15 minutes
(This exercise should be assigned only if E4–10 is also assigned.) Refer to the data for Helox Ltd in E4–10 and to the equivalent units and costs per equivalent unit you have computed there.

Required

Complete the following cost reconciliation for the first process:

Cost reconciliation

	Total cost	Equivalent units Materials	Conversion
Cost accounted for as follows:			
Transferred to the next process: (? units × £?)	£?		
Work in progress, 31 May:			
Materials, at — per EU	?	?	
Conversion, at — per EU	?		?
Total work in progress	?		
Total cost	£?		

E4–12 Time allowed: 20 minutes
(Appendix 4A) Refer to the data for Helox Ltd in E4–10. Assume that the company uses the FIFO cost method.

Required

1 Prepare a quantity schedule and a computation of equivalent units for the month for the first process.
2 Compute the costs per equivalent unit for the month for the first process.

E4–13 Time allowed: 20 minutes
(Appendix 4A) (This exercise should be assigned only if E4–12 is also assigned.) Refer to the data for Helox Ltd in E4–10 and to the equivalent units and costs per equivalent unit that you computed in E4–12.

Required

Complete the following cost reconciliation for the first process:

Cost reconciliation

	Total cost	Equivalent units Materials	Conversion
Cost accounted for as follows:			
Transferred to the next process:			
From the beginning stock:			
Cost in the beginning stock	£?		
Cost to complete these units:			
Materials, at — per EU	?	?	
Conversion, at — per EU	?		?
Total cost	?		
Units started and completed this month: units × each	?	?	?
Total cost transferred	?		
Work in progress, 31 May:			
Materials, at — per EU	?	?	
Conversion, at — per EU	?		?
Total work in progress	?		
Total cost	£?		

Problems

P4–14 Weighted-average method; step-by-step production report Time allowed: 45 minutes
Builder Products Ltd manufactures a caulking compound that goes through three processing stages prior to completion. Information on work in the first department, Cooking, is given below for May:

Production data:	
Units in process, 1 May; 100% complete as to materials and 80% complete as to labour and overhead	10,000
Units started into production during May	100,000
Units completed and transferred out	95,000
Units in process, 31 May; 60% complete as to materials and 20% complete as to labour and overhead	?
Cost data:	
Work in progress stock, 1 May:	
Materials cost	£1,500
Labour cost	1,800
Overhead cost	5,400
Cost added during May:	
Materials cost	154,500
Labour cost	22,700
Overhead cost	68,100

Materials are added at several stages during the cooking process, whereas labour and overhead costs are incurred uniformly. The company uses the weighted-average method.

Required

Prepare a production report for the Cooking Department for May. Use the following three steps in preparing your report:

1 Prepare a quantity schedule and a computation of equivalent units.

2 Compute the costs per equivalent unit for the month.

3 Using the data from Questions 1 and 2 above, prepare a cost reconciliation.

P4–15 Weighted-average method; basic production report Time allowed: 45 minutes
Sunspot Beverages Ltd of Fiji makes blended tropical fruit drinks in two stages. Fruit juices are extracted from fresh fruits and then blended in the Blending Department. The blended juices are then bottled and packed for shipping in the Bottling Department. The following information pertains to the operations of the Blending Department for June. (The currency in Fiji is the Fijian dollar.)

		Percentage completed	
	Units	**Materials**	**Conversion**
Work in progress, beginning	20,000	100%	75%
Started into production	180,000		
Completed and transferred out	160,000		
Work in progress, ending	40,000	100%	25%

Cost in the beginning work in progress stock and cost added during June were as follows for the Blending Department:

	Materials	Conversion
Work in progress, beginning	$25,200	$24,800
Cost added during June	334,800	238,700

Required

Prepare a production report for the Blending Department for June assuming that the company uses the weighted-average method.

P4–16 FIFO method; basic production report Time allowed: 45 minutes
(Appendix 4A) Refer to the data for the Blending Department of Sunspot Beverages, Ltd in P4–15. Assume that the company uses the FIFO method to compute unit costs rather than the weighted-average method.

Required

Prepare a production report for the Blending Department for June.

P4–17 Weighted-average method; interpreting a production report Time allowed: 30 minutes
Cooperative San José of southern Sonora state in Mexico makes a unique syrup using cane sugar and local herbs. The syrup is sold in small bottles and is prized as a flavouring for drinks and for use in desserts. The bottles are sold for $12 each. (The Mexican currency is the peso and is denoted by $.) The first stage in the production process is carried out in the Mixing Department, which removes foreign matter from the raw materials and mixes them in the proper proportions in large vats. The company uses the weighted-average method in its process costing system.

A hastily prepared report for the Mixing Department for April appears below:

Quantity schedule	
Units to be accounted for:	
Work in progress, 1 April (90% materials, 80% conversion cost added last month)	30,000
Started into production	200,000
Total units	230,000
Units accounted for as follows:	
Transferred to the next department	190,000
Work in progress, 30 April (75% materials, 60% conversion cost added this month	40,000
Total units	230,000
Total cost	
Cost to be accounted for:	
Work in progress, 1 April	$98,000
Cost added during the month	827,000
Total cost	$925,000
Cost reconciliation	
Cost accounted for as follows:	
Transferred to the next department	$805,600
Work in progress, 30 April	119,400
Total cost	$925,000

Cooperative San José has just been acquired by another company, and the management of the acquiring company wants some additional information about Cooperative San José's operations.

Required

1 What were the equivalent units for the month?

2 What were the costs per equivalent unit for the month? The beginning stock consisted of the following costs: materials, $67,800; and conversion cost, $30,200. The costs added during the month consisted of: materials, $579,000; and conversion cost, $248,000.

3 How many of the units transferred to the next department were started and completed during the month?

4 The manager of the Mixing Department, anxious to make a good impression on the new owners, stated, 'Materials prices jumped from about $2.50 per unit in March to $3.00 per unit in April, but due to good cost control I was able to hold our materials cost to less than $3.00 per unit for the month.' Should this manager be rewarded for good cost control? Explain.

Cases

C4–18 Weighted-average method; production report: second department Time allowed: 45 minutes

'I think we blundered when we hired that new assistant accountant', said Ruth Scarpino, Managing Director of Provost Industries. 'Just look at this production report that he prepared last month for the Finishing Department. I can't make head nor tail of it.'

Finishing Department costs:	
Work in progress, stock, 1 April, 450 units;	
100% complete as to materials; 60% complete as to conversion costs	£8,208*
Costs transferred in during the month from the preceding department, 1,950 units	17,940
Materials cost added during the month (materials are added when processing is 50% complete in the Finishing Department)	6,210
Conversion costs incurred during the month	13,920
Total departmental costs	£46,278
Finishing Department costs assigned to:	
Units completed and transferred to finished goods, 1,800 units at £25.71 per unit	£46,278
Work in progress stock, 30 April,600 units; 0% complete as to materials; 35% complete as to processing	0
Total departmental costs assigned	£46,278

*Consists of: cost transferred in, £4,068; materials cost, £1,980; and conversion cost, £2,160.

'He's struggling to learn our system,' replied Frank Harrop, the operations manager. 'The problem is that he's been away from process costing for a long time, and it's coming back slowly.'

'It's not just the format of his report that I'm concerned about. Look at that £25.71 unit cost that he's come up with for April. Doesn't that seem high to you?' said Ms Scarpino.

'Yes, it does seem high; but on the other hand, I know we had an increase in materials prices during April, and that may be the explanation,' replied Mr Harrop. 'I'll get someone else to redo this report and then we may be able to see what's going on.'

Provost Industries manufactures a ceramic product that goes through two processing departments – Moulding and Finishing. The company uses the weighted-average method to account for units and costs.

Required

1 Prepare a revised production report for the Finishing Department.

2 Explain to the Managing Director why the unit cost on the new assistant accountant's report is so high.

C4–19 FIFO method, production report: second department Time allowed: 45 minutes
(Appendix 4A) Refer to the data for Provost Industries in the preceding case. Assume that the company uses the FIFO method to account for units and costs.

Required

1 Prepare a production report for the Finishing Department for April.

2 As stated in the case, the company experienced an increase in materials prices during April. Would the effects of this price increase tend to show up more under the weighted-average method or under the FIFO method? Why?

Endnote

1 There is another method called LIFO (last in, first out) but this is unacceptable for taxation purposes according to the accounting standard (SSAP 9) on stocks and work in progress.

Chapter 5
Cost behaviour: analysis and use

Learning objectives

After studying Chapter 5, you should be able to:

1 Explain the effect of a change in activity on both total variable costs and per unit variable costs
2 Explain the effect of a change in activity on both total fixed costs and fixed costs expressed on a per unit basis
3 Use a cost formula to predict costs at a new level of activity
4 Analyse a mixed cost using the high–low method
5 Analyse a mixed cost using the scattergraph method
6 Explain the least-squares regression method of analysing a mixed cost
7 Prepare profit and loss statements using the contribution format
8 (Appendix 5A) Analyse a mixed cost using the least-squares regression method
9 (Appendix 5B) Analyse the impact of learning and experience curves
10 (Appendix 5C) Analyse the behaviour of costs in service organizations

Concepts in Context

The labour laws in the country in which the company operates often affect whether employee staff costs are fixed or variable. In Europe, banks have historically had very large numbers of branches, some of which serve very small villages. These branches are expensive to staff and maintain, and banks have argued that they are a drain on profits. In Denmark and the United Kingdom, the numbers of branches were cut by 34% and 22%, respectively, over a span of ten years. In both cases, this led to a 15% reduction in staff employees. In contrast, countries with more restrictive labour laws that make it difficult to lay off workers have been unable to reduce staff or the number of branches significantly. For example, in Germany the number of branches was reduced by only 2% and the number of staff by only two-tenths of a per cent during the same period.[1]

In our discussion of cost terms and concepts in Chapter 2, we stated that one way in which costs can be classified is by behaviour. We defined cost behaviour as meaning how a cost will react or change as changes take place in the level of business activity. An understanding of cost behaviour is the key to many decisions in an organization. Managers who understand how costs behave are better able to predict what costs will be under various operating circumstances. Attempts at decision making without a thorough understanding of the costs involved – and how these costs may change with the activity level – can lead to disaster. For example, a decision to drop a particular product line might result in far less cost savings than managers had assumed – leading to a decline in profits. To avoid such problems, a manager must be able accurately to predict what costs will be at various activity levels. In this chapter, we shall find that the key to effective cost prediction lies in understanding cost behaviour patterns.

We briefly review in this chapter the definitions of variable costs and fixed costs and then discuss the behaviour of these costs in greater depth than we were able to do in Chapter 2. After this review and discussion, we turn our attention to the analysis of mixed costs. We conclude the chapter by introducing a new profit format – called the contribution format – in which costs are organized by behaviour rather than by the traditional functions of production, sales and administration.

Types of cost behaviour patterns

In our brief discussion of cost behaviour in Chapter 2, we mentioned only variable and fixed costs. There is a third behaviour pattern, generally known as a *mixed* or *semivariable* cost. All three cost behaviour patterns – variable, fixed and mixed – are found in most organizations. The relative proportion of each type of cost present in a firm is known as the firm's **cost structure**. For example, a firm might have many fixed costs but few variable or mixed costs. Alternatively, it might have many variable costs but few fixed or mixed costs. A firm's cost structure can have a significant impact on decisions. We must reserve a detailed discussion of cost structures for later chapters, however, and concentrate for the moment on gaining a fuller understanding of the behaviour of each type of cost.

Variable costs

We found in Chapter 2 that a variable cost is a cost whose total amount varies in direct proportion to changes in the activity level. If the activity level doubles, the total amount of the variable costs also doubles. If the activity level increases by only 10%, then the total amount of the variable costs increases by 10% as well.

We also found in Chapter 2 that a variable cost remains constant if expressed on a *per unit* basis. To provide an example, consider Wildmoor, a small company that provides day-long pony trekking excursions on the North Yorkshire Moors. The company provides all necessary equipment and experienced guides, and serves gourmet meals to its guests. The meals are purchased from an exclusive caterer for £30 a person for a day-long excursion. If we look at the cost of the meals on a *per person* basis, the cost remains constant at £30. This £30 cost per person will not change, regardless of how many people participate in a day-long excursion. The behaviour of this variable cost, on both a per unit and a total basis, is tabulated below:

Number of guests	Cost of meals per guest	Total cost of meals
250	£30	£7,500
500	30	15,000
750	30	22,500
1,000	30	30,000

The idea that a variable cost is constant per unit but varies in total with the activity level is crucial to an understanding of cost behaviour patterns. We shall rely on this concept again and again in this chapter and in chapters ahead.

Exhibit 5.1 provides a graphic illustration of variable cost behaviour. Note that the graph of the total cost of the meals slants upward to the right. This is because the total cost of the meals is directly proportional to the number of guests. In contrast, the graph of the per unit cost of meals is flat. This is because the cost of the meals per guest is constant at £30 per guest.

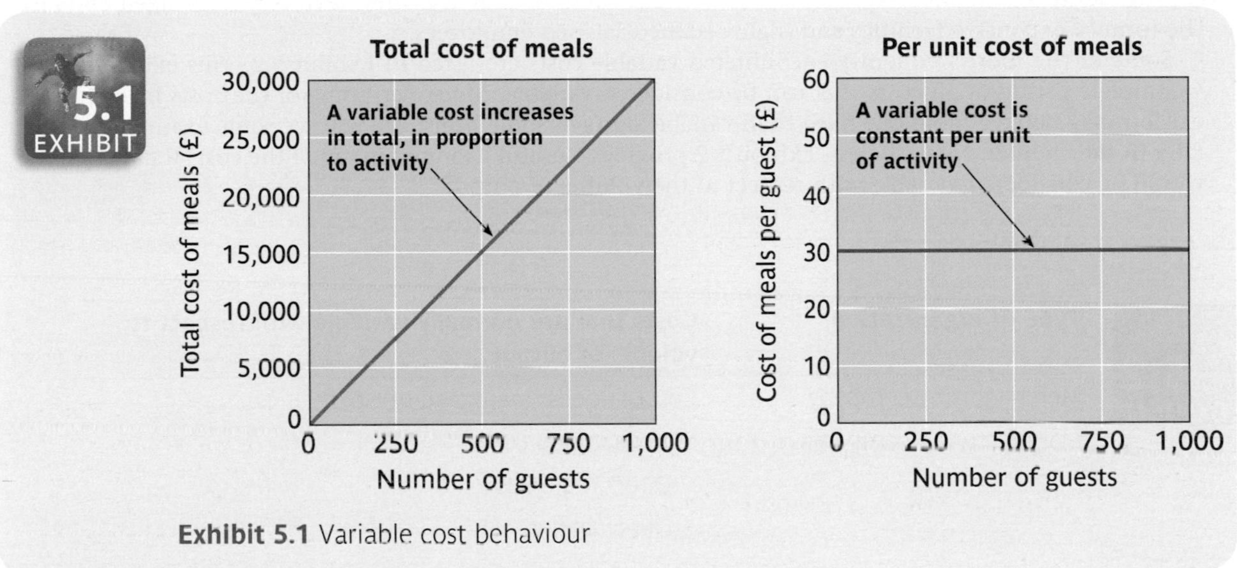

Exhibit 5.1 Variable cost behaviour

The activity base

For a cost to be variable, it must be variable with *respect to something*. That 'something' is its *activity base*. An **activity base** is a measure of whatever causes the incurrence of variable cost. In Chapter 3, we mentioned that an activity base is sometimes referred to as a *cost driver*. Some of the most common activity bases are direct labour-hours, machine-hours, units produced and units sold. Other activity bases (cost drivers) might include the number of miles driven by salespersons, the number of kilos of laundry processed by a hotel, the number of letters typed by a secretary, and the number of occupied beds in a hospital.

To plan and control variable costs, a manager must be well acquainted with the various activity bases within the firm. People sometimes get the notion that if a cost doesn't vary with production or with sales, then it is not really a variable cost. This is not correct. As suggested by the range of bases listed above, costs are caused by many different activities within an organization. Whether a cost is considered to be variable depends on whether it is caused by the activity under consideration. For example, if a manager is analysing the cost of service calls under a product warranty, the relevant activity measure will be the number of service calls made. Those costs that vary in total with the number of service calls made are the variable costs of making service calls.

Nevertheless, unless stated otherwise, you can assume that the activity base under consideration is the total volume of goods and services provided by the organization. So, for example, if we ask whether direct materials at Ford is a variable cost, the answer is yes, since the cost of direct materials is variable with respect to Ford's total volume of output. We will specify the activity base only when it is something other than total output.

Extent of variable costs

The number and type of variable costs present in an organization will depend in large part on the organization's structure and purpose. A public utility like Powergen, with large investments in equipment, will tend to have few variable costs. Most of the costs are associated with its plant, and these costs tend to be insensitive to changes in levels of service provided. A manufacturing company like Black and Decker, by contrast, will often have many variable costs; these costs will be associated with both the manufacture and distribution of its products to customers.

A merchandising company like Next will usually have a high proportion of variable costs in its cost structure. In most merchandising companies, the cost of merchandise purchased for resale, a variable cost, constitutes a very large component of total cost. Service companies, by contrast, have diverse cost structures. Some service companies, such as the Café Rouge restaurant chain, have fairly large variable costs because of the costs of their raw materials. On the other hand, service companies involved in consulting, auditing, engineering, dental, medical and architectural activities have very large fixed costs in the form of expensive facilities and highly trained salaried employees.

Some of the more frequently encountered variable costs are listed in Exhibit 5.2. This exhibit is not a complete listing of all costs that can be considered variable. Moreover, some of the costs listed in the exhibit may behave more like fixed than variable costs in some firms. We will see some examples of this later in the chapter. Nevertheless, Exhibit 5.2 provides a useful listing of many of the costs that normally would be considered variable with respect to the volume of output.

5.2 EXHIBIT

Type of organization	Costs that are normally variable with respect to volume of output
Merchandising company	Cost of goods (merchandise) sold
Manufacturing company	Manufacturing costs:
	Direct materials
	Direct labour*
	Variable portion of manufacturing overhead:
	Indirect materials
	Lubricants
	Supplies
	Power
Both merchandising and manufacturing companies	Selling, general, and administrative costs:
	Commissions
	Clerical costs, such as invoicing
	Shipping costs
Service organizations	Supplies, travel clerical

*Direct labour may or may not be variable in practice. See the discussion later in this chapter.

Exhibit 5.2 Examples of variable costs

True variable versus step-variable costs

Not all variable costs have exactly the same behaviour pattern. Some variable costs behave in a *true variable* or *proportionately variable* pattern. Other variable costs behave in a *step-variable* pattern.

True variable costs

Direct materials is a true or proportionately variable cost because the amount used during a period will vary in direct proportion to the level of production activity. Moreover, any amounts purchased but not used can be stored and carried forward to the next period as stock.

Step-variable costs

The wages of maintenance workers are often considered to be a variable cost, but this labour cost does not behave in quite the same way as the cost of direct materials. Unlike direct materials, the time of maintenance workers is obtainable only in large chunks. Moreover, any maintenance time not utilized cannot be stored as inventory and carried forward to the next period. If the time is not used effectively, it is gone for ever. Furthermore, a maintenance crew can work at a fairly leisurely pace if pressures are light but intensify its efforts if pressures build up. For this reason, somewhat small changes in the level of production may have no effect on the number of maintenance people needed to properly carry on maintenance work.

A cost that is obtainable only in large chunks (such as the labour cost of maintenance workers) and that increases or decreases only in response to fairly wide changes in the activity level is known as a **step-variable cost**. The behaviour of a step-variable cost, contrasted with the behaviour of a true variable cost, is illustrated in Exhibit 5.3.

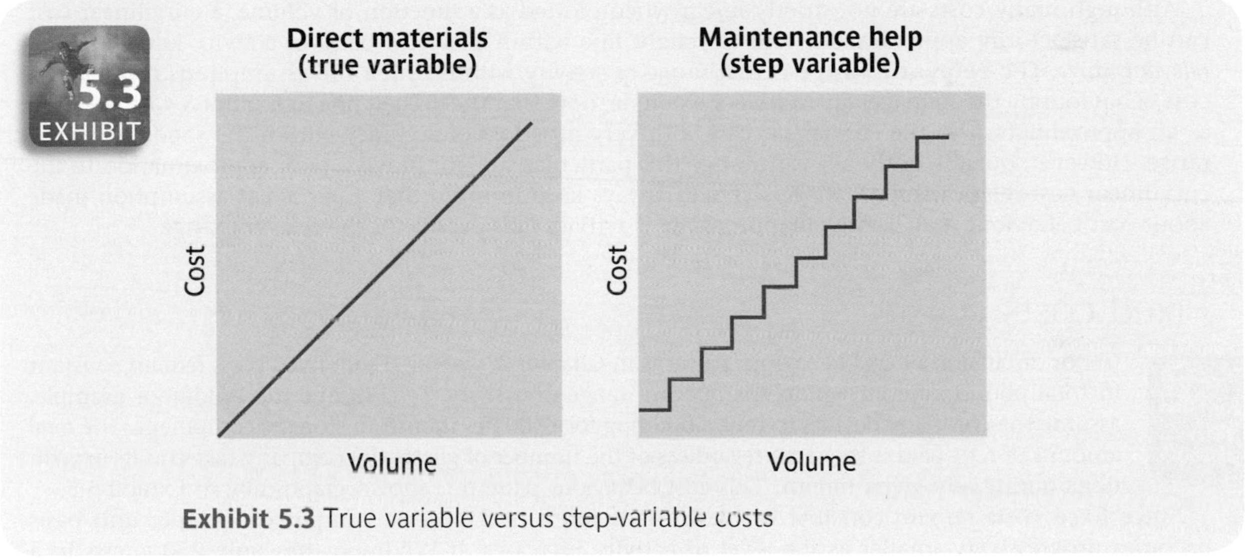

Exhibit 5.3 True variable versus step-variable costs

Notice that the need for maintenance help changes only with fairly wide changes in volume and that when additional maintenance time is obtained, it comes in large, indivisible chunks. The strategy of management in dealing with step-variable costs must be to obtain the fullest use of services possible for each separate step. Great care must be taken in working with these kinds of costs to prevent 'fat' from building up in an organization. There may be a tendency to employ additional help more quickly than needed, and there is a natural reluctance to lay people off when volume declines.

The linearity assumption and the relevant range

In dealing with variable costs, we have assumed a strictly linear relationship between cost and volume, except in the case of step-variable costs. Economists correctly point out that many costs that the accountant classifies as variable actually behave in a curvilinear fashion. The behaviour of a **curvilinear cost** is shown in Exhibit 5.4.

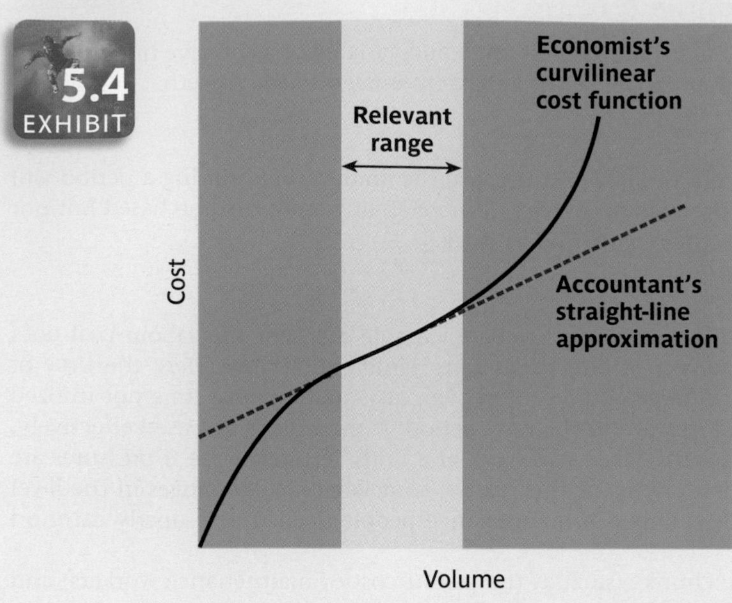

Exhibit 5.4 Curvilinear costs and the relevant range

Although many costs are not strictly linear when plotted as a function of volume, a curvilinear cost can be satisfactorily approximated with a straight line within a narrow band of activity known as the *relevant range*. The **relevant range** is that range of activity within which the assumptions made about cost behaviour by the manager are valid. For example, note that the dashed line in Exhibit 5.4 can be used as an approximation to the curvilinear cost with very little loss of accuracy within the shaded relevant range. However, outside of the relevant range this particular straight line is a poor approximation to the curvilinear cost relationship. Managers should always keep in mind that a particular assumption made about cost behaviour may be very inappropriate if activity falls outside of the relevant range.

Fixed costs

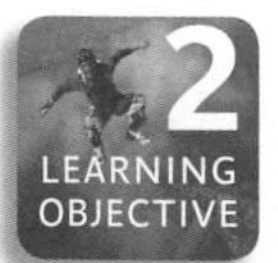

In our discussion of cost behaviour patterns in Chapter 2, we stated that fixed costs remain constant in total pound amount within the relevant range of activity. To continue the Wildmoor example, assume the company decides to rent a building for £500 per month to store its equipment. The *total* amount of rent paid is the same regardless of the number of guests the company takes on its expeditions during any given month. This cost behaviour pattern is shown graphically in Exhibit 5.5.

Since fixed costs remain constant in total, the amount of fixed cost computed on a per unit basis becomes progressively smaller as the level of activity increases. If Wildmoor has only 250 guests in a month, the £500 fixed rental cost would amount to £2 per guest. If there are 1,000 guests, the fixed rental cost would amount to only 50 pence per guest. This aspect of the behaviour of fixed costs is also displayed in Exhibit 5.5. Note that as the number of guests increases, the average unit cost drops, but it drops at a decreasing rate. The first guests have the biggest impact on unit costs.

As we noted in Chapter 2, this aspect of fixed costs can be confusing, although it is necessary in some contexts to express fixed costs on an average per unit basis. We found in Chapter 3, for example, that a broad unit cost figure containing both variable and fixed cost elements is used in *external* financial statements. For *internal* uses, however, fixed costs should not be expressed on a per unit basis because of the potential confusion. Experience has shown that for internal uses, fixed costs are most easily (and most safely) dealt with on a total basis rather than on a per unit basis.

Types of fixed costs

Fixed costs are sometimes referred to as a capacity cost, since they result from outlays made for buildings, equipment, skilled professional employees and other items needed to provide the basic capacity

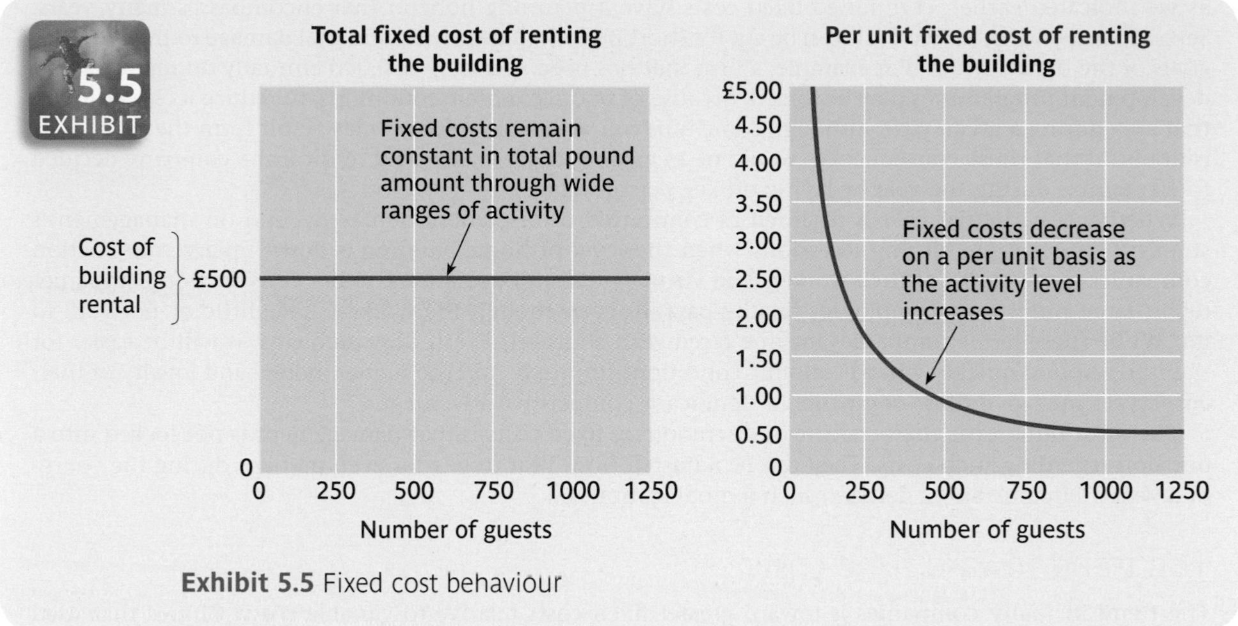

Exhibit 5.5 Fixed cost behaviour

for sustained operations. For planning purposes, fixed costs can be viewed as being either *committed* or *discretionary*.

Committed fixed costs

Committed fixed costs relate to the investment in facilities, equipment and the basic organizational structure of a firm. Examples of such costs include depreciation of buildings and equipment, taxes on real estate, insurance, and salaries of top management and operating personnel.

The two key factors about committed fixed costs are that first, they are long term in nature, and second, they cannot be reduced to zero even for short periods of time without seriously impairing the profitability or long-run goals of the organization. Even if operations are interrupted or cut back, the committed fixed costs will still continue largely unchanged. During a recession, for example, a firm will not usually discharge key executives or sell off key facilities. The basic organizational structure and facilities ordinarily are kept intact. The costs of restoring them later are likely to be far greater than any short-run savings that might be realized.

Since it is difficult to change a committed fixed cost once the commitment has been made, management should approach these decisions with particular care. Decisions to acquire major equipment or to take on other committed fixed costs involve a long planning horizon. Management should make such commitments only after careful analysis of the available alternatives. Once a decision is made to build a certain size facility, a firm becomes locked into that decision for many years to come. Decisions relating to committed fixed costs will be examined in Chapter 9.

While not much can be done about committed fixed costs in the short run, management is generally very concerned about how these resources are *utilized*. The strategy of management must be to utilize the capacity of the organization as effectively as possible.

Discretionary fixed costs

Discretionary fixed costs (often referred to as *managed fixed costs*) usually arise from *annual* decisions by management to spend in certain fixed cost areas. Examples of discretionary fixed costs include advertising, research, public relations, management development programmes and internships for students.

Basically, two key differences exist between discretionary fixed costs and committed fixed costs. First, the planning horizon for a discretionary fixed cost is fairly short term – usually a single year. By contrast, as we indicated earlier, committed fixed costs have a planning horizon that encompasses many years. Second, discretionary fixed costs can be cut for short periods of time with minimal damage to the long-run goals of the organization. For example, a firm that has been spending £50,000 annually on management development programmes may be forced, because of poor economic conditions, to reduce its spending in that area during a given year. Although some unfavourable consequences may result from the cutback, it is doubtful that these consequences would be as great as those that would result if the company decided to economize during the year by laying off key personnel.

Whether a particular cost is regarded as committed or discretionary may depend on management's strategy. For example, during recessions when the level of home building is down, many construction companies lay off most of their workers and virtually disband operations. Other construction companies retain large numbers of employees on the payroll, even though the workers have little or no work to do. While these latter companies may be faced with short-term cash flow problems, it will be easier for them to respond quickly when economic conditions improve. And the higher morale and loyalty of their employees may give these companies a significant competitive advantage.

The most important characteristic of discretionary fixed costs is that management is not locked into a decision regarding such costs. They can be adjusted from year to year or even perhaps during the course of a year if circumstances demand such a modification.

The trend toward fixed costs

The trend in many companies is toward greater fixed costs relative to variable costs. Chores that used to be performed by hand have been taken over by machines. For example, retail checkout staff used to key in prices by hand on cash registers. Now, most supermarkets are equipped with barcode readers that enter price and other product information automatically. In general, competition has created pressure to give customers more value for their money – a demand that often can only be satisfied by automating business processes.

As machines take over more and more of the tasks that were performed by humans, the overall demand for human workers has not diminished. The demand for 'knowledge' workers – those who work primarily with their minds rather than their muscles – has grown tremendously. And knowledge workers tend to be salaried, highly trained and difficult to replace. As a consequence, the costs of compensating knowledge workers are often relatively fixed and are committed rather than discretionary costs.

Is labour a variable or a fixed cost?

As the preceding discussion suggests, wages and salaries may be fixed or variable. The concepts in context example at the beginning of the chapter illustrates that the behaviour of wage and salary costs will differ from one country to another, depending on labour regulations, labour contracts and custom. In some countries, such as France, Germany, China and Japan, management has little flexibility in adjusting the labour force to changes in business activity. In countries such as the United Kingdom and the United States, management typically has much greater latitude. However, even in these less restrictive environments, managers may choose to treat employee compensation as a fixed cost for several reasons.

First, companies have become much more reluctant to adjust the workforce in response to short-term fluctuations in sales. Most companies realize that their employees are a very valuable asset. More and more, highly skilled and trained employees are required to run a successful business, and these workers are not easy to replace. Trained workers who are laid off may never return, and layoffs undermine the morale of those workers who remain.

In addition, managers do not want to be caught with a bloated payroll in an economic downturn. Therefore, there is an increased reluctance to add workers when sales activity picks up. Many companies are turning to temporary and part-time workers to take up the slack when their permanent, full-time employees are unable to handle all the demand for the company's products and services. In such companies, labour costs are a curious mixture of fixed and variable costs.

Many major companies have undergone waves of downsizing in recent years in which large numbers of employees – particularly middle managers – have lost their jobs. It may seem that this downsizing proves that even management salaries should be regarded as variable costs, but this would not be a valid conclusion. Downsizing has been the result of attempts to re-engineer business processes and cut costs rather than a response to a decline in sales activity. This underscores an important, but subtle, point. Fixed costs can change – they just do not change in response to small changes in activity.

In sum, we cannot provide a clear-cut answer to the question 'Is labour a variable or fixed cost?' It depends on how much flexibility management has and management's strategy. Nevertheless, we will assume in this text that, unless otherwise stated, direct labour is a variable cost. This assumption is more likely to be valid for companies in the United Kingdom than in countries where employment laws permit much less flexibility.

Fixed costs and the relevant range

The concept of the relevant range, which was introduced in the discussion of variable costs, is also important in understanding fixed costs – particularly discretionary fixed costs. The levels of discretionary fixed costs are typically decided at the beginning of the year and depend on the support needs of the planned programmes such as advertising and training. The scope of these programmes will depend, in turn, on the overall anticipated level of activity for the year. At very high levels of activity, programmes are usually broadened or expanded. For example, if the company hopes to increase sales by 25%, it would probably plan for much larger advertising costs than if no sales increase was planned. So the *planned* level of activity may affect total discretionary fixed costs. However, once the total discretionary fixed costs have been budgeted, they are unaffected by the actual level of activity. For example, once the advertising budget has been decided on and has been spent, it will not be affected by how many units are actually sold. Therefore, the cost is fixed with respect to the actual number of units sold.

Discretionary fixed costs are easier to adjust than committed fixed costs. They also tend to be less 'lumpy'. Committed fixed costs tend to consist of costs of buildings, equipment and the salaries of key personnel. It is difficult to buy half a piece of equipment or to hire a quarter of a product-line manager, so the step pattern depicted in Exhibit 5.6 is typical for such costs. The relevant range of activity for a fixed cost is the range of activity over which the graph of the cost is flat as in Exhibit 5.6. As a company expands its level of activity, it may outgrow its present facilities, or the key management team may need to be expanded. The result, of course, will be increased committed fixed costs as larger facilities are built and as new management positions are created.

One reaction to the step pattern depicted in Exhibit 5.6 is to say that discretionary and committed fixed costs are really just step-variable costs. To some extent this is true, since almost *all* costs can be adjusted in the long run. There are two major differences, however, between the step-variable costs depicted earlier in Exhibit 5.3 and the fixed costs depicted in Exhibit 5.6.

The first difference is that the step-variable costs can often be adjusted quickly as conditions change, whereas once fixed costs have been set, they often cannot be changed easily. A step-variable cost such as maintenance labour, for example, can be adjusted upward or downward by hiring and laying off maintenance workers. By contrast, once a company has signed a lease for a building, it is locked into that level of lease cost for the life of the contract.

The second difference is that the *width of the steps* depicted for step-variable costs is much narrower than the width of the steps depicted for the fixed costs in Exhibit 5.6. The width of the steps relates to volume or level of activity. For step-variable costs, the width of a step may be 40 hours of activity or less if one is dealing, for example, with maintenance labour cost. For fixed costs, however, the width of a step may be *thousands* or even *tens of thousands* of hours of activity. In essence, the width of the steps for step-variable costs is generally so narrow that these costs can be treated essentially as variable costs for most purposes. The width of the steps for fixed costs, on the other hand, is so wide that these costs must generally be treated as being entirely fixed within the relevant range.

Mixed costs

A **mixed cost** is one that contains both variable and fixed cost elements. Mixed costs are also known as semivariable costs. To continue the Wildmoor example, the company must pay a licence fee of £25,000 per year plus £3 per pony party to the North Yorkshire National Park. If the company runs 1,000 pony treks this year, then the total fees paid to the Park authority would be £28,000, made up of £25,000 in fixed cost plus £3,000 in variable cost. The behaviour of this mixed cost is shown graphically in Exhibit 5.7.

Even if Wildmoor fails to attract any customers and there are no rafting parties, the company will still have to pay the licence fee of £25,000. This is why the cost line in Exhibit 5.7 intersects the vertical cost axis at the £25,000 point. For each trekking party the company organizes, the total cost of the Park fees will increase by £3. Therefore, the total cost line slopes upward as the variable cost element is added to the fixed cost element.

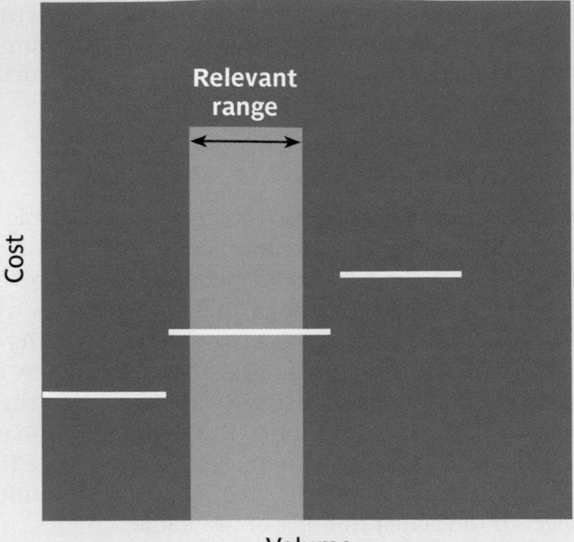

Exhibit 5.6 Fixed costs and the relevant range

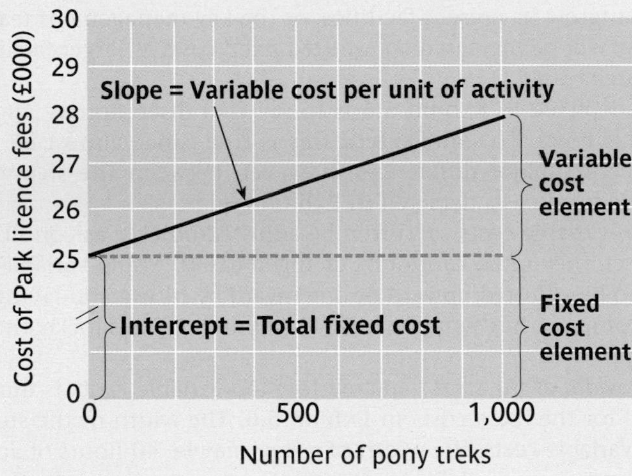

Exhibit 5.7 Mixed cost behaviour

Since the mixed cost in Exhibit 5.7 is represented by a straight line, the following equation for a straight line can be used to express the relationship between mixed cost and the level of activity:

$$Y = a + bX$$

In this equation

Y = The total mixed cost

a = The total fixed cost (the vertical intercept of the line)

b = The variable cost per unit of activity (the slope of the line)

X = The level of activity

In the case of the Park fees paid by Wildmoor, the equation is written as follows:

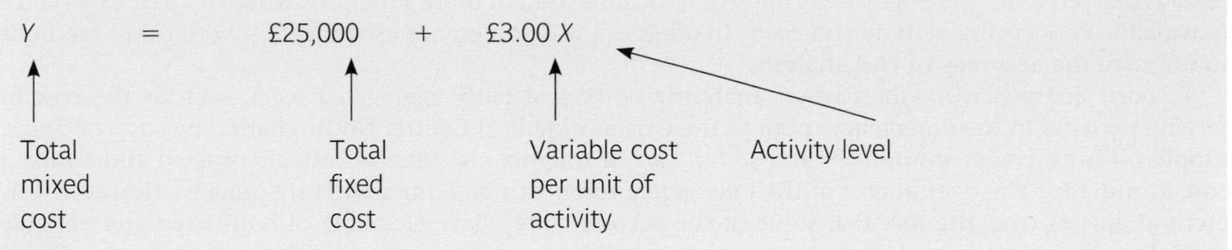

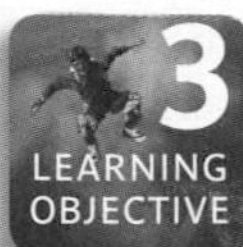

This equation makes it very easy to calculate what the total mixed cost would be for any level of activity within the relevant range. For example, suppose that the company expects to organize 800 pony treks in the next year. Then the total licence fees would be £27,400, calculated as follows:

$$Y = £25{,}000 + (£3.00 \times 800 \text{ pony treks}) = £27{,}400$$

The analysis of mixed costs

In practice, mixed costs are very common. For example, the cost of providing X-ray services to patients at St Bartholomew's Hospital is a mixed cost. There are substantial fixed costs for equipment depreciation and for salaries for radiologists and technicians, but there are also variable costs for X-ray film, power and supplies. At easyJet, maintenance costs are a mixed cost. The company must incur fixed costs for renting maintenance facilities and for keeping skilled mechanics on the payroll, but the costs of replacement parts, lubricating oils, tyres and so forth, are variable with respect to how often and how far the company's aircraft are flown.

FOCUS

Focus on current practice

Lowcost airlines such as Ryanair and easyJet have exploited deregulation and new technology to drive down costs. However, even before airlines began dramatically to reduce their operating costs, they exploited the principles of fixed and variable costs. Through forecasting likely load factors – the percentage of seats occupied – well in advance of flights, airlines can offer low prices that just cover variable costs in order to sell the excess capacity. Further savings depend on understanding how their costs behave and changing the perceived cost drivers.

The fixed portion of a mixed cost represents the basic, minimum cost of just having a service *ready and available* for use. The variable portion represents the cost incurred for *actual consumption* of the service. The variable element varies in proportion to the amount of service that is consumed.

How does management go about actually estimating the fixed and variable components of a mixed cost? The most common methods used in practice are *account analysis* and the *engineering approach*. These methods are used most often in later chapters of this text.

In **account analysis**, each account under consideration is classified as either variable or fixed based on the analyst's prior knowledge of how the cost in the account behaves. For example, direct materials would be classified as variable and a building lease cost would be classified as fixed because of the nature of those costs. The total fixed cost is the sum of the costs for the accounts that have been classified as fixed. The variable cost per unit is estimated by dividing the sum of the costs for the accounts that have been classified as variable by the total activity.

The **engineering approach** to cost analysis involves a detailed analysis of what cost behaviour should be, based on an industrial engineer's evaluation of the production methods to be used, the materials specifications, labour requirements, equipment usage, efficiency of production, power consumption, and so on. For example, Pizza Hut might use the engineering approach to estimate the cost of serving a particular take-out pizza. The cost of the pizza would be estimated by carefully costing the specific ingredients used to make the pizza, the power consumed to cook the pizza, and the cost of the container the pizza is delivered in. The engineering approach must be used in those situations where no past experience is available concerning activity and costs. In addition, it is sometimes used together with other methods to improve the accuracy of cost analysis.

Account analysis works best when analysing costs at a fairly aggregated level, such as the cost of serving patients in the emergency room of the Queen's Medical Centre, Nottingham. The costs of drugs, supplies, forms, wages, equipment and so on, can be roughly classified as variable or fixed and a mixed cost formula for the overall cost of the emergency room can be estimated fairly quickly. However, this method glosses over the fact that some of the accounts may have elements of both fixed and variable costs. For example, the cost of electricity for the Accident and Emergency (A&E) department is a mixed cost. Most of the electricity is used for heating and lighting and is a fixed cost. However, the consumption of electricity increases with activity in A&E since diagnostic equipment, operating theatre lights, defibrillators, and so on, all consume electricity. The most effective way to estimate the fixed and variable elements of such a mixed cost may be to analyse past records of cost and activity data. These records should reveal whether electrical costs vary significantly with the number of patients and if so, by how much. The remainder of this section will be concerned with how to conduct such an analysis of past cost and activity data.

Management accounting in action: the issue

Dr Derek Chalmers, the chief executive officer of Brentline Hospital, motioned Nigel Barker, the chief financial officer of the hospital, into his office.

Derek: Nigel, come on in.

Nigel: What can I do for you?

Derek: Well for one, could you get the government to rescind the bookcase full of regulations against the wall over there?

Nigel: Sorry, that's a bit beyond my authority.

Derek: Just wishing, Nigel. Actually, I wanted to talk to you about our maintenance expenses. I used not to have to pay attention to such things, but these expenses seem to be bouncing around a lot. Over the last half year or so they have been as low as £7,400 and as high as £9,800 per month.

Nigel: Actually, that's a pretty normal variation in those expenses.

Derek: Well, we budgeted a constant £8,400 a month. Can't we do a better job of predicting what these costs are going to be? And how do we know when we've spent too much in a month? Shouldn't there be some explanation for these variations?

Nigel: Now that you mention it, we are in the process right now of tightening up our budgeting process. Our first step is to break all of our costs down into fixed and variable components.

Derek: How will that help?

Nigel: Well, that will permit us to predict what the level of costs will be. Some costs are fixed and shouldn't change much. Other costs go up and down as our activity goes up and down. The trick is to figure out what is driving the variable component of the costs.

Derek: What about the maintenance costs?

Nigel: My guess is that the variations in maintenance costs are being driven by our overall level of activity. When we treat more patients, our equipment is used more intensively, which leads to more maintenance expense.

Derek: How would you measure the level of overall activity? Would you use patient-days?

Nigel: I think so. Each day a patient is in the hospital counts as one patient-day. The greater the number of patient-days in a month, the busier we are. Besides, our budgeting is all based on projected patient-days.

Derek: Okay, so suppose you are able to break the maintenance costs down into fixed and variable components. What will that do for us?

Nigel: Basically, I will be able to predict what maintenance costs should be as a function of the number of patient-days.

Derek: I can see where that would be useful. We could use it to predict costs for budgeting purposes.

Nigel: We could also use it as a benchmark. Based on the actual number of patient-days for a period, I can predict what the maintenance costs should have been. We can compare this to the actual spending on maintenance.

Derek: Sounds good to me. Let me know when you get the results.

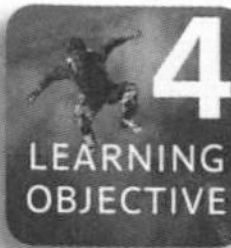

LEARNING OBJECTIVE

We will examine three methods that Nigel Barker might use to break down mixed costs into their fixed and variable elements – the *high–low* method, the *scattergraph* method and the *least-squares regression* method. All three methods are based on analysing cost and activity records from a number of prior periods. In the case of Brentline Hospital, we will use the following records of maintenance costs and patient-days for the first seven months of the year to estimate the fixed and variable elements of maintenance costs:

Month	Activity level: patient-days	Maintenance cost incurred
January	5,600	£7,900
February	7,100	8,500
March	5,000	7,400
April	6,500	8,200
May	7,300	9,100
June	8,000	9,800
July	6,200	7,800

The high–low method

To analyse mixed costs with the **high-low method**, one begins by identifying the period with the lowest level of activity and the period with the highest level of activity. The difference in cost observed at the two extremes is divided by the change in activity between the extremes in order to estimate the variable cost per unit of activity.

Since total maintenance cost at Brentline Hospital appears generally to increase as the activity level increases, it is likely that some variable cost element is present. Using the high–low method, we first identify the periods with the highest and lowest activity – in this case, June and March. We then use the activity and cost data from these two periods to estimate the variable cost component as follows:

	Patient-days	Maintenance cost incurred
High activity level (June)	8,000	£9,800
Low activity level (March)	5,000	7,400
Change	3,000	£2,400

$$\text{Variable cost} = \frac{\text{Change in cost}}{\text{Change in activity}} = \frac{£2400}{3000} = £0.8 \text{ per patient day}$$

Having determined that the variable rate for maintenance cost is 80 pence per patient-day, we can now determine the amount of fixed cost. This is done by taking total cost at *either* the high *or* the low activity level and deducting the variable cost element. In the computation below, total cost at the high activity level is used in computing the fixed cost element:

Fixed cost element = Total cost − Variable cost element

= £9,800 − (£0.80 per patient-day × per 8,000 patient-days)

= £3,400

Both the variable and fixed cost elements have now been isolated. The cost of maintenance can be expressed as £3,400 per month plus 80 pence per patient-day.

The cost of maintenance can also be expressed in terms of the equation for a straight line as follows:

$$Y = £3{,}400 + £0.80X$$

where Y = Total maintenance cost and X = Total patient-days.

The data used in this illustration are shown graphically in Exhibit 5.8. Three things should be noted in relation to this exhibit:

1 Notice that cost, Y, is plotted on the vertical axis. Cost is known as the **dependent variable**, since the amount of cost incurred during a period depends on the level of activity for the period. (That is, as the level of activity increases, total cost will also increase.)

2 Notice that activity, X (patient-days in this case), is plotted on the horizontal axis. Activity is known as the **independent variable**, since it causes variations in the cost.

3 Notice that a straight line has been drawn through the points corresponding to the low and high levels of activity. In essence, that is what the high–low method does – it draws a straight line through those two points. The formula for the variable cost,

$$\frac{\text{Change in cost (i.e., change in } Y)}{\text{Change in activity (i.e., change in } X)}$$

is basically the same as the formula for the slope of the line,

$$\frac{\text{Rise (i.e., change in } Y)}{\text{Run (i.e., change in } X)}$$

that is familiar from school algebra. This is because the slope of the line is the variable cost per unit. The higher the variable cost per unit, the steeper the line.

Sometimes the high and low levels of activity do not coincide with the high and low amounts of cost. For example, the period that has the highest level of activity may not have the highest amount of cost. Nevertheless, the highest and lowest levels of *activity* are always used to analyse a mixed cost under the high–low method. The reason is that the activity presumably causes costs, so the analyst would like to use data that reflects the greatest possible variation in activity.

The high–low method is very simple to apply, but it suffers from a major (and sometimes critical) defect in that it utilizes only two data points. Generally, two points are not enough to produce accurate results in cost analysis work. Additionally, periods in which the activity level is unusually low or unusually high will tend to produce inaccurate results. A cost formula that is estimated solely using data from these unusual periods may seriously misrepresent the true cost relationship that holds during normal periods. Such a distortion is evident in Exhibit 5.8. The straight line should probably be shifted down somewhat so that it is closer to more of the data points. For these reasons, other methods of cost analysis that utilize a greater number of points will generally be more accurate than the high–low method. If a manager chooses to use the high–low method, he or she should do so with a full awareness of the method's limitations.

The scattergraph method

A more accurate way of analysing mixed costs is to use the **scattergraph method**, which takes into account all of the cost data. A graph like the one we used in Exhibit 5.8 is constructed in which cost is shown on the vertical axis and the level of activity is shown on the horizontal axis. Costs observed at various levels of activity are then plotted on the graph, and a line is fitted to the plotted points. However, rather than just fitting the line to the high and low points, all points are considered when the line is drawn. This is done through simple visual inspection of

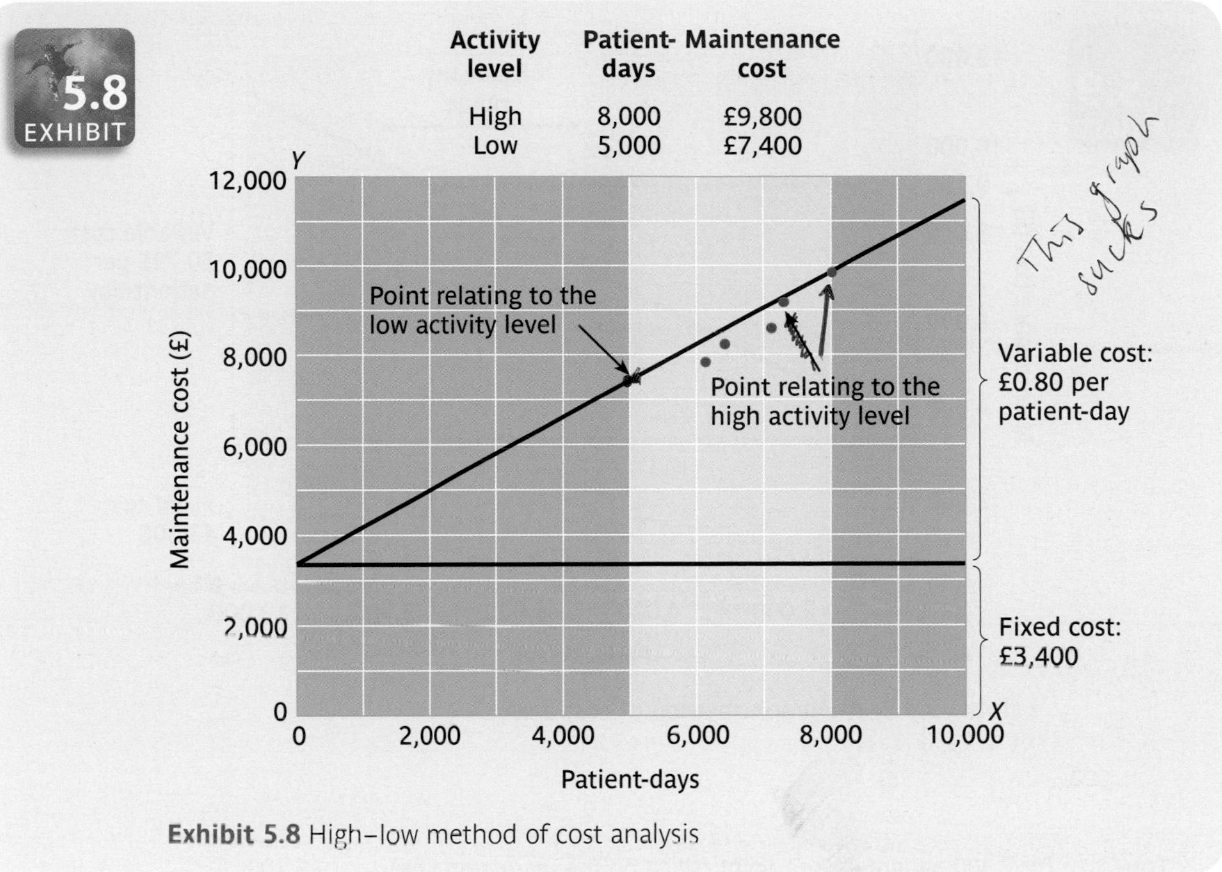

Exhibit 5.8 High–low method of cost analysis

the data, with the analyst taking care that the placement of the line is representative of all points, not just the high and low ones. Typically, the line is placed so that approximately equal numbers of points fall above and below it.

A graph of this type is known as a *scattergraph*, and the line fitted to the plotted points is known as a **regression line**. The regression line, in effect, is a line of averages, with the average variable cost per unit of activity represented by the slope of the line and the average total fixed cost represented by the point where the regression line intersects the cost axis.

The scattergraph approach using the Brentline Hospital maintenance data is illustrated in Exhibit 5.9. Note that the regression line has been placed in such a way that approximately equal numbers of points fall above and below it. Also note that the line has been drawn so that it goes through one of the points. This is not absolutely necessary, but it makes subsequent calculations a little easier.

Since the regression line strikes the vertical cost axis at £3,300, that amount represents the fixed cost element. The variable cost element can be computed by subtracting the fixed cost of £3,300 from the total cost for any point lying on the regression line. Since the point representing 7,300 patient-days lies on the regression line, we can use it. The variable cost (to the nearest tenth of a penny) would be 79.5 pence per patient-day, computed as follows:

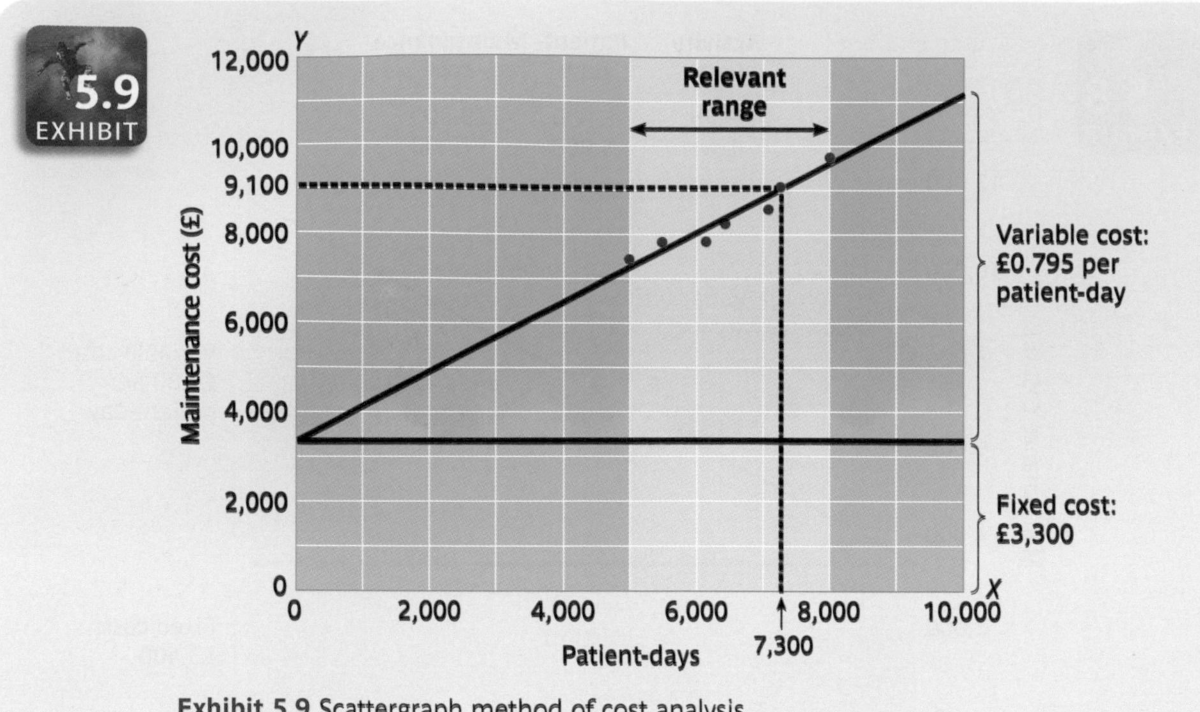

Exhibit 5.9 Scattergraph method of cost analysis

Total cost for 7,300 patient-days (a point falling on the regression line)	£9,100
Less fixed cost element	3,300
Variable cost element	£5,800
£5,800/7,300 patient-days = £0.795 per patient-day	

Thus, the cost formula using the regression line in Exhibit 5.9 would be £3,300 per month plus 79.5 pence per patient-day.

In this example, there is not a great deal of difference between the cost formula derived using the high–low method and the cost formula derived using the scattergraph method. However, sometimes there *will* be a big difference. In those situations, more reliance should ordinarily be placed on the results of the scattergraph approach.

Also note that all of the points in Exhibit 5.9 lie reasonably close to the straight line. In other words, the estimates of the fixed and variable costs are reasonably accurate within this range of activity, so the relevant range extends at least from 5,000 to 8,000 patient-days. It may also be accurate below 5,000 patient-days and above 8,000 patient-days – we cannot tell for sure without looking at more data.

A scattergraph can be an extremely useful tool in the hands of an experienced analyst. Quirks in cost behaviour due to strikes, bad weather, breakdowns and so on, become immediately apparent to the trained observer, who can make appropriate adjustments to the data when fitting the regression line. Some cost analysts would argue that a scattergraph should be the beginning point in all cost analyses, due to the benefits to be gained from having the data visually available in graph form.

There are, however, two major drawbacks to the scattergraph method. First, it is subjective. No two analysts who look at the same scattergraph are likely to draw exactly the same regression line. Second, the estimates of fixed costs are not as precise as they are with other methods, since it is difficult to measure precisely the pound amount where the regression line intersects the vertical cost axis. Some managers are uncomfortable with these elements of subjectivity and imprecision and desire a method that will yield a precise answer that will be the same no matter who does the analysis. Fortunately, modern computer software makes it very easy to use sophisticated statistical methods, such as *least-squares regression*, that are capable of providing much more information than just the estimates of variable and fixed costs. The details of these statistical methods are beyond the scope of this text, but the basic approach is discussed below. Nevertheless, even if the least-squares regression approach is used, it is always a good idea to plot the data in a scattergraph. By simply looking at the scattergraph, one can quickly verify whether it makes sense to fit a straight line to the data using least-squares regression or some other method.

The least-squares regression method

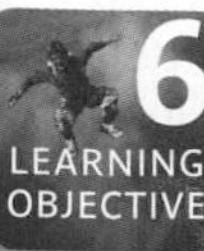

The **least-squares regression method** is a more objective and precise approach to estimating the regression line than the scattergraph method. Rather than fitting a regression line through the scattergraph data by visual inspection, the least-squares regression method uses mathematical formulas to fit the regression line. Also, unlike the high–low method, the least-squares regression method takes all of the data into account when estimating the cost formula.

The basic idea underlying the least-squares regression method is illustrated in Exhibit 5.10 using hypothetical data points. Notice from the exhibit that the deviations from the plotted points to the regression line are measured vertically on the graph. These vertical deviations are called the regression errors and are the key to understanding what least-squares does. There is nothing mysterious about the least-squares regression method. It simply computes the regression line that minimizes the sum of these squared errors. The formulas that accomplish this are fairly complex and involve numerous calculations, but the principle is simple.

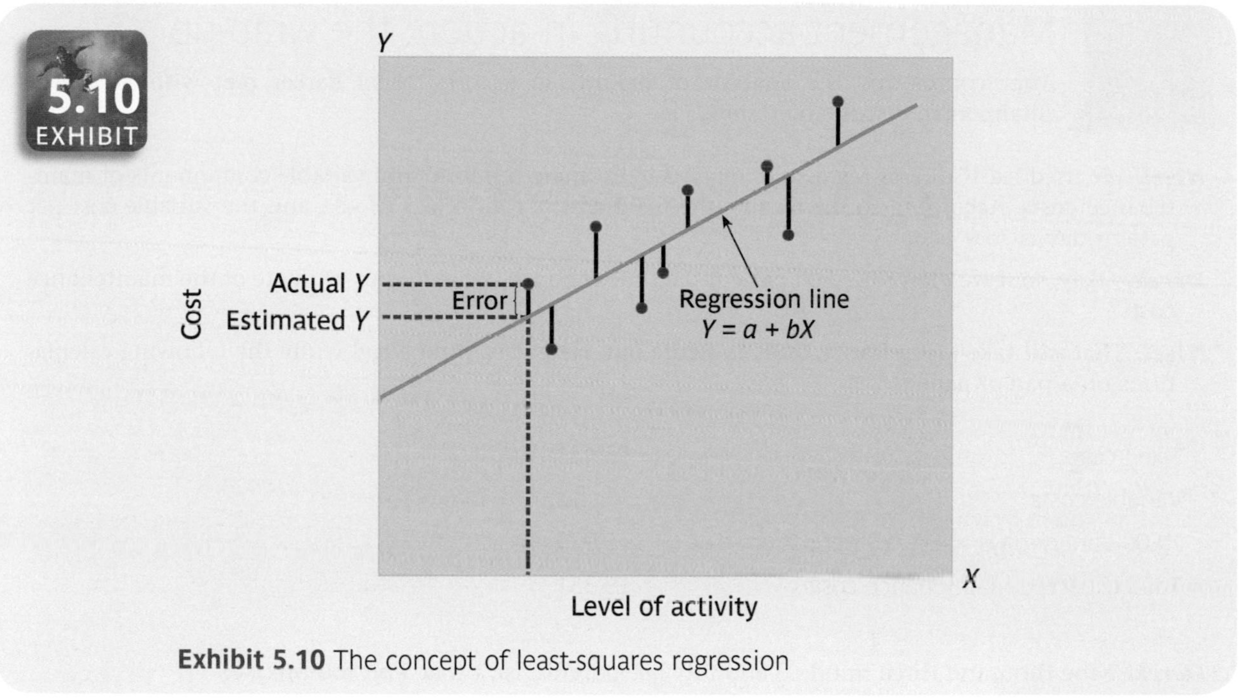

Exhibit 5.10 The concept of least-squares regression

Fortunately, computers are adept at carrying out the computations required by the least-squares regression formulas. The data – the observed values of X and Y – are entered into the computer, and software does the rest. In the case of the Brentline Hospital maintenance cost data, we used a statistical software package on a personal computer to calculate the following least-squares regression estimates of the total fixed cost a and the variable cost per unit of activity b:

a = £3,431

b = £0.759

Therefore, using the least-squares regression method, the fixed element of the maintenance cost is £3,431 per month and the variable portion is 75.9 pence per patient-day.

In terms of the linear equation $Y = a = bX$, the cost formula can be written as:

$Y = £3{,}431 = £0.759X$

where activity (X) is expressed in patient-days.

While we used a personal computer to calculate the values of a and b in this example, they can also be calculated by hand. In Appendix 5A to this chapter, we show how this can be done.

In addition to estimates of the intercept (fixed cost) and slope (variable cost per unit), least-squares regression software ordinarily provides a number of other very useful statistics. One of these statistics is the *adjusted* R^2, which is a measure of 'goodness of fit'. The **adjusted** $\mathbf{R^2}$ tells us the percentage of the variation in the dependent variable (cost) that is explained by variation in the independent variable (activity). The adjusted R^2 varies from 0% to 100%, and the higher the percentage, the better. In the case of the Brentline Hospital maintenance cost data, the adjusted R^2 is 88%, which indicates that 88% of the variation in maintenance costs is explained by the variation in patient-days. This is reasonably high and is an indication of a good fit. On the other hand, a low adjusted R^2 would be an indication that there is a poor fit. You should always plot the data in a scattergraph, but it is particularly important to check the data visually when there is a low adjusted R^2. A quick look at the scattergraph can reveal that there is little real relation between the cost and the activity or that the relation is something other than a simple straight line. In such cases, additional analysis would be required.

Management accounting in action: the wrap-up

After completing the analysis of maintenance costs, Nigel Barker met with Dr Derek Chalmers to discuss the results.

Nigel: We used least-squares regression analysis to estimate the fixed and variable components of maintenance costs. According to the results, the fixed cost per month is £3,431 and the variable cost per patient-day is 75.9 pence.

Derek: Okay, so if we plan for 7,800 patient-days next month, what is your estimate of the maintenance costs?

Nigel: That will take just a few seconds to figure out. Here it is. [And Nigel wrote the following calculations on a pad of paper.]

Fixed costs	£3,431
Variable costs:	
7,800 patient-days × £0.759 per patient-day	5,920
Total expected maintenance costs	£9,351

Derek: Nine thousand three hundred and fifty *one* pounds; isn't that a bit too precise?

Nigel: I don't really believe the maintenance costs will be exactly this figure. However, based on the information we have, this is the best estimate we can come up with.

Derek: Don't let me give you a hard time. Even if it is an estimate, it will be a lot better than just guessing as we have done in the past. Thanks. I hope to see more of this kind of analysis.

Multiple regression analysis

In the discussion thus far, we have assumed that a single factor such as patient-days drives the variable cost component of a mixed cost. This assumption is acceptable for many mixed costs, but in some situations there may be more than one causal factor driving the variable cost element. For example, shipping costs may depend on both the number of units shipped *and* the weight of the units. In a situation such as this, *multiple regression* is necessary. **Multiple regression** is an analytical method that is used when the dependent variable (i.e., cost) is caused by more than one factor. Although adding more factors, or variables, makes the computations more complex, the principles involved are the same as in the simple least-squares regressions discussed above. Because of the complexity of the calculations, multiple regression is nearly always done with a computer.

The contribution format

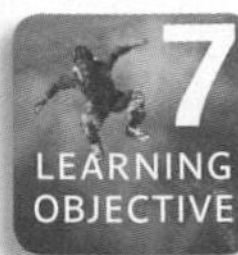

Once the manager has separated costs into fixed and variable elements, what is done with the data? We have already answered this question somewhat by showing how a cost formula can be used to predict costs. To answer this question more fully would require most of the remainder of this text, since much of what the manager does rests in some way on an understanding of cost behaviour. One immediate and very significant application of the ideas we have developed, however, is found in a new profit statement format known as the **contribution approach**. The unique thing about the contribution approach is that it provides the manager with a profit statement geared directly to cost behaviour.

Why a new profit and loss statement format?

The *traditional approach* to the profit and loss statement, as illustrated in Chapter 2, is not organized in terms of cost behaviour. Rather, it is organized in a 'functional' format – emphasizing the functions of production, administration and sales in the classification and presentation of cost data. No attempt is made to distinguish between the behaviour of costs included under each functional heading. Under the heading 'Administrative expense', for example, one can expect to find both variable and fixed costs lumped together.

Although a profit and loss statement prepared in the functional format may be useful for external reporting purposes, it has serious limitations when used for internal purposes. Internally, the manager needs cost data organized in a format that will facilitate planning, control and decision making. As we have seen in past chapters, these tasks are much easier when cost data are available in a fixed and variable format. The contribution approach to the profit and loss statement has been developed in response to this need.

The contribution approach

Exhibit 5.11 illustrates the contribution approach to the profit and loss statement with a simple example, along with the traditional approach discussed in Chapter 2.

Notice that the contribution approach separates costs into fixed and variable categories, first deducting variable expenses from sales to obtain what is known as the *contribution margin*. The **contribution margin** is the amount remaining from sales revenues after variable expenses have been deducted. This amount *contributes* toward covering fixed expenses and then toward profits for the period.

The contribution approach to the profit and loss statement is used as an internal planning and decision-making tool. Its emphasis on costs by behaviour facilitates cost-volume-profit analysis, which we will tackle in Chapter 7. The approach is also very useful in appraising management performance, in segmented reporting of profit data, and in budgeting. Moreover, the contribution approach helps managers organize data pertinent to all kinds of special decisions such as product-line analysis, pricing, use of scarce resources, and make or buy analysis. All of these topics are covered in later chapters.

Managers use costs organized by behaviour as a basis for many decisions. To facilitate this use, the profit statement can be prepared in a contribution format. The contribution format classifies costs on the profit and loss statement by cost behaviour (i.e., variable versus fixed) rather than by the functions of production, administration, and sales.

Traditional approach (costs organized by function)			**Contribution approach (costs organized by behaviour)**		
Sales		£12,000	Sales		£12,000
Less cost of goods sold		6,000*	Less variable expenses:		
Gross margin		6,000	Variable production	£2,000	
Less operating expenses:			Variable selling	600	
Selling	£3,100*		Variable administrative	400	3,000
Administrative	1,900*	5,000	Contribution margin		9,000
Net profit		£1,000	Less fixed expenses:		
			Fixed production	4,000	
			Fixed selling	2,500	
			Fixed administrative	1,500	8,000
			Net profit		£1,000

*Contains both variable and fixed expenses. This is the profit statement for a manufacturing company; thus, when the profit statement is placed in the contribution format, the 'cost of goods sold' figure is divided between variable production costs and fixed production costs. If this were the profit statement for a *merchandising* company (which simply purchases completed goods from a supplier), then the cost of goods sold would *all* be variable.

Exhibit 5.11 Comparison of the contribution profit statement with the traditional profit statement

Summary

- The ability to predict how costs will respond to changes in activity is critical for making decisions and for other major management functions. Three major classifications of costs were discussed – variable, fixed and mixed. Mixed costs consist of a mixture of variable and fixed elements.
- There are three major methods of analysing mixed costs that rely on past records of cost and activity data – the high-low method, the scattergraph approach, and least-squares regression. The high–low method is the simplest of the three methods and can yield estimates of fixed and variable costs very quickly, but it suffers from relying on just two data points.
- In most situations, the least-squares regression method should be used to derive a cost formula, although the scattergraph method can also give good results. The least-squares method is objective, and a variety of useful statistics are automatically produced by most software packages along with estimates of the intercept (fixed cost) and slope (variable cost per unit). Nevertheless, even when least-squares regression is used, the data should be plotted to confirm that the relationship is really a straight line.

Key terms for review

Account analysis (p. 165).

Activity base (p. 157).

Adjusted R^2 (p. 172).

Committed fixed costs (p. 161).

Contribution approach (p. 173).

Contribution margin (p. 173).

Cost structure (p. 156).
Curvilinear costs (p. 159).
Dependent variable (p. 168).
Discretionary fixed costs (p. 161).
Engineering approach (p. 165).
High–low method (p. 166).
Independent variable (p. 168).
Least-squares regression method (p. 171).
Mixed cost (p. 163).
Multiple regression (p. 173).
Regression line (p. 169).
Relevant range (p. 160).
Scattergraph method (p. 168).
Step-variable cost (p. 159).

Appendix 5A: Least-squares regression calculations

The least-squares regression method for estimating a linear relationship is based on the equation for a straight line:

$$Y = a + Bx$$

The following formulas are used to calculate the values of the vertical intercept (a) and the slope (b) that minimize the sum of the squared errors:

$$b = \frac{n(\Sigma XY) - (X)(\Sigma Y)}{n(\Sigma X^2) - (\Sigma X)^2}$$

$$a = \frac{(\Sigma Y) - b(\Sigma X)}{n}$$

where:

X = The level of activity (independent variable)
Y = The total mixed cost (dependent variable)
a = The total fixed cost (the vertical intercept of the line)
b = The variable cost per unit of activity (the slope of the line)
n = Number of observations
Σ = Sum across all n observations

To illustrate how these calculations are accomplished, we will use the Brentline Hospital data from page 166.

Step 1. Compute ΣX, ΣY, ΣXY, ΣX^2, and n.

Month	Patient-days X	Maintenance costs Y	XY	X^2
January	5,600	£7,900	£44,240,000	31,360,000
February	7,100	8,500	60,350,000	50,410,000
March	5,000	7,400	37,000,000	25,000,000
April	6,500	8,200	53,300,000	42,250,000
May	7,300	9,100	66,430,000	53,290,000
June	8,000	9,800	78,400,000	64,000,000
July	6,200	7,800	48,360,000	38,440,000
Total Σ	45,700	£58,700	£388,080,000	304,750,000

From this table:

$\Sigma X = 45,700$

$\Sigma Y = £58,700$

$\Sigma XY = £388,080,000$

$\Sigma X^2 = 304,750,000$

$n = 7$

Step 2. Insert the values computed in step 1 into the formula for the slope b.

$$b = \frac{n(\Sigma YX) - (\Sigma X)(\Sigma Y)}{n(\Sigma X^2) - (\Sigma X)^2}$$

$$b = \frac{7(£388,080,000) - (45,700)(£58,700)}{7(304,750,000) - (45,700)^2}$$

$$b = £0.759$$

Therefore, the maintenance cost is 75.9 pence per patient-day.

Step 3. Insert the values computed in step 1 and the value of b computed in step 2 into the formula for the intercept a.

$$a = \frac{(\Sigma X) - b(\Sigma X)}{n}$$

$$a = \frac{(£58,700) - £0.759(45,700)}{7}$$

$$a = £3,431$$

Therefore, the fixed maintenance cost is £3,431 per month. The cost formula for maintenance cost is as follows:

$$Y = a = bX$$

$$Y = £3,431 = £0.759X.$$

Appendix 5B: Non-linear cost functions and the learning curve

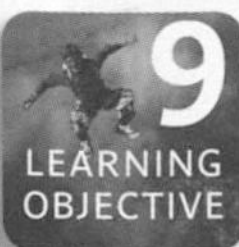
LEARNING OBJECTIVE 9

As more units of output are produced over time there may be a tendency for costs to lower as work processes become more efficient. This tendency is known as the *learning effect* and produces a non-linear cost function known as the *learning curve* (see Exhibit 5B.1). Workers become more used to their tasks and find more efficient ways to work. Indeed, a whole set of processes all along the supply chain may improve as experience grows.[2] Typically, the improvements are most dramatic in the early stages of production where the curve is steepest. At the steady-state production level, the curve levels out as no further efficiency gains can be made.

The learning curve may be modelled and used to predict cost behaviour. In the cumulative average time learning model, the improvements in efficiency are reflected in progressive reductions in the labour time taken to produce a unit of output. The rate of time reduction may be measured so that different types of learning curves may be specified quite precisely. For example, with an 80% learning curve, the cumulative time per unit falls to 80% each time output is doubled. So if the average time taken per unit for the first batch is 100 hours, with the next batch the average time is 80 hours (100 × 80%), the third batch (80 × 80%), and so on.

Mathematically, the relationship is expressed as follows:

$$Y = tX^{1}$$

where:

y = cumulative average labour hours per unit

X = cumulative number of units produced

t = time required to produce the first unit

l = rate of learning

and where

$$l = \frac{\ln(\%\ \text{learning})}{\ln 2}$$

The exponent l is defined as the ratio of the logarithm of the learning curve improvement rate divided by the logarithm of 2. Thus for an 80% learning curve

$$l = \frac{\text{Log}0.8}{\text{Log}2}$$

$$= -0.322$$

If the cumulative average time for unit 1 is 100 hours, then for 10 units the cumulative average time is

$$\begin{aligned} Y_{10} &= 100 \times 10^{-0.322} \\ &= 100 \times 0.476431 \\ &= \underline{47} \end{aligned}$$

And for 20 units the cumulative average time will be

$$\begin{aligned} Y_{20} &= 100 \times 20^{-0.322} \\ &= 100 \times 0.381126 \\ &= \underline{38} \end{aligned}$$

Putting these numbers into a graph we have the learning curve shown in Exhibit 5B.1.

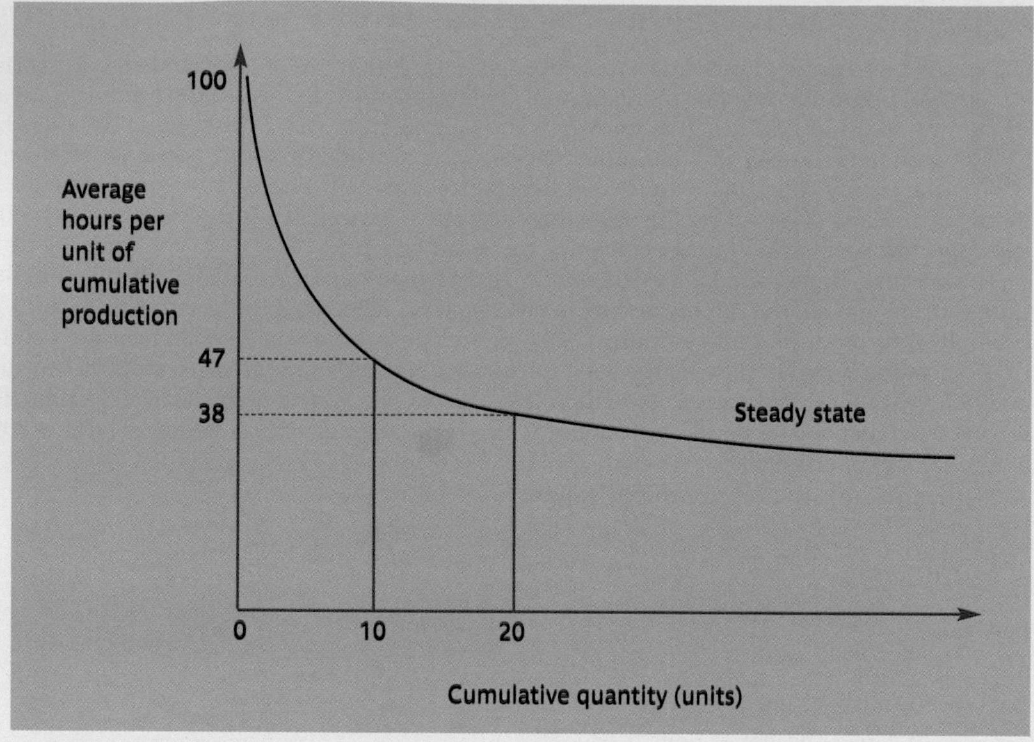

Exhibit 5B.1 An 80% learning curve

Appendix 5C: Cost measurement in service industries

In Chapter 2, we argued that although many of the principles of costing could be applied similarly to manufacturing and services, there are some special characteristics of service activities which can affect the measurement of costs. One particular issue relates to the definition of *service volume* in order to estimate cost behaviour. One way of dealing with this problem is to classify service industries into three archetypes: *professional services, service shops* and *mass services.*[3] These categories are themselves characterized in terms of six main dimensions: (1) Equipment or people focus; (2) Customer contact time; (3) Degree of customization; (4) Degree of discretion by front-line staff/freedom from supervision; (5) Front-office versus back-office orientation/source of value added; (6) Product-oriented service versus process-oriented service.

For example, professional service organization like a management consultancy would tend to have a people focus, have high customer contact time, a high degree of customization, a high degree of discretion by front-line staff, a front-office source of value added and a process rather than a product emphasis. A mass service organization such as an airline would have the opposite features while a hotel might be seen as a service shop.

Each archetype may also be ranked according to *volume of customers processed by a typical unit per day.* A professional service would tend to have a relatively low number of customers processed by a typical unit per day while a mass services organization such as an airline would expect to process a relatively high number of customers per unit per day. These classifications and relationships also seem to capture other cost structures and behaviours. First, mass services seem to have a higher proportion of fixed costs to variable costs. Second, cost traceability decreases from a high level with professional services to a low level with mass services.

The difficulties of defining output and tracing costs partly explain why some service organizations, such as banks, have generally seen the department rather than the product as the key cost object. It also explains why banks and other service organizations have been keen to implement activity-based cost systems, as we shall see in Chapter 8.

Review problem 1: cost behaviour

Neptune Rentals offers a boat rental service. Consider the following costs of the company over the relevant range of 5,000 to 8,000 hours of operating time for its boats:

	Hours of operating time			
	5,000	**6,000**	**7,000**	**8,000**
Total costs:				
Variable costs	£20,000	£?	£?	£?
Fixed costs	168,000	?	?	?
Total costs	£188,000	£?	£?	£?
Cost per hour:				
Variable cost	£?	£?	£?	£?
Fixed cost	?	?	?	?
Total cost per hour	£?	£?	£?	£?

Required

Compute the missing amounts, assuming that cost behaviour patterns remain unchanged within the relevant range of 5,000 to 8,000 hours.

Solution to review problem 1

The variable cost per hour can be computed as follows:

£20,000/5,000 hours = £4 per hour

Therefore, in accordance with the behaviour of variable and fixed costs, the missing amounts are as follows:

	Hours of operating time			
	5,000	**6,000**	**7,000**	**8,000**
Total costs:				
Variable costs	£20,000	£24,000	£28,000	£32,000
Fixed costs	168,000	168,000	168,000	168,000
Total costs	£188,000	£192,000	£196,000	£200,000
Cost per hour:				
Variable cost	£4.00	£4.00	£4.00	£4.00
Fixed cost	33.60	28.00	24.00	21.00
Total cost per hour	£37.60	£32.00	£28.00	£25.00

Observe that the total variable costs increase in proportion to the number of hours of operating time, but that these costs remain constant at £4 if expressed on a per hour basis.

In contrast, the total fixed costs do not change with changes in the level of activity. They remain constant at £168,000 within the relevant range. With increases in activity, however, the fixed costs decrease on a per hour basis, dropping from £33.60 per hour when the boats are operated 5,000 hours a period to only £21.00 per hour when the boats are operated 8,000 hours a period. *Because of this troublesome aspect of fixed costs, they are most easily (and most safely) dealt with on a total basis, rather than on a unit basis, in cost analysis work.*

Review problem 2: high–low method

The administrator of Azalea Hills Hospital would like a cost formula linking the costs involved in admitting patients to the number of patients admitted during a month. The admission department's costs and the number of patients admitted during the immediately preceding eight months are given in the following table:

Month	Number of patients admitted	Admission Department costs (in £s)
May	1,800	14,700
June	1,900	15,200
July	1,700	13,700
August	1,600	14,000
September	1,500	14,300
October	1,300	13,100
November	1,100	12,800
December	1,500	14,600

Required

1 Use the high–low method to establish the fixed and variable components of admitting costs.

2 Express the fixed and variable components of admitting costs as a cost formula in the linear equation form $Y = a = bX$.

Solution to review problem 2

1 The first step in the high–low method is to identify the periods of the lowest and highest activity. Those periods are November (1,100 patients admitted) and June (1,900 patients admitted).

The second step is to compute the variable cost per unit using those two points:

Month	Number of patients admitted	Admission Department costs
High activity level (June)	1,900	£15,200
Low activity level (November)	1,100	12,800
Change	800	£2,400

$$\text{Variable cost} = \frac{\text{Change in cost}}{\text{Change in activity}} = \frac{£2{,}400}{800} = £3 \text{ per patient admitted}$$

The third step is to compute the fixed cost element by deducting the variable cost element from the total cost at either the high or low activity. In the computation below, the high point of activity is used:

Fixed cost element = Total cost – Variable cost element = £15,200 – (£3 × 1,900 patients admitted) = £9,500

2 The cost formula expressed in the linear equation form is $Y = £9{,}500 + £3X$.

Questions

5–1 Distinguish between (a) a variable cost, (b) a fixed cost, and (c) a mixed cost.

5–2 What effect does an increase in volume have on
- **(a)** Unit fixed costs?
- **(b)** Unit variable costs?
- **(c)** Total fixed costs?
- **(d)** Total variable costs?

5–3 Define the following terms (a) cost behaviour, and (b) relevant range.

5–4 What is meant by an activity base when dealing with variable costs? Give several examples of activity bases.

5–5 Distinguish between (a) a variable cost, (b) a mixed cost and (c) a step-variable cost. Chart the three costs on a graph, with activity plotted horizontally and cost plotted vertically.

5–6 Managers often assume a strictly linear relationship between cost and volume. How can this practice be defended in light of the fact that many costs are curvilinear?

5–7 Distinguish between discretionary fixed costs and committed fixed costs.

5–8 Classify the following fixed costs as normally being either committed or discretionary:
- **(a)** Depreciation on buildings
- **(b)** Advertising
- **(c)** Research
- **(d)** Long-term equipment leases
- **(e)** Pension payments to the firm's retirees
- **(f)** Management development and training.

5–9 Does the concept of the relevant range apply to fixed costs? Explain.

5–10 What is the major disadvantage of the high–low method?

5–11 What methods are available for separating a mixed cost into its fixed and variable elements using past records of cost and activity data? Which method is considered to be most accurate? Why?

5–12 What is meant by a regression line? Give the general formula for a regression line. Which term represents the variable cost? The fixed cost?

5–13 Once a regression line has been drawn, how does one determine the fixed cost element? The variable cost element?

5–14 What is meant by the term least-squares regression?

5–15 What is the difference between ordinary least-squares regression analysis and multiple regression analysis?

5–16 What is the difference between the contribution approach to the profit and loss statement and the traditional approach to the profit and loss statement?

5–17 What is the contribution margin?

5–18 Why do average costs per unit tend to fall over time?

Exercises

E5–1 Time allowed: 20 minutes

The Lakeshore Hotel's guest-days of occupancy and custodial supplies expense over the last seven months were:

Month	Guest-days of occupancy	Custodial supplies expense
March	4,000	£7,500
April	6,500	8,250
May	8,000	10,500
June	10,500	12,000
July	12,000	13,500
August	9,000	10,750
September	7,500	9,750

Guest-days is a measure of the overall activity at the hotel. For example, a guest stay at the hotel lasting for three days is counted as three guest-days.

Required

1 Using the high–low method, estimate a cost formula for custodial supplies expense.

2 Using the cost formula you derived above, what amount of custodial supplies expense would you expect to be incurred at an occupancy level of 11,000 guest-days?

E5–2 Time allowed: 25 minutes
Refer to the data in E5–1.

Required

1 Prepare a scattergraph using the data from E5–1. Plot cost on the vertical axis and activity on the horizontal axis. Fit a regression line to your plotted points by visual inspection.

2 What is the approximate monthly fixed cost? The approximate variable cost per guest-day?

3 Scrutinize the points on your graph and explain why the high–low method would or would not yield an accurate cost formula in this situation.

E5–3 Time allowed: 30 minutes
The following data relating to units shipped and total shipping expense have been assembled by Archer Company, a manufacturer of large, custom-built air-conditioning units for commercial buildings:

Month	Units shipping	Total shipped expense
January	3	£1,800
February	6	2,300
March	4	1,700
April	5	2,000
May	47	2,300
June	8	2,700
July	2	1,200

Required

1 Using the high–low method, estimate a cost formula or shipping expense.

2 For the scattergraph method, do the following:

(a) Prepare a scattergraph, using the data given above. Plot cost on the vertical axis and activity on the horizontal axis. Fit a regression line to your plotted points by visual inspection.

(b) Using your scattergraph, estimate the approximate variable cost per unit shipped and the approximate fixed cost per month.

3 What factors, other than the number of units shipped, are likely to affect the company's total shipping expense? Explain.

E5–4 Time allowed: 25 minutes
(Appendix 5A) Refer to the data in E5–3.

Required

1 Using the least-squares regression method, estimate a cost formula for shipping expense.

2 If you also completed E5–3, prepare a simple table comparing the variable and fixed-cost elements of shipping expense as computed under the high–low method, the scattergraph method and the least-squares regression method.

E5–5 Time allowed: 20 minutes
St Mark's Hospital contains 450 beds. The average occupancy rate is 80% per month. In other words, on average, 80% of the hospital's beds are occupied by patients. At this level of occupancy, the hospital's operating costs are £32 per occupied bed per day, assuming a 30-day month. This £32 figure contains both variable and fixed cost elements.

During June, the hospital's occupancy rate was only 60%. A total of £326,700 in operating cost was incurred during the month.

Required

1 Using the high–low method, estimate:

(a) The variable cost per occupied bed on a daily basis.

(b) The total fixed operating costs per month.

2 Assume an occupancy rate of 70% per month. What amount of total operating cost would you expect the hospital to incur?

E5–6 Time allowed: 20 minutes
Hoi Chong Transport Ltd operates a fleet of delivery trucks in Singapore. The company has determined that if a truck is driven 105,000 kilometres during a year, the average operating cost is 11.4 pence per kilometre. If a truck is driven only 70,000 kilometres during a year, the average operating cost increases to 13.4 pence per kilometre. (The Singapore dollar is the currency used.)

Required

1 Using the high–low method, estimate the variable and fixed cost elements of the annual cost of truck operation.

2 Express the variable and fixed costs in the form $Y = a + bX$.

3 If a truck were driven 80,000 kilometres during a year, what total cost would you expect to be incurred?

E5–7 Time allowed: 20 minutes
Oki Products Ltd has observed the following processing costs at various levels of activity over the last fifteen months:

Month	Units produced	Processing cost
1	4,500	£38,000
2	11,000	52,000
3	12,000	56,000
4	5,500	40,000
5	9,000	47,000
6	10,500	52,000
7	7,500	44,000
8	5,000	41,000
9	11,500	52,000
10	6,000	43,000
11	8,500	48,000
12	10,000	50,000
13	6,500	44,000
14	9,500	48,000
15	8,000	46,000

Required

1 Prepare a scattergraph by plotting the above data on a graph. Plot cost on the vertical axis and activity on the horizontal axis. Fit a line to your plotted points by visual inspection.

2 What is the approximate monthly fixed cost? The approximate variable cost per unit processed? Show your computations.

E5–8 Time allowed: 20 minutes
(Appendix 5A) George Caloz & Frères, located in Grenchen, Switzerland, makes prestige high-quality custom watches in small lots. The company has been in operation since 1856. One of the company's products, a platinum diving watch, goes through an etching process. The company has observed etching costs as follows over the last six weeks:

Week	Units	Total etching cost
1	4	SFr18
2	3	17
3	8	25
4	6	20
5	7	24
6	2	16
	30	SFr120

The Swiss currency is the Swiss franc, which is denoted by SFr.

For planning purposes, management would like to know the amount of variable etching cost per unit and the total fixed etching cost per week.

Required

1 Using the least-squares regression method, estimate the variable and fixed elements of etching cost.

2 Express the cost data in Question 1 above in the form $Y = a + bX$.

3 If the company processes five units next week, what would be the expected total etching cost?

E5–9 Time allowed: 20 minutes

Harris Company manufactures and sells a single product. A partially completed schedule of the company's total and per unit costs over the relevant range of 30,000 to 50,000 units produced and sold annually is given below:

	Units produced and sold		
	30,000	40,000	50,000
Total costs:			
Variable costs	£180,000	?	?
Fixed costs	300,000	?	?
Total costs	£480,000	?	?
Cost per unit:			
Variable cost	?	?	?
Fixed cost	?	?	?
Total cost per unit	?	?	?

Required

1 Complete the schedule of the company's total and unit costs above.

2 Assume that the company produces and sells 45,000 units during a year at a selling price of £16 per unit. Prepare a profit statement in the contribution format for the year.

E5–10 Time allowed: 15 minutes

The Alpine House Ltd is a large retailer of winter sports equipment. A profit statement for the company's Ski Department for a recent quarter is presented below:

The Alpine House Ltd Profit and loss statement – Ski Department
For the quarter ended 31 March

Sales		£150,000
Less cost of goods sold		90,000
Gross margin		60,000
Less operating expenses:		
Selling expenses	£30,000	
Administrative expenses	10,000	40,000
Net profit		£20,000

Skis sell, on the average, for £750 per pair. Variable selling expenses are £50 per pair of skis sold. The remaining selling expenses are fixed. The administrative expenses are 20% variable and 80% fixed. The company does not manufacture its own skis; it purchases them from a supplier for £450 per pair.

Required

1 Prepare a profit statement for the quarter using the contribution approach.

2 For every pair of skis sold during the quarter, what was the contribution toward covering fixed expenses and toward earning profits?

Problems

P5–11 High–low method; contribution profit statement Time allowed: 30 minutes

Morrisey & Brown Ltd of Sydney is a merchandising firm that is the sole distributor of a product that is increasing in popularity among Australian consumers. The company's profit statements for the three most recent months follow:

Morrisey & Brown Ltd Profit and loss statements
For the three months ending 30 September

	July	August	September
Sales in units	4,000	4,500	5,000
Sales revenue	A$400,000	A$450,000	A$500,000
Less cost of goods sold	240,000	270,000	300,000
Gross margin	160,000	180,000	200,000
Less operating expenses:			
Advertising expense	21,000	21,000	21,000
Shipping expense	34,000	36,000	38,000
Salaries and commissions	78,000	84,000	90,000
Insurance expense	6,000	6,000	6,000
Depreciation expense	15,000	15,000	15,000
Total operating expenses	154,000	162,000	170,000
Net income	A$6,000	A$18,000	A$30,000

(*Note:* The Australian dollar is denoted by A$.)

Required

1 Identify each of the company's expenses (including cost of goods sold) as being either variable, fixed, or mixed.

2 By use of the high–low method, separate each mixed expense into variable and fixed elements. State the cost formula for each mixed expense.

3 Redo the company's profit statement at the 5,000-unit level of activity using the contribution format.

P5–12 Identifying cost behaviour patterns Time allowed: 20 minutes

On the next page are a number of cost behaviour patterns that might be found in a company's cost structure. The vertical axis on each graph represents total cost, and the horizontal axis on each graph represents level of activity (volume).

Required

1 For each of the following situations, identify the graph from the next page that illustrates the cost pattern involved. Any graph may be used more than once.

(a) Cost of raw materials used.

(b) Electricity bill – a flat fixed charge, plus a variable cost after a certain number of kilowatt-hours are used.

(c) City water bill, which is computed as follows:

First 1,000,000 litres or less	£1,000 flat fee
Next 10,000 litres	0.003 per litre used
Next 10,000 litres	0.006 per litre used
Next 10,000 litres	0.009 per litre used
Etc.	Etc.

(d) Depreciation of equipment, where the amount is computed by the straight-line method. When the depreciation rate was established, it was anticipated that the obsolescence factor would be greater than the wear and tear factor.

(e) Rent on a factory building donated by the city, where the agreement calls for a fixed-fee payment unless 200,000 labour-hours or more are worked, in which case no rent need be paid.

(f) Salaries of maintenance workers, where one maintenance worker is needed for every 1,000 hours of machine-hours or less (that is, 0 to 1,000 hours requires one maintenance worker, 1,001 to 2,000 hours requires two maintenance workers, etc.)

(g) Cost of raw materials, where the cost decreases by 5 pence per unit for each of the first 100 units purchased, after which it remains constant at £2.50 per unit.

(h) Rent on a factory building donated by the county, where the agreement calls for rent of £100,000 less £1 for each direct labour-hour worked in excess of 200,000 hours, but where a minimum rental payment of £20,000 must be paid.

(i) Use of a machine under a lease, where a minimum charge of £1,000 is paid for up to 400 hours of machine time. After 400 hours of machine time, an additional charge of £2 per hour is paid up to a maximum charge of £2,000 per period.

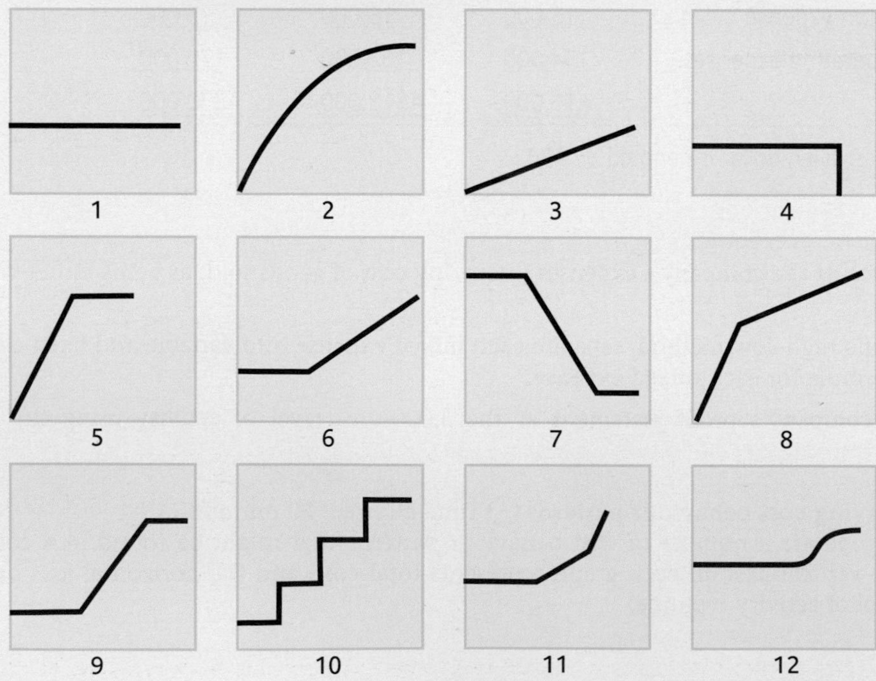

2 How would a knowledge of cost behaviour patterns such as those above be of help to a manager in analysing the cost structure of his or her firm?

(*CPA*, adapted)

P5–13 High–low method of cost analysis Time allowed: 35 minutes
Nova Company's total overhead costs at various levels of activity are presented below.

Month	Machine-hours	Total overhead costs
April	70,000	£198,000
May	60,000	174,000
June	80,000	222,000
July	90,000	246,000

Assume that the total overhead costs above consist of utilities, supervisory salaries and maintenance. The breakdown of these costs at the 60,000 machine-hour level of activity is:

Utilities (V)	£48,000
Supervisory salaries (F)	21,000
Maintenance (M)	105,000
Total overhead costs	£174,000

V = variable; F = fixed; M = mixed.

Nova Company's management wants to break down the maintenance cost into its basic variable and fixed cost elements.

Required

1 As shown above, overhead costs in July amounted to £246,000. Determine how much of this consisted of maintenance cost. (*Hint:* to do this, it may be helpful first to determine how much of the £246,000 consisted of utilities and supervisory salaries. Think about the behaviour of variable and fixed costs!)

2 By means of the high–low method, estimate a cost formula for maintenance.

3 Express the company's total overhead costs in the linear equation form $Y = a = bX$.

4 What total overhead costs would you expect to be incurred at an operating activity level of 75,000 machine-hours?

P5–14 High–low method of cost analysis Time allowed: 30 minutes
Sawaya Co. Ltd of Japan is a manufacturing company whose total factory overhead costs fluctuate considerably from year to year according to increases and decreases in the number of direct labour-hours worked in the factory. Total factory overhead costs (in Japanese yen, denoted ¥) at high and low levels of activity for recent years are given below:

	Level of activity	
	Low	High
Direct labour-hours	50,000	75,000
Total factory overhead costs	¥14,250,000	¥17,625,000

The factory overhead costs above consist of indirect materials, rent and maintenance. The company has analysed these costs at the 50,000-hour level of activity as follows:

Indirect materials (V)	¥5,000,000
Rent (F)	6,000,000
Maintenance (M)	3,250,000
Total factory overhead costs	¥14,250,000

V = variable; F = fixed; M = mixed.

To have data available for planning, the company wants to break down the maintenance cost into its variable and fixed cost elements.

Required

1 Estimate how much of the ¥17,625,000 factory overhead cost at the high level of activity consists of maintenance cost. (*Hint:* To do this, it may be helpful to first determine how much of the ¥17,625,000 consists of indirect materials and rent. Think about the behaviour of variable and fixed costs!)

2 By means of the high–low method of cost analysis, estimate a cost formula for maintenance.

3 What total factory overhead costs would you expect the company to incur at an operating level of 70,000 direct labour-hours?

P5–15 Manufacturing statements; high–low method of cost analysis Time allowed: 40 minutes

Amfac Company manufactures a single product. The company keeps careful records of manufacturing activities from which the following information has been extracted:

	Level of activity	
	March-low	**June-high**
Number of units produced	6,000	9,000
Cost of goods manufactured	£168,000	£257,000
Work in progress inventory, beginning	£9,000	£32,000
Work in progress inventory, ending	£15,000	£21,000
Direct materials cost per unit	£6	£6
Direct labour cost per unit	£10	£10
Manufacturing overhead cost, total	?	?

The company's manufacturing overhead cost consists of both variable and fixed cost elements. To have data available for planning, management wants to determine how much of the overhead cost is variable with units produced and how much of it is fixed per month.

Required

1 For both March and June, determine the amount of manufacturing overhead cost added to production. The company had no under- or overapplied overhead in either month. (*Hint:* A useful way to proceed might be to construct a schedule of cost of goods manufactured.)

2 By means of the high–low method of cost analysis, estimate a cost formula for manufacturing overhead. Express the variable portion of the formula in terms of a variable rate per unit of product.

3 If 7,000 units are produced during a month, what would be the cost of goods manufactured? (Assume that work in progress inventories do not change and that there is no under- or overapplied overhead cost for the month.)

P5–16 Cost function estimation Time allowed: 35 minutes

A factory's monthly production costs and output from a production line for circuit boards are as follows:

	Jan	Feb	Mar	April	May	June	July	Aug	Sept	Oct
Output X (units)	200	150	400	450	50	500	150	350	100	250
Costs Y (£000)	10	9	12	14	5	16	10	14	6	10

$\Sigma X = 2,600$ $\Sigma Y = 106$ $\Sigma X^2 = 895,000$ $\Sigma Y^2 = 1,234$ $\Sigma XY = 32,200$

Required

1

(a) Draw on graph paper a scatter diagram of costs against output.
[Do *not* draw in your 'line of best fit'.] *(6 marks)*

(b) Comment on your diagram. *(2 marks)*

2

(a) Calculate the least-squares regression of costs on output and plot this line on the diagram. *(6 marks)*

(b) Explain the meaning of your regression line. *(3 marks)*

3 Estimate approximate values for the correlation coefficient, and R-squared, and explain their meanings.
[Do not calculate the value of R-squared.] *(3 marks)*

4 The planned output of the factory for November is 300 circuit boards.

(a) Forecast the costs for November. *(2 marks)*

(b) Discuss the reliability of your forecast. *(3 marks)*

(Total = 25 marks)

CIMA Business Mathematics, November 2001

P5–17 High–low method Time allowed: 30 minutes
The following information is available for a company:

	Year 1	Year 2	Year 3	Year 4
Sales/production (units)	67,200	71,300	75,600	75,100
Total costs (£)	135,000	144,072	156,090	158,950
Cost inflation index	100	103.5	107.5	110.0

Required

1 Determine a linear function for total costs per annum (at Year 1 prices) from the above data, using the high–low method (unit costs should be calculated to three decimal places of £). *(5 marks)*

2 Using the function in Question 1 and the data above, evaluate and comment upon the accuracy of the function as a predictor of costs. *(5 marks)*

3 Using the function in Question 1, forecast the total costs in Year 5 based on a volume of 77,200 units and a cost inflation index of 112.9. *(2 marks)*

4 Selling prices in Year 5 are expected to be 15% higher than those in Year 1, when total sales revenue was £159,936. Draw a profit-volume chart for Year 5, showing sales up to 90,000 units per annum. *(8 marks)*

(20 marks)

ACCA Management information, December 1999

P5–18 Learning/experience curve Time allowed: 45 minutes

Armourco Ltd manufactures and fits a range of armoured attachments to standard army vehicles to protect them against attacks by guerrillas and damage from land mines. Due to worsening conflicts in Rhodambia, the British Army is to form part of a United Nations peace-keeping force to be sent into the area.

Armourco has been invited by the Government to tender for a special contract to supply and fit armoured kits to four-wheel drive vehicles, which are to be airlifted to the trouble-spot. The ultimate size of the order is not yet known, but the company has been asked to quote selling prices for orders of 50 kits and 100 kits assuming the size of the order will be known when the contract is placed; and also to quote a separate price for an extra 100 kits subsequent to the initial order.

The following data are relevant:

Armourco estimates costs for an initial order of 50 kits to be:

Direct materials:

X	2000 kilograms at £10.00 per kilogram			
Y	500 metres at £25.00 per metre			

Direct wages:

Department:	1	160 hours	at	£12.50 per hour
	2	1000 hours	at	£15.00 per hour
	3	2000 hours	at	£10.00 per hour

Variable Overhead: 25% of direct wages

Fixed overhead rates per hour:

Department:	1	£10.00 per hour
	2	£20.00 per hour
	3	£10.00 per hour

The nature of the work in the three departments is as follows:

Department 1	uses highly automated machines. The efficiency of the operators can have little impact on the quantity of output
Department 2	employs skilled operators. Experience has shown that an 80% learning curve can be expected to operate
Department 3	also employs skilled operators. Here a 75% learning curve is expected

On orders of this type, it is the company's practice to add the following margins on cost in arriving at selling prices:

Direct materials	20%
Conversion costs	40%

Required

Calculate the price per kit for:

1 an initial order of 50 kits;

2 an initial order of 100 kits;

3 a separate order for an extra 100 kits subsequent to the order for 100 in (2) above

(Thanks to Alan Coad, University of Birmingham)

CASE

Cases

C5–19 Analysis of mixed costs, job-cost system and activity-based costing Time allowed: 90 minutes

Hokuriku-Seika Co. Ltd of Yokohama, Japan, is a subcontractor to local manufacturing firms. The company specializes in precision metal cutting using focused high-pressure water jets and high-energy lasers. The company has a traditional job-cost system in which direct labour and direct materials costs are assigned directly to jobs, but factory overhead is applied using direct labour-hours as a base. Management uses this job-cost data for valuing cost of goods sold and inventories for external reports. For internal decision making, management has largely ignored this cost data since direct labour costs are basically fixed and management believes overhead costs actually have little to do with direct labour-hours. Recently, management has become interested in activity-based costing (ABC) as a way of estimating job costs and other costs for decision-making purposes.

Management assembled a cross-functional team to design a prototype ABC system. Electrical cost was one of the factory overhead costs first investigated by the team. Electricity is used to provide light, to power equipment and to heat the building in the winter and cool it in the summer. The ABC team proposed allocating electrical costs to jobs based on machine-hours since running the machines consumes significant amounts of electricity. Data assembled by the team concerning actual direct labour-hours, machine-hours and electrical costs over a recent eight-week period appear below. (The Japanese currency is the yen, which is denoted by ¥.)

	Direct labour-hours	Machine-hours	Electrical costs
Week 1	8,920	7,200	¥77,100
Week 2	8,900	8,200	84,400
Week 3	8,950	8,700	80,400
Week 4	8,990	7,200	75,500
Week 5	8,840	7,400	81,100
Week 6	8,890	8,800	83,300
Week 7	8,950	6,400	79,200
Week 8	8,990	7,700	85,500
Total	71,340	61,600	¥646,500

To help assess the effect of the proposed change to machine-hours as allocation base, the eight-week totals were converted to annual figures by multiplying them by six.

	Direct labour-hours	Machine-hours	Electrical costs
Estimated annual total (eight-week total above × 6)	428,040	369,600	¥3,879,000

Required

1 Assume that the estimated annual totals from the above table are used to compute the company's predetermined overhead rate. What would be the predetermined overhead rate for electrical costs if the allocation base is direct labour-hours? Machine-hours?

2 Hokuriku-Seika Co. intends to bid on a job for a shipyard that would require 350 direct labour-hours and 270 machine-hours. How much electrical cost would be charged to this job using the predetermined overhead rate computed in 1 above if the allocation base is direct labour-hours? Machine-hours?

3 Prepare a scattergraph in which you plot direct labour-hours on the horizontal axis and electrical costs on the vertical axis. Prepare another scattergraph in which you plot machine-hours on the horizontal

axis and electrical costs on the vertical axis. Do you agree with the ABC team that machine-hours is a better allocation base for electrical costs than direct labour-hours? Why?

4 Using machine-hours as the measure of activity, estimate the fixed and variable components of electrical costs using either the scattergraph (i.e., visual fit) method or least-squares regression.

5 How much electrical cost do you think would actually be caused by the shipyard job in Question 2 above? Explain.

6 What factors, apart from direct labour-hours and machine-hours, are likely to affect consumption of electrical power in the company?

C5–20 Analysis of mixed costs in a pricing decision Time allowed: 90 minutes

Maria Chavez owns a catering company that serves food and beverages at parties and business functions. Chavez's business is seasonal, with a heavy schedule during the summer months and holidays and a lighter schedule at other times.

One of the major events Chavez's customers request is a cocktail party. She offers a standard cocktail party and has estimated the cost per guest as follows:

Food and beverages	£15.00
Labour (0.5 hrs @ £10.00/hr)	5.00
Overhead (0.5 hrs @ £13.98/hr)	6.99
Total cost per guest	£26.99

The standard cocktail party lasts three hours and Chavez hires one worker for every six guests, so that works out to one-half hour of labour per guest. These workers are hired only as needed and are paid only for the hours they actually work.

When bidding on cocktail parties, Chavez adds a 15% markup to yield a price of about £31 per guest. She is confident about her estimates of the costs of food and beverages and labour but is not as comfortable with the estimate of overhead cost. The £13.98 overhead cost per labour hour was determined by dividing total overhead expenses for the last twelve months by total labour hours for the same period. Monthly data concerning overhead costs and labour-hours appear below:

Month expenses	Labour-hours	Overhead
January	2,500	£55,000
February	2,800	59,000
March	3,000	60,000
April	4,200	64,000
May	4,500	71,000
July	6,500	74,000
August	7,500	477,000
September	7,000	75,000
October	4,500	68,000
November	3,100	62,000
December	6,500	73,000
Total	52,100	£738,000

Chavez has received a request to bid on a 180-guest fund-raising cocktail party to be given next month by an important local charity. (The party would last the usual three hours.) She would really like to win this contract; the guest list for the charity event includes many prominent individuals she would like to land as future clients. Maria is confident that these potential customers would be favourably impressed by her company's services at the charity event.

Required

1 Estimate the contribution to profit of a standard 180-guest cocktail party if Chavez charges her usual price of £31 per guest. (In other words, by how much would her overall profit increase?)

2 How low could Chavez bid for the charity event in terms of a price per guest and still not lose money on the event itself?

3 The individual who is organizing the charity's fund-raising event has indicated that he has already received a bid under £30 from another catering company. Do you think Chavez should bid below her normal £31 per guest price for the charity event? Why or why not?

(*CMA*, adapted)

Endnotes

1 Fingleton (1995).

2 For further reading see Chen and Manes (1985).

3 See Silvestro, Fitzgerald, Johnston and Voss (1992) and Brignall, Fitzgerald, Johnston and Silvestro (1991).

Part II
Information for decision making

Chapter 6
Profit reporting under variable costing and absorption costing

Learning objectives

After studying Chapter 6, you should be able to:

1. Explain how variable costing differs from absorption costing and compute the unit product cost under each method
2. Describe how fixed manufacturing overhead costs are deferred in stock and released from stock under absorption costing
3. Prepare profit and loss accounts using both variable and absorption costing, and reconcile the two profit figures
4. Explain the effect of changes in production on the profit reported under both variable and absorption costing
5. Explain the advantages and limitations of both the variable and absorption costing methods
6. Explain how the use of JIT reduces the difference in profit reported under the variable and absorption costing methods

Concepts in Context

Oliver is employed by a large pension fund as an investment analyst. His job is to closely monitor the performance of companies in the electrical equipment industry and to recommend which of these companies the fund should invest in.

Before Oliver joined the company, the fund had invested heavily in Power Transformers plc. Oliver knew that he should be alert for any signs of trouble at Power Transformers. He had just received the company's annual report and was puzzled by several items in the report.

First, Power Transformer's profit for the year was higher than the previous year, but not as high as many investment analysts had predicted. Second, the company's sales had actually fallen a little from the previous year. Third, the company's stocks had risen substantially. Oliver wondered if these three facts might be related and if he should issue a warning about the share price to his pension fund's investment committee.

Two general approaches are used for costing products for the purposes of valuing stock and cost of goods sold. One approach, called *absorption costing*, was discussed in Chapter 3. Absorption costing is generally used for external financial reports. The other approach, called *variable costing*, is preferred by some managers for internal decision making and must be used when a profit and loss account is prepared in the contribution format. Ordinarily, absorption costing and variable costing produce different figures for profit, and the difference can be quite large. In addition to showing how these two methods differ, we will consider the arguments for and against each costing method and we will show how management decisions can be affected by the costing method chosen.

Overview of absorption and variable costing

In the next two chapters, we will learn that the contribution format profit and loss account and cost-volume-profit (CVP) analysis are valuable management tools. Both of these tools emphasize cost behaviour and require that managers carefully distinguish between variable and fixed costs. Absorption costing, which was discussed in Chapters 2 and 3, assigns both variable and fixed costs to products – mingling them in a way that makes it difficult for managers to distinguish between them. This has led to the development of variable costing, which focuses on *cost behaviour*. One of the strengths of variable costing is that it harmonizes fully with both the contribution approach and the CVP concepts.

Absorption costing

In Chapter 3, we learned that absorption costing treats *all* costs of production as product costs, regardless of whether they are variable or fixed. The cost of a unit of product under the absorption costing method therefore consists of direct materials, direct labour, and both variable and fixed overhead. Thus, absorption costing allocates a portion of *fixed manufacturing overhead cost* to each unit of product, along with the variable manufacturing costs. Because absorption costing includes all costs of production as product costs, it is frequently referred to as the full cost method.

Variable costing

Under **variable costing**, only those costs of production that vary with output are treated as product costs. This would generally include direct materials, direct labour and the variable portion of manufacturing overhead. Fixed manufacturing overhead is not treated as a product cost under this method. Rather, fixed manufacturing overhead is treated as a period cost and, like selling and administrative expenses, it is charged off in its entirety against revenue each period. Consequently, the cost of a unit of product in stock or in cost of goods sold under the variable costing method contains no element of fixed overhead cost.

Variable costing is sometimes referred to as **direct costing** or **marginal costing**. The term *direct costing* was popular for many years, but is slowly disappearing from day-to-day use. The term *variable costing* is more descriptive of the way in which product costs are computed when a contribution profit and loss account is prepared.

To complete this summary comparison of absorption and variable costing, we need to consider briefly the handling of selling and administrative expenses. These expenses are never treated as product costs, regardless of the costing method in use. Thus, under either absorption or variable costing, selling and administrative expenses are always treated as period costs and deducted from revenues as incurred.

The concepts discussed so far in this section are illustrated in Exhibit 6.1, which shows the classification of costs under both absorption and variable costing.

6.1 EXHIBIT

Absorption costing		**Variable costing**
Product costs	Direct materials	Product costs
	Direct labour	
	Variable manufacturing overhead	
	Fixed manufacturing overhead	Period costs
Period costs	Selling and alternative expenses	

Exhibit 6.1 Cost classifications – absorption versus variable costing

Unit cost computations

To illustrate the computation of unit costs under both absorption and variable costing, consider Boley Company, a small company that produces a single product and has the following cost structure:

Number of units produced each year	6,000
Variable costs per unit:	
Direct materials	£2
Direct labour	4
Variable manufacturing overhead	1
Variable selling and administrative expenses	3
Fixed costs per year:	
Fixed manufacturing overhead	30,000
Fixed selling and administrative expenses	10,000

Required

1 Compute the unit product cost under absorption costing.

2 Compute the unit product cost under variable costing.

Absorption costing	
Direct materials	£2
Direct labour	4
Variable manufacturing overhead	1
Total variable production cost	7
Fixed manufacturing overhead (£30,000/6,000 units of product)	5
Unit product cost	£12
Variable costing	
Direct materials	£2
Direct labour	4
Variable manufacturing overhead	1
Unit product cost	£7

(The £30,000 fixed manufacturing overhead will be charged off in total against profit as a period expense along with the selling and administrative expenses.)

Under the absorption costing method, notice that all production costs, variable and fixed, are included when determining the unit product cost. Thus, if the company sells a unit of product and absorption costing is being used, then £12 (consisting of £7 variable cost and £5 fixed cost) will be deducted on the profit and loss account as cost of goods sold. Similarly, any unsold units will be carried as stock on the balance sheet at £12 each.

Under the variable costing method, notice that only the variable production costs are included in product costs. Thus, if the company sells a unit of product, only £7 will be deducted as cost of goods sold, and unsold units will be carried in the balance sheet stock account at only £7 each.

Profit comparison of absorption and variable costing

Profit and loss accounts prepared under the absorption and variable costing approaches are shown in Exhibit 6.2. In preparing these statements, we use the data for Boley Company presented earlier, along with other information about the company as given below:

Units in beginning stock	0
Units produced	6,000
Units sold	5,000
Units in ending stock	1,000
Selling price per unit	£20
Selling and administrative expenses:	
Variable per unit	3
Fixed per year	10,000

	Absorption costing	Variable costing
Unit product cost:		
Direct materials	£2	£2
Direct labour	4	4
Variable manufacturing overhead	1	1
Fixed manufacturing overhead (30,000/6,000 units)	5	—
	£12	£7

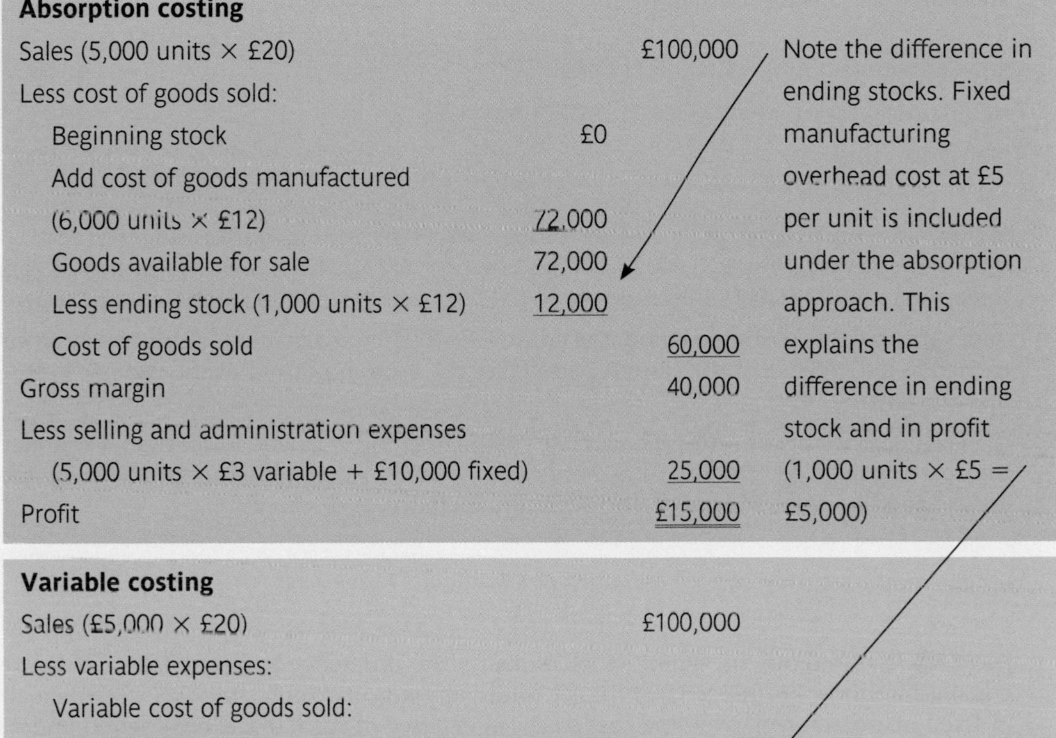

Absorption costing

Sales (5,000 units × £20)		£100,000	Note the difference in ending stocks. Fixed manufacturing overhead cost at £5 per unit is included under the absorption approach. This explains the difference in ending stock and in profit (1,000 units × £5 = £5,000)
Less cost of goods sold:			
Beginning stock	£0		
Add cost of goods manufactured (6,000 units × £12)	72,000		
Goods available for sale	72,000		
Less ending stock (1,000 units × £12)	12,000		
Cost of goods sold		60,000	
Gross margin		40,000	
Less selling and administration expenses (5,000 units × £3 variable + £10,000 fixed)		25,000	
Profit		£15,000	

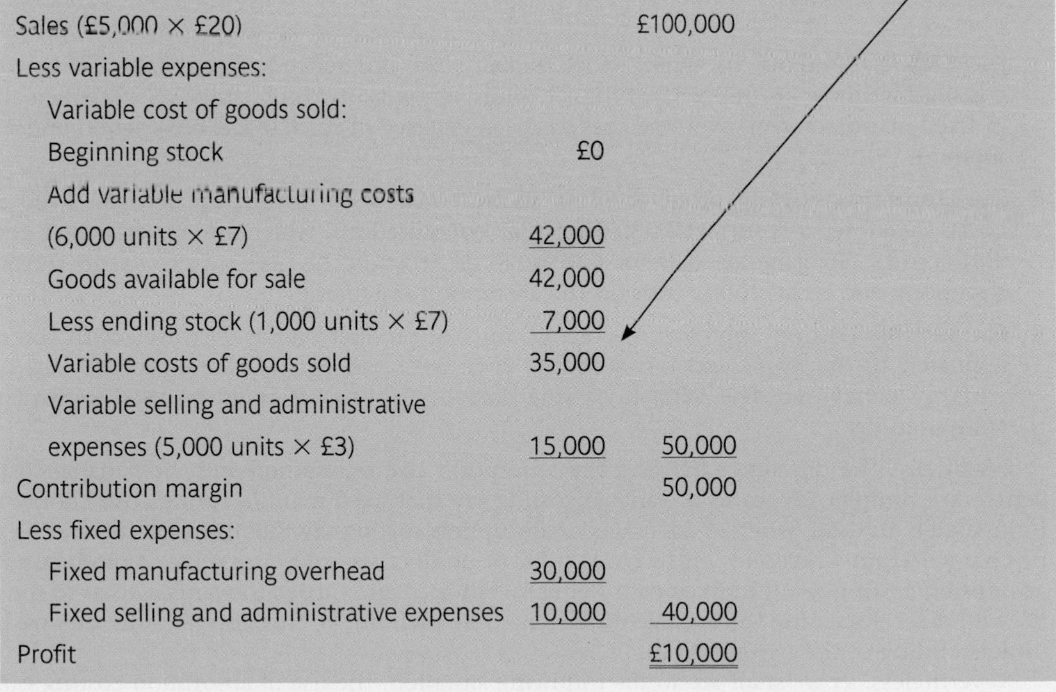

Variable costing

Sales (£5,000 × £20)		£100,000
Less variable expenses:		
Variable cost of goods sold:		
Beginning stock	£0	
Add variable manufacturing costs (6,000 units × £7)	42,000	
Goods available for sale	42,000	
Less ending stock (1,000 units × £7)	7,000	
Variable costs of goods sold	35,000	
Variable selling and administrative expenses (5,000 units × £3)	15,000	50,000
Contribution margin		50,000
Less fixed expenses:		
Fixed manufacturing overhead	30,000	
Fixed selling and administrative expenses	10,000	40,000
Profit		£10,000

Exhibit 6.2 Comparison of absorption and variable costing – Boley Company

Several points can be made from the financial statements in Exhibit 6.2:

1 Under the absorption costing method, if there is an increase in stock then some of the fixed manufacturing costs of the current period will not appear on the profit and loss account as part of cost of goods sold. Instead, these costs are deferred to a future period and are carried on the balance sheet as part of the stock count. Such a deferral of costs is known as **fixed manufacturing overhead cost deferred in stock**. The process involved can be explained by referring to the data for Boley Company. During the current period, Boley Company produced 6,000 units but sold only 5,000 units, thus leaving 1,000 unsold units in the ending stock. Under the absorption costing method, each unit produced was assigned £5 in fixed overhead cost (see the unit cost computations above). Therefore, each of the 1,000 units going into stock at the end of the period has £5 in fixed manufacturing overhead cost attached to it, or a total of £5,000 for the 1,000 units. *This fixed manufacturing overhead cost of the current period is deferred in stock to the next period, when, hopefully, these units will be taken out of stock and sold.* The deferral of £5,000 of fixed manufacturing overhead costs can be seen clearly by analysing the ending stock under the absorption costing method:

Variable manufacturing costs: 1,000 units × £7	£7,000
Fixed manufacturing overhead costs: 1,000 units × £5	5,000
Total stock value	£12,000

In summary, under absorption costing, of the £30,000 in fixed manufacturing overhead costs incurred during the period, only £25,000 (5,000 units sold × £5) has been included in cost of goods sold. The remaining £5,000 (1,000 units not sold × £5) has been deferred in stock to the next period.

2 Under the variable costing method, the entire £30,000 in fixed manufacturing overhead costs has been treated as an expense of the current period (see the bottom portion of the variable costing profit and loss account).

3 The ending stock figure under the variable costing method is £5,000 lower than it is under the absorption costing method. The reason is that under variable costing, only the variable manufacturing costs are assigned to units of product and therefore included in stock:

Variable manufacturing costs: 1,000 units × £7	£7,000

The £5,000 difference in ending stock explains the difference in profit reported between the two costing methods. Profit is £5,000 higher under absorption costing since, as explained above, £5,000 of fixed manufacturing overhead cost has been deferred in stock to the next period under that costing method.

4 The absorption costing profit and loss account makes no distinction between fixed and variable costs; therefore, it is not well suited for CVP computations, which are important for good planning and control. To generate data for CVP analysis, it would be necessary to spend considerable time reworking and reclassifying costs on the absorption statement.

5 The variable costing approach to costing units of product blends very well with the contribution approach to the profit and loss account, since both concepts are based on the idea of classifying costs by behaviour. The variable costing data in Exhibit 6.2 could be used immediately in CVP computations.

Essentially, the difference between the absorption costing method and the variable costing method centres on timing. Advocates of variable costing say that fixed manufacturing costs should be expensed immediately in total, whereas advocates of absorption costing say that fixed manufacturing costs should be charged against revenues bit by bit as units of product are sold. Any units of product not sold under absorption costing result in fixed costs being inventoried and carried forward *as assets* to the next period. We will defer discussing the arguments presented by each side in this dispute until after we have a better understanding of the two methods.

Nevertheless, as we shall see in the following situation, the use of absorption costing can sometimes produce strange effects on profit and loss accounts.

Extended comparison of profit data

Management accounting in action: the issue

Mary O'Meara is the owner and manager of Emerald Isle Knitters Ltd of Galway, Republic of Ireland. The company is very small, with only ten employees. Mary started the company three years ago with cash loaned to her by a local bank. The company manufactures a traditional wool fisherman's sweater from a pattern Mary learned from her grandmother. Like most clothing manufacturers, Emerald Isle Knitters sells its product to department stores and clothing store chains rather than to retail customers.

The sweater was an immediate success, and the company sold all of the first year's production. However, in the second year of operations, one of the company's major customers cancelled its order due to bankruptcy, and the company ended the year with large stocks of unsold sweaters. The third year of operations was a great year in contrast to that disastrous second year. Sales rebounded dramatically, and all of the unsold production carried over from the second year was sold by the end of the third year.

Shortly after the close of the third year, Mary met with her accountant Sean MacLafferty to discuss the results for the year.

Mary: Sean, the results for this year look a lot better than for last year, but I am frankly puzzled why this year's results aren't even better than the profit and loss account shows.

Sean: I know what you mean. The profit for this year is just €90,000. Last year it was €30,000. That is a huge improvement, but it seems that profits this year should have been even higher and profits last year should have been much less. We were in big trouble last year. I was afraid we might not even break even – yet we showed a healthy €30,000 profit. Somehow it doesn't seem quite right.

Mary: I wondered about that €30,000 profit last year, but I didn't question it since it was the only good news I'd had for quite some time.

Sean: In case you're wondering, I didn't invent that profit last year just to make you feel better. Our auditor required that I follow certain accounting rules in preparing those reports for the bank. This may sound heretical, but we could use different rules for our own internal reports.

Mary: Wait a minute, rules are rules – especially in accounting.

Sean: Yes and no. For our internal reports, it might be better to use different rules than we use for the reports we send to the bank.

Mary: As I said, rules are rules. Still, I'm willing to listen if you want to show me what you have in mind.

Sean: It's a deal.

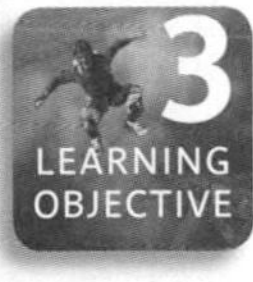

Immediately after the meeting with Mary, Sean put together the data and financial reports that appear in Exhibit 6.3. To make the principles clearer, Sean simplified the data so that the illustrations all use round figures.

EXHIBIT 6.3

Basic data

Selling price	€20
Variable manufacturing cost per unit produced	7
Fixed manufacturing overhead costs per year	150,000
Variable selling and administrative expenses per unit sold	1
Fixed selling and administrative expenses per year	90,000

	Year 1	Year 2	Year 3	Three years together
Units in beginning stock	0	0	5,000	0
Units produced	25,000	25,000	25,000	75,000
Units sold	25,000	20,000	30,000	75,000
Units in ending stock	0	5,000	0	0

Unit product costs

	Year 1	Year 2	Year 3
Under variable costing (variable manufacturing costs only)	€7	€7	€7
Under absorption costing:			
Variable manufacturing costs	€7	€7	€7
Fixed manufacturing overhead costs (€150,000 spread over the number of units produced in each year)	6	6	6
Total absorption cost per unit	€13	€13	€13

	Year 1	Year 2	Year 3	Three years together
Absorption costing				
Sales	€500,000	€400,000	€600,000	€1,500,000
Less cost of goods sold:				
Beginning stock	€0	€0	€65,000	€0
Add cost of goods manufactured (25,000 units × €13)	325,000	325,000	325,000	975,000
Goods available for sale	325,000	325,000	390,000	975,000
Less ending stock (5,000 units × €13)	0	65,000	0	0

Gross margin	175,000	140,000	210,000	525,000
Less selling and administrative expenses	115,000*	110,000*	120,000*	345,00
Profit	€60,000	€30,000	€90,000	€180,000

*The selling and administrative expenses are computed as follows:

Year 1: 25,000 units × €1 variable plus €90,000 fixed = €115,000.

Year 2: 20,000 units × €1 variable plus €90,000 fixed = €110,000.

Year 3: 30,000 units × €1 variable plus €90,000 fixed = €120,000.

Variable costing								
Sales		€500,000		€100,000		€600,000		€1,500,000
Less variable expenses:								
Variable cost of goods sold:								
Beginning stock	0		0		35,000		0	
Add variable manufacturing costs (25,000 units × €7)	175,000		175,000		175,000		525,000	
Goods available for sale	175,000		175,000		210,000		525,000	
Less ending stock (5,000 units × €7)	0		35,000		0		0	
Variable costs of goods sold	175,000*		140,000*		210,000*		525,000	
Variable selling and administrative expenses (€1 per unit sold)	25,000	200,000	20,000	160,000	30,000	240,000	75,000	600,000
Contribution margin		300,000		240,000		360,000		900,000
Less fixed expenses:								
Fixed manufacturing overhead	150,000		150,000		150,000		450,000	
Fixed selling and administrative expenses	90,000	240,000	90,000	240,000	90,000	240,000	270,000	720,000
Profit		€60,000		€0		€120,000		€180,000

*The variable cost of goods sold could have been computed more simply as follows:

Year 1: 25,000 units sold × €7 = €175,000.

Year 2: 20,000 units sold × €7 = €140,000.

Exhibit 6.3 Absorption and variable costing statements – Emerald Isle Knitters Ltd

The basic data appear at the top of Exhibit 6.3, and the absorption costing profit and loss accounts as reported to the bank for the last three years appear on the following page. Sean decided to try using the variable costing approach to see what effect that might have on profit. The variable costing profit and loss accounts for the last three years appear on the next page.

Note that Emerald Isle Knitters maintained a steady rate of production of 25,000 sweaters per year. However, sales varied from year to year. In Year 1, production and sales were equal. In Year 2, production exceeded sales due to the cancelled order. In Year 3, sales recovered and exceeded production. As a consequence, there was no change in stock during Year 1, stock increased during Year 2, and stock decreased during Year 3. The change in stock during the year is the key to understanding how absorption costing differs from variable costing. Note that when stock increased in Year 2, absorption costing profit exceeds variable costing profit. When stock decreased in Year 3, the opposite occurs – variable costing profit exceeds absorption costing profit. And when there is no change in stock as in Year 1, there is no difference in profit between the two methods. Why is this? The reasons are discussed below and are briefly summarized in Exhibit 6.4.

Relation between production and sales for the period	Effect on stocks	Relation between absorption and variable costing profit
Production = Sales	No change in stocks	Absorption costing profit = Variable costing profit
Production > Sales	Stocks increase	Absorption costing profit > Variable costing profit*
Production < Sales	Stocks decrease	Absorption costing profit < Variable costing profit†

*Profit is higher under absorption costing, since fixed manufacturing overhead cost is deferred in stock under absorption costing as stocks increase.

†Profit is lower under absorption costing, since fixed manufacturing overhead cost is released from stock under absorption costing as stocks decrease.

Exhibit 6.4 Comparative profit effects – absorption and variable costing

1 When production and sales are equal, as in Year 1 for Emerald Isle Knitters, profit will generally be the same regardless of whether absorption or variable costing is used. The reason is as follows: the *only* difference that can exist between absorption and variable costing profit is the amount of fixed manufacturing overhead recognized as expense on the profit and loss account. When everything that is produced in the year is sold, all of the fixed manufacturing overhead assigned to units of product under absorption costing become part of the year's cost of goods sold. Under variable costing, the total fixed manufacturing overhead flows directly to the profit and loss account as an expense. So under either method, when production equals sales (and hence there is no change in stock), all the fixed manufacturing overhead incurred during the year flows through to the profit and loss account as expense. And, therefore, the profit under the two methods is the same.

2 When production exceeds sales, the profit reported under absorption costing will generally be greater than the profit reported under variable costing (see Year 2 in Exhibit 6.3). This occurs because under absorption costing, part of the fixed manufacturing overhead costs of the current period is deferred in stock. In Year 2, for example, €30,000 of fixed manufacturing overhead costs (5,000 units × €6 per unit) has been applied to units in ending stock. These costs are excluded from cost of goods sold.

Under variable costing, however, *all* of the fixed manufacturing overhead costs of Year 2 have been charged immediately against income as a period cost. As a result, the profit for Year 2 under variable costing is €30,000 *lower* than it is under absorption costing. Exhibit 6.5 contains a reconciliation of the variable costing and absorption costing profit figures.

	Year 1	Year 2	Year 3
Variable costing profit	€60,000	€0	€120,000
Add fixed manufacturing overhead costs deferred in stock under absorption costing (5,000 units × €6 per unit)	0	30,000	0
Deduct fixed manufacturing overhead costs released from stock under absorption costing (5,000 units × €6 per unit)	0	0	(30,000)
Absorption costing profit	€60,000	€30,000	€90,000

Exhibit 6.5 Reconciliation of variable costing and absorption costing – profit data from Exhibit 6.3

3 When production is less than sales, the profit reported under the absorption costing approach will generally be less than the profit reported under the variable costing approach (see Year 3 in Exhibit 6.3). This happens because stock is drawn down and fixed manufacturing overhead costs that were previously deferred in stock under absorption costing are released and charged against profit (known as **fixed manufacturing overhead cost released from stock**). In Year 3, for example, the €30,000 in fixed manufacturing overhead costs deferred in stock under the absorption approach from Year 2 to Year 3 is released from stock because these units were sold. As a result, the cost of goods sold for Year 3 contains not only all of the fixed manufacturing overhead costs for Year 3 (since all that was produced in Year 3 was sold in Year 3) but €30,000 of fixed manufacturing overhead costs from Year 2 as well.

By contrast, under variable costing only the fixed manufacturing overhead costs of Year 3 have been charged against Year 3. The result is that profit under variable costing is €30,000 *higher* than it is under absorption costing. Exhibit 6.5 contains a reconciliation of the variable costing and absorption costing profit figures for Year 3.

4 Over an *extended* period of time, the profit figures reported under absorption costing and variable costing will tend to be the same. The reason is that over the long run sales cannot exceed production, nor can production much exceed sales. The shorter the time period, the more the profit figures will tend to differ.

Effect of changes in production on profit

4 LEARNING OBJECTIVE

In the Emerald Isle Knitters example in the preceding section, production was constant and sales fluctuated over the three-year period. Since sales fluctuated, the data Sean MacLafferty presented in Exhibit 6.3 allowed us to see the effect of changes in sales on profit under both variable and absorption costing.

To further investigate the differences between variable and absorption costing, Sean next put together the hypothetical example in Exhibit 6.6. In this hypothetical example, sales are constant and production fluctuates (the opposite of Exhibit 6.3). The purpose of Exhibit 6.6 is to illustrate for Mary O'Meara the effect of changes in *production* on profit under both variable and absorption costing.

Variable costing

Profit is *not* affected by changes in production under variable costing. Notice from Exhibit 6.6 that profit is the same for all three years under the variable costing approach, although production exceeds sales in one year and is less than sales in another year. In short, a change in production has no impact on profit when variable costing is in use.

EXHIBIT 6.6

Basic data

Selling price per unit sold		€25	
Variable manufacturing cost per unit produced		10	
Fixed manufacturing overhead costs per year		300,000	
Variable selling and administrative expenses per unit sold		1	
Fixed selling and administrative expenses per year		200,000	
	Year 1	**Year 2**	**Year 3**
Units in beginning stock	0	0	10,000
Units produced	40,000	50,000	30,000
Units sold	40,000	40,000	40,000
Units in ending stock	0	10,000	0
Unit product costs			
Under variable costing (variable manufacturing costs only	€10.00	€10.00	€10.00
Under absorption costing			
Variable manufacturing costs	€10.00	€10.00	€10.00
Fixed manufacturing overhead costs (€300,000 total spread over the number of units produced in each year)	7.50	6.00	10.00
Total absorption cost per unit	€17.50	€16.00	€20.00

	Year 1		Year 2		Year 3	
Absorption costing						
Sales (40,000 units)		€1,000,000		€1,000,000		€1,000,000
Less cost of goods sold:						
Beginning stock	€0		€0		€150,000	
Add cost of goods manufactured	700,000*		800,000*		600,000*	
Goods available for sale	700,000		800,000		760,000	
Less ending stock	0		160,000†		0	
Cost of goods sold		700,000		640,000		760,000
Gross margin		300,000		360,000		240,000
Less selling and administrative expenses (400 units × †1 plus †200,000)		240,000		240,000		240,000

*Cost of goods manufactured:

Year 1: 40,000 units × €17.50 = €700,000.

Year 2: 50,000 units × €16.00 = €800,000.

Year 3: 30,000 units × €20.00 = €600,000.

† Ending stock, Year 2: 10,000 units × €16 = €160,000.

Variable costing						
Sales (40,000 units)		€1,000,000		€1,000,000		€1,000,000
Less variable expenses:						
Variable cost of goods sold:						
Beginning stock	€0		€0		€100,000	
Add variable manufacturing costs at €10 per unit produced	400,000		500,000		300,000	
Goods available for sale	400,000		500,000		400,000	
Less ending stock	0		100,000*		0	
Variable cost of goods sold	400,000		400,000		400,000	
Variable selling and administrative expenses	40,000	440,000	40,000	440,000	40,000	440,000
Contribution margin		560,000		560,000		560,000
Less fixed expenses:						
Fixed manufacturing expenses	300,000		300,000		300,000	
Fixed selling and administrative expenses	200,000	500,000	200,000	500,000	200,000	500,000
Profit		€60,000		€60,000		€60,000

*Ending stock, Year 2: 10,000 units × €10 = €100,000.

Exhibit 6.6 Sensitivity of costing methods to changes in production – hypothetical data

Management accounting in action: the wrap-up

After checking all of his work, Sean took the exhibits he had prepared to Mary's office where the following conversation took place:

Sean: I have some calculations I would like to show you.

Mary: Will this take long? I only have a few minutes before I have to meet with the buyer from Neiman Marcus.

Sean: Well, we can at least get started. These exhibits should help explain why our profit didn't increase this year as much as you thought it should have.

Mary: This first exhibit [i.e., Exhibit 6.3] looks like it just summarizes our profit and loss accounts for the last three years.

Sean: Not exactly. There are actually two sets of profit and loss accounts on this exhibit. The absorption costing profit and loss accounts are the ones I originally prepared and we submitted to the bank. Below the absorption costing profit and loss accounts are another set of profit and loss accounts.

Mary: Those are the ones labelled variable costing.

Sean: That's right. You can see that the profits are the same for the two sets of profit and loss accounts in our first year of operations, but they differ for the other two years.

Mary: I'll say! The variable costing statements indicate that we just broke even in the second year instead of earning a €30,000 profit. And the increase in profit between the second and third years is €120,000 instead of just €60,000. I don't know how you come up with two different profit figures, but the variable costing profit seems to be much closer to the truth. The second year was almost a disaster. We barely sold enough sweaters to cover all of our fixed costs.

Sean: You and I both know that, but the accounting rules view the situation a little differently. If we produce more than we sell, the accounting rules require that we take some of the fixed cost and assign it to the units that end up in stock at year-end.

Mary: You mean that instead of appearing on the profit and loss account as an expense, some of the fixed costs wind up on the balance sheet as stock?

Sean: Precisely.

Mary: I thought accountants were conservative. Since when was it conservative to call an expense an asset?

Sean: We accountants have been debating whether fixed production costs are an asset or an expense for over 50 years.

Mary: It must have been a fascinating debate.

Sean: I have to admit that it ranks right up there with watching grass grow in terms of excitement level.

Mary: I don't know what the arguments are, but I can tell you for sure that we don't make any money by just producing sweaters. If I understand what you have shown me, I can increase my profit under absorption costing by simply making more sweaters – we don't have to sell them.

Sean: Correct.

Mary: So all I have to do to enjoy the lifestyle of the rich and famous is to hire every unemployed knitter in Ireland to make sweaters I can't sell.

Sean: We would have a major cash flow problem, but our profit would certainly go up.

Mary: Well, if the banks want us to use absorption costing so be it. I don't know why they would want us to report that way, but if that's what they want, that's what they'll get. Is there any reason why we can't use this variable costing method ourselves? The statements are easier to understand, and the profit figures make more sense to me. Can't we do both?

Sean: I don't see why not. Making the adjustment from one method to the other is very simple.

Mary: Good. Let's talk about this some more after I get back from the meeting with Neiman Marcus.

Absorption costing

Profit *is* affected by changes in production when absorption costing is in use, however. As shown in Exhibit 6.6, profit under the absorption approach goes up in Year 2, in response to the increase in production for that year, and then goes down in Year 3, in response to the drop in production for that year. Note particularly that profit goes up and down between these two years *even though the same number of units is sold in each year*. The reason for this effect can be traced to the shifting of fixed manufacturing overhead costs between periods under the absorption costing method as a result of changes in stock.

As shown in Exhibit 6.6, production exceeds sales in Year 2, resulting in an increase of 10,000 units in stock. Each unit produced during Year 2 has €6 in fixed manufacturing overhead costs attached to it (see the unit cost computations at the top of Exhibit 6.6). Therefore, €60,000 (10,000 units × €6) of the fixed manufacturing overhead costs of Year 2 are not charged against that year but rather are added to the stock account (along with the variable manufacturing costs). The profit of Year 2 rises sharply, because of the deferral of these costs in stock, even though the same number of units is sold in Year 2 as in the other years.

The reverse effect occurs in Year 3. Since sales exceed production in Year 3, that year is forced to cover all of its own fixed manufacturing overhead costs as well as the fixed manufacturing overhead costs carried forward in stock from Year 2. A substantial drop in profit during Year 3 results from the release of fixed manufacturing overhead costs from stock despite the fact that the same number of units is sold in that year as in the other years.

The variable costing and absorption costing profits are reconciled in Exhibit 6.7. This exhibit shows that the differences in profit can be traced to the effects of changes in stock on absorption costing profit. Under absorption costing, fixed manufacturing overhead costs are deferred in stock when stocks increase and are released from stock when stocks decrease.

	Year 1	Year 2	Year 3
Variable costing profit	€60,000	€60,000	€60,000
Add fixed manufacturing overhead costs deferred in stock under absorption costing (10,000 units × €6 per unit)	0	60,000	0
Deduct fixed manufacturing overhead costs released from stock under absorption costing (10,000 units × €6 per unit)	0	0	(60,000)
Absorption costing profit	€60,000	€120,000	€0

Exhibit 6.7 Reconciliation of variable costing and absorption costing – profit data from Exhibit 6.6

The impact on the manager

Like Mary O'Meara, opponents of absorption costing argue that shifting fixed manufacturing overhead cost between periods can be confusing and can lead to misinterpretations and even to faulty decisions. Look again at the data in Exhibit 6.6; a manager might wonder why profit went up substantially in Year 2 under absorption costing when sales remained the same as in the prior year. Was it a result of lower selling costs, more efficient operations, or was some other factor involved? The manager is unable to tell, looking simply at the absorption costing profit and loss account. Then in Year 3, profit drops sharply, even though again the same number of units is sold as in the other two years. Why would income rise in one year and then drop in the next? The figures seem erratic and contradictory and can lead to confusion and a loss of confidence in the integrity of the statement data.

By contrast, the variable costing profit and loss accounts in Exhibit 6.6 are clear and easy to understand. Sales remain constant over the three-year period covered in the exhibit, so both contribution margin and profit also remain constant. The statements are consistent with what the manager would expect to happen under the circumstances, so they tend to generate confidence rather than confusion. To avoid mistakes when absorption costing is used, readers of financial statements should be alert to changes in stock levels. Under absorption costing, if there is an increase in stock, fixed manufacturing overhead costs are deferred in stock and profit is elevated. If there is a decrease in stock, fixed manufacturing overhead costs are released from stock and profit is depressed. Thus, fluctuations in profit can be due to changes in stock rather than to changes in sales.

Focus on current practice

While managers can artificially increase profit under absorption costing by producing more than is really necessary and building up stock, a few unscrupulous managers have stepped over the line into the area of outright fraud. By claiming stock that do not exist, an unethical manager can produce instant profits and dress up the balance sheet. Since the value of ending stock is subtracted from the cost of goods available for sale in order to arrive at the cost of goods sold, phantom stock directly reduce cost of goods sold. Phantom stock also beef up the balance sheet by increasing assets.

Auditors attempt to uncover such fraud by physically verifying the existence of stock reported on the balance sheet. This is done by counting random samples of perhaps 5% to 10% of reported stock items. However, this audit approach is not always effective. For example, managers at failing Laribee Wire Manufacturing Co attempted to keep the company afloat by creating fictitious stocks. Investigations following the company's bankruptcy revealed that managers had fraudulently overstated income by claiming stocks of over 4 million pounds of copper rod that did not exist. Such stock fraud at Laribee turned a loss of $6.5 million into an operating profit of $5.5 million in one year alone.[1]

Choosing a costing method

In choosing between variable and absorption costing, several factors should be considered by the manager. These factors are discussed in this section.

Decision making

A basic problem with absorption costing is that fixed manufacturing overhead costs appear to be variable with respect to the number of units sold, but they are not. For example, in Exhibit 6.3, the absorption unit product cost is €13, but the variable portion of this cost is only €7. Since the product costs are stated in terms of a per unit figure, managers may mistakenly believe that if another unit is produced, it will cost the company €13.

The misperception that absorption unit product costs are variable can lead to many managerial problems, including inappropriate pricing decisions and decisions to drop products that are in fact profitable. These problems with absorption costing product costs will be discussed more fully in later chapters when we develop CVP and ABC in more detail.

External reporting

A company that attempts to use variable costing on its external financial reports runs the risk that its auditors may not accept the financial statements as conforming to internationally accepted accounting principles. Even if a company must use absorption costing for its external reports, a manager can, as Mary O'Meara suggests, use variable costing statements for internal reports. No particular accounting problems are created by using *both* costing methods – the variable costing method for internal reports and the absorption costing method for external reports. As we demonstrated earlier in Exhibits 6.5 and 6.7, the adjustment from variable costing profit to absorption costing profit is a simple one that can easily be made at year-end.

We must note, however, that using two sets of accounting data can create a problem for the top executives of publicly held corporations. The problem is that these executives are usually evaluated based on the external reports prepared for shareholders. It is difficult for managers to make decisions based on one set of accounting statements when they will be evaluated with a different set of accounting statements.

Advantages of variable costing and the contribution approach

As stated earlier, even if the absorption approach is used for external reporting purposes, variable costing, together with the contribution margin format profit and loss account, is an appealing alternative for internal reports. The advantages of variable costing can be summarized as follows:

1. The data that are required for CVP analysis (see Chapter 7) can be taken directly from a contribution margin format profit and loss account. These data are not available on a conventional profit and loss account based on absorption costing.
2. Under variable costing, the profit for a period is not affected by changes in stock. Other things remaining equal (i.e., selling prices, costs, sales mix, etc.), profits move in the same direction as sales when variable costing is in use.
3. Managers often assume that unit product costs are variable costs. This is a problem under absorption costing, since unit product costs are a combination of both fixed and variable costs. Under variable costing, unit product costs do not contain fixed costs.
4. The impact of fixed costs on profits is emphasized under the variable costing and contribution approach. The total amount of fixed costs appears explicitly on the profit and loss account. Under absorption costing, the fixed costs are mingled together with the variable costs and are buried in cost of goods sold and in ending stock.
5. Variable costing data make it easier to estimate the profitability of products, customers, and other segments of the business. With absorption costing, profitability is obscured by arbitrary allocations of fixed costs. These issues will be discussed in later chapters.
6. Variable costing ties in with cost control methods such as standard costs and flexible budgets, which will be covered in later chapters.
7. Variable costing profit is closer to net cash flow than absorption costing profit. This is particularly important for companies having cash flow problems.

With all of these advantages, one might wonder why absorption costing continues to be used almost exclusively for external reporting and why it is the predominant choice for internal reports as well. This is partly due to tradition, but absorption costing is also attractive to many accountants and managers because they believe it better matches costs with revenues. Advocates of absorption costing argue that all manufacturing costs must be assigned to products in order properly to match the costs of producing units of product with the revenues from the units when they are sold. The fixed costs of depreciation, taxes, insurance, supervisory salaries, and so on, are just as essential to manufacturing products as are the variable costs.

Advocates of variable costing argue that fixed manufacturing costs are not really the costs of any particular unit of product. These costs are incurred in order to have the capacity to make products during a particular period and will be incurred even if nothing is made during the period. Moreover, whether a unit is made or not, the fixed manufacturing costs will be exactly the same. Therefore, variable costing advocates argue that fixed manufacturing costs are not part of the costs of producing a particular unit of product and thus the matching principle dictates that fixed manufacturing costs should be charged to the current period.

At any rate, absorption costing is the generally accepted method for preparing mandatory external financial reports and income tax returns. Probably because of the cost and possible confusion of maintaining two separate costing systems – one for external reporting and one for internal reporting – most companies use absorption costing for both external and internal reports.

Impact of JIT methods

As discussed in this chapter, variable and absorption costing will produce different profit figures whenever the number of units produced is different from the number of units sold – in other words, whenever there is a change in the number of units in stock. We have also learned that the absorption costing profit figure can be erratic, sometimes moving in a direction that is opposite from the movement in sales.

When companies use just-in-time (JIT) methods, these problems are reduced. The erratic movement of profit under absorption costing and the difference in profit between absorption and variable costing occur because of changes in the number of units in stock. Under JIT, goods are produced to customers' orders and the goal is to eliminate finished goods stock entirely and reduce work in progress stock almost to nothing. If there is very little stock, then changes in stock will be very small and both variable and absorption costing will show basically the same profit figure. In that case, absorption costing profit will move in the same direction as movements in sales.

Of course, the cost of a unit of product will still be different between variable and absorption costing, as explained earlier in the chapter. But when JIT is used, the differences in profit will largely disappear.

Summary

- Variable and absorption costing are alternative methods of determining unit product costs. Under variable costing, only those production costs that vary with output are treated as product costs. This includes direct materials, variable overhead and, ordinarily, direct labour. Fixed manufacturing overhead is treated as a period cost and charged off against revenue as it is incurred, the same as selling and administrative expenses.
- By contrast, absorption costing treats fixed manufacturing overhead as a product cost, along with direct materials, direct labour and variable overhead. Since absorption costing treats fixed manufacturing overhead as a product cost, a portion of fixed manufacturing overhead is assigned to each unit as it is produced.
- If units of product are unsold at the end of a period, then the fixed manufacturing overhead cost attached to the units is carried with them into the stock account and deferred to the next period. When these units are later sold, the fixed manufacturing overhead cost attached to them is released from the stock account and charged against revenues as a part of cost of goods sold. Thus, under absorption costing, it is possible to defer a portion of the fixed manufacturing overhead cost of one period to the next period through the stock account.
- Unfortunately, this shifting of fixed manufacturing overhead cost between periods can cause profit to move in an erratic manner and can result in confusion and unwise decisions on the part of management. To guard against mistakes when they interpret profit and loss account data, managers should be alert to any changes that may have taken place in stock levels or in unit product costs during the period.
- Practically speaking, variable costing cannot be used externally for either financial reporting or tax purposes. However, it may be used internally for planning purposes. The variable costing approach dovetails well with CVP concepts that are often indispensable in profit planning and decision making.

Key terms for review

Direct costing (p. 200).

Fixed manufacturing overhead cost deferred in stock (p. 204).

Fixed manufacturing overhead cost released from stock (p. 209).

Marginal costing (p. 200).

Variable costing (p. 200).

Review problem: reporting effects of different costing methods

Dexter Company produces and sells a single product, a wooden hand loom for weaving small items such as scarves. Selected cost and operating data relating to the product for two years are given below:

Selling price per unit	£ 50
Manufacturing costs:	
Variable per unit produced:	
Direct materials	11
Direct labour	6
Variable overhead	3
Fixed per year	120,000
Selling and administrative costs:	
Variable per unit sold	5
Fixed per year	70,000

	Year 1	Year 2
Units in beginning stock	0	2,000
Units produced during the year	10,000	6,000
Units sold during the year	8,000	8,000
Units in ending stock	2,000	0

Required

1 Assume that the company uses absorption costing.

(a) Compute the unit product cost in each year.

(b) Prepare a profit and loss account for each year.

2 Assume that the company uses variable costing.

(a) Compute the unit product cost in each year.

(b) Prepare a profit and loss account for each year.

3 Reconcile the variable costing and absorption costing profit figures.

Solution to review problem: reporting effects of different costing methods

1 (a) Under absorption costing, all manufacturing costs, variable and fixed, are included in unit product costs:

	Year 1	Year 2
Direct materials	£11	£11
Direct labour	6	6
Variable manufacturing overhead	3	3
Fixed manufacturing overhead		
(£120,000/10,000 units)	12	
(£120,000/6,000 units)		20
Unit product cost	£32	£40

(b) The absorption costing profit and loss accounts follow:

	Year 1		Year 2	
Sales (8,000 units × £50)		£400,000		£400,000
Less cost of goods sold:				
Beginning stock	£0		£64,000	
Add cost of goods manufactured (10,000 units × £32)	320,000			
(6,000 units × £40)			240,000	
Goods available for sale	320,000		304,000	
Less ending stock (2,000 units × £32; 0 units)	64,000	256,000	0	304,000
Gross margin		144,000		96,000
Less selling and administrative expenses		110,000*		110,000*
Profit		£34,000		£(14,000)

*Selling and administrative expenses:

Variable (8,000 units × £5)	£40,000
Fixed per year	70,000
Total	£110,000

2 (a) Under variable costing, only the variable manufacturing costs are included in unit product costs:

	Year 1	Year 2
Direct materials	£11	£11
Direct labour	6	6
Variable manufacturing overhead	3	3
Unit product cost	£20	£20

(b) The variable costing profit and loss accounts follow. Notice that the variable cost of goods sold is computed in a simpler, more direct manner than in the examples provided earlier. On a variable costing profit and loss account, either approach to computing the cost of goods sold followed in this chapter is acceptable.

		Year 1		Year 2
Sales (8,000 units × £50)		£400,000		£400,000
Less variable expenses:				
Variable cost of goods sold (8,000 units × £20)	£160,000		£160,000	
Variable selling and administrative expenses (8,000 units × £5)	40,000		40,000	
Contribution margin		200,000		200,000
Less fixed expenses:				
Fixed manufacturing overhead	120,000		120,000	
Fixed selling and administrative expenses	70,000	190,000	70,000	190,000
Profit		£10,000		£10,000

3 The reconciliation of the variable and absorption costing profit figures follows:

	Year 1	Year 2
Variable costing profit	£10,000	£10,000
Add fixed manufacturing overhead costs deferred in stock under absorption costing (2,000 units × £12 per unit)	24,000	
Deduct fixed manufacturing overhead costs released from stock under absorption costing (2,000 units × £12 per unit)		24,000
Absorption costing profit	£34,000	£(14,000)

Questions

6–1 What is the basic difference between absorption costing and variable costing?

6–2 Are selling and administrative expenses treated as product costs or as period costs under variable costing?

6–3 Explain how fixed manufacturing overhead costs are shifted from one period to another under absorption costing.

6–4 What arguments can be advanced in favour of treating fixed manufacturing overhead costs as product costs?

6–5 What arguments can be advanced in favour of treating fixed manufacturing overhead costs as period costs?

6–6 If production and sales are equal, which method would you expect to show the higher profit, variable costing or absorption costing? Why?

6–7 If production exceeds sales, which method would you expect to show the higher profit, variable costing or absorption costing? Why?

6–8 If fixed manufacturing overhead costs are released from stock under absorption costing, what does this tell you about the level of production in relation to the level of sales?

6–9 Under absorption costing, how is it possible to increase profit without increasing sales?

6–10 How is the use of variable costing limited?

6–11 How does the use of JIT stock methods reduce or eliminate the difference in reported profit between absorption and variable costing?

Exercises

EXERCISES

E6–1 Time allowed: 10 minutes

Ida Sidha Karya Company is a family-owned company located in the village of Gianyar on the island of Bali in Indonesia. The company produces a handcrafted Balinese musical instrument called a gamelan that is similar to a xylophone. The sounding bars are cast from brass and hand-filed to attain just the right sound. The bars are then mounted on an intricately hand-carved wooden base. The gamelans are sold for 850 (thousand) rupiahs. (The currency in Indonesia is the rupiah, which is denoted by Rp.) Selected data for the company's operations last year follow (all currency values are in thousands of rupiahs):

Units in beginning stock	0
Units produced	250
Units sold	225
Units in ending stock	25
Variable costs per unit:	
Direct materials	Rp100
Direct labour	320
Variable manufacturing overhead	40
Variable selling and administrative	20
Fixed costs:	
Fixed manufacturing overhead	Rp60,000
Fixed selling and administrative	20,000

Required

1 Assume that the company uses absorption costing. Compute the unit product cost for one gamelan.

2 Assume that the company uses variable costing. Compute the unit product cost for one gamelan.

E6–2 Time allowed: 20 minutes

Refer to the data in E6–1 for Ida Sidha Karya Company. A profit and loss account prepared under the absorption costing method by the company's accountant appears below (all currency values are in thousands of rupiahs):

Sales (225 units × Rp850)		Rp191,250
Less cost of goods sold:		
Beginning stock	Rp0	
Add cost of goods manufactured (250 units × Rp ?)	175,000	
Goods available for sale	175,000	
Less ending stock (25 units × Rp ?)	17,500	157,500
Gross margin		33,750
Less selling and administrative expenses:		
Variable selling and administrative	4,500	
Fixed selling and administrative	20,000	24,500
Profit		Rp9,250

Required

1 Determine how much of the ending stock of Rp17,500 above consists of fixed manufacturing overhead cost deferred in stock to the next period.

2 Prepare a profit and loss account for the year using the variable costing method.

Explain the difference in profit between the two costing methods.

Problems

P6–3 Straightforward variable costing statements Time allowed: 25 minutes

During Heaton Company's first two years of operations, the company reported profit as follows (absorption costing basis):

	Year 1	Year 2
Sales (@ £25)	£1,000,000	£1,250,000
Less cost of goods sold:		
Beginning stock	0	90,000
Add cost of goods manufactured (@ £18)	810,000	810,000
Goods available for sale	810,000	900,000
Less ending stock (@ £18)	90,000	0
Cost of goods sold	720,000	900,000
Gross margin	280,000	350,000
Less selling and administrative expenses*	210,000	230,000
Profit	£70,000	£120,000

*£2 per unit variable; £130,000 fixed each year.

The company's £18 unit product cost is computed as follows:

Direct materials	£4
Direct labour	7
Variable manufacturing overhead	1
Fixed manufacturing overhead (£270,000/45,000 units)	6
Unit product cost	£18

Production and cost data for the two years are:

	Year 1	Year 2
Units produced	45,000	45,000
Units sold	40,000	50,000

Required

1 Prepare a profit and loss account for each year in the contribution format using variable costing.

2 Reconcile the absorption costing and the variable costing profit figures for each year.

P6–4 Prepare and reconcile variable costing statements Time allowed: 40 minutes
Denton Company manufactures and sells a single product. Cost data for the product are given below:

Variable costs per unit:	
Direct materials	£7
Direct labour	10
Variable manufacturing overhead	5
Variable selling and administrative	3
Total variable cost per unit	£25
Fixed costs per month:	
Fixed manufacturing overhead	£315,000
Fixed selling and administrative	245,000
Total fixed cost per month	£560,000

The product sells for £60 per unit. Production and sales data for July and August, the first two months of operations, follow:

	Units produced	Units sold
July	17,500	15,000
August	17,500	20,000

The company's Accounting Department has prepared profit and loss accounts for both July and August. These statements, which have been prepared using absorption costing, are presented below:

	July	August
Sales	£900,000	£1,200,000
Less cost of goods sold:		
Beginning stock	0	100,000
Add cost of goods manufactured	700,000	700,000
Goods available for sale	700,000	800,000
Less ending stock	100,000	0
Cost of goods sold	600,000	800,000
Gross margin	300,000	400,000
Less selling and administrative expences	290,000	305,000
Profit	£10,000	£95,000

Required

1 Determine the unit product cost under:

(a) Absorption costing;

(b) Variable costing.

2 Prepare profit and loss accounts for July and August using the contribution approach, with variable costing.

3 Reconcile the variable costing and absorption costing profit figures. The company's Accounting Department has determined the company's break-even point to be 16,000 units per month, computed as follows:

$$\frac{\text{Fixed cost per month, £560,000}}{\text{Unit contribution margin, £35}} = \text{16,000 units}$$

'I'm confused,' said the managing director. 'The accounting people say that our break-even point is 16,000 units per month, but we sold only 15,000 units in July, and the profit and loss account they prepared shows a £10,000 profit for that month. Either the profit and loss account is wrong or the break-even point is wrong.' Prepare a brief memo for the managing director, explaining what happened on the July profit and loss account.

P6–5 Variable and absorption costing Time allowed: 30 minutes
Chew Ltd manufactures and sells a single product. The summarized data below relate to its first two years of operation.

Required

1 Briefly explain what is meant by:

(a) Marginal (variable) costing; and

(b) Full (absorption) costing. *(2 marks)*

2 Briefly explain why the operating profits resulting from the use of the two costing methods will usually differ. Under what circumstances will the operating profit under marginal (variable) costing be identical to that under full (absorption) costing. *(3 marks)*

	Year ended 30 June 2000	**Year ended 30 June 2001**
Sales (units)	7,500	7,400
Production (units)	9,200	6,000
Selling price (per unit)	£35.00	£37.50
Costs:		
Variable manufacturing	£92,000	£63,000
Fixed manufacturing	£33,488	£23,220
Variable marketing and administration	£16,200	£17,950
Fixed marketing and administration	£19,076	£21,772

Chew Ltd values closing stock on a first-in, first-out basis.

3 Calculate, for each of the two years, the operating profit and the closing stock value using:

(a) Marginal (variable) costing; and

(b) Full (absorption) costing. *(7 marks)*

4 Prepare, for each of the two years, a reconciliation which explains the difference in the operating profits resulting from the use of the two costing methods. *(3 marks)*

(Total = 15 marks)

ICAEW Accounting, September 2001

P6–6 Variable versus absorption costing Time allowed: 30 minutes

Jaime plc manufactures and sells a single product. You are given the following information concerning its operations for the year ended 30 November 2000:

	Units	£
Sales	30,000	
Opening stock	1,200	
Closing stock	6,000	
Selling price per unit		
		37.00
Fixed costs:		
Manufacturing overhead		139,200
Marketing and administrative overhead		170,000
Variable costs per unit:		
Direct materials		7.00
Direct manufacturing labour		7.50
Manufacturing overhead		3.00
Marketing and administrative overhead		1.35

In the year ended 30 November 1999, the company produced 22,000 units. Variable costs per unit were as shown above while fixed manufacturing overheads totalled £110,000.

Required

1 State what is meant by each of the following terms:

(a) Direct costs
(b) Indirect costs
(c) Fixed costs
(d) Variable costs
(e) Marginal (variable) costing
(f) Full (absorption) costing
(g) Activity based costing
(h) Standard cost. *(8 marks)*

2 Calculate the profit for the year ended 30 November 2000 and the stock value at that date using (a) marginal (variable) costing and (b) full (absorption) costing. *(7 marks)*

(Total = 15 marks)

ICAEW Accounting, December 2000

P6–7 Prepare and interpret statements; changes in both sales and production; automation; JIT Time allowed: 60 minutes

Starfax manufactures a small part that is widely used in various electronic products such as home computers. Operating results for the first three years of activity were as follows (absorption costing basis):

	Year 1	Year 2	Year 3
Sales	£800,000	£640,000	£800,000
Cost of goods sold:			
Beginning stock	0	0	200,000
Add cost of goods manufactured	580,000	600,000	560,000
Goods available for sale	580,000	600,000	760,000
Less ending stock	0	200,000	140,000
Cost of goods sold	580,000	400,000	620,000
Gross margin	220,000	240,000	180,000
Selling and administrative expenses	190,000	180,000	190,000
Profit (loss)	£30,000	£60,000	£(10,000)

In the latter part of Year 2, a competitor went out of business and in the process dumped a large number of units on the market. As a result, Starfax's sales dropped by 20% during Year 2 even though production increased during that year. Management had expected sales to remain constant at 50,000 units; the increased production was designed to provide the company with a buffer of protection against unexpected spurts in demand. By the start of Year 3, management could see that stock was excessive and that spurts in demand were unlikely. To work off the excessive stock, Starfax cut back production during Year 3, as shown below:

	Year 1	Year 2	Year 3
Production in units	50,000	60,000	40,000
Sales in units	50,000	40,000	50,000

Additional information about the company follows:

(a) The company's plant is highly automated. Variable manufacturing costs (direct materials, direct labour and variable manufacturing overhead) total only £2 per unit, and fixed manufacturing costs total £480,000 per year.

(b) Fixed manufacturing costs are applied to units of product on the basis of each year's production. (That is, a new fixed manufacturing overhead rate is computed each year, as in Exhibit 6.6.)

(c) Variable selling and administrative expenses were £1 per unit sold in each year. Fixed selling and administrative expenses totalled £140,000 each year.

(d) The company uses a FIFO stock flow assumption. Starfax's management cannot understand why profits doubled during Year 2 when sales dropped by 20% and why a loss was incurred during Year 3 when sales recovered to previous levels.

Required

1 Prepare a new profit and loss account for each year using the contribution approach, with variable costing.

2 Refer to the absorption costing profit and loss accounts above.

(a) Compute the unit product cost in each year under absorption costing. (Show how much of this cost is variable and how much is fixed.)

(b) Reconcile the variable costing and absorption costing profit figures for each year.

3 Refer again to the absorption costing profit and loss accounts. Explain why profit was higher in Year 2 than it was in Year 1 under the absorption approach, in light of the fact that fewer units were sold in Year 2 than in Year 1.

4 Refer again to the absorption costing profit and loss accounts. Explain why the company suffered a loss in Year 3 but reported a profit in Year 1 although the same number of units was sold in each year.

(a) Explain how operations would have differed in Year 2 and Year 3 if the company had been using JIT stock methods.

(b) If JIT had been in use during Year 2 and Year 3, what would the company's profit (or loss) have been in each year under absorption costing? Explain the reason for any differences between these income figures and the figures reported by the company in the statements above.

P6–8 Prepare variable costing statements; sales constant, production varies; JIT impact Time allowed: 40 minutes

'This makes no sense at all,' said Bill Sharp, managing director of Essex Company. 'We sold the same number of units this year as we did last year, yet our profits have more than doubled. Who made the goof – the computer or the people who operate it?' The statements to which Mr Sharp was referring are shown below (absorption costing basis):

	Year 1	Year 2
Sales (20,000 units each year)	£700,000	£700,000
Less cost of goods sold	460,000	400,000
Gross margin	240,000	300,000
Less selling and administrative expenses	200,000	200,000
Profit	£40,000	£100,000

The statements above show the results of the first two years of operation. In the first year, the company produced and sold 20,000 units; in the second year, the company again sold 20,000 units, but it increased production in order to have a stock of units on hand, as shown below:

	Year 1	Year 2
Production in units	20,000	25,000
Sales in units	20,000	20,000
Variable production cost per unit	£8	£8
Fixed manufacturing overhead costs (total)	£300,000	£300,000

Essex Company produces a single product; fixed manufacturing overhead costs are applied to the product on the basis of each year's production. (Thus, a new fixed manufacturing overhead rate is computed each year, as in Exhibit 6.6.) Variable selling and administrative expenses are £1 per unit sold.

Required

1 Compute the unit product cost for each year under:

(a) Absorption costing.

(b) Variable costing.

2 Prepare a profit and loss account for each year, using the contribution approach with variable costing.

3 Reconcile the variable costing and absorption costing profit figures for each year.

4 Explain to the managing director why, under absorption costing, the profit for Year 2 was higher than the profit for Year 1, although the same number of units was sold in each year.

5 (a) Explain how operations would have differed in Year 2 if the company had been using JIT stock methods.

(b) If JIT has been in use during Year 2, what would the company's profit have been under absorption costing? Explain the reason for any difference between this income figure and the figure reported by the company in the statements above.

CASE

Cases

C6–9 The case of the plummeting profits; just-in-time (JIT) impact Time allowed: 90 minutes

'These statements can't be right,' said Ben Yoder, managing director of Rayco Ltd. 'Our sales in the second quarter were up by 25 per cent over the first quarter, yet these profit and loss accounts show a precipitous drop in profit for the second quarter. Those accounting people have fouled something up.' Mr Yoder was referring to the following statements:

Rayco Ltd
Profit and loss accounts
For the first two quarters

	First quarter		Second quarter	
Sales		£480,000		£600,000
Less cost of goods sold:				
Beginning stock	£80,000		£140,000	
Add cost of goods manufactured	300,000		180,000	
Goods available for sale	380,000		320,000	
Less ending stock	140,000		20,000	
Cost of goods sold	240,000		300,000	
Add underapplied overhead	–	240,000	72,000	372,000
Gross margin		240,000		228,000
Less selling and administrative expenses		200,000		215,000
Profit		£40,000		£13,000

After studying the statements briefly, Mr Yoder called in the accountant to see if the mistake in the second quarter could be located before the figures were released to the press. The accountant stated, 'I'm sorry to say that those figures are correct, Ben. I agree that sales went up during the second quarter, but the problem is in production. You see, we budgeted to produce 15,000 units each quarter, but a strike on the west coast among some of our suppliers forced us to cut production in the second quarter back to only 9,000 units. That's what caused the drop in profit.'

Mr Yoder was confused by the accountant's explanation. He replied, 'This doesn't make sense. I ask you to explain why profit dropped when sales went up and you talk about production! So what if we had to cut back production? We still were able to increase sales by 25%. If sales go up, then profit should go up. If your statements can't show a simple thing like that, then it's time for some changes in your area!'

Budgeted production and sales for the year, along with actual production and sales for the first two quarters, are given in the following table:

	Quarter First	Second	Third	Fourth
Budgeted sales (units)	12,000	15,000	15,000	18,000
Actual sales (units)	12,000	15,000	–	–
Budgeted production (units)	15,000	15,000	15,000	15,000
Actual production (units)	15,000	9,000	–	–

The company's plant is heavily automated, and fixed manufacturing overhead amounts to £180,000 each quarter. Variable manufacturing costs are £8 per unit. The fixed manufacturing overhead is applied to units of product at a rate of £12 per unit (based on the budgeted production shown above). Any under- or overapplied overhead is taken directly to cost of goods sold for the quarter. The company had 4,000 units in stock to start the first quarter and uses the FIFO stock flow assumption. Variable selling and administrative expenses are £5 per unit.

Required

1 What characteristic of absorption costing caused the drop in profit for the second quarter and what could the accountant have said to explain the problem more fully?

2 Prepare profit and loss accounts for each quarter using the contribution approach, with variable costing.

3 Reconcile the absorption costing and the variable costing profit figures for each quarter.

4 Identify and discuss the advantages and disadvantages of using the variable costing method for internal reporting purposes.

5 Assume that the company had introduced JIT stock methods at the beginning of the second quarter. (Sales and production during the first quarter remain the same.)

   (a) How many units would have been produced during the second quarter under JIT?

   (b) Starting with the third quarter, would you expect any difference between the profit reported under absorption costing and under variable costing? Explain why there would or would not be any difference.

Endnotes

1 Burton (1992).

Chapter 7
Cost–volume–profit relationships

Learning objectives

After studying Chapter 7, you should be able to:

1 Explain how changes in activity affect contribution margin and profit

2 Compute the contribution margin ratio (CM ratio) and use it to compute changes in contribution margin and profit

3 Show the effects on contribution margin of changes in variable costs, fixed costs, selling price, and volume

4 Compute the break-even point by both the equation method and the contribution margin method

5 Prepare a cost–volume–profit (CVP) graph and explain the significance of each of its components

6 Use the CVP formulas to determine the activity level needed to achieve a desired target profit

7 Compute the margin of safety and explain its significance

8 Compute the degree of operating leverage at a particular level of sales and explain how the degree of operating leverage can be used to predict changes in profit

9 Compute the break-even point for a multiple product company and explain the effects of shifts in the sales mix on contribution margin and the break-even point

Concepts in Context

Since CVP analysis shows that levels of activity can have a big effect on profits, choices on the best way of compensating salespersons must be chosen with a great deal of care.

Digital Equipment Corporation's founder believed that salespersons should never sell customers something they do not need and, accordingly, Digital paid them salaries rather than sales commissions. This approach worked fine for many years because 'Digital's products were the hottest alternative to expensive mainframe computers, and because they were cheaper, they almost sold themselves. But when competition arrived, the Digital sales staff was hopelessly outclassed.' When commissions were introduced in an attempt to stem the tide, the new system backfired. 'Some salesmen sold product at little or no profit to pump up volume – and their commission.'[1]

CVP analysis is one of the most powerful tools that managers have at their command. It helps them understand the interrelationship between cost, volume and profit in an organization by focusing on interactions between the following five elements:

1. Prices of products
2. Volume or level of activity
3. Per unit variable costs
4. Total fixed costs
5. Mix of products sold.

Because CVP analysis helps managers understand the interrelationship between cost, volume and profit, it is a vital tool in many business decisions. These decisions include, for example, what products to manufacture or sell, what pricing policy to follow, what marketing strategy to employ, and what type of productive facilities to acquire.

Management accounting in action: the issue

Acoustic Concepts Ltd was founded by Prem Narayan, a graduate student in engineering, to market a radical new speaker he had designed for car sound systems. The speaker, called the Sonic Blaster, uses an advanced microprocessor chip to boost amplification to high levels. Prem contracted with a Taiwanese electronics manufacturer to produce the speaker. With seed money provided by his family, Prem placed an order with the manufacturer for completed units and ran advertisements in car magazines.

The Sonic Blaster was an almost immediate success, and sales grew to the point that Prem moved the company's headquarters out of his apartment and into rented quarters in a neighbouring industrial park. He also hired a receptionist, an accountant, a sales manager, and a small sales staff to sell the speakers to retail stores. The accountant, Bob White, had worked for several small companies where he had acted as a business adviser as well as accountant and bookkeeper. The following discussion occurred soon after Bob was hired:

Prem: Bob, I've got a lot of questions about the company's finances that I hope you can help answer.

Bob: We're in great shape. The loan from your family will be paid off within a few months.

Prem: I know, but I am worried about the risks I've taken on by expanding operations.

What would happen if a competitor entered the market and our sales slipped? How far could sales drop without putting us into the red? Another question I've been trying to resolve is how much our sales would have to increase in order to justify the big marketing campaign the sales staff is pushing for.

Bob: Marketing always wants more money for advertising.

Prem: And they are always pushing me to drop the selling price on the speaker. I agree with them that a lower price will boost our volume, but I'm not sure the increased volume will offset the loss in revenue from the lower price.

Bob: **It sounds like these questions all are related in some way to the relationships between our selling prices, our costs and our volume. We shouldn't have a problem coming up with some answers. I'll need a day or two, though, to gather some data.**

Prem: **Why don't we set up a meeting for three days from now? That would be Thursday.**

Bob: **That'll be fine. I'll have some preliminary answers for you as well as a model you can use for answering similar questions in the future.**

Prem: **Good. I'll be looking forward to seeing what you come up with.**

The basics of cost–volume–profit (CVP) analysis

Bob White's preparation for the Thursday meeting begins where our study of cost behaviour in Chapter 5 left off – with the contribution profit and loss account. The contribution profit and loss account emphasizes the behaviour of costs and therefore is extremely helpful to a manager in judging the impact on profits of changes in selling price, cost or volume. Bob will base his analysis on the following contribution profit and loss account he prepared last month:

Acoustic Concepts Ltd
Contribution profit and loss account
For the month of June

	Total	**Per unit**
Sales (400 speakers)	£100,000	£250
Less variable expenses	60,000	150
Contribution margin	40,000	£100
Less fixed expenses	35,000	
Profit	£5,000	

Notice that sales, variable expenses and contribution margin are expressed on a per unit basis as well as in total. This is commonly done on profit and loss accounts prepared for management's own use, since, as we shall see, it facilitates profitability analysis.

Contribution margin

Contribution margin is the amount remaining from sales revenue after variable expenses have been deducted. Thus, it is the amount available to cover fixed expenses and then to provide profits for the period. Notice the sequence here – contribution margin is used *first* to cover the fixed expenses, and then whatever remains goes toward profits. If the contribution margin is not sufficient to cover the fixed expenses, then a loss occurs for the period. To illustrate with an extreme example, assume that by the middle of a particular month Acoustic Concepts has been able to sell only one speaker. At that point, the company's profit and loss account will appear as follows:

	Total	**Per unit**
Sales (1 speakers)	£250	£250
Less variable expenses	150	150
Contribution margin	100	£100
Less fixed expenses	35,000	
Net loss	£(34,900)	

For each additional speaker that the company is able to sell during the month, £100 more in contribution margin will become available to help cover the fixed expenses. If a second speaker is sold, for example, then the total contribution margin will increase by £100 (to a total of £200) and the company's loss will decrease by £100, to £34,800:

	Total	Per unit
Sales (2 speakers)	£500	£250
Less variable expenses	300	150
Contribution margin	200	£100
Less fixed expenses	35,000	
Net loss	£(34,800)	

If enough speakers can be sold to generate £35,000 in contribution margin, then all of the fixed costs will be covered and the company will have managed to at least *break even* for the month – that is, to show neither profit nor loss but just cover all of its costs. To reach the break-even point, the company will have to sell 350 speakers in a month, since each speaker sold yields £100 in contribution margin:

	Total	Per unit
Sales (350 speakers)	£87,500	£250
Less variable expenses	52,500	150
Contribution margin	35,000	£100
Less fixed expenses	35,000	
Profit	£0	

Computation of the **break-even point** is discussed in detail later in the chapter; for the moment, note that the break-even point can be defined as the level of sales at which profit is zero.

Once the break-even point has been reached, profit will increase by the unit contribution margin for each additional unit sold. If 351 speakers are sold in a month, for example, then we can expect that the profit for the month will be £100, since the company will have sold one speaker more than the number needed to break even:

	Total	Per unit
Sales (351 speakers)	£87,750	£250
Less variable expenses	52,650	150
Contribution margin	35,100	£100
Less fixed expenses	35,000	
Profit	£100	

If 352 speakers are sold (2 speakers above the break-even point), then we can expect that the profit for the month will be £200, and so forth. To know what the profits will be at various levels of activity, therefore, it is not necessary for a manager to prepare a whole series of profit and loss accounts. The manager can simply take the number of units to be sold over the break-even point and multiply that number by the unit contribution margin. The result represents the anticipated profits for the period. Or, to estimate the effect of a planned increase in sales on profits, the manager can simply multiply the increase in units sold by the unit contribution margin. The result will be the expected increase in profits. To illustrate, if

Acoustic Concepts is currently selling 400 speakers per month and plans to increase sales to 425 speakers per month, the anticipated impact on profits can be computed as follows:

Increased number of speakers to be sold	25
Contribution margin per speaker	× £100
increase in profit	£2,500

These calculations can be verified as follows:

	Sales volume			
	400 speakers	425 speakers	Difference 25 speakers	Per unit
Sales	£100,000	£106,250	£6,250	£250
Less variable expenses	60,000	63,750	3,750	150
Contribution margin	40,000	42,500	2,500	£100
Less fixed expenses	35,000	35,000	0	
Profit	£5,000	£7,500	£2,500	

To summarize the series of examples given above, if there were no sales, the company's loss would equal its fixed expenses. Each unit that is sold reduces the loss by the amount of the unit contribution margin. Once the break-even point has been reached, each additional unit sold increases the company's profit by the amount of the unit contribution margin.

Contribution margin ratio (CM ratio)

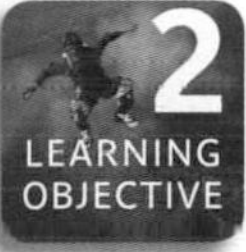

In addition to being expressed on a per unit basis, sales revenues, variable expenses, and contribution margin for Acoustic Concepts can also be expressed as a percentage of sales:

	Total	Per unit	Percentage of sales
Sales (400 speakers)	£100,000	£250	100
Less variable expenses	60,000	150	60
Contribution margin	40,000	£100	40
Less fixed expenses	35,000		
Profit	£5,000		

The contribution margin as a percentage of total sales is referred to as the **contribution margin ratio (CM ratio)**. This ratio is computed as follows:

$$\text{CM ratio} = \frac{\text{Contribution margin}}{\text{Sales}}$$

For Acoustic Concepts, the computations are as follows:

$$\frac{\text{Total contribution margin, £40,000}}{\text{total sales, £100,000}} = 40\%$$

or

$$\frac{\text{Per unit contribution margin, £100}}{\text{Per unit sales, £250}} = 40\%$$

The CM ratio is extremely useful since it shows how the contribution margin will be affected by a change in total sales. To illustrate, notice that Acoustic Concepts has a CM ratio of 40%. This means that for each pound increase in sales, total contribution margin will increase by 40 pence (£1 sales × CM ratio of 40%). Profit will also increase by 40 pence, assuming that there are no changes in fixed costs.

As this illustration suggests, the impact on profit of any given pound change in total sales can be computed in seconds by simply applying the CM ratio to the pound change. If Acoustic Concepts plans a £30,000 increase in sales during the coming month, for example, management can expect contribution margin to increase by £12,000 (£30,000 increased sales × CM ratio of 40%). As we noted above, profit will also increase by £12,000 if fixed costs do not change.

This is verified by the following table:

	Sales volume			
	Present	**Expected**	**Increase**	**Percentage of sales**
Sales	£100,000	£130,000	£30,000	100%
Less variable expenses	60,000	78,000*	18,000	60%
Contribution margin	40,000	52,000	12,000	40%
Less fixed expenses	35,000	35,000	0	
Profit	£5,000	£17,000	£12,000	

*£130,000 expected sales/£250 per unit = 520 units. 520 units × £150 per unit = £78,000.

Some managers prefer to work with the CM ratio rather than the unit contribution margin figure. The CM ratio is particularly valuable in those situations where the manager must make trade-offs between more pound sales of one product versus more pound sales of another. Generally speaking, when trying to increase sales, products that yield the greatest amount of contribution margin per pound of sales should be emphasized.

Some applications of CVP concepts

Bob White, the accountant at Acoustic Concepts, wanted to demonstrate to the company's president, Prem Narayan, how the concepts developed on the preceding pages of this text can be used in planning and decision making. Bob gathered the following basic data:

	Per unit	**Percentage of sales**
Sales price	£250	100%
Less variable expenses	150	60%
Contribution margin	£100	40%

Recall that fixed expenses are £35,000 per month. Bob White will use these data to show the effects of changes in variable costs, fixed costs, sales price and sales volume on the company's profitability.

Change in fixed cost and sales volume

Acoustic Concepts is currently selling 400 speakers per month (monthly sales of £100,000). The sales manager feels that a £10,000 increase in the monthly advertising budget would increase monthly sales by £30,000. Should the advertising budget be increased?

The following table shows the effect of the proposed change in monthly advertising budget:

	Current sales	Advertising budget	Sales with additional difference	Percentage of sales
Sales	£100,000	£130,000	£30,000	100%
Less variable expenses	60,000	78,000	18,000	60%
Contribution margin	40,000	52,000	12,000	40%
Less fixed expenses	35,000	45,000*	10,000	
Profit	£5,000	£7,000	£2,000	

*£35,000 plus additional £10,000 monthly advertising budget = £45,000.

Assuming there are no other factors to be considered, the increase in the advertising budget should be approved since it would lead to an increase in profit of £2,000. There are two shorter ways to present this solution. The first alternative solution follows:

Expected total contribution margin:	
£130,000 × 40% CM ratio	£52,000
Present total contribution margin:	
£100,000 × 40% CM ratio	40,000
Incremental contribution margin	12,000
Change in fixed costs:	
Less incremental advertising expense	10,000
Increased profit	£2,000

Since, in this case, only the fixed costs and the sales volume change, the solution can be presented in an even shorter format, as follows:

Incremental contribution margin:	
£30,000 × 40% CM ratio	£12,000
Less incremental advertising expense	10,000
Increased profit	£2,000

Notice that this approach does not depend on a knowledge of previous sales. Also notice that it is unnecessary under either shorter approach to prepare a profit and loss account. Both of the solutions above involve an **incremental analysis** in that they consider only those items of revenue, cost and volume that will change if the new programme is implemented. Although in each case a new profit and loss account could have been prepared, most managers would prefer the incremental approach. The reason is that it is simpler and more direct, and it permits the decision maker to focus attention on the specific items involved in the decision.

Change in variable costs and sales volume

Refer to the original data. Recall that Acoustic Concepts is currently selling 400 speakers per month. Management is contemplating the use of higher-quality components, which would increase variable costs (and thereby reduce the contribution margin) by £10 per speaker. However, the sales manager predicts that the higher overall quality would increase sales to 480 speakers per month. Should the higher-quality components be used?

The £10 increase in variable costs will cause the unit contribution margin to decrease from £100 to £90. So the solution is:

Expected total contribution margin with higher-quality components:	
480 speakers × £90	£43,200
Present total contribution margin:	
400 speakers × £100	40,000
Increase in total contribution margin	£3,200

Yes, based on the information above, the higher-quality components should be used. Since fixed costs will not change, profit should increase by the £3,200 increase in contribution margin shown above.

Change in fixed cost, sales price and sales volume

Refer to the original data and recall again that the company is currently selling 400 speakers per month. To increase sales, the sales manager would like to cut the selling price by £20 per speaker and increase the advertising budget by £15,000 per month.

The sales manager argues that if these two steps are taken, unit sales will increase by 50% to 600 speakers per month. Should the changes be made?

A decrease of £20 per speaker in the selling price will cause the unit contribution margin to decrease from £100 to £80. The solution is:

Expected total contribution margin with lower selling price:	
600 speakers × £80	£48,000
Present total contribution margin:	
400 speakers × £100	40,000
Incremental contribution margin	8,000
Change in fixed costs:	
Less incremental advertising expense	15,000
Reduction in profit	£(7,000)

No, based on the information above, the changes should not be made. The same solution can be obtained by preparing comparative profit and loss accounts:

	Present 400 speakers per month		Expected 600 speakers per month		
	Total	**Per unit**	**Total**	**Per unit**	**Difference**
Sales	£100,000	£250	£138,000	£230	£38,000
Less variable expenses	60,000	150	90,000	£150	30,000
Contribution margin	40,000	£100	48,000	£80	8,000
Less fixed expenses	35,000		50,000*		15,000
Profit (loss)	£5,000		£(2,000)		£(7,000)

*£35,000 + Additional monthly advertising budget of £15,000 = £50,000.

Notice that the effect on profit is the same as that obtained by the incremental analysis above.

Change in variable cost, fixed cost and sales volume

Refer to the original data. As before, the company is currently selling 400 speakers per month. The sales manager would like to place the sales staff on a commission basis of £15 per speaker sold, rather than on flat salaries that now total £6,000 per month. The sales manager is confident that the change will increase monthly sales by 15% to 460 speakers per month. Should the change be made?

Changing the sales staff from a salaried basis to a commission basis will affect both fixed and variable costs. Fixed costs will decrease by £6,000, from £35,000 to £29,000. Variable costs will increase by £15, from £150 to £165, and the unit contribution margin will decrease from £100 to £85.

Expected total contribution margin with sales staff on commissions:	
460 speakers × £85	£39,100
Present total contribution margin:	
400 speakers × £100	40,000
Decrease in total contribution margin	(900)
Change in fixed costs:	
Add salaries avoided if a commission is paid	6,000
Increase in profit	£5,100

Yes, based on the information above, the changes should be made. Again, the same answer can be obtained by preparing comparative profit and loss accounts:

	Present 400 speakers per month		Expected 600 speakers per month		
	Total	Per unit	Total	Per unit	Difference: increase or (decrease) in profit
Sales	£100,000	£250	£115,000	£250	£15,000
Less variable expenses	60,000	150	75,900	165	(15,900)
Contribution margin	40,000	£100	39,100	£85	(900)
Less fixed expenses	35,000		29,000		6,000
Profit	£5,000		£10,100		£5,100

Change in regular sales price

Refer to the original data where Acoustic Concepts is currently selling 400 speakers per month. The company has an opportunity to make a bulk sale of 150 speakers to a wholesaler if an acceptable price can be worked out. This sale would not disturb the company's regular sales. What price per speaker should be quoted to the wholesaler if Acoustic Concepts wants to increase its monthly profits by £3,000? The solution is:

Variable cost per speaker	£150
Desired profit per speaker:	
£3,000/150 speakers	20
Quoted price per speaker	£170

Notice that no element of fixed cost is included in the computation. This is because fixed costs are not affected by the bulk sale, so all additional revenue in excess of variable costs goes to increasing the profits of the company.

Importance of the contribution margin

As stated in the introduction to the chapter, CVP analysis seeks the most profitable combination of variable costs, fixed costs, selling price and sales volume. The above examples show that the effect on the contribution margin is a major consideration in deciding on the most profitable combination of these factors. We have seen that profits can sometimes be improved by reducing the contribution margin if fixed costs can be reduced by a greater amount. More commonly, however, we have seen that the way to improve profits is to increase the total contribution margin figure. Sometimes this can be done by reducing the selling price and thereby increasing volume; sometimes it can be done by increasing the fixed costs (such as advertising) and thereby increasing volume; and sometimes it can be done by trading off variable and fixed costs with appropriate changes in volume. Many other combinations of factors are possible.

The size of the unit contribution margin figure (and the size of the CM ratio) will have a heavy influence on what steps a company is willing to take to improve profits. For example, the greater the unit contribution margin for a product, the greater is the amount that a company will be willing to spend in order to increase unit sales of the product by a given percentage. This explains in part why companies with high unit contribution margins (such as car manufacturers) advertise so heavily, while companies with low unit contribution margins (such as dishware manufacturers) tend to spend much less for advertising.

In short, the effect on the contribution margin holds the key to many decisions.

Break-even analysis

CVP analysis is sometimes referred to simply as break-even analysis. This is unfortunate because break-even analysis is only one element of CVP analysis – although an important element. Break-even analysis is designed to answer questions such as those asked by Prem Narayan, the president of Acoustic Concepts, concerning how far sales could drop before the company begins to lose money.

Break-even computations

Earlier in the chapter we defined the break-even point to be the level of sales at which the company's profit is zero. The break-even point can be computed using either the *equation method* or the *contribution margin method* – the two methods are equivalent.

The equation method

The **equation method** centres on the contribution approach to the profit and loss account illustrated earlier in the chapter. The format of this profit and loss account can be expressed in equation form as follows:

Profits = Sales – (Variable expenses + Fixed expenses)

Rearranging this equation slightly yields the following equation, which is widely used in CVP analysis:

Sales = Variable expenses + Fixed expenses + Profits

At the break-even point, profits are zero. Therefore, the break-even point can be computed by finding that point where sales just equal the total of the variable expenses plus the fixed expenses. For Acoustic Concepts, the break-even point in unit sales, Q, can be computed as follows:

Sales = Variable expenses + Fixed expenses + Profits

£250Q = £150Q + £35,000 + £0

£100Q = £35,000

Q = £35,000/100

Q = 350 speakers

where:

Q = Number (quantity) of speakers sold
£250 = Unit sales price
£150 = Unit variable expenses
£35,000 = Total fixed expenses

The break-even point in sales can be computed by multiplying the break-even level of unit sales by the selling price per unit:

350 speakers × £250 = £87,500

The break-even in total sales pounds, X, can also be directly computed as follows:

$$\text{Sales} = \text{Variable expenses} + \text{Fixed expenses} + \text{Profits}$$

$$X = 0.60X + £35,000 + £0$$

$$0.40X - £35,000$$

$$X = £35,000/0.40$$

$$X = £87,500$$

where:

X = Total sales
0.60 = Variable expenses as a percentage of sales
£35,000 = Total fixed expenses

Firms often have data available only in percentage form, and the approach we have just illustrated must then be used to find the break-even point. Notice that use of percentages in the equation yields a break-even point in sales rather than in units sold. The break-even point in units sold is the following:

£87,500 = £250 × 350 speakers

The contribution margin method

The **contribution margin method** is actually just a shortcut version of the equation method already described. The approach centres on the idea discussed earlier that each unit sold provides a certain amount of contribution margin that goes towards covering fixed costs. To find how many units must be sold to break even, divide the total fixed costs by the unit contribution margin:

$$\text{Break-even point in units sold} = \frac{\text{Fixed expenses}}{\text{Unit contribution margin}}$$

Each speaker generates a contribution margin of £100 (£250 selling price, less £150 variable expenses). Since the total fixed expenses are £35,000, the break-even point is as follows:

$$\frac{\text{Fixed expenses}}{\text{Unit contribution margin}} = \frac{£35,000}{£100} = 350 \text{ speakers}$$

A variation of this method uses the CM ratio instead of the unit contribution margin. The result is the break-even in total sales pounds rather than in total units sold.

$$\text{Break-even point in total sales} = \frac{\text{Fixed expenses}}{\text{CM ratio}}$$

In the Acoustic Concepts example, the calculations are as follows:

$$\frac{\text{Fixed expenses}}{\text{CM ratio}} = \frac{£35,000}{40\%} = £87,500$$

This approach, based on the CM ratio, is particularly useful in those situations where a company has multiple product lines and wishes to compute a single break-even point for the company as a whole. More is said on this point in a later section on the concept of sales mix, page 248.

CVP relationships in graphic form

5 LEARNING OBJECTIVE

The relationships among revenue, cost, profit and volume can be expressed graphically by preparing a **cost–volume–profit (CVP) graph**. A CVP graph highlights CVP relationships over wide ranges of activity and can give managers a perspective that can be obtained in no other way. To help explain his analysis to Prem Narayan, Bob White decided to prepare a CVP graph for Acoustic Concepts.

Preparing the CVP graph

Preparing a CVP graph (sometimes called a *break-even chart*) involves three steps. These steps are keyed to the graph in Exhibit 7.1:

1 Draw a line parallel to the volume axis to represent total fixed expenses. For Acoustic Concepts, total fixed expenses are £35,000.

2 Choose some volume of sales and plot the point representing total expenses (fixed and variable) at the activity level you have selected. In Exhibit 7.1, Bob White chose a volume of 600 speakers. Total expenses at that activity level would be as follows:

Fixed expenses	£35,000
Variable expenses (600 speakers × £150)	90,000
Total expenses	£125,000

7.1 EXHIBIT

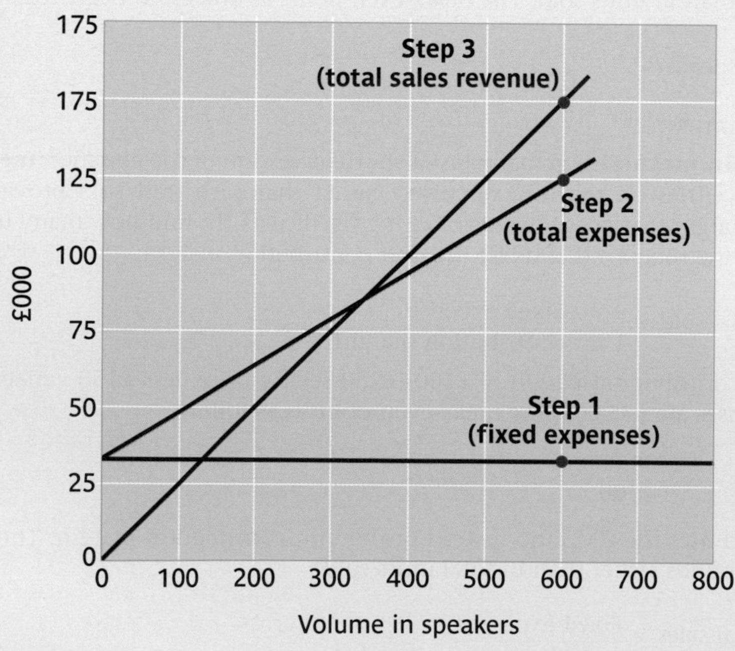

Exhibit 7.1 Preparing the CVP graph

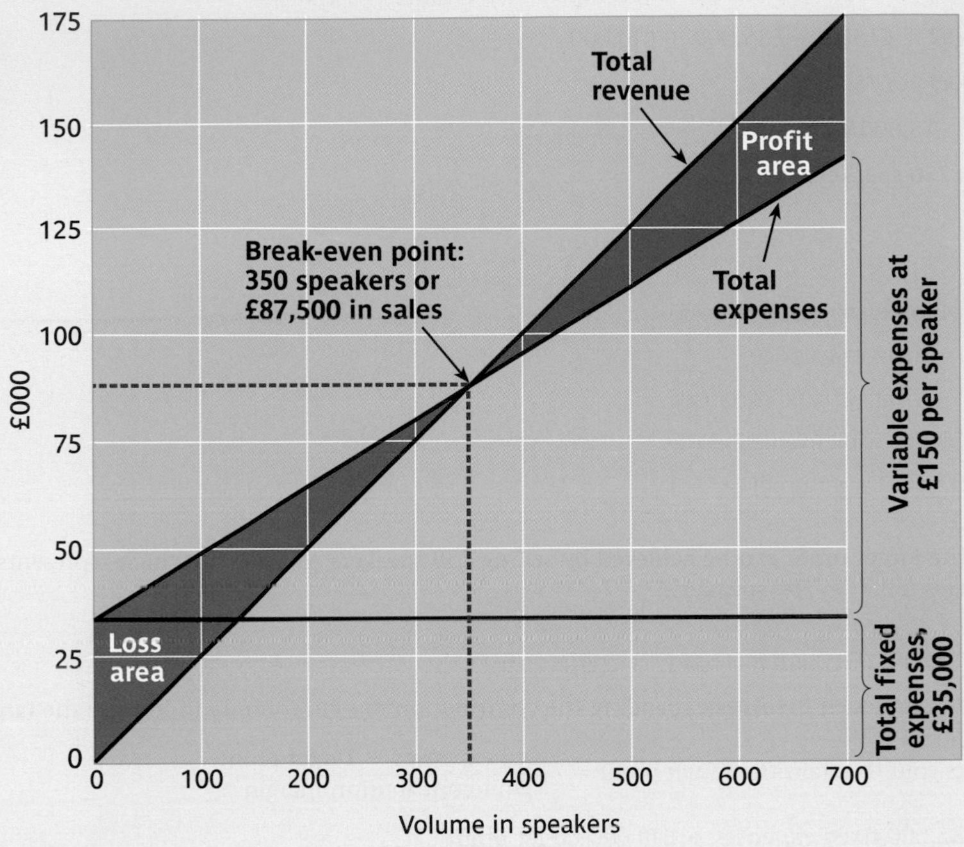

Exhibit 7.2 The completed CVP graph

After the point has been plotted, draw a line through it back to the point where the fixed expenses line intersects the pounds axis.

3 Choose some volume of sales and plot the point representing total sales pounds at the activity level you have selected. In Exhibit 7.1, Bob White again chose a volume of 600 speakers. Sales at that activity level total £150,000 (600 speakers × £250). Draw a line through this point back to the origin.

The interpretation of the completed CVP graph is given in Exhibit 7.2. The anticipated profit or loss at any given level of sales is measured by the vertical distance between the total revenue line (sales) and the total expenses line (variable expenses plus fixed expenses).

The break-even point is where the total revenue and total expenses lines cross. The break-even point of 350 speakers in Exhibit 7.2 agrees with the break-even point obtained for Acoustic Concepts in earlier computations.

Target profit analysis

CVP formulas can be used to determine the sales volume needed to achieve a target profit. Suppose that Prem Narayan of Acoustic Concepts would like to earn a target profit of £40,000 per month. How many speakers would have to be sold?

The CVP equation

One approach is to use the equation method discussed on page 238. Instead of solving for the unit sales where profits are zero, you instead solve for the unit sales where profits are £40,000.

Sales = Variable expenses + Fixed expenses + Profits

£250Q = £150Q + £35,000 + £40,000

£100Q = £75,000

Q = £75,000/£100

Q = 750 speakers

where:

Q = Number of speakers sold

£250 = Unit sales price

£150 = Unit variable expenses

£35,000 = Total fixed expenses

£40,000 = Target profit

Thus, the target profit can be achieved by selling 750 speakers per month, which represents £187,500 in total sales (£250 × 750 speakers).

The contribution margin approach

A second approach involves expanding the contribution margin formula to include the target profit:

$$\text{Units sold to attain the target profit} = \frac{\text{Fixed expenses} + \text{Target profit}}{\text{Unit contribution margin}}$$

$$= \frac{\text{£35,000 fixed expenses} + \text{£40,000 target profit}}{\text{£100 contribution margin per speaker}} = 750 \text{ speakers}$$

This approach gives the same answer as the equation method since it is simply a shortcut version of the equation method.

The margin of safety

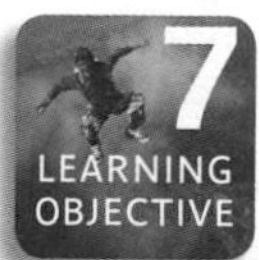

The **margin of safety** is the excess of budgeted (or actual) sales over the break-even volume of sales. It states the amount by which sales can drop before losses begin to be incurred. The formula for its calculation is as follows:

Margin of safety = Total budgeted (or actual) sales − Break-even sales

The margin of safety can also be expressed in percentage form. This percentage is obtained by dividing the margin of safety in pound terms by total sales:

$$\text{Margin of safety percentage} = \frac{\text{Margin of safety in pounds}}{\text{Total budgeted (or actual) sales}}$$

The calculations for the margin of safety for Acoustic Concepts are as follows:

Sales (at the current volume of 400 speakers) (a)	£100,000
Break-even sales (at 350 speakers)	87,500
Margin of safety (in pounds) (b)	£12,500
Margin of safety as a percentage of sales, (b)/(a)	12.5%

This margin of safety means that at the current level of sales and with the company's current prices and cost structure, a reduction in sales of £12,500, or 12.5%, would result in just breaking even.

In a single-product firm like Acoustic Concepts, the margin of safety can also be expressed in terms of the number of units sold by dividing the margin of safety in pounds by the selling price per unit. In this case, the margin of safety is 50 units (£12,500/£250 per unit = 50 units).

Management accounting in action: the wrap-up

It is Thursday morning, and Prem Narayan and Bob White are discussing the results of Bob's analysis.

Prem: Bob, everything you have shown me is pretty clear. I can see what impact some of the sales manager's suggestions would have on our profits. Some of those suggestions are quite good and some are not so good. I also understand that our break-even is 350 speakers, so we have to make sure we don't slip below that level of sales. What really bothers me is that we are only selling 400 speakers a month now. What did you call the 50-speaker cushion?

Bob: That's the margin of safety.

Prem: Such a small cushion makes me very nervous. What can we do to increase the margin of safety?

Bob: We have to increase total sales or decrease the break-even point or both.

Prem: And to decrease the break-even point, we have either to decrease our fixed expenses or increase our unit contribution margin?

Bob: Exactly.

Prem: And to increase our unit contribution margin, we have to either increase our selling price or decrease the variable cost per unit?

Bob: Correct.

Prem: So what do you suggest?

Bob: Well, the analysis doesn't tell us which of these to do, but it does indicate we have a potential problem here.

Prem: If you don't have any immediate suggestions, I would like to call a general meeting next week to discuss ways we can work on increasing the margin of safety. I think everyone will be concerned about how vulnerable we are to even small downturns in sales.

Bob: I agree. This is something everyone will want to work on.

CVP considerations in choosing a cost structure

We stated in the preceding chapter that *cost structure* refers to the relative proportion of fixed and variable costs in an organization. We also stated that an organization often has some latitude in trading off between fixed and variable costs. Such a trade-off is possible, for example, by automating facilities rather than using direct labour workers.

In this section, we discuss various considerations involved in choosing a cost structure. We look first at the matter of cost structure and profit stability, and then we discuss an important concept known as *operating leverage*. Finally, we conclude the section by comparing capital-intensive (automated) and labour-intensive companies in terms of the potential risks and rewards that are inherent in the cost structures these companies have chosen.

Cost structure and profit stability

When a manager has some latitude in trading off between fixed and variable costs, which cost structure is better – high variable costs and low fixed costs, or the opposite? No categorical answer to this question is possible; there may be advantages either way, depending on the specific circumstances. To show what we mean by this statement, refer to the profit and loss accounts given below for two blackberry farms.

Bogside Farm depends on migrant workers to pick its berries by hand, whereas Sterling Farm has invested in expensive berry-picking machines. Consequently, Bogside Farm has higher variable costs, but Sterling Farm has higher fixed costs:

	Bogside Farm		**Sterling Farm**	
	Amount	**Percentage**	**Amount**	**Percentage**
Sales	£100,000	100%	£100,000	100%
Less variable expenses	60,000	60%	303,000	30%
Contribution margin	40,000	40%	70,000	70%
Less fixed expenses	30,000		60,000	
Profit	£10,000		£10,000	

The question as to which farm has the better cost structure depends on many factors, including the long-run trend in sales, year-to-year fluctuations in the level of sales, and the attitude of the owners toward risk. If sales are expected to be above £100,000 in the future, then Sterling Farm probably has the better cost structure. The reason is that its CM ratio is higher, and its profits will therefore increase more rapidly as sales increase. To illustrate, assume that each farm experiences a 10% increase in sales without any increase in fixed costs. The new profit and loss accounts would be as follows:

	Bogside Farm		**Sterling Farm**	
	Amount	**Percentage**	**Amount**	**Percentage**
Sales	£110,000	100%	£110,000	100%
Less variable expenses	66,000	60%	33,000	30%
Contribution margin	44,000	40%	77,000	70%
Less fixed expenses	30,000		60,000	
Profit	£14,000		£17,000	

Sterling Farm has experienced a greater increase in profit due to its higher CM ratio even though the increase in sales was the same for both farms.

What if sales drop below £100,000 from time to time? What are the break-even points of the two farms? What are their margins of safety? The computations needed to answer these questions are carried out below using the contribution margin method:

	Bogside Farm	**Sterling Farm**
Fixed expenses	£30,000	£60,000
Contribution margin ratio	÷ 40%	÷ 70%
Break-even in total sales pounds	£75,000	£85,714
Total current sales (a)	£100,000	£100,000
Break-even sales	75,000	85,714
Margin of safety in sales pounds (b)	£25,000	£14,286
Margin of safety as a percentage of sales, (b)/(a)	25.0%	14.3%

This analysis makes it clear that Bogside Farm is less vulnerable to downturns than Sterling Farm. We can identify two reasons why it is less vulnerable. First, due to its lower fixed expenses, Bogside Farm has a lower break-even point and a higher margin of safety, as shown by the computations above. Therefore, it will not incur losses as quickly as Sterling Farm in periods of sharply declining sales. Secondly, due to its lower CM ratio, Bogside Farm will not lose contribution margin as rapidly as Sterling Farm when sales fall off. Thus, Bogside Farm's profit will be less volatile. We saw earlier that this is a drawback when sales increase, but it provides more protection when sales drop.

To summarize, without knowing the future, it is not obvious which cost structure is better. Both have advantages and disadvantages. Sterling Farm, with its higher fixed costs and lower variable costs, will experience wider swings in profit as changes take place in sales, with greater profits in good years and greater losses in bad years. Bogside Farm, with its lower fixed costs and higher variable costs, will enjoy greater stability in profit and will be more protected from losses during bad years, but at the cost of lower profit in good years.

Operating leverage

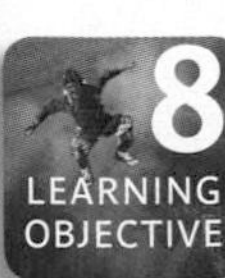

A lever is a tool for multiplying force. Using a lever, a massive object can be moved with only a modest amount of force. In business, *operating leverage* serves a similar purpose. **Operating leverage** is a measure of how sensitive profit is to percentage changes in sales. Operating leverage acts as a multiplier. If operating leverage is high, a small percentage increase in sales can produce a much larger percentage increase in profit.

Operating leverage can be illustrated by returning to the data given above for the two blackberry farms. We previously showed that a 10% increase in sales (from £100,000 to £110,000 in each farm) results in a 70% increase in the profit of Sterling Farm (from £10,000 to £17,000) and only a 40% increase in the profit of Bogside Farm (from £10,000 to £14,000). Thus, for a 10% increase in sales, Sterling Farm experiences a much greater percentage increase in profits than does Bogside Farm. Therefore, Sterling Farm has greater operating leverage than Bogside Farm.

The **degree of operating leverage** at a given level of sales is computed by the following formula:

$$\text{Degree of operating leverage} = \frac{\text{Contribution margin}}{\text{Profit}}$$

The degree of operating leverage is a measure, at a given level of sales, of how a percentage change in sales volume will affect profits. To illustrate, the degree of operating leverage for the two farms at a £100,000 sales level would be as follows:

$$\text{Bogside Farm: } \frac{£40{,}000}{£10{,}000} = 4$$

$$\text{Sterling Farm: } \frac{£70{,}000}{£10{,}000} = 7$$

Since the degree of operating leverage for Bogside Farm is four, the farm's profit grows four times as fast as its sales. Similarly, Sterling Farm's profit grows seven times as fast as its sales. Thus, if sales increase by 10%, then we can expect the profit of Bogside Farm to increase by four times this amount, or by 40%, and the profit of Sterling Farm to increase by seven times this amount, or by 70%.

	1 Percentage increase in sales	2 Degree of operating leverage	3 Percentage increase in profit (1 × 2)
Bogside Farm	10	4	40%
Sterling Farm	10	7	70%

What is responsible for the higher operating leverage at Sterling Farm? The only difference between the two farms is their cost structure. If two companies have the same total revenue and same total expense but different cost structures, then the company with the higher proportion of fixed costs in its cost structure will have higher operating leverage. Referring back to the original example on page 244, when both farms have sales of £100,000 and total expenses of £90,000, one-third of Bogside Farm's costs are fixed but two-thirds of Sterling Farm's costs are fixed. As a consequence, Sterling's degree of operating leverage is higher than Bogside's.[2]

The degree of operating leverage is greatest at sales levels near the break-even point and decreases as sales and profits rise. This can be seen from the tabulation below, which shows the degree of operating leverage for Bogside Farm at various sales levels. (Data used earlier for Bogside Farm are shown in colour.)

Sales	£75,000	£80,000	£100,000	£150,000	£225,000
Less variable expenses	45,000	48,000	60,000	90,000	135,000
Contribution margin (a)	30,000	32,000	40,000	60,000	90,000
Less fixed expenses	30,000	30,000	30,000	30,000	30,000
Profit (b)	£0	£2,000	£10,000	£30,000	£60,000
Degree of operating leverage, (a)/(b)	∞	16	4	2	1.5

Thus, a 10% increase in sales would increase profits by only 15% (10% × 1.5) if the company were operating at a £225,000 sales level, as compared to the 40% increase we computed earlier at the £100,000 sales level. The degree of operating leverage will continue to decrease the farther the company moves from its break-even point. At the break-even point, the degree of operating leverage will be infinitely large (£30,000 contribution margin/£0 profit = ∞).

A manager can use the degree of operating leverage quickly to estimate what impact various percentage changes in sales will have on profits, without the necessity of preparing detailed profit and loss accounts. As shown by our examples, the effects of operating leverage can be dramatic. If a company is near its break-even point, then even small percentage increases in sales can yield large percentage increases in profits.

This explains why management will often work very hard for only a small increase in sales volume. If the degree of operating leverage is five, then a 6% increase in sales would translate into a 30% increase in profits.

Automation: risks and rewards from a CVP perspective

Several factors, including the move towards flexible manufacturing systems and other uses of automation, have resulted in a shift towards greater fixed costs and less variable costs in organizations. In turn, this shift in cost structure has had an impact on the CM ratio, the break-even point, and the degree of operating leverage. Some of this impact has been favourable and some has not, as shown in Exhibit 7.3.

Many benefits can accrue from automation, but as shown in the exhibit, certain risks are introduced when a company moves towards greater amounts of fixed costs. These risks suggest that management must be careful as it automates to ensure that investment decisions are made in accordance with a carefully devised long-run strategy. This point is discussed further in Chapter 16 where we consider the strategic issues concerning an investment decision in an automated environment.

Structuring sales commissions

Companies generally reward salespeople by paying them either a commission based on sales or a salary plus a sales commission. Commissions based on sales pounds can lead to lower profits in a company. To illustrate, consider Pipeline Unlimited, a producer of surfing equipment. Salespeople for the company sell the company's product to retail sporting goods stores throughout North America and the Pacific Basin. Data for two of the company's surfboards, the XR7 and Turbo models, appear below:

	Model XR7	Turbo
Selling price	£100	£150
Less variable expenses	75	132
Contribution margin	£25	£18

Item	Capital-intensive (automated) company	Labour-intensive Company	Comments
The CM ratio will tend to be relatively	High	Low	Variable costs in an automated company will tend to be lower than in a labour-intensive company, thereby causing the CM ratio for a given product to be higher.
Operating leverage will tend to be	High	Low	Operating leverage is higher in the automated company because the companies are identical except for their cost structures and the automated company has lower variable costs and hence a larger contribution margin.
In periods of increasing sales, profit will tend to iincrease	Rapidly	Slowly	Since both operating leverage and CM ratios tend to be high in automated companies, profit will increase more rapidly.
In periods of decreasing sales, profit will tend to decrease	Rapidly	Slowly	Just as profit increases more rapidly in an automated company, so will profit decrease more rapidly as sales decrease.
The volatility of profit with changes in sales will tend to be	Greater	Less	Due to its higher operating leverage, the profit in an automated company will tend to be more sensitive to changes in sales than in a labour-intensive company.
The break-even point will tend to be	Higher	Lower	The break-even point in an automated company will tend to be higher because of its greater fixed costs, although this is offset to some extent by the higher CM ratio.
The margin of safety at a given level of sales will tend to be break-even point.	Lower	Higher	The margin of safety in an automated company will tend to be lower because of its higher
The latitude available to management in times of economic stress will tend to be	Less	Greater	With high committed fixed costs in an automated company, management is more locked when dealing with changing economic conditions.

Exhibit 7.3 CVP comparison of capital-intensive (automated) and labour-intensive companies

Which model will salespeople push hardest if they are paid a commission of 10% of sales revenue? The answer, clearly, is the Turbo, since it has the higher selling price. On the other hand, from the standpoint of the company, profits will be greater if salespeople steer customers toward the XR7 model since it has the higher contribution margin.

To eliminate such conflicts, some companies base salespersons' commissions on contribution margin rather than on sales. The reasoning goes like this: since contribution margin represents the amount of sales revenue available to cover fixed expenses and profits, a firm's well-being will be maximized when contribution margin is maximized. By tying salesperson's commissions to contribution margin, the salespersons are automatically encouraged to concentrate on the element that is of most importance to the firm. There is no need to worry about what mix of products the salespersons sell because they will automatically sell the mix of products that will maximize the contribution margin. In effect, by maximizing their own well-being, they automatically maximize the well-being of the firm – assuming there is no change in fixed expenses.

The comparison below is between two profitable companies that have different cost structures but are otherwise identical. They sell the same products and services and have the same total sales revenues and the same total expenses. One of the companies has chosen to automate, resulting in a capital-intensive facility. The other company has chosen to rely more on human labour, resulting in a labour-intensive facility. Assuming that labour is a variable cost, the company that has automated has a higher proportion of fixed costs in its cost structure.

The concept of sales mix

The preceding sections have given us some insights into the principles involved in CVP analysis, as well as some selected examples of how these principles are used by the manager. Before concluding our discussion, it will be helpful to consider one additional application of the ideas that we have developed – the use of CVP concepts in analysing sales mix.

The definition of sales mix

The term **sales mix** means the relative proportions in which a company's products are sold. Managers try to achieve the combination, or mix, that will yield the greatest amount of profits. Most companies have several products, and often these products are not equally profitable. Where this is true, profits will depend to some extent on the company's sales mix. Profits will be greater if high-margin rather than low-margin items make up a relatively large proportion of total sales.

Changes in the sales mix can cause interesting (and sometimes confusing) variations in a company's profits. A shift in the sales mix from high-margin items to low-margin items can cause total profits to decrease even though total sales may increase. Conversely, a shift in the sales mix from low-margin items to high-margin items can cause the reverse effect – total profits may increase even though total sales decrease. It is one thing to achieve a particular sales volume; it is quite a different thing to sell the most profitable mix of products.

Sales mix and break-even analysis

If a company sells more than one product, break-even analysis is somewhat more complex than discussed earlier in the chapter. The reason is that different products will have different selling prices, different costs and different contribution margins. Consequently, the break-even point will depend on the mix in which the various products are sold. To illustrate, consider Sound Unlimited, a small company that imports CD-ROMs from France for use in personal computers. At present, the company distributes the following to retail computer stores: the Le Louvre CD, a multimedia free-form tour of the famous art museum in Paris; and the Le Vin CD, which features the wines and wine-growing regions of France. Both multimedia products have sound, photos, video clips, and sophisticated software. The company's September sales, expenses and break-even point are shown in Exhibit 7.4.

As shown in the exhibit, the break-even point is £60,000 in sales. This is computed by dividing the fixed costs by the company's *overall* CM ratio of 45%. But £60,000 in sales represents the break-even point for the company only as long as the sales mix does not change. *If the sales mix changes, then the break-even point will also change.* This is illustrated by the results for October in which the sales mix shifted away from the more profitable Le Vin CD (which has a 50% CM ratio) towards the less profitable Le Louvre CD (which has only a 25% CM ratio). These results appear in Exhibit 7.5.

7.4 EXHIBIT

Sound Unlimited
Contribution profit statement
For the month of September

	Le Louvre CD		Le Vin CD		Total	
	Amount	**%**	**Amount**	**%**	**Amount**	**%**
Sales	£20,000	100	£80,000	100	£100,000	100
Less variable expenses	15,000	75	40,000	50	55,000	55
Contribution margin	£5,000	25	£40,000	50	45,000	45
Less fixed expenses					27,000	
Profit					£18,000	

Computation of the break-even point:

$$\frac{\text{Fixed expenses, £27,000}}{\text{Overall CM ratio, 45\%}} = \text{£60,000}$$

Verification of the break-even:

	Le Louvre CD		Le Vin CD		Total	
	Amount	**%**	**Amount**	**%**	**Amount**	**%**
Sales	£12,000	100	£48,000	100	£60,000	100
Less variable expenses	9,000	75	24,000	50	33,000	55
Contribution margin	£3,000	25	£24,000	50	27,000	45
Less fixed expenses					27,000	
Profit					£0	

Exhibit 7.4 Multiple product break-even analysis

7.5 EXHIBIT

Sound Unlimited
Contribution profit statement
For the month of October

	Le Louvre CD		Le Vin CD		Total	
	Amount	**%**	**Amount**	**%**	**Amount**	**%**
Sales	£80,000	100	£20,000	100	£100,000	100
Less variable expenses	60,000	75	10,000	50	70,000	70
Contribution margin	£20,000	25	£10,000	50	30,000	30
Less fixed expenses					27,000	
Profit					£3,000	

Computation of the break-even point:

$$\frac{\text{Fixed expenses, £27,000}}{\text{Overall CM ratio, 30\%}} = \text{£90,000}$$

Exhibit 7.5 Multiple product break-even analysis: a shift in sales mix (see Exhibit 7.4)

Although sales have remained unchanged at £100,000, the sales mix is exactly the reverse of what it was in Exhibit 7.4, with the bulk of the sales now coming from the less profitable Le Louvre CD. Notice that this shift in the sales mix has caused both the overall CM ratio and total profits to drop sharply from the prior month – the overall CM ratio has dropped from 45% in September to only 30% in October, and profit has dropped from £18,000 to only £3,000. In addition, with the drop in the overall CM ratio, the company's break-even point is no longer £60,000 in sales. Since the company is now realizing less average contribution margin per pound of sales, it takes more sales to cover the same amount of fixed costs. Thus, the break-even point has increased from £60,000 to £90,000 in sales per year.

In preparing a break-even analysis, some assumption must be made concerning the sales mix. Usually the assumption is that it will not change. However, if the manager knows that shifts in various factors (consumer tastes, market share and so forth) are causing shifts in the sales mix, then these factors must be explicitly considered in any CVP computations. Otherwise, the manager may make decisions on the basis of outmoded or faulty data.

Assumptions of CVP analysis

A number of assumptions typically underlie CVP analysis:

1 Selling price is constant throughout the entire relevant range. The price of a product or service will not change as volume changes.

2 Costs are linear throughout the entire relevant range, and they can be accurately divided into variable and fixed elements. The variable element is constant per unit, and the fixed element is constant in total over the entire relevant range.

3 In multiproduct companies, the sales mix is constant.

4 In manufacturing companies, stocks do not change. The number of units produced equals the number of units sold.

While some of these assumptions may be technically violated, the violations are usually not serious enough to call into question the basic validity of CVP analysis. For example, in most multiproduct companies, the sales mix is constant enough for the results of CVP analysis to be reasonably valid.

Perhaps the greatest danger lies in relying on simple CVP analysis when a manager is contemplating a large change in volume that lies outside the relevant range. For example, a manager might contemplate increasing the level of sales far beyond what the company has ever experienced before. However, even in these situations a manager can adjust the model as we have done in this chapter to take into account anticipated changes in selling prices, fixed costs and the sales mix that would otherwise violate the assumptions. For example, in a decision that would affect fixed costs, the change in fixed costs can be explicitly taken into account as illustrated earlier in the chapter in the Acoustic Concepts example on page 234.

Summary

- CVP analysis involves finding the most favourable combination of variable costs, fixed costs, selling price, sales volume, and mix of products sold.
- Trade-offs are possible between types of costs, as well as between costs and selling price, and between selling price and sales volume.
- Sometimes these trade-offs are desirable, and sometimes they are not. CVP analysis provides the manager with a powerful tool for identifying those courses of action that will improve profitability.
- The concepts developed in this chapter represent *a way of thinking* rather than a mechanical set of procedures. That is, to put together the optimum combination of costs, selling price and sales volume, the manager must be trained to think in terms of the unit contribution margin, the break-even point, the CM ratio, the sales mix, and the other concepts developed in this chapter.
- These concepts are dynamic in that a change in one will trigger changes in others – changes that may not be obvious on the surface.

Key terms for review

Break-even point (p. 232).

Contribution margin method (p. 239).

Contribution margin ratio (CM ratio) (p. 233).

Cost–volume–profit (CVP) graph (p. 240).

Degree of operating leverage (p. 245).

Equation method (p. 238).

Incremental analysis (p. 235).

Margin of safety (p. 242).

Operating leverage (p. 245).

Sales mix (p. 248).

Review problem: CVP relationships

Voltar Company manufactures and sells a telephone answering machine. The company's contribution format profit and loss account for the most recent year is given below:

	Total	Per unit	% of sales
Sales (20,000 units)	£1,200,000	£60	100%
Less variable expenses	900,000	45	?%
Contribution margin	300,000	£15	?%
Less fixed expenses	240,000		
Profit	£60,000		

Management is anxious to improve the company's profit performance and has asked for several items of information.

Required

1 Compute the company's CM ratio and variable expense ratio.

2 Compute the company's break-even point in both units and sales pounds. Use the equation method.

3 Assume that sales increase by £400,000 next year. If cost behaviour patterns remain unchanged, by how much will the company's profit increase? Use the CM ratio to determine your answer.

4 Refer to original data. Assume that next year management wants the company to earn a minimum profit of £90,000. How many units will have to be sold to meet this target profit figure?

5 Refer to the original data. Compute the company's margin of safety in both pound and percentage form.

6 (a) Compute the company's degree of operating leverage at the present level of sales.

(b) Assume that through a more intense effort by the sales staff the company's sales increase by 8% next year. By what percentage would you expect profit to increase? Use the operating leverage concept to obtain your answer.

(c) Verify your answer to (b) by preparing a new profit and loss account showing an 8% increase in sales.

7 In an effort to increase sales and profits, management is considering the use of a higher-quality speaker. The higher-quality speaker would increase variable costs by £3 per unit, but management could eliminate one quality inspector who is paid a salary of £30,000 per year. The sales manager estimates that the higher-quality speaker would increase annual sales by at least 20%.

(a) Assuming that changes are made as described above, prepare a projected profit and loss account for next year. Show data on a total, per unit, and percentage basis.

(b) Compute the company's new break-even point in both units and pounds of sales. Use the contribution margin method.

(c) Would you recommend that the changes be made?

Solution to review problem: CVP relationships

1 CM ratio:

$$\frac{\text{Contribution margin, £15}}{\text{Selling price, £60}} = 25\%$$

Variable expense ratio:

$$\frac{\text{Variable expense, £45}}{\text{Selling price, £60}} = 75\%$$

2 Sales = Variable expenses + Fixed expenses = Profits

$$£60Q = £45Q + £240{,}000 + £0$$

$$£15Q = £240{,}000$$

$$Q = £240{,}000/£15$$

$Q = 16{,}000$ units; or at £60 per unit, £960,000

Alternative solution:

$$X = 0.75X + £240{,}000 + £0$$

$$0.25X = £240{,}000$$

$$X = £240{,}000/0.25$$

$X = £960{,}000$; or at £60 per unit, 16,000 units

3

Increase in sales	£400,000
Multiply by the CM ratio	× 25%
Expected increase in contribution margin	£100,000

Since the fixed expenses are not expected to change, profit will increase by the entire £100,000 increase in contribution margin computed above.

4 Equation method:

Sales = Variable expenses + Fixed expenses + Profits

$£60Q = £45Q + £240{,}000 + £90{,}000$

$£15Q = £330{,}000$

$Q = £330{,}000/£15$

$Q = 22{,}000$ units

Contribution margin method:

$$\frac{\text{Fixed expenses + Target profit}}{\text{Contribution margin per unit}} = \frac{£240{,}000 + £90{,}000}{£15} = 22{,}000 \text{ units}$$

5 Total sales – Break-even sales = Margin of safety in pounds

$£1{,}200{,}000 - £960{,}000 = £240{,}000$

$$\frac{\text{Margin of safety in pounds, £240,000}}{\text{Total sales, £1,200,000}} = 20\%$$

6 (a)

$$\frac{\text{Contribution margin, £300,000}}{\text{Profit, £60,000}} = 5 \text{ (degree of operating leverage)}$$

(b)

Expected increase in sales	8%
Degree of operating leverage	× 5
Expected increase in profit	40%

(c) If sales increase by 8%, then 21,600 units (20,000 × 1.08 = 21,600) will be sold next year. The new profit and loss account will be as follows:

	Total	**Per unit**	**Percentage of sales**
Sales (21,600 units)	£1,296,000	£60	100
Less variable expenses	972,000	45	75
Contribution margin	324,000	£15	25
Less fixed expenses	240,000		
Profit	£84,000		

Thus, the £84,000 expected profit for next year represents a 40% increase over the £60,000 profit earned during the current year:

$$\frac{£84{,}000 - £60{,}000}{£60{,}000} = £24{,}000 = 40\%$$

Note from the profit and loss account above that the increase in sales from 20,000 to 21,600 units has resulted in increases in both total sales and total variable expenses. It is a common error to overlook the increase in variable expenses when preparing a projected profit and loss account.

7 (a) A 20% increase in sales would result in 24,000 units being sold next year: 20,000 units × 1.20 = 24,000 units.

	Total	Per unit	Percentage of sales
Sales (24,000 units)	£1,440,000	£60	100
Less variable expenses	1,152,000	48*	80
Contribution margin	288,000	£12	20
Less fixed expenses	210,000†		
Profit	£78,000		

*£45 + £3 = £48; £48/£60 = 80%

†£240,000 – £30,000 = £210,000

Note that the change in per unit variable expenses results in a change in both the per unit contribution margin and the CM ratio.

(b)

$$\frac{\text{Fixed expenses, £210,000}}{\text{Contribution margin per unit, £12}} = 17{,}500 \text{ units}$$

$$\frac{\text{Fixed expenses, £210,000}}{\text{CM ratio, 20\%}} = \text{£1,050,000 break-even sales}$$

(c) Yes, based on these data the changes should be made. The changes will increase the company's profit from the present £60,000 to £78,000 per year. Although the changes will also result in a higher break-even point (17,500 units as compared to the present 16,000 units), the company's margin of safety will actually be wider than before:

Total sales – Break-even sales = Margin of safety in pounds

£1,400,000 – £1,050,000 = £390,000

As shown in (5) above, the company's present margin of safety is only £240,000. Thus, several benefits will result from the proposed changes.

Questions

7–1 What is meant by a product's CM ratio? How is this ratio useful in planning business operations?

7–2 Often the most direct route to a business decision is to make an incremental analysis based on the information available. What is meant by an *incremental analysis*?

7–3 Company A's cost structure includes costs that are mostly variable, whereas Company B's cost structure includes costs that are mostly fixed. In a time of increasing sales, which company will tend to realize the most rapid increase in profits? Explain.

7–4 What is meant by the term *operating leverage*?

7–5 A 10% decrease in the selling price of a product will have the same impact on profit as a 10% increase in the variable expenses. Do you agree? Why or why not?

7–6 What is meant by the term *break-even point*?

7–7 Name three approaches to break-even analysis. Briefly explain how each approach works.

7–8 In response to a request from your immediate supervisor, you have prepared a CVP graph portraying the cost and revenue characteristics of your company's product and operations. Explain how the lines on the graph and the break-even point would change if (a) the selling price per unit decreased, (b) fixed costs increased throughout the entire range of activity portrayed on the graph, and (c) variable costs per unit increased.

7–9 Al's Car Wash charges £4 to wash a car. The variable costs of washing a car are 15% of sales. Fixed expenses total £1,700 monthly. How many cars must be washed each month for Al to break even?

7–10 What is meant by the margin of safety?

7–11 Companies X and Y are in the same industry. Company X is highly automated, whereas Company Y relies primarily on labour to make its products. If sales and total expenses in the two companies are about the same, which would you expect to have the lower margin of safety? Why?

7–12 What is meant by the term sales mix? What assumption is usually made concerning sales mix in CVP analysis?

7–13 Explain how a shift in the sales mix could result in both a higher break-even point and a lower profit.

Exercises

E7–1 Time allowed: 20 minutes

Menlo Company manufactures and sells a single product. The company's sales and expenses for the last quarter follow:

	Total	Per unit
Sales	£450,000	£30
Less variable expenses	180,000	12
Contribution margin	270,000	£18
Less fixed expenses	216,000	
Profit	£54,000	

Required

1 What is the quarterly break-even point in units sold and in sales pounds?

2 Without resorting to computations, what is the total contribution margin at the break-even point?

3 How many units would have to be sold each quarter to earn a target profit of £90,000? Use the unit contribution method. Verify your answer by preparing a contribution profit and loss account at the target level of sales.

4 Refer to the original data. Compute the company's margin of safety in both pound and percentage terms.

5 What is the company's CM ratio? If sales increase by £50,000 per quarter and there is no change in fixed expenses, by how much would you expect quarterly profit to increase? (Do not prepare a profit and loss account; use the CM ratio to compute your answer.)

E7–2 Time allowed: 20 minutes

Lindon Company is the exclusive distributor for an automotive product. The product sells for £40 per unit and has a CM ratio of 30%. The company's fixed expenses are £180,000 per year.

Required

1 What are the variable expenses per unit?

2 Using the equation method:

(a) What is the break-even point in units and sales pounds?

(b) What sales level in units and in sales pounds is required to earn an annual profit of £60,000?

(c) Assume that by using a more efficient shipper, the company is able to reduce its variable expenses by £4 per unit. What is the company's new break-even point in units and sales pounds?

3 Repeat Question 2 above using the unit contribution method.

E7–3 Time allowed: 25 minutes

The Hartford Symphony Guild is planning its annual dinner-dance. The dinner-dance committee has assembled the following expected costs for the event:

Dinner (per person)	£18
Favours and programme (per person)	2
Band	2,800
Rental of ballroom	900
Professional entertainment during intermission	1,000
Tickets and advertising	1,300

The committee members would like to charge £35 per person for the evening's activities.

Required

1 Compute the break-even point for the dinner-dance (in terms of the number of persons that must attend).

2 Assume that last year only 300 persons attended the dinner-dance. If the same number attend this year, what price per ticket must be charged in order to break even?

3 Refer to the original data (£35 ticket price per person). Prepare a CVP graph for the dinner-dance from a zero level of activity up to 900 tickets sold. Number of persons should be placed on the horizontal (x) axis, and pounds should be placed on the vertical (z) axis.

E7–4 Time allowed: 15 minutes

Magic Realm Ltd has developed a new fantasy board game. The company sold 15,000 games last year at a selling price of £20 per game. Fixed costs associated with the game total £182,000 per year, and variable costs are £6 per game. Production of the game is entrusted to a printing contractor. Variable costs consist mostly of payments to this contractor.

Required

1 Prepare a profit and loss account for the game last year and compute the degree of operating leverage.

2 Management is confident that the company can sell 18,000 games next year (an increase of 3,000 games, or 20%, over last year). Compute:

(a) The expected percentage increase in profit for next year.

(b) The expected total pound profit for next year. (Do not prepare a profit and loss account; use the degree of operating leverage to compute your answer.)

E7–5 Time allowed: 20 minutes
Miller Company's most recent profit and loss account is shown below:

	Total	Per unit
Sales (20,000 units)	£300,000	£15.00
Less variable expenses	180,000	9.00
Contribution margin	120,000	£6.00
Less fixed expenses	70,000	
Profit	£50,000	

Required

Prepare a new profit and loss account under each of the following conditions (consider each case independently):

1 The sales volume increases by 15%.

2 The selling price decreases by £1.50 per unit, and the sales volume increases by 25%.

3 The selling price increases by £1.50 per unit, fixed expenses increase by £20,000, and the sales volume decreases by 5%.

4 The selling price increases by 12%, variable expenses increase by 60 pence per unit, and the sales volume decreases by 10%.

E7–6 Time allowed: 20 minutes
Fill in the missing amounts in each of the eight case situations below. Each case is independent of the others. (*Hint*: One way to find the missing amounts would be to prepare a contribution profit and loss account for each case, enter the known data, and then compute the missing items.)

(a) Assume that only one product is being sold in each of the four following case situations:

Case	Units sold	Sales	Variable expenses	Contribution margin per unit	Fixed expenses	Net profit (loss)
1	15,000	£180,000	£120,000	£?	£50,000	£?
2	?	100,000	?	10	32,000	8,000
3	10,000	?	70,000	13	?	12,000
4	6,000	300,000	?	?	100,000	(10,000)

(b) Assume that more than one product is being sold in each of the four following case situations:

Case	Sales	Variable expenses	Contribution margin (%)	Average expenses	Net profit (loss)
1	£500,000	£?	20	£?	£7,000
2	400,000	260,000	?	100,000	?
3	?	?	60	130,000	20,000
4	600,000	420,000	?	?	(5,000)

E7–7 Time allowed: 25 minutes
Olongapo Sports Corporation is the distributor in the Philippines of two premium golf balls – the Flight Dynamic and the Sure Shot. Monthly sales and the contribution margin ratios for the two products follow:

	Product		
	Flight Dynamic	Sure Shot	Total
Sales	P150,000	P250,000	P400,000
CM ratio	80%	36%	?

Fixed expenses total P183,750 per month (the currency in the Philippines is the peso, which is denoted by P).

Required

1 Prepare a profit and loss account for the company as a whole. Use the format shown in Exhibit 7.4 and carry computations to one decimal place.

2 Compute the break-even point for the company based on the current sales mix.

3 If sales increase by P100,000 a month, by how much would you expect profit to increase? What are your assumptions?

E7–8 Time allowed: 25 minutes
Outback Outfitters manufactures and sells recreational equipment. One of the company's products, a small camp stove, sells for £50 per unit. Variable expenses are £32 per stove, and fixed expenses associated with the stove total £108,000 per month.

Required

1 Compute the break-even point in number of stoves and in total sales pounds.

2 If the variable expenses per stove increase as a percentage of the selling price, will it result in a higher or a lower break-even point? Why? (Assume that the fixed expenses remain unchanged.)

3 At present, the company is selling 8,000 stoves per month. The sales manager is convinced that a 10% reduction in the selling price would result in a 25% increase in monthly sales of stoves. Prepare two contribution profit and loss accounts, one under present operating conditions, and one as operations would appear after the proposed changes. Show both total and per unit data on your statements.

4 Refer to the data in Question 3 above. How many stoves would have to be sold at the new selling price to yield a minimum profit of £35,000 per month?

PROBLEMS

Problems

P7–9 Basic CVP analysis; graphing Time allowed: 60 minutes
The Fashion Shoe Company operates a chain of women's shoe shops around the country. The shops carry many styles of shoes that are all sold at the same price. Sales personnel in the shops are paid a substantial commission on each pair of shoes sold (in addition to a small basic salary) in order to encourage them to be aggressive in their sales efforts.

The following cost and revenue data relate to Shop 48 and are typical of one of the company's many outlets:

	Per pair of shoes
Sales price	£30.00
Variable expenses:	
Invoice cost	£13.50
Sales commission	4.50
Total variable expenses	£18.00
	Annual
Fixed expenses:	
Advertising	£30,000
Rent	20,000
Salaries	100,000
Total fixed expenses	£150,000

Required

1. Calculate the annual break-even point in pound sales and in unit sales for Shop 48.
2. Prepare a CVP graph showing cost and revenue data for Shop 48 from a zero level of activity up to 20,000 pairs of shoes sold each year. Clearly indicate the break-even point on the graph.
3. If 12,000 pairs of shoes are sold in a year, what would be Shop 48's profit or loss?
4. The company is considering paying the store manager of Shop 48 an incentive commission of 75 pence per pair of shoes (in addition to the salesperson's commission). If this change is made, what will be the new break-even point in pound sales and in unit sales?
5. Refer to the original data. As an alternative to (4) above, the company is considering paying the store manager 50 pence commission on each pair of shoes sold in excess of the break-even point. If this change is made, what will be the shop's profit or loss if 15,000 pairs of shoes are sold?
6. Refer to the original data. The company is considering eliminating sales commissions entirely in its shops and increasing fixed salaries by £31,500 annually. If this change is made, what will be the new break-even point in pound sales and in unit sales for Shop 48? Would you recommend that the change be made? Explain.

P7–10 Basics of CVP analysis; cost structure Time allowed: 60 minutes
Due to erratic sales of its sole product – a high-capacity battery for laptop computers –PEM Ltd has been experiencing difficulty for some time. The company's profit and loss account for the most recent month is given below:

Sales (19,500 units x £30)	£585,000
Less variable expenses	409,500
Contribution margin	175,500
Less fixed expenses	180,000
Net loss	£(4,500)

Required

1. Compute the company's CM ratio and its break-even point in both units and pounds.
2. The president believes that a £16,000 increase in the monthly advertising budget, combined with an intensified effort by the sales staff, will result in an £80,000 increase in monthly sales. If the president

is right, what will be the effect on the company's monthly profit or loss? (Use the incremental approach in preparing your answer.)

3 Refer to the original data. The sales manager is convinced that a 10% reduction in the selling price, combined with an increase of £60,000 in the monthly advertising budget, will cause unit sales to double. What will the new profit and loss account look like if these changes are adopted?

4 Refer to the original data. The Marketing Department thinks that a fancy new package for the laptop computer battery would help sales. The new package would increase packaging costs by 75 pence per unit. Assuming no other changes, how many units would have to be sold each month to earn a profit of £9,750?

5 Refer to the original data. By automating certain operations, the company could reduce variable costs by £3 per unit. However, fixed costs would increase by £72,000 each month.

(a) Compute the new CM ratio and the new break-even point in both units and pounds.

(b) Assume that the company expects to sell 26,000 units next month. Prepare two profit and loss accounts, one assuming that operations are not automated and one assuming that they are. (Show data on a per unit and percentage basis, as well as in total, for each alternative.)

(c) Would you recommend that the company automate its operations? Explain.

P7–11 Sales mix assumptions; break-even analysis Time allowed: 35 minutes

Gold Star Rice Ltd of Thailand exports Thai rice throughout Asia. The company grows three varieties of rice – Fragrant, White and Loonzain. (The currency in Thailand is the baht, which is denoted by B.) Budgeted sales by product and in total for the coming month are shown below:

	Product							
	White		**Fragrant**		**Loonzain**		**Total**	
Percentage of total sales	20%		52%		28%		100%	
Percentage of sales	B150,000	100%	B390,000	100%	B210,000	100%	B750,000	100%
Less variable expenses	108,000	72%	78,000	20%	84,000	40%	270,000	36%
Contribution margin	B42,000	28%	B312,000	80%	B126,000	60%	480,000	64%
Less fixed expenses							449,280	
Profit							B30,720	

$$\frac{\text{Break-even sales: Fixed Expenses, B449,280}}{\text{CM Ratio, 0.64}} = \text{B702,000}$$

As shown by these data, profit is budgeted at B30,720 for the month and break-even sales at B702,000.

Assume that actual sales for the month total B750,000 as planned. Actual sales by product are: White, B300,000; Fragrant, B180,000; and Loonzain, B270,000.

Required

1 Prepare a contribution profit and loss account for the month based on actual sales data. Present the profit and loss account in the format shown above.

2 Compute the break-even sales for the month based on your actual data.

3 Considering the fact that the company met its B750,000 sales budget for the month, the managing director is shocked at the results shown on your profit and loss account in Question 1 above. Prepare a brief memo for the MD explaining why both the operating results and break-even sales are different from what was budgeted.

P7–12 Basics of CVP analysis Time allowed: 20 minutes

Feather Friends Ltd makes a high-quality wooden birdhouse that sells for £20 per unit. Variable costs are £8 per unit, and fixed costs total £180,000 per year.

Required

Answer the following independent questions:

1 What is the product's CM ratio?

2 Use the CM ratio to determine the break-even point in sales pounds.

3 Due to an increase in demand, the company estimates that sales will increase by £75,000 during the next year. By how much should profit increase (or net loss decrease) assuming that fixed costs do not change?

4 Assume that the operating results for last year were:

Sales	£400,000
Less variable expenses	160,000
Contribution margin	240,000
Less fixed expenses	180,000
Profit	£60,000

(a) Compute the degree of operating leverage at the current level of sales.

(b) The MD expects sales to increase by 20% next year. By what percentage should profit increase?

5 Refer to the original data. Assume that the company sold 18,000 units last year. The sales manager is convinced that a 10% reduction in the selling price, combined with a £30,000 increase in advertising, would cause annual sales in units to increase by one-third. Prepare two contribution profit and loss accounts, one showing the results of last year's operations and one showing the results of operations if these changes are made. Would you recommend that the company do as the sales manager suggests?

6 Refer to the original data. Assume again that the company sold 18,000 units last year. The president does not want to change the selling price. Instead, he wants to increase the sales commission by £1 per unit. He thinks that this move, combined with some increase in advertising, would increase annual sales by 25%. By how much could advertising be increased with profits remaining unchanged? Do not prepare a profit and loss account; use the incremental analysis approach.

P7–13 The case of the elusive contribution margin Time allowed: 30 minutes

The Shirt Works sells a large variety of tee shirts and sweat shirts. Steve Hooper, the owner, is thinking of expanding his sales by hiring local high school students, on a commission basis, to sell sweat shirts bearing the name and mascot of the local high school.

These sweat shirts would have to be ordered from the manufacturer six weeks in advance, and they could not be returned because of the unique printing required. The sweat shirts would cost Mr Hooper £8 each with a minimum order of 75 sweat shirts. Any additional sweat shirts would have to be ordered in increments of 75.

Since Mr Hooper's plan would not require any additional facilities, the only costs associated with the project would be the costs of the sweat shirts and the costs of the sales commissions. The selling price of the sweat shirts would be £13.50 each. Mr Hooper would pay the students a commission of £1.50 for each shirt sold.

Required

1 To make the project worth while, Mr Hooper would require a £1,200 profit for the first three months of the venture. What level of sales in units and in pounds would be required to reach this target profit? Show all computations.

2 Assume that the venture is undertaken and an order is placed for 75 sweat shirts. What would be Mr Hooper's break-even point in units and in sales pounds? Show computations and explain the reasoning behind your answer.

P7–14 Interpretive questions on the CVP graph time allowed: 30 minutes

A CVP graph such as the one shown below is a useful technique for showing relationships between costs, volume and profits in an organization.

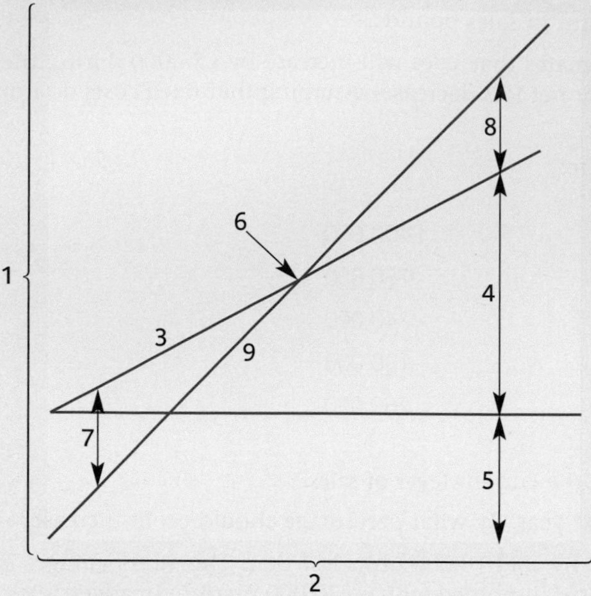

Required

1 Identify the numbered components in the CVP graph.

2 State the effect of each of the following actions on line 3, line 9, and the break-even point. For line 3 and line 9, state whether the action will cause the line to:

Remain unchanged
Shift upward
Shift downward
Have a steeper slope (i.e., rotate upwards)
Have a flatter slope (i.e., rotate downwards)
Shift upwards *and* have a steeper slope
Shift upwards *and* have a flatter slope
Shift downwards *and* have a steeper slope
Shift downwards *and* have a flatter slope.

In the case of the break-even point, state whether the action will cause the break-even point to:

Remain unchanged
Increase
Decrease
Probably change, but the direction is uncertain.

Treat each case independently.

(x) Example: fixed costs are reduced by £5,000 per period

Answer (see choices above): Line 3: Shift downwards

Line 9: remain unchanged

Break-even point: decrease

(a) The unit selling price is increased from £18 to £20.

(b) Unit variable costs are decreased from £12 to £10.

(c) Fixed costs are increased by £3,000 per period.

(d) Two thousand more units are sold during the period than were budgeted.

(e) Due to paying salespersons a commission rather than a flat salary, fixed costs are reduced by £8,000 per period and unit variable costs are increased by £3.

(f) Due to an increase in the cost of materials, both unit variable costs and the selling price are increased by £2.

(g) Advertising costs are increased by £10,000 per period, resulting in a 10% increase in the number of units sold.

(h) Due to automating an operation previously done by workers, fixed costs are increased by £12,000 per period and unit variable costs are reduced by £4.

P7–15 Sensitivity analysis of profit; changes in volume Time allowed: 30 minutes

Minden Company introduced a new product last year for which it is trying to find an optimal selling price. Marketing studies suggest that the company can increase sales by 5,000 units for each £2 reduction in the selling price. The company's present selling price is £70 per unit, and variable expenses are £40 per unit. Fixed expenses are £540,000 per year. The present annual sales volume (at the £70 selling price) is 15,000 units.

Required

1 What is the present yearly profit or loss?

2 What is the present break-even point in units and in pound sales?

3 Assuming that the marketing studies are correct, what is the maximum profit that the company can earn yearly? At how many units and at what selling price per unit would the company generate this profit?

4 What would be the break even point in units and in pound sales using the selling price you determined in Question 3 above (e.g., the selling price at the level of maximum profits)? Why is this break even point different from the break-even point you computed in Question 2 above?

P7–16 Graphing; incremental analysis; operating leverage Time allowed: 60 minutes

Angie Silva has recently opened The Sandal Shop in Brisbane, Australia, a store that specializes in fashionable sandals. Angie has just received a degree in business and she is anxious to apply the principles she has learned to her business. In time, she hopes to open a chain of sandal shops. As a first step, she has prepared the following analysis for her new store:

Sales price per pair of sandals	£40
Variable expenses per pair of sandals	16
Contribution margin per pair of sandals	£24
Fixed expenses per year:	
Building rental	£15,000
Equipment depreciation	7,000
Selling	20,000
Administrative	18,000
Total fixed expenses	£60,000

Required

1 How many pairs of sandals must be sold each year to break even? What does this represent in total pound sales?

2 Prepare a CVP graph for the store from a zero level of activity up to 5,000 pairs of sandals sold each year. Indicate the break-even point on your graph.

3 Angie has decided that she must earn at least £18,000 the first year to justify her time and effort. How many pairs of sandals must be sold to reach this target profit?

4 Angie now has two salespersons working in the store – one full time and one part time. It will cost her an additional £8,000 per year to convert the part-time position to a full-time position. Angie believes that the change would bring in an additional £25,000 in sales each year. Should she convert the position? Use the incremental approach (do not prepare a profit and loss account).

5 Refer to the original data. During the first year, the store sold only 3,000 pairs of sandals and reported the following operating results:

Sales (3,000 pairs)	£120,000
Less variable expenses	48,000
Contribution margin	72,000
Less fixed expenses	60,000
Profit	£12,000

(a) What is the store's degree of operating leverage?

(b) Angie is confident that with a more intense sales effort and with a more creative advertising programme she can increase sales by 50% next year. What would be the expected percentage increase in profit? Use the degree of operating leverage to compute your answer.

P7–17 Sales mix; commission structure; break-even point Time allowed: 60 minutes

Carbex Ltd produces cutlery sets out of high-quality wood and steel. The company makes a standard cutlery set and a deluxe set and sells them to retail department stores throughout the country. The standard set sells for £60, and the deluxe set sells for £75.

The variable expenses associated with each set are given below (in cost per set):

	Standard	Deluxe
Production costs	£15.00	£30.00
Sales commissions (15% of sales price)	9.00	11.25
The company's fixed		
Advertising	£105,000	
Depreciation	21,700	
Administrative	63,000	

Salespersons are paid on a commission basis to encourage them to be aggressive in their sales efforts. Mary Parsons, the financial vice president, watches sales commissions carefully and has noted that they have risen steadily over the last year. For this reason, she was shocked to find that even though sales have increased, profits for the current month – May – are down substantially from April. Sales, in sets, for the last two months are given below:

	Standard	Deluxe	Total
April	4,000	2,000	6,000
May	1,000	5,000	6,000

Required

1 Prepare a profit and loss account for April and a profit and loss account for May. Use the contribution format, with the following headings:

Standard		Deluxe		Total	
Amount	Percentage	Amount	Percentage	Amount	Percentage
Sales etc.					

Place the fixed expenses only in the Total column. Carry percentage computations to one decimal place. Do not show percentages for the fixed expenses.

2 Explain why there is a difference in profit between the two months, even though the same total number of sets was sold in each month.

3 What can be done to the sales commissions to optimize the sales mix?

4 (a) Using April's figures, what was the break-even point for the month in sales pounds?

(b) Has May's break-even point gone up or down from that of April? Explain your answer without calculating the break-even point for May.

P7–18 Various CVP questions: break-even point; cost structure; target sales Time allowed: 60 minutes

Northwood Company manufactures basketballs. The company has a standard ball that sells for £25. At present, the standard ball is manufactured in a small plant that relies heavily on direct labour workers. Thus, variable costs are high, totalling £15 per ball.

Last year, the company sold 30,000 standard balls, with the following results:

Sales (30,000 standard balls)	£750,000
Less variable expenses	450,000
Contribution margin	300,000
Less fixed expenses	210,000
Profit	£90,000

Required

1 Compute (a) the CM ratio and the break-even point in balls, and (b) the degree of operating leverage at last year's level of sales.

2 Due to an increase in labour rates, the company estimates that variable costs will increase by £3 per ball next year. If this change takes place and the selling price per ball remains constant at £25, what will be the new CM ratio and break-even point in balls?

3 Refer to the data in Question 2 above. If the expected change in variable costs takes place, how many balls will have to be sold next year to earn the same profit (£90,000) as last year?

4 Refer again to the data in Question 2 above. The managing director feels that the company must raise the selling price on the standard balls. If Northwood Company wants to maintain the same CM ratio as last year, what selling price per ball must it charge next year to cover the increased labour costs?

5 Refer to the original data. The company is discussing the construction of a new, automated plant to manufacture the standard balls. The new plant would slash variable costs per ball by 40%, but it would cause fixed costs to double in amount per year. If the new plant is built, what would be the company's new CM ratio and new break-even point in balls?

6 Refer to the data in Question 5 above.

(a) If the new plant is built, how many balls will have to be sold next year to earn the same profit (£90,000) as last year?

(b) Assume the new plant is built and that next year the company manufactures and sells 30,000 balls (the same number as sold last year). Prepare a contribution profit and loss account and compute the degree of operating leverage.

(c) If you were a member of top management, would you have voted in favour of constructing the new plant? Explain.

P7–19 Changing levels of fixed and variable costs Time allowed: 30 minutes

Neptune Company produces toys and other items for use in beach and resort areas. A small, inflatable toy has come onto the market that the company is anxious to produce and sell. Enough capacity exists in the company's plant to produce 16,000 units of the toy each month. Variable costs to manufacture and sell one unit would be £1.25, and fixed costs associated with the toy would total £35,000 per month.

The company's Marketing Department predicts that demand for the new toy will exceed the 16,000 units that the company is able to produce. Additional manufacturing space can be rented from another company at a fixed cost of £1,000 per month. Variable costs in the rented facility would total £1.40 per unit, due to somewhat less efficient operations than in the main plant. The new toy will sell for £3 per unit.

Required

1 Compute the monthly break-even point for the new toy in units and in total pound sales. Show all computations in good form.

2 How many units must be sold each month to make a monthly profit of £12,000?

3 If the sales manager receives a bonus of 10 pence for each unit sold in excess of the break-even point, how many units must be sold each month to earn a return of 25% on the monthly investment in fixed costs?

P7–20 Changes in cost structure Time allowed: 60 minutes

Morton Company's profit and loss account for last month is given below:

Sales (15,000 units × £30)	£450,000
Less variable expenses	315,000
Contribution margin	135,000
Less fixed expenses	90,000
Profit	£45,000

The industry in which Morton Company operates is quite sensitive to cyclical movements in the economy. Thus, profits vary considerably from year to year according to general economic conditions. The company has a large amount of unused capacity and is studying ways of improving profits.

Required

1 New equipment has come onto the market that would allow Morton Company to automate a portion of its operations. Variable costs would be reduced by £9 per unit. However, fixed costs would increase to a total of £225,000 each month. Prepare two contribution-type profit and loss accounts, one showing present operations and one showing how operations would appear if the new equipment is purchased. Show an Amount column, a Per Unit column, and a Percentage column on each statement. Do not show percentages for the fixed costs.

2 Refer to the profit and loss accounts in Question 1 above. For both present operations and the proposed new operations, compute (a) the degree of operating leverage, (b) the break-even point in pounds, and (c) the margin of safety in both pound and percentage terms.

3 Refer again to the data in Question 1 above. As a manager, what factor would be paramount in your mind in deciding whether to purchase the new equipment? (You may assume that ample funds are available to make the purchase.)

4 Refer to the original data. Rather than purchase new equipment, the president is thinking about changing the company's marketing method. Under the new method, sales would increase by 20% each month and profit would increase by one-third. Fixed costs could be slashed to only £48,000 per month. Compute the break-even point for the company after the change in marketing method.

Cases

CASE

C7–21 Cost structure; break-even; target profits Time allowed: 75 minutes

Pittman Company is a small but growing manufacturer of telecommunications equipment. The company has no sales force of its own; rather, it relies completely on independent sales agents to market its products. These agents are paid a commission of 15% of selling price for all items sold.

Barbara Cheney, Pittman's controller, has just prepared the company's budgeted profit and loss account for next year. The statement follows:

As Barbara handed the statement to Karl Vecci, Pittman's managing director, she commented, 'I went ahead and used the agents' 15% commission rate in completing these statements, but we've just learned that they refuse to handle our products next year unless we increase the commission rate to 20%.'

'That's the last straw,' Karl replied angrily. 'Those agents have been demanding more and more, and this time they've gone too far. How can they possibly defend a 20% commission rate?'

'They claim that after paying for advertising, travel and the other costs of promotion, there's nothing left over for profit,' replied Barbara.

'I say it's just plain robbery,' retorted Karl. 'And I also say it's time we dumped those guys and got our own sales force. Can you get your people to work up some cost figures for us to look at?'

'We've already worked them up,' said Barbara. 'Several companies we know about pay a 7.5% commission to their own salespeople, along with a small salary. Of course, we would have to handle all promotion costs, too. We figure our fixed costs would increase by £2,400,000 per year, but that would be more than offset by the £3,200,000 (20% × £16,000,000) that we would avoid on agents' commissions.'

Pittman Company
Budgeted profit and loss account
For the year ended 31 December

Sales		£16,000,000
Manufacturing costs:		
Variable	£7,200,000	
Fixed overhead	2,340,000	9,540,000
Gross margin		6,460,000
Selling and administrative costs:		
Commissions to agents	2,400,000	
Fixed marketing costs	120,000*	
Fixed administrative costs	1,800,000	4,320,000
Net profit		2,140,000
Less fixed interest cost		540,000
Income before income taxes		1,600,000
Less income taxes (30%)		480,000
Profit		£1,120,000

* Primarily depreciation on storage facilities.

The breakdown of the £2,400,000 cost figure follows:

Salaries:	
Sales manager	£100,000
Salespersons	600,000
Travel and entertainment	400,000
Advertising	1,300,000
Total	£2,400,000

'Super,' replied Karl. 'And I note that the £2,400,000 is just what we're paying the agents under the old 15% commission rate.'

'It's even better than that,' explained Barbara. 'We can actually save £75,000 a year because that's what we're having to pay the auditing firm now to check out the agents' reports. So our overall administrative costs would be less.'

'Pull all of these numbers together and we'll show them to the executive committee tomorrow,' said Karl. 'With the approval of the committee, we can move on the matter immediately.'

Required

1 Compute Pittman Company's break-even point in sales pounds for next year assuming:
   - **(a)** That the agents' commission rate remains unchanged at 15%
   - **(b)** That the agents' commission rate is increased to 20%
   - **(c)** That the company employs its own sales force.

2 Assume that Pittman Company decides to continue selling through agents and pays the 20% commission rate. Determine the volume of sales that would be required to generate the same profit as contained in the budgeted profit and loss account for next year.

3 Determine the volume of sales at which profit would be equal regardless of whether Pittman Company sells through agents (at a 20% commission rate) or employs its own sales force.

4 Compute the degree of operating leverage that the company would expect to have on 31 December at the end of next year assuming:
   - **(a)** That the agents' commission rate remains unchanged at 15%
   - **(b)** That the agents' commission rate is increased to 20%
   - **(c)** That the company employs its own sales force.

   Use income before income taxes in your operating leverage computation.

5 Based on the data in Questions 1–4 above, make a recommendation as to whether the company should continue to use sales agents (at a 20% commission rate) or employ its own sales force. Give reasons for your answer.

(*CMA*, adapted)

C7–22 Detailed profit and loss account; CVP sensitivity analysis Time allowed: 60 minutes

The most recent profit and loss account for Whitney Company appears below:

Whitney Company
Profit and loss account
For the year ended 31 December

Sales (45,000 units at £10)		£450,000
Less cost of goods sold:		
Direct materials	£90,000	
Direct labour	78,300	
Manufacturing overhead	98,500	266,800
Gross margin	183,200	
Less operating expenses:		
Selling expenses:		
Variable:		
Sales commissions	£27,000	
Shipping	5,400	32,400
Fixed (advertising, salaries)	120,000	
Administrative:		
Variable (billing and other)	1,800	
Fixed (salaries and other)	48,000	202,200
Net loss		£(19,000)

All variable expenses in the company vary in terms of unit sold, except for sales commissions, which are based on sales pounds. Variable manufacturing overhead is 30 pence per unit. There were no beginning or ending inventories. Whitney Company's plant has a capacity of 75,000 units per year.

The company has been operating at a loss for several years. Management is studying several possible courses of action to determine what should be done to make next year profitable.

Required

1 Redo Whitney Company's profit and loss account in the contribution format. Show both a Total column and a Per Unit column on your statement. Leave enough space to the right of your numbers to enter the solution to both parts of Question 2 below.

2 The managing director is considering two proposals prepared by members of his staff:

(a) For next year, the operating manager would like to reduce the unit selling price by 20%. She is certain that this would fill the plant to capacity.

(b) For next year, the sales manager would like to increase the unit selling price by 20%, increase the sales commission to 9% of sales, and increase advertising by £100,000. Based on marketing studies, he is confident this would increase unit sales by one-third.

Prepare two contribution profit and loss accounts, one showing what profits would be under the operating manager's proposal and one showing what profits would be under the sales manager's proposal. On each statement, include both Total and Per Unit columns (do not show per unit data for the fixed costs).

3 Refer to the original data. The managing director believes it would be a mistake to change the unit selling price. Instead, he wants to use less costly materials in manufacturing units of product, thereby reducing unit costs by 70 pence. How many units would have to be sold next year to earn a target profit of £30,200?

4 Refer to the original data. Whitney Company's board of directors believes that the company's problem lies in inadequate promotion. By how much can advertising be increased and still allow the company to earn a target return of 4.5% on sales of 60,000 units?

5 Refer to the original data. The company has been approached by an overseas distributor who wants to purchase 9,500 units on a special price basis. There would be no sales commission on these units. However, shipping costs would be increased by 50% and variable administrative costs would be reduced by 25%. In addition, a £5,700 special insurance fee would have to be paid by Whitney Company to protect the goods in transit. What unit price would have to be quoted on the 9,500 units by Whitney Company to allow the company to earn a profit of £14,250 on total operations? Regular business would not be disturbed by this special order.

C7–23 Individual product break evens in a multiproduct company Time allowed: 60 minutes
Cheryl Montoya picked up the phone and called her boss, Wes Chan, the director of marketing at Piedmont Fasteners Corporation: 'Wes, I'm not sure how to go about answering the questions that came up at the meeting with the CEO yesterday.'

'What's the problem?'

'The CEO wanted to know each product's break even, but I am having trouble figuring them out.'

'I'm sure you can handle it, Cheryl. And, by the way, I need your analysis on my desk tomorrow morning at 8:00 sharp in time for the follow-up meeting at 9:00.'

Piedmont Fasteners Corporation makes three different clothing fasteners in its manufacturing facility in Birmingham. Data concerning these products appear below:

	Velcro	Metal	Nylon
Normal annual sales volume	100,000	200,000	400,000
Unit selling price	£1.65	£1.50	£0.85
Variable cost per unit	£1.25	£0.70	£0.25

Total fixed expenses are £400,000 per year.

All three products are sold in highly competitive markets, so the company is unable to raise its prices without losing unacceptable numbers of customers.

The company has an extremely effective just-in-time manufacturing system, so there are no beginning or ending work in progress or finished goods inventories.

Required

1 What is the company's overall break-even in total sales?

2 Of the total fixed costs of £400,000, £20,000 could be avoided if the Velcro product were dropped, £80,000 if the Metal product were dropped, and £60,000 if the Nylon product were dropped. The remaining fixed costs of £240,000 consist of common fixed costs such as administrative salaries and rent on the factory building that could be avoided only by going out of business entirely.

(a) What is the break-even quantity of each product?

(b) If the company sells exactly the break-even quantity of each product, what will be the overall profit of the company?

C7–24 Break-even analysis Time allowed: 60 minutes
Peter Wilkinson owns and manages The Three Tuns Hotel in Reigate. Peter recently bought the hotel for £700,000 and then spent a further £800,000 on renovations, fixtures, fittings and equipment. The hotel has 60 twin-bedded rooms, a bar restaurant, and a leisure facility which is available free for use by hotel guests.

Peter estimates the costs of operating the hotel over a year as follows:

Business rates	£160,000
Maintenance and repairs	25,000
Depreciation of fixtures, fittings and equipment	60,000
Salaries – assistant managers, bar/restaurant and facilities managers	150,000
Wages – full-time staff	140,000
Electricity and utilities	
(includes average variable cost of £1 per guest per night)	67,000
Administration	
(includes average variable cost of £2 per guest per night)	114,000
Advertising	40,000
Part-time reception, bar, kitchen and housekeeping staff	
(average variable cost per guest per night)	5
Other costs (average variable cost per guest per night)	1

Rooms are let on a half-board basis and the average variable cost per meal served is :

Breakfast	£3
Evening meal	£8

Required

1 Determine the maximum possible number of 'guest nights' that the hotel can accommodate (a) per year, (b) per week, and (c) per night (assume a 50-week year and twin-bedded occupation).

2 Identify which costs of operating the hotel you would recognize as:

(a) fixed costs

(b) variable costs and

(c) semi-variable costs.

3 Determine the total fixed costs of operating the hotel for a period of one year.

4 Determine the variable cost per 'guest night'.

5 Peter operates a standard charge of £40 per 'guest night', and on average each guest generates a further £5 per night in net income from spending at the bar. Determine the number of bookings required to achieve break-even: (a) over the year, and (b) per night. What percentage occupancy does this represent?

6 Sketch a diagram to illustrate a break-even position over a full year.

7 Assume that during the year Peter's hotel averaged 70% guest capacity. How much profit in total did the hotel make over a full year? What 'margin of safety' does this occupancy represent?

8 If Peter requires a 10% return on capital employed/return on investment (ROCE/ROI), determine the number of bookings required per year to achieve this target return.

9 Assume that weekdays Peter introduces a 'business user' tariff of £50 per 'person night' and as a result, during the weekdays his hotel has 90% room occupancy, but on the basis of 1 guest per room. On a weekend he proposes a special tariff of £30 per person and anticipates a 75% room occupancy per night, but on the basis of 2 guests per room. Would you recommend that Peter pursue this price discrimination proposal?

10 What alternative pricing and promotion strategies could you suggest Peter consider to raise the profit profile of his hotel?

(With thanks to Bill Hughill, University of Kent)

C7-25 Break-even, product mix. Time allowed 50 minutes.

Home Trends sells kitchenware, wooden flooring and cane furniture at a single store location in trendy Kinvara, Co. Galway, mainly to customers living in apartments, townhouses and holiday homes. With regard to cane furniture, rapidly changing consumer taste in furniture has seen a decline in sales and rising inward transportation costs from the Far East causing larger order quantities to be purchased with ensuing problems in finding space for slow-moving stock have depressed margins. Recent figures for the last quarter were:

	Kitchenware Department	Wooden flooring Department	Cane Furniture Department	Total
	€	€	€	€
Sales	120,000	170,000	150,000	440,000
Variable costs	(72,000)	(109,000)	(90,000)	(271,000)
Separable fixed costs (staffing, display units and stock-holding costs, excluding central costs)	(30,000)	(40,000)	(95,000)	(165,000)
Total costs	(102,000)	(149,000)	(185,000)	(436,000)
Departmental profits	18,000	21,000	(35,000)	4,000
Advertising				(2,000)
Part-time accounts				(15,000)
Total operating profit/(loss)				(13,000)

Management are evaluating whether to drop cane furniture because of changing consumer trends and accompanying losses and replace it with a selection of artisan products, made by the local community. If the cane line is dropped, the following changes are expected to occur:

(a) The vacated space will be remodelled at a cost of €2,500 and some of this space will be devoted to artisan gift products, made by the local community. These products are expected to generate extra sales revenues of €25,000 and an incremental contribution (before remodelling cost) of €15,000 per annum.

(b) The remaining vacated space will be given to some new product ranges in wooden flooring and more space for customers to walk around the display stands. These changes are expected to increase sales of wooden flooring by €35,000, and the line's overall average contribution to sales ratio will rise by 5% on all sales.

(c) Home Trends will save 70% of the separable fixed costs of cane furniture (not counting the remodelling cost), having been replaced with new artisan products which are small, require less floor space, cheaper display and junior sales staff. The separable fixed costs of kitchenware and wooden flooring will continue to be incurred at the same level.

(d) The firm will increase advertising expenditures by €2,500 to promote the artisan products.

Required

1 Draft a report to the commercial director of Home Trends giving your calculations and recommendations for the following questions:

(a) Should Home Trends close its cane furniture department? Show your relevant costing calculations and state your advice.

(b) Compute the weighted average break-even point, for the existing three product lines. Compute the new weighted average break-even point with the new total sales revenues of €350,000 and the substitution of €25,000 sales of artisan products and an extra €35,000 of sales from new wooden floor lines, into the overall mix. Interpret this information for the commercial director.

(c) Irrespective of whether the cane furniture department is closed or not, management are considering providing a 'mornings only' interior design consultant. A new studio would be set up in the foyer of the store; a van with a logo would be hired for home visits, some new display fixtures would be installed. The total cost of running the interior design consultancy would be a mixed cost. The consultation fee is projected at €75 per hour per customer (per service unit) for the next month. The sales and associated total costs of the service projected for the next month are as follows:-

Projected interior design consultation hours sold per month	40	50	60	70
Average mixed cost per consultation hour	€39.25	€33	€28.83	€25.857
Consultation fee per customer hour	€75			

2 Use the high–low method to estimate the cost equation for the interior design service. Compute the projected break-even point for the interior design service and the total profit from 50 consultations (most likely level) for the next month. Advise the management on this proposed development.

(With thanks to Dr R. Mattimoe, Dublin City University Business School)

Endnotes

1 Wilke (1994).

2 See Lord (1995) for an extensive discussion of the impact of cost structure on the degree of operating leverage.

Chapter 8
Activity-based costing

Learning objectives

After studying Chapter 8, you should be able to:

1. Explain the major differences between activity-based costing and a traditional costing system
2. Distinguish between unit-level, batch-level, product-level, customer-level, and organization-sustaining activities
3. Assign costs to cost pools using a first-stage allocation
4. Compute activity rates for cost pools and explain how they can be used to target process improvements
5. Assign costs to a cost object using a second-stage allocation
6. Prepare a report showing activity-based costing product margins from an activity view
7. Prepare an action analysis report using activity-based costing data and interpret the report
8. Understand why activity-based costing is particularly suitable for service-providing companies
9. Use the simplified approach to compute activity-based costs and margins

Concepts in Context

As well as costing products more accurately, activity-based costing offers a way of assessing customer profitability by analysing the huge chunk of overhead and non-manufacturing costs that traditional cost systems can struggle to measure. Take, for example, a large consumer goods manufacturer that has two distinct customer segments – major multiple/superstores and corner shop independents. The gross margins are good in the independent sector but the costs of service make the true profitability much lower than in the multiples. Why? With multiples there are a small number of large orders, a small number of drop points at the multiples' own distribution centres, and transactions are expedited electronically through EDI links. In contrast, the independents are served 'by an army of direct sales forces, each generating thousands of small paper-based orders ... [D]elivery goes to thousands of drop-off points ... payment is often by cheque (inefficient and expensive to handle) and payment is frequently late'.[1]

The cost accounting systems described in Chapters 2, 3 and 4 were designed primarily to provide unit product costs for external reporting purposes. Variable costing, which was described in Chapters 5 and 6, is intended to provide managers with product cost and other information for decisions that do not affect fixed costs and capacity. Recently, there has been tremendous interest in activity-based costing. **Activity-based costing (ABC)** is a costing method that is designed to provide managers with cost information for strategic and other decisions that potentially affect capacity and therefore 'fixed' costs. Activity-based costing is also used as an element of activity-based management, an approach to management that focuses on activities.

In practice, there are many 'flavours' of activity-based costing. Consultants emphasize different aspects of activity-based costing, and companies interpret activity-based costing differently. Since so much variation occurs in practice, we focus our attention in this chapter on what we consider to be 'the best practice' – those techniques that provide managers with the most useful information for making strategic decisions. We will assume that the ABC system is used as a supplement to, rather than as a replacement for, the company's formal cost accounting system. The cost accounting methods described in Chapters 2, 3 and 4 would continue to be used to determine product costs for external financial reports. Activity-based costing would be used to determine product and other costs for special management reports. To keep the discussion simple, we gloss over some of the relatively unimportant details that can add enormously to the complexity of activity-based costing. Even so, you are likely to find this chapter especially challenging.

In the traditional cost accounting systems described in Chapters 2, 3 and 4, the objective is to properly value stocks and cost of goods sold for external financial reports. In activity-based costing, the objective is to understand overhead and the profitability of products and customers. As a consequence of these differences in objectives, 'best practice' activity-based costing differs in a number of ways from traditional cost accounting.

In activity-based costing:

1 Non-manufacturing as well as manufacturing costs may be assigned to products
2 Some manufacturing costs may be excluded from product costs
3 There are a number of overhead cost pools, each of which is allocated to products and other costing objects using its own unique measure of activity
4 The allocation bases often differ from those used in traditional costing systems
5 The overhead rates, or *activity rates*, may be based on the level of activity at capacity rather than on the budgeted level of activity.

As we will see later in the chapter, these differences from traditional cost accounting systems can have dramatic impacts on the apparent costs of products and the profitability of products and customers. But first, we will briefly discuss the reasons for these departures from traditional cost accounting practices.

How costs are treated under activity-based costing

Non-manufacturing costs and activity-based costing

In traditional cost accounting, only manufacturing costs are assigned to products. Selling, general and administrative expenses are treated as period expenses and are not assigned to products. However, many of these non-manufacturing costs are also part of the costs of producing, selling, distributing and servicing products. For example, commissions paid to salespersons, shipping costs and warranty repair costs can easily be traced to individual products. To determine the profitability of products and services, such non-manufacturing costs are assigned to products in activity-based costing.

Manufacturing costs and activity-based costing

In traditional cost accounting, *all* manufacturing costs are assigned to products – even manufacturing costs that are not caused by the products. For example, a portion of the factory security guard's wages would be allocated to each product even though the guard's wages are totally unaffected by which products are made or not made during a period. In activity-based costing, a cost is assigned to a product only if there is good reason to believe that the cost would be affected by decisions concerning the product.

Plantwide overhead rate

Our discussion in Chapter 3 assumed that a single overhead rate, called a *plantwide overhead* rate, was being used throughout an entire factory and that the allocation base was direct labour-hours or machine-hours. This simple approach to overhead assignment can result in distorted unit product costs when it is used for decision-making purposes.

When cost systems were developed in the 1800s, direct labour was a larger component of product costs than it is today. Data relating to direct labour were readily available and convenient to use, and managers believed there was a high positive correlation between direct labour and overhead costs. (A positive correlation between two things means that they tend to move in tandem.) Consequently, direct labour was a useful allocation base for overhead.

However, a plantwide overhead rate based on direct labour may no longer be satisfactory. First, in many companies, direct labour may no longer be highly correlated with (i.e., move in tandem with) overhead costs. Second, because of the large variety of activities encompassed in overhead, no single allocation base may be able to reflect adequately the demands that products place on overhead resources.

On an economy-wide basis, direct labour and overhead costs have been moving in opposite directions for a long time. As a percentage of total cost, direct labour has been declining, whereas overhead has been increasing.[2] Many tasks that used to be done by hand are now done with largely automated equipment – a component of overhead. Furthermore, product diversity has increased. Companies are creating new products and services at an ever-accelerating rate that differ in volume, batch size and complexity. Managing and sustaining this product diversity requires many more overhead resources such as production schedulers and product design engineers, and many of these overhead resources have no obvious connection with direct labour.

Nevertheless, direct labour remains a viable base for applying overhead to products in many companies – particularly for external reports. In some companies there is still a high positive correlation between overhead costs and direct labour. And most companies throughout the world continue to base overhead allocations on direct labour or machine-hours. However, in those instances in which overhead costs do not move in tandem with direct labour, some other means of assigning costs must be found or product costs will be distorted. Furthermore, in service industries activity-based costing offers the chance to understand those product and customer costs which were not measured under traditional costing systems.[3]

Departmental overhead rates

Rather than use a plantwide overhead rate, many companies use departmental overhead rates. The allocation bases used in these departmental overhead rates depend on the nature of the work performed in each department. For example, overhead costs in a machining department may be allocated on the basis of the machine-hours in that department. In contrast, the overhead costs in an assembly department may be allocated on the basis of direct labour-hours in that department.

Unfortunately, even departmental overhead rates will not correctly assign overhead costs in situations where a company has a range of products that differ in volume, batch size or complexity of production.[4] This is because the departmental approach usually relies on volume as the factor in allocating overhead cost to products. For example, if the machining department's overhead is applied to products on the basis of machine-hours, it is assumed that the department's overhead costs are caused by, and are directly proportional to, machine-hours. However, the department's overhead costs are probably more complex than this and are caused by a variety of factors, including the range of products processed in the department, the number of batch set-ups that are required, the complexity of the products, and so on. Activity-based costing is a technique that is designed to reflect these diverse factors more accurately when costing products. It attempts to accomplish this goal by identifying the major *activities* such as batch set-ups, purchase order processing and so on, that consume overhead resources. An **activity** is any event that causes the consumption of overhead resources. The costs of carrying out these activities are assigned to the products that cause the activities.

The costs of idle capacity in activity-based costing

In traditional cost accounting, predetermined overhead rates are computed by dividing budgeted overhead costs by a measure of budgeted activity such as budgeted direct labour-hours. This practice results in applying the costs of unused, or idle, capacity to products, and it results in unstable unit product costs as discussed in Chapter 3. If budgeted activity falls, the overhead rate increases because the fixed components of overhead are spread over a smaller base, resulting in increased unit product costs.

In contrast to traditional cost accounting, activity-based costing means that products are charged for the costs of capacity they use – not for the costs of capacity they don't use. In other words, the costs of idle capacity are not charged to products. This results in more stable unit costs and is consistent with the objective of assigning only those costs to products that are actually caused by the products.

Designing an activity-based costing (ABC) system

Experts agree on several essential characteristics of any successful implementation of activity-based costing. First, the initiative to implement activity-based costing must be strongly supported by top management. Second, the design and implementation of an ABC system should be the responsibility of a cross-functional team rather than of the accounting department. The team should include representatives from each area that will use the data provided by the ABC system. Ordinarily, this would include representatives from marketing, production, engineering and top management as well as technically trained accounting staff. Sometimes an outside consultant who specializes in activity-based costing acts as an adviser to the team.

The reason for insisting on strong top-management support and a multifunction team approach is rooted in the fact that it is difficult to implement changes in organizations unless those changes have the full support of those who are affected. Activity-based costing changes 'the rules of the game' since it changes some of the key measures that managers use for their decision-making and for evaluating individuals' performance. Unless the managers who are directly affected by the changes in the rules have a say, there will inevitably be resistance. In addition, designing a good ABC system requires intimate knowledge of many parts of the organization's overall operations. This knowledge can only come from the people who are familiar with those operations.

Top managers must support the initiative for two reasons. First, without leadership from top management, some managers may not see any reason to change. Second, if top managers do not support the ABC system and continue to play the game by the old rules, their subordinates will quickly get the message and abandon the ABC system. Time after time, when accountants have attempted to implement an ABC system on their own without top-management support and active co-operation from other managers, the results have been ignored.

Management accounting in action: the issue

Classic Brass Ltd makes finely machined brass fittings for a variety of applications including stanchions, cleats and helms for luxury yachts. The CEO of the company, John Towers, recently attended a management conference at which activity-based costing was discussed. Following the conference, he called a meeting of top managers in the company to discuss what he had learned. Attending the meeting were the production manager Susan Ritcher, the marketing manager Tom Olafson and the accounting manager Mary Goodman.

John: I'm glad we could all get together this morning. The conference I have just attended dealt with some issues that we have all been wondering about for some time.

Susan: Did anyone at the conference explain why my equipment always breaks down at the worst possible moment?

John: Sorry Susan, I suppose it must be bad karma or something.

Tom: Did the conference tell you why we've been losing all those bids lately on our high-volume routine work?

John: Tom, you probably weren't expecting this answer, but, yes, there may be a simple reason why we've been losing those bids.

Tom: Let me guess. We've been losing the bids because we have more competition.

John: Yes, the competition has a lot to do with it. But Tom, we may have been shooting ourselves in the foot.

Tom: What do you mean? I don't know about anyone else, but my salespeople have been busting their guts to get more business for the company.

Susan: Wait a minute, Tom, my production people have been turning in tremendous improvements in defect rates, on-time delivery, and so on.

John: Whoa everybody. Calm down. I don't think anyone is to blame for losing the bids. Tom, when you talk with our customers, what reasons do they give for taking their business to our competitors? Is it a problem with the quality of our products or our on-time delivery?

Tom: No, they don't have any problem with our products or with our service – our customers readily admit we're among the best in the business.

Susan: Too right!

John: Then what's the problem?

Tom: Price. The competition is undercutting our prices on the high-volume work.

John: Why are our prices too high?

Tom: Our prices aren't too high. Theirs are too low. Our competitors must be pricing below their cost.

John: Tom, why do you think that?

Tom: Well, if we charged the prices on high-volume work that our competitors are quoting, we'd be pricing below our cost, and I know we are just as efficient as any competitor.

Susan: Tom, why would our competitors price below their cost?

Tom: They are out to grab market share.

Susan: Does that make any sense? What good does more market share do if they are pricing below their cost?

John: I think Susan has a point, Tom. Mary, you're the expert with the numbers. Can you suggest another explanation?

Mary: I was afraid you would ask that. Those unit product cost figures in our department reports to you are primarily intended to be used to value stocks and determine cost of goods sold for our external financial statements. I am awfully uncomfortable about using them for bidding. In fact, I have mentioned this several times, but no one was interested.

John: Now I'm interested. Mary, are you telling us that the product cost figures we have been using for bidding are wrong? Perhaps the competition isn't pricing below our cost – we just don't know what our cost is?

Mary: Yes, that could be the problem. I just wish someone had listened earlier.

John: Does everyone agree with Mary that this is a problem we should work on?

Tom: Sure, if it means we can win more bids.

John: Okay, I want each of you to appoint one of your top people to a special team to investigate how we cost products.

Susan: Isn't this something Mary can handle with her staff?

John: Perhaps she could, but you know more about your operations than she does and besides, I want to make sure you agree with the results of the study and use them. Mary, do you agree?

Mary: Absolutely.

After studying the existing cost accounting system at Classic Brass and reviewing articles in professional and trade journals, the special team decided to implement an activity-based costing (ABC) system. Like most other ABC implementations, the new ABC system would supplement, rather than replace, the existing cost accounting system, which would continue to be used for external financial reports.

The new ABC system would be used to prepare special reports for management decisions such as bidding for new business. The accounting manager drew the chart appearing in Exhibit 8.1 to explain the general structure of the ABC model. In activity-based costing it is assumed that cost objects such as products generate activities. For example, a customer order for a brass spittoon generates a production order, which is an activity. It is further assumed that activities consume resources. For example, a production order uses a sheet of paper and takes time for a manager to fill out. And it is assumed that consumption of resources leads to costs. The greater the number of sheets used to fill out production orders and the greater the amount of time devoted to filling out such orders, the greater the cost. Activity-based costing attempts to trace through these relationships to identify how products and customers affect costs.

8.1 EXHIBIT

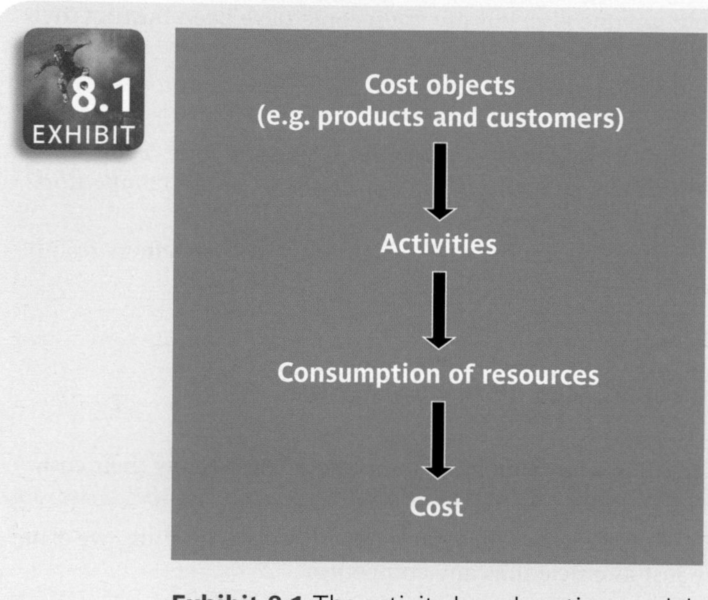

Exhibit 8.1 The activity-based costing model

As in most other companies, the ABC team at Classic Brass felt that the company's traditional cost accounting system adequately measures the *direct material* and *direct labour* costs of products. Therefore, the ABC study would be concerned solely with the other costs of the company – *manufacturing overhead* and *selling, general* and *administrative costs*.

The team felt it was important to plan carefully how it would go about implementing the new ABC system at Classic Brass. Accordingly, the implementation process was broken down into the following six basic steps:

1. Identify and define activities and activity pools
2. Wherever possible, directly trace costs to activities and cost objects
3. Assign costs to activity cost pools
4. Calculate activity rates
5. Assign costs to cost objects using the activity rates and activity measures
6. Prepare management reports.

Identifying activities to include in the ABC system

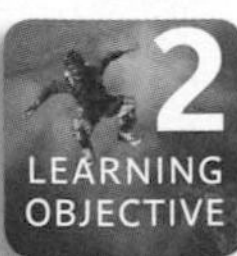

The first major step in implementing an ABC system is to identify the activities that will form the foundation for the system. This can be difficult, time-consuming and involves a great deal of judgement. A common procedure is for the individuals on the ABC implementation team to interview everyone – or at least all supervisors and managers – in overhead departments and ask them to describe their major activities. Ordinarily, this results in a very long list of activities. The length of such lists of activities poses a problem. On the one hand, the greater the number of activities tracked in the ABC system, the more accurate the costs are likely to be. On the other hand, it is costly to design, implement, maintain and use a complex system involving large numbers of activities. Consequently, the original lengthy list of activities is usually reduced to a handful by combining similar activities. For example, several actions may be involved in handling and moving raw materials – from receiving raw materials on the loading dock to sorting them into the appropriate bins in the storeroom. All of these activities might be combined into a single activity called material handling.

A useful way to think about activities and how to combine them is to organize them into five general levels: **unit-level**, **batch-level**, **product-level**, **customer-level**, and **organization-sustaining activities**. These levels are described as follows:[4]

1 **Unit-level activities** are performed each time a unit is produced. The costs of unit-level activities should be proportional to the number of units produced. For example, providing power to run processing equipment would be a unit-level activity since power tends to be consumed in proportion to the number of units produced.

2 **Batch-level activities** are performed each time a batch is handled or processed, regardless of how many units are in the batch. For example, tasks such as placing purchase orders, setting up equipment and arranging for shipments to customers are batch-level activities. They are incurred each time there is a batch (or a customer order). Costs at the batch level depend on the number of batches processed rather than on the number of units produced, the number of units sold or other measures of volume. For example, the cost of setting up a machine for batch processing is the same regardless of whether the batch contains one or 5,000 items.

3 **Product-level activities** relate to specific products and typically must be carried out regardless of how many batches are run or units of product are produced or sold. For example, activities such as designing a product, advertising a product and maintaining a product manager and staff are all product-level activities.

4 **Customer-level activities** relate to specific customers and include activities such as sales calls, catalogue mailings and general technical support that are not tied to any specific product.

5 **Organization-sustaining activities** are carried out regardless of which customers are served, which products are produced, how many batches are run, or how many units are made. This category includes activities such as cleaning executive offices, providing a computer network, arranging for loans, preparing annual reports to shareholders, and so on.

When combining activities in an ABC system, activities should be grouped together at the appropriate level. Batch-level activities should not be combined with unit-level activities or product-level activities with batch-level activities and so on. In general, it is best to combine only those activities that are highly correlated with each other within a level. Activities are correlated with each other if they tend to move in tandem. For example, the number of customer orders received is likely to be highly correlated with the number of completed customer orders shipped, so these two batch-level activities (receiving and shipping orders) can usually be combined with little loss of accuracy.

At Classic Brass, the ABC team, in consultation with top managers, selected the following *activity cost pools* and *activity measures*.

Activity cost pools at Classic Brass

Activity cost pool	Activity measure
Customer orders	Number of customer orders
Product design	Number of product designs
Order size	Machine-hours
Customer relations	Number of active customers
Other	Not applicable

An **activity cost pool** is a 'bucket' in which costs are accumulated that relate to a single activity in the ABC system. For example, the Customer Orders cost pool will be assigned all costs of resources that are consumed by taking and processing customer orders, including costs of processing paperwork and any costs involved in setting up machines. The measure of activity for this cost pool is simply the number of customer orders received. This is a batch-level activity, since each order generates work that occurs regardless of whether the order is for one unit or 1,000 units. The number of customer orders received is an example of an *activity measure*. An **activity measure** is an allocation base in an activity-based costing system.

The Product Design cost pool will be assigned all costs of resources consumed by designing products. The activity measure for this cost pool is the number of products designed. This is a product-level activity, since the amount of design work on a new product does not depend on the number of units ultimately ordered or batches ultimately run.

The Order Size cost pool will be assigned all costs of resources consumed as a consequence of the number of units produced, including the costs of miscellaneous factory supplies, power to run machines, and some equipment depreciation. This is a unit-level activity since each unit requires some of these resources. The activity measure for this cost pool is machine-hours.

The Customer Relations cost pool will be assigned all costs associated with maintaining relations with customers, including the costs of sales calls and the costs of entertaining customers. The activity measure for this cost pool is the number of customers the company has on its active customer list.

The Other cost pool will be assigned all overhead costs that are not associated with customer orders, product design, the size of the orders, or customer relations. These costs mainly consist of organization-sustaining costs and the costs of unused, idle capacity. These costs *will not* be assigned to products since they represent resources that are *not* consumed by products.

It is unlikely that any other company would use exactly the same activity cost pools and activities as those selected by Classic Brass. Because of the amount of judgement involved, there is considerable variation in the number and definitions of the activity cost pools and activity measures used by companies.

The mechanics of activity-based costing

After the ABC system had been designed, the team was ready to begin the process of actually computing the costs of products, customers and other objects of interest.

Tracing overhead costs to activities and cost objects

The second step in implementing an ABC system is to directly trace as many overhead costs as possible to the ultimate cost objects. At Classic Brass, the ultimate cost objects are products, customer orders, and customers. The company's manufacturing overhead and selling, general and administrative costs are listed in Exhibit 8.2. In the ABC system at Classic Brass all of these costs are considered to be 'overhead' and will be assigned to cost objects as appropriate.

One of these overhead costs – shipping – can be traced directly to customer orders. Classic Brass is directly billed for each customer order it ships, so it is a simple matter to trace these costs to the customer orders. Customers do not pay these actual shipping costs; instead they pay a standard shipping charge that can differ substantially from the actual bill that Classic Brass receives from the freight company.

No other overhead costs could be directly traced to products, customer orders, or customers. Consequently, the remainder of the overhead costs would be assigned to cost objects using the ABC system.

Assigning costs to activity cost pools

3 LEARNING OBJECTIVE

Most overhead costs are originally classified in the company's basic accounting system according to the departments in which they are incurred. For example, salaries, supplies, rent, and so forth, incurred by the marketing department are charged to that department. In some cases, some or all of these costs can be directly traced to one of the activity cost pools in the ABC system, which is the third step in implementing activity-based costing. For example, if the ABC system has an activity called *purchase order processing*, then all of the costs of the purchasing department could probably be traced to that activity. To the extent possible, costs should be traced directly to the activity cost pools. However, it is quite common for an overhead department to be involved in several of the activities that are tracked in the ABC system. In such situations, the costs of the department are divided among the activity cost pools via an allocation process called *first-stage allocation*. The **first-stage allocation** in an ABC system is the process by which overhead costs are assigned to activity cost pools.

The immediate problem is to figure out how to divide, for example, the £500,000 of indirect factory wages at Classic Brass shown in Exhibit 8.2 among the various activity cost pools in the ABC system. The point of activity-based costing is to determine the resources consumed by cost objects. Since indirect factory worker time is a resource, we need some way of estimating the amount of indirect factory worker time that is consumed by each activity in the ABC system. Often, the best way to get this kind of information is to ask the people who are directly involved. Members of the ABC team interview indirect factory workers (e.g., supervisors, engineers, quality inspectors, etc.) and ask them what percentage of time they spend dealing with customer orders, with product design, with processing units of product (i.e., order size), and with customer relations. These interviews are conducted with considerable care. Those who are interviewed must thoroughly understand what the activities encompass and what is expected of them in the interview. In addition, departmental managers are interviewed to determine how the non-personnel costs should be distributed across the activity cost pools. In each case the key question is 'What percentage of the available resource is consumed by this activity?' For example, the production manager would be asked, 'What percentage of the available machine capacity is consumed as a consequence of the number of units processed (i.e., size of orders)?'

Production Department:		
Indirect factory wages	£500,000	
Factory equipment depreciation	300,000	
Factory utilities	120,000	
Factory building lease	80,000	£1,000,000
Shipping costs*		40,000
General Administrative Department:		
Administrative wages and salaries	400,000	
Office equipment depreciation	50,000	
Administrative building lease	60,000	510,000
Marketing Department:		
Marketing wages and salaries	250,000	
Selling expenses	50,000	300,000
Total overhead costs		£1,850,000

*Shipping costs can be traced directly to customer orders.

Exhibit 8.2 Overhead costs (both manufacturing and non-manufacturing) at Classic Brass

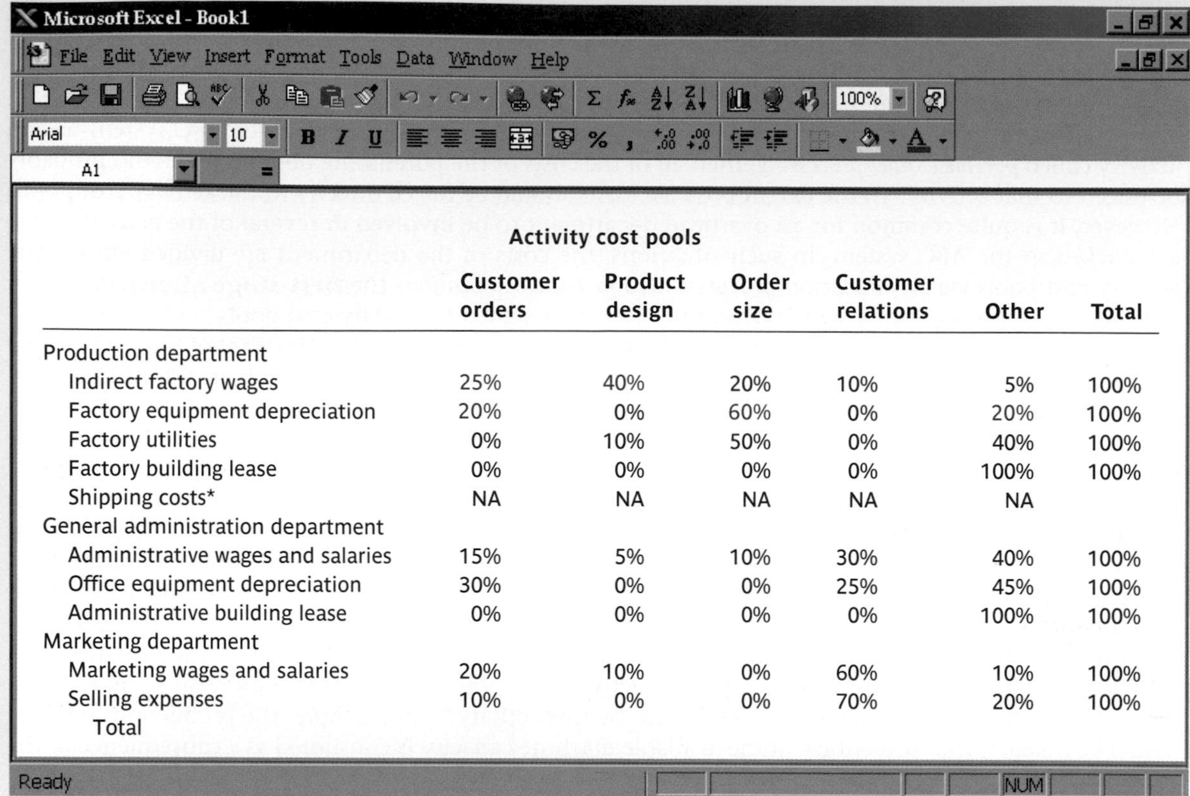

	Activity cost pools					
	Customer orders	Product design	Order size	Customer relations	Other	Total
Production department						
Indirect factory wages	25%	40%	20%	10%	5%	100%
Factory equipment depreciation	20%	0%	60%	0%	20%	100%
Factory utilities	0%	10%	50%	0%	40%	100%
Factory building lease	0%	0%	0%	0%	100%	100%
Shipping costs*	NA	NA	NA	NA	NA	
General administration department						
Administrative wages and salaries	15%	5%	10%	30%	40%	100%
Office equipment depreciation	30%	0%	0%	25%	45%	100%
Administrative building lease	0%	0%	0%	0%	100%	100%
Marketing department						
Marketing wages and salaries	20%	10%	0%	60%	10%	100%
Selling expenses	10%	0%	0%	70%	20%	100%
Total						

*Shipping costs are not included in this and subsequent tables because they are directly traced to customer orders rather than being allocated using the ABC system.

NA = Not applicable.

Exhibit 8.3 Results of interviews: distribution of activities

The results of the interviews at Classic Brass are displayed in Exhibit 8.3. For example, factory equipment depreciation is distributed 20% to Customer Orders, 60% to Order Size, and 20% to the Other cost pool. The resource in this instance is machine time. According to the estimate made by the production manager, 60% of the total available time was actually used to process units to fill orders. Each customer order requires setting up, which also requires machine time. This activity consumes 20% of the total available machine time and is entered under the Customer Orders column. The remaining 20% of available machine time represents idle time and is entered under the Other column.

Exhibit 8.3 and many of the other exhibits in this chapter are presented in the form of Excel spreadsheets. It is often a good idea to use spreadsheet software in activity-based costing because of the large number of calculations involved. You *can* do all the calculations by hand, by setting up an activity-based costing system on a spreadsheet or you can use special ABC software which can save a lot of work in the long run – particularly in companies that intend periodically to update their ABC systems.

We will not go into the details of how all of the percentages in Exhibit 8.3 were determined. However, note that 100% of the factory building lease has been assigned to the Other cost pool. Classic Brass has a single production facility. It has no plans to expand or to sublease any excess space. The cost of this production facility is treated as an organization-sustaining cost since there is no way to avoid even a portion of this cost if a product or customer were dropped. (Remember that organization-sustaining

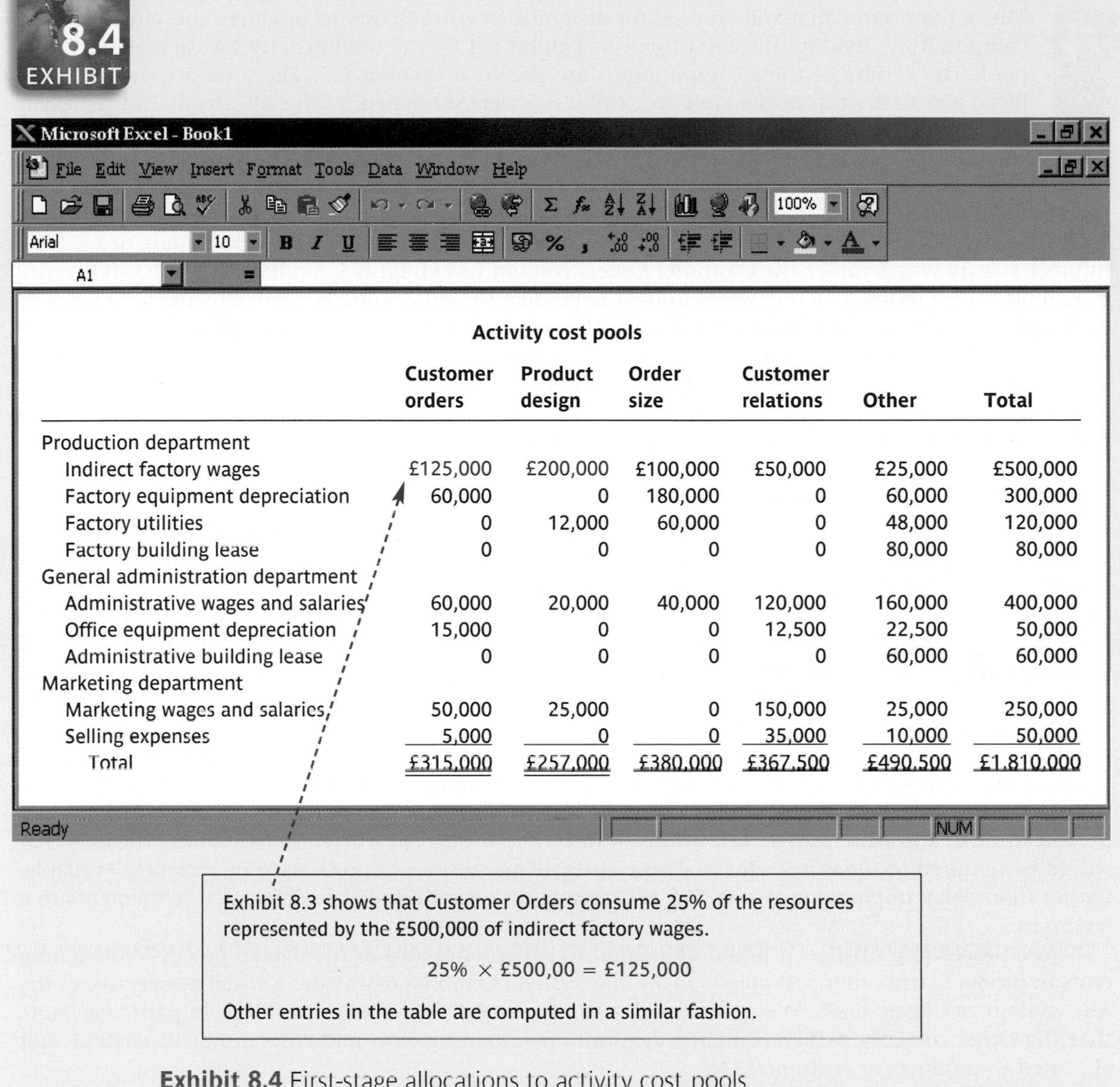

	Activity cost pools					
	Customer orders	Product design	Order size	Customer relations	Other	Total
Production department						
Indirect factory wages	£125,000	£200,000	£100,000	£50,000	£25,000	£500,000
Factory equipment depreciation	60,000	0	180,000	0	60,000	300,000
Factory utilities	0	12,000	60,000	0	48,000	120,000
Factory building lease	0	0	0	0	80,000	80,000
General administration department						
Administrative wages and salaries	60,000	20,000	40,000	120,000	160,000	400,000
Office equipment depreciation	15,000	0	0	12,500	22,500	50,000
Administrative building lease	0	0	0	0	60,000	60,000
Marketing department						
Marketing wages and salaries	50,000	25,000	0	150,000	25,000	250,000
Selling expenses	5,000	0	0	35,000	10,000	50,000
Total	£315,000	£257,000	£380,000	£367,500	£490,500	£1,810,000

Exhibit 8.3 shows that Customer Orders consume 25% of the resources represented by the £500,000 of indirect factory wages.

25% × £500,00 = £125,000

Other entries in the table are computed in a similar fashion.

Exhibit 8.4 First-stage allocations to activity cost pools

costs are assigned to the Other cost pool and are not allocated to products.) In contrast, some companies have separate facilities for manufacturing specific products. The costs of these separate facilities could be directly traced to the specific products.

Once the percentage distributions in Exhibit 8.3 have been established, it is a simple matter to allocate costs to the activity cost pools. The results of this first stage allocation are displayed in Exhibit 8.4. Each cost is allocated across the activity cost pools by multiplying it by the percentages in Exhibit 8.3. For example, the indirect factory wages of £500,000 are multiplied by the 25% entry under Customer Orders in Exhibit 8.3 to arrive at the £125,000 entry under Customer Orders in Exhibit 8.4. Similarly, the indirect factory wages of £500,000 are multiplied by the 40% entry under Product Design in Exhibit 8.3 to arrive at the £200,000 entry under Product Design in Exhibit 8.4. All of the entries in Exhibit 8.4 are computed in this way.

Now that the first-stage allocations to the activity cost pools have been completed, the fourth step is to compute the activity rates.

Computation of activity rates

The activity rates that will be used for assigning overhead costs to products and customers are computed by dividing the costs listed in Exhibit 8.4 by the total activity for each activity cost pool. The results of these computations are shown in Exhibit 8.5. The total activity numbers listed across the top of the table in Exhibit 8.5 were estimated by the ABC team and represent the amount of activity actually required to produce the company's present product mix and to serve its present customers. The activity at the top of each column was divided into each of the costs in the corresponding column in Exhibit 8.4 to arrive at the activity rates in Exhibit 8.5. For example, the £125,000 entry in Exhibit 8.4 for indirect factory wages under the Customer Orders column is divided by the total of 1,000 customer orders listed at the top of Exhibit 8.5 to arrive at the activity rate of £125 for indirect factory wages under the Customer Orders column in Exhibit 8.5. Similarly, the £200,000 entry in Exhibit 8.4 for indirect factory wages under the Product Design column is divided by the total number of designs (i.e., 200 product designs) to arrive at the activity rate of £1,000 per design for indirect factory wages. Note that activity rates are not computed for the Other category of costs. This is because these organization-sustaining costs and costs of idle capacity are not allocated to products and customers.

We urge you to study Exhibit 8.5 with care so that you are sure you know how each entry in the table was computed. Take each column in turn and divide each of the cost entries in Exhibit 8.4 under that column by the total activity at the top of the column in Exhibit 8.5. Once you see how the numbers were computed, it is really easy, although there are a lot of computations.

The entries at the bottom of Exhibit 8.5 indicate that on average a customer order consumes resources that cost £315; a product design consumes resources that cost £1,285; a unit of product consumes resources that cost £19 per machine-hour; and maintaining relations with a customer consumes resources that cost £3,675. Note that these are *average* figures. Some members of the ABC design team at Classic Brass argued that it would be unfair to charge all new products the same £1,285 product design cost regardless of how much design time they actually require. After discussing the pros and cons, the team concluded that it would not be worth the effort at the present time to keep track of actual design time spent on each new product. Similarly, some team members were uncomfortable assigning the same £3,675 cost to each customer. Some customers are undemanding – ordering standard products well in advance of their needs. Others are very demanding and consume large amounts of marketing and administrative staff time. These are generally customers who order customized products, who tend to order at the last minute, and who change their minds. While everyone agreed with this observation, the data that would be required to measure individual customers' demands on resources was not currently available. Rather than delay implementation of the ABC system, the team decided to defer such refinements to a later date.

Before proceeding further, it would be helpful to get a better idea of the overall process of assigning costs to products and other cost objects in an ABC system. Exhibit 8.6 provides a visual perspective of the ABC system at Classic Brass. We recommend that you carefully go over this exhibit. In particular, note that the Other category, which contains organization-sustaining costs and costs of idle capacity, is not allocated to products or customers.

Targeting process improvements: activity-based management

Activity-based costing can be used to identify areas that would benefit from process improvements. Indeed, managers often cite this as the major benefit of activity-based costing.[5] When used in this way, activity-based costing is often called *activity-based management*. Basically, **activity-based management (ABM)** focuses on managing activities as a way of eliminating waste and reducing delays and defects. Activity-based management is used in organizations as diverse as manufacturing companies, hospitals and banks.

The first step in any improvement programme is to decide what to improve. Activity-based management provides an approach. The activity rates computed in activity-based costing can provide valuable clues concerning where there is waste and scope for improvement in an organization. For example, managers at Classic Brass were surprised at the high cost of customer orders. Some customer orders are for less than £100 worth of products, and yet it costs, on average, £315 to process an order according to the activity rates calculated in Exhibit 8.5. This seemed like an awful lot of money for an activity that adds no value to the product. As a consequence, the customer order processing activity was targeted for

Microsoft Excel - Book1

File Edit View Insert Format Tools Data Window Help

	Activity cost pools				
	Customer orders	Product design	Order size	Customer relations	Other
Total activity	1,000 orders	200 designs	20,000 machine-hours	100 customers	NA*
Production department					
Indirect factory wages	£125	£1,000	£5	£500	
Factory equipment depreciation	60	0	9	0	
Factory utilities	0	60	3	0	
Factory building lease	0	0	0	0	
General administration department					
Administrative wages and salaries	60	100	2	1,200	
Office equipment depreciation	15	0	0	125	
Administrative building lease	0	0	0	0	
Marketing department					
Marketing wages and salaries	50	125	0	1,500	
Selling expenses	5	0	0	350	
Total	£315	£1,285	£19	£3,675	

Ready NUM

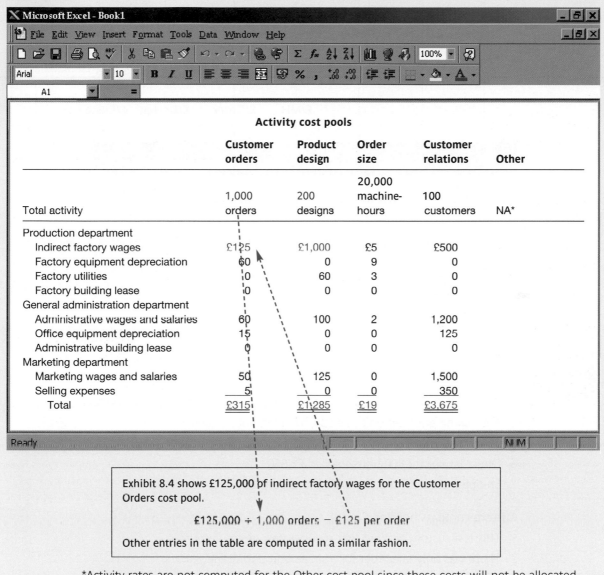

Exhibit 8.4 shows £125,000 of indirect factory wages for the Customer Orders cost pool.

£125,000 ÷ 1,000 orders = £125 per order

Other entries in the table are computed in a similar fashion.

*Activity rates are not computed for the Other cost pool since these costs will not be allocated further. NA = Not applicable.

Exhibit 8.5 Computation of activity rates

improvement. In Chapter 18, we examine how techniques such as quality management, benchmarking and business process re-engineering may be used together with ABM in order to improve operations.

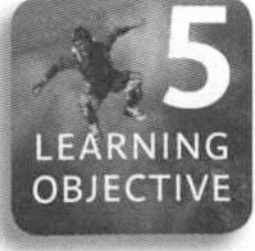

Assigning costs to cost objects

The fifth step in the implementation of activity-based costing is called *second-stage allocation*. In **second-stage allocation**, activity rates are used to apply costs to products and customers. At Classic Brass, the ABC system might be used to apply activity costs to all of the company's

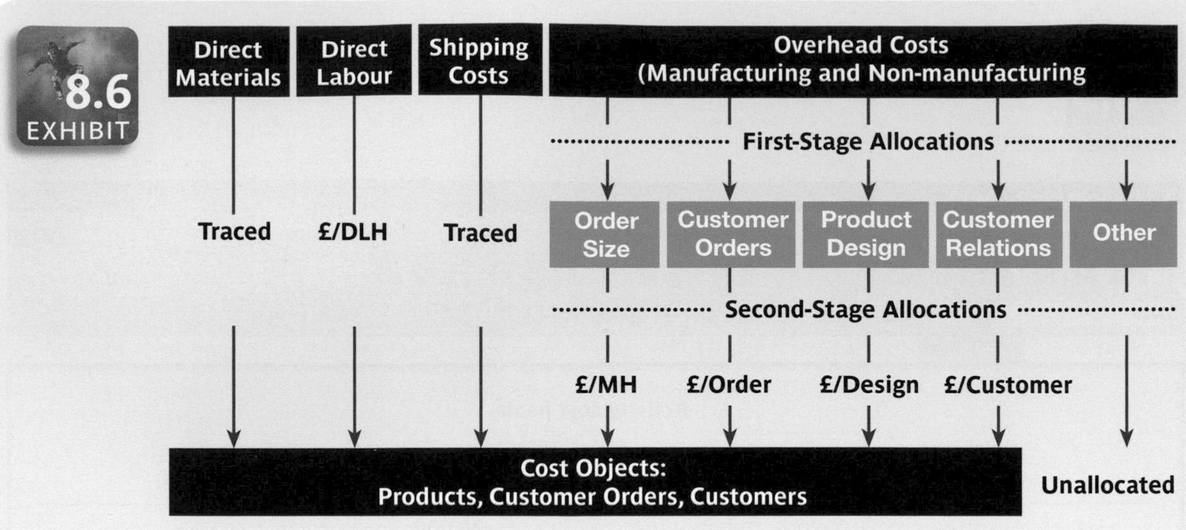

Exhibit 8.6 The activity-based costing model at Classic Brass

products, customer orders and customers. For purposes of illustration, we will consider only one customer – Windward Yacht. This customer ordered two different products – stanchions and a compass housing. The stanchions are a standard product that does not require any design work. In contrast, the compass housing is a custom product that required extensive designing. Data concerning these two products appear in Exhibit 8.7.

Standard stanchions

1. This is a standard design that does not require any new design resources.
2. Four hundred units were ordered during the year, comprising two separate orders.
3. Each stanchion required 0.5 machine-hours, for a total of 200 machine-hours.
4. The selling price per unit was £34, for a total of £13,600.
5. Direct materials for 400 units totalled £2,110.
6. Direct labour for 400 units totalled £1,850.
7. Shipping costs for the two orders totalled £180.

Custom compass housing

1. This is a custom product that requires new design resources.
2. There was only one order for a single unit during the year.
3. The compass housing required 4 machine-hours.
4. The selling price was £650.
5. Direct materials were £13.
6. Direct labour was £50.
7. Shipping costs were £25.

Exhibit 8.7 Data concerning the products ordered by Windward Yachts

Overhead costs computed using the ABC system

Direct materials and direct labour costs are the same under traditional cost accounting systems and the new ABC system. However, the two systems handle overhead very differently.

Microsoft Excel - Book1

File Edit View Insert Format Tools Data Window Help

	Activity cost pools				
	Customer orders	Product design	Order size	Customer relations	Total (action analysis)
Total activity for stanchions	2 orders	No new designing	200 machine-hours	NA	
Production department					
Indirect factory wages	£250	£0	£1,000	£0	£1,250
Factory equipment depreciation	120	0	£1,800	0	£1,920
Factory utilities	0	0	600	0	600
Factory building lease	0	0	0	0	0
General administration department					
Administrative wages and salaries	120	0	400	0	520
Office equipment depreciation	30	0	0	0	30
Administrative building lease	0	0	0	0	0
Marketing department					
Marketing wages and salaries	100	0	0	0	100
Selling expenses	10	0	0	0	10
Total	£630	£0	£3,800	£0	£4,430

Ready NUM

Exhibit 8.5 shows an activity rate of £125 for indirect factory wages for the Customer Orders cost pool.

£125 per order × 2 orders = £250

Other entries in the table are computed in a similar fashion.

NA = Not applicable.

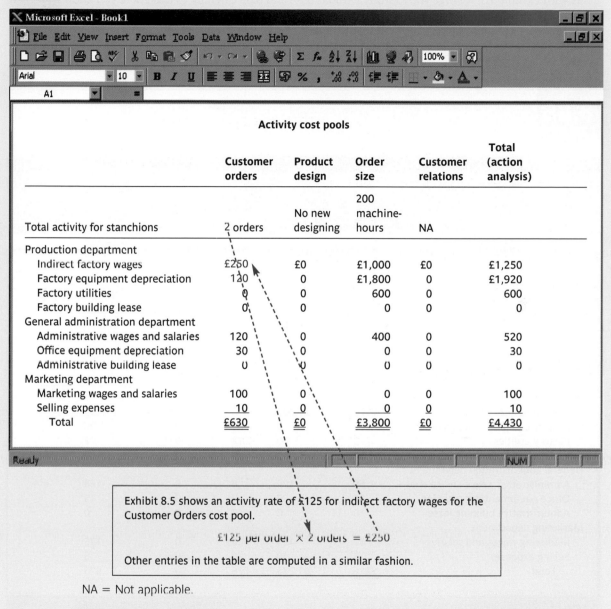

Exhibit 8.8A Computation of the overhead cost of two orders for standard stanchions totalling four hundred units

The overhead calculations for the stanchions and compass housings are carried out in Exhibits 8.8A and 8.8B, respectively. Let's examine the ABC overhead calculations for the stanchions in Exhibit 8.8A. First note that none of the Customer Relations costs has been allocated to the stanchions. A customer-level cost is assigned to customers directly; it is not assigned to products. The activities required to fill the two orders for stanchions totalling 400 units are listed across the top of the exhibit. Since this is a standard product, no new designing is required and hence no design costs are allocated to the order. However, there are two orders, so each of the activity rates under the Customer Orders column in Exhibit 8.5 is multiplied by 2 to determine the Customer Orders costs for this product. For example, the activity rate for indirect factory wages for Customer Orders in Exhibit 8.5 is £125 per order. Since there are two orders, 2 × £125 = £250 is allocated to this product and appears as the first entry under the Customer Orders column in Exhibit 8.8A. Similarly, the activity rate for factory equipment depreciation for Customer Orders in Exhibit 8.5 is £60 per order. Since there are two orders, the product is charged £120. This appears as the second entry under Customer Orders in Exhibit 8.8A.

As with Exhibit 8.5, we urge you to study Exhibits 8.8A and 8.8B carefully to make sure you know how each entry in the table was computed. Take each column in turn and multiply each of the activity rates in Exhibit 8.5 under that column by the total activity at the top of the column in Exhibit 8.8A (and 8.8B). As before, once you see how the numbers are computed, it is not difficult, although there are a lot of computations.

8.8B EXHIBIT

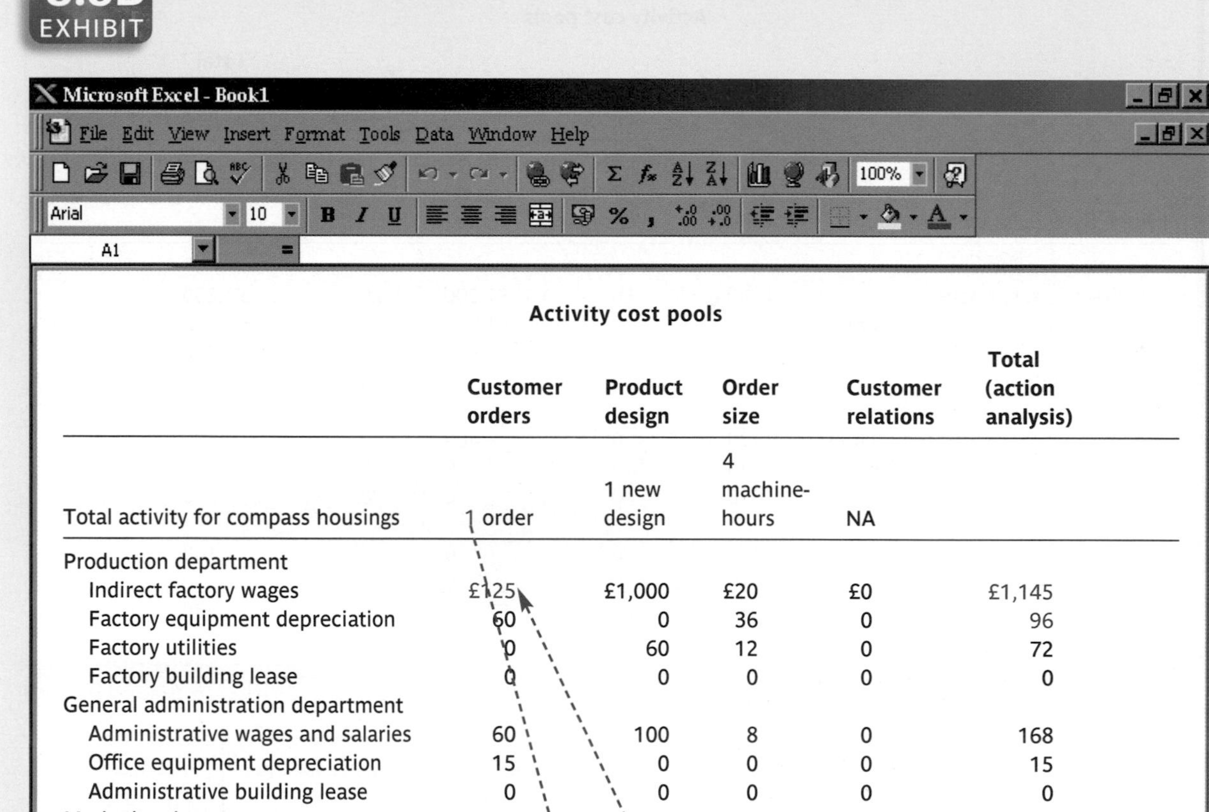

Microsoft Excel - Book1

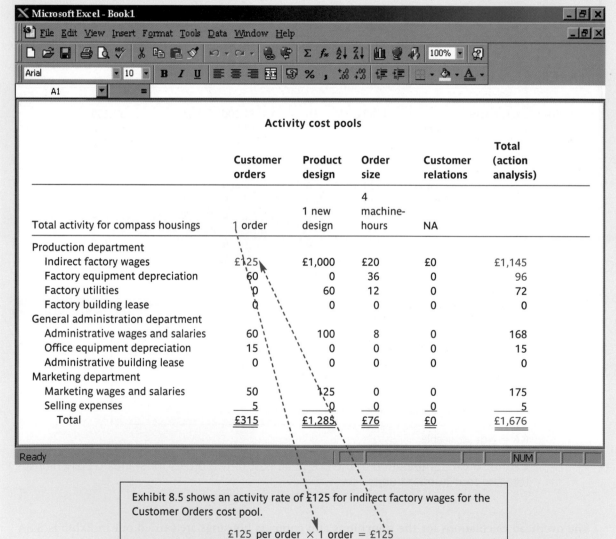

	Activity cost pools				
	Customer orders	Product design	Order size	Customer relations	Total (action analysis)
Total activity for compass housings	1 order	1 new design	4 machine-hours	NA	
Production department					
Indirect factory wages	£125	£1,000	£20	£0	£1,145
Factory equipment depreciation	60	0	36	0	96
Factory utilities	0	60	12	0	72
Factory building lease	0	0	0	0	0
General administration department					
Administrative wages and salaries	60	100	8	0	168
Office equipment depreciation	15	0	0	0	15
Administrative building lease	0	0	0	0	0
Marketing department					
Marketing wages and salaries	50	125	0	0	175
Selling expenses	5	0	0	0	5
Total	£315	£1,285	£76	£0	£1,676

Exhibit 8.5 shows an activity rate of £125 for indirect factory wages for the Customer Orders cost pool.

£125 per order × 1 order = £125

Other entries in the table are computed in a similar fashion.

NA = Not applicable.

Exhibit 8.8B Computation of the overhead cost of one order for one unit of the custom compass housing

Product margins and customer profitability computed using the ABC system

6 LEARNING OBJECTIVE

In Exhibit 8.9, the overhead costs computed from Exhibits 8.8A and 8.8B are combined with direct materials, direct labour and shipping cost data. For each of the products, these combined costs are deducted from sales to arrive at product margins. Under the ABC system, the stanchions show a profit of £5,030, whereas the compass housing shows a loss of £1,114.

Note from Exhibit 8.9 that the new ABC system also includes a profitability analysis of Windward Yachts, the customer that ordered the stanchions and the custom compass housing. Such customer analyses can be easily accomplished by adding together the product margins for each of the products a customer has ordered and then subtracting the average charge of £3,675 for Customer Relations.

8.9 EXHIBIT

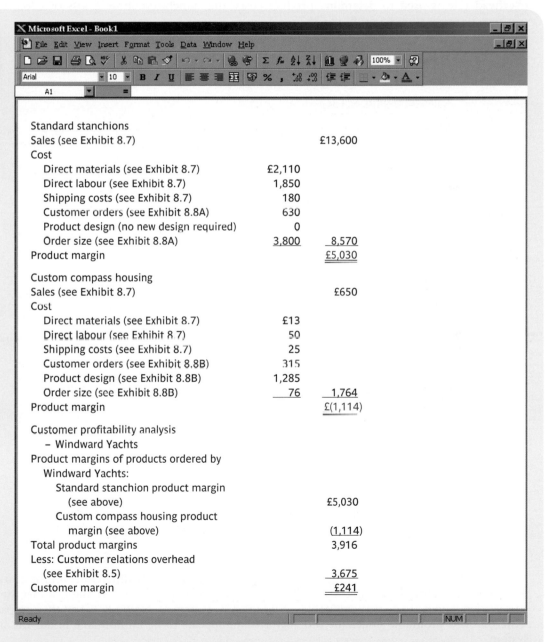

Standard stanchions		
Sales (see Exhibit 8.7)		£13,600
Cost		
Direct materials (see Exhibit 8.7)	£2,110	
Direct labour (see Exhibit 8.7)	1,850	
Shipping costs (see Exhibit 8.7)	180	
Customer orders (see Exhibit 8.8A)	630	
Product design (no new design required)	0	
Order size (see Exhibit 8.8A)	3,800	8,570
Product margin		£5,030
Custom compass housing		
Sales (see Exhibit 8.7)		£650
Cost		
Direct materials (see Exhibit 8.7)	£13	
Direct labour (see Exhibit 8.7)	50	
Shipping costs (see Exhibit 8.7)	25	
Customer orders (see Exhibit 8.8B)	315	
Product design (see Exhibit 8.8B)	1,285	
Order size (see Exhibit 8.8B)	76	1,764
Product margin		£(1,114)
Customer profitability analysis – Windward Yachts		
Product margins of products ordered by Windward Yachts:		
Standard stanchion product margin (see above)		£5,030
Custom compass housing product margin (see above)		(1,114)
Total product margins		3,916
Less: Customer relations overhead (see Exhibit 8.5)		3,675
Customer margin		£241

Exhibit 8.9 Product margins – activity-based costing system (activity view)

Comparison of traditional and ABC product costs

Now that the product margins have been computed using activity-based costing, it would be interesting to compare them to the product margins computed using the company's traditional cost system.

Product margins computed using the traditional cost system

The costs of the two products ordered by Windward Yachts are computed under the company's traditional cost accounting system in Exhibit 8.10. The company's traditional system uses a plantwide predetermined overhead rate based on machine-hours. Since the total manufacturing overhead cost is £1,000,000 (see Exhibit 8.2) and the total machine time is 20,000 machine-hours (see Exhibit 8.5), the predetermined manufacturing overhead rate for the company is £50 per machine-hour (£1,000,000/20,000 machine-hours = £50 per machine-hour). From Exhibit 8.10, we see that when this predetermined manufacturing overhead rate is used to determine product costs, the stanchions show a loss of £360, whereas the compass housing shows a profit of £387.

Standard stanchions		
Margin computed using the company's old cost accounting system:		
Sales (400 units × £34)		£13,600
Cost:		
Direct materials	£2,110	
Direct labour	1,850	
Manufacturing overhead (400 units × 0.5 machine-hours per unit × £50 per machine-hour*)	10,000	13,960
Product margin		£(360)
Custom compass housing		
Margin computed using the company's old cost accounting system:		
Sales (1 unit × £650)		£650
Cost:		
Direct materials	13	
Direct labour	50	
Manufacturing overhead (1 unit × 4.0 machine-hours per unit 3 £50 per machine-hour)	200	263
Product margin		£387

*Predetermined manufacturing overhead rate:

$$\frac{\text{Total manufacturing overhead, £1,000,000}}{\text{Total machine-hours, 20,000}} = \text{£50 per machine-hour}$$

Exhibit 8.10 Product margins – traditional cost accounting system

The differences between ABC and traditional product costs

The costs of the products under the new ABC system are dramatically different from the costs computed using the old traditional costing system. The stanchions, which looked unprofitable under the traditional cost system, appear to be very profitable under the ABC system in Exhibit 8.9. And the compass housing, which looked profitable under the old cost system, appears to be unprofitable under the new costing system.

There are two major reasons for these changes in apparent profitability. First, under the old cost system the costs of designing products were spread across all products without regard to whether they actually required design work. Under the new ABC system, these costs are assigned only to products that actually require design work. Consequently, under the ABC system, design costs have been shifted from standard products like stanchions, which do not require any design work, to custom products like the compass housing.

Second, the Customer Orders costs, which are batch-level costs, were applied on the basis of machine-hours, a unit-level base, under the old cost system. Therefore, under the old cost system, high-volume products absorbed the bulk of these batch-level costs even though they caused no more of these costs than low-volume products that are ordered as frequently. Under the new cost system, these batch-level costs are assigned as a lump sum to each customer order. Consequently, the new cost system shifts these costs from high-volume orders like the stanchions to low-volume orders like the compass housing.

When there are batch-level or product-level costs, activity-based costing will ordinarily shift costs from high-volume products produced in large batches to low-volume products produced in small batches. This cost shifting will usually have a greater impact on the *per unit* costs of low-volume products than on the per unit costs of high-volume products. For example, suppose that a total of £100 in batch-level cost is shifted from a high-volume, 100-unit product to a low-volume, 1-unit product. This shifting of cost will decrease the cost of the high-volume product by £1 per unit, on average, but will increase the cost of the low-volume product by £100 for the single unit. In sum, implementing activity-based costing will typically shift costs from high-volume to low-volume products, but the effects will be much more dramatic on the per unit costs of the low-volume products. The per unit costs of the low-volume products will increase far more than the per unit costs of the high-volume products will decrease.

It is important to remember another major difference between the costs of products as computed under the new ABC system at Classic Brass and product costs as computed under the old traditional cost system. Under a traditional system, only manufacturing costs are assigned to products. Under the new ABC system at Classic Brass, non-manufacturing costs are assigned to products as well as the manufacturing costs. In addition, the organization-sustaining manufacturing costs and the costs of idle capacity are *not* assigned to products under the ABC system, whereas they are assigned to products under the old traditional costing system. For these reasons, the term 'product cost' in this chapter has a different meaning than it had in Chapters 2, 3 and 4. In the context of an ABC system like the one implemented at Classic Brass, product costs include the costs of *all* resources consumed by the product, whether they are manufacturing costs or not.

ABC product costs – an action analysis

7 LEARNING OBJECTIVE

The sixth step in implementing an ABC system is preparing management reports. The activity view of product and customer margins, as illustrated in Exhibit 8.9, may be one of those reports. However, the overhead computations in Exhibits 8.8A and 8.8B allow another view of the ABC product costs that emphasizes who in the organization is responsible for the costs and how easy it would be to actually adjust the costs in the event that the products were dropped. To help in this supplemental analysis, the ABC team applied a simple colour coding scheme to the company's costs.

Ease of adjustment codes

The ABC team constructed Exhibit 8.11 to aid managers in the use of the ABC data. In this exhibit, each cost has been assigned an *ease of adjustment code* – Green, Yellow or Red. The **ease of adjustment code** reflects how easily the cost could be adjusted to changes in activity.[6] 'Green' costs are those costs that would adjust more or less automatically to changes in activity without any action by managers. For example, direct materials costs would adjust to changes in orders without any action being taken by managers. If a customer does not order stanchions, the direct materials for the stanchions would not be required and would not be ordered. 'Yellow' costs are those costs that could be adjusted in response to changes in activity, but such adjustments require management action; the adjustment is not automatic. The ABC team believes, for example, that direct labour costs should be included in the Yellow category. Managers must make difficult decisions and take explicit action to increase or decrease, in aggregate, direct labour costs – particularly since the company has a no lay-off policy. 'Red' costs are costs that could be adjusted to changes in activity only with a great deal of difficulty, and the adjustment would require management action. The building leases fall into this category, since it would be very difficult and expensive to break the leases.

Green: Costs that adjust automatically to changes in activity without management action.

Direct materials

Shipping costs

Yellow: Costs that could, in principle, be adjusted to changes in activity, but management action would be required.

Direct labour

Indirect factory wages

Factory utilities

Administrative wages and salaries

Office equipment depreciation

Marketing wages and salaries

Selling expenses

Red: Costs that would be very difficult to adjust to changes in activity and management action would be required.

Factory equipment depreciation

Factory building lease

Administrative building lease

Exhibit 8.11 Ease of adjustment codes

The action analysis view of the ABC data

Looking at Exhibit 8.8B, the totals on the right-hand side of the table indicate that the £1,676 of overhead cost for the custom housing consists of £1,145 of indirect factory wages, £96 of factory equipment depreciation, and so on. These data are displayed in Exhibit 8.12, which shows an *action analysis* of the custom compass housing product. An **action analysis report** is a report showing what costs have been assigned to the cost object, such as a product or customer, and how difficult it would be to adjust the cost if there is a change in activity. Note that the Red margin at the bottom of Exhibit 8.12 (£1,114) is exactly the same as the product margin for the custom compass housing in Exhibit 8.9.

The cost data in the action analysis in Exhibit 8.12 are arranged by the colour coded ease of adjustment. All of the Green costs – those that adjust more or less automatically to changes in activity – appear together at the top of the list of costs. These costs total £38 and are subtracted from the sales of £650 to yield a Green margin of £612. The same procedure is followed for the Yellow and Red costs. This action analysis indicates exactly what costs would have to be cut and how difficult it would be to cut them if the custom compass housing product were dropped. Prior to making any decision about dropping products, the managers responsible for the costs must agree to either eliminate the resources represented by those costs or to transfer the resources to an area in the organization that really needs the resources – namely, a constraint. *If managers do not make such a commitment, it is likely that the costs would continue to be incurred. As a result, the company would lose the sales from the products without really saving the costs.*

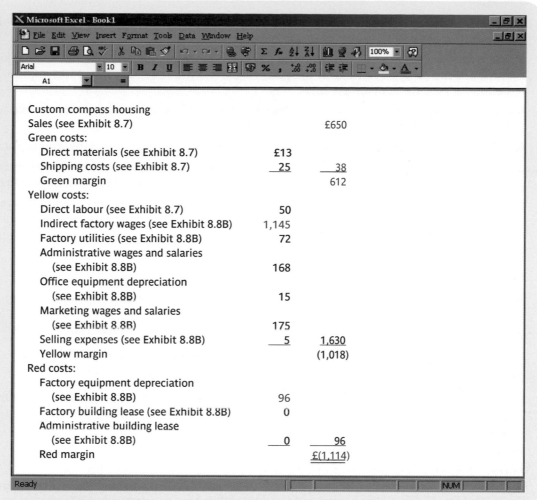

Custom compass housing		
Sales (see Exhibit 8.7)		£650
Green costs:		
Direct materials (see Exhibit 8.7)	£13	
Shipping costs (see Exhibit 8.7)	25	38
Green margin		612
Yellow costs:		
Direct labour (see Exhibit 8.7)	50	
Indirect factory wages (see Exhibit 8.8B)	1,145	
Factory utilities (see Exhibit 8.8B)	72	
Administrative wages and salaries (see Exhibit 8.8B)	168	
Office equipment depreciation (see Exhibit 8.8B)	15	
Marketing wages and salaries (see Exhibit 8.8B)	175	
Selling expenses (see Exhibit 8.8B)	5	1,630
Yellow margin		(1,018)
Red costs:		
Factory equipment depreciation (see Exhibit 8.8B)	96	
Factory building lease (see Exhibit 8.8B)	0	
Administrative building lease (see Exhibit 8.8B)	0	96
Red margin		£(1,114)

Exhibit 8.12 Action analysis of custom compass housing: activity-based costing system

Management accounting in action: the wrap-up

The ABC design team presented the results of its work in a meeting attended by all of the top managers of Classic Brass, including the CEO John Towers, the production manager Susan Richter, the marketing manager Tom Olafson, and the accounting manager Mary Goodman. The ABC team brought with them to the meeting copies of the chart showing the ABC design (Exhibit 8.6), the tables showing the product margins for the stanchions and compass housing under the company's old cost accounting system (Exhibit 8.7), the tables showing the ABC analysis of the same products (Exhibit 8.9), and the action analysis (Exhibit 8.12). After the formal presentation by the ABC team, the following discussion took place:

John: I would like to thank personally the ABC team for all of the work they have done and for an extremely interesting presentation. I am now beginning to wonder about a lot of the decisions we have made in the past using our old cost accounting system.

Mary: I hope I don't have to remind anyone that I have been warning for quite some time about this problem.

John: No, you don't have to remind us, Mary. I suppose we just didn't understand the problem before.

John: Tom, why did we accept this order for standard stanchions in the first place if our old cost accounting system was telling us it was a big money loser?

Tom: Windward Yachts, the company that ordered the stanchions, has asked us to do a lot of custom work like the compass housing in the past. To get that work, we felt we had to accept their orders for box-money-losing standard products.

John: According to this ABC analysis, we had it all backwards. We are losing money on the custom products and making a fistful on the standard products.

Susan: I never did believe we were making a lot of money on the custom jobs. You ought to see all of the problems they create for us in production.

Tom: I hate to admit it, but the custom jobs always seem to give us headaches in marketing too.

John: Why don't we just stop soliciting custom work? This seems like a non-starter to me. If we are losing money on custom jobs like the compass housing, why not suggest to our customers that they go elsewhere for that kind of work?

Tom: Wait a minute, we would lose a lot of sales.

Susan: So what, we would save a lot more costs.

Mary: Maybe yes, maybe no. Some of the costs would not disappear if we were to drop all of those products.

Tom: Like what?

Mary: Well Tom, part of your salary is included in the costs of the ABC model.

Tom: Where? I don't see anything listed that looks like my salary.

Mary: Tom, when the ABC team interviewed you they asked you what percentage of your time was spent in handling customer orders and how much was spent dealing with new product design issues. Am I correct?

Tom: Yeah, but what's the point?

Mary: I believe you said that about 10% of your time is spent dealing with new products. As a consequence, 10% of your salary was allocated to the Product Design cost pool. If we were to drop all of the products requiring design work, would you be willing to take a 10% pay cut?

Tom: I trust you're joking.

Mary: Do you see the problem? Just because 10% of your time is spent on custom products doesn't mean that the company would save 10% of your salary if the custom products were dropped. Before we take a drastic action like dropping the custom products, we should identify which costs are really relevant.

John: I think I see what you are driving at. We wouldn't want to drop a lot of products just to find that our costs really haven't changed much. It is true that dropping the products would free up resources like Tom's time, but we had better be sure we have some good use for those resources *before* we take such an action.

Mary: That's why we put together the action analysis.

John: What's this red margin at the bottom of the action analysis? Isn't that a product margin?

Mary: Yes, it is. However, we call it a red margin because we should stop and think very, very carefully before taking any actions based on that margin.

John: Why is that?

Mary: We subtracted the costs of factory equipment depreciation to arrive at that red margin. We doubt that we could avoid any of that cost if we were to drop custom orders. We use the same machines on custom orders that we use on standard products. The factory equipment has no resale value, and it does not wear out through use.

John: What about this yellow margin?

Mary: Yellow means proceed with a great deal of caution. To get to the yellow margin we deducted from sales a lot of costs that could be adjusted only if the managers involved are willing to eliminate resources or shift them elsewhere in the organization.

John: If I understand the yellow margin correctly, the apparent loss of £1,018 on the custom stanchions is the result of the indirect factory wages of £1,145?

Susan: Right, that's basically the wages of our design engineers.

John: I wouldn't want to lay off any of our designers. Could we turn them into salespeople?

Tom: I'd love to have Shueli Park join our marketing team.

Susan: No way, she's our best designer.

John: Okay, I get the picture. We are not going to be cutting anyone's wages, we aren't going to be laying off anyone, and it looks like we may have problems getting agreement about moving people around. Where does that leave us?

Mary: What about raising prices on our custom products?

Tom: We should be able to do that. We have been undercutting the competition to make sure we got custom work. We were doing that because we thought custom work was very profitable.

John: Why don't we just charge directly for design work?

Tom: Some of our competitors already charge for design work. However, I don't think we would be able to charge enough to cover our design costs.

John: What about design work? Can we do anything to make it more efficient so it costs us less? I'm not going to lay anyone off, but if we make the design process more efficient, we could lower the charge for design work and spread those costs across more customers.

Susan: That may be possible. I'll form a TQM team to look at it.

John: Let's get some benchmark data on design costs. If we set our minds to it, I'm sure we can be world class in no time.

Susan: Okay. Mary, will you help with the benchmark data?

Mary: Sure.

Tom: There is another approach we can take too. Windward Yachts probably doesn't really need a custom compass housing. One of our standard compass housings would work just fine. If we start charging for the design work, I think they will see that it would be in their own interests to use the lower-cost standard product.

John: Let's meet again in about a week to discuss our progress. Is there anything else on the agenda for today?

The points raised in the preceding discussion are extremely important. By measuring the resources consumed by products (and other cost objects), a 'best practice' ABC system provides a much better basis for decision making than a traditional cost accounting system that spreads overhead costs around without much regard for what might be causing the overhead. A well-designed ABC system provides managers with estimates of potentially relevant costs that can be a very useful starting point for management analysis.

Service costing and management: the benefits of an ABC approach

As discussed in earlier chapters, service companies have tended to rely on rather crude or underdeveloped cost systems. Although there was often some form of budgetary control of responsibility centres such as departments or branches there was a lack of detailed product cost systems.[7] Partly, this gap was due to the lack of a financial reporting imperative to measure stocks.[8] But it also reflected a lack of awareness of products and customers. For example, in banking, an awareness of product cost was preceded by a marketing drive to develop a product consciousness and move away from a branch focus.[9] To some extent the traditionally high levels of regulation in sectors such as banking, airlines and telecommunications protected companies from serious competition and a need to access detailed cost and revenue information.

Apart from this past neglect, there are technical reasons as to why activity-based costing is particularly suitable. First, service companies appear to have a very large proportion of fixed costs compared to manufacturing where material costs comprise the bulk of their variable costs. Second, the marginal cost in service companies is often zero because capacity is provided in advance of demand but costs eventually need to be recovered. Third, there is a lack of a direct link between decisions by customers that generate revenues (making a phone call, making a flight) and decisions by companies that incur costs (e.g. adding a new city to airline routes; building a new university). ABC links indirect costs incurred across the organization in order to supply products and customers when the resources used often cut across departmental boundaries. ABC provides an end-to-end process analysis.[10]

Finally, service companies cannot usually rely on a proprietary technology in order to gain and hold on to customers, but customized service is both important and expensive. ABC offers much greater detail on customer profitability and a much greater understanding on what is driving costs. It is consequently much easier to make informed decisions about developing specific approaches to specific customers. ABC could be part of a customer relationship management system which is a 'method of coordinating an organization's culture, internal processes and IT systems to satisfy its customers' needs'.[11] One way of understanding the value of a customer relationship is to rank them as in Exhibit 8.13. This exhibit shows that while some customers are profitable and highly valuable, others may be only marginally profitable to serve. Indeed, if according to some estimates, 80% of customers generate 125% of firm profit, then 20% of customers are unprofitable.[12] With the latter, decisions about increasing prices or altering the way the customers are served may be in order. ABC analysis may reveal that some customers are expensive to serve because they are constantly requesting after sales service or insist on small orders and/or expensive methods of payment.

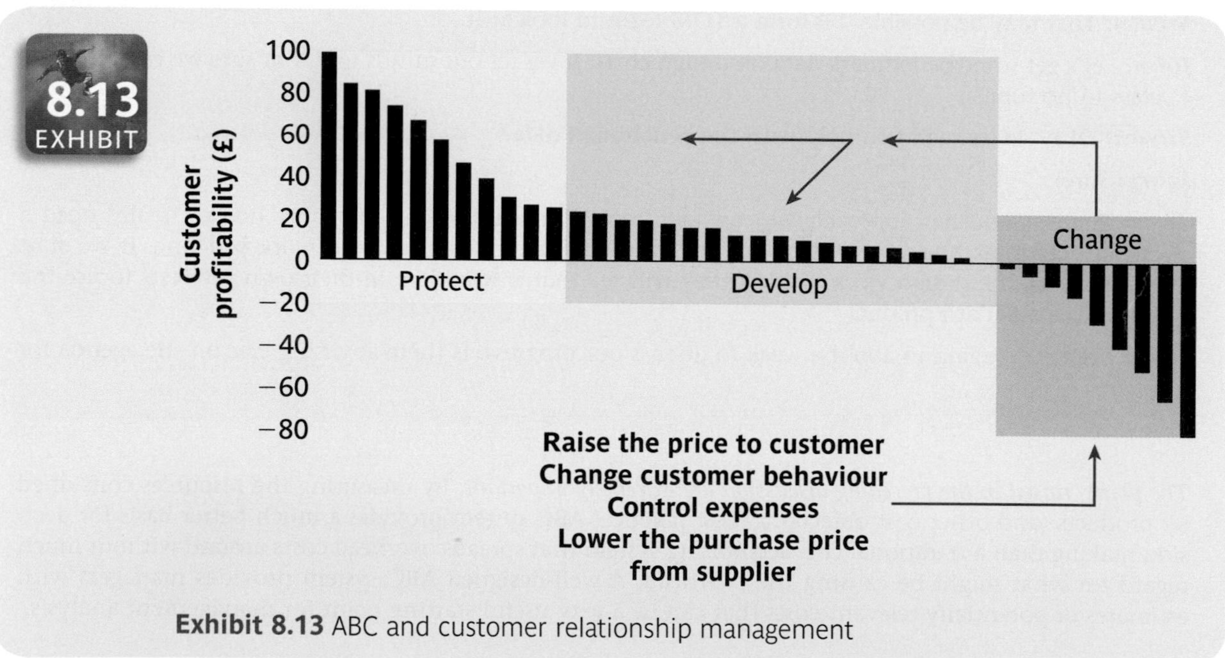

Exhibit 8.13 ABC and customer relationship management

Activity-based costing and external reports

Since activity-based costing generally provides more accurate product costs than traditional costing methods, why isn't it used for external reports? Some companies *do* use activity-based costing in their external reports, but most do not. There are a number of reasons for this. First, external reports are less detailed than internal reports prepared for decision making. On the external reports, individual product costs are not reported. Cost of goods sold and inventory valuations are disclosed, but there is no breakdown of these accounts by product. If some products are under-costed and some are over-costed, the errors tend to cancel each other when the product costs are added together.

Second, it is often very difficult to make changes in a company's accounting system. The official cost accounting systems in most large companies are usually embedded in complex computer programs that have been modified in-house over the course of many years. It is extremely difficult to make changes in such computer programs without causing numerous bugs.

Third, an ABC system such as the one described in this chapter does not conform to externally regulated accounting principles. As discussed in Chapter 2, product costs computed for external reports must include all of the manufacturing costs and only manufacturing costs; but in an ABC system as described in this chapter, product costs exclude some manufacturing costs and include some non-manufacturing costs. It is possible to adjust the ABC data at the end of the period to conform to regulations, but that requires more work.

Fourth, auditors are likely to be uncomfortable with allocations that are based on interviews with the company's personnel. Such subjective data can easily be manipulated by management to make earnings and other key variables look more favourable.

For all of these reasons, most companies confine their ABC efforts to special studies for management, and they do not attempt to integrate activity-based costing into their formal cost accounting systems.

A simplified approach to activity-based costing

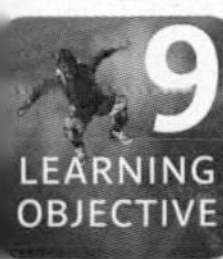

If an action analysis like Exhibit 8.12 is not prepared, the process of computing product margins under activity-based costing can be considerably simplified. The first-stage allocation shown in Exhibit 8.4 is still necessary, but the remainder of the computations can be streamlined.

To use the simplified approach after the first-stage allocation is completed, compute activity rates for each activity cost pool as shown for each cost pool as follows in Exhibit 8.14.

EXHIBIT 8.14

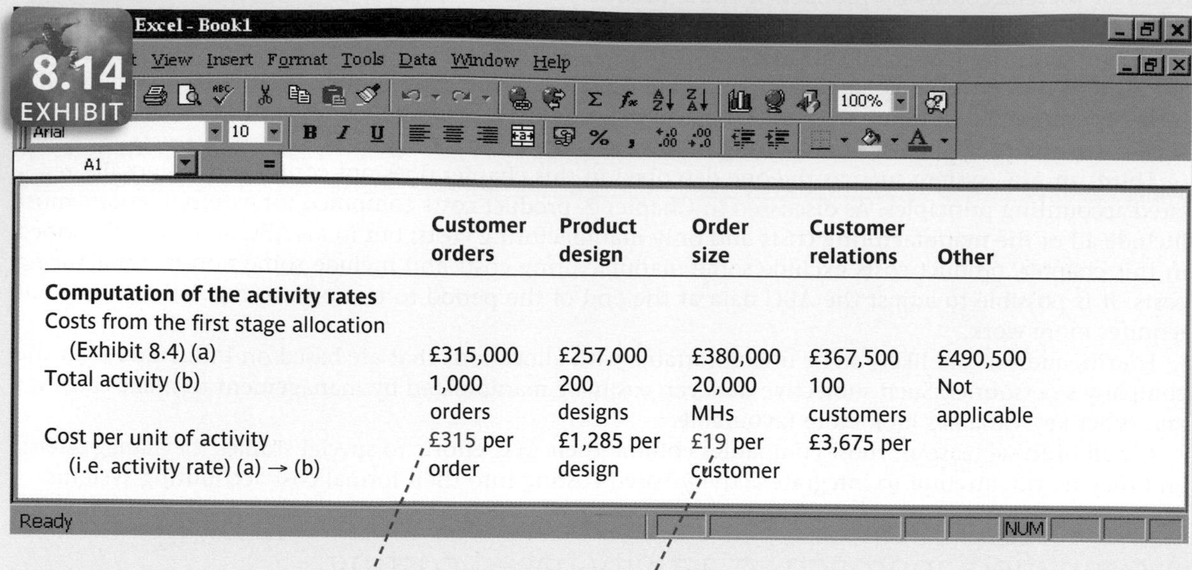

	Customer orders	Product design	Order size	Customer relations	Other
Computation of the activity rates					
Costs from the first stage allocation (Exhibit 8.4) (a)	£315,000	£257,000	£380,000	£367,500	£490,500
Total activity (b)	1,000 orders	200 designs	20,000 MHs	100 customers	Not applicable
Cost per unit of activity (i.e. activity rate) (a) → (b)	£315 per order	£1,285 per design	£19 per customer	£3,675 per	

Note that these activity rates are exactly the same as the activity rates at the bottom of Exhibit 8.5. If there is to be no activity analysis, the other numbers in Exhibit 8.5 are not needed and do not have to be computed.

Using these activity rates, the product and customer margins can be directly computed as follows.

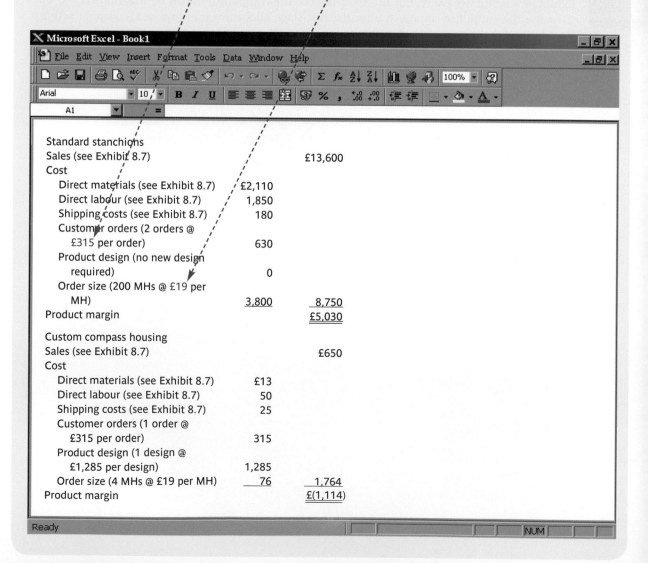

Standard stanchions		
Sales (see Exhibit 8.7)		£13,600
Cost		
Direct materials (see Exhibit 8.7)	£2,110	
Direct labour (see Exhibit 8.7)	1,850	
Shipping costs (see Exhibit 8.7)	180	
Customer orders (2 orders @ £315 per order)	630	
Product design (no new design required)	0	
Order size (200 MHs @ £19 per MH)	3,800	8,750
Product margin		£5,030
Custom compass housing		
Sales (see Exhibit 8.7)		£650
Cost		
Direct materials (see Exhibit 8.7)	£13	
Direct labour (see Exhibit 8.7)	50	
Shipping costs (see Exhibit 8.7)	25	
Customer orders (1 order @ £315 per order)	315	
Product design (1 design @ £1,285 per design)	1,285	
Order size (4 MHs @ £19 per MH)	76	1,764
Product margin		£(1,114)

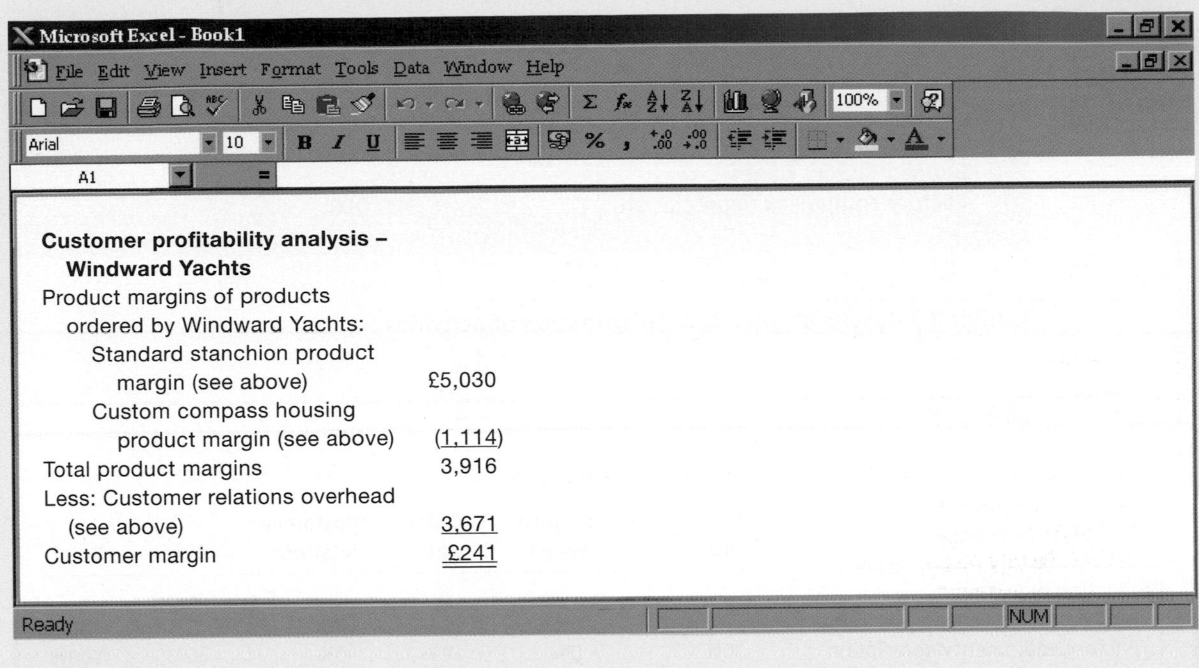

Customer profitability analysis – Windward Yachts	
Product margins of products ordered by Windward Yachts:	
Standard stanchion product margin (see above)	£5,030
Custom compass housing product margin (see above)	(1,114)
Total product margins	3,916
Less: Customer relations overhead (see above)	3,671
Customer margin	£241

Exhibit 8.14 ABC: a simplified approach

Note that the numbers in this report match the numbers that appear in Exhibit 8.9. This simplified approach allows one to compute product and customer margins without having to do the detailed computations in all of the cells of Exhibit 8.5 and Exhibits 8.8A and 8.8B. However, this simplified approach does not provide the data that are needed to construct an action analysis.

Exhibit 8.2 Overhead costs (both manufacturing and non-manufacturing) at Classic Brass

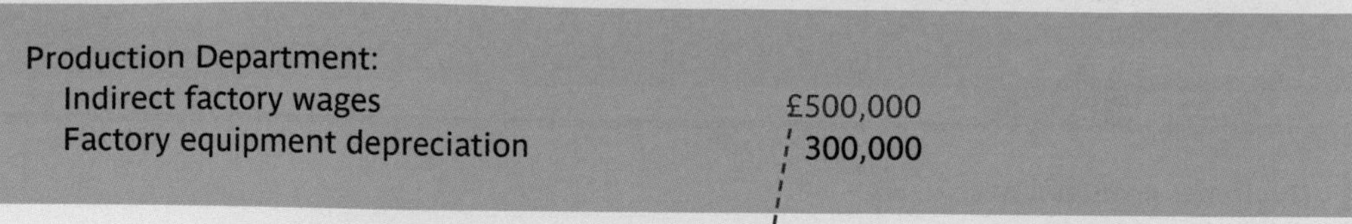

Production Department:	
Indirect factory wages	£500,000
Factory equipment depreciation	300,000

Exhibit 8.3 Results of interviews: distribution of activities

	Activity cost pools					
	Customer orders	Product design	Order size	Customer relations	Other	Total
Production department						
Indirect factory wages	25%	40%	20%	10%	5%	100%
Factory equipment depreciation	20%	0%	60%	0%	20%	100%

25% × £500,000

Exhibit 8.4 First-stage allocations to activity cost pools

	Activity cost pools					
	Customer orders	Product design	Order size	Customer relations	Other	Total
Production department						
Indirect factory wages	£125,000	£200,000	£100,000	£50,000	£25,000	£500,000
Factory equipment depreciation	60,000	0	180,000	0	60,000	300,000

£125,000 ÷ 1,000 orders

Exhibit 8.5 Computation of activity rates

	Activity cost pools				
	Customer orders	Product design	Order size	Customer relations	Other
Total activity	1,000 orders	200 designs	20,000 machine-hours	100 customers	NA*
Production department					
Indirect factory wages	£125	£1,000	£5	£500	
Factory equipment depreciation	60	0	9	0	
Factory utilities	0	60	3	0	
Factory building lease	0	0	0	0	

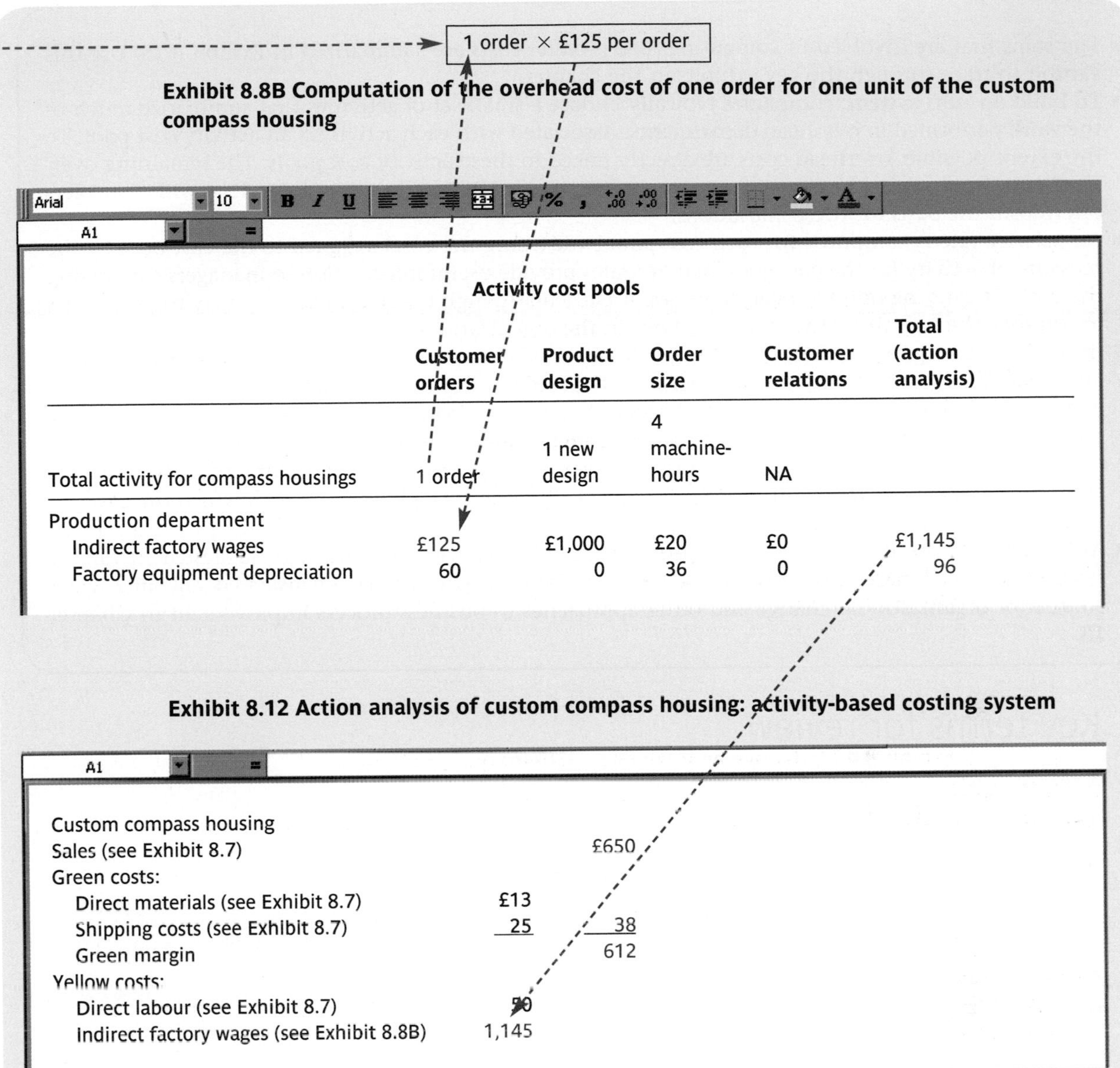

1 order × £125 per order

Exhibit 8.8B Computation of the overhead cost of one order for one unit of the custom compass housing

	Activity cost pools				
	Customer orders	Product design	Order size	Customer relations	Total (action analysis)
Total activity for compass housings	1 order	1 new design	4 machine-hours	NA	
Production department					
Indirect factory wages	£125	£1,000	£20	£0	£1,145
Factory equipment depreciation	60	0	36	0	96

Exhibit 8.12 Action analysis of custom compass housing: activity-based costing system

Custom compass housing		
Sales (see Exhibit 8.7)		£650
Green costs:		
Direct materials (see Exhibit 8.7)	£13	
Shipping costs (see Exhibit 8.7)	25	38
Green margin		612
Yellow costs:		
Direct labour (see Exhibit 8.7)	50	
Indirect factory wages (see Exhibit 8.8B)	1,145	

Exhibit 8.15 How the ABC steps fit together

Summary

- Traditional cost accounting methods suffer from several defects that can result in distorted costs for decision-making purposes. All manufacturing costs – even those that are not caused by any specific product – are allocated to products. And non-manufacturing costs that are caused by products are not assigned to products. Traditional methods also allocate the costs of idle capacity to products. In effect, products are charged for resources that they do not use. And finally, traditional methods tend to place too much reliance on unit-level allocation bases such as direct labour and machine-hours. This results in over-costing high-volume products and under-costing low-volume products and can lead to mistakes when making decisions.
- Activity-based costing estimates the costs of the resources consumed by cost objects such as products and customers. The approach taken in activity-based costing assumes that cost objects generate activities that in turn consume costly resources. Activities form the link between costs and cost objects. Activity-based costing is concerned with overhead – both manufacturing overhead and selling, general and administrative overhead. The accounting for direct labour and direct material is usually unaffected.

- The steps that are involved in computing ABC product costs are summarized in Exhibit 8.15. Use this exhibit to trace through the key exhibits in the chapter.
- To build an ABC system, companies typically choose a small set of activities that summarize much of the work performed in overhead departments. Associated with each activity is an activity cost pool. To the extent possible, overhead costs are directly traced to these activity cost pools. The remaining overhead costs are assigned to the activity cost pools in the first-stage allocation. Interviews with managers often form the basis for these allocations.
- An activity rate is computed for each cost pool by dividing the costs assigned to the cost pool by the measure of activity for the cost pool. Activity rates provide useful information to managers concerning the costs of carrying out overhead activities. A particularly high cost for an activity may trigger efforts to improve the way the activity is carried out in the organization.
- In the second-stage allocation, the activity rates are used to apply costs to cost objects such as products and customers. The costs computed under activity-based costing are often quite different from the costs generated by a company's traditional cost accounting system. While the ABC system is almost certainly more accurate, managers should nevertheless exercise caution before making decisions based on the ABC data. A vital part of any activity-based analysis of product or customer profitability is an action analysis that identifies who is ultimately responsible for each cost and the ease with which the cost can be adjusted.
- ABC and ABM are not without their critics, as may be seen in the references suggested in further reading. Some of these criticisms may be better understood after we have considered ABC in a wider context of organizational change and other approaches to business process improvement in Chapter 18.

Key terms for review

Action analysis report (p. 294).

Activity (p. 278).

Activity-based costing (ABC) (p. 276).

Activity-based management (ABM) (p. 286).

Activity cost pool (p. 282).

Activity measure (p. 282).

Batch-level activities (p. 281).

Customer-level activities (p. 281).

Ease of adjustment codes (p. 293).

First-stage allocation (p. 283).

Organization-sustaining activities (p. 281).

Product-level activities (p. 281).

Second-stage allocation (p. 287).

Unit-level activities (p. 281).

Review problem: activity-based costing

Ferris Corporation makes a single product – a fire-resistant commercial filing cabinet – that it sells to office furniture distributors. The company has a simple ABC system that it uses for internal decision making. The company has two overhead departments whose costs are listed below:

Manufacturing overhead	£500,000
Selling and administrative overhead	300,000
Total overhead costs	£800,000

The company's ABC system has the following activity cost pools and activity measures:

Activity cost pool	Activity measure
Volume related	Number of units
Order related	Number of orders
Customer support	Number of customers
Other	Not applicable

Costs assigned to the 'Other' activity cost pool have no activity measure; they consist of the costs of unused capacity and organization-sustaining costs – neither of which are assigned to products, orders or customers.

Ferris Corporation distributes the costs of manufacturing overhead and of selling and administrative overhead to the activity cost pools based on employee interviews, the results of which are reported below:

Distribution of resource consumption across activities	Volume related	Order related	Customer support	Other	Total
Manufacturing overhead	50%	35%	5%	10%	100%
Selling and administrative overhead	10%	45%	25%	20%	100%
Total activity	1,000 units	250 orders	100 customers		

Required

1 Perform the first-stage allocations of overhead costs to the activity cost pools as in Exhibit 8.4.

2 Compute activity rates for the activity cost pools as in Exhibit 8.5.

3 OfficeMart is one of Ferris Corporation's customers. Last year, OfficeMart ordered filing cabinets four different times. OfficeMart ordered a total of 80 filing cabinets during the year. Construct a table as in Exhibit 8.8A showing the overhead costs of these 80 units and four orders.

4 The selling price of a filing cabinet is £595. The cost of direct materials is £180 per filing cabinet, and direct labour is £50 per filing cabinet. What is the product margin on the 80 filing cabinets ordered by OfficeMart? How profitable is OfficeMart as a customer? See Exhibit 8.9 for an example of how to complete this report.

5 Management of Ferris Corporation has assigned ease of adjustment codes to the various costs as follows:

Cost	Ease of adjustment code
Direct materials	Green
Direct labour	Yellow
Manufacturing overhead	Yellow
Selling and administrative overhead	Red

Prepare an activity analysis of the OfficeMart orders as in Exhibit 8.12.

Solution to review problem: activity-based costing

1 The first-stage allocation of costs to the activity cost pools appears below:

	Activity cost pools				
	Volume related	Order-related cost	Customer support	Other	Total
Manufacturing overhead	£250,000	£175,000	£25,000	£50,000	£500,000
Selling and administrative overhead	30,000	135,000	75,000	60,000	300,000
Total cost	£280,000	£310,000	£100,000	£110,000	£800,000

2 The activity rates for the activity cost pools are:

	Volume related	Order related	Customer support
Manufacturing overhead	£250	£700	£250
Selling and administrative overhead	30	540	750
Total cost	£280	£1,240	£1,000

3 The overhead cost for the four orders of a total of 80 filing cabinets would be computed as follows:

	Volume related	Order related	Total
Activity	80 units	4 orders	
Manufacturing overhead	£20,000	£2,800	£22,800
Selling and administrative overhead	2,400	2,160	4,560
Total cost	£22,400	£4,960	£27,360

4 The product and customer margins can be computed as follows:

Filing cabinet product margin

Sales (£595 × 80)		£47,600
Cost:		
Direct materials (£180 × 80)	£14,400	
Direct labour (£50 × 80)	4,000	
Volume-related overhead (above)	22,400	
Order-related overhead (above)	4,960	45,760
Product margin		£1,840
Customer profitability analysis – OfficeMart		
Product margin (above)	£1,840	
Less: Customer support overhead (above)	1,000	
Customer margin	£840	

5 The activity analysis of the four orders for 80 filing cabinets in total is

Action analysis report for four orders totalling 80 units

Sales		£47,600
Green costs:		
Direct materials	£14,400	14,400
Green margin		33,200
Yellow costs:		
Direct labour	4,000	
Manufacturing overhead	22,800	26,800
Yellow margin		6,400
Red costs:		
Selling and administrative overhead	4,560	4,560
Red margin		£1,840

Note: An action analysis report can also be completed for OfficeMart as a customer. The first step would be to calculate the overhead costs for OfficeMart as follows:

	Volume Related	**Order related**	**Customer support**	**Total**
Activity	80 units	4 orders	1 customer	
Manufacturing overhead	£20,000	£2,800	£250	£23,050
Selling and administrative overhead	2,400	2,160	750	5,310
Total cost	£22,400	£4,960	£1,000	£28,360

The action analysis report can then be easily prepared as follows:

Action analysis report for OfficeMart as a customer

Sales		£47,600
Green costs:		
Direct materials	£14,400	14,400
Green margin		33,200
Yellow costs:		
Direct labour	4,000	
Manufacturing overhead	23,050	27,050
Yellow margin		6,150
Red costs:		
Selling and administrative overhead	5,310	5,310
Red margin		£840

Questions

8–1 In what fundamental ways does activity-based costing differ from traditional costing methods such as those described in Chapters 2 and 3?

8–2 Why is direct labour a poor base for allocating overhead in many companies?

8–3 Why are overhead rates in activity-based costing based on the level of activity at capacity rather than on the budgeted level of activity?

8–4 Why is top management support crucial when attempting to implement an activity-based costing system?

8–5 What are unit-level, batch-level, product-level, customer-level and organization-sustaining activities?

8–6 What types of costs should not be assigned to products in an activity-based costing system?

8–7 Why are there two stages of allocation in activity-based costing?

8–8 Why is the first stage of the allocation process in activity-based costing often based on interviews?

8–9 How can the activity rates (i.e., cost per activity) for the various activities be used to target process improvements?

8–10 When activity-based costing is used, why are manufacturing overhead costs often shifted from high-volume products to low-volume products?

8–11 Why should an activity view of product margins such as in Exhibit 8.9 be supplemented with an action analysis such as in Exhibit 8.12 when making decisions about products or customers?

8–12 Why is the activity-based costing described in this chapter probably unacceptable for external financial reports?

8-13 Why is ABC particularly suitable for managing costs in service industries?

EXERCISES

Exercises

E8–1 Time allowed: 10 minutes

CD Express Ltd provides CD duplicating services to software companies. The customer provides a master CD from which CD Express makes copies. An order from a customer can be for a single copy or for thousands of copies. Most jobs are broken down into batches to allow smaller jobs, with higher priorities, to have access to the machines.

Below are listed a number of activities carried out at CD Express.

(a) Sales representatives' periodic visits to customers to keep them informed about the services provided by CD Express

(b) Ordering labels from the printer for a particular CD

(c) Setting up the CD duplicating machine to make copies from a particular master CD

(d) Loading the automatic labelling machine with labels for a particular CD

(e) Visually inspecting CDs and placing them by hand into protective plastic cases prior to shipping

(f) Preparation of the shipping documents for the order

(g) Periodic maintenance of equipment

(h) Lighting and heating the company's production facility

(i) Preparation of quarterly financial reports.

Required

Classify each of the activities above as either a unit-level, batch-level, product-level, customer-level, or organization-sustaining activity. (An order to duplicate a particular CD is a product-level activity.) Assume the order is large enough that it must be broken down into batches.

E8–2 Time allowed: 10 minutes

Listed below are a number of activities that you have observed at Ming Company, a manufacturing company. Each activity has been classified as a unit-level, batch-level, product-level, or customer-level activity.

Activity	Level of activity	Examples of activity measures
(a) Direct labour workers assemble a product	Unit	
(b) Products are designed by engineers	Product	
(c) Equipment is set up	Batch	
(d) Machines are used to shape and cut materials	Unit	
(e) Monthly bills are sent out to regular customers	Customer	
(f) Materials are moved from the receiving dock to production lines	Batch	
(g) All completed units are inspected for defects	Unit	

Required

Complete the table by providing examples of activity measures for each activity that could be used to allocate its costs to products or customers.

E8–3 Time allowed: 15 minutes

Listed below are a number of activities that you have observed at Vapo Ingman Oy, a Finnish manufacturing company. The company makes a variety of products at its plant outside Helsinki.

(a) Machine settings are changed between batches of different products

(b) Parts inventories are maintained in the storeroom (each product requires unique parts)

(c) Products are milled on a milling machine

(d) New employees are hired by the personnel office

(e) New products are designed

(f) Periodic maintenance is performed on general-purpose production equipment

(g) A bill is sent to a customer who is late in making payments

(h) Yearly taxes are paid on the company's facilities

(i) Purchase orders are issued for materials to be used in production.

Required

1 Classify each of the activities above as either a unit-level, batch-level, product-level, customer-level, or organization-sustaining activity.

2 Where possible, for each activity name one or more activity measures that might be used to assign costs generated by the activity to products or customers.

E8–4 Time allowed: 10 minutes

The operations manager of Security Home Bank has been interested in investigating the efficiency of the bank's operations. She has been particularly concerned about the costs of handling routine transactions at the bank and would like to compare these costs at the bank's various branches. If the branches with the most efficient operations can be identified, their methods can be studied and then replicated elsewhere. While the bank maintains meticulous records of wages and other costs, there has been no attempt thus far to show how those costs are related to the various services provided by the bank. The operations manager has asked your help in conducting an activity-based costing study of bank operations. In particular, she would like to know the cost of opening an account, the cost of processing deposits and withdrawals, and the cost of processing other customer transactions.

The Westfield branch of Security Home Bank has submitted the following cost data for last year:

Teller wages	£160,000
Assistant branch manager salary	75,000
Branch manager salary	80,000
Total	£315,000

Virtually all of the other costs of the branch – rent, depreciation, utilities and so on – are organization-sustaining costs that cannot be meaningfully assigned to individual customer transactions such as depositing cheques.

In addition to the cost data above, the employees of the Westfield branch have been interviewed concerning how their time was distributed last year across the activities included in the activity-based costing study. The results of those interviews appear below:

Distribution of resource consumption across activities

	Opening accounts	Processing deposits and Withdrawals	Processing other customer transactions	Other activities	Total
Teller wages	5%	65%	20%	10%	100%
Assistant branch manager salary	15%	5%	30%	50%	100%
Branch manager salary	5%	0%	10%	85%	100%

Required

Prepare the first-stage allocation for the activity-based costing study. (See Exhibit 8.4 for an example of a first-stage allocation.)

E8–5 Time allowed: 20 minutes

(This exercise is a continuation of E8–4; it should be assigned only if E8–4 is also assigned.) The manager of the Westfield branch of Security Home Bank has provided the following data concerning the transactions of the branch during the past year:

Activity	**Total activity at the Westfield Branch**
Opening accounts	500 new accounts opened
Processing deposits and withdrawals	100,000 deposits and withdrawals processed
Processing other customer transactions	5,000 other customer transactions processed

The lowest costs reported by other branches for these activities are displayed below:

Activity	**Lowest cost among all Security Home Bank Branches**
Opening accounts	£26.75 per new account
Processing deposits and withdrawals	£1.24 per deposit or withdrawal
Processing other customer transactions	£11.86 per other customer transaction

Required

1 Using the first-stage allocation from E8–4 and the above data, compute the activity rates for the activity-based costing system. (Use Exhibit 8.5 as a guide.) Round all computations to the nearest whole cent.

2 What do these results suggest to you concerning operations at the Westfield branch?

E8–6 Time allowed: 20 minutes

Durban Metal Products Ltd of the Republic of South Africa makes speciality metal parts used in applications ranging from the cutting edges of bulldozer blades to replacement parts for Land Rovers. The company uses an activity-based costing system for internal decision-making purposes. The company has four activity cost pools as listed below:

Activity cost pool	**Activity measure**
Order size	Number of direct labour-hours
Customer orders	Number of customer orders
Product testing	Number of testing hours
Selling	Number of sales calls

The results of the first-stage allocation of the activity-based costing system, in which the activity rates were computed, appear below:

	Order size	Customer orders	Product testing	Selling
Manufacturing:				
Indirect labour	R8.25	R180.00	R30.00	R0.00
Factory depreciation	8.00	0.00	40.00	0.00
Factory utilities	0.10	0.00	1.00	0.00
Factory administration	0.00	48.00	18.00	30.00
General selling and administrative:				
Wages and salaries	0.50	80.00	0.00	800.00
Depreciation	0.00	12.00	0.00	40.00
Taxes and insurance	0.00	0.00	0.00	20.00
Selling expenses	0.00	0.00	0.00	200.00
Overhead cost	R16.85	R320.00	R89.00	R1,090.00

Note: The currency in South Africa is the Rand, denoted here by R.

The managing director of the company would like information concerning the cost of a recently completed order for heavy-duty trailer axles. The order required 200 direct labour-hours, 4 hours of product testing, and 2 sales calls.

Required

1 Prepare a report showing the overhead cost of the order for heavy-duty trailer axles according to the activity-based costing system. (Use Exhibit 8.8A as a guide.) What is the total overhead cost of the order according to the activity-based costing system?

2 Explain the two different perspectives this report gives to managers concerning the nature of the overhead costs involved in the order. (*Hint*: Look at the row and column totals of the report you have prepared.)

PROBLEMS

Problems

P8–7 Activity rates and pricing job Time allowed: 45 minutes

Mercer Asbestos Removal Company is in the business of removing potentially toxic asbestos insulation and related products from buildings. There has been a long-simmering dispute between the company's estimator and the work supervisors. The on-site supervisors claim that the estimators do not take enough care in distinguishing between routine work such as removal of asbestos insulation around heating pipes in older homes and non-routine work such as removing asbestos-contaminated ceiling plaster in industrial buildings. The on-site supervisors believe that non-routine work is far more expensive than routine work and should bear higher customer charges. The estimator sums up his position in this way: 'My job is to measure the area to be cleared of asbestos. As directed by top management, I simply multiply the square meterage by £2.50 to determine the bid price. Since our average cost is only £2.175 per square metre, that leaves enough cushion to take care of the additional costs of non-routine work that shows up. Besides, it is difficult to know what is routine or not routine until you actually start tearing things apart.'

Partly to shed light on this controversy, the company initiated an activity-based costing study of all of its costs. Data from the activity-based costing system follow:

Activity cost pool	Activity measure
Job size	Thousands of square metres
Estimating and job set-up	Number of jobs
Dealing with non-routine jobs	Number of non-routine jobs
Other (costs of idle capacity and organization-sustaining costs)	Not applicable; these costs are not allocated to jobs

	Costs for the year
Wages and salaries	£300,000
Disposal fees	700,000
Equipment depreciation	90,000
On-site supplies	50,000
Office expenses	200,000
Licensing and insurance	400,000
Total cost	£1,740,000

Distribution of resource consumption across activities

	Job size	Estimating and job set-up	Dealing with non-routine jobs	Other	Total
Wages and salaries	50%	10%	30%	10%	100%
Disposal fees	60%	0%	40%	0%	100%
Equipment depreciation	40%	5%	20%	35%	100%
On-site supplies	60%	30%	10%	0%	100%
Office expenses	10%	35%	25%	30%	100%
Licensing and insurance	30%	0%	50%	20%	100%

Activity cost pool	Activity for the year
Job size	800 thousand square metres
Estimating and job set-up	500 jobs
Dealing with non-routine jobs	100 non-routine jobs

Note: The 100 non-routine jobs are included in the total of 500 jobs. Both non-routine jobs and routine jobs require estimating and setup.

Required

1 Perform the first-stage allocation of costs to the activity cost pools. (Use Exhibit 8.4 as a guide.)

2 Compute the activity rates for the activity cost pools. (Use Exhibit 8.5 as a guide or the simpler approach described at the end of the chapter.)

3 Using the activity rates you have computed, determine the total cost and the average cost per thousand square metres of each of the following jobs according to the activity-based costing system.

(You will not be able to do an activity analysis because the ease of adjustment codes have not been provided.)

(a) A routine 1,000-square-metre asbestos removal job.

(b) A routine 2,000-square-metre asbestos removal job.

(c) A non-routine 2,000-square-metre asbestos removal job.

4 Given the results you obtained in Question 3 above, do you agree with the estimator that the company's present policy for bidding on jobs is adequate?

P8–8 Activity rates and activity-based management Time allowed: 30 minutes

Aerotraiteur SA is a French company that provides passenger and crew meals to airlines operating out of the two international airports of Paris – Orly and Charles de Gaulle (CDG). The operations at Orly and CDG are managed separately, and top management believes that there may be benefits in greater sharing of information between the two operations.

To better compare the two operations, an activity-based costing system has been designed with the active participation of the managers at both Orly and CDG. The activity-based costing system is based on the following activity cost pools and activity measures:

Activity cost pool	Activity measure
Meal preparation	Number of meals
Flight-related activities	Number of flights
Customer service	Number of customers
Other (costs of idle capacity and organization-sustaining costs)	Not applicable

The operation at CDG airport serves 1.5 million meals annually on 7,500 flights for ten different airlines. (Each airline is considered one customer.) The annual cost of running the CDG airport operation, excluding only the costs of raw materials for meals, totals €29,400,000.

Annual cost of the CDG operation	
Cooks and delivery personnel wages	€24,000,000
Kitchen supplies	300,000
Chef salaries	1,800,000
Equipment depreciation	600,000
Administrative wages and salaries	1,500,000
Building costs	1,200,000
Total cost	€29,400,000

The results of employee interviews at CDG are displayed below:

Distribution of resource consumption across activities at the CDG operation (percentages)

	Meal preparation	Flight related	Customer service	Other	Total
Cooks and delivery personnel wages	75%	20%	0%	5%	100%
Kitchen supplies	100%	0%	0%	0%	100%
Chef salaries	30%	20%	40%	10%	100%
Equipment depreciation	60%	0%	0%	40%	100%
Administrative wages and salaries	0%	20%	60%	20%	100%
Building costs	0%	0%	0%	100%	100%

Required

1 Perform the first-stage allocation of costs to the activity cost pools. (Use Exhibit 8.4 as a guide.)

2 Compute the activity rates for the activity cost pools. (Use Exhibit 8.5 as a guide.)

3 The Orly operation has already concluded its activity-based costing study and has reported the following costs of carrying out activities at Orly:

	Meal preparation	Flight related	Customer service
Cooks and delivery personnel wages	€12.20	€780	
Kitchen supplies	0.25		
Chef salaries	0.18	32	€54,000
Equipment depreciation	0.23		
Administrative wages and salaries		45	67,000
Building costs	0.00	0	0
Total cost	€12.86	€857	€122,000

Comparing the activity rates for the CDG operation you computed in (2) above to the activity rates for Orly, do you have any suggestions for the top management of Aerotraiteur SA?

P8–9 Activity-based costing as an alternative to traditional product costing: simplified method Time allowed: 45 minutes

This chapter emphasizes the use of activity-based costing in internal decisions. However, a modified form of activity-based costing can also be used to develop product costs for external financial reports. For this purpose, product costs include all manufacturing overhead costs and exclude all non-manufacturing costs. This problem illustrates such a costing system.

Siegel Company manufactures a product that is available in both a deluxe model and a regular model. The company has manufactured the regular model for years. The deluxe model was introduced several years ago to tap a new segment of the market. Since introduction of the deluxe model, the company's profits have steadily declined and management has become increasingly concerned about the accuracy of its costing system. Sales of the deluxe model have been increasing rapidly.

Manufacturing overhead is assigned to products on the basis of direct labour-hours. For the current year, the company has estimated that it will incur £900,000 in manufacturing overhead cost and produce 5,000 units of the deluxe model and 40,000 units of the regular model. The deluxe model requires two hours of direct labour time per unit, and the regular model requires one hour. Material and labour costs per unit are as follows:

	Model	
	Deluxe	Regular
Direct materials	£40	£25
Direct labour	14	7

Required

1 Using direct labour-hours as the base for assigning overhead cost to products, compute the predetermined overhead rate. Using this rate and other data from the problem, determine the unit product cost of each model.

2 Management is considering using activity-based costing to apply manufacturing overhead cost to products for external financial reports. The activity-based costing system would have the following four activity cost centres:

Activity cost pool	Activity measure	Estimated overhead cost
Purchasing	Purchase orders issued	£204,000
Processing	Machine-hours	182,000
Scrap/rework	Scrap/rework orders issued	379,000
Shipping	Number of shipments	135,000
		£900,000

	Expected activity		
Activity measure	Deluxe	Regular	Total
Purchase orders issued	200	400	600
Machine-hours	20,000	15,000	35,000
Scrap/rework orders issued	1,000	1,000	2,000
Number of shipments	250	650	900

Using the simplified approach described at the end of the chapter, determine the predetermined overhead rate for each of the four activity cost pools.

3 Using the predetermined overhead rates you computed in Question 2 above, do the following:

(a) Compute the total amount of manufacturing overhead cost that would be applied to each model using the activity-based costing system. After these totals have been computed, determine the amount of manufacturing overhead cost per unit of each model.

(b) Compute the unit product cost of each model.

4 From the data you have developed in Questions 1–3 above, identify factors that may account for the company's declining profits.

P8–10 ABC profit statement, ABM and implementation of ABC Time allowed: 35 minutes
Admer owns several home furnishing stores. In each store, consultations, if needed, are undertaken by specialists, who also visit potential customers in their homes, using specialist software to help customers realize their design objectives. Customers visit the store to make their selections from the wide range of goods offered, after which sales staff collect payment and raise a purchase order. Customers then collect their self-assembly goods from the warehouse, using the purchase order as authority to collect. Administration staff process purchase orders and also arrange consultations.

Each store operates an absorption costing system and costs other than the cost of goods sold are apportioned on the basis of sales floor area.

Results for one of Admer's stores for the last three months are as follows:

Department	Kitchens	Bathrooms	Dining Rooms	Total
	£	£	£	£
Sales	210,000	112,500	440,000	762,500
Cost of goods sold	63,000	37,500	176,000	276,500
Other costs	130,250	81,406	113,968	325,624
Profit	16,750	(6,406)	150,032	160,376

The management accountant of Admer is concerned that the bathrooms department of the store has been showing a loss for some time, and is considering a proposal to close the bathrooms department in order to concentrate on the more profitable kitchens and dining rooms departments. He has found that other costs for this store for the last three months are made up of:

	£	Employees
Sales staff wages	64,800	12
Consultation staff wages	24,960	4
Warehouse staff wages	30,240	6
Administration staff wages	30,624	4
General overheads (light, heat, rates, etc.)	175,000	
	325,624	

He has also collected the following information for the last three months:

Department	Kitchens	Bathrooms	Dining Rooms
Number of items sold	1,000	1,500	4,000
Purchase orders	1,000	900	2,500
Floor area (square metres)	16,000	10,000	14,000
Number of consultations	798	200	250

The management accountant believes that he can use this information to review the store's performance in the last three months from an activity-based costing (ABC) perspective.

Required

(a) Discuss the management accountant's belief that the information provided can be used in an activity-based costing analysis. *(4 marks)*

(b) Explain and illustrate, using supporting calculations, how an ABC profit statement might be produced from the information provided. Clearly explain the reasons behind your choice of cost drivers. *(8 marks)*

(c) Evaluate and discuss the proposal to close the bathrooms department. *(6 marks)*

(d) Discuss the advantages and disadvantages that may arise for Admer from introducing activity-based costing in its stores. *(7 marks)*

(Total = 25 marks)

ACCA Financial Management and Information, June 2004

Cases

CASE

C8–11 Evaluating the profitability of customers Time allowed: 90 minutes

Classic Windows is a small company that builds speciality wooden windows for local builders. For years the company has relied on a simple costing system based on direct labour-hours (DLHs) for determining the costs of its products. However, the company's president became interested in activity-based costing after reading an article about ABC in a trade journal. An activity-based costing design team was put together, and within a few months a simple system consisting of four activity cost pools had been designed.

The activity cost pools and their activity measures appear below:

Activity cost pool	Activity measure	Activity for the year
Making windows	Direct labour-hours	100,000 DLHs
Processing orders	Number of orders	2,000 orders
Customer relations	Number of customers	100 customers
Other (costs of idle capacity and organization-sustaining costs)	None	Not applicable

The Processing Orders activity cost pool includes order taking, job set-up, job scheduling and so on. Direct materials and direct labour are directly assigned to jobs in both the traditional and activity-based costing systems. The total overhead cost (both non-manufacturing and manufacturing) for the year is £1,370,000 and includes the following costs:

Manufacturing overhead costs:		
Indirect factory wages	£400,000	
Production equipment depreciation	300,000	
Other factory costs	80,000	£780,000
Selling and administrative expenses:		
Administrative wages and salaries	300,000	
Office expenses	40,000	
Marketing expenses	250,000	590,000
Total overhead cost		£1,370,000

Based largely on interviews with employees, the distribution of resource consumption across the activities has been estimated as follows:

Distribution of resource consumption across activities (percentages)

	Making windows	Processing orders	Customer relations	Other	Total
Indirect factory wages	30	40	10	20	100
Production equipment depreciation	90	0	0	10	100
Other factory costs	30	0	0	70	100
Administrative wages and salaries	0	20	30	50	100
Office expenses	0	30	10	60	100
Marketing expenses	0	0	60	40	100

Management of the company is particularly interested in measuring the profitability of two customers. One of the customers, Kuszik Builders, is a low-volume purchaser. The other, Western Homes, is a relatively high-volume purchaser. Details of these two customers' orders for the year appear below:

	Kuszik Builders	Western Homes
Number of orders during the year	2 orders	3 orders
Total direct labour hours	300 DLHs	2,000 DLHs
Total sales	£12,500	£68,000
Total direct materials	£4,200	£18,500
Total direct labour cost	£5,400	£36,000

Required

1 The company's traditional costing system applies manufacturing overhead to jobs strictly on the basis of direct labour-hours. Using this traditional approach, carry out the following steps:

(a) Compute the predetermined manufacturing overhead rate.

(b) Compute the total margin for all of the windows ordered by Kuszik Builders according to the traditional costing system. Do the same for Western Homes.

2 Using activity-based costing, carry out the following steps:

(a) Perform the first-stage allocation of costs to the activity cost pools (use Exhibit 8.4 as a guide).

(b) Compute the activity rates for the activity cost pools (use Exhibit 8.5 as a guide).

(c) Compute the overhead costs of serving each of the two customers. (You will need to construct a table like Exhibit 8.8A for each of the customers. However, unlike Exhibit 8.8A, you should fill in the column for Customer Relations as well as the other columns. Exhibit 8.8A was constructed for a product; in this case we are interested in a customer.)

(d) Prepare an action analysis report showing the margin on business with Kuszik Builders. (The ease of adjustment codes appear below.) Repeat for Western Homes.

	Ease of adjustment code
Direct materials	Green
Direct labour	Yellow
Indirect factory wages	Yellow
Production equipment depreciation	Yellow
Other factory costs	Yellow
Administrative wages and salaries	Red
Office expenses	Yellow
Marketing expenses	Yellow

3 Does Classic Windows appear to be losing money on either customer? Do the traditional and activity-based costing systems agree concerning the profitability of the customers? If they do not agree, which costing system do you believe? Why?

C8–12 Activity-based costing as an alternative to traditional product costing: simplified method Time allowed: 90 minutes

'A pound of gross margin per briefcase? That's ridiculous!' roared Jack Dejans, managing director of CarryAll Ltd. 'Why do we go on producing those standard briefcases when we're able to make over £15 per unit on our speciality items? Maybe it's time to get out of the standard line and focus the whole plant on speciality work.'

Mr Dejans is referring to a summary of unit costs and revenues that he had just received from the company's Accounting Department:

	Standard briefcases	Speciality briefcases
Selling price per unit	£36	£40
Unit product cost	35	25
Gross margin per unit	£1	£15

CarryAll produces briefcases from leather, fabric and synthetic materials in a single plant. The basic product is a standard briefcase that is made from leather lined with fabric. The standard briefcase is a high-quality item and has sold well for many years.

Last year, the company decided to expand its product line and produce speciality briefcases for special orders. These briefcases differ from the standard in that they vary in size, they contain the finest synthetic materials, and they are imprinted with the buyer's name. To reduce labour costs on the speciality briefcases, most of the cutting and stitching is done by automated machines. These machines are used to a much lesser degree in the production of standard briefcases.

'I agree that the speciality business is looking better and better,' replied Sally Henrie, the company's marketing manager. 'And there seems to be plenty of speciality work out there, particularly since the competition hasn't been able to touch our price. Did you know that Armour Company, our biggest competitor, charges over £50 a unit for its speciality items? Now that's what I call gouging the customer!'

A breakdown of the manufacturing cost for each of CarryAll's product lines is given below:

	Standard briefcases		Speciality briefcases	
Units produced each month	10,000		2,500	
Direct materials:				
Leather	1.0 sq. m.	£15.00	0.5 sq. m.	£7.50
Fabric	1.0 sq. m.	5.00	1.0 sq. m.	5.00
Synthetic		–		5.00
Total materials		20.00		17.50
Direct labour	0.5 hr.@ £12	6.00	0.25 hr.@ £12	3.00
Manufacturing overhead	0.5 hr.@ £18	9.00	0.25 hr.@ £18	4.50
Unit product cost		£35.00		£25.00

Manufacturing overhead is applied to products on the basis of direct labour-hours. The rate of £18 per direct labour-hour is determined by dividing the total manufacturing overhead cost for a month by the direct labour-hours:

$$\frac{\text{Manufacturing overhead cost, £101,250}}{\text{Direct labour-hours, 5,625}} = \text{£18 per DLH}$$

The following additional information is available about the company and its products:

(a) Standard briefcases are produced in batches of 200 units, and speciality briefcases are produced in batches of 25 units. Thus, the company does 50 set-ups for the standard items each month and 100 set-ups for the speciality items. A set-up for the standard items requires one hour of time, whereas a set-up for the speciality items requires two hours of time.

(b) All briefcases are inspected to ensure that quality standards are met. A total of 300 hours of inspection time is spent on the standard briefcases and 500 hours of inspection time is spent on the speciality briefcases each month.

(c) A standard briefcase requires 0.5 hour of machine time, and a speciality briefcase requires 2 hours of machine time.

(d) The company is considering the use of activity-based costing as an alternative to its traditional costing system for computing unit product costs. Since these unit product costs will be used for external financial reporting, all manufacturing overhead costs are to be allocated to products and non-manufacturing costs are to be excluded from product costs. The activity-based costing system has already been designed and costs allocated to the activity cost pools. The activity cost pools and activity measures are detailed below:

Activity cost pool	Activity measure	Estimated overhead cost
Purchasing	Number of orders	£12,000
Material handling	Number of receipts	15,000
Production orders and setup	Set-up hours	20,250
Inspection	Inspection-hours	16,000
Frame assembly	Assembly-hours	8,000
Machine related	Machine-hours	30,000
		£101,250

Activity measure	Expected activity Standard briefcase	Speciality briefcase	Total
Number of orders:			
Leather	34	6	40
Fabric	48	12	60
Synthetic material	–	100	100
Number of receipts:			
Leather	52	8	60
Fabric	64	16	80
Synthetic material	–	160	160
Set-up hours	?	?	?
Inspection-hours	?	?	?
Assembly-hours	800	800	1,600
Machine-hours	?	?	?

Required

1 Using activity-based costing and the simplified approach described at the end of the chapter, determine the amount of manufacturing overhead cost that would be applied to each standard briefcase and each speciality briefcase.

2 Using the data computed in 1 above and other data from the case as needed, determine the unit product cost of each product line from the perspective of the activity-based costing system.

3 Ideally, what changes should be made in CarryAll's activity-based costing system if it is to be used for making decisions about products?

4 Within the limitations of the data that have been provided, evaluate the managing director's concern about the profitability of the two product lines. Would you recommend that the company shift its resources entirely to production of speciality briefcases? Explain.

5 Sally Henrie stated that 'the competition hasn't been able to touch our price' on speciality business. Why do you suppose the competition hasn't been able to touch CarryAll's price?

(Adapted from a case written by Harold P. Roth and Imogene Posey, 'Management Accounting Case Study: CarryAll Company', *Management Accounting Campus Report*, Institute of Management Accountants, Fall 1991, p. 9. Used by permission.)

Further reading

There is a huge and growing literature on ABC in both academic and practitioner journals. Some recent articles have tried to put this literature into some perspective. See, for example, Bjornenak and Mitchell (2000); Kaplan and Cooper (1998); Jones and Dugdale (2002).

For some more critical interpretations see Armstrong (2002); Johnson (1992).

Endnotes

1 Greco (1996).

2 Böer (1994) provides some data concerning these trends. Data maintained by the US Department of Commerce shows that since 1849, on average, material cost as a percentage of manufacturing cost has been fairly constant at 55% of sales. Labour cost has always been relatively less important and has declined steadily from 23% in 1849 to about 10% in 1987. Overhead has grown from about 18% of sales in 1947 to about 33% of sales 50 years later.

3 Brignall, Fitzgerald, Johnston and Silvestro (1991).

4 See Cooper and Kaplan (1988).

5 Merz and Hardy (1993).

6 King (1993).

7 Brignall *et al.* (1991).

8 Kaplan and Cooper (1998).

9 See Seal and Croft (1997); Cressey and Scott (1992).

10 Kaplan and Cooper (1998).

11 Miner (2002).

12 Cobbold (2003).

Chapter 9
Relevant costs for decision making

Learning objectives

After studying Chapter 9, you should be able to:

1 Distinguish between relevant and irrelevant costs in decisions

2 Prepare an analysis showing whether to keep or replace old equipment

3 Prepare an analysis showing whether a product line or other organizational segment should be dropped or retained

4 Prepare a well-organized make or buy analysis

5 Prepare an analysis showing whether a special order should be accepted

6 Determine the most profitable use of a constrained resource

7 Prepare an analysis showing whether joint products should be sold at the split-off point or processed further

Concepts in Context

The costing used in routine accounting may be difficult to reconcile with costs that have been developed for decision making in *ad hoc* projects. Why? The main reason is that traditional accounting is period-oriented while project budgets are task- or decision-oriented. As Arthur explains: 'Project managers and project planners tend to think in terms of tasks, task costs, and planning-based forecasts. They are used to being able to produce *ad hoc* reports at any time of the month and to being able to do extensive "what if?" analysis on the project plan. They are unaware of the data collection and reporting processes that underlie accounting reports, and tend to be unsympathetic to the restrictions these impose. ...' Accountants, on the other hand, tend to think in terms of time periods and cost types – they ask, 'What did we spend on labour in May?', rather than, 'What did it cost us to build module 4?' If accountants want to be relevant to project decision making then they need to adjust their orientation and their accounting models.[1]

Making decisions is one of the basic functions of a manager. Managers are constantly faced with problems of deciding what products to sell, what production methods to use, whether to make or buy component parts, what prices to charge, what channels of distribution to use, whether to accept special orders at special prices, and so forth. Decision making is often a difficult task that is complicated by the existence of numerous alternatives and massive amounts of data, only some of which may be relevant.

Every decision involves choosing from among at least two alternatives. In making a decision, the costs and benefits of one alternative must be compared to the costs and benefits of other alternatives. Costs that differ between alternatives are called **relevant costs**. Distinguishing between relevant and irrelevant cost and benefit data is critical for two reasons. First, irrelevant data can be ignored and need not be analysed. This can save decision makers tremendous amounts of time and effort. Second, bad decisions can easily result from erroneously including irrelevant cost and benefit data when analysing alternatives. To be successful in decision making, managers must be able to tell the difference between relevant and irrelevant data and must be able to correctly use the relevant data in analysing alternatives. The purpose of this chapter is to develop these skills by illustrating their use in a wide range of decision-making situations. We hasten to add that these decision-making skills are as important in your personal life as they are to managers. After completing your study of the material in this chapter, you should be able to think more clearly about decisions in all facets of your life.

Cost concepts for decision making

Four cost terms discussed in Chapter 2 are particularly applicable to this chapter. These terms are *differential costs, incremental costs, opportunity costs* and *sunk costs*. You may find it helpful to turn back to Chapter 2 and refresh your memory concerning these terms before reading on.

Identifying relevant costs and benefits

Only those costs and benefits that differ in total between alternatives are relevant in a decision. If a cost will be the same regardless of the alternative selected, then the decision has no effect on the cost and it can be ignored. For example, if you are trying to decide whether to go to a film or to rent a videotape for the evening, the rent on your apartment is irrelevant. Whether you go to a film or rent a videotape, the rent on your apartment will be exactly the same and is therefore irrelevant in the decision. On the other hand, the cost of the film ticket and the cost of renting the videotape would be relevant in the decision since they are *avoidable* costs.

An **avoidable cost** is a cost that can be eliminated in whole or in part by choosing one alternative over another. By choosing the alternative of going to the film, the cost of renting the videotape can be avoided. By choosing the alternative of renting the videotape, the cost of the film ticket can be avoided. Therefore, the cost of the film ticket and the cost of renting the videotape are both avoidable costs. On the other hand, the rent on the apartment is not an avoidable cost of either alternative. You would continue to rent your apartment under either alternative. Avoidable costs are relevant costs. Unavoidable costs are irrelevant costs.

Two broad categories of costs are never relevant in decisions. These irrelevant costs are:

1 Sunk costs
2 Future costs that do not differ between the alternatives.

As we learned in Chapter 2, a **sunk cost** is a cost that has already been incurred and that cannot be avoided regardless of what a manager decides to do. Sunk costs are always the same, no matter what alternatives are being considered, and they are therefore always irrelevant and should be ignored. On the other hand, future costs that do differ between alternatives are relevant. For example, when deciding whether to go to a film or rent a videotape, the cost of buying a film ticket and the cost of renting a videotape have not yet been incurred. These are future costs that differ between alternatives when the decision is being made and therefore are relevant.

Along with sunk cost, the term **differential cost** was introduced in Chapter 2. In management accounting, the terms *avoidable cost, differential cost, incremental cost*, and *relevant cost* are often used interchangeably. To identify the costs that are avoidable (differential) in a particular decision situation and are therefore relevant, these steps can be followed:

1 Eliminate costs and benefits that do not differ between alternatives. These irrelevant costs consist of (a) sunk costs and (b) future costs that do not differ between alternatives.
2 Use the remaining costs and benefits that do differ between alternatives in making the decision. The costs that remain are the differential, or avoidable, costs.

Different costs for different purposes

We need to recognize from the outset of our discussion that costs that are relevant in one decision situation are not necessarily relevant in another. Simply put, this means that *the manager needs different costs for different purposes*. For one purpose, a particular group of costs may be relevant; for another purpose, an entirely different group of costs may be relevant. Thus, in each decision situation the manager must examine the data at hand and isolate the relevant costs. Otherwise, the manager runs the risk of being misled by irrelevant data.

The concept of 'different costs for different purposes' is basic to managerial accounting; we shall see its application frequently in the pages that follow.

Sunk costs are not relevant costs

One of the most difficult conceptual lessons that managers have to learn is that sunk costs are never relevant in decisions. The temptation to include sunk costs in the analysis is especially strong in the case of book value of old equipment. We focus on book value of old equipment below, and then we consider other kinds of sunk costs in other parts of the chapter. We shall see that regardless of the kind of sunk cost involved, the conclusion is always the same – sunk costs are not avoidable, and therefore they should be ignored in decisions.

Management accounting in action: the issue

SoaringWings Ltd is a small manufacturer of high-quality hang gliders. The most critical component of a hang glider is its metal frame, which must be very strong and yet very light. The frames are made by brazing together tubes of high-strength, but lightweight, metal alloys. Most of the brazing must be done by hand, but some can be done in an automated process by machine. Pete Fisher, the production manager of SoaringWings Ltd has been trying to convince Jim Marker, the company's managing director, to purchase a new brazing machine from Furimoro Industries. This machine would replace an old brazing machine from Bryston Ltd that generates a large amount of scrap and waste.

On a recent blustery morning, Pete and Jim happened to drive into the company's car park at the same time. The following conversation occurred as they walked together into the building.

Pete: Morning, Jim. Have you had a chance to look at the specifications on the new brazing machine from Furimoro Industries that I gave you last week?

Jim: Are you still pestering me about the brazing machine?

Pete: You know it's almost impossible to keep that old Bryston brazing machine working within tolerances.

Jim: I know, I know. But we're carrying the Bryston machine on the books for £140,000.

Pete: That's right. But I've done some investigating, and we could sell it for £90,000 to a plumbing company in town that doesn't require as tight tolerances as we do.

Jim: Pete, that's just brilliant! You want me to sell a £140,000 machine for £90,000 and take a loss of £50,000. Do you have any other great ideas this morning?

Pete: Jim, I know it sounds far-fetched, but we would actually save money buying the new machine.

Jim: I'm sceptical. However, if you can show me the hard facts, I'll listen.

Pete: Fair enough. I'll do it.

Book value of old equipment

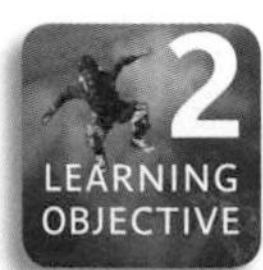

Pete first gathered the following data concerning the old machine and the proposed new machine:

Old machine		**Proposed new machine**	
Original cost	£175,000	List price new	£200,000
Remaining book value	140,000	Expected life	4 years
Remaining life	4 years	Disposal value in four years	£0
Disposal value now	£90,000	Annual variable expenses to operate	300,000
Disposal value in four years	£0	Annual revenue from sales	500,000
Annual variable expenses to operate	345,000		
Annual revenue from sales	500,000		

Should the old machine be disposed of and the new machine purchased? The first reaction of SoaringWings' managing director was to say no, since disposal of the old machine would result in a 'loss' of £50,000:

Old machine	
Remaining book value	£140,000
Disposal value now	90,000
Loss if disposed of now	£50,000

Given this potential loss if the old machine is sold, a manager may reason, 'We've already made an investment in the old machine, so now we have no choice but to use it until our investment has been fully recovered.' A manager may tend to think this way even though the new machine is clearly more efficient than the old machine. An error made in the past cannot be corrected by simply using the machine. The investment that has been made in the old machine is a sunk cost. The portion of this investment that remains on the company's books (the book value of £140,000) should not be considered in a decision about whether to buy the new machine. Pete Fisher verified the irrelevance of the book value of the old machine by the following analysis:[2]

	Total cost and revenues – four years		
	Keep old machine	Purchase new machine	Differential costs and benefits
Sales	£2,000,000	£2,000,000	£0
Variable expenses	(1,380,000)	(1,200,000)	180,000
Cost (depreciation) of the new machine	–	(200,000)	(200,000)
Depreciation of the old machine or book value write-off	(140,000)	(140,000)*	0
Disposal value of the old machine	–	90,000*	90,000
Total net operating profit over the four years	£480,000	£550,000	£70,000

*For external reporting purposes, the £140,000 remaining book value of the old machine and the £90,000 disposal value would be netted together and deducted as a single £50,000 'loss' figure.

Looking at all four years together, notice that the firm will be £70,000 better off by purchasing the new machine. Also notice that the £140,000 book value of the old machine had no effect on the outcome of the analysis. Since this book value is a sunk cost, it must be absorbed by the firm regardless of whether the old machine is kept and used or whether it is sold. If the old machine is kept and used, then the £140,000 book value is deducted in the form of depreciation. If the old machine is sold, then the £140,000 book value is deducted in the form of a lump-sum write-off. Either way, the company bears the same £140,000 cost and the differential cost is zero.

Focusing on relevant costs

What costs in the example above are relevant in the decision concerning the new machine? Looking at the original cost data, we should eliminate first the sunk costs and second the future costs and benefits that do not differ between the alternatives at hand.

1 The sunk costs:

   (a) The remaining book value of the old machine (£140,000).

2 The future costs and benefits that do not differ

   (a) The sales revenue (£500,00 per year)

   (b) The variable expenses (to the extent of £300,000 per year).

The costs and benefits that remain will form the basis for a decision. The analysis is as follows:

	Differential costs and benefits over four years
Reduction in variable expense promised by the new machine (£45,000* per year × 4 years)	£180,000
Cost of the new machine	(200,000)
Disposal value of the old machine	90,000
Net advantage of the new machine	£70,000

*£345,000 – £300,000 = £45,000

Note that the items above are the same as those in the last column of the earlier analysis and represent those costs and benefits that differ between the two alternatives. Armed with this analysis, Pete felt confident that he would be able to explain the financial advantages of the new machine to the managing director of the company.

Management accounting in action: the issue

Pete Fisher took his analysis to the office of Jim Marker, the managing director of SoaringWings, where the following conversation took place.

Pete: Jim, do you remember that discussion we had about the proposed new brazing machine?

Jim: Of course I remember. Did you find out that I'm right?

Pete: Not exactly. Here's the analysis where I compare the profit with the old machine over the next four years to the profit with the new machine.

Jim: I see you're claiming the profit is £70,000 higher with the new machine. Are you assuming higher sales with the new machine?

Pete: No, I have assumed total sales of £2,000,000 over the four years in either situation. The real advantage comes with the reduction in variable expenses of £180,000.

Jim: Where are those reductions going to come from?

Pete: The new brazing machine should cut our scrap and rework rate at least in half. That results in substantial savings in materials and labour costs.

Jim: What about the £50,000 loss on the old machine?

Pete: What really matters is the £200,000 cost of the new machine and the £90,000 salvage value of the old machine. The book value of the old machine is irrelevant. No matter what we do, that cost will eventually flow through the income statement as a charge in one form or another.

Jim: I find that hard to accept, but it is difficult to argue with your analysis.

Pete: The analysis actually understates the advantages of the new machine. We don't catch all of the defects caused by the old machine, and defective products are sometimes sold to customers. With the new machine, I expect our warranty costs to decrease and our repeat sales to increase. And I would hate to be held responsible for any accidents caused by defective brazing by our old machine.

Jim: Okay, I'm convinced. Put together a formal proposal, and we'll present it at the next meeting of the board of directors.

Future costs that do not differ are not relevant costs

We stated above that people often have difficulty accepting the idea that sunk costs are never relevant in a decision. Some people also have difficulty accepting the principle that future costs that do not differ between alternatives are never relevant in a decision. An example will help illustrate how future costs *should* be handled in a decision.

An example of irrelevant future costs

A company is contemplating the purchase of a new labour-saving machine that will cost £30,000 and have a 10-year useful life. Data concerning the company's annual sales and costs with and without the new machine are shown below:

	Current situation	**Situation with the new machine**
Units produced and sold	5,000	5,000
Selling price per unit	£40	£40
Direct materials cost per unit	14	14
Direct labour cost per unit	8	5
Variable overhead cost per unit	2	2
Fixed costs, other	62,000	62,000
Fixed costs, new machine	–	3,000

The new machine promises a saving of £3 per unit in direct labour costs (£8 − £5 = £3), but it will increase fixed costs by £3,000 per year. All other costs, as well as the total number of units produced and sold, will remain the same. Following the steps outlined earlier, the analysis is as follows:

1 Eliminate the sunk costs. (No sunk costs are included in this example.)

2 Eliminate the future costs and benefits that do not differ between the alternatives:

   (a) The selling price per unit and the number of units sold do not differ between the alternatives. (Therefore, total future sales revenues will not differ.)

   (b) The direct materials cost per unit, the variable overhead cost per unit, and the number of units produced do not differ between the alternatives. (Therefore, total future direct materials costs and variable overhead costs will not differ.)

   (c) The 'Fixed costs, other' do not differ between the alternatives.

The remaining costs – direct labour costs and the fixed costs associated with the new machine – are the only relevant costs.

Savings in direct labour costs (5,000 units at a cost saving of £3 per unit)	£15,000
Less increase in fixed costs	3,000
Net annual cost savings promised by the new machine	£12,000

This solution can be verified by looking at all of the cost data (both those that are relevant and those that are not) under the two alternatives. This is done in Exhibit 9.1. Notice from the exhibit that the net advantage in favour of buying the machine is £12,000 – the same answer we obtained by focusing on just the relevant costs. Thus, we can see that future costs that do not differ between alternatives are indeed irrelevant in the decision-making process and can safely be eliminated from the analysis.

	5,000 units produced and sold		
	Present method	**New machine**	**Differential costs and benefits**
Sales	£200,000	£200,000	£0
Variable expenses:			
Direct materials	70,000	70,000	0
Direct labour	40,000	25,000	15,000
Variable overhead	10,000	10,000	0
Total variable expenses	120,000	105,000	
Contribution margin	80,000	95,000	
Less fixed expenses:			
Other	62,000	62,000	0
New machine	0	3,000	(3,000)
Total fixed expenses	62,000	65,000	
Net operating profit	£18,000	£30,000	£12,000

Exhibit 9.1 Differential cost analysis

Why isolate relevant costs?

In the preceding example, we used two different approaches to analyse the alternatives. First, we considered only the relevant costs; and, second, we considered all costs, both those that were relevant and those that were not. We obtained the same answer under both approaches. It would be natural to ask, 'Why bother to isolate relevant costs when total costs will do the job just as well?' Isolating relevant costs is desirable for at least two reasons.

First, only rarely will enough information be available to prepare a detailed profit statement for both alternatives such as we have done in the preceding examples. Assume, for example, that you are called on to make a decision relating to a single operation of a multidepartmental, multiproduct firm. Under these circumstances, it would be virtually impossible to prepare a profit statement of any type. You would have to rely on your ability to recognize which costs are relevant and which are not in order to assemble that data necessary to make a decision.

Second, mingling irrelevant costs with relevant costs may cause confusion and distract attention from the matters that are really critical. Furthermore, the danger always exists that an irrelevant piece of data may be used improperly, resulting in an incorrect decision. The best approach is to ignore irrelevant data and base the decision entirely on the relevant data.

Relevant cost analysis, combined with the contribution approach to the profit statement, provides a powerful tool for making decisions. We will investigate various uses of this tool in the remaining sections of this chapter.

Adding and dropping product lines and other segments

Decisions relating to whether old product lines or other segments of a company should be dropped and new ones added are among the most difficult that a manager has to make. In such decisions, many qualitative and quantitative factors must be considered. Ultimately, however, any final decision to drop an old segment or to add a new one is going to hinge primarily on the impact the decision will have on net profit. To assess this impact, it is necessary to make a careful analysis of the costs involved.

An illustration of cost analysis

Consider the three major product lines of the Discount Drug Company – drugs, cosmetics and house-

			Product line	
	Total	Drugs	Cosmetics	Housewares
Sales	£250,000	£125,000	£75,000	£50,000
Less variable expenses	105,000	50,000	25,000	30,000
Contribution margin	145,000	75,000	50,000	20,000
Less fixed expenses:				
Salaries	50,000	29,500	12,500	8,000
Advertising	15,000	1,000	7,500	6,500
Utilities	2,000	500	500	1,000
Depreciation – fixtures	5,000	1,000	2,000	2,000
Rent	20,000	10,000	6,000	4,000
Insurance	3,000	2,000	500	500
General administrative	30,000	15,000	9,000	6,000
Total fixed expenses	125,000	59,000	38,000	28,000
Net operating profit (loss)	£20,000	£16,000	£12,000	£(8,000)

Exhibit 9.2 Discount Drug Company product lines

wares. Sales and cost information for the preceding month for each separate product line and for the store in total are given in Exhibit 9.2.

What can be done to improve the company's overall performance? One product line – housewares – shows a net operating loss for the month. Perhaps dropping this line would cause profits in the company as a whole to improve. In deciding whether the line should be dropped, management should reason as follows:

If the housewares line is dropped, then the company will lose £20,000 per month in contribution margin. By dropping the line, however, it may be possible to avoid some fixed costs. It may be possible, for example, to discharge certain employees, or it may be possible to reduce advertising costs. If by dropping the housewares line the company is able to avoid more in fixed costs than it loses in contribution margin, then it will be better off if the line is eliminated, since overall profit should improve. On the other hand, if the company is not able to avoid as much in fixed costs as it loses in contribution margin, then the housewares line should be retained. In short, the manager should ask, 'What costs can I avoid if I drop this product line?'

As we have seen from our earlier discussion, not all costs are avoidable. For example, some of the costs associated with a product line may be sunk costs. Other costs may be allocated common costs that will not differ in total regardless of whether the product line is dropped or retained. As discussed in Chapter 8, an activity-based costing analysis may be used to help identify the relevant costs.

To show how the manager should proceed in a product-line analysis, suppose that the management of the Discount Drug Company has analysed the costs being charged to the three product lines and has determined the following:

1 The salaries expense represents salaries paid to employees working directly in each product-line area. All the employees working in housewares would be discharged if the line is dropped.

2 The advertising expense represents direct advertising of each product line and is avoidable if the line is dropped.

3 The utilities expense represents utilities costs for the entire company. The amount charged to each product line is an allocation based on space occupied and is not avoidable if the product line is dropped.

4 The depreciation expense represents depreciation on fixtures used for display of the various product lines. Although the fixtures are nearly new, they are custom-built and will have little resale value if the housewares line is dropped.

5 The rent expense represents rent on the entire building housing the company; it is allocated to the product lines on the basis of sales. The monthly rent of £20,000 is fixed under a long-term lease agreement.

6 The insurance expense represents insurance carried on inventories within each of the three product-line areas.

7 The general administrative expense represents the costs of accounting, purchasing and general management, which are allocated to the product lines on the basis of sales. Total administrative costs will not change if the housewares line is dropped.

With this information, management can identify costs that can and cannot be avoided if the product line is dropped:

	Cost	**Not avoidable***	**Avoidable**
Salaries	£8,000		£8,000
Advertising	6,500		6,500
Utilities	1,000	£1,000	
Depreciation – fixtures	2,000	2,000	
Rent	4,000	4,000	
Insurance	500		500
General administrative	6,000	6,000	
Total fixed expenses	£28,000	£13,000	£15,000

*These costs represent either (1) sunk costs or (2) future costs that will not change if the housewares line is retained or discontinued.

To determine how dropping the line will affect the overall profits of the company, we can compare the contribution margin that will be lost to the costs that can be avoided if the line is dropped:

Contribution margin lost if the housewares line is discontinued (see Exhibit 9.2)	£(20,000)
Less fixed costs that can be avoided if the housewares line is discontinued (see above)	15,000
Decrease in overall company net operating profit	£(5,000)

In this case, the fixed costs that can be avoided by dropping the product line are less than the contribution margin that will be lost. Therefore, based on the data given, the housewares line should not be discontinued unless a more profitable use can be found for the floor and counter space that it is occupying.

A comparative format

Some managers prefer to approach decisions of this type by preparing comparative profit statements showing the effects on the company as a whole of either keeping or dropping the product line in question. A comparative analysis of this type for the Discount Drug Company is shown in Exhibit 9.3.

9.3 EXHIBIT

	Keep housewares	Drop housewares	Difference: profit increase or (decrease)
Sales	£50,000	£0	£(50,000)
Less variable expenses	30,000	0	30,000
Contribution margin	20,000	0	(20,000)
Less fixed expenses:			
Salaries	8,000	0	8,000
Advertising	6,500	0	6,500
Utilities	1,000	1,000	0
Depreciation – fixtures	2,000	2,000	0
Rent	4,000	4,000	0
Insurance	500	0	500
General administrative	6,000	6,000	0
Total fixed expenses	28,000	13,000	15,000
Net operating profit (loss)	£(8,000)	£(13,000)	£(5,000)

Exhibit 9.3 A comparative format for product-line analysis

As shown by column 3 in the exhibit, overall company profit will decrease by £5,000 each period if the housewares line is dropped. This is the same answer, of course, as we obtained in our earlier analysis.

Beware of allocated fixed costs

Our conclusion that the housewares line should not be dropped seems to conflict with the data shown earlier in Exhibit 9.2. Recall from the exhibit that the housewares line is showing a loss rather than a profit. Why keep a line that is showing a loss? The explanation for this apparent inconsistency lies at least in part with the common fixed costs that are being allocated to the product lines. One of the great dangers in allocating common fixed costs is that such allocations can make a product line (or other segment of a business) look less profitable than it really is. By allocating the common fixed costs among all product lines, the housewares line has been made to look as if it were unprofitable, whereas, in fact, dropping the line would result in a decrease in overall company net operating profit. This point can be seen clearly if we recast the data in Exhibit 9.2 and eliminate the allocation of the common fixed costs. This recasting of data – using the segmented approach from Chapter 14 – is shown in Exhibit 9.4.

		Product line		
	Total	Drugs	Cosmetics	Housewares
Sales	£250,000	£125,000	£75,000	£50,000
Less variable expenses	105,000	50,000	25,000	30,000
Contribution margin	145,000	75,000	50,000	20,000
Less traceable fixed expenses:				
Salaries	50,000	29,500	12,500	8,000
Advertising	15,000	1,000	7,500	6,500
Depreciation – fixtures	5,000	1,000	2,000	2,000
Insurance	3,000	2,000	500	500
Total	73,000	33,500	22,500	17,000
Product-line segment margin	72,000	£41,500	£27,500	£3,000*
Less common fixed expenses:				
Utilities	2,000			
Rent	20,000			
General administrative	30,000			
Total	52,000			
Net operating profit	£20,000			

*If the housewares line is dropped this £3,000 in segment margin will be lost to the company. In addition, we have seen that the £2,000 depreciation on the fixtures is a sunk cost that cannot be avoided. The sum of these two figures (£3,000 + £2,000 = £5,000) would be the decrease in the company's overall profits if the housewares line were discontinued.

Exhibit 9.4 Discount Drug Company product lines – recast in contribution format (from Exhibit 9.2)

Exhibit 9.4 gives us a much different perspective of the housewares line than does Exhibit 9.2. As shown in Exhibit 9.4, the housewares line is covering all of its own traceable fixed costs and is generating a £3,000 segment margin toward covering the common fixed costs of the company. Unless another product line can be found that will generate a greater segment margin than this, the company would be better off keeping the housewares line. By keeping the line, the company's overall profit will be higher than if the product line was dropped.

Additionally, we should note that managers may choose to retain an unprofitable product line if the line is necessary to the sale of other products or if it serves as a 'magnet' or 'loss-leader' to attract customers. Bread, for example, is not an especially profitable line in food stores, but customers expect it to be available, and many would undoubtedly shift their buying elsewhere if a particular store decided to stop carrying it.

FOCUS

Focus on current practice

The Amazon group was deciding between investing in television advertising and offering free delivery on large orders as a tactic for growing sales and profits. To evaluate the first option, Amazon.com invested in television advertising in two markets in the US. The company quantified the profit impact of this choice by subtracting the increase in fixed advertising costs from the increase in contribution margin. The profit impact of television advertising paled in comparison to the free 'super saver' delivery programme. This was introduced by Amazon.co.uk in 2003 on all orders over £39 and was so popular and profitable that they soon dropped the qualifying threshold to £25 and then again to £15 as it is today. At each stage of this progression, the Amazon group used cost–volume–profit analysis to determine whether the extra volume from liberalizing the free delivery offer more than offset the associated increase in shipping costs.

The make or buy decision

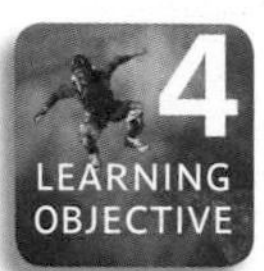

4 LEARNING OBJECTIVE

A decision to produce a fabricated part internally, rather than to buy the part externally from a supplier, is called a **make or buy decision**. Actually, any decision relating to **vertical integration** is a make or buy decision, since the company is deciding whether to meet its own needs internally or to buy externally.

An example of make or buy

To provide an illustration of a make or buy decision, consider Mountain Goat Cycles. The company is now producing the heavy-duty gear shifters used in its most popular line of mountain bikes. The company's Accounting Department reports the following costs of producing the shifter internally:

	Per unit	8,000 units
Direct materials	£6	£48,000
Direct labour	4	32,000
Variable overhead	1	8,000
Supervisor's salary	3	24,000
Depreciation of special equipment	2	16,000
Allocated general overhead	5	40,000
Total cost	£21	£168,000

An outside supplier has offered to sell Mountain Goat Cycles 8,000 changers a year at a price of only £19 each. Should the company stop producing the shifters internally and start purchasing them from the outside supplier? To approach the decision from a financial point of view, the manager should again focus on the differential costs. As we have seen, the differential costs can be obtained by eliminating those costs that are not avoidable – that is, by eliminating first the sunk costs and second the future costs that will continue regardless of whether the shifters are produced internally or purchased outside. The costs that remain after making these eliminations are the costs that are avoidable to the company by purchasing outside. If these avoidable costs are less than the outside purchase price, then the company should continue to manufacture its own changers and reject the outside supplier's offer. That is, the company should purchase outside only if the outside purchase price is less than the costs that can be avoided internally as a result of stopping production of the changers.

Looking at the above data, note first that depreciation of special equipment is listed as one of the costs of producing the changers internally. Since the equipment has already been purchased, this depreciation is a sunk cost and is therefore irrelevant. If the equipment could be sold, its salvage value would be relevant. Or if the machine could be used to make other products, this could be relevant as well. However, we will assume that the equipment has no salvage value and that it has no other use except making the heavy-duty gear changers.

Also note that the company is allocating a portion of its general overhead costs to the changers. Any portion of this general overhead cost that would actually be eliminated if the gear changers were purchased rather than made would be relevant in the analysis. However, it is likely that the general overhead costs allocated to the gear changers are in fact common to all items produced in the factory and would continue unchanged even if the changers are purchased from the outside. Such allocated common costs are not differential costs (since they do not differ between the make or buy alternatives) and should be eliminated from the analysis along with the sunk costs.

The variable costs of producing the changers (materials, labour and variable overhead) are differential costs, since they can be avoided by buying the changers from the outside supplier. If the supervisor can be discharged and his or her salary avoided by buying the changers, then it too will be a differential cost and relevant to the decision. Assuming that both the variable costs and the supervisor's salary can be avoided by buying from the outside supplier, then the analysis takes the form shown in Exhibit 9.5.

9.5 EXHIBIT

		Per unit differential costs		**Total differential costs – 8,000 units**	
	Production 'cost' per unit	**Make**	**Buy**	**Make**	**Buy**
Direct materials	£6	£6		£48,000	£1
Direct labour	4	4		32,000	
Variable overhead	1	1		8,000	
Supervisor's salary	3	3		24,000	
Depreciation of special equipment	2	–		–	
Allocated general overhead	5	–		–	
Outside purchase price			£19		£152,000
Total cost	£21	£14	£19	£112,000	£152,000
Difference in favour of continuing to make		£5		£40,000	

Exhibit 9.5 Mountain Goat Cycles make or buy analysis

Since it costs £5 less per unit to continue to make the changers, Mountain Goat Cycles should reject the outside supplier's offer. However, there is one additional factor that the company may wish to consider before coming to a final decision. This factor is the opportunity cost of the space now being used to produce the changers.

The matter of opportunity cost

If the space now being used to produce the changers *would otherwise be idle*, then Mountain Goat Cycles should continue to produce its own changers and the supplier's offer should be rejected, as stated above. Idle space that has no alternative use has an opportunity cost of zero.

But what if the space now being used to produce changers could be used for some other purpose? In that case, the space would have an opportunity cost that would have to be considered in assessing the desirability of the supplier's offer. What would this opportunity cost be? It would be the segment margin that could be derived from the best alternative use of the space.

To illustrate, assume that the space now being used to produce changers could be used to produce a new cross-country bike that would generate a segment margin of £60,000 per year. Under these conditions, Mountain Goat Cycles would be better off to accept the supplier's offer and to use the available space to produce the new product line:

	Make	Buy
Differential cost per unit (see prior example)	£14	£19
Number of units needed annually	× 8,000	× 8,000
Total annual cost	112,000	152,000
Opportunity cost – segment margin forgone on a potential new product line	60,000	
Total cost	£172,000	£152,000
Difference in favour of purchasing from the outside supplier	£20,000	

Opportunity costs are not recorded in accounts of an organization. They do not represent actual cash outlays. Rather, they represent economic benefits that are *forgone* as a result of pursuing some course of action. The opportunity costs of Mountain Goat Cycles are sufficiently large in this case to make continued production of the changers very costly from an economic point of view.

Special orders

Managers often must evaluate whether a special order should be accepted, and if the order is accepted, the price that should be charged. A **special order** is a one-time order that is not considered part of the company's normal ongoing business. To illustrate, Mountain Goat Cycles has just received a request from the Nottingham Police Department to produce 100 specially modified mountain bikes at a price of £179 each. The bikes would be used to patrol some of the more densely populated residential sections of the city. Mountain Goat Cycles can easily modify its City Cruiser model to fit the specifications of the Nottingham Police. The normal selling price of the City Cruiser bike is £249, and its unit product cost is £182 as shown below:

Direct materials	£86
Direct labour	45
Manufacturing overhead	51
Unit product cost	£182

The variable portion of the above manufacturing overhead is £6 per unit. The order would have no effect on the company's total fixed manufacturing overhead costs.

The modifications to the bikes consist of welded brackets to hold radios, handcuffs and other gear. These modifications would require £17 in incremental variable costs. In addition, the company would have to pay a graphics design studio £1,200 to design and cut stencils that would be used for spray painting the Nottingham Police Department's logo and other identifying marks on the bikes.

This order should have no effect on the company's other sales. The production manager says that she can handle the special order without disrupting any of the regular scheduled production.

What effect would accepting this order have on the company's profit?

Only the incremental costs and benefits are relevant. Since the existing fixed manufacturing overhead costs would not be affected by the order, they are not incremental costs and are therefore not relevant. The incremental profit can be computed as follows:

	Per unit	Total 100 bikes
Incremental revenue	£179	£17,900
Incremental costs:		
Variable costs:		
Direct materials	86	8,600
Direct labour	45	4,500
Variable manufacturing overhead	6	600
Special modifications	17	1,700
Total variable cost	£154	15,400
Fixed cost:		
Purchase of stencils		1,200
Total incremental cost		16,600
Incremental net operating profit		£1,300

Therefore, even though the price on the special order (£179) is below the normal unit product cost (£182) and the order would require incurring additional costs, the order would result in an increase in net operating profit. In general, a special order is profitable as long as the incremental revenue from the special order exceeds the incremental costs of the order. We must note, however, that it is important to make sure that there is indeed idle capacity and that the special order does not cut into normal sales. For example, if the company was operating at capacity, opportunity costs would have to be taken into account as well as the incremental costs that have already been detailed above.

Utilization of a constrained resource

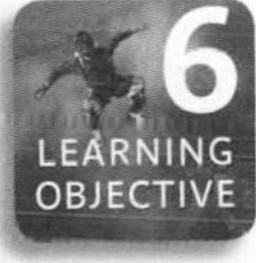

Managers are routinely faced with the problem of deciding how constrained resources are going to be utilized. A department store, for example, has a limited amount of floor space and therefore cannot stock every product that may be available. A manufacturing firm has a limited number of machine-hours and a limited number of direct labour-hours at its disposal. When a limited resource of some type restricts the company's ability to satisfy demand, the company is said to have a **constraint**. Because of the constrained resource, the company cannot fully satisfy demand, so the manager must decide how the constrained resource should be used. Fixed costs are usually unaffected by such choices, so the manager should select the course of action that will maximize the firm's total contribution margin.

Contribution in relation to a constrained resource

To maximize total contribution margin, a firm should not necessarily promote those products that have the highest *unit* contribution margins. Rather, total contribution margin will be maximized by promoting those products or accepting those orders that provide the highest unit contribution margin *in relation to the constrained resource*. To illustrate, Mountain Goat Cycles makes a line of panniers – a saddlebag for bicycles. There are two models of panniers – a touring model and a mountain model. Cost and revenue data for the two models of panniers are given below:

	Model	
	Mountain pannier	Touring pannier
Selling price per unit	£25	£30
Variable cost per unit	10	18
Contribution margin per unit	£15	£12
Contribution margin (CM) ratio	60%	40%

The mountain pannier appears to be much more profitable than the touring pannier. It has a £15 per unit contribution margin as compared to only £12 per unit for the touring model, and it has a 60% CM ratio as compared to only 40% for the touring model.

But now let us add one more piece of information – the plant that makes the panniers is operating at capacity. Ordinarily this does not mean that every machine and every person in the plant is working at the maximum possible rate. Because machines have different capacities, some machines will be operating at less than 100% of capacity. However, if the plant as a whole cannot produce any more units, some machine or process must be operating at capacity. The machine or process that is limiting overall output is called the **bottleneck** – it is the constraint.

At Mountain Goat Cycles, the bottleneck is a particular stitching machine. The mountain pannier requires two minutes of stitching time, and each unit of the touring pannier requires one minute of stitching time. Since this stitching machine already has more work than it can handle, something will have to be cut back. In this situation, which product is more profitable? To answer this question, the manager should look at the contribution margin per unit of the constrained resource. This figure is computed by dividing the contribution margin by the amount of the constrained resource a unit of product requires. These calculations are carried out below for the mountain and touring panniers.

	Model	
	Mountain pannier	Touring pannier
Contribution margin per unit (above) (a)	£15.00	£12.00
Time on the stitching machine required to produce one unit (b)	2 min.	1 min.
Contribution margin per unit of the constrained resource, (a)/(b)	£7.50/min.	£12.00/min.

It is now easy to decide which product is less profitable and should be de-emphasized. Each minute of processing time on the stitching machine that is devoted to the touring pannier results in an increase of £12 in contribution margin and profits. The comparable figure for the mountain pannier is only £7.50 per minute. Therefore, the touring model should be emphasized. Even though the mountain model has the larger per unit contribution margin and the larger CM ratio, the touring model provides the larger contribution margin in relation to the constrained resource.

To verify that the touring model is indeed the more profitable product, suppose an hour of additional stitching time is available and that there are unfilled orders for both products. The additional hour on the stitching machine could be used to make either 30 mountain panniers (60 minutes/2 minutes) or 60 touring panniers (60 minutes/1 minute), with the following consequences:

	Model	
	Mountain pannier	**Touring pannier**
Contribution margin per unit (above) (a)	£15	£12
Additional units that can be processed in one hour	× 30	× 60
Additional contribution margin	£450	£720

This example clearly shows that looking at unit contribution margins alone is not enough; the contribution margin must be viewed in relation to the amount of the constrained resource each product requires.

Joint product costs and the contribution approach

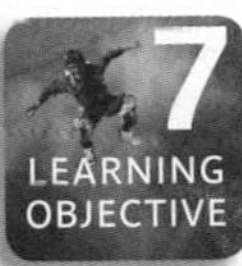

In some industries, a number of end products are produced from a single raw material input. A grisly, but apt, example is provided by the meat-packing industry. A great variety of end products – bacon, ham, spareribs, pork roasts, and so on – are produced from a single pig. Firms that produce several end products from a common input (e.g., a pig) are faced with the problem of deciding how the cost of that input is going to be divided among the end products. Before we address this problem, it will be helpful to define three terms – joint products, joint product costs and split-off point.

Two or more products that are produced from a common input are known as **joint products**. The term **joint product costs** is used to describe those manufacturing costs that are incurred in producing joint products up to the split-off point. The **split-off point** is that point in the manufacturing process at which the joint products (bacon, ham, spareribs, and so on) can be recognized as separate products. At that point, some of the joint products will be in final form, ready to be marketed to the consumer. Others will still need further processing on their own before they are in marketable form. These concepts are presented graphically in Exhibit 9.6.

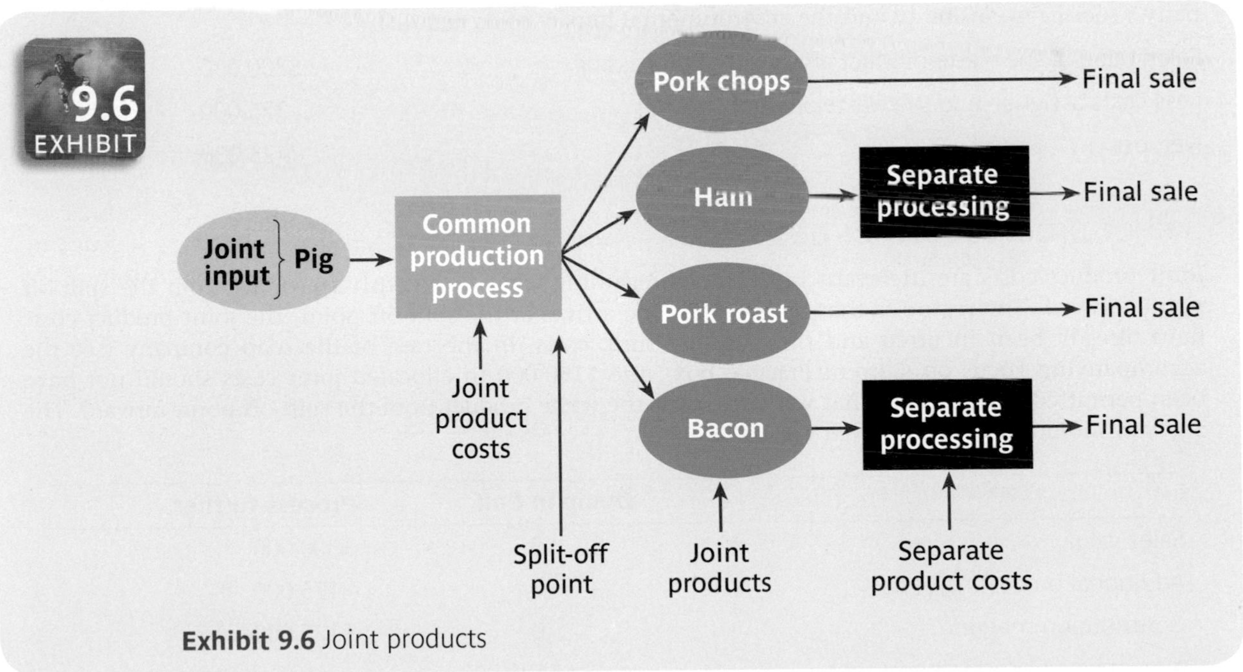

Exhibit 9.6 Joint products

The pitfalls of allocation

Joint product costs are really common costs incurred to simultaneously produce a variety of end products. Traditional cost accounting books contain various approaches to allocating these common costs among the different products at the split-off point. A typical approach is to allocate the joint product costs according to the relative sales value of the end products.

Although allocation of joint product costs is needed for some purposes, such as balance sheet stock valuation, allocations of this kind should be viewed with great caution internally in the decision-making process. Unless a manager proceeds with care, he or she may be led into incorrect decisions as a result of relying on allocated common costs. The Focus on Current Practice box below discusses an actual business situation illustrating an incorrect decision that resulted from using allocated costs.

Focus on current practice

FOCUS

A company located on the Gulf of Mexico is a producer of soap products. Its six main soap product lines are produced from common inputs. Joint product costs up to the split-off point constitute the bulk of the production costs for all six product lines. These joint product costs are allocated to the six product lines on the basis of the relative sales value of each line at the split-off point.

The company has a waste product that results from the production of the six main product lines. Until a few years ago, the company loaded the waste onto barges and dumped it into the Gulf of Mexico, since the waste was thought to have no commercial value. The dumping was stopped, however, when the company's research division discovered that with some further processing the waste could be made commercially saleable as a fertilizer ingredient. The further processing was initiated at a cost of $175,000 per year. The waste was then sold to fertilizer manufacturers at a total price of $300,000 per year.

The accountants responsible for allocating manufacturing costs included the sales value of the waste product along with the sales value of the six main product lines in their allocation of the joint product costs at the split-off point. This allocation resulted in the waste product being allocated $150,000 in joint product cost. This $150,000 allocation, when added to the further processing costs of $175,000 for the waste, caused the waste product to show the net loss computed in the table below.

When presented with this analysis, the company's management decided that further processing of the waste was not desirable after all. The company went back to dumping the waste in the Gulf. In addition to being unwise from an economic viewpoint, this dumping also raises questions regarding the company's social responsibility and the environmental impact of its actions.

Sales value of the waste product after further processing	$300,000
Less costs assignable to the waste product	325,000
Net loss	$(25,000)

Sell or process further decisions

Joint product costs are irrelevant in decisions regarding what to do with a product from the split-off point forward. The reason is that by the time one arrives at the split-off point, the joint product costs have already been incurred and therefore are sunk costs. In the case of the soap company (see the accompanying Focus on Current Practice box), the $150,000 in allocated joint costs should not have been permitted to influence what was done with the waste product from the split-off point forward. The analysis should have been as follows:

	Dump in Gulf	Process further
Sales value	0	$300,000
Additional processing costs	0	175,000
Contribution margin	0	$125,000
Advantage of processing further	$125,000	

Decisions of this type are known as **sell or process further decisions**. It will always be profitable to continue processing a joint product after the split-off point as long as the incremental revenue from such processing exceeds the incremental processing cost incurred after the split-off point. Joint product costs that have already been incurred up to the split-off point are sunk costs, which are always irrelevant in decisions concerning what to do from the split-off point forward.

To provide a detailed example of a sell or process further decision, assume that three products are derived from a single raw material input. Cost and revenue data relating to the products are presented in Exhibit 9.7 along with an analysis of which products should be sold at the split-off point and which should be processed further. As shown in the exhibit, products B and C should both be processed further; product A should be sold at the split-off point.

	Product		
	A	B	C
Sales value at the split-off point	£120,000	£150,000	£60,000
Sales value after further processing	160,000	240,000	90,000
Allocated joint product costs	80,000	100,000	40,000
Cost of further processing	50,000	60,000	10,000
Analysis of sell or process further:			
Sales value after further processing	£160,000	£240,000	£90,000
Sales value at the split-off point	120,000	150,000	60,000
Incremental revenue from further processing	40,000	90,000	30,000
Cost of further processing	50,000	60,000	10,000
Profit (loss) from further processing	£(10,000)	£30,000	£20,000

Exhibit 9.7 Sell or process further decision

Activity-based costing and relevant costs

As discussed in Chapter 8, activity-based costing can be used to help identify potentially relevant costs for decision-making purposes. Activity-based costing improves the traceability of costs by focusing on the activities caused by a product or other segment. Managers should exercise caution against reading more into this 'traceability' than really exists. People have a tendency to assume that if a cost is traceable to a segment, then the cost is automatically an avoidable cost. That is not true. As emphasized in Chapter 8, the costs provided by a well-designed activity-based costing system are only potentially relevant. Before making a decision, managers must still decide which of the potentially relevant costs are actually avoidable. Only those costs that are avoidable are relevant and the others should be ignored.

To illustrate, refer again to the data relating to the housewares line in Exhibit 9.4 on page 333. The £2,000 depreciation on fixtures is a traceable cost of the houseware lines because it relates to activities in that department. We found, however, that the £2,000 is not avoidable if the housewares line is dropped. The key lesson here is that the method used to assign a cost to a product or other segment does not change the basic nature of the cost. A sunk cost such as depreciation of old equipment is still a sunk cost regardless of whether it is traced directly to a particular segment on an activity basis, allocated to all segments on the basis of labour-hours, or treated in some other way in the costing process. Regardless of the method used to assign costs to products or other segments, the manager must still apply the principles discussed in this chapter to determine the costs that are avoidable in each situation.[3]

Summary

- All of the material in this chapter consists of applications of one simple but powerful idea. Only those costs and benefits that differ between alternatives are relevant in a decision. All other costs and benefits are irrelevant and can and should be ignored. In particular, sunk costs are irrelevant as are future costs that do not differ between alternatives.
- This simple idea was applied in a variety of situations including decisions that involve replacing equipment, making or buying a component, adding or dropping a product line, processing a joint product further, and using a constrained resource.
- This list includes only a tiny sample of the possible applications of the relevant cost concept. Indeed, *any* decision involving costs hinges on the proper identification and analysis of the costs that are relevant.
- We will continue to focus on the concept of relevant costs in the following chapter where long-run investment decisions are considered.

Key terms for review

Avoidable cost (p. 324).

Bottleneck (p. 338).

Constraint (p. 337).

Differential cost (p. 325).

Joint product costs (p. 339).

Joint products (p. 339).

Make or buy decision (p. 334).

Relevant costs (p. 324).

Sell or process further decision (p. 341).

Special order (p. 336).

Split-off point (p. 339).

Sunk cost (p. 325).

Vertical integration (p. 334).

Review problem: relevant costs

Charter Sports Equipment manufactures round, rectangular, and octagonal trampolines. Data on sales expenses for the past month follow:

		Trampoline		
	Total	Round	Rectangular	Octagonal
Sales	£1,000,000	£140,000	£500,000	£360,000
Less variable expenses	410,000	60,000	200,000	150,000
Contribution margin	590,000	80,000	300,000	210,000
Less fixed expenses:				
Advertising – traceable	216,000	41,000	110,000	65,000
Depreciation of special equipment	95,000	20,000	40,000	35,000
Line supervisors' salaries	19,000	6,000	7,000	6,000
General factory overhead*	200,000	28,000	100,000	72,000
Total fixed expenses	530,000	95,000	257,000	178,000
Net operating profit (loss)	£60,000	£(15,000)	£43,000	£32,000

*A common cost that is allocated on the basis of sales.

Management is concerned about the continued losses shown by the round trampolines and wants a recommendation as to whether or not the line should be discontinued. The special equipment used to produce the trampolines has no resale value. If the round trampoline model is dropped, the two line supervisors assigned to the model would be discharged.

Required

1 Should production and sale of the round trampolines be discontinued? You may assume that the company has no other use for the capacity now being used to produce the round trampolines. Show computations to support your answer.

2 Recast the above data in a format that would be more usable to management in assessing the long-run profitability of the various product lines.

Solution to review problem: relevant costs

1 No, production and sale of the round trampolines should not be discontinued. Computations to support this answer follow:

Contribution margin lost if the round trampolines are discontinued		£(80,000)
Less fixed costs that can be avoided:		
Advertising – traceable	£41,000	
Line supervisors' salaries	6,000	47,000
Decrease in net operating profit for the company as a whole		£(33,000)

The depreciation of the special equipment represents a sunk cost, and therefore it is not relevant to the decision. The general factory overhead is allocated and will presumably continue regardless of whether or not the round trampolines are discontinued; thus, neither is this relevant to the decision.

Alternative solution to Question 1:

	Keep round tramps	Drop round tramps	Difference: profit increase (or (decrease)
Sales	£140,000	£0	£(140,000)
Less variable expenses	60,000	0	60,000
Contribution margin	80,000	0	(80,000)
Less fixed expenses:			
Advertising – traceable	41,000	0	41,000
Depreciation of special equipment	20,000	20,000	0
Line supervisors' salaries	6,000	0	6,000
General factory overhead	28,000	28,000	0
Total fixed expenses	95,000	48,000	47,000
Net operating profit (loss)	£(15,000)	£(48,000)	£(33,000)

2 If management wants a clear picture of the profitability of the segments, the general factory overhead should not be allocated. It is a common cost and therefore should be deducted from the total product-line segment margin, as shown in Chapter 14. A more useful profit statement format would be as follows:

		Trampoline		
	Total	Round	Rectangular	Octagonal
Sales	£1,000,000	£140,000	£500,000	£360,000
Less variable expenses	410,000	60,000	200,000	150,000
Contribution margin	590,000	80,000	300,000	210,000
Less traceable fixed expenses:				
Advertising – traceable	216,000	41,000	110,000	65,000
Depreciation of special equipment	95,000	20,000	40,000	35,000
Line supervisors' salaries	19,000	6,000	7,000	6,000
Total traceable fixed expenses	330,000	67,000	157,000	106,000
Product-line segment margin	260,000	£13,000	£143,000	£104,000
Less common fixed expenses	200,000			
Net operating profit (loss)	£60,000			

Questions

9–1 What is a relevant cost?

9–2 Define the following terms: *incremental cost, opportunity cost*, and *sunk cost*.

9–3 Are variable costs always relevant costs? Explain.

9–4 The book value of a machine (as shown on the balance sheet) is an asset to a company, but this same book value is irrelevant in decision making. Explain why this is so.

9–5 'Sunk costs are easy to spot – they're simply the fixed costs associated with a decision.' Do you agree? Explain.

9–6 'Variable costs and differential costs mean the same thing.' Do you agree? Explain.

9–7 'All future costs are relevant in decision making.' Do you agree? Why?

9–8 Prentice Company is considering dropping one of its product lines. What costs of the product line would be relevant to this decision? Irrelevant?

9–9 'If a product line is generating a loss, then that's pretty good evidence that the product line should be discontinued.' Do you agree? Explain.

9–10 What is the danger in allocating common fixed costs among product lines or other segments of an organization?

9–11 How does opportunity cost enter into the make or buy decision?

9–12 Give four examples of possible constraints.

9–13 How will relating product contribution margins to the constrained resource they require help a company ensure that profits will be maximized?

9–14 Define the following terms: *joint products, joint product costs*, and *split-off point*.

9–15 From a decision-making point of view, what pitfalls are there in allocating common costs among joint products?

9–16 What guideline can be used in determining whether a joint product should be sold at the split-off point or processed further?

9–17 Airlines sometimes offer reduced rates during certain times of the week to members of a businessperson's family if they accompany him or her on trips. How does the concept of relevant costs enter into the decision to offer reduced rates of this type?

Exercises

EXERCISES

E9–1 Time allowed: 15 minutes

Listed below are a number of costs that may be relevant in decisions faced by the management of Svahn, AB, a Swedish manufacturer of sailing yachts:

Item	Case 1		Case 2	
	Relevant	**Not relevant**	**Relevant**	**Not relevant**
(a) Sales revenue				
(b) Direct materials				
(c) Direct labour				
(d) Variable manufacturing overhead				
(e) Depreciation – Model B100 machine				
(f) Book value – Model B100 machine				
(g) Disposal value – Model B100 machine				
(h) Market value – Model B300 machine (cost)				
(i) Depreciation – Model B300 machine				
(j) Fixed manufacturing overhead (general)				
(k) Variable selling expense				
(l) Fixed selling expense				
(m) General administrative overhead.				

Required

Copy the information above onto your answer sheet and place an X in the appropriate column to indicate whether each item is relevant or not relevant in the following situations (requirement 1 relates to Case 1 above, and requirement 2 relates to Case 2):

1 Management is considering purchasing a Model B300 machine to use in addition to the company's present Model B100 machine. This will increase the company's production and sales. The increase in volume will be large enough to require increases in fixed selling expenses and in general administrative overhead, but not in the fixed manufacturing overhead.

2 Management is, instead, considering replacing its present Model B100 machine with a new Model B300 machine. The Model B100 machine would be sold.

This change will have no effect on production or sales, other than some savings in direct materials costs due to less waste.

E9–2 Time allowed: 20 minutes

Bill has just returned from a duck hunting trip. He has brought home eight ducks. Bill's friend, John, disapproves of duck hunting and, to discourage Bill from further hunting, John has presented him with the following cost estimate per duck:

Camper and equipment:	
Cost, £12,000; usable for eight seasons; 10 hunting trips per season	£150
Travel expense (pickup van):	
100 miles at £0.12 per mile (gas, oil and tyres – £0.07 per mile: depreciation and insurance – £0.05 per mile)	12
Shotgun shells (two boxes)	20
Boat:	
Cost, £2,320, usable for eight seasons; 10 hunting trips per season	29
Hunting licence:	
Cost, £30 for the season; 10 hunting trips per season	3
Money lost playing poker:	
Loss, £18 (Bill plays poker every weekend)	18
A fifth of Old Grandad:	
Cost, £8 (used to ward off the cold)	8
Total cost	£240
Cost per duck (£240/8 ducks)	£30

Required

1 Assuming that the duck hunting trip Bill has just completed is typical, what costs are relevant to a decision as to whether Bill should go duck hunting again this season?

2 Suppose that Bill gets lucky on his next hunting trip and shoots 10 ducks in the amount of time it took him to shoot 8 ducks on his last trip. How much would it have cost him to shoot the last two ducks?

3 Which costs are relevant in a decision of whether Bill should give up hunting? Explain.

E9–3 Time allowed: 20 minutes

Thalassines Kataskeves SA of Greece makes marine equipment. The company has been experiencing losses on its bilge pump product line for several years. The most recent quarterly profit statement for the bilge pump product line is given below:

Thalassines Kataskeves SA
Profit statement – bilge pump
For the quarter ended 31 March

Sales		€850,000
Less variable expenses:		
Variable manufacturing expenses	€330,000	
Sales commissions	42,000	
Shipping	18,000	
Total variable expenses		390,000
Contribution margin		460,000
Less fixed expenses:		
Advertising	270,000	
Depreciation of equipment (no resale value)	80,000	
General factory overhead	105,000*	
Salary of product-line manager	32,000	
Insurance on inventories	8,000	
Purchasing department expenses	45,000†	
Total fixed expenses		540,000†
Net loss		€ (80,000)

*Common costs allocated on the basis of machine-hours.

†Common costs allocated on the basis of sales.

The discontinuance of the bilge pump product line would not affect sales of other product lines and would have no noticeable effect on the company's total general factory overhead or total Purchasing Department expenses.

Required

Would you recommend that the bilge pump product line be discontinued? Support your answer with appropriate computations.

E9–4 Time allowed: 20 minutes

Hollings Company sells office furniture. As part of its service, it delivers furniture to customers.

The costs associated with the acquisition and annual operation of a delivery van are given below:

Insurance	£1,600
Licences	250
Taxes (vehicle)	150
Garage rent for parking (per van)	1,200
Depreciation (£9,000/5 years)	1,800*
Petrol, oil, tyres, and repairs	0.07 per mile

*Based on obsolescence rather than on wear and tear.

Required

1 Assume that Hollings Company has purchased one van and that the van has been driven 50,000 miles during the first year. Compute the average cost per mile of owning and operating the van.

2 At the beginning of the second year, Hollings Company is unsure whether to use the van or leave it parked in the garage and have all hauling done commercially. (The state requires the payment of vehicle taxes even if the vehicle is not used.) What costs from the previous list are relevant to this decision? Explain.

3 Assume that the company decides to use the van during the second year. Near year-end an order is received from a customer over 1,000 miles away. What costs from the previous list are relevant in a decision between using the van to make the delivery and having the delivery done commercially? Explain.

4 Occasionally, the company could use two vans at the same time. For this reason, some thought is being given to purchasing a second van. The total miles driven would be the same as if only one van were owned. What costs from the previous list are relevant to a decision over whether to purchase the second van? Explain.

E9–5 Time allowed: 20 minutes

Barlow Company manufactures three products: A, B and C. The selling price, variable costs and contribution margin for one unit of each product follow:

	Product		
	A	B	C
Selling price	£180	£270	£240
Less variable expenses:			
Direct materials	24	72	32
Other variable expenses	102	90	148
Total variable expenses	126	162	180
Contribution margin	£54	£108	£60
Contribution margin ratio	30%	40%	25%

The same raw material is used in all three products. Barlow Company has only 5,000 kilos of material on hand and will not be able to obtain any more material for several weeks due to a strike in its supplier's plant. Management is trying to decide which product(s) to concentrate on next week in filling its backlog of orders. The material costs £8 per kilo.

Required

1 Compute the amount of contribution margin that will be obtained per kilo of material used in each product.

2 Which orders would you recommend that the company work on next week – the orders for product A, product B, or product C? Show computations.

3 A foreign supplier could furnish Barlow with additional stocks of the raw material at a substantial premium over the usual price. If there is unfilled demand for all three products, what is the highest price that Barlow Company should be willing to pay for an additional kilo of materials?

E9–6 Time allowed: 20 minutes

Troy Engines Ltd manufactures a variety of engines for use in heavy equipment. The company has always produced all of the necessary parts for its engines, including all of the carburettors. An outside supplier has offered to produce and sell one type of carburettor to Troy Engines for a cost of £35 per unit. To evaluate this offer, Troy Engines has gathered the following information relating to its own cost of producing the carburettor internally:

	Per unit	15,000 units per year
Direct materials	£14	£210,000
Direct labour	10	150,000
Variable manufacturing overhead	3	45,000
Fixed manufacturing overhead, traceable	6*	90,000
Fixed manufacturing overhead, allocated	9	135,000
Total cost	£42	£630,000

*One-third supervisory salaries; two-thirds depreciation of special equipment (no resale value).

Required

1 Assuming that the company has no alternative use for the facilities that are now being used to produce the carburettors, should the outside supplier's offer be accepted? Show all computations.

2 Suppose that, if the carburettors were purchased, Troy Engines, could use the freed capacity to launch a new product. The segment margin of the new product would be £150,000 per year. Should Troy Engines Ltd accept the offer to buy the carburettors for £35 per unit? Show all computations.

E9–7 Time allowed: 10 minutes

Waukee Railroad is considering the purchase of a powerful, high-speed wheel grinder to replace a standard wheel grinder that is now in use. Selected information on the two machines is given below:

	Standard wheel grinder	High-speed wheel grinder
Original cost new	£20,000	£30,000
Accumulated depreciation to date	6,000	–
Current salvage value	9,000	–
Estimated cost per year to operate	15,000	7,000
Remaining years of useful life	5 years	5 years

Required

Prepare a computation covering the five-year period that will show the net advantage or disadvantage of purchasing the high-speed wheel grinder. Use only relevant costs in your analysis.

E9–8 Time allowed: 20 minutes

The Regal Cycle Company manufactures three types of bicycles – a dirt bike, a mountain bike and a racing bike. Data on sales and expenses for the past quarter follow:

	Total	Dirt bikes	Mountain bikes	Racing bikes
Sales	£300,000	£90,000	£150,000	£60,000
Less variable manufacturing and selling expenses	120,000	27,000	60,000	33,000
Contribution margin	180,000	63,000	90,000	27,000
Less fixed expenses:				
Advertising, traceable	30,000	10,000	14,000	6,000
Depreciation of special equipment	23,000	6,000	9,000	8,000
Salaries of product-line managers	35,000	12,000	13,000	10,000
Common allocated costs*	60,000	18,000	30,000	12,000
Total fixed expenses	148,000	46,000	66,000	36,000
Net operating income (loss)	£32,000	£17,000	£24,000	£(9,000)

*Allocated on the basis of sales.

Management is concerned about the continued losses shown by the racing bikes and wants a recommendation as to whether or not the line should be discontinued. The special equipment used to produce racing bikes has no resale value and does not wear out.

Required

1 Should production and sale of the racing bikes be discontinued? Show computations to support your answer.

2 Recast the above data in a format that would be more usable to management in assessing the long-run profitability of the various product lines.

E9–9 Time allowed: 10 minutes

Han Products manufactures 30,000 units of part S–6 each year for use on its production line. At this level of activity, the cost per unit for part S–6 is as follows:

Direct materials	£3.60
Direct labour	10.00
Variable overhead	2.40
Fixed overhead	9.00
Total cost per part	£25.00

An outside supplier has offered to sell 30,000 units of part S–6 each year to Han Products for £21 per part. If Han Products accepts this offer, the facilities now being used to manufacture part S–6 could be rented to another company at an annual rental of £80,000. However, Han Products has determined that two-thirds of the fixed overhead being applied to part S–6 would continue even if part S–6 were purchased from the outside supplier.

Required

Prepare computations to show the net advantage or disadvantage of accepting the outside supplier's offer.

E9–10 Time allowed: 10 minutes

Dorsey Company manufactures three products from a common input in a joint processing operation.

Joint processing costs up to the split-off point total £350,000 per quarter. The company allocates these costs to the joint products on the basis of their total sales value at the split-off point. Unit selling prices and total output at the split-off point are as follows:

Product	Quarterly selling price	Output
A	£16 per kilo	15,000 kilos
B	8 per kilo	20,000 kilos
C	25 per litre	4,000 litres

Each product can be processed further after the split-off point. Additional processing requires no special facilities. The additional processing costs (per quarter) and unit selling prices after further processing are given below:

Product	Additional processing costs	Selling price
A	£63,000	£20 per kilo
B	80,000	13 per kilo
C	36,000	32 per litre

Required

Which product or products should be sold at the split-off point and which product or products should be processed further? Show computations.

E9–11 Special order Time allowed: 10 minutes

Cosi Ltd produces and sells a single product, a fan called a tutte. Annual production capacity is 100,000 machine hours. Annual demand for tuttes is 80,000 fans. The selling price is expected to remain at £12 per fan. Cost data for producing and selling tuttes are as follows:

Variable costs (per unit)	**£**
Direct materials, labour and overhead	5.80
Selling costs	2.00
Fixed costs (per year)	**£'000**
Fixed production costs	70,000
Fixed selling costs	40,000

Cosi Ltd has 2,000 tuttes in stock that were incorrectly painted. The company has two choices:

1 sell these lower quality fans through the normal distribution channels at a reduced price

or

2 scrap them at a net cost of zero.

Sales of these lower quality fans are not expected to affect regular sales of tuttes.

Required

Determine and justify the minimum price per fan that would have to be received in order to make it worth while selling the lower quality fans rather than scrapping them.

(3 marks)

ICAEW Business Management, September 2001

PROBLEMS

Problems

P9–12 Relevant cost analysis; book value Time allowed: 25 minutes

Murl Plastics Ltd purchased a new machine one year ago at a cost of £60,000. Although the machine operates well, the managing director (MD) wondered if the company should replace it with a new electronically operated machine that has just come on the market. The new machine would slash annual operating costs by two-thirds, as shown in the comparative data below:

	Present machine	Proposed New machine
Purchase cost new	£60,000	£90,000
Estimated useful life new	6 years	5 years
Annual operating costs	£42,000	£14,000
Annual straight-line depreciation	10,000	18,000
Remaining book value	50,000	–
Salvage value now	10,000	–
Salvage value in 5 years	0	0

In trying to decide whether to purchase the new machine, the MD has prepared the following analysis:

Book value of the old machine	£50,000
Less salvage value	10,000
Net loss from disposal	£40,000

'Even though the new machine looks good,' said the managing director, 'we can't get rid of the old one if it means taking a huge loss on it. We'll have to use it for at least a few more years.'

Sales are expected to be £200,000 per year, and selling and administrative expenses are expected to be £126,000 per year, regardless of which machine is used.

Required

1 Prepare a summary profit statement covering the next five years, assuming:

(a) That the new machine is not purchased.

(b) That the new machine is purchased.

2 Determine the desirability of purchasing the new machine using only relevant costs in your analysis.

P9–13 Dropping a flight; analysis of operating policy Time allowed: 25 minutes

Profits have been decreasing for several years at Pegasus Airlines. In an effort to improve the company's performance, consideration is being given to dropping several flights that appear to be unprofitable.

A typical income statement for one such flight (flight 482) is given below (per flight):

Ticket revenue (175 seats × 40% occupancy × £200 ticket price)	£14,000	100.0%
Less variable expenses (£15 per person)	1,050	7.5%
Contribution margin	12,950	92.5%
Less flight expenses:		
Salaries, flight crew	1,800	
Flight promotion	750	
Depreciation of aircraft	1,550	
Fuel for aircraft	6,800	
Liability insurance	4,200	
Salaries, flight assistants	500	
Baggage loading and flight preparation	1,700	
Overnight costs for flight crew and assistants at destination	300	
Total flight expenses	17,600	
Net operating loss	£(4,650)	

The following additional information is available about flight 482:

(a) Members of the flight crew are paid fixed annual salaries, whereas the flight assistants are paid by the flight.

(b) One-third of the liability insurance is a special charge assessed against flight 482 because in the opinion of the insurance company, the destination of the flight is in a 'high-risk' area. The remaining two-thirds would be unaffected by a decision to drop flight 482.

(c) The baggage loading and flight preparation expense is an allocation of ground crews' salaries and depreciation of ground equipment. Dropping flight 482 would have no effect on the company's total baggage loading and flight preparation expenses.

(d) If flight 482 is dropped, Pegasus Airlines has no authorization at present to replace it with another flight.

(e) Depreciation of aircraft is due entirely to obsolescence. Depreciation due to wear and tear is negligible.

(f) Dropping flight 482 would not allow Pegasus Airlines to reduce the number of aircraft in its fleet or the number of flight crew on its payroll.

Required

1 Prepare an analysis showing what impact dropping flight 482 would have on the airline's profits.

2 The airline's scheduling officer has been criticized because only about 50% of the seats on Pegasus' flights are being filled compared to an average of 60% for the industry. The scheduling officer has explained that Pegasus' average seat occupancy could be improved considerably by eliminating about 10% of the flights, but that doing so would reduce profits. Explain how this could happen.

P9–14 Relevant cost potpourri Time allowed: 60 minutes
Unless otherwise indicated, each of the following parts is independent. In all cases, show computations to support your answer.

1 A merchandising company has two departments, A and B. A recent monthly income statement for the company follows:

	Total	Department A	B
Sales	£4,000,000	£3,000,000	£1,000,000
Less variable expenses	1,300,000	900,000	400,000
Contribution margin	2,700,000	2,100,000	600,000
Less fixed expenses	2,200,000	1,400,000	800,000
Net operating profit (loss)	£500,000	£700,000	£(200,000)

A study indicates that £340,000 of the fixed expenses being charged to Department B are sunk costs or allocated costs that will continue even if B is dropped. In addition, the elimination of Department B will result in a 10% decrease in the sales of Department A. If Department B is dropped, what will be the effect on the net operating profit of the company as a whole?

2 For many years Futura Company has purchased the starters that it installs in its standard line of farm tractors. Due to a reduction in output of certain of its products, the company has idle capacity that could be used for producing the starters. The chief engineer has recommended against this move, however, pointing out that the cost to produce the starters would be greater than the current £8.40 per unit purchase price:

	Per unit	Total
Direct materials	£3.10	
Direct labour	2.70	
Supervision	1.50	£60,000
Depreciation	1.00	40,000
Variable manufacturing overhead	0.60	
Rent	0.30	12,000
Total production cost	£9.20	

A supervisor would have to be hired to oversee production of the starters. However, the company has sufficient idle tools and machinery that no new equipment would have to be purchased. The rent charge above is based on space utilized in the plant. The total rent on the plant is £80,000 per period. Depreciation is due to obsolescence rather than wear and tear. Prepare computations to show the financial advantage or disadvantage per period of making the starters.

3 Wexpro Ltd produces several products from processing 1 ton of clypton, a rare mineral. Material and processing costs total £60,000 per ton, a quarter of which is allocated to product X. Seven thousand units of product X are produced from each ton of clypton. The units can either be sold at the split-off point for £9 each, or processed further at a total cost of £9,500 and then sold for £12 each. Should product X be processed further or sold at the split-off point?

4 Benoit Company produces three products, A, B and C. Data concerning the three products follows (per unit):

	Product		
	A	B	C
Selling price	£80	£56	£70
Less variable expenses:			
Direct materials	24	15	9
Other variable expenses	24	27	40
Total variable expenses	48	42	49
Contribution margin	£32	£14	£21
Contribution margin ratio	40%	25%	30%

Demand for the company's products is very strong, with far more orders each month than the company has raw materials available to produce. The same material is used in each product. The material costs £3 per kilo with a maximum of 5,000 kilos available each month. Which orders would you advise the company to accept first, those for A, for B, or for C? Which orders second? Third?

5 Delta Company produces a single product. The cost of producing and selling a single unit of this product at the company's normal activity level of 60,000 units per year is:

Direct materials	£5.10
Direct labour	3.80
Variable manufacturing overhead	1.00
Fixed manufacturing overhead	4.20
Variable selling and administrative expense	1.50
Fixed selling and administrative expense	2.40

The normal selling price is £21 per unit. The company's capacity is 75,000 units per year. An order has been received from a mail-order house for 15,000 units at a special price of £14 per unit. This order would not affect regular sales. If the order is accepted, by how much will annual profits be increased or decreased? (The order will not change the company's total fixed costs.)

6 Refer to the data in Question 5 above. Assume the company has 1,000 units of this product left over from last year that are vastly inferior to the current model. The units must be sold through regular channels at reduced prices. What unit cost figure is relevant for establishing a minimum selling price for these units? Explain.

P9–15 Sell or process further decision Time allowed: 15 minutes
(Prepared from a situation suggested by Professor John W. Hardy.)

Lone Star Meat Packers is a major processor of beef and other meat products. The company has a large amount of T-bone steak on hand, and it is trying to decide whether to sell the T-bone steaks as they are initially cut or to process them further into filet mignon and the New York cut.

If the T-bone steaks are sold as initially cut, the company figures that a 1-pound T-bone steak would yield the following profit:

Selling price (£2.25 per pound)	£2.25
Less joint product cost	1.80
Profit per pound	£0.45

Instead of being sold as initially cut, the T-bone steaks could be further processed into filet mignon and New York cut steaks. Cutting one side of a T-bone steak provides the filet mignon, and cutting the other side provides the New York cut. One 16-oz (16 oz = 1 pound) T-bone steak thus cut will yield one 6-oz filet mignon and one 8-oz New York cut; the remaining ounces are waste. The cost of processing the T-bone steaks into these cuts is £0.25 per pound. The filet mignon can be sold for £4.00 per pound, and the New York cut can be sold for £2.80 per pound.

Required

1 Determine the profit per pound from further processing the T-bone steaks.

2 Would you recommend that the T-bone steaks be sold as initially cut or processed further? Why?

P9–16 Make or buy analysis Time allowed: 45 minutes

'In my opinion, we ought to stop making our own drums and accept that outside supplier's offer,' said Wim Niewindt, managing director of Antilles Refining NV of Aruba. 'At a price of 18 florins per drum, we would be paying 5 florins less than it costs us to manufacture the drums in our own plant. (The currency in Aruba is the florin, denoted below by fl.) Since we use 60,000 drums a year, that would be an annual cost saving of 300,000 florins.' Antilles Refining's present cost to manufacture one drum is given below (based on 60,000 drums per year)

Direct material	fl10.35
Direct labour	6.00
Variable overhead	1.50
Fixed overhead (fl2.80 general company overhead, fl1.60 depreciation and, fl0.75 supervision)	5.15
Total cost per drum	fl23.00

A decision about whether to make or buy the drums is especially important at this time since the equipment being used to make the drums is completely worn out and must be replaced. The choices facing the company are:

Alternative 1	Purchase new equipment and continue to make the drums. The equipment would cost fl810,000; it would have a six-year useful life and no salvage value. The company uses straight-line depreciation.
Alternative 2	Purchase the drums from an outside supplier at fl18 per drum under a six-year contract.

The new equipment would be more efficient than the equipment that Antilles Refining has been using and, according to the manufacturer, would reduce direct labour and variable overhead costs by 30%. The old equipment has no resale value. Supervision cost (fl45,000 per year) and direct materials cost per drum would not be affected by the new equipment. The new equipment's capacity would be 90,000 drums per year. The company has no other use for the space being used to produce the drums.

The company's total general company overhead would be unaffected by this decision.

Required

1 To assist the managing director in making a decision, prepare an analysis showing what the total cost and the cost per drum would be under each of the alternatives given above. Assume that 60,000 drums are needed each year. Which course of action would you recommend to the managing director?

2 Would your recommendation in Question 1 above be the same if the company's needs were: (a), 75,000 drums per year or (b), 90,000 drums per year? Show computations to support your answer, with costs presented on both a total and a per unit basis.

3 What other factors would you recommend that the company consider before making a decision?

P9–17 Selected relevant cost questions Time allowed: 30 minutes
Andretti Company has a single product called a Dak. The company normally produces and sells 60,000 Daks each year at a selling price of £32 per unit. The company's unit costs at this level of activity are given below:

Direct materials	£10.00	
Direct labour	4.50	
Variable manufacturing overhead	2.30	
Fixed manufacturing overhead	5.00	(£300,000 total)
Variable selling expenses	1.20	
Fixed selling expenses	3.50	(£210,000 total)
Total cost per unit	£26.50	

A number of questions relating to the production and sale of Daks follow. Each question is independent.

Required

1 Assume that Andretti Company has sufficient capacity to produce 90,000 Daks each year without any increase in fixed manufacturing overhead costs. The company could increase its sales by 25% above the present 60,000 units each year if it were willing to increase the fixed selling expenses by £80,000. Would the increase fixed expenses be justified?

2 Assume again that Andretti Company has sufficient capacity to produce 90,000 Daks each year. A customer in a foreign market wants to purchase 20,000 Daks. Import duties on the Daks would be £1.70 per unit, and costs for permits and licences would be £9,000. The only selling costs that would be associated with the order would be £3.20 per unit shipping cost. You have been asked by the managing director to compute the per unit break-even price on this order.

3 The company has 1,000 Daks on hand that have some irregularities and are therefore considered to be 'seconds'. Due to the irregularities, it will be impossible to sell these units at the normal price through regular distribution channels. What unit cost figure is relevant for setting a minimum selling price?

4 Due to a strike in its supplier's plant, Andretti Company is unable to purchase more material for the production of Daks. The strike is expected to last for two months. Andretti Company has enough material on hand to continue to operate at 30% of normal levels for the two-month period. As an alternative, Andretti could close its plant down entirely for the two months. If the plant were closed, fixed overhead costs would continue at 60% of their normal level during the two-month period; the fixed selling costs would be reduced by 20% while the plant was closed. What would be the financial advantage or disadvantage of closing the plant for the two-month period?

5 An outside manufacturer has offered to produce Daks for Andretti Company and to ship them directly to Andretti's customers. If Andretti Company accepts this offer, the facilities that it uses to produce Daks would be idle; however, fixed overhead costs would be reduced by 75% of their present level. Since the outside manufacturer would pay for all the costs of shipping, the variable selling costs would be only two-thirds of their present amount. Compute the unit cost figure that is relevant for comparison to whatever quoted price is received from the outside manufacturer.

P9–18 Discontinuance of a store Time allowed: 60 minutes
Superior Markets Ltd operates three stores in a large metropolitan area. A segmented profit statement for the company for the last quarter is given below:

Superior Markets Ltd
Profit statement for the quarter ended 30 September

	Total	North store	South store	East store
Sales	£3,000,000	£720,000	£1,200,000	£1,080,000
Cost of goods sold	1,657,200	403,200	660,000	594,000
Gross margin	1,342,800	316,800	540,000	486,000
Operating expenses:				
Selling expenses	817,000	231,400	315,000	270,600
Administrative expenses	383,000	106,000	150,900	126,100
Total expenses	1,200,000	337,400	465,900	396,700
Net operating profit (loss)	£142,800	£(20,600)	£74,100	£89,300

The North store has consistently shown losses over the past two years. For this reason, management is giving consideration to closing the store. The company has retained you to make a recommendation as to whether the store should be closed or kept open. The following additional information is available for your use:

(a) The breakdown of the selling and administrative expenses is as follows:

	Total	North store	South store	East store
Selling expenses:				
Sales salaries	£239,000	£70,000	£89,000	£80,000
Direct advertising	187,000	51,000	72,000	64,000
General advertising*	45,000	10,800	18,000	16,200
Store rent	300,000	85,000	120,000	95,000
Depreciation of store fixtures	16,000	4,600	6,000	5,400
Delivery salaries	21,000	7,000	7,000	7,000
Depreciation of delivery equipment	9,000	3,000	3,000	3,000
Total selling expenses	£817,000	£231,400	£315,000	£270,600

*Allocated on the basis of sales.

	Total	North store	South store	East store
Administrative expenses:				
Store management salaries	£70,000	£21,000	£30,000	£19,000
General office salaries*	50,000	12,000	20,000	18,000
Insurance on fixtures and inventory	25,000	7,500	9,000	8,500
Utilities	106,000	31,000	40,000	35,000
Employment taxes	57,000	16,500	21,900	18,600
General office – other*	75,000	18,000	30,000	27,000
Total administrative expenses	£383,000	£106,000	£150,900	£126,100

*Allocated on the basis of sales.

(b) The lease on the building housing the North store can be broken with no penalty.

(c) The fixtures being used in the North store would be transferred to the other two stores if the North store were closed.

(d) The general manager of the North store would be retained and transferred to another position in the company if the North store were closed. She would be filling a position that would otherwise be filled by hiring a new employee at a salary of £11,000 per quarter. The general manager of the North store would be retained at her normal salary of £12,000 per quarter. All other employees in the store would be discharged.

(e) The company has one delivery crew that serves all three stores. One delivery person could be discharged if the North store were closed. This person's salary is £4,000 per quarter. The delivery equipment would be distributed to the other stores. The equipment does not wear out through use but does, eventually, become obsolete.

(f) The company's employment taxes are 15% of salaries.

(g) One-third of the insurance in the North store is on the store's fixtures.

(h) The 'General office salaries' and 'General office – other' relate to the overall management of Superior Markets. If the North store were closed, one person in the general office could be discharged because of the decrease in overall workload. This person's salary is £6,000 per quarter.

Required

1 Prepare a schedule showing the change in revenues and expenses and the impact on the company's overall profit that would result if the North store were closed.

2 Assuming that the store space can't be subleased, what recommendation would you make to the management of Superior Markets?

3 Assume that if the North store were closed, at least one-fourth of its sales would transfer to the East store, due to strong customer loyalty to Superior Markets. The East store has ample capacity to handle the increased sales. You may assume that the increased sales in the East store would yield the same gross margin rate as present sales in that store. What effect would these factors have on your recommendation concerning the North store? Show all computations to support your answer.

P9–19 Shutdown versus continue-to-operate decision Time allowed: 30 minutes
(Note: This type of decision is similar to that of dropping a product line.)

Birch Company normally produces and sells 30,000 units of RG–6 each month. RG–6 is a small electrical relay used in the automotive industry as a component part in various products. The selling price is £22 per unit, variable costs are £14 per unit, fixed manufacturing overhead costs total £150,000 per month, and fixed selling costs total £30,000 per month.

Employment-contract strikes in the companies that purchase the bulk of the RG–6 units have caused Birch Company's sales to temporarily drop to only 8,000 units per month. Birch Company estimates that the strikes will last for about two months, after which time sales of RG–6 should return to normal. Due to the current low level of sales, however, Birch Company is thinking about closing down its own plant during the two months that the strikes are on. If Birch Company does close down its plant, it is estimated that fixed manufacturing overhead costs can be reduced to £105,000 per month and that fixed selling costs can be reduced by 10%. Start-up costs at the end of the shutdown period would total £8,000. Since Birch Company uses just-in-time (JIT) production methods, no inventories are on hand.

Required

1 Assuming that the strikes continue for two months, as estimated, would you recommend that Birch Company close its own plant? Show computations in good form.

2 At what level of sales (in units) for the two-month period should Birch Company be indifferent between closing the plant or keeping it open? Show computations. (*Hint*: This is a type of break-even analysis, except that the fixed cost portion of your break-even computation should include only those fixed costs that are relevant [i.e., avoidable] over the two-month period.)

P9–20 Make or buy decision Time allowed: 40 minutes

Silven Industries, which manufactures and sells a highly successful line of summer lotions and insect repellents, has decided to diversify in order to stabilize sales throughout the year. A natural area for the company to consider is the production of winter lotions and creams to prevent dry and chapped skin.

After considerable research, a winter products line has been developed. However, Silven's president has decided to introduce only one of the new products for this coming winter. If the product is a success, further expansion in future years will be initiated.

The product selected (called Chap-Off) is a lip balm that will be sold in a lipstick-type tube. The product will be sold to wholesalers in boxes of 24 tubes for £8 per box. Because of excess capacity, no additional fixed overhead costs will be incurred to produce the product. However, a £90,000 charge for fixed overhead will be absorbed by the product under the company's absorption costing system. Using the estimated sales and production of 100,000 boxes of Chap-Off, the Accounting Department has developed the following cost per box:

Direct material	£3.60
Direct labour	2.00
Manufacturing overhead	1.40
Total cost	£7.00

The costs above include costs for producing both the lip balm and the tube into which the lip balm is to be placed. As an alternative to making the tubes, Silven has approached a supplier to discuss the possibility of purchasing the tubes for Chap-Off. The purchase price of the empty tubes from the supplier would be £1.35 per box of 24 tubes. If Silven Industries accepts the purchase proposal, it is predicted that direct labour and variable manufacturing overhead costs per box of Chap-Off would be reduced by 10% and that direct materials costs would be reduced by 25%.

Required

1 Should Silven Industries make or buy the tubes? Show calculations to support your answer.

2 What would be the maximum purchase price acceptable to Silven Industries? Support your answer with an appropriate explanation.

3 Instead of sales of 100,000 boxes, revised estimates show sales volume at 120,000 boxes. At this new volume, additional equipment at an annual rental of £40,000 must be acquired to manufacture the tubes. Assuming that the outside supplier will not accept an order for less than 100,000 boxes, should Silven Industries make or buy the tubes? Show computations to support your answer.

4 Refer to the data in Question 3 above. Assume that the outside supplier will accept an order of any size for the tubes at £1.35 per box. How, if at all, would this change your answer? Show computations.

5 What qualitative factors should Silven Industries consider in determining whether they should make or buy the tubes?

(*CMA*, heavily adapted)

P9–21 Accept or reject special order Time allowed: 30 minutes

Polaski Company manufactures and sells a single product called a Ret. Operating at capacity, the company can produce and sell 30,000 Rets per year. Costs associated with this level of production and sales are given below:

	Unit	Total
Direct materials	£15	£450,000
Direct labour	8	240,000
Variable manufacturing overhead	3	90,000
Fixed manufacturing overhead	9	270,000
Variable selling expense	4	120,000
Fixed selling expense	6	180,000
Total cost	£45	£1,350,000

The Rets normally sell for £50 each. Fixed manufacturing overhead is constant at £270,000 per year within the range of 25,000 through 30,000 Rets per year.

Required

1 Assume that due to a recession, Polaski Company expects to sell only 25,000 Rets through regular channels next year. A large retail chain has offered to purchase 5,000 Rets if Polaski is willing to accept a 16% discount off the regular price. There would be no sales commissions on this order; thus, variable selling expenses would be slashed by 75%. However, Polaski Company would have to purchase a special machine to engrave the retail chain's name on the 5,000 units. This machine would cost £10,000. Polaski Company has no assurance that the retail chain will purchase additional units any time in the future. Determine the impact on profits next year if this special order is accepted.

2 Refer to the original data. Assume again that Polaski Company expects to sell only 25,000 Rets through regular channels next year. The US Army would like to make a one-time-only purchase of 5,000 Rets. The Army would pay a fixed fee of £1.80 per Ret, and in addition it would reimburse Polaski Company for all costs of production (variable and fixed) associated with the units. Since the army would pick up the Rets with its own vans, there would be no variable selling expenses of any type associated with this order. If Polaski Company accepts the order, by how much will profits be increased or decreased for the year?

3 Assume the same situation as that described in Question 2 above, except that the company expects to sell 30,000 Rets through regular channels next year. Thus, accepting the US Army's order would require giving up regular sales of 5,000 Rets. If the Army's order is accepted, by how much will profits be increased or decreased from what they would be if the 5,000 Rets were sold through regular channels?

P9–22 Utilization of a constrained resource Time allowed: 45 minutes

The Walton Toy Company manufactures a line of dolls and a doll dress sewing kit. Demand for the dolls is increasing, and management requests assistance from you in determining an economical sales and production mix for the coming year. The company's Sales Department provides the following information:

Product	Demand next year (units)	Estimated selling price per unit
Debbie	50,000	£13.50
Trish	42,000	5.50
Sarah	35,000	21.00
Mike	40,000	10.00
Sewing kit	325,000	8.00

The standard costs for direct materials and direct labour per unit are as follows:

Direct product	Direct materials	Labour
Debbie	£4.30	£3.20
Trish	1.10	2.00
Sarah	6.44	5.60
Mike	2.00	4.00
Sewing kit	3.20	1.60

The following additional information is available:

(a) The company's plant has a capacity of 130,000 direct labour-hours per year on a single-shift basis. The company's present employees and equipment can produce all five products.

(b) The direct labour rate is £8 per hour; this rate is expected to remain unchanged during the coming year.

(c) Fixed costs total £520,000 per year. Variable overhead costs are £2 per direct labour-hour.

(d) All of the company's non manufacturing costs are fixed.

(e) The company's present inventory of finished products is negligible and can be ignored.

Required

1 Determine the contribution margin per direct labour-hour expended on each product.

2 Prepare a schedule showing the total direct labour-hours that will be required to produce the units estimated to be sold during the coming year.

3 Examine the data you have computed in (1) and (2) above. Indicate how much of each product should be made so that total production time is equal to the 130,000 hours available.

4 What is the highest price, in terms of a rate per hour, that Walton Toy Company would be willing to pay for additional capacity (that is, for added direct labour time)?

5 Assume again that the company does not want to reduce sales of any product. Identify ways in which the company could obtain the additional output.

(*CPA*, heavily adapted)

P9–23 Evaluating the profitability of a product; break even Time allowed: 30 minutes

Tracey Douglas is the owner and managing director of Heritage Garden Furniture Ltd, a South African company that makes museum quality reproductions of antique outdoor furniture. Ms Douglas would like advice concerning the advisability of eliminating the model C3 lawnchair. These lawnchairs have been among the company's best-selling products, but they seem to be unprofitable.

A condensed statement of operating income for the company and for the model C3 lawnchair for the quarter ended 30 June follows:

	All products	Model C3 lawnchair
Sales	R2,900,000	R300,000
Cost of sales:		
Direct materials	759,000	122,000
Direct labour	680,000	72,000
Fringe benefits (20% of direct labour)	136,000	14,400
Variable manufacturing overhead	28,000	3,600
Building rent and maintenance	30,000	4,000
Depreciation	75,000	19,100
Total cost of sales	1,708,000	235,100
Gross margin	1,192,000	64,900
Selling and administrative expenses:		
Product managers' salaries	75,000	10,000
Sales commissions (5% of sales)	145,000	15,000
Fringe benefits (20% of salaries and commissions)	44,000	5,000
Shipping	120,000	10,000
General administrative expenses	464,000	48,000
Total selling and administrative expenses	848,000	88,000
Net operating profit (loss)	R344,000	R(23,100)

The currency in South Africa is the rand, denoted here by R.

The following additional data have been supplied by the company:

(a) Direct labour is a variable cost at Heritage Garden Furniture.

(b) All of the company's products are manufactured in the same facility and use the same equipment. Building rent and maintenance and depreciation are allocated to products using various bases. The equipment does not wear out through use; it eventually becomes obsolete.

(c) There is ample capacity to fill all orders.

(d) Dropping the model C3 lawnchair would have no effect on sales of other product lines.

(e) Stocks of work in progress or finished goods are insignificant.

(f) Shipping costs are traced directly to products.

(g) General administrative expenses are allocated to products on the basis of sales. There would be no effect on the total general administrative expenses if the model C3 lawnchair were dropped.

(h) If the model C3 lawnchair were dropped, the product manager would be laid off.

Required

1 Given the current level of sales, would you recommend that the model C3 lawnchair be dropped? Prepare appropriate computations to support your answer.

2 What would sales of the model C3 lawnchair have to be, at minimum, in order to justify retaining the product? (*Hint*: Set this up as a break-even problem but include only the relevant costs from Question 1 above.)

P9–24 Sell or process further decision Time allowed: 30 minutes

Cleanit Corporation produces a variety of cleaning compounds and solutions for both industrial and household use. While most of its products are processed independently, a few are related, such as the company's Grit 337 and its Sparkle silver polish.

Grit 337 is a coarse cleaning powder with many industrial uses. It costs £1.60 a kilo to make, and it has a selling price of £2.00 a kilo. A small portion of the annual production of Grit 337 is retained in the factory for further processing. It is combined with several other ingredients to form a paste that is marketed as Sparkle silver polish. The silver polish sells for £4.00 per jar. This further processing requires a quarter kilo of Grit 337 per jar of silver polish. The additional direct costs involved in the processing of a jar of silver polish are:

Other ingredients	£0.65
Direct labour	1.48
Total direct cost	£2.13

Overhead costs associated with the processing of the silver polish are:

Variable manufacturing overhead cost	25% of direct labour cost
Fixed manufacturing overhead cost (per month):	
Production supervisor	£1,600
Depreciation of mixing equipment	1,400

The production supervisor has no duties other than to oversee production of the silver polish. The mixing equipment is special-purpose equipment acquired specifically to produce the silver polish. It has only negligible resale value.

Direct labour is a variable cost at Cleanit Corporation.

Advertising costs for the silver polish total £4,000 per month. Variable selling costs associated with the silver polish are 7.5% of sales.

Due to a recent decline in the demand for silver polish, the company is wondering whether its continued production is advisable. The sales manager feels that it would be more profitable to just sell all of the Grit 337 as a cleaning powder.

Required

1 What is the incremental contribution margin per jar from further processing of Grit 337 into silver polish?

2 What is the minimum number of jars of silver polish that must be sold each month to justify the continued processing of Grit 337 into silver polish? Show all computations in good form.

(*CMA*, heavily adapted)

Cases

C9–25 Sell or process further decision Time allowed: 30 minutes

The Scottie Sweater Company produces sweaters under the 'Scottie' label. The company buys raw wool on the market and processes it into wool yarn from which the sweaters are woven. One spindle of wool yarn is required to produce one sweater. The costs and revenues associated with the sweaters are given below:

		Per sweater
Selling price		£30.00
Cost to manufacture:		
Raw materials:		
Buttons, thread, lining	£2.00	
Wool yarn	16.00	
Total raw materials	18.00	
Direct labour	5.80	
Manufacturing overhead	8.70	32.50
Manufacturing profit (loss)		£(2.50)

Originally, all the wool yarn was used to produce sweaters, but in recent years a market has developed for the wool yarn itself. The yarn is purchased by other companies for use in production of wool blankets and other wool products. Since the development of the market for the wool yarn, a continuing dispute has existed in the Scottie Sweater Company as to whether the yarn should be sold simply as yarn or processed into sweaters. Current cost and revenue data on the yarn are given below:

		Per spindle of yarn
Selling price		£20.00
Cost to manufacture:		
Raw materials (raw wool)	£7.00	
Direct labour	3.60	
Manufacturing overhead	5.40	16.00
Manufacturing profit		£4.00

The market for sweaters is temporarily depressed, due to unusually warm weather in the western states where the sweaters are sold. This has made it necessary for the company to discount the selling price of the sweaters to £30 from the normal £40 price. Since the market for wool yarn has remained strong, the dispute has again surfaced over whether the yarn should be sold outright rather than processed into sweaters. The sales manager thinks that the production of sweaters should be discontinued; she is upset about having to sell sweaters at a £2.50 loss when the yarn could be sold for a £4.00 profit. However, the production superintendent is equally upset at the suggestion that he close down a large portion of the factory. He argues that the company is in the sweater business, not the yarn business, and that the company should focus on its core strength.

Due to the nature of the production process, virtually all the manufacturing overhead costs are fixed and would not be affected even if sweaters were discontinued. Manufacturing overhead is assigned to products on the basis of 150% of direct labour cost.

Required

1 Would you recommend that the wool yarn be sold outright or processed into sweaters? Show computations in good form to support your answer and explain your reasoning.

2 What is the lowest price that the company should accept for a sweater? Show computations in good form to support your answer and explain your reasoning.

C9–26 Make or buy; optimal use of a constrained resource Time allowed: 45 minutes

Sportway is a wholesale distributor supplying a wide range of moderately priced sporting equipment to large chain stores. About 60% of Sportway's products are purchased from other companies while the remainder of the products are manufactured by Sportway. The company has a Plastics Department that is currently manufacturing moulded fishing tackle boxes. Sportway is able to manufacture and sell 8,000 tackle boxes annually, making full use of its direct labour capacity at available workstations. Presented below are the selling price and costs associated with Sportway's tackle boxes.

Selling price per box		£86.00
Cost per box:		
Moulded plastic	£8.00	
Hinges, latches, handle	9.00	
Direct labour (£15 per hour)	18.75	
Manufacturing overhead	12.50	
Selling and administrative cost	17.00	65.25
Net operating profit per box		£20.75

Because Sportway believes it could sell 12,000 tackle boxes if it had sufficient manufacturing capacity, the company has looked into the possibility of purchasing the tackle boxes for distribution. Maple Products, a steady supplier of quality products, would be able to provide up to 9,000 tackle boxes per year at a price of £68 per box delivered to Sportway's facility.

Traci Kader, Sportway's production manager, has suggested that the company could make better use of its Plastics Department by manufacturing skateboards. To support her position, Traci has a market study that indicates an expanding market for skateboards. Traci believes that Sportway could expect to sell 17,500 skateboards annually at a price of £45 per skateboard. Traci's estimate of the costs to manufacture the skateboards is presented below:

Selling price per skateboard		£45.00
Cost per skateboard:		
Moulded plastic	£5.50	
Wheels, hardware	7.00	
Direct labour (£15 per hour)	7.50	
Manufacturing overhead	5.00	
Selling and administrative cost	9.00	34.00
Net operating profit per skateboard		£11.00

In the Plastics Department, Sportway uses direct labour-hours as the application base for manufacturing overhead. Included in the manufacturing overhead for the current year is £50,000 of fixed overhead costs, of which 40% is traceable to the Plastics Department and 60% is allocated as factorywide manufacturing overhead cost. The remaining manufacturing overhead cost is variable with respect to direct labour-hours. The skateboards could be produced with existing equipment and personnel in the Plastics Department.

For each unit of product that Sportway sells, regardless of whether the product has been purchased or is manufactured by Sportway, there is an allocated £6 fixed cost per unit for distribution. This £6 per unit is included in the selling and administrative cost for all products. The remaining amount of selling and administrative cost for all products – purchased or manufactured – is variable. The total selling and administrative cost figure for the purchased tackle boxes would be £10 per unit.

Required

1 Determine the number of direct labour-hours per year being used to manufacture tackle boxes.

2 Compute the contribution margin per unit for:

(a) Purchased tackle boxes.

(b) Manufactured tackle boxes.

(c) Manufactured skateboards.

3 Determine the number of tackle boxes (if any) that Sportway should purchase and the number of tackle boxes and/or skateboards that it should manufacture, and compute the improvement in profit that will result from this product mix over current operations.

(*CMA*, adapted)

C9–27 Plant closing decision Time allowed: 20 minutes

GianAuto Corporation manufactures cars, vans and trucks. Among the various GianAuto plants around the United States is the Denver Cover Plant. Coverings made primarily of vinyl and upholstery fabric are sewn at the Denver Cover Plant and used to cover interior seating and other surfaces of GianAuto products.

Ted Vosilo is the plant manager for Denver Cover. The Denver Cover Plant was the first GianAuto plant in the region. As other area plants were opened, Vosilo, in recognition of his management ability, was given responsibility for managing them. Vosilo functions as a regional manager, although the budget both for him and also for his staff is charged to the Denver Cover Plant.

Vosilo has just received a report indicating that GianAuto could purchase the entire annual output of Denver Cover from outside suppliers for £35 million. Vosilo was astonished at the low outside price because the budget for Denver Cover's operating costs for the coming year was set at £52 million. Vosilo believes that GianAuto will have to close down operations at Denver Cover in order to realize the £22 million in annual cost savings.

The budget for Denver Cover's operating costs for the coming year is presented below. Additional facts regarding the plant's operations are as follows:

1 Due to Denver Cover's commitment to use high-quality fabrics in all its products, the Purchasing Department was instructed to place blanket purchase orders with major suppliers to ensure the receipt of sufficient materials for the coming year. If these orders are cancelled as a consequence of the plant closing, termination charges would amount to 20% of the cost of direct materials.

2 Approximately 800 plant employees will lose their jobs if the plant is closed. This includes all the direct labourers and supervisors as well as the plumbers, electricians and other skilled workers classified as indirect plant workers. Some would be able to find new jobs while many others would have difficulty. All employees would have difficulty matching Denver Cover's base pay of £9.40 per hour, which is the highest in the area. A clause in Denver Cover's contract with the union may help some employees; the company must provide employment assistance to its former employees for twelve months after a plant closing. The estimated cost to administer this service would be £1.5 million for the year.

3 Some employees would probably choose early retirement because GianAuto has an excellent pension plan. In fact, £3 million of the annual pension expense would continue whether Denver Cover is open or not.

4 Vosilo and his staff would not be affected by the closing of Denver Cover. They would still be responsible for administering three other area plants.

5 Denver Cover considers equipment depreciation to be a variable cost and uses the units-of-production method to depreciate its equipment; Denver Cover is the only GianAuto plant to use this depreciation method. However, Denver Cover uses the customary straight-line method to depreciate its building.

Denver Cover plant
Annual budget for operating costs

Materials		£14,000,000
Labour:		
Direct	£13,100,000	
Supervision	900,000	
Indirect plant	4,000,000	18,000,000
Overhead:		
Depreciation – equipment	3,200,000	
Depreciation – building	7,000,000	
Pension expense	5,000,000	
Plant manager and staff	800,000	
Corporate allocation	4,000,000	20,000,000
Total budgeted costs		£52,000,000

Required

1 Without regard to costs, identify the advantages to GianAuto Corporation of continuing to obtain covers from its own Denver Cover Plant.

2 GianAuto Corporation plans to prepare a financial analysis that will be used in deciding whether or not to close the Denver Cover Plant. Management has asked you to identify:

(a) The annual budgeted costs that are relevant to the decision regarding closing the plant (show the monetary amounts).

(b) The annual budgeted costs that are not relevant to the decision regarding closing the plant, and explain why they are not relevant (again show the monetary amounts).

(c) Any non-recurring costs that would arise due to the closing of the plant, and explain how they would affect the decision (again show any monetary amounts).

3 Looking at the data you have prepared in Question 2 above, should the plant be closed? Show computations and explain your answer.

4 Identify any revenues or costs not specifically mentioned in the problem that GianAuto should consider before making a decision.

(*CMA, adapted*)

Further reading

Considerable evidence exists that once a manager commits to an action such as the purchase of a machine, rational decision making often takes a back seat to wishful thinking and an unwillingness to acknowledge mistakes. Long after an original decision is seen to be a mistake, most managers will continue to support an action with even more resources. Accounting systems reinforce this 'head in the sand' tendency. Recognition of a loss is delayed until an asset is disposed of, creating a bias against disposing of assets when they should be retired or replaced.

For an interesting discussion (and disagreement) of relevant costs in different decision contexts, read Kaplan, Shank, Horngren, Böer, Ferrara and Robinson (1990).

Endnotes

1 Arthur (2000).

2 The computations involved in this example are taken one step further in Chapter 10 when we discuss the time value of money and the use of present value in decision making.

3 For further discussion, see Sharp and Christensen (1991) and Hirsch and Nibbelin (1992).

Chapter 10
Capital investment decisions

Learning objectives

After studying Chapter 10, you should be able to:

1. Determine the acceptability of an investment project using the net present value method
2. Determine the acceptability of an investment project using the internal rate of return method
3. Explain how the cost of capital is used as a screening tool
4. Prepare a net present value analysis of two competing investment projects using either the incremental-cost approach or the total-cost approach
5. Rank investment projects in order of preference
6. Determine the payback period for an investment
7. Compute the simple rate of return for an investment
8. (Appendices 10A and C) Understand the impact of inflation and corporate taxation on investment decisions
9. (Appendix 10D) Analyse the impact of uncertainty and risk on investment appraisal

Concepts in Context

When Steven Burd became the CEO of Safeway, he slashed annual capital spending from $550 million to $290 million. Burd gave the following reason: 'We had projects that were not returning the cost of money. So we cut spending back, which made the very best projects come to the surface.'

Safeway set a minimum 22.5% pretax return on investment in all new store and remodelling projects. With that discipline in place, Safeway again increased capital spending. It spent about $1 billion in a single year, adding 40 to 45 new stores and remodelling more than 200. Burd says he has emphasized expanding existing stores because the older stores generally have excellent real estate locations and the added size brings strong increases in sales.[1]

The term 'investment decision making' or, alternatively, 'capital budgeting', is used to describe how managers plan significant outlays on projects that have long-term implications such as the purchase of new equipment and the introduction of new products. Most companies have many more potential projects than can actually be funded. Hence, managers must carefully select those projects that promise the greatest future return. How well managers make these capital budgeting decisions is a critical factor in the long-run profitability of the company.

Capital budgeting involves *investment* – a company must commit funds now in order to receive a return in the future. Investments are not limited to shares and bonds. Purchase of stock or equipment is also an investment. For example, PepsiCo makes an investment when it opens a new Pizza Hut restaurant. Powergen makes an investment when it installs a new computer to handle customer billing. Ford makes an investment when it redesigns a product such as the Range Rover and must retool its production lines. GSK invests in medical research. All of these investments are characterized by a commitment of funds today in the expectation of receiving a return in the future in the form of additional cash inflows or reduced cash outflows.

Capital budgeting – planning investments

Typical capital budgeting decisions

What types of business decisions require capital budgeting analysis? Virtually any decision that involves an outlay now in order to obtain some return (increase in revenue or reduction in costs) in the future. Typical capital budgeting decisions include:

1 Cost reduction decisions. Should new equipment be purchased to reduce costs?

2 Expansion decisions. Should a new plant, warehouse, or other facility be acquired to increase capacity and sales?

3 Equipment selection decisions. Which of several available machines would be the most cost effective to purchase?

4 Lease or buy decisions. Should new equipment be leased or purchased?

5 Equipment replacement decisions. Should old equipment be replaced now or later?

Capital budgeting decisions tend to fall into two broad categories – *screening decisions* and *preference decisions*. **Screening decisions** are those relating to whether a proposed project meets some preset standard of acceptance. For example, a firm may have a policy of accepting projects only if they promise a return of, say, 20% on the investment. The required rate of return is the minimum rate of return a project must yield to be acceptable.

Preference decisions, by contrast, relate to selecting from among several *competing* courses of action. To illustrate, a firm may be considering five different machines to replace an existing machine on the assembly line. The choice of which machine to purchase is a *preference* decision.

In this chapter, we initially discuss ways of making screening decisions. Preference decisions are discussed toward the end of the chapter.

The time value of money

As stated earlier, business investments commonly promise returns that extend over fairly long periods of time. Therefore, in approaching capital budgeting decisions, it is necessary to employ techniques that recognize *the time value of money*. A pound today is worth more than a pound a year from now. The same concept applies in choosing between investment projects. Those projects that promise returns earlier in time are preferable to those that promise returns later in time.

The capital budgeting techniques that recognize the two above characteristics of business investments most fully are those that involve discounted cash flows. We will spend most of this chapter illustrating the use of discounted cash flow methods in making *capital budgeting decisions*.

Discounted cash flows – the net present value method

There are two approaches to making capital budgeting decisions by means of discounted cash flows. One is the *net present value* method, and the other is the *internal rate of return method* (sometimes called the *time-adjusted rate of return method*). The net present value method is discussed in this section; the internal rate of return method is discussed in the next section.

The net present value method illustrated

Under the net present value method, the present value of all cash inflows is compared to the present value of all cash outflows that are associated with an investment project. The difference between the present value of these cash flows, called the **net present value**, determines whether or not the project is an acceptable investment. To illustrate, let us assume the following data:

Harper Company is contemplating the purchase of a machine capable of performing certain operations that are now performed manually. The machine will cost £5,000, and it will last for five years. At the end of the five-year period, the machine will have a zero scrap value. Use of the machine will reduce labour costs by £1,800 per year.

Harper Company requires a minimum return of 20% before taxes on all investment projects.[2]

Should the machine be purchased? Harper Company must determine whether a cash investment now of £5,000 can be justified if it will result in an £1,800 reduction in cost each year over the next five years. It may appear that the answer is obvious since the total cost savings is £9,000 (5 × £1,800). However, the company can earn a 20% return by investing its money elsewhere. It is not enough that the cost reductions cover just the original cost of the machine; they must also yield at least a 20% return or the company would be better off investing the money elsewhere.

To determine whether the investment is desirable, it is necessary to discount the stream of annual £1,800 cost savings to its present value and then to compare this discounted present value with the

Initial cost	£5,000
Life of the project (years)	5
Annual cost savings	£1,800
Salvage value	0
Required rate of return	20%

Item Year	Year(s)	Amount of cash flow	20% factor	Present value of cash flows
Annual cost savings	1–5	£1,800	2.991*	£5,384
Initial investment	Now	(5,000)	1.000	(5,000)
Net present value				£384

*From Exhibit 10B.4 in Appendix 10B at the end of this chapter.

Exhibit 10.1 Net present value analysis of a proposed project

cost of the new machine. Since Harper Company requires a minimum return of 20% on all investment projects, this rate is used in the discounting process. Exhibit 10.1 shows how this analysis is done.

According to the analysis, Harper Company should purchase the new machine. The present value of the cost savings is £5,384, as compared to a present value of only £5,000 for the investment required (cost of the machine). Deducting the present value of the investment required from the present value of the cost savings gives a net present value of £384. Whenever the net present value is zero or greater, as in our example, an investment project is acceptable. Whenever the net present value is negative (the present value of the cash outflows exceeds the present value of the cash inflows), an investment project is not acceptable. In sum:

If the net present value is ...	Then the project is ...
Positive	Acceptable, since it promises a return greater than a required rate of return
Zero	Acceptable, since it promises a return equal to the required rate of return
Negative	Not acceptable, since it promises a return less than the required rate of return

A full interpretation of the solution would be as follows: The new machine promises more than the required 20% rate of return. This is evident from the positive net present value of £384. Harper Company could spend up to £5,384 for the new machine and still obtain the minimum required 20% rate of return. The net present value of £384, therefore, shows the amount of 'cushion' or 'margin of error'. One way to look at this is that the company could underestimate the cost of the new machine by up to £384, or overestimate the net present value of the future cash savings by up to £384, and the project would still be financially attractive.

Emphasis on cash flows

In capital budgeting decisions, the focus is on cash flows and not on accounting profit. The reason is that accounting profit is based on accrual concepts that ignore the timing of cash flows into and out of an organization. From a capital budgeting standpoint the timing of cash flows is important, since a pound received today is more valuable than a pound received in the future. Therefore, even though the accounting profit figure is useful for many things, it is not used in discounted cash flow analysis. Instead of determining accounting profit, the manager must concentrate on identifying the specific cash flows associated with an investment project.

What kinds of cash flows should the manager look for? Although the specific cash flows will vary from project to project, certain types of cash flows tend to recur, as explained in the following paragraphs.

Typical cash outflows

Most projects will have an immediate cash outflow in the form of an initial investment in equipment or other assets. Any salvage value realized from the sale of old equipment can be recognized as a cash inflow or as a reduction in the required investment. In addition, some projects require that a company expand its working capital. **Working capital** is current assets (cash, debtors and stock) less current liabilities. When a company takes on a new project, the balances in the current asset accounts will often increase. For example, opening a new Tesco store would require additional cash in sales registers, increased debtors for new customers, and more stock to fill the shelves. These additional working capital needs should be treated as part of the initial investment in a project. Also, many projects require periodic outlays for repairs and maintenance and for additional operating costs. These should all be treated as cash outflows for capital budgeting purposes.

Typical cash inflows

On the cash inflow side, a project will normally either increase revenues or reduce costs. Either way, the amount involved should be treated as a cash inflow for capital budgeting purposes. (In regard to this point, notice that so far as cash flows are concerned, *a reduction in costs is equivalent to an increase in rev-*

enues.) Cash inflows are also frequently realized from salvage of equipment when a project is terminated. In addition, upon termination of a project, any working capital that was tied up in the project can be released for use elsewhere and should be treated as a cash inflow. Working capital is released, for example, when a company sells off its stock or collects its receivables. (If the released working capital is not shown as a cash inflow at the termination of a project, then the project will go on being charged for the use of the funds forever!)

In summary, the following types of cash flows are common in business investment projects:

Cash outflows:

- Initial investment (including installation costs)
- Increased working capital needs
- Repairs and maintenance
- Incremental operating costs.

Cash inflows:

- Incremental revenues
- Reduction in costs
- Salvage value
- Release of working capital.

Recovery of the original investment

When computing the present value of a project, depreciation is not deducted for two reasons.

First, depreciation is not a current cash outflow. Second, as discussed above, discounted cash flow methods of making capital budgeting decisions focus on *cash flows*. Although depreciation is a vital concept in computing profit for financial statements, it is not relevant in an analytical framework that focuses on cash flows.

A second reason for not deducting depreciation is that discounted cash flow methods *automatically* provide for return of the original investment, thereby making a deduction for depreciation unnecessary. To demonstrate this point, let us assume the following data:

Carver Hospital is considering the purchase of an attachment for its X-ray machine that will cost £3,170. The attachment will be usable for four years, after which time it will have no salvage value. It will increase net cash inflows by £1,000 per year in the X-ray department. The hospital's board of directors has instructed that no investments are to be made unless they have an annual return of at least 10%.

A present value analysis of the desirability of purchasing the X-ray attachment is presented in Exhibit 10.2. Notice that the attachment promises exactly a 10% return on the original investment, since the net present value is zero at a 10% discount rate.

Each annual £1,000 cash inflow arising from use of the attachment is made up of two parts. One part represents a recovery of a portion of the original £3,170 paid for the attachment, and the other part represents a return on this investment. The breakdown of each year's £1,000 cash inflow between recovery of investment and return on investment is shown in Exhibit 10.3.

10.2 EXHIBIT

Initial cost	£3,170
Life of the project (years)	4
Annual cost savings	£1,000
Salvage value	0
Required rate of return	10%

Item	Year(s)	Amount of cash flow	10% factor	Present value of cash flows
Annual cost savings	1–4	£1,000	3.170*	£3,170
Initial investment	Now	(3,170)	1.000	(3,170)
Net present value				£0

*From Exhibit 10B.4 in Appendix 10B.

Exhibit 10.2 Carver Hospital – net present value analysis of X-ray attachment

Year	(1) Investment outstanding during the year	(2) Cash inflow	(3) Return on investment (1) × 10%	(4) Recovery of investment during the year (2) − (3)	(5) Unrecovered investment at the end of the year (1) − (4)
1	£3,170	£1,000	£317	£683	£2,487
2	2,487	1,000	249	751	1,736
3	1,736	1,000	173	827	909
4	909	1,000	91	909	0
Total investment recovered				£3,170	

Exhibit 10.3 Carver Hospital – breakdown of annual cash inflows

The first year's £1,000 cash inflow consists of a £317 interest return (10%) on the £3,170 original investment, plus a £683 return of that investment. Since the amount of the unrecovered investment decreases over the four years, the pound amount of the interest return also decreases. By the end of the fourth year, all £3,170 of the original investment has been recovered.

Simplifying assumptions

In working with discounted cash flows, at least two simplifying assumptions are usually made.

The first assumption is that all cash flows other than the initial investment occur at the end of a period. This is somewhat unrealistic in that cash flows typically occur somewhat uniformly throughout a period. The purpose of this assumption is just to simplify computations.

The second assumption is that all cash flows generated by an investment project are immediately reinvested. It is further assumed that the reinvested funds will yield a rate of return equal to the discount rate. Unless these conditions are met, the return computed for the project will not be accurate. To illustrate, we used a discount rate of 10% for the Carver Hospital in Exhibit 10.2. Unless the funds released each period are immediately reinvested at a 10% return, the net present value computed for the X-ray attachment will be misstated.

Choosing a discount rate

To use the net present value method, we must choose some rate of return for discounting cash flows to their present value. In Example A we used a 20% rate of return, and in Example B we used a 10% rate of return. These rates were chosen somewhat arbitrarily simply for the sake of illustration.

The firm's cost of capital is usually regarded as the most appropriate choice for the discount rate. The **cost of capital** is the average rate of return the company must pay to its long-term creditors and shareholders for the use of their funds. The mechanics involved in cost of capital computations are covered in finance texts and will not be considered here.

An extended example of the net present value method

To conclude our discussion of the net present value method, we present below an extended example of how it is used in analysing an investment proposal. This example will also help to tie together (and to reinforce) many of the ideas developed thus far.

Under a special licensing arrangement, Swinyard Company has an opportunity to market a new product in western Europe for a five-year period. The product would be purchased from the manufacturer, with Swinyard Company responsible for all costs of promotion and distribution. The licensing arrangement could be renewed at the end of the five-year period at the option of the manufacturer. After careful study, Swinyard Company has estimated that the following costs and revenues would be associated with the new product:

Cost of equipment needed	£60,000
Working capital needed	100,000
Overhaul of the equipment in four years	5,000
Salvage value of the equipment in five years	10,000
Annual revenues and costs:	
Sales revenues	200,000
Cost of goods sold	125,000
Out-of-pocket operating costs (for salaries, advertising and other direct costs)	35,000

At the end of the five-year period, the working capital would be released for investment elsewhere if the manufacturer decided not to renew the licensing arrangement. Swinyard Company's discount rate and cost of capital is 20%. Would you recommend that the new product be introduced?

This example involves a variety of cash inflows and cash outflows. The solution is given in Exhibit 10.4.

Sales revenues	£200,000
Less cost of goods sold	125,000
Less out-of-pocket costs for salaries, advertising, etc.	35,000
Annual net cash inflows	£40,000

Item	Year(s)	Amount of cash flows	20% factor	Present value of cash flows
Purchase of equipment	Now	£(60,000)	1.000	£(60,000)
Working capital needed	Now	(100,000)	1.000	(100,000)
Overhaul of equipment	4	(5,000)	0.482*	(2,410)
Annual net cash inflows from sales of the product line	1–5	40,000	2.991†	119,640
Salvage value of the equipment	5	10,000	0.402*	4,020
Working capital released	5	100,000	0.402*	40,200
Net present value				£1,450

*From Exhibit 10B.3 in Appendix 10B.

†From Exhibit 10B.4 in Appendix 10B.

Exhibit 10.4 The net present value method – an extended example

Notice, particularly, how the working capital is handled in this exhibit. It is counted as a cash outflow at the beginning of the project and as a cash inflow when it is released at the end of the project. Also notice how the sales revenues, cost of goods sold and out-of-pocket costs are handled. **Out-of-pocket costs** are actual cash outlays for salaries, advertising and other operating expenses. Depreciation would not be an out-of-pocket cost, since it involves no current cash outlay.

Since the overall net present value is positive, the new product should be added assuming the company has no better use for the investment funds.

Discounted cash flows – the internal rate of return method

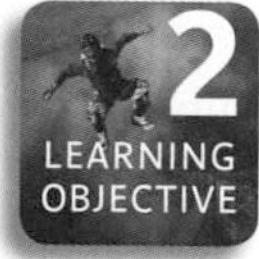

The **internal rate of return** (or **time-adjusted rate of return**) can be defined as the interest yield promised by an investment project over its useful life. It is sometimes referred to simply as the **yield** on a project. The internal rate of return is computed by finding the discount rate that equates the present value of a project's cash outflows with the present value of its cash inflows. In other words, the internal rate of return is that discount rate which will cause the net present value of a project to be equal to zero.

The internal rate of return method illustrated

To illustrate the internal rate of return method, let us assume the following data:

Glendale School is considering the purchase of a large tractor-pulled lawn mower. At present, the lawn is mowed using a small hand-pushed petrol mower. The large, tractor-pulled mower will cost £16,950 and will have a useful life of 10 years. It will have only a negligible scrap value, which can be ignored. The tractor-pulled mower would do the job much more quickly than the old mower and would result in a labour saving of £3,000 per year.

To compute the internal rate of return promised by the new mower, we must find the discount rate that will cause the net present value of the project to be zero. How do we do this? The simplest and most direct approach *when the net cash inflow is the same every year* is to divide the investment in the project by the expected net annual cash inflow. This computation will yield a factor from which the internal rate of return can be determined. The formula is as follows:

$$\text{Factor of the internal rate of return} = \frac{\text{Investment required}}{\text{Net annual cash flow}} \quad \textbf{(1)}$$

The factor derived from formula (1) is then located in the present value tables to see what rate of return it represents. Using formula (1) and the data for Glendale School's proposed project, we get:

$$\frac{\text{Investment required}}{\text{Net annual cash flow}} = \frac{£16,950}{£3,000} = £5,650$$

Thus, the discount factor that will equate a series of £3,000 cash inflows with a present investment of £16,950 is 5.650. Now we need to find this factor in Table 10B.4 in Appendix 10C to see what rate of return it represents. We should use the 10-period line in Table 10B.4 since the cash flows for the project continue for 10 years. If we scan along the 10-period line, we find that a factor of 5.650 represents a 12% rate of return. Therefore, the internal rate of return promised by the mower project is 12%. We can verify this by computing the project's net present value using a 12% discount rate. This computation is made in Exhibit 10.5.

10.5 EXHIBIT

Initial cost	£16,950
Life of the project (years)	10
Annual cost savings	£3,000
Salvage value	0

Item	Year(s)	Amount of cash flow	20% factor	Present value of cash flows
Annual cost savings	1–10	£3,000	5.650*	£16,950
Initial investment	Now	(16,950)	1.000	(16,950)
Net present value				£0

*From Exhibit 10B.4 in Appendix 10B.

Exhibit 10.5 Evaluation of the mower purchase using a 12% discount rate

Notice from Exhibit 10.5 that using a 12% discount rate equates the present value of the annual cash inflows with the present value of the investment required in the project, leaving a zero net present value. The 12% rate therefore represents the internal rate of return promised by the project.

Salvage value and other cash flows

The technique just demonstrated works very well if a project's cash flows are identical every year. But what if they are not? For example, what if a project will have some salvage value at the end of its life in addition to the annual cash inflows? Under these circumstances, a trial-and-error process is necessary to find the rate of return that will equate the cash inflows with the cash outflows. This trial-and-error process can be carried out by hand, or it can be carried out by means of computer software programs such as spreadsheets that perform the necessary computations in seconds. In short, erratic or uneven cash flows should not prevent a manager from determining a project's internal rate of return.

The process of interpolation

Interpolation is used to find rates of return that do not appear in published interest tables. Interest tables are usually printed in terms of whole percentages (10%, 12%, and so forth), whereas projects often have fractional rates of return. To illustrate the process of interpolation, assume the following data:

Investment required	£6,000
Annual cost savings	£1,500
Life of the project	10 years

What is the internal rate of return promised by this project? Using formula (1), the appropriate factor is 4.000:

$$\frac{\text{Investment required}}{\text{Net annual cash flow}} = \frac{£6,000}{£1,500} = 4.000$$

Looking at Exhibit 10B.4 in Appendix 10B and scanning along the 10-period line, we find that a factor of 4.000 represents a rate of return somewhere between 20% and 22%. To find the rate we are after, we must interpolate, as follows:

	Present value factors	
20% factor	4.192	4.192
True factor	4.000	
22% factor		3.923
Difference	0.192	0.269

$$\text{Internal rate of return} = 20\% + (\frac{0.192}{0.269} \times 2\%)$$

$$\text{Internal rate of return} = 21.4\%.$$

Using the internal rate of return

Once the internal rate of return has been computed, what does the manager do with the information? The internal rate of return is compared to the company's *required rate of return*. The **required rate of return** is the minimum rate of return that an investment project must yield to be acceptable. If the internal rate of return is *equal* to or *greater than* the required rate of return, then the project is acceptable. If it is less than the required rate of return, then the project is rejected. Quite often, the company's cost of capital is used as the required rate of return. The reasoning is that if a project cannot provide a rate of return at least as great as the cost of the funds invested in it, then it is not profitable.

In the case of the Glendale School example used earlier, let us assume that the district has set a minimum required rate of return of 15% on all projects. Since the large mower promises a rate of return of only 12%, it does not clear this hurdle and would therefore be rejected as a project.

The cost of capital as a screening tool

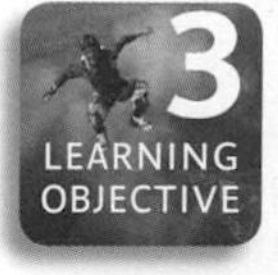

As we have seen in preceding examples, the cost of capital often operates as a screening device, helping the manager screen out undesirable investment projects. This screening is accomplished in different ways, depending on whether the company is using the internal rate of return method or the net present value method in its capital budgeting analysis.

When the internal rate of return method is used, the cost of capital is used as the hurdle rate that a project must clear for acceptance. If the internal rate of return of a project is not great enough to clear the cost of capital hurdle, then the project is ordinarily rejected. We saw the application of this idea in the Glendale School example, where the hurdle rate was set at 15%.

When the net present value method is used, the cost of capital is the discount rate used to compute the net present value of a proposed project. Any project yielding a negative net present value is rejected unless other factors are significant enough to require its acceptance. (This point is discussed further in a following section, Investments in automated equipment.)

The use of the cost of capital as a screening tool is summarized in Exhibit 10.6.

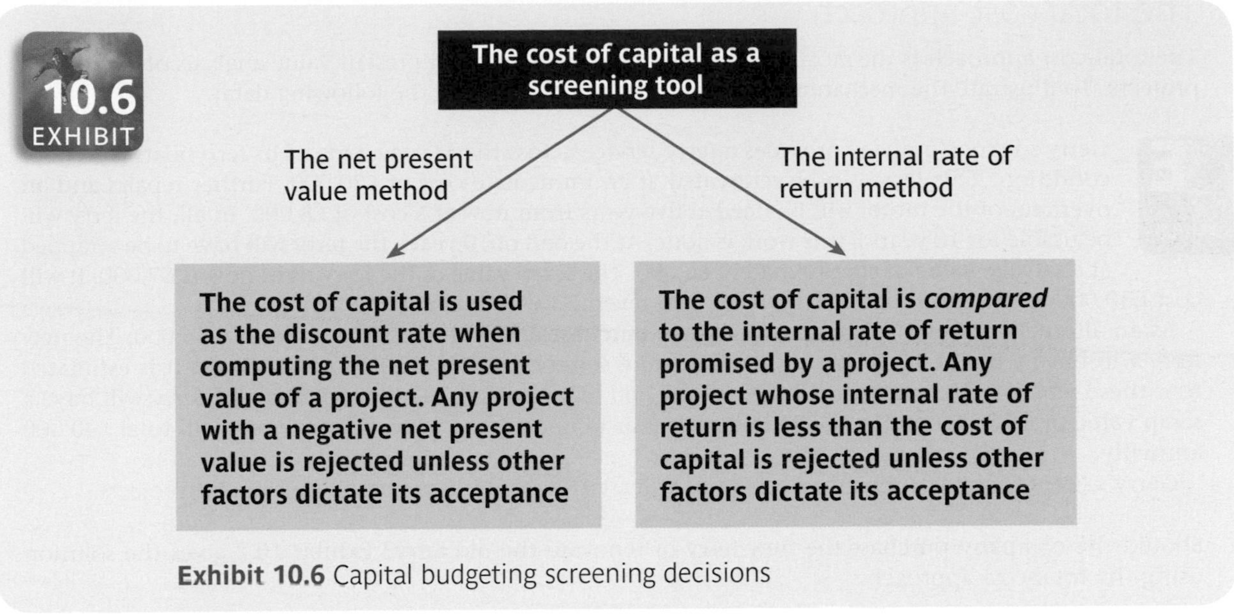

Exhibit 10.6 Capital budgeting screening decisions

Comparison of the net present value and the internal rate of return methods

The net present value method has several important advantages over the internal rate of return method.

First, the net present value method is often simpler to use. As mentioned earlier, the internal rate of return method may require hunting for the discount rate that results in a net present value of zero. This can be a very laborious trial-and-error process, although it can be automated to some degree using a computer spreadsheet.

Second, a key assumption made by the internal rate of return method is questionable. Both methods assume that cash flows generated by a project during its useful life are immediately reinvested elsewhere. However, the two methods make different assumptions concerning the rate of return that is earned on those cash flows. The net present value method assumes the rate of return is the discount rate, whereas the internal rate of return method assumes the rate of return is the internal rate of return on the project. Specifically, if the internal rate of return of the project is high, this assumption may not be realistic. It is generally more realistic to assume that cash inflows can be reinvested at a rate of return equal to the discount rate – particularly if the discount rate is the company's cost of capital or an opportunity rate of return. For example, if the discount rate is the company's cost of capital, this rate of return can actually be realized by paying off the company's creditors and buying back the company's stock with cash flows from the project. In short, when the net present value method and the internal rate of return method do not agree concerning the attractiveness of a project, it is best to go with the net present value method. Of the two methods, it makes the more realistic assumption about the rate of return that can be earned on cash flows from the project.

Expanding the net present value method

4 LEARNING OBJECTIVE

So far, all of our examples have involved only a single investment alternative. We will now expand the net present value method to include two alternatives. In addition, we will integrate the concept of relevant costs into the discounted cash flow analysis.

The net present value method can be used to compare competing investment projects in two ways. One is the *total-cost approach*, and the other is the *incremental-cost approach*. Each approach is illustrated below.

The total-cost approach

The total-cost approach is the most flexible method of making a net present value analysis of competing projects. To illustrate the mechanics of the approach, let us assume the following data:

EXAMPLE

Gerry's Ferry Company provides a ferry service across the Mersey. One of its ferryboats is in poor condition. This ferry can be renovated at an immediate cost of £20,000. Further repairs and an overhaul of the motor will be needed five years from now at a cost of £8,000. In all, the ferry will be usable for 10 years if this work is done. At the end of 10 years, the ferry will have to be scrapped at a salvage value of approximately £6,000. The scrap value of the ferry right now is £7,000. It will cost £30,000 each year to operate the ferry, and revenues will total £40,000 annually.

As an alternative, Gerry's Ferry Company can purchase a new ferryboat at a cost of £36,000. The new ferry will have a life of 10 years, but it will require some repairs at the end of five years. It is estimated that these repairs will amount to £3,000. At the end of 10 years, it is estimated that the ferry will have a scrap value of £6,000. It will cost £21,000 each year to operate the ferry, and revenues will total £40,000 annually.

Gerry's Ferry Company requires a return of at least 18% before taxes on all investment projects.

Should the company purchase the new ferry or renovate the old ferry? Exhibit 10.7 gives the solution using the total-cost approach.

10.7 EXHIBIT

	New ferry	Old ferry
Annual revenues	£40,000	£40,000
Annual cash operating costs	21,000	30,000
Net annual cash inflows	£19,000	£10,000

Item	Year(s)	Amount of cash flows	18% factor*	Present value of cash flows
Buy the new ferry:				
Initial investment	Now	£(36,000)	1.000	£(36,000)
Repairs in five years	5	(3,000)	0.437	(1,311)
Net annual cash inflows	1–10	19,000	4.494	85,386
Salvage of the old ferry	Now	7,000	1,000	7,000
Salvage of the new ferry	10	6,000	0.191	1,146
Net present value				56,221
Keep the old ferry:				
Initial repairs	Now	£(20,000)	1.000	(20,000)
Repairs in five years	5	(8,000)	0.437	(3,496)
Net annual cash inflows	1–10	10,000	4.494	44,940
Salvage of the old ferry	10	6,000	0.191	1,146
Net present value				22,590
Net present value in favour of buying the new ferry				£33,631

*All factors are from Exhibits 10B.3 and 10B.4 in Appendix 10B.

Exhibit 10.7 The total-cost approach to project selection

Two points should be noted from the exhibit. First, observe that *all* cash inflows and all cash outflows are included in the solution under each alternative. No effort has been made to isolate those cash flows that are relevant to the decision and those that are not. The inclusion of all cash flows associated with each alternative gives the approach its name – the *total-cost* approach.

Second, notice that a net present value figure is computed for each of the alternatives. This is a distinct advantage of the total-cost approach in that an unlimited number of alternatives can be compared side by side to determine the best action. For example, another alternative for Gerry's Ferry Company would be to get out of the ferry business entirely. If management desired, the net present value of this alternative could be computed to compare with the alternatives shown in Exhibit 10.7. Still other alternatives might be open to the company. Once management has determined the net present value of each alternative it wishes to consider, it can select the course of action that promises to be the most profitable. In the case at hand, given only the two alternatives, the data indicate that the most profitable course is to purchase the new ferry.[3]

The incremental-cost approach

When only two alternatives are being considered, the incremental-cost approach offers a simpler and more direct route to a decision. Unlike the total-cost approach, it focuses only on differential costs.[4] The procedure is to include in the discounted cash flow analysis only those costs and revenues that *differ* between the two alternatives being considered. To illustrate, refer again to the data in Example E relating to Gerry's Ferry Company. The solution using only differential costs is presented in Exhibit 10.8.

10.8 EXHIBIT

Item	Year(s)	Amount of cash flows	18% factor*	Present value of cash flows
Incremental investment required to purchase the new ferry	Now	£(16,000)	1.000	£(16,000)
Repairs in five years avoided	5	5,000	0.437	2,185
Increased net annual cash inflows	1–10	9,000	4.494	40,446
Salvage of the old ferry	Now	7,000	1.000	7,000
Difference in salvage value in 10 years	10	0	–	0
Net present value in favour of buying the new ferry				£33,631

*All factors are from Exhibits 10B.3 and 10B.4 in Appendix 10B.

Exhibit 10.8 The incremental cost approach to project selection

Two things should be noted from the data in this exhibit. First, notice that the net present value of £33,631 shown in Exhibit 10.8 agrees with the net present value shown under the total-cost approach in Exhibit 10.7. This agreement should be expected, since the two approaches are just different roads to the same destination.

Second, notice that the costs used in Exhibit 10.8 are just mathematical differences between the costs shown for the two alternatives in the prior exhibit. For example, the £16,000 incremental investment required to purchase the new ferry in Exhibit 10.8 is the difference between the £36,000 cost of the new ferry and the £20,000 cost required to renovate the old ferry from Exhibit 10.7. The other figures in Exhibit 10.8 have been computed in the same way.

Least-cost decisions

Revenues are not directly involved in some decisions. For example, a company that does not charge for delivery service may need to replace an old delivery truck, or a company may be trying to decide whether to lease or to buy its fleet of executive cars. In situations such as these, where no revenues are involved, the most desirable alternative will be the one that promises the *least total cost* from the present value perspective. Hence, these are known as least-cost decisions. To illustrate a least-cost decision, assume the following data:

EXAMPLE

Val-Tek Company is considering the replacement of an old threading machine. A new threading machine is available that could substantially reduce annual operating costs. Selected data relating to the old and the new machines are presented below:

	Old machine	New machine
Purchase cost when new	£20,000	£25,000
Salvage value now	3,000	–
Annual cash operating costs	15,000	9,000
Overhaul needed immediately	4,000	–
Salvage value in six years	0	5,000
Remaining life	6 years	6 years

Val-Tek Company's cost of capital is 10%.

Exhibit 10.9 provides an analysis of the alternatives using the total-cost approach.

10.9 EXHIBIT

Item	Year(s)	Amount of cash flows	18% factor*	Present value of cash flows
Buy the new machine:				
Initial investment	Now	£(25,000)	1.000	£(25,000)†
Salvage of the old machine	Now	3,000	1.000	3,000†
Annual cash operating costs	1–6	(9,000)	4.355	(39,195)
Salvage of the new machine	6	5,000	0.564	2,820
Present value of net cash outflows				(58,375)
Keep the old machine:				
Overhaul needed now	Now	£(4,000)	1,000	£(4,000)
Annual cash operating costs	1–6	(15,000)	4.355	(65,325)
Present value of net cash outflows				(69,325)
Net present value in favour of buying the new machine				£10,950

*All factors are from Exhibits 10B.3 and 10B.4 in Appendix 10B.

†These two items could be netted into a single £22,000 incremental-cost figure (£25,000 – £3,000 = £22,000).

Exhibit 10.9 The total-cost approach (least-cost decision)

As shown in the exhibit, the new machine has the lowest total cost when the present value of the net cash outflows is considered. An analysis of the two alternatives using the incremental-cost approach is presented in Exhibit 10.10. As before, the data in this exhibit represent the differences between the alternatives as shown under the total-cost approach.

Item	Year(s)	Amount of cash flows	18% factor*	Present value of cash flows
Incremental investment required to purchase the new machine	Now	£(21,000)	1.000	£(21,000)†
Salvage of the old machine	Now	3,000	1.000	3,000†
Savings in annual cash operating costs	1–6	6,000	4.355	26,130
Difference in salvage value in six years	6	5,000	0.564	2,820
Net present value in favour of buying the new machine				£10,950

*All factors are from Exhibits 10B.3 and 10B.4 in Appendix 10B.

†These two items could be netted into a single £18,000 incremental-cost figure (£21,000 – £3,000 = £18,000).

Exhibit 10.10 The incremental-cost approach (least-cost decision)

Capital budgeting and non-profit organizations

Capital budgeting concepts can be applied in all types of organizations. Note, for example, the different types of organizations used in the examples in this chapter. These organizations include a hospital, a company working under a licensing agreement, a school, a company operating a ferryboat service and a manufacturing company. The diversity of these examples shows the range and power of discounted cash flow methods.

One problem faced by *non-profit* organizations in capital budgeting is determining the proper discount rate. Some non-profit organizations use the rate of interest paid on special bond issues (such as an issue for street improvements or an issue to build a school) as their discount rate; others use the rate of interest that could be earned by placing money in an endowment fund rather than spending it on capital improvements; and still others use discount rates that are set somewhat arbitrarily by governing boards.

The greatest danger lies in using a discount rate that is too low. Most government agencies, for example, at one time used the interest rate on government bonds as their discount rate. It is now recognized that this rate is too low and has resulted in the acceptance of many projects that should not have been undertaken. To resolve this problem, the UK Treasury has specified that the public sector must use a discount rate of at least 6% on all projects.

Preference decisions – the ranking of investment projects

Recall that when considering investment opportunities, managers must make two types of decisions – screening decisions and preference decisions. Screening decisions pertain to whether or not some proposed investment is acceptable. Preference decisions come *after* screening decisions and attempt to answer the following question: 'How do the remaining investment proposals, all of which have been screened and provide an acceptable rate of return, rank in terms of preference? That is, which one(s) would be *best* for the firm to accept?'

Preference decisions are more difficult to make than screening decisions because investment funds are usually limited. This often requires that some (perhaps many) otherwise very profitable investment opportunities must be passed up.

Sometimes preference decisions are called ranking decisions, or rationing decisions, because they ration limited investment funds among many competing alternatives, or there may be many alternatives that must be ranked. Either the internal rate of return method or the net present value method can be used in making preference decisions. However, as discussed earlier, if the two methods are in conflict, it is best to use the net present value method, which is more reliable.

Internal rate of return method

When using the internal rate of return method to rank competing investment projects, the preference rule is: *the higher the internal rate of return, the more desirable the project.* An investment project with an internal rate of return of 18% is preferable to another project that promises a return of only 15%. Internal rate of return is widely used to rank projects.

Net present value method

If the net present value method is used to rank projects, the net present value of one project cannot be compared directly to the net present value of another project unless the investments in the projects are of equal size. For example, assume that a company is considering two competing investments, as shown below:

	Investment	
	A	B
Investment required	£(80,000)	£(5,000)
Present value of cash inflows	81,000	6,000
Net present value	£1,000	£1,000

Each project has a net present value of £1,000, but the projects are not equally desirable. The project requiring an investment of only £5,000 is much more desirable when funds are limited than the project requiring an investment of £80,000. To compare the two projects on a valid basis, the present value of the cash inflows should be divided by the investment required. The result is called the **profitability index**. The formula for the profitability index follows:

$$\text{Profitability index} = \frac{\text{Present value of cash inflows}}{\text{Investment required}} \qquad (2)$$

The profitability indexes for the two investments above would be computed as follows:

	Investment	
	A	B
Present value of cash inflows (a)	£81,000	£6,000
Investment required (b)	£80,000	£5,000
Profitability index, (a)/(b)	1.01	1.20

When using the profitability index to rank competing investments projects, the preference rule is: *the higher the profitability index, the more desirable the project.* Applying this rule to the two investments above, investment B should be chosen over investment A.

The profitability index is an application of the techniques for utilizing scarce resources discussed in Chapter 9. In this case, the scarce resource is the limited funds available for investment, and the profitability index is similar to the contribution margin per unit of the scarce resource.

A few details should be clarified with respect to the computation of the profitability index. The 'investment required' refers to any cash outflows that occur at the beginning of the project, reduced by any salvage value recovered from the sale of old equipment. The 'investment required' also includes any investment in working capital that the project may need. Finally, we should note that the 'present value of cash inflows' is net of all outflows that occur after the project starts.

Other approaches to capital budgeting decisions

Discounted cash flow methods have gained widespread acceptance as decision-making tools. Other methods of making capital budgeting decisions are also used, however, and are preferred by some managers. In this section, we discuss two such methods known as *payback* and *simple rate of return*. Both methods have been in use for a hundred years or more, but they are now declining in popularity as primary tools for project evaluation.

The payback method

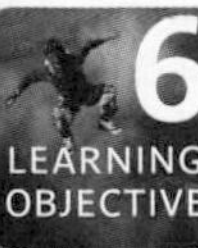

The payback method centres on a span of time known as the payback period. The **payback period** can be defined as the length of time that it takes for a project to recoup its initial cost out of the cash receipts that it generates. This period is sometimes referred to as 'the time that it takes for an investment to pay for itself'. The basic premise of the payback method is that the more quickly the cost of an investment can be recovered, the more desirable is the investment.

The payback period is expressed in years. *When the net annual cash inflow is the same every year*, the following formula can be used to compute the payback period:

$$\text{Payback period} = \frac{\text{Investment required}}{\text{Net annual cash flow*}} \quad \textbf{(3)}$$

*If new equipment is replacing old equipment, this becomes incremental net annual cash inflow.

To illustrate the payback method, assume the following data:

York Company needs a new milling machine. The company is considering two machines: machine A and machine B. Machine A costs £15,000 and will reduce operating costs by £5,000 per year. Machine B costs only £12,000 but will also reduce operating costs by £5,000 per year.

Which machine should be purchased according to the payback method?

$$\text{Machine A payback period} = \frac{£15{,}000}{£5{,}000} = 3.0 \text{ years}$$

$$\text{Machine B payback period} = \frac{£12{,}000}{£5{,}000} = 2.4 \text{ years}$$

According to the payback calculations, York Company should purchase machine B, since it has a shorter payback period than machine A.

Evaluation of the payback method

The payback method is not a true measure of the profitability of an investment. Rather, it simply tells the manager how many years will be required to recover the original investment. Unfortunately, a shorter payback period does not always mean that one investment is more desirable than another.

To illustrate, consider again the two machines used in the example above. Since machine B has a shorter payback period than machine A, it *appears* that machine B is more desirable than machine A. But, if we add one more piece of data, this illusion quickly disappears. Machine A has a projected 10-year life, and machine B has a projected 5-year life. It would take two purchases of machine B to provide the same length of service as a single purchase of machine A. Under these circumstances, machine A would be a much better investment than machine B, even though machine B has a shorter payback period. Unfortunately, the payback method has no inherent mechanism for highlighting differences in useful life between investments. Such differences can be very important, and relying on payback alone may result in incorrect decisions.

A further criticism of the payback method is that it does not consider the time value of money. A cash inflow to be received several years in the future is weighed equally with a cash inflow to be received right now. To illustrate, assume that for an investment of £8,000 you can purchase either of the two following streams of cash inflows:

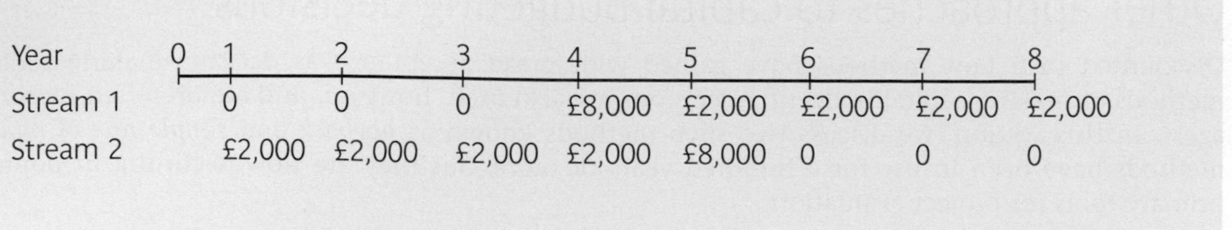

Year	0	1	2	3	4	5	6	7	8
Stream 1		0	0	0	£8,000	£2,000	£2,000	£2,000	£2,000
Stream 2		£2,000	£2,000	£2,000	£2,000	£8,000	0	0	0

Which stream of cash inflows would you prefer to receive in return for your £8,000 investment? Each stream has a payback period of 4.0 years. Therefore, if payback alone were relied on in making the decision, you would be forced to say that the streams are equally desirable. However, from the point of view of the time value of money, stream 2 is much more desirable than stream 1.

On the other hand, under certain conditions the payback method can be very useful. For one thing, it can help identify which investment proposals are in the 'ballpark'. That is, it can be used as a screening tool to help answer the question, 'Should I consider this proposal further?' If a proposal does not provide a payback within some specified period, then there may be no need to consider it further. In addition, the payback period is often of great importance to new firms that are 'cash poor'. When a firm is cash poor, a project with a short payback period but a low rate of return might be preferred over another project with a high rate of return but a long payback period. The reason is that the company may simply need a faster return of its cash investment. And finally, the payback method is sometimes used in industries where products become obsolete very rapidly – such as consumer electronics. Since products may last only a year or two, the payback period on investments must be very short.

An extended example of payback

As shown by formula (3) given earlier, the payback period is computed by dividing the investment in a project by the net annual cash inflows that the project will generate. If new equipment is replacing old equipment, then any salvage to be received on disposal of the old equipment should be deducted from the cost of the new equipment, and only the *incremental* investment should be used in the payback computation. In addition, any depreciation deducted in arriving at the project's profit must be added to obtain the project's expected net annual cash inflow. To illustrate, assume the following data:

Bevco Ltd operates many outlets in the European Union. Some of the vending machines in one of its outlets provide very little revenue, so the company is considering removing the machines and installing equipment to dispense soft ice cream. The equipment would cost £80,000 and have an eight-year useful life. Incremental annual revenues and costs associated with the sale of ice cream would be as follows:

Sales	£150,000
Less cost of ingredients	90,000
Contribution margin	60,000
Less fixed expenses:	
Salaries	27,000
Maintenance	3,000
Depreciation	10,000
Total fixed expenses	40,000
Profit	£20,000

The vending machines can be sold for £5,000 scrap value. The company will not purchase equipment unless it has a payback of three years or less. Should the equipment to dispense ice cream be purchased?

An analysis as to whether the proposed equipment meets the company's payback requirements is given in Exhibit 10.11. Several things should be noted from the data in this exhibit. First, notice that

Step 1: *Compute the net annual cash inflow.* Since the net annual cash inflow is not given, it must be computed before the payback period can be determined.

Net income (given above)	£20,000
Add: Non-cash deduction for depreciation	10,000
Net annual cash inflow	£30,000

Step 2: *Compute the payback period.* Using the net annual cash inflow figure from above, the payback period can be determined as follows:

Cost of the new equipment	£80,000
Less salvage value of old equipment	5,000
Investment required	£75,000

$$\text{Payback period} = \frac{\text{Investment required}}{\text{New annual cash inflow}} = \frac{£75{,}000}{£30{,}000} = 2.5 \text{ years}$$

Exhibit 10.11 Computation of the payback period

depreciation is added to profit to obtain the net annual cash inflow from the new equipment. As stated earlier in the chapter, depreciation is not a cash outlay; thus, it must be added to profit in order to adjust profit to a cash basis. Second, notice in the payback computation that the salvage value from the old machines has been deducted from the cost of the new equipment, and that only the incremental investment has been used in computing the payback period.

Since the proposed equipment has a payback period of less than three years, the company's payback requirement has been met.

Payback and uneven cash flows

When the cash flows associated with an investment project change from year to year, the simple payback formula that we outlined earlier is no longer usable, and the computations involved in deriving the payback period can be fairly complex. Consider the following data:

Year	Investment	Cash inflow
1	£4,000	£1,000
2		0
3		2,000
4	2,000	1,000
5		500
6		3,000
7		2,000
8		2,000

What is the payback period on this investment? The answer is 5.5 years, but to obtain this figure it is necessary to track the unrecovered investment year by year. The steps involved in this process are shown in Exhibit 10.12. By the middle of the sixth year, sufficient cash inflows will have been realized to recover the entire investment of £6,000 (£4,000 + £2,000).

10.12 EXHIBIT

Year	(1) Beginning unrecovered investment	(2) Additional investment	(3) Total Unrecovered Investment (1) + (2)	(4) Cash inflow	(5) Ending unrecovered investment (3) − (4)
1	£4,000		£4,000	£1,000	£3,000
2	3,000		3,000	0	3,000
3	3,000		3,000	2,000	1,000
4	1,000	£2,000	3,000	1,000	2,000
5	2,000		2,000	500	1,500
6	1,500		1,500	3,000	0
7	0		0	2,000	0
8	0		0	2,000	0

Exhibit 10.12 Payback and uneven cash flows

The simple rate of return method

7 LEARNING OBJECTIVE

The **simple rate of return** method is another capital budgeting technique that does not involve discounted cash flows. The method is also known as the accounting rate of return, the unadjusted rate of return, and the financial statement method.

Unlike the other capital budgeting methods that we have discussed, the simple rate of return method does not focus on cash flows. Rather, it focuses on accounting profit. The approach is to estimate the revenues that will be generated by a proposed investment and then to deduct from these revenues all of the projected operating expenses associated with the project. This profit figure is then related to the initial investment in the project, as shown in the following formula:

$$\text{Simple rate of return} = \frac{\text{Incremental revenues} - \text{Incremental expenses including depreciation} = \text{Incremental net profit}}{\text{Initial investment*}} \quad (4)$$

* The investment should be reduced by any salvage from the sale of old equipment. Or, if a cost reduction project is involved, formula (4) becomes:

$$\text{Simple rate of return} = \frac{\text{Cost savings} - \text{Depreciation on new equipment}}{\text{Initial investment*}} \quad (5)$$

* The investment should be reduced by any salvage from the sale of old equipment.

I EXAMPLE

Brigham Tea Ltd is a processor of a non-tannic acid tea. The company is contemplating purchasing equipment for an additional processing line. The additional processing line would increase revenues by £90,000 per year. Incremental cash operating expenses would be £40,000 per year. The equipment would cost £180,000 and have a nine-year life. No salvage value is projected.

Required

1 Compute the simple rate of return.

2 Compute the internal rate of return and compare it to the simple rate of return.

Solution

1 By applying the formula for the simple rate of return found in equation (4), we can compute the simple rate of return:

$$\text{Simple rate of return} = \frac{\begin{bmatrix}\text{£90,000 incremental} \\ \text{revenues}\end{bmatrix} - \begin{bmatrix}\text{£40,000 cash operating expenses} \\ \text{+ £20,000 depreciation}\end{bmatrix}}{\text{£180,000 initial investment}}$$

$$= \text{£30,000/£180,000}$$

$$= 16.7\%$$

2 The rate computed in (1) above, however, is far below the internal rate of return of approximately 24%:

$$\text{Factor of the internal rate of return} = \frac{\text{£180,000}}{\text{£50,000}} = 3.600$$

*£30,000 profit + £20,000 depreciation = £50,000; or the annual cash inflow can be computed as £90,000 increased revenues − £40,000 cash expenses = £50,000.

By scanning across the nine-year line in Exhibit 10B.4 in Appendix 10B, we can see that the internal rate of return is approximately 24%.

Midshires Farms Ltd hires people on a part-time basis to sort eggs. The cost of this hand-sorting process is £30,000 per year. The company is investigating the purchase of an egg-sorting machine that would cost £90,000 and have a 15-year useful life. The machine would have negligible salvage value, and it would cost £10,000 per year to operate and maintain. The egg-sorting equipment currently being used could be sold now for a scrap value of £2,500.

Required

Compute the simple rate of return on the new egg-sorting machine.

A cost reduction project is involved in this situation. By applying the formula for the simple rate of return found in equation (5), we can compute the simple rate of return as follows:

Solution

$$\text{Simple rate of return} = \frac{\text{£20,000* cost savings} - \text{£6,000† depreciation on new equipment}}{\text{£90,000} - \text{£2,500}}$$

$$= 16.0\%$$

* £30,000 − £10,000 = £20,000 cost savings.

† £90,000 ÷ 15 years = £6,000 depreciation.

Criticisms of the simple rate of return

The most damaging criticism of the simple rate of return method is that it does not consider the time value of money. A pound received ten years from now is viewed as being just as valuable as a pound received today. Thus, the manager can be misled if the alternatives being considered have different cash flow patterns. For example, assume that project A has a high simple rate of return but yields the bulk of its cash flows many years from now. Another project, B, has a somewhat lower simple rate of return but yields the bulk of its cash flows over the next few years. Project A has a higher simple rate of return than project B; however, project B might in fact be a much better investment if the time value of money were considered.

Postaudit of investment projects

A **postaudit** of an investment project involves a follow-up after the project has been approved to see whether or not expected results are actually realized. This is a key part of the capital budgeting process in that it provides management with an opportunity, over time, to see if realistic data are being submitted to support capital budgeting proposals. It also provides an opportunity to reinforce successful projects as needed, to strengthen or perhaps salvage projects that are encountering difficulty, to terminate unsuccessful projects before losses become too great, and to improve the overall quality of future investment proposals. In performing a postaudit, the same technique should be used as was used in the original approval process. That is, if a project was approved on the basis of a net present value analysis, then the same procedure should be used in performing the postaudit. However, the data used in the postaudit analysis should be actual observed data rather than estimated data. This affords management with an opportunity to make a side-by-side comparison to see how well the project has worked out. It also helps assure that estimated data received on future proposals will be carefully prepared, since the persons submitting the data will know that their estimates will be given careful scrutiny in the postaudit process. Actual results that are far out of line with original estimates should be carefully reviewed by management, and corrective action taken as necessary. Those managers responsible for the original estimates should be required to provide a full explanation of any major differences between estimated and actual results.

Summary

- Investment decisions should take into account the time value of money since a pound today is more valuable than a pound received in the future. The net present value and internal rate of return methods both reflect this fact. In the net present value method, future cash flows are discounted to their present value so that they can be compared on a valid basis with current cash outlays.
- The difference between the present value of the cash inflows and the present value of the cash outflows is called the project's net present value. If the net present value of the project is negative, the project is rejected.
- The discount rate in the net present value method is usually a minimum required rate of return such as the company's cost of capital.
- The internal rate of return is the rate of return that equates the present value of the cash inflows and the present value of the cash outflows, resulting in a zero net present value. If the internal rate of return is less than the company's minimum required rate of return, the project is rejected.
- After rejecting projects whose net present values are negative or whose internal rates of return are less than the minimum required rate of return, the company may still have more projects than can be supported with available funds. The remaining projects can be ranked using either the profitability index or their internal rates of return. The profitability index is computed by dividing the present value of the project's future net cash inflows by the required initial investment.
- Some companies prefer to use either payback or the simple rate of return to evaluate investment proposals. The payback period is the number of periods that are required to recover the initial investment in the project. The simple rate of return is determined by dividing a project's accounting profit by the initial investment in the project.

Key terms for review

Capital budgeting (p. 372).

Cost of capital (p. 377).

Internal rate of return (p. 378).

Net present value (p. 373).

Out-of-pocket costs (p. 378).

Payback period (p. 387).

Postaudit (p. 391).

Preference decision (p. 372).

Profitability index (p. 386).

Required rate of return (p. 380).

Screening decisions (p. 372).

Simple rate of return (p. 390).

Time-adjusted rate of return (p. 378).

Working capital (p. 374).

Yield (p. 378).

Review problem 1: basic present value computations

Each of the following situations is independent. Work out your own solution to each situation, and then check it against the solution provided.

1 John has just reached age 58. In 12 years he plans to retire. Upon retiring, he would like to take an extended vacation, which he expects will cost at least £4,000. What lump-sum amount must he invest now to have the needed £4,000 at the end of 12 years if the rate of return is:

(a) 8%?

(b) 12%?

2 The Morgans would like to send their daughter to an expensive music camp at the end of each of the next five years. The camp costs £1,000 a year. What lump-sum amount would have to be invested now to have the £1,000 at the end of each year if the rate of return is:

(a) 8%?

(b) 12%?

3 You have just received an inheritance from a relative. You can invest the money and either receive a £20,000 lump-sum amount at the end of ten years or receive £1,400 at the end of each year for the next ten years. If your minimum desired rate of return is 12%, which alternative would you prefer?

Solution to review problem 1: basic present value computations

1 **(a)** The amount that must be invested now would be the present value of the £4,000, using a discount rate of 8%. From Exhibit 10B.3 in Appendix 10B, the factor for a discount rate of 8% for 12 periods is 0.397. Multiplying this discount factor by the £4,000 needed in 12 years will give the amount of the present investment required: £4,000 × 0.397 = £1,588.

(b) We will proceed as we did in (a) above, but this time we will use a discount rate of 12%. From Table 10B.3 in Appendix 10B, the factor for a discount rate of 12% for 12 periods is 0.257. Multiplying this discount factor by the £4,000 needed in 12 years will give the amount of the present investment required: £4,000 × 0.257 = £1,028.

Notice that as the discount rate (desired rate of return) increases, the present value decreases.

2 This part differs from Question 1 above in that we are now dealing with an annuity rather than with a single future sum. The amount that must be invested now will be the present value of the £1,000 needed at the end of each year for five years. Since we are dealing with an annuity, or a series of annual cash flows, we must refer to Exhibit 10B.4 in Appendix 10B for the appropriate discount factor.

(a) From Exhibit 10B.4 in Appendix 10B, the discount factor for 8% for five periods is 3.993. Therefore, the amount that must be invested now to have £1,000 available at the end of each year for five years is £1,000 × 3.993 = £3,993.

(b) From Exhibit 10B.4 in Appendix 10B, the discount factor for 12% for five periods is 3.605.

Therefore, the amount that must be invested now to have £1,000 available at the end of each year for five years is £1,000 × 3.605 = £3,605.

Again, notice that as the discount rate (desired rate of return) increases, the present value decreases. At a higher rate of return we can invest less than would have been needed if a lower rate of return were being earned.

3 For this part we will need to refer to both Exhibits 10B.3 and 10B.4 in Appendix 10B. From Exhibit 10B.3, we will need to find the discount factor for 12% for 10 periods, then apply it to the £20,000 lump sum to be received in 10 years. From Exhibit 10B.4, we will need to find the discount factor for 12% for 10 periods, then apply it to the series of £1,400 payments to be received over the 10-year period. Whichever alternative has the higher present value is the one that should be selected.

£20,000 × 0.322 = £6,440

£1,400 × 5.650 = £7,910

Thus, you would prefer to receive the £1,400 per year for 10 years rather than the £20,000 lump sum.

Review problem 2: comparison of capital budgeting methods

Lamar Company is studying a project that would have an eight-year life and require a £1,600,000 investment in equipment. At the end of eight years, the project would terminate and the equipment would have no salvage value. The project would provide profit each year as follows:

Sales		£3,000,000
Less variable expenses		1,800,000
Contribution margin		1,200,000
Less fixed expenses:		
Advertising, salaries, and other fixed out-of-pocket costs	£700,000	
Depreciation	200,000	
Total fixed expenses		900,000
Profit		£300,000

The company's discount rate is 18%.

Required

1 Compute the net annual cash inflow from the project.
2 Compute the project's net present value. Is the project acceptable?
3 Compute the project's internal rate of return. Interpolate to one decimal place.
4 Compute the project's payback period. If the company requires a maximum payback of three years, is the project acceptable?
5 Compute the project's simple rate of return.

Solution to review problem 2: comparison of capital budgeting methods

1 The net annual cash inflow can be computed by deducting the cash expenses from sales:

Sales	£3,000,000	
Less variable expenses	1,800,000	
Contribution margin	1,200,000	
Less advertising, salaries, and other fixed out-of-pocket costs	700,000	
Net annual cash inflow	£500,000	
Or it can be computed by adding depreciation back to profit:		
Profit		£300,000
Add: Non-cash deduction for depreciation		200,000
Net annual cash inflow		£500,000

2 The net present value can be computed as follows:

Item	Year(s)	Amount of cash flows	18% factor	Present value of cash flows
Cost of new equipment	Now	£(1,600,000)	1.000	£(1,600,000)
Net annual cash inflow	1–8	500,000	4.078	2,039,000
Net present value				£439,000

Yes, the project is acceptable since it has a positive net present value.

3 The formula for computing the factor of the internal rate of return is:

$$\text{Factor of the internal rate of return} = \frac{\text{Investment required}}{\text{Net annual cash flow}} = \frac{£1,600,000}{£500,000} = 3.200$$

Looking in Exhibit 10B.4 in Appendix 10B at the end of the chapter and scanning along the 8-period line, we find that a factor of 3.200 represents a rate of return somewhere between 26 and 28%. To find the rate we are after, we must interpolate as follows:

26% factor	3.241	3.241
True factor	3.200	
28% factor		3.076
Difference	0.041	0.165

$$\text{Internal rate of return} = 26\% + \left(\frac{0.041}{0.165}\right) \times 2\% = 26.5\%$$

4 The formula for the payback period is:

$$\text{Payback period} = \frac{\text{Investment required}}{\text{Net annual cash flow*}} = \frac{£1,600,000}{£500,000} = 3.2 \text{ years}$$

No, the project is not acceptable when measured by the payback method. The 3.2 years payback period is greater than the maximum 3 years set by the company.

5 The formula for the simple rate of return is:

Simple rate of return =

$$\frac{\text{Incremental revenues} - \text{Incremental expenses, including depreciation} = \text{Incremental net profit}}{\text{Initial investment*}}$$

$$= \frac{£300,000}{£1,600,000}$$

= 18.75%

Appendix 10A: Inflation and capital budgeting

Does inflation have an impact in a capital budgeting analysis? The answer is a qualified 'yes' in that inflation does have an impact on the *numbers* that are used in a capital budgeting analysis, but it does not have an impact on the *results* of the analysis if certain conditions are satisfied. To show what we mean by this statement, we will use the following data:

Martin Company wants to purchase a new machine that costs £36,000. The machine would provide annual cost savings of £20,000, and it would have a three-year life with no salvage value. For each of the next three years, the company expects a 10% inflation rate in the cash flows associated with the new machine. If the company's cost of capital is 23.2%, should the new machine be purchased?

To answer this question, it is important to know how the cost of capital was derived. Ordinarily, it is based on the market rates of return on the company's various sources of financing – both debt and equity. This market rate of return includes expected inflation; the higher the expected rate of inflation, the higher the market rate of return on debt and equity. When the inflationary effect is removed from the market rate of return, the result is called a real rate of return. For example, if the inflation rate of 10% is removed from Martin's cost of capital of 23.2%, the 'real cost of capital' is only 12%, as shown in Exhibit 10A.1. (You cannot simply subtract the inflation rate from the market cost of capital to obtain the real cost of capital. The computations are a bit more complex than that.)

When performing a net present value analysis, one must be consistent. The market-based cost of capital reflects inflation. Therefore, if a market-based cost of capital is used to discount cash flows, then the cash flows should be adjusted upwards to reflect the effects of inflation in forthcoming periods. Computations for Martin Company under this approach are given in solution B in Exhibit 10A.1.

On the other hand, there is no need to adjust the cash flows upward if the 'real cost of capital' is used in the analysis (since the inflationary effects have been taken out of the discount rate). Computations for Martin Company under this approach are given in solution A in Exhibit 10A.1. Note that under solutions A and B the answer will be the same (within rounding error) regardless of which approach is used, as long as one is consistent and all of the cash flows associated with the project are affected in the same way by inflation.

Several points should be noted about solution B, where the effects of inflation are explicitly taken into account. First, note that the annual cost savings are adjusted for the effects of inflation by multiplying each year's cash savings by a price-index number that reflects a 10% inflation rate. (Observe from the footnotes to the exhibit how the index number is computed for each year.) Second, note that the net present value obtained in solution B, where inflation is explicitly taken into account, is the same, within rounding error, to that obtained in solution A, where the inflation effects are ignored. This result may seem surprising, but it is logical. The reason is that we have adjusted both the cash flows and the discount rate so that they are consistent, and these adjustments cancel each other out across the two solutions.

Throughout the chapter we assume for simplicity that there is no inflation. In that case, the market-based and real costs of capital are the same, and there is no reason to adjust the cash flows for inflation since there is none. When there is inflation, the unadjusted cash flows can be used in the analysis if all

Reconciliation of the market-based and real costs of capital

The real cost of capital	12.0%
The inflation factor	10.0%
The combined effect (12% × 10% = 1.2%)	1.2%
The market-based cost of capital	23.2%

Solution A: inflation not considered

Item	Year(s)	Amount of cash flows	12% Factor	Present value of cash flows
Initial investment	Now	£(36,000)	1.000	£(36,000)
Annual cost savings	1–3	20,000	2.402	48,040
Net present value				£12,040‡

Solution B: inflation not considered

Item	Year(s)	Amount of cash flows	Price index number*	Price-adjusted cash	23.2% factor †	Present cash flows
Initial investment	Now	£(36,000)	1.000	£(36,000)	1.000	£(36,000)
Annual cost savings	1	20,000	1.100	22,000	0.812	17,864
	2	20,000	1.210	24,200	0.659	15,948
	3	20,000	1.331	26,620	0.535	14,242
Net present value						£12,050‡

*Computation of the price-index numbers, assuming a 10% inflation rate each year: Year 1, (1.10)1 = 1.10; Year 2, (1.10)2 =1.21; and Year 3, (1.10)3 =1.331.

†Discount formulas are computed using the formula 1/(1 + *r*)*n*, where *r* is the discount factor and *n* is the number of years. The computations are 1/1.232 = 0.812 for Year 1; 1/(1.232)2 = 0.659 for Year 2; and 1/(1.232)3 = 0.535 for Year 3.

‡These amounts are different only because of rounding error.

Exhibit 10A.1 Capital budgeting and inflation

of the cash flows are affected identically by inflation and the real cost of capital is used to discount the cash flows. Otherwise, the cash flows should be adjusted for inflation and the market-based cost of capital should be used in the analysis.

Appendix 10B: Future value and present value tables

Periods	4%	6%	8%	10%	12%	14%	20%
1	1.040	1.060	1.080	1.100	1.120	1.140	1.200
2	1.082	1.124	1.166	1.210	1.254	1.300	1.440
3	1.125	1.191	1.260	1.331	1.405	1.482	1.728
4	1.170	1.263	1.361	1.464	1.574	1.689	2.074
5	1.217	1.338	1.469	1.611	1.762	1.925	2.488
6	1.265	1.419	1.587	1.772	1.973	2.195	2.986
7	1.316	1.504	1.714	1.949	2.211	2.502	3.583
8	1.369	1.594	1.851	2.144	2.476	2.853	4.300
9	1.423	1.690	1.999	2.359	2.773	3.252	5.160
10	1.480	1.791	2.159	2.594	3.106	3.707	6.192
11	1.540	1.898	2.332	2.853	3.479	4.226	7.430
12	1.601	2.012	2.518	3.139	3.896	4.818	8.916
13	1.665	2.133	2.720	3.452	4.364	5.492	10.699
14	1.732	2.261	2.937	3.798	4.887	6.261	12.839
15	1.801	2.397	3.172	4.177	5.474	7.138	15.407
20	2.191	3.207	4.661	6.728	9.646	13.473	38.338
30	3.243	5.744	10.063	17.450	29.960	50.950	237.380
40	4.801	10.286	21.275	45.260	93.051	199.880	1469.800

Exhibit 10B.1 Future value of £1; $F_n = P(1 + r)^n$

Periods	4%	6%	8%	10%	12%	14%	20%
1	1.000	1.000	1.000	1.000	1.000	1.000	1.000
2	2.040	2.060	2.080	2.100	2.120	2.140	2.220
3	3.122	3.184	3.246	3.310	3.374	3.440	3.640
4	4.247	4.375	4.506	4.641	4.779	4.921	5.368
5	5.416	5.637	5.867	6.105	6.353	6.610	7.442
6	6.633	6.975	7.336	7.716	8.115	8.536	9.930
7	7.898	8.394	8.923	9.487	10.089	10.730	12.916
8	9.214	9.898	10.637	11.436	12.300	13.233	16.499
9	10.583	11.492	12.488	13.580	14.776	16.085	20.799
10	12.006	13.181	14.487	15.938	17.549	19.337	25.959
11	13.486	14.972	16.646	18.531	20.655	23.045	32.150
12	15.026	16.870	18.977	21.385	24.133	27.271	39.580
13	16.627	18.882	21.495	24.523	28.029	32.089	48.497
14	18.282	21.015	24.215	27.796	32.393	37.581	59.196
15	20.024	23.276	27.152	31.773	37.280	43.842	72.035
20	29.778	36.778	45.762	57.276	75.052	91.025	186.690
30	56.085	79.058	113.283	164.496	241.330	356.790	1181.900
40	95.026	154.762	259.057	442.597	767.090	1342.000	7343.900

Exhibit 10B.2 Future value of an annuity of £1 in arrears;

$$F_n = \frac{(1 + r)_n - 1}{r}$$

Period	4%	5%	6%	8%	10%	12%	14%	16%	18%	20%	22%	24%	26%	28%	30%	40%
1	0.962	0.952	0.926	0.943	0.909	0.893	0.877	0.862	0.847	0.833	0.820	0.806	0.794	0.781	0.769	0.714
2	0.925	0.907	0.857	0.890	0.826	0.797	0.769	0.743	0.718	0.684	0.672	0.650	0.630	0.610	0.592	0.510
3	0.889	0.864	0.794	0.840	0.751	0.712	0.675	0.641	0.609	0.579	0.551	0.524	0.500	0.477	0.455	0.364
4	0.855	0.823	0.735	0.792	0.683	0.636	0.592	0.552	0.516	0.482	0.451	0.423	0.397	0.373	0.350	0.260
5	0.822	0.784	0.681	0.747	0.621	0.567	0.519	0.476	0.437	0.402	0.370	0.341	0.315	0.291	0.269	0.186
6	0.790	0.746	0.630	0.705	0.564	0.507	0.456	0.410	0.370	0.335	0.303	0.275	0.250	0.227	0.207	0.133
7	0.760	0.711	0.583	0.665	0.513	0.452	0.400	0.352	0.314	0.279	0.249	0.222	0.198	0.178	0.159	0.095
8	0.731	0.677	0.540	0.627	0.467	0.404	0.351	0.305	0.266	0.233	0.204	0.179	0.157	0.139	0.123	0.068
9	0.703	0.645	0.500	0.592	0.424	0.361	0.308	0.263	0.225	0.194	0.167	0.144	0.125	0.108	0.094	0.048
10	0.676	0.614	0.463	0.558	0.386	0.322	0.270	0.227	0.191	0.162	0.137	0.116	0.099	0.085	0.073	0.035
11	0.650	0.585	0.429	0.527	0.350	0.287	0.237	0.195	0.162	0.135	0.112	0.094	0.079	0.066	0.056	0.025
12	0.625	0.557	0.397	0.497	0.319	0.257	0.208	0.168	0.137	0.112	0.092	0.076	0.062	0.052	0.043	0.018
13	0.601	0.530	0.368	0.469	0.290	0.229	0.182	0.145	0.116	0.093	0.075	0.061	0.050	0.040	0.033	0.013
14	0.577	0.505	0.340	0.442	0.263	0.205	0.160	0.125	0.099	0.078	0.062	0.049	0.039	0.032	0.025	0.009
15	0.555	0.481	0.315	0.417	0.239	0.183	0.140	0.108	0.084	0.065	0.051	0.040	0.031	0.025	0.020	0.006
16	0.534	0.458	0.292	0.394	0.218	0.163	0.123	0.093	0.071	0.054	0.042	0.032	0.025	0.019	0.015	0.005
17	0.513	0.436	0.270	0.371	0.198	0.146	0.108	0.080	0.060	0.045	0.034	0.026	0.020	0.015	0.012	0.003
18	0.494	0.416	0.250	0.350	0.180	0.130	0.095	0.069	0.051	0.038	0.027	0.021	0.016	0.012	0.009	0.002
19	0.476	0.396	0.232	0.331	0.164	0.116	0.083	0.060	0.043	0.031	0.023	0.017	0.012	0.009	0.007	0.002
20	0.456	0.377	0.215	0.312	0.149	0.104	0.073	0.051	0.037	0.026	0.019	0.014	0.010	0.007	0.005	0.001
21	0.439	0.359	0.199	0.294	0.135	0.093	0.064	0.044	0.031	0.022	0.015	0.011	0.008	0.006	0.004	0.001
22	0.422	0.342	0.184	0.278	0.123	0.083	0.056	0.038	0.026	0.018	0.013	0.009	0.006	0.004	0.003	0.001
23	0.406	0.328	0.170	0.262	0.112	0.074	0.049	0.033	0.022	0.015	0.010	0.007	0.005	0.003	0.002	
24	0.390	0.310	0.158	0.247	0.102	0.066	0.043	0.028	0.019	0.013	0.008	0.006	0.004	0.003	0.002	
25	0.375	0.295	0.146	0.233	0.092	0.059	0.038	0.024	0.016	0.010	0.007	0.005	0.003	0.002	0.001	
26	0.361	0.281	0.135	0.220	0.084	0.053	0.033	0.021	0.014	0.009	0.006	0.004	0.002	0.002	0.001	
27	0.347	0.268	0.125	0.207	0.076	0.047	0.029	0.018	0.011	0.007	0.005	0.003	0.002	0.001	0.001	
28	0.333	0.255	0.116	0.196	0.069	0.042	0.026	0.016	0.010	0.006	0.004	0.002	0.002	0.001	0.001	
29	0.321	0.243	0.107	0.185	0.063	0.037	0.022	0.014	0.008	0.005	0.003	0.002	0.001	0.001	0.001	
30	0.308	0.231	0.099	0.174	0.057	0.033	0.020	0.012	0.007	0.004	0.003	0.002	0.001	0.001		
40	0.208	0.142	0.046	0.097	0.022	0.011	0.005	0.003	0.001	0.001						

Exhibit 10B.3 Present value of £1;

$$F_n = \frac{F_n}{(1 + r)^n}$$

Period	4%	5%	6%	8%	10%	12%	14%	16%	18%	20%	22%	24%	26%	28%	30%	40%
1	0.962	0.952	0.943	0.926	0.909	0.893	0.877	0.862	0.847	0.833	0.820	0.806	0.781	0.794	0.769	0.714
2	1.886	1.859	1.833	1.783	1.736	1.690	1.647	1.605	1.566	1.528	1.492	1.457	1.424	1.392	1.361	1.224
3	2.775	2.723	2.673	2.577	2.487	2.402	2.322	2.246	2.174	2.106	2.042	1.981	1.923	1.868	1.816	1.589
4	3.630	3.546	3.465	3.312	3.170	3.037	2.914	2.798	2.690	2.589	2.494	2.404	2.320	2.241	2.166	1.879
5	4.452	4.330	4.212	3.993	3.791	3.605	3.433	3.274	3.127	2.991	2.864	2.745	2.635	2.532	2.436	2.035
6	5.242	5.076	4.917	4.623	4.355	4.111	3.889	3.685	3.498	3.326	3.167	3.030	2.885	2.759	2.643	2.168
7	6.002	5.786	5.582	5.206	4.868	4.564	4.288	4.039	3.812	3.605	3.416	3.242	3.083	2.937	2.802	2.263
8	6.733	6.463	6.210	5.747	5.335	4.968	4.639	4.344	4.078	3.837	3.619	3.421	3.421	3.076	2.925	2.331
9	7.435	7.108	6.802	6.247	7.759	5.328	4.946	4.607	4.303	4.031	3.786	3.566	3.366	3.184	3.019	2.379
10	8.111	7.722	7.360	6.710	6.145	5.650	5.216	4.833	4.494	4.192	3.923	3.682	3.465	3.629	3.092	2.414
11	8.760	8.306	7.887	7.139	6.495	5.988	5.453	5.029	4.656	4.327	4.035	3.776	3.544	3.335	3.147	2.438
12	9.385	8.863	8.384	7.536	6.814	6.194	5.660	5.197	4.793	4.430	4.127	3.851	3.606	3.387	3.190	2.456
13	9.986	9.394	8.853	7.904	7.103	6.424	5.842	5.342	4.910	4.533	4.203	3.912	3.656	3.427	3.223	2.468
14	10.563	9.899	9.295	8.244	7.367	6.628	6.002	5.468	5.008	4.611	4.265	3.962	3.695	3.459	3.249	2.477
15	11.118	10.380	9.712	8.559	7.606	6.811	6.142	5.575	5.092	4.675	4.315	4.001	3.726	3.483	3.268	2.484
16	11.652	10.838	10.106	8.851	7.824	6.974	6.265	5.669	5.162	4.730	4.357	4.033	3.751	3.503	3.283	2.489
17	12.166	11.274	10.477	9.122	8.022	7.120	6.373	5.749	5.222	4.775	4.391	4.059	3.771	3.518	3.295	2.492
18	12.659	11.690	10.828	9.372	8.201	7.250	6.467	5.818	5.273	4.812	4.419	4.080	3.786	3.529	3.304	2.494
19	13.134	12.085	11.158	9.604	8.365	7.366	6.550	5.877	5.316	4.844	4.442	4.097	3.799	3.539	3.311	2.496
20	13.590	12.462	11.470	9.818	8.514	7.469	6.623	5.929	5.353	4.870	4.460	4.110	3.808	3.546	3.316	2.497
21	14.029	12.821	11.764	10.017	8.649	7.562	6.687	5.973	5.384	4.891	4.476	4.121	3.186	3.551	3.320	2.498
22	14.451	13.163	12.042	10.201	8.772	7.645	6.743	6.011	5.410	4.909	4.499	4.130	3.822	3.556	3.323	2.498
23	14.857	13.489	12.303	10.371	8.883	7.718	6.792	6.044	5.432	4.295	4.499	4.137	3.827	3.559	3.325	2.499
24	15.247	13.799	12.550	10.529	8.985	7.784	6.835	6.073	5.451	4.937	4.507	4.143	3.831	3.562	3.327	2.499
25	15.622	14.094	12.783	10.675	9.077	7.843	6.873	6.097	5.467	4.948	4.514	4.147	3.834	3.564	3.329	2.499
26	15.983	14.375	13.003	10.810	9.161	7.896	6.906	6.118	5.480	4.956	4.520	4.151	3.837	3.566	3.330	2.500
27	16.330	14.643	13.211	10.935	9.237	7.943	6.935	6.136	5.492	4.964	4.525	4.154	3.839	3.567	3.331	2.500
28	16.663	14.898	13.406	11.051	9.307	7.984	6.961	6.152	5.502	4.970	4.528	4.157	3.840	3.568	3.331	2.500
29	16.984	15.141	13.591	11.158	9.370	8.022	6.983	6.166	5.510	4.975	4.531	4.159	3.841	3.569	3.332	2.500
30	17.292	15.373	13.765	11.258	9.427	8.055	7.003	6.177	5.517	4.979	4.534	4.160	3.842	3.569	3.332	2.500
40	19.793	17.159	15.046	11.925	9.779	8.244	7.105	6.234	5.548	4.997	4.544	4.166	3.846	3.571	3.333	2.500

Exhibit 10B.4 Present value of an annuity of £1 in arrears;

$$P_n = \frac{1}{r}\left(\frac{1-1}{(1+r)^n}\right)$$

Appendix 10C: The impact of corporate taxation

Businesses, like individuals, must pay income/corporation taxes. In the case of businesses, the amount of income tax that must be paid is determined by the company's net taxable income/profit. Tax deductible expenses (tax deductions) decrease the company's net taxable income and hence reduce the taxes the company must pay. For this reason, expenses are often stated on an after-tax basis. For example, if a company pays rent of £10 million a year but this expense results in a reduction in income taxes of £3 million, the after-tax cost of the rent is £7 million. An expenditure net of its tax effect is known as after-tax cost.

To illustrate, assume that a company with a tax rate of 30% is contemplating a training programme that costs £60,000. What impact will this have on the company's taxes? To keep matters simple, let us suppose the training programme has no immediate effect on sales. How much does the company actually pay for the training programme after taking into account the impact of this expense on taxes? The answer is £42,000 as shown in Exhibit 10C.1. While the training programme costs £60,000 before taxes, it would reduce the company's taxes by £18,000, so its after-tax cost would be only £42,000.

	Without training programme		With training programme
Sales	£850,000		£850,000
Less tax deductible expenses:			
Salaries, insurance and other	700,000		700,000
New training programme			60,000
Total expenses	700,000		760,000
Taxable income	£150,000		£90,000
Income taxes (30%)	£45,000		£27,000
Cost of new training programme		£60,000	
Less: Reduction in income taxes (£45.000 – £27,000)		£18,000	
After-tax cost of the new training programme		£42,000	

Exhibit 10C.1 The computation of after-tax cost

The after-tax cost of any tax-deductible cash expense can be determined using the following formula:

$$\text{After-tax cost (net cash outflow)} = (1 - \text{Tax rate}) \times \text{Tax-deductible cash expense} \tag{6}$$

We can verify the accuracy of this formula by applying it to the £60,000 training programme expenditure:

$$(1 - 0.30) \times £60,000 = £42,000 \text{ after-tax cost of the training programme}$$

This formula is very useful since it provides the actual amount of cash a company must pay after taking into consideration tax effects. It is this actual, after-tax, cash outflow that should be used in capital budgeting decisions.

Similar reasoning applies to revenues and other taxable cash inflows. Since these cash receipts are taxable, the company must pay out a portion of them in taxes. The *after-tax benefit*, or *net cash inflow*, realized from a particular cash receipt can be obtained by applying a simple variation of the *cash expenditure formula* used above:

After-tax benefit (net cash inflow) = (1 − Tax rate) × Taxable cash receipt **(10)**

We emphasize the term *taxable cash receipts* because not all cash inflows are taxable. For example, the release of working capital at the termination of an investment project would not be a taxable cash inflow, since it simply represents a return of original investment.

Depreciation is not a cash flow and has been ignored in all discounted cash flow computations. However, depreciation allowances affect the taxes that must be paid and therefore has an indirect effect on the company's cash flows. In the UK, depreciation allowances are known as *capital* or *writing down allowances*. They are set by taxation authorities rather than being based on the opinion of the company's accountants. The impact of taxation, capital allowances and inflation are shown in Exhibit 10C.2.

Problem: Estimate the relevant after-tax cash flows from the following investment in a machine costing £4.5m assuming that the taxation rate is 33% payable 1 year in arrears and capital allowances are allowable at 25% per year on a reducing balance basis. The machine is assumed to have no scrap value. The investment generates additional cash flows of £2m per year for 5 years. What are the after-tax cash flows?

Step 1: Work out the writing down allowances (WDA):

Initial cost	4,500	
WDA year 1	1,125	
	3,375	
WDA year 2	844	
	2,531	
WDA year 3	633	
	1,898	
WDA year 4	475	
	1,423	
Balancing allowance	1,423	Year 5
Sales proceeds	0	

Step 2: Work out relevant after-tax cash flows

	Net cash flows: (in £000s)						
	Year 0	**1**	**2**	**3**	**4**	**5**	**6**
Annual profits		2,000	2,000	2,000	2,000	2,000	
Less write downs		1,125	844	633	475	1,423	
Taxable profits		875	1,156	1,367	1,525	577	
Tax at 33%			(289)	(382)	(451)	(503)	(190)
Net cash flows	(4,500)	2,000	1,711	1,618	1,549	1,497	(190)

Exhibit 10C.2 Impact of corporation tax and capital allowances on net cash flows

Appendix 10D: Investment decision making and risk

Risk and uncertainty

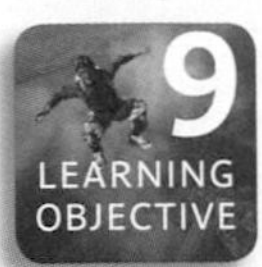

Some of the techniques of managing **risk** and return are used almost unconsciously by ordinary people who are assessing the best gamble to take. Let's consider the case of Jimmy who is down to his last few pounds before his next payday. Instead of buying an evening paper as he usually does, he decides to get a lottery ticket. Dreaming of a win to take him away from his dreary job, he is faced with a choice between a jackpot ticket and, also costing a pound, a 'cannon-ball extra' ticket. The jackpot winners get the headlines for the really big wins but he knows that he has a better chance with a 'cannon-ball extra'. Jimmy is an inveterate gambler, he 'likes a flutter', but he also likes to know the odds facing him.

Jimmy knows that bookmakers offer odds to tempt gamblers to look beyond the favourite by balancing the possible pay-off against the chances of a particular horse winning the race. Yet although the odds may make the expected outcomes roughly equal and that, 'the bookie always wins', there is also some incalculable **uncertainty** about a horse race that excites him. Jimmy may have thought that he had about a one in 14 million chance of winning the lottery jackpot. If the jackpot is £7 million then the expected value of his ticket is:

7,000,000/14,000,000 = £0.50!

Jimmy obviously likes a gamble because if he weighted the pay-off of his bet with the probability of winning with one ticket then he would find that the **expected value** of the ticket is less than the £1 cost of the ticket!

Some academics argue that businesses should distinguish between risks that can be calculated and uncertainty when it is not possible to formally calculate the risks. Decisions with calculable risks may be described using statistical terms such as the expected value as in our lottery ticket example. With some knowledge of a range of outcomes with their associated probabilities, a decision can be modelled in terms of what might be expected 'according to the law of averages'. The most basic descriptive statistic is the *average* or *mean*. In business decisions, objective probabilities can be determined using historical data. For example, insurance companies use past records of life expectancy to work out life insurance premiums.

Investment decision making and risk

Rather than producing a single estimate of NPV as we did in the previous chapter, we can model the risk characteristics of an investment decision by attaching probabilities to a number of possible outcomes. For example, we may find that a company, Pipeco Ltd, is faced with two, mutually exclusive, investment opportunities. One investment has the following probability distribution, that is, pay-offs with associated probabilities:

Project A **Probability**	**NPV (in £000)**
0.25	200
0.50	600
0.25	1,000
1.00	

The expected or mean NPV is:

200 × 0.25 + 600 × 0.50 + 1000 × 0.25 = £600

Compare that investment with project B:

Project B Probability	NPV (in £000)
0.1	300
0.8	400
0.1	500
1.00	

The expected value of this investment is:

$$300 \times 0.1 + 400 \times 0.8 + 500 \times 0.1 = £400$$

Diagrammatically, the two investment profiles are shown in Exhibit 10D.1.

Which investment should the company choose? Without considering risk, the company should choose project A as it gives it the highest NPV. However, with risk taken into consideration, project B looks better because although it has a lower expected value, it is less risky in the sense that the *spread* of outcomes is narrower. The risk, or spread, of a project can be formally calculated as the **standard deviation** around the mean or the expected value.

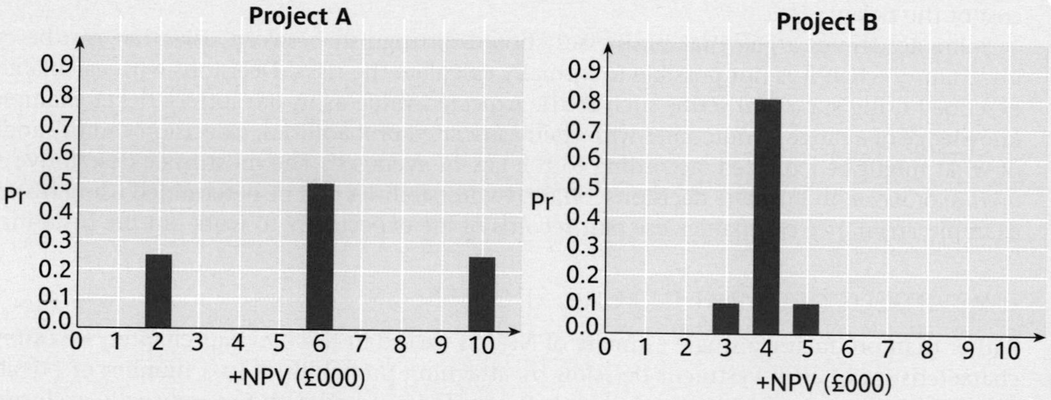

With more observations it may be possible to compare smoother distributions.

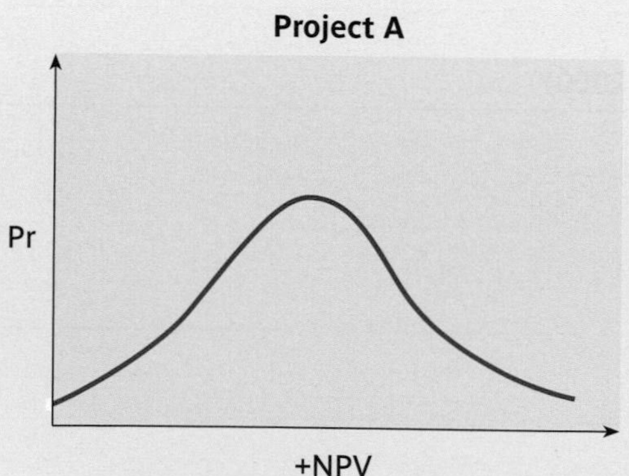

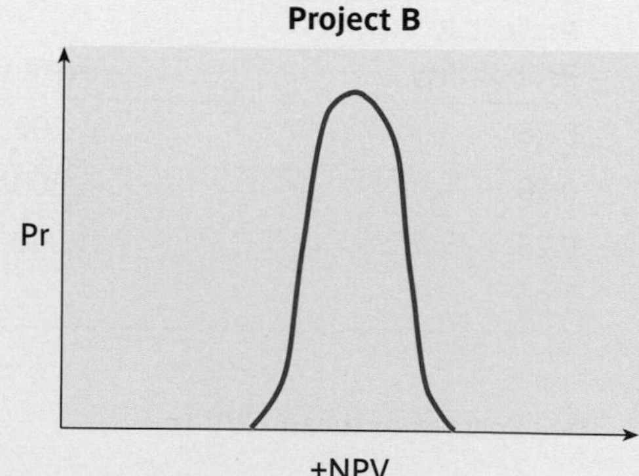

Exhibit 10D.1 Probability distributions and risk

The formula for calculating the standard deviation is:

$$\sigma = \sqrt{\sum_{i=1}^{n} (A_i - \bar{A})^2 P_i}$$

Project A has a wider 'spread', i.e. is more risky than Project B. The spread is calculated using the formula for standard deviation.

where $\bar{A}$ is the mean, A_i is a particular observation, P_i is the probability of each outcome and n is the total number of observations. The lower the standard deviation of a project, the lower the risk.

Attitudes to risk

The choice between the two investments in the above example is not immediately obvious. Neither project *dominates* the other in the sense of having *both* a higher expected value *and* a lower risk. Pipeco is facing a common situation where there is a *trade-off* between *risk* and *return* – the higher the risk, the higher the pay-off. The formal analysis of this problem through portfolio theory is beyond the scope of this book but is covered in finance textbooks.[5] In less formal terms, the three attitudes to risk-taking may be described as *risk preferring, risk averting* and *risk neutral*. When faced by two projects with the same expected value, a *risk preferrer* chooses the project with the highest risk. Faced with the same choice, the *risk-averter* chooses the less risky while the *risk-neutral* person is indifferent between the two risks. Of course, the choice may not just be a matter of pure, psychological, risk preference. For example, when decisions are made by managers on behalf of shareholders, the risks of the project are different for each party. In some situations managers may be more risk-averse than shareholders – sometimes, managers seems to be risk-preferrers because the downside of failure is borne by the owners.[6]

Interrelated risks: the decision tree

We have seen how to calculate the pay-off in choosing between independent projects. A more complicated problem arises when a decision depends on a sequence of linked risky states. This problem may be modelled using a technique known as a *decision tree*. The aim of the decision tree approach is to clarify the relationships between each set of alternatives and outcomes by modelling the *action* alternatives. A step-by-step procedure is followed until a complex problem is broken down into decisions, probabilities and pay-offs. Consider the problem in Exhibit 10D.2.

The decision tree provides the decision maker with rich information on the three alternatives. First, if the decision maker wants to maximize the annual expected value, Product M is the best alternative because its expected value of £240,000 is the highest. However, there is a risk of having a negative pay off of £16,000 if Product M was launched. This risk of a negative pay-off does not exist with the other two products.

The decision tree provides the decision maker with information related to the probability of achieving a certain level of pay-off. For example, the decision maker wants to maximize the probability of achieving a pay-off of at least £100,000. First, add up all probabilities of a pay off of £100,000 or more (look at columns 5 and 6 in Exhibit 10D.3) of each alternative (product) as follows:

Product Y = 0.28 + 0.12 = 0.40

Product Z = 0.30 + 0.20 + 0.30 = 0.80

Product M = 0.18 + 0.12 + 0.30 + 0.20 + 0.06 + 0.04 = 0.90

Second, choose Product M (the highest total probability).

Alternatively, the decision maker wants to minimize the probability of having a negative pay-off. Add up all the probabilities associated with each alternative and then choose the alternative with the lowest total probability. In this case, Product Z would be the best because there is a probability of 0 to get a negative pay-off. Although Product Y's probability is 0 as well, Product Z is better because it gives more total expected value.

10D.2 EXHIBIT

MHA Ltd is currently manufacturing at only 65% of full practical capacity due to a reduction in market share. The company is seeking to launch a new product – Y, Z or M – which it is hoped will recover some lost sales. Only one new product may be launched. The new product will be made by either machine Aye or machine Bee. Because the demand is uncertain the manager of MHA decided to hire the machine. The annual cost of hiring the machines is £350,000 and £280,000 respectively. Machine Aye is flexible and can be used in making either product Y or product Z while machine Bee specializes in making only product M. The current products will not be affected by the new one.

The company's marketing manager has estimated the demand levels of each product and the probabilities of those levels, as follows:

Product Y		Product Z		Product M	
Probability	**Demand level (units)**	**Probability**	**Demand level (units)**	**Probability**	**Demand level (units)**
0.60	60,000	0.50	50,000	0.10	20,000
0.40	90,000	0.50	60,000	0.30	30,000
				0.50	40,000
				0.10	50,000

Each product is made of the same material but requires different amounts of work. The company's production manager has estimated the variable costs per unit of making each product and the related probabilities as follows:

	Product Y		Product Z		Product M	
	Probability	**Var. cost per unit**	**Probability**	**Var. cost per unit**	**Probability**	**Var. cost per unit**
Low cost	0.70	£15	0.40	£22	0.60	£33
High cost	0.30	£18	0.60	£26	0.40	£38

The new product will be allocated a £25,000 share of fixed overheads. The company pricing policy is to cover all variable costs plus 40% as a contribution.

The problem is that MHA faces two risks – a risk associated with demand and a risk associated with cost and production. The overall problem can be modelled using a decision tree, which illustrates the alternative courses of action and their possible outcomes. The decision tree for MHA is shown in Exhibit 10D.3.

Exhibit 10D.2 An example of interrelated risks

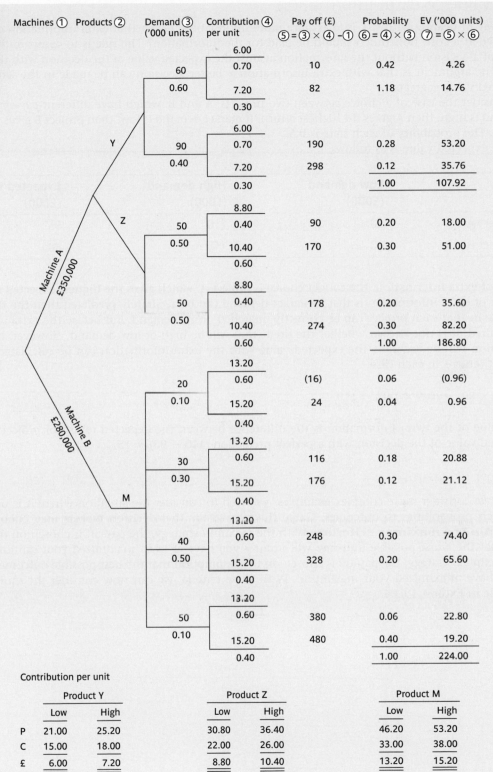

Machines ①	Products ②	Demand ③ ('000 units)	Probability	Contribution ④ per unit	Probability	Pay off (£) ⑤ = ③ × ④ − ①	Probability ⑥ = ④ × ③	EV ('000 units) ⑦ = ⑤ × ⑥
Machine A £350,000	Y	60	0.60	6.00	0.70	10	0.42	4.26
				7.20	0.30	82	1.18	14.76
		90	0.40	6.00	0.70	190	0.28	53.20
				7.20	0.30	298	0.12	35.76
							1.00	107.92
	Z	50	0.50	8.80	0.40	90	0.20	18.00
				10.40	0.60	170	0.30	51.00
		50	0.50	8.80	0.40	178	0.20	35.60
				10.40	0.60	274	0.30	82.20
							1.00	186.80
Machine B £280,000	M	20	0.10	13.20	0.60	(16)	0.06	(0.96)
				15.20	0.40	24	0.04	0.96
		30	0.30	13.20	0.60	116	0.18	20.88
				15.20	0.40	176	0.12	21.12
		40	0.50	13.20	0.60	248	0.30	74.40
				15.20	0.40	328	0.20	65.60
		50	0.10	13.20	0.60	380	0.06	22.80
				15.20	0.40	480	0.40	19.20
							1.00	224.00

Contribution per unit

	Product Y Low	Product Y High	Product Z Low	Product Z High	Product M Low	Product M High
P	21.00	25.20	30.80	36.40	46.20	53.20
C	15.00	18.00	22.00	26.00	33.00	38.00
£	6.00	7.20	8.80	10.40	13.20	15.20

Exhibit 10D.3 MHA solution using a decision tree

The value of extra information

One way of dealing with risk is to acquire more information. Given that extra information can only be acquired at a cost, how much should be paid for the information? The rule is to compare the expected value of a decision without the information against the expected value of the decision with the information. The argument is that with extra information a 'better' decision can be made in the sense that the expected value is greater.

Consider the case of a choice between two projects, A and B, which have different *pay-offs*. If market demand is high, then A gives the highest return. If market demand is low, then project B gives the highest return. The probability of each state is 0.5.

The expected value is as follows:

	Low demand (£000)	High demand (£000)	Expected value (£000)
Project A	80	110	95
Project B	20	140	80

Without extra information, the correct choice is project A, which gives the highest expected return. The benefit of extra information is that if market demand can be accurately predicted then the right choice is made in that each project can be correctly 'matched' to its demand. But before the extra information is acquired, it is not known whether the prediction will be high or low demand. However, because the prediction will be accurate, the expected value with the extra information can be calculated using the highest returns in each case:

$$(0.5 \times 80) + (0.5 \times 140) = 110$$

The value of the extra information is the difference between the expected return of project A and the expected value of the decision with a perfect prediction $(110 - 95) = 15$.

Pay-off strategies

Before we consider more complex examples, we need to consider the situation where it is not possible to attach probabilities to outcomes. Game theory suggests that decision makers may choose either a **maximin** or a **maximax criterion**. With the maximin strategy, the pay-off is chosen on the assumption that the worst possible outcome will occur – you have at least 'maximized your minimum'. With the maximax strategy, the pay-off is chosen on the assumption that the best possible outcome will occur – you have 'maximized your maximum'. With these criteria, we can now consider the more complex example in Exhibit 10D.4.

Fluffy's Enterprises (FE) specializes in late-booking skiing holidays. The business takes block bookings of 250 seats on return flights to Vienna with coach transfer to Austrian ski resorts. Demand for the holidays over the 12-week season is dependent on snow reports during the week before travel. The reports are classified as Good or Bad and the probability of the states and the related demand has been found to be as follows:

Snow reports:	**Good**	**Bad**
Probability	0.7	0.3
Demand	250	70

Revenue, net of travel agents' commission and related costs, is £500 per person and variable costs per person are £300. The cost of each block booking is £35,000 per flight (payable only if the flight is booked) while the fixed cost of running the office is £75,000 per year. The optimal strategy, in the absence of further information, was to book the flight for every week of the season and just hope that the snow reports are good.

FE, however, makes use in summer months of the services of a specialist weather forecasting agency, which has been found to make accurate forecasts 65% of the time. The agency would be prepared to extend their service to Austrian winter weather for a fee of £1,000 per week. The forecast would be available immediately before the decision on whether or not to book the flight. If FE is risk neutral, should the company use the agency to forecast snow conditions?

Solution: Fluffy's Enterprises

Revenue per person	£500
Variable costs	£300
Contribution	200

Block booking £35,000

Fixed costs are not relevant

If merely go ahead each week:

E(V) = 0.7 × 250 × 200 + 0.3 × 70 × 200 − 35,000
= 0.7 × 50,000 + 0.3 × 14,000 − 35,000
= £4,200

If forecasters are employed:

Φ Good | F Forecast = Φ Good × Φ Correct signal / GF
= 0.7 × 65%/0.56 = 0.813
Φ Good | B Forecast = 0.7 × 35%/0.44 = 0.557
Φ Bad | BF = 0.3 × 65%/0.44 = 0.443
Φ Bad | GF = 0.3 × 35%/0.56 = 0.187
Φ GF = 65% × 0.7 + 35% × 0.3 = 0.56
Φ BF = 65% × 0.3 + 35% × 0.7 = 0.44

Therefore, if a good forecast is received, the
E(V) = 0.813 × 50,000 + 0.187 × 4,200 − 35,000 = £6,435
If a bad forecast is received the
E(V) = 0.443 × 4,200 + 0.557 × 50,000 − 35,000 = £5,289
therefore, if a bad forecast is received, do not book and overall E(V)
= £6,435 × 0.56
= £3,604

Since the E(V) if forecasters are employed (£3,604) is less than the E(V) of merely booking each week, it is not worth paying £1,000 per week for the forecast.

Exhibit 10D.4 The value of information

10-1 What is the difference between capital budgeting screening decisions and capital budgeting preference decisions?

10-2 What is meant by the term *time value of money*?

10-3 What is meant by the term *discounting*?

10-4 Why can't accounting profit figures be used in the net present value and internal rate of return methods of making capital budgeting decisions?

10-5 Why are discounted cash flow methods of making capital budgeting decisions superior to other methods?

10-6 What is net present value? Can it ever be negative? Explain.

10-7 Identify two simplifying assumptions associated with discounted cash flow methods of making capital budgeting decisions.

10-8 If a firm has to pay interest of 14% on long-term debt, then its cost of capital is 14%. Do you agree? Explain.

10-9 What is meant by an investment project's internal rate of return? How is the internal rate of return computed?

10-10 Explain how the cost of capital serves as a screening tool when dealing with (a) the net present value method and (b) the internal rate of return method.

10-11 As the discount rate increases, the present value of a given future cash flow also increases. Do you agree? Explain.

10-12 Refer to Exhibit 10.4. Is the return on this investment proposal exactly 20%, slightly more than 20%, or slightly less than 20%? Explain.

10-13 Frontier Company is investigating the purchase of a piece of automated equipment, but after considering the savings in labour costs the machine has a negative net present value. If no other cost savings can be identified, should the company reject the equipment? Explain.

10-14 Why are preference decisions sometimes called *rationing* decisions?

10-15 How is the profitability index computed, and what does it measure?

10-16 What is the preference rule for ranking investment projects under the net present value method?

10-17 Can an investment with a profitability index of less than 1.00 be an acceptable investment? Explain.

10-18 What is the preference rule for ranking investment projects using the internal rate of return?

10-19 What is meant by the term *payback period*? How is the payback period determined?

10-20 How can the payback method be useful to the manager?

10-21 What is the major criticism of the payback and simple rate of return methods of making capital budgeting decisions?

Key terms for review (Appendix 10D)

Expected value (p. 403).

Maximin/maximax criterion (p. 408).

Uncertainty (p. 403).

Exercises

E10–1 Consider each of the following situations independently. (Ignore income taxes.) Time allowed: 10 minutes

1 In three years, when he is discharged from the Air Force, Steve wants to buy a power boat that will cost £8,000. What lump-sum amount must he invest now to have the £8,000 at the end of three years if he can invest money at:

(a) 10%?

(b) 14%?

2 Annual cash inflows that will arise from two competing investment projects are given below:

	Investment	
Year	**A**	**B**
1	£3,000	£12,000
2	6,000	9,000
3	9,000	6,000
4	12,000	3,000
	£30,000	£30,000

Each investment project will require the same investment outlay. You can invest money at an 18% rate of return. Compute the present value of the cash inflows for each investment.

3 Julie has just retired. Her company's retirement programme has two options as to how retirement benefits can be received. Under the first option, Julie would receive a lump sum of £150,000 immediately as her full retirement benefit. Under the second option, she would receive £14,000 each year for 20 years plus a lump-sum payment of £60,000 at the end of the 20-year period. If she can invest money at 12%, which option would you recommend that she accept? Use present value analysis.

E10–2 Time allowed: 15 minutes

Each of the following parts is independent. (Ignore income/corporation taxes.)

1 The Atlantic Medical Clinic can purchase a new computer system that will save £7,000 annually in billing costs. The computer system will last for eight years and have no salvage value. What is the maximum purchase price that the Atlantic Medical Clinic would be willing to pay for the new computer system if the clinic's required rate of return is:

(a) 16%?

(b) 20%?

2 The Caldwell *Herald* newspaper reported the following story:

Frank Ormsby of Caldwell is the state's newest millionaire. By choosing the six winning numbers on last week's state lottery, Mr Ormsby has won the week's grand prize totalling £1.6 million. The State Lottery Commission has indicated that Mr Ormsby will receive his prize in 20 annual instalments of £80,000 each.

(a) If Mr Ormsby can invest money at a 12% rate of return, what is the present value of his winnings?

(b) Is it correct to say that Mr Ormsby is the 'state's newest millionaire'?

Explain your answer.

3 Fraser Company will need a new warehouse in five years. The warehouse will cost £500,000 to build. What lump-sum amount should the company invest now to have the £500,000 available at the end of the five-year period? Assume that the company can invest money at:

(a) 10%

(b) 14%.

E10–3 Time allowed: 15 minutes
Kathy Myers frequently purchases stocks and bonds, but she is uncertain how to determine the rate of return she is earning. For example, three years ago she paid £13,000 for 200 shares of the common stock of Malti Company. She received a £420 cash dividend on the stock at the end of each year for three years. At the end of three years, she sold the stock for £16,000. Kathy would like to earn a return of at least 14% on all of her investments. She is not sure whether the Malti Company stock provided a 14% return and would like some help with the necessary computations.

Using the net present value method, determine whether or not the Malti Company stock provided a 14% return. Use the general format illustrated in Exhibit 10.4 and round all computations to the nearest whole pound.

E10–4 Time allowed: 15 minutes
Labeau Products Ltd of Perth, Australia, has £35,000 to invest. The company is trying to decide between two alternative uses for the funds. The alternatives are:

	Invest in Project X	Invest in Project Y
Investment required	£35,000	£35,000
Annual cash inflows	9,000	–
Single cash inflow at the end of 10 years	–	150,000
Life of the project	10 years	10 years

The company's discount rate is 18%. Which alternative would you recommend that the company accept? Show all computations using the net present value approach. Prepare a separate computation for each project.

E10–5 Time allowed: 15 minutes
Perot Industries has £100,000 to invest. The company is trying to decide between two alternative uses of the funds. The alternatives are:

	Project	
	A	B
Cost of equipment required	£100,000	–
Working capital investment required	–	£100,000
Annual cash inflows	21,000	16,000
Salvage value of equipment in six years	8,000	–
Life of the project	6 years	6 years

The working capital needed for project B will be released at the end of six years for investment elsewhere. Perot Industries' discount rate is 14%.

Which investment alternative (if either) would you recommend that the company accept? Show all computations using the net present value format. Prepare a separate computation for each project.

E10–6 Time allowed: 30 minutes
Complete the following cases (ignore income taxes).

1 Preston Company requires a minimum return of 14% on all investments. The company can purchase a new machine at a cost of £84,900. The new machine would generate cash inflows of £15,000 per year and have a 12-year useful life with no salvage value. Compute the machine's net present value. (Use the format shown in Exhibit 10.1.) Is the machine an acceptable investment? Explain.

2 The Walton *Daily News* is investigating the purchase of a new auxiliary press that has a projected life of 18 years. It is estimated that the new press will save £30,000 per year in cash operating costs. If the

new press costs £217,500, what is its internal rate of return? Is the press an acceptable investment if the company's required rate of return is 16%? Explain.

3 Refer to the data above for the Walton *Daily News*. How much would the annual cash inflows (cost savings) have to be for the new press to provide the required 16% rate of return? Round your answer to the nearest whole pound.

E10–7 Time allowed: 30 minutes

Solve the three following present value exercises:

1 The Cambro Foundation, a non-profit organization, is planning to invest £104,950 in a project that will last for three years. The project will provide cash inflows as follows:

Year 1	£30,000
Year 2	40,000
Year 3	?

Assuming that the project will yield exactly a 12% rate of return, what is the expected cash inflow for Year 3?

2 Lukow Products is investigating the purchase of a piece of automated equipment that will save £400,000 each year in direct labour and stock carrying costs. This equipment costs £2,500,000 and is expected to have a 15-year useful life with no salvage value. The company requires a minimum 20% return on all equipment purchases. Management anticipates that this equipment will provide intangible benefits such as greater flexibility, higher quality of output, and experience in automation. What pound value per year would management have to attach to these intangible benefits to make the equipment an acceptable investment?

3 The Matchless Dating Service has made an investment in video and recording equipment that costs £106,700. The equipment is expected to generate cash inflows of £20,000 per year. How many years will the equipment have to be used to provide the company with a 10% rate of return on its investment?

E10–8 Time allowed: 10 minutes

Information on four investment proposals is given below:

	Investment proposal			
	A	**B**	**C**	**D**
Investment required	£(90,000)	£(100,000)	£(70,000)	£(120,000)
Present value of cash inflows	126,000	90,000	105,000	160,000
Net present value	£36,000	£(10,000)	£35,000	£40,000
Life of the project	5 years	7 years	6 years	6 years

Required

1 Compute the profitability index for each investment proposal.

2 Rank the proposals in terms of preference.

E10–9 Time allowed: 10 minutes

A piece of labour-saving equipment has just come onto the market that Mitsui Electronics Ltd could use to reduce costs in one of its plants in Japan. Relevant data relating to the equipment follow (currency is in thousands of yen, denoted by ¥).

Purchase cost of the equipment	¥432,000
Annual cost savings that will be provided by the equipment	¥90,000
Life of the equipment	12 years

Required

1 Compute the payback period for the equipment. If the company requires a payback period of four years or less, would the equipment be purchased?

2 Compute the simple rate of return on the equipment. Use straight-line depreciation based on the equipment's useful life. Would the equipment be purchased if the company requires a rate of return of at least 14%?

E10–10 Time allowed: 10 minutes

Nick's Novelties Ltd is considering the purchase of electronic pinball machines to place in amusement houses. The machines would cost a total of £300,000, have an eight-year useful life, and have a total salvage value of £20,000. Based on experience with other equipment, the company estimates that annual revenues and expenses associated with the machines would be as follows:

Revenues from use		£200,000
Less operating expenses:		
Commissions to amusement houses	£100,000	
Insurance	7,000	
Depreciation	35,000	
Maintenance	18,000	160,000
Profit		£40,000

Required (ignore taxes)

1 Assume that Nick's Novelties Ltd will not purchase new equipment unless it provides a payback period of four years or less. Would the company purchase the pinball machines?

2 Compute the simple rate of return promised by the pinball machines. If the company requires a simple rate of return of at least 12%, will the pinball machines be purchased?

PROBLEMS

Problems

P10–11 Investment and taxation Time allowed: 40 minutes

Benland plc manufacture and fit a variety of children's playground equipment. The company at present purchases the rubber particles used in the playground surfacing from an outside supplier, but is considering investing in equipment which would process and shred used vehicle tyres to produce equivalent rubber particles. One tonne of purchased particles is saved per tonne of tyres processed. Disposal of used tyres is becoming an environmental problem, and Benland believes that it could charge £40 per tonne to garages/tyre distributors wishing to dispose of their old tyres. This price would be 20% lower than the cost of the landfill sites currently being used, and so Benland believes that it would face no risk or shortage of supply of what would be a key raw material for the business. The price charged by Benland for tyre disposal (£40 per tonne) remains fixed for the next five years.

The cost to Benland of purchased particles is £3.50 per tonne for each of the next five years, and the price has been contractually guaranteed. If the contract is terminated within the next two years, Benland will be charged an immediate termination penalty of £100,000, which will not be allowed as a tax deductible expense.

The machine required to process the tyres will cost £1.06 million, and it is estimated that at the end of year five the machine will have a second-hand value of £120,000 before selling costs of £5,000.

Sales of the playground surfacing which uses rubber particles are forecast to be £1.2 million in year one, rising by 10% per year until year five but prices will remain constant. The new equipment will result in Benland incurring additional maintenance costs of £43,000 per year.

80,000 tonnes of tyres need to be processed in order to meet the raw material requirement for the forecast sales in year one. Processing costs are estimated at £37 per tonne (excluding additional depreciation and maintenance).

Benland is subject to corporation tax at a rate of 33%, payable one year in arrears. Capital expenditure is eligible for 25% allowances on a reducing balance basis, and sales proceeds of assets are subject to tax. Benland has sufficient profits to fully utilize all available capital allowances.

Required

1 Using 12% as the after-tax discount rate, advise Benland on the desirability of purchasing the tyre processing equipment. *(12 marks)*

2 Discuss which cash flows are most important in determining the outcome of the proposed investment and how Benland might seek to minimize the risk of large changes in predicted cash flows. *(8 marks)*

(Total = 20 marks)

ACCA Managerial Finance, December 1999

P10–12 Basic net present value analysis Time allowed: 20 minutes

Windhoek Mines Ltd of Namibia is contemplating the purchase of equipment to exploit a mineral deposit that is located on land to which the company has mineral rights. An engineering and cost analysis has been made, and it is expected that the following cash flows would be associated with opening and operating a mine in the area:

Cost of new equipment and timbers	R275,000
Working capital required	100,000
Net annual cash receipts	120,000*
Cost to construct new roads in three years	40,000
Salvage value of equipment in four years	65,000

*Receipts from sales of ore, less out-of-pocket costs for salaries, utilities, insurance, and so forth.

The currency in Namibia is the rand, here denoted by R.

It is estimated that the mineral deposit would be exhausted after four years of mining. At that point, the working capital would be released for reinvestment elsewhere. The company's discount rate is 20%.

Required (ignore taxes)

Determine the net present value of the proposed mining project. Should the project be accepted? Explain.

P10–13 Basic net present value analysis Time allowed: 20 minutes

The Sweetwater Candy Company would like to buy a new machine that would automatically 'dip' chocolates. The dipping operation is currently done largely by hand. The machine the company is considering costs £120,000. The manufacturer estimates that the machine would be usable for 12 years but would require the replacement of several key parts at the end of the sixth year. These parts would cost £9,000, including installation. After 12 years, the machine could be sold for about £7,500.

The company estimates that the cost to operate the machine will be only £7,000 per year. The present method of dipping chocolates costs £30,000 per year. In addition to reducing costs, the new machine will increase production by 6,000 boxes of chocolates per year. The company realizes a contribution margin of £1.50 per box. A 20% rate of return is required on all investments.

Required (ignore taxes)

1 What are the net annual cash inflows that will be provided by the new dipping machine?

2 Compute the new machine's net present value. Use the incremental cost approach and round all pound amounts to the nearest whole pound.

P10–14 Preference ranking of investment projects Time allowed: 30 minutes

The management of Revco Products is exploring five different investment opportunities. Information on the five projects under study is given below:

	Project number				
	1	2	3	4	5
Investment required	£(270,000)	£(450,000)	£(400,000)	£(360,000)	£(480,000)
Present value of cash inflows at a 10% discount rate	336,140	522,970	379,760	433,400	567,270
Net present value	£66,140	£72,970	£(20,240)	£73,400	£87,270
Life of the project	6 years	3 years	5 years	12 years	6 years
Internal rate of return	18%	19%	8%	14%	16%

The company's required rate of return is 10%; thus, a 10% discount rate has been used in the present value computations above. Limited funds are available for investment, so the company cannot accept all of the available projects.

Required (ignore taxes)

1 Compute the profitability index for each investment project.

2 Rank the five projects according to preference, in terms of:

   (a) Net present value.

   (b) Profitability index.

   (c) Internal rate of return.

3 Which ranking do you prefer? Why?

P10–15 Simple rate of return; payback Time allowed: 30 minutes

Paul Swanson has an opportunity to acquire a franchise from The Yogurt Place plc to dispense frozen yogurt products under The Yogurt Place name. Mr Swanson has assembled the following information relating to the franchise:

1 A suitable location in a large shopping mall can be rented for £3,500 per month.

2 Remodelling and necessary equipment would cost £270,000. The equipment would have an estimated 15-year life and an estimated £18,000 salvage value. Straight-line depreciation would be used, and the salvage value would be considered in computing depreciation deductions.

3 Based on similar outlets elsewhere, Mr Swanson estimates that sales would total £300,000 per year. Ingredients would cost 20% of sales.

4 Operating costs would include £70,000 per year for salaries, £3,500 per year for insurance, and £27,000 per year for utilities. In addition, Mr Swanson would have to pay a commission to The Yogurt Place plc of 12.5% of sales.

Rather than obtain the franchise, Mr Swanson could invest his funds in long-term corporate bonds that would yield a 12% annual return.

Required (ignore taxes)

1 Prepare a profit statement that shows the expected profit each year from the franchise outlet. Use the contribution format.

2 Compute the simple rate of return promised by the outlet. If Mr Swanson requires a simple rate of return of at least 12%, should he obtain the franchise?

3 Compute the payback period on the outlet. If Mr Swanson wants a payback of four years or less, should the outlet be opened?

P10–16 Net present value analysis of a new product Time allowed: 50 minutes
Matheson Electronics has just developed a new electronic device which, when mounted on a car, will tell the driver how many miles the car is travelling per gallon of petrol.

The company is anxious to begin production of the new device. To this end, marketing and cost studies have been made to determine probable costs and market potential. These studies have provided the following information:

1 New equipment would have to be acquired to produce the device. The equipment would cost £315,000 and have a 12-year useful life. After 12 years, it would have a salvage value of about £15,000.

2 Sales in units over the next 12 years are projected to be as follows:

Year	Sales in units
1	6,000
2	12,000
3	15,000
4–12	18,000

3 Production and sales of the device would require working capital of £60,000 to finance debtors, inventories and day-to-day cash needs. This working capital would be released at the end of the project's life.

4 The devices would sell for £35 each; variable costs for production, administration and sales would be £15 per unit.

5 Fixed costs for salaries, maintenance, property taxes, insurance and straight-line depreciation on the equipment would total £135,000 per year. (Depreciation is based on cost less salvage value.)

6 To gain rapid entry into the market, the company would have to advertise heavily. The advertising programme would be:

Year	Amount of yearly advertising
1–2	£180,000
3	150,000
4–12	120,000

7 Matheson Electronics' board of directors has specified that all new products must have a return of at least 14% to be acceptable.

Required (ignore taxes)

1 Compute the net cash inflow (cash receipts less yearly cash operating expenses) anticipated from sale of the device for each year over the next 12 years.

2 Using the data computed in Question 1 above and other data provided in the problem, determine the net present value of the proposed investment. Would you recommend that Matheson accepts the device as a new product?

P10–17 Opening a small business; net present value Time allowed: 30 minutes
In eight years, Kent Duncan will retire. He has £150,000 to invest, and is exploring the possibility of opening a self-service car wash. The car wash could be managed in the free time he has available from his regular occupation, and it could be closed easily when he retires. After careful study, Mr Duncan has determined the following:

1 A building in which a car wash could be installed is available under an eight-year lease at a cost of £1,700 per month.

2 Purchase and installation costs of equipment would total £150,000. In eight years the equipment could be sold for about 10% of its original cost.

3 An investment of an additional £2,000 would be required to cover working capital needs for cleaning supplies, change funds, and so forth. After eight years, this working capital would be released for investment elsewhere.

4 Both a car wash and a vacuum service would be offered with a wash costing £1.50 and the vacuum costing 25 pence per use.

5 The only variable costs associated with the operation would be 23 pence per wash for water and 10 pence per use of the vacuum for electricity.

6 In addition to rent, monthly costs of operation would be: cleaning, £450; insurance, £75; and maintenance, £500.

7 Gross receipts from the car wash would be about £1,350 per week. According to the experience of other car washes, 70% of the customers using the wash would also use the vacuum.

Mr Duncan will not open the car wash unless it provides at least a 10% return, since this is the amount that could be earned by simply placing the £150,000 in high-grade securities.

Required (ignore taxes)

1 Assuming that the car wash will be open 52 weeks a year, compute the expected net annual cash receipts (gross cash receipts less cash disbursements) from its operation. (Do not include the cost of the equipment, the working capital, or the salvage value in these computations.)

2 Would you advise Mr Duncan to open the car wash? Show computations using the net present value method of investment analysis. Round all pound figures to the nearest whole pound.

P10–18 Replacement decision ⏱ Time allowed: 30 minutes
Bilboa Freightlines SA of Panama has a small truck that it uses for intra-city deliveries. The truck is in bad repair and must be either overhauled or replaced with a new truck. The company has assembled the following information. (Panama uses the US dollar as its currency):

	Present truck	**New truck**
Purchase cost new	$21,000	$30,000
Remaining book value	11,500	–
Overhaul needed now	7,000	–
Annual cash operating costs	10,000	6,500
Salvage value – now	9,000	–
Salvage value – eight years from now	1,000	4,000

If the company keeps and overhauls its present delivery truck, then the truck will be usable for eight more years. If a new truck is purchased, it will be used for eight years, after which it will be traded in for another truck. The new truck would be diesel-operated, resulting in a substantial reduction in annual operating costs, as shown above.

The company computes depreciation on a straight-line basis. All investment projects are evaluated using a 16% discount rate.

Required (ignore taxes)

1 Should Bilboa Freightlines keep the old truck or purchase the new one? Use the total-cost approach to net present value in making your decision. Round to the nearest whole pound.

2 Redo Question 1 above, this time using the incremental-cost approach.

P10–19 Internal rate of return; sensitivity analysis Time allowed: 60 minutes

'In my opinion, a tanning salon would be a natural addition to our spa and very popular with our customers,' said Stacey Winder, manager of the Lifeline Spa. 'Our figures show that we could remodel the building next door to our spa and install all of the necessary equipment for £330,000. I have contacted tanning salons in other areas, and I am told that the tanning beds will be usable for about nine years. I am also told that a four-bed salon such as we are planning would generate a cash inflow of about £80,000 per year after all expenses.'

'It does sound very appealing,' replied Kevin Leblanc, the spa's accountant. 'Let me push the numbers around a bit and see what kind of a return the salon would generate.'

Required (ignore taxes)

1 Compute the internal rate of return promised by the tanning salon. Interpolate to the nearest tenth of a per cent.

2 Assume that Ms Winder will not open the salon unless it promises a return of at least 14%. Compute the amount of annual cash inflow that would provide this return on the £330,000 investment.

3 Although nine years is the average life of tanning salon equipment, Ms Winder has found that this life can vary substantially. Compute the internal rate of return if the life were (a) 6 years and (b) 12 years rather than 9 years. Interpolate to the nearest tenth of a per cent. Is there any information provided by these computations that you would be particularly anxious to show Ms Winder?

4 Ms Winder has also found that although £80,000 is an average cash inflow from a four-bed salon, some salons vary as much as 20% from this figure. Compute the internal rate of return if the annual cash inflows were (a) 20% less and (b) 20% greater than £80,000. Interpolate to the nearest tenth of a per cent.

5 Assume that the £330,000 investment is made and that the salon is opened as planned. Because of concerns about the effects of excessive tanning, however, the salon is not able to attract as many customers as planned. Cash inflows are only £50,000 per year, and after eight years the salon equipment is sold to a competitor for £135,440. Compute the internal rate of return (to the nearest whole per cent) earned on the investment over the eight-year period. (*Hint*: A useful way to proceed is to find the discount rate that will cause the net present value to be equal to, or near, zero.)

P10–20 Simple rate of return; payback Time allowed: 30 minutes

Sharkey's Fun Centre contains a number of electronic games as well as a miniature golf course and various rides located outside the building. Paul Sharkey, the owner, would like to construct a water slide on one portion of his property. Mr Sharkey has gathered the following information about the slide:

1 Water slide equipment could be purchased and installed at a cost of £330,000. According to the manufacturer, the slide would be usable for 12 years after which it would have no salvage value.

2 Mr Sharkey would use straight-line depreciation on the slide equipment.

3 To make room for the water slide, several rides would be dismantled and sold. These rides are fully depreciated, but they could be sold for £60,000 to an amusement park in a nearby city.

4 Mr Sharkey has concluded that about 50,000 more people would use the water slide each year than have been using the rides. The admission price would be £3.60 per person (the same price that the Fun Centre has been charging for the rides).

5 Based on experience at other water slides, Mr Sharkey estimates that incremental operating expenses each year for the slide would be: salaries, £85,000; insurance, £4,200; utilities, £13,000; and maintenance, £9,800.

Required

1 Prepare a profit statement showing the expected profit each year from the water slide.

2 Compute the simple rate of return expected from the water slide. Based on this computation, should the water slide be constructed if Mr Sharkey requires a simple rate of return of at least 14% on all investments?

3 Compute the payback period for the water slide. If Mr Sharkey requires a payback period of five years or less, would the water slide be constructed?

P10–21 Simple rate of return; payback; internal rate of return Time allowed: 30 minutes
Honest John's Used Cars plc has always hired students from the local university to wash the cars on the lot. Honest John is considering the purchase of an automatic car wash that would be used in place of the students. The following information has been gathered by Honest John's accountant to help Honest John make a decision on the purchase:

1 Payments to students for washing cars total £15,000 per year at present.
2 The car wash would cost £21,000 installed, and it would have a 10-year useful life. Honest John uses straight-line depreciation on all assets. The car wash would have a negligible salvage value in 10 years.
3 Annual out-of-pocket costs associated with the car wash would be: wages of students to operate the wash, keep the soap bin full and so forth, £6,300; utilities, £1,800; and insurance and maintenance, £900.
4 Honest John now earns a return of 20% on the funds invested in his stock of used cars. He feels that he would have to earn an equivalent rate on the car wash for the purchase to be attractive.

Required (ignore taxes)

1 Determine the annual savings that would be realized in cash operating costs if the car wash were purchased.
2 Compute the simple rate of return promised by the car wash. (*Hint:* Note that this is a cost reduction project.) Will Honest John accept this project if he expects a 20% return?
3 Compute the payback period on the car wash. Honest John (who has a reputation for being something of a penny-pincher) will not purchase any equipment unless it has a payback of four years or less. Will he purchase the car wash equipment?
4 Compute (to the nearest whole per cent) the internal rate of return promised by the car wash. Based on this computation, does it appear that the simple rate of return would normally be an accurate guide in investment decisions?

P10–22 Simple rate of return; payback Time allowed: 40 minutes
Westwood Furniture Company is considering the purchase of two different items of equipment, as described below.

Machine A. A compacting machine has just come onto the market that would permit Westwood Furniture Company to compress sawdust into various shelving products. At present the sawdust is disposed of as a waste product. The following information is available on the machine:

1 The machine would cost £420,000 and would have a 10% salvage value at the end of its 12-year useful life. The company uses straight-line depreciation and considers salvage value in computing depreciation deductions.
2 The shelving products manufactured from use of the machine would generate revenue of £300,000 per year. Variable manufacturing costs would be 20% of sales.
3 Fixed expenses associated with the new shelving products would be (per year): advertising, £40,000; salaries, £110,000; utilities, £5,200; and insurance, £800.

Machine B. A second machine has come onto the market that would allow Westwood Furniture Company to automate a sanding process that is now largely done by hand. The following information is available:

1 The new sanding machine would cost £234,000 and would have no salvage value at the end of its 13-year useful life. The company would use straight-line depreciation on the new machine.
2 Several old pieces of sanding equipment that are fully depreciated would be disposed of at a scrap value of £9,000.

3 The new sanding machine would provide substantial annual savings in cash operating costs. It would require an operator at an annual salary of £16,350 and £5,400 in annual maintenance costs. The current, hand-operated sanding procedure costs the company £78,000 per year in total.

Westwood Furniture Company requires a simple rate of return of 15% on all equipment purchases. Also, the company will not purchase equipment unless the equipment has a payback period of four years or less.

Required (ignore taxes)

1 For machine A:
   - **(a)** Prepare an income statement showing the expected profit each year from the new shelving products. Use the contribution format.
   - **(b)** Compute the simple rate of return.
   - **(c)** Compute the payback period.

2 For machine B:
   - **(a)** Compute the simple rate of return.
   - **(b)** Compute the payback period.

3 According to the company's criteria, which machine, if either, should the company purchase?

P10–23 NPV and investment appraisal Time allowed: 35 minutes
Beaters Ltd makes plastic kits for building model sailing ships. The company's designer has just developed a new product, a kit for making a model of the *Golden Hind*, the ship in which Drake circumnavigated the world. To make the kits, a new plastic-moulding machine will have to be bought for £50,000.

A net present value appraisal has been carried out that indicates a positive net present value (NPV) of £2,983. This appraisal was followed up with an assessment of the riskiness of the project. This was achieved by taking each of the input factors, in turn, and estimating the value for it at which the project would have a zero NPV. In looking at each input factor, it was assumed that the other factors would be as originally estimated.

Data on the original estimates and on the values of each of them that generate a zero NPV are as follows:

	Original estimate	**Value to generate a zero NPV**
Cost of moulding machine	£50,000	£52,983
Selling price (per unit)	£20	£19.60
Material cost (per unit)	£6	£6.40
Labour cost (per unit)	£5	£5.40
Variable overheads (per unit)	£2	£2.40
Sales life	6 years	5.5 years

The above assessment is based on the assumptions of a discount rate of 15% and of constant sales of 2,000 units per annum. It has been reliably established that the new production would not affect fixed costs or working capital to any significant extent. There are no other input factors for the decision.

The risk-free rate of interest over the six years has been estimated to be 6%.

Required (ignore taxes)

1 Estimate the values for:
   - **(a)** The discount rate, and
   - **(b)** The annual sales volume to generate a zero NPV. *(4 marks)*

2 Comment on the results of both the NPV appraisal and the subsequent quantitative analysis. Discuss

how the managers might proceed to put themselves in a position to reach a decision on whether to go ahead with the new product. Your discussion should include some consideration of the usefulness of the quantitative analysis already undertaken and how this might usefully be extended. *(9 marks)*

(Total = 13 marks)

ICAEW Business Finance, December 2000

P10–24 Capital allowances Time allowed: 30 minutes

Profitis plc has a continuing need for a machine. At the level of intensity that the company uses the machine, after four years from new it is not capable of efficient working. It has been the company's practice to replace the machine every four years. The production manager has pointed out that in the fourth year the machine needs additional maintenance to keep it working at normal efficiency. The question has, therefore, arisen as to whether to replace the machine after three years instead of the usual four years.

Relevant information is as follows:

1 The machine costs £80,000 to buy new. If the machine is retained for four years it will have a zero scrap value at the end of the period. If it is retained for three years, it would have an estimated disposal value of £10,000.

The machine will attract capital allowances. For the purposes of this analysis assume that it will be excluded from the general pool. This means that it will attract a 25% (reducing balance) tax allowance in the year of acquisition and in every subsequent year of being owned by the company, except the last. In the last year, the difference between the machine's written down value for tax purposes and its disposal proceeds will either be allowed to the company as an additional tax relief, if the disposal proceeds are less than the written down value, or be charged to the company if the disposal proceeds are more than the tax written down value.

Assume that the machine will be bought and disposed of on the last day of the company's accounting year.

2 The company's corporation tax rate is 30%. Tax is payable on the last day of the accounting year concerned.

3 During the first year of ownership, the supplier takes responsibility for any maintenance work which is necessary. In the second and third years, maintenance costs average £10,000 a year. During the fourth year this rises to £20,000. Maintenance charges are payable on the first day of the company's accounting year and are allowable for tax.

4 The company's cost of capital is estimated at 15%.

Required

1 Prepare calculations that show whether it would be more economically desirable to replace the machine after three years or four years

(11 marks)

2 Discuss any other issues that could influence the company's replacement decision. This should include any weaknesses in the approach taken in Question 1. *(3 marks)*

(Total = 14 marks)

ICAEW Business Finance, December 2001

P10–25 ARR and NPV Time allowed: 35 minutes

Penar plc assesses investment projects using the accounting rate of return (ARR) approach. The company's auditor has pointed out that this is a theoretically flawed approach to investment appraisal, but it continues to be used.

The company is considering an investment in some plant that will enable it to provide a new service. The plant will be bought using funds that will be raised from a five-year loan at a fixed interest rate of 7% p.a. (before tax). It has been decided to assess the project assuming a five-year life.

The following is a schedule of the revenues and expenses relating to the new plant that has been prepared by one of the company's finance staff:

	Year ending 31 December				
	2002	**2003**	**2004**	**2005**	**2006**
	£000	**£000**	**£000**	**£000**	**£000**
Sales	220	270	300	300	250
Labour	(90)	(110)	(120)	(120)	(100)
Other costs	(10)	(10)	(10)	(10)	(10)
Depreciation	(80)	(80)	(80)	(80)	(80)
Operating profit	40	70	90	90	60
Loan interest	(35)	(35)	(35)	(35)	(35)
Managers' bonus	(1)	(7)	(11)	(11)	(5)
Profit before tax	4	28	44	44	20

The member of staff who prepared the schedule argued that since the average pre-tax profit from the new product is projected to be £28,000 and the average investment is £300,000, this represents a return greater than the 7% cost of finance.

The following information relates to the project:

1 The plant will cost £500,000, payable on 31 December 2001. It will be sold for an estimated £100,000 on 31 December 2006.

The plant will attract capital allowances, but for the purposes of this analysis will be assumed to be excluded from the general pool. This means that it attracts 25% (reducing balance) tax allowances in the year of acquisition and in every subsequent year of being owned by the company, except the last year. In the last year, the difference between the plant's written down value for tax purposes and its disposal proceeds will either be allowed to the company as an additional tax relief, if the disposal proceeds are less than the written down value, or be charged to the company if the disposal proceeds are more than the tax written down value.

2 Labour will be employed on a flexible basis and so staff will be paid only for the hours that they work and will be employed only for the five years of the project.

3 'Other costs', in the schedule, represent a share of the company's general administrative costs.

4 To motivate the managers, their remuneration packages all have relatively low basic salaries, but generous bonuses. Between them, the managers receive bonuses of 20% of the company's net profit after interest.

5 The company's weighted average cost of capital (after tax) is estimated at 15%.

6 The project's working capital requirement represents about 10% of annual sales. This needs to be in place by the beginning of the year concerned and it will all be released at the end of the project.

7 Work to develop the new service cost £100,000 during 2001. This will attract full corporation tax relief during that year.

8 The company's accounting year end is 31 December and its corporation tax rate is 30%. Assume that tax is payable at the end of the year to which it relates.

Required

1 Assess whether, on the basis of net present value, the project is viable. *(12 marks)*

2 Discuss whether the auditor is correct to argue that the approach to project appraisal adopted by the company is flawed. *(3 marks)*

3 Suggest why the managers might persist with the use of ARR, what problem underlies this and what might be done to overcome the problem. *(3 marks)*

(Total = 18 marks)

ICAEW Business Finance, September 2001

P10–26 Time allowed: 30 minutes
DigitPP owns 20 print and computer shops in the UK. At present it hires its 35 photocopying machines from Rentit at an annual rental of £5,600 each, payable monthly. (Assume year-end cash flows for simplicity.) The rental agreement covers a 24-hour repair service which assists DigitPP to maintain its high reputation for a quick and reliable service. DigitPP estimates that each machine generates £7,600 of contribution each year.

XX Company is trying to break into the UK market and offers to sell to DigitPP new machines for £18,000 each, payable on installation. DigitPP is considering this and has found some research that suggests that each machine stands a 0.7 chance of being reliable and a 0.3 chance of being unreliable. The reliability of the machines will be discovered by the end of the first year. All machines that are reliable at the end of year 1 will still be reliable at the end of year 4. If a machine proves reliable, DigitPP will keep it for 4 years in total and it will generate a contribution of £8,000 each year, after which time the machine will be scrapped and sold for £600. If the machine proves unreliable, it will be scrapped after a year and sold for £400. An unreliable machine is expected to generate a contribution of £5,000 each year.

The company's annual cost of capital is 8%. The management at DigitPP considers that a time horizon of no longer than 6 years should be used when evaluating decisions on photocopiers, as beyond that date photocopying machines are likely to be outdated technology.

Required

(Ignore taxation in parts (a) and (b).)

(a) Prepare calculations to show whether a rented or purchased machine is the financially better option. *(5 marks)*

XX Company has now made an alternative introductory, once only, offer. It will buy back 30% of the machines at the end of either the first or second year, if required. The buy-back price will be 60% of the original purchase price at the end of year 1 and 50% at the end of year 2. DigitPP must nominate in advance which replacement option it prefers. If DigitPP agrees to either of XX Company's proposals, it would remain with the company during the life of the purchased and replaced photocopiers. Because most shops have two photocopiers available, the management of DigitPP has now agreed that further replacements after either year 1 or year 2 would be unnecessary.

(b) Advise DigitPP whether or not it should accept the revised offer. *(11 marks)*

CIMA Decision Making, November 2001

P10–27 Investment decision making and risk Time allowed: 35 minutes
Broadham Hotels Ltd (BH) owns and manages a hotel in a major Midlands city. The hotel has 500 identical, twin-bedded rooms for which a standard rate of £50 per night is charged, irrespective of whether the room is occupied by one or two people. Occupancy rates have fallen below that which was envisaged when the hotel was built five years ago.

Septo, a Japanese-owned business, which is shortly to open a local manufacturing plant, has approached the hotel's management with a proposal that it takes over 100 of the hotel's rooms, in effect the whole of the top two floors of the hotel, to accommodate its staff and guests when they visit the plant. Septo wishes to take over the rooms for a five-year period starting on 1 July 2002. Under the proposal, Septo would employ its own staff to service and manage the rooms.

On the basis of past experience and taking account of future developments in the market, the hotel's management believes that future average nightly demand will be:

Rooms	Probability (%)
380	20
400	20
420	30
440	20
460	10

The hotel is open for 360 nights each year.

It is estimated that the variable costs of having a room occupied average 10% of the room rate. All staff costs are effectively fixed costs and no staff cost savings are expected to be made by the hotel should the Septo proposal be accepted. The total fixed costs of running the hotel are estimated at £4 million a year.

Under the proposal Septo would pay a fixed fee annually on 1 July from 2002 to 2006, inclusive. There is expected to be a general annual rate of inflation of 3% running throughout the five-year period. This will affect the room rate, the variable costs and the fixed costs, all of which are stated above at 1 July 2002 prices.

BH has a corporation tax rate of 30% and an accounting year that ends on 30 June. Tax will be payable on the last day of the accounting year in which the relevant transactions occur. You should assume that all operating cash flows occur on the last day of the relevant accounting year, except any receipt from Septo, which will be received on the first day. BH's cost of capital, in real terms, is 10% per annum.

Required

1 Determine, on the basis of net present value and the information given in the question, the minimum fixed annual payment that Septo must make so that BH is as well off in expected value terms as it would be without the Septo proposal. (*Note*: Work in 'money' terms. Assume for this requirement that neither Septo's new plant, nor the proposal to BH, would affect the projected nightly demand figures given in the question.) *(11 marks)*

2 State and explain any other items of information, not mentioned in the question, that should have been brought into the determination of the minimum annual payment in Question 1. *(3 marks)*

3 Discuss briefly whether from Septo's perspective, in principle, the planned provision of accommodation seems a good idea. *(4 marks)*

(Total = 18 marks)

ICAEW Business Finance, December 2001

P10–28 Time allowed: 40 minutes

C Ltd excavates, mixes, processes and then distributes a variety of materials that are used to surface roads and pedestrian walkways. The business works to capacity every year and usually earns annual profits of £24 million.

Another company, Z Ltd, has developed a new product, 'Flexicrete', which can be used to provide a softer and safer surface than traditional coverings. Flexicrete is made by passing traditional coverings through an additional process. Z Ltd has developed this finishing process, but does not have access to the earlier stages of the process or a distribution network. Consequently, Z Ltd has offered to lease the machinery needed for the finishing process to C Ltd.

There are three sizes of machinery that could be leased. However, the machines are not reliable. Their possible annual outputs and associated probabilities are shown in the table below. The annual lease payments are also shown.

Annual output (m^3)	Probability Machine A	Machine B	Machine C
1 million	0.8	0.4	–
5 million	0.2	0.3	0.6
8 million	–	0.3	0.4
Annual lease (£ million)	£20	£30	£40

If C Ltd processed Flexicrete, it would not be able to sell any of its traditional products. Due to the unreliability of the machinery, rectification problems, overtime working and possibly the need to reduce the output of the earlier processing plants, the costs per cubic metre (m^3) will vary with the type of machine and its output. The uncertainty is so great that even for a given output there is a range of possible costs.

Z Ltd will dictate the selling price of Flexicrete. The accountant for C Ltd has produced the following forecasts of profit per cubic metre and their probabilities.

Annual output (m^3)	Machine A Profit (£ per m^3)	Prob	Machine B Profit (£ per m^3)	Prob	Machine C Profit (£ per m^3)	Prob
1 million	35	0.7	5	0.4	–	–
1 million	25	0.3	−5	0.6	–	–
5 million	35	0.4	25	0.4	10	0.3
5 million	15	0.3	15	0.3	5	0.5
5 million	5	0.3	5	0.3	−5	0.2
8 million	–	–	25	0.5	25	0.6
8 million	–	–	5	0.5	5	0.4

Note: The profit per cubic metre is after charging all costs except the lease payments.

Required

1 Draw a decision tree that shows the situation facing C Ltd. *(7 marks)*

2 Using the decision tree, or any other method, calculate for each machine

(a) the expected value of the total profit;

(b) the probability of at least breaking even. *(9 marks)*

3 As a management accountant, write a report to the management of C Ltd that recommends the action it should take. The report must support your recommendation by evaluating the situation and include a discussion of the appropriateness of the methodologies used in Question 2 above. *(9 marks)*

(Total = 25 marks)

CIMA Management Accounting – Decision making, November 2004

CASE

Cases

C10–29 Lease or buy decision Time allowed: 40 minutes

Top-Quality Stores Ltd owns a nationwide chain of supermarkets. The company is going to open another store soon, and a suitable building site has been located in an attractive and rapidly growing area. In discussing how the company can acquire the desired building and other facilities needed to open the new store, Sam Watkins, the company's director in charge of sales, stated, 'I know most of our competitors are starting to lease facilities rather than buy, but I just can't see the economics of it. Our development people tell me that we can buy the building site, put a building on it, and get all the store fixtures we need for just £850,000. They also say that property taxes, insurance and repairs would run at £20,000 a year. When you figure that we plan to keep a site for 18 years, that's a total cost of £1,210,000. But then when you realize that the property will be worth at least a half million in 18 years, that's a net cost to us of only £710,000. What would it cost to lease the property?'

'I understand that Beneficial Insurance Company is willing to purchase the building site, construct a building and install fixtures to our specifications, and then lease the facility to us for 18 years at an annual lease payment of £120,000,' replied Lisa Coleman, the company's executive manager.

'That's just my point,' said Sam. 'At £120,000 a year, it would cost us a cool £2,160,000 over the 18 years. That's three times what it would cost to buy, and what would we have left at the end? Nothing! The building would belong to the insurance company!'

'You're overlooking a few things,' replied Lisa. 'For one thing, the treasurer's office says that we could only afford to put £350,000 down if we buy the property, and then we would have to pay the other £500,000 off over four years at £175,000 a year. So there would be some interest involved on the purchase side that you haven't figured in.'

'But that little bit of interest is nothing compared to over 2 million pounds for leasing,' said Sam. 'Also, if we lease I understand we would have to put up a £8,000 security deposit that we wouldn't get back until the end. And besides that, we would still have to pay all the yearly repairs and maintenance costs just as if we owned the property. No wonder those insurance companies are so rich if they can swing deals like this.'

'Well, I'll admit that I don't have all the figures sorted out yet,' replied Lisa. 'But I do have the operating cost breakdown for the building, which includes £7,500 annually for property taxes, £8,000 for insurance, and £4,500 for repairs and maintenance. If we lease, Beneficial will handle its own insurance costs and of course the owner will have to pay the property taxes. I'll put all this together and see if leasing makes any sense with our required rate of return of 16%. The managing director wants a presentation and recommendation in the executive committee meeting tomorrow. Let's see, development said the first lease payment would be due now and the remaining ones due in years 1–17. Development also said that this store should generate a net cash inflow that's well above the average for our stores.'

Required

1. Using the net present value approach, determine whether Top-Quality Stores Ltd should lease or buy the new facility. Assume that you will be making your presentation before the company's executive committee, and remember that the managing director detests sloppy, disorganized reports.
2. What reply will you make in the meeting if Sam Watkins brings up the issue of the building's future sales value?

C10–30 Equipment acquisition: uneven cash flows Time allowed: 60 minutes

Kingsley Products Ltd is using a model 400 shaping machine to make one of its products. The company is expecting to have a large increase in demand for the product and is anxious to expand its productive capacity. Two possibilities are under consideration:

1. Purchase another model 400 shaping machine to operate along with the currently owned model 400 machine.
2. Purchase a model 800 shaping machine and use the currently owned model 400 machine as standby equipment. The model 800 machine is a high-speed unit with double the capacity of the model 400 machine.

The following additional information is available on the alternatives:

1. Both the model 400 machine and the model 800 machine have a 10-year life from the time they are first used in production. The scrap value of both machines is negligible and can be ignored. Straight-line depreciation is used.
2. The cost of a new model 800 machine is £300,000.
3. The model 400 machine now in use cost £160,000 three years ago. Its present book value is £112,000, and its present market value is £90,000.
4. A new model 400 machine costs £170,000 now. If the company decides not to buy the model 800 machine, then the currently owned model 400 machine will have to be replaced in seven years at a cost of £200,000. The replacement machine will be sold at the end of the tenth year for £140,000.
5. Production over the next 10 years is expected to be:

Year	Production in units
1	40,000
2	60,000
3	80,000
4–10	90,000

6 The two models of machines are not equally efficient. Comparative variable costs per unit are:

	Model	
	400	**800**
Materials per unit	£0.25	£0.40
Direct labour per unit	0.49	0.16
Supplies and lubricants per unit	0.06	0.04
Total variable cost per unit	£0.80	£0.60

7 The model 400 machine is less costly to maintain than the model 800 machine. Annual repairs and maintenance costs on a model 400 machine are £2,500.

8 Repairs and maintenance costs on a model 800 machine, with a model 400 machine used as standby, would total £3,800 per year.

9 No other factory costs will change as a result of the decision between the two machines.

Kingsley Products requires a 20% rate of return on all investments.

Required

1 Which alternative should the company choose? Use the net present value approach.

2 Suppose that the cost of labour increases by 10%. Would this make the model 800 machine more or less desirable? Explain. No computations are needed.

3 Suppose that the cost of materials doubles. Would this make the model 800 machine more or less desirable? Explain. No computations are needed.

C10–31 Time allowed: 50 minutes

The Independent Film Company plc is a film distribution company which purchases distribution rights on films from small independent producers, and sells the films on to cinema chains for national and international screening. In recent years the company has found it difficult to source sufficient films to maintain profitability. In response to the problem, the Independent Film Company has decided to invest in commissioning and producing films in its own right. In order to gain the expertise for this venture, the Independent Film Company is considering purchasing an existing film-making concern, at a cost of £400,000.

The main difficulty that is anticipated for the business is the increasing uncertainty as to the potential success/failure rate of independently produced films. Many cinema chains are adopting a policy of only buying films from large international film companies, as they believe that the market for independent films is very limited and specialist in nature. The Independent Film Company is prepared for the fact that they are likely to have more films that fail than succeed, but believe that the proposed film production business will nonetheless be profitable.

Using data collected from the existing distribution business and discussions with industry experts, they have produced cost and revenue forecasts for the five years of operation of the proposed investment. The company aims to complete the production of three films per year. The after-tax cost of capital for the company is estimated to be 14%.

Year 1 sales for the new business are uncertain, but expected to be in the range of £4–10 million. Probability estimates for different forecast values are given in the table below.

Sales are expected to grow at an annual rate of 5%.

Sales (£ million)	Probability
4	0.2
5	0.4
7	0.3
10	0.1

Anticipated costs related to the new business are as follows:

Cost type	£000
Purchase of film-making company	400
Annual legal and professional costs	20
Annual lease rental (office equipment)	12
Studio and set hire (per film)	180
Camera/specialist equipment hire (per film)	40
Technical staff wages (per film)	520
Screenplay (per film)	50
Actors' salaries (per film)	700
Costumes and wardrobe hire (per film)	60
Set design and painting (per film)	150
Annual non-production staff wages	60

Additional information

(i) No capital allowances are available.

(ii) Tax is payable one year in arrears, at a rate of 33% and full use can be made of tax refunds as they fall due.

(iii) Staff wages (technical and non-production staff) and actors' salaries, are expected to rise by 10% per annum.

(iv) Studio hire costs will be subject to an increase of 30% in Year 3.

(v) Screenplay costs per film are expected to rise by 15% per annum due to a shortage of skilled writers.

(vi) The new business will occupy office accommodation which has to date been let out for an annual rent of £20,000. Demand for such accommodation is buoyant and the company anticipates no problems in finding future tenants at the same annual rent.

(vii) A market research survey into the potential for the film production business cost £25,000.

Required

1 Using DCF analysis, calculate the expected net present value of the proposed investment. (Workings should be rounded to the nearest £000.) *(15 marks)*

2 Outline the main limitations of using expected values when making investment decisions. *(6 marks)*

3 In addition to the possible purchase of the film-making business, the company has two other investment opportunities, the details of which are given below:

	Post-tax cash flows, £000						
	Year 0	**Year 1**	**Year 2**	**Year 3**	**Year 4**	**Year 5**	**Year 6**
Investment X	(200)	200	200	150	100	100	100
Investment Y	(100)	80	80	40	40	40	40

The Independent Film Company has a total of £400,000 available for capital investment in the current year. No project can be invested in more than once.

(a) Define the term profitability index, and briefly explain how it may be used when a company faces a problem of capital rationing in any single accounting period. *(4 marks)*

(b) Calculate the profitability index for each of the investment projects available to the Independent Film Company, i.e. purchase of the film production company, Investment X and Investment Y, and outline the optimal investment strategy. Assume that all of the projects are indivisible. *(6 marks)*

(c) Explain the limitations of using a profitability index in a situation where there is capital rationing. *(4 marks)*

4 Briefly explain how the tax treatment of capital purchases can affect an investment decision. *(5 marks)*

(Total = 40 marks)

ACCA Managerial Finance, June 1999

Endnotes

1 Adapted from Berner (1998).

2 For simplicity, we assume initially in this chapter that there is no inflation. The impact of inflation on discounted cash flow analysis is discussed in Appendix 10A to this chapter. Also, initially we ignore income/corporation taxes. The impact of taxes on capital budgeting decisions will be covered later in the chapter, in Appendix 10C.

3 The alternative with the highest net present value is not always the best choice, although it is the best choice in this case. For further discussion, see the section 'Preference decisions – the ranking of investment projects', pp. 385–87.

4 Technically, the incremental-cost approach is misnamed, since it focuses on differential costs (that is, on both cost increases and decreases) rather than just on incremental costs. As used here, the term incremental costs should be interpreted broadly to include both cost increases and cost decreases.

5 The seminal work was associated with Markowitz (1959).

6 These issues are discussed more fully in the principal–agent literature. See, e.g., Jensen and Meckling (1976).

Part III
Planning and control

Chapter 11
Profit planning and the role of budgeting

Learning objectives

After studying Chapter 11, you should be able to:

1. Understand why organizations budget and the processes they use to create budgets
2. Prepare a sales budget, including a schedule of expected cash receipts
3. Prepare a production budget
4. Prepare a direct materials budget
5. Prepare a direct labour budget
6. Prepare a manufacturing overhead budget
7. Prepare an ending finished stock budget
8. Prepare a selling and administrative expense budget
9. Prepare a cash budget
10. Prepare a budgeted profit and loss statement and a budgeted balance sheet

Concepts in Context

After an initial boom, many early dotcom companies have now failed. One reason seems to be that some companies thought that the old business practices such as budgeting were obsolete. The emphasis was on speed, being the first-mover and working out detailed business plans as the business developed. Frequently, many companies squandered their start-up resources before they had established a sustainable business. The collapse of dotcoms and the high tech sector around the turn of the millennium seemed to suggest that the disciplines of planning and control inherent in budgeting should not just be the concern of 'fuddy-duddy', bricks-and-mortar organizations.[1]

In this chapter, we focus our attention on those steps taken by business organizations to achieve their desired levels of profits – a process that is generally called profit planning. We shall see that profit planning is accomplished through the preparation of a number of budgets, which, when brought together, form an integrated business plan known as the master budget. The master budget is an essential management tool that communicates management's plans throughout the organization, allocates resources and co-ordinates activities.

The basic framework of budgeting

Definition of budgeting

1 LEARNING OBJECTIVE

A **budget** is a detailed plan for the acquisition and use of financial and other resources over a specified time period. It represents a plan for the future expressed in formal quantitative terms. The act of preparing a budget is called *budgeting*. The use of budgets to control a firm's activities is known as *budgetary control*.

The *master budget* is a summary of a company's plans that sets specific targets for sales, production, distribution and financing activities. It generally culminates in a *cash budget*, a *budgeted profit and loss account*, and a *budgeted balance sheet*. In short, it represents a comprehensive expression of management's plans for the future and how these plans are to be accomplished.

Personal budgets

Nearly everyone budgets to some extent, even though many of the people who use budgets do not recognize what they are doing as budgeting. For example, most people make estimates of their income and plan expenditures for food, clothing, housing and so on. As a result of this planning, people restrict their spending to some predetermined, allowable amount. While they may not be conscious of the fact, these people clearly go through a budgeting process. Income is estimated, expenditures are planned, and spending is restricted in accordance with the plan. Individuals also use budgets to forecast their future financial condition for purposes such as purchasing a home, financing college education, or setting aside funds for retirement. These budgets may exist only in the mind of the individual, but they are budgets nevertheless.

The budgets of a business firm serve much the same functions as the budgets prepared informally by individuals. Business budgets tend to be more detailed and to involve more work, but they are similar to the budgets prepared by individuals in most other respects. Like personal budgets, they assist in planning and controlling expenditures; they also assist in predicting operating results and financial condition in future periods.

Differences between planning and control

The terms *planning* and *control* are often confused, and occasionally these terms are used in such a way as to suggest that they mean the same thing. Actually, planning and control are two quite distinct concepts. **Planning** involves developing objectives and preparing various budgets to achieve these objectives. **Control** involves the steps taken by management to increase the likelihood that the objectives set down at the planning stage are attained, and to ensure that all parts of the organization function in a manner consistent with organizational policies. To be completely effective, a good budgeting system must provide for *both* planning and control. Good planning without effective control is time wasted. On the other hand, unless plans are laid down in advance, there are no objectives toward which control can be directed.

Budgeting systems often serve multiple purposes with two of the more important functions being planning and control. Management must decide which role is more appropriate. For example, large firms concerned with operational efficiency should focus on the control and co-ordination aspects of budgeting, while small, innovative companies should be more concerned with the planning aspects of budgeting.[2]

Advantages of budgeting

There is an old saying to the effect that 'a man is usually down on what he isn't up on'. Managers who have never tried budgeting are usually quick to state that budgeting is a waste of time. These managers may argue that even though budgeting may work well in some situations, it would never work well in their companies because operations are too complex or because there are too many uncertainties. In reality, however, managers who argue this way usually will be deeply involved in planning (albeit on an informal basis). These managers will have clearly defined thoughts about what they want to accomplish and when they want it accomplished. The difficulty is that unless they have some way of communicating their thoughts and plans to others, the only way their companies will ever attain the desired objectives will be through accident. In short, even though companies may attain a certain degree of success without budgets, they never attain the heights that could have been reached with a co-ordinated system of budgets.

Companies realize many benefits from a budgeting programme. Among these benefits are the following:

1. Budgets provide a means of *communicating* management's plans throughout the organization.
2. Budgets force managers to *think about* and plan for the future. In the absence of the necessity to prepare a budget, too many managers would spend all their time dealing with daily emergencies.
3. The budgeting process provides a means of *allocating resources* to those parts of the organization where they can be used most effectively.
4. The budgeting process can uncover potential *bottlenecks* before they occur.
5. Budgets *co-ordinate* the activities of the entire organization by integrating the plans of the various parts. Budgeting helps to ensure that everyone in the organization is pulling in the same direction.
6. Budgets define goals and objectives that can serve as *benchmarks* for evaluating subsequent performance.

Focus on current practice

FOCUS

Consider the following situation encountered by one of the authors at a mortgage banking firm: For years, the company operated with virtually no system of budgets whatever. Management contended that budgeting was not well suited to the firm's type of operation. Moreover, management pointed out that the firm was already profitable. Indeed, outwardly the company gave every appearance of being a well-managed, smoothly operating organization. A careful look within, however, disclosed that day-to-day operations were far from smooth, and often approached chaos. The average day was nothing more than an exercise in putting out one brush fire after another. The Cash account was always at crisis levels. At the end of a day, no one ever knew whether enough cash would be available the next day to cover required loan closings. Departments were uncoordinated, and it was not uncommon to find that one department was pursuing a course that conflicted with the course pursued by another department. Employee morale was low, and turnover was high. Employees complained bitterly that when a job was well done, nobody ever knew about it.

The company was bought out by a new group who required that an integrated budgeting system be established to control operations. Within one year's time, significant changes were evident. Brush fires were rare. Careful planning virtually eliminated the problems that had been experienced with cash, and departmental efforts were co-ordinated and directed toward predetermined overall company goals.

Although the employees were wary of the new budgeting programme initially, they became 'converted' when they saw the positive effects that it brought about. The more efficient operations caused profits to jump dramatically. Communication increased throughout the organization. When a job was well done everybody knew about it. As one employee stated, 'For the first time, we know what the company expects of us.'

In the past, some managers have avoided budgeting because of the time and effort involved in the budgeting process. It can be argued that budgeting is actually 'free' in that the manager's time and effort are more than offset by greater profits. Moreover, with the advent of computer spreadsheet programs, *any* company – large or small – can implement and maintain a budgeting programme at minimal cost. Budgeting lends itself well to readily available spreadsheet application programs.

Responsibility accounting

Most of what we say in this chapter and in the next three chapters centres on the concept of *responsibility accounting*. The basic idea behind **responsibility accounting** is that a manager should be held responsible for those items – and only those items – that the manager can actually control to a significant extent. Each line item (i.e., revenue or cost) in the budget is made the responsibility of a manager, and that manager is held responsible for subsequent deviations between budgeted goals and actual results. In effect, responsibility accounting *personalizes* accounting information by looking at costs from a *personal control* standpoint. This concept is central to any effective profit planning and control system. Someone must be held responsible for each cost or else no one will be responsible, and the cost will inevitably grow out of control.

Being held responsible for costs does not mean that the manager is penalized if the actual results do not measure up to the budgeted goals. However, the manager should take the initiative to correct any unfavourable discrepancies, should understand the source of significant favourable or unfavourable discrepancies, and should be prepared to explain the reasons for discrepancies to higher management. The point of an effective responsibility system is to make sure that nothing 'falls through the cracks', that the organization reacts quickly and appropriately to deviations from its plans, and that the organization learns from the feedback it gets by comparing budgeted goals to actual results. The point is *not* to penalize individuals for missing targets.

We will look at responsibility accounting in more detail in the next three chapters. For the moment, we can summarize the overall idea by noting that it rests on three basic premises. The first premise is that costs can be organized in terms of levels of management responsibility. The second premise is that the costs charged to a particular level are controllable at that level by its managers. And the third premise is that effective budget data can be generated as a basis for evaluating actual performance. This chapter on profit planning is concerned with the third of these premises in that the purpose of the chapter is to show the steps involved in budget preparation.

Choosing a budget period

Operating budgets are ordinarily set to cover a one-year period. The one-year period should correspond to the company's fiscal year so that the budget figures can be compared with the actual results. Many companies divide their budget year into four quarters. The first quarter is then subdivided into months, and monthly budget figures are established. These *near-term* figures can often be established with considerable accuracy. The last three quarters are carried in the budget as quarterly totals only. As the year progresses, the figures for the second quarter are broken down into monthly amounts, then the third-quarter figures are broken down, and so forth. This approach has the advantage of requiring periodic review and reappraisal of budget data throughout the year.

Continuous, perpetual or *rolling budgets* are used by a significant number of organizations. A **continuous or perpetual budget** is a 12-month budget that rolls forward one month (or quarter) as the current month (or quarter) is completed. In other words, one month (or quarter) is added to the end of the budget as each month (or quarter) comes to a close. This approach keeps managers focused on the future at least one year ahead. Advocates of continuous budgets argue that with this approach there is less danger that managers will become too focused on short-term results as the year progresses.

In this chapter, we will focus on one-year operating budgets. However, using basically the same techniques, operating budgets can be prepared for periods that extend over many years. It may be difficult accurately to forecast sales and required data much beyond a year, but even rough estimates can be invaluable in uncovering potential problems and opportunities that would otherwise be overlooked.

The self-imposed or participative budget

The success of a budget programme will be determined in large part by the way in which the budget is developed. The most successful budget programmes involve managers with cost control responsibilities in preparing their own budget estimates – rather than having a budget imposed from above. This approach to preparing budget data is particularly important if the budget is to be used to control and evaluate a manager's activities. If a budget is imposed on a manager from above, it will probably generate resentment and ill will rather than co-operation and increased productivity.

This budgeting approach, in which managers prepare their own budget estimates – called a *self-imposed budget* – is generally considered to be the most effective method of budget preparation. A **self-imposed budget** or **participative budget** is a budget that is prepared with the full co-operation and participation of managers at all levels. Exhibit 11.1 illustrates this approach to budget preparation.

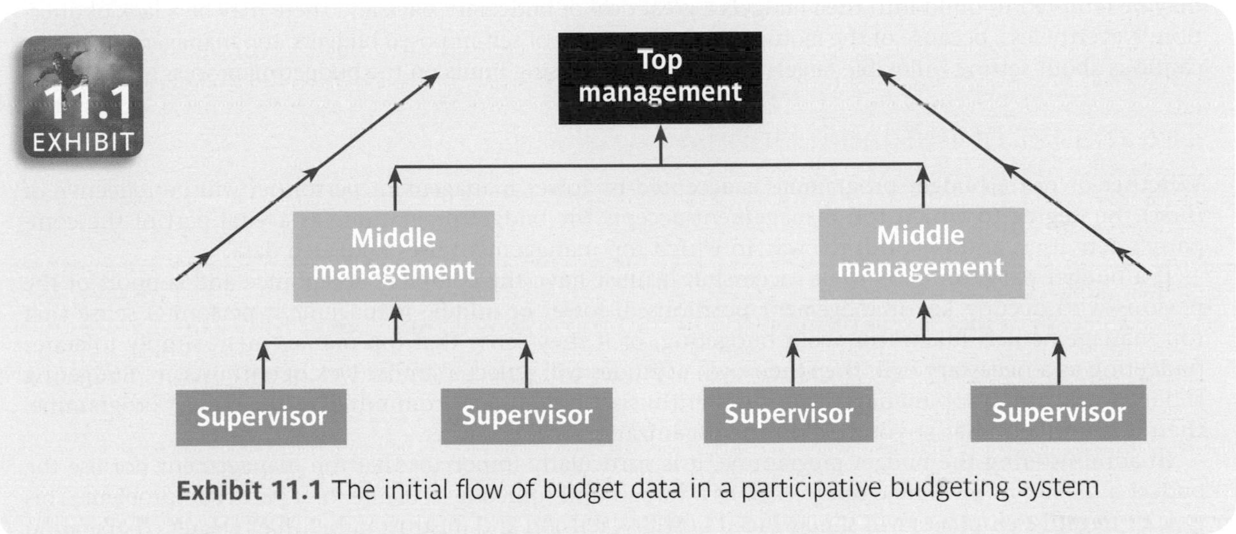

Exhibit 11.1 The initial flow of budget data in a participative budgeting system

A number of advantages are commonly cited for such self-imposed budgets:

1 Individuals at all levels of the organization are recognized as members of the team whose views and judgements are valued by top management.

2 The person in direct contact with an activity is in the best position to make budget estimates. Therefore, budget estimates prepared by such persons tend to be more accurate and reliable.

3 People are more likely to work at fulfilling a budget that they have participated in setting than they are to work at fulfilling a budget that is imposed from above.

4 A self-imposed budget contains its own unique system of control in that if people are not able to meet budget specifications, they have only themselves to blame. On the other hand, if a budget is imposed from above, they can always say that the budget was unreasonable or unrealistic to start with, and therefore was impossible to meet.

Once self-imposed budgets are prepared, are they subject to any kind of review? The answer is yes. Budget estimates prepared by lower-level managers cannot necessarily be accepted without question by higher levels of management. If no system of checks and balances is present, self-imposed budgets may be too loose and allow too much 'budgetary slack'. The result will be inefficiency and waste. Therefore, before budgets are accepted, they must be carefully reviewed by immediate superiors. If changes from the original budget seem desirable, the items in question are discussed and modified as necessary by mutual consent.

In essence, all levels of an organization should work together to produce the budget. Since top management is generally unfamiliar with detailed, day-to-day operations, it should rely on subordinates to provide detailed budget information. On the other hand, top management has a perspective on the company as a whole that is vital in making broad policy decisions in budget preparation. Each level of responsibility in an organization should contribute in the way that it best can in a *co-operative* effort to develop an integrated budget document.

To be successful, a self-imposed approach to setting budgets requires that all managers understand and agree with the organization's strategy. Otherwise, the budgets proposed by the lower-level managers will lack coherent direction. We will discuss in greater detail in Chapters 16 and 17 how a company can go about formulating its strategy and then communicating it throughout the organization.

We have described an ideal budgetary process that involves self-imposed budgets prepared by the managers who are directly responsible for revenues and costs. Most companies deviate from this ideal. Typically, top managers initiate the budget process by issuing broad guidelines in terms of overall target profits or sales. Lower-level managers are directed to prepare budgets that meet those targets. The difficulty is that the targets set by top managers may be unrealistically high or may allow too much slack. If the targets are too high and employees know they are unrealistic, motivation will suffer. If the targets allow too much slack, waste will occur. And, unfortunately, top managers are often not in a position to know whether the targets they have set are appropriate. Admittedly, however, in a pure self-imposed budgeting system, lower-level managers may be tempted to build into their budgets a great deal of budgetary slack and there may be a lack of direction. Nevertheless, because of the motivational advantages of self-imposed budgets, top managers should be cautious about setting inflexible targets or otherwise imposing limits on the budgeting process.

The matter of human relations

Whether or not a budget programme is accepted by lower management personnel will be reflective of (first) the degree to which top management accepts the budget programme as a vital part of the company's activities, and (second) the way in which top management uses budgeted data.

If a budget programme is to be successful, it must have the complete acceptance and support of the persons who occupy key management positions. If lower or middle management personnel sense that top management is lukewarm about budgeting, or if they sense that top management simply tolerates budgeting as a necessary evil, then their own attitudes will reflect a similar lack of enthusiasm. Budgeting is hard work, and if top management is not enthusiastic about and committed to the budget programme, then it is unlikely that anyone else in the organization will be either.

In administering the budget programme, it is particularly important that top management not use the budget as a club to pressure employees or as a way to find someone to blame for a particular problem. This type of negative emphasis will simply breed hostility, tension and mistrust rather than greater co-operation and productivity. Unfortunately, research suggests that the budget is often used as a pressure device and that great emphasis is placed on 'meeting the budget' under all circumstances.[3] Rather than being used as a pressure device, the budget should be used as a positive instrument to assist in establishing goals, in measuring operating results, and in isolating areas that are in need of extra effort or attention. Any misgivings that employees have about a budget programme can be overcome by meaningful involvement at all levels and by proper use of the programme over a period of time. Administration of a budget programme requires a great deal of insight and sensitivity on the part of management. The ultimate object must be to develop the realization that the budget is designed to be a positive aid in achieving both individual and company goals.

Management must keep clearly in mind that the human dimension in budgeting is of key importance. It is easy for the manager to become preoccupied with the technical aspects of the budget programme to the exclusion of the human aspects. Indeed, the use of budget data in a rigid and inflexible manner is the greatest single complaint of persons whose performance is being evaluated through the budget process.[4] Management should remember that the purposes of the budget are to motivate employees and to co-ordinate efforts. Preoccupation with the pounds and pence in the budget, or being rigid and inflexible in budget administration, can only lead to frustration of these purposes.

The budget committee

A standing **budget committee** will usually be responsible for overall policy matters relating to the budget programme and for co-ordinating the preparation of the budget itself. This committee generally consists of the managing director; directors in charge of various functions such as sales, production and purchasing; and the controller. Difficulties and disputes between segments of the organization in matters relating to the budget are resolved by the budget committee. In addition, the budget committee approves the final budget and receives periodic reports on the progress of the company in attaining budgeted goals.

Disputes can (and do) erupt over budget matters. Because budgets allocate resources, the budgeting process, to a large extent, determines which departments get more resources and which get relatively less. Also, the budget sets the benchmarks by which managers and their departments will be at least partially evaluated. Therefore, it should not be surprising that managers take the budgeting process very seriously and invest considerable energy and even emotion in ensuring that their interests, and those of their departments, are protected. Because of this, the budgeting process can easily degenerate into an inter-office brawl in which the ultimate goal of working together toward common goals is forgotten.

Running a successful budgeting programme that avoids inter-office battles requires considerable inter-personal skills in addition to purely technical skills. But even the best inter-personal skills will fail if, as discussed earlier, top management uses the budget process inappropriately as a club or as a way to find blame.

Focus on current practice

Budgeting is often an intensely political process in which managers jockey for resources and relaxed goals for the upcoming year. One group of consultants describes the process in this way: Annual budgets 'have a particular urgency in that they provide the standard and most public framework against which managers are assessed and judged. It is, therefore, not surprising that budget-setting is taken seriously ... Often budgets are a means for managers getting what they want. A relaxed budget will secure a relatively easy twelve months, a tight one means that their names will constantly be coming up in the monthly management review meeting. Far better to shift the burden of cost control and financial discipline to someone else. Budgeting is an intensely political exercise conducted with all the sharper managerial skills not taught at business school, such as lobbying and flattering superiors, forced haste, regretted delay, hidden truth, half-truths, and lies.'[5]

The master budget interrelationships

The master budget consists of a number of separate but interdependent budgets. Exhibit 11.2 provides an overview of the various parts of the master budget and how they are related.

The sales budget

A **sales budget** is a detailed schedule showing the expected sales for the budget period; typically, it is expressed in both pounds and units of product. An accurate sales budget is the key to the entire budgeting process. All other parts of the master budget are dependent on the sales budget in some way, as illustrated in Exhibit 11.2. Thus, if the sales budget is sloppily done, then the rest of the budgeting process is largely a waste of time.

The sales budget will help determine how many units will have to be produced. Thus, the *production budget* is prepared after the sales budget. The production budget in turn is used to determine the budgets for manufacturing costs including the *direct materials budget*, the *direct labour budget*, and the *manufacturing overhead budget*. These budgets are then combined with data from the sales budget and the selling and administrative expense budget to determine the cash budget. In essence, the sales budget triggers a chain reaction that leads to the development of the other budgets.

As shown in Exhibit 11.2, the selling and administrative expense budget is both dependent on and a determinant of the sales budget. This reciprocal relationship arises because sales will in part be determined by the funds committed for advertising and sales promotion.

The cash budget

Once the operating budgets (sales, production, and so on) have been established, the cash budget and other financial budgets can be prepared. A **cash budget** is a detailed plan showing how cash resources

11.2 EXHIBIT

Sales budget

Ending stock budget

Production budget

Selling and administrative expense budget

Direct materials budget

Direct labour budget

Manufacturing overhead budget

Cash budget

Budgeted profit statement

Budget balance sheet

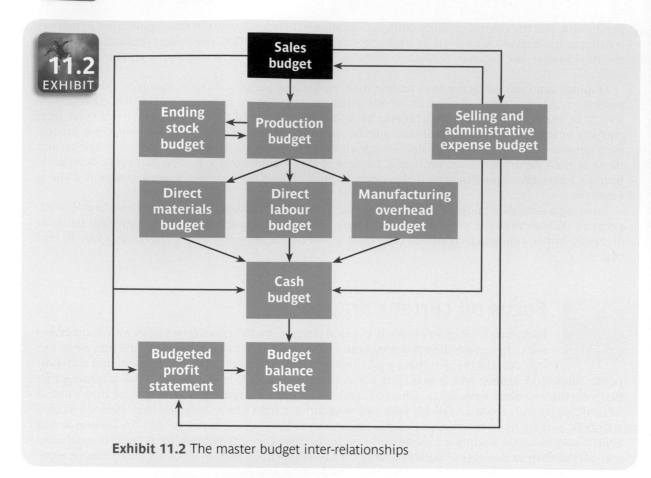

Exhibit 11.2 The master budget inter-relationships

will be acquired and used over some specified time period. Observe from Exhibit 11.2 that all of the operating budgets have an impact on the cash budget. In the case of the sales budget, the impact comes from the planned cash receipts to be received from sales. In the case of the other budgets, the impact comes from the planned cash expenditures within the budgets themselves.

Sales forecasting – a critical step

The sales budget is usually based on the company's *sales forecast.* Sales from prior years are commonly used as a starting point in preparing the sales forecast. In addition, the manager may examine the company's unfilled back orders, the company's pricing policy and marketing plans, trends in the industry and general economic conditions. Sophisticated statistical tools may be used to analyse the data and to build models that are helpful in predicting key factors influencing the company's sales.

Preparing the master budget

Management accounting in action: the issue

Tom Wills is the majority shareholder and managing director of Hampton Freeze Ltd, a company he started in 1998. The company makes premium ice lollies using only natural ingredients and featuring exotic flavours such as tangy tangerine and minty mango. The company's business is highly seasonal, with most of the sales occurring in spring and summer.

In 1999, the company's second year of operations, there was a major cash crunch in the first and second quarters that almost forced the company into bankruptcy. In spite of this cash crunch, 1999 turned out to be overall a very successful year in terms of both cashflow and profit. Partly as a result of that harrowing experience, Tom decided towards the end of 1999 to hire a professional financial manager. Tom interviewed several promising candidates for the job and settled on Larry Moore, who had considerable experience in the packaged foods industry. In the job interview, Tom questioned Larry about the steps he would take to prevent a recurrence of the 1999 cash crunch:

Tom: As I mentioned earlier, we are going to wind up 1999 with a very nice profit. What you may not know is that we had some very big financial problems this year.

Larry: Let me guess. You ran out of cash sometime in the first or second quarter.

Tom: How did you know?

Larry: Most of your sales are in the second and third quarter, right?

Tom: Spot on, everyone wants to buy ice lollies in the spring and summer, but nobody wants them when the weather turns cold.

Larry: So you don't have many sales in the first quarter?

Tom: Right.

Larry: And in the second quarter, which is the spring, you are producing like mad to fill orders?

Tom: Yes.

Larry: Do your customers pay you the day you make your deliveries?

Tom: You must be joking? Of course not.

Larry: So in the first quarter, you don't have many sales. In the second quarter, you are producing like mad, which eats up cash, but you aren't paid by your customers until long after you have paid your employees and suppliers. No wonder you had a cash problem. I see this pattern all the time in food processing because of the seasonality of the business.

Tom: So what can we do about it?

Larry: The first step is to predict the magnitude of the problem before it occurs. If we can predict early in the year what the cash shortfall is going to be, we can go to the bank and arrange for credit before we really need it. Bankers tend to be wary of panicky people who show up begging for emergency loans. They are much more likely to make the loan if you look like you know what you are doing, you have done your homework, and you are in control of the situation.

Tom: How can we predict the cash shortfall?

Larry: You can put together a cash budget. While you're at it, you might as well do a master budget. You'll find it is well worth the effort.

Tom: I don't like budgets. They are too confining. My wife budgets everything at home, and I can't spend what I want.

Larry: May I ask a personal question?

Tom: What?

Larry: Where did you get the money to start this business?

Tom: Mainly from our family's savings. I get your point. We wouldn't have had the money to start the business if my wife hadn't been forcing us to save every month.

Larry: Exactly. I suggest you use the same discipline in your business. It is even more important here because you can't expect your employees to spend your money as carefully as you would.

Tom: I'm sold. Welcome aboard.

With the full backing of Tom Wills, Larry Moore set out to create a **master budget** for the company for the year 2000. In his planning for the budgeting process, Larry drew up the following list of documents that would be a part of the master budget:

1 A sales budget, including a schedule of expected cash collections
2 A production budget (or merchandise purchases budget for a merchandising company)
3 A direct materials budget, including a schedule of expected cash disbursements for raw materials
4 A direct labour budget
5 A manufacturing overhead budget
6 An ending finished goods stock budget

7 A selling and administrative expense budget

8 A cash budget

9 A budgeted profit and loss account

10 A budgeted balance sheet.

Larry felt it was important to get everyone's co-operation in the budgeting process, so he asked Tom to call a companywide meeting in which the budgeting process would be explained. At the meeting there was initially some grumbling, but Tom was able to convince nearly everyone of the necessity for planning and getting better control over spending. It helped that the cash crisis earlier in the year was still fresh in everyone's minds. As much as some people disliked the idea of budgets, they liked their jobs even more.

In the months that followed, Larry worked closely with all the managers involved in the master budget, gathering data from them and making sure that they understood and fully supported the parts of the master budget that would affect them. In subsequent years, Larry hoped to turn the whole budgeting process over to the managers and to take a more advisory role.

The interdependent documents that Larry Moore prepared for Hampton Freeze are Schedules 1 to 10 of his company's master budget. In this section, we will study these schedules.

The sales budget

2 LEARNING OBJECTIVE

The sales budget is the starting point in preparing the master budget. As shown earlier in Exhibit 11.2, all other items in the master budget, including production, purchases, stocks and expenses, depend on it in some way.

The sales budget is constructed by multiplying the budgeted sales in units by the selling price. Schedule 1 contains the sales budget for Hampton Freeze Ltd for the year 2000, by quarters. Notice from the schedule that the company plans to sell 100,000 cases of ice lollies during the year, with sales peaking in the third quarter.

A schedule of expected *cash collections*, such as the one that appears in Schedule 1 for Hampton Freeze, is prepared after the sales budget. This schedule will be needed later to prepare the cash budget. Cash collections consist of collections on sales made to customers in prior periods plus collections on sales made in the current budget period. At Hampton Freeze, experience has shown that 70% of sales are collected in the quarter in which the sale is made and the remaining 30% are collected in the following quarter. So, for example, 70% of the first quarter sales of £200,000 (or £140,000) is collected during the first quarter and 30% (or £60,000) is collected during the second quarter.

The production budget

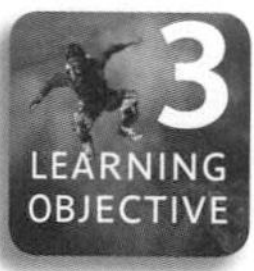

The production budget is prepared after the sales budget. The **production budget** lists the number of units that must be produced during each budget period to meet sales needs and to provide for the desired ending stock. Production needs can be determined as follows:

Budgeted sales in units	XXXX
Add desired ending stock	XXXX
Total needs	XXXX
Less beginning stock	XXXX
Required production	XXXX

Schedule 2 contains the production budget for Hampton Freeze.

Note that production requirements for a quarter are influenced by the desired level of the ending stock. Stocks should be carefully planned. Excessive stocks tie up funds and create storage problems. Insufficient stocks can lead to lost sales or crash production efforts in the following period. At Hampton Freeze, management believes that an ending stock equal to 20% of the next quarter's sales strikes the appropriate balance.

Schedule 1

Microsoft Excel - Book1

Hampton Freeze Ltd.
Sales budget
for the year ended 31 December 2000

	Quarter 1	2	3	4	Year
Budgeted sales in units (cases of lollies)	10,000	30,000	40,000	20,000	100,000
Selling price per unit	× £20	× £20	× £20	× £20	× £20
Total sales	£200,000	£600,000	£800,000	£400,000	£2,000,000
Schedule of expected cash collections					
Debtors, beginning balance*	£90,000				£90,000
First-quarter sales (£200,000 × 70%, 30%)†	140,000	60,000			200,000
Second-quarter sales (£600,000 × 70%, 30%)		420,000	180,000		600,000
Third-quarter sales (£800,000 × 70%, 30%)			560,000	240,000	800,000
Fourth-quarter sales (£400,000 × 70%)‡				280,000	280,000
Total cash collections	£230,000	£480,000	£740,000	£520,000	£1,970,000

*Cash collections from last year's fourth-quarter sales. See the beginning-of-year balance sheet on page 450.

†Cash collections from sales are as follows: 70% collected in the quarter of sale, and the remaining 30% collected in the following year.

‡Uncollected fourth-quarter sales appear as debtors on the company's end-of-year balance sheet (see Schedule 10 on page 453).

Stock purchases – merchandising firm

Hampton Freeze prepares a production budget, since it is a manufacturing firm. If it were a merchandising firm, then instead of a production budget it would prepare a **merchandise purchases budget** showing the amount of goods to be purchased from its suppliers during the period. The merchandise purchases budget is in the same basic format as the production budget, except that it shows goods to be purchased rather than goods to be produced, as shown below:

Budgeted cost of goods sold (in units or in pounds)	XXXXX
Add desired ending merchandise stock	XXXXX
Total needs	XXXXX
Less beginning merchandise stock	XXXXX
Required purchases (in units or in pounds)	XXXXX

The merchandising firm would prepare a stock purchases budget such as the one above for each item carried in stock. Some large retail organizations make such computations on a frequent basis (particularly at peak seasons) to ensure that adequate stocks are on hand to meet customer needs.

Schedule 2

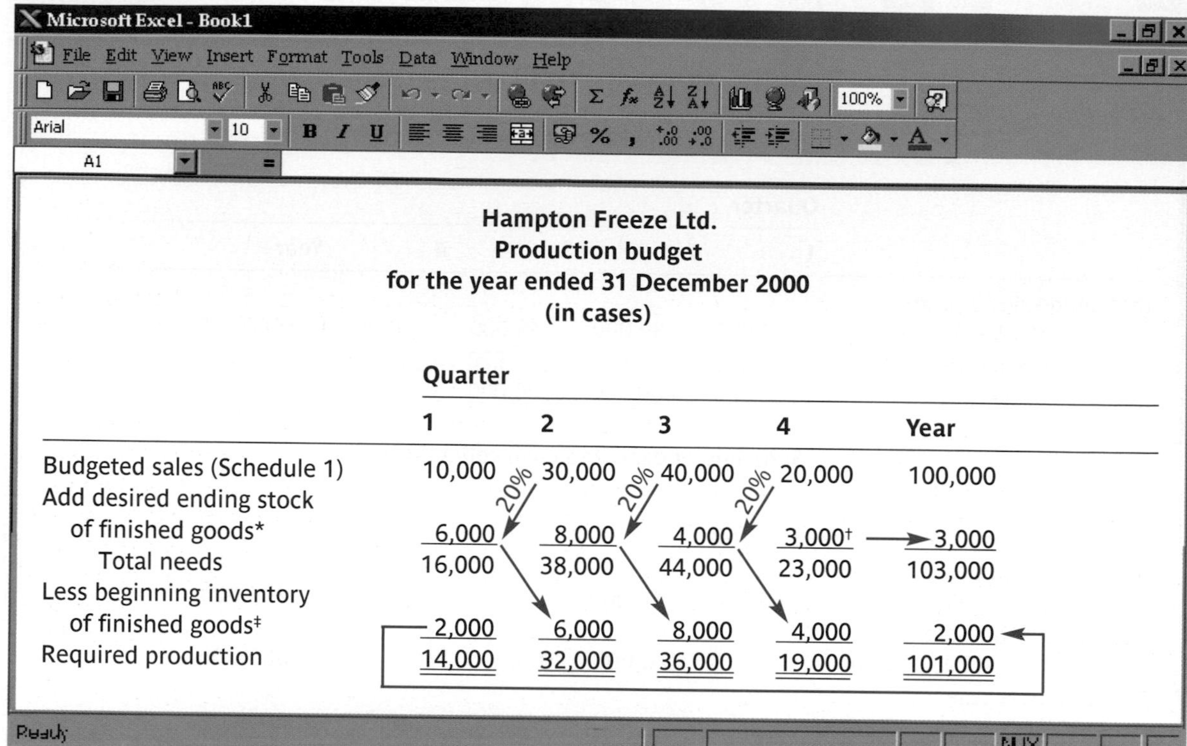

Hampton Freeze Ltd.
Production budget
for the year ended 31 December 2000
(in cases)

	Quarter 1	2	3	4	Year
Budgeted sales (Schedule 1)	10,000	30,000	40,000	20,000	100,000
Add desired ending stock of finished goods*	6,000	8,000	4,000	3,000†	3,000
Total needs	16,000	38,000	44,000	23,000	103,000
Less beginning inventory of finished goods‡	2,000	6,000	8,000	4,000	2,000
Required production	14,000	32,000	36,000	19,000	101,000

*20% cent of next quarter's sales.

†Estimated.

‡The same as the prior quarter's *ending* stock.

The direct materials budget

Returning to Hampton Freeze's budget data, after the production requirements have been computed, a *direct materials budget* can be prepared. The **direct materials budget** details the raw materials that must be purchased to fulfil the production budget and to provide for adequate stocks. The required purchases of raw materials are computed as follows:

Raw materials needed to meet the production schedule	XXXXX
Add desired ending stock of raw materials	XXXXX
Total raw materials needs	XXXXX
Less beginning stock of raw materials	XXXXX
Raw materials to be purchased	XXXXX

Preparing a budget of this kind is one step in a company's overall **material requirements planning (MRP)**. MRP is an operations management tool that uses a computer to help manage materials and stocks. The objective of MRP is to ensure that the right materials are on hand, in the right quantities, and at the right time to support the production budget. The detailed operation of MRP is covered in most operations management books.

Schedule 3 contains the direct materials budget for Hampton Freeze. The only raw material included in that budget is high fructose sugar, which is the major ingredient in ice lollies other than water. The remaining raw materials are relatively insignificant and are included in variable manufacturing overhead. Notice that materials requirements are first determined in units (kilos, litres, and so on) and then translated into pounds by multiplying by the appropriate unit cost. Also note that the management of Hampton Freeze desires to maintain ending stocks of sugar equal to 10% of the following quarter's production needs.

The direct materials budget is usually accompanied by a schedule of expected cash disbursements for raw materials. This schedule is needed to prepare the overall cash budget. Disbursements for raw materials consist of payments for purchases on account in prior periods plus any payments for purchases in the current budget period. Schedule 3 contains such a schedule of cash disbursements.

The direct labour budget

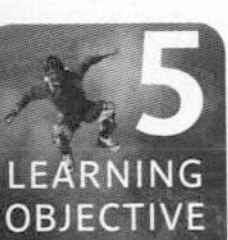

The **direct labour budget** is also developed from the production budget. Direct labour requirements must be computed so that the company will know whether sufficient labour time is available to meet production needs. By knowing in advance just what will be needed in the way of labour time throughout the budget year, the company can develop plans to adjust the labour force as the situation may require. Firms that neglect to budget run the risk of facing labour shortages, or having to hire and lay off at awkward times. Erratic labour policies lead to insecurity and inefficiency on the part of employees.

To compute direct labour requirements, the number of units of finished product to be produced each period (month, quarter, and so on) is multiplied by the number of direct labour-hours required to produce a single unit. Many different types of labour may be involved. If so, then computations should be by type of labour needed. The direct labour requirements can then be translated into expected direct labour costs. How this is done will depend on the labour policy of the firm. In Schedule 4, the management of Hampton Freeze has assumed that the direct labour force will be adjusted as the work requirements change from quarter to quarter. In that case, the total direct labour cost is computed by simply multiplying the direct labour-hour requirements by the direct labour rate per hour as was done in Schedule 4.

However, many companies have employment policies or contracts that prevent them from laying off and rehiring workers as needed. Suppose, for example, that Hampton Freeze has fifty workers who are classified as direct labour and each of them is guaranteed at least 480 hours of pay each quarter at a rate of £7.50 per hour. In that case, the minimum direct labour cost for a quarter would be as follows:

$$50 \text{ workers} \times 480 \text{ hour} \times £7.50 = £180{,}000$$

Note that in Schedule 4 the direct labour costs for the first and fourth quarters would have to be increased to a £180,000 level if Hampton Freeze's labour policy did not allow it to adjust the workforce at will.

The manufacturing overhead budget

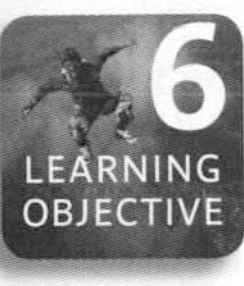

The **manufacturing overhead budget** provides a schedule of all costs of production other than direct materials and direct labour. Schedule 5 shows the manufacturing overhead budget for Hampton Freeze. Note how the production costs are separated into variable and fixed components. The variable component is £2 per direct labour-hour. The fixed component is £60,600 per quarter.

The last line of Schedule 5 for Hampton Freeze shows its budgeted cash disbursements for manufacturing overhead. Since some of the overhead costs are not cash outflows, the total budgeted manufacturing overhead costs must be adjusted to determine the cash disbursements for manufacturing overhead. At Hampton Freeze, the only significant non-cash manufacturing overhead cost is depreciation, which is £15,000 per quarter. These non-cash depreciation charges are deducted from the total budgeted manufacturing overhead to determine the expected cash disbursements. Hampton Freeze pays all overhead costs involving cash disbursements in the quarter incurred.

The ending finished goods stock budget

After completing Schedules 1–5, Larry Moore had all of the data he needed to compute unit product costs. This computation was needed for two reasons: first, to determine cost of goods sold on the budgeted profit and loss account; and second, to know what amount to put on the balance sheet stock account for unsold units. The carrying cost of the unsold units is computed on the **ending finished goods stock budget**.

Larry Moore considered using variable costing in preparing Hampton Freeze's budget statements, but he decided to use absorption costing instead since the bank would very likely require that absorption costing be used. He also knew that it would be easy to convert the absorption costing financial statements to a variable costing basis later. At this point, the primary concern was to determine what financing, if any, would be required in the year 2000 and then to arrange for that financing from the bank.

The unit product cost computations are shown in Schedule 6. For Hampton Freeze, the absorption costing unit product cost is £13 per case of ice lollies – consisting of £3 of direct materials, £6 of direct labour and £4 of manufacturing overhead. For convenience, the manufacturing overhead is applied to units of product on the basis of direct labour-hours. The budgeted carrying cost of the expected ending stock is £39,000.

8 LEARNING OBJECTIVE

The selling and administrative expense budget

The **selling and administrative expense budget** lists the budgeted expenses for areas other than manufacturing. In large organizations, this budget would be a compilation of many smaller, individual budgets submitted by department heads and other persons responsible for selling and administrative expenses. For example, the marketing manager in a large organization would submit a budget detailing the advertising expenses for each budget period.

Schedule 7 contains the selling and administrative expense budget for Hampton Freeze.

The cash budget

As illustrated in Exhibit 11.2, the cash budget pulls together much of the data developed in the preceding steps. It is a good idea to restudy Exhibit 11.2 to get the big picture firmly in mind before moving on.

The cash budget is composed of four major sections:

1. The receipts section.
2. The disbursements section.
3. The cash excess or deficiency section.
4. The financing section.

The receipts section consists of a listing of all of the cash inflows, except for financing, expected during the budget period. Generally, the major source of receipts will be from sales.

The disbursements section consists of all cash payments that are planned for the budget period. These payments will include raw materials purchases, direct labour payments, manufacturing overhead costs, and so on, as contained in their respective budgets. In addition, other cash disbursements such as equipment purchases, dividends and other cash withdrawals by owners are listed. For instance, we see in Schedule 8 that management plans to spend £130,000 during the budget period on equipment purchases and £32,000 on dividends to the owners. This is additional information that does not appear on any of the earlier schedules.

The cash excess or deficiency section is computed as follows:

Cash balance, beginning	XXXX
Add receipts	XXXX
Total cash available before financing	XXXX
Less disbursements	XXXX
Excess (deficiency) of cash available over disbursements	XXXX

Schedule 3

Microsoft Excel - Book1

File Edit View Insert Format Tools Data Window Help

Hampton Freeze Ltd.
Direct materials budget
for the year ended 31 December 2000

	Quarter 1	2	3	4	Year
Required production (units) (Schedule 2)	14,000	32,000	36,000	19,000	101,000
Raw materials needed per unit (kilos)	× 15	× 15	× 15	× 15	× 10
Production needs (kilos)	210,000	480,000	540,000	285,000	1,515,000
Add desired stock of raw materials (kilos)*	48,000	54,000	28,500	22,500	22,500
Total needs (kilos)	258,000	534,000	568,500	307,500	1,537,500
Less beginning stock of raw materials (kilos)	21,000	48,000	54,000	28,500	21,000
Raw materials to be purchased (kilos)	237,000	486,000	514,500	279,000	1,516,500
Cost of raw materials to be purchased at £0.20 per kilo	£47,400	£97,200	£102,900	£55,800	£303,300

Schedule of expected cash disbursements for materials

	1	2	3	4	Year
Creditors, beginning balance†	£25,800				£25,800
First quarter purchases (£47,000 × 50%, 50%)‡	23,700	£23,700			47,400
Second-quarter purchases (£97,200 × 50%, 50%)		48,600	£48,600		97,200
Third-quarter purchases (£102,900 × 50%, 50%)			51,450	£51,450	102,900
Fourth-quarter purchases (£55,800 × 50%)§				27,900	27,900
Total cash disbursements	£49,500	£72,300	£100,500	£79,350	£301,200

Ready

*10% of the next quarter's production needs. For example, the second-quarter production needs are 480,000 kilos. Therefore, the desired ending inventory for the first quarter would be 10% × 480,000 kilos – 48,000 kilos. The ending stock of 22,500 kilos for the fourth quarter is estimated.

‡Cash payments for last year's fourth-quarter material purchases. See the beginning-of-year balance sheet on page 450.

‡Cash payments for purchases are as follows: 50% paid for in the quarter of purchase, and the remaining 50% paid for in the following quarter.

§Unpaid fourth-quarter purchases appear as creditors on the company's end-of-year balance sheet (see Schedule 10 on page 453).

Schedule 4

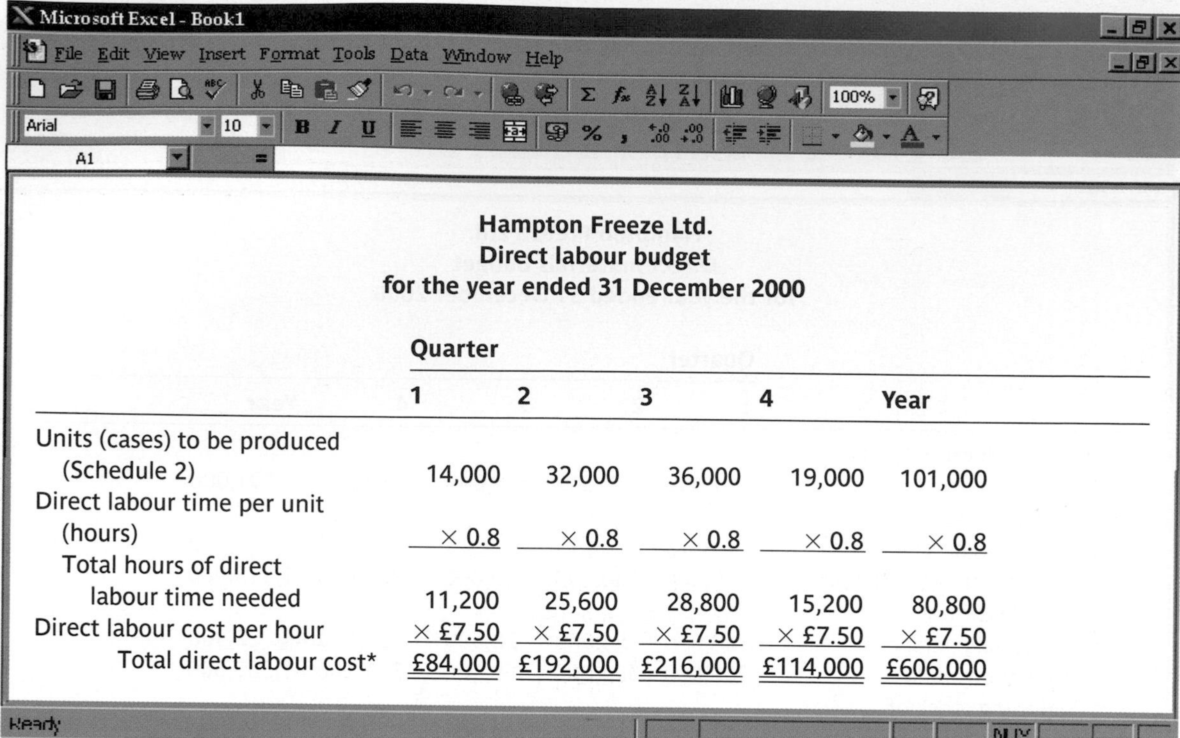

Microsoft Excel - Book1

File Edit View Insert Format Tools Data Window Help

Hampton Freeze Ltd.
Direct labour budget
for the year ended 31 December 2000

	Quarter 1	2	3	4	Year
Units (cases) to be produced (Schedule 2)	14,000	32,000	36,000	19,000	101,000
Direct labour time per unit (hours)	× 0.8	× 0.8	× 0.8	× 0.8	× 0.8
Total hours of direct labour time needed	11,200	25,600	28,800	15,200	80,800
Direct labour cost per hour	× £7.50	× £7.50	× £7.50	× £7.50	× £7.50
Total direct labour cost*	£84,000	£192,000	£216,000	£114,000	£606,000

Ready

*This schedule assumes that the direct labour workforce will be fully adjusted to the workload (i.e., 'total hours of direct labour time needed') each quarter.

Schedule 5

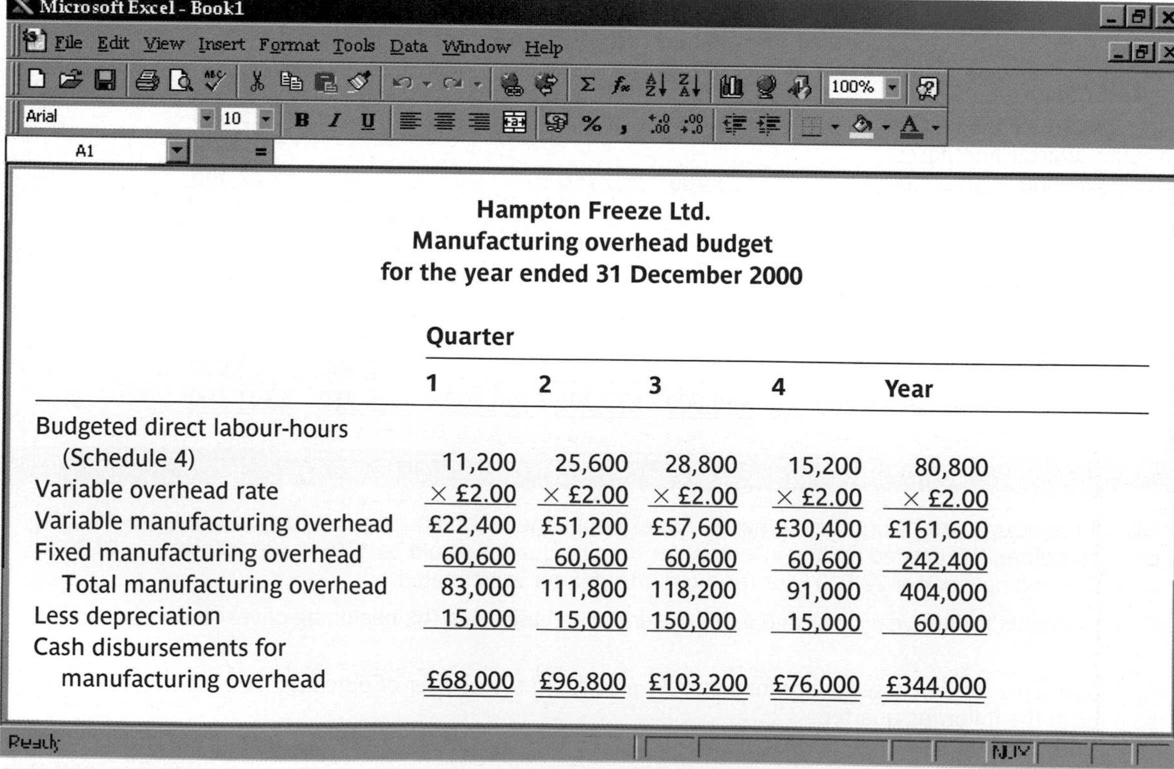

Microsoft Excel - Book1

File Edit View Insert Format Tools Data Window Help

Hampton Freeze Ltd.
Manufacturing overhead budget
for the year ended 31 December 2000

	Quarter 1	2	3	4	Year
Budgeted direct labour-hours (Schedule 4)	11,200	25,600	28,800	15,200	80,800
Variable overhead rate	× £2.00	× £2.00	× £2.00	× £2.00	× £2.00
Variable manufacturing overhead	£22,400	£51,200	£57,600	£30,400	£161,600
Fixed manufacturing overhead	60,600	60,600	60,600	60,600	242,400
Total manufacturing overhead	83,000	111,800	118,200	91,000	404,000
Less depreciation	15,000	15,000	150,000	15,000	60,000
Cash disbursements for manufacturing overhead	£68,000	£96,800	£103,200	£76,000	£344,000

Ready

£404,000 ÷ 80,000 hours = £5.

Schedule 6

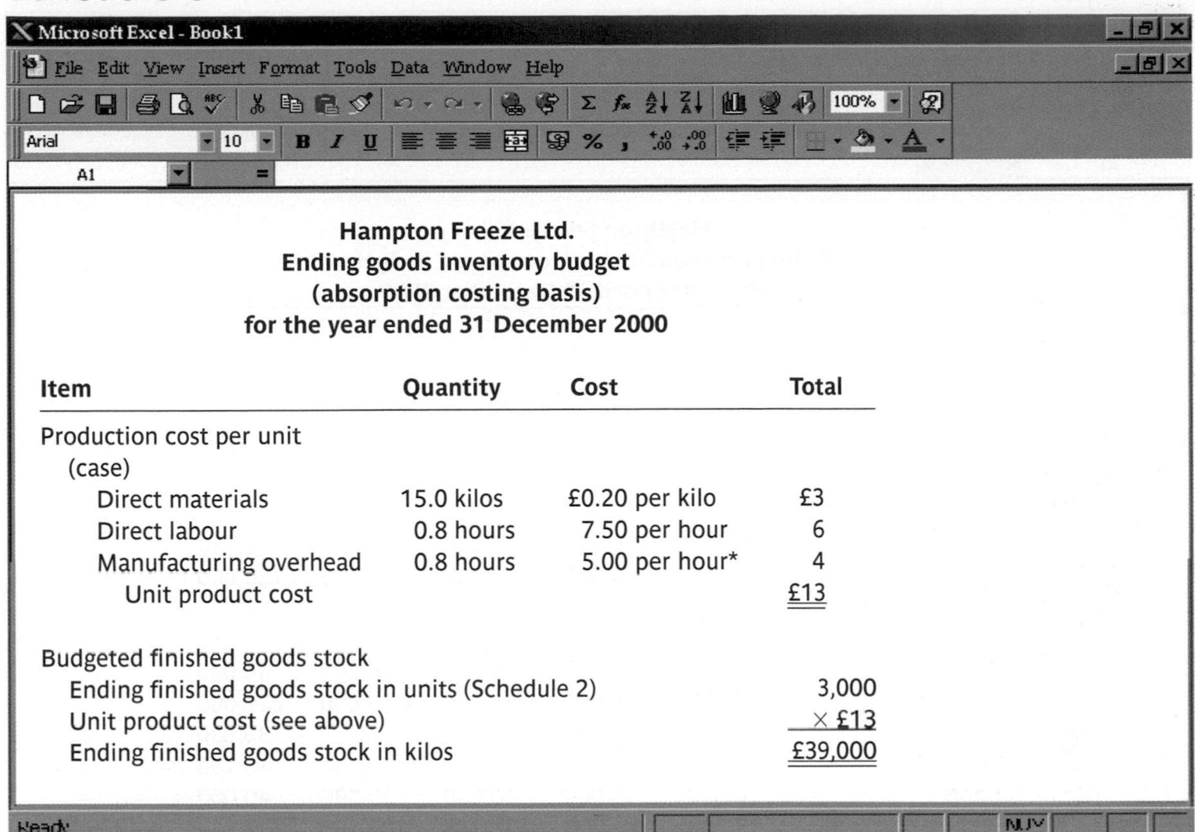

Hampton Freeze Ltd.
Ending goods inventory budget
(absorption costing basis)
for the year ended 31 December 2000

Item	**Quantity**	**Cost**	**Total**
Production cost per unit (case)			
Direct materials	15.0 kilos	£0.20 per kilo	£3
Direct labour	0.8 hours	7.50 per hour	6
Manufacturing overhead	0.8 hours	5.00 per hour*	4
Unit product cost			£13
Budgeted finished goods stock			
Ending finished goods stock in units (Schedule 2)			3,000
Unit product cost (see above)			× £13
Ending finished goods stock in kilos			£39,000

*£404,000 ÷ 80,000 hours = £5.

If there is a cash deficiency during any budget period, the company will need to borrow funds. If there is a cash excess during any budget period, funds borrowed in previous periods can be repaid or the idle funds can be placed in short-term or other investments.

The financing section provides a detailed account of the borrowings and repayments projected to take place during the budget period. It also includes a detail of interest payments that will be due on money borrowed. Generally speaking, the cash budget should be broken down into time periods that are as short as feasible. There can be considerable fluctuations in cash balances that would be hidden by looking at a longer time period. While a monthly cash budget is most common, many firms budget cash on a weekly or even daily basis. Larry Moore has prepared a quarterly cash budget for Hampton Freeze that can be further refined as necessary. This budget appears in Schedule 8. Larry has assumed in the budget that an open line of credit can be arranged with the bank that can be used as needed to bolster the company's cash position. He has also assumed that the interest on any loans taken out with this line of credit would carry an interest rate of 10% per year. For simplicity, Larry has assumed that all borrowings and repayments are in round £1,000 amounts and that all borrowing occurs at the beginning of a quarter and all repayments are made at the end of a quarter.

In the case of Hampton Freeze, all loans have been repaid by year-end. If all loans are not repaid and a budgeted profit and loss account or balance sheet is being prepared, then interest must be accrued on the unpaid loans. This interest will *not* appear on the cash budget (since it has not yet been paid), but it will appear as part of interest expense on the budgeted profit and loss account and as a liability on the budgeted balance sheet.

10 LEARNING OBJECTIVE

The budgeted profit and loss account

A budgeted profit and loss account can be prepared from the data developed in Schedules 1–8. The budgeted profit and loss account is one of the key schedules in the budget process. It shows the company's planned profit for the upcoming budget period, and it stands as a benchmark against which subsequent company performance can be measured. Schedule 9 contains the budgeted profit and loss account for Hampton Freeze.

Schedule 7

Microsoft Excel - Book1

File Edit View Insert Format Tools Data Window Help

Hampton Freeze Ltd.
Selling and administrative expense budget
for the year ended 31 December 2000

	Quarter 1	2	3	4	Year
Budgeted sales in units (cases)	10,000	30,000	40,000	20,000	100,000
Variable selling and administrative expense per unit*	× £1.80	× £1.80	× £1.80	× £1.80	× £1.80
Variable expense	£18,000	£54,000	£72,000	£36,000	£180,000
Fixed selling and administrative expenses:					
Advertising	20,000	20,000	20,000	20,000	80,000
Executive salaries	55,000	55,000	55,000	55,000	220,000
Insurance		1,900	37,750		39,650
Property taxes				18,150	18,150
Depreciation	10,000	10,000	10,000	10,000	40,000
Total	85,000	86,900	122,750	103,150	397,800
Total selling and administrative expenses	103,000	140,900	194,750	139,150	577,800
Less depreciation	10,000	10,000	10,000	10,000	40,000
Cash disbursements for selling and administrative expenses	£93,000	£130,900	£184,750	£129,150	£537,800

Ready

*Commissions, clerical and shipping.

The budgeted balance sheet

The budgeted balance sheet is developed by beginning with the current balance sheet and adjusting it for the data contained in the other budgets. Hampton Freeze's budgeted balance sheet is presented in Schedule 10. Some of the data on the budgeted balance sheet have been taken from the company's end-of-year balance sheet for 1999 which appears below:

Hampton Freeze Ltd
Balance sheet
31 December 1999

Assets		
Current assets:		
Cash	£42,500	
Debtors	90,000	
Raw materials stock (21,000 kilos)	4,200	
Finished goods stock (2,000 cases)	26,000	
Total current assets		£162,700
Plant and equipment:		
Land	80,000	

Buildings and equipment	700,000	
Accumulated depreciation	(292,000)	
Plant and equipment, net		488,000
Total assets		£650,700
Liabilities and shareholders' equity		
Current liabilities:		
Creditors (raw materials)		£25,800
Shareholders' equity:		
Common stock, no par	£175,000	
Retained earnings	449,900	
Total shareholders' equity		624,900
Total liabilities and shareholders' equity		£650,700

Schedule 8

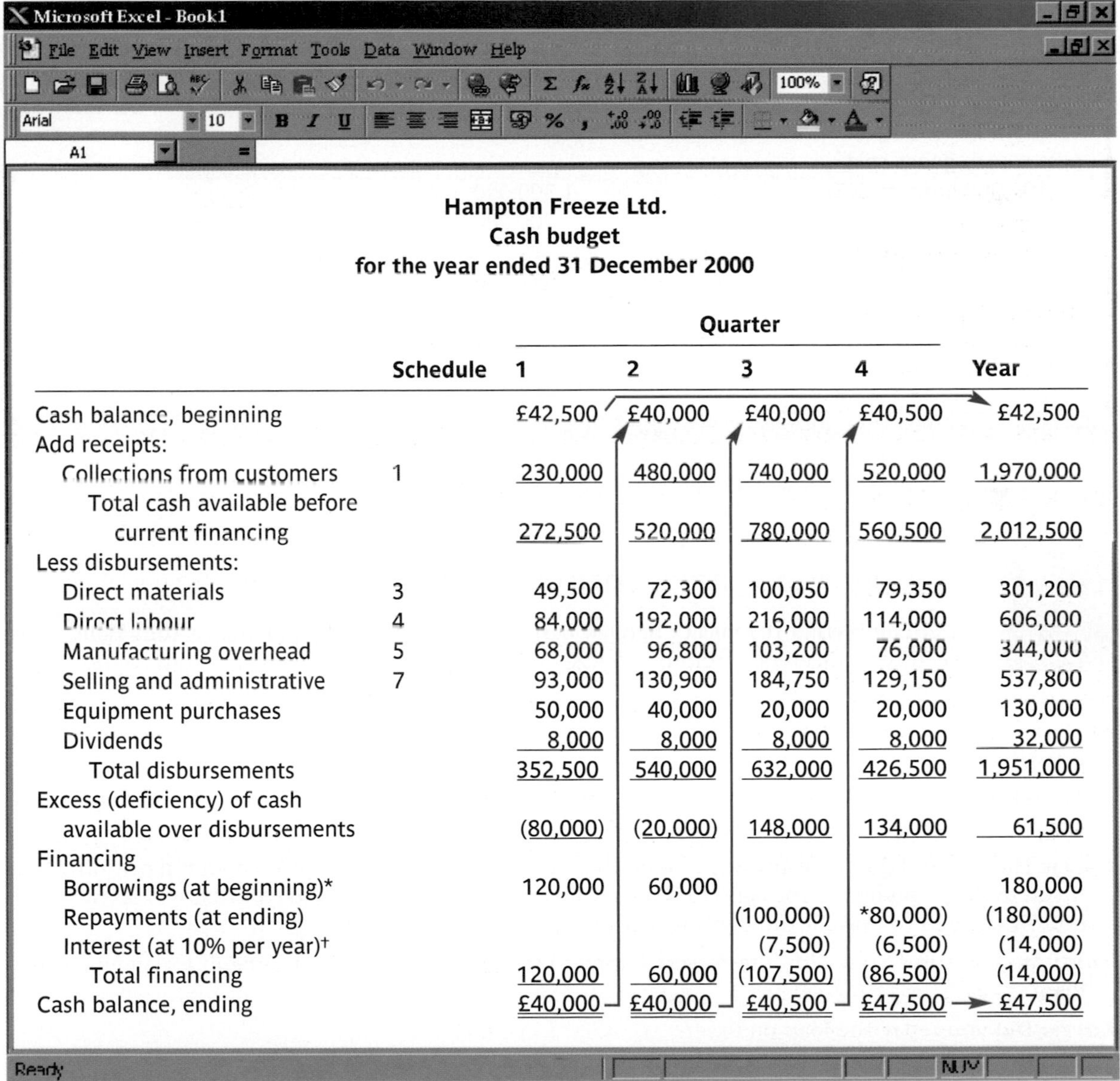

Hampton Freeze Ltd.
Cash budget
for the year ended 31 December 2000

	Schedule	Quarter 1	2	3	4	Year
Cash balance, beginning		£42,500	£40,000	£40,000	£40,500	£42,500
Add receipts:						
Collections from customers	1	230,000	480,000	740,000	520,000	1,970,000
Total cash available before current financing		272,500	520,000	780,000	560,500	2,012,500
Less disbursements:						
Direct materials	3	49,500	72,300	100,050	79,350	301,200
Direct labour	4	84,000	192,000	216,000	114,000	606,000
Manufacturing overhead	5	68,000	96,800	103,200	76,000	344,000
Selling and administrative	7	93,000	130,900	184,750	129,150	537,800
Equipment purchases		50,000	40,000	20,000	20,000	130,000
Dividends		8,000	8,000	8,000	8,000	32,000
Total disbursements		352,500	540,000	632,000	426,500	1,951,000
Excess (deficiency) of cash available over disbursements		(80,000)	(20,000)	148,000	134,000	61,500
Financing						
Borrowings (at beginning)*		120,000	60,000			180,000
Repayments (at ending)				(100,000)	*80,000)	(180,000)
Interest (at 10% per year)†				(7,500)	(6,500)	(14,000)
Total financing		120,000	60,000	(107,500)	(86,500)	(14,000)
Cash balance, ending		£40,000	£40,000	£40,500	£47,500	£47,500

*The company requires a minimum cash balance of £40,000. Therefore, borrowing must be sufficient to cover the cash deficiency of £80,000 in quarter 1 and to provide for the minimum cash balance of £40,000. All borrowings and all repayments of principal are in round £1,000 amounts.

†The interest payments relate only to the principal being repaid at the time it is repaid. For example, the interest in quarter 3 relates only to the interest due on the £100,000 principal being repaid from quarter 1 borrowing £100,00 × ½ × 10% – £7,500. The interest paid in quarter 4 is computed as follows:

£20,000 × 10% × 1 year	£2,000
£60,000 × 10% × ½	4,500
Total interest paid	£6,500

Schedule 9

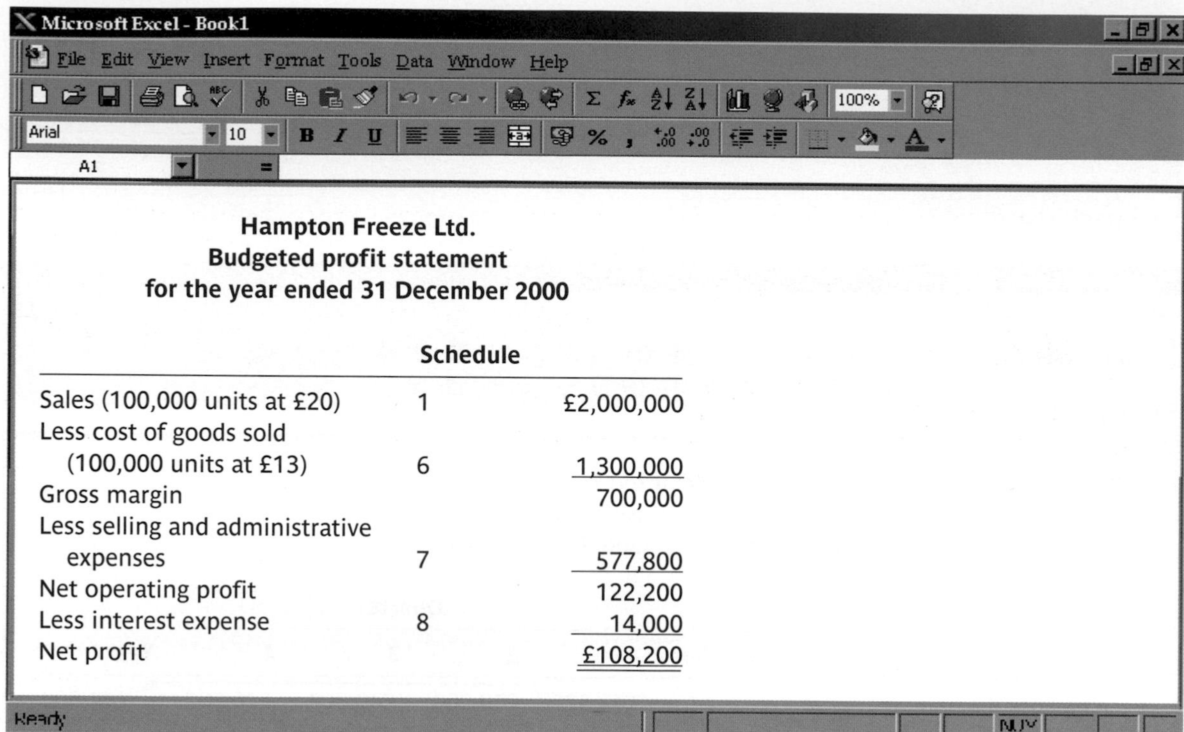

Hampton Freeze Ltd.
Budgeted profit statement
for the year ended 31 December 2000

	Schedule	
Sales (100,000 units at £20)	1	£2,000,000
Less cost of goods sold (100,000 units at £13)	6	1,300,000
Gross margin		700,000
Less selling and administrative expenses	7	577,800
Net operating profit		122,200
Less interest expense	8	14,000
Net profit		£108,200

Management accounting in action: the wrap-up

After completing the master budget, Larry Moore took the documents to Tom Wills, chief executive officer of Hampton Freeze, for his review. The following conversation took place:

Larry: Here's the budget. Overall, the net income is excellent, and the net cash flow for the entire year is positive.

Tom: Yes, but I see on this cash budget that we have the same problem with negative cash flows in the first and second quarters that we had last year.

Larry: That's true. I don't see any way around that problem. However, there is no doubt in my mind that if you take this budget to the bank today, they'll approve an open line of credit that will allow you to borrow enough to make it through the first two quarters without any problem.

Tom: Are you sure? They didn't seem very happy to see me last year when I came in for an emergency loan.

Larry: Did you repay the loan on time?

Tom: Sure.

Larry: I don't see any problem. You won't be asking for an emergency loan this time. The bank will have plenty of warning. And with this budget, you have a solid plan that shows when and how you are going to pay off the loan. Trust me, they'll go for it.

Tom: Fantastic! It would sure make life a lot easier this year.

Schedule 10

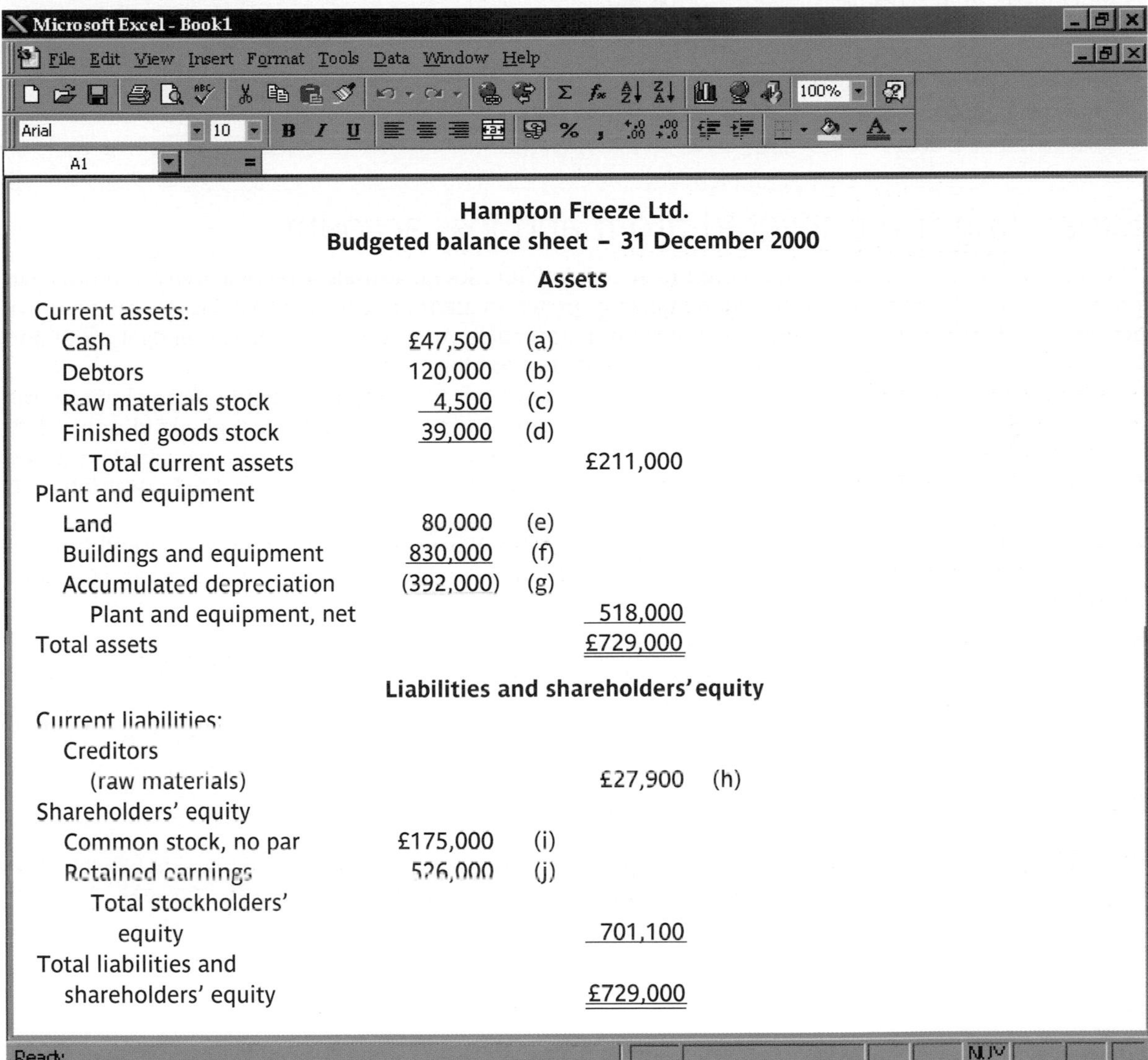

Hampton Freeze Ltd.
Budgeted balance sheet – 31 December 2000

Assets				
Current assets:				
Cash	£47,500	(a)		
Debtors	120,000	(b)		
Raw materials stock	4,500	(c)		
Finished goods stock	39,000	(d)		
Total current assets			£211,000	
Plant and equipment				
Land	80,000	(e)		
Buildings and equipment	830,000	(f)		
Accumulated depreciation	(392,000)	(g)		
Plant and equipment, net			518,000	
Total assets			£729,000	
Liabilities and shareholders' equity				
Current liabilities:				
Creditors (raw materials)			£27,900	(h)
Shareholders' equity				
Common stock, no par	£175,000	(i)		
Retained earnings	526,000	(j)		
Total stockholders' equity			701,100	
Total liabilities and shareholders' equity			£729,000	

Explanation of 31 December 2000 balance sheet figures:

a The ending cash balance, as projected by the cash budget in Schedule 8.

b 30% of fourth-quarter sales, from Schedule 1 (£400,000 × 30% = £120,000).

c From Schedule 3, the ending raw materials stock will be 22,500 kilos. This material costs £0.20 per kilo. Therefore, the ending stock in kilos, will be 22,500 kilos × £0.20 = £4,500.

d From Schedule 6.

e From the 31 December 1999 balance sheet (no change).

f The 31 December 1999 balance sheet indicated a balance of £700,000. During 2000, £130,000 additional equipment will be purchased (see Schedule 8), bringing the 31 December 2000 balance to £830,000.

g The 31 December 1999 balance sheet indicated a balance sheet of £292,000. During 2000, £100,000 of depreciation will be taken (£60,000 on Schedule 5 and £40,000 on Schedule 7), bringing the 31 December 2000 balance to £392,000.

h One-half of the fourth-quarter raw materials purchases, from Schedule 3.

i From the 31 December 1999 balance sheet (no change).

j 31 December 1999 balance	£449,000
Add net profit, from Schedule 9	108,200
	558,100
Deduct dividends paid, from Schedule 8	32,000
31 December 2000 balance	£526,100

Expanding the budgeted profit and loss account

The master budget profit and loss account in Schedule 9 focuses on a single level of activity and has been prepared using absorption costing. Some managers prefer an alternative format that focuses on a *range of* activity and that is prepared using the contribution approach. An example of a master budget profit and loss account using this alternative format is presented in Exhibit 11.3.

A statement such as that in Exhibit 11.3 is flexible, since it is geared to more than one level of activity. If, for example, the company planned to sell 2,000 units during a period but actually sold only 1,900 units, then the budget figures at the 1,900-unit level would be used to compare against actual costs and revenues. Other columns could be added to the budget as needed by simply applying the budget formulas provided.

In short, a master budget profit and loss account in this expanded format can be very useful in planning and controlling operations. The concepts underlying a flexible approach to budgeting are discussed in later chapters.

Microsoft Excel - Book1

File Edit View Insert Format Tools Data Window Help

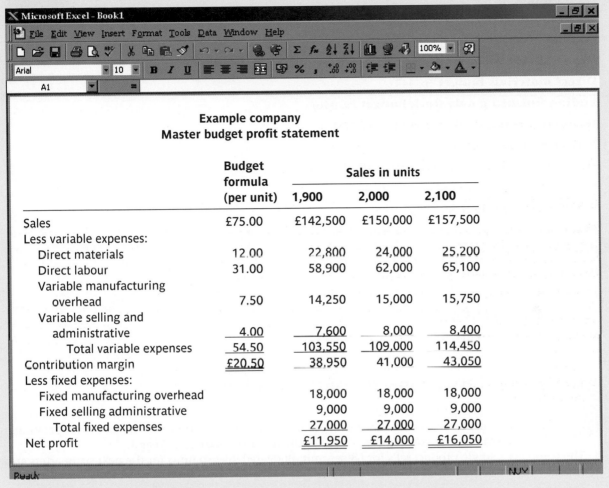

Example company
Master budget profit statement

	Budget formula (per unit)	Sales in units		
		1,900	2,000	2,100
Sales	£75.00	£142,500	£150,000	£157,500
Less variable expenses:				
Direct materials	12.00	22,800	24,000	25,200
Direct labour	31.00	58,900	62,000	65,100
Variable manufacturing overhead	7.50	14,250	15,000	15,750
Variable selling and administrative	4.00	7,600	8,000	8,400
Total variable expenses	54.50	103,550	109,000	114,450
Contribution margin	£20.50	38,950	41,000	43,050
Less fixed expenses:				
Fixed manufacturing overhead		18,000	18,000	18,000
Fixed selling administrative		9,000	9,000	9,000
Total fixed expenses		27,000	27,000	27,000
Net profit		£11,950	£14,000	£16,050

Ready

Exhibit 11.3 Flexible budget profit statement

Summary

- Our purpose has been to present an overview of the budgeting process and to show how the various operating budgets relate to each other.
- We have seen how the sales budget forms the foundation for profit planning. Once the sales budget has been set, the production budget and the selling and administrative budget can be prepared since they depend on how many units are to be sold.
- The production budget determines how many units are to be produced, so after it is prepared, the various manufacturing cost budgets can be prepared. All of these various budgets feed into the cash budget and the budgeted profit and loss account and balance sheet.
- There are many connections between these various parts of the master budget. For example, the schedule of expected cash collections, which is completed in connection with the sales budget, provides data for both the cash budget and the budgeted balance sheet.
- The material in this chapter is just an introduction to budgeting and profit planning. In the next two chapters, we will see how budgets are used to control day-to-day operations and how they are used in performance evaluation. We will look at how a firm performs through a comparison of actual performance with budgeted performance.

Key terms for review

Budget (p. 434).
Budget committee (p. 438).
Cash budget (p. 439).
Continuous or perpetual budget (p. 436).
Control (p. 434).
Direct labour budget (p. 445).
Direct materials budget (p. 444).
Ending finished goods stock budget (p. 446).
Manufacturing overhead budget (p. 445).
Master budget (p. 441).
Material requirements planning (MRP) (p. 444).
Merchandise purchases budget (p. 443).
Participative budget (p. 437).
Planning (p. 434).
Production budget (p. 442).
Responsibility accounting (p. 436).
Sales budget (p. 439).
Self-imposed budget (p. 437).
Selling and administrative expense budget (p. 446).

Review problem: budget schedules

Mylar Company manufactures and sells a product that has seasonal variations in demand, with peak sales coming in the third quarter. The following information concerns operations for Year 2 – the coming year – and for the first two quarters of Year 3:

1 The company's single product sells for £8 per unit. Budgeted sales in units for the next six quarters are as follows:

	Year 2 quarter				Year 3 quarter	
	1	2	3	4	1	2
Budgeted sales in units	40,000	60,000	100,000	50,000	70,000	80,000

2 Sales are collected in the following pattern: 75% in the quarter the sales are made, and the remaining 25% in the following quarter. On 1 January, Year 2, the company's balance sheet showed £65,000 in debtors, all of which will be collected in the first quarter of the year. Bad debts are negligible and can be ignored.

3 The company desires an ending stock of finished units on hand at the end of each quarter equal to 30% of the budgeted sales for the next quarter. This requirement was met on 31 December, Year 1, in that the company had 12,000 units on hand to start the new year.

4 Five kilos of raw materials are required to complete one unit of product. The company requires an ending stock of raw materials on hand at the end of each quarter equal to 10% of the production needs of the following quarter. This requirement was met on 31 December, Year 1, in that the company had 23,000 kilos worth of raw materials on hand to start the new year.

5 The raw material costs £0.80 per kilo. Purchases of raw material are paid for in the following pattern: 60% paid in the quarter the purchases are made, and the remaining 40% paid in the following quarter.

On 1 January, Year 2, the company's balance sheet showed £81,500 in creditors for raw material purchases, all of which will be paid for in the first quarter of the year.

Required

Prepare the following budgets and schedules for the year, showing both quarterly and total figures:

1 A sales budget and a schedule of expected cash collections.

2 A production budget.

3 A direct materials purchases budget and a schedule of expected cash payments for material purchases.

Solution to review problem: budget schedules

1 The sales budget is prepared as follows:

	Year 2 quarter				
	1	2	3	4	Year
Budgeted sales in units	40,000	60,000	100,000	50,000	250,000
Selling price per unit	× £8	× £8	× £8	× £8	× £8
Total sales	£320,000	£480,000	£800,000	£400,000	£2,000,000

Based on the budgeted sales above, the schedule of expected cash collections is prepared as follows:

	Year 2 quarter				
	1	2	3	4	Year
Debtors, beginning balance	£65,000				£65,000
First-quarter sales (£320,000 × 75%, 25%)	240,000	£80,000			320,000
Second-quarter sales (£480,000 × 75%, 25%)		360,000	£120,000		480,000
Third-quarter sales (£800,000 × 75%, 25%)			600,000	£200,000	800,000
Fourth-quarter sales (£400,000 × 75%)				300,000	300,000
Total cash collections	£305,000	£440,000	£720,000	£500,000	£1,965,000

2 Based on the sales budget in units, the production budget is prepared as follows:

	Year 2 quarter					Year 3 quarter	
	1	2	3	4	Year	1	2
Budgeted sales (units)	40,000	60,000	100,000	50,000	250,000	70,000	80,000
Add desired ending stock of finished goods*	18,000	30,000	15,000	21,000†	21,000	24,000	
Total needs	58,000	90,000	115,000	71,000	271,000	94,000	
Less beginning stock of finished goods	12,000	18,000	30,000	15,000	12,000	21,000	
Required production	46,000	72,000	85,000	56,000	259,000	73,000	

*30% of the following quarter's budgeted sales in units.

†30% of the budgeted Year 3 first-quarter sales.

3 Based on the production budget figures, raw materials will need to be purchased as follows during the year:

	Year 2 quarter					Year 3 quarter
	1	2	3	4	Year 2	1
Required production (units)	46,000	72,000	85,000	56,000	259,000	73,000
Raw materials needed per unit (kilos)	× 5	× 5	× 5	× 5	× 5	× 5
Production needs (kilos)	230,000	360,000	425,000	280,000	1,295,000	365,000
Add desired ending stock of raw materials kilos*	36,000	42,500	28,000	36,500†	36,500	
Total needs (kilos)	266,000	402,500	453,000	316,500	1,331,500	
Less beginning stock of raw materials (kilos)	23,000	36,000	42,500	28,000	23,000	
Raw materials to be purchased (kilos)	243,000	366,500	410,500	288,500	1,308,500	

*10% of the following quarter's production needs in kilos.

†10% of the Year 3 first-quarter production needs in kilos.

Based on the raw material purchases above, expected cash payments are computed as follows:

	Year 2 quarter				
	1	2	3	4	Year 2
Cost of raw materials to be purchased at £0.80 per kilo	£194,400	£293,200	£328,400	£ 230,800	£1,046,800
Creditors, beginning balance	£81,500	£81,500			
First-quarter purchases (£194,400 × 60%, 40%)	116,640	£77,760			194,400
Second-quarter purchases (£293,200 × 60%, 40%)		175,920	£117,280		293,200
Third-quarter purchases (£328,400 × 60%, 40%)			197,040	£131,360	328,400
Fourth-quarter purchases (£230,800 × 60%)				138,480	138,480
Total cash disbursements	£198,140	£253,680	£314,320	£269,840	£1,035,980

Questions

11–1 What is a budget? What is budgetary control?

11–2 Discuss some of the major benefits to be gained from budgeting.

11–3 What is meant by the term responsibility accounting?

11–4 What is a master budget? Briefly describe its contents.

11–5 Why is the sales forecast the starting point in budgeting?

11–6 'As a practical matter, planning and control mean exactly the same thing.' Do you agree? Explain.

11–7 Describe the flow of budget data in an organization. Who are the participants in the budgeting process, and how do they participate?

11–8 What is a self-imposed budget? What are the major advantages of self-imposed budgets? What caution must be exercised in their use?

11–9 How can budgeting assist a firm in its employment policies?

11–10 'The principal purpose of the cash budget is to see how much cash the company will have in the bank at the end of the year.' Do you agree? Explain.

11–11 How does zero-based budgeting differ from traditional budgeting?

Exercises

E11–1 Time allowed: 20 minutes

Silver Company makes a product that is very popular as a Mother's Day gift. Thus, peak sales occur in May of each year. These peak sales are shown in the company's sales budget for the second quarter given below:

	April	May	June	Total
Budgeted sales	£300,000	£500,000	£200,000	£1,000,000

From past experience, the company has learned that 20% of a month's sales are collected in the month of sale, that another 70% is collected in the month following sale, and that the remaining 10% is collected in the second month following sale. Bad debts are negligible and can be ignored. February sales totalled £230,000 and March sales totalled £260,000.

Required

1 Prepare a schedule of expected cash collections from sales, by month and in total, for the second quarter.

2 Assume that the company will prepare a budgeted balance sheet as of 30 June. Compute the debtors as of that date.

E11–2 Time allowed: 10 minutes

Down Under Products Ltd of Australia has budgeted sales of its popular boomerang for the next four months as follows:

	Sales in units
April	50,000
May	75,000
June	90,000
July	80,000

The company is now in the process of preparing a production budget for the second quarter. Past experience has shown that end-of-month stock levels must equal 10% of the following month's sales. The stock at the end of March was 5,000 units.

Required

Prepare a production budget for the second quarter. In your budget, show the number of units to be produced each month and for the quarter in total.

E11–3 Time allowed: 15 minutes

Three grams of musk oil are required for each bottle of Mink Caress, a very popular perfume made by a small company in western Siberia. The cost of the musk oil is 150 roubles per gram. (Siberia is located in Russia, whose currency is the rouble.) Budgeted production of Mink Caress is given below by quarters for Year 2 and for the first quarter of Year 3.

	Year 2 quarter				Year 3 quarter
	First	Second	Third	Fourth	First
Budgeted production, in bottles	60,000	90,000	150,000	100,000	70,000

Musk oil has become so popular as a perfume base that it has become necessary to carry large inventories as a precaution against stock-outs. For this reason, the stock of musk oil at the end of a quarter must be equal to 20% of the following quarter's production needs. Some 36,000 grams of musk oil will be on hand to start the first quarter of Year 2.

Required

Prepare a materials purchases budget for musk oil, by quarter and in total, for Year 2. At the bottom of your budget, show the amount of purchases in roubles for each quarter and for the year in total.

E11–4 Time allowed: 25 minutes

You have been asked to prepare a December cash budget for Ashton Company, a distributor of exercise equipment. The following information is available about the company's operations:

1 The cash balance on 1 December will be £40,000.

2 Actual sales for October and November and expected sales for December are as follows:

	October	November	December
Cash sales	£65,000	£70,000	£83,000
Sales on account	400,000	525,000	600,000

Sales on account are collected over a three-month period in the following ratio: 20% collected in the month of sale, 60% collected in the month following sale, and 18% collected in the second month following sale. The remaining 2% is uncollectable.

3 Purchases of stock will total £280,000 for December and 30% of a month's stock purchases are paid during the month of purchase. The accounts payable remaining from November's stock purchases total £161,000, all of which will be paid in December.

4 Selling and administrative expenses are budgeted at £420,000 for December. Of this amount, £50,000 is for depreciation.

5 A new web server for the Marketing Department costing £76,000 will be purchased for cash during December, and dividends totalling £9,000 will be paid during the month.

6 The company must maintain a minimum cash balance of £20,000. An open line of credit is available from the company's bank to bolster the cash position as needed.

Required

1 Prepare a schedule of expected cash collections for December.

2 Prepare a schedule of expected cash disbursements during December to suppliers for materials for stock purchases.

3 Prepare a cash budget for December. Indicate in the financing section any borrowing that will be needed during the month.

PROBLEMS

Problems

P11–5 Budgeting and costing Time allowed: 40 minutes
P Ltd manufactures a specialist photocopier. Increased competition from a new manufacturer has meant that P Ltd has been operating below full capacity for the last two years.

The *budgeted information* for the last two years was as follows:

	Year 1	Year 2
Annual sales demand (units)	70	70
Annual production (units)	70	70
Selling price (for each photocopier)	£50,000	£50,000
Direct costs (for each photocopier)	£20,000	£20,000
Variable production overheads (for each photocopier)	£11,000	£12,000
Fixed production overheads	£525,000	£525,000

Actual results for the last two years were as follows:

	Year 1	Year 2
Annual sales demand (units)	30	60
Annual production (units)	40	60
Selling price (for each photocopier)	£50,000	£50,000
Direct costs (for each photocopier)	£20,000	£20,000
Variable production overheads (for each photocopier)	£11,000	£12,000
Fixed production overheads	£500,000	£530,000

There was no opening stock at the beginning of Year 1.

Required

1 Prepare the actual profit and loss statements for each of the two years using:
   (a) absorption costing;
   (b) marginal costing. *(14 marks)*

2 Calculate the budgeted break-even point in units and the budgeted margin of safety as a percentage of sales for Year 1 and then again for Year 2. *(6 marks)*

3 Explain how the change in cost structure (as detailed in the budgeted information) has affected the values you have calculated in your answer to Question 1. *(5 marks)*

(Total = 25 marks)

CIMA Management Accounting Fundamentals, November 2001

P11–6 Production and purchases budgets Time allowed: 40 minutes
Pearl Products Limited of Shenzhen, China, manufactures and distributes toys throughout South East Asia. Three cubic centimetres (cc) of solvent H300 are required to manufacture each unit of Supermix, one of the company's products. The company is now planning raw materials needs for the third quarter, the quarter in which peak sales of Supermix occur. To keep production and sales moving smoothly, the company has the following stock requirements:

1 The finished goods stock on hand at the end of each month must be equal to 3,000 units of Supermix plus 20% of the next month's sales. The finished goods stock on 30 June is budgeted to be 10,000 units.

2 The raw materials stock on hand at the end of each month must be equal to one-half of the following month's production needs for raw materials. The raw materials stock on 30 June is budgeted to be 54,000 cc of solvent H300.

3 The company maintains no work in progress stocks.

A sales budget for Supermix for the last six months of the year follows.

	Budgeted sales in units
July	35,000
August	40,000
September	50,000
October	30,000
November	20,000
December	10,000

Required

1 Prepare a production budget for Supermix for the months July–October.

2 Examine the production budget that you prepared in Question 1 above. Why will the company produce more units than it sells in July and August, and fewer units than it sells in September and October?

3 Prepare a budget showing the quantity of solvent H300 to be purchased for July, August and September, and for the quarter in total.

P11–7 Evaluating a company's budget procedures Time allowed: 30 minutes

Springfield Corporation operates on a calendar-year basis. It begins the annual budgeting process in late August, when the managing director establishes targets for the total pound sales and net income before taxes for the next year.

The sales target is given to the Marketing Department, where the marketing manager formulates a sales budget by product line in both units and pounds. From this budget, sales quotas by product line in units and pounds are established for each of the corporation's sales districts.

The marketing manager also estimates the cost of the marketing activities required to support the target sales volume and prepares a tentative marketing expense budget.

The operations manager uses the sales and profit targets, the sales budget by product line, and the tentative marketing expense budget to determine the pound amounts that can be devoted to manufacturing and corporate office expense. The operations manager prepares the budget for corporate expenses, and then forwards to the Production Department the product-line sales budget in units and the total pound amount that can be devoted to manufacturing.

The production manager meets with the factory managers to develop a manufacturing plan that will produce the required units when needed within the cost constraints set by the operations manager. The budgeting process usually comes to a halt at this point because the Production Department does not consider the financial resources allocated to be adequate.

When this standstill occurs, the director of finance, the operations manager, the marketing manager and the production manager meet to determine the final budgets for each of the areas. This normally results in a modest increase in the total amount available for manufacturing costs, while the marketing expense and corporate office expense budgets are cut. The total sales and profit figures proposed by the managing director are seldom changed. Although the participants are seldom pleased with the compromise, these budgets are final. Each executive then develops a new detailed budget for the operations in his or her area.

None of the areas has achieved its budget in recent years. Sales often run below the target. When budgeted sales are not achieved, each area is expected to cut costs so that the managing director's profit target can still be met. However, the profit target is seldom met because costs are not cut enough. In fact, costs often run above the original budget in all functional areas. The managing director is disturbed that Springfield has not been able to meet the sales and profit targets. He hired a consultant with considerable experience with companies in Springfield's industry. The consultant reviewed the budgets for the past four years. He concluded that the product-line sales budgets were reasonable and that the cost and expense budgets were adequate for the budgeted sales and production levels.

Required

1 Discuss how the budgeting process as employed by Springfield Corporation contributes to the failure to achieve the managing director's sales and profit targets.

2 Suggest how Springfield Corporation's budgeting process could be revised to correct the problem.

3 Should the functional areas be expected to cut their costs when sales volume falls below budget? Explain your answer.

(CMA, adapted)

P11–8 Budgeting, learning curve Time allowed: 45 minutes

PR plc is a marketing consultancy company that offers three different types of service. It is preparing the budget for the year ending 31 December 2002. The details for each type of service are as follows:

	Service A	Service B	Service C
Estimated demand (number of services)	150	800	200
	£ per service	£ per service	£ per service
Fee income	2,500	2,000	3,200
Consultant (£300 per day)	900	750	1,500
Specialists' report	400	200	500
Variable overhead	200	160	300

It has been estimated that the consultants will be able to work for a total of 2,400 days during the year. PR plc estimates that the fixed overhead for the year will be £600,000.

Required

1 (a) Prepare calculations that show how many of each type of service should be undertaken in order for PR plc to maximize its profits.

(b) Prepare a statement that shows the budgeted profit for the year 2002 based on your answer to (a) above. *(8 marks)*

2 The Managing Director has received the service schedule and budget statement that you prepared but would like it to be amended to reflect the following additional information:

- There is a 90% learning curve operating on the consultants' times for service C. The budgeted consultants' time of 5 days per service C was based on the time taken for the very first service C performed. By the end of December 2001, a total of 100 type C services will have been performed.
- The consultants' salaries will rise by 8% with effect from 1 January 2002.
- Overhead costs will rise by 5% with effect from 1 January 2002.

(a) Calculate the revised optimal service plan and prepare the associated profit statement for the year ending 31 December 2002. *Note:* The formula for a 90% learning curve is $y = ax - 0.1520$. *(12 marks)*

(b) Prepare a report to the Managing Director that explains the implications of the learning curve effect on service C for PR plc. *(10 marks)*

(Total = 30 marks)

CIMA Management Accounting – Performance Management, May 2001

P11–9 Master budget preparation Time allowed: 60 minutes

Minden Company is a wholesale distributor of premium European chocolates. The company's balance sheet as of 30 April is given below:

Minden Company
Balance sheet
30 April

Assets	
Cash	£9,000
Debtors, customers	54,000
Stock	30,000
Buildings and equipment, net of depreciation	207,000
Total assets	£300,000
Liabilities and shareholders' equity	
Creditors, suppliers	£63,000
Note payable	14,500
Capital stock, no par	180,000
Retained earnings	42,500
Total liabilities and shareholders' equity	£300,000

The company is in the process of preparing budget data for May. A number of budget items have already been prepared, as stated below:

1 Sales are budgeted at £200,000 for May. Of these sales, £60,000 will be for cash; the remainder will be credit sales. One-half of a month's credit sales are collected in the month the sales are made, and the remainder is collected in the following month. All of the 30 April receivables will be collected in May.

2 Purchases of stock are expected to total £120,000 during May. These purchases will all be on account: 40% of all purchases are paid for in the month of purchase; the remainder is paid in the following month. All of the 30 April creditors to suppliers will be paid during May.

3 The 31 May stock balance is budgeted at £40,000.

4 Operating expenses for May are budgeted at £72,000, exclusive of depreciation. These expenses will be paid in cash. Depreciation is budgeted at £2,000 for the month.

5 The note payable on the 30 April balance sheet will be paid during May, with £100 in interest. (All of the interest relates to May.)

6 New refrigerating equipment costing £6,500 will be purchased for cash during May.

7 During May, the company will borrow £20,000 from its bank by giving a new note payable to the bank for that amount. The new note will be due in one year.

Required

1 Prepare a cash budget for May. Support your budget with schedules showing budgeted cash receipts from sales and budgeted cash payments for stock purchases.

2 Prepare a budgeted profit and loss account for May. Use the traditional profit and loss account format.

3 Prepare a budgeted balance sheet as of 31 May.

P11–10 Time allowed: 50 minutes

The management team at MN Limited is considering the budgets it prepared for the year ending 31 December 2003. It has now been revealed that in June 2003 the company will be able to purchase only 10,000 litres of material Q (all other resources will be fully available). In the light of this new information, the management team wants to revise its plans for June to ensure that profits are maximized for that month.

MN Limited can produce three products from the same labour and main raw material Q, though different amounts are required for each product. The standard resource requirements, costs and selling prices, and the customer demand for delivery in June (including those orders already accepted) for each of its finished products are as follows:

	Product V	Product S	Product T
Resources per unit:			
Material Q	10 litres	8 litres	5 litres
Direct labour	8 hours	9 hours	6 hours
Selling prices and costs:	**£ per unit**	**£ per unit**	**£ per unit**
Selling price	145.00	134.00	99.00
Material Q	25.00	20.00	12.50
Other materials	10.00	4.00	8.50
Direct labour	40.00	45.00	30.00
Overheads:			
Variable	10.00	11.25	7.50
Fixed*	24.00	30.00	12.00
	109.00	110.25	70.50
Customer demand	1,100 units	950 units	1,450 units

* Based on budgeted costs of £95,000 per month.

MN Limited has already accepted customer orders for delivery in June 2003 as follows:

Product V	34 units
Product S	75 units
Product T	97 units

The management team has decided that these customer orders must be satisfied as the financial and non-financial penalties that would otherwise arise are very significant.

Given the shortage of material Q, the management team has now set the following stock levels for June:

	Opening stock	Closing stock
Material Q*	621 litres	225 litres
Product V	20 units	10 units
Product S	33 units	25 units
Product T	46 units	20 units

* This would mean that 10.396 litres of material Q would be available during the period.

Required

1 Prepare a production budget for June 2003 that clearly shows the number of units of each product that should be produced to maximize the profits of MN Limited for June 2003. *(12 marks)*

2 Using your answer to requirement 1 above, calculate the number of units of each product that will be sold in June 2003. *(3 marks)*

3 Using your answer to requirement 2 above, calculate the profit for June 2003 using:

(a) marginal costing;

(b) absorption costing. *(5 marks)*

The Managing Director of MN Limited is concerned about the effect on cashflow caused by the scarcity of material Q during June 2003. She is aware that monthly profit and cashflow are often unequal and has heard that marginal costing profits more closely resemble cashflow than do absorption costing profits.

4 **(a)** Explain briefly why there is a difference between cashflow and profit.

(b) Briefly discuss the assertion that marginal costing profits are a better indicator of cashflow than absorption costing profits. *(5 marks)*

(Total = 25 marks)

CIMA Management Accounting – Performance Management, May 2003

Cases

C11–11 Evaluating a company's budget procedures Time allowed: 45 minutes

Tom Emory and Jim Morris strolled back to their plant from the administrative offices of Ferguson & Son Mfg Company. Tom is manager of the machine shop in the company's factory; Jim is manager of the equipment maintenance department.

The men had just attended the monthly performance evaluation meeting for plant department heads. These meetings had been held on the third Tuesday of each month since Robert Ferguson, the owner's son, had become plant manager a year earlier.

As they were walking, Tom Emory spoke: 'Wow, I hate those meetings! I never know whether my department's accounting reports will show good or bad performance. I'm beginning to expect the worst. If the accountants say I saved the company a pound, I'm called "Sir", but if I spend even a little too much – boy, do I get in trouble. I don't know if I can hold on until I retire.' Tom had just been given the worst evaluation he had ever received in his long career with Ferguson & Son. He was the most respected of the experienced machinists in the company. He had been with Ferguson & Son for many years and was promoted to supervisor of the machine shop when the company expanded and moved to its present location. The owner (James Ferguson) had often stated that the company's success was due to the high quality of the work of machinists like Tom. As supervisor, Tom stressed the importance of craftsmanship and told his workers that he wanted no sloppy work coming from his department.

When Robert Ferguson became the plant manager, he directed that monthly performance comparisons be made between actual and budgeted costs for each department. The departmental budgets were intended to encourage the supervisors to reduce inefficiencies and to seek cost reduction opportunities. The company controller was instructed to have his staff 'tighten' the budget slightly whenever a department attained its budget in a given month; this was done to reinforce the plant manager's desire to reduce costs. The young plant manager often stressed the importance of continued progress toward attaining the budget; he also made it known that he kept a file of these performance reports for future reference when he succeeded his father.

Tom Emory's conversation with Jim Morris continued as follows:

Emory: I really don't understand. We've worked so hard to get up to budget, and the minute we make it they tighten the budget on us. We can't work any faster and still maintain quality. I think my men are ready to quit trying. Besides, those reports don't tell the whole story. We always seem to be interrupting the big jobs for all those small rush orders. All that set-up and machine adjustment time is killing us. And quite frankly, Jim, you were no help. When our hydraulic press broke down last month, your people were nowhere to be found. We had to take it apart ourselves and got stuck with all that idle time.

Morris: I'm sorry about that, Tom, but you know my department has had trouble making budget, too. We were running well behind at the time of that problem, and if we'd spent a day on that old machine, we would never have made it up. Instead we made the scheduled inspections of the forklift trucks because we knew we could do those in less than the budgeted time.

Emory: Well, Jim, at least you have some options. I'm locked into what the scheduling department assigns me and you know they're being harassed by sales for those special orders. Incidentally, why didn't your report show all the supplies you guys wasted last month when you were working in Bill's department?

Morris: We're not out of the woods on that deal yet. We charged the maximum we could to other work and haven't even reported some of it yet.

Emory: Well, I'm glad you have a way of getting out of the pressure. The accountants seem to know everything that's happening in my department, sometimes even before I do. I thought all that budget and accounting stuff was supposed to help, but it just gets me into trouble. It's all a big pain. I'm trying to put out quality work; they're trying to save pence.

Required

1 Identify the problems that appear to exist in Ferguson & Son Mfg Company's budgetary control system and explain how the problems are likely to reduce the effectiveness of the system.

2 Explain how Ferguson & Son Mfg Company's budgetary control system could be revised to improve its effectiveness.

(*CMA*, adapted)

C11–12 Cash budget for a growing company Time allowed: 75 minutes

CrossMan Corporation, a rapidly expanding crossbow distributor to retail outlets, is in the process of formulating plans for next year. Joan Caldwell, director of marketing, has completed her sales budget and is confident that sales estimates will be met or exceeded. The following budgeted sales figures show the growth expected and will provide the planning basis for other corporate departments.

Budgeted sales		Budgeted sales	
January	£1,800,000	July	£3,000,000
February	2,000,000	August	3,000,000
March	1,800,000	September	3,200,000
April	2,200,000	October	3,200,000
May	2,500,000	November	3,000,000
June	2,800,000	December	3,400,000

George Brownell, assistant chief accountant, has been given the responsibility for formulating the cash budget, a critical element during a period of rapid expansion. The following information provided by operating managers will be used in preparing the cash budget.

1 CrossMan has experienced an excellent record in debtors collection and expects this trend to continue. Sixty per cent of billings are collected in the month after the sale and 40% in the second month after the sale. Uncollectable accounts are negligible and will not be considered in this analysis.

2 The purchase of the crossbows is CrossMan's largest expenditure; the cost of these items equals 50% of sales. Sixty per cent of the crossbows are received one month prior to sale and 40% are received during the month of sale.

3 Prior experience shows that 80% of creditors are paid by CrossMan one month after receipt of the purchased crossbows, and the remaining 20% are paid the second month after receipt.

4 Hourly wages, including fringe benefits, depend on sales volume and are equal to 20% of the current month's sales. These wages are paid in the month incurred.

5 General and administrative expenses are budgeted to be £2,640,000 for the year. The composition of these expenses is given below. All of these expenses are incurred evenly throughout the year except the property taxes. Property taxes are paid in four equal instalments in the last month of each quarter.

Salaries	£480,000
Promotion	660,000
Property taxes	240,000
Insurance	360,000
Utilities	300,000
Depreciation	600,000
Total	£2,640,000

6 Corporation tax payments are made by CrossMan in the first month of each quarter based on the profit for the prior quarter. CrossMan's tax rate is 40%. CrossMan's net profit for the first quarter is projected to be £612,000.

7 Equipment and warehouse facilities are being acquired to support the company's rapidly growing sales. Purchases of equipment and facilities are budgeted at £28,000 for April and £324,000 for May.

8 CrossMan has a corporate policy of maintaining an end-of-month cash balance of £100,000. Cash is borrowed or invested monthly, as needed, to maintain this balance. Interest expense on borrowed funds is budgeted at £8,000 for the second quarter, all of which will be paid during June.

9 CrossMan uses a calendar year reporting period.

Required

1 Prepare a cash budget for CrossMan Corporation by month and in total for the second quarter. Be sure that all receipts, disbursements and borrowing investing amounts are shown for each month. Ignore any interest income associated with amounts invested.

2 Discuss why cash budgeting is particularly important for a rapidly expanding company such as CrossMan Corporation.

(*CMA*, adapted)

C11–13 Master budget with supporting schedules Time allowed: 120 minutes or longer

You have just been hired as a new management trainee by Earrings Unlimited, a distributor of earrings to various retail outlets located in shopping centres across the country. In the past, the company has done very little in the way of budgeting and at certain times of the year has experienced a shortage of cash.

Since you are well trained in budgeting, you have decided to prepare comprehensive budgets for the upcoming second quarter in order to show management the benefits that can be gained from an integrated budgeting programme. To this end, you have worked with accounting and other areas to gather the information assembled below. The company sells many styles of earrings, but all are sold for the same price – £10 per pair. Actual sales of earrings for the last three months and budgeted sales for the next six months follow (in pairs of earrings)

January (actual)	20,000	June (budget)	50,000
February (actual)	26,000	July (budget)	30,000
March (actual)	40,000	August (budget)	28,000
April (budget)	65,000	September (budget)	25,000
May (budget)	100,000		

The concentration of sales before and during May is due to Mother's Day. Sufficient stock should be on hand at the end of each month to supply 40% of the earrings sold in the following month.

Suppliers are paid £4 for a pair of earrings. Half of a month's purchases is paid for in the month of purchase; the other half is paid for in the following month. All sales are on credit, with no discount, and are payable within 15 days. The company has found, however, that only 20% of a month's sales are collected in the month of sale. An additional 70% is collected in the following month, and the remaining 10% is collected in the second month following sale. Bad debts have been negligible.

Monthly operating expenses for the company are given below:

Variable:	
Sales commissions	4% of sales
Fixed:	
Advertising	£200,000
Rent	18,000
Salaries	106,000
Utilities	7,000
Insurance expired	3,000
Depreciation	14,000

Insurance is paid on an annual basis, in November of each year.

The company plans to purchase £16,000 in new equipment during May and £40,000 in new equipment during June; both purchases will be for cash. The company declares dividends of £15,000 each quarter, payable in the first month of the following quarter.

A listing of the company's ledger accounts as of 31 March is given below:

Assets	
Cash	£74,000
Debtors (£26,000 February sales; £320,000 March sales)	346,000
Stock	104,000
Prepaid insurance	21,000
Property and equipment (net)	950,000
Total assets	£1,495,000
Liabilities and shareholders' equity	
Creditors	£100,000
Dividends payable	15,000
Capital stock	800,000
Retained earnings	580,000
Total liabilities and shareholders' equity	£1,495,000

Part of the use of the budgeting programme will be to establish an ongoing line of credit at a local bank. Therefore, determine the borrowing that will be needed to maintain a minimum cash balance of £50,000. All borrowing will be done at the beginning of a month; any repayments will be made at the end of a month.

The annual interest rate will be 12%. Interest will be computed and paid at the end of each quarter on all loans outstanding during the quarter. Compute interest on whole months (1/12, 2/12, and so forth).

Required

Prepare a master budget for the three-month period ending 30 June. Include the following detailed budgets:

1 (a) A sales budget, by month and in total.
 (b) A schedule of expected cash collections from sales, by month and in total.
 (c) A merchandise purchases budget in units and in pounds. Show the budget by month and in total.
 (d) A schedule of expected cash disbursements for merchandise purchases, by month and in total.
2 A cash budget. Show the budget by month and in total.
3 A budgeted profit and loss account for the three-month period ending 30 June. Use the contribution approach.
4 A budgeted balance sheet as of 30 June.

Further reading

For a classic study on budgeting see Hofstede (1967). Although we will be considering critical and behavioural issues in Chapter 17, see Hopwood (1980).

Endnotes

1 Bates, Rizvi, Tewari, and Vardan (2001).
2 See Churchill (1984).
3 Carruth, McClendon and Ballard (1983).
4 Carruth *et al.* (1983), p. 91.
5 Morrow (1992), p. 91.

Chapter 12
Standard costs and variance analysis

Learning objectives

After studying Chapter 12, you should be able to:

1 Explain how direct materials standards and direct labour standards are set.

2 Compute the direct materials price and quantity variances and explain their significance

3 Compute the direct labour rate and efficiency variances and explain their significance

4 Compute the variable manufacturing overhead spending and efficiency variances

5 Understand the advantages of and the potential problems with using standard costs

6 (Appendix 12A) Prepare journal entries to record standard costs and variances

Concepts in Context

Industrie Natuzzi SpA, founded and run by Pasquale Natuzzi, produces handmade leather furniture for the world market in Santaeramo Del Colle in southern Italy. Natuzzi is export-oriented and has, for example, about 25% of the US leather furniture market. The company's furniture is handmade by craftsmen, each of whom has a computer terminal that is linked to a sophisticated computer network. The computer terminal provides precise instructions on how to accomplish a particular task in making a piece of furniture. And the computer keeps track of how quickly the craftsman completes the task. If the craftsman beats the standard time to complete the task, the computer adds a bonus to the craftsman's pay.

The company's computers know exactly how much thread, screws, foam, leather, labour, and so on, is required for every model. 'Should the price of Argentinian hides or German dyes rise one day, employees in Santaeramo enter the new prices into the computer, and the costs for all sofas with that leather and those colours are immediately recalculated. "Everything has to be clear for me," says Natuzzi. "Why this penny? Where is it going?"'[1]

In this chapter we begin our study of management control and performance measures. Quite often, these terms carry with them negative connotations – we may have a tendency to think of performance measurement as something to be feared. And indeed, performance measurements can be used in negative ways – to cast blame and to punish. However, that is not the way they should be used. As explained in the following quotation, performance measurement serves a vital function in both personal life and in organizations:

> Imagine someone engaging in a weight loss programme. A normal step in such programmes is to purchase some scales to be able to track one's progress: Is this programme working? Am I losing weight? A positive answer would be encouraging and would motivate me to keep up the effort, while a negative answer might lead me to reflect on the process: Am I working on the right diet and exercise programme? Am I doing everything I am supposed to? Suppose you don't want to set up a sophisticated measurement system and decide to forgo the scales. You would still have some idea of how well you are doing from simple methods such as clothes feeling looser, a belt that fastens at a different hole, or simply via observation in a mirror! Now, imagine trying to sustain a weight loss programme without any feedback on how well you are doing.
>
> In this example, availability of quantitative measures of performance can yield two types of benefits: First, performance feedback can help improve the 'production process' through a better understanding of what works and what doesn't. Second, feedback on performance can sustain motivation and effort, because it is encouraging and/or because it suggests that more effort is required for the goal to be met.[2]

In the same way, performance measurement can be helpful in an organization. It can provide feedback concerning what works and what does not work, and it can help motivate people to sustain their efforts.

Our study of performance measurement begins in this chapter with the lowest levels in the organization. We work our way up the organizational ladder in subsequent chapters. In this chapter we see how various measures are used to control operations and to evaluate performance. Even though we are starting with the lowest levels in the organization, keep in mind that the performance measures used should be derived from the organization's overall strategy.

Companies in highly competitive industries like Ryanair, Dell Computer, Shell Oil and Toyota[3] must be able to provide high-quality goods and services at low cost. If they do not, they will perish. Stated in the starkest terms, managers must obtain inputs such as raw materials and electricity at the lowest possible prices and must use them as effectively as possible – while maintaining or increasing the quality of the output. If inputs are purchased at prices that are too high or more input is used than is really necessary, higher costs will result.

How do managers control the prices that are paid for inputs and the quantities that are used? They could examine every transaction in detail, but this obviously would be an inefficient use of management time. For many companies, the answer to this control problem lies at least partially in standard costs.[4]

Standard costs – management by exception

A *standard* is a *benchmark* or *'norm'* for measuring performance. Standards are found everywhere. Your doctor evaluates your weight using standards that have been set for individuals of your age, height and gender. The food we eat in restaurants must be prepared under specified standards of cleanliness. The buildings we live in must conform to standards set in building codes. Standards are also used widely in management accounting where they relate to the *quantity* and *cost* of inputs used in manufacturing goods or providing services.

Managers – often assisted by engineers and accountants – set quantity and cost standards for each major input such as raw materials and labour time. *Quantity standards* indicate how much of an input should be used in manufacturing a unit of product or in providing a unit of service. *Cost (price) standards* indicate what the cost, or purchase price, of the input should be. Actual quantities and actual costs of inputs are compared to these standards. If either the quantity or the cost of inputs departs significantly from the standards, managers investigate the discrepancy. The purpose is to find the cause of the problem and then eliminate it so that it does not recur. This process is called **management by exception**.

In our daily lives, we operate in a management by exception mode most of the time. Consider what happens when you sit down in the driver's seat of your car. You put the key in the ignition, you turn the key, and your car starts. Your expectation (standard) that the car will start is met; you do not have to open the car bonnet and check the battery, the connecting cables, the fuel lines and so on. If you turn the key and the car does not start, then you have a discrepancy (variance). Your expectations are not met, and you need to investigate why. Note that even if the car starts after a second try, it would be wise to investigate anyway. The fact that the expectation was not met should be viewed as an opportunity to uncover the cause of the problem rather than as simply an annoyance. If the underlying cause is not discovered and corrected, the problem may recur and become much worse.

Who uses standard costs?

Manufacturing, service, food, and not-for-profit organizations all make use of standards to some extent; car service centres, for example, often set specific labour time standards for the completion of certain work tasks, such as installing a carburettor or doing a valve job, and then measure actual performance against these standards. Fastfood outlets such as McDonald's have exacting standards as to the quantity of meat going into a sandwich, as well as standards for the cost of the meat. In short, you are likely to run into standard costs in virtually any line of business that you enter.

Manufacturing companies often have highly developed standard costing systems in which standards relating to materials, labour and overhead are developed in detail for each separate product. These standards are listed on a **standard cost card** that provides the manager with a great deal of information concerning the inputs that are required to produce a unit and their costs. In the following section, we provide a detailed example of the setting of standard costs and the preparation of a standard cost card.

Setting standard costs

Setting price and quantity standards is more an art than a science. It requires the combined expertise of all persons who have responsibility over input prices and over the effective use of inputs. In a manufacturing setting, this might include accountants, purchasing managers, engineers, production supervisors, line managers and production workers. Past records of purchase prices and of input usage can be helpful in setting standards. However, the standards should be designed to encourage efficient *future* operations, not a repetition of past inefficient operations.

Ideal versus practical standards

Should standards be attainable all of the time, should they be attainable only part of the time, or should they be so tight that they become, in effect, 'the impossible dream'? Opinions among managers vary, but standards tend to fall into one of two categories – either ideal or practical.

Ideal standards are those that can be attained only under the best circumstances. They allow for no machine breakdowns or other work interruptions, and they call for a level of effort that can be attained only by the most skilled and efficient employees working at peak effort 100% of the time. Some managers feel that such standards have a motivational value. These managers argue that even though employees know they will rarely meet the standard, it is a constant reminder of the need for ever increasing efficiency and effort. Few firms use ideal standards. Most managers feel that ideal standards tend to discourage even the most diligent workers. Moreover, when ideal standards are used, variances from the standards have little meaning. Because of these ideal standards, large variances are normal and it is difficult to 'manage by exception'.

Practical standards are defined as standards that are 'tight but attainable'. They allow for normal machine downtime and employee rest periods, and they can be attained through reasonable, though highly efficient, efforts by the average worker. Variances from such a standard are very useful to management in that they represent deviations that fall outside of normal operating conditions and signal a need for management attention. Furthermore, practical standards can serve multiple purposes. In addition to signalling abnormal conditions, they can also be used in forecasting cash flows and in planning stocks. By contrast, ideal standards cannot be used in forecasting and planning; they do not allow for normal inefficiencies, and therefore they result in unrealistic planning and forecasting figures.

Throughout the remainder of this chapter, we will assume the use of practical rather than ideal standards.

Management accounting in action: the issue

The Colonial Pewter Company was organized a year ago. The company's only product at present is a reproduction of an eighteenth-century pewter bookend. The bookend is largely made by hand, using traditional metal-working tools. Consequently, the manufacturing process is labour intensive and requires a high level of skill.

Colonial Pewter has recently expanded its workforce to take advantage of unexpected demand for the bookends as gifts. The company started with a small cadre of experienced pewter workers but has had to hire less experienced workers as a result of the expansion. The managing director of the company, J.D. Wriston, has called a meeting to discuss production problems. Attending the meeting are Tom Kuchel, the production manager; Janet Warner, the purchasing manager; and Terry Sherman, the finance director.

JD: I've got a feeling that we aren't getting the production we should out of our new people.

Tom: Give us a chance. Some of the new people have been on board for less than a month.

Janet: Let me add that production seems to be wasting an awful lot of material – particularly pewter. That stuff is very expensive.

Tom: What about the shipment of defective pewter you bought a couple of months ago – the one with the iron contamination? That caused us major problems.

Janet: That's ancient history. How was I to know it was off-grade? Besides, it was a great deal.

JD: Calm down everybody. Let's get the facts before we start sinking our fangs into each other.

Tom: I agree. The more facts the better.

JD: Okay, Terry, it's your turn. Facts are the financial director's department.

Terry: I'm afraid I can't provide the answers off the top of my head, but it won't take me too long to set up a system that can routinely answer questions relating to worker productivity, material waste and input prices.

JD: How long is 'not too long'?

Terry: I will need all of your co-operation, but how about a week from today?

JD: That's okay with me. What about everyone else?

Tom: Sure.

Janet: Fine with me.

JD: Let's mark it on our calendars.

Setting direct materials standards

Terry Sherman's first task was to prepare price and quantity standards for the company's only significant raw material, pewter ingots. The **standard price per unit** for direct materials should reflect the final, delivered cost of the materials, net of any discounts taken. After consulting with purchasing manager Janet Warner, Terry prepared the following documentation for the standard price of a kilo of pewter in ingot form:

Purchase price, top-grade pewter ingots, in 40-kilo ingots	£3.60
Freight, by truck, from the supplier's warehouse	0.44
Receiving and handling	0.05
Less purchase discount	(0.09)
Standard price per kilo	£4.00

Notice that the *standard price* reflects a particular grade of material (top grade), purchased in particular lot sizes (40-kilo ingots), and delivered by a particular type of carrier (truck). Allowances have also been made for handling and discounts. If everything proceeds according to these expectations, the net standard price of a kilo of pewter should therefore be £4.00.

The **standard quantity per unit** for direct materials should reflect the amount of material going into each unit of finished product, as well as an allowance for unavoidable waste, spoilage and other normal inefficiencies. After consulting with the production manager, Tom Kuchel, Terry Sherman prepared the following documentation for the standard quantity of pewter going into a pair of bookends:

Material requirements as specified in the bill of materials for a pair of bookends, in kilos	2.7
Allowance for waste and spoilage, in kilos	0.2
Allowance for rejects, in kilos	0.1
Standard quantity per pair of bookends, in kilos	3.0

A **bill of materials** is a list that shows the type and quantity of each item of material going into a unit of finished product. It is a handy source for determining the basic material input per unit, but it should be adjusted for waste and other factors, as shown above, when determining the standard quantity per unit of product. 'Waste and spoilage' in the table above refers to materials that are wasted as a normal part of the production process or that spoil before they are used. 'Rejects' refers to the direct material contained in units that are defective and must be scrapped.

Although it is common to recognize allowances for waste, spoilage and rejects when setting standard costs, this practice is now coming into question. Those involved in *TQM (total quality management)* and similar management approaches argue that no amount of waste or defects should be tolerated (see Chapter 18). If allowances for waste, spoilage and rejects are built into the standard cost, the levels of those allowances should be periodically reviewed and reduced over time to reflect improved processes, better training and better equipment.

Once the price and quantity standards have been set, the standard cost of material per unit of finished product can be computed as follows:

3.0 kilos per unit × £4.00 per kilo = £12 per unit

This £12 cost figure will appear as one item on the standard cost card of the product.

Setting direct labour standards

Direct labour price and quantity standards are usually expressed in terms of a labour rate and labour-hours. The **standard rate per hour** for direct labour would include not only wages earned but also fringe benefits and other labour costs. Using last month's wage records and in consultation with the production manager, Terry determined the standard rate per hour at the Colonial Pewter Company as follows:

Basic wage rate per hour	£10
Employment taxes at 10% of the basic rate	1
Fringe benefits at 30% of the basic rate	3
Standard rate per direct labour-hour	£14

Many companies prepare a single standard rate for all employees in a department. This standard rate reflects the expected 'mix' of workers, even though the actual wage rates may vary somewhat from individual to individual due to differing skills or seniority. A single standard rate simplifies the use of standard costs and also permits the manager to monitor the use of employees within departments. More is said on this point a little later. According to the standard computed above, the direct labour rate for Colonial Pewter should average £14 per hour.

The standard direct labour time required to complete a unit of product (generally called the **standard hours per unit**) is perhaps the single most difficult standard to determine. One approach is to divide each operation performed on the product into elemental body movements (such as reaching, pushing, and turning over). Published tables of standard times for such movements are available. These times can be applied to the movements and then added together to determine the total standard time allowed per operation. Another approach is for an industrial engineer to do a time and motion study, actually clocking the time required for certain tasks. As stated earlier, the standard time should include allowances for coffee breaks, personal needs of employees, cleanup, and machine downtime. After consulting with the production manager, Terry prepared the following documentation for the standard hours per unit:

Basic labour time per unit, in hours	1.9
Allowance for breaks and personal needs	0.1
Allowance for cleanup and machine downtime	0.3
Allowance for rejects	0.2
Standard labour-hours per unit of product	2.5

Once the rate and time standards have been set, the standard labour cost per unit of product can be computed as follows:

2.5 hours per unit × £14 per hour = £35 per unit

This £35 cost figure appears along with direct materials as one item on the standard cost card of the product.

Setting variable manufacturing overhead standards

As with direct labour, the price and quantity standards for variable manufacturing overhead are generally expressed in terms of rate and hours. The rate represents *the variable portion of the predetermined overhead rate* discussed in Chapter 3; the hours represent whatever hours base is used to apply overhead to units of product (usually machine-hours or direct labour-hours, as we learned in Chapter 3). At Colonial Pewter, the variable portion of the predetermined overhead rate is £3 per direct labour-hour. Therefore, the standard variable manufacturing overhead cost per unit is computed as follows:

2.5 hours per unit × £3 per hour = £7.50 per unit

This £7.50 cost figure appears along with direct materials and direct labour as one item on the standard cost card in Exhibit 12.1. Observe that the **standard cost per unit** is computed by multiplying the standard quantity or hours by the standard price or rate.

Are standards the same as budgets?

Standards and *budgets* are very similar. The major distinction between the two terms is that a standard is a *unit* amount, whereas a budget is a *total* amount. The standard cost for materials at Colonial Pewter is £12 per pair of bookends. If 1,000 pairs of bookends are to be manufactured during a budgeting period, then the budgeted cost of materials would be £12,000. In effect, *a standard can be viewed as the budgeted cost for one unit of product.*

Input	(1) Standard quantity or hours	(2) Standard price or rate	(3) Standard cost (1) × (2)
Direct materials	3.0 kilos	£4.00	£12.00
Direct labour	2.5 hours	14.00	35.00
Variable manufacturing overhead	2.5 hours	3.00	7.50
Total standard cost per unit			£54.50

Exhibit 12.1 Standard cost card – variable production cost

A general model for variance analysis

An important reason for separating standards into two categories – price and quantity – is that different managers are usually responsible for buying and for using inputs and these two activities occur at different points in time. In the case of raw materials, for example, the purchasing manager is responsible for the price, and this responsibility is exercised at the time of purchase. In contrast, the production manager is responsible for the amount of the raw material used, and this responsibility is exercised when the materials are used in production, which may be many weeks or months after the purchase date. It is important, therefore, that we cleanly separate discrepancies due to deviations from price standards from those due to deviations from quantity standards. Differences between *standard* prices and *actual* prices and *standard* quantities and *actual* quantities are called **variances**. The act of computing and interpreting variances is called *variance analysis*.

Price and quantity variances

A general model for computing standard cost variances for variable costs is presented in Exhibit 12.2. This model isolates price variances from quantity variances and shows how each of these is computed.[5] We will be using this model throughout the chapter to compute variances in direct materials, direct labour and variable manufacturing overhead.

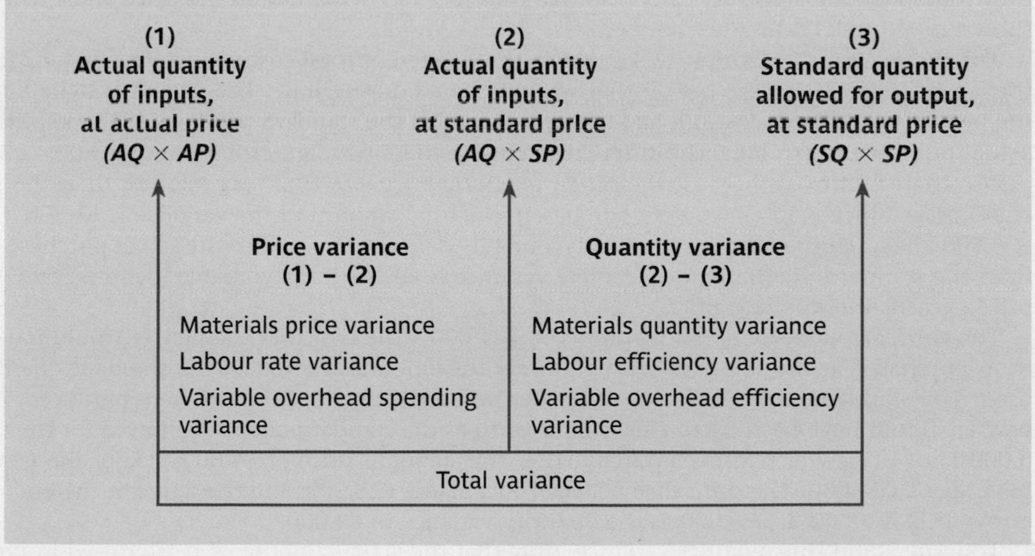

Exhibit 12.2 A general model for variance analysis – variable production costs

Three things should be noted from Exhibit 12.2. First, note that a price variance and a quantity variance can be computed for all three variable cost elements – direct materials, direct labour and variable manufacturing overhead – even though the variance is not called by the same name in all cases. For example, a price variance is called a *materials price variance* in the case of direct materials but a *labour rate variance* in the case of direct labour and an *overhead spending variance* in the case of variable manufacturing overhead.

Second, note that even though a price variance may be called by different names, it is computed in exactly the same way regardless of whether one is dealing with direct materials, direct labour or variable manufacturing overhead. The same is true with the quantity variance.

Third, note that *variance analysis* is actually a type of input–output analysis. The inputs represent the actual quantity of direct materials, direct labour and variable manufacturing overhead used; the output represents the good production of the period, expressed in terms of the *standard quantity (or the standard hours) allowed for the actual output* (see column 3 in Exhibit 12.2). By **standard quantity allowed** or **standard hours allowed**, we mean the amount of direct materials, direct labour or variable manufacturing overhead *that should have been used to* produce the actual output of the period. This could be more or could be less materials, labour or overhead than was *actually* used, depending on the efficiency or inefficiency of operations. The standard quantity allowed is computed by multiplying the actual output in units by the standard input allowed per unit.

With this general model as a foundation, we will now examine the price and quantity variances in more detail.

Using standard costs – direct materials variances

After determining Colonial Pewter Company's standard costs for direct materials, direct labour, and variable manufacturing overhead, Terry Sherman's next step was to compute the company's variances for June, the most recent month. As discussed in the preceding section, variances are computed by comparing standard costs to actual costs. To facilitate this comparison, Terry referred to the standard cost data contained in Exhibit 12.1. This exhibit shows that the standard cost of direct materials per unit of product is as follows:

3.0 kilos per unit × £4.00 per kilo = £12 per unit

Colonial Pewter's purchasing records for June showed that 6,500 kilos of pewter were purchased at a cost of £3.80 per kilo. This cost figure included freight and handling and was net of the quantity discount. All of the material purchased was used during June to manufacture 2,000 pairs of pewter bookends. Using these data and the standard costs from Exhibit 12.1, Terry computed the price and quantity variances shown in Exhibit 12.3.

The three arrows in Exhibit 12.3 point to three different total cost figures. The first, £24,700, refers to the actual total cost of the pewter that was purchased during June. The second, £26,000, refers to what the pewter would have cost if it had been purchased at the standard price of £4.00 a kilo rather than the actual price of £3.80 a kilo. The difference between these two figures, £1,300 (£26,000 – £24,700), is the price variance. It exists because the actual purchase price was £0.20 per kilo less than the standard purchase price. Since 6,500 kilos were purchased, the total amount of the variance is £1,300 (£0.20 per kilo × 6,500 kilos). This variance is labelled favourable (denoted by F), since the actual purchase price was less than the standard purchase price. A price variance is labelled unfavourable (denoted by U) if the actual price exceeds the standard price.

The third arrow in Exhibit 12.3 points to £24,000 – the cost that the pewter would have been had it been purchased at the standard price and only the amount allowed by the standard quantity had been used. The standards call for 3 kilos of pewter per unit. Since 2,000 units were produced, 6,000 kilos of pewter should have been used. This is referred to as the standard quantity allowed for the output. If this 6,000 kilos of pewter had been purchased at the standard price of £4.00 per kilo, the company would have spent £24,000. The difference between this figure, £24,000, and the figure at the end of the middle arrow in Exhibit 12.3, £26,000, is the quantity variance of £2,000.

To understand this quantity variance, note that the actual amount of pewter used in production was 6,500 kilos. However, the standard amount of pewter allowed for the actual output is only 6,000 kilos. Therefore, a total of 500 kilos too much pewter was used to produce the actual output. To express this in

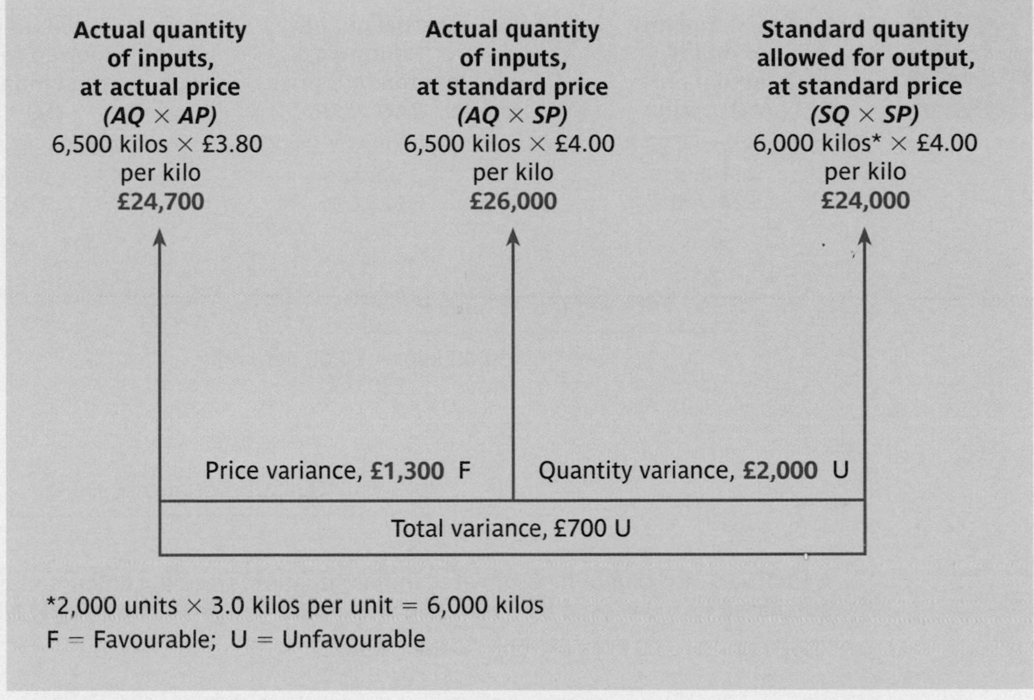

Exhibit 12.3 Variance analysis – direct materials

monetary terms, the 500 kilos is multiplied by the standard price of £4.00 per kilo to yield the quantity variance of £2,000. Why is the standard price, rather than the actual price, of the pewter used in this calculation? The production manager is ordinarily responsible for the quantity variance. If the actual price were used in the calculation of the quantity variance, the production manager would be held responsible for the efficiency or inefficiency of the purchasing manager. Apart from being unfair, fruitless arguments between the production manager and purchasing manager would occur every time the actual price of an input is above its standard price. To avoid these arguments, the standard price is used when computing the quantity variance.

The quantity variance in Exhibit 12.3 is labelled unfavourable (denoted by U). This is because more pewter was used to produce the actual output than is called for by the standard. A quantity variance is labelled unfavourable if the actual quantity exceeds the standard quantity and is labelled favourable if the actual quantity is less than the standard quantity.

The computations in Exhibit 12.3 reflect the fact that all of the material purchased during June was also used during June. How are the variances computed if a different amount of material is purchased than is used? To illustrate, assume that during June the company purchased 6,500 kilos of materials, as before, but that it used only 5,000 kilos of material during the month and produced only 1,600 units. In this case, the price variance and quantity variance would be as shown in Exhibit 12.4.

Most firms compute the materials price variance, for example, when materials *are purchased* rather than when the materials are placed into production. This permits earlier isolation of the variance, since materials may remain in storage for many months before being used in production. Isolating the price variance when materials are purchased also permits the company to carry its raw materials in the stock accounts at standard cost. This greatly simplifies assigning raw materials costs to work in progress when raw materials are later placed into production.[6]

Note from the exhibit that the price variance is computed on the entire amount of material purchased (6,500 kilos), as before, whereas the quantity variance is computed only on the portion of this material used in production during the month (5,000 kilos). A quantity variance on the 1,500 kilos of material that was purchased during the month but not used in production (6,500 kilos purchased − 5,000 kilos used = 1,500 kilos unused) will be computed in a future period when these materials are drawn out of

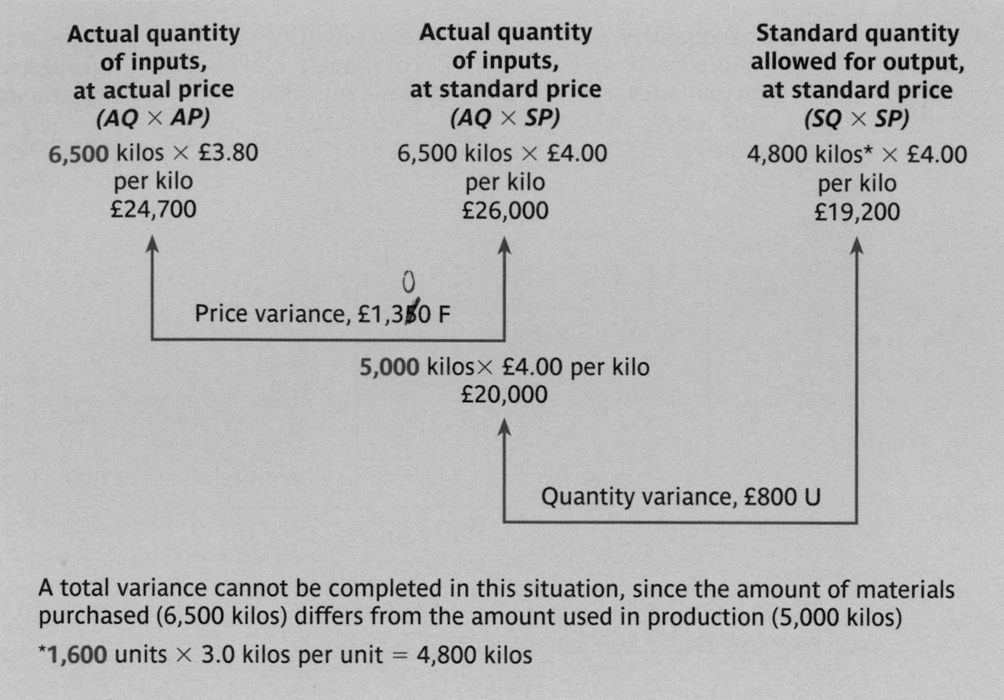

Exhibit 12.4 Variance analysis – direct materials, when the amount purchased differs from the amount used

stocks and used in production. The situation illustrated in Exhibit 12.4 is common for companies that purchase materials well in advance of use and store the materials in warehouses while awaiting the production process.

Materials price variance – a closer look

A **materials price variance** measures the difference between what is paid for a given quantity of materials and what should have been paid according to the standard that has been set. From Exhibit 12.3, this difference can be expressed by the following formula:

$$\text{Materials price variance} = (AQ \times AP) - (AQ \times SP)$$

Actual quantity — Actual price — Standard price

The formula can be factored into simpler form as follows:

$$\text{Materials price variance} = AQ(AP - SP)$$

Some managers prefer this simpler formula, since it permits variance computations to be made very quickly. Using the data from Exhibit 12.3 in this formula, we have the following:

6,500 kilos (£3.80 per kilo − £4.00 per kilo) = £1,300 F

Notice that the answer is the same as that yielded in Exhibit 12.3. If the company wanted to put these data into a performance report, the data might appear as follows:

Colonial Pewter Company
Performance report – purchasing department

Item purchased	(1) Quantity purchased	(2) Actual price	(3) Standard price	(4) Difference in price (2) − (3)	(5) Total price variance (1) × (4)	Explanation
Pewter	6,500 kilos	£3.80	£4.00	£0.20	£1,300 F	Bargained for an especially favourable price

F = Favourable; U = Unfavourable.

Isolation of variances

At what point should variances be isolated and brought to the attention of management? The answer is, the earlier the better. The sooner deviations from standard are brought to the attention of management, the sooner problems can be evaluated and corrected.

Once a performance report has been prepared, what does management do with the price variance data? The most significant variances should be viewed as 'red flags', calling attention to the fact that an exception has occurred that will require some explanation and perhaps follow-up effort. Normally, the performance report itself will contain some explanation of the reason for the variance, as shown above. In the case of Colonial Pewter Company, the purchasing manager, Janet Warner, said that the favourable price variance resulted from bargaining for an especially favourable price.

Responsibility for the variance

Who is responsible for the materials price variance? Generally speaking, the purchasing manager has control over the price paid for goods and is therefore responsible for any price variances. Many factors influence the prices paid for goods, including how many units are ordered in a lot, how the order is delivered, whether the order is a rush order, and the quality of materials purchased. A deviation in any of these factors from what was assumed when the standards were set can result in a price variance. For example, purchase of second-grade materials rather than top-grade materials may result in a favourable price variance, since the lower-grade materials would generally be less costly (but perhaps less suitable for production).

There may be times, however, when someone other than the purchasing manager is responsible for a materials price variance. Production may be scheduled in such a way, for example, that the purchasing manager must request delivery by airfreight, rather than by truck. In these cases, the production manager would bear responsibility for the resulting price variances.

A word of caution is in order. Variance analysis should not be used as an excuse to conduct witch hunts or as a means of beating line managers and workers over the head. The emphasis must be on the control function in the sense of *supporting* the line managers and *assisting* them in meeting the goals that they have participated in setting for the company. In short, the emphasis should be positive rather than negative. Excessive dwelling on what has already happened, particularly in terms of trying to find someone to blame, can be destructive to the functioning of an organization.

Materials quantity variance – a closer look

The **materials quantity variance** measures the difference between the quantity of materials used in production and the quantity that should have been used according to the standard that has been set. Although the variance is concerned with the physical usage of materials, it is generally stated in monetary terms, as shown in Exhibit 12.3. The formula for the materials quantity variance is as follows:

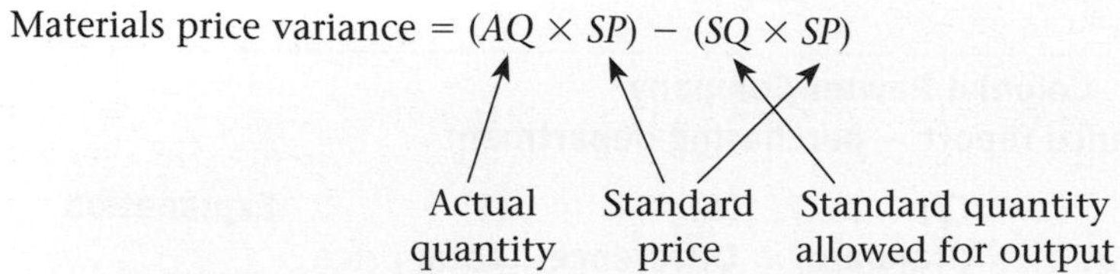

Materials price variance = (AQ × SP) − (SQ × SP)
Actual quantity
Standard price
Standard quantity allowed for output

Again, the formula can be factored into simpler terms:

Materials quantity variance = $SP\ (AQ - SQ)$

Using the data from Exhibit 12.3 in the formula, we have the following:

£4.00 per kilo (6,500 kilos − 6,000 kilos*) = £2,000 U

*2,000 units × 3.0 kilos per unit = 6,000 kilos.

The answer, of course, is the same as that yielded in Exhibit 12.3. The data might appear as follows if a formal performance report were prepared:

Colonial Pewter Company
Performance report – purchasing department

Type of materials	(1) Standard price	(2) Actual quantity	(3) Standard quantity allowed	(4) Difference in quantity (2) − (3)	(5) Total price variance (1) × (4)	Explanation
Pewter	£4.00	6,500 kilos	6,000 kilos	500 Kilos	£2,000 U	Second-grade materials unsuitable for production

F = Favourable; U = Unfavourable.

The materials quantity variance is best isolated at the time that materials are placed into production. Materials are drawn for the number of units to be produced, according to the standard bill of materials for each unit. Any additional materials are usually drawn with an excess materials requisition slip, which is different in colour from the normal requisition slips. This procedure calls attention to the excessive usage of materials *while production is still in process* and provides an opportunity for early control of any developing problem.

Excessive usage of materials can result from many factors, including faulty machines, inferior quality of materials, untrained workers and poor supervision. Generally speaking, it is the responsibility of the production department to see that material usage is kept in line with standards. There may be times, however, when the purchasing department may be responsible for an unfavourable materials quantity variance. If the purchasing department obtains inferior quality materials in an effort to economize on price, the materials may be unsuitable for use and may result in excessive waste. Thus, purchasing rather than production would be responsible for the quantity variance. At Colonial Pewter, the production manager, Tom Kuchel, said that second-grade materials were the cause of the unfavourable materials quantity variance for June.

Using standard costs – direct labour variances

Terry's next step in determining Colonial Pewter's variances for June was to compute the direct labour variances for the month. Recall from Exhibit 12.1 that the standard direct labour cost per unit of product is £35, computed as follows:

2.5 hours per unit × £14.00 per hour = £35 per unit

During June, the company paid its direct labour workers £74,250, including employment taxes and fringe benefits, for 5,400 hours of work. This was an average of £13.75 per hour. Using these data and the standard costs from Exhibit 12.1, Terry computed the direct labour rate and efficiency variances that appear in Exhibit 12.5.

Notice that the column headings in Exhibit 12.5 are the same as those used in the prior two exhibits, except that in Exhibit 12.5 the terms *hours* and *rate* are used in place of the terms *quantity* and *price*.

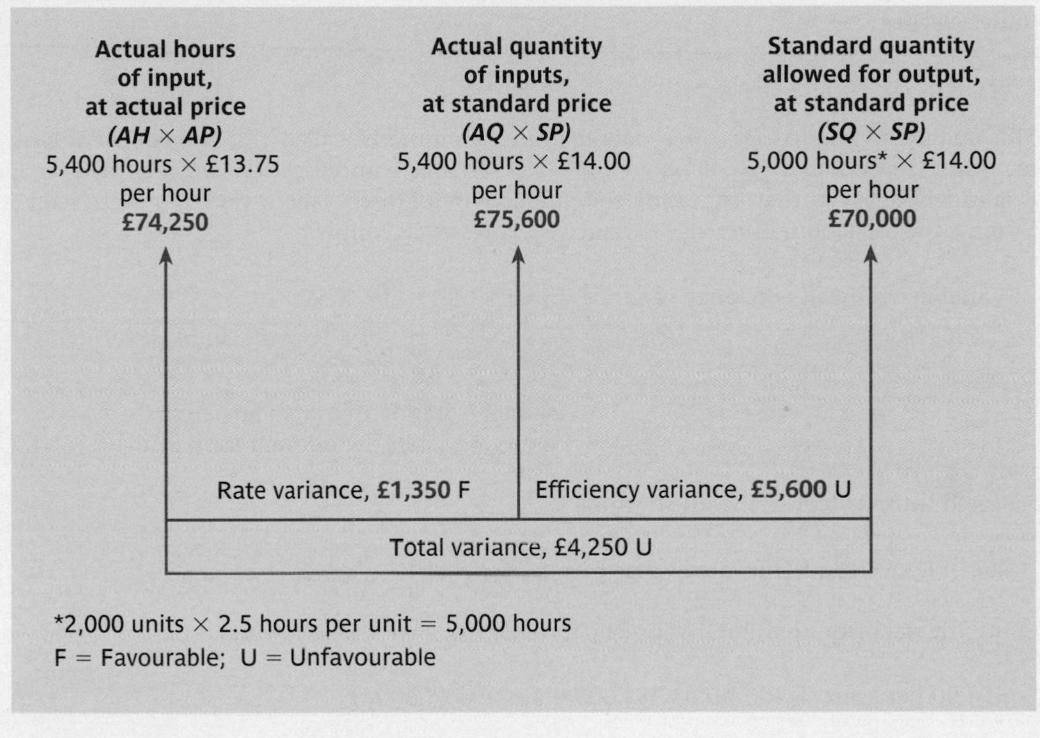

Exhibit 12.5 Variance analysis – direct labour

Labour rate variance – a closer look

As explained earlier, the price variance for direct labour is commonly termed a **labour rate variance**. This variance measures any deviation from standard in the average hourly rate paid to direct labour workers. The formula for the labour rate variance is expressed as follows:

$$\text{Labour rate variance} = (AH \times AR) - (AH \times SR)$$

Actual hours   Actual rate   Standard rate

The formula can be factored into simpler form as follows:

$$\text{Labour rate variance} = AH\,(AR - SR)$$

Using the data from Exhibit 12.5 in the formula, we have the following:

5,400 hours (£13.75 per hour − £14.00 per hour) = £1,350 F

In most firms, the rates paid to workers are quite predictable. Nevertheless, rate variances can arise through the way labour is used. Skilled workers with high hourly rates of pay may be given duties that require little skill and call for low hourly rates of pay. This will result in unfavourable labour rate variances, since the actual hourly rate of pay will exceed the standard rate specified for the particular task being performed. A reverse situation exists when unskilled or untrained workers are assigned to jobs that require some skill or training. The lower pay scale for these workers will result in favourable rate variances, although the workers may be inefficient. Finally, unfavourable rate variances can arise from overtime work at premium rates if any portion of the overtime premium is added to the direct labour account.

Who is responsible for controlling the labour rate variance? Since rate variances generally arise as a result of how labour is used, supervisors bear responsibility for seeing that labour rate variances are kept under control.

Labour efficiency variance – a closer look

The quantity variance for direct labour, more commonly called the **labour efficiency variance**, measures the productivity of labour time. No variance is more closely watched by management, since it is widely believed that increasing the productivity of direct labour time is vital to reducing costs. The formula for the labour efficiency variance is expressed as follows:

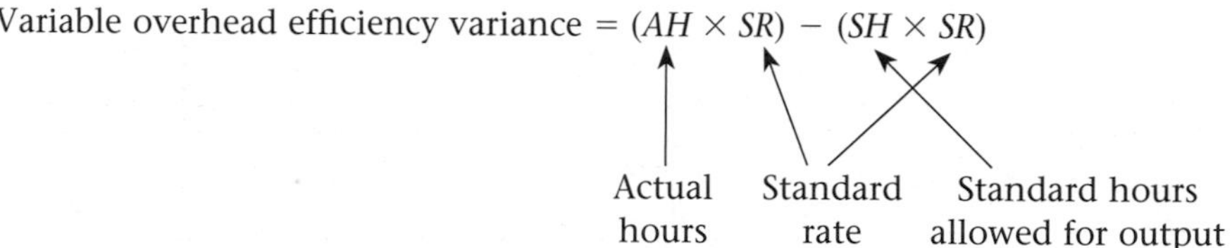

Variable overhead efficiency variance = (AH × SR) − (SH × SR)
Actual hours
Standard rate
Standard hours allowed for output

Factored into simpler terms, the formula is:

$$\text{Variable overhead efficiency variance} = SR(AH - SH)$$

Using the data from Exhibit 12.5 in the formula, we have the following:

£14.00 per hour (5,400 hours − 5,000 hours*) = £5,600 U

*2,000 units × hours per unit = 5,000 hours.

Possible causes of an unfavourable labour efficiency variance include poorly trained or motivated workers; poor quality materials, requiring more labour time in processing; faulty equipment, causing breakdowns and work interruptions; poor supervision of workers; and inaccurate standards. The managers in charge of production would generally be responsible for control of the labour efficiency variance. However, the variance might be chargeable to purchasing if the acquisition of poor materials resulted in excessive labour processing time.

When the labour force is essentially fixed in the short term, another important cause of an unfavourable labour efficiency variance is insufficient demand for the output of the factory. In some firms, the actual labour-hours worked is basically fixed – particularly in the short term. Managers in these firms argue that it is difficult, and perhaps even unwise, constantly to adjust the workforce in response to changes in the workload. Therefore, the only way a work centre manager can avoid an unfavourable labour efficiency variance in such firms is by keeping everyone busy all the time. The option of reducing the number of workers on hand is not available.

Thus, if there are insufficient orders from customers to keep the workers busy, the work centre manager has two options – either accept an unfavourable labour efficiency variance or build stocks. A central lesson of just-in-time (JIT) (see Chapter 18) is that building stocks with no immediate prospect of sale is a bad idea. Stocks – particularly work in progress stocks – lead to high defect rates, obsolete goods and generally inefficient operations. As a consequence, when the workforce is basically fixed in the short term, managers must be cautious about how labour efficiency variances are used. Some managers advocate dispensing with labour efficiency variances entirely in such situations – at least for the purposes of motivating and controlling workers on the shop floor.

Using standard costs – variable manufacturing overhead variances

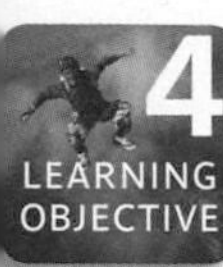

The final step in Terry's analysis of Colonial Pewter's variances for June was to compute the variable manufacturing overhead variances. The variable portion of manufacturing overhead can be analysed using the same basic formulas that are used to analyse direct materials and direct labour. Recall from Exhibit 12.1 that the standard variable manufacturing overhead is £7.50 per unit of product, computed as follows:

2.5 hours per unit × £3.00 per hour = £7.50 per unit

Colonial Pewter's cost records showed that the total actual variable manufacturing overhead cost for June was £15,390. Recall from the earlier discussion of the direct labour variances that 5,400 hours of direct labour time were recorded during the month and that the company produced 2,000 pairs of bookends. Terry's analysis of this overhead data appears in Exhibit 12.6.

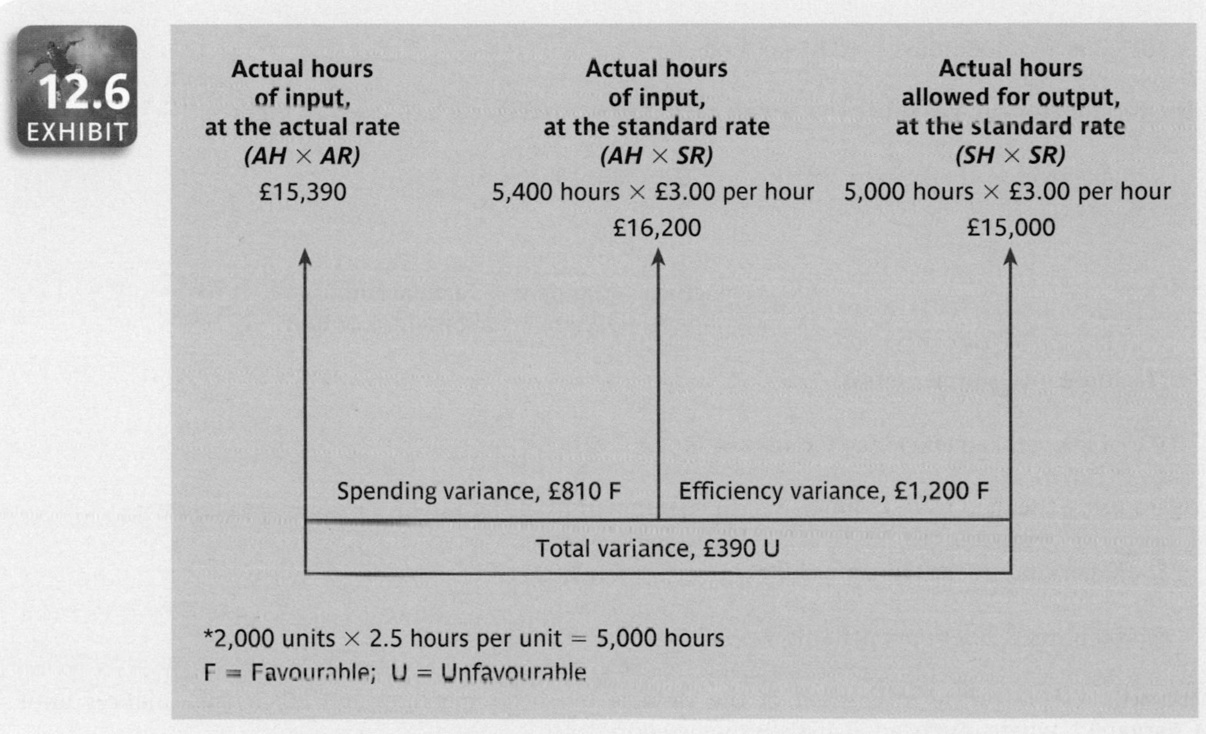

Exhibit 12.6 Variance analysis – variable manufacturing overhead

Notice the similarities between Exhibits 12.5 and 12.6. These similarities arise from the fact that direct labour-hours are being used as a base for allocating overhead cost to units of product; thus, the same hourly figures appear in Exhibit 12.6 for variable manufacturing overhead as in Exhibit 12.5 for direct labour. The main difference between the two exhibits is in the standard hourly rate being used, which in this company is much lower for variable manufacturing overhead.

Manufacturing overhead variances – a closer look

The formula for **variable overhead spending variance** is expressed as follows:

$$\text{Variable overhead spending variance} = (AH \times AR) - (AH \times SR)$$

Actual hours | Actual rate | Standard rate

Or, factored into simpler terms:

$$\text{Variable overhead spending variance} = AH(AR - SR)$$

Using the data from Exhibit 12.6 in the formula, we have the following:

5,400 hours (£2.85 per hour* − £3.00 per hour) = £810 F

*£15,390 ÷ 5,400 hours = £2.85 per hour.

The formula for the **variable overhead efficiency variance** is expressed as follows:

$$\text{Variable overhead efficiency variance} = (AH \times SR) - (SH \times SR)$$

Actual hours | Standard rate | Standard hours allowed for output

Or, factored into simpler terms:

$$\text{Variable overhead efficiency variance} = SR(AH - SH)$$

Again using the data from Exhibit 12.6, the computation of the variance would be as follows:

£3.00 per hour (5,400 hours − 5,000 hours*) = £1,200 U

*2,000 units × 2.5 hours per unit = 5,000 hours.

We will reserve further discussion of the variable overhead spending and efficiency variances until Chapter 13, where overhead analysis is discussed in depth.

Before proceeding further, we suggest that you pause at this point and go back to review the data contained in Exhibits 12.1 to 12.6. These exhibits and the accompanying text discussion provide a comprehensive, integrated illustration of standard setting and variance analysis.

Management accounting in action: the wrap-up

In preparation for the scheduled meeting to discuss Terry's analysis of Colonial Pewter's standard costs and variances, Terry distributed Exhibits 12.1 to 12.6, with supporting explanations, to the management group of Colonial Pewter. This included J.D. Wriston, the managing director of the company; Tom Kuchel, the production manager; and Janet Warner, the purchasing manager. J.D. Wriston opened the meeting with the following question:

JD: Terry, I think I understand the report you distributed, but just to make sure, would you mind summarizing the highlights of what you found?

Terry: As you can see, the biggest problems are the unfavourable materials quantity variance of £2,000 and the unfavourable labour efficiency variance of £5,600.

JD: Tom, you're the production boss. What do you think is responsible for the unfavourable labour efficiency variance?

Tom: It pretty much has to be the new production workers. Our experienced workers shouldn't have much problem meeting the standard of 2.5 hours per unit. We all knew that there would be some inefficiency for a while as we brought new people on board.

JD: No one is disputing that, Tom. However, £5,600 is a lot of money. Is this problem likely to go away very soon?

Tom: I hope so. If we were to contrast the last two weeks of June with the first two weeks, I'm sure we would see some improvement.

JD: I don't want to beat up on you, Tom, but this is a significant problem. Can you do something to accelerate the training process?

Tom: Sure. I could pair up each of the new guys with one of our old-timers and have them work together for a while. It would slow down our older guys a bit, but I'll bet the new workers would learn a lot.

JD: Let's try it. Now, what about that £2,000 unfavourable materials quantity variance?

Tom: Are you asking me?

JD: Well, I would like someone to explain it.

Tom: Don't look at me. It's that iron-contaminated pewter that Janet bought on her 'special deal'.

Janet: We got rid of that stuff months ago.

JD: Hold your horses. We're not trying to figure out who to blame here. I just want to understand what happened. If we can understand what happened, maybe we can fix it.

Terry: Tom, are the new workers generating a lot of scrap?

Tom: Yeah, I guess so.

JD: I think that could be part of the problem. Can you do anything about it?

Tom: I can watch the scrap really closely for a few days to see where it's being generated. If it is the new workers, I can have the old-timers work with them on the problem when I team them up.

JD: Good. Let's reconvene in a few weeks and see what has happened. Hopefully, we can get those unfavourable variances under control.

Structure of performance reports

On preceding pages we have learned that performance reports are used in a standard cost system to communicate variance data to management. Exhibit 12.7 provides an example of how these reports can be integrated in a responsibility reporting system.

Note from the exhibit that the performance reports *start at the bottom and build upwards*, with managers at each level receiving information on their own performance as well as information on the performance of each manager under them in the chain of responsibility. This variance information flows upward from level to level in a pyramid fashion, with the managing director finally receiving a summary of all activities in the organization. If the manager at a particular level (such as the production superintendent) wants to know the reasons behind a variance, he or she can ask for the detailed performance reports prepared by the various operations or departments.

In the following section, we turn our attention to the question of how a manager can determine which variances on these reports are significant enough to warrant further attention.

Variance analysis and management by exception

Variance analysis and performance reports are important elements of *management by exception*. Simply put, management by exception means that the manager's attention should be directed toward those parts of the organization where plans are not working out for one reason or another. Time and effort should not be wasted attending to those parts of the organization where things are going smoothly.

12.7 EXHIBIT

Managing director's report
The managing director's performance report summarizes all company data. The managing director can trace the variances downwards through the company as needed to determine where top management time should be spent.

	Budget	Actual	Variance
Responsibility centre:			
Sales manager	X	X	X
Production superintendent	£26,000	£29,000	£3,000 U
Engineering head	X	X	X
Personnel supervisor	X	X	X
Controller	X	X	X
	£54,000	£61,000	£7,000 U

Production superintendent
The performance of each department head is summarized for the production superintendent. The totals on the superintendent's performance report are then passed upwards to the next level of responsibility.

	Budget	Actual	Variance
Responsibility centre:			
Cutting department	X	X	X
Machining department	X	X	X
Finishing department	£11,000	£12,500	£1,500 U
Packing department	X	X	X
	£26,000	£29,000	£3,000 U

Finishing department head
The performance report of each supervisor is summarized on the performance report of the department head. The department totals are then passed upwards to the production superintendent.

	Budget	Actual	Variance
Responsibility centre:			
Sanding operation	X	X	X
Wiring operatio	£5,000	£5,800	£800 U
Assembly operation	X	X	X
	£11,000	£12,500	£1,500 U

Wiring operation supervisor
The supervisor of each operation receives a performance report. The totals on these reports are then communicated upwards to the next higher level of responsibility.

	Budget	Actual	Variance
Variable costs:			
Direct materials	X	X	X
Direct labour	X	X	X
Manufacturing overhead	X	X	X
	£5,000	£5,890	£800 U

Exhibit 12.7 Upward flow of performance reports

The budgets and standards discussed in this chapter and in the preceding chapter reflect management's plans. If all goes according to plan, there will be little difference between actual results and the results that would be expected according to the budgets and standards. If this happens, managers can concentrate on other issues. However, if actual results do not conform to the budget and to standards, the performance reporting system sends a signal to the manager that an 'exception' has occurred. This signal is in the form of a variance from the budget or standards.

However, are all variances worth investigating? The answer is no. Differences between actual results and what was expected will almost always occur. If every variance were investigated, management would waste a great deal of time tracking down trivial differences. Variances may occur for any of a variety of reasons – only some of which are significant and warrant management attention. For example, hotter-than normal weather in the summer may result in higher than-expected electrical bills for air conditioning. Or, workers may work slightly faster or slower on a particular day. Because of unpredictable random factors, one can expect that virtually every cost category will produce a variance of some kind.

How should managers decide which variances are worth investigating? One clue is the size of the variance. A variance of £5 is probably not big enough to warrant attention, whereas a variance of £5,000 might well be worth tracking down. Another clue is the size of the variance relative to the amount of spending involved. A variance that is only 0.1% of spending on an item is likely to be well within the bounds one would normally expect due to random factors. On the other hand, a variance of 10% of spending is much more likely to be a signal that something is basically wrong.

A more dependable approach is to plot variance data on a statistical control chart, such as illustrated in Exhibit 12.8. The basic idea underlying a statistical control chart is that some random fluctuations in variances from period to period are normal and to be expected even when costs are well under control. A variance should only be investigated when it is unusual relative to that normal level of random fluctuation. Typically the standard deviation of the variances is used as the measure of the normal level of fluctuations. A rule of thumb is adopted such as 'investigate all variances that are more than *X* standard deviations from zero.' In the control chart in Exhibit 12.8, *X* is 1.0. That is, the rule of thumb in this company is to investigate all variances that are more than one standard deviation in either direction (favourable or unfavourable) from zero. This means that the variances in weeks 7, 11 and 17 would have been investigated, but none of the others.

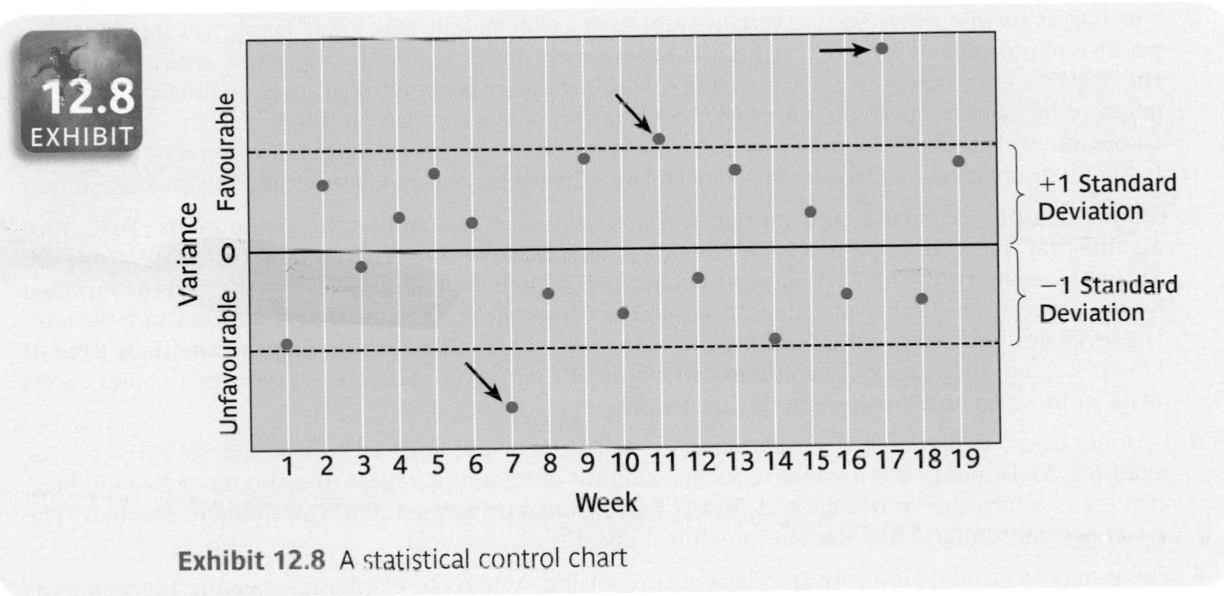

Exhibit 12.8 A statistical control chart

What value of *X* should be chosen? The bigger the value of *X*, the wider the band of acceptable variances that would not be investigated. Thus, the bigger the value of *X*, the less time will be spent tracking down variances, but the more likely it is that a real out-of-control situation would be overlooked. Ordinarily, if *X* is selected to be 1.0, roughly 30% of all variances will trigger an investigation even when there is no real problem. If *X* is set at 1.5, the figure drops to about 13%. If *X* is set at 2.0, the figure drops all the way to about 5%. Don't forget, however, that selecting a big value of *X* will result not only in fewer investigations but also a higher probability that a real problem will be overlooked.

In addition to watching for unusually large variances, the pattern of the variances should be monitored. For example, a run of steadily mounting variances should trigger an investigation even though none of the variances is large enough by itself to warrant investigation.

Evaluation of controls based on standard costs

Advantages of standard costs

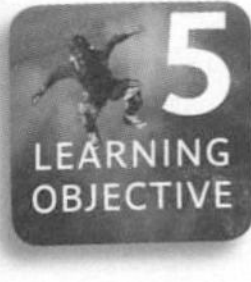

Standard cost systems have a number of advantages.

1 As stated earlier, the use of standard costs is a key element in a management by exception approach. So long as costs remain within the standards, managers can focus on other issues. When costs fall significantly outside the standards, managers are alerted that there may be problems requiring attention. This approach helps managers focus on important issues.

2 So long as standards are viewed as reasonable by employees, they can promote economy and efficiency. They provide benchmarks that individuals can use to judge their own performance.

3 Standard costs can greatly simplify bookkeeping. Instead of recording actual costs for each job, the standard costs for materials, labour and overhead can be charged to jobs.

4 Standard costs fit naturally in an integrated system of 'responsibility accounting'. The standards establish what costs should be, who should be responsible for them, and whether actual costs are under control.

Potential problems with the use of standard costs

The use of standard costs can present a number of potential problems. Most of these problems result from improper use of standard costs and the management by exception principle or from using standard costs in situations in which they are not appropriate.[7]

1 Standard cost variance reports are usually prepared on a monthly basis and often are released days or even weeks after the end of the month. As a consequence, the information in the reports may be so stale that it is almost useless. Timely, frequent reports that are approximately correct are better than infrequent reports that are very precise but out of date by the time they are released. As mentioned earlier, some companies are now reporting variances and other key operating data daily or even more frequently.

2 If managers are insensitive and use variance reports as a club, morale may suffer. Employees should receive positive reinforcement for work well done. Management by exception, by its nature, tends to focus on the negative. If variances are used as a club, subordinates may be tempted to cover up unfavourable variances or take actions that are not in the best interests of the company to make sure the variances are favourable. For example, workers may put on a crash effort to increase output at the end of the month to avoid an unfavourable labour efficiency variance. In the rush to produce output, quality may suffer.

3 Labour quantity standards and efficiency variances make two important assumptions. First, they assume that the production process is labour-paced; if labour works faster, output will go up. However, output in many companies is no longer determined by how fast labour works; rather, it is determined by the processing speed of machines. Second, the computations assume that labour is a variable cost. However, as discussed in earlier chapters, in many companies, direct labour may be essentially fixed. If labour is fixed, then an undue emphasis on labour efficiency variances creates pressure to build excess work in progress and finished goods inventories.

4 In some cases, a 'favourable' variance can be as bad or worse than an 'unfavourable' variance. For example, McDonald's has a standard for the amount of hamburger meat that should be in a Big Mac. If there is a 'favourable' variance, it means that less meat was used than the standard specifies. The result is a substandard Big Mac and possibly a dissatisfied customer.

5 There may be a tendency with standard cost reporting systems to emphasize meeting the standards to the exclusion of other important objectives such as maintaining and improving quality, on-time delivery, and customer satisfaction. This tendency can be reduced by using supplemental performance measures that focus on these other objectives.

6 Just meeting standards may not be sufficient; continual improvement may be necessary to survive in the current competitive environment. For this reason, some companies focus on the trends in the standard cost variances – aiming for continual improvement rather than just meeting the standards. In other companies, engineered standards are being replaced either by a rolling average of actual costs, which is expected to decline, or by very challenging target costs. This approach is sometimes known as **kaizen costing** which involves the reduction of cost during production through continuous gradual improvements that reduce waste and increase efficiency. While continuous improvement can be built into the costing system by setting small percentage reductions in cost, kaizen involves more than just technical changes because the philosophy relies on the development of a motivated and empowered workforce.[8]

In sum, managers should exercise considerable care in their use of a standard cost system. It is particularly important that managers go out of their way to focus on the positive, rather than just on the negative, and to be aware of possible unintended consequences.

Nevertheless, standard costs are still found in the vast majority of manufacturing companies and in many service companies, although their use is changing. For evaluating performance, standard cost variances may be supplanted in the future by a particularly interesting development known as the *balanced scorecard*, which is discussed in Chapter 16.

Summary

- A standard is a benchmark or 'norm' for measuring performance. In business organizations, standards are set for both the cost and the quantity of inputs needed to manufacture goods or to provide services. Quantity standards indicate how much of a cost element, such as labour time or raw materials, should be used in manufacturing a unit of product or in providing a unit of service. Cost standards indicate what the cost of the time or the materials should be.
- Standards are normally practical in nature, meaning that they can be attained by reasonable, though highly efficient, efforts. Such standards are generally felt to have a favourable motivational impact on employees.
- When standards are compared to actual performance, the difference is referred to as a variance. Variances are computed and reported to management on a regular basis for both the price and the quantity elements of materials, labour and overhead. Price and rate variances for inputs are computed by taking the difference between the actual and standard prices of the inputs and multiplying the result by the amount of input purchased. Quantity and efficiency variances are computed by taking the difference between the actual amount of the input used and the amount of input that is allowed for the actual output, and then multiplying the result by the standard price of the input.
- Not all variances require management time or attention. Only unusual or particularly significant variances should be investigated – otherwise a great deal of time would be spent investigating unimportant matters. Additionally, it should be emphasized that the point of the investigation should not be to find someone to blame. The point of the investigation is to pinpoint the problem so that it can be fixed and operations improved.
- Traditional standard cost variance reports should often be supplemented with other performance measures. Overemphasis on standard cost variances may lead to problems in other critical areas such as product quality, stocks levels, and on-time delivery.

Key terms for review

Bill of materials (p. 475).

Ideal standards (p. 473).

Kaizen costing (p. 490).

Labour efficiency variance (p. 484).

Labour rate variance (p. 483).

Management by exception (p. 473).

Materials price variance (p. 480).

Materials quantity variance (p. 481).

Practical standards (p. 474).

Standard cost card (p. 473).

Standard cost per unit (p. 476).

Standard hours allowed (p. 478).

Standard hours per unit (p. 476).

Standard price per unit (p. 474).

Standard quantity allowed (p. 478).

Standard quantity per unit (p. 475).

Standard rate per hour (p. 475).

Variable overhead efficiency variance (p. 486).

Variable overhead spending variance (p. 486).

Variances (p. 477).

Review problem: standard costs

Xavier Company produces a single product. Variable manufacturing overhead is applied to products on the basis of direct labour-hours. The standard costs for one unit of product are as follows:

Direct material: 6 grams at £0.50 per gram	£3
Direct labour: 1.8 hours at £10 per hour	18
Variable manufacturing overhead: 1.8 hours at £5 per hour	9
Total standard variable cost per unit	£30

During June, 2,000 units were produced. The costs associated with June's operations were as follows:

Material purchased: 18,000 grams at £0.60 per gram	£10,800
Material used in production: 14,000 grams	–
Direct labour: 4,000 hours at £9.75 per hour	39,000
Variable manufacturing overhead costs incurred	20,800

Required

Compute the materials, labour and variable manufacturing overhead variances.

Solution to review problem: standard costs

Materials variances

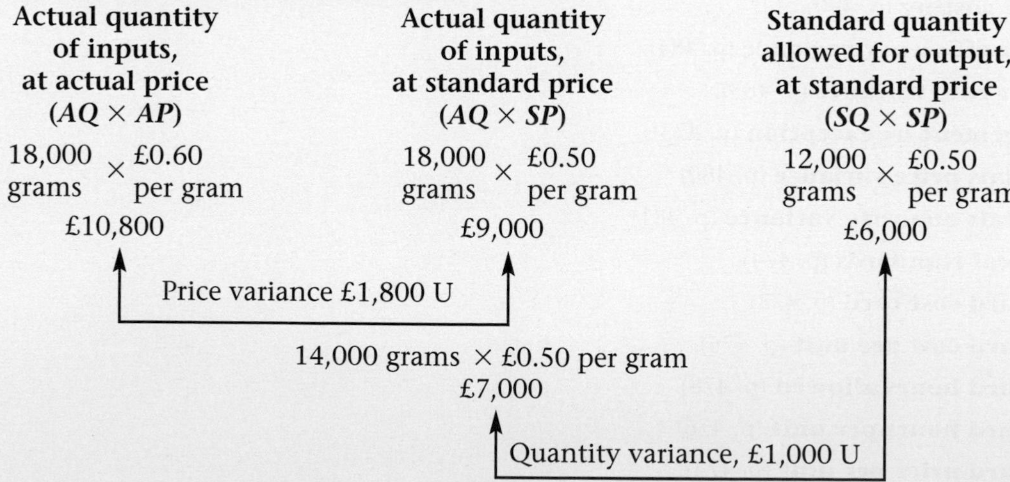

*2,000 units × 6 grams per unit = 12,000 grams.

A total variance cannot be computed in this situation, since the amount of materials purchased (18,000 grams) differs from the amount of materials used in production (14,000 grams).

Using the formulas in the chapter, the same variances would be computed as:

Materials price variance = $AQ(AP - SP)$

18,000 grams × (£0.60 per gram − £0.50 per gram) = £1,800 U

Materials quantity variance = $SP(AQ - SQ)$

£0.50 per gramme × (14,000 grams − 12,000 grams) = £1,000 U

Labour variances

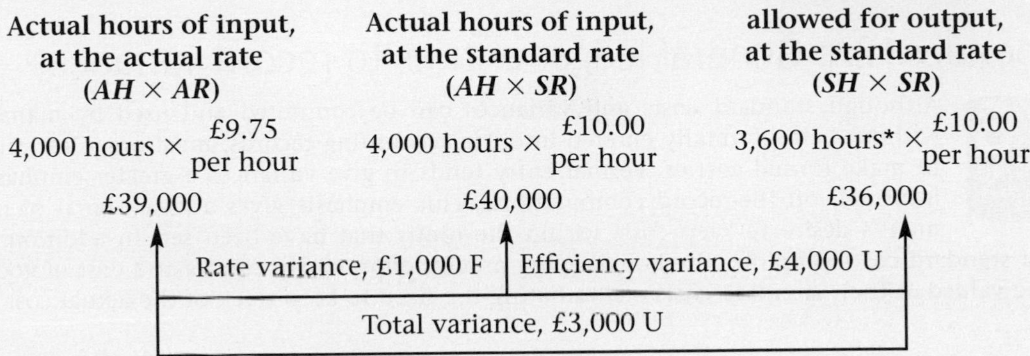

*2,000 units × 1.8 hours per unit = 3,600 hours.

Using the formulas in the chapter, the same variances would be computed as:

Labour rate variance = $AH(AR - SR)$

4,000 hours × (£9.75 per hour − £10.00 per hour) = £1,000 F

Labour efficiency variance = $SR(AH - SH)$

£10.00 per hour × (4,000 hours − 3,600 hours) = £4,000 U

Variable manufacturing overhead variances

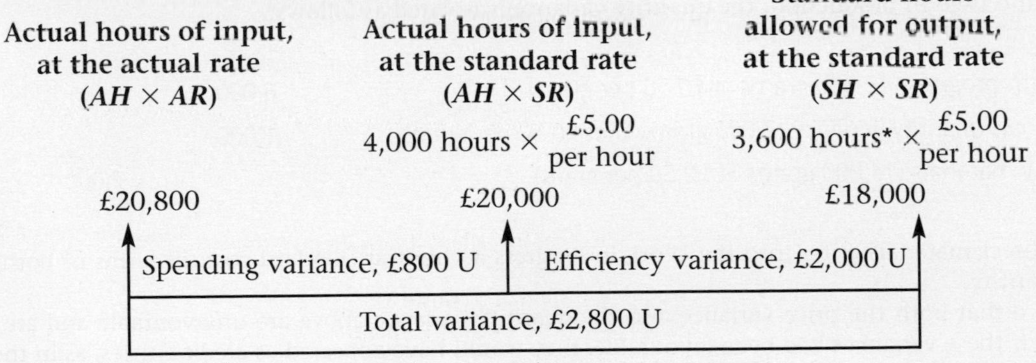

*2,000 units × 1.8 hours per unit = 3,600 hours.

Using the formulas in the chapter, the same variances would be computed as:

Variable overhead spending variance = *AH*(*AR* − *SR*)

4,000 hours × (£5.20 per hour* − £5.00 per hour) = £800 U

*£20,800 / 4,000 hours = £5.20 per hour.

Variable overhead efficiency variance = *SR*(*AH* − *SH*)

£5.00 per hour × (4,000 hours − 3,600 hours) = £2,000 U

Appendix 12A: General ledger entries to record variances

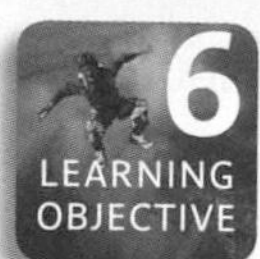

LEARNING OBJECTIVE 6

Although standard costs and variances can be computed and used by management without being formally entered into the accounting records, most organizations prefer to make formal entries. Formal entry tends to give variances a greater emphasis than informal, off-the-record computations. This emphasis gives a clear signal of management's desire to keep costs within the limits that have been set. In addition, formal use of standard costs simplifies the bookkeeping process enormously. Stocks and cost of goods sold can be valued at their standard costs – eliminating the need to keep track of the actual cost of each unit.

Direct materials variances

To illustrate the general ledger entries needed to record standard cost variances, we will return to the data contained in the review problem at the end of the chapter. The entry to record the purchase of direct materials would be as follows:

Raw materials (18,000 grams at £0.50 per gram)	9,000	
Materials price variance (18,000 grams at £0.10 per gram U)	1,800	
Creditors (18,000 grams at £0.60 per gram)		10,800

Notice that the price variance is recognized when purchases are made, rather than when materials are actually used in production. This permits the price variance to be isolated early, and it also permits the materials to be carried in the stocks account at standard cost. As direct materials are later drawn from stocks and used in production, the quantity variance is isolated as follows:

Work in progress (12,000 grams at £0.50 per gram)	6,000	
Materials quantity variance (2,000 grams U at £0.50 per gram)	1,000	
Raw materials (14,000 grams at £0.50 per gram)		7,000

Thus, direct materials enter into the Work in Progress account at standard cost, in terms of both price and quantity.

Notice that both the price variance and the quantity variance above are unfavourable and are debit entries. If these variances had been favourable, they would have appeared as credit entries, as in the case of the direct labour rate variance below.

Direct labour variances

Referring again to the cost data in the review problem at the end of the chapter, the general ledger entry to record the incurrence of direct labour cost would be:

Work in progress (3,600 hours at £10.00 per hour)	36,000	
Labour efficiency variance (400 hours U at £10.00 per hour)	4,000	
Labour rate variance (4,000 hours at £0.25 per hour F)		1,000
Wages payable (4,000 hours at £9.75 per hour)		39,000

Thus, as with direct materials, direct labour costs enter into the Work in Progress account at standard, both in terms of the rate and in terms of the hours allowed for the actual production of the period.

Variable manufacturing overhead variances

Variable manufacturing overhead variances generally are not recorded in the accounts separately but rather are determined as part of the general analysis of overhead, which is discussed in Chapter 13.

Cost flows in a standard cost system

The flows of costs through the company's accounts are illustrated in Exhibit 12A.1. Note that entries into the various stocks accounts are made at standard cost – not actual cost. The differences between actual and standard costs are entered into special accounts that accumulate the various standard cost variances. Ordinarily, these standard cost variance accounts are closed out to Cost of Goods Sold at the end of the period. Unfavourable variances increase Cost of Goods Sold, and favourable variances decrease Cost of Goods Sold.

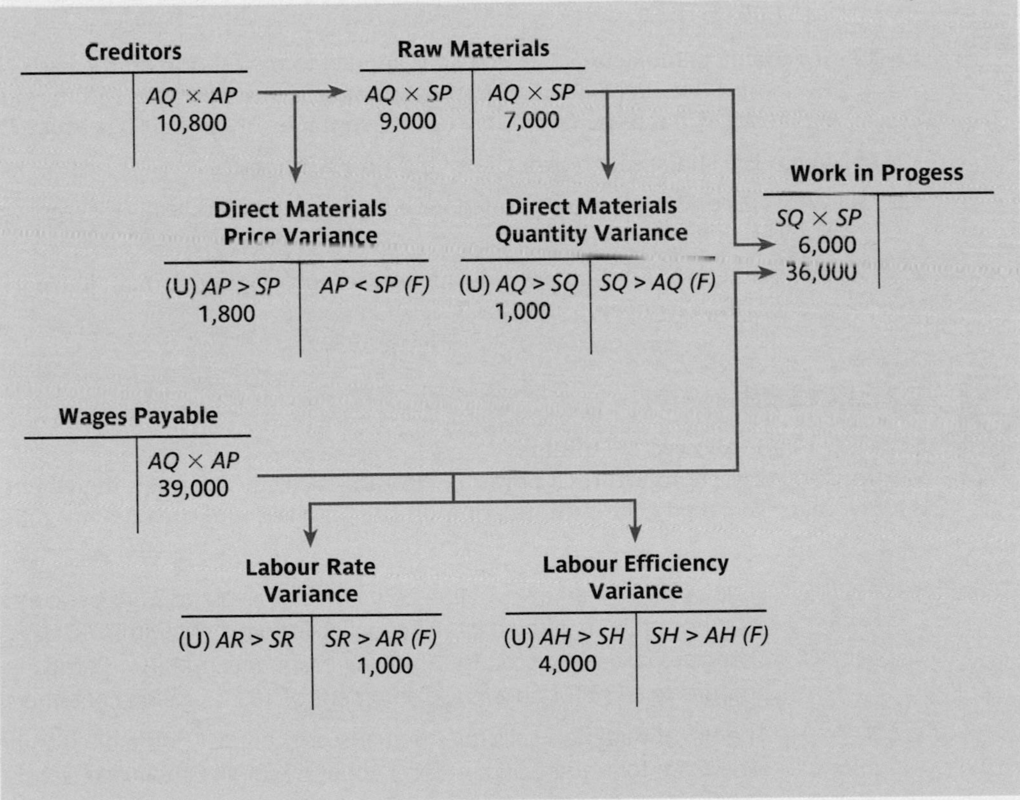

*The authors would like to thank Professor Rick French for suggesting this exhibit.

Exhibit 12A.1 Cost flows in a standard cost system*

Questions

12–1 What is a quantity standard? What is a price standard?

12–2 Distinguish between ideal and practical standards.

12–3 If employees are chronically unable to meet a standard, what effect would you expect this to have on their productivity?

12–4 What is the difference between a standard and a budget?

12–5 What is meant by the term *variance*?

12–6 What is meant by the term *management by exception*?

12–7 Why are variances generally segregated in terms of a price variance and a quantity variance?

12–8 Who is generally responsible for the materials price variance? The materials quantity variance? The labour efficiency variance?

12–9 The materials price variance can be computed at what two different points in time? Which point is better? Why?

12–10 An examination of the cost records of the Chittenden Furniture Company reveals that the materials price variance is favourable but that the materials quantity variance is unfavourable by a substantial amount. What might this indicate?

12–11 What dangers lie in using standards as punitive tools?

12–12 'Our workers are all under labour contracts; therefore, our labour rate variance is bound to be zero.' Discuss.

12–13 What effect, if any, would you expect poor quality materials to have on direct labour variances?

12–14 If variable manufacturing overhead is applied to production on the basis of direct labour-hours and the direct labour efficiency variance is unfavourable, will the variable overhead efficiency variance be favourable or unfavourable, or could it be either? Explain.

12–15 What is a statistical control chart, and how is it used?

12–16 Why can undue emphasis on labour efficiency variances lead to excess work in progress stocks?

12–17 (Appendix 12A) What are the advantages of making formal journal entries in the accounting records for variances?

Exercises

E12–1 Time allowed: 20 minutes

Martin Company manufactures a powerful cleaning solvent. The main ingredient in the solvent is a raw material called Echol. Information on the purchase and use of Echol follows:

Purchase of echol — Echol is purchased in 15-gallon containers at a cost of £115 per container. A discount of 2% is offered by the supplier for payment within 10 days, and Martin Company takes all discounts. Shipping costs, which Martin Company must pay, amount to £130 for an average shipment of 100 15-gallon containers of Echol.

Use of echol — The bill of materials calls for 7.6 quarts of Echol per bottle of cleaning solvent. (There are four quarts in a gallon.) About 5% of all Echol used is lost through spillage or evaporation (the 7.6 quarts above is the actual content per bottle). In addition, statistical analysis has shown that every 41st bottle is rejected at final inspection because of contamination.

Required

1 Compute the standard purchase price for one quart of Echol.

2 Compute the standard quantity of Echol (in quarts) per saleable bottle of cleaning solvent.

3 Using the data from Questions 1 and 2 above, prepare a standard cost card showing the standard cost of Echol per bottle of cleaning solvent.

E12–2 Time allowed: 15 minutes
Bandar Industries Berhad of Malaysia manufactures sporting equipment. One of the company's products, a football helmet for the North American market, requires a special plastic. During the quarter ending 30 June, the company manufactured 35,000 helmets, using 22,500 kilograms of plastic in the process. The plastic cost the company RM 171,000. (The currency in Malaysia is the ringgit, which is denoted here by RM.)

According to the standard cost card, each helmet should require 0.6 kilograms of plastic, at a cost of RM 8 per kilogram.

Required

1 What cost for plastic should have been incurred in the manufacture of the 35,000 helmets? How much greater or less is this than the cost that was incurred?

2 Break down the difference computed in Question 1 above in terms of a materials price variance and a materials quantity variance.

E12–3 Time allowed: 15 minutes
Huron Company produces a commercial cleaning compound known as Zoom. The direct materials and direct labour standards for one unit of Zoom are given below:

	Standard quantity or hours	Standard price or rate	Standard cost
Direct materials	4.6 kilos	£2.50 per kilo	£11.50
Direct labour	0.2 hours	12.00 per hour	2.40

During the most recent month, the following activity was recorded:

1 Twenty thousand kilos of material were purchased at a cost of £2.35 per kilo.

2 All of the material purchased was used to produce 4,000 units of Zoom.

3 A total of 750 hours of direct labour time was recorded at a total labour cost of £10,425.

Required

1 Compute the direct materials price and quantity variances for the month.

2 Compute the direct labour rate and efficiency variances for the month.

E12–4 Time allowed: 10 minutes
Refer to the data in E12–3. Assume that instead of producing 4,000 units during the month, the company produced only 3,000 units, using 14,750 kilos of material in the production process. (The rest of the material purchased remained in stocks.)

Required

Compute the direct materials price and quantity variances for the month.

E12–5 Time allowed: 20 minutes
Erie Company manufactures a small cassette player called the Jogging Mate. The company uses standards to control its costs. The labour standards that have been set for one Jogging Mate cassette player are as follows:

Standard hours	Standard rate per hour	Standard cost
18 minutes	£12.00	£3.60

During August, 5,750 hours of direct labour time were recorded in the manufacture of 20,000 units of the Jogging Mate. The direct labour cost totalled £73,600 for the month.

Required

1 What direct labour cost should have been incurred in the manufacture of the 20,000 units of the Jogging Mate? By how much does this differ from the cost that was incurred?

2 Break down the difference in cost from Question 1 above into a labour rate variance and a labour efficiency variance.

3 The budgeted variable manufacturing overhead rate is £4 per direct labour-hour. During August, the company incurred £21,850 in variable manufacturing overhead cost. Compute the variable overhead spending and efficiency variances for the month.

E12–6 Time allowed: 30 minutes

Dawson Toys Ltd produces a toy called the Maze. The company has recently established a standard cost system to help control costs and has established the following standards for the Maze toy:

Direct materials: 6 microns per toy at £0.50 per micron

Direct labour: 1.3 hours per toy at £8 per hour

During July, the company produced 3,000 Maze toys. Production data for the month on the toy follow:

Required

1 Compute the following variances for July:

(a) Direct materials price and quantity variances.

(b) Direct labour rate and efficiency variances.

2 Prepare a brief explanation of the significance and possible causes of each variance.

E12–7 Time allowed: 20 minutes

The repair shop of Quality Motor Company uses standards to control the labour time and labour cost in the shop. The standard labour cost for a motor tune-up is given below:

Job	Standard hours	Standard rate	Standard cost
Motor tune-up	2.5	£9	£22.50

The record showing the time spent in the shop last week on motor tune-ups has been misplaced. However, the shop supervisor recalls that 50 tune-ups were completed during the week, and the controller recalls the following variance data relating to tune-ups:

Labour rate variance	£87 F
Total labour variance	93 U

Required

1 Determine the number of actual labour-hours spent on tune-ups during the week.

2 Determine the actual hourly rate of pay for tune-ups last week.
(*Hint*: A useful way to proceed would be to work from known to unknown data either by using the variance formulas or by using the columnar format shown in Exhibit 12.5.)

E12–8 Time allowed: 30 minutes
(Appendix 12A) Genola Fashions began production of a new product on 1 June. The company uses a standard cost system and has established the following standards for one unit of the new product:

	Standard quantity or hours	Standard price or rate	Standard cost
Direct materials	2.5 metres	£14 per metre	£35.00
Direct labour	1.6 hours	8 per hour	12.80

During June, the following activity was recorded relative to the new product:

1 Purchasing acquired 10,000 metres of material at a cost of £13.80 per metre.

2 Production used 8,000 metres of the material to manufacture 3,000 units of the new product.

3 Production reported 5,000 hours of labour time worked directly on the new product; the cost of this labour time was £43,000.

Required

1 For materials

(a) Compute the direct materials price and quantity variances.

(b) Prepare journal entries to record the purchase of materials and the use of materials in production.

2 For direct labour:

(a) Compute the direct labour rate and efficiency variances.

(b) Prepare a journal entry to record the incurrence of direct labour cost for the month.

3 Post the entries you have prepared to the following T-accounts:

Raw materials

	?	?
Bal.	?	

Creditors

	138,000

Materials price variance

Wages payable

	43,000

Materials quantity variance

Labour rate variance

Work in progress – Product A

Materials used	?	
Labour cost	?	

Labour efficiency variance

PROBLEMS

Problems

P12–9 Standard costing Time allowed: 50 minutes

SS Ltd makes and sells a single product 'PP'. The company uses a standard absorption costing system.

The budgeted production and sales for the year ended 31 October 2001 were 59,500 units with a selling price of £2 each unit. The standard time for producing each unit was 3 minutes. The standard labour rate was £10 an hour. The standard material cost for one unit of PP was £0.75 per unit.

Production overhead absorption rates were based on direct labour cost and were as follows:

Overheads	Labour costs
Variable overhead	35% of direct labour cost
Fixed overhead	40% of direct labour cost

For the year under review, the actual results were as follows:

Production and sales of PP	62,000 units £
Selling price for one unit	2.00
Labour cost incurred – for 3,500 hours	38,500
Material cost for each unit	0.75
Variable production overhead incurred	9,500
Fixed production overhead incurred	9,500

There were no changes in any stock levels during the period.

Required

1 Prepare a statement that reconciles budgeted profit with actual profit for the year ended 31 October 2001, showing the analysis of variances in as much detail as possible from the information given. *(14 marks)*

2 Referring to your analysis in Question 1, suggest two possible reasons for the labour efficiency variance and two possible reasons for the labour rate variance that you have calculated. *(4 marks)*

3 Explain the factors that should be considered when selecting the most appropriate base to use for an overhead absorption rate. Your answer should include a discussion of the method used by SS Ltd. *(7 marks)*

(Total = 25 marks)

CIMA Management Accounting Fundamentals, November 2001

P12–10 Standard costing Time allowed: 45 minutes

As a recently appointed assistant management accountant you are attending a monthly performance meeting. You have with you a statement of monthly actual costs, a summary of cost variances and other pieces of information you have managed to collect, as shown below:

	£
Actual cost of direct material purchased and used	62,700
Actual direct wages paid	97,350
Variable overheads incurred	19,500
Fixed overheads incurred	106,500

The variances from standard cost were:

Direct material price variance	5,700 Adv.
Direct material usage variance	3,000 Fav.
Direct labour rate variance	1,650 Fav.
Direct labour efficiency variance	9,000 Fav.
Variable overhead variance	1,500 Adv.
Fixed overhead expenditure variance	1,500 Adv.
Fixed overhead volume variance	15,000 Adv.

The actual wage rate paid for the period was £8.85 per hour. It takes three standard hours to produce one unit of the finished product.

The single direct material used in the period cost 30p per kilogram above the standard price. Five kilograms of raw material input is allowed for as standard for one unit of output.

All figures relate to the single product which is manufactured at the plant. There were no stocks at the beginning or end of the accounting period. Variable and fixed overhead absorption rates are based on standard hours produced.

Managers from various functions have brought to the meeting measures which they have collected for their own areas of responsibility. In order to demonstrate the link between the accounting values and their measures you decide to work from the variances to confirm some of them.

Required

1 The formula for the calculation of the labour cost variance is:

$(SH \times SR) - (AH \times AR)$

Provide formulae for the calculation of the labour rate variance and labour efficiency variance using similar notation to that above. Demonstrate how they will sum to the labour cost variance given above. *(2 marks)*

2 Using variance formulae, such as those above, or otherwise, determine:

(a) the actual number of direct labour hours worked

(b) the standard rate of pay per direct labour hour

(c) the standard hours of production

(d) the actual production in units

(e) the actual quantity of direct material consumed

(f) the actual price paid for the direct material (per kilogram)

(g) the standard direct material usage in kilograms for the actual number of units produced. *(10 marks)*

3 From Question 2 above and any other calculations which may be appropriate, compute the standard cost per unit of finished product. Show separately standard prices and standard quantities for each element of cost. *(4 marks)*

4 Briefly interpret the overhead variances given in the question. *(4 marks)*

(Total = 20 marks)

ACCA Managerial Finance, June 1999

P12–11 Hospital; basic variance analysis Time allowed: 45 minutes

John Fleming, chief administrator for Valley View Hospital, is concerned about costs for tests in the hospital's lab. Charges for lab tests are consistently higher at Valley View than at other hospitals and have resulted in many complaints. Also, because of strict regulations on amounts reimbursed for lab tests, payments received from insurance companies and governmental units have not been high enough to provide an acceptable level of profit for the lab.

Mr Fleming has asked you to evaluate costs in the hospital's lab for the past month. The following information is available:

1 Basically, two types of tests are performed in the lab – blood tests and smears. During the past month, 1,800 blood tests and 2,400 smears were performed in the lab.

2 Small glass plates are used in both types of tests. During the past month, the hospital purchased 12,000 plates at a cost of £28,200. This cost is net of a 6% quantity discount. Some 1,500 of these plates were still on hand unused at the end of the month; there were no plates on hand at the beginning of the month.

3 During the past month, 1,150 hours of labour time were recorded in the lab. The cost of this labour time was £13,800.

4 Variable overhead cost last month in the lab for utilities and supplies totalled £7,820.

Valley View Hospital has never used standard costs. By searching industry literature, however, you have determined the following nationwide averages for hospital labs:

Plates:	Two plates are required per lab test. These plates cost £2.50 each and are disposed of after the test is completed.
Labour:	Each blood test should require 0.3 hours to complete, and each smear should require 0.15 hours to complete. The average cost of this lab time is £14 per hour.
Overhead:	Overhead cost is based on direct labour-hours. The average rate for variable overhead is £6 per hour.

Mr Fleming would like a complete analysis of the cost of plates, labour and overhead in the lab for the last month so that he can get to the root of the lab's cost problem.

Required

1 Compute a materials price variance for the plates purchased last month and a materials quantity variance for the plates used last month.

2 For labour cost in the lab:

(a) Compute a labour rate variance and a labour efficiency variance.

(b) In most hospitals, one-half of the workers in the lab are senior technicians and one-half are assistants. In an effort to reduce costs, Valley View Hospital employs only one-quarter senior technicians and three-quarters assistants. Would you recommend that this policy be continued? Explain.

3 Compute the variable overhead spending and efficiency variances. Is there any relationship between the variable overhead efficiency variance and the labour efficiency variance? Explain.

P12–12 Straightforward variance analysis Time allowed: 45 minutes
Becton Labs Ltd produces various chemical compounds for industrial use. One compound, called Fludex, is prepared by means of an elaborate distilling process. The company has developed standard costs for one unit of Fludex, as follows:

	Standard quantity	Standard price or rate	Standard cost
Direct materials	2.5 grams	£20.00 per gram	£50.00
Direct labour	1.4 hours	12.50 per hour	17.50
Variable manufacturing overhead	1.4 hours	3.50 per hour	4.90
			£72.40

During November, the following activity was recorded by the company relative to production of Fludex:

1 Materials purchased, 12,000 grams at a cost of £225,000.

2 There was no beginning stocks of materials on hand to start the month; at the end of the month, 2,500 grams of material remained in the warehouse unused.

3 The company employs 35 lab technicians to work on the production of Fludex. During November, each worked an average of 160 hours at an average rate of £12 per hour.

4 Variable manufacturing overhead is assigned to Fludex on the basis of direct labour-hours. Variable manufacturing overhead costs during November totalled £18,200.

5 During November, 3,750 good units of Fludex were produced. The company's management is anxious to determine the efficiency of the activities surrounding the production of Fludex.

Required

1 For materials used in the production of Fludex:

(a) Compute the price and quantity variances.

(b) The materials were purchased from a new supplier who is anxious to enter into a long-term purchase contract. Would you recommend that the company sign the contract? Explain.

2 For direct labour employed in the production of Fludex:

(a) Compute the rate and efficiency variances.

(b) In the past, the 35 technicians employed in the production of Fludex consisted of 20 senior technicians and 15 assistants. During November, the company experimented with only 15 senior technicians and 20 assistants in order to save costs. Would you recommend that the new labour mix be continued? Explain.

3 Compute the variable overhead spending and efficiency variances. What relationship can you see between this efficiency variance and the labour efficiency variance?

P12–13 Basic variance analysis Time allowed: 45 minutes
Miller Toy Company manufactures a plastic swimming pool at its Westwood Plant. The plant has been experiencing problems for some time as shown by its June profit statement below:

	Budgeted	Actual
Sales (15,000 pools)	£450,000	£450,000
Less variable expenses:		
Variable cost of goods sold*	180,000	196,290
Variable selling expenses	20,000	20,000
Total variable expenses	200,000	216,290
Contribution margin	250,000	233,710
Less fixed expenses:		
Manufacturing overhead	130,000	130,000
Selling and administrative	84,000	84,000
Total fixed expenses	214,000	214,000
Net profit	£36,000	£19,710

*Contains direct materials, direct labour and variable manufacturing overhead.

Janet Dunn, who has just been appointed general manager of the Westwood Plant, has been given instructions to 'get things under control'. Upon reviewing the plant's profit statement, Ms Dunn has concluded that the major problem lies in the variable cost of goods sold. She has been provided with the following standard cost per swimming pool:

	Standard quantity	Standard price or rate	Standard cost
Direct materials	3.0 kilos	£2.00 per kilo	£6.00
Direct labour	0.8 hours	6.00 per hour	4.80
Variable manufacturing overhead	0.4 hours*	3.00 per hour	1.20
Total standard cost			£12.00

* Based on machine-hours.

Ms Dunn has determined that during June the plant produced 15,000 pools and incurred the following costs:

1 Purchased 60,000 kilos of materials at a cost of £1.95 per kilo.

2 Used 49,200 kilos of materials in production. (Finished goods and work in progress stocks are insignificant and can be ignored.)

3 Worked 11,800 direct labour-hours at a cost of £7.00 per hour.

4 Incurred variable manufacturing overhead cost totalling £18,290 for the month. A total of 5,900 machine-hours was recorded.

It is the company's policy to close all variances to cost of goods sold on a monthly basis.

Required

1 Compute the following variances for June:
   (a) Direct materials price and quantity variances.
   (b) Direct labour rate and efficiency variances.
   (c) Variable overhead spending and efficiency variances.

2 Summarize the variances that you computed in Question 1 above by showing the net overall favourable or unfavourable variance for the month. What impact did this figure have on the company's profit statement? Show computations.

3 Pick out the two most significant variances that you computed in Question 1 above. Explain to Ms Dunn possible causes of these variances.

P12–14 Variances; unit costs; journal entries Time allowed: 50 minutes
(Appendix 12A) Trueform Products Ltd produces a broad line of sports equipment and uses a standard cost system for control purposes. Last year the company produced 8,000 of its footballs. The standard costs associated with this football, along with the actual costs incurred last year, are as follows (per football):

	Standard cost	Actual cost
Direct materials:		
Standard: 3.7 metres at £5.00 per metre	£18.50	
Actual: 4.0 metres at £4.80 per metre		£19.20
Direct labour:		
Standard: 0.9 hours at £7.50 per hour	6.75	
Actual: 0.8 hours at £8.00 per hour		6.40
Variable manufacturing overhead:		
Standard: 0.9 hours at £2.50 per hour	2.25	
Actual: 0.8 hours at £2.75 per hour		2.20
Total cost per football	£27.50	£27.80

The managing director was elated when he saw that actual costs exceeded standard costs by only £0.30 per football. He stated, 'I was afraid that our unit cost might get out of hand when we gave out those raises last year in order to stimulate output. But it's obvious our costs are well under control.'

There were no stocks of materials on hand to start the year. During the year, 32,000 metres of materials were purchased and used in production.

Required

1 For direct materials:
   (a) Compute the price and quantity variances for the year.
   (b) Prepare journal entries to record all activity relating to direct materials for the year.
2 For direct labour:
   (a) Compute the rate and efficiency variances.
   (b) Prepare a journal entry to record the incurrence of direct labour cost for the year.
3 Compute the variable overhead spending and efficiency variances.
4 Was the managing director correct in his statement that 'our costs are well under control'? Explain.
5 State possible causes of each variance that you have computed.

P12–15 Developing standard costs Time allowed: 40 minutes
Danson Company is a chemical manufacturer that supplies various products to industrial users. The company plans to introduce a new chemical solution, called Nysap, for which it needs to develop a standard product cost. The following information is available on the production of Nysap:

1 Nysap is made by combining a chemical compound (nyclyn) and a solution (salex), and boiling the mixture. A 20% loss in volume occurs for both the salex and the nyclyn during boiling. After boiling, the mixture consists of 9.6 litres of salex and 12 kilograms of nyclyn per 10-litre batch of Nysap.
2 After the boiling process is complete, the solution is cooled slightly before 5 kilograms of protet are added per 10-litre batch of Nysap. The addition of the protet does not affect the total liquid volume. The resulting solution is then bottled in 10-litre containers.
3 The finished product is highly unstable, and one 10-litre batch out of six is rejected at final inspection. Rejected batches have no commercial value and are thrown out.
4 It takes a worker 35 minutes to process one 10-litre batch of Nysap. Employees work an eight-hour day, including one hour per day for rest breaks and clean-up.

Required

1 Determine the standard quantity for each of the raw materials needed to produce an acceptable 10-litre batch of Nysap.

2 Determine the standard labour time to produce an acceptable 10-litre batch of Nysap.

3 Assuming the following purchase prices and costs, prepare a standard cost card for materials and labour for one acceptable 10-litre batch of Nysap:

Salex	£1.50	per litre
Nyclyn	2.80	per kilogram
Protet	3.00	per kilogram
Direct labour cost	9.00	per hour

(*CMA*, adapted)

P12–16 Standards and variances from incomplete data Time allowed: 45 minutes
Highland Company produces a lightweight backpack that is popular with students. Standard variable costs relating to a single backpack are given below:

During March, 1,000 backpacks were manufactured and sold. Selected information relating to the month's production is given below:

	Standard quantity	Standard price or rate	Standard cost
Direct materials	?	£6 per metre	£?
Direct labour	?	?	?
Variable manufacturing overhead	?	£3 per hour	?
Total standard cost			£?

	Materials used	Direct labour	Variable manufacturing overhead
Total standard cost allowed*	£16,800	£10,500	£4,200
Actual costs incurred	15,000	?	3,600
Materials price variance	?		
Materials quantity variance	1,200 U		
Labour rate variance		?	
Labour efficiency variance		?	
Variable overhead spending variance			?
Variable overhead efficiency variance			?

*For the month's production.

The following additional information is available for March's production:

Actual direct labour-hours	1,500
Standard overhead rate per hour	£3.00
Standard price of one metre of materials	£6.00
Difference between standard and actual cost per backpack produced during March	0.15 F

Overhead is applied to production on the basis of direct labour-hours.

Required

1 What is the standard cost of a single backpack?

2 What was the actual cost per backpack produced during March?

3 How many metres of material are required at standard per backpack?

4 What was the materials price variance for March?

5 What is the standard direct labour rate per hour?

6 What was the labour rate variance for March? The labour efficiency variance?

7 What was the variable overhead spending variance for March? The variable overhead efficiency variance?

8 Prepare a standard cost card for one backpack.

P12–17 Computations from incomplete data Time allowed: 30 minutes
Sharp Company manufactures a product for which the following standards have been set:

	Standard quantity or hours	Standard price or rate	Standard cost
Direct materials	3 metres	£5 per metre	£15
Direct labour	? hours	? per hour	?

During March, the company purchased direct materials at a cost of £55,650, all of which were used in the production of 3,200 units of product. In addition, 4,900 hours of direct labour time were worked on the product during the month. The cost of this labour time was £36,750. The following variances have been computed for the month:

Required

1 For direct materials:

(a) Compute the actual cost per metre for materials for March.

(b) Compute the materials price variance and a total variance for materials.

2 For direct labour:

(a) Compute the standard direct labour rate per hour.

(b) Compute the standard hours allowed for the month's production.

(c) Compute the standard hours allowed per unit of product.

(*Hint:* In completing the problem, it may be helpful to move from known to unknown data either by using the columnar format shown in Exhibits 12.3 and 12.5 or by using the variance formulas.)

P12–18 Variance analysis with multiple lots Time allowed: 45 minutes
Hillcrest Leisure Wear Ltd manufactures men's clothing. The company has a single line of slacks that is produced in lots, with each lot representing an order from a customer. As a lot is completed, the customer's store label is attached to the slacks before shipment.

Hillcrest has a standard cost system and has established the following standards for a dozen slacks:

	Standard quantity or hours	Standard price or rate	Standard cost
Direct materials	32 metres	£2.40 per metre	£7680
Direct labour	6 hours	7.50 per hour	£4500

During October, Hillcrest worked on three orders for slacks. The company's job cost records for the month reveal the following:

Lot	Units in lot (dozens)	Materials used (metres)	Hours worked
48	1,500	48,300	8,900
49	950	30,140	6,130
50	2,100	67,250	10,270

The following additional information is available:

1 Hillcrest purchased 180,000 metres of material during October at a cost of £424,800.

2 Direct labour cost incurred during the month for production of slacks amounted to £192,280.

3 There was no work in progress stocks on 1 October. During October, lots 48 and 49 were completed, and lot 50 was 100% complete as to materials and 80% complete as to labour.

Required

1 Compute the materials price variance for the materials purchased during October.

2 Determine the materials quantity variance for October in both metres and pounds:
 (a) For each lot worked on during the month.
 (b) For the company as a whole.

3 Compute the labour rate variance for October.

4 Determine the labour efficiency variance for the month in both hours and pounds:
 (a) For each lot worked on during the month.
 (b) For the company as a whole.

5 In what situations might it be better to express variances in units (hours, metres, and so on) rather than in pounds? In pounds rather than in units?

(*CPA*, adapted)

P12–19 Variance analysis; incomplete data; journal entries Time allowed: 50 minutes
(Appendix 12A) Maple Products Ltd manufactures a hockey stick that is used worldwide. The standard cost of one hockey stick is:

	Standard quantity	Standard price or rate	Standard cost
Direct materials	? metre	£3.00 per metre	£?
Direct labour	2 hours	? per hour	?
Variable manufacturing overhead	? hours	1.30 per hour	?
Total standard cost			£27.00

Last year 8,000 hockey sticks were produced and sold. Selected cost data relating to last year's operations follow:

	Dr	Cr
Direct materials purchased (60,000 metres)	£174,000	
Wages payable (? hours)		£79,200*
Work in progress – direct materials	115,200	
Direct labour rate variance		3,300
Variable overhead efficiency variance	650	

*Relates to the actual direct labour cost for the year.

The following additional information is available for last year's operations:

1 No materials were on hand at the start of last year. Some of the materials purchased during the year were still on hand in the warehouse at the end of the year.

2 The variable manufacturing overhead rate is based on direct labour-hours. Total actual variable manufacturing overhead cost for last year was £19,800.

3 Actual direct materials usage for last year exceeded the standard by 0.2 metres per stick.

Required

1 For direct materials:

(a) Compute the price and quantity variances for last year.

(b) Prepare journal entries to record all activities relating to direct materials for last year.

2 For direct labour:

(a) Verify the rate variance given above and compute the efficiency variance for last year.

(b) Prepare a journal entry to record activity relating to direct labour for last year.

3 Compute the variable overhead spending variance for last year and verify the variable overhead efficiency variance given above.

4 State possible causes of each variance that you have computed.

5 Prepare a completed standard cost card for one hockey stick.

P12–20 Developing standard costs Time allowed: 30 minutes

ColdKing Company is a small producer of fruit-flavoured frozen desserts. For many years, ColdKing's products have had strong regional sales on the basis of brand recognition; however, other companies have begun marketing similar products in the area, and price competition has become increasingly important. John Wakefield, the company's chief accountant, is planning to implement a standard cost system for ColdKing and has gathered considerable information from his co-workers on production and material requirements for ColdKing's products. Wakefield believes that the use of standard costing will allow ColdKing to improve cost control and make better pricing decisions.

ColdKing's most popular product is raspberry sherbet. The sherbet is produced in 10-litre batches, and each batch requires 6 litres of good raspberries. The fresh raspberries are sorted by hand before they enter the production process. Because of imperfections in the raspberries and normal spoilage, 1 litre of berries is discarded for every 4 litres of acceptable berries. Three minutes is the standard direct labour time for the sorting that is required to obtain 1 litre of acceptable raspberries. The acceptable raspberries are then blended with the other ingredients; blending requires 12 minutes of direct labour time per batch. After blending, the sherbet is packaged in litre containers. Wakefield has gathered the following pricing information:

1 ColdKing purchases raspberries at a cost of £0.80 per litre. All other ingredients cost a total of £0.45 per litre.

2 Direct labour is paid at the rate of £9.00 per hour.

3 The total cost of material and labour required to package the sherbet is £0.38 per litre.

Required

1 Develop the standard cost for the direct cost components (materials, labour and packaging) of a 10-litre batch of raspberry sherbet. The standard cost should identify the standard quantity, standard rate and standard cost per batch for each direct cost component of a batch of raspberry sherbet.

2 As part of the implementation of a standard cost system at ColdKing, John Wakefied plans to train those responsible for maintaining the standards on how to use variance analysis. Wakefield is particularly concerned with the causes of unfavourable variances.

   (a) Discuss possible causes of unfavourable materials price variances and identify the individual(s) who should be held responsible for these variances.

   (b) Discuss possible causes of unfavourable labour efficiency variances and identify the individual(s) who should be held responsible for these variances.

(*CMA*, adapted)

P12–21 Standard costs and variance analysis Time allowed: 40 minutes
Marvel Parts Ltd manufactures car accessories. One of the company's products is a set of seat covers that can be adjusted to fit nearly any small car. The company has a standard cost system in use for all of its products. According to the standards that have been set for the seat covers, the factory should work 2,850 hours each month to produce 1,900 sets of covers. The standard costs associated with this level of production activity are:

	Total	Per set of covers
Direct materials	£42,560	£22.40
Direct labour	17,100	9.00
Variable manufacturing overhead (based on direct labour-hours)	6,840	3.60
		£35.00

During August, the factory worked only 2,800 direct labour-hours and produced 2,000 sets of covers. The following actual costs were recorded during the month:

	Total	Per set of covers
Direct materials (12,000 metres)	£45,600	£22.80
Direct labour	18,200	9.10
Variable manufacturing overhead	7,000	3.50
		£35.40

At standard, each set of covers should require 5.6 metres of material. All of the materials purchased during the month were used in production.

Required

Compute the following variances for August:

1 The materials price and quantity variances.

2 The labour rate and efficiency variances.

3 The variable overhead spending and efficiency variances.

P12–22 Time allowed: 40 minutes

R plc is an engineering company that repairs machinery and manufactures replacement parts for machinery used in the building industry. There are a number of different departments in the company including a foundry, a grinding department, a milling department and a general machining department. R plc prepared its budget for the year ending 31 December 2003 using an incremental budgeting system.

The budget is set centrally and is then communicated to each of the managers who have responsibility for achieving their respective targets. The following report has been produced for the general machining department for October 2003:

	Budget	Actual	Variance	
Number of machine-hours	9,000	11,320	2,320	(F)
Cleaning materials	$1,350	$1,740	$390	(A)
Steel	45,000	56,000	11,000	(A)
Other direct materials	450	700	250	(A)
Direct labour	29,000	32,400	3,400	(A)
Production overheads	30,000	42,600	12,600	(A)
Total	105,800	133,440	27,640	(A)

The Manager of the general machining department has received a memo from the Financial Controller requiring him to explain the serious overspending within his department.

The Manager has sought your help and, after some discussion, you have ascertained the following:

1 The cleaning materials, steel and other direct materials vary in proportion to the number of machine hours;

2 The budgeted direct labour costs include fixed salary costs of $4,250, the balance is variable in proportion to the number of machine hours;

3 The production overhead costs include a variable cost that is constant per machine hour at all activity levels, and a stepped fixed cost which changes when the activity level exceeds 10,000 machine hours. A further analysis of this cost is shown below:

Activity (machine hours)	3,000	7,000	14,000
Costs ($)	13,500	24,500	45,800

Required

1 Prepare a revised budgetary control statement using the additional information that you have obtained from the Manager of the general machining department. *(10 marks)*

2 **(a)** Explain the differences between an incremental budgeting system and a zero based budgeting system. *(4 marks)*

(b) Explain why R plc and similar organizations would find it difficult to introduce a system of zero based budgeting. *(4 marks)*

3 Explain the benefits of involving the managers of R plc in the budget setting process, rather than setting the budget centrally as is R plc's current policy. *(7 marks)*

(Total = 25 marks)

CIMA Management Accounting – Performance Management, November 2003

CASE

Cases

C12–23 Behavioural impact of standard costs and variances Time allowed: 30 minutes

Terry Travers is the manufacturing supervisor of Aurora Manufacturing Company, which produces a variety of plastic products. Some of these products are standard items that are listed in the company's catalogue, while others are made to customer specifications. Each month, Travers receives a performance report showing the budget for the month, the actual activity, and the variance between budget and actual. Part of Travers' annual performance evaluation is based on his department's performance against budget. Aurora's purchasing manager, Sally Christensen, also receives monthly performance reports and she, too, is evaluated in part on the basis of these reports.

The monthly reports for June had just been distributed when Travers met Christensen in the hallway outside their offices. Scowling, Travers began the conversation, 'I see we have another set of monthly performance reports hand delivered by that not very nice junior employee in the budget office. He seemed pleased to tell me that I'm in trouble with my performance again.'

Christensen: I got the same treatment. All I ever hear about are the things I haven't done right. Now I'll have to spend a lot of time reviewing the report and preparing explanations. The worst part is that it's now the 21st of July so the information is almost a month old, and we have to spend all this time on history.

Travers: My biggest gripe is that our production activity varies a lot from month to month, but we're given an annual budget that's written in stone. Last month we were shut down for three days when a strike delayed delivery of the basic ingredient used in our plastic formulation, and we had already exhausted our stocks. You know about that problem, though, because we asked you to call all over the country to find an alternate source of supply. When we got what we needed on a rush basis, we had to pay more than we normally do.

Christensen: I expect problems like that to pop up from time to time – that's part of my job – but now we'll both have to take a careful look at our reports to see where the charges are reflected for that rush order. Every month I spend more time making sure I should be charged for each item reported than I do making plans for my department's daily work. It's really frustrating to see charges for things I have no control over.

Travers: The way we get information doesn't help, either. I don't get copies of the reports you get, yet a lot of what I do is affected by your department, and by most of the other departments we have. Why do the budget and accounting people assume that I should only be told about my operations even though the president regularly gives us pep talks about how we all need to work together as a team?

Christensen: I seem to get more reports than I need, and I am never asked to comment on them until top management calls me on the carpet about my department's shortcomings. Do you ever hear comments when your department shines?

Travers: I guess they don't have time to review the good news. One of my problems is that all the reports are in pounds and pence. I work with people, machines and materials. I need information to help me this month to solve this month's problems – not another report of the pounds expended last month or the month before.

Required

1 Based on the conversation between Terry Travers and Sally Christensen, describe the likely motivation and behaviour of these two employees resulting from Aurora Manufacturing Company's standard cost and variance reporting system.

2 When properly implemented, both employees and companies should benefit from a system involving standard costs and variances.

(a) Describe the benefits that can be realized from a standard cost system.

(b) Based on the situation presented above, recommend ways for Aurora Manufacturing Company to improve its standard cost and variance reporting system so as to increase employee motivation.

(*CMA*, adapted)

C12–24 Unit costs, variances, and journal entries from incomplete data Time allowed: 90 minutes (Appendix 12A) You are employed by Olster Company, which manufactures products for the senior citizen market. As a rising young executive in the company, you are scheduled to make a presentation in a few hours to your superior. This presentation relates to last week's production of Maxitol, a popular health tonic that is manufactured by Olster Company. Unfortunately, while studying ledger sheets and variance summaries by the poolside in the company's fitness area, you were bumped and dropped the papers into the pool. In desperation, you fished the papers from the water, but you have discovered that only the following fragments are readable:

Maxitol – standard cost card

	Standard quantity or hours	Standard price or rate	Standard cost
Material A	6 litres	£8 per litre	£?
Material B	?	per kilo	?
Direct labour	?	per hour	? 0
Standard cost per batch	?		£99.50

Raw materials – A

	Debit		Credit
Bal. 3/1	0		
Bal. 3.7	2,000		

Work in progress

	Debit		Credit
Bal 3/1	0		
Material A	5,760		
Bal 3/7	0		

Material A – price variance

	Debit		Credit
			300

Wages payable

	Debit		Credit
			41,000

Raw materials – B

	Debit		Credit
Bal. 3/1	700		2,500
Bal. 3/7	1,400		

Labour rate variance

	Debit		Credit
	500		

Material B – quantity variance

	Debit		Credit
	100		

Creditors

	Debit		Credit
			11,460

Maxitol – General ledger accounts

You remember that the creditors are for purchases of both material A and material B. You also remember that only 10 direct labour workers are involved in the production of Maxitol and that each worked 40 hours last week. The wages payable above are for wages earned by these workers.

You realize that to be ready for your presentation, you must reconstruct all data relating to Maxitol very quickly. As a start, you have called purchasing and found that 1,000 litres of material A and 800 kilos of material B were purchased last week.

Required

1 How many batches of Maxitol were produced last week? (This is a key figure; be sure it is right before going on.)

2 For material A:
   (a) What was the cost of material A purchased last week?
   (b) How many litres were used in production last week?
   (c) What was the quantity variance?
   (d) Prepare journal entries to record all activity relating to material A for last week.

3 For material B:
   (a) What is the standard cost per kilo for material B?
   (b) How many kilos of material B were used in production last week? How many kilos should have been used at standard?
   (c) What is the standard quantity of material B per batch?
   (d) What was the price variance for material B last week?
   (e) Prepare journal entries to record all activity relating to material B for last week.

4 For direct labour:
   (a) What is the standard rate per direct labour-hour?
   (b) What are the standard hours per batch?
   (c) What were the standard hours allowed for last week's production?
   (d) What was the labour efficiency variance for last week?
   (e) Prepare a journal entry to record all activity relating to direct labour for last week.

5 Complete the standard cost card shown above for one batch of Maxitol.

Endnotes

1 Morais (1997).

2 Dutta and Manzoni (1999), Chapter IV.

3 Toyota is also particularly noted for its use of kaizen costing or continuous improvement. See end of chapter.

4 Standard costing has been around for such a long time that recent articles are not that common. See, however, Fleischmann and Tyson (1996).

5 Variance analysis of fixed costs is reserved until Chapter 13.

6 See Appendix 12A at the end of the chapter for an illustration of journal entries in a standard cost system.

7 While the evils of standard cost systems are recounted in many articles and books, two particularly thorough accounts of their drawbacks can be found in Johnson (1990) and Kaplan (1986b).

8 Monden and Hamada (1991).

Chapter 13

Flexible budgets and overhead analysis

Learning objectives

After studying Chapter 13, you should be able to:

1. Prepare a flexible budget and explain the advantages of the flexible budget approach
2. Prepare a performance report for variable and fixed overhead costs using a flexible budget
3. Prepare a variable overhead performance report containing only a spending variance
4. Prepare a variable overhead performance report containing both a spending and an efficiency variance
5. Explain the role of the denominator activity figure in determining the standard cost of a unit of product
6. Apply overhead cost to units of product in a standard cost system
7. Compute and interpret the fixed overhead budget and volume variances
8. Appreciate an activity-based budgeting approach
9. (Appendix 13A) Compute and evaluate sales mix, quantity variances, production mix and yield variances
10. (Appendix 13B) Apply the variance analysis model to service organizations

Concepts in Context

Dr Finlay had just been unexpectedly appointed director of Providence Hospital Trust. The previous director, who had instituted tight budgetary controls, had been extremely unpopular with the hospital's staff. This had led to his sacking by the hospital's board of directors. Dr Finlay suspected that he had been chosen for the job because of his popularity rather than any innate management ability. He thought of himself as a doctor rather than as a manager.

Shortly after taking over as director, the hospital's lab supervisor came storming into Dr Finlay's office, threw a computer-generated report on Dr Finlay's desk, and angrily stated: 'Here, look at this report. It says we spent too much money in the Lab Department. We spent 5% more than had been authorized in the annual budget. Well, of course we did! Practically every department in the hospital asked for more tests than they had predicted at budget time! What are we supposed to do, refuse to run tests once we ran over budget?' Dr Finlay responded: 'Of course not. You have to run the tests. However, we also have to keep some control over our spending. On the other hand, I agree it isn't fair to hold you to the original budget. I don't see the solution right now, but I will work on it.'

Controlling overhead costs is a major preoccupation of managers in business, in government, and in not-for-profit organizations. Overhead is a major cost, if not *the* major cost, in most large organizations. It costs Microsoft very little to download copies of its software onto hard disks and to provide purchasers with software manuals; almost all of Microsoft's costs are in research and development and marketing – elements of overhead. Or consider Disney World. The only direct cost of serving a particular guest is the cost of the food the guest consumes at the park; virtually all of the other costs of running the amusement park are overhead. At Boeing, there are far more direct costs, but there are still huge amounts of overhead in the form of engineering salaries, buildings, insurance, administrative salaries and marketing costs.

Control of overhead costs poses special problems. Costs like direct materials and direct labour are often easier to understand, and therefore to control, than overhead, which can include everything from the disposable coffee cup in the visitors' waiting area to the CEO's salary. Overhead is usually made up of many separate costs – many of which may be small. This makes it impractical to control them in the same way that costs such as direct materials and direct labour are controlled. And some overhead costs are variable, some are fixed, and some are a mixture of fixed and variable. These particular problems can be largely overcome by the use of flexible budgets – a topic that was briefly discussed in Chapter 11. In this chapter, we study flexible budgets in greater detail and learn how they can be used to control costs. We also expand the study of overhead variances that we started in Chapter 12.

Flexible budgets

Characteristics of a flexible budget

The budgets that we studied in Chapter 11 were *static budgets*. A **static budget** is prepared for only the planned level of activity. This approach is suitable for planning purposes, but it is inadequate for evaluating how well costs are controlled. If the actual activity during a period differs from what was planned, it would be misleading to simply compare actual costs to the static budget. If activity is higher than expected, the variable costs should be higher than expected; and if activity is lower than expected, the variable costs should be lower than expected.

Flexible budgets take into account changes in costs that should occur as a consequence of changes in activity. A **flexible budget** provides estimates of what cost should be for any level of activity within a specified range. When a flexible budget is used in performance evaluation, actual costs are compared to what the *costs should have been for the actual level of activity during the period* rather than to the budgeted costs from the original budget. This is a very important distinction – particularly for variable costs. If adjustments for the level of activity are not made, it is very difficult to interpret discrepancies between budgeted and actual costs.

Deficiencies of the static budget

To illustrate the difference between a static budget and a flexible budget, we will consider the case of Rick's Hairstyling, a hairstyling salon located in Beverly Hills that is owned and managed by Rick Manzi.

The salon has very loyal customers – many of whom are associated with the film industry. Despite the glamour associated with his salon, Rick is a very shrewd businessman. Recently he has been attempting to get better control over his overhead, and at the urging of his accounting and business adviser Victoria Kho, he has begun to prepare monthly budgets. Victoria Kho is a qualified accountant in independent practice who specializes in small service-oriented businesses like Rick's Hairstyling.

At the end of February, Rick carefully prepared the March budget for overhead items that appears in Exhibit 13.1. Rick believes that the number of customers served in a month is the best way to measure the overall level of activity in his salon. Rick refers to these visits as client-visits. A customer who comes into the salon and has his or her hair styled is counted as one client-visit. After some discussion with Victoria Kho, Rick identified three major categories of variable overhead costs – hairstyling supplies, client gratuities and electricity – and four major categories of fixed costs – support staff wages and salaries, rent, insurance, and utilities other than electricity. Client gratuities consist of flowers, sweets and glasses of champagne that Rick gives to his customers while they are in the salon. Rick considers electricity to be a variable cost, since almost all of the electricity in the salon is consumed in running blow-dryers, curling irons and other hairstyling equipment.

Rick's Hairstyling
Static budget
For the month ended 31 March

Budgeted number of client-visits	5,000
Budget variable overhead costs:	
Hairstyling supplies	$6,000
Client gratuities	20,000
Electricity	1,000
Total variable overhead cost	27,000
Budgeted fixed overhead costs:	
Support staff wages and salaries	8,000
Rent	12,000
Insurance	1,000
Utilities other than electricity	500
Total fixed overhead cost	21,500
Total budgeted overhead cost	$48,500

Exhibit 13.1

To develop the budget for variable overhead, Rick estimated that the average cost per client-visit should be $1.20 for hairstyling supplies, $4.00 for client gratuities, and $0.20 for electricity. Based on his estimate of 5,000 client-visits in March, Rick budgeted for $6,000 ($1.20 per client-visit × 5,000 client-visits) in hairstyling supplies, $20,000 ($4.00 per client-visit × 5,000 client-visits) in client gratuities, and $1,000 ($0.20 per client-visit × 5,000 client-visits) in electricity.

The budget for fixed overhead items was based on Rick's records of how much he had spent on these items in the past. The budget included $8,000 for support staff wages and salaries, $12,000 for rent, $1,000 for insurance and $500 for utilities other than electricity.

At the end of March, Rick prepared a report comparing actual to budgeted costs. That report appears in Exhibit 13.2. The problem with that report, as Rick immediately realized, is that it compares costs at one level of activity (5,200 client-visits) to costs at a different level of activity (5,000 client-visits). Since Rick had 200 more client-visits than expected, his variable costs *should* be higher than budgeted. The static budget performance report confuses control over activity and control over costs. From Rick's standpoint, the increase in activity was good and should be counted as a favourable variance, but the increase in activity has an apparently negative impact on the costs in the report. Rick knew that something would have to be done to make the report more meaningful, but he was unsure of what to do. So he made an appointment to meet with Victoria Kho to discuss the next step.

13.2 EXHIBIT

Rick's Hairstyling
Static budget performance report
For the month ended 31 March

	Actual	Budgeted	Variance
Client-visits	5,200	5,000	200 F
Variable overhead costs:			
Hairstyling supplies	$6,400	$6,000	$400 U*
Client gratuities	22,300	20,000	2,300 U*
Electricity	1,020	1,000	20 U*
Total variable overhead cost	29,720	27,000	2,720 U*
Fixed overhead costs:			
Support staff wages and salaries	8,100	8,000	100 U
Rent	12,000	12,000	0
Insurance	1,000	1,000	0
Utilities other than electricity	470	500	30 F
Total fixed overhead cost	21,570	21,500	70 U
Total overhead cost	$51,290	48,500	$2,790 U*

The cost variances for variable costs and for total overhead are useless for evaluating how well costs were controlled since they have been derived by comparing actual costs at one level of activity to budgeted costs at a different level of activity.

Exhibit 13.2

IN ACTION

Management accounting in action: the issue

Victoria: How is the budgeting going?

Rick: Pretty well. I didn't have any trouble putting together the overhead budget for March. I also made out a report comparing the actual costs for March to the budgeted costs, but that report isn't giving me what I really want to know.

Victoria: Because your actual level of activity didn't match your budgeted activity?

Rick: Right. I know that shouldn't affect my fixed costs, but we had a lot more client-visits than I had expected and that had to affect my variable costs.

Victoria: So you want to know whether the actual costs are justified by the actual level of activity you had in March?

Rick: Precisely.

Victoria: If you leave your reports and data with me, I can work on it later today, and by tomorrow I'll have a report to show to you. Actually, I have a styling appointment for later this week. Why don't I move my appointment up to tomorrow, and I will bring along the analysis so we can discuss it.

Rick: That's great.

How a flexible budget works

2 LEARNING OBJECTIVE

The basic idea of the flexible budget approach is that a budget does not have to be static. Depending on the actual level of activity, a budget can be adjusted to show what costs *should be* for that specific level of activity. To illustrate how flexible budgets work, Victoria wrote a report for Rick that is simple to prepare (Exhibit 13.3). It shows how overhead costs can be expected to change, depending on the monthly level of activity. Within the activity range of 4,900 to 5,200 client-visits, the fixed costs are expected to remain the same. For the variable overhead costs, Victoria multiplied Rick's per client costs ($1.20 for hairstyling supplies, $4.00 for client gratuities and $0.20 for electricity) by the appropriate number of client-visits in each column. For example, the $1.20 cost of hairstyling supplies was multiplied by 4,900 client-visits to give the total cost of $5,880 for hairstyling supplies at that level of activity.

Rick's Hairstyling
Flexible budget
For the month ended 31 March

Budgeted number of client-visits		5,000			
Overheads costs	**Cost formula (per client-visit)**	**Activity (in client-visits)**			
		4,900	**5,000**	**5,100**	**5,200**
Variable overhead costs:					
Hairstyling supplies	$1.20	$5,880	$6,000	$6,120	$6,240
Client gratuities	4.00	19,600	20,000	20,400	20,800
Electricity (variable)	0.20	980	1,000	1,020	1,040
Total variable overhead cost	$5.40	26,460	27,000	27,540	28,080
Fixed overhead costs:					
Support staff wages and salaries		8,000	8,000	8,000	8,000
Rent		12,000	12,000	12,000	12,000
Insurance		1,000	1,000	1,000	1,000
Utilities other than electricity		500	500	500	500
Total fixed overhead cost		21,500	21,500	21,500	21,500
Total overhead cost		$47,960	$48,500	$49,040	$49,580

Exhibit 13.3 Illustration of the flexible budgeting concept

Using the flexible budgeting concept in performance evaluation

To get a better idea of how well Rick's variable overhead costs were controlled in March, Victoria applied the flexible budgeting concept to create a new performance report (Exhibit 13.4). Using the flexible budget approach, Victoria constructed a budget based on the *actual* number of client-visits for the month. The budget is prepared by multiplying the actual level of activity by the cost formula for each of the variable cost categories. For example, using the $1.20 per client-visit for hairstyling supplies, the total cost for this item *should* be $6,240 for 5,200 client-visits ($1.20 × 5,200). Since the actual cost for hairstyling supplies was $6,400, the unfavourable variance was $160.

Contrast the performance report in Exhibit 13.4 with the static budget approach in Exhibit 13.2. The variance for hairstyling supplies was $400 unfavourable using the static budget approach. In that exhibit, apples were being compared to oranges in the case of the variable cost items. Actual costs at one level of activity were being compared to budgeted costs at a different level of activity. Because actual activity was higher by 200 client-visits than budgeted activity, the total cost of hairstyling supplies *should* have been \$240 (\$1.20 per client-visit × 200 client-visits) higher than budgeted. As a result, \$240 of the \$400 'unfavourable' variance in the static budget performance report in Exhibit 13.2 was spurious.

In contrast, the flexible budget performance report in Exhibit 13.4 provides a more valid assessment of performance. Apples are compared to apples. Actual costs are compared to what costs should have been at the actual level of activity. When this is done, we see that the variance is \$160 unfavourable rather than \$400 unfavourable as it was in the original static budget performance report. In some cases, as with electricity in Rick's report, an unfavourable variance may be transformed into a favourable variance when an increase in activity is properly taken into account in a performance report.

13.4 EXHIBIT

Rick's Hairstyling
Flexible budget performance report
For the month ended 31 March

Budgeted number of client-visits	5,000			
Actual number of client-visits	5,200			
Overhead costs	**Cost formula (per client-visit)**	**Actual Costs Incurred for 5,200 client-visits**	**Budget based on 5,200 client-visits**	**Variance**
Variable overhead costs:				
Hairstyling supplies	\$1.20	\$6,400	\$6,240	\$160 U
Client gratuities	4.00	22,300	20,800	1,500 U
Electricity (variable)	0.20	1,020	1,040	20 F
Total variable overhead cost	\$5.40	29,720	28,080	1,640 U
Fixed overhead costs:				
Support staff wages and salaries		8,100	8,000	100 U
Rent		12,000	12,000	0
Insurance		1,000	1,000	0
Utilities other than electricity		470	500	30 F
Total fixed overhead cost		21,570	21,500	70 U
Total overhead cost		\$51,290	\$49,580	\$1,710 U

Exhibit 13.4

IN ACTION

Management accounting in action: the wrap-up

The following discussion took place the next day at Rick's salon.

Victoria: Let me show you what I've got. [Victoria shows the report contained in Exhibit 13.4.] All I did was multiply the costs per client-visit by the number of client-visits you actually had in March for the variable costs. That allowed me to come up with a better benchmark for what the variable costs should have been.

Rick: That's what you labelled the 'budget based on 5,200 client-visits'?

Victoria: That's right. Your original budget was based on 5,000 client-visits, so it understated what the variable overhead costs should be when you actually serve 5,200 customers.

Rick: That's clear enough. These variances aren't quite as shocking as the variances on my first report.

Victoria: Yes, but you still have an unfavourable variance of $1,500 for client gratuities.

Rick: I know how that happened. In March there was a big Democratic Party fundraising dinner that I forgot about when I prepared the March budget. Everyone in the film industry was there.

Victoria: Even Arnold Schwarzeneger?

Rick: Well, all the Democrats were there. At any rate, to fit all of our regular clients in, we had to push them through here pretty fast. Everyone still got top rate service, but I felt pretty bad about not being able to spend as much time with each customer. I wanted to give my customers a little extra something to compensate them for the less personal service, so I ordered a lot of flowers which I gave away by the bunch.

Victoria: With the prices you charge, Rick, I am sure the gesture was appreciated.

Rick: One thing bothers me about the report. Why are some of my actual fixed costs different from what I budgeted? Doesn't fixed mean that they are not supposed to change?

Victoria: We call these costs *fixed* because they shouldn't be affected by *changes in the level of activity*. However, that doesn't mean that they can't change for other reasons. For example, your utilities bill, which includes natural gas for heating, varies with the weather.

Rick: I can see that. March was warmer than normal, so my utilities bill was lower than I had expected.

Victoria: The use of the term *fixed* also suggests to people that the cost can't be controlled, but that isn't true. It is often easier to control fixed costs than variable costs. For example, it would be fairly easy for you to change your insurance bill by adjusting the amount of insurance you carry. It would be much more difficult for you to have much of an impact on the variable electric bill, which is a necessary part of serving customers.

Rick: I think I understand, but it is confusing.

Victoria: Just remember that a cost is called variable if it is proportional to activity; it is called fixed if it does not depend on the level of activity. However, fixed costs can change for reasons having nothing to do with changes in the level of activity. And controllability has little to do with whether a cost is variable or fixed. Fixed costs are often more controllable than variable costs.

Using the flexible budget approach, Rick Manzi now has a much better way of assessing whether overhead costs are under control. The analysis is not so simple, however, in companies that provide a variety of products and services. The number of units produced or customers served may not be an adequate measure of overall activity. For example, does it make sense to count a Sony floppy diskette, worth only a few dollars, as equivalent to a large-screen Sony TV? If the number of units produced is used as a measure of overall activity, then the floppy diskette and the large-screen TV would be counted as equivalent. Clearly, the number of units produced (or customers served) may not be appropriate as an overall measure of activity when the organization has a variety of products or services; a common denominator may be needed.

The measure of activity – a critical choice

What should be used as the measure of activity when the company produces a variety of products and services? At least three factors are important in selecting an activity base for an overhead flexible budget:

1 There should be a causal relationship between the activity base and variable overhead costs. Changes in the activity base should cause, or at least be highly correlated with, changes in the variable overhead costs in the flexible budget. Ideally, the variable overhead costs in the flexible budget should vary in direct proportion to changes in the activity base. For example, in a carpentry shop specializing in handmade wood furniture, the costs of miscellaneous supplies such as glue, wooden dowels and sandpaper can be expected to vary with the number of direct labour-hours. Direct labour-hours would therefore be a good measure of activity to use in a flexible budget for the costs of such supplies.

2 The activity base should not be expressed in pounds sterling or other currency. For example, direct labour cost is usually a poor choice for an activity base in flexible budgets. Changes in wage rates affect the activity base but do not usually result in a proportionate change in overhead. For example, we would not ordinarily expect to see a 5% increase in the consumption of glue in a carpentry shop if the workers receive a 5% increase in pay. Therefore, it is normally best to use physical rather than financial measures of activity in flexible budgets.

3 The activity base should be simple and easily understood. A base that is not easily understood will probably result in confusion and misunderstanding. It is difficult to control costs if people do not understand the reports or do not accept them as valid.

Variable overhead variances – a closer look

A special problem arises when the flexible budget is based on *hours* of activity (such as direct labour-hours) rather than on units of product or number of customers served. The problem relates to whether actual hours or standard hours should be used to develop the flexible budget on the performance report.

The problem of actual versus standard hours

The nature of the problem can best be seen through a specific example. MicroDrive Corporation is an automated manufacturer of precision personal computer diskdrive motors. Data concerning the company's variable manufacturing overhead costs are shown in Exhibit 13.5.

13.5 EXHIBIT

Budgeted production	25,000 motors
Actual production	20,000 motors
Standard machine-hours per motor	2 machine-hours per motor
Budgeted machine-hours (2 × 25,000)	50,000 machine-hours
Standard machine-hours allowed for the actual production (2 × 20,000)	40,000 machine-hours
Actual machine-hours	42,000 machine-hours
Variable overhead costs per machine-hour:	
Indirect labour	£0.80 per machine-hour
Lubricants	0.30 per machine-hour
Power	0.40 per machine-hour
Actual total variable overhead costs:	
Indirect labour	£36,600
Lubricants	11,000
Power	24,000
Total actual variable overhead cost	£71,000

Exhibit 13.5 MicroDrive Corporation data

MicroDrive Corporation uses machine-hours as the activity base in its flexible budget. Based on the budgeted production of 25,000 motors and the standard of 2 machine-hours per motor, the budgeted level of activity was 50,000 machine-hours. However, actual production for the year was only 20,000 motors, and 42,000 hours of machine time were used to produce these motors. According to the standard, only 40,000 hours of machine time should have been used (40,000 hours = 2 hours per motor × 20,000 motors).

In preparing an overhead performance report for the year, MicroDrive could use the 42,000 machine-hours actually worked during the year *or* the 40,000 machine-hours that should have been worked according to the standard. If the actual hours are used, only a spending variance will be computed. If the standard hours are used, both a spending *and* an efficiency variance will be computed. Both of these approaches are illustrated in the following sections.

Spending variance alone

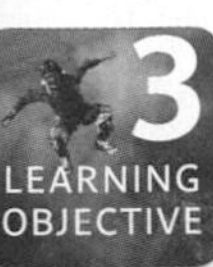

If MicroDrive Corporation bases its overhead performance report on the 42,000 machine-hours actually worked during the year, then the performance report will show only a spending variance for variable overhead. A performance report prepared in this way is shown in Exhibit 13.6.

13.6 EXHIBIT

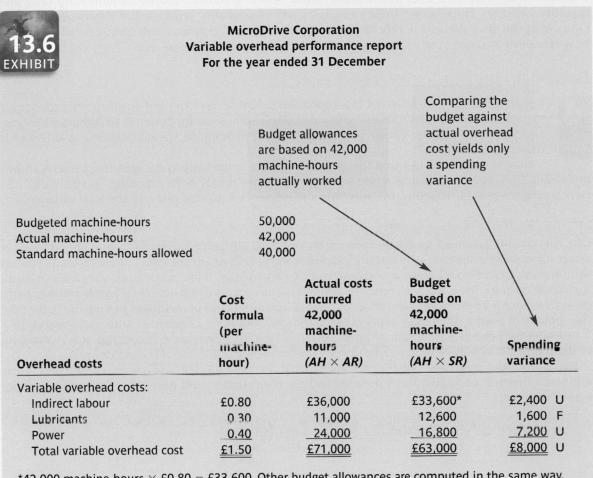

MicroDrive Corporation
Variable overhead performance report
For the year ended 31 December

Budget allowances are based on 42,000 machine-hours actually worked

Comparing the budget against actual overhead cost yields only a spending variance

Budgeted machine-hours	50,000
Actual machine-hours	42,000
Standard machine-hours allowed	40,000

Overhead costs	**Cost formula (per machine-hour)**	**Actual costs incurred 42,000 machine-hours *(AH × AR)***	**Budget based on 42,000 machine-hours *(AH × SR)***	**Spending variance**
Variable overhead costs:				
Indirect labour	£0.80	£36,000	£33,600*	£2,400 U
Lubricants	0.30	11,000	12,600	1,600 F
Power	0.40	24,000	16,800	7,200 U
Total variable overhead cost	£1.50	£71,000	£63,000	£8,000 U

*42,000 machine-hours × £0.80 = £33,600. Other budget allowances are computed in the same way.

Exhibit 13.6

The formula for the spending variance was introduced in the preceding chapter. That formula is:

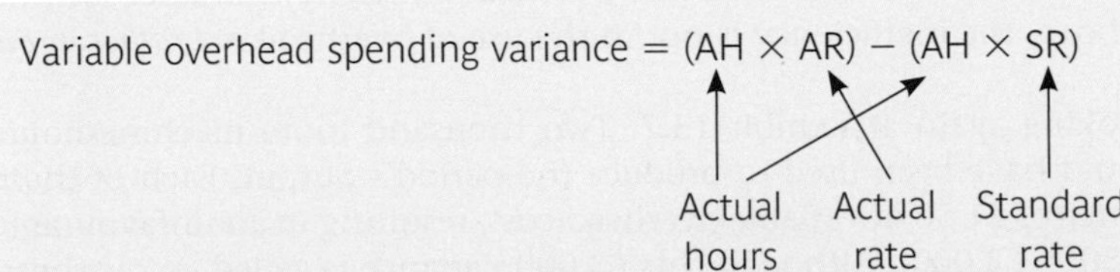

Variable overhead spending variance = (AH × AR) − (AH × SR)
Actual hours
Actual rate
Standard rate

Or, in factored form:

$$\text{Variable overhead spending variance} = AH(AR - SR)$$

The report in Exhibit 13.6 is structured around the first, or unfactored, format.

Interpreting the spending variance

The variable overhead spending variance is useful only if the cost driver for variable overhead really is the actual hours worked. Then the flexible budget based on the actual hours worked is a valid benchmark that tells us how much *should* have been spent in total on variable overhead items during the period. The actual overhead costs would be larger than this benchmark, resulting in an unfavourable variance, if either (1) the variable overhead items cost more to purchase than the standards allow or (2) more variable overhead items were used than the standards allow. So the spending variance includes both price and quantity variances. In principle, these variances could be separately reported, but this is seldom done. Ordinarily, the price element in this variance will be small, so the variance will mainly be influenced by how efficiently variable overhead resources such as production supplies are used.

Both spending and efficiency variances

4 LEARNING OBJECTIVE

If management of MicroDrive Corporation wants both a spending and an efficiency variance for variable overhead, then it should compute budget allowances for both the 40,000 machine-hour and the 42,000 machine-hour levels of activity. A performance report prepared in this way is shown in Exhibit 13.7.

Note from Exhibit 13.7 that the spending variance is the same as the spending variance shown in Exhibit 13.6. The performance report in Exhibit 13.7 has simply been expanded to include an efficiency variance as well. Together, the spending and efficiency variances make up the total variance.

Interpreting the efficiency variance

Like the variable overhead spending, the variable overhead efficiency variance is useful only if the cost driver for variable overhead really is the actual hours worked. Then any increase in hours actually worked should result in additional variable overhead costs. Consequently, if too many hours were used to create the actual output, this is likely to result in an increase in variable overhead. The variable overhead efficiency variance is an estimate of the effect on variable overhead costs of inefficiency in the use of the base (i.e., hours). In a sense, the term *variable overhead efficiency variance* is a misnomer. It seems to suggest that it measures the efficiency with which variable overhead resources were used. It does not. It is an estimate of the indirect effect on variable overhead costs of inefficiency in the use of the activity base.

Recall from the preceding chapter that the variable overhead efficiency variance is a function of the difference between the actual hours incurred and the hours that should have been used to produce the period's output:

$$\text{Variable overhead efficiency variance} = (AH \times SR) - (SH \times SR)$$

Actual hours · Standard rate · Standard hours allowed for output

$$\text{Variable overhead efficiency variance} = SR\,(AH - SH)$$

If more hours are worked than are allowed at standard, then the overhead efficiency variance will be unfavourable. However, as discussed above, the inefficiency is not in the use of overhead *but rather in the use of the base itself*.

This point can be illustrated by looking again at Exhibit 13.7. Two thousand more machine-hours were used during the period than should have been used to produce the period's output. Each of these hours presumably required the incurrence of £1.50 of variable overhead cost, resulting in an unfavourable variance of £3,000 (2,000 hours × £1.50 = £3,000). Although this £3,000 variance is called an overhead

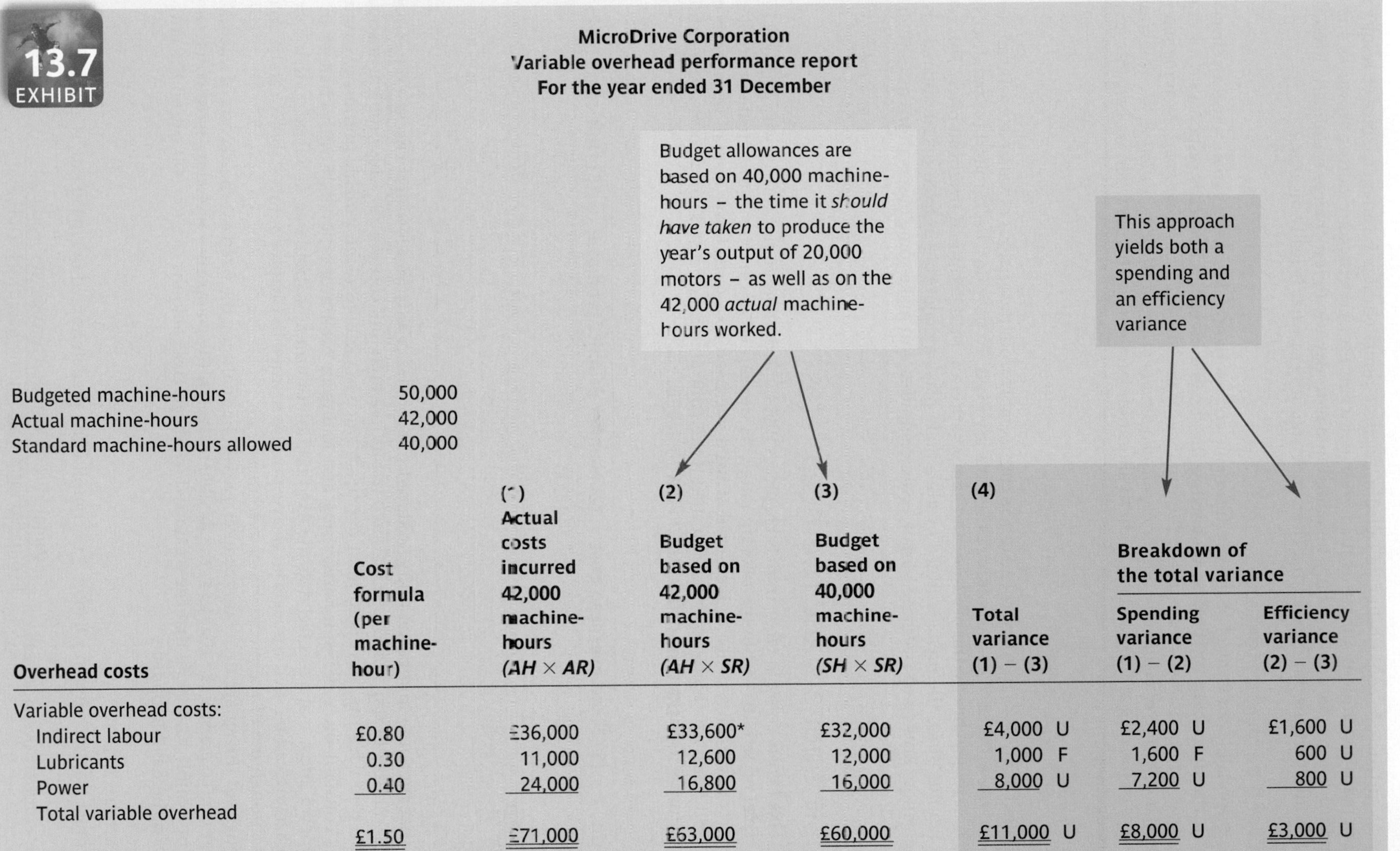

13.7 EXHIBIT

MicroDrive Corporation
Variable overhead performance report
For the year ended 31 December

Budget allowances are based on 40,000 machine-hours – the time it *should have taken* to produce the year's output of 20,000 motors – as well as on the 42,000 *actual* machine-hours worked.

This approach yields both a spending and an efficiency variance

Budgeted machine-hours	50,000
Actual machine-hours	42,000
Standard machine-hours allowed	40,000

		(1)	(2)	(3)	(4)	Breakdown of the total variance	
Overhead costs	**Cost formula (per machine-hour)**	**Actual costs incurred 42,000 machine-hours** ***(AH × AR)***	**Budget based on 42,000 machine-hours** ***(AH × SR)***	**Budget based on 40,000 machine-hours** ***(SH × SR)***	**Total variance (1) − (3)**	**Spending variance (1) − (2)**	**Efficiency variance (2) − (3)**
Variable overhead costs:							
Indirect labour	£0.80	£36,000	£33,600*	£32,000	£4,000 U	£2,400 U	£1,600 U
Lubricants	0.30	11,000	12,600	12,000	1,000 F	1,600 F	600 U
Power	0.40	24,000	16,800	16,000	8,000 U	7,200 U	800 U
Total variable overhead	£1.50	£71,000	£63,000	£60,000	£11,000 U	£8,000 U	£3,000 U

*42,000 machine-hours × £0.80 = £33,600. Other budget allowances are computed in the same way.

Exhibit 13.7

efficiency variance, it could better be called a machine-hours efficiency variance, since it results from using too many machine-hours rather than from inefficient use of overhead resources. However, the term *overhead efficiency variance* is so firmly ingrained in day-to-day use that a change is unlikely. Even so, be careful to interpret the variance with a clear understanding of what it really measures.

Control of the efficiency variance

Who is responsible for control of the overhead efficiency variance? Since the variance really reflects efficiency in the utilization of the base underlying the flexible budget, whoever is responsible for control of this base is responsible for control of the variance. *If the base is direct labour-hours, then the supervisor responsible for the use of labour time will be responsible for any overhead efficiency variance.* We will consider other ways of looking at the bases of overhead allocation later in this chapter when we consider activity-based budgeting.

Overhead rates and fixed overhead analysis

The detailed analysis of fixed overhead differs considerably from the analysis of variable overhead, simply because of the difference in the nature of the costs involved. To provide a background for our discussion, we will first review briefly the need for, and computation of, predetermined overhead rates. This review will be helpful, since the predetermined overhead rate plays a major role in fixed overhead analysis. We will then show how fixed overhead variances are computed and make some observations as to their usefulness to managers.

Flexible budgets and overhead rates

Fixed costs come in large, indivisible pieces that by definition do not change with changes in the level of activity within the relevant range. As we learned in Chapter 3, this creates a problem in product costing, since a given level of fixed overhead cost spread over a small number of units will result in a higher cost per unit than if the same amount of cost is spread over a large number of units. Consider the data in the following table:

Months	(1) Fixed overhead cost	(2) Number of units produced	(3) Unit cost (1)/(2)
January	£6,000	1,000	£6.00
February	6,000	1,500	4.00
March	6,000	800	7.50

Notice that the large number of units produced in February results in a low unit cost (£4.00), whereas the small number of units produced in March results in a high unit cost (£7.50). This problem arises only in connection with the fixed portion of overhead, since by definition the variable portion of overhead remains constant on a per unit basis, rising and falling in total proportionately with changes in the activity level. Most managers feel that the fixed portion of unit cost should be stabilized so that a single unit cost figure can be used throughout the year. As we learned in Chapter 3, this stability can be accomplished through use of the predetermined overhead rate.

Throughout the remainder of this chapter, we will be analysing the fixed overhead costs of MicroDrive Corporation. To assist us in that task, the flexible budget of the company – including fixed costs – is displayed in Exhibit 13.8. Note that the total fixed overhead costs amount to £300,000 within the range of activity in the flexible budget.

Denominator activity

The formula that we used in Chapter 3 to compute the predetermined overhead rate is given below:

$$\text{Predetermined overhead rate} = \frac{\text{Estimated total manufacturing overhead cost}}{\text{Estimated total units in the base (MH, DLH, etc.)}}$$

MicroDrive Corporation
Flexible budgets at various levels of activity

Overhead costs	Cost formula (per machine-hour)	Activity (in machine-hours) 40,000	45,000	50,000	55,000
Variable overhead costs:					
Indirect labour	£0.80	£32,000	£36,000	£40,000	£44,000
Lubricants	0.30	12,000	13,500	15,000	16,500
Power	0.40	16,000	18,000	20,000	22,000
Total variable overhead cost	£1.50	60,000	67,500	**75,000**	82,500
Fixed overhead costs:					
Depreciation		100,000	100,000	100,000	100,000
Supervisory salaries		160,000	160,000	160,000	160,000
Insurance		40,000	40,000	40,000	40,000
Total fixed overhead cost		300,000	300,000	**300,000**	300,000
Total overhead cost		£360,000	£367,000	**£375,000**	£382,500

Exhibit 13.8

The estimated total units in the base in the formula for the predetermined overhead rate is called the **denominator activity**. Recall from our discussion in Chapter 3 that once an estimated activity level (denominator activity) has been chosen, it remains unchanged throughout the year, even if the actual activity turns out to be different from what was estimated. The reason for not changing the denominator is to maintain stability in the amount of overhead applied to each unit of product regardless of when it is produced during the year.

Computing the overhead rate

When we discussed predetermined overhead rates in Chapter 3, we did not explain how the estimated total manufacturing cost was determined. This figure can be derived from the flexible budget. Once the denominator level of activity has been chosen, the flexible budget can be used to determine the total amount of overhead cost that should be incurred at that level of activity. The predetermined overhead rate can then be computed using the following variation on the basic formula for the predetermined overhead rate:

$$\text{Predetermined overhead rate} = \frac{\text{Overhead from the flexible budget at the demoninator level of activity}}{\text{Denominator level of activity}}$$

To illustrate, refer to MicroDrive Corporation's flexible budget for manufacturing overhead in Exhibit 13.8. Suppose that the budgeted activity level for the year is 50,000 machine-hours and that this will be used as the denominator activity in the formula for the predetermined overhead rate. The numerator in the formula is the estimated total overhead cost of £375,000 when the activity is 50,000 machine-hours. This figure is taken from the flexible budget in Exhibit 13.8. In sum, the predetermined overhead rate for MicroDrive Corporation will be computed as follows:

$$\frac{\text{£375,000}}{\text{50,000 MH}} = \text{£7,50 per machine-hour}$$

Or the company can break its predetermined overhead rate down into variable and fixed elements rather than using a single combined figure:

$$\frac{\text{Variable element: £75,000}}{\text{50,000 MH}} = \text{£1.50 per machine-hour (MH)}$$

$$\frac{\text{Fixed element: £300,000}}{\text{50,000 MH}} = \text{£6 per machine-hour (MH)}$$

For every *standard machine-hour* of operation, work in progress will be charged with £7.50 of overhead, of which £1.50 will be *variable overhead* and £6.00 will be *fixed overhead*. If a disk-drive motor should take two machine-hours to complete, then its cost will include £3 variable overhead and £12 fixed overhead, as shown on the following standard cost card:

Standard cost card – per motor	
Direct materials (assumed)	£14
Direct labour (assumed)	6
Variable overhead (2 machine-hours at £1.50)	3
Fixed overhead (2 machine-hours at £6)	12
Total standard cost per motor	£35

In sum, the flexible budget provides the estimated overhead cost needed to compute the predetermined overhead rate. Thus, the flexible budget plays a key role in determining the amount of fixed and variable overhead cost that will be charged to units of product.

Overhead application in a standard cost system

6 LEARNING OBJECTIVE

To understand the fixed overhead variances, it is necessary first to understand how overhead is applied to work in progress in a standard cost system. In Chapter 3, recall that we applied overhead to work in progress on the basis of actual hours of activity (multiplied by the predetermined overhead rate). This procedure was correct, since at the time we were dealing with a normal cost system.[1] However, we are now dealing with a standard cost system. In such a system, overhead is applied to work in progress on the basis of the standard hours allowed for the output of the period rather than on the basis of the actual number of hours worked. This point is illustrated in Exhibit 13.9. In a standard cost system, every unit of product moving along the production line bears the same amount of overhead cost, regardless of any variations in efficiency that may have been involved in its production.

13.9 EXHIBIT

Normal Cost System Manufacturing Overhead	
Actual overhead costs incurred	Applied overhead costs: Actual hours × Predetermined overhead rate
Under- or overapplied overhead	

Standard Cost System Manufacturing Overhead	
Actual overhead costs incurred	Applied overhead costs: Standard hours allowed for output × Predetermined overhead rate
Under- or overapplied overhead	

Exhibit 13.9 Applied overhead costs: normal cost system versus standard cost system

The fixed overhead variances

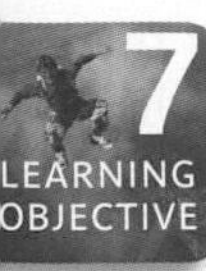
7 LEARNING OBJECTIVE

To illustrate the computation of fixed overhead variances, we will refer again to the data for MicroDrive Corporation.

Denominator activity in machine-hours	50,000
Budgeted fixed overhead costs	£300,000
Fixed portion of the predetermined overhead rate (computed earlier)	£6

Let us assume that the following actual operating results were recorded for the year:

Actual machine-hours	42,000
Standard machine-hours allowed*	40,000
Actual fixed overhead costs:	
Depreciation	£100,000
Supervisory salaries	172,000
Insurance	36,000
Total actual cost	£308,000

*For the actual production of the year.

From these data, two variances can be computed for fixed overhead – a *budget variance* and a *volume variance*. The variances are shown in Exhibit 13.10.

13.10 EXHIBIT

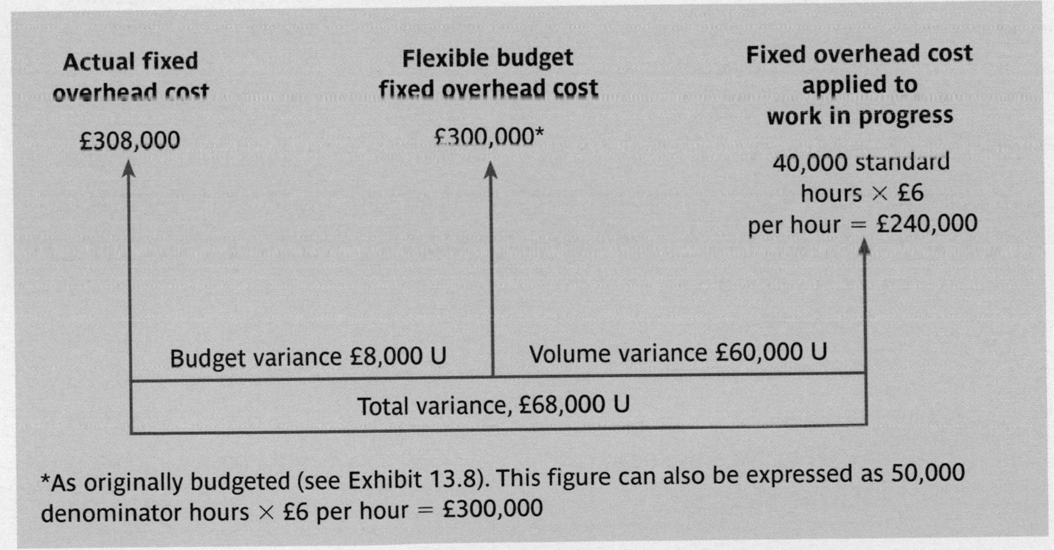

Exhibit 13.10 Computation of the fixed overhead variances

Notice from the exhibit that overhead has been applied to work in progress on the basis of 40,000 standard hours allowed for the output of the year rather than on the basis of 42,000 actual hours worked. As stated earlier, this keeps unit costs from being affected by any variations in efficiency.

The budget variance – a closer look

The **budget variance** is the difference between the actual fixed overhead costs incurred during the period and the budgeted fixed overhead costs as contained in the flexible budget. It can be computed as shown in Exhibit 13.10 or by using the following formula:

Budget variance = Actual fixed overhead cost − Flexible budget fixed overhead cost

Applying this formula to MicroDrive Corporation, the budget variance would be as follows:

£308,000 − £300,000 = £8,000 U

The variances computed for the fixed costs at Rick's Hairstyling in Exhibit 13.4 are all budget variances, since they represent the difference between the actual fixed overhead cost and the budgeted fixed overhead cost from the flexible budget.

An expanded overhead performance report for MicroDrive Corporation appears in Exhibit 13.11. This report now includes the budget variances for fixed overhead as well as the spending variances for variable overhead that were in Exhibit 13.6.

13.11 EXHIBIT

MicroDrive Corporation
Overhead performance report
For the year ended 31 December

Budgeted machine-hours		50,000		
Actual machine-hours		42,000		
Standard machine-hours allowed		40,000		
Overhead costs	**Cost formula (per machine-hour)**	**Actual costs 42,000 machine-hours**	**Budget based on 42,000 machine-hours**	**Spending or budget variance**
Variable overhead costs:				
Indirect labour	£0.80	£36,000	£33,600	£2,400 U
Lubricants	0.30	11,000	12,600	1,600 F
Power	0.40	24,000	16,800	7,200 U
Total variable overhead cost	£1.50	71,000	63,000	8,000 U
Fixed overhead costs:				
Depreciation		100,000	100,000	–
Supervisory salaries		172,000	160,000	12,000 U
Insurance		36,000	40,000	4,000 F
Total fixed overhead cost		308,000	300,000	8,000 U
Total overhead cost		£379,000	£363,000	£16,000 U

Exhibit 13.11 Fixed overhead costs on the overhead performance report

The budget variances for fixed overhead can be very useful, since they represent the difference between how much should have been spent (according to the flexible budget) and how much was actually spent. For example, supervisory salaries has a £12,000 unfavourable variance. There should be some explanation for this large variance. Was it due to an increase in salaries? Was it due to overtime? Was another supervisor hired? If so, why was another supervisor hired – this was not included in the budget when activity for the year was planned.

The volume variance – a closer look

The **volume variance** is a measure of utilization of plant facilities. The variance arises whenever the standard hours allowed for the output of a period are different from the denominator activity level that was planned when the period began. It can be computed as shown in Exhibit 13.10 or by means of the following formula:

$$\text{Volume Variance} = \begin{array}{c}\text{Fixed portion of the}\\ \text{predetermined Overhead rate}\end{array} \times \left(\begin{array}{c}\text{Denominator}\\ \text{hours}\end{array} - \begin{array}{c}\text{Standard hours}\\ \text{allowed}\end{array}\right)$$

Applying this formula to MicroDrive Corporation, the volume variance would be computed as follows:

£6 per MH (50,000 MH – 40,000 MH) = £60,000 U

Note that this computation agrees with the volume variance as shown in Exhibit 13.10. As stated earlier, the volume variance is a measure of utilization of available plant facilities. An unfavourable variance, as above, means that the company operated at an activity level *below* that planned for the period. A favourable variance would mean that the company operated at an activity level *greater* than that planned for the period.

It is important to note that the volume variance does not measure over- or underspending. A company normally would incur the same monetary amount of fixed overhead cost regardless of whether the period's activity was above or below the planned (denominator) level. In short, the volume variance is an activity-related variance. It is explainable only by activity and is controllable only through activity.

To summarize:

1 If the denominator activity and the standard hours allowed for the output of the period are the same, then there is no volume variance.

2 If the denominator activity is greater than the standard hours allowed for the output of the period, then the volume variance is unfavourable, signifying an underutilization of available facilities.

3 If the denominator activity is less than the standard hours allowed for the output of the period, then the volume variance is favourable, signifying a higher utilization of available facilities than was planned.

Graphic analysis of fixed overhead variances

Some insights into the budget and volume variances can be gained through graphic analysis. A graph containing these variances is presented in Exhibit 13.12.

As shown in the graph, fixed overhead cost is applied to work in progress at the predetermined rate of £6 for each standard hour of activity. (The applied-cost line is the upward-sloping line on the graph.) Since a denominator level of 50,000 machine-hours was used in computing the £6 rate, the applied-cost line crosses the budget-cost line at exactly the 50,000 machine-hour point. Thus, if the denominator hours and the standard hours allowed for the output are the same, there can be no volume variance, since the applied-cost line and the budget-cost line will exactly meet on the graph. It is only when the standard hours differ from the denominator hours that a volume variance can arise.

In the case at hand, the standard hours allowed for the actual output (40,000 hours) are less than the denominator hours (50,000 hours); the result is an unfavourable volume variance, since less cost was applied to production than was originally budgeted. If the situation had been reversed and the standard hours allowed for the actual output had exceeded the denominator hours, then the volume variance on the graph would have been favourable.

Cautions in fixed overhead analysis

The reason we get a volume variance for fixed overhead is that the total fixed cost does not depend on activity; yet when applying the costs to work in progress, we act *as if* the fixed costs were variable and depended on

13.12 EXHIBIT

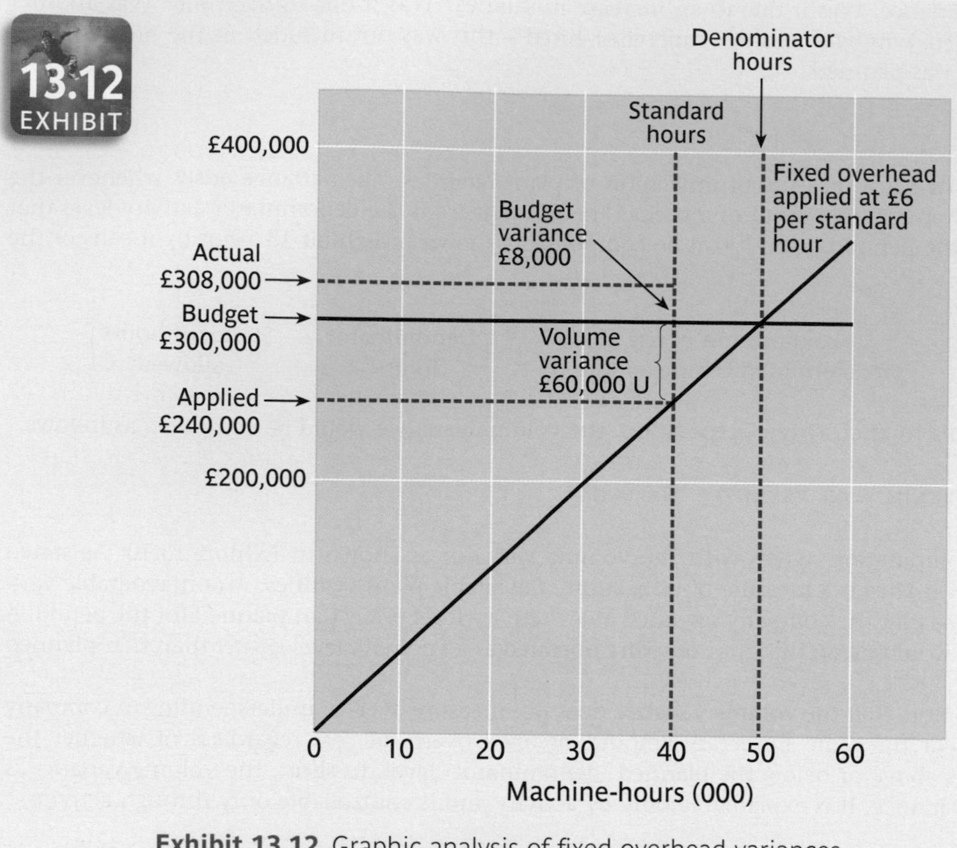

Exhibit 13.12 Graphic analysis of fixed overhead variances

activity. This point can be seen from the graph in Exhibit 13.12. Notice from the graph that the fixed overhead costs are applied to work in progress at a rate of £6 per hour *as if* they were variable. Treating these costs as if they were variable is necessary for product costing purposes, but there are some real dangers here. The manager can easily become misled and start thinking of the fixed costs as if they were *in fact* variable.

The manager must keep clearly in mind that fixed overhead costs come in large, indivisible pieces. Expressing fixed costs on a unit or per hour basis, though necessary for product costing for external reports, is artificial. Increases or decreases in activity in fact have no effect on total fixed costs within the relevant range of activity. Even though fixed costs are expressed on a unit or per hour basis, they are *not* proportional to activity. In a sense, the volume variance is the error that occurs as a result of treating fixed costs as variable costs in the costing system.

Because of the confusion that can arise concerning the interpretation of the volume variance, some companies present the volume variance in physical units (hours) rather than in pounds sterling. These companies feel that stating the variance in physical units gives management a clearer signal concerning the cause of the variance.

Overhead variances and under- or overapplied overhead cost

Four variances relating to overhead cost have been computed for MicroDrive Corporation in this chapter. These four variances are as follows:

Variable overhead spending variance (p. 523)	£8,000 U
Variable overhead efficiency variance (p. 524)	3,000 U
Fixed overhead budget variance (p. 529)	8,000 U
Fixed overhead volume variance (p. 531)	60,000 U
Total overhead variance	£79,000 U

Recall from Chapter 3 that under- or overapplied overhead is the difference between the amount of overhead applied to products and the actual overhead costs incurred during a period. Basically, the overhead variances we have computed in this chapter break the under- or overapplied overhead down into variances that can be used by managers for control purposes. Consequently, *the sum of the overhead variances equals the under- or overapplied overhead cost for a period.*

Furthermore, in a standard cost system, unfavourable variances are equivalent to underapplied overhead and favourable variances are equivalent to overapplied overhead. Unfavourable variances occur because more was spent on overhead than the standards allow. Underapplied overhead occurs when more was spent on overhead than was applied to products during the period. But in a standard costing system, the standard amount of overhead allowed is exactly the same amount of overhead applied to products. Therefore, *in a standard costing system, unfavourable variances and underapplied overhead are the same thing, as are favourable variances and overapplied overhead.*

For MicroDrive Corporation, the total overhead variance was £79,000 unfavourable. Therefore, its overhead cost was underapplied by £79,000 for the year. To solidify this point in your mind, *carefully study the review problem at the end of the chapter*! This review problem provides a comprehensive summary of overhead analysis, including the computation of under- or overapplied overhead cost in a standard cost system.

Activity-based budgeting

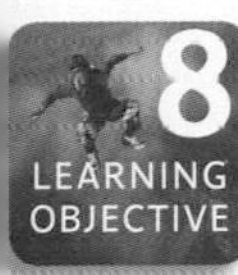

It is unlikely that all variable overhead in a complex organization is driven by a single factor such as the number of units produced or the number of labour-hours or machine-hours. Traditionally there has been little understanding of what drives costs that do not vary with volume. Activity-based costing provides a way of recognizing a variety of overhead cost drivers and thereby increasing the accuracy of the costing system. In activity-based costing, each overhead cost pool has its own measure of activity. The actual spending in each overhead cost pool can be independently evaluated using the techniques discussed in this chapter. The only difference is that the cost formulas for variable overhead costs will be stated in terms of different kinds of activities instead of all being stated in terms of units or a common measure of activity such as direct labour-hours or machine-hours. If done properly, activity-based costing can greatly enhance the usefulness of overhead performance reports by recognizing multiple causes of overhead costs. But the usefulness of overhead performance reports depends on how carefully the reports are done. In particular, managers must take care to separate the variable from the fixed costs in the flexible budgets.

Activity analysis may be used to develop *activity-based budgeting* (ABB) in which the aim is that financial systems should *derive from the business* rather than drive it. Thus an **activity-based budgeting (ABB)** model is generally seen as being comprised of two stages, as shown in Exhibit 13.13. In stage 1, the aim is to develop an operational model of business processes *before* moving on to stage 2 which derives a financial model that is based on the operational plan. The operational plan starts with estimating the demands for products and services and then uses activity consumption rates to determine resource consumption rates. As with ABC, the activity based budget is derived from a more detailed knowledge of the demand for indirect and support activities such as machine set-ups, materials ordering and handling, customer ordering and so on. In contrast to ABC, however, which begins by assigning resources to activities and activity cost drivers through to products and customers, ABB *starts* with the analysis of product and customer demand and works through to resource requirements.[2]

The **activity consumption rate** is the quantity of each activity required to produce a unit of demand and the **resource consumption rate** is the quantity of each resource that produces one instance of an activity. The operational and financial plans are reconciled through the adjustment of one or more of the following items: activity and resource consumption rates; the resource capacity; the resource cost; the product/service demand and product service price. In conventional, one stage budgeting, a balance can only be achieved by changing the quantity of demand and/or the capacity (resources available).

In comparison with conventional budgeting, ABB offers a more sophisticated approach to capacity adjustment issues as well as improving communication across departments and up and down the organization. The advantage of ABB is that it both avoids unnecessary financial balancing and incorporates operational issues such as inefficiencies and bottlenecks that are usually left out of traditional budgets. Crucially, managers and employees talk in *operational* rather than *financial* terms.

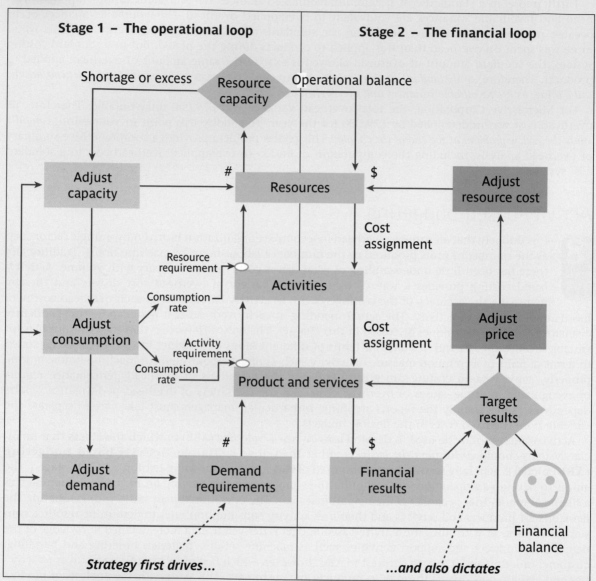

Exhibit 13.13 Activity-based budgeting

Reproduced with permission from p. 100 of Hansen, S., Otley, D. and Van der Stede, W. 2003. Practice developments in budgeting: an overview and research perspective, *Journal of Management Accounting Research*, 15, pp. 95–116.

Advocates of ABB argue that in traditional budgeting, discussions are characterized by a trial-and-error, negotiating process, up and down the organization that encourages both gaming and incrementalism. A correctly designed and implemented ABB system 'offers the opportunity for such discussions to be based more on facts and less on power, influence and negotiating ability'.[3]

Summary

- When analysing overhead costs, it is vital to distinguish between variable overhead and fixed overhead. Variable overhead costs vary in proportion to changes in activity whereas total fixed costs do not change within the relevant range. This distinction is important when constructing flexible budgets and computing variances for overhead.
- A flexible budget shows what cost should be for various levels of activity. If a cost is variable, the flexible budget amount is computed by multiplying the cost per unit of activity by the level of activity specified for the flexible budget. If the cost is fixed, the original total budgeted fixed cost is used as the flexible budget amount.
- The two variances discussed in the chapter are the variable overhead spending and variable overhead efficiency variances.
- Two variances for fixed overheads are covered in the chapter. The budget variance is the difference between the actual total fixed overhead cost incurred and the total amount of fixed overhead cost that was originally budgeted. The volume variance is the difference between the amount of fixed overhead cost applied to inventory and the total amount of fixed overhead cost that was originally budgeted.
- The budget variance is a measure of the degree to which fixed overhead spending was under control. The volume variance is the consequence of treating a fixed cost as if it was variable and is more difficult to interpret meaningfully.
- The sum of all four overhead variances equals the overhead over- or underapplied for the period. Unfavourable variances are equivalent to underapplied overhead and favourable variances are equivalent to overapplied overhead.

Key terms for review

Activity-based budgeting (p. 533).

Activity consumption rate (p. 533).

Budget variance (p. 530).

Denominator activity (p. 527).

Flexible budget (p. 516).

Resource consumption rate (p. 533).

Static budget (p. 516).

Volume variance (p. 531).

Review problem: overhead analysis

(This problem provides a comprehensive review of the computation of under- or overapplied overhead and its breakdown into the four overhead variances.)

Data for the manufacturing overhead of Aspen Company are given below:

Overhead costs	Cost formula (per machine-hour)	Machine hours		
		5,000	6,000	7,000
Variable overhead costs:				
Supplies	£0.20	£1,000	£1,200	£1,400
Indirect labour	0.30	1,500	1,800	2,100
Total variable overhead cost	£0.50	2,500	3,000	3,500
Fixed overhead costs:				
Depreciation		4,000	4,000	4,000
Supervision		5,000	5,000	5,000
Total fixed overhead cost		9,000	9,000	9,000
Total overhead cost		£11,500	£12,000	£12,500

Five hours of machine time are required per unit of product. The company has set denominator activity for the coming period at 6,000 machine-hours (or 1,200 units). The computation of the predetermined overhead rate would be as follows:

$$\text{Total: } \frac{£12,000}{6,000 \text{ MH}} = £2.00 \text{ per machine-hour}$$

$$\text{Variable element: } \frac{£3,000}{6,000 \text{ MH}} = £0.50 \text{ per machine-hour}$$

$$\text{Fixed element: } \frac{£9,000}{6,000 \text{ MH}} = £1.50 \text{ per machine-hour}$$

Assume the following *actual* results for the period:

Number of units produced	1,300 units
Actual machine-hours	6,800 machine-hours
Standard machine-hours allowed*	6,500 machine-hours
Actual variable overhead cost	£4,200
Actual fixed overhead cost	9,400

*1,300 units 3 5 machine-hours per unit.

Therefore, the company's Manufacturing Overhead account would appear as follows at the end of the period:

	Manufacturing overhead		
Actual overhead costs	13,600*	13,000†	Applied overhead costs
Underapplied overhead	600		

* £4,200 variable + £94,000 fixed = £13,600

† 6,500 standard hours × £2 per machine hour = £13,000. In a standard cost system, overhead is applied on the basis of standard hours, not actual hours.

Required

Analyse the £600 underapplied overhead in terms of:

1. A variable overhead spending variance.
2. A variable overhead efficiency variance.
3. A fixed overhead budget variance.
4. A fixed overhead volume variance.

Solution to review problem: overhead analysis

Variable overhead variances

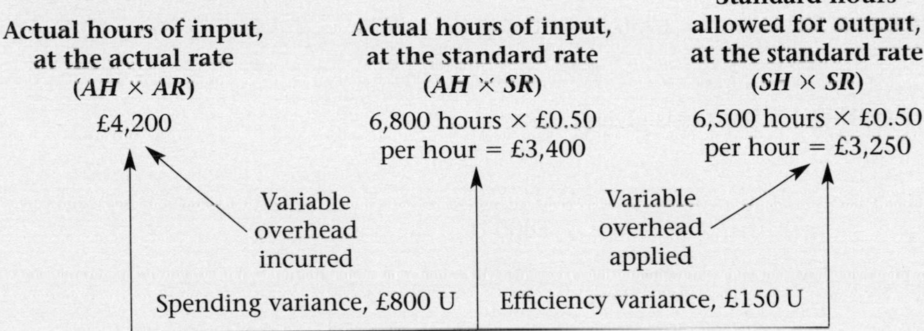

These same variances in the alternative format would be as follows:

Variable overhead spending variance:

Spending variance = (*AH* × *AR*) − (*AH* × *SR*)
(£4,200*) − (6,800 hours × £0.50 per hour) = £800 U

**AH* × *AR* equals the total actual cost for the period.

Variable overhead efficiency variance:

Efficiency variance = *SR*(*AH* − *SH*)
£0.50 per hour (6,800 hours − 6,500 hours) = £150 U

Fixed overhead variances

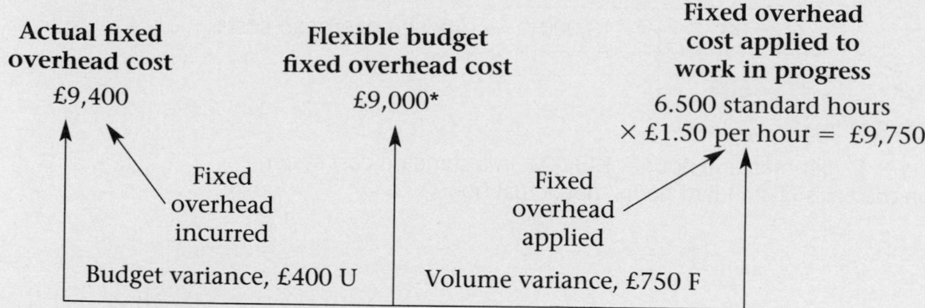

*Can be expressed as: 6,000 denominator hours × £1.50 per hour = £9,000.

These same variances in the alternative format would be as follows:
Fixed overhead budget variance:

Budget variance = Actual fixed overhead cost − Flexible budget fixed overhead cost
£9,400 − £9,000 = £400 U

Fixed overhead volume variance:

Volume variance = Fixed portion of Predetermined overhead rate × (denominator hours − standard hours)

£1.50 per hour (6,000 − 6,500 hours) = £750 F

Summary of variances
A summary of the four overhead variances is given below:

Variable overhead:	
Spending variance	£800 U
Efficiency variance	150 U
Fixed overhead:	
Budget variance	400 U
Volume variance	750 F
Underapplied overhead	£600

Notice that the £600 summary variance figure agrees with the underapplied balance in the company's Manufacturing Overhead account. This agreement verifies the accuracy of our variance analysis.

Appendix 13A: Sales mix, quantity variances, production mix and yield variances

Sales mix variances with multiple products

A **sales mix variance** provides useful information when a company sells multiple products and the products are (imperfect) substitutes for each other. For example, a computer dealer sells two types of computers, graphics professional (*Pro*) and *Consumer*. For May, the company estimated sales of 500 computers, 100 *Pro* models and 400 *Consumer* models. The per computer contribution margin expected was £100 for the *Pro* and £20 for the *Consumer* model. Thus, the budgeted total contribution for May was as follows:

Pro: 100 at £100	£10,000
Consumer: 400 at £20	8,000
Total contribution	£18,000

When the May results were tabulated, the company had sold 500 computers, and each model had provided the predicted contribution margin per unit. The total contribution was a disappointing £14,000, however, because instead of the predicted 20% *Pro* to 80% *Consumer* mix sold, the actual mix sold was 10% *Pro* and 90% *Consumer*, with the following results:

Pro: 50 at £100	£5,000
Consumer: 450 at £20	9,000
Total contribution	£14,000

The £4,000 decrease from the budgeted contribution margin is the sales mix variance. In this case, it occurred because 50 fewer *Pro* models were sold (for a loss of 50 × £100 = £5,000) while 50 more Consumer models were sold (for a gain of 50 × £20 = £1,000). The net effect is a loss of £80 (= £100 – £20) in contribution margin for each *Consumer* model that was sold instead of a *Pro* model. (This emphasizes the importance of assuming the products are substitutes. If a store sells, among other things, jewellery and garden tractors, the mix variance is probably not as useful as when comparing two products that are close substitutes.)

Evaluating sales mix and sales quantity

Assume that Custom Electronics makes and sells two models of electrical switches, Industrial and standard. Data on the two models for February are shown in the following table.

Although there are several approaches to calculating a sales mix variance, our computation allows us to break down the sales activity variance into two components: sales mix and sales quantity. The *sales mix variance measures the impact of substitution* (it appears that the industrial model has been substituted for the standard model) while the sales quantity variance *measures the variance in sales quantity, holding the sales mix constant.*

See Exhibit 13A.1 for calculations for this example. The sales price variance is unaffected by our analysis; the sales activity variance is broken down into the mix and quantity variances.

	A	B	C	D	E	F	G	H
1		Industrial		Standard		Total		
2	Standard selling price	£15.00		£5.00				
3	Standard variable costs	8.00		2.00				
4	Standard contribution margin per unit	£7.00		£3.00				
5								
6	Budgeted sales quantity	10,000		40,000		50,000		
7	Budgeted sales mix	20%		80%				
8	Budgeted contribution margin	£70,000		£120,000		£190,000		
9								
10	Actual sales mix	23%		77%				
11	Actual sales quantity	9,200		30,800		40,000		
12	Budgeted contribution margin at actual quantities	£64,400	(a)	£92,400	(a)	£156,800		
13	Sales activity variance					£33,200	U	(b)
14								
15								
16	(a) £ 64,400 = £ 7 per unit × 9,200 units; £ 92,400 = £ 3 per unit × 30,800 units.							
17	(b) £ 33,200 U = £ 156,800 − £ 190,000.							
18								

13A.1 EXHIBIT

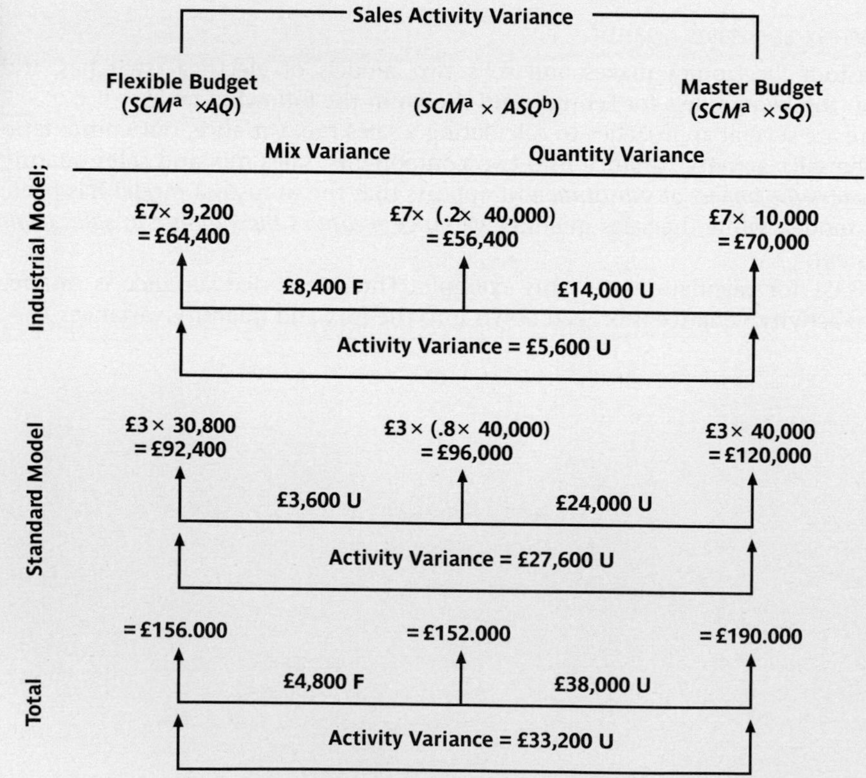

Exhibit 13A.1 Sales mix and sales quantity variances, February – Custom Electronics

By separating the activity variance into its mix and quantity components, we have isolated the pure mix effect by holding constant the quantity effects, and we have isolated the pure quantity effect by holding constant the mix effect.

Source of the sales mix variance

Although we have calculated the mix variance of each product sold to show the exact source, the total mix variance (£4,800 F) is most frequently used. In this example, the favourable mix variance results from the substitution of the higher contribution industrial model for the lower contribution standard model.

Production mix and yield variances

Our analysis of mix and quantity variances for sales also can be applied to production. Often a mix of inputs is used in production. Chemicals, steel, fabrics, plastics, and many other products require a mix of direct materials, some of which can be substituted for each other without affecting product quality.

Mix and yield variances in manufacturing

Wigan Chemicals, a division of Newfoundland Enterprises, makes a cleaning product, EZ-Foam, which is made up of two chemicals, C-30 and D-12. The standard costs and quantities are as follows:

Direct Materials	Standard Price per Litre	Standard Number of Litres of Chemical per Litre of Finished Product
C-30	£ 5	0.6
D-12	15	0.4
		1.0

The standard cost per unit of finished product is as follows:

C-30:0.6 litres @ £5	£3
D-12:0.4 litres @ £15	6
	£9

During September, Wigan Chemicals had the following results:

Units produced	100,000 litres of finished product
Materials purchased and used	
C-30	55,000 litres @ £5.20
D-12	49,000 litres @ £14.00
	104,000 litres

Our computation of the mix variance breaks down the direct materials efficiency variance into two components, mix and yield. The mix variance for costs is conceptually the same as the mix variance for sales, and the yield variance is conceptually the same as the sales quantity variance. The **production mix variance** measures the impact of substitution (material D-12 appears to have been substituted for material C-30); the **production yield variance** measures the input-output relationship holding the standard mix inputs constant. Standards called for 100,000 litres of materials to produce 100,000 litres of output; however, 104,000 litres of input were actually used. The overuse of 4,000 litres is a physical measure of the yield variance.

To derive mix and yield variances, we use the term *ASQ*, which is the actual amount of input used at the standard mix. Calculations for the three variances (price, mix, yield) for Wigan Chemicals are shown in Exhibit 13A.2. Note that the sum of the mix and yield variances equals the materials efficiency variance. In examining these calculations, recall that the standard proportions (mix) of direct materials are C-30, 60%, and D-12, 40%; 104,000 litres were used in total. Thus, *ASQ* for each material is as follows:

C-30:	0.6 × 104,000 =	62,400 litres
D-12:	0.4 × 104,000 =	41,600 litres
		104,000 litres

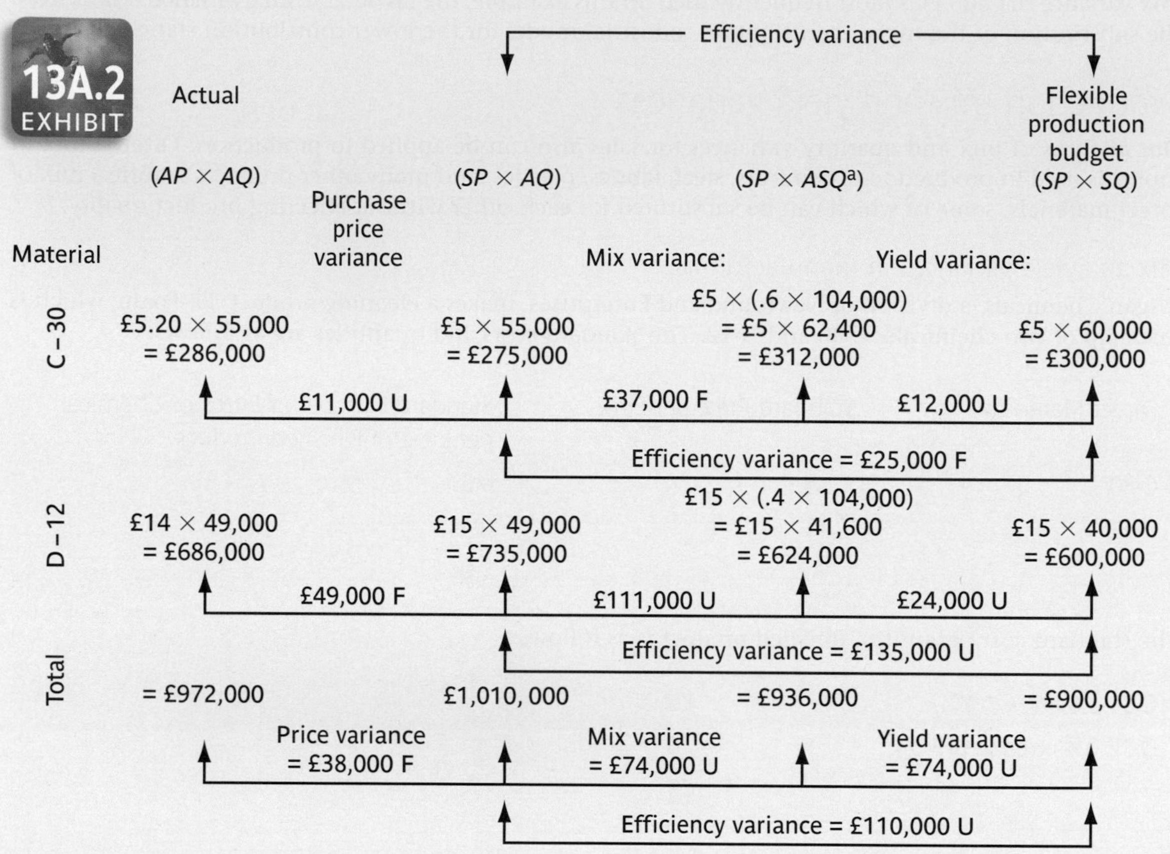

Exhibit 13A.2 Production mix and yield variances – Wigan Chemicals

By separating the efficiency variance into its mix and yield components, we have isolated the pure mix effect by holding constant the yield effect, and we have isolated the pure yield effect by holding constant the mix effect.

We have calculated the mix variance for each direct material to demonstrate its exact source. However, it is the total mix variance (£74,000 U) that is used most commonly. In this example, the unfavourable mix is caused by a substitution of the more expensive direct material D-12 for the less expensive direct material C-30. To be precise, the substitutions are as follows:

Decrease in C-30 (55,000 − 62,400)	= 7,400 litres @ £ 5 =	£ 37,000 decrease
Increase in D-12 (49,000 − 41,600)	= 7,400 litres @ £15 =	£111,000 increase
Net effect in litres	−0−	
Net effect in £		£ 74,000 increase

As previously indicated, the yield variance results from the overuse of 4,000 litres, or more precisely,

Material C-30: (62,400 − 60,000) = 2,400 litres @ £ 5 =	£12,000 U
Material D-12: (41,600 − 40,000) = 1,600 litres @ £15 =	24,000 U
	£36,000 U

The journal entry to record the purchase and use of materials at Wigan Chemicals follows:

Work-in-Progress Inventory	900,000	
Material Price Variance – C-30	11,000	
Material Yield Variance – C-30	12,000	
Material Mix Variance – D-12	111,000	
Material Yield Variance – D-12	24,000	
Material Price Variance – D-12		49,000
Material Mix Variance – C-30		37,000
Creditors		972,000

To record the purchase and use of 55,000 litres of C-30, with an actual price of £5.20 per litre and a standard price of £5.00 per litre, and 49,000 litres of D-12, with an actual price of £14 per litre and a standard price of £15 per litre. Standard usage to produce 100,000 litres of EZ-Foam is 60,000 litres of C-30 and 40,000 litres of D-12.

Appendix 13B: Variance analysis in service settings

The comparison of the master budget, the flexible budget, and actual results also can be used in service and merchandising organizations. The basic framework in Chapters 11 and 12 are retained. *Output* is usually defined as sales units in merchandising, but service organizations use other measures, such as the following:

Organization	Units of Activity in Number of
Public accounting, legal, and consulting firms	Professional staff hours
Hotel	Room-nights, guests
Airline	Seat-miles, revenue-miles
Hospital	Patient-days

Merchandising and service organizations focus on marketing and administrative costs to measure efficiency and control costs. The key items to control are labour costs, particularly for service organizations, and occupancy costs per sales-pound, particularly for merchandising organizations.

Efficiency measures

The need for analysis of price and efficiency variances in non-manufacturing settings is increasing. Banks, fast-food outlets, hospitals, consulting firms, retail stores, and many other organizations apply the variance analysis techniques discussed in this chapter to their labour and overhead costs. In some cases, an efficiency variance can be used to analyse variable non-manufacturing costs; its computation requires a reliable measure of output activity. Ideally, this requires some quantitative input that can be linked to output.

For example, personnel in the purchasing department of Bayou Division are expected to process ten transactions per day. The standard labour cost is £175 per day including benefits. During August, personnel worked 120 staff-days and processed 1,130 transactions. The actual labour cost was £20,040. For 1,130 transactions, the number of standard staff-days allowed is 113 (= 1,130 transactions ÷ 10 transactions per day). Favourable price and unfavourable efficiency variances were computed (Exhibit 13B.1). The calculations in the exhibit are similar to the ones used for labour variances in manufacturing.

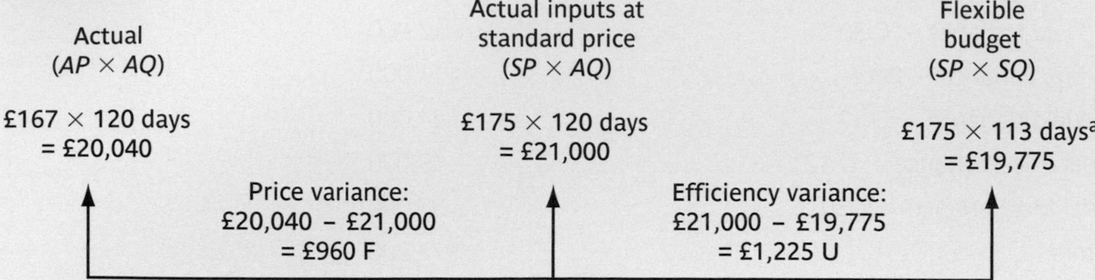

[a] 113 staff days = 1,130 transactions ÷ 10 transactions per staff-days.

Exhibit 13B.1 Non-manufacturing variance analysis, purchasing department – Bayou Division

Computing non-manufacturing efficiency variances requires some assumed relationship between input and output activity. Some examples include:

Department	Input in Number of	Output in Number of
Mailing	Labour-hours worked	Pieces handled
Personnel	Labour-hours worked	Requests processed
Food service	Labour-hours worked	Meals served
Consulting	Billable hours worked	Customer revenues
Nursing	Labour-hours worked	Patient-days
Cheque processing	Computer-hours worked	Cheques processed

In general, jobs with routine tasks lend themselves to efficiency measures, and jobs with nonroutine tasks, such as most administrative positions, do not.

Mix and yield variances in service organizations

Companies also substitute different types of labour. An accounting company might substitute partner time for staff time on a particular audit job, for example. Suppose the Birmingham office has bid a job for 3,000 hours: 900 hours of partner time at a cost of £300 per hour and 2,100 hours of staff time at a cost of £100 per hour. Due to scheduling problems, both the partner and the staff member spend 1,500 hours on the job. If the actual costs are £300 and £100 for partner and staff time, respectively, there is no labour price variance. But even though the 3,000 hours required were exactly what was bid, the job cost is £120,000 over budget:

Actual cost = (1,500 hours × £300) + (1,500 hours × £100)
= £450,000 + £150,000
= £600,000

Budgeted cost = (900 hours × £300) + (2,100 hours × £100)
= £270,000 + £210,000
= £480,000

The £120,000 variance results from the substitution of 600 hours of partner time at £300 per hour for 600 hours of staff time at £100 per hour. The production mix variance is the difference in labour costs per hour (£300 − £100 = £200) times the number of hours substituted (600): £200 × 600 hours = £120,000.

Two factors are important when considering mix variances. First, there is an assumed *substitutability of inputs,* just as there was an assumed substitutability of sales products to make the sales mix variance meaningful. Although partner time may have been substitutable for staff time, the reverse may not have been true. Second, the input costs must be different for a mix variance to exist. If the hourly costs of both partners and staff were the same, the substitution of hours would have no effect on the total cost of the job.

Questions

13–1 What is a static budget?

13–2 What is a flexible budget and how does it differ from a static budget?

13–3 Name three criteria that should be considered in choosing an activity base on which to construct a flexible budget.

13–4 In comparing budgeted data with actual data in a performance report for variable overhead, what variance(s) will be produced if the budgeted data are based on actual hours worked? On both actual hours worked and standard hours allowed?

13–5 What is meant by the term standard hours allowed?

13–6 How does the variable manufacturing overhead spending variance differ from the materials price variance?

13–7 Why is the term overhead efficiency variance a misnomer?

13–8 In what way is the flexible budget involved in product costing?

13–9 What is meant by the term denominator level of activity?

13–10 Why do we apply overhead to work in progress on the basis of standard hours allowed in Chapter 11 when we applied it on the basis of actual hours in Chapter 3? What is the difference in costing systems between the two chapters?

13–11 In a standard cost system, what two variances are computed for fixed manufacturing overhead?

13–12 What does the fixed overhead budget variance measure?

13–13 Under what circumstances would you expect the volume variance to be favourable? Unfavourable? Does the variance measure deviations in spending for fixed overhead items? Explain.

13–14 How might the volume variance be measured, other than in pounds?

13–15 What dangers are there in expressing fixed costs on a per unit basis?

13–16 In Chapter 3, you became acquainted with the concept of under- or overapplied variances. The under- or overapplied overhead can be broken down into what four variances?

13–17 If factory overhead is overapplied for August, would you expect the total of the overhead variances to be favourable or unfavourable?

Exercises

E13–1 Time allowed: 10 minutes

An incomplete flexible budget is given below for Lavage Rapide, a Swiss company that owns and operates a large automatic carwash facility near Geneva. The Swiss currency is the Swiss franc, which is denoted by SFr.

Lavage Rapide Flexible budget for the month ended 31 August				
Overhead costs	**Cost formula (per car)**	**Activity (cars)**		
		8,000	**9,000**	**10,000**
Variable overhead costs:				
Cleaning supplies	?	?	7,200 SFr	?
Electricity	?	?	2,700	?
Maintenance	?	?	1,800	?
Total variable overhead cost	?	?	?	?
Fixed overhead costs:				
Operator wages		?	9,000	?
Depreciation		?	6,000	?
Rent		?	8,000	?
Total fixed overhead cost		?	?	?
Total overhead cost		?	?	?

Required

Fill in the missing data.

E13–2 Time allowed: 10 minutes

Refer to the data in Exercise 13.1. Lavage Rapide's owner-manager would like to prepare a budget for August assuming an activity level of 8,800 cars.

Required

Prepare a static budget for August. Use Exhibit 13.1 in the chapter as your guide.

E13–3 Time allowed: 10 minutes

Refer to the data in Exercise 13.1. Lavage Rapide's actual level of activity during August was 8,900 cars, although the owner had constructed his static budget for the month assuming the level of activity would be 8,800 cars. The actual overhead costs incurred during August are given below:

	Actual costs incurred for 8,900 cars
Variable overhead costs:	
Cleaning supplies	7,080 SFr
Electricity	2,460
Maintenance	1,550
Fixed overhead costs:	
Operator wages	9,100
Depreciation	7,000
Rent	8,000

Required

Prepare a flexible budget performance report for both the variable and fixed overhead costs for August. Use Exhibit 13.4 in the chapter as your guide.

E13–4 Time allowed: 10 minutes
The cost formulas for Emory Company's manufacturing overhead costs are given below. These cost formulas cover a relevant range of 15,000 to 25,000 machine-hours each year.

Overhead costs	Cost formula
Utilities	£0.30 per machine-hour
Indirect labour	£52,000 plus £1.40 per machine-hour
Supplies	£0.20 per machine-hour
Maintenance	£18,000 plus £0.10 per machine-hour
Depreciation	£90,000

Required
Prepare a flexible budget in increments of 5,000 machine-hours. Include all costs in your budget.

E13–5 Time allowed: 20 minutes
The variable portion of Murray Company's flexible budget for manufacturing overhead is given below:

Variable overhead costs	Cost formula (per machine-hour)	Machine-hours 10,000M	12,000	14,000
Supplies	£0.20	£2,000	£2,400	£2,800
Maintenance	0.80	8,000	9,600	11,200
Utilities	0.10	1,000	1,200	1,400
Rework time	0.40	4,000	4,800	5,600
Total variable overhead cost	£1.50	£15,000	£18,000	£21, 000

During a recent period, the company recorded 11,500 machine-hours of activity. The variable overhead costs incurred were:

Supplies	£2,400
Maintenance	8,000
Utilities	1,100
Rework time	5,300

The budgeted activity for the period had been 12,000 machine-hours.

Required

1 Prepare a variable overhead performance report for the period. Indicate whether variances are favourable (F) or unfavourable (U). Show only a spending variance on your report.

2 Discuss the significance of the variances. Might some variances be the result of others? Explain.

E13–6 Time allowed: 15 minutes
The cheque-clearing office of Columbia National Bank is responsible for processing all cheques that come to the bank for payment. Managers at the bank believe that variable overhead costs are essentially proportional to the number of labour-hours worked in the office, so labour-hours is used as the activity

base for budgeting and for performance reports for variable overhead costs in the department. Data for September, the most recent month, appear below:

Budgeted labour-hours		3,080
Actual labour-hours		3,100
Standard labour-hours allowed for the actual number of cheques processed		3,200

	Cost formula (per labour-hour)	**Actual costs incurred in September**
Variable overhead costs:		
Office supplies	£0.10	£365
Staff coffee lounge	0.20	520
Indirect labour	0.90	2,710
Total variable overhead cost	£1.20	£3,595

Required

Prepare a variable overhead performance report for September for the cheque-clearing office that includes both spending and efficiency variances. Use Exhibit 13.7 as a guide.

E13–7 Time allowed: 10 minutes

Operating at a normal level of 30,000 direct labour-hours, Lasser Company produces 10,000 units of product each period. The direct labour wage rate is £6 per hour. Two-and-a-half metres of direct materials go into each unit of product; the material costs £8.60 per metre. The flexible budget used to plan and control manufacturing overhead costs is given below (in condensed form):

Overhead costs	**Cost formula**	**Direct labour hours**		
	(per direct labour-hour)	**20,000**	**30,000**	**40,000**
Variable costs	£1.90	£38,000	£57,000	£76,000
Fixed costs		168,000	168,000	168,000
Total overhead cost		£206,000	£225,000	£244,000

Required

1 Using 30,000 direct labour-hours as the denominator activity, compute the predetermined overhead rate and break it down into variable and fixed elements.

2 Complete the standard cost card below for one unit of product:

Direct materials, 2.5 metres at £8.60	£21.50
Direct labour, ?	?
Variable overhead, ?	?
Fixed overhead, ?	?
Total standard cost per unit	£?

E13–8 Time allowed: 20 minutes

Norwall Company's flexible budget for manufacturing overhead (in condensed form) is given below:

Overhead costs	Cost formula (per machine-hour)	Machine-hours		
		50,000	60,000	70,000
Variable costs	£3	£150,000	£180,000	£210,000
Fixed costs		300,000	300,000	300,000
Total overhead cost		£450,000	£480,000	£510,000

The following information is available for a recent period:

1 A denominator activity of 60,000 machine-hours is used to compute the predetermined overhead rate.

2 At the 60,000 standard machine-hours level of activity, the company should produce 40,000 units of product.

3 The company's actual operating results were:

Number of units produced	42,000
Actual machine-hours	64,000
Actual variable overhead costs	£185,000
Actual fixed overhead costs	302,400

Required

1 Compute the predetermined overhead rate and break it down into variable and fixed cost elements.

2 Compute the standard hours allowed for the actual production.

3 Compute the variable overhead spending and efficiency variances and the fixed overhead budget and volume variances.

E13–9 Time allowed: 10 minutes

Selected operating information on three different companies for a recent year is given below:

	Company		
	A	B	C
Full-capacity machine-hours	10,000	18,000	20,000
Budgeted machine-hours*	9,000	17,000	20,000
Actual machine-hours	9,000	17,800	19,000
Standard machine-hours allowed for actual production	9,500	16,000	20,000

* Denominator activity for computing the predetermined overhead rate.

Required

For each company, state whether the company would have a favourable or unfavourable volume variance and why.

E13–10 Time allowed: 20 minutes The standard cost card for the single product manufactured by Cutter Ltd is given below:

Standard cost card – per unit	
Direct materials, 3 metres at £6	£18
Direct labour, 4 hours at £7.75	31
Variable overhead, 4 hours at £1.50	6
Fixed overhead, 4 hours at £5	20
Total standard cost per unit	£75

Manufacturing overhead is applied to production on the basis of direct labour-hours. During the year, the company worked 37,000 hours and manufactured 9,500 units of product. Selected data relating to the company's fixed manufacturing overhead cost for the year are shown below:

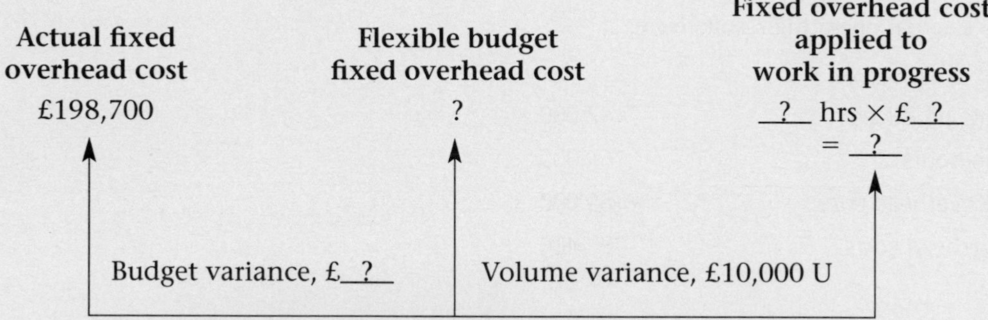

Required

1 What were the standard hours allowed for the year's production?

2 What was the amount of fixed overhead cost contained in the flexible budget for the year?

3 What was the fixed overhead budget variance for the year?

4 What denominator activity level did the company use in setting the predetermined overhead rate for the year?

E13–11 Time allowed: 15 minutes
Selected information relating to Yost Company's operations for the most recent year is given below:

Activity:	
Denominator activity (machine-hours)	45,000
Standard hours allowed per unit	3
Number of units produced	14,000
Costs:	
Actual fixed overhead costs incurred	£267,000
Fixed overhead budget variance	3,000 F

The company applies overhead cost to products on the basis of machine-hours.

Required

1 What were the standard hours allowed for the actual production?

2 What was the fixed portion of the predetermined overhead rate?

3 What was the volume variance?

PROBLEMS

Problems

P13–12 Preparing a revised performance report Time allowed: 30 minutes

Several years ago, Westmont Company developed a comprehensive budgeting system for profit planning and control purposes. The line supervisors have been very happy with the system and with the reports being prepared on their performance, but both middle and upper management have expressed considerable dissatisfaction with the information being generated by the system. A typical manufacturing overhead performance report for a recent period is shown below:

Westmont Company
Overhead performance report – Assembly department
for the quarter ended 31 March

	Actual	Budget	Variance
Machine-hours	35,000	40,000	
Variable overhead costs:			
Indirect materials	£29,700	£32,000	£2,300 F
Rework time	7,900	8,000	100 F
Utilities	51,800	56,000	4,200 F
Machine setup	11,600	12,000	400 F
Total variable overhead cost	101,000	108,000	7,000 F
Fixed overhead costs:			
Maintenance	79,200	80,000	800 F
Inspection	60,000	60,000	–
Total fixed overhead cost	139,200	140,000	800 F
Total overhead cost	£240,200	£248,000	£7,800 F

After receiving a copy of this overhead performance report, the supervisor of the Assembly Department stated, 'These reports are super. It makes me feel really good to see how well things are going in my department. I can't understand why those people upstairs complain so much.'

The budget data above are for the original planned level of activity for the quarter.

Required

1 The company's managing director is uneasy about the performance reports being prepared and would like you to evaluate their usefulness to the company.

2 What changes, if any, would you recommend be made in the overhead performance report above in order to give better insight into how well the supervisor is controlling costs?

3 Prepare a new overhead performance report for the quarter, incorporating any changes you suggested in Question 2 above. (Include both the variable and the fixed costs in your report.)

P13–13 Applying the flexible budget approach Time allowed: 30 minutes

The St Lucia Blood Bank, a private charity partly supported by government grants, is located on the Caribbean island of St Lucia. The Blood Bank has just finished its operations for September, which was a particularly busy month due to a powerful hurricane that hit neighbouring islands causing many injuries. The hurricane largely bypassed St Lucia, but residents of St Lucia willingly donated their blood to help people on other islands. As a consequence, the blood bank collected and processed over 20% more blood than had been originally planned for the month.

A report prepared by a government official comparing actual costs to budgeted costs for the Blood Bank appears below. (The currency on St Lucia is the East Caribbean dollar.) Continued support from the government depends on the Blood Bank's ability to demonstrate control over their costs.

St Lucia Blood Bank
Cost control report
For the month ended 30 September

	Actual	**Budget**	**Variance**
Litres of blood collected	620	500	120 F
Variable costs:			
Medical supplies	$9,350	$7,500	$1,850 U
Lab tests	6,180	6,000	180 U
Refreshments for donors	1,340	1,000	340 U
Administrative supplies	400	250	150 U
Total variable cost	17,270	14,750	2,520 U
Fixed costs:			
Staff salaries	10,000	10,000	–
Equipment depreciation	2,800	2,500	300 U
Rent	1,000	1,000	–
Utilities	570	500	70 U
Total fixed cost	14,370	14,000	370 U
Total cost	$31,640	$28,750	$2,890 U

The managing director of the Blood Bank was very unhappy with this report, claiming that his costs were higher than expected due to the emergency on the neighbouring islands. He also pointed out that the additional costs had been fully covered by payments from grateful recipients on the other islands. The government official who prepared the report countered that all of the figures had been submitted by the Blood Bank to the government; he was just pointing out that actual costs were a lot higher than promised in the budget.

Required

1 Prepare a new performance report for September using the flexible budget approach. (*Note*: Even though some of these costs might be classified as direct costs rather than as overhead, the flexible budget approach can still be used to prepare a flexible budget performance report.)

2 Do you think any of the variances in the report you prepared should be investigated? Why?

P13–14 Standard cost card: materials, labour, and all overhead variances Time allowed: 30 minutes
Flandro Company uses a standard cost system and sets predetermined overhead rates on the basis of direct labour-hours. The following data are taken from the company's budget for the current year:

Denominator activity (direct labour-hours)	10,000
Variable manufacturing overhead cost	£25,000
Fixed manufacturing overhead cost	59,000

The standard cost card for the company's only product is given below:

Direct materials, 3 metres at £4.40	£13.20
Direct labour, 2 hours at £6	12.00
Manufacturing overhead, 140% of direct labour cost	16.80
Standard cost per unit	£42.00

During the year, the company produced 6,000 units of product and incurred the following costs:

Materials purchased, 24,000 metres at £4.80	£115,200
Materials used in production (in metres)	18,500
Direct labour cost incurred, 11,600 hours at £6.50	£75,400
Variable manufacturing overhead cost incurred	29,580
Fixed manufacturing overhead cost incurred	60,400

Required

1 Redo the standard cost card in a clearer, more usable format by detailing the variable and fixed overhead cost elements.
2 Prepare an analysis of the variances for materials and labour for the year.
3 Prepare an analysis of the variances for variable and fixed overhead for the year.
4 What effect, if any, does the choice of a denominator activity level have on unit standard costs? Is the volume variance a controllable variance from a spending point of view? Explain.

P13–15 Basic overhead analysis Time allowed: 40 minutes
Chilczuk SA of Gdansk, Poland, is a major producer of classic Polish sausage. The company uses a standard cost system to help in the control of costs. Overhead is applied to production on the basis of labour-hours. According to the company's flexible budget, the following manufacturing overhead costs should be incurred at an activity level of 35,000 labour-hours (the denominator activity level):

Variable overhead costs	87,500
Fixed overhead costs	210,000
Total overhead cost	€297,500

During the most recent year, the following operating results were recorded:

Activity:	
Actual labour-hours worked	30,000
Standard labour-hours allowed for output	32,000
Cost:	
Actual variable overhead cost incurred	€78,000
Actual fixed overhead cost incurred	209,400

At the end of the year, the company's Manufacturing overhead account contained the following data:

Manufacturing overhead			
Actual	287,000	Applied	272,000
	15,400		

Management would like to determine the cause of the €15,400 underapplied overhead.

Required

1 Compute the predetermined overhead rate. Break the rate down into variable and fixed cost elements.

2 Show how the €272,000 Applied figure in the Manufacturing overhead account was computed.

3 Analyse the €15,400 underapplied overhead figure in terms of the variable overhead spending and efficiency variances and the fixed overhead budget and volume variances.

4 Explain the meaning of each variance that you computed in Question 3 above.

P13–16 Integration of materials, labour, and overhead variances Time allowed: 45 minutes
'Wonderful! Not only did our salespeople do a good job in meeting the sales budget this year, but our production people did a good job in controlling costs as well,' said Kim Clark, managing director of Martell Company. 'Our £18,000 overall manufacturing cost variance is only 1.5% of the £1,200,000 standard cost of products sold during the year. That's well within the 3% parameter set by management for acceptable variances. It looks like everyone will be in line for a bonus this year.'

The company produces and sells a single product. A standard cost card for the product follows:

Standard cost card – per unit of product	
Direct materials, 2 metres at £8.45	£16.90
Direct labour, 1.4 hours at £8	11.20
Variable overhead, 1.4 hours at £2.50	3.50
Fixed overhead, 1.4 hours at £6	8.40
Standard cost per unit	£40.00

The following additional information is available for the year just completed:

1 The company manufactured 30,000 units of product during the year.

2 A total of 64,000 metres of material was purchased during the year at a cost of £8.55 per metre. All of this material was used to manufacture the 30,000 units. There were no beginning or ending inventories for the year.

3 The company worked 45,000 direct labour-hours during the year at a cost of £7.80 per hour.

4 Overhead is applied to products on the basis of direct labour-hours. Data relating to manufacturing overhead costs follow:

Denominator activity level (direct labour-hours)	35,000
Budgeted fixed overhead costs (from the overhead flexible budget)	£210,000
Actual variable overhead costs incurred	108,000
Actual fixed overhead costs incurred	211,800

Required

1 Compute the direct materials price and quantity variances for the year.

2 Compute the direct labour rate and efficiency variances for the year.

3 For manufacturing overhead compute:

(a) The variable overhead spending and efficiency variances for the year.

(b) The fixed overhead budget and volume variances for the year.

4 Total the variances you have computed, and compare the net amount with the £18,000 mentioned by the managing director. Do you agree that bonuses should be given to everyone for good cost control during the year? Explain.

P13–17 Flexible budget and overhead performance report Time allowed: 35 minutes

You have just been hired by FAB Company, the manufacturer of a revolutionary new garage door opening device. John Foster, the managing director, has asked that you review the company's costing system and 'do what you can to help us get better control of our manufacturing overhead costs'. You find that the company has never used a flexible budget, and you suggest that preparing such a budget would be an excellent first step in overhead planning and control.

After much effort and analysis, you are able to determine the following cost formulas for the company's normal operating range of 20,000 to 30,000 machine-hours each month:

Overhead costs	Cost formula
Utilities	£0.90 per machine-hour
Maintenance	£1.60 per machine-hour plus £40,000 per month
Machine set-up	£0.30 per machine-hour
Indirect labour	£0.70 per machine-hour plus £130,000 per month
Depreciation	£70,000 per month

To show the managing director how the flexible budget concept works, you have gathered the following actual cost data for the most recent month, March, in which the company worked 26,000 machine-hours and produced 15,000 units:

Utilities	£24,200
Maintenance	78,100
Machine set-up	8,400
Indirect labour	149,600
Depreciation	71,500
Total cost	£331,800

The only variance in the fixed costs for the month was with depreciation, which was increased as a result of a purchase of new equipment.

The company had originally planned to work 30,000 machine-hours during March.

Required

1 Prepare a flexible budget for the company in increments of 5,000 hours.

2 Prepare an overhead performance report for the company for March. (Use the format illustrated in Exhibit 13.11.)

3 What additional information would you need to compute an overhead efficiency variance for the company?

P13–18 Spending and efficiency variances; evaluating an overhead performance report Time allowed: 30 minutes

Frank Western, supervisor of the Machining Department for Freemont Company, was visibly upset after being reprimanded for his department's poor performance over the prior month. The department's performance report is given below:

Freemont Company
Performance report – Machining department

	Cost formula (per machine-hour)	Actual	Budget	Variance
Machine-hours		38,000	35,000	
Variable overhead costs:				
Utilities	£0.40	£15,700	£14,000	£1,700 U
Indirect labour	2.30	86,500	80,500	6,000 U
Supplies	0.60	26,000	21,000	5,000 U
Maintenance	1.20	44,900	42,000	2,900 U
Total variable overhead cost	£4.50	173,100	157,500	15,600 U
Fixed overhead costs:				
Supervision		38,000	38,000	–
Maintenance		92,400	92,000	400 U
Depreciation		80,000	80,000	–
Total fixed overhead cost		210,400	210,000	400 U
Total overhead cost		£383,500	£367,500	£16,000 U

'I just can't understand all the red ink,' said Western to Sarah Mason, supervisor of another department. 'When the boss called me in, I thought he was going to give me a pat on the back because I know for a fact that my department worked more efficiently last month than it has ever worked before. Instead, he tore me apart. I thought for a minute that it might be over the supplies that were stolen out of our warehouse last month. But they only amounted to a couple of thousand pounds, and just look at this report. Everything is unfavourable, and I don't even know why.'

The budget for the Machining Department had called for production of 14,000 units last month, which is equal to a budgeted activity level of 35,000 machine-hours (at a standard time of 2.5 hours per unit). Actual production in the Machining Department for the month was 16,000 units.

Required

1 Evaluate the overhead performance report given above and explain why the variances are all unfavourable.

2 Prepare a new overhead performance report that will help Mr Western's superiors assess efficiency and cost control in the Machining Department (*Hint*: Exhibit 13.7 may be helpful in structuring your report; however, the report you prepare should include both variable and fixed costs.)

3 Would the supplies stolen out of the warehouse be included as part of the variable overhead spending variance or as part of the variable overhead efficiency variance for the month? Explain.

P13–19 Detailed performance report Time allowed: 20 minutes

The cost formulas for variable overhead costs in a machining operation are as follows:

Variable overhead costs	Cost formula (per machine-hour)
Power	£0.30
Set-up time	0.20
Polishing wheels	0.16
Maintenance	0.18
Total variable overhead cost	£0.84

During August, the machining operation was scheduled to work 11,250 machine hours and to produce 4,500 units of product. The standard machine time per unit of product is 2.5 hours. A strike near the end of the month forced a cutback in production. Actual results for the month were:

Actual machine-hours worked	9,250
Actual number of units produced	3,600

Actual costs for the month were:

Variable overhead costs	Total actual costs	Per machine-hour
Power	£2,405	£0.26
Set-up time	2,035	0.22
Polishing wheels	1,110	0.12
Maintenance	925	0.10
Total variable overhead cost	£6,475	£0.70

Required

Prepare an overhead performance report for the machining operation for August. Use column headings in your report as shown below:

Overhead costs	Cost formula (per machine-hour)	Actual cost incurred 9,250 machine-hours	Budget costs on ? machine-hours	Budget based on ? machine-hours	Total variance	Breakdown of total variance: Spending variance	Breakdown of total variance: Efficiency variance

E13–20 Standard cost card and overhead analysis Time allowed: 45 minutes

Lane Company manufactures a single product that requires a great deal of hand labour. Overhead cost is applied on the basis of direct labour-hours. The company's condensed flexible budget for manufacturing overhead is given overleaf:

Overhead costs	Cost formula (per direct labour-hour)	Direct labour-hours		
		45,000	60,000	75,000
Variable costs	£2	£90,000	£120,000	£150,000
Fixed costs		480,000	480,000	480,000
Total overhead cost		£570,000	£600,000	£630,000

The company's product requires 3 kilos of material that has a standard cost of £7 per kilo and 1.5 hours of direct labour time that has a standard rate of £6 per hour.

The company planned to operate at a denominator activity level of 60,000 direct labour-hours and to produce 40,000 units of product during the most recent year. Actual activity and costs for the year were as follows:

Number of units produced	42,000
Actual direct labour-hours worked	65,000
Actual variable overhead cost incurred	£123,500
Actual fixed overhead cost incurred	483,000

Required

1 Compute the predetermined overhead rate for the year. Break the rate down into variable and fixed elements.

2 Prepare a standard cost card for the company's product; show the details for all manufacturing costs on your standard cost card.

3 Do the following:

(a) Compute the standard hours allowed for the year's production.

(b) Complete the following Manufacturing overhead T-account for the year:

Manufacturing overhead

?	?
?	?

4 Determine the reason for any under- or overapplied overhead for the year by computing the variable overhead spending and efficiency variances and the fixed overhead budget and volume variances.

5 Suppose the company had chosen 65,000 direct labour-hours as the denominator activity rather than 60,000 hours. State which, if any, of the variances computed in Question 4 above would have changed, and explain how the variance(s) would have changed. No computations are necessary.

P13–21 Standard cost card; fixed overhead analysis; graphing Time allowed: 45 minutes
When planning operations for the year, Southbrook Company chose a denominator activity of 40,000 direct labour-hours. According to the company's flexible budget, the following manufacturing overhead costs should be incurred at this activity level:

Variable overhead costs	£72,000
Fixed overhead costs	360,000

The company produces a single product that requires 2.5 hours to complete. The direct labour rate is £6 per hour. Eight metres of material are needed to complete one unit of product; the material has a standard cost of £4.50 per metre. Overhead is applied to production on the basis of direct labour-hours.

Required

1 Compute the predetermined overhead rate. Break the rate down into variable and fixed cost elements.

2 Prepare a standard cost card for one unit of product using the following format:

Direct materials, 8 metres at £4.50	£36
Direct labour, ?	?
Variable overhead, ?	?
Fixed overhead, ?	?
Standard cost per unit	£?

3 Prepare a graph with cost on the vertical (y) axis and direct labour-hours on the horizontal (x) axis. Plot a line on your graph from a zero level of activity to 60,000 direct labour-hours for each of the following costs:

(a) Budgeted fixed overhead (in total).

(b) Applied fixed overhead (applied at the hourly rate computed in Question 1 above).

4 Assume that during the year actual activity is as follows:

Number of units produced	14,000
Actual direct labour-hours worked	33,000
Actual fixed overhead cost incurred	£361,800

(a) Compute the fixed overhead budget and volume variances for the year.

(b) Show the volume variance on the graph you prepared in Question 3 above.

5 Disregard the data in Question 4 above. Assume instead that actual activity during the year is as follows:

Number of units produced	20,000
Actual direct labour-hours worked	52,000
Actual fixed overhead costs incurred	£361,800

(a) Compute the fixed overhead budget and volume variances for the year.

(b) Show the volume variance on the graph you prepared in Question 3 above.

P13–22 Flexible budget and overhead analysis Time allowed: 45 minutes

Harper Company assembles all of its products in the Assembly department. Budgeted costs for the operation of this department for the year have been set as follows:

Variable overhead costs:	
Direct materials	£900,000
Direct labour	675,000
Utilities	45,000
Indirect labour	67,500
Supplies	22,500
Total variable overhead cost	1,710,000
Fixed overhead costs:	
Insurance	8,000
Supervisory salaries	90,000
Depreciation	160,000
Equipment rental	42,000
Total fixed overhead cost	300,000
Total budgeted overhead cost	£2,010,000
Budgeted direct labour-hours	75,000

Since the assembly work is done mostly by hand, operating activity in this department is best measured by direct labour-hours. The cost formulas used to develop the budgeted costs above are valid over a relevant range of 60,000 to 90,000 direct labour-hours per year.

Required

1 Prepare a manufacturing overhead flexible budget in good form for the Assembly department. Make your budget in increments of 15,000 direct labour-hours. (The company does not include direct materials and direct labour costs in the flexible budget.)

2 Assume that the company computes predetermined overhead rates by department. Compute the rates that will be used by the Assembly department to apply overhead costs to production. Break this rate down into variable and fixed cost elements.

3 Suppose that during the year the following actual activity and costs are recorded by the Assembly department:

Actual direct labour-hours worked	73,000
Standard direct labour-hours allowed for the output of the year	70,000
Actual variable overhead cost incurred	£124,100
Actual fixed overhead cost incurred	301,600

Complete the following:

(a) A T-account for manufacturing overhead costs in the Assembly Department for the year is given below. Determine the amount of applied overhead cost for the year, and compute the under- or overapplied overhead.

Manufacturing overhead

Actual cost 425,700	

(b) Analyse the under- or overapplied overhead figure in terms of the variable overhead spending and efficiency variances and the fixed overhead budget and volume variances.

P13–23 Flexible budget; overhead performance report Time allowed: 45 minutes
Gant Products Ltd has recently introduced budgeting as an integral part of its corporate planning process. The company's first effort at constructing a flexible budget for manufacturing overhead is shown below:

Percentage of capacity	80%	100%
Machine-hours	4,800	6,000
Maintenance	£1,480	£1,600
Supplies	1,920	2,400
Utilities	1,940	2,300
Supervision	3,000	3,000
Machine set-up	960	1,200
Total overhead cost	£9,300	£10,500

The budgets above are for costs over a relevant range of 80 to 100% of capacity on a monthly basis. The managers who will be working under these budgets have control over both fixed and variable costs.

Required

1 Redo the company's flexible budget, presenting it in better format. Show the budget at 80%, 90%, and 100% levels of capacity. (Use the high–low method to separate fixed and variable costs.)

2 Express the budget prepared in Question 1 above in cost formula form using a single cost formula to express all overhead costs.

3 The company operated at 95% of capacity during April in terms of actual hours of machine time recorded in the factory. 5,600 standard machine-hours were allowed for the output of the month. Actual overhead costs incurred were:

Maintenance	£2,083
Supplies	3,420
Utilities	2,666
Supervision	3,000
Machine set up	855
Total overhead cost	£12,024

The fixed costs had no variances. Prepare an overhead performance report for April. Structure your report so that it shows only a spending variance for overhead. You may assume that the master budget for April called for an activity level during the month of 6,000 machine-hours.

4 Upon receiving the performance report you have prepared, the production manager commented, 'I have two observations to make. First, I think there's an error on your report. You show an unfavourable spending variance for supplies, yet I know that we paid exactly the budgeted price for all the supplies we used last month. Pat Stevens, the purchasing agent, made a comment to me that our supplies prices haven't changed in over a year. Second, I wish you would modify your report to include an efficiency variance for overhead. The reason is that waste has been a problem in the factory for years and the efficiency variance would help us get overhead waste under control.'

(a) Explain the probable cause of the unfavourable spending variance for supplies.

(b) Compute an efficiency variance for total variable overhead and explain to the production manager why it would or would not contain elements of overhead waste.

P13–24 Activity-based costing and the flexible budget approach Time allowed: 60 minutes
The Little Theatre is a non-profit organization devoted to staging theatre productions of plays for children in Manchester. The theatre has a very small full-time professional administrative staff. Through a special arrangement with the actors' union, actors and directors rehearse without pay and are paid only for actual performances.

The costs of 1998's operations appear below. During 1998, The Little Theatre had six different productions – each of which was performed 18 times. For example, one of the productions was Peter the Rabbit, which had the usual six-week run with three performances on each weekend.

The Little Theatre
Cost report
for the year ended 31 December 1998

Number of productions	6
Number of performance of each production	18
Total number of performances	108
Actual costs incurred:	
Actors' and directors' wages	£216,000
Stagehands' wages	32,400
Ticket booth personnel and ushers' wages	16,200
Scenery, costumes and props	108,000
Theatre hall rent	54,000
Printed programmes	27,000
Publicity	12,000
Administrative expenses	43,200
Total cost	£508,800

Some of the costs vary with the number of productions, some with the number of performances, and some are relatively fixed and depend on neither the number of productions nor the number of performances. The costs of scenery, costumes and props, and of publicity vary with the number of productions. It does not make any difference how many times Peter the Rabbit is performed, the cost of the scenery is the same. Likewise, the cost of publicizing a play with posters and radio commercials is the same whether there are 10, 20 or 30 performances of the play. On the other hand, the wages of the actors, directors, stagehands, ticket booth personnel, and ushers vary with the number of performances. The greater the number of performances, the higher the wage costs will be. Similarly, the costs of renting the hall and printing the programmes will vary with the number of performances. Administrative expenses are more difficult to pin down, but the best estimate is that approximately 75% of these costs are fixed, 15% depend on the number of productions staged, and the remaining 10% depend on the number of performances.

At the end of 1998, the board of directors of the theatre authorized expanding the theatre's programme in 1999 to seven productions, with 24 performances each. Not surprisingly, actual costs for 1999 were considerably higher than the costs for 1998. (Grants from donors and ticket sales were also correspondingly higher.) Data concerning 1999's operations are as follows:

The Little Theatre Cost report for the year ended 31 December 1999	
Number of productions	7
Number of performances of each production	24
Total number of performances	168
Actual costs incurred:	
Actors' and directors' wages	£341,800
Stagehands' wages	49,700
Ticket booth personnel and ushers' wages	25,900
Scenery, costumes and props	130,600
Theatre hall rent	78,000
Printed programmes	38,300
Publicity	15,100
Administrative expenses	47,500
Total cost	£726,900

Even though many of the costs above may be considered direct costs rather than overhead, the flexible budget approach covered in the chapter can still be used to evaluate how well these costs are controlled. The principles are the same whether a cost is a direct cost or is overhead.

Required

1 Use the actual results from 1998 to estimate the cost formulas for the flexible budget for The Little Theatre. Keep in mind that the theatre has two measures of activity – the number of productions and the number of performances.

2 Prepare a performance report for 1999 using the flexible budget approach and both measures of activity. Assume there was no inflation. (*Note*: To evaluate administrative expenses, first determine the flexible budget amounts for the three elements of administrative expenses. Then compare the total of the three elements to the actual administrative expense of £47,500.)

3 If you were on the board of directors of the theatre, would you be pleased with how well costs were controlled during 1999? Why or why not?

4 The cost formulas provide figures for the average cost per production and average cost per performance. How accurate do you think these figures would be for predicting the cost of a new production or of an additional performance of a particular production?

P13–25 Selection of a denominator; overhead analysis Time allowed: 45 minutes
Morton Company's condensed flexible budget for manufacturing overhead is given below:

Overhead costs	Cost formula (per direct labour-hour)	Direct labour-hours		
		20,000	30,000	45,000
Variable costs	£4.50	£90,000	£135,000	£180,000
Fixed costs		270,000	270,000	270,000
Total overhead cost		£360,000	£405,000	£450,000

The company manufactures a single product that requires two direct labour-hours to complete. The direct labour wage rate is £5 per hour. Four metres of raw material are required for each unit of product; the standard cost of the material is £8.75 per metre.

Although long-run normal activity is 30,000 direct labour-hours each year, the company expects to operate at a 40,000-hour level of activity this year.

Required

1 Assume that the company chooses 30,000 direct labour-hours as the denominator level of activity. Compute the predetermined overhead rate, breaking it down into variable and fixed cost elements.

2 Assume that the company chooses 40,000 direct labour-hours as the denominator level of activity. Repeat the computations in Question 1 above.

3 Complete two standard cost cards as outlined below. Each card should relate to a single unit of product.

Denominator activity: 30,000 direct labour-hours	
Direct materials, 4 metres at £8.75	£35.00
Direct labour, ?	?
Variable overhead, ?	?
Fixed overhead, ?	?
Standard cost per unit	£?
Denominator activity: 40,000 direct labour-hours	
Direct materials, 4 metres at £8.75	£35.00
Direct labour, ?	?
Variable overhead, ?	?
Fixed overhead, ?	?
Standard cost per unit	£?

4 Assume that the company produces 18,000 units and works 38,000 actual direct labour-hours during the year. Actual manufacturing overhead costs for the year are:

Variable costs	£174,800
Fixed costs	271,600
Total overhead cost	£446,400

Do the following:

(a) Compute the standard hours allowed for this year's production.

(b) Complete the Manufacturing Overhead account below. Assume that the company uses 30,000 direct labour-hours (long-run normal activity) as the denominator activity figure in computing predetermined overhead rates, as you have done in Question 1 above.

Manufacturing overhead

Actual cost 446,400	?
?	?

(c) Determine the cause of the under- or overapplied overhead for the year by computing the variable overhead spending and efficiency variances and the fixed overhead budget and volume variances.

5 Looking at the variances you have computed, what appears to be the major disadvantage of using long-run normal activity rather than expected actual activity as a denominator in computing the predetermined overhead rate? What advantages can you see to offset this disadvantage?

P13–26 Standard costing and budgeting Time allowed: 20 minutes
Sunbird Ltd manufactures and sells a single product. The company uses a standard marginal (variable) costing system and absorbs variable manufacturing overheads on the basis of direct labour hours. No stocks of raw materials, work in progress or finished goods are held.

For the month of May 2001, the budgeted sales volume was 1,200 units at a standard selling price of £86.00; budgeted fixed overheads were £10,700, while the standard cost information for the product was as follows:

		£
Direct materials	5 kg @ £7.30 per kg	36.50
Direct labour	4 hours @ £6.00 per hour	24.00
Variable overheads		16.00
Total		76.50

You are given the following information regarding the actual results for the month:

		£
Sales revenue	1,100 units	99,000
Direct materials	6,000 kg	48,000
Direct labour	4,100 hours	25,420
Variable overheads		16,810
Fixed overheads		7,350

Required

1 Explain what is meant by a standard cost and briefly outline the main purposes of a standard costing system. *(4 marks)*

2 Prepare a statement which reconciles budgeted and actual profit for Sunbird Ltd for the month of May 2001 which separately identifies the following variances:

(a) sales price and volume

(b) direct materials price and usage

(c) direct labour rate and efficiency

(d) variable overheads expenditure and efficiency

(e) fixed overheads expenditure. *(11 marks)*

(Total = 15 marks)

ICAEW Accounting, June 2001

P13–27 Standard costing and budgeting Time allowed: 20 minutes
Wild Ltd manufactures and sells a single product. The company uses a standard marginal (variable) costing system and absorbs variable manufacturing overheads on the basis of direct labour-hours. No stocks of raw materials, work in progress or finished goods are held.

For the month of November 2001, the standard selling price was £135.00 while the standard cost card for the product was as follows:

		£
Direct materials	8 kg @ £10.10 per kg	80.80
Direct labour	3 hours @ £8.20 per hour	24.60
Variable overheads		15.00
Total		120.40

The company's trainee cost accountant was asked to prepare an operating statement reconciling budgeted profit for the month to actual profit. Unfortunately, before completing the task, the trainee fell ill and you have been asked to complete this task. After searching through the trainee's desk, you have been able to find the following rough workings:

Operating statement for November 2001
Workings

1 Sales volume 10% higher than budgeted; multiplying this increase by the standard selling price of £135.00 gives sales quantity variance of £16,200.

2 Fixed overheads of £10,185 are 5% higher than budgeted.

3 Actual selling price £132.00.

4

		£
Direct materials	10,490 kg	103,851
Direct labour	4,200 hours	33,390
Variable overheads		20,700

Required

1 Comment critically on the trainee's approach to calculating the sales quantity variance. *(3 marks)*

2 Prepare a statement which reconciles budgeted and actual profit for Wild Ltd for the month of November 2001, separately identifying the following variances:
   (a) sales price and quantity
   (b) direct materials price and usage
   (c) direct labour rate and efficiency
   (d) variable overheads expenditure and efficiency
   (e) fixed overheads expenditure.

(12 marks)
(Total = 15 marks)
ICAEW Accounting, December 2001

P13–28 Standard costing and flexible budgets Time allowed: 30 minutes
A food manufacturer specializes in the production of frozen cakes and sweet products, selling mainly to supermarkets. The following monthly budget applies to one of its products.

	Original budget	
	£000	**£000**
Sales		1,000
Costs:		
Ingredients	400	
Labour and energy	100	
Fixed overheads	300	
		800
Profit		200

For the ingredients, a standard quantity of 5 kg per pack is required; a standard price of 40p per kg applies in the original budget.

Considerable attention has been given to increasing the market share of this product while attempting to maintain its profitability. Consequently, since the preparation of the budget the management team implemented some changes to the manufacture and sale of this product. These changes were:

1. The product was budgeted to sell for £5.00 per pack but, to promote sales, a price reduction on all sales to £4.50 per pack was made.
2. The supplier of ingredients was changed and this secured a price reduction to 37.5p per kg on all ingredient supplies in return for a long-term contract.
3. The method of working was changed in order to reduce the direct labour and energy costs which are regarded as variable.

All of the above changes applied for the whole of the month just ended and are reflected in the actual results shown below.

The management intend, however, to use the original budget, for both cost and volume, as a reference point until the effect of the changes has been evaluated. The following actual results have just been reported for the month:

	Actual results	
	£000	**£000**
Sales		1,080
Costs:		
Ingredients	520	
Labour and energy	110	
Fixed overheads	340	
		970
Profit		110

Required

1. Prepare a flexible budget (for the actual quantity sold in the month just ended) based on the original budgeted unit costs and selling price. *(3 marks)*
2. Using variances, reconcile the original budget profit with the actual profit. You should use a contribution approach to variance analysis. *(9 marks)*

3 Provide a commentary on the variances you have produced. Within this commentary refer to possible interrelationships between the variances and how the level of fixed overheads may be reduced. *(8 marks)*

(Total = 20 marks)

ACCA Managerial Finance, December 1999

P13–29 Activity-based budgeting Time allowed: 45 minutes

ST plc produces three types of processed foods for a leading food retailer. The company has three processing departments (Preparation, Cooking and Packaging). After recognizing that the overheads incurred in these departments varied in relation to the activities performed, the company switched from a traditional absorption costing system to a budgetary control system that is based on activity-based costing.

The foods are processed in batches. The budgeted output for April was as follows:

	Output
Food A	100 batches
Food B	30 batches
Food C	200 batches

The number of activities and processing hours budgeted to process a batch of foods in each of the departments are as follows:

	Food A Activities per batch	Food B Activities per batch	Food C Activities per batch
Preparation	5	9	12
Cooking	2	1	4
Packaging	15	2	6
Processing time	10 hours	375 hours	80 hours

The budgeted departmental overhead costs for April were:

	Overheads $
Preparation	100,000
Cooking	350,000
Packaging	50,000

Required

1 For food A only, calculate the budgeted overhead cost per batch:

(a) using traditional absorption costing, based on a factory-wide absorption rate per processing hour; and

(b) using activity-based costing. *(6 marks)*

2 Comment briefly on the advantages of using an activity-based costing approach to determine the cost of each type of processed food compared to traditional absorption costing approaches. You should make reference to your answers to Question 1 where appropriate. *(4 marks)*

3 The actual output for April was:

	Output
Food A	120 batches
Food B	45 batches
Food C	167 batches

Prepare a flexed budget for April using an activity-based costing approach. Your statement must show the total budgeted overhead for each department and the total budgeted overhead absorbed by each food. *(10 marks)*

4 Discuss the advantages that ST plc should see from the activity-based control system compared to the traditional absorption costing that it used previously. *(5 marks)*

CIMA Performance Management, May 2004

P13–30 Time allowed: 45 minutes

TBS produces two products in a single factory. The following details have been extracted from the standard marginal cost cards of the two products:

Product	**S3** **$/unit**	**S5** **$/unit**
Selling price	100	135
Variable costs:		
Material X ($3 per kg)	30	39
Liquid Z ($4.50 per litre)	27	45
Direct labour ($6 per hour)	18	24
Overheads	12	16

TBS uses a standard marginal costing system linked with budgets.

Required

1 Calculate the budgeted profit/loss for October. *(2 marks)*

2 Calculate the actual profit/loss for October. *(3 marks)*

3 As a management accountant in TBS you will be attending the monthly management team meeting. In preparation for that meeting you are required to:

(a) Prepare a statement that reconciles the budgeted and actual profit/loss for October, showing the variances in as much detail as is possible from the data provided. *(15 marks)*

(b) State, and then briefly explain, the main issues in your profit reconciliation statement. *(5 marks)*

(Total 25 marks)

CIMA Management Accounting – Performance management, November 2004

Budgeted data for the month of October included:	S3	S5
Sales (units)	10,000	10,000
Production (units)	12,000	13,500
Fixed costs:		
Production	$51,000	
Administration	$34,000	
Actual data for the month of October was as follows:		
Sales (units)	12,200	8,350
Production (units)	13,000	9,400
Selling prices per unit	$96	$145
Variable costs:		
Material X 270,000 kgs costing	$786,400	
Liquid Z 150,000 litres costing	$763,200	
Direct labour 73,200 hours costing	$508,350	
Overheads	$347,000	
Fixed costs:		
Production	$47,550	
Administration	$36,870	

Cases

C13–31 Incomplete data Time allowed: 35 minutes for each company; 70 minutes in total
Each of the cases below is independent. You may assume that each company uses a standard cost system and that each company's flexible budget for manufacturing overhead is based on standard machine-hours.

Item		Company A	Company B
1	Denominator activity in hours	?	40,000
2	Standard hours allowed for units produced	32,000	?
3	Actual hours worked	30,000	?
4	Flexible budget variable overhead per machine-hour	£?	£2.80
5	Flexible budget fixed overhead (total)	?	?
6	Actual variable overhead cost incurred	54,000	117,000
7	Actual fixed overhead cost incurred	209,400	302,100
8	Variable overhead cost applied to production*	?	117,600
9	Fixed overhead cost applied to production*	192,000	?
10	Variable overhead spending variance	?	?
11	Variable overhead efficiency variance	3,500 F	8,400 U
12	Fixed overhead budget variance	?	2,100 U

13 Fixed overhead volume variance	18,000 U	?
14 Variable portion of the predetermined overhead rate	?	?
15 Fixed portion of the predetermined overhead rate	?	?
16 Underapplied (or overapplied) overhead	?	?

* Based on standard hours allowed for units produced

Required

Compute the unknown amounts. (*Hint*: One way to proceed would be to use the format for variance analysis found in Exhibit 13.6 for variable overhead and in Exhibit 13.10 for fixed overhead.)

C13–32 Preparing a performance report using activity-based costing Time allowed: 45 minutes

Boyne University offers an extensive continuing education programme in many cities throughout the country. For the convenience of its faculty and administrative staff and to save costs, the university employs a supervisor to operate a motor pool. The motor pool operated with 20 vehicles until February, when an additional car was acquired. The motor pool furnishes petrol, oil and other supplies for its cars. A mechanic does routine maintenance and minor repairs. Major repairs are done at a nearby commercial garage.

Each year, the supervisor prepares an operating budget that informs the university administration of the funds needed for operating the motor pool. Depreciation (straight line) on the cars is recorded in the budget in order to determine the cost per mile of operating the vehicles.

The following schedule presents the operating budget for the current year, which has been approved by the university. The schedule also shows actual operating costs for March of the current year compared to one-twelfth of the annual operating budget.

University Motor Pool
Budget report for March

	Annual operating budget	Monthly budget*	March actual	(Over) under budget
Petrol	£42,000	£3,500	£4,300	£(800)
Oil, minor repairs, parts	3,600	300	380	(80)
Outside repairs	2,700	225	50	175
Insurance	6,000	500	525	(25)
Salaries and benefits	30,000	2,500	2,500	–
Depreciation of vehicles	26,400	2,200	2,310	(110)
Total costs	£110,700	£9,225	£10,065	£(840)
Total miles	600,000	50,000	63,000	
Cost per mile	£0.1845	£0.1845	£0.1598	
Number of cars in use	20	20	21	

* Annual operating budget/12 months.

The annual operating budget was constructed on the following assumptions:

1 Twenty cars in the motor pool.
2 Thirty thousand miles driven per year per car.
3 Fifteen miles per litre per car.

4 £1.05 per litre of petrol.

5 £0.006 cost per mile for oil, minor repairs and parts.

6 £135 cost per car per year for outside repairs.

7 £300 cost per car per year for insurance.

The supervisor of the motor pool is unhappy with the monthly report comparing budget and actual costs for March, claiming it presents an unfair picture of performance. A previous employer used flexible budgeting to compare actual costs to budgeted amounts.

Required

1 Prepare a new performance report for March showing budgeted costs, actual costs, and variances. In preparing your report, use flexible budgeting techniques to compute the monthly budget figures.

2 What are the deficiencies in the performance report presented above? How does the report that you prepared in Question 1 above overcome these deficiencies?

(*CMA*, adapted)

C13–33 Flexible budgeting Time allowed: 60 minutes

The Management Control Association is an academy that organizes a major conference each year. Its conference for 2004 will be held in the Edinburgh Business School (EBS), which is located in the grounds of Heriot-Watt University, 7 miles west of the city of Edinburgh. The conference will begin with lunch at 12.30 on Monday 12 July, which will be followed by a series of presentations over the next two days, and will end with a buffet lunch on Wednesday 14 July 2004.

The registration fee for conference delegates includes attendance at the conference, 2 nights' accommodation, meals, and conference materials such as copies of conference papers. The fee to be charged to delegates will depend on their grade of overnight accommodation. Luxury en-suite accommodation is available in the Paul Stobart Building, while standard en-suite accommodation is available in Robert Bryson Hall. All meals, with the exception of the Scottish Banquet (see below) will be served in the Bistro within EBS, which is serviced by an outside contractor. Conference fees have been set at £410 per delegate for luxury accommodation and £350 per delegate for standard accommodation.

A special feature of Management Control Association conferences is an organized social event. Because this year's conference is in Edinburgh, the organizing committee has decided that the social event will be held at the Scotch Whisky Heritage Centre on the Royal Mile. It will comprise a tour of the Whisky Heritage Centre, followed by a Scottish Banquet, with entertainment by Piper and Highland Dancers. The cost of this event, including coach transport from EBS, is included in the registration fee.

You have obtained the following additional information:

EBS manage the luxury en-suite accommodation in the Paul Stobart Building. The cost of these rooms will be £60 per room per night, including breakfast. A maximum of 20 rooms are available for use by conference attendees. Demand for this accommodation is likely to be relatively high, so if conference numbers exceed 50 delegates, it may reasonably be assumed that all 20 rooms will be taken.

The Heriot-Watt University manage the standard en-suite accommodation in the Robert Bryson Hall. The cost of these rooms will be £40 per room per night, including breakfast. As several conferences may take place at the University at the same time, the general demand for accommodation during July might be very high. So it is essential that the conference organizing committee book accommodation well in advance. The terms and conditions of business of Heriot-Watt University are such that the full fee for the rooms must be paid if notification of cancellation occurs within 6 weeks of commencement of the event. As a result of these conditions, the conference organizing committee feels it has no option but to book 80 rooms in Robert Bryson Hall, which it expects to have to pay for in full.

As co-organizers of the conference, EBS will provide conference theatres for the event, free of charge. The size of the main conference theatre limits the maximum number of delegates to 100.

Outside contractors provide catering in the Bistro of EBS. They have sufficient flexibility so as to require notification of conference numbers only a few days before the event. They will provide lunch on each of the three days, Monday 12 July to Wednesday 14 July, at £16 per head. They will also manage the Conference Dinner on Monday 12 July at £22 per head. The dinner will be preceded by a drinks reception, expected to cost £6 per head. In addition, table wines, water etc. are expected to cost another £6 per head. The contractors will also cater for four tea and coffee breaks during the conference programme, each costing £2 per head.

The social event at the Whisky Heritage Centre on the evening of Tuesday 13 July must be booked well in advance. The Centre requires a booking for a minimum of 70 people at £70 per head. Half of the cost for minimum numbers must be paid at the time of booking as a non-returnable deposit. The final invoice for actual numbers will be issued to the conference organizing committee after the event. The terms and conditions of the Centre mean that payment for the minimum number of 70 people must be made, even if conference numbers fall below that level. But for numbers in excess of 70, the Centre requires only a few days' notice. In addition to the basic fee, it is expected that drinks will be provided at £12 per person attending the social event. Return transport to the social event will be provided by a local coach company in 35-seater coaches at a cost of £280 each.

Following a buffet lunch, the conference proper will open with a plenary lecture by a guest speaker from France. The guest will attend the remainder of the conference, the social event, and be provided with 2 nights' accommodation in the Paul Stobart Building, free of charge. In addition, she will be paid travelling expenses, which are expected to be £500.

Sundry expenses for the conference, including compact discs with copies of conference papers, folders, name badges, pens and miscellaneous photocopying are expected to cost £20 per person. Most of these will have to be bought well in advance of the conference when conference numbers are uncertain. Given the relatively low cost per person, the conference organizing committee have decided to purchase 100 of these items, irrespective of actual numbers attending the conference.

Required

1. Produce a flexible budget for the conference to show revenue and expenditure for 50, 70 and 100 delegates.
2. Discuss the value of the flexible budget to the conference organizing committee.
3. More generally, discuss the extent to which flexible budgets can help to mitigate risk in organizations.

(Thanks to Alan Coad, University of Birmingham, for this case)

Further reading

Understanding and managing discretionary fixed costs is one of the most difficult challenges facing management accountants, especially since so little is known about the optimum levels of discretionary costs. Donald Ramcy (1993) discusses a number of approaches for managing discretionary costs.

While the evils of standard cost systems are recounted in many articles and books, two particularly thorough accounts of their drawbacks can be found in Johnson (1990) and Kaplan (1986b). See also Kaplan and Cooper (1998).

Endnotes

1 Normal costs are discussed in Chapter 3.

2 Kaplan and Cooper (1998).

3 Kaplan and Cooper (1998) p. 302.

Chapter 14
Segment reporting and decentralization

Learning objectives

After studying Chapter 14, you should be able to:

1. Differentiate between performance measurement in cost centres, profit centres and investment centres
2. Prepare a segmented profit and loss account using the contribution format
3. Identify three business practices that hinder proper cost assignment
4. Compute the return on investment (ROI)
5. Show how changes in sales, expenses and assets affect an organization's ROI
6. Compute residual income and understand its strengths and weaknesses
7. Compute economic value added (EVA) and other value management metrics

Concepts in Context

Quaker Oats provides an example of how use of a specific performance measure can change the way a company operates. Prior to adopting EVA, 'its businesses had one overriding goal – increasing quarterly earnings. To do it, they guzzled capital. They offered sharp price discounts at the end of each quarter, so plants ran overtime turning out huge shipments of Gatorade, Rice-A-Roni, 100 per cent Natural Cereal, and other products. Managers led the late rush, since their bonuses depended on raising operating profits each quarter ... Pumping up sales requires many warehouses (capital) to hold vast temporary inventories (more capital). But who cared? Quaker's operating businesses paid no charge for capital in internal accounting, so they barely noticed. It took EVA to spotlight the problem. ... One plant has trimmed inventories from $15 million to $9 million, even though it is producing much more, and Quaker has closed five of 15 warehouses, saving $6 million a year in salaries and capital costs.'[1]

Once an organization grows beyond a few people, it becomes impossible for the top manager to make decisions about everything. For example, the managing director of the Novotel Hotel chain cannot be expected to decide whether a particular hotel guest at the Novotel in Sheffield should be allowed to check out later than the normal checkout time. To some degree, managers have to delegate decisions to those who are at lower levels in the organization. However, the degree to which decisions are delegated varies from organization to organization.

Decentralization in organizations

A **decentralized organization** is one in which decision making is not confined to a few top executives but rather is spread throughout the organization, with managers at various levels making *key operating decisions* relating to their sphere of responsibility. Decentralization is a matter of degree, since all organizations are decentralized to some extent out of necessity. At one extreme, a strongly decentralized organization is one in which there are few, if any, constraints on the freedom of even the lowest-level managers and employees to make decisions. At the other extreme, in a strongly centralized organization, lower-level managers have little freedom to make a decision. Although most organizations fall somewhere between these two extremes, there is a pronounced trend toward more and more decentralization.

Advantages and disadvantages of decentralization

Decentralization has many benefits, including:

1 Top management is relieved of much day-to-day problem solving and is left free to concentrate on strategy, on higher-level decision making, and on co-ordinating activities.

2 Decentralization provides lower-level managers with vital experience in making decisions. Without such experience, they would be ill-prepared to make decisions when they are promoted.

3 Added responsibility and decision-making authority often result in increased job satisfaction. It makes the job more interesting and provides greater incentives for people to put out their best efforts.

4 Lower-level managers generally have more detailed and up-to-date information about conditions in their own area of responsibility than top managers. Therefore, the decisions of lower-level managers are often based on better information.

5 It is difficult to evaluate a manager's performance if the manager is not given much latitude in what he or she can do.

Decentralization has four major disadvantages:

1 Lower-level managers may make decisions without fully understanding the 'big picture'. While top-level managers typically have less detailed information about operations than the lower-level managers, they usually have more information about the company as a whole and may have a better understanding of the company's strategy. This situation can be avoided to some extent with the use of modern management information systems that can, in principle, give every manager at every level the same information that goes to the managing director and other top-level managers.

2 In a truly decentralized organization, there may be a lack of co-ordination among autonomous managers. This problem can be reduced by clearly defining the company's strategy and communicating it effectively throughout the organization.

3 Lower-level managers may have objectives that are different from the objectives of the entire organization. For example, some managers may be more interested in increasing the sizes of their departments than in increasing the profits of the company.[2] To some degree, this problem can be overcome by designing performance evaluation systems that motivate managers to make decisions that are in the best interests of the company.

4 In a strongly decentralized organization, it may be more difficult effectively to spread innovative ideas. Someone in one part of the organization may have a terrific idea that would benefit other parts of the organization, but without strong central direction the idea may not be shared with and adopted by other parts of the organization.

Decentralization and segment reporting

Effective decentralization requires *segmental reporting*. In addition to the companywide profit and loss account, reports are needed for individual segments of the organization. A **segment** is a part or activity of an organization about which managers would like cost, revenue or profit data. Examples of segments include divisions of a company, sales territories, individual stores, service centres, manufacturing plants, marketing departments, individual customers and product lines. As we shall see, a company's operations can be segmented in many ways. For example, a supermarket chain like Tesco or Sainsbury can segment their businesses by geographic region, by individual store, by the nature of the merchandise (i.e., green groceries, canned goods, paper goods), by brand name, and so on. In this chapter, we learn how to construct profit and loss accounts for such business segments. These segmented profit and loss accounts are useful in analysing the profitability of segments and in measuring the performance of segment managers.

Cost, profit and investment centres

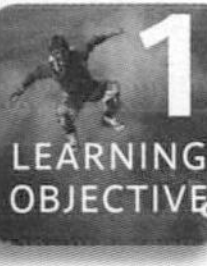

Decentralized companies typically categorize their business segments into cost centres, profit centres and investment centres – depending on the responsibilities of the managers of the segments.[3]

Cost centre

A **cost centre** is a business segment whose manager has control over costs but not over revenue or investment funds. Service departments such as accounting, finance, general administration, legal, personnel and so on, are usually considered to be cost centres. In addition, manufacturing facilities are often considered to be cost centres. The managers of cost centres are expected to minimize cost while providing the level of services or the amount of products demanded by other parts of the organization. For example, the manager of a production facility would be evaluated at least in part by comparing actual costs to how much the costs should have been for the actual number of units produced during the period.

Profit centre

In contrast to a cost centre, a **profit centre** is any business segment whose manager has control over both cost and revenue. Like a cost centre, however, a profit centre generally does not have control over investment funds. For example, the manager in charge of an amusement park would be responsible for both the revenues and costs, and hence the profits, of the amusement park but may not have control over major investments in the park. Profit centre managers are often evaluated by comparing actual profit to targeted or budgeted profit.

Investment centre

An **investment centre** is any segment of an organization whose manager has control over cost, revenue and investments in operating assets. For example, the managing director of the Truck Division at General Motors (one of the companies that pioneered decentralization in the last century)[4] would have a great deal of discretion over investments in the division. The managing director of the Truck Division would be responsible for initiating investment proposals, such as funding research into more fuel-efficient engines for sport-utility vehicles. Once the proposal has been approved by the top level of managers at General Motors and the board of directors, the managing director of the Truck Division would then be responsible for making sure that the investment pays off. Investment centre managers are usually evaluated using return on investment or residual income measures as discussed later in the chapter.

Responsibility centres

2 LEARNING OBJECTIVE

A **responsibility centre** is broadly defined as any part of an organization whose manager has control over cost, revenue or investment funds. Cost centres, profit centres and investment centres are all known as responsibility centres.

A partial organization chart for Universal Foods Corporation, a company in the snack food and beverage industry, appears in Exhibit 14.1. This partial organization chart indicates how the various business segments of the company are classified in terms of responsibility. Note that the cost centres are the departments and work centres that do not generate significant revenues by themselves. These are staff departments such as finance, legal and personnel, and operating units such as the bottling plant, warehouse and beverage distribution centre. The profit centres are business segments that generate revenues and include the beverage, salty snacks and confections product segments. The managing director of operations oversees allocation of investment funds across the product segments and is responsible for revenues and costs and so is treated as an investment centre. And finally, corporate headquarters is an investment centre, since it is responsible for all revenues, costs and investments.

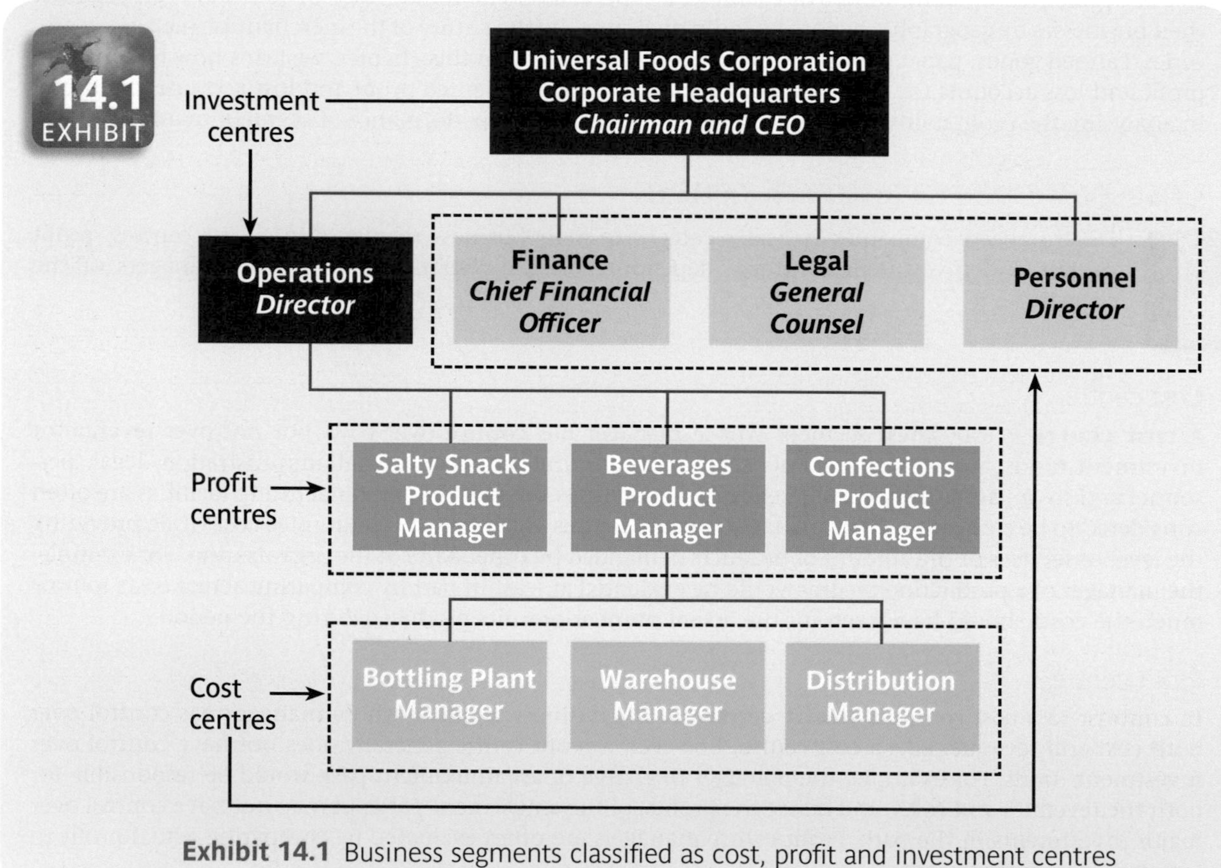

Exhibit 14.1 Business segments classified as cost, profit and investment centres

Segment reporting and profitability analysis

As previously discussed, a different kind of profit and loss account is required for evaluating the performance of business segments – a profit and loss account that emphasizes segments rather than the performance of the company as a whole. This point is illustrated in the following discussion.

Management accounting in action: the issue

SoftSolutions Ltd is a rapidly growing computer software company founded by Stephanie Evans, who had previously worked in a large software company, and Marjorie Price, who had previously worked in the hotel industry as a general manager. They formed the company to develop and market user-friendly accounting and operations software designed specifically for hotels. They quit their jobs, pooled their savings, hired several programmers, and got down to work.

The first sale was by far the most difficult. No hotel wanted to be the first to use an untested product from an unknown company. After overcoming this obstacle with persistence, good luck, dedication to customer service and a very low introductory price, the company's sales burgeoned.

The company quickly developed similar business software for other specialized markets and then branched out into clip art and computer games. Within four years of its founding, the organization had grown to the point where Evans and Price were no longer able personally to direct all of the company's activities. Decentralization had become a necessity.

Accordingly, the company was split into two divisions – Business Products and Consumer Products. By mutual consent, Price took the title chief executive officer and Evans took the title managing director of the Business Products Division. Chris Worden, a programmer who had spearheaded the drive into the clip art and computer games markets, was designated managing director of the Consumer Products Division.

Almost immediately, the issue arose of how best to evaluate the performance of the divisions. Price called a meeting to consider this issue and asked Evans, Worden and the chief accountant, Bill Carson, to attend. The following discussion took place at that meeting:

Marjorie Price: We need to find a better way to measure the performance of the divisions.

Chris Worden: I agree. Consumer Products has been setting the pace in this company for the last two years, and we should be getting more recognition.

Stephanie Evans: Chris, we are delighted with the success of the Consumer Products Division.

Chris Worden: I know. But it is hard to work out just how successful we are with the present accounting reports. All we have are sales and cost of goods sold figures for the division.

Bill Carson: What's the matter with those figures? They are prepared using internationally accepted accounting principles.

Chris Worden: The sales figures are fine. However, cost of goods sold includes some costs that really aren't the costs of our division, and it excludes some costs that are. Let's take a simple example. Everything we sell in the Consumer Products Division has to pass through the automatic bar-coding machine, which applies a unique bar code to the product.

Stephanie Evans: We know. Every item we ship must have a unique identifying bar code. That's true for items from the Business Products Division as well as for items from the Consumer Products Division.

Chris Worden: That's precisely the point. Whether an item comes from the Business Products Division or the Consumer Products Division, it must pass through the automatic bar-coding machine after the software has been packaged. How much of the cost of the automatic bar coder would be saved if we didn't have any consumer products?

Marjorie Price: Since we have only one automatic bar coder and we would need it anyway to code the business products, I guess none of the cost would be saved.

Chris Worden: That's right. And since none of the cost could be saved even if the entire Consumer Products Division were eliminated, how can we logically say that some of the cost of the automatic bar coder is a cost of the Consumer Products Division?

Stephanie Evans: Just a minute, Chris, are you saying that my Business Products Division should be charged with the entire cost of the automatic bar coder?

Chris Worden: No, that's not what I am saying.

Marjorie Price:But Chris, I don't see how we can have sensible performance reports without making someone responsible for costs like the cost of the automatic bar coder. Bill, as our accounting expert, what do you think?

Bill Carson: I have some ideas for handling issues like the automatic bar coder. The best approach would probably be for me to put together a draft performance report. We can discuss it at the next meeting when everyone has something concrete to look at.

Marjorie Price: Okay, let's see what you come up with.

Bill Carson, the chief accountant of SoftSolutions, realized that segmented profit and loss accounts would be required to evaluate more appropriately the performance of the two divisions. To construct the segmented reports, he would have to segregate carefully costs that are attributable to the two divisions from costs that are not. Since most of the disputes over costs would be about fixed costs such as the automatic bar-coding machine, he knew he would also have to separate fixed from variable costs. Under the conventional absorption costing profit and loss account prepared for the entire company, variable and fixed production costs were being commingled in the cost of goods sold.

Largely for these reasons, Bill Carson decided to use the contribution format profit and loss account discussed in earlier chapters. Recall that when the contribution format is used: (1) the cost of goods sold consists only of the variable manufacturing costs; (2) the variable and fixed costs are listed in separate sections; and (3) a contribution margin is computed. When such a statement is segmented as in this chapter, fixed costs are broken down further into what are called traceable and common costs as discussed later. This breakdown allows a *segment margin* to be computed for each segment of the company. The segment margin is a valuable tool for assessing the long-run profitability of a segment and is also a much better tool for evaluating performance than the usual absorption costing reports.

Levels of segmented statements

A portion of the segmented report Bill Carson prepared is shown in Exhibit 14.2. The contribution format profit and loss account for the entire company appears at the very top of the exhibit under the column labelled Total company. Immediately to the right of this column are two columns – one for each of the two divisions. We can see that the divisional segment margin is £60,000 for the Business Products Division and £40,000 for the Consumer Products Division. This is the portion of the report that was specifically requested by the company's divisional managers. They wanted to know how much each of their divisions was contributing to the company's profits.

However, segmented profit and loss accounts can be prepared for activities at many levels in a company. To provide more information to the company's divisional managers, Bill Carson has further segmented the divisions according to their *major product lines*. In the case of the Consumer Products Division, the product lines are clip art and computer games. Going even further, Bill Carson has segmented each of the product lines according to how they are sold – in retail computer stores or by catalogue sales. In Exhibit 14.2, this further segmentation is illustrated for the computer games product line. Notice that as we go from one segmented statement to another, we look at smaller and smaller pieces of the company. While

Segments defined as divisions

	Total company	Divisions: Business Products Division	Divisions: Consumer Products Division
Sales	£500,000	£300,000	£200,000
Less variable expenses:			
Variable cost of goods sold	180,000	120,000	60,000
Other variable expenses	50,000	30,000	20,000
Total variable expenses	230,000	150,000	80,000
Contribution margin	270,000	150,000	120,000
Less traceable fixed expenses	170,000	90,0000	80,000*
Divisional segment margin	100,000	£60,000	£40,000
Less common fixed expenses not traceable to the individual divisions	£85,000		
Net Profit	£15,000		

Segments defined as product lines of the Consumer Products Division

	Consumer Products Division	Product line: Clip art	Product line: Computer games
Sales	£200,000	£75,000	£125,000
Less variable expenses:			
Variable cost of goods sold	60,000	20,000	40,000
Other variable expenses	£20,000	5,000	15,000
Total variable expenses	£80,000	£25,000	£55,000
Contribution margin	120,000	50,000	70,000
Less traceable expenses	£70,000	30,000	£40,000
Product-line segment margin	50,000	£20,000	£30,000
Less common fixed expenses not traceable to the individual product lines	£10,000		
Divisional segment margin	£40,000		

Segments defined as sales channels for one product line, computer games, of the Consumer Products Division

	Computer games	Sales channels: Retail stores	Sales channels: Catalogue sales
Sales	£125,000	£100,000	£25,000
Less variable expenses:			
Variable cost of goods sold	40,000	32,000	8,000
Other variable expenses	15,000	5,000	10,000
Total variable expenses	55,000	37,000	18,000
Contribution margin	70,000	63,000	7,000
Less traceable expenses	25,000	15,000	10,000
Sales-channel segment margin	45,000	£48,000	£(3,000)
Less common fixed expenses Not traceable to the individual sales channels	15,000		
Product-line segment margin	£30,000		

*Notice that this £80,000 in traceable fixed expenses is divided into two parts – £70,000 traceable and £10,000 common – when the Consumer Products Division is broken down into product lines. The reasons for this are discussed later under Traceable costs can become common costs.

Exhibit 14.2 SoftSolutions Ltd – segmented profit statements in the contribution format

not shown in Exhibit 14.2, Bill Carson also prepared segmented profit and loss accounts for the major product lines in the Business Products Division.

Substantial benefits are received from a series of statements such as those contained in Exhibit 14.2. By carefully examining trends and results in each segment, a manager is able to gain considerable insight into the company's operations viewed from many different angles. And advanced computer-based information systems are making it easier and easier to construct such statements and to keep them current.

Sales and contribution margin

To prepare a profit and loss account for a particular segment, variable expenses are deducted from the sales to yield the contribution margin for the segment. It is important to keep in mind that the contribution margin tells us what happens to profits as volume changes – holding a segment's capacity and fixed costs constant. The contribution margin is especially useful in decisions involving temporary uses of capacity such as special orders. Decisions concerning the most effective uses of existing capacity often involve only variable costs and revenues, which, of course, are the very elements involved in contribution margin. Such decisions were discussed in detail in Chapter 9.

Traceable and common fixed costs

The most puzzling aspect of Exhibit 14.2 is probably the treatment of fixed costs. The report has two kinds of fixed costs – *traceable* and *common*. Only the *traceable fixed costs* are charged to the segments in the segmented profit and loss accounts in the report. If a cost is not traceable to a segment, then it is not assigned to the segment.

A **traceable fixed cost** of a segment is a fixed cost that is incurred because of the existence of the segment – if the segment had never existed, the fixed cost would not have been incurred; and/or if the segment were eliminated, the fixed cost would disappear. Examples of traceable fixed costs include the following:

- The salary of the Fritos product manager at PepsiCo is a *traceable* fixed cost of the Fritos business segment of PepsiCo.
- The maintenance cost for the building in which Boeing 747s are assembled is a *traceable* fixed cost of the 747 business segment of Boeing.
- The liability insurance at Disney World is a *traceable* fixed cost of the Disney World business segment of the Disney Corporation.

A **common fixed cost** is a fixed cost that supports the operations of more than one segment but is not traceable in whole or in part to any one segment. Even if a segment were entirely eliminated, there would be no change in a true common fixed cost. Note the following:

- The salary of the Managing Director of General Motors is a *common* fixed cost of the various divisions of General Motors.
- The cost of the automatic bar-coding machine at SoftSolutions is a *common* fixed cost of the Consumer Products Division and of the Business Products Division.
- The cost of the receptionist's salary at an office shared by a number of doctors is a *common* fixed cost of the doctors. The cost is traceable to the office, but not to any one of the doctors individually.

Identifying traceable fixed costs

The distinction between traceable and common fixed costs is crucial in segment reporting, since traceable fixed costs are charged to the segments, whereas common fixed costs are not. In an actual situation, it is sometimes hard to determine whether a cost should be classified as traceable or common.

The general guideline is to treat as traceable costs *only those costs that would disappear over time if the segment itself disappeared*. For example, if the Consumer Products Division were sold or discontinued, it would no longer be necessary to pay the division manager's salary. Therefore the division manager's salary should be classified as a traceable fixed cost of the division. On the other hand, the managing director of the company undoubtedly would continue to be paid even if the Consumer Products Division were dropped. In fact, he or she might even be paid more if dropping the division was a good idea. Therefore, the managing director's salary is common to both divisions. The same idea can be expressed in another way: *treat as traceable costs only those costs that are added as a result of the creation of a segment.*

Activity-based costing

Some costs are easy to identify as traceable costs. For example, the costs of advertising Crest toothpaste on television are clearly traceable to Crest. A more difficult situation arises when a building, machine, or other resource is shared by two or more segments. For example, assume that a multi-product company leases warehouse space that is used for storing the full range of its products. Would the lease cost of the warehouse be a traceable or a common cost of the products? Managers familiar with activity-based costing might argue that the lease cost is traceable and should be assigned to the products according to how much space the products use in the warehouse. In like manner, these managers would argue that order processing costs, sales support costs and other *selling, general and administrative (SG&A) expenses* should also be charged to segments according to the segments' consumption of SG&A resources.

To illustrate, consider Holt Corporation, a company that manufactures concrete pipe for industrial uses. The company has three products – 9-centimetre pipe, 12-centimetre pipe and 18-centimetre pipe. Space is leased in a large warehouse on a yearly basis as needed. The lease cost of this space is £4 per square metre per year. The 9-centimetre pipe occupies 1,000 square metres of space, 12-centimetre pipe occupies 4,000 square metres, and 18-centimetre pipe occupies 5,000 square metres. The company also has an order processing department that incurred £150,000 in order processing costs last year. Management believes that order processing costs are driven by the number of orders placed by customers in a year. Last year 2,500 orders were placed, of which 1,200 were for 9-centimetre pipe, 800 were for 12-centimetre pipe, and 500 were for 18-centimetre pipe. Given these data, the following costs would be assigned to each product using the activity-based costing approach:

Warehouse space cost:	
9-centimetre pipe: £4 × 1,000 square metres	£4,000
12-centimetre pipe: £4 × 4,000 square metres	16,000
18-centimetre pipe: £4 × 5,000 square metres	20,000
Total cost assigned	£40,000
Order processing costs:	
£150,000/2,500 orders = £60 per order	
9-centimetre pipe: £60 × 1,200 orders	£72,000
12-centimetre pipe: £60 × 800 orders	48,000
18-centimetre pipe: £60 × 500 orders	30,000
Total cost assigned	£150,000

This method of assigning costs combines the strength of activity-based costing with the power of the contribution approach and greatly enhances the manager's ability to measure the profitability and performance of segments. However, managers must still ask themselves if the costs would in fact disappear over time if the segment itself disappeared. In the case of Holt Corporation, it is clear that the £20,000 in warehousing costs for the 18-centimetre pipe would be eliminated if 18-centimetre pipes were no longer being produced. The company would simply rent less warehouse space the following year. However, suppose the company owns the warehouse. Then it is not so clear that £20,000 of the cost of the warehouse would really disappear if the 18-centimetre pipes were discontinued as a product. The company might be able to sublease the space, or use it for other products, but then again the space might simply be empty while the costs of the warehouse continue to be incurred.

In assigning costs to segments, the key point is to resist the temptation to allocate costs (such as depreciation of corporate facilities) that are clearly common in nature and that would continue regardless of whether the segment exists or not. *Any allocation of common costs to segments will reduce the value of the segment margin as a guide to long-run segment profitability and segment performance.* This point will be discussed at length later in the chapter.

Traceable costs can become common costs

Fixed costs that are traceable to one segment may be a common cost of another segment. For example, an airline might want a segmented profit and loss account that shows the segment margin for a particular flight from Los Angeles to Paris, further broken down into first-class, business-class and economy-class *segment margins*. The airline must pay a substantial landing fee at Charles DeGaulle airport in Paris. This fixed landing fee is a traceable cost of the flight, but it is a common cost of the first-class, business-class and economy-class segments. Even if the first-class cabin is empty, the entire landing fee must be paid. So the landing fee is not a traceable cost of the first-class cabin. But on the other hand, paying the fee is necessary in order to have any first-class, business-class, or economy-class passengers. So the landing fee is a common cost of these three classes.

The dual nature of some of the fixed costs can be seen from the diagram in Exhibit 14.3. Notice from the diagram that when segments are defined as divisions, the Consumer Products Division has £80,000 in traceable fixed expenses. Only £70,000 of this amount remains traceable, however, when we narrow the definition of a segment from divisions to product lines. Notice that the other £10,000 then becomes a common cost of the two product lines of the Consumer Products Division.

14.3 EXHIBIT

	Total company	Segment: Business Products Division	Segment: Consumer Products Division
Contribution margin	£270,000	£150,000	£120,000
Less traceable fixed expenses	170,000	90,000	**80,000**

	Consumer Products Division	Segment: Clip art	Segment: Computer games
Contribution margin	£120,000	£50,000	£70,000
Less traceable fixed expenses	**70,000**	30,000	40,000
Product-line segment margin	50,000	£20,000	£30,000
Less common fixed expenses	**10,000**		
Divisional segment margin	£40,000		

Exhibit 14.3 Reclassification of traceable fixed expenses from Exhibit 14.2

Why would £10,000 of traceable fixed cost become a common cost when the division is divided into product lines? The £10,000 is the monthly salary of the manager of the Consumer Products Division. This salary is a traceable cost of the division as a whole, but it is a common cost of the division's product lines. The manager's salary is a necessary cost of having the two product lines, but even if one of the product lines were discontinued entirely, the manager's salary would probably not be cut. Therefore, none of the manager's salary can be really traced to the individual products.

The £70,000 traceable fixed cost of the product lines consists of the costs of product-specific advertising. A total of £30,000 was spent on advertising clip art and £40,000 was spent on advertising computer games. These costs can clearly be traced to the individual product lines.

Segment margin

Observe from Exhibit 14.2 that the **segment margin** is obtained by deducting the traceable fixed costs of a segment from the segment's contribution margin. It represents the margin available after a segment has covered all of its own costs. *The segment margin is the best gauge of the long-run profitability of a segment,* since it includes only those costs that are caused by the segment. If a segment cannot cover its own costs, then that segment probably should not be retained (unless it has important side effects on other segments). Notice from Exhibit 14.2, for example, that Catalogue sales has a negative segment margin. This means that the segment is not covering its own costs; it is generating more costs than it collects in revenue.

From a decision-making point of view, the segment margin is most useful in major decisions that affect capacity such as dropping a segment. By contrast, as we noted earlier, the contribution margin is most useful in decisions relating to short-run changes in volume, such as pricing special orders that involve utilization of existing capacity.

Management accounting in action: the wrap-up

Shortly after Bill Carson, SoftSolutions Ltd's chief accountant, completed the draft segmented profit and loss account, he sent copies to the other managers and scheduled a meeting in which the report could be explained. The meeting was held on the Monday following the first meeting; and Marjorie Price, Stephanie Evans and Chris Worden were all in attendance.

Stephanie Evans: I think these segmented profit and loss accounts are fairly self-explanatory. However, there is one thing I wonder about.

Bill Carson: What's that?

Stephanie Evans: What is this common fixed expense of £85,000 listed under the total company? And who is going to be responsible for it if neither Chris nor I have responsibility?

Bill Carson: The £85,000 of common fixed expenses represents expenses like general administrative salaries and the costs of common production equipment such as the automatic bar-coding machine. Marjorie, do you want to respond to the question about responsibility for these expenses?

Marjorie Price: Sure. Since I'm the managing director of the company, I'm responsible for those costs. Some things can be delegated, others cannot. It wouldn't make any sense for either you or Chris to make decisions about the bar coder, since it affects both of you. That's an important part of my job – Segment making decisions about resources that affect all parts of the organization. This report makes it much clearer who is responsible for what. I like it.

Chris Worden: So do I – my division's segment margin is higher than the net profit for the entire company.

Marjorie Price: Don't get carried away, Chris. Let's not misinterpret what this report means. The segment margins have to be big to cover the common costs of the company. We can't let the big segment margins lull us into a sense of complacency. If we use these reports, we all have to agree that our objective is to increase all of the segment margins over time.

Stephanie Evans: I'm willing to give it a try.

Chris Worden: The reports make sense to me.

Marjorie Price: So be it. Then the first item of business would appear to be a review of catalogue sales of computer games, where we appear to be losing money. Chris, could you brief us on this at our next meeting?

Chris Worden: I'd be happy to. I have been suspecting for some time that our catalogue sales strategy could be improved.

Marjorie Price: We look forward to hearing your analysis. Meeting's adjourned.

There is more than one way to segment a company

SoftSolutions segmented its sales by division, by product line within each division, and by sales channel. An organization can be segmented in many ways. For example, two different ways of segmenting the sales of the General Electric Company are displayed in Exhibit 14.4. In the first diagram, the company's sales are segmented by geographic region. In the second diagram, they are segmented by products. Note that each of the diagrams could be continued, providing progressively more detailed segment data. For example, the sales in France could be broken down by major product line, then by product. Similar breakdowns could be done of General Electric's costs and segment margins, although that would

14.4 EXHIBIT

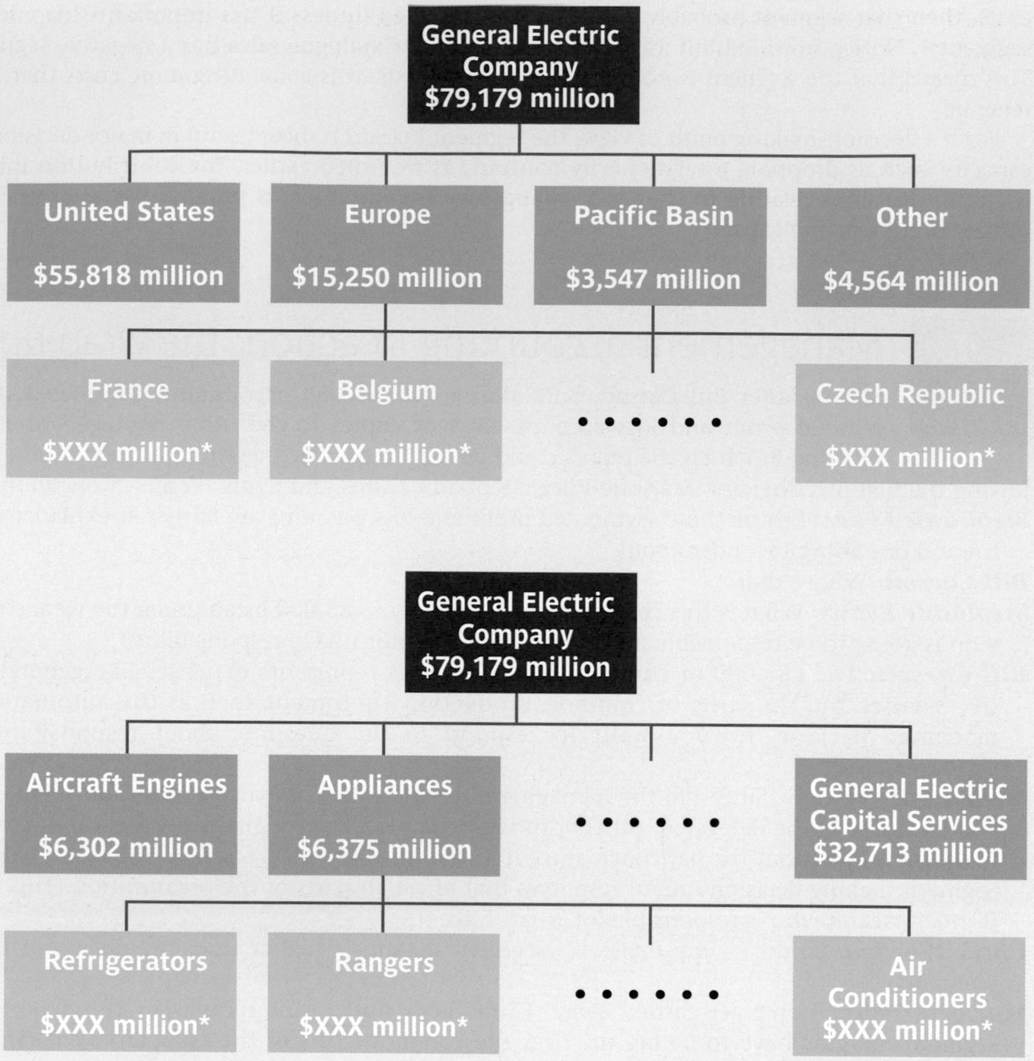

General Electric Company
$79,179 million

- **United States** — $55,818 million
- **Europe** — $15,250 million
  - **France** — $XXX million*
  - **Belgium** — $XXX million*
  - • • • • • •
  - **Czech Republic** — $XXX million*
- **Pacific Basin** — $3,547 million
- **Other** — $4,564 million

General Electric Company
$79,179 million

- **Aircraft Engines** — $6,302 million
- **Appliances** — $6,375 million
  - **Refrigerators** — $XXX million*
  - **Rangers** — $XXX million*
  - • • • • • •
  - **Air Conditioners** — $XXX million*
- • • • • • •
- **General Electric Capital Services** — $32,713 million

*These sales figures are not publicly disclosed by GE, but they are readily available within the company to managers.

Exhibit 14.4 General Electric Company's revenues segmented by geographic region and products

require substantial additional analytical work to identify the segments to which various costs should be assigned.

Segment breakdowns such as those shown in Exhibit 14.4 give a company's managers the ability to look at the company from many different directions. With the increasing availability of companywide databases and sophisticated management information system software, detailed segmental reports of revenues, costs, and margins are becoming much easier to do.

Hindrances to proper cost assignment

For segment reporting to accomplish its intended purposes, costs must be properly assigned to segments. If the purpose is to determine the profits being generated by a particular division, then all of the costs attributable to that division – and only those costs – should be assigned to it.

Unfortunately, three business practices greatly hinder proper cost assignment: (1) omission of some costs in the assignment process, (2) the use of inappropriate methods for allocating costs among segments of a company, and (3) assignment to segments of costs that are really common costs.

Omission of costs

The costs assigned to a segment should include all costs attributable to that segment from the company's entire *value chain*. The value chain, which is illustrated in Exhibit 14.5, consists of the major business functions that add value to a company's products and services. All of these functions, from research and development, through product design, manufacturing, marketing, distribution and customer service, are required to bring a product or service to the customer and generate revenues.

14.5 EXHIBIT

Research and Development	Product Design	Manufacturing	Marketing	Distribution	Customer Service

Exhibit 14.5 Business functions making up the value chain

However, as discussed in Chapters 2, 3 and 6, only manufacturing costs are included in product costs for financial reporting purposes. Consequently, when trying to determine product profitability for internal decision-making purposes, some companies deduct only manufacturing costs from product revenues. As a result, such companies omit from their profitability analysis part or all of the 'upstream' costs in the value chain, which consist of research and development and product design, and the 'downstream' costs, which consist of marketing, distribution and customer service. Yet these non-manufacturing costs are just as essential in determining product profitability as are the manufacturing costs. These upstream and downstream costs, which are usually titled *Selling, General, and Administrative (SG&A)* on the profit and loss account, can represent half or more of the total costs of an organization. If either the upstream or downstream costs are omitted in profitability analysis, then the product is undercosted and management may unwittingly develop and maintain products that in the long run result in losses rather than profits for the company.

Inappropriate methods for allocating costs among segments

Cross-subsidization, or cost distortion, occurs when costs are improperly assigned among a company's segments. Cross-subsidization can occur in two ways; first, when companies fail to trace costs directly to segments in those situations where it is feasible to do so; and second, when companies use inappropriate bases to allocate costs.

Failure to trace costs directly

Costs that can be traced directly to a specific segment of a company should not be allocated to other segments. Rather, such costs should be charged directly to the responsible segment. For example, the rent for a branch office of an insurance company should be charged directly against the branch to which it relates rather than included in a companywide overhead pool and then spread throughout the company.

Inappropriate allocation base

Some companies allocate costs to segments using arbitrary bases such as sales or cost of goods sold. For example, under the sales approach, costs are allocated to the various segments according to the percentage of company sales generated by each segment. Thus, if a segment generates 20% of total company sales, it would be allocated 20% of the company's SG&A expenses as its 'fair share'. This same basic procedure is followed if costs of goods sold or some other measure is used as the allocation base.

For this approach to be valid, the allocation base must actually drive the overhead cost. (Or at least the allocation base should be highly correlated with the cost driver of the overhead cost.) For example, when sales are used as the allocation base for SG&A expenses, it is implicitly assumed that SG&A expenses change in proportion to changes in total sales. If that is not true, the SG&A expenses allocated to segments will be misleading.

Arbitrarily dividing common costs among segments

The third business practice that leads to distorted segment costs is the practice of assigning non-traceable costs to segments. For example, some companies allocate the costs of the corporate headquarters building to products on segment reports. However, in a multi-product company, no single product is likely to be responsible for any significant amount of this cost. Even if a product were eliminated entirely, there would usually be no significant effect on any of the costs of the corporate headquarters building. In short, there is no cause-and-effect relation between the cost of the corporate headquarters building and the existence of any one product. As a consequence, any allocation of the cost of the corporate headquarters building to the products must be arbitrary.

Common costs like the costs of the corporate headquarters building are necessary, of course, to have a functioning organization. The common practice of arbitrarily allocating these costs to segments is often justified on the grounds that 'someone' has to 'cover the common costs'. While it is undeniably true that the common costs must be covered, arbitrarily allocating common costs to segments does not ensure that this will happen. In fact, adding a share of common costs to the real costs of a segment may make an otherwise profitable segment appear to be unprofitable. If a manager erroneously eliminates the segment, the revenues will be lost, the real costs of the segment will be saved, but the common costs will still be there. The net effect will be to reduce the profits of the company as a whole and make it even more difficult to 'cover the common costs'.

In sum, the way many companies handle segment reporting results in *cost distortion*. This distortion results from three practices – the failure to trace costs directly to a specific segment when it is feasible to do so, the use of inappropriate bases for allocating costs and the allocation of common costs to segments. These practices are widespread. One study found that 60% of the companies surveyed made no attempt to assign SG&A costs to segments on a cause-and-effect basis.[5]

Rate of return for measuring managerial performance

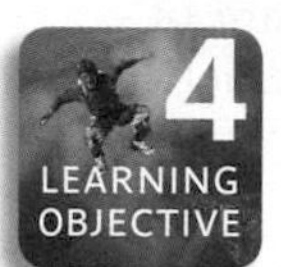

When a company is truly decentralized, segment managers are given a great deal of autonomy. So great is this autonomy that the various profit and investment centres are often viewed as being virtually independent businesses, with their managers having about the same control over decisions as if they were in fact running their own independent firms. With this autonomy, fierce competition often develops among managers, with each striving to make his or her segment the 'best' in the company.

Competition between investment centres is particularly keen for investment funds. How do top managers in corporate headquarters go about deciding who gets new investment funds as they become available, and how do these managers decide which investment centres are most profitably using the funds that have already been entrusted to their care? One of the most popular ways of making these judgements is to measure the rate of return that investment centre managers are able to generate on their assets. This rate of return is called *the return on investment (ROI)*.

The return on investment (ROI) formula

The **return on investment (ROI)** is defined as net operating profit divided by average operating assets:

$$\text{ROI} = \frac{\text{Net operating profit}}{\text{Average operating assets}}$$

There are some issues about how to measure net operating profit and average operating assets, but this formula seems clear enough. The higher the return on investment of a business segment, the greater the *profit generated per pound invested* in the segment's operating assets.

Net operating profit and operating assets defined

Note that *net operating profit*, rather than net profit, is used in the ROI formula. **Net operating profit** is profit before interest and taxes and is sometimes referred to as EBIT (earnings before interest and taxes).

The reason for using net operating profit in the formula is that the profit figure used should be consistent with the base to which it is applied. Notice that the base (i.e., denominator) consists of *operating assets*. Thus, to be consistent we use net operating profit in the numerator.

Operating assets include cash, debtors, inventory, plant and equipment, and all other assets held for productive use in the organization. Examples of assets that would not be included in the operating assets category (i.e., examples of non-operating assets) would include land held for future use, an investment in another company, or a factory building rented to someone else. The operating assets base used in the formula is typically computed as the average of the operating assets between the beginning and the end of the year.

Plant and equipment: net book value or gross cost?

A major issue in ROI computations is the monetary measure of plant and equipment that should be included in the operating assets base. To illustrate the problem involved, assume that a company reports the following amounts for plant and equipment on its balance sheet:

Plant and equipment	£3,000,000
Less accumulated depreciation	900,000
Net book value	£2,100,000

What amount of plant and equipment should the company include with its operating assets in computing ROI? One widely used approach is to include only the plant and equipment's *net book value* – that is, the plant's original cost less accumulated depreciation (£2,100,000 in the example above). A second approach is to ignore depreciation and include the plant's entire *gross cost* in the operating assets base (£3,000,000 in the example above). Both of these approaches are used in actual practice, even though they will obviously yield very different operating asset and ROI figures.

The following arguments can be raised for using *net book value* to measure *operating assets* and for using *gross cost* to measure operating assets in ROI computation.

Arguments for using net book value to measure operating assets in ROI computations:

1 The net book value method is consistent with how plant and equipment are reported on the balance sheet (i.e., cost less accumulated depreciation to date).

2 The net book value method is consistent with the computation of operating profit, which includes depreciation as an operating expense.

Arguments for using gross cost to measure operating assets in ROI computations:

1 The gross cost method eliminates both the age of equipment and the method of depreciation as factors in ROI computations. (Under the net book value method, ROI will tend to increase over time as net book value declines due to depreciation.)

2 The gross cost method does not discourage replacement of old, worn out equipment. (Under the net book value method, replacing fully depreciated equipment with new equipment can have a dramatic, adverse effect on ROI.)

Managers generally view consistency as the most important of the considerations above. As a result, a majority of companies use the net book value approach in ROI computations. In this text, we will also use the net book value approach unless a specific exercise or problem directs otherwise.

Controlling the rate of return

When we first defined the return on investment, we used the following formula:

$$\text{ROI} = \frac{\text{Net operating profit}}{\text{Average operating assets}}$$

We can modify this formula slightly by introducing sales as follows:

$$\text{ROI} = \frac{\text{Net operating profit}}{\text{Sales}} \times \frac{\text{Sales}}{\text{Average operating assets}}$$

The first term on the right-hand side of the equation is the *margin*, which is defined as follows:

$$\text{Margin} = \frac{\text{Net operating profit}}{\text{Sales}}$$

The **margin** is a measure of management's ability to control operating expenses in relation to sales. The lower the operating expenses per pound of sales, the higher the margin earned.

The second term on the right-hand side of the preceding equation is *turnover* which is defined as follows:

$$\text{Turnover} = \frac{\text{Sales}}{\text{Average operating assets}}$$

Turnover is a measure of the sales that are generated for each pound invested in operating assets.

The following alternative form of the ROI formula, which we will use most frequently, combines margin and turnover:

$$\text{ROI} = \text{Margin} \times \text{Turnover}$$

Which formula for ROI should be used – the original one stated in terms of net operating profit and average operating assets or this one stated in terms of margin and turnover? Either can be used – they will always give the same answer. However, the margin and turnover formulation provides some additional insights.

Some managers tend to focus too much on margin and ignore turnover. To some degree at least, the margin can be a valuable indicator of a manager's performance. Standing alone, however, it overlooks one crucial area of a manager's responsibility – the investment in operating assets. Excessive funds tied up in operating assets, which depresses turnover, can be just as much of a drag on profitability as excessive operating expenses, which depresses margin. One of the advantages of ROI as a performance measure is that it forces the manager to control the investment in operating assets as well as to control expenses and the margin.

Du Pont pioneered the ROI concept and recognized the importance of looking at both margin and turnover in assessing the performance of a manager. The ROI formula is now widely used as the key measure of the performance of an investment centre. The ROI formula blends together many aspects of the manager's responsibilities into a single figure that can be compared to the returns of competing investment centres, the returns of other firms in the industry, and to the past returns of the investment centre itself.

Du Pont also developed the diagram that appears in Exhibit 14.6. This exhibit helps managers understand how they can control ROI. An investment centre manager can increase ROI in basically three ways:

1 Increase sales
2 Reduce expenses
3 Reduce assets.

To illustrate how the rate of return can be improved by each of these three actions, consider how the manager of the Raffles Burger Grill is evaluated. Burger Grill is a small chain of upmarket casual restaurants that has been rapidly adding outlets via franchising. The Raffles franchise is owned by a group of local surgeons who have little time to devote to management and little expertise in business matters. Therefore, they delegate operating decisions – including decisions concerning investment in operating assets such as inventories – to a professional manager they have hired. The manager is evaluated largely based on the ROI the franchise generates.

The following data represent the results of business activity for the most recent month:

Net operating profit	£10,000
Sales	100,000
Average operating assets	50,000

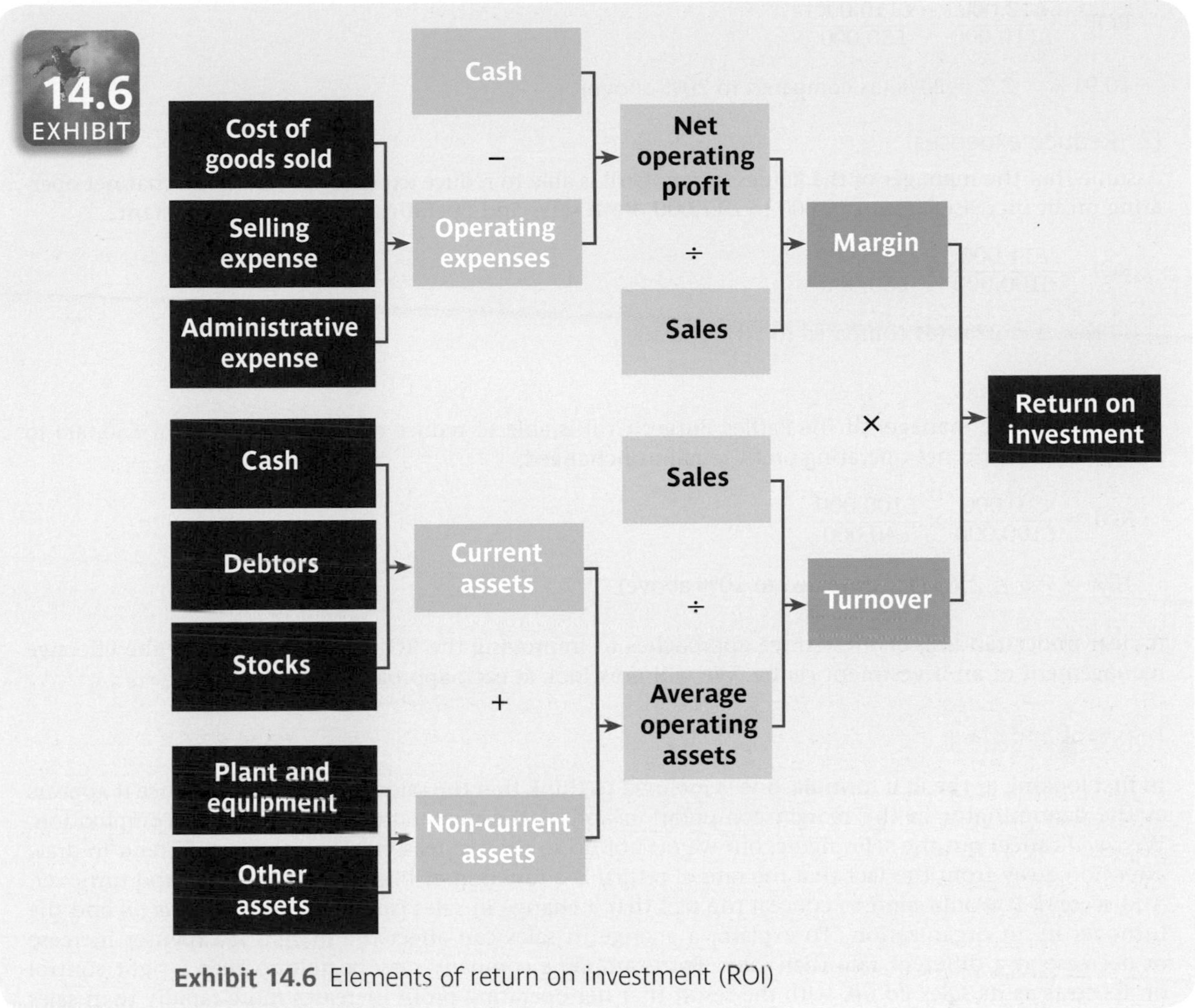

Exhibit 14.6 Elements of return on investment (ROI)

The rate of return generated by the Raffles Burger Grill investment centre is as follows:

$$\text{ROI} = \text{Margin} \times \text{Turnover}$$

$$\frac{\text{Net operating profit}}{\text{Sales}} \times \frac{\text{Sales}}{\text{Average operating assets}}$$

$$\frac{£10{,}000}{£1{,}000{,}000} \times \frac{£100{,}000}{£50{,}000}$$

$$10\% \times 2 = 20\%$$

As we stated above, to improve the ROI figure, the manager can (1) increase sales, (2) reduce expenses, or (3) reduce the operating assets.

(1) Increase sales

Assume that the manager of the Raffles Burger Grill is able to increase sales from £100,000 to £110,000. Assume further that either because of good cost control or because some costs in the company are fixed, the net operating profit increases even more rapidly, going from £10,000 to £12,000 per period. The operating assets remain constant.

$$\text{ROI} = \frac{£12{,}000}{£110{,}000} \times \frac{£110{,}000}{£50{,}000}$$

10.91% × 2.2 = 24% (as compared to 20% above)

(2) Reduce expenses

Assume that the manager of the Raffles Burger Grill is able to reduce expenses by £1,000 so that net operating profit increases from £10,000 to £11,000. Both sales and operating assets remain constant.

$$\text{ROI} = \frac{£11{,}000}{£100{,}000} \times \frac{£100{,}000}{£50{,}000}$$

11% × 2 = 22% (as compared to 20% above)

(3) Reduce assets

Assume that the manager of the Raffles Burger Grill is able to reduce operating assets from £50,000 to £40,000. Sales and net operating profit remain unchanged.

$$\text{ROI} = \frac{£10{,}000}{£100{,}000} \times \frac{£100{,}000}{£40{,}000}$$

10% × 2.5 = 25% (as compared to 20% above)

A clear understanding of these three approaches to improving the ROI figure is critical to the effective management of an investment centre. We will now look at each approach in more detail.

Increase sales

In first looking at the ROI formula, one is inclined to think that the sales figure is neutral, since it appears as the denominator in the margin computation and as the numerator in the turnover computation. We *could* cancel out the sales figure, but we do not do so for two reasons. First, this would tend to draw attention away from the fact that the rate of return is a function of *two* variables, margin and turnover. And second, it would tend to conceal the fact that a change in sales can affect both the *margin* and the turnover in an organization. To explain, a change in sales can affect the margin if expenses increase or decrease at a different rate than sales. For example, a company may be able to keep a tight control on its costs as its sales go up, with the result that net operating profit increases more rapidly than sales and increases the margin. Or a company may have fixed expenses that remain constant as sales go up, resulting in an increase in the net operating profit and in the margin. Either (or both) of these factors could have been responsible for the increase in the margin percentage from 10 to 10.91 illustrated in (1) above.

Further, a change in sales can affect the *turnover* if sales either increase or decrease without a proportionate increase or decrease in the operating assets. In the first approach above, for example, sales increased from £100,000 to £110,000, but the operating assets remained unchanged. As a result, the turnover increased from 2 to 2.2 for the period.

Reduce expenses

Often the easiest route to increased profitability and to a stronger ROI figure is simply to cut the 'fat' out of an organization through a concerted effort to control expenses. When margins begin to be squeezed, this is generally the first line of attack by a manager. Discretionary fixed costs usually come under scrutiny first, and various programmes are either curtailed or eliminated in an effort to cut costs. Managers must be careful, however, not to cut out muscle and bone along with the fat. Also, they must remember that frequent cost-cutting binges can destroy morale. Most managers now agree that it is best to stay 'lean and mean' all the time.

Reduce operating assets

Managers have always been sensitive to the need to control sales, operating expenses and operating margins. However, they have not always been equally sensitive to the need to control investment in operating assets. Firms that have adopted the ROI approach to measuring managerial performance report that one of the first reactions of investment centre managers is to trim their investment in operating assets. The reason, of course, is that these managers soon realize that an excessive investment in operating assets reduces turnover and hurts the ROI. As these managers reduce their investment in operating assets, funds are released that can be used elsewhere in the organization.

How can an investment centre manager control the investment in operating assets? One approach is to eliminate unneeded stock. Just-in-time (JIT) purchasing and JIT manufacturing have been extremely helpful in reducing stocks of all types, with the result that ROI figures have improved dramatically in some companies. Another approach is to devise various methods of speeding up the collection of debtors. For example, many firms now employ the lockbox technique by which customers in distant states send their payments directly to post office boxes in their area. The funds are received and deposited by a local bank on behalf of the payee firm. This speeds up the collection process, since the payments are not delayed in the postal system. As a result of the speedup in collection, the Debtors balance is reduced and the asset turnover is increased.

Criticisms of ROI

Although ROI is widely used in evaluating performance, it is not a perfect tool. The method is subject to the following criticisms:

1 Just telling managers to increase ROI may not be enough. Managers may not know how to increase ROI; they may increase ROI in a way that is inconsistent with the company's strategy; or they may take actions that increase ROI in the short run but harm the company in the long run (such as cutting back on research and development). This is why ROI is best used as part of a balanced scorecard, as we will discuss in Chapter 16. A balanced scorecard can provide concrete guidance to managers, make it more likely that actions taken are consistent with the company's strategy, and reduce the likelihood that short-run performance will be enhanced at the expense of long-term performance.

2 A manager who takes over a business segment typically inherits many committed costs over which the manager has no control. These committed costs may be relevant in assessing the performance of the business segment as an investment but make it difficult fairly to assess the performance of the manager relative to other managers.

3 As discussed in the next section, a manager who is evaluated based on ROI may reject profitable investment opportunities.

Residual income[6] – another measure of performance

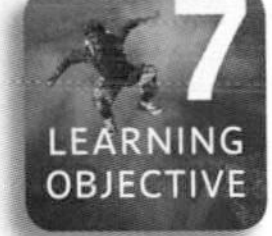

Another approach to measuring an investment centre's performance focuses on a concept known as *residual income*. **Residual income** is the net operating profit that an investment centre earns above the minimum required return on its operating assets. **Economic value added (EVA)** is a similar concept that differs in some details from residual income.[7] For example, under the economic value added concept, funds used for research and development are treated as investments rather than as expenses.[8] However, for our purposes, we will not draw any distinction between residual income and economic value added.

When residual income or economic value added is used to measure performance, the purpose is to maximize the total amount of residual income or economic value added, not to maximize overall ROI. For purposes of illustration, consider the following data for an investment centre – the Scottish Division of Alaskan Marine Services Corporation.

Alaskan Marine Services Corporation
Scottish Division
Basic data for performance evaluation

Average operating assets	£100,000
Net operating profit	£20,000
Minimum required rate of return	15%

Alaskan Marine Services Corporation has long had a policy of evaluating investment centre managers based on ROI, but it is considering a switch to residual income. The finance director of the company, who is in favour of the change to residual income, has provided the following table that shows how the performance of the division would be evaluated under each of the two methods:

Marine Services Corporation
Scottish Division
Alternative performance measures

	ROI	Residual income
Average operating assets	£100,000 (a)	£100,000
Net operating profit	£20,000 (b)	£20,000
ROI, (b) ÷ (a)	20%	
Minimum required return (15% × £100,000)		15,000
Residual income		£5,000

The reasoning underlying the residual income calculation is straightforward. The company is able to earn a rate of return of at least 15% on its investments. Since the company has invested £100,000 in the Scottish Division in the form of operating assets, the company should be able to earn at least £15,000 (15% × £100,000) on this investment. Since the Scottish Division's net operating profit is £20,000, the residual income above and beyond the minimum required return is £5,000. If *residual income* is adopted as the performance measure to replace ROI, the manager of the Scottish Division would be evaluated based on the growth from year to year in residual income.

Motivation and residual income

One of the primary reasons why the chief accountant of Marine Services Corporation would like to switch from ROI to residual income has to do with how managers view new investments under the two performance measurement schemes. The residual income approach encourages managers to make investments that are profitable for the entire company but that would be rejected by managers who are evaluated by the ROI formula.

To illustrate this problem, suppose that the manager of the Scottish Division is considering purchasing a computerized diagnostic machine to aid in servicing marine diesel engines. The machine would cost £25,000 and is expected to generate additional operating profit of £4,500 a year. From the standpoint of the company, this would be a good investment since it promises a rate of return of 18% (£4,500/£25,000), which is in excess of the company's minimum required rate of return of 15%.

If the manager of the Scottish Division is evaluated based on residual income, she would be in favour of the investment in the diagnostic machine as shown below:

Marine Services Corporation
Scottish Division
Performance evaluated using residual income

	Present	New project	Overall
Average operating assets	£100,000	£25,000	£125,000
Net operating profit	£20,000	£4,500	£24,500
Minimum required return	15,000	3,750*	18,750
Residual income	£5,000	£750	£5,750

*£25,000 × 15% = £3,750.

Since the project would increase the residual income of the Scottish Division, the manager would want to invest in the new diagnostic machine.

Now suppose that the manager of the Scottish Division is evaluated based on ROI. The effect of the diagnostic machine on the division's ROI is computed below:

Marine Services Corporation
Scottish Division
Performance evaluated using ROI

	Present	New project	Overall
Average operating assets (a)	£100,000	£25,000	£125,000
Net operating profit (b)	£20,000	£4,500†	
ROI, (b)/(a)	20%	18%	19.6%

†£25,000 × 18% = £4,500.

The new project reduces the division's ROI from 20% to 19.6%. This happens because the 18% rate of return on the new diagnostic machine, while above the company's 15% minimum rate of return, is below the division's present ROI of 20%. Therefore, the new diagnostic machine would drag the division's ROI down even though it would be a good investment from the standpoint of the company as a whole. If the manager of the division is evaluated based on ROI, she will be reluctant even to propose such an investment.

Basically, a manager who is evaluated based on ROI will reject any project whose rate of return is below the division's current ROI even if the rate of return on the project is above the minimum required rate of return for the entire company. In contrast, any project whose rate of return is above the minimum required rate of return for the company will result in an increase in residual income. Since it is in the best interests of the company as a whole to accept any project whose rate of return is above the minimum required rate of return, managers who are evaluated based on residual income will tend to make better decisions concerning investment projects than managers who are evaluated based on ROI.

Divisional comparison and residual income

The residual income approach has one major disadvantage. It cannot be used to compare the performance of divisions of different sizes. You would expect larger divisions to have more residual income than smaller divisions, not necessarily because they are better managed but simply because of the bigger numbers involved.

As an example, consider the following residual income computations for Division X and Division Y:

	Division	
	X	Y
Average operating assets (a)	£1,000,000	£250,000
Net operating profit	£120,000	£40,000
Minimum required return: 10% × (a)	100,000	25,000
Residual income	£20,000	£15,000

Observe that Division X has slightly more residual income than Division Y, but that Division X has £1,000,000 in operating assets as compared to only £250,000 in operating assets for Division Y. Thus, Division X's greater residual income is probably more a result of its size than the quality of its management. In fact, it appears that the smaller division is better managed, since it has been able to generate nearly as much residual income with only a quarter as much in operating assets to work with. This problem can be reduced to some degree by focusing on the percentage change in residual income from year to year rather than on the absolute amount of the residual income.

ROI, RI and the balanced scorecard

Simply exhorting managers to increase ROI is not sufficient. Managers who are told to increase ROI will naturally wonder how this is to be accomplished. The Du Pont scheme, which is illustrated in Exhibit 14.6, provides managers with some guidance. Generally speaking, ROI can be increased by increasing sales, decreasing costs, and/or decreasing investments in operating assets. However, it may not be obvious to managers how they are supposed to increase sales, decrease costs and decrease investments in a way that is consistent with the company's strategy. For example, a manager who is given inadequate guidance may cut back on investments that are critical to implementing the company's strategy.

For that reason, as will be discussed in Chapter 16, when managers are evaluated based on ROI, a *balanced scorecard* approach is advised. And indeed, ROI, or residual income, is typically included as one of the financial performance measures on a company's balanced scorecard. The balanced scorecard provides a way of communicating a company's strategy to managers throughout the organization. The scorecard indicates how the company intends to improve its financial performance. A well-constructed balanced scorecard should answer questions such as: 'What internal business processes should be improved?' and 'Which customer should be targeted and how will they be attracted and retained at a profit?' In short, a well-constructed balanced scorecard can provide managers with a road map that indicates how the company intends to increase its ROI. In the absence of such a road map of the company's strategy, managers may have difficulty understanding what they are supposed to do to increase ROI and they may work at cross-purposes rather than in harmony with the overall strategy of the company. Other critics of EVA are also concerned that a single top-down metric will not be enough to guide the generation of corporate wealth.[9] We will discuss these broader issues in Chapter 17 when we review techniques that help organizational learning.[10]

The problem of single period metrics: the bonus bank approach

The problem with ROI, RI and EVA is that they are all single period metrics. Thus, although it can be shown that under certain assumptions the capitalized value of residual income equals the net present value of the company,[11] a one-period measure cannot capture the economic value of a division or investment. From this point of view, investment decisions based on these techniques will not be identical to those based on the 'correct' NPV rule.

Advocates of EVA have tried to respond to this problem by basing executive remuneration on a 'bonus bank' system. The aim of this approach is that bonuses are not just based on a single year's performance but may be accumulated over a number of years. The aim is to discourage managers who may be able to boost EVA in the very short term, take a bonus and then leave the company. In fact, one of the distinguishing features of EVA over RI, is the great care that is devoted to designing managerial compensation schemes that are aligned with shareholder wealth objectives.[12]

Summary

- Segment reports can provide information for evaluating the profitability and performance of divisions, product lines, sales territories and other segments of a company. Under the contribution approach to segment reporting, only those costs that are traceable are assigned to a segment. Fixed common costs and other non-traceable costs are not allocated to a segment. A cost is considered to be traceable to a segment only if the cost is caused by the segment and eliminating the segment would result in avoiding the cost.
- Costs that are traceable to a segment are further classified as either variable or fixed. The contribution margin is sales less variable costs. The segment margin is the contribution margin less the traceable fixed costs of the segment.
- For purposes of evaluating the performance of managers, there are at least three kinds of business segments – cost centres, profit centres and investment centres.
- Return on investment (ROI) is widely used to evaluate investment centre performance. However, there is a trend towards using residual income or economic value added instead of ROI.
- The residual income and economic value added approaches encourage profitable investments in many situations where the ROI approach would discourage investment.

Key terms for review

Common fixed cost (p. 582).
Cost centre (p. 577).
Decentralized organization (p. 576).
Economic value added (EVA) (p. 593).
Investment centre (p. 577).
Margin (p. 590).
Net operating profit (p. 588).
Operating assets (p. 589).
Profit centre (p. 577).
Residual income (p. 593).
Responsibility centre (p. 578).
Return on investment (ROI) (p. 588).
Segment (p. 577).
Segment margin (p. 584).
Traceable fixed cost (p. 582).
Turnover (p. 590).
Value chain (p. 587).

Review problem 1: segmented statements

The business staff of the legal firm Frampton, Davis & Smythe has constructed the following report which breaks down the firm's overall results for last month in terms of its two main business segments – family law and commercial law:

	Total	Family law	Commercial law
Revenues from clients	£1,000,000	£400,000	£600,000
Less variable expenses	220,000	100,000	120,000
Contribution margin	780,000	300,000	480,000
Less traceable fixed expenses	670,000	280,000	390,000
Segment margin	110,000	20,000	90,000
Less common fixed expenses	60,000	24,000	36,000
Net profit	£50,000	£(4,000)	£54,000

However, this report is not quite correct. The common fixed expenses such as the managing partner's salary, general administrative expenses, and general firm advertising have been allocated to the two segments based on revenues from clients.

Required

1 Redo the segment report, eliminating the allocation of common fixed expenses. Show both amount and percentage columns for the firm as a whole and for each of the segments. Would the firm be

better off financially if the family law segment were dropped? (*Note*: Many of the firm's commercial law clients also use the firm for their family law requirements such as drawing up wills.)

2 The firm's advertising agency has proposed an ad campaign targeted at boosting the revenues of the family law segment. The ad campaign would cost £20,000, and the advertising agency claims that it would increase family law revenues by £100,000. The managing partner of Frampton, Davis & Smythe believes this increase in business could be accommodated without any increase in fixed expenses. What effect would this ad campaign have on the family law segment margin and on overall net profit of the firm?

Solution to review problem 1: segmented statements

1 The corrected segmented profit and loss account appears below:

	Total		Family law		Commercial law	
	Amount	**%**	**Amount**	**%**	**Amount**	**%**
Revenues from clients	£1,000,000	100	£400,000	100	£600,000	100
Less variable expenses	220,000	22	100,000	25	120,000	20
Contribution margin	780,000	78	300,000	75	480,000	80
Less traceable fixed expenses	670,000	67	280,000	70	390,000	65
Segment margin	110,000	11	£20,000	5	£90,000	15
Less common fixed expenses	60,000	6				
Net profit	£50,000	5				

No, the firm would not be financially better off if the family law practice were dropped. The family law segment is covering all of its own costs and is contributing £20,000 per month to covering the common fixed expenses of the firm. While the segment margin as a percentage of sales is much lower for family law than for commercial law, it is still profitable; and it is likely that family law is a service that the firm must provide to its commercial clients in order to remain competitive.

2 The ad campaign would be expected to add £55,000 to the family law segment as follows:

Increased revenues from clients	£100,000
Family law contribution margin ratio	×75%
Incremental contribution margin	75,000
Less cost of the ad campaign	20,000
Increased segment margin	£55,000

Since there would be no increase in fixed expenses (including common fixed expenses), the increase in overall net profit should also be £55,000.

Review problem 2: return on investment (ROI) and residual income

The Magnetic Imaging Division of Medical Diagnostics plc has reported the following results for last year's operations:

Sales	£25 million
Net operating profit	3 million
Average operating assets	10 million

Required

1 Compute the margin, turnover and ROI for the Magnetic Imaging Division.

2 Top management of Medical Diagnostics plc has set a minimum required rate of return on average operating assets of 25%. What is the Magnetic Imaging Division's residual income for the year?

Solution to review problem 2: return on investment (ROI) and residual income

1 The required calculations appear below:

$$\text{Margin} = \frac{\text{Net operating profit, £3,000,000}}{\text{Sales, £25,000,000}}$$

$$= 12\%$$

$$\text{Turnover} = \frac{\text{Sales, £25,000,000}}{\text{Average operating assets, £10,000,000}}$$

$$= 2.5\%$$

$$\text{ROI} = \text{Margin} \times \text{Turnover}$$

$$= 12\% \times 2.5$$

$$= 30\%$$

2 The residual income for the Magnetic Imaging Division is computed as follows:

Average operating assets	£10,000,000
Net operating income	£3,000,000
Minimum required return (25% × £10,000,000)	2,500,000
Residual income	£500,000

Questions

14–1 What is meant by the term *decentralization*?

14–2 What benefits result from decentralization?

14–3 Distinguish between a cost centre, a profit centre and an investment centre.

14–4 Define a segment of an organization. Give several examples of segments.

14–5 How does the contribution approach assign costs to segments of an organization?

14–6 Distinguish between a traceable cost and a common cost. Give several examples of each.

14–7 Explain how the segment margin differs from the contribution margin.

14–8 Why aren't common costs allocated to segments under the contribution approach?

14–9 How is it possible for a cost that is traceable to a segment to become a common cost if the segment is divided into further segments?

14–10 What is meant by the terms *margin* and *turnover*?

14–11 What are the three basic approaches to improving return on investment (ROI)?

14–12 What is meant by residual income?

14–13 In what way can the use of ROI as a performance measure for investment centres lead to bad decisions? How does the residual income approach overcome this problem?

Exercises

E14–1 Time allowed: 15 minutes

Royal Lawncare Company produces and sells two packaged products, Weedban and Greengrow. Revenue and cost information relating to the products follow:

	Product	
	Weedban	**Greengrow**
Selling price per unit	£6.00	£7.50
Variable expenses per unit	2.40	5.25
Traceable fixed expenses per year	45,000	21,000

Common fixed expenses in the company total £33,000 annually. Last year the company produced and sold 15,000 units of Weedban and 28,000 units of Greengrow.

Required

Prepare a profit and loss account segmented by product lines. Show both amount and percentage columns for the company as a whole and for each of the products.

E14–2 Time allowed: 20 minutes

Raner, Harris & Chan is a consulting firm that specializes in information systems for medical and dental clinics. The firm has two offices – one in Chicago and one in Minneapolis. The firm classifies the direct costs of consulting jobs as variable costs. A segmented profit and loss account for the company's most recent year follows:

	Total company		Segment			
			Chicago		Minneapolis	
	Amount	%	Amount	%	Amount	%
Sales	£450,000	100	£150,000	100	£300,000	100
Less variable expenses	225,000	50	45,000	30	180,000	60
Contribution margin	225,000	50	105,000	70	120,000	40
Less traceable fixed expenses	126,000	28	78,000	52	48,000	16
Office segment margin	99,000	22	£27,000	18	£72,000	24
Less common fixed expenses not traceable to segments	63,000	14				
Net profit	£36,000	8				

Required

1 By how much would the company's net profit increase if Minneapolis increased its sales by £75,000 per year? Assume no change in cost behaviour patterns.

2 Refer to the original data. Assume that sales in Chicago increase by £50,000 next year and that sales in Minneapolis remain unchanged. Assume no change in fixed costs.

(a) Prepare a new segmented profit and loss account for the company using the format above. Show both amounts and percentages.

(b) Observe from the profit and loss account you have prepared that the contribution margin ratio for Chicago has remained unchanged at 70% (the same as in the data above) but that the segment margin ratio has changed. How do you explain the change in the segment margin ratio?

E14–3 Time allowed: 15 minutes

Refer to the data in E14–2. Assume that Minneapolis' sales by major market are:

	Minneapolis		Segment			
			Medical		Dental	
	Amount	%	Amount	%	Amount	%
Sales	£300,000	100	£200,000	100	£100,000	100
Less variable expenses	180,000	60	128,000	64	52,000	52
Contribution margin	120,000	40	72,000	36	48,000	48
Less traceable fixed expenses	33,000	11	12,000	6	21,000	21
Product-line segment margin	87,000	29	£60,000	30	£27,000	27
Less common fixed expenses not traceable to markets	15,000	5				
Divisional segment margin	£72,000	24				

The company would like to initiate an intensive advertising campaign in one of the two market segments during the next month. The campaign would cost £5,000. Marketing studies indicate that such a campaign would increase sales in the medical market by £40,000 or increase sales in the dental market by £35,000.

Required

1 In which of the markets would you recommend that the company focus its advertising campaign? Show computations to support your answer.

2 In E14–2, Minneapolis shows £48,000 in traceable fixed expenses. What happened to the £48,000 in this exercise?

E14–4 Time allowed: 20 minutes

Wingate Company, a wholesale distributor of videotapes, has been experiencing losses for some time, as shown by its most recent monthly profit and loss account below:

Sales	£1,000,000
Less variable expense	390,000
Contribution margin	610,000
Less fixed expenses	625,000
Net profit (loss)	£(15,000)

In an effort to isolate the problem, the managing director has asked for a profit and loss account segmented by division. Accordingly, the Accounting Department has developed the following information:

	Division		
	East	**Central**	**West**
Sales	£250,000	£400,000	£350,000
Variable expenses as a percentage of sales	52%	30%	40%
Traceable fixed expenses	£160,000	£200,000	£175,000

Required

1 Prepare a profit and loss account segmented by divisions, as desired by the managing director. Show both amount and percentage columns for the company as a whole and for each division.

2 As a result of a marketing study, the managing director believes that sales in the West Division could be increased by 20% if advertising in that division was increased by £15,000 each month. Would you recommend the increased advertising? Show computations.

E14–5 Time allowed: 15 minutes

You have a client who operates a large upmarket grocery store that has a full range of departments. The management has encountered difficulty in using accounting data as a basis for decisions as to possible changes in departments operated, products, marketing methods, and so forth. List several overhead costs, or costs not applicable to a particular department, and explain how the existence of such costs (sometimes called *common costs*) complicates and limits the use of accounting data in making decisions in such a store.

(*CPA*, adapted)

E14–6 Time allowed: 15 minutes

Selected operating data for two divisions of Outback Brewing Ltd of Australia are given below:

	Division	
	Queensland	**New South Wales**
Sales	£4,000,000	£7,000,000
Average operating assets	2,000,000	2,000,000
Net operating profit	360,000	420,000
Property, plant, and equipment (net)	950,000	800,000

Required

1 Compute the rate of return for each division using the return on investment (ROI) formula stated in terms of margin and turnover.

2 As far as you can tell from the data, which divisional manager seems to be doing the better job? Why?

E14–7 Time allowed: 15 minutes

Provide the missing data in the following tabulation:

	Division		
	Alpha	**Bravo**	**Charlie**
Sales	£?	£11,500,000	£?
Net operating profit	?	920,000	210,000
Average operating assets	800,000	?	?
Margin	4%	?	7%
Turnover	5	?	?
Return on investment (ROI)	?	20%	14%

E14–8 Time allowed: 20 minutes

Meiji Isetan Corp. of Japan has two regional divisions with headquarters in Osaka and Yokohama. Selected data on the two divisions follow (in millions of yen, denoted by ¥):

	Division	
	Osaka	**Yokohama**
Sales	¥3,000,000	¥9,000,000
Net operating profit	210,000	720,000
Average operating assets	1,000,000	4,000,000

Required

1 For each division, compute the return on investment (ROI) in terms of margin and turnover. Where necessary, carry computations to two decimal places.

2 Assume that the company evaluates performance by use of residual profit and that the minimum required return for any division is 15%. Compute the residual profit for each division.

3 Is Yokohama's greater amount of residual profit an indication that it is better managed? Explain.

E14–9 Time allowed: 30 minutes
Selected sales and operating data for three divisions of a multinational structural engineering firm are given below:

	Division		
	Asia	**Europe**	**North America**
Sales	£12,000,000	£14,000,000	£25,000,000
Average operating assets	3,000,000	7,000,000	5,000,000
Net operating profit	600,000	560,000	800,000
Minimum required rate of return	14%	10%	16%

Required

1 Compute the return on investment (ROI) for each division using the formula stated in terms of margin and turnover.

2 Compute the residual income for each division.

3 Assume that each division is presented with an investment opportunity that would yield a 15% rate of return.

(a) If performance is being measured by ROI, which division or divisions will probably accept the opportunity? Reject? Why?

(b) If performance is being measured by residual income, which division or divisions will probably accept the opportunity? Reject? Why?

Problems

P14–10 Restructuring a segmented statement Time allowed: 60 minutes
Losses have been incurred in Millard Company for some time. In an effort to isolate the problem and improve the company's performance, management has requested that the monthly profit and loss account be segmented by sales region. The company's first effort at preparing a segmented statement is given below. This statement is for May, the most recent month of activity.

Cost of goods sold and shipping expense are both variable; other costs are all fixed.

Millard Company is a wholesale distributor of office products. It purchases office products from manufacturers and distributes them in the three regions given above. The three regions are about the same size, and each has its own manager and sales staff. The products that the company distributes vary widely in profitability.

Required

1 List any disadvantages or weaknesses that you see to the statement format illustrated above.

2 Explain the basis that is apparently being used to allocate the corporate expenses to the regions. Do you agree with these allocations? Explain.

3 Prepare a new segmented profit and loss account for May using the contribution approach. Show a Total column as well as data for each region. Include percentages on your statement for all columns.

	Sales region		
	West	**Central**	**East**
Sales	£450,000	£800,000	£750,000
Less regional expenses (traceable):			
Cost of goods sold	162,900	280,000	376,500
Advertising	108,000	200,000	210,000
Salaries	90,000	88,000	135,000
Utilities	13,500	12,000	15,000
Depreciation	27,000	28,000	30,000
Shipping expense	17,100	32,000	28,500
Total regional expenses	418,500	640,000	795,000
Regional profit (loss) before corporate expenses	31,500	160,000	(45,000)
Less corporate expenses:			
Advertising (general)	18,000	32,000	30,000
General administrative expense	50,000	50,000	50,000
Total corporate expenses	68,000	82,000	80,000
Net profit (loss)	£(36,500)	£78,000	£(125,000)

4 Analyse the statement that you prepared in Question 3 above. Which points that might help to improve the company's performance would you be particularly anxious to bring to the attention of management?

P14–11 Segment reporting Time allowed: 30 minutes
Vulcan Company's profit and loss account for last month is given below:

Vulcan Company Profit and loss account for the month ended 30 June	
Sales	£750,000
Less variable expenses	336,000
Contribution margin	414,000
Less fixed expenses	378,000
Net profit	£36,000

Management is disappointed with the company's performance and is wondering what can be done to improve profits. By examining sales and cost records, you have determined the following:

1 The company is divided into two sales territories – Northern and Southern. The Northern territory recorded £300,000 in sales and £156,000 in variable expenses during June; the remaining sales and variable expenses were recorded in the Southern territory. Fixed expenses of £120,000 and £108,000 are traceable to the Northern and Southern territories, respectively. The rest of the fixed expenses are common to the two territories.

2 The company sells two products – Paks and Tibs. Sales of Paks and Tibs totalled £50,000 and £250,000, respectively, in the Northern territory during June. Variable expenses are 22% of the selling price for

Paks and 58% for Tibs. Cost records show that £30,000 of the Northern territory's fixed expenses are traceable to Paks and £40,000 to Tibs, with the remainder common to the two products.

Required

1 Prepare segmented profit and loss accounts first showing the total company broken down between sales territories and then showing the Northern territory broken down by product line. Show both amount and percentage columns for the company in total and for each segment.

2 Look at the statement you have prepared showing the total company segmented by sales territory. Which points revealed by this statement should be brought to the attention of management?

3 Look at the statement you have prepared showing the Northern territory segmented by product lines. Which points revealed by this statement should be brought to the attention of management?

P14–12 Segment reporting; activity-based cost assignment Time allowed: 60 minutes
Diversified Products plc has recently acquired a small publishing company that Diversified Products intends to operate as one of its investment centres. The newly acquired company has three books that it offers for sale – a cookbook, a travel guide and a handy speller. Each book sells for £10. The publishing company's most recent monthly profit and loss account is given below:

			Product line		
	Total company		**Cookbook**	**Travel guide**	**Handy speller**
Sales	£300,000	100%	£90,000	£150,000	£60,000
Less expenses:					
Printing costs	102,000	34%	27,000	63,000	12,000
Advertising	36,000	12%	13,500	19,500	3,000
General sales	18,000	6%	5,400	9,000	3,600
Salaries	33,000	11%	18,000	9,000	6,000
Equipment depreciation	9,000	3%	3,000	3,000	3,000
Sales commissions	30,000	10%	9,000	15,000	6,000
General administration	42,000	14%	14,000	14,000	14,000
Warehouse rent	12,000	4%	3,600	6,000	2,400
Depreciation – office facilities	3,000	1%	1,000	1,000	1,000
Total expenses	285,000	95%	94,500	139,500	51,000
Net profit (loss)	£15,000	5%	£(4,500)	£10,500	£9,000

The following additional information is available about the company:

1 Only printing costs and sales commissions are variable; all other costs are fixed. The printing costs (which include materials, labour and variable overhead) are traceable to the three product lines as shown in the statement above. Sales commissions are 10% of sales for any product.

2 The same equipment is used to produce all three books, so the equipment depreciation cost has been allocated equally among the three product lines. An analysis of the company's activities indicates that the equipment is used 30% of the time to produce cookbooks, 50% of the time to produce travel guides, and 20% of the time to produce handy spellers.

3 The warehouse is used to store finished units of product, so the rental cost has been allocated to the product lines on the basis of sales. The warehouse rental cost is £3 per square metre per year. The warehouse contains 48,000 square metres of space, of which 7,200 square metres is used by the cookbook

line, 24,000 square metres by the travel guide line, and 16,800 square metres by the handy speller line.

4 The general sales cost above includes the salary of the sales manager and other sales costs not traceable to any specific product line. This cost has been allocated to the product lines on the basis of sales pounds.

5 The general administration cost and depreciation of office facilities both relate to overall administration of the company as a whole. These costs have been allocated equally to the three product lines.

6 All other costs are traceable to the three product lines in the amounts shown on the statement above.

The management of Diversified Products plc is anxious to improve the new investment centre's 5% return on sales.

Required

1 Prepare a new segmented profit and loss account for the month using the contribution approach. Show both an amount column and a percentage column for the company as a whole and for each product line. Adjust allocations of equipment depreciation and of warehouse rent as indicated by the additional information provided.

2 After seeing the profit and loss account in the main body of the problem, management has decided to eliminate the cookbook, since it is not returning a profit, and to focus all available resources on promoting the travel guide.

(a) Based on the statement you have prepared, do you agree with the decision to eliminate the cookbook? Explain.

(b) Based on the statement you have prepared, do you agree with the decision to focus all available resources on promoting the travel guide? Explain. (You may assume that an ample market is available for all three product lines.)

3 What additional points would you bring to the attention of management that might help to improve profits?

P14–13 Return on investment (ROI); comparison of company performance Time allowed: 30 minutes

Comparative data on three companies in the same industry are given below:

	Company		
	A	B	C
Sales	£600,000	£500,000	£?
Net operating profit	84,000	70,000	?
Average operating assets	300,000	?	1,000,000
Margin	?	?	3.5%
Turnover	?	?	2
ROI	?	7%	?

Required

1 What advantages can you see in breaking down the ROI computation into two separate elements, margin and turnover?

2 Fill in the missing information above, and comment on the relative performance of the three companies in as much detail as the data permit. Make specific recommendations on steps to be taken to improve the return on investment, where needed.

(Adapted from National Association of Accountants, Research Report No. 35, p. 34)

P14–14 Return on investment (ROI) and residual income Time allowed: 20 minutes
Financial data for Joel de Paris plc for last year follow:

Joel de Paris plc
Balance sheet

Assets	**Ending balance**	**Beginning balance**
Cash	£120,000	£140,000
Debtors	530,000	450,000
Stock	380,000	320,000
Plant and equipment, net	620,000	680,000
Investment in Buisson SA	280,000	250,000
Land (undeveloped)	170,000	180,000
Total assets	£2,100,000	£2,020,000
Liabilities and shareholders' equity		
Creditors	£310,000	£360,000
Long-term debt	1,500,000	1,500,000
Shareholders' equity	290,000	160,000
Total liabilities and shareholders' equity	£2,100,000	£2,020,000

Joel de Paris plc
Profit and loss account

Sales		£4,050,000
Less operating expenses		3,645,000
Net operating profit		405,000
Less interest and taxes:		
Interest expense	£150,000	
Tax expense	110,000	260,000
Net profit		£145,000

The company paid dividends of £15,000 last year. The 'Investment in Buisson', on the balance sheet represents an investment in the shares of another company.

Required

1 Compute the company's margin, turnover and ROI for last year.

2 The board of directors of Joel de Paris Inc has set a minimum required return of 15%. What was the company's residual income last year?

P14–15 Return on investment (ROI) and residual income Time allowed: 30 minutes
'I know headquarters wants us to add on that new product line', said Dell Havasi, manager of Billings Company's Office Products Division. 'But I want to see the numbers before I make any move. Our division has led the company for three years, and I don't want any letdown.'

Billings Company is a decentralized organization with five autonomous divisions. The divisions are evaluated on the basis of the return that they are able to generate on invested assets, with year-end bonuses given to the divisional managers who have the highest ROI figures. Operating results for the company's Office Products Division for the most recent year are given below:

Sales	£10,000,000
Less variable expenses	6,000,000
Contribution margin	4,000,000
Less fixed expenses	3,200,000
Net operating profit	£800,000
Divisional operating assets	£4,000,000

The company had an overall ROI of 15% last year (considering all divisions). The Office Products Division has an opportunity to add a new product line that would require an additional investment in operating assets of £1,000,000. The cost and revenue characteristics of the new product line per year would be:

Sales	£2,000,000
Variable expenses	60% of sales
Fixed expenses	£640,000

Required

1 Compute the Office Products Division's ROI for the most recent year; also compute the ROI as it will appear if the new product line is added.

2 If you were in Dell Havasi's position, would you be inclined to accept or reject the new product line? Explain.

3 Why do you suppose headquarters is anxious for the Office Products Division to add the new product line?

4 Suppose that the company views a return of 12% on invested assets as being the minimum that any division should earn and that performance is evaluated by the residual income approach.

(a) Compute the Office Products Division's residual income for the most recent year; also compute the residual income as it will appear if the new product line is added.

(b) Under these circumstances, if you were in Dell Havasi's position, would you accept or reject the new product line? Explain.

P14–16 Activity-based segment reporting Time allowed: 60 minutes

'That commercial market has been dragging us down for years,' complained Shanna Reynolds, managing director of Morley Products. 'Just look at that anaemic profit figure for the commercial market. That market had three million pounds more in sales than the home market, but only a few thousand pounds more in profits. What a loser it is!'

The profit and loss account to which Ms Reynolds was referring follows:

	Total company		Commercial market	Home market	School market
Sales	£20,000,000	100.0%	£8,000,000	£5,000,000	£7,000,000
Less expenses:					
Cost of goods sold	9,500,000	47.5%	3,900,000	2,400,000	3,200,000
Sales support	3,600,000	18.0%	1,440,000	900,000	1,260,000
Order processing	1,720,000	8.6%	688,000	430,000	602,000
Warehousing	940,000	4.7%	376,000	235,000	329,000
Packing and shipping	520,000	42.6%	208,000	130,000	182,000
Advertising	1,690,000	8.5%	676,000	422,500	591,500
General management	1,310,000	6.6%	524,000	327,500	458,500
Total expenses	19,280,000	96.4%	7,812,000	4,845,000	6,623,000
Net profit	£720,000	3.6%	£188,000	£155,000	£377,000

'I agree,' said Walt Divot, the company's deputy managing director. 'We need to focus more of our attention on the school market, since it's our best segment. Maybe that will bolster profits and get the shareholders off our backs.'

The following additional information is available about the company:

1 Morley Products is a wholesale distributor of various goods; the cost of goods sold figures above are traceable to the markets in the amounts shown.

2 Sales support, order processing, and packing and shipping are considered by management to be variable costs. Warehousing, general management and advertising are fixed costs. These costs have all been allocated to the markets on the basis of sales pounds – a practice that the company has followed for years.

3 You have compiled the following data:

Cost pool and allocation base	Total cost	Amount of activity			
		Total	Commercial market	Home market	School market
Sales support (number of calls)	£3,600,000	24,000	8,000	5,000	11,000
Order processing (number of orders)	1,720,000	8,600	1,750	5,200	1,650
Warehousing (square metres of space)	940,000	117,500	35,000	65,000	17,500
Packing and shipping (kilos shipped)	520,000	104,000	24,000	16,000	64,000

4 You have determined the following breakdown of the company's advertising expense and general management expense:

		Market		
	Total	Commercial	Home	School
Advertising:				
Traceable	£1,460,000	£700,000	£180,000	£580,000
Common	230,000			
General management:				
Traceable – salaries	410,000	150,000	120,000	140,000
Common	900,000			

The company is searching for ways to improve profit, and you have suggested that a segmented statement in which costs are assigned on the basis of activities might provide some useful insights for management.

Required

1 Refer to the data in (3) above. Determine a rate for each cost pool. Then, using this rate, compute the amount of cost assignable to each market.

2 Using the data from Question 1 above and other data from the problem, prepare a revised segmented statement for the company. Use the contribution format. Show an amount column and a percentage column for the company as a whole and for each market segment. Carry percentage figures to one decimal place. (Remember to include warehousing among the fixed expenses.)

3 What, if anything, in your segmented statement should be brought to the attention of management? Explain.

P14–17 Multiple segmented profit and loss accounts Time allowed: 60 minutes
Companhia Bradesco SA of Brazil has two divisions. The company's profit and loss account segmented by divisions for last year is given below (the currency in Brazil is the real, denoted here by R):

		Division	
	Total company	Plastic	Glass
Sales	R1,500,000	R900,000	R600,000
Less variable expenses	700,000	400,000	300,000
Contribution margin	800,000	500,000	300,000
Less traceable fixed expenses:			
Advertising	300,000	180,000	120,000
Depreciation	140,000	92,000	48,000
Administration	220,000	118,000	102,000
Total	660,000	390,000	270,000
Divisional segment margin	140,000	R 110,000	R 30,000
Less common fixed expenses	100,000		
Net profit	R 40,000		

Top management does not understand why the Glass Division has such a low segment margin when its sales are only one-third less than sales in the Plastics Division. Accordingly, management has directed that the Glass Division be further segmented into product lines. The following information is available on the product lines in the Glass Division:

	Glass Division product lines		
	Flat glass	**Auto glass**	**Speciality glass**
Sales	R200,000	R300,000	R100,000
Traceable fixed expenses:			
Advertising	30,000	42,000	48,000
Depreciation	10,000	24,000	14,000
Administration	14,000	21,000	7,000
Variable expenses as a percentage of sales	65%	40%	50%

Analysis shows that R60,000 of the Glass Division's administration expenses are common to the product lines.

Required

1 Prepare a segmented profit and loss account for the Glass Division with segments defined as product lines. Use the contribution approach. Show both an amount column and a percentage column for the division in total and for each product line.

2 Management is surprised by Speciality Glass's poor showing and would like to have the product line segmented by market. The following information is available about the two markets in which speciality glass is sold:

	Speciality glass markets	
	Domestic	**Foreign**
Sales	R60,000	R40,000
Traceable fixed expenses:		
Advertising	18,000	30,000
Variable expenses as a percentage of sales	50%	50%

All of Speciality Glass's depreciation and administration expenses are common to the markets in which the product is sold. Prepare a segmented profit and loss account for Speciality Glass with segments defined as markets. Again use the contribution approach and show both amount and percentage columns.

3 Refer to the statement prepared in Question 1 above. The sales manager wants to run a special promotional campaign on one of the products over the next month. A market study indicates that such a campaign would increase sales of Flat Glass by R40,000 or sales of Auto Glass by R30,000. The campaign would cost R8,000. Show computations to determine which product line should be chosen.

P14–18 Return on investment (ROI) analysis Time allowed: 30 minutes
The profit and loss account for Huerra Company for last year is given below:

	Total	Unit
Sales	£4,000,000	£80.00
Less variable expenses	2,800,000	56.00
Contribution margin	1,200,000	24.00
Less fixed expenses	840,000	16.80
Net operating profit	360,000	7.20
Less profit taxes (30%)	108,000	2.16
Net profit	£252,000	£5.04

The company had average operating assets of £2,000,000 during the year.

Required

1 Compute the company's ROI for the period using the ROI formula stated in terms of margin and turnover.

For each of the following questions, indicate whether the margin and turnover will increase, decrease, or remain unchanged as a result of the events described, and then compute the new ROI figure. Consider each question separately, starting in each case from the data used to compute the original ROI in Question 1 above.

2 By use of just-in-time (JIT), the company is able to reduce the average level of inventory by £400,000. (The released funds are used to pay off short-term creditors.)

3 The company achieves a cost savings of £32,000 per year by using less costly materials.

4 The company issues bonds and uses the proceeds to purchase £500,000 in machinery and equipment. Interest on the bonds is £60,000 per year. Sales remain unchanged. The new, more efficient equipment reduces production costs by £20,000 per year.

5 As a result of a more intense effort by salespeople, sales are increased by 20%; operating assets remain unchanged.

6 Obsolete items of inventory carried on the records at a cost of £40,000 are scrapped and written off as a loss since they are unsaleable.

7 The company uses £200,000 of cash (received on debtors) to repurchase and retire some of its common stock.

P14–19 Return on investment (ROI) and residual income Time allowed: 30 minutes
Raddington Industries produces tool and die machinery for manufacturers. The company expanded vertically several years ago by acquiring Reigis Steel Company, one of its suppliers of alloy steel plates. Raddington decided to maintain Reigis' separate identity and therefore established the Reigis Steel Division as one of its investment centres.

Raddington evaluates its divisions on the basis of ROI. Management bonuses are also based on ROI. All investments in operating assets are expected to earn a minimum rate of return of 11%.

Reigis' ROI has ranged from 14% to 17% since it was acquired by Raddington. During the past year, Reigis had an investment opportunity that would yield an estimated rate of return of 13%. Reigis' management decided against the investment because it believed the investment would decrease the division's overall ROI.

Last year's profit and loss account for Reigis Steel Division is given below. The division's operating assets employed were £12,960,000 at the end of the year, which represents an 8% increase over the previous year-end balance.

Reigis Steel Division
Divisional profit and loss account
for the year ended 31 December

Sales		£31,200,000
Cost of goods sold		16,500,000
Gross margin		14,700,000
Less operating expenses:		
Selling expenses	£5,620,000	
Administrative expenses	7,208,000	12,828,000
Net operating profit		£1,872,000

Required

1 Compute the following performance measures for the Reigis Steel Division:

(a) ROI. (Remember, ROI is based on the average operating assets, computed from the beginning-of-year and end-of-year balances.) State ROI in terms of margin and turnover.

(b) Residual profit.

2 Would the management of Reigis Steel Division have been more likely to accept the investment opportunity it had last year if residual profit were used as a performance measure instead of ROI? Explain.

3 The Reigis Steel Division is a separate investment centre within Raddington Industries. Identify the items Reigis must be free to control if it is to be evaluated fairly by either the ROI or residual profit performance measures.

(*CMA*, adapted)

P14–20 Cost-volume-profit analysis; return on investment (ROI); transfer pricing Time allowed: 45 minutes

The Valve Division of Bendix plc produces a small valve that is used by various companies as a component part in their products. Bendix plc operates its divisions as autonomous units, giving its divisional managers great discretion in pricing and other decisions. Each division is expected to generate a rate of return of at least 14% on its operating assets. The Valve Division has average operating assets of £700,000. The valves are sold for £5 each. Variable costs are £3 per valve, and fixed costs total £462,000 per year. The division has a capacity of 300,000 valves each year.

Required

1 How many valves must the Valve Division sell each year to generate the desired rate of return on its assets?

(a) What is the margin earned at this level of sales?

(b) What is the turnover at this level of sales?

2 Assume that the Valve Division's current ROI is just equal to the minimum required 14%. In order to increase the division's ROI, the divisional manager wants to increase the selling price per valve by 4%. Market studies indicate that an increase in the selling price would cause sales to drop by 20,000 units each year. However, operating assets could be reduced by £50,000 due to decreased needs for debtors and inventory. Compute the margin, turnover and ROI if these changes are made.

3 Refer to the original data. Assume again that the Valve Division's current ROI is just equal to the minimum required 14%. Rather than increase the selling price, the sales manager wants to reduce the selling price per valve by 4%. Market studies indicate that this would fill the plant to capacity. In order to carry the greater level of sales, however, operating assets would increase by £50,000.

Compute the margin, turnover and ROI if these changes are made.

4 Refer to the original data. Assume that the normal volume of sales is 280,000 valves each year at a price of £5 per valve. Another division of the company is currently purchasing 20,000 valves each year from an overseas supplier, at a price of £4.25 per valve. The manager of the Valve Division has adamantly refused to meet this price, pointing out that it would result in a loss for his division:

Selling price per valve		£4.25
Cost per valve:		
Variable	£3.00	
Fixed (£462,000 ÷ 300,000 valves)	1.54	4.54
Net loss per valve		£(0.29)

The manager of the Valve Division also points out that the normal £5 selling price barely allows his division the required 14% rate of return. 'If we take on some business at only £4.25 per unit, then our ROI is obviously going to suffer', he reasons, 'and maintaining that ROI figure is the key to my future. Besides, taking on these extra units would require us to increase our operating assets by at least £50,000 due to the larger inventories and receivables we would be carrying.' Would you recommend that the Valve Division sell to the other division at £4.25? Show ROI computations to support your answer.

P14–21 Segmented statements; product-line analysis Time allowed: 90 minutes

'At last, I can see some light at the end of the tunnel', said Steve Adams, managing director of Jelco Products. 'Our losses have shrunk from over £75,000 a month at the beginning of the year to only £26,000 for August. If we can just isolate the remaining problems with products A and C, we'll be in the black by the first of next year.'

The company's profit and loss account for the latest month (August) is presented below (absorption costing basis):

Jelco Products
Profit and loss account
for August

		Product		
	Total company	**A**	**B**	**C**
Sales	£1,500,000	£600,000	£400,000	£500,000
Less cost of goods sold	922,000	372,000	220,000	330,000
Gross margins	578,000	228,000	180,000	170,000
Less operating expenses:				
Selling	424,000	162,000	112,000	150,000
Administrative	180,000	72,000	48,000	60,000
Total operating expenses	604,000	234,000	160,000	210,000
Net profit (loss)	£(26,000)	£(6,000)	£20,000	£(40,000)

'What recommendations did that business consultant make?' asked Mr Adams. 'We paid the guy £100 an hour; surely he found something wrong.' 'He says our problems are concealed by the way we make up our statements', replied Sally Warren, the deputy managing director. 'He left us some data on what he calls "traceable" and "common" costs that he says we should be isolating in our reports.' The data to which Ms Warren was referring are shown as follows:

	Total company	Product A	Product B	Product C
Variable costs:*				
Production (materials, labour, and variable overhead)	–	18%	32%	20%
Selling	–	10%	8%	10%
Traceable fixed costs:				
Production	£376,000	£180,000	£36,000	£160,000
Selling	282,000	102,000	80,000	100,000
Common fixed costs:				
Production	210,000	–	–	–
Administrative	180,000	–	–	–

*As a percentage of sales.

'I don't see anything wrong with our statements', said Mr Adams. 'Bill, our chief accountant, says that he has been using this format for over 30 years. He's also very careful to allocate all of our costs to the products.'

'I'll admit that Bill always seems to be on top of things', replied Ms Warren. 'By the way, purchasing says that the X7 chips we use in products A and B are on back order and won't be available for several weeks. From the looks of August's profit and loss account, we had better concentrate our remaining inventory of X7 chips on product B.' (Two X7 chips are used in both product A and product B.)

The following additional information is available on the company:

1 Work in progress and finished goods inventories are negligible and can be ignored.

2 Products A and B each sell for £250 per unit, and product C sells for £125 per unit. Strong market demand exists for all three products.

Required

1 Prepare a new profit and loss account for August, segmented by product and using the contribution approach. Show both amount and percentage columns for the company in total and for each product.

2 Assume that Mr Adams is considering the elimination of product C due to the losses it is incurring. Based on the statement you prepared in Question 1 above, what points would you make for or against elimination of product C?

3 Do you agree with the company's decision to concentrate the remaining stock of X7 chips on product B? Why or why not?

4 Product C is sold in both a vending and a home market with sales and cost data as follows:

	Total	Market	
		Vending	Home
Sales	£500,000	£50,000	£450,000
Variable costs:*			
Production	–	20%	20%
Selling	–	28%	8%
Traceable fixed costs:			
Selling	£75,000	£45,000	£30,000

*As a percentage of sales.

The remainder of product C's fixed selling costs and all of product C's fixed production costs are common to the markets in which product C is sold.

(a) Prepare a profit and loss account showing product C segmented by market. Use the contribution approach and show both amount and percentage columns for the product in total and for each market.

(b) Which points revealed by this statement would you be particularly anxious to bring to the attention of management?

P14–22 Decentralization Time allowed: 50 minutes

PQR is a company that develops bespoke educational computer software. The company is based in Germany. It has recently acquired two companies: W and Z. W is a well-established company that is also based in Germany. It develops educational computer software and was a direct competitor of PQR. Z, which is based in Malaysia, is a new but rapidly growing company that develops off-the-shelf educational software and also produces CD ROMs. Z was acquired so that it could produce CD ROMs for PQR and W.

The Managing Director of PQR has now realized that the acquisition of these two companies will cause problems for him in terms of planning, control and decision making. He is thinking of implementing a decentralized structure but is unsure of the advantages and disadvantages of such a structure, of how much autonomy to grant the new companies, and also which performance measure to use to appraise their performance. Consequently he has contacted you, the Finance Director of PQR, for help.

Required

Write a report to the Managing Director which:

(a) explains the advantages and disadvantages that would be experienced by PQR in operating a decentralized structure; *(6 marks)*

(b) explains which types of responsibility centres you would recommend as being most appropriate for W and Z in a decentralized structure; *(6 marks)*

(c) critically evaluates the possible use of the financial performance measures 'return on capital employed' and 'residual income' for the decentralized structure of PQR; *(8 marks)*

(d) discusses the issues that need to be considered in relation to setting transfer prices for transfers made from Z to PQR and W. *(5 marks)*

(Total = 25 marks)

CIMA Management Accounting – Decision making, May 2004

P14–23 ROI, RI and NPV Time allowed: 35 minutes

NCL plc, which has a divisionalized structure, undertakes civil engineering and mining activities. All applications by divisional management teams for funds with which to undertake capital projects require the authorization of the board of directors of NCL plc. Once authorization has been granted to a capital application, divisional management teams are allowed to choose the project for investment.

Under the terms of the management incentive plan, which is currently in operation, the managers of each division are eligible to receive annual bonus payments which are calculated by reference to the return on investment (ROI) earned during each of the first two years by new investments. ROI is calculated using the average capital employed during the year. NCL plc depreciates its investments on a straight-line basis.

One of the most profitable divisions during recent years has been the IOA Division, which is engaged in the mining of precious metals. The management of the IOA Division is currently evaluating three projects relating to the extraction of substance 'xxx' from different areas in its country of operation. The management of the IOA Division has been given approval by the board of directors of NCL plc to spend £24 million on one of the three proposals it is considering (i.e. North, East and South projects).

The following net present value (NPV) calculations have been prepared by the management accountant of the IOA Division.

	North Project		East Project		South Project	
	Net cash inflow/ (outflow) £'000	Present value at 12% £'000	Net cash inflow/ (outflow) £'000	Present value at 12% £'000	Net cash inflow/ (outflow) £'000	Present value at 12% £'000
Year 0	(24,000.0)	(24,000.0)	(24,000.0)	(24,000.0)	(24,000.0)	(24,000.0)
Year 1	6,000.0	5,358.0	11,500.0	10,269.5	12,000.0	10,716.0
Year 2	8,000.0	6,376.0	11,500.0	9,165.5	10,000.0	7,970.0
Year 3	13,500.0	9,612.0	11,500.0	8,188.0	9,000.0	6,408.0
Year 4	10,500.0	6,678.0	–	–	3,000.0	1,908.0
NPV		4,024.0		3,623.0		3,002.0

The following additional information concerning the three projects is available:

1 Each of the above projects has a nil residual value.

2 The life of the East project is three years. The North and South projects are expected to have a life of four years.

3 The three projects have a similar level of risk.

4 Ignore taxation.

Required

1 Explain (with relevant calculations) why the interests of the management of the IOA Division might conflict with those of the board of directors of NCL plc. *(10 marks)*

2 Explain how the adoption of residual income (RI) using the annuity method of depreciation might prove to be a superior basis for the management incentive plan operated by NCL plc.

(N.B. No illustrative calculations should be incorporated into your explanation). *(4 marks)*

The IOA Division is also considering whether to undertake an investment in the West of the country (the West Project). An initial cash outlay investment of £12 million will be required and a net cash inflow amounting to £5 million is expected to arise in each of the four years of the life of the project.

The activities involved in the West project will cause the local river to become polluted and discoloured due to the discharge of waste substances from mining operations.

It is estimated that at the end of year four a cash outlay of £2 million would be required to restore the river to its original colour. This would also clear 90% of the pollution caused as a result of the mining activities of the IOA Division.

The remaining 10% of the pollution caused as a result of the mining activities of the IOA Division could be cleared up by a further cash outlay of £2 million.

3 Evaluate the West project and, stating your reasons, comment on whether the board of directors of NCL plc should spend the further £2 million in order to eliminate the remaining 10% of pollution. *(6 marks)*

(Ignore taxation).

(Total = 20 marks)

ACCA Performance Management, June 2004

CASE

Cases

C14–24 Comparison and critical appraisal of ROI and residual income Time allowed: 90 minutes

Culharb plc is a large, long-established, and now widely diversified UK company mainly engaged in manufacturing industrial products in more than ten divisions. There is a significant bias towards 'traditional industries' in its strategic portfolio. In recent years earnings per share, sales growth rates and rate of return on investment levels achieved by the company have been disappointing. There has recently been a major restructuring of the corporate management team, including the replacement of the Chief Executive and several other senior managers, with new managers recruited from outside the company. One senior management position remains unfilled and an effort has been made to recruit from the existing divisional general managers (DGM) in the first instance. The DGMs of the Pumps and Forging Divisions have been short-listed.

A summary of the financial performance of the company is given in Appendix 1. The generally improved projected results for next year reflect the effect of planned profit improvement programmes. The projected results have caused central management to revise upwards the capital expenditure budget for next year, and they have invited DGMs to make additional capital project proposals.

Company headquarters are located in a major city in the English Midlands while each division has its own head office in various cities and towns around the UK where their major facilities are located. A division is managed by a team of senior functional managers headed by a DGM. Each division is a subsidiary with corporate legal status and enjoys a significant degree of autonomy over operational and managerial decision making but all financing is provided by headquarters. The company operates comprehensive long-term and short-term financial planning systems, which include long-term financial forecasts and budgets for sales, costs, expenditures and rate of return on investment. Both long-term financial forecasting and budgeting are based on annual planning cycles. Management reports (each division has its own balance sheet and income statement supported by detailed schedules of financial and other statistics) are submitted by divisions to headquarters and reviewed by headquarters' executives on a monthly basis.

The new corporate management team has placed increased emphasis on the monthly report: the DGMs are required each month to explain the financial performance of their division. To provide a stimulus to improve profitability, the minimum required rate of return for the company and any new capital expenditure proposals has been raised to 15% before tax. Return on investment and the annual budgeted returns to be achieved by divisions have also been raised. This reinforces a traditional stress on financial results as regards divisional performance evaluation and on the rate of return on investment as a key indicator. However, for the next and subsequent financial years, the reward systems for senior divisional managers will include a bonus element, which will largely depend on achievement of budgeted financial results.

Capital budgeting system

The capital budgeting system (CBS) is highly formalized and standardized across all the divisions. The timing of the submission of capital expenditure requests from divisions to headquarters is set to follow the submission and approval of their strategic plans and objectives. Operating budget requests are submitted at the same time as capital expenditure requests. In the light of the capital expenditure requests approved, operating budgets are subsequently revised by divisions and resubmitted to headquarters for approval.

Capital expenditure requests are classified as follows:

(a) Cost reduction, plant replacement and product improvement projects. Justification is on the basis of payback period and return on investment, and if the project is large enough, DCF analysis. There is scope for flexibility in the application of these criteria particularly where quality improvements are claimed. However, the latter must be both identifiable and necessary.

(b) Expansion projects. These are justified on the basis of payback period, return on investment, and DCF analysis.

(c) New product proposals. Two types of project are distinguished – extensions to product lines and diversifications. While both are justified on the basis of return on investment and DCF analysis, they are also subject to sensitivity analysis and tested for consistency with strategic plans.

(d) Proposals not justified on profitability criteria. These encompass safety, convenience, non-productive and necessity projects, and so on. Where appropriate and feasible a financial analysis is performed and alternative ways of carrying out the project are assessed. At a minimum the full cost consequences over time must be identified.

On average, proposals falling into groups (a) and (d) have dominated the capital expenditure bids from divisions, with the emphasis falling on group (a) proposals.

DGMs have some discretionary authority as regards capital expenditure. Up to £250,000 per year can be authorized by a DGM, without reference to headquarters, for purposes which have general approval from headquarters. However, there is an upper limit on individual discretionary expenditures of £25,000. Approximately 25% of capital expenditure per year is accounted for by discretionary spending by divisions.

The divisions

Divisions have made their budget submissions and capital expenditure proposals for the next financial year. Characteristics of three of the divisions and summaries of their actual and projected financial performance now follow.

Pumps Division

This division manufactures and assembles pumps that are widely used in manufacturing, construction and primary industries. It is one of the original core businesses of the group and operates in an industry which has seen a slow pace of technical change in both products and production methods. Competition is relatively low-key and the division enjoys a reputation as a good quality reliable supplier. Three factories are operated by the division using plant that is long lasting and not prone to obsolescence.

The average age of plant is ten years old. As indicated by the financial summary in Appendix 2, there has been only a low rate of growth in the sales and asset base of the division even though demand for the products of this industry has been quite buoyant for several years. Most capital expenditure proposals in the last three years had been for cost-reduction projects, with the remainder being necessity projects. Although all capital requests had been granted by headquarters, no large expansion projects had been proposed and annual additions to assets had approximately equalled retirements.

The product line of the division, which involves a large number of standard products as well as a significant amount of specialty contract work, is divided into five product groups so that the profitability of each group can be examined. There is a significant degree of specificity between types of pump and the equipment needed to produce them.

Details of the additional capital project proposals being considered for submission to headquarters for approval are given in Appendix 3.

Forging Division

This division also has a long history within the group. Since the severe trading difficulties of the early 1990s, when sales fell 40% in real terms in two years and employee numbers from all levels were reduced by 50%, the division had pursued a major shift in strategy. The majority of the high-volume, low value-added product range had been discontinued and emphasis placed on highly specialized, large-size, high-quality, lower-volume products for two main unrelated groups of customers. Demand is more predictable in these market areas and there is less competition but the market is still subject to major cyclical fluctuations. Since the early 1990s demand has steadily strengthened. The division enjoys formally recognized status as a high-quality supplier with several of its major customers.

Each new product needs expensive specially developed design work and tooling that is carried out under contract for a customer. Because of this there is a need to maintain the design and technical capability of the division.

One factory is operated and the plant for the most part comprises large-scale traditional forging equipment, the majority of which is well over 20 years old but is still reliable. However, the very expensive, largely hand-made, dies which are used are largely manufactured in-house by highly skilled but ageing toolmakers who are in increasingly short supply. Relative to other long-established divisions based on traditional industries, this division has performed quite well (see Appendix 4 for a summary of financial results) and almost all of its capital expenditure proposals in the past have been accepted.

The technology of the product design, die making and forging processes, and the quality standards demanded by customers have changed markedly in recent years. The last major investment in new-technology forging equipment cost the equivalent of 60% of annual gross sales revenue and took two years to install and commission. It is predicted that several more years will be needed to explore the learning curve and develop sales to a level that fully exploits its potential. Only one other company in the world has a plant to match the new investment made by this division. More recently the division has made significant investments in computer-aided design and integrated automated manufacture of dies. The Engineering Manager is now arguing for a major new investment in forging equipment that would give a world lead to the company but the rest of the divisional management team are resisting the proposal (see Appendix 5 for the additional major capital investment proposals the division is considering).

Visicon Systems Division

This is a new division, small in size relative to other divisions, but achieving high growth in a market that is already expanding rapidly and is expected to continue to do so for many years. There are as yet few competing companies.

A Visicon system is a computer-based visual recognition system used in automated manufacturing systems. Images of product components, usually obtained by video cameras, are electronically processed and identified. The information is fed to automated handling equipment, which then selects the appropriate component and feeds it to automated assembly systems. The system can distinguish different components and guide handling equipment to select appropriate ones.

The technology is developing rapidly and each customer has somewhat different needs. A high investment is needed in research, technical development, systems design, marketing and engineering services. The majority of physical components are bought-in so the essential nature of provision to customers is advice, system design and system installation services.

As indicated in Appendix 6, the division, although it is growing rapidly, cannot yet be regarded as financially successful and future market prospects are far from clear although independent commentators on the industry appear confident that there will be sustained rapid growth in combination with an increasing pace of technological change and diversity.

Appendix 1: Summary of corporate financial results

	Budget				
	1998 **£m**	**1999** **£m**	**2000** **£m**	**2001** **£m**	**2002** **£m**
Net sales	499	556	548	557	601
Cost of goods sold	368	410	390	387	407
Gross profit	131	146	158	170	194
Period expenses	104	115	123	130	141
Operating profit	27	31	35	40	53
Financing costs	2	2	2	2	4
Taxation	7	9	11	11	12
Profit after tax	18	20	22	27	37
Net current assets	122	120	139	156	189
Net fixed assets	207	187	218	225	252
Net assets	329	307	357	381	441
Equity	196	197	216	228	239
Long-term liabilities	133	110	141	153	202
Capital employed	329	307	357	381	441
ROI	8.2%	10.1%	9.8%	10.5%	12.0%
Earnings per share (EPS)	4.5	5.0	5.5	6.75	9.25

During the period to which these results relate the annual rate of increase in a generally accepted price index has averaged 5%.

Appendix 2: Summary of Pumps Division financial results

	Budget				
	1998 £m	1999 £m	2000 £m	2001 £m	2002 £m
Net sales	70	67	69	76	92
Cost of goods sold	46	42	45	48	59
Gross profit	24	25	24	28	33
Selling and administration	13	12	12	13	16
Research, development and technical services	2	2	2	3	3
Allocation of central overhead	3	3	2	3	4
Operating profit	6	8	8	9	10
Financing costs	–	1	2	3	2
Taxation	2	3	1	1	2
Profit after tax	4	4	5	5	6
Net current assets	15	17	18	19	20
Net fixed assets	18	20	21	25	26
Net assets	33	37	39	44	46
Equity	31	35	34	36	39
Long-term liabilities	2	2	5	8	7
Capital employed	33	37	39	44	46
ROI	18%	21.7%	20.4%	20.4%	21.7%
Target ROI					25%

Appendix 3: Pumps Division – Additional capital project proposals

Proposal A: Pump assembly automation

The automation of the pump assembly operation for one of the main product groups includes the installation of an automated part handling system relying on a Visicon system that would be supplied by the Visicon Division (estimated cost to Pumps Division £250,000). Existing assembly equipment, which has a zero net book value, would become redundant if the project proceeds, as would the majority of its supporting workforce.

Financial projections:	
Initial investment	£4.9m
Net cash flows	£1.862m per year for 5 years
NPV at 15%	£1.341m
ROI	18%

Proposal B: Product termination

One of several proposed terminations, this product was launched five years ago and had an expected six-year life. The original cost of the assets was £3.6m, the project profit for 2002 is £102,000 and its current realizable value is estimated to be £600,000.

The divisional management has decided to proceed, with the request for approval for Proposal B but not A.

Appendix 4: Summary of Forging Division financial results

	Budget				
	1998	**1999**	**2000**	**2001**	**2002**
Volume index	100	110	132	151	165
	£m	**£m**	**£m**	**£m**	**£m**
Net sales	38	46	58	70	83
Cost of goods sold	16	30	35	37	41
Gross profit	22	16	23	33	42
Selling and administration	7	7	9	10	11
Research, development and technical services	9	10	13	15	17
Allocation of central overhead	1	2	2	3	4
Operating profit	5	3	1	5	10
Financing costs	–	3	2	2	1
Taxation	2	–	–	–	4
Profit after tax	3	6	1	3	5
Net current assets	11	6	4	1	10
Net fixed assets	21	49	44	49	61
Other assets	2	2	2	4	5
Net assets	34	57	50	52	76
Equity	34	28	27	30	60
Long-term liabilities	–	29	23	22	16
Capital employed	34	57	50	52	76
ROI	14.7%	–	–	9.6%	13.1%
Target ROI					15%

Appendix 5: Forging Division – Additional capital project proposals

Proposal 1: Energy Saving Project

This proposal is expected to produce significant economies in the consumption of gas in die preparation and use.

Financial projections:	
Initial Investment	£3m
Net cash flows	£1.091m per year for 5 years
NPV at 15%	£0.657m
ROI	16.4%

Proposal 2: 32,000 ton screw press

This project would equip the division with a technical forging capability unmatched by any other company in the world and would help to develop markets for precision production of large part sizes, which have been beyond the range of existing equipment.

Financial projections:

		£m
Initial investment		38
Net cash flows	Year 1	8
	Year 2	8
	Year 3	13
	Year 4	33
	Year 5	10
NPV at 15%		7.41
ROI		17.9%

The major decline at the end of Year 5 is due to the predicted development of new casting and forging processes for the precision forging market. From Year 5 onwards the net cash flows are expected to stabilize at around £5m p.a.

Divisional management has decided to support Proposal 1 but not Proposal 2.

Appendix 6: Summary of Visicon Division financial results

	Budget				
	1998 £000	**1999 £000**	**2000 £000**	**2001 £000**	**2002 £000**
Net sales	98	240E	356	540	810
Cost of goods sold	27	66	98	149	223
Gross profit	71	174	258	391	587
Selling and administration	33	58	71	93	116
Research, development and technical services	96	136	182	284	401
Allocation of central overhead	2	6	8	20	29
Operating profit	60	26	3	4	41
Financing costs	24	30	35	42	84
Taxation	–	–	–	–	–
Profit after tax	84	56	38	38	43
Net current assets	129	147	178	221	388
Net fixed assets	48	65	70	85	137
Other assets	23	38	42	64	85
Net assets	200	250	290	370	610
Net equity balance	200	144	176	250	362
Long-term liabilities	–	106	114	120	248
Capital employed	200	250	290	370	610
ROI	–	–	–	1.1%	6.7%
Target ROI – short and medium term					12%
Target ROI – long term					25%

No additional capital expenditures are proposed. Rather, approval of the 2002 budget proposals is requested, which implies a major expansion of the staffing of the technical core of the division and its supporting services and equipment.

Required

1 Using the information provided, critically evaluate the use by Culharb plc of return on investment (ROI) as the measure of divisional performance.

2 Demonstrate whether a move to residual income as the key indicator of divisional performance would resolve any of the conflicts relating to the capital expenditure proposals being considered for both the Pumps Division and the Forging Division.

3 Suggest and evaluate alternative methods of measuring divisional performance that may be appropriate for Culharb plc.

[Thanks to Keith Harrison (Sheffield Hallam University), John Cullen (Sheffield University) and Mick Broadbent (University of Hertfordshire)]

C14–25 Service organization; segment reporting Time allowed: 75 minutes
Music Teachers is an educational association for music teachers that has 20,000 members. The association operates from a central headquarters but has local membership chapters throughout the United States. Monthly meetings are held by the local chapters to discuss recent developments on topics of interest to music teachers. The association's journal, *Teachers' Forum*, is issued monthly with features about recent developments in the field. The association publishes books and reports and also sponsors professional courses that qualify for continuing professional education credit. The association's statement of revenues and expenses for the current year is presented below.

Music Teachers
Statement of revenues and expenses
for the year ended 30 November

Revenues	$3,275,000
Less expenses:	
Salaries	920,000
Personnel costs	230,000
Occupancy costs	280,000
Reimbursement of member costs to local chapters	600,000
Other membership services	500,000
Printing and paper	320,000
Postage and shipping	176,000
Instructors' fees	80,000
General and administrative	38,000
Total expenses	3,144,000
Excess of revenues over expenses	$131,000

The board of directors of Music Teachers has requested that a segmented statement of operations be prepared showing the contribution of each profit centre to the association. The association has four profit centres: Membership Division, Magazine Subscriptions Division, Books and Reports Division, and Continuing Education Division. Mike Doyle has been assigned responsibility for preparing the segmented statement, and he has gathered the following data prior to its preparation.

1 Membership dues are $100 per year, of which $20 is considered to cover a one-year subscription to the association's journal. Other benefits include membership in the association and chapter affiliation. The portion of the dues covering the magazine subscription ($20) should be assigned to the Magazine Subscription Division.

2 One-year subscriptions to Teachers' Forum were sold to non-members and libraries at $30 per subscription. A total of 2,500 of these subscriptions were sold last year.

   In addition to subscriptions, the magazine generated $100,000 in advertising revenues.

   The costs per magazine subscription were $7 for printing and paper and $4 for postage and shipping.

3 A total of 28,000 technical reports and professional texts were sold by the Books and Reports Division at an average unit selling price of $25. Average costs per publication were $4 for printing and paper and $2 for postage and shipping.

4 The association offers a variety of continuing education courses to both members and non-members. The one-day courses had a tuition cost of $75 each and were attended by 2,400 students. A total of 1,760 students took two-day courses at a tuition cost of $125 for each student. Outside instructors were paid to teach some courses.

5 Salary costs and space occupied by division follow:

	Salaries	Space occupied (square metres)
Membership	210,000	2,000
Magazine Subscriptions	150,000	2,000
Books and Reports	300,000	3,000
Continuing Education	180,000	2,000
Corporate staff	80,000	1,000
Total	$920,000	10,000

Personnel costs are 25% of salaries in the separate divisions as well as for the corporate staff. The $280,000 in occupancy costs includes $50,000 in rental cost for a warehouse used by the Books and Reports Division for storage purposes.

6 Printing and paper costs other than for magazine subscriptions and for books and reports relate to the Continuing Education Division.

7 General and administrative expenses include costs relating to overall administration of the association as a whole. The company's corporate staff does some mailing of materials for general administrative purposes.

The expenses that can be traced or assigned to the corporate staff, as well as any other expenses that are not traceable to the profit centres, will be treated as common costs. It is not necessary to distinguish between variable and fixed costs.

Required

1 Prepare a segmented statement of revenues and expenses for Music Teachers. This statement should show the segment margin for each division as well as results for the association as a whole.

2 Give arguments for and against allocating all costs of the association to the four divisions.

(*CMA*, adapted)

Endnotes

1 Tully (1993).

2 There is a similar problem with top-level managers as well, as we shall see in Chapter 17.

3 Some companies classify business segments that are responsible mainly for generating revenue, such as an insurance sales office, as revenue centres. Other companies would consider this to be just another type of profit centre, since costs of some kind (salaries, rent, utilities) are usually deducted from the revenues in the segment's profit statement.

4 See Johnson and Kaplan (1987).

5 Emore and Ness (1991) p. 39.

6 Since residual income was developed in the United States, the term 'income' rather than 'profit' is used.

7 The basic idea underlying residual income and economic value added has been around for over 100 years. In recent years, economic value added has been popularized and trademarked by the consulting firm Stern, Stewart & Co.

8 Over 100 different adjustments could be made for deferred taxes, LIFO reserves, provisions for future liabilities, mergers and acquisitions, gains or losses due to changes in accounting rules, operating leases, and other accounts, but most companies make only a few. For further details, see Young and O'Byrne (2001).

9 See, for example, Mouritsen (1998).

10 See also Bouwens and Spekle (2007).

11 O'Hanlon and Peasnell (1998).

12 See, for example, Young and O'Byrne (2001).

Chapter 15
Pricing and intra-company transfers

Learning objectives

After studying Chapter 15, you should be able to:

1 Compute the profit-maximizing price using the price elasticity of demand and variable cost
2 Compute the selling price of a product using the absorption costing approach
3 Compute the mark-up percentage under the absorption costing approach
4 Compute the target cost for a new product or service
5 Compute and use the billing rates used in time and material pricing
6 Understand the basics of revenue management in capacity constrained businesses
7 Understand the main issues in transfer pricing in decentralized companies

Concepts in Context

Airlines and hotels are industries with very high fixed costs and 'perishable products'. Since an unfilled seat or empty bedroom is a lost contribution, these industries make use of revenue maximizing models whereby the price of an airline ticket or a room is altered according to the time of booking relative to departure time or hotel stay. These sectors have learned the importance of altering prices in order to operate at much higher capacities than they would if prices remained fixed.[1]

Some businesses have no pricing problems. They make a product that is in competition with other, identical products for which a market price already exists. Customers will not pay more than this price, and there is no reason for any company to charge less. Under these circumstances, the company simply charges the prevailing market price. Markets for basic raw materials such as farm products and minerals follow this pattern.

In this chapter, we are concerned with the more common situation in which a company is faced with the problem of setting its own prices. Clearly, the pricing decision can be critical. If the price is set too high, customers will avoid purchasing the company's products. If the price is set too low, the company's costs may not be covered.

The usual approach in pricing is to *mark up* cost. A product's **mark-up** is the difference between its selling price and its cost. The mark-up is usually expressed as a percentage of cost. This approach is called **cost-plus pricing** because the predetermined mark-up percentage is applied to the cost base to determine a target selling price.

Selling price = Cost + (Mark-up percentage × Cost)

For example, if a company uses a mark-up of 50%, it adds 50% to the costs of its products to determine the selling price. If a product costs £10, then it would charge £15 for the product.

There are two key issues when the cost-plus approach to pricing is used. First, what cost should be used? Second, how should the mark-up be determined? Several alternative approaches are considered in this chapter, starting with the approach generally favoured by economists.

The economists' approach to pricing

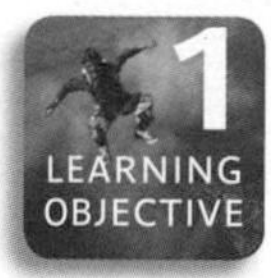

If a company raises the price of a product, unit sales ordinarily fall. Because of this, pricing is a delicate balancing act in which the benefits of higher revenues per unit are traded off against the lower volume that results from charging higher prices. The sensitivity of unit sales to changes in price is called the *price elasticity of demand*.

Elasticity of demand

A product's price elasticity should be a key element in setting its price. The **price elasticity of demand** measures the degree to which the volume of unit sales for a product or service is affected by a change in price. Demand for a product is said to be *inelastic* if a change in price has little effect on the number of units sold. The demand for designer perfumes sold by trained personnel at cosmetic counters in department stores is relatively inelastic. Lowering prices on these luxury goods has little effect on sales volume; factors other than price are more important in generating sales. On the other hand, demand for a product is said to be *elastic* if a change in price has a substantial effect on the volume of units sold. An example of a product whose demand is elastic is petrol. If a petrol station raises its price for petrol, there will usually be a substantial drop in volume as customers seek lower prices elsewhere.

Price elasticity is very important in determining prices. Managers should set higher mark-ups over cost when customers are relatively insensitive to price (i.e., demand is inelastic) and lower mark-ups when customers are relatively sensitive to price (i.e., demand is elastic). This principle is followed in department stores. Merchandise sold in the bargain basement has a much lower mark-up than merchandise sold elsewhere in the store because customers who shop in the bargain basement are much more sensitive to price (i.e., demand is elastic).

The price elasticity of demand for a product or service, εd, can be estimated using the following formula.[2]

$$\varepsilon_d = \frac{\ln(1 + \%\text{ change in quantity sold})}{\ln(1 + \%\text{ change in price})}$$

For example, suppose that the managers of Nature's Garden believe that every 10% increase in the selling price of their apple-almond shampoo would result in a 15% decrease in the number of bottles of shampoo sold.[3] The price elasticity of demand for this product would be computed as follows:

$$\varepsilon_d = \frac{\ln(1 + (-0.15))}{\ln(1 + (0.10))} = \frac{\ln(0.85)}{\ln(1.10)} = -1.71$$

For comparison purposes, the managers of Nature's Garden believe that another product, strawberry glycerine soap, would experience a 20% drop in unit sales if its price were increased by 10%. (Purchasers of this product are more sensitive to price than the purchasers of the apple-almond shampoo.) The price elasticity of demand for the strawberry glycerine soap is:

$$\varepsilon_d = \frac{\ln(1 + (-0.20))}{\ln(1 + (0.10))} = \frac{\ln(0.80)}{\ln(1.10)} = -2.34$$

Both of these products, like other products, have a price elasticity that is less than −1. Note also that the price elasticity of demand for the strawberry glycerine soap is larger (in absolute value) than the price elasticity of demand for the apple-almond shampoo. The more sensitive customers are to price, the larger (in absolute value) is the price elasticity of demand. In other words, a larger (in absolute value) price elasticity of demand indicates a product whose demand is more elastic.

In the next subsection, the price elasticity of demand will be used to compute the selling price that maximizes the profits of the company.

The profit-maximizing price

Under certain conditions, it can be shown that the *profit-maximizing price* can be determined by marking up *variable cost* using the following formula:[4]

$$\text{Profit-maximizing mark-up on variable cost} = \left(\frac{\varepsilon_d}{1 + \varepsilon_d}\right) - 1$$

Using the above mark-up is equivalent to setting the selling price using this formula:

$$\text{Profit-maximizing price on variable cost} = \left(\frac{\varepsilon_d}{1 + \varepsilon_d}\right) \text{Variable cost per unit}$$

The profit-maximizing prices for the two Nature's Garden products are computed below using these formulas:

	Apple-almond shampoo	**Strawberry glycerine soap**
Price elasticity of demand (ε_d)	−1.71	−2.34
Profit-maximizing mark-up on variable cost (a)	$\left(\frac{-1.71}{-1.71 + 1}\right) - 1$	$\left(\frac{-2.34}{-2.34 + 1}\right) - 1$
	= 2.41 − 1 = 1.41	= 1.75 − 1 = 0.75
	or 141%	or 75%
Variable cost per unit – given (b)	£2.00	£0.40
Mark-up, (a) × (b)	2.82	0.30
Profit-maximizing price	£4.82	£0.70

Note that the 75% mark-up for the strawberry glycerine soap is lower than the 141% mark-up for the apple-almond shampoo. The reason for this is that purchasers of strawberry glycerine soap are more sensitive to price than the purchasers of apple-almond shampoo. This could be because strawberry glycerine soap is a relatively common product with close substitutes available in nearly every grocery store.

Exhibit 15.1 shows how the profit-maximizing mark-up is affected by how sensitive unit sales are to price. For example, if a 10% increase in price leads to a 20% decrease in unit sales, then the optimal mark-up on variable cost according to the exhibit is 75% – the figure computed above for the strawberry glycerine soap. Note that the optimal mark-up drops as unit sales become more sensitive to price.

15.1 EXHIBIT

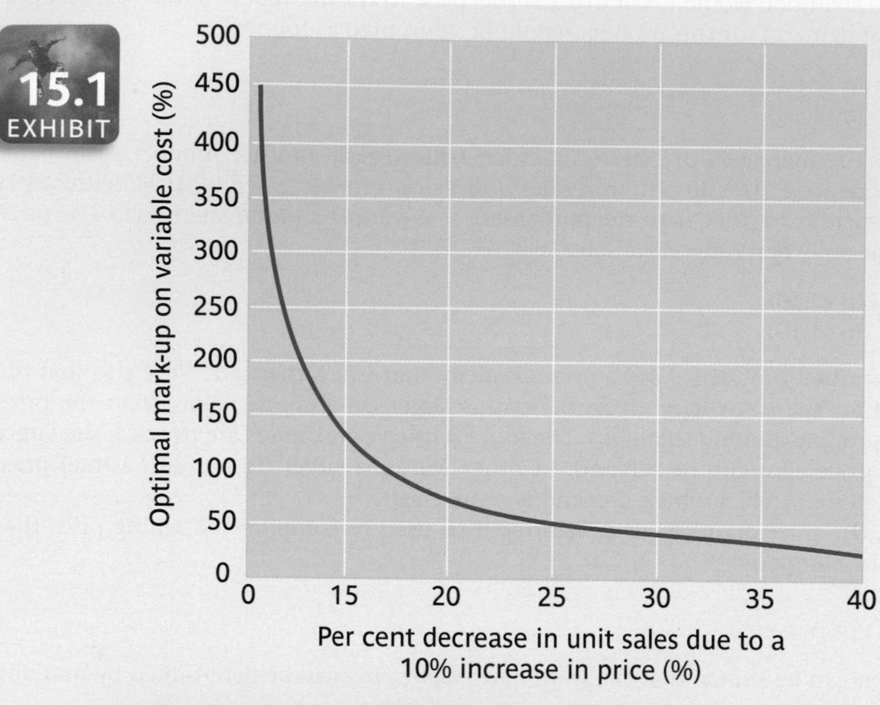

Exhibit 15.1 The optimal mark-up on variable cost as a function of the sensitivity of unit sales to price

Caution is advised when using these formulas to establish a selling price. The assumptions underlying the formulas are probably not completely true, and the estimate of the percentage change in unit sales that would result from a given percentage change in price is likely to be inexact. Nevertheless, the formulas can provide valuable clues regarding whether prices should be increased or decreased. Suppose, for example, that the strawberry glycerine soap is currently being sold for £0.60 per bar. The formula indicates that the profit-maximizing price is £0.70 per bar. Rather than increasing the price by £0.10, it would be prudent to increase the price by a more modest amount to observe what happens to unit sales and to profits.

The formula for the profit-maximizing price also conveys a very important lesson. The optimal selling price should depend on two factors – the variable cost per unit and how sensitive unit sales are to changes in price. In particular, fixed costs play no role in setting the optimal price. If the total fixed costs are the same whether the company charges £0.60 or £0.70, they cannot be relevant in the decision of which price to charge for the soap. Fixed costs are relevant when deciding whether to offer a product but are not relevant when deciding how much to charge for the product.

Incidentally, we can directly verify that an increase in selling price for the strawberry glycerine soap from the current price of £0.60 per bar is warranted, based just on the forecast that a 10% increase in selling price would lead to a 20% decrease in unit sales. Suppose, for example, that Nature's Garden is currently selling 200,000 bars of the soap per year at the price of £0.60 a bar. If the change in price has no effect on the company's fixed costs or on other products, the effect on profits of increasing the price by 10% can be computed as follows:

	Present price	Higher price
Selling price	£0.60	£0.60 + (0.10 × £0.60)
		= £0.66
Unit sales	200,000	200,000 − (0.20 × 200,000)
		= 160,000
Sales	£120,000	£105,600
Variable cost	80,000	64,000
Contribution margin	£40,000	£41,600

Despite the apparent optimality of prices based on marking up variable costs according to the price elasticity of demand, surveys consistently reveal that most managers approach the pricing problem from a completely different perspective. They prefer to mark up some version of full, not variable, costs, and the mark-up is based on desired profits rather than on factors related to demand.

The absorption costing approach to cost-plus pricing

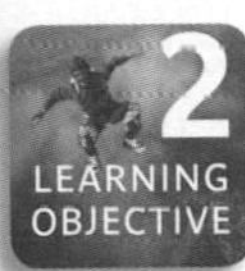

The absorption costing approach to cost-plus pricing differs from the economists' approach both in what costs are marked up and in how the mark-up is determined. Under the absorption approach to cost-plus pricing, the cost base is the absorption costing unit product cost as defined in Chapters 2, 3 and 4 rather than variable cost.

Setting a target selling price using the absorption costing approach

To illustrate, let us assume that the management of Ritter Company wants to set the selling price on a product that has just undergone some design modifications. The Accounting Department has provided cost estimates for the redesigned product as shown below:

	Per unit	Total
Direct materials	£6	
Direct labour	4	
Variable manufacturing overhead	3	
Fixed manufacturing overhead	–	£70,000
Variable selling, general and administrative expenses	2	
Fixed selling, general and administrative expenses	–	60,000

The first step in the absorption costing approach to cost-plus pricing is to compute the unit product cost. For Ritter Company, this amounts to £20 per unit at a volume of 10,000 units, as computed below:

Direct materials	£6
Direct labour	4
Variable manufacturing overhead	3
Fixed manufacturing overhead (£70,000 ÷ 10,000 units)	7
Unit product cost	£20

Ritter Company has a general policy of marking up unit product costs by 50%. A price quotation sheet for the company prepared using the absorption approach is presented in Exhibit 15.2. Note that selling, general and administrative (SG&A) costs are not included in the cost base. Instead, the mark-up is supposed to cover these expenses. Let us see how some companies compute these mark-up percentages.

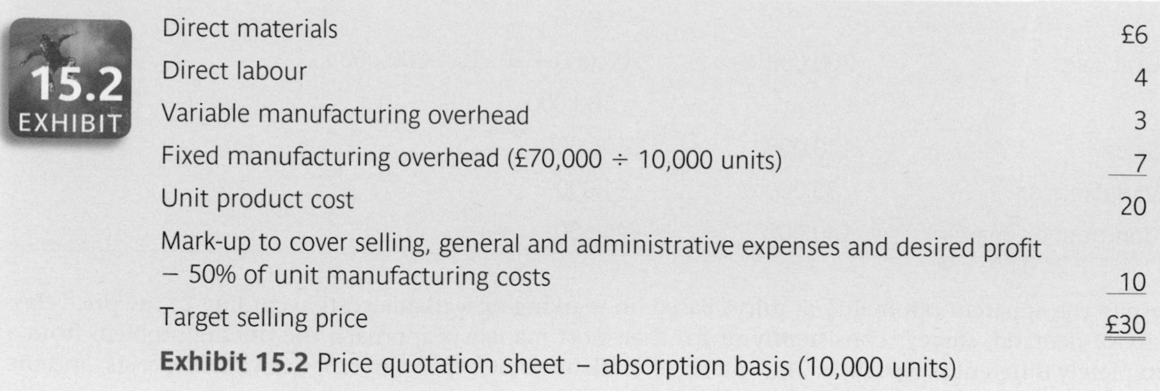

Direct materials	£6
Direct labour	4
Variable manufacturing overhead	3
Fixed manufacturing overhead (£70,000 ÷ 10,000 units)	7
Unit product cost	20
Mark-up to cover selling, general and administrative expenses and desired profit – 50% of unit manufacturing costs	10
Target selling price	£30

Exhibit 15.2 Price quotation sheet – absorption basis (10,000 units)

Determining the mark-up percentage

3 LEARNING OBJECTIVE

How did Ritter Company arrive at its mark-up percentage of 50%? This figure could be a widely used rule of thumb in the industry or just a company tradition that seems to work. The mark-up percentage may also be the result of an explicit computation.

As we have discussed, the mark-up over cost ideally should be largely determined by market conditions. However, a popular approach is to at least start with a mark-up based on cost and desired profit. The reasoning goes like this. The mark-up must be large enough to cover SG&A expenses and provide an adequate return on investment (ROI). Given the forecasted unit sales, the mark-up can be computed as follows:

$$\text{Mark-up percentage on absorption cost} = \frac{(\text{Required ROI} \times \text{Investment}) + \text{SG\&A expenses}}{\text{Unit sales} \times \text{Unit product cost}}$$

To show how the formula above is applied, assume Ritter Company must invest £100,000 to produce and market 10,000 units of the product each year. The £100,000 investment covers purchase of equipment and funds needed to carry stocks and debtors. If Ritter Company requires a 20% ROI, then the mark-up for the product would be determined as follows:

$$\text{Mark-up percentage on absorption cost} = \frac{(£20{,}000 \times 100{,}000) + (£2 \times 10{,}000 + £60{,}000)}{10{,}000 \times £20}$$

$$\text{Mark-up percentage on absorption cost} = \frac{(£20{,}000) + £80{,}000)}{£200{,}000} = 50\%$$

As shown earlier, this mark-up of 50% leads to a target selling price of £30 for Ritter Company. As shown in Exhibit 15.3, *if the company actually sells 10,000 units* of the product at this price, the company's ROI on this product will indeed be 20%. If it turns out that more than 10,000 units are sold at this price, the ROI will be greater than 20%. If less than 10,000 units are sold, the ROI will be less than 20%. *The required ROI will be attained only if the forecasted unit sales volume is attained.*

Problems with the absorption costing approach

Using the absorption costing approach, the pricing problem looks deceptively simple. All you have to do is compute your unit product cost, decide how much profit you want, and then set your price. It appears that you can ignore demand and arrive at a price that will safely yield whatever profit you want. However, as noted above, the absorption costing approach relies on a forecast of unit sales. Neither the mark-up nor the unit product cost can be computed without such a forecast.

The absorption costing approach essentially assumes that customers *need* the forecasted unit sales and will pay whatever price the company decides to charge. However, customers have a choice. If the price is too high, they can buy from a competitor or they may choose not to buy at all. Suppose, for example, that

Direct materials	£6
Direct labour	4
Variable manufacturing overhead	3
Fixed manufacturing overhead (£70,000 ÷ 10,000 units)	7
Unit product cost	£20

Ritter Company Absorption costing profit statement

Sales (£30 × 10,000 units)	£300,000
Less cost of goods sold (£20 × 10,000 units)	200,000
Gross margin	100,000
Less selling, general and administration expenses (£2 × 10,000 units £60,000)	80,000
Net operating profit	£20,000

ROI

$$\text{ROI} = \frac{\text{Net operating profit}}{\text{Average operating assets}}$$

$$= \frac{£20{,}000}{£100{,}000}$$

$$= 20\%$$

Exhibit 15.3 Profit statement and ROI analysis – Ritter Company actual unit sales = 10,000 units; selling price = £30

when Ritter Company sets its price at £30, it sells only 7,000 units rather than the 10,000 units forecasted. As shown in Exhibit 15.4, the company would then have a loss of £25,000 on the product instead of a profit of £20,000. Some managers believe that the absorption costing approach to pricing is safe. This is an illusion. The absorption costing approach is safe only as long as customers choose to buy at least as many units as managers forecasted they would buy.

Target costing

Our discussion thus far has presumed that a product has already been developed, has been costed, and is ready to be marketed as soon as a price is set. In many cases, the sequence of events is just the reverse. That is, the company will already *know* what price should be charged, and the problem will be to *develop* a product that can be marketed profitably at the desired price. Even in this situation, where the normal sequence of events is reversed, cost is still a crucial factor. The company's approach will be to employ *target costing*. **Target costing** is the process of determining the maximum allowable cost for a new product and then developing a prototype that can be profitably made for that maximum target cost figure. Many companies use target costing, including Compaq, Cummins Engine, Daihatsu Motors, Ford, Isuzu Motors, ITT Automotive, Komatsu, Matsushita Electric, Mitsubishi Kasei, NEC, Nippodenso, Nissan, Olympus, Sharp, Texas Instruments and Toyota.

The target costing approach was developed in recognition that many companies have less control over price than they would like to think. The market (i.e., supply and demand) really determines prices, and a company that attempts to ignore this does so at its peril. Therefore, the anticipated market price is taken as a given in target costing. Second, as we shall see in Chapters 16 and 19, target costing is more than just an approach to pricing – it takes a *strategic approach to cost management* by linking a whole series of organizational functions such as marketing, design, production and procurement.

The target cost for a product is computed by starting with the product's anticipated selling price and then deducting the desired profit, as follows:

Target cost = Anticipated selling price – Desired profit

15.4 EXHIBIT

Direct materials	£6
Direct labour	4
Variable manufacturing overhead	3
Fixed manufacturing overhead (£70,000 ÷ 10,000 units)	10
Unit product cost	£23

Ritter Company Absorption costing profit statement

Sales (£30 × 7,000 units)	£210,000
Less cost of goods sold (£20 × 7,000 units)	161,000
Gross margin	49,000
Less selling, general and administration expenses (£2 × 10,000 units £60,000)	74,000
Net operating profit	£(25,000)

ROI

$$\text{ROI} = \frac{\text{Net operating profit}}{\text{Average operating assets}}$$

$$= \frac{(£25,000)}{£100,000}$$

$$= -25\%$$

Exhibit 15.4 Profit statement and ROI analysis – Ritter Company actual unit sales = 7,000 units; selling price = £30

The product development team is given the responsibility of designing the product so that it can be made for no more than the target cost.

An example of target costing

To provide a simple numerical example of target costing, assume the following situation: Handy Appliance Company feels that there is a market niche for a hand mixer with certain new features. Surveying the features and prices of hand mixers already on the market, the Marketing Department believes that a price of £30 would be about right for the new mixer. At that price, Marketing estimates that 40,000 of the new mixers could be sold annually. To design, develop, and produce these new mixers, an investment of £2,000,000 would be required. The company desires a 15% ROI. Given these data, the target cost to manufacture, sell, distribute, and service one mixer is £22.50 as shown below.

Projected sales (40,000 mixers × £30)	£1,200,000
Less desired profit (15% × £2,000,000)	300,000
Target cost for 40,000 mixers	£900,000
Target cost per mixer (£900,000/40,000 mixers)	£22.50

This £22.50 target cost would be broken down into target costs for the various functions: manufacturing, marketing, distribution, after-sales service, and so on. Each functional area would be responsible for keeping its actual costs within target.

Service companies – time and material pricing

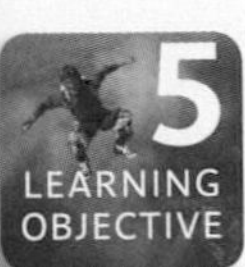

Some companies – particularly in service industries – use a variation on cost-plus pricing called **time and material pricing**. Under this method, two pricing rates are established – one based on direct labour time and the other based on the cost of direct material used. This pricing method is widely used in repair shops, in printing shops, and by many professionals such as doctors and dentists. The time and material rates are usually market-determined. In other words, the rates are determined by the interplay of supply and demand and by competitive conditions in the industry. However, some companies set the rates using a process similar to the process followed in the absorption costing approach to cost-plus pricing. In this case, the rates include allowances for selling, general and administrative expenses; for other direct and indirect costs; and for a desired profit. This section will show how the rates might be set using the cost-plus approach.

Time component

The time component is typically expressed as a rate per hour of labour. The rate is computed by adding together three elements: (1) the direct costs of the employee, including salary and fringe benefits; (2) a pro rata allowance for selling, general and administrative expenses of the organization; and (3) an allowance for a desired profit per hour of employee time. In some organizations (such as a repair shop), the same hourly rate will be charged regardless of which employee actually works on the job; in other organizations, the rate may vary by employee. For example, in a public accounting firm, the rate charged for a new assistant accountant's time will generally be less than the rate charged for an experienced senior accountant or for a partner.

Material component

The material component is determined by adding a **material loading charge** to the invoice price of any materials used on the job. The material loading charge is designed to cover the costs of ordering, handling and carrying materials in stock, plus a profit margin on the materials themselves.

An example of time and material pricing

To provide a numerical example of time and material pricing, assume the following data.

The Quality Auto Shop uses time and material pricing for all of its repair work. The following costs have been budgeted for the coming year:

	Repairs	Parts
Mechanics' wages	£300,000	£–
Service manager – salary	40,000	–
Parts manager – salary	–	36,000
Clerical assistant – salary	18,000	15,000
Pensions and insurance – 16% of salaries and wages	57,280	8,160
Supplies	720	540
Utilities	36,000	20,800
Property taxes	8,400	1,900
Depreciation	91,600	37,600
Invoice cost of parts used	–	400,000
Total budgeted cost	£552,000	£520,000

The company expects to bill customers for 24,000 hours of repair time. A profit of £7 per hour of repair time is considered to be feasible, given the competitive conditions in the market. For parts, the competitive mark-up on the invoice cost of parts used is 15%.

15.5 EXHIBIT

	Time component: repairs		Parts: material loading charge	
	Total	Per hour*	Total	Per cent†
Cost of mechanics' time:				
Mechanics' wages	£300,000			
Retirement and insurance (16% of wages)	48,000			
Total cost	348,000	£14.50		
For repairs – other cost of repair service.				
For parts – costs of ordering, handling and storing parts:				
Repairs service manager – salary	40,000		£–	
Parts manager – salary	–		36,000	
Clerical assistant – salary	18,000		15,000	
Retirement and insurance (16% of salaries)	9,280		8,160	
Supplies	720		540	
Utilities	36,000		20,800	
Property taxes	8,400		1,900	
Depreciation	91,600		37,600	
Total cost	204,000	8.50	120,000	30%
Desired profit:				
24,000 hours × £7	168,000	7.00	–	
15% × £400,000	–		60,000	15%
Total amount to be billed	£720,000	£30.00	£180,000	45%

*Based on 24,000 hours.

†Based on £400,000 invoice cost of parts. The charge for ordering, handling and storing parts, for example, is computed as follows: £120,000 cost ÷ £400,000 invoice cost = 30%.

Exhibit 15.5 Time and material pricing

Exhibit 15.5 shows the computation of the billing rate and the material loading charge to be used over the next year. Note that the billing rate, or time component, is £30 per hour of repair time and the material loading charge is 45% of the invoice cost of parts used. Using these rates, a repair job that requires 4.5 hours of mechanics time and £200 in parts would be billed as follows:

Labour time: 4.5 hours × £30		£135
Parts used:		
Invoice cost	£200	
Material loading charge: 45% × £200	90	290
Total price of the job		£425

Rather than using labour-hours as the basis for computing the time rate, a machine shop, a printing shop or a similar organization might use machine-hours.

This method of setting prices is a variation of the absorption costing approach. As such, it is not surprising that it suffers from the same problem. Customers may not be willing to pay the rates that have been computed. If actual business is less than the forecasted 24,000 hours and £400,000 worth of parts, the profit objectives will not be met and the company may not even break even.

Revenue and yield management

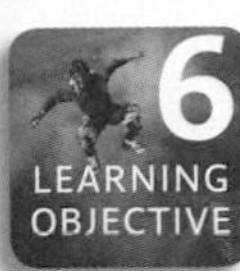

Some industries such as hotels and airlines are characterized by high fixed costs and perishability. The capacity of a plane or a hotel is fixed in the short run. Furthermore, an empty bedroom at night or an empty seat in a plane that has taken off represent a sale that is lost forever. Ideally, hotel managers would like to sell all rooms at the highest (rack) rate but they know that there is a trade-off between high occupancy and high room rates. The problem becomes one of determining how much to sell, at what price and to which market segment, so as to maximize revenue. The resolution lies in control over rates (being price restrictive if demand is high and more flexible if it low) and restrictions to occupancy (blocking of rooms in advance) in order to maximize overall gross revenue per period of time. These are the principles behind the technique of *yield management*. **Yield management (YM)** is a practice of achieving high capacity utilization through varying prices according to market segments and time of booking.[5]

To use YM, a hotel must know its market segments and why guests need to stay and develop appropriate marketing strategies for each market segment. To ensure the optimization of the total revenues from the room stock of a group of hotels, for example, and to allow access to its demand history, a centralized reservations system is needed. There should be some return from linking YM systems to marketing expenditure plans. For example, predicted periods of low demand from YM team meetings can trigger the need to advertise short-break packages. The overall effectiveness of a YM system is dependent on the implementation of the following market-focused principles: identification of a customer base using a detailed segmentation strategy; developing an awareness of customers' changing needs and expectations; estimating the price elasticity of demand per market segment; responsiveness of management to cope with changing market conditions; and accurate historical demand analysis, combined with a reliable forecasting method. The key performance metric in this model is the *yield percentage*:

$$\text{Yield percentage} = \frac{\text{Actual revenue}}{\text{Maximum potential revenue}}$$

The **yield percentage** will depend on the average price × the number of units sold (hotel rooms, airline seats). The maximum potential revenue is a full hotel or plane charging the maximum price.[6]

Transfer pricing

There are special problems in evaluating pricing goods or services transferred from one division/segment of a company to another. The problems revolve around the question of what transfer price to charge between the segments. A **transfer price** is the price charged when one segment of a company provides goods or services to another segment of the company. For example, most companies in the oil industry, such as BP, Exxon, Shell and Texaco, have petroleum refining and retail sales divisions that are evaluated on the basis of ROI or residual income. The petroleum refining division processes crude oil into petrol, kerosene, lubricants and other end products. The retail sales division takes petrol and other products from the refining division and sells them through the company's chain of service stations. Each product has a price for transfers within the company. Suppose the transfer price for petrol is £0.80 a litre. Then the refining division gets credit for £0.80 a litre of revenue on its segment report and the retailing division must deduct £0.80 a litre as an expense on its segment report. Clearly, the refining division would like the transfer price to be as high as possible, whereas the retailing division would like the transfer price to be as low as possible. However, the transaction has no direct effect on the entire company's reported profit. It is like taking money out of one pocket and putting it into the other.

Managers are intensely interested in how transfer prices are set, since they can have a dramatic effect on the apparent profitability of a division. Three common approaches are used to set transfer prices:

1 Allow the managers involved in the transfer to negotiate their own transfer price.

2 Set transfer prices at cost using:

(a) Variable cost.

(b) Full (absorption) cost.

3 Set transfer prices at the market price.

We will consider each of these transfer pricing methods in turn, beginning with negotiated transfer prices. Throughout the discussion we should keep in mind that *the fundamental objective in setting transfer prices is to motivate the managers to act in the best interests of the overall company*. In contrast, **sub-optimization** occurs when managers do not act in the best interests of the overall company or even in the best interests of their own segment.

Negotiated transfer prices

A **negotiated transfer price** is a transfer price that is agreed on between the selling and purchasing divisions. Negotiated transfer prices have several important advantages. First, this approach preserves the autonomy of the divisions and is consistent with the spirit of decentralization. Second, the managers of the divisions are likely to have much better information about the potential costs and benefits of the transfer than others in the company.

When negotiated transfer prices are used, the managers who are involved in a proposed transfer within the company meet to discuss the terms and conditions of the transfer. They may decide not to go through with the transfer, but if they do, they must agree to a transfer price. Generally speaking, we cannot predict the exact transfer price they will agree to. However, we can confidently predict two things: (1) the selling division will agree to the transfer only if the profits of the selling division increase as a result of the transfer, and (2) the purchasing division will agree to the transfer only if the profits of the purchasing division also increase as a result of the transfer. This may seem obvious, but it is an important point.

Clearly, if the transfer price is below the selling division's cost, a loss will occur on the transaction and the selling division will refuse to agree to the transfer. Likewise, if the transfer price is set too high, it will be impossible for the purchasing division to make any profit on the transferred item. For any given proposed transfer, the transfer price has both a lower limit (determined by the situation of the selling division) and an upper limit (determined by the situation of the purchasing division). The actual transfer price agreed to by the two division managers can fall anywhere between those two limits. These limits determine the **range of acceptable transfer prices** – the range of transfer prices within which the profits of both divisions participating in a transfer would increase.

An example will help us to understand negotiated transfer prices. Harris & Louder Ltd owns fast-food restaurants and snack food and beverage manufacturers in the United Kingdom. One of the restaurants, Pizza Maven, serves a variety of beverages along with pizzas. One of the beverages is ginger beer, which is served on tap. Harris & Louder has just purchased a new division, Imperial Beverages, that produces ginger beer. The managing director of Imperial Beverages has approached the managing director of Pizza Maven about purchasing Imperial Beverages' ginger beer for sale at Pizza Maven restaurants rather than its usual brand of ginger beer. Managers at Pizza Maven agree that the quality of Imperial Beverages' ginger beer is comparable to the quality of their regular brand. It is just a question of price. The basic facts are listed below:

Imperial Beverages:	
Ginger beer production capacity per month	10,000 barrels
Variable cost per barrel of ginger beer	£8 per barrel
Fixed costs per month	£70,000
Selling price of Imperial Beverages' ginger beer on outside market	£20 per barrel
Pizza Maven:	
Purchase price of regular brand of ginger beer	£18 per barrel
Monthly consumption of ginger beer	2,000 barrels

The selling division's lowest acceptable transfer price

The selling division, Imperial Beverages, will be interested in a proposed transfer only if its profit increases. Clearly, the transfer price must not fall below the variable cost per barrel of £8. In addition, if Imperial Beverages has insufficient capacity to fill the Pizza Maven order, then it would have to give up some of its regular sales. Imperial Beverages would expect to be compensated for the contribution margin on these lost sales. In sum, if the transfer has no effect on fixed costs, then from the selling division's standpoint, the transfer price must cover both the variable costs of producing the transferred units and any opportunity costs from lost sales.

Seller's perspective:

$$\text{Transfer price} \geq \text{Variable cost per unit} + \frac{\text{Total contribution margin on lost sales}}{\text{Number of units transferred}}$$

The purchasing division's highest acceptable transfer price

The purchasing division, Pizza Maven, will be interested in the proposal only if its profit increases. In cases like this where a purchasing division has an outside supplier, the purchasing division's decision is simple. Buy from the inside supplier if the price is less than the price offered by the outside supplier.

Purchaser's perspective:

$$\text{Transfer price} \leq \text{Cost of buying from outside supplier}$$

We will consider several different hypothetical situations and see what the range of acceptable transfer prices would be in each situation.

Selling division with idle capacity

Suppose that Imperial Beverages has sufficient idle capacity to satisfy the demand for ginger beer from Pizza Maven without cutting into sales of ginger beer to its regular customers. To be specific, let's suppose that Imperial Beverages is selling only 7,000 barrels of ginger beer a month on the outside market. That leaves unused capacity of 3,000 barrels a month – more than enough to satisfy Pizza Maven's requirement of 2,000 barrels a month. What range of transfer prices, if any, would make both divisions better off with the transfer of 2,000 barrels a month?

1 The selling division, Imperial Beverages, will be interested in the proposal only if:

$$\text{Transfer price} \geq \text{Variable cost per unit} + \frac{\text{Total contribution margin on lost sales}}{\text{Number of units transferred}}$$

Since Imperial Beverages has ample idle capacity, there are no lost outside sales. And since the variable cost per unit is £8, the lowest acceptable transfer price as far as the selling division is concerned is also £8.

$$\text{Transfer price} \geq £8 + \frac{£0}{2{,}000} = £8$$

2 The purchasing division, Pizza Maven, can buy similar ginger beer from an outside vendor for £18. Therefore, Pizza Maven would be unwilling to pay more than £18 per barrel for Imperial Beverages' ginger beer.

$$\text{Transfer price £20 per barrel} \leq \text{Cost of buying from outside supplier} = £18$$

3 Combining the requirements of both the selling division and the purchasing division, the acceptable range of transfer prices in this situation is:

$$£8 \leq \text{Transfer price} \leq £18$$

Assuming that the managers understand their own businesses and that they are co-operative, they should be able to agree on a transfer price within this range.

Selling division with no idle capacity

Suppose that Imperial Beverages has no idle capacity; it is selling 10,000 barrels of ginger beer a month on the outside market at £20 per barrel. To fill the order from Pizza Maven, Imperial Beverages would have to divert 2,000 barrels from its regular customers. What range of transfer prices, if any, would make both divisions better off transferring the 2,000 barrels within the company?

1 The selling division, Imperial Beverage, will be interested in the proposal only if:

$$\text{Transfer price} \geq \text{Variable cost per unit} + \frac{\text{Total contribution margin on lost sales}}{\text{Number of units transferred}}$$

Since Imperial Beverage has no idle capacity, there *are* lost outside sales. The contribution margin per barrel on these outside sales is £12 (£20 − £8).

$$\text{Transfer price} \geq £8 + \frac{(20 - £8) \times 2{,}000}{2{,}000} = £8 + (£20 - £8) = £20$$

Thus, as far as the selling division is concerned, the transfer price must at least cover the revenue on the lost sales, which is £20 per barrel. This makes sense since the cost of producing the 2,000 barrels is the same whether they are sold on the inside market or on the outside. The only difference is that the selling division loses the revenue of £20 per barrel if it transfers the barrels to Pizza Maven.

2 As before, the purchasing division, Pizza Maven, would be unwilling to pay more than the £18 per barrel it is already paying for similar ginger beer from its regular supplier.

$$\text{Transfer price} \leq \text{Cost of buying from outside supplier} = £18$$

3 Therefore, the selling division would insist on a transfer price of at least £20. But the purchasing division would refuse any transfer price above £18. It is impossible to satisfy both division managers simultaneously; there can be no agreement on a transfer price and no transfer will take place. Is this good? The answer is yes. From the standpoint of the entire company, the transfer doesn't make sense. Why give up sales of £20 to save £18?

Basically, the transfer price is a mechanism for dividing between the two divisions any profit the entire company earns as a result of the transfer. If the company loses money on the transfer, there will be no profit to divide up, and it will be impossible for the two divisions to come to an agreement. On the other hand, if the company makes money on the transfer, there will be a potential profit to share, and it will always be possible for the two divisions to find a mutually agreeable transfer price that increases the profits of both divisions. If the pie is bigger, it is always possible to divide it up in such a way that everyone has a bigger piece.

Selling division has some idle capacity

Suppose now that Imperial Beverages is selling 9,000 barrels of ginger beer a month on the outside market. Pizza Maven can only sell one kind of ginger beer on tap. They cannot buy 1,000 barrels from Imperial Beverages and 1,000 barrels from their regular supplier; they must buy all their ginger beer from one source.

To fill the entire 2,000-barrel a month order from Pizza Maven, Imperial Beverages would have to divert 1,000 barrels from its regular customers who are paying £20 per barrel. The other 1,000 barrels can be made using idle capacity. What range of transfer prices, if any, would make both divisions better off transferring the 2,000 barrels within the company?

1 As before, the selling division, Imperial Beverage, will insist on a transfer price that at least covers their variable cost and opportunity cost:

$$\text{Transfer price} \geq \text{Variable cost per unit} + \frac{\text{Total contribution margin on lost sales}}{\text{Number of units transferred}}$$

Since Imperial Beverage does not have enough idle capacity to fill the entire order for 2,000 barrels, there *are* lost outside sales. The contribution margin per barrel on the 1,000 barrels of lost outside sales is £12 (£20 − £8).

$$\text{Transfer price} \geq £8 + \frac{(£20 - £8) \times 1{,}000}{2{,}000} = £8 + £6 = £14$$

Thus, as far as the selling division is concerned, the transfer price must cover the variable cost of £8 plus the average opportunity cost of lost sales of £6.

2 As before, the purchasing division, Pizza Maven, would be unwilling to pay more than the £18 per barrel it pays its regular supplier.

Transfer price $\leq$ Cost of buying from outside suppliers = £18

3 Combining the requirements for both the selling and purchasing divisions, the range of acceptable transfer prices is:

£14 $\leq$ Transfer price $\leq$ £18

Again, assuming that the managers understand their own businesses and that they are co-operative, they should be able to agree on a transfer price within this range.

No outside supplier

If Pizza Maven has no outside supplier for the ginger beer, the highest price the purchasing division would be willing to pay depends on how much the purchasing division expects to make on the transferred units – excluding the transfer price. If, for example, Pizza Maven expects to earn £30 per barrel of ginger beer after paying its own expenses, then it should be willing to pay up to £30 per barrel to Imperial Beverages. Remember, however, that this assumes Pizza Maven cannot buy ginger beer from other sources.

Evaluation of negotiated transfer prices

As discussed earlier, if a transfer within the company would result in higher overall profits for the company, there is always a range of transfer prices within which both the selling and purchasing division would also have higher profits if they agree to the transfer. Therefore, if the managers understand their own businesses and are co-operative, then they should always be able to agree on a transfer price if it is in the best interests of the company that they do so.

The difficulty is that not all managers understand their own businesses and not all managers are co-operative. As a result, negotiations often break down even when it would be in the managers' own best interests to come to an agreement. Sometimes that is the fault of the way managers are evaluated. If managers are pitted against each other rather than against their own past performance or reasonable benchmarks, a non-cooperative atmosphere is almost guaranteed. Nevertheless, it must be admitted that even with the best performance evaluation system, some people by nature are not co-operative.

Possibly because of the fruitless and protracted bickering that often accompanies disputes over transfer prices, most companies rely on some other means of setting transfer prices. Unfortunately, as we will see below, all the alternatives to negotiated transfer prices have their own serious drawbacks.

Transfers at the cost to the selling division

Many companies set transfer prices at either the variable cost or full (absorption) cost incurred by the selling division. Although the cost approach to setting transfer prices is relatively simple to apply, it has some major defects.

First, the use of cost – particularly full cost – as a transfer price can lead to bad decisions and thus sub-optimization. Return to the example involving the ginger beer. The full cost of ginger beer can never be less than £15 per barrel (£8 per barrel variable cost + £7 per barrel fixed cost at capacity). What if the cost of buying the ginger beer from an outside supplier is less than £15 – for example, £14 per barrel? If the transfer price were bureaucratically set at full cost, then Pizza Maven would never want to buy ginger beer from Imperial Beverages, since it could buy its ginger beer from the outside supplier at less cost. However, from the standpoint of the company as a whole, ginger beer should be transferred from Imperial Beverages to Pizza Maven whenever Imperial Beverages has idle capacity. Why? Because when Imperial Beverage has idle capacity, it only costs the company £8 in variable cost to produce a barrel of ginger beer, but it costs £14 per barrel to buy from outside suppliers.

Secondly, if cost is used as the transfer price, the selling division will never show a profit on any internal transfer. The only division that shows a profit is the division that makes the final sale to an outside party.

A third problem with cost-based prices is that they do not provide incentives to control costs. If the costs of one division are simply passed on to the next, then there is little incentive for anyone to work to reduce costs. This problem can be overcome to some extent by using standard costs rather than actual costs for transfer prices.

Despite these shortcomings, cost-based transfer prices are commonly used in practice. Advocates argue that they are easily understood and convenient to use.

Transfers at market price

Some form of competitive **market price** (i.e., the price charged for an item on the open market) is often regarded as the best approach to the transfer pricing problem – particularly if transfer price negotiations routinely become bogged down.

The market price approach is designed for situations in which there is an *intermediate market* for the transferred product or service. By **intermediate market**, we mean a market in which the product or service is sold in its present form to outside customers. If the selling division has no idle capacity, the market price in the intermediate market is the perfect choice for the transfer price. The reason for this is that if the selling division can sell a transferred item on the outside market instead, then the real cost of the transfer as far as the company is concerned is the opportunity cost of the lost revenue on the outside sale. Whether the item is transferred internally or sold on the outside intermediate market, the production costs are exactly the same. If the market price is used as the transfer price, the selling division manager will not lose anything by making the transfer, and the purchasing division manager will get the correct signal about how much it really costs the company for the transfer to take place.

While the market price works beautifully when there is no idle capacity, difficulties occur when the selling division has idle capacity. Recalling once again the ginger beer example, the outside market price for the ginger beer produced by Imperial Beverages is £20 per barrel. However, Pizza Maven can purchase all of the ginger beer it wants from outside suppliers for £18 per barrel. Why would Pizza Maven ever buy from Imperial Beverages if Pizza Maven is forced to pay Imperial Beverages' market price? In some market price-based transfer pricing schemes, the transfer price would be lowered to £18, the outside vendor's market price, and Pizza Maven would be directed to buy from Imperial Beverages as long as Imperial Beverages is willing to sell. This scheme can work reasonably well, but a drawback is that managers at Pizza Maven will regard the cost of ginger beer as £18 rather than the £8, which is the real cost to the company when the selling division has idle capacity. Consequently, the managers of Pizza Maven will make pricing and other decisions based on an incorrect cost.

Unfortunately, none of the possible solutions to the transfer pricing problem are perfect – not even market-based transfer prices.

Divisional autonomy and sub-optimization

A question often arises as to how much autonomy should be granted to divisions in setting their own transfer prices and in making decisions concerning whether to sell internally or to sell outside. Should the divisional heads have complete authority to make these decisions, or should top corporate management step in if it appears that a decision is about to be made that would result in sub-optimization? For example, if the selling division has idle capacity and divisional managers are unable to agree on a transfer price, should top corporate management step in and *force* a settlement?

Efforts should always be made, of course, to bring disputing managers together. But the almost unanimous feeling among top corporate executives is that divisional heads should not be forced into an agreement over a transfer price. That is, if a manager flatly refuses to change his or her position in a dispute, *then this decision should be respected even if it results in sub-optimization*. This is simply the price that is paid for divisional autonomy. If top corporate management steps in and forces the decisions in difficult situations, then the purposes of decentralization are defeated and the company simply becomes a centralized operation with decentralization of only minor decisions and responsibilities. In short, if a division is to be viewed as an autonomous unit with independent profit responsibility, then it must have control over its own destiny – even to the extent of having the right to make bad decisions.

We should note, however, that if a division consistently makes bad decisions, the results will sooner or later reduce its profit and rate of return, and the divisional manager may find that he or she has to defend the division's performance. Even so, the manager's right to get into an embarrassing situation must be respected if decentralization is to operate successfully. Divisional autonomy and independent profit responsibility generally lead to much greater success and profitability than do closely controlled, centrally administered operations. Part of the price of this success is occasional sub-optimization due to pettiness, bickering or just plain stubbornness.

Furthermore, one of the major reasons for decentralizing is that top managers cannot know enough about every detail of operations to make every decision themselves. To impose the correct transfer price, top managers would have to know details about the intermediate market, variable costs and capacity utilization. If top managers have all of this information, it is not clear why they decentralized in the first place.

International aspects of transfer pricing

The objectives of transfer pricing change are when a multinational corporation (MNC) is involved and the goods and services being transferred cross international borders. The objectives of international transfer pricing, as compared to domestic transfer pricing, are summarized in Exhibit 15.6.[7]

As shown in the exhibit, the objectives of international transfer pricing focus on minimizing taxes, duties and foreign exchange risks, along with enhancing a company's competitive position and improving its relations with foreign governments. Although domestic objectives such as managerial motivation and divisional autonomy are always important, they often become secondary when international transfers are involved. Companies will focus instead on charging a transfer price that will slash its total tax bill or that will strengthen a foreign subsidiary.

For example, charging a low transfer price for parts shipped to a foreign subsidiary may reduce customs duty payments as the parts cross international borders, or it may help the subsidiary to compete in foreign markets by keeping the subsidiary's costs low. On the other hand, charging a high transfer price may help an MNC draw profits out of a country that has stringent controls on foreign remittances, or it may allow an MNC to shift income from a country that has high income tax rates to a country that has low rates.

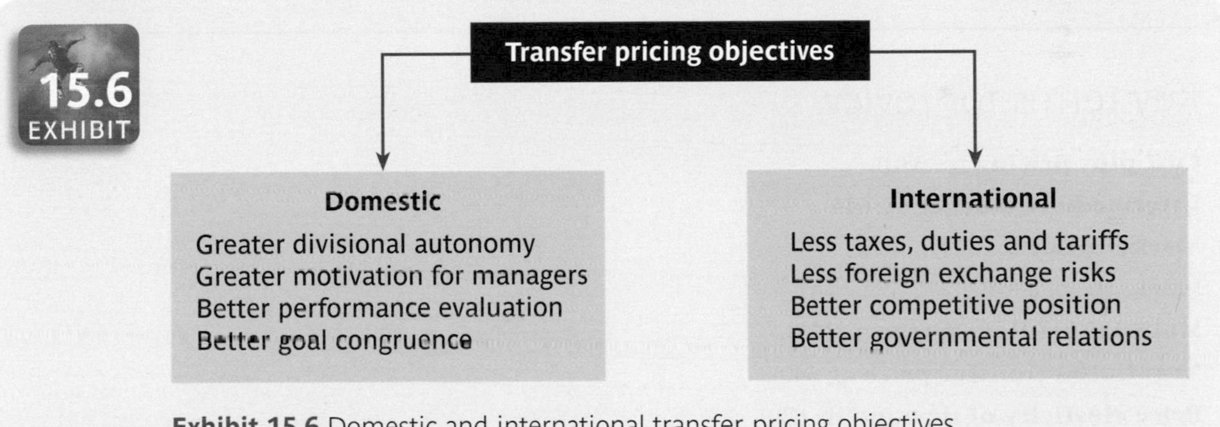

Exhibit 15.6 Domestic and international transfer pricing objectives

FOCUS

Focus on current practice

There is a potential clash of interest between national tax authorities who want to raise revenue and multinational companies who wish to pay as little tax as possible. International transfer pricing may be used to reduce a company's tax burden in at least one country. Even more dramatically, profits from a high tax regime may be shifted to a zero tax regime in an offshore tax haven. The Organization for Economic Co-operation and Development (OECD) has calculated that 60% of world trade consists of transfers within multinationals which effectively result in profits being made by anonymous subsidiaries in tax-free jurisdictions.[8] Oxfam estimates that offshore tax havens cost the United Kingdom nearly £85 billion in lost tax revenue every year.[9]

In an attempt to curb the abuse of such international transfer pricing, legislation tries to ensure that 'arm's length' prices are charged in transactions between related parties. An arm's length relationship between two related parties should exhibit the characteristics that would be found if the same relationship existed between two unrelated parties. Taxation authorities ask themselves 'Would the transaction have been entered into between comparable independent enterprises?' If so, then the next question is: 'Is the price charged compatible with the arm's length principle?'[10]

Summary

- Pricing involves a delicate balancing act. Higher prices result in more revenue per unit sold but drive down unit sales. Exactly where to set prices to maximize profit is a difficult problem, but, in general, the mark-up over cost should be highest for those products where customers are least sensitive to price. The demand for such products is said to be price inelastic.
- Managers often rely on cost-plus formulas to set target prices. In the absorption costing approach, the cost base is absorption costing unit product cost and the mark-up is computed to cover both non-manufacturing costs and to provide an adequate return on investment. However, costs will not be covered and there will not be an adequate return on investment unless the unit sales forecast used in the cost-plus formula is accurate. If applying the cost-plus formula results in a price that is too high, the unit sales forecast will not be attained.
- Some companies take a different approach to pricing. Instead of starting with costs and then determining prices, they start with prices and then determine allowable costs. Companies that use target costing estimate what a new product's market price is likely to be based on its anticipated features and prices of products already on the market. They subtract desired profit from the estimated market price to arrive at the product's target cost. The design and development team is then given the responsibility of ensuring that the actual cost of the new product does not exceed the target cost.
- A special approach to pricing is required when goods or services are being transferred between segments or divisions of the same company. The theoretically optimal market price may not be appropriate if the company has spare capacity. Overall the aim should be to determine a price that maximizes the profit for the whole company. International transfer prices in multinational companies raise important taxation issues where the interests of the company and national taxation authorities may be in conflict.

Key terms for review

Cost-plus pricing (p. 630).

Intermediate market (p. 644).

Market price (p. 644).

Mark-up (p. 630).

Material loading charge (p. 637).

Negotiated transfer price (p. 640).

Price elasticity of demand (p. 630).

Range of acceptable transfer prices (p. 640).

Sub-optimization (p. 640).

Target costing (p. 635).

Time and material pricing (p. 637).

Transfer price (p. 639).

Yield management (YM) (p 639)

Yield percentage (p 639).

Review problem: transfer pricing

Situation A

Collyer Products plc has a Valve Division that manufactures and sells a standard valve as follows:

Capacity in units	100,000
Selling price to outside customers on the intermediate market	£30
Variable costs per unit	16
Fixed costs per unit (based on capacity)	9

The company has a Pump Division that could use this valve in the manufacture of one of its pumps. The Pump Division is currently purchasing 10,000 valves per year from an overseas supplier at a cost of £29 per valve.

Required

1 Assume that the Valve Division has ample idle capacity to handle all of the Pump Division's needs. What is the acceptable range, if any, for the transfer price between the two divisions?

2 Assume that the Valve Division is selling all that it can produce to outside customers on the intermediate market. What is the acceptable range, if any, for the transfer price between the two divisions?

3 Assume again that the Valve Division is selling all that it can produce to outside customers on the intermediate market. Also assume that £3 in variable expenses can be avoided on transfers within the company, due to reduced selling costs. What is the acceptable range, if any, for the transfer price between the two divisions?

Solution to situation A

1 Since the Valve Division has idle capacity, it does not have to give up any outside sales to take on the Pump Division's business. Applying the formula for the lowest acceptable transfer price from the viewpoint of the selling division, we get:

$$\text{Transfer price} \geq \text{Variable cost per unit} + \frac{\text{Total contribution margin on lost sales}}{\text{Number of units transferred}}$$

$$\text{Transfer price} \geq £16 + \frac{£0}{10{,}000} = £16$$

The Pump Division would be unwilling to pay more that £29, the price it is currently paying an outside supplier for its valves. Therefore, the transfer price must fall within the range:

$$£16 \leq \text{Transfer price} \leq £29$$

2 Since the Valve Division is selling all that it can produce on the intermediate market, it would have to give up some of these outside sales to take on the Pump Division's business. Thus, the Valve Division has an opportunity cost that is the total contribution margin on lost sales:

$$\text{Transfer price} \geq \text{Variable cost per unit} + \frac{\text{Total contribution margin on lost sales}}{\text{Number of units transferred}}$$

$$\text{Transfer price} \geq £16 + \frac{(£30 - £16) \times 10{,}000}{10{,}000} = £16 + £14 = £30$$

Since the Pump Division can purchase valves from an outside supplier at only £29 per unit, no transfers will be made between the two divisions.

3 Applying the formula for the lowest acceptable price from the viewpoint of the selling division, we get:

$$\text{Transfer price} \geq \text{Variable cost per unit} + \frac{\text{Total contribution margin on lost sales}}{\text{Number of units transferred}}$$

$$\text{Transfer price} \geq (£16 - £3) + \frac{(30 - £16) \times 10{,}000}{10{,}000} = £13 + £14 = £27$$

In this case, the transfer price must fall within the range:

£27 ≤ Transfer price ≤ £29.

Situation B Review problem transfer pricing

Refer to the original data in situation A above. Assume that the Pump Division needs 20,000 special high-pressure valves per year. The Valve Division's variable costs to manufacture and ship the special valve would be £20 per unit. To produce these special valves, the Valve Division would have to reduce its production and sales of regular valves from 100,000 units per year to 70,000 units per year.

Required

As far as the Valve Division is concerned, what is the lowest acceptable transfer price?

Solution to situation B

To produce the 20,000 special valves, the Valve Division will have to give up sales of 30,000 regular valves to outside customers. Applying the formula for the lowest acceptable price from the viewpoint of the selling division, we get:

$$\text{Transfer price} \geq \text{Variable cost per unit} + \frac{\text{Total contribution margin on lost sales}}{\text{Number of units transferred}}$$

$$\text{Transfer price} \geq (£20) + \frac{(30 - £16) \times 30{,}000}{20{,}000} = £20 + £21 = £41$$

Questions

15–1 What is meant by cost-plus pricing?

15–2 What does the price elasticity of demand measure? What is meant by inelastic demand? What is meant by elastic demand?

15–3 According to the economists' approach to setting prices, the profit-maximizing price should depend on which two factors?

15–4 Which product should have a larger mark-up over variable cost, a product whose demand is elastic or a product whose demand is inelastic?

15–5 When the absorption costing approach to cost-plus pricing is used, what is the mark-up supposed to cover?

15–6 What assumption does the absorption costing approach make about how consumers react to prices?

15–7 Discuss the following statement: 'Full cost can be viewed as a floor of protection. If a firm always sets its prices above full cost, it will never have to worry about operating at a loss.'

15–8 What is target costing? How do target costs enter into the pricing decision?

15–9 What is time and material pricing?

15–10 From the standpoint of a selling division that has idle capacity, what is the minimum acceptable transfer price for an item?

15–11 From the standpoint of a selling division that has no idle capacity, what is the minimum acceptable transfer price for an item?

15–12 What are the advantages and disadvantages of cost-based transfer prices?

15–13 If a market price for a product can be determined, why isn't it always the best transfer price?

Exercises

E15–1 Time allowed: 15 minutes

Maria Lorenzi owns an ice cream stand that she operates during the summer months in West Yellowstone, Montana. Her store caters primarily to tourists passing through town on their way to Yellowstone National Park.

Maria is unsure of how she should price her ice cream cones and has experimented with two prices in successive weeks during the busy August season. The number of people who entered the store was roughly the same in the two weeks. During the first week, she priced the cones at $1.89 and 1,500 cones were sold. During the second week, she priced the cones at $1.49 and 2,340 cones were sold. The variable cost of a cone is $0.43 and consists solely of the costs of the ice cream and of the cone itself. The fixed expenses of the ice cream stand are $675 per week.

Required

1 Did Maria make more money selling the cones for $1.89 or for $1.49?

2 Estimate the price elasticity of demand for the ice cream cones.

3 Estimate the profit-maximizing price for ice cream cones.

E15–2 Time allowed: 10 minutes

Martin Company is considering the introduction of a new product. To determine a target selling price, the company has gathered the following information:

Number of units to be produced and sold each year	14,000
Unit product cost	£25
Projected annual selling, general, and administrative expenses	50,000
Estimated investment required by the company	750,000
Desired return on investment (ROI)	12%

Required

The company uses the absorption costing approach to cost-plus pricing.

1 Compute the mark-up the company will have to use to achieve the desired ROI.

2 Compute the target selling price per unit.

E15–3 Time allowed: 5 minutes

Shimada Products Corporation of Japan is anxious to enter the electronic calculator market. Management believes that in order to be competitive in world markets, the electronic calculator that the company is developing cannot be priced at more than £15. Shimada requires a minimum return of 12% on all investments. An investment of £5,000,000 would be required to acquire the equipment needed to produce the 300,000 calculators that management believes can be sold each year at the £15 price.

Required

Compute the target cost of one calculator.

E15–4 Time allowed: 15 minutes
The Reliable TV Repair Shop had budgeted the following costs for next year:

Repair technicians:	
Wages	£120,000
Fringe benefits	30,000
Repairs operation per year	90,000
Materials:	
Costs of ordering, handling, and storing parts	20% of invoice cost

In total, the company expects 10,000 hours of repair time it can bill to customers. According to competitive conditions, the company believes it should aim for a profit of £6 per hour of repair time. The competitive mark-up on materials is 40% of invoice cost. The company uses time and material pricing.

Required

1 Compute the time rate and the material loading charge that would be used to bill jobs.

2 One of the company's repair technicians has just completed a repair job that required 2.5 hours of time and £80 in parts (invoice cost). Compute the amount that would be billed for the job.

E15–5 Time allowed: 30 minutes
Sako Company's Audio Division produces a speaker that is widely used by manufacturers of various audio products. Sales and cost data on the speaker follow:

Selling price per unit on the intermediate market	£60
Variable costs per unit	42
Fixed costs per unit (based on capacity)	8
Capacity in units	25,000

Sako Company has just organized a Hi-Fi Division that could use this speaker in one of its products. The Hi-Fi Division will need 5,000 speakers per year. It has received a quote of £57 per speaker from another manufacturer. Sako Company evaluates divisional managers on the basis of divisional profits.

Required

1 Assume that the Audio Division is now selling only 20,000 speakers per year to outside customers on the intermediate market.

(a) From the standpoint of the Audio Division, what is the lowest acceptable transfer price for speakers sold to the Hi-Fi Division?

(b) From the standpoint of the Hi-Fi Division, what is the highest acceptable transfer price for speakers purchased from the Audio Division?

(c) If left free to negotiate without interference, would you expect the division managers to voluntarily agree to the transfer of 5,000 speakers from the Audio Division to the Hi-Fi Division? Why or why not?

(d) From the standpoint of the entire company, should the transfer take place? Why or why not?

2 Assume that the Audio Division is selling all of the speakers it can produce to outside customers on the intermediate market.

(a) From the standpoint of the Audio Division, what is the lowest acceptable transfer price for speakers sold to the Hi-Fi Division?

(b) From the standpoint of the Hi-Fi Division, what is the highest acceptable transfer price for speakers purchased from the Audio Division?

(c) If left free to negotiate without interference, would you expect the division managers to voluntarily agree to the transfer of 5,000 speakers from the Audio Division to the Hi-Fi Division? Why or why not?

(d) From the standpoint of the entire company, should the transfer take place? Why or why not?

E15–6 Time allowed: 20 minutes

In each of the cases below, assume that Division X has a product that can be sold either to outside customers on an intermediate market or to Division Y of the same company for use in its production process. The managers of the divisions are evaluated based on their divisional profits.

	Case A	Case B
Division X:		
Capacity in units	200,000	200,000
Number of units being sold on the intermediate market	200,000	160,000
Selling price per unit on the intermediate market	£90	£75
Variable costs per unit	70	60
Fixed costs per unit (based on capacity)	13	8
Division Y:		
Number of units needed for production	40,000	40,000
Purchase price per unit now being paid to an outside supplier	£86	£74

Required

1 Refer to the data in case A above. Assume in this case that £3 per unit in variable costs can be avoided on intra-company sales. If the managers are free to negotiate and make decisions on their own, will a transfer take place? If so, within what range will the transfer price fall? Explain.

2 Refer to the data in case B above. In this case there will be no savings in variable costs on intra-company sales. If the managers are free to negotiate and make decisions on their own, will a transfer take place? If so, within what range will the transfer price fall? Explain.

E15–7 Time allowed: 15 minutes

Division A manufactures electronic circuit boards. The boards can be sold either to Division B of the same company or to outside customers. Last year, the following activity occurred in Division A:

Selling price per circuit board	£125
Production cost per circuit board	90
Number of circuit boards:	
Produced during the year	20,000
Sold to outside customers	16,000
Sold to Division B	4,000

Sales to Division B were at the same price as sales to outside customers. The circuit boards purchased by Division B were used in an electronic instrument manufactured by that division (one board per instrument). Division B incurred £100 in additional cost per instrument and then sold the instruments for £300 each.

Required

1 Prepare profit statements for Division A, Division B, and the company as a whole.

2 Assume that Division A's manufacturing capacity is 20,000 circuit boards. Next year, Division B wants to purchase 5,000 circuit boards from Division A rather than 4,000. (Circuit boards of this type are not available from outside sources.) From the standpoint of the company as a whole, should Division A sell the 1,000 additional circuit boards to Division B or continue to sell them to outside customers? Explain.

PROBLEMS

Problems

P15–8 Economists' approach to pricing Time allowed: 30 minutes

The postal service of St Vincent, an island in the West Indies, obtains a significant portion of its revenues from sales of special souvenir sheets to stamp collectors. The souvenir sheets usually contain several high-value St Vincent stamps depicting a common theme, such as the life of Princess Diana. The souvenir sheets are designed and printed for the postal service by Imperial Printing, a stamp agency service company in the United Kingdom. The souvenir sheets cost the postal service $0.80 each. (The currency in St Vincent is the East Caribbean dollar.) St Vincent has been selling these souvenir sheets for $7.00 each and ordinarily sells about 100,000 units. To test the market, the postal service recently priced a new souvenir sheet at $8.00 and sales dropped to 85,000 units.

Required

1 Does the postal service of St Vincent make more money selling souvenir sheets for $7.00 each or $8.00 each?

2 Estimate the price elasticity of demand for the souvenir sheets.

3 Estimate the profit-maximizing price for souvenir sheets.

4 If Imperial Printing increases the price it charges to the St Vincent postal service for souvenir sheets to $1.00 each, how much should the St Vincent postal service charge its customers for the souvenir sheets?

P15–9 Standard costs; mark-up computations; pricing decisions Time allowed: 30 minutes

Wilderness Products plc has designed a self-inflating sleeping pad for use by backpackers and campers. The following information is available about the new product:

1 An investment of £1,350,000 will be necessary to carry stocks and debtors and to purchase some new equipment needed in the manufacturing process. The company requires a 24% return on investment for new products.

2 A standard cost card has been prepared for the sleeping pad, as shown below:

	Standard quantity or hours	Standard price or rate	Standard cost
Direct materials	4.0 metres	£2.70 per metre	£10.80
Direct labour	2.4 hours	8.00 per hour	19.20
Manufacturing overhead (1/5 variable)	2.4 hours	12.50 per hour	30.00
Total standard cost per pad			£60.00

3 The only variable selling, general and administrative expenses on the pads will be £9 per pad sales commission. Fixed selling, general and administrative expenses will be (per year):

Salaries	£82,000
Warehouse rent	50,000
Advertising and other	600,000
Total	£732,000

4 Since the company manufactures many products, it is felt that no more than 38,400 hours of direct labour time per year can be devoted to production of the new sleeping pads.

5 Manufacturing overhead costs are allocated to products on the basis of direct labour-hours.

Required

1 Assume that the company uses the absorption approach to cost-plus pricing.

(a) Compute the mark-up that the company needs on the pads to achieve a 24% return on investment (ROI) if it sells all of the pads it can produce.

(b) Using the mark-up you have computed, prepare a price quotation sheet for a single sleeping pad.

(c) Assume that the company is able to sell all of the pads that it can produce. Prepare an income statement for the first year of activity and compute the company's ROI for the year on the pads.

2 After marketing the sleeping pads for several years, the company is experiencing a fall-off in demand due to an economic recession. A large retail outlet will make a bulk purchase of pads if its label is sewn in and if an acceptable price can be worked out. What is the absolute minimum price that would be acceptable for this special order?

P15–10 Pricing Time allowed: 30 minutes

A small company is engaged in the production of plastic tools for the garden. Subtotals on the spreadsheet of budgeted overheads for a year reveal:

	Moulding Department	Finishing Department	General factory overhead
Variable overhead (£000)	1,600	500	1,050
Fixed overhead (£000)	2,500	850	1,750
Budgeted activity			
Machine-hours (000)	800	600	
Practical capacity			
Machine-hours (000)	1,200	800	

For the purposes of reallocation of general factory overhead it is agreed that the variable overheads accrue in line with the machine-hours worked in each department. General factory fixed overhead is to be reallocated on the basis of the practical machine hour capacity of the two departments.

It has been a long-standing company practice to establish selling prices by applying a mark-up on full manufacturing cost of between 25% and 35%.

A possible price is sought for one new product which is in a final development stage. The total market for this product is estimated at 200,000 units per annum. Market research indicates that the company could expect to obtain and hold about 10% of the market. It is hoped the product will offer some improvement over competitors' products, which are currently marketed at between £90 and £100 each.

The product development department has determined that the direct material content is £9 per unit. Each unit of the product will take two labour-hours (four machine-hours) in the moulding department and three labour-hours (three machine-hours) in finishing. Hourly labour rates are £5.00 and £5.50 respectively.

Management estimate that the annual fixed costs which would be specifically incurred in relation to the product are: supervision £20,000, depreciation of a recently acquired machine £120,000 and advertising £27,000. It may be assumed that these costs are included in the budget given above. Given the state of development of this new product, management do not consider it necessary to make revisions, to the budgeted activity levels given above, for any possible extra machine-hours involved in its manufacture.

Required

1 Briefly explain the role of costs in pricing. *(6 marks)*

2 Prepare full cost and marginal cost information which may help with the pricing decision. *(9 marks)*

3 Comment on the cost information and suggest a price range which should be considered. *(5 marks)*

(Total = 20 marks)
ACCA Managerial Finance, December, 1999

P15–11 Pricing, experience curve Time allowed: 45 minutes
VI plc produces a number of mobile telephone products. It is an established company with a good reputation that has been built on well-engineered, reliable and good quality products. It is currently developing a product called Computel and has spent £1.5 million on development so far. The company has to decide whether it should proceed further and launch the product in one year's time.

If VI plc decides to continue with the project, it will incur further development costs of £0.75 million straight away. Assets worth £3.5 million will be required immediately prior to the product launch, and working capital of £1.5 million would be required. VI plc expects that it could sell Computel for three years before the product becomes out of date.

It is estimated that the first 500 Computels produced and sold would cost an average of £675 each unit, for production, marketing and distribution costs. The fixed costs associated with the project are expected to amount to £2.4 million (cash out flow) for each year the product is in production.

Because of the cost estimates, the Chief Executive expected the selling price to be in the region of £950. However, the Marketing Director is against this pricing strategy; he says that this price is far too high for this type of product and that he could sell only 6,000 units in each year at this price. He suggests a different strategy: setting a price of £425, at which price he expects sales to be 15,000 units each year.

VI plc has found from past experience that a 70% experience curve applies to production, marketing and distribution costs. The company's cost of capital is 7% a year.

Required

1 The Chief Executive has asked you to help sort out the pricing dilemma. Prepare calculations that demonstrate:

(a) which of the two suggestions is the better pricing strategy;

(b) the financial viability of the better strategy. *(15 marks)*

2 Discuss other issues that VI plc should consider in relation to the two pricing strategies. *(5 marks)*

3 Calculate and comment on the sensitivity of the financially better pricing strategy to changes in the selling price. *(4 marks)*

4 Discuss the usefulness of the experience curve in gaining market share. Illustrate your answer with specific instances/examples. *(6 marks)*

(Total = 30 marks)
CIMA Management Accounting – Decision-making, May 2001

P15–12 Transfer pricing, divisional performance Time allowed: 45 minutes
Division A, which is part of the ACF Group, manufactures only one type of product, a Bit, which it sells to external customers and also to division C, another member of the group. ACF Group's policy is that divisions have the freedom to set transfer prices and choose their suppliers.

The ACF Group uses residual income (RI) to assess divisional performance and each year it sets each division a target RI. The group's cost of capital is 12% a year.

Division A
Budgeted information for the coming year is:

Maximum capacity	150,000 Bits
External sales	110,000 Bits
External selling price	£35 per Bit
Variable cost	£22 per Bit
Fixed costs	£1,080,000
Capital employed	£3,200,000
Target residual income	£180,000

Division C

Division C has found two other companies willing to supply Bits:

X could supply at £28 per Bit, but only for annual orders in excess of 50,000 Bits.

Z could supply at £33 per Bit for any quantity ordered.

Required

(*Note:* Ignore tax for parts a and b.)

1 Division C provisionally requests a quotation for 60,000 Bits from division A for the coming year.

(a) Calculate the transfer price per Bit that division A should quote in order to meet its residual income target. *(6 marks)*

(b) Calculate the two prices division A would have to quote to division C, if it became group policy to quote transfer prices based on opportunity costs. *(2 marks)*

2 Evaluate and discuss the impact of the group's current and proposed policies on the profits of divisions A and C, and on group profit. Illustrate your answer with calculations. *(11 marks)*

3 Assume that divisions A and C are based in different countries and consequently pay taxes at different rates: division A at 55% and division C at 25%. Division A has now quoted a transfer price of £30 per Bit for 60,000 Bits. Calculate whether it is better for the group if division C purchases 60,000 Bits from division A or from supplier X. *(6 marks)*

(Total = 25 marks)

CIMA Management Accounting – Decision-making, May 2001

P15–13 Transfer pricing Time allowed: 20 minutes

1 Alpha division has an external market for product A which fully utilizes its production capacity.

(a) Explain the principle which would suggest that Alpha division should transfer product A to Beta division of the same group of companies at the existing market price.

(b) Explain circumstances in which Alpha division may offer to transfer product A to Beta division at less than the external market price and yet report the same total profit. *(4 marks)*

2 The transfer pricing method to be used for an intermediate product between two divisions in a group is under debate. The supplying division wishes to use actual cost plus a 25% profit mark-up. The receiving division suggests the use of standard cost plus a 25% profit mark-up. A suggested compromise is to use revised standard cost plus 25% profit mark-up. The revised standard cost is arrived at after taking into account the appropriate elements of a planning and operational variance analysis at the supplying division.

Discuss the impact of EACH of the above transfer pricing methods and their acceptability to the supplying and receiving divisions. *(6 marks)*

3 An intermediate product is manufactured in limited quantities at three divisions of a group and is available in limited quantities from an external source. The intermediate product is required by four divisions in the group as an input for products to be sold externally. The total quantity of intermediate product which is available is insufficient to satisfy demand at the four user divisions.

Explain the procedure which should lead to a transfer pricing and deployment policy which will result in group profit maximization. *(5 marks)*

(Total = 15 marks)

ACCA Information for Control and Decision-making, December, 1999

P15–14 Target costing Time allowed: 45 minutes

National Restaurant Supply Inc sells restaurant equipment and supplies throughout most of the United States. Management of the company is considering adding a machine that makes sorbet to its line of ice cream making machines. Management is preparing to enter into negotiations with the Swedish manufacturer of the sorbet machine concerning the price at which the machine would be sold to National Restaurant Supply.

Management of National Restaurant Supply believes the sorbet machine can be sold to its customers in the United States for $4,950. At that price, annual sales of the sorbet machine should be 100 units. If the sorbet machine is added to National Restaurant Supply's product lines, the company will have to invest $600,000 in inventories and special warehouse fixtures. The variable cost of selling the sorbet machines would be $650 per machine.

Required

1 If National Restaurant Supply requires a 15% return on investment (ROI), what is the maximum amount the company would be willing to pay the Swedish manufacturer for the sorbet machines?

2 The manager who is flying to Sweden to negotiate the purchase price of the machines would like to know how the purchase price of the machines would affect National Restaurant Supply's ROI. Construct a chart that shows National Restaurant Supply's ROI as a function of the purchase price of the sorbet machine. Put the purchase price on the X-axis and the resulting ROI on the Y-axis. Plot the ROI for purchase prices between $3,000 and $4,000 per machine.

3 After many hours of negotiations, management has concluded that the Swedish manufacturer is unwilling to sell the sorbet machine at a low enough price so that National Restaurant Supply is able to earn its 15% required ROI. Apart from simply giving up on the idea of adding the sorbet machine to National Restaurant Supply's product lines, what could management do?

P15–15 Time and material pricing Time allowed: 45 minutes

City Appliance Ltd operates an appliance service business with a fleet of trucks dispatched by radio in response to calls from customers. The company's profit margin has dropped steadily over the last two years, and management is concerned that pricing rates for time and material may be out of date. According to industry trade magazines, the company should be earning £8.50 per hour of repair service time, and a profit of 10% of the invoice cost of parts used. The company maintains a large parts inventory in order to give prompt repair service to customers.

Costs associated with repair work and with the parts inventory over the past year are provided below:

	Repairs	**Parts**
Repair service manager – salary	£25,000	£–
Parts manager – salary	–	20,000
Repair technicians – wages	180,000	–
Office assistant – salary	9,000	3,000
Depreciation – trucks and equipment	15,400	–
Depreciation – buildings and fixtures	6,000	17,500
Retirement benefits (15% of salaries and wages)	32,100	3,450
Health insurance (5% of salaries and wages)	10,700	1,150
Utilities	2,600	12,000
Truck operating costs	36,000	–
Property taxes	900	3,400
Liability and fire insurance	1,500	1,900
Supplies	800	600
Invoice cost of parts used	–	210,000
Total cost	£320,000	£273,000

During the past year, customers were billed for 20,000 hours of repair time.

Required

1 Using the data above, compute the following:
   (a) The rate that would be charged per hour of repair service time using time and material pricing.
   (b) The material loading charge that would be used in billing jobs. The material loading charge should be expressed as a percentage of the invoice cost of parts.

2 Assume that the company adopts the rates that you have computed in Question 1 above. What would be the total price charged on a repair that requires 112 hours of service time and £108 in parts?

3 During the past year, the company billed repair service time at £20 per hour and added a material loading charge of 35% to parts. If the company adopts the rates that you have computed in Question 1 above, would you expect the company's profits to improve? Explain.

P15–16 Missing data; mark-up computations: return on investment (ROI); pricing Time allowed: 45 minutes

South Seas Products plc has designed a new surfboard to replace its old surfboard line. Because of the unique design of the new surfboard, the company anticipates that it will be able to sell all the boards that it can produce. On this basis, the following incomplete budgeted profit statement for the first year of activity is available:

Sales (? boards at ? per board)	£?
Less cost of goods sold (? boards at ? per board)	1,600,000
Gross margin	?
Less selling, general, and administrative expenses	1,130,000
Profit	£?

Additional information on the new surfboard is given below:

1 An investment of £1,500,000 will be necessary to carry stocks and debtors and to purchase some new equipment needed in the manufacturing process. The company requires an 18% return on investment for all products.

2 A partially completed standard cost card for the new surfboard follows:

	Standard quantity or hours	Standard price	Standard cost
Direct materials	6 feet	£4.50 per foot	£27
Direct labour	2 hours	? per hour	?
Manufacturing overhead	?	? per hour	?
Total standard cost per surfboard			£?

3 The company will employ 20 workers in the manufacture of the new surfboards. Each will work a 40-hour week, 50 weeks a year.

4 Other information relating to production and costs follows:

Variable manufacturing overhead cost (per board)	£5
Variable selling cost (per board)	10
Fixed manufacturing overhead cost (total)	600,000
Fixed selling, general, and administrative cost (total)	?
Number of boards produced and sold (per year)	?

5 Overhead costs are allocated to production on the basis of direct labour-hours.

Required

1 Complete the standard cost card for a single surfboard.

2 Assume that the company uses the absorption costing approach to cost-plus pricing.

  (a) Compute the mark-up that the company needs on the surfboards to achieve an 18% ROI.

  (b) Using the mark-up you have computed, prepare a price quotation sheet for a single surfboard.

  (c) Assume, as stated, that the company is able to sell all of the surfboards that it can produce. Complete the profit statement for the first year of activity, and then compute the company's ROI for the year.

3 Assuming that direct labour is a variable cost, how many units would the company have to sell at the price you computed in Question 2 above to achieve the 18% ROI? How many units would have to be sold to just break even without achieving the 18% ROI?

P15–17 Economist's model of cost/volume price Time allowed: 45 minutes
The per unit average revenue (AR) and average cost (AC) functions for a business have been determined as follows:

$$AR = -x/100 + 29$$

$$AC = 15 + 3{,}000/x$$

where x is the level of output in units (between 200 and 1,200 units).

Required

1 Determine the functions for total revenue (TR) and total costs (TC), and demonstrate that the total profit function (TP) is given by:

$$TP = -x^2/100 + 14x - 3{,}000$$ *(4 marks)*

2 Using the total profit function (TP) in Question 1 above, draw a graph of the function (plotting units in 250 unit intervals between 200 and 1,200). *(5 marks)*

3 By equation, establish the roots of the total profit function. *(4 marks)*

4 Using differential calculus, establish the profit maximizing output. *(4 marks)*

5 Explain briefly the relationship between the roots of the total profit function and the profit maximizing output. Use the results to Questions 3 and 4 to demonstrate this relationship. *(3 marks)*

(Total = 20 marks)

ACCA Management Information, June 2000

P15–18 Economists' approach to pricing; absorption costing approach to costplus pricing Time allowed: 60 minutes
Software Solutions plc was started by two young software engineers to market SpamBlocker, a software application they had written that screens incoming email messages and eliminates unsolicited mass mailings. Sales of the software have been good at 50,000 units a month, but the company has been losing money as shown below:

Sales (50,000 units × £25 per unit)	£1,250,000
Variable cost (50,000 units × £6 per unit)	300,000
Contribution margin	950,000
Fixed expenses	960,000
Net operating profit (loss)	£(10,000)

The company's only variable cost is the £6 fee it pays to another company to reproduce the software on floppy diskettes, print manuals, and package the result in an attractive box for sale to consumers. Monthly fixed selling, general and administrative expenses total £960,000.

The company's marketing manager has been arguing for some time that the software is priced too high. She estimates that every 5% decrease in price will yield an 8% increase in unit sales. The marketing manager would like your help in preparing a presentation to the company's owners concerning the pricing issue.

Required

1 To help the marketing manager prepare for her presentation, she has asked you to fill in the blanks in the following table. The selling prices in the table were computed by successively decreasing the selling price by 5%. The estimated unit sales were computed by successively increasing the unit sales by 8%. For example, £23.75 is 5% less than £25.00 and 54,000 units is 8% more than 50,000 units.

Selling price	Estimated unit sales	Sales	Variable Cost	Fixed expenses	Net operating
£25.00	50,000	£1,250,000	£300,000	£960,000	£(10,000)
£23.75	54,000	£1,282,500	£324,000	£960,000	£(1,500)
£22.56	58,320	?	?	?	?
£21.43	62,986	?	?	?	?
£20.36	68,025	?	?	?	?
£19.34	73,467	?	?	?	?
£18.37	79,344	?	?	?	?
£17.45	85,692	?	?	?	?
£16.58	92,547	?	?	?	?
£15.75	99,951	?	?	?	?

2 Using the data from the table, construct a chart that shows the net operating profit as a function of the selling price. Put the selling price on the x-axis and the net operating profit on the y-axis. Using the chart, determine the approximate selling price at which net operating profit is maximized.

3 Compute the price elasticity of demand for the SpamBlocker software. Based on this calculation, what is the profit-maximizing price?

4 The owners have invested £400,000 in the company and feel that they should be earning at least 10% on these funds. If the absorption costing approach to pricing were used, what would be the target selling price based on the current sales of 50,000 units? What do you think would happen to the net operating profit of the company if this price were charged?

5 If the owners of the company are dissatisfied with the net operating profit and return on investment at the selling price you computed in Question 3 above, should they increase the selling price? Explain.

P15–19 Transfer price; well-defined intermediate market Time allowed: 45 minutes

Hrubec Products plc operates a Pulp Division that manufactures wood pulp for use in the production of various paper goods. Revenue and costs associated with a ton of pulp follow:

Selling price		£70
Less expenses:		
Variable	£42	
Fixed (based on a capacity of 50,000 tons per year)	18	60
Net profit		£10

Hrubec Products has just acquired a small company that manufactures paper cartons. This company will be treated as a division of Hrubec with full profit responsibility. The newly formed Carton Division is currently purchasing 5,000 tons of pulp per year from a supplier at a cost of £70 per ton, less a 10% quantity discount. Hrubec's managing director is anxious for the Carton Division to begin purchasing its pulp from the Pulp Division if an acceptable transfer price can be worked out.

Required

For Questions 1 and 2 below, assume that the Pulp Division can sell all its pulp to outside customers at the normal £70 price.

1 Are the managers of the Carton and Pulp Divisions likely to agree to a transfer price for 5,000 tons of pulp next year? Why or why not?

2 If the Pulp Division meets the price that the Carton Division is currently paying to its supplier and sells 5,000 tons of pulp to the Carton Division each year, what will be the effect on the profits of the Pulp Division, the Carton Division, and the company as a whole?

For Questions 3–6 below, assume that the Pulp Division is currently selling only 30,000 tons of pulp each year to outside customers at the stated £70 price.

3 Are the managers of the Carton and Pulp Divisions likely to agree to a transfer price for 5,000 tons of pulp next year? Why or why not?

4 Suppose that the Carton Division's outside supplier drops its price (net of the quantity discount) to only £59 per ton. Should the Pulp Division meet this price? Explain. If the Pulp Division does not meet the £59 price, what will be the effect on the profits of the company as a whole?

5 Refer to Question 4 above. If the Pulp Division refuses to meet the £59 price, should the Carton Division be required to purchase from the Pulp Division at a higher price for the good of the company as a whole?

6 Refer to Question 4 above. Assume that due to inflexible management policies, the Carton Division is required to purchase 5,000 tons of pulp each year from the Pulp Division at £70 per ton. What will be the effect on the profits of the company as a whole?

P15–20 Basic transfer pricing Time allowed: 60 minutes

Alpha and Beta are divisions within the same company. The managers of both divisions are evaluated based on their own division's return on investment (ROI). Assume the following information relative to the two divisions:

	Case			
	1	**2**	**3**	**4**
Alpha Division:				
Capacity in units	80,000	400,000	150,000	300,000
Number of units now being sold to outside customers on the intermediate market	80,000	400,000	100,000	300,000
Selling price per unit on the intermediate market	£30	£90	£75	£50
Variable costs per unit	18	65	40	26
Fixed costs per unit (based on capacity)	6	15	20	9
Beta Division:				
Number of units needed annually	5,000	30,000	20,000	120,000
Purchase price now being paid to an outside supplier	£27	£89	£75*	–

* Before any quantity discount.

Managers are free to decide if they will participate in any internal transfers. All transfer prices are negotiated.

Required

1 Refer to Case 1 above. Alpha Division can avoid £2 per unit in commissions on any sales to Beta Division. Will the managers agree to a transfer and if so, within what range will the transfer price be? Explain.

2 Refer to Case 2 above. A study indicates that Alpha Division can avoid £5 per unit in shipping costs on any sales to Beta Division.

(a) Would you expect any disagreement between the two divisional managers over what the transfer price should be? Explain.

(b) Assume that Alpha Division offers to sell 30,000 units to Beta Division for £88 per unit and that Beta Division refuses this price. What will be the loss in potential profits for the company as a whole?

3 Refer to Case 3 above. Assume that Beta Division is now receiving an 8% quantity discount from the outside supplier.

(a) Will the managers agree to a transfer? If so, what is the range within which the transfer price would be?

(b) Assume that Beta Division offers to purchase 20,000 units from Alpha Division at £60 per unit. If Alpha Division accepts this price, would you expect its ROI to increase, decrease, or remain unchanged? Why?

4 Refer to Case 4 above. Assume that Beta Division wants Alpha Division to provide it with 120,000 units of a different product from the one that Alpha Division is now producing. The new product would require £21 per unit in variable costs and would require that Alpha Division cut back production of its present product by 45,000 units annually. What is the lowest acceptable transfer price from Alpha Division's perspective?

P15–21 Divisional performance and transfer pricing Time allowed: 45 minutes

G&P plc (hereafter G&P) is a manufacturer of chemical-based products and is a major listed company on the London Stock Exchange. It has two separate operating divisions: the *retailing division* which sells a range of chemical-based cleaning products to supermarkets and the *industrial division* which sells bulk chemicals to other chemical companies for further processing. These divisions are both operated as investment centres.

The company also has three service divisions: marketing, information technology, and research and development. The service divisions charge their services to the two main operating divisions at full standard operating cost, thereby aiming to break even. The service divisions do not currently generate any revenue from other companies.

The Marketing Division

The directors of G&P have been pleased by the growth in company sales in recent years but they are unsure how much of this is due to the marketing division and how much is due to other factors, such as new products. Two further concerns have now arisen:

- The directors are uncertain how to measure the performance of the marketing division
- A number of key marketing personnel have left the company recently complaining of a lack of performance-based motivation and incentives.

Strategic solutions

The following two strategies have been proposed to the directors of G&P with respect to the marketing division:

Strategy 1 A change in the transfer pricing system would be introduced to make the marketing division a profit centre as a means of measuring performance and providing incentives.

Strategy 2 The marketing division would become a separate company, Marketo Ltd, with G&P holding a controlling equity stake. The new company would then be operated independently and thus be free to offer its services at commercial prices not only to G&P, but also to external clients. The G&P operating divisions would similarly be free to purchase marketing services from outside the company.

Under the existing transfer pricing system the budgeted summary profit and loss account for the year to 30 June 2002 for the marketing division would be as follows:

	£m	£m
Revenue		36
Variable costs	30	
Fixed costs		
Use of G&P premises	2	
Fixed overheads	4	
Profit		36
		Nil

The company is considering measuring performance using residual income. In this case the divisional capital employed would be £20 million and the annual rate of interest 10%. Interest has not been included in the above summary profit and loss account.

Required

1 Assess, and critically appraise, how performance measures can be used in respect of the marketing division in each of the following circumstances:

(a) The current system

(b) Strategy 1

(c) Strategy 2. *(11 marks)*

2 Evaluate the incentives that can be given to marketing division managers under each of the performance measures identified in Question 1. *(6 marks)*

3 Assume that Strategy 2 is implemented and that external sales of £10 million per year are expected by Marketo Ltd, priced on the basis of variable cost plus 25%.

Calculate the annual revenue that must be generated from sales with G&P to achieve an overall residual income for Marketo Ltd of £3 million. Assume for this purpose that fixed costs are £6 million and that the mark-up on variable costs in respect of sales to G&P is as per the original budget. *(5 marks)*

(Total = 22 marks)

ICAEW Business Management, September 2001

P15–22 Pricing Time allowed: 45 minutes

Just over two years ago, R Ltd was the first company to produce specific 'off-the-shelf' accounting software packages. The pricing strategy, decided on by the Managing Director, for the packages was to add a 50% mark-up to the budgeted full cost of the packages. The company achieved and maintained a significant market share and high profits for the first two years.

Budgeted information for the current year (Year 3) was as follows:

Production and sales	15,000 packages
Full cost	£400 per package

At a recent Board meeting, the Finance Director reported that although costs were in line with the budget for the current year, profits were declining. He explained that the full cost included £80 for fixed overheads. This figure had been calculated by using an overhead absorption rate based on labour-hours and the budgeted level of production which, he pointed out, was much lower than the current capacity of 25,000 packages.

The Marketing Director stated that competitors were beginning to increase their market share. He also reported the results of a recent competitor analysis which showed that when R Ltd announced its prices for the current year, the competitors responded by undercutting them by 15%. Consequently, he commissioned an investigation of the market. He informed the Board that the market research showed that at a price of £750 there would be no demand for the packages but for every £10 reduction in price the demand would increase by 1,000 packages. The Managing Director appeared to be unconcerned about the loss of market share and argued that profits could be restored to their former level by increasing the mark-up.

Note: If price $= a - bx$ then marginal revenue $= a - 2bx$

Required

1 Discuss the Managing Director's pricing strategy in the circumstances described above. Your appraisal must include a discussion of the alternative strategies that could have been implemented at the launch of the packages. *(10 marks)*

2

(a) Based on the data supplied by the market research, calculate the maximum annual profit that can be earned from the sale of the packages from year 3 onwards. *(6 marks)*

(b) A German computer software distribution company, L, which is interested in becoming the sole distributor of the accounting software packages, has now approached R Ltd. It has offered to purchase 25,000 accounting packages per annum at a fixed price of €930 per package. If R Ltd were to sell the packages to L, then the variable costs would be £300 per package. The current exchange rate is €1 = £0.60.

Draw a diagram to illustrate the sensitivity of the proposal from the German company to changes in the exchange rate and then state and comment on the minimum exchange rate needed for the proposal to be worth while. *(7 marks)*

3 R Ltd has signed a contract with L to supply the accounting packages. However, there has been a fire in one of the software manufacturing departments and a machine has been seriously damaged and requires urgent replacement.

The replacement machine will cost £1 million and R Ltd is considering whether to lease or buy the machine. A lease could be arranged under which R Ltd would pay £300,000 per annum for four years with each payment being made annually in advance. The lease payments would be an allowable expense for taxation purposes.

Corporation tax is payable at the rate of 30% per annum in two equal instalments: one in the year that profits are earned and the other in the following year. Writing-down allowances are allowed at 25% each year on a reducing balance basis. It is anticipated that the machine will have a useful economic life of four years, at the end of which there will be no residual value.

The after-tax cost of capital is 12%.

Evaluate the acquisition of the new machine from a financial viewpoint. *(7 marks)*

(Total = 30 marks)

CIMA Management Accounting – Decision-making, May 2003

P15–23 Time allowed: 50 minutes

X manufactures and sells audio-visual products. Over the last two years it has developed a DVD recorder (the DVDR). The company is currently deciding whether it should manufacture the DVDR itself or sell the design to another manufacturer for $3 million net of tax. Information relating to the in-house manufacture and sale of the DVDR is as follows.

Investment

The equipment needed to manufacture the DVDR would cost $5.12 million and could be sold for $1.12 million at the end of year four. The equipment would be depreciated in equal amounts over four years.

Working capital of $1.2 million will be needed.

Sales

The Managing Director of X thinks that a target costing based approach should be adopted. As a result of a market research survey that has already been conducted at a cost of $750,000, it has been decided that the selling price of the DVDR will be set, and held, at $180 per unit. It is thought that this price will be lower than that charged by competitors.

The annual unit sales forecasts for the DVDR are:

Year	Unit sales
1	190,000
2	200,000
3	150,000
4	100,000

It is thought that the DVDR will be obsolete in year 5 due to further advances in audiovisual technology.

Costs

The Management Accountant expects that the variable costs will reduce as a result of the impact of a learning curve. She has forecast the following relationship between the unit variable cost of a DVDR and the selling price:

Year	Variable cost/Selling price
1	105%
2	85%
3	60%
4	60%

The annual fixed costs directly attributable to the DVDR project are forecast to be:

Depreciation	$1.00 million
Manufacturing overhead	$0.90 million
Administration overhead	$0.10 million
Marketing and distribution overhead	$0.35 million

Taxation

X pays tax at 30%. This is payable at the end of the year after that in which profits are earned. An annual writing down allowance of 25% on a reducing balance basis will be available on the manufacturing equipment. The company has sufficient profits from other activities to offset any losses that may arise on the DVDR project.

Cost of capital

X has an after-tax cost of capital of 14% per year.

Required

1 Prepare calculations that show, from a financial perspective, whether X should manufacture the DVDR. State clearly your recommendation based upon your calculations. *(17 marks)*

2 Discuss any other factors that the management of X should consider before making the decision. *(6 marks)*

3

(a) Briefly explain 'target costing'. *(2 marks)*

(b) Identify and explain evidence from the scenario that X has adopted 'target costing'. *(5 marks)*

(Total = 30 marks)

CIMA Management Accounting – Decision-making, November 2004

P15–24 Pricing and transfer pricing Time allowed: 45 minutes

Part (a)

The Premier Cycle Company has two divisions: the Frame Division and the Assembly Division. One type of frame produced by the Frame Division is a high-quality carbon frame for racing bicycles. The Frame Division can sell the frames directly to external customers as 'frame only' or the frames can be transferred to the Assembly Division where they are assembled into complete racing bicycles.

Company policy

It is current company policy for the managers of each division to seek to maximize their own divisional profits. Consequently, the transfer price of a carbon frame is set by the manager of the Frame Division to be the same as the external selling price.

Frame Division

The relationship between the selling price of carbon frames and the annual quantity demanded by external customers is such that at a price of £4,000 there will be no demand, but demand will increase by 500 frames for every £250 decrease in price. The variable cost of producing a carbon frame is £1,000. The division has a maximum annual output of 10,000 frames and fixed costs of £2 million each year.

Assembly Division

The relationship between selling price and annual demand for a complete bicycle is such that at a price of £7,000 there will be no demand, but demand will increase by 300 bicycles for every £100 decrease in price. The Assembly Division has a maximum annual capacity of 30,000 assemblies and fixed costs of £1.2 million each year. The total variable costs of additional parts and assembling are £1,750 for each bicycle.

Note: If the relationship between Price (P) and quantity demanded (x) is represented by the equation $Pa - bx$ then Marginal Revenue (MR) will be given by $MR = a - 2bx$.

Required

1 Calculate the unit selling price of an assembled bicycle and the quantity that would be demanded given the current company policy. *(8 marks)*

2 Calculate the unit selling price, and quantity demanded, of an assembled bicycle that would maximize the profit of the Premier Cycle Company. *(4 marks)*

Total for requirement (a) = 12 marks)

Part (b)

Freezer Foods Ltd is a divisionalized company that specializes in the production of frozen foods. Each division is a profit centre. The Pizza Division produces frozen pizzas. In order to ensure a regular supply of suitable packaging, Freezer Foods Ltd recently acquired a company that produces high-quality packaging. This company is now the Box Division.

Bonus scheme

Freezer Foods Ltd will pay a fixed bonus to each Divisional Manager next year if he/she earns a minimum profit equivalent to at least 12% of his/her division's fixed costs.

Pizza Division

The manager of the Pizza Division has just won a fixed price contract to supply 7 million pizzas to a chain of food shops. This contract will fully utilize all of the capacity of the Pizza Division for the next year.

Budget details for the next year are:

Variable cost per pizza	£0.89 (this does *not* include the box)
Fixed costs	£4.50 million
Revenue	£11.55 million
Capacity	7 million pizzas

Box Division

Budget details for the Box Division for the next year are:

Variable production cost	£0.025 per box
Fixed costs	£1 million
External market demand	32 million boxes

Required

1 Calculate the price per box that the Box Division will want to charge the Pizza Division if this is to equal the budgeted external selling price. *(3 marks)*

2 Calculate the maximum price per box that the Pizza Division would be willing to pay. *(3 marks)*

3 Discuss the validity of using relevant costs as a basis to set transfer prices for internal performance measurement. You should use data from Freezer Foods Ltd to illustrate your answer. *(7 marks)*

Total for requirement (b) = 13 marks)

(Total = 25 marks)

CIMA Management Accounting – Decision-making, November 2004

Cases

C15–25 Pricing and ROI Time allowed: 70 minutes

Cinque Division produces three types of wooden container which it sells to external customers and transfers to other divisions within its own group of companies. Relevant budget information for the period ended 31 December 1999 on which the unit costs per container are based is as follows:

	Container type		
	Uno	**Due**	**Tre**
Total production/sales (units)	50,000	25,000	75,000
Direct material per container (sq. metres)	1.2	0.8	2.4
Material cost per sq. metre is £30			

Overhead costs for the division are:

	£ 000
Production conversion cost	6,000
Administration cost	1,800
Selling/marketing cost	1,000
Distribution cost	1,400

The current policy in Cinque Division is to compile unit cost per container on the basis of production cost plus distribution cost. Administration and selling/marketing costs are considered general divisional costs which are not product specific.

The budgeted unit costs per container are calculated as the sum of:

- Direct material cost
- Production conversion cost absorbed on the basis of an overall percentage on direct material cost
- Distribution cost as an overall average cost per container unit.

Product pricing is based on the achievement of an overall return on capital employed of 15% (ignore taxation). A single mark-up percentage applicable to all container types is applied to product specific unit cost in order to achieve this ROCE level. The resulting selling prices form the basis of selling and marketing strategy. Capital employed is taken as £16,800,000.

Required

1 Prepare calculations which show the detailed unit cost and selling price calculations for each container type. *(9 marks)*

2 Activity-based unit costs are prepared for the period ended 31 December 1999. These differ from the original unit costs in a number of cost areas. The relevant amended elements of product specific unit costs are:

	Uno	**Due**	**Tre**
	£	**£**	**£**
Production conversion cost	42.81	30.69	41.23
Distribution cost	2.40	8.00	14.40
Selling/marketing cost (see note)	1.20	6.00	1.20

Note: 30% of the budgeted selling and marketing cost has been identified as product specific. This has been charged to container types after taking into account relevant activities. The balance of selling and marketing cost is still considered a divisional cost.

(a) Prepare a summary which compares original and activity-based information per container for cost, profit and selling price for each type of container, where selling prices remain as calculated in above. *(6 marks)*

(b) A substantial proportion of sales of Uno are transfers to other divisions within the group. This business is obtained in competition with potential external suppliers. In addition, Cinque Division is experiencing problems in retaining the level of market which it has budgeted for Tre. Using this additional information together with the original versus activity-based unit cost/profit/price analysis, suggest possible action by management for *each* of the three types of container in order to improve divisional and group profitability. *(6 marks)*

3 Cinque Division has a proposed strategy to redesign container Uno. There is some controversy as to the effect of the redesign on the number of cuts required per unit, which is seen as a key cost driver in the production process and also on the quantity of direct material which will be required per product unit. Probabilities have been estimated for the level at which these key variables will occur. Number of cuts and quantity of material are independent of each other. The estimates are as follows:

Direct material per unit (sq. m)	Probability	Number of cuts per unit	Probability
1.6	0.3	40	0.3
1.2	0.4	35	0.2
0.8	0.3	25	0.5

(a) Prepare a summary which shows the range of possible activity-based unit cost outcomes for Uno showing the combined probability of each outcome, using Appendix 1 as appropriate. *(6 marks)*

(b) Comment on the likely impact of management's attitude to risk on their decision whether or not to implement the redesign strategy for Uno on financial grounds. You should include the calculation of, and comment on, the expected value of the product specific cost for Uno in your answer. *(8 marks)*

Appendix 1

Two Way data table to monitor the effect on the activity-based product unit cost for product Uno of a proposed redesign. This may affect the direct material per unit – range 1.6 to 0.8 sq. m – and the number of cuts required – range 25 to 50:

		Number of cuts				
		25	**30**	**35**	**40**	**50**
Material required (sq. m)	1.6	94.31	95.38	96.30	97.10	98.42
	1.4	87.00	88.08	89.00	89.80	91.12
	1.2	79.62	80.69	81.61	82.41	83.73
	1.0	72.14	73.21	74.13	74.93	76.25
	0.8	64.56	65.63	66.55	67.35	68.67

(35 marks)

ACCA Information for Control and Decision making, June 1999

C15–26 Transfer pricing; divisional performance Time allowed: 45 minutes

Weller Industries is a decentralized organization with six divisions. The company's Electrical Division produces a variety of electrical items, including an X52 electrical fitting. The Electrical Division (which is operating at capacity) sells this fitting to its regular customers for £7.50 each; the fitting has a variable manufacturing cost of £4.25.

The company's Brake Division has asked the Electrical Division to supply it with a large quantity of X52 fittings for only £5 each. The Brake Division, which is operating at 50% of capacity, will put the fitting into a brake unit that it will produce and sell to a large commercial airline manufacturer. The cost of the brake unit being built by the Brake Division follows:

Purchased parts (from outside vendors)	£22.50
Electrical fitting X52	5.00
Other variable costs	14.00
Fixed overhead and administration	8.00
Total cost per brake unit	£49.50

Although the £5 price for the X52 fitting represents a substantial discount from the regular £7.50 price, the manager of the Brake Division believes that the price concession is necessary if his division is to get the contract for the airplane brake units. He has heard 'through the grapevine' that the airplane manufacturer plans to reject his bid if it is more than £50 per brake unit. Thus, if the Brake Division is forced to pay the regular £7.50 price for the X52 fitting, it will either not get the contract or it will suffer a substantial loss at a time when it is already operating at only 50% of capacity. The manager of the Brake Division argues that the price concession is imperative to the well-being of both his division and the company as a whole.

Weller Industries uses return on investment (ROI) and profits in measuring divisional performance.

Required

1 Assume that you are the manager of the Electrical Division. Would you recommend that your division supply the X52 fitting to the Brake Division for £5 each as requested? Why or why not? Show all computations.

2 Would it be to the economic advantage of the company as a whole for the Electrical Division to supply the fittings to the Brake Division if the airplane brakes can be sold for £50? Show all computations, and explain your answer.

3 In principle, should it be possible for the two managers to agree to a transfer price in this particular situation? If so, within what range would that transfer price lie?

4 Discuss the organizational and manager behaviour problems, if any, inherent in this situation. What would you advise the company's managing director to do in this situation?

(CMA, adapted)

C15–27 ROI versus RI. International Transfer pricing and taxation Time allowed: 90 minutes

The NAW Group manufactures healthcare products which it markets both under its own brand and in unbranded packs. The group has adopted a divisional structure. Division O, which is based in a country called Homeland, manufactures three pharmaceutical products for sale in the domestic market. Budgeted information in respect of Division O for the year ending 31 May 2005 is as follows:

Sales information:

Product		'Painfree'	'Digestisalve'	'Awaysafe'
Sales packs (000's)	NAW Brand	5,000	15,000	15,000
	Unbranded	15,000	20,000	–
Selling price per pack (£)	NAW Brand	2·40	4·80	8·00
Unbranded		1·20	3·60	–

Cost of sales information:

Variable manufacturing costs per pack:	Material and conversion costs	Packaging costs
	£	£
'Painfree'		
NAW Brand	0·85	0·15
Unbranded	0·85	0·05
'Digestisalve'		
NAW Brand	1·85	0·25
Unbranded	1·85	0·15
'Awaysafe'		
NAW Brand	2·80	0·40

Other relevant information is as follows:

1 Each of the three products is only sold in tablet form in a single pack-size which contains 12 tablets. During the year to 31 May 2005 it is estimated that a maximum of 780 million tablets could be manufactured. All three products are manufactured by the same process therefore management have the flexibility to alter the product-mix. Management expect that sales volume will increase by 10% in the year ending 31 May 2006.

2 Advertising expenditure has been committed to under a fixed term contract with a leading consultancy and is therefore regarded as a fixed cost by management. Advertising expenditure in respect of the turnover of branded products in the year ending 31 May 2005 is apportioned as follows:

Product:	Advertising expenditure as a percentage of turnover
Painfree	5%
Digestisalve	10%
Awaysafe	12%

3 The average capital employed in the year to 31 May 2005 is estimated to be £120 million. The company's cost of capital is 10%.

4 The management of the NAW Group use both return on investment (ROI) and residual income (RI) to assess divisional performance.

5 Budgeted fixed overheads (excluding advertising) for Division O during the year ended 31 May 2005 amount to £81,558,000.

6 There is no planned change in manufacturing capacity between the years ended 31 May 2005 and 31 May 2006.

7 Ignore taxation for all calculations other than those in part (c).

Required

(a) (i) Prepare a statement of budgeted profit in respect of Division O for the year ending 31 May 2005.

Your answer should show the annual budgeted contribution of each branded and unbranded product.

Calculate BOTH the residual income (RI) and Return on Investment (ROI) for Division O.

(7 marks)

(ii) Name and comment on THREE factors, other than profit maximization, that the management of the NAW Group ought to consider when deciding upon the product mix strategy for the year ending 31 May 2006. *(3 marks)*

(iii) Suggest THREE reasons why the management of the NAW Group may have chosen to use residual income (RI) in addition to return on investment (ROI) in order to assess divisional performance. *(3 marks)*

Division L of the NAW Group is based in Farland. The management of Division L purchases products from various sources, including other divisions of the group, for subsequent resale. The manager of Division L has requested two alternative quotations from Division O in respect of the year ended 31 May 2005:

1. Quotation 1 – Purchasing five million packs of 'Awaysafe'.
2. Quotation 2 – Purchasing nine million packs of 'Awaysafe'.

The management of the NAW Group has made a decision that a minimum of 15 million packs of 'Awaysafe' must be reserved for Homeland customers in order to ensure that customer demand can be satisfied and the product's competitive position is further established in the Homeland market.

The management of the NAW Group is willing, if necessary, to reduce the budgeted sales quantities of other products in order to satisfy the requirements of Division L. They wish, however, to minimize the loss of contribution to the group.

The management of Division L is aware of the availability of another product that competes with 'Awaysafe' which could be purchased at a local currency price that is equivalent to £5.50 per pack. The NAW Group's policy is that all divisions are allowed the autonomy to set transfer prices and purchase from whatever sources they choose. The management of Division O intend to use market price less 30% as the basis for each of the quotations.

(b) (i) From the viewpoint of the NAW Group, comment on the appropriateness of the decision by the management of Division O to use an adjusted market price as a basis for the preparation of Quotations 1 and 2, and the implications of the likely decision by the management of Division L. *(3 marks)*

(ii) Recommend the prices that should be quoted by Division O for 'Awaysafe', in respect of Quotations 1 and 2, which will ensure that the profitability of the NAW Group as a whole is not adversely affected by the decision of the management of Division L. *(3 marks)*

(iii) Discuss the proposition that transfer prices should be based on opportunity costs.

(4 marks)

(c) (i) After much internal discussion concerning Quotation 2 by the management of the NAW Group, Division O is not prepared to supply nine million packs of 'Awaysafe' to Division L at a price lower than market price less 30%. All profits earned in Farland are subject to taxation at a rate of 20%. Division O pays tax in Homeland at a rate of 40% on all profits.

Advise the management of the NAW Group whether the management of Division L should be directed to purchase 'Awaysafe' from Division O, or purchase a similar product from a local supplier. Supporting calculations should be provided. *(6 marks)*

(ii) Identify and comment on the major issues that can arise with regard to transfer pricing in a multinational organisztion. *(5 marks)*

(d) Evaluate the extent to which the management of the NAW Group could make use of the product life cycle model in the determination of its product pricing strategy. *(6 marks)*

(Total = 40 marks)

ACCA Performance Management, June 2004

Endnotes

1 Harris (1999).

2 The term 'ln()' is the natural log function. You can compute the natural log of any number using the LN or lnx key on your calculator. For example, ln(0.85) = 20.1625.

This formula assumes that the price elasticity of demand is constant. This occurs when the relation between the selling price, p, and the unit sales, q, can be expressed in the following form: $\ln(q) = a = \varepsilon_d \ln(p)$. Even if this is not precisely true, the formula provides a useful way to estimate a product's real price elasticity.

3 The estimated change in unit sales should take into account competitors' responses to a price change.

4 The formula assumes that (a) the price elasticity of demand is constant; (b) Total cost = Total fixed cost = Variable cost per unit × q; and (c) the price of the product has no effect on the sales or costs of any other product. The formula can be derived using calculus.

5 Kimes (1989).

6 Harris (1999).

7 The exhibit is adapted from Abdallah (1988).

8 Davies (2002).

9 Sikka (2002). For other examples, see AABA website, www.visar.csustan.edu/aaba/home.htm

10 Brick (2001).

Part IV
Value metrics and performance management in a strategic context

Chapter 16

Value-based management and strategic management accounting

Learning objectives

After studying Chapter 16, you should be able to:

1. Define the concepts of strategy and strategic management accounting
2. Understand the impact of corporate strategy on management accounting
3. Understand the relationship between profit-planning and value-based management
4. Understand some basic strategic models and their relationship with management accounting techniques
5. Examine the impact of lean technologies
6. Understand how a balanced scorecard fits together and how it supports a company's strategy
7. Consider the impact of emergent strategies and organizational learning on management accounting

Concepts in Context

The term strategic management accounting (SMA) has been used to describe the process of 'provision and analysis of management accounting data about a business and its competitors for use in developing and monitoring business strategy'.[1] We may illustrate the basic ideas of SMA by looking at one of the leading retailers in the United Kingdom, Tesco, which has tailored its key performance indicators to the economics of its business. For example, rather than maximize EVA, Tesco has realized that its main fixed assets are its stores. With this type of asset base, the company aims to reduce the cost of building good quality new stores through strategic partnering with construction companies. In order to check its market positioning, the company is constantly monitoring the prices of its merchandise relative to the prices charged by its main competitors. As well as promoting customer loyalty, it uses its store card as a database for targeting the specific needs of individual customers as revealed through their purchase patterns. It also keeps a close eye on non-financial indicators such as the length of queues at the check-outs.

In this chapter we will review both short- and long-term financial planning but in the context of *strategic choice*. **Strategic choice** means that companies can *choose* which industries and products they want to compete in but it also means that different companies in the *same* industry may decide to adopt different strategies with quite different implications for management accounting and control. For example, a company's strategy may determine whether management will be concentrating on a tight control of costs, maintaining quality or generating new product ideas.

As more and more reliance is placed on bought-in goods and services, a higher proportion of costs are generated by a firm's suppliers, which suggests that major improvements in cost, quality and innovation are potentially available through the effective management of the firm's supply chain. In *strategic* as opposed to *traditional* management accounting, there is a recognition that managers may have some freedom to choose which industry they operate in, which technology is used and how the organization is structured. Thus, rather than passively adapting to given competitive, technological and organizational circumstances, **strategic management accounting (SMA)** helps managers make choices through information support. Strategic management accounting is also concerned with the *implementation* of strategies by setting up control systems that drive through the chosen strategies. For example, if a company wishes to pursue a low-cost strategy then traditional budgetary control may help implementation. However, few companies compete on price alone so additional performance measures may be non-financial, such as delivery or queueing time.

As described in this chapter's 'Concepts in context' feature, Tesco's approach in linking its goals and its management information systems demonstrates many of the principles of SMA. The company has decided how it is going to compete, reviewed its internal and external operations and chosen key performance indicators that enable it to monitor the development of its chosen business model. The search for data is driven by decision needs rather than by what is simply easily available.

Finally, in some businesses, strategy is seen as involving **organizational learning** rather than as a top-down, centralized process. In this business model, management accounting may be used as part of an interactive communication process both within the organization and between the organization and its customers and suppliers.

The chapter begins by showing how the techniques developed in Chapters 2–15 can be used to plan and control profit and shareholder value. We will then consider the limitations of this framework and argue that these techniques can be further enhanced by putting them in a strategic context. While traditional management accounting focuses on the analysis of existing activities, with SMA there is a concern with the analysis of data about the organization in relation to its competitors in order to monitor and develop business options. Performance indicators should be relative, with a continuous recognition of *rivalry* with competitors. For example, market share has intrinsic value because a high market share may reflect weaker competition. As in a game of chess, there is a need not only to develop your own strategy but also to understand the strategy of your opponent. In many instances, strategic management accounting may involve new applications of existing approaches rather than new techniques. For example, strategic management accounting that attempts to measure competitors' or suppliers' costs may well use the same sort of techniques that we have already covered in the earlier parts of the book. Yet the context of the cost analysis will be different because strategic management seeks to establish *relative* market positions and *relative* costs.

Profit planning with a given industry and product: cost structure and business orientation

3 LEARNING OBJECTIVE

Traditionally, management accounting is presented as a matter of fitting cost systems to particular business environments and technological tasks. As we saw in Chapters 3 and 4, process or job costing systems are applied according to batch sizes and the nature of the product. We may decide that a given cost structure of a business will help to determine its profit planning orientation as discussed in our work on flexible budgeting in Chapter 13. The first steps to profit planning can be based on a combination of the techniques introduced in earlier chapters – particularly, *cost behaviour, CVP analysis, flexible budgeting* and *pricing* as shown in Exhibit 16.1. Thus cost behaviour analysis may help determine whether a business is 'market-oriented' or 'cost-oriented'.[2] If, for example, the business has a high proportion of fixed costs relative to variable costs, then it may be seen as being 'market-oriented' because, as CVP analysis indicates, it has to achieve high levels of capacity utilization in order to break even.

Profit planning techniques not only may help the choice of business orientation but they also lend themselves to the possibility of 'what-if' sensitivity exercises. For example, given a firm's cost and revenue structure, how would the firm's profits change with a 10% cut in price or 10% cut in fixed costs? As shown in Chapter 15, techniques such as *yield management* may also be used as they are in the airline and hotel industries, to segment the market and offer different prices to different segments at different booking times. Finally, the practice of flexible budgeting ensures that variance analysis is based on variable levels of activity rather than a single estimate as with static budgeting.

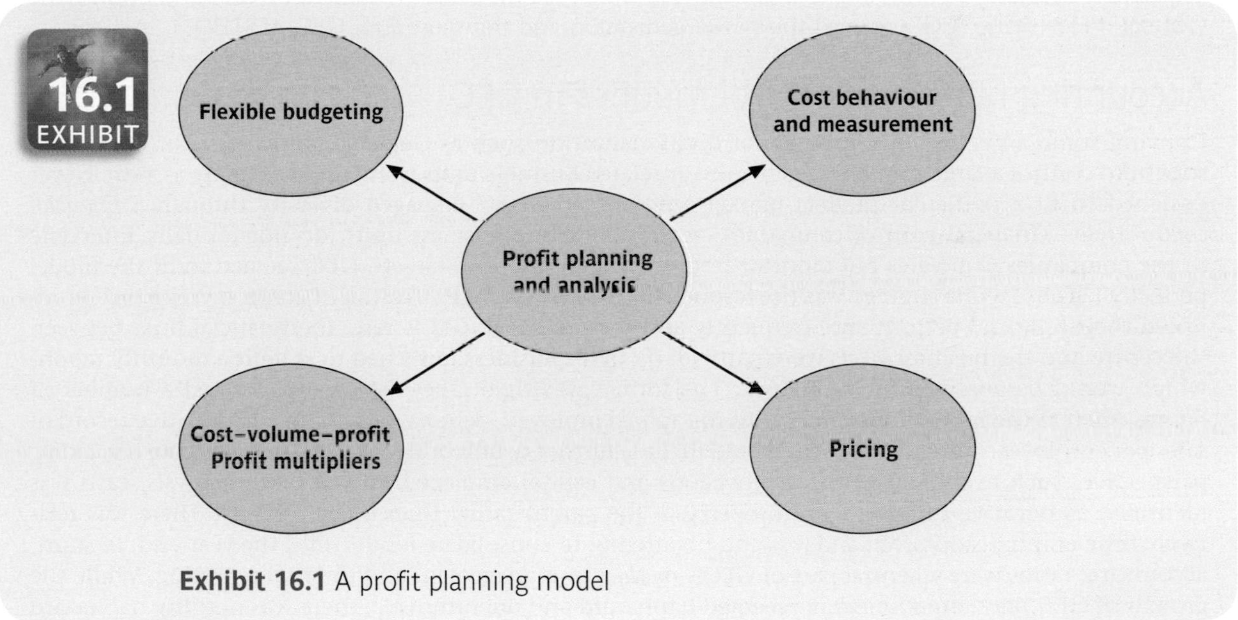

Exhibit 16.1 A profit planning model

Value-based management

Useful as they are for short-term decision making there are a number of limitations to the techniques in the basic profit planning model. First, short-term profit increases may be made at the expense of long-term profit.[3] Second, there is no analysis of the use of capital resources. Indeed, from a *shareholder perspective*, a 'company only makes a real or economic profit after it has repaid the cost of capital that was used to generate it'.[4] Third, the approach is inward- rather than outward-looking – for example, how would the firm's competitors react to a 10% cut in price? Is it realistic to just assume that they will not also respond with similar cuts? Finally, a focus on profit by definition limits the applicability of the approach to for-profit organizations and neglects the interests of other *stakeholders* such as consumers, employees or regulators.

The criticisms that profit-seeking is short-termist and ignores the cost and allocation of capital have been explicitly addressed in for-profit firms by focusing on the goal of increasing shareholder wealth through the application of *value-based management*. In its narrowest form, **value-based management (VBM)** focuses on how to increase a shareholder wealth metric such as *residual income* (see Chapter 14) or *net present value* (see Chapter 10) through the identification and management of value-drivers.[5] In its wider form, value-based management is 'an integrated framework for measuring and managing businesses, with the explicit objective of creating superior long-term value for shareholders'.[6] In this chapter, we prefer to adopt the narrower definition of VBM as it enables us to distinguish between VBM and SMA with the latter emphasizing the importance of *competitor analysis*. Indeed, as our *Management accounting in action* section illustrates below, companies that have embraced VBM have not always analysed their competitors' actions very carefully.

IN ACTION

Management accounting in action: a lesson from business history

Arnold Weinstock became GEC's Managing Director in 1963 and was behind the big expansion and diversification with the take-over of Associated Electrical Industries (AEI) in 1967 and, in 1968, with the merger with English Electric. At this point, GEC was the fourth largest industrial company in the UK and the second largest electrical company in the world outside the USA. GEC continued to expand and diversify with the acquisition of Yarrow Shipbuilders in 1974 and Avery in 1979. The late 1980s witnessed further mergers and joint ventures, with the creation of GPT by GEC and Plessey in 1988, and the joint acquisition of Plessey by GEC and Siemens the following year. An equal investment by GEC and Compagnie General d'Electricitie (CGE) formed the power generation and transport arm, GEC ALSTHOM, in 1989.

Accounting ratios and control routines in GEC

Copying some aspects of the pioneers of divisionalization such as General Motors and Du Pont, GEC sought to control a large number of generally unrelated business units (sometimes as many as 140). Never designed to fit a particular product-market environment, GEC managed diversity through a *financial control style*.[7] Financial control companies create standalone business units, do not formally intervene in the companies' strategies but monitor results through financial targets. GEC seemed to fit the model perfectly because while strategy was the responsibility of the various investment centres, Weinstock monitored their financial performance frequently and personally. In GEC's case, the financial links between the centre and the business units were particularly tight. Business units had to submit a monthly report, which would be analysed by Weinstock. The format was rigid. The first page contained a number of figures, such as the ratio of sales and profit to capital employed, debtors' ratios and a cumulative record of sales per employee. Subsequent pages would include further details of significance in a *financial accounting* perspective, such as a breakdown of provisions and capital employed. In the latter analysis, cash was identified as negative funding – the property of the parent rather than the subsidiary! There was relatively little emphasis on profit and loss and no attempt to consolidate results until the year-end. In short, accounting ratios were a central part of GEC's *routines* of management and internal reporting. While the growth of GEC may sometimes have seemed haphazard and opportunistic, there was nothing haphazard about the 'Weinstock system' based on financial ratios and a monthly internal reporting system.

Marconi (1996–2001) boom …

The retirement of Weinstock and changes in some major customers in the defence and telecom industries plus an emerging preference in the City for focused companies led to a change in management style that affected both the nature and corporate role of its management accounting. The appointment of George Simpson as Chief Executive together with a number of other strategic appointments was accompanied by a new management ethos of 'GEC to be no. 1 or no. 2 in the world in particular industries'. As a symbol of the policy of focus, GEC changed its name to Marconi, a name reminiscent of the pioneer of radio.[8]

The new strategic direction involved different ways of working. In particular, the old source of expansion through largely unrelated acquisition had been abandoned. The company was seeking organic growth and acquisition that would enhance its market and technological capability. Acquisitions were intended to be integrated to fully exploit cross-selling and technological synergies.

Other changes were:

- Globalization, with acquisitions in Europe, North America and the Asia–Pacific region.
- Integration of acquisitions. Financial reports that were sent to the group finance office were arrayed in a matrix structure so that items such as sales, profit and loss, and so on, could be viewed from both product and regional perspectives.
- The introduction of an EVA-style value management system that signalled a continuous awareness of the company's stock market performance.
- More outsourcing, with a new emphasis on process and multi-functional teams in supply chain management.
- More diversity in reporting and decision-making innovations. In particular, non-financial performance indicators were reported directly to the finance group by a specially designated Performance Improvement function.

... and bust!

Marconi's rise and fall was not untypical of many companies in the global telecom sector. From a share price that peaked at over £12 in 2000, a series of profit warnings culminated in huge losses and a collapse in the share price to a few pence in 2002. The difference between Marconi and many other high-tech bubble companies was its transformation from a cash-rich conglomerate as GEC to a company that is now non-existent as an independent business entity.

There are a number of points to note in this case. It could be argued that it illustrates the limitations of the narrow view of value-based management which focuses on a shareholder value metric such as residual income but does little to indicate how value is to be created or sustained. GEC/Marconi *did* change from ROI to value-based management and it *did* introduce some improved operational innovations in its business processes and supply chain. But as the case demonstrates so dramatically, it is no good being world class at producing a product when the market for that product is so overcrowded with competitors! With the benefit of hindsight, the company's adoption of management innovations was incomplete. In particular, the *strategic management accounting information* that could monitor developments in the industry as a whole was either not collected or was not analysed in a systematic way.

The next section of the chapter will show how SMA can be used to help to *choose, implement* and *monitor* a company's strategy. It will introduce a number of ways of developing strategy and some new metrics, non-financial as well as financial, in order to implement and monitor strategy. As will be shown in Chapter 17, the basic ideas of SMA and scorecards can also be applied to not-for-profit organizations and accommodate social and environmental objectives.

Some basic techniques of strategic management accounting

SMA has an orientation towards the firm's environment. The relevant environment may be in its value chain, that is, its 'upstream' relations with suppliers and 'downstream' relations with its customers. The other relevant environment is its competitive position relative to both existing and potential competitors. Its competitive position will not just depend on price but on a **marketing mix**.

Sometimes SMA will use existing information and sometimes new information will be sought. For example, the increased emphasis on marketing may involve the use of techniques such as **attribute costing** that costs product attributes that appeal to customers, using brand value as a basis for managerial decisions and measuring the costs of quality. The competitive position is monitored through competitor cost assessment through estimates of competitors' costs based on an appraisal of facilities, technology, economies of scale, market share, volume, unit costs and return on sales. Strategic management accounting is also concerned with the long run through the use of target and **life-cycle costing**[9] that looks at the costs incurred throughout the life of a product as it goes through various stages such as development and full production.

SMA and the concept of strategic positioning

Both the choice of strategic options and the ongoing search for strategic information may be informed by a variety of corporate strategy models. In short, a further development of SMA integrates the more outward and forward-looking aspects of the strategic intelligence approach with some well-known models of strategic choice.

Some strategic choice models involve deciding on a company's *strategic position*. For example, following Miles and Snow,[10] should the company be a **defender** concentrating on reducing costs and/or improving quality, a **prospector** continually searching for market opportunities or an analyser which combines the defender and prospector positions? Or, following Michael Porter,[11] should the company concentrate on **cost leadership** (aiming to be the lowest-cost producer in an industry) or **product differentiation** (maintain a price premium based on superior product quality)? Porter argues that: '(T)he worst strategic error is to be *stuck in the middle* or to try simultaneously to pursue all the strategies. This is a recipe for strategic mediocrity and below-average performance, because pursuing all strategies simultaneously means that a firm is not able to achieve any of them because of their inherent contradictions.'[12]

The implications for management accounting of these positional strategies could be that a company that seeks cost leadership may use standard costing with flexible budgets for manufacturing cost control. With product cost being the key input to pricing decisions, it may also analyse costs of competitors in order to review its positioning. If the company is a differentiator then traditional costing may be less important, and more attention is paid to new product development and marketing expenditures.

Porter's generic strategy model may be linked to another of his innovations, the concept of the value chain. The **value chain**,[13] which is illustrated in Exhibit 16.2, consists of the major business functions that add value to a company's products and services. All these functions, from research and development through product design, manufacturing, marketing, distribution and customer service, are required to bring a product or service to the customer and generate revenues.

Exhibit 16.2 Business functions making up the value chain

With value-chain analysis, the aim is to find linkages between value-creating activities, which result in lower costs and/or enhanced differentiation. John Shank's *strategic cost management*[14] approach shows how Porter's ideas on strategic positioning and gaining competitive advantage can have an impact on management accounting. Shank advocates a cost-driver analysis, which suggests that costs are driven by *structural* and *executional* factors. **Structural drivers** consider factors such as scale, scope, experience, technology and complexity, while **executional drivers** include factors such as work force involvement, quality management capacity utilization, plant lay-out efficiency, product configuration effectiveness, and exploitation of linkages.

Strategic investment appraisal: investment appraisal with strategic 'bolt-ons'?

In Chapter 10, we considered the various techniques of investment appraisal such as net present value and internal rate of return. In principle, many strategic decisions, such as acquisitions or major marketing initiatives, could be analysed using these techniques by estimating and discounting future net cash flows and choosing the option that seems to give the highest return or largest NPV. As we also saw in Chapter 10, the risks attached to the various options may also be analysed using mathematical techniques. Yet some advocates of more strategic approaches have argued that the conventional investment appraisal approach may set up business problems in a misleading way with an overemphasis on financial calculation leaving strategic issues either neglected or treated in an *ad hoc*, 'bolt-on' manner. John Shank argues that the NPV model follows four steps:

Step 1	Identifying spending proposals
Step 2	Quantitative analysis of incremental cash flows
Step 3	Qualitative issues that cannot be fitted into NPV are then treated in an *ad hoc* manner
Step 4	Decision – *Yes/No.*

According to Shank, in conventional capital budgeting/investment appraisals, *Step 1* is hardly analysed since the investment proposals just appear out of thin air. *Step 2,* in contrast, gets a great deal of attention with elaborate considerations of relevant cash flows and sophisticated treatments of risk. *Step 3* is a 'step-child' concerned with 'soft-issues' that cannot be handled in *Step 2*. *Step 4*, the decision, *then generally flows out of Step 2.*

Shank[15] argues that the finance framework sets up strategic problems in a misleading way and argues that pure NPV analysis misses the richness of real business problems and is often merely set up to rationalize a prior decision. He illustrates the point with a case study, *Mavis Machines.*

The Mavis Machines case

Mavis Machine shop is a small metal working company producing drill bits for oil exploration. At present, the shop has four large manual lathes each operated by a skilled worker. The question facing the Managing Director of Mavis Machines is whether the company should install a numerically controlled lathe to replace all manual lathes. The numerical lathe would require only one operator but with different skills in computerized automation.

The decision can be set up using an NPV model and produces a very high rate of internal rate of return, as shown in Exhibit 16.3.

The main cash savings stem from the need for fewer workers. However, other significant savings can be made in the net cost of the initial investment because of the healthy trade-in value of the relatively modern manual lathes. Indeed, 60% of the attractiveness of the project comes from the scrap value of the old machines, which suggests that the previous replacement decision might have been faulty. In an NPV approach other factors such as *flexibility, marketing* and *corporate image* are treated in rather an *ad hoc* manner.

An alternative strategic approach suggests a different perspective on the choice. Indeed when explicit strategic models are used to explore the issues the emphasis on a positive NPV in the financial analysis is eclipsed by other factors. *Competitive analysis* suggests that as a small machine shop, Mavis is best positioned as a *niche* player rather than a cost leader. The manual lathes and the skilled operators give it more product flexibility and greater security than one numerical lathe. Its strength lies in its flexibility to vary its products and sources of raw material. *Value chain analysis* suggested that it would lose both buyer and seller power because it would be more dependent only on those suppliers that could meet stringent quality requirements and would be more dependent on a single customer. There were also questions concerning the ease of maintenance of the new machine and the likely impact that firing eight workers out of a small workforce would have on morale and the firm's local reputation.

Strategic investment appraisal: an iterative model

Does the criticism of NPV by Shank and others mean that the material in Chapter 10 is of limited relevance for strategic decisions? Not according to Tomkins and Carr,[16] who suggest that strategic investment decisions may be modelled to include both financial and strategic analysis as shown in Exhibit 16.4. They suggest that a three-stage approach is followed:

1. The firm decides which markets to be in, by assessing both customer requirements and the relative ability of rivals to meet them. The firm will generate a number of investment possibilities based on product attributes related to volume of sales.
2. Analysis of the value chain assesses the means by which the attributes of the product can be delivered. This analysis will review possible suppliers and distributors as part of an iterative process to check on performance throughout the whole product life cycle.
3. The first two steps may then be modelled in terms of a cost and attribute driver analysis to see if the attributes can be delivered at an acceptable profit. The process is iterative in that a first assessment

Net Investment

Purchase price		$680,000
Less:		
Trade-in value of old machines		(240,000)
Tax saving from trade-in (46%)		(108,000)
Book value	476,000	
Selling price	240,000	
Loss on resale	236,000	
Investment tax credit (10%)		(68,000)
Net		**($263,400)**
Annual cash savings		
Labour – six operators (3/shift × 2 shifts) × $20,800 each		($124,800)
Factory space savings (no difference in cash flows)		0
Other cash savings (supplies, maintenance and power)		20,000
Total, pre-tax		$144,800
Less additional taxes (46%)		(60,600)
Cash saved – pre-tax	144,800	
Additional depreciation	(13,000)*	
Additional taxable income	131,800	
Annual after tax cash savings		**$84,200**
(ignoring inflation in savings in future years)		

*Old depreciation = $590–$20/15 = $38,000

New depreciation = $680–$68/12 = $51,000

Difference = $13,000

Summary of cash flows*

Period 0 (263,400) 12 year IRR = 32 + %, real

Periods 1–12 $84,200

*Ignoring the minor impact from the lost salvage values in year 12.

Shank, J. 1996. 'Analyzing technology investments – from NPV to Strategic Cost Management', *Management Accounting Research*, 7, 185–97.

Exhibit 16.3 Summary of the quantitative analysis of the automation project in Mavis Machines

may suggest unacceptable low levels of profitability. The next assessment may then consider whether the profitability can be improved through piecemeal cost savings or whether existing delivery systems must be changed more radically through process re-engineering. Tomkins and Carr call this search for improvement, a process of 'probing' that uses discounted cash flow analysis but which also draws on an array of market, technological and other data.[17]

16.4 EXHIBIT

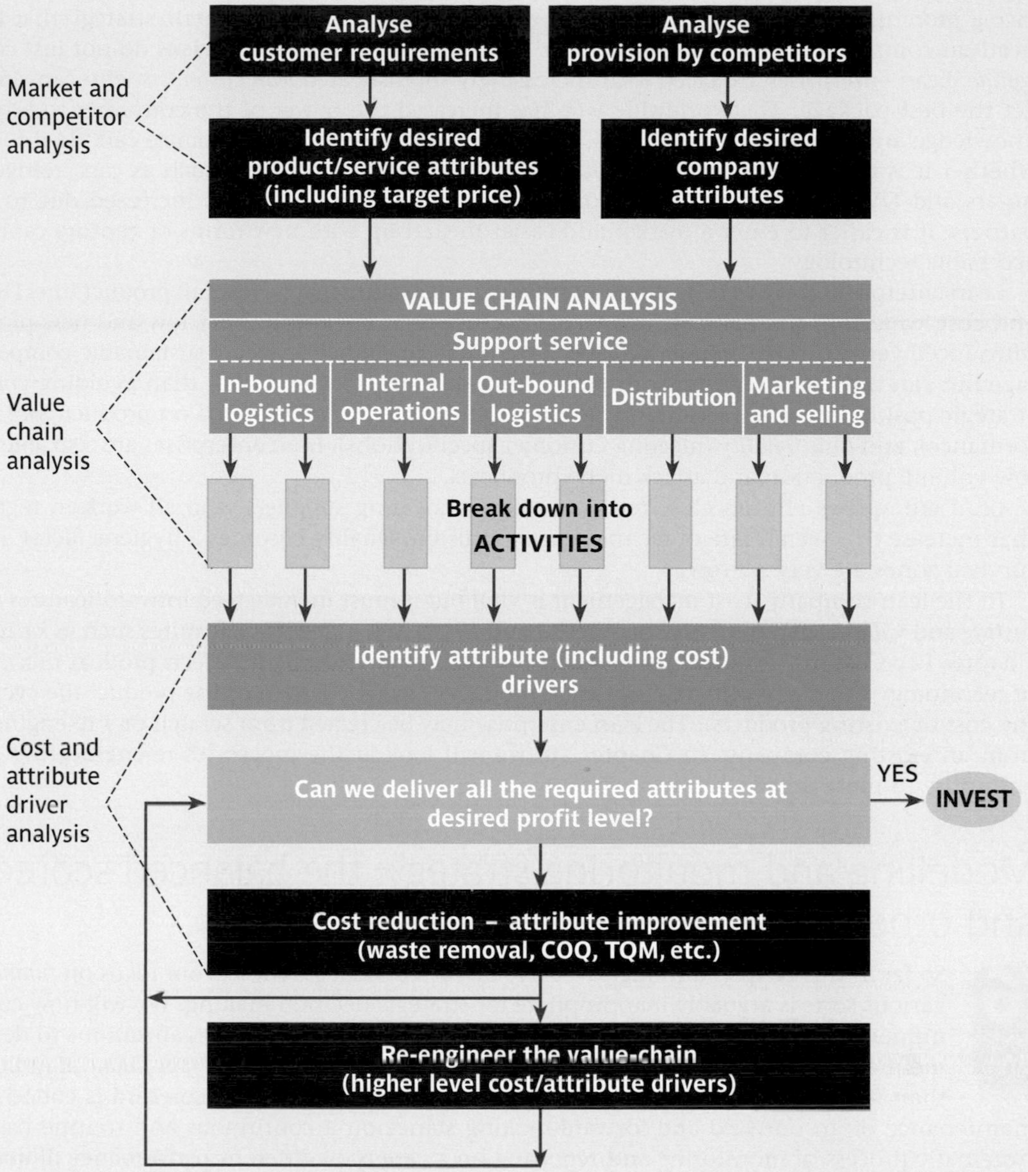

Market and competitor analysis

Analyse customer requirements

Analyse provision by competitors

Identify desired product/service attributes (including target price)

Identify desired company attributes

Value chain analysis

VALUE CHAIN ANALYSIS

Support service

In-bound logistics | Internal operations | Out-bound logistics | Distribution | Marketing and selling

Break down into ACTIVITIES

Cost and attribute driver analysis

Identify attribute (including cost) drivers

Can we deliver all the required attributes at desired profit level?

YES → INVEST

Cost reduction – attribute improvement (waste removal, COQ, TQM, etc.)

Re-engineer the value-chain (higher level cost/attribute drivers)

Exhibit 16.4 A systematic formal analysis for strategic investment decisions

Tomkins, C. and Carr, C. 1996. 'Reflections on the papers in this issue and a commentary on the state of strategic management accounting', *Management Accounting Research*, 7, 271–80.

Strategy as collision: lean enterprises and business process re-engineering

There have been some criticisms of the strategic positioning models by those who argue that some companies seem to have done quite well by being 'stuck-in-the middle' and that firms that have failed were not stuck in the middle but just bad at what they were doing.[18] It has also been argued that strategic positioning models were appropriate in the 1970s and 80s but that recently firms face a more hectic form of competition where they cannot choose a generic strategy that tries to avoid head-on competition. According to Cooper[19] the emerging **lean enterprises** do not just compete, they *collide*. Lean enterprises are faced with increasingly sophisticated *lean customers* who can shop around to get the best package. The worldwide web has increased the power of the consumer to acquire product knowledge and search for the best deal. New technology also means customers can 'do it for themselves' whether it is buying air tickets or choosing a new car. Many products such as cars, refrigerators, computers and DVD players have matured. Competition between firms has increased due to falling trade barriers. It is easier to enter a market and easier to start-up with new forms of venture capital and more accessible technology.

Lean enterprises have to be technologically up to date and must have a full product line. Differentiation and cost leadership strategies are less viable because costs are already very low and new products can be introduced very quickly. Lean enterprises do not have a chance to create sustainable competitive advantage but can only seek repeatedly to create *temporary* advantages. Rather than avoiding competition by strategic positioning, they seek it out, working on the *survival triplet* based on product *price, quality* (conformance), and *functionality* (meeting customer specifications). Lean enterprises are also able to cope with low volume production and attack niche producers.

Lean enterprises rely on close relations with innovating suppliers who all work in regional clusters that increase the overall rate of technological diffusion. Quality becomes a hygiene factor and the firms' survival zones are very narrow.

In the lean company, cost management is vital but it must include feed forward features such as *target costing* and *value engineering* (see Chapters 15 and 19) as well as feedback features such as *kaizen costing* (see Chapter 12). Cost management depends on competitive environment (affects product mix), the maturity of technology (managing the cost of future products) and the length of the product life cycle (managing the cost of existing products). The lean enterprise may be created from scratch or a re-engineered version from an existing company. In Chapter 18, we will look at the process of re-engineering and the lean enterprise in more detail.

Modelling and monitoring strategy: the balanced scorecard and other non-financial measures

So far in this chapter although we have discussed strategic choice, our focus on *financial metrics* of various sorts is arguably inappropriate for strategic decision making. We will now consider a very influential model, the *balanced scorecard*, which may be used by organizations to develop, implement and control strategy through a balanced use of financial and *non-financial* indicators. Rather than focus on an individual strategic investment, the balanced scorecard is concerned with the maintenance of an outward and forward-looking stance on a continuous and routine basis through a systematic process of monitoring and reporting on a variety of different performance dimensions.

A **balanced scorecard (BSC)** consists of an integrated set of performance measures that are derived from the company's strategy and that support the company's strategy throughout the organization.[20] A strategy is essentially a theory about how to achieve the organization's goals. For example, low-cost European carriers such as easyJet, Ryanair and Go have copied Southwestern Airlines' strategy of offering passengers low prices and fun on short-haul jet service. The low prices result from the absence of costly frills such as meals, assigned seating and interline baggage checking. The fun is provided by flight attendants who go out of their way to entertain passengers with their antics. This is an interesting strategy. Southwestern Airlines consciously hires people who have a sense of humour and who enjoy their work. Hiring and retaining such employees probably costs no more – and may cost less – than retaining grumpy flight attendants who view their jobs as a chore. Southwestern Airlines' strategy is to build loyal customers through a combination of 'fun' – which does not cost anything to provide – and low prices that are possible because of the lack of costly frills offered by competing airlines. The theory is that low prices and fun[21] will lead to loyal customers, which, in combination with low costs, will lead to high profits. So far, this theory has worked.

Under the balanced scorecard approach, top management translates its strategy into performance measures that employees can understand and can do something about. For example, the amount of time passengers have to wait in line to have their baggage checked might be a performance measure for a supervisor in charge of the check-in counter at an airport. This performance measure is easily understood by the supervisor, and can be improved by the supervisor's actions.

Common characteristics of balanced scorecards

Performance measures used in the balanced scorecard approach tend to fall into the four groups illustrated in Exhibit 16.5: financial, customer, internal business processes, and learning and growth. Internal business processes are what the company does in an attempt to satisfy customers. For example, in a manufacturing company, assembling a product is an internal business process. In an airline, handling baggage is an internal business process. The basic idea is that learning is necessary to improve internal business processes; improving business processes is necessary to improve customer satisfaction; and improving customer satisfaction is necessary to improve financial results.

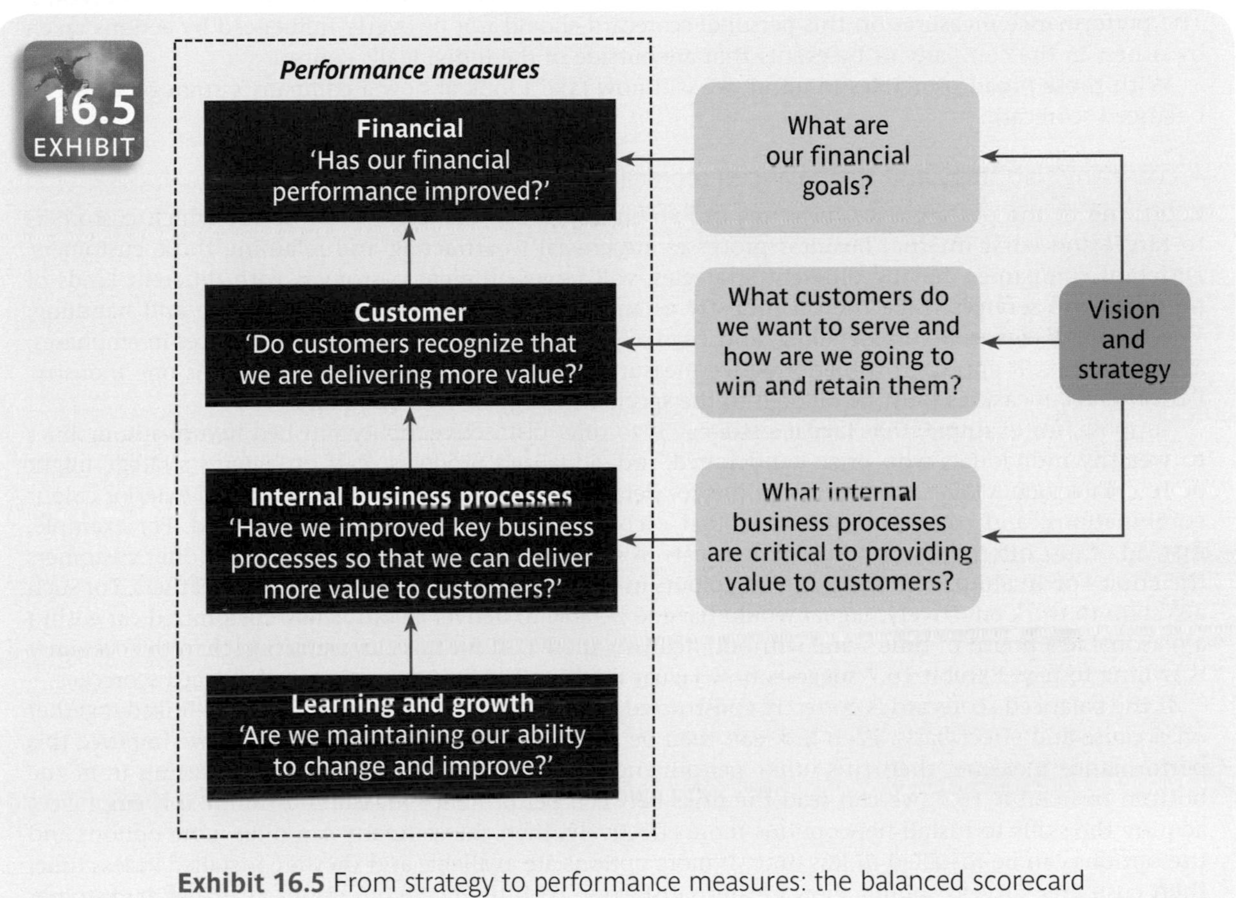

Exhibit 16.5 From strategy to performance measures: the balanced scorecard

Note that the emphasis in Exhibit 16.5 is on *improvement* – not on just attaining some specific objective such as profits of £10 million. In the balanced scorecard approach, continual improvement is encouraged. In many industries, this is a matter of survival. If an organization does not continually improve, it will eventually lose out to competitors that do.

Financial performance measures appear at the top of Exhibit 16.5. Ultimately, most companies exist to provide financial rewards to owners. There are exceptions. Some companies – for example, The Body Shop – may have loftier goals, such as providing environmentally friendly products to consumers. However, even non-profit organizations must generate enough financial resources to stay in operation.

Ordinarily, top managers are responsible for the financial performance measures – not lower level managers. The supervisor in charge of checking in passengers can be held responsible for how long passengers have to queue. However, this supervisor cannot reasonably be held responsible for the entire company's profit. That is the responsibility of the airline's top managers.

Exhibit 16.6 lists some examples of performance measures that can be found on the balanced scorecards of companies. However, few companies, if any, would use all of these performance measures, and almost all companies would add other performance measures. Managers should carefully select the performance measures for their company's balanced scorecard, keeping the following points in mind. First and foremost, the performance measures should be consistent with, and follow from, the company's strategy. If the performance measures are not consistent with the company's strategy, people will find themselves working at cross-purposes. Second, the scorecard should not have too many performance measures. This can lead to a lack of focus and confusion.

While the entire organization will have an overall balanced scorecard, each responsible individual will have his or her own personal scorecard as well. This scorecard should consist of items the individual can personally influence that relate directly to the performance measures on the overall balanced scorecard. The performance measures on this personal scorecard should not be overly influenced by actions taken by others in the company or by events that are outside of the individual's control.

With those broad principles in mind, we will now take a look at how a company's strategy affects its balanced scorecard.

A company's strategy and the balanced scorecard

Returning to the performance measures in Exhibit 16.6, each company must decide which customers to target and what internal business processes are crucial to attracting and retaining those customers. Different companies, having different strategies, will target different customers with different kinds of products and services. Take the car industry as an example. BMW stresses engineering and handling; Volvo, safety; Jaguar, luxury detailing; and Toyota,[22] reliability. Because of these differences in emphases, a one-size-fits-all approach to performance measurement will not work even within this one industry. Performance measures must be tailored to the specific strategy of each company.

Suppose, for example, that Jaguar's strategy is to offer distinctive, richly finished luxury automobiles to wealthy individuals who prize handcrafted, individualized products. Part of Jaguar's strategy might be to create such a large number of options for details, such as leather seats, interior and exterior colour combinations, and wooden dashboards, that each car becomes virtually one of a kind. For example, instead of just offering tan or blue leather seats in standard cowhide, the company may offer customers the choice of an almost infinite palate of colours in any of a number of different exotic leathers. For such a system to work effectively, Jaguar would have to be able to deliver a completely customized car within a reasonable amount of time – and without incurring more cost for this customization than the customer is willing to pay. Exhibit 16.7 suggests how Jaguar might reflect this strategy in its balanced scorecard.

If the balanced scorecard is correctly constructed, the performance measures should be linked together on a cause-and-effect basis. Each link can then be read as a hypothesis in the form 'If we improve this performance measure, then this other performance measure should also improve.' Starting from the bottom of Exhibit 16.7, we can read the links between performance measures as follows. If employees acquire the skills to install new options more effectively, then the company can offer more options and the options can be installed in less time. If more options are available and they are installed in less time, then customer surveys should show greater satisfaction with the range of options available. If customer satisfaction improves, then the number of cars sold should increase. In addition, if customer satisfaction improves, the company should be able to maintain or increase its selling prices, and if the time to install options decreases, the costs of installing the options should decrease. Together, this should result in an increase in the contribution margin per car. If the contribution margin per car increases and more cars are sold, the result should be an increase in profits.

In essence, the balanced scorecard articulates a theory of how the company can attain its desired outcomes (financial, in this case) by taking concrete actions. While the strategy laid out in Exhibit 16.7 seems plausible, it should be regarded as only a theory that should be discarded if it proves to be invalid. For example, if the company succeeds in increasing the number of options available and in decreasing the time required to install options and yet there is no increase in customer satisfaction, the number of cars sold, the contribution margin per car, or profits, the strategy would have to be reconsidered. One of the advantages of the balanced scorecard is that it continually tests the theories underlying manage-

Customer perspective Performance measure	Desired change
Customer satisfaction as measured by survey results	+
Number of customer complaints	–
Market share	+
Product returns as a percentage of sales	–
Percentage of customers retained from last period	+
Number of new customers	+
Internal business processes perspective Performance measure	**Desired change**
Percentage of sales from new products	+
Time to introduce new products to market	–
Percentage of customer calls answered within 20 seconds	+
On-time deliveries as a percentage of all deliveries	+
Work in progress inventory as a percentage of sales	–
Unfavourable standard cost variances	–
Defect-free units as a percentage of completed units	+
Delivery cycle time*	–
Throughput time*	–
Manufacturing cycle efficiency*	+
Quality costs†	–
Set-up time	–
Time from call by customer to repair of product	–
Percentage of customer complaints settled on first contact	+
Time to settle a customer claim	–
Learning and growth perspective Performance measure	**Desired change**
Suggestions per employee	+
Value-added employee†	+
Employee turnover	–
Hours of in-house training per employee	+

*Explained later in this chapter.

†See cost of quality in Chapter 18.

‡Value-added is revenue less externally purchased materials, supplies and services

Exhibit 16.6 Examples of performance measures for balanced scorecards

ment's strategy. If a strategy is not working, it should become evident when some of the predicted effects (i.e. more car sales) do not occur. Without this feedback, management may drift on indefinitely with an ineffective strategy based on faulty assumptions.

Advantages of timely feedback

Whatever performance measures are used, they should be reported on a frequent and timely basis. For example, data about defects should be reported to the responsible managers at least once a day so that action can quickly be taken if an unusual number of defects occurs. In the most advanced companies,

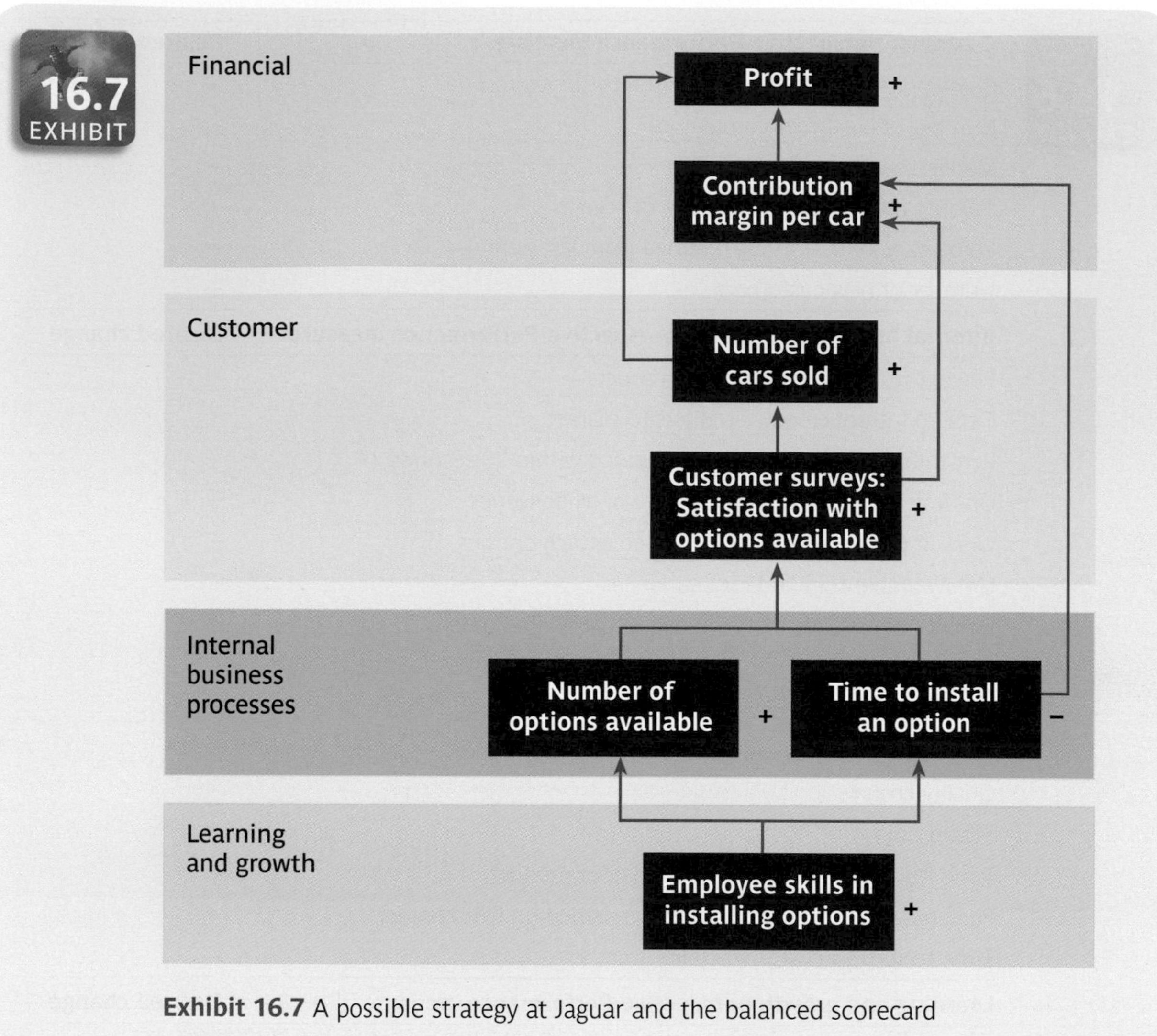

Exhibit 16.7 A possible strategy at Jaguar and the balanced scorecard

any defect is reported *immediately*, and its cause is tracked down before any more defects can occur. Another common characteristic of the performance measures under the balanced scorecard approach is that managers focus on trends in the performance measures over time. The emphasis is on progress and *improvement* rather than on meeting any specific standard.

Some measures of internal business process performance

Most of the performance measures listed in Exhibit 16.6 are self-explanatory. However, three are not – *delivery cycle time, throughput time* and *manufacturing cycle efficiency* (MCE). These three important performance measures are discussed next.

Delivery cycle time

The amount of time between when an order is received from a customer to when the completed order is shipped is called **delivery cycle time**. This time is clearly a key concern to many customers, who would like the delivery cycle time to be as short as possible. Cutting the delivery cycle time may give a company a key competitive advantage – and may be necessary for survival – and therefore many companies would include this performance measure on their balanced scorecard.

Throughput (manufacturing cycle) time

The amount of time required to turn raw materials into completed products is called **throughput time**, or manufacturing cycle time. The relationship between the delivery cycle time and the throughput (manufacturing cycle) time is illustrated in Exhibit 16.8.

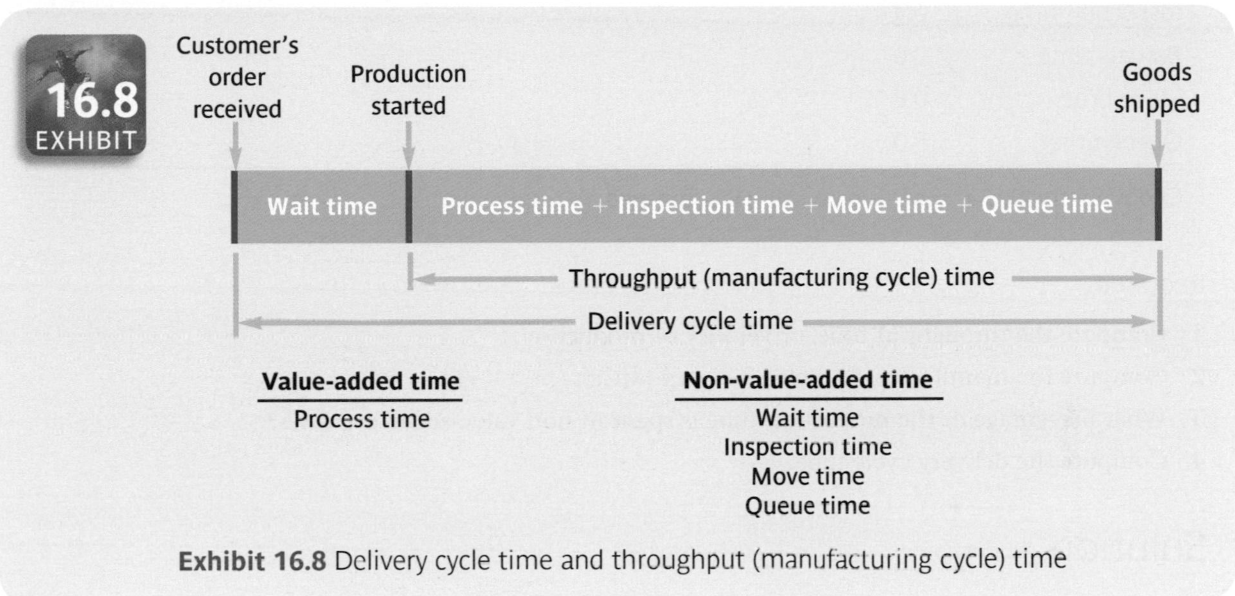

Exhibit 16.8 Delivery cycle time and throughput (manufacturing cycle) time

Note that, as shown in Exhibit 16.8, the throughput time, or manufacturing cycle time, is made up of process time, inspection time, move time and queue time. Process time is the amount of time in which work is actually done on the product. Inspection time is the amount of time spent ensuring that the product is not defective. Move time is the time required to move materials or partially completed products from workstation to workstation. Queue time is the amount of time a product spends waiting to be worked on, to be moved, to be inspected, or in storage waiting to be shipped.

As shown at the bottom of Exhibit 16.8, the only one of these four activities that adds value to the product is process time. The other three activities – inspecting, moving and queueing – add no value and should be eliminated as much as possible.

Manufacturing cycle efficiency (MCE)

Through concerted efforts to eliminate the non-value-added activities of inspecting, moving and queueing, some companies have reduced their throughput time to only a fraction of previous levels. In turn, this has helped to reduce the delivery cycle time from months to only weeks or hours. The throughput time, which is considered to be a key measure in delivery performance, can be put into better perspective by computing the **manufacturing cycle efficiency (MCE)**. The MCE is computed by relating the value-added time to the throughput time. The formula is as follows:

$$\text{MCE} = \frac{\text{Value-added time}}{\text{Throughput (manufacturing cycle) time}}$$

If the MCE is less than 1, then non-value-added time is present in the production process. An MCE of 0.5, for example, would mean that half of the total production time consisted of inspection, moving and similar non-value-added activities. In many manufacturing companies, the MCE is less than 0.1 (10%), which means that 90% of the time a unit is in process is spent on activities that do not add value to the product. By monitoring the MCE, companies are able to reduce non-value-added activities and thus get products into the hands of customers more quickly and at a lower cost.

To provide a numeric example of these measures, assume the following data for Novex Company.

Novex Company keeps careful track of the time relating to orders and their production. During the most recent quarter, the following average times were recorded for each unit or order:

	Days
Wait time	17.0
Inspection time	0.4
Process time	2.0
Move time	0.6
Queue time	5.0

Goods are shipped as soon as production is completed.

Required

1 Compute the throughput time, or velocity of production.

2 Compute the manufacturing cycle efficiency (MCE).

3 What percentage of the production time is spent in non-value-added activities?

4 Compute the delivery cycle time.

Solution

1 Throughput time = Process time + Inspection time + Move time + Queue time

= 2.0 days + 0.4 days + 0.6 days + 5.0 days

= 8.0 days

2 Only process time represents value-added time; therefore, the computation of the MCE would be as follows:

$$\text{MCE} = \frac{\text{Value-added time, 2.0 days}}{\text{Throughput time, 8.0 days}}$$

= 0.25

Thus, once put into production, a typical unit is actually being worked on only 25% of the time.

3 Since the MCE is 25%, the complement of this figure, or 75% of the total production time, is spent in non-value-added activities.

Delivery cycle time = Wait time + Throughput time

= 17.0 days + 8.0 days

= 25.0 days.

7 LEARNING OBJECTIVE

We would like to emphasize a few points concerning the balanced scorecard. First, the balanced scorecard should be tailored to the company's strategy; each company's balanced scorecard should be unique. The examples given in this chapter are just that – examples. They should not be interpreted as general templates to be fitted to each company. Second, the balanced scorecard reflects a particular strategy, or theory, about how a company can further its objectives by taking specific actions. The theory should be viewed as tentative and subject to change if the actions do not in fact lead to attaining the company's financial and other goals. If the theory (i.e. strategy) changes, then the performance measures on the balanced scorecard should also change. The balanced scorecard should be viewed as a dynamic system that evolves as the company's strategy evolves.[23,24]

The balanced scorecard should not be seen just as a 'four bucket' model[25] with four boxes that must be filled. Organizations may choose to have five main dimensions. For example, banks may wish to have an extra box labelled risk management. As we have seen recently with the worldwide 'credit crunch', banks that have failed to manage risk have suffered financially or even gone out of business completely. The role of the balanced scorecard in a management control model will be reviewed in the next chapter.

Strategy as an emergent process: interactive control systems and the learning organization

The balanced scorecard fits in with a more sophisticated view that sees strategy as an emergent process and which is less a top-down, keep-on-track approach to organizational control. The organization is seen as engaged in a learning process both through internal communication and through contact with its customers and suppliers. The balanced scorecard can facilitate this learning process as can other techniques such as **benchmarking** (see Chapter 18) through a consciously interactive relationship between performance indicators and management action.[26] We will develop these ideas more fully in Chapter 17 when we look at the relationship between strategy and organizational control.

In a learning system, information is used to encourage debate up and down organizations. Rather than being the product of a 'central plan', strategy is seen as a more emergent process[27] linking up strategy with tactics. The aim of management accounting in this approach to strategy is to aid the development of double-loop learning. In contrast with a single-loop control model such as standard costing, which simply requires conformance to existing policies, double-loop learning constantly questions both standards and policies. Another source of learning comes from benchmarking against the best practices in other organizations. Benchmarking may be based on cost performance (see Chapter 18 for ABM examples) or on processes to improve quality (see Chapter 18). The key to successful benchmarking is to adopt a learning orientation rather than the blame culture that can sometimes develop from a league-table approach. Sometimes a company will change its strategy unintentionally, whereby successive adaptations to changing markets, competitive position and technology leads to a new organizational identity, a new realization of where the company's core competences[28] actually lie.

Some obstacles to SMA

Strategic management accounting has not become a branded technique widely marketed by consultants in the same way as ABC,[29] EVA and the BSC. One obstacle to the development of an SMA perspective by accountants may be that, traditionally, accountants have a *performance* rather than a *learning* orientation. Thus, rather than look for new data (outside the organization and traditional accounting systems) and fearing failure, accountants stick to the familiar.[30] To accountants, the familiar usually means financial data.[31] Furthermore, although the data for SMA may be held in different functional areas of the organization (such as marketing), there may be a reluctance to share with other functional areas such as management accounting.

Some sceptical commentators have suggested that companies may actually respond to business challenges by following the principles that comprise SMA but without a conscious adoption of an SMA package. Identifying the key principles of SMA as the *collection of competitor information, the exploitation of cost reduction opportunities* and *the matching of accounting emphasis with strategic position,* Lord[32] argues that:

> ...the characteristics that have been ascribed to strategic management accounting are likely to be already operating in many firms. However, it appears that the management accountant does not need to be involved in their operation, nor do they need to be quantified in accounting figures. Perhaps the widely touted 'strategic management accounting' is but a figment of academic imagination.

In short, the data for SMA are usually available somewhere, the difficulty is pulling them together in an organizational context. Indeed, the advantage of the BSC is that it offers a neat format for integrating financial and non-financial data into organizational reporting systems. As we shall see in the next chapter, scorecard models in general may be used to enhance corporate accountability from both shareholder and wider stakeholder perspectives.

Summary

- Profit and shareholder value metrics may be used for business planning but they may not provide sufficient information for developing and implementing strategies.
- Strategic management accounting has evolved from the collection of competitor information to attempts to match management accounting systems with an organization's strategic position.
- As competition has become tougher and strategic positions seem harder to sustain, the managerial emphasis has shifted to supporting the lean enterprise.
- A balanced scorecard consists of an integrated system of performance measures that are derived from and support the company's strategy. Different companies will have different balanced scorecards because they have different strategies. A well-constructed balanced scorecard provides a means for guiding the company and also provides feedback concerning the effectiveness of the company's strategy.
- As competitive advantage becomes based on the development of corporate knowledge rather than the simple ownership of tangible assets, we may use the balanced scorecard as a flexible model that can help the organization learn from its customers and suppliers.

Key terms for review

Attribute costing (p. 679).

Balanced scorecard (BSC) (p. 684).

Benchmarking (p. 691).

Cost leadership (p. 680).

Defender (p. 680).

Delivery cycle time (p. 688).

Double-loop learning (p. 691).

Executional drivers (p. 680).

Lean enterprises (p. 684).

Life-cycle costing (p. 679).

Manufacturing cycle efficiency (MCE) (p. 689).

Marketing mix (p. 679).

Organizational learning (p. 676).

Product differentiation (p. 680).

Prospector (p. 680).

Strategic choice (p. 676).

Strategic management accounting (SMA) (p. 676).

Structural drivers (p. 680).

Throughput time (p. 689).

Value-based management (VBM) (p. 678).

Value chain (p. 680).

Questions

16–1 Why is market share an important indicator to monitor?

16–2 What aspects of a competitor's costs should be analysed in a strategic assessment?

16–3 What sources are useful for strategic intelligence gathering?

16–4 What is the difference between a prospector and a defender company?

16–5 What is the difference between a cost leader and a product differentiator?

16–6 What are the three steps/dimensions that combine financial and strategic analysis as proposed by Tomkins and Carr?

16–7 What are the implications of the 'strategy as collision' model?

16–8 Why does the balanced scorecard include financial performance measures as well as measures of how well internal business processes are doing?

16–9 What is the difference between the delivery cycle time and the throughput time? What four elements make up the throughput time? Into what two classes can these four elements be placed?

16–10 If a company has a manufacturing cycle efficiency (MCE) of less than 1, what does it mean? How would you interpret an MCE of 0.40?

16–11 How can a balanced scorecard aid organizational learning?

16–12 Why does the balanced scorecard differ from company to company?

16–13 Which views of strategy would you expect to provoke the most resistance from the 'traditional' management accountants?

Exercises

E16–1 Time allowed: 20 minutes

Management of Mittel Rhein AG of Köln, Germany, would like to reduce the amount of time between when a customer places an order and when the order is shipped. For the first quarter of operations during the current year the following data were reported:

	Days
Inspection time	0.3
Wait time (from order to start of production)	14.0
Process time	2.7
Move time	1.0
Queue time	5.0

Required

1 Compute the throughput time, or velocity of production.

2 Compute the manufacturing cycle efficiency (MCE) for the quarter.

3 What percentage of the throughput time was spent in non-value-added activities?

4 Compute the delivery cycle time.

5 If by use of just-in-time (JIT) all queue time during production is eliminated, what will be the new MCE?

Problems

P16–2 Perverse effects of some performance measures Time allowed: 30 minutes

There is often more than one way to improve a performance measure. Unfortunately, some of the actions taken by managers to make their performance look better may actually harm the organization. For example, suppose the marketing department is held responsible only for increasing the performance measure 'total revenues'. Increases in total revenues may be achieved by working harder and smarter, but they can also usually be achieved by simply cutting prices. The increase in volume from cutting prices almost always results in greater total revenues; however, it does not always lead to greater total profits. Those who design performance measurement systems need to keep in mind that managers who are under pressure to perform may take actions to improve performance measures that have negative consequences elsewhere.

Required

For each of the following situations, describe actions that managers might take to show improvement in the performance measure but which do not actually lead to improvement in the organization's overall performance.

1 Concerned with the slow rate at which new products are brought to market, top management of a consumer electronics company introduces a new performance measure – speed-to-market. The research and development department is given responsibility for this performance measure, which measures the average amount of time a product is in development before it is released to the market for sale.

2 The Chief Executive of a telephone company has been under public pressure from city officials to fix the large number of public pay phones that do not work. The company's repair people complain that the problem is vandalism and damage caused by theft of coins from coin boxes – particularly in high crime areas in the city. The Chief Executive says she wants the problem solved and has pledged to city officials that there will be substantial improvement by the end of the year. To ensure that this is done, she makes the managers in charge of installing and maintaining pay phones responsible for increasing the percentage of public pay phones that are fully functional.

3 A manufacturing company has been plagued by the chronic failure to ship orders to customers by the promised date. To solve this problem, the production manager has been given the responsibility of increasing the percentage of orders shipped on time. When a customer calls in an order, the production manager and the customer agree to a delivery date. If the order is not completed by that date, it is counted as a late shipment.

4 Concerned with the productivity of employees, the board of directors of a large multinational corporation has dictated that the manager of each subsidiary will be held responsible for increasing the revenue per employee of his or her subsidiary.

P16–3 Use of quantitative techniques and non-financial indicators Time allowed: 45 minutes

PMF plc is a long-established public transport operator that provides a commuter transit link between an airport and the centre of a large city.

The following data has been taken from the sales records of PMF plc for the last two years:

Quarter	Number of passengers carried	
	Year 1	Year 2
1	15,620	34,100
2	15,640	29,920
3	16,950	29,550
4	34,840	56,680

The trend equation for the number of passengers carried has been found to be:

$$x = 10{,}000 + 4{,}200q$$

where x = number of passengers carried per quarter

and q = time period (year 1 quarter 1: $q = 1$)
(year 1 quarter 2: $q = 2$)
(year 2 quarter 1: $q = 5$).

Based on data collected over the last two years, PMF plc has found that its quarterly costs have the following relationships with the number of passengers carried:

Cost item	Relationship
Premises costs	$y = 260{,}000$
Premises staff	$y = 65{,}000 + 0.5x$
Power	$y = 13{,}000 + 4x$
Transit staff	$y = 32{,}000 + 3x$
Other	$y = 9{,}100 + x$

where y = the cost per quarter (£)
and x = number of passengers per quarter.

Required

1 Using the trend equation for the number of passengers carried and the multiplicative (proportional) time series model, determine the expected number of passengers to be carried in the third quarter of year 3. *(7 marks)*

2 Explain why you think that the equation for the Transit staff cost is in the form $y = 32{,}000 + 3x$. *(3 marks)*

3 Using your answer to Question 1 and the cost relationships equations, calculate for each cost item and in total, the costs expected to be incurred in the third quarter of year 3. *(3 marks)*

4 Explain briefly why there may be differences between the actual data for the third quarter of year 3 and the values you have predicted. *(5 marks)*

5 Prepare a report, addressed to the Board of Directors of PMF plc, that briefly explains the following in the context of measuring the *effectiveness* of the transport service:
- Why the company should consider the use of non-financial performance measures;
- Three non-financial performance measures that could be used. *(7 marks)*

(Total = 25 marks)

CIMA Management Accounting – Performance Management, November 2001

P16–4 Strategic analysis Time allowed: 45 minutes
M-HK provides a passenger ferry service between two large cities separated by the mouth of a major river. The ferries are frequent, well supported by passengers and cover the distance between the cities in one hour. M-HK also transports passengers and goods by water ferry to other cities located on the river mouth. There are other ferry operators providing services between each of these locations besides M-HK.

Required

1 Explain what strategic information is required by M-HK's management in respect of customer demand, competition, competitiveness, and finance in order to plan its future ferry services. *(10 marks)*

2 Using the information in your answer to Question 1, discuss how M-HK's Chartered Management Accountant should provide reports to M-HK's senior management for operational and strategic planning purposes. *(15 marks)*

(Total = 25 marks)

CIMA Management Accounting – Business Strategy, May 2001

P16–5 Strategic analysis Time allowed: 45 minutes

R is a large high-class hotel situated in a thriving city. It is part of a worldwide hotel group owned by a large number of shareholders. The majority of the shares are held by individuals, each holding a small number; the rest are owned by financial institutions. The hotel provides full amenities, including a heated swimming pool, as well as the normal facilities of bars, restaurants and good-quality accommodation. There are many other hotels in the city which all compete with R. The city in which R is situated is old and attracts many foreign visitors, particularly in its summer season.

Required

1 State the main stakeholders with whom relationships need to be established and maintained by the management of R. Explain why it is important that relationships are developed and maintained with each of these stakeholders. *(10 marks)*

2 Explain how the management of R should carry out a benchmarking exercise on its services, and recommend ways in which the outcomes should be evaluated. *(15 marks)*

Note: Do NOT describe different methods of benchmarking in answering this question.

(Total = 25 marks)

CIMA Management Accounting – Business Strategy, May 2001

P16–6 Strategic management accounting Time allowed: 60 minutes

The Y Corporation is based in the USA. It was founded in the early part of the last century when Mr Y produced cartoon films. These soon proved very popular as a form of family entertainment and the characters in the films became household names. The Corporation established a theme park (based around the film characters) in southern USA, where there was a warm and mainly dry climate. The theme park, known as Yland, proved to be an immediate success, attracting millions of visitors each year. A whole range of family entertainment flourished, based on the original theme of the cartoon characters. These included shops, restaurants, hotels and amusement rides.

Following the success of Y-land in the USA, the directors of the Corporation established another Y theme park based in northern Europe. The rationale behind this was that although many Europeans visited Y-land in the USA, the cost of travel made visiting the attraction very expensive. The directors believed that establishing a Y-land in northern Europe would enable European people to visit the attraction without incurring high travel expenses. Y-land Europe was built in a highly populated area of northern Europe which is easily accessible. A factor which differentiates Y-land Europe from the theme park in the USA is that it is located in a region which is frequently affected by rain and it does not enjoy a guaranteed warm climate.

Y-land Europe did not in fact attract the volume of visitors that were expected and almost went bankrupt before receiving a massive cash injection from a wealthy donor who took part shares in the theme park.

Further strategic development

The Y Corporation is now considering building another theme park, this time in a tropical area in the Far East. Y-land FE will be part-funded by the host government in the Far East, which will take a 60% share in the park. The Y Corporation will fund the remaining 40%. Profits and losses will be shared in direct proportion to the shareholding of each of the joint venture partners. It is believed that local tourism and related sectors of the entertainment industry will benefit from the development as the theme park will attract more visitors to the region. Similar to the other two Y-land theme parks, the development will include many facilities such as hotels, bars and restaurants as well as the entertainment attractions.

It will take two years to build Y-land FE before any paying visitors enter the park. The Y Corporation has based its estimates of visitors in the first year of operation (that is, after the two years of construction) on the following probabilities:

	Visitors	Probability
Optimistic	8 million	0.25
Most likely	3 million	0.50
Pessimistic	2 million	0.25

After the first year of operation, it is expected that the number of visitors will increase by 50% in the next year. The Y Corporation directors consider that this number of visitors will be the maximum and after that the theme park will suffer a reduction in the number of visitors (marketing decay) of 5% compounded each year for the next two years. After two years, the directors expect the number of visitors each year to remain constant at this level. The host government believes that the theme park will create about 15,000 new jobs in the area through servicing the facilities. It expects the construction of the park to create about 5,000 jobs in addition to the 8,000 who will be employed in land reclamation and other necessary infrastructural work associated with the project.

Cost and revenue estimates

It is expected that the overall capital cost of the theme park will be $2,200 million. This sum will be spread evenly over the construction period and, for the purposes of calculation, the actual cash outflow may be assumed to arise at the end of each of the two years. The Y Corporation will be responsible for raising 40% of this sum.

In any year, the visitors are expected to be in the proportion of 40% adults and 60% children or people who will obtain a concession (reduction) on their entrance fees. For simplicity, the entrance charges will be set at a flat rate of $50 for each adult and $30 for each child or concession. There will be no further fees for entertainment after the entrance charge has been made to the visitor.

Past experience has shown that running expenses of the theme park show a certain level of consistency. In terms of labour, the costs follow the pattern of a 90% learning curve which applies on average to every million visitors. This lasts for the first two years, after which the labour costs for each visitor become constant. The cost of labour at the time the park will open is expected to be $3 for each visitor. The effects of this are that the cumulative average direct labour costs in the first year of operation (that is, year 3 of the project) are estimated to be $972 million (after being multiplied by the number of expected visitors in that year). The cumulative average labour costs for both the first and second years of operation (that is, years 3 and 4 of the project) are expected to be $2,114 million (after being multiplied by the total number of visitors for the first two years of operation). After this point the learning effect is expected to cease.

The other direct costs, which are not subject to learning, can be assumed to be incurred at the rate of $2 for each visitor. Attributable fixed running expenses are estimated to be $100 million each year in cash terms. In addition, the Y Corporation expects that its joint venture with the host government will earn average net contribution of $10 from the sale of souvenirs and refreshments and $100 from accommodation charges for each adult, child or concessionary visitor each year.

The cost of capital for the whole project is expected to be 15%.

Shareholder value

The Y Corporation believes that its main objective is to increase the wealth of its owners. The corporation requires a gross return on investment of 22% after eight years of income generated from the venture. It has been recommended to the directors of the Y Corporation that the return is calculated by taking the net present value of the project after eight years of operation and dividing this by the gross initial undiscounted capital outlay of $2,200 million.

Ignore taxation, inflation and variations due to exchange rates.

Required

1 Produce a discounted cash flow (DCF) calculation for Y-land FE from the start of building work in the first year until eight years of cash inflows have been generated (that is, ten years in total), and calculate the return on investment in accordance with the method recommended. *(15 marks)*

2 Analyse and critically appraise the DCF calculation and the resulting return on investment as defined by the method recommended to the directors of the Y Corporation, and advise the directors as to whether they should proceed with Yland FE. You should consider financial and non-financial factors in providing your advice. *(15 marks)*

(Total = 30 marks)

(Abbreviated version from *CIMA Management Accounting* – Business Strategy, November 2001)

P16–7 Uncertainty, strategic management accounting Time allowed: 50 minutes

Lipo plc ('Lipo') manufactures labels for consumer goods. The company obtained a listing on the Alternative Investment Market in 1998, having been established in 1955.

Basic labels

Lipo's sole manufacturing site is in Newcastle in the north-east of England. For many years the company produced only basic, low technology labels ('basic labels') for a range of consumer goods. It has a market share in the UK of about 3%. These are mainly stick-on labels for plastic containers including those for soft drinks, detergents and food products. In common with its competitors, which are of similar size to Lipo, manufacturing takes place using low-tech machinery and a standardized process.

Historically, about half of the basic labels were sold in the UK and half overseas, mainly to the Far East. Selling prices are determined in sterling and are the same in all markets. The strength of sterling in recent years relative to most Far Eastern currencies, however, has caused the overseas market to decline significantly to around 25% of total sales and, as a consequence, company profitability also fell.

Within the UK, sales have remained stable, being strongest in northern England and southern Scotland. Good relations have been developed with a wide ranging and loyal customer base.

Hi-tech labels

The significant decline in Far Eastern markets forced the company to search for an additional product market. After some internal debate it was decided in 1998 to set up a separate division and heavily invest in new machinery to make high-tech security labels ('hi-tech labels') with embedded microchips. These could be used with a wide range of goods (including electrical goods, motor vehicles and, even, animals) to prevent theft, but also to enable police to identify ownership if stolen goods are subsequently recovered.

Large-scale investment was required as it is necessary to make large volumes for the production of hi-tech labels to be viable. The new investment is financed by borrowing and, as a result, the company has reached its debt capacity. Raising further equity finance is not currently feasible.

Lipo sells hi-tech labels only in the UK market. In contrast with basic labels, however, it competes against both small and large competitors.

Microchips are imported from a major international company based in Japan, as few other manufacturers can match their price. Recently, however, the Japanese company patented, and commenced production of, a second generation microchip for security labels. This new microchip significantly improves performance, but it also costs much more than the first generation microchip.

The industry background

The labels industry has a number of small companies similar to Lipo, but there are also a few high volume producers, and some consumer goods manufacturers make their own labels in-house. The market tends to segment with the smaller companies making basic labels and selling to smaller manufacturers. Conversely, the large labelling companies sell good quality basic labels, but also high-tech labels, targeting larger manufacturers in each case.

The market for high-tech labels has grown very significantly in recent years at about 75% per annum, as new applications and new technology have been developed. While the prices were initially high, greater production volumes have lowered both costs and prices over the past year. The increase in demand has also drawn in many new entrants to the industry. This means that the customers of high-tech labelling companies are constantly switching suppliers as competitive conditions change.

Draft profit and loss accounts for the year to 30 September 2001

	Basic labels		Hi-tech labels	
		£0'00		£0'00
Turnover		15,000		22,000
Variable manufacturing costs	4,500		5,000	
Fixed manufacturing costs	2,000		10,000	
Administration	3,000		4,000	
Selling costs	1,000		2,750	
		10,500		21,750
Operating profit		4,500		250

The board meeting

A board meeting was held to review the strategic direction of the company, and particularly to review hi-tech label production.

The director in charge of the Hi-Tech Division was enthusiastic. 'This division is the future. We started from nothing four years ago and we now have a much greater turnover than the Basic Labels Division. What is more, we have achieved 50% growth in each of the last two years, and this year we won some major contracts at the expense of much larger competitors.'

The finance director commented 'Hi-Tech Division is certainly achieving growth and market share, but it is not generating any profit. It has cut prices to win contracts but winning a contract and making a profit on it are two different things.'

The director in charge of basic labels agreed: 'Hi-Tech Division has had all the investment recently. My division has had nothing. In short, the core business is being squeezed in favour of a new technique which can only compete in the market by cutting prices with the result that it makes no profit. In contrast, since the disastrous few years following currency devaluations in the Far East, our division has been quite stable in terms of both turnover and operating profit.'

Required

1 So far as the information permits, evaluate the causes and consequences of environmental uncertainty in the labelling industry for:

(a) Basic labels

(b) Hi-tech labels. *(10 marks)*

2 As a strategic consultant write a memorandum to the board of Lipo which assesses each of the following issues in determining the future direction of the company:

(a) Future development of Basic Labels Division

(b) Hi-tech security labels:

Competitor analysis

Pricing policy

Viability. *(20 marks)*

(Total = 30 marks)

ICAEW Business Management, December 2001

P16–8 Balanced scorecard Time allowed: 45 minutes

The Royal Hotel Ltd is privately owned and situated in Keswick, an inland resort in the English Lake District. It is a medium-sized hotel with 50 bedrooms. Whilst high standards of building maintenance exist, the hotel has been conservatively managed by William Wordsworth, who owns 100% of its share capital. The hotel currently offers accommodation and restaurant facilities only, and has experienced little innovation in services offered during recent years.

William Wordsworth intends to retire in five years' time, so he has invited Pam Ayres to join him in partnership, with a view to her taking a controlling interest in the hotel on his retirement. She has recently qualified with a Masters Degree from the University of Birmingham, and has some knowledge of the latest approaches to the measurement of business performance. She has conducted a preliminary investigation of the hotel's performance over the past two years, to form a basis for taking a decision on joining William in partnership. The data she has gathered, based on the balanced scorecard approach to performance measurement, is presented in Appendix 1 and Appendix 2.

Appendix 1: Financial data

	Current year	Previous year
Estimated market value of the business	£2,000,000	£2,000,000
Turnover	£1,000,000	£950,000
Net profit	£200,000	£188,000
Current assets (cash, stock and credit card debtors)	£30,000	£25,000
Current liabilities (trade creditors)	£7,000	£10,000

Appendix 2: Non-financial data

Customer perspective

	Current year	Previous year
Room occupancy (during the 300 days the hotel is open each year)	55%	65%
Market share of overnight hotel accommodation in Keswick	4.33%	3.67%
Customer satisfaction rating (score maximum 100%)	55%	65%
Customers indicating they would return to the Royal Hotel if visiting Keswick again	25%	45%

Internal business processes

	Current year	Previous year
Audited percentage of procedures done according to job specification	75%	85%
Year on year employee retention rate	30%	50%
Customer rating of staff responsiveness (score maximum 100%)	60%	85%
Customer rating of staff competence (score maximum 100%)	50%	90%
Customer rating of staff courtesy (score maximum 100%)	60%	78%

Learning and growth perspective

	Current year	Previous year
Royal Hotel percentage of revenue from accommodation and restaurant	100%	100%
Keswick hotels industry average percentage of revenue from accommodation and restaurants	65%	75%
Average percentage of staff with hotel and restaurant qualifications	55%	65%

Required

1 Assess the financial performance of the Royal Hotel based only on the information provided in Appendix 1.

2 Explain why the information in Appendix 2 is likely to give a better indication of future success than the information in Appendix 1.

3 Using all the information at your disposal, assess the future prospects of the Royal Hotel, and advise Pam Ayres on the desirability of becoming a partner in the business.

(Thanks to Alan Coad, University of Birmingham)

CASE

Cases

C16–9 The Balanced Scorecard Time allowed: 60 minutes

Weierman Department Store is located in the downtown area of a medium-sized city in the American Midwest. While the store had been profitable for many years, it is facing increasing competition from large national chains that have set up stores in the city's suburbs. Recently the downtown area has been undergoing revitalization, and the owners of Weierman Department Store are somewhat optimistic that profitability can be restored.

In an attempt to accelerate the return to profitability, the management of Weierman Department Store is in the process of designing a balanced scorecard for the company. Management believes the company should focus on two key problems. First, customers are taking longer and longer to pay the bills they incur on the department store's charge card and they have far more bad debts than are normal for the industry. If this problem were solved, the company would have more cash to make much needed renovations. Investigation has revealed that much of the problem with late payments and unpaid bills is apparently due to disputed bills that are the result of incorrect charges on the customer bills. These incorrect charges usually occur because sales assistants enter data incorrectly on the charge account slip. Secondly, the company has been incurring large losses on unsold seasonal apparel. Such items are ordinarily resold at a loss to discount stores that specialize in such distress items.

The meeting in which the balanced scorecard approach was discussed was disorganized and ineffectively led – possibly because no one other than one of the vice presidents had read anything about how to put a balanced scorecard together. Nevertheless, a number of potential performance measures were suggested by various managers. These potential performance measures are listed below:

- Total sales revenue
- Percentage of sales clerks trained to correctly enter data on charge account slips
- Customer satisfaction with accuracy of charge account bills from monthly customer survey
- Sales per employee
- Travel expenses for buyers for trips to fashion shows
- Average age of debtors
- Courtesy shown by junior staff members to senior staff members based on surveys of senior staff
- Unsold inventory at the end of the season as a percentage of total cost of sales
- Sales per square metre of floor space
- Percentage of suppliers making just-in-time deliveries
- Quality of food in the staff cafeteria based on staff surveys
- Written-off debtors (bad debts) as a percentage of sales
- Percentage of charge account bills containing errors
- Percentage of employees who have attended the city's cultural diversity workshop
- Total profit
- Profit per employee.

Required

1 As someone with more knowledge of the balanced scorecard than almost anyone else in the company, you have been asked to build an integrated balanced scorecard. In your scorecard, use only performance measures suggested by the managers above. You do not have to use them all, but you should build a balanced scorecard that reveals a strategy for dealing with the problems with accounts receivable and with unsold merchandise. Construct the balanced scorecard following the format used in Exhibit 16.7. Do not be particularly concerned with whether a specific performance measure falls within the learning and growth, internal business process, customer or financial perspective. However, clearly show the causal links between the performance measures with arrows and whether the performance measures should show increases or decreases.

2 Assume that the company adopts your balanced scorecard. After operating for a year, there are improvements in some performance measures but not in others. What should management do next?

3

(a) Suppose that customers express greater satisfaction with the accuracy of their charge account bills but the performance measures for the average age of receivables and for bad debts do not improve. Explain why this might happen.

(b) Suppose that the performance measures for the average age of accounts receivable, bad debts, and unsold inventory improve, but total profits do not. Explain why this might happen. Assume in your answer that the explanation lies within the company.

C16–10 Strategic management accounting Time allowed: 90 minutes

Bernard Mason has just been appointed as Commercial Manager of the Salchester Theatre. The theatre has just completed a disappointing year with low attendances, culminating in a loss of £57,000. Details of the financial position of Salchester Theatre are given in Table 1. The current Artistic Director had, until now, been responsible for both the commercial and creative activities of the theatre. Mason has been brought in to improve the financial health of the theatre. His previous experience has been in the financial function within the manufacturing industry, and more recently as a finance manager at the town's university. Bernard considers himself to be a man of culture and not just a hard, bottom-line oriented businessman. He has welcomed this challenge to improve the fortunes of Salchester Theatre. Salchester is situated about 50 miles from London, has a population of about 200,000 people, and is home to one of the newer universities. The main sources of employment are in the commercial sector, including the headquarters of a large insurance company, and in the computing industry. There are also a significant number of commuters who travel daily to work in London. The theatre is reasonably modern, built in the early 1980s, and is located in the centre of town, having a seating capacity of 350. There is also a restaurant/coffee shop which is open throughout the day. However, this facility is poorly supported and is only ever busy for pre-theatre meals in the evening. There is also a rehearsal stage which is adjacent to the theatre. The theatre employs 20 full-time actors and actresses and a stage crew of twelve – which includes set designers and builders, carpenters, electricians and painters. Ticket sales and administration are handled by two full-time employees. Much of the work done during performances is by the 'Friends of Salchester Theatre' – a small group of active volunteers, many of whom are retired. These people act as bar and restaurant staff. They deal with mailing lists and also collect tickets, show people to their seats, and sell ice cream and confectionery to the audience at the interval. The 20 actors and actresses are usually divided into two groups, each performing a play for three weeks. While one group is performing, the other group is rehearsing for its next three-week commitment. Occasionally when a larger cast is required, such as for a performance of Shakespeare, members of one group will supplement the other. In fact when requirements are for a large number of actors they are helped by volunteers from the drama department of the university. The theatre company operates for 42 weeks in a year. The theatre is closed for one week each year for refurbishment and decoration. The remaining nine weeks are used by touring companies for shows such as opera, ballet and musicals, the Christmas show targeted at young children for the holiday period, and by the local choral society for its concerts.

The funding of the theatre is typical of many regional theatres. The Arts Council (a central government-funded body to support cultural activities throughout the country) provides an annual grant of £180,000, subject to the programme being artistically acceptable. The Arts Council aims to encourage both artistic

Table 1 Financial Details of Salchester Theatre (financial year September–August) (£000)

	1996/97	1997/98	1998/99
Income			
Theatre Group	410.00	390.00	340.00
Touring Companies	118.00	120.00	140.00
Restaurant	31.00	36.00	32.00
Arts Council	180.00	180.00	180.00
Local Authority	130.00	130.00	130.00
University	5.00	5.00	5.00
Hire to Local Choral Groups	3.50	3.50	4.00
Total Income	877.50	864.50	831.00
Expenditure			
Wages and Salaries	500.00	520.00	550.00
Materials and Other Costs	100.00	103.00	120.00
Restaurant (food etc.)	28.50	30.00	35.00
Fixed Costs (rent, lighting, heating)	30.00	33.00	38.00
Cost of Touring Companies	110.00	115.00	145.00
Total Expenditure	768.50	801.00	888.00
Surplus/Deficit	109.00	63.50	−57.00

and cultural development. The town council in Salchester provides another subsidy of £130,000 each year. They believe that the existence of a theatre in Salchester is valuable for a number of reasons. It provides both culture and entertainment for the population of Salchester. Furthermore it enhances the reputation of the town. This is thought to be particularly important in attracting students. The university has 8,000 students who provide valuable income to the town, including shopkeepers and providers of student accommodation. With increasing competition for students Salchester does not want to lose a potential attraction. In addition, the university has a drama department and the theatre provides both resources and support to this department. Although there is only a nominal charge for this (about £5,000 a year) the theatre does receive help from the graphics and advertising department of the university in the form of posters and publicity material, as well as tapes for local radio advertising. The rest of the income has to be generated by the theatre itself. Box office receipts have been falling over the past three years and in the financial year just completed amounted to only £340,000. Until last year ticket prices had been £8 for weekday performances (Monday–Thursday) and £10 for weekends (Fridays and Saturdays). In order to cut the deficit the prices have been increased to £10 for midweek and £12.50 for weekends. The strategy does not appear to have worked and the receipts have continued to fall.

Mason has decided that there must be a review of the theatre's operations. Attendances are continuing to fall. He has reviewed the productions over the past year and has discovered that on average attendances were less than a third of capacity. There were few shows which could be considered to be financially successful. The twice-yearly Shakespeare productions are always popular because the management wisely choose to perform the plays which are being used as the examination texts by the local schools. Naturally the local students take the opportunity to see these plays. The Christmas show is successful for about two weeks but unfortunately the performances are scheduled for three weeks. Some of the touring groups for opera and ballet are well supported but the cost of attracting these companies is very high and although the attendance is almost at capacity the revenue does not cover the operating costs. However, the main problem appears to be with the resident theatre group. Their costs are escalating but they do not appear to be attracting the public to their productions.

Mason called a meeting with the various groups who have an interest in the theatre's future to look at alternative approaches for improving the situation. The outcome of this meeting has not resulted in an agreed plan of action for the future. The actors and actresses who are looking for challenging modern plays are suggesting that future programmes be more adventurous and modern. One of them said 'We need to educate the audience to accept more creative material. The old favourites are boring and provide no interest for us.' However, this view has been totally rejected by the theatre supporters club who do most of the voluntary work. They are looking for an increase in established and popular plays with which the audience are familiar. They want comedies and easy-to-understand detective plays. This request has met with total opposition from the performers, who have said that this type of material is both uninteresting and unacceptable to them. Finally, the members of the local council, who appear to enjoy the privilege of free entry to the theatre as a result of their patronage, seem more concerned with attracting outside companies to the theatre. The presence of nationally known theatre groups and performers apparently enhances the town's reputation.

Bernard Mason is unhappy at this inability to agree a way to resolve the current unacceptable position. There has to be some agreed strategy if the theatre is to survive and yet most of the groups, who have a stake in the theatre, cannot reach an understanding. Unless a viable solution can be found and agreed upon, Salchester Theatre will have to close, just as have many other regional theatres. This job is going to be more difficult and challenging than Mason originally had thought.

Required

1 It appears that the stakeholders in the theatre cannot agree on a strategic direction to solve the financial problems. Mason believes that a mission statement for the theatre could draw the conflicting parties closer together. With reference to the problems of Salchester Theatre, identify the major characteristics of a good mission statement, and comment on the problems which Mason may experience in drawing up such a statement. *(13 marks)*

2 Evaluate the current position at Salchester Theatre and critically review the solutions which the various parties have suggested might improve the financial position of the theatre. *(20 marks)*

3 Discuss what actions Mason might take in order to correct the worrying deterioration in the financial position. *(17 marks)*

(Total = 50 marks)

ACCA Management and Strategy, December 1999

C16–11 Strategic management accounting time allowed: 75 minutes

Sports & Leisure Ltd (SL) is a private company which operates two private health and fitness clubs in Yorkshire.

The company history

SL was formed in 1986 by its two shareholders and directors, Mike Conn and Archie Moon, who opened the first fitness club in Toddmartin. This is a prosperous commuter town of about 25,000 people just outside Leeds. Mike and Archie had been physiotherapists with a major football club and had used savings and mortgaged their houses to finance their shares in the company. They took an active role in supervising club members and advertised their previous professional experience.

The Toddmartin leisure club prospered with growth stabilizing over the past three years at the current level of about 1,000 members. Each member currently pays an annual subscription fee of £500. This has risen in excess of inflation for a number of years.

The success of the business was due to a number of factors. First, it is the only fitness club in the town; second, it has the personal day-to-day involvement of the owners, both of whom have a good local reputation; and, third, the staff has a good knowledge of health and fitness and is paid premium rates.

In order to expand further, SL opened a second fitness club in 1999 in Dingledown, a town near Sheffield, of some 45,000 people, mainly in the low to middle income groups. It is about 30 miles from the Toddmartin club and adopted the same general approach and level of fees as in Toddmartin. Dingledown has no other fitness clubs.

The fitness club industry

Health and fitness has experienced a significant increase in demand in the UK, with annual membership growth figures of over 10% over recent years, despite an average increase in fees above inflation. Currently, it is estimated that some 5% of the UK population are members of fitness clubs, but membership is more concentrated in the higher income group.

On the supply side there are several major health and fitness chains which have a national reputation and are operated by subsidiaries of the major brewing and hotel groups. These tend to have the best equipment, largest memberships and highest fees. They are usually located in major cities.

There are also many smaller chains or single club organizations around the country. Market surveys suggest that there is still an undersupply with a potential to attain the US level of fitness club membership of 7% of the total population.

Strategic issues

The shareholders are concerned about two issues which developed this year.

Issue 1: Rival competition at Toddmartin

A rival, medium-sized company, Premier Leisure Ltd, has announced that it is to open a new fitness club in Toddmartin in six months' time. It will use the latest equipment, in contrast to SL's facilities which are in need of some updating.

Premier Leisure Ltd will offer discounted membership fees for the first three months, but the long-term annual fees charged by Premier Leisure Ltd at existing clubs are around £450. This is possible as they operate with fewer and less qualified staff than SL.

Issue 2: Establishing the Dingledown Club

The performance of the Dingledown Club is disappointing. The membership is growing, but more slowly than had been anticipated. The manager originally employed to run the club had focused more on operational activities and less on marketing and expanding membership. A replacement manager has recently been appointed. His remuneration package is yet to be decided but some incentive to expand membership, while maintaining the long-term reputation, is being considered. Additionally, an approach has been made by a large industrial company, Filochem plc. It is offering to pay a lump sum of £50,000 if SL offers half-price membership to any of its employees and ex-employees joining over the next year. Initial estimates are that 250 people would join the club under this scheme. Filochem plc provides a significant amount of employment in the town, but recently it received adverse publicity having made some employees redundant.

Draft accounts

The directors prepared the following draft accounts for the year to 31 March 2001.

	Toddmartin £000	Dingledown £000	Total £000
Fitness Activities			
Fees	500	100	600
Fitness salaries	230	90	320
Net income	270	10	280
Overheads			
Lease rentals – building	50	50	100
Depreciation	15	20	35
Other	20	25	45
Net profit/(loss)	185	(85)	100

Required

1 Analyse and justify the strategic position of each of SL's two fitness clubs according to their positions in the product life cycle and in the Boston Consulting Group Matrix. *(6 marks)*

2 Write a memorandum to the directors, as an external adviser, which assesses and advises upon each of the two strategic issues. In so doing use the following headings:

Issue 1 Competition at Toddmartin

(a) Competitive strategy, market segmentation and pricing

(b) Long-term viability of two fitness clubs in Toddmartin

(c) Determining the circumstances under which SL should exit the Toddmartin market *(11 marks)*

Issue 2 Establishing the Dingledown Club

(a) The relationship between costs, revenues and profitability

(b) The Filochem contract

(c) Marketing strategy and incentives (excluding Filochem)

(d) Long-term viability. *(15 marks)*

(Total = 32 marks)

ICAEW Business Management, June 2001

C16–12 Strategic management accounting Time allowed: 80 minutes

Saxex plc (hereafter Saxex) is listed on the London Stock Exchange and is the largest jewellery retailer in the UK.

Company profile

Saxex operates some 600 jewellery outlets in the UK. Products include: traditional jewellery of gold and gem stones, costume jewellery, watches, clocks and silverware. Saxex's turnover makes up about 17% of the UK jewellery market which is valued at around £2.7 billion per year. Its brand name, used in all outlets, is 'Jewel in the Crown' and is well recognized as a sign of good value and reasonable quality.

The company currently manufactures some jewellery from gold and rough gem stones, but it also buys in jewellery ready for sale. Given the volume of its purchases it obtains significant discounts from all types of supplier.

While the company is profitable, its rate of growth has slowed significantly in recent years. The major reasons for this are:

1 There is an outlet in every city and most major towns in the UK and Saxex has thus reached the point of market saturation.

2 The 'Jewel in the Crown' stores are essentially mid-market and this has not been a growth area for the industry in recent years. It is particularly susceptible to a downturn in the economy.

An industry profile

Jewellery in the UK is retailed through a variety of outlets including shops, mail order, jewellery counters in department stores, market stalls and catalogue showrooms.

Retailers include large listed companies with many branches, smaller private companies (normally with a limited number of branches in a particular region) and independent single outlets. There is also a very wide range of quality and prices in the industry.

Strategies for growth

The board of Saxex is considering two strategies to return the business to higher growth. The company does not have significant liquid resources and thus intends to use debt to finance strategic development.

Strategy A – Open a new, up-market jewellery division

The board is considering opening shops under a new name to sell up-market jewellery at a higher price and at a much greater profit margin than the existing business. As yet it is unsure whether to buy retailing space and create a new brand or to buy an existing up-market jewellery chain.

Strategy B – Expand Overseas

Saxex is considering opening up further outlets in Europe under its existing brand name and selling its existing product range. It is unsure whether to buy existing overseas companies and re-brand them with the 'Jewel in the Crown' label or merely to buy retailing space.

Required

1 Assume the following with respect to an existing outlet and a new outlet under *Strategy A*.

	Existing	Up-market
Annual Fixed Costs	£240,000	£360,000
Expected sales volume	37,500	24,000
Average variable cost per item	£24	£36

Assume that existing outlets generate a contribution margin (i.e. contribution divided by sales) of 25%.

Calculate the average price that the new up-market outlet must charge per item in order to earn the same overall profit as the existing outlet. *(5 marks)*

2 Evaluate each of the proposed development strategies under the following headings:

(a) Marketing strategy

(b) Risk

(c) Growth by acquisition or by internal development; and conclusions.

Where appropriate, refer to relevant strategic models. *(23 marks)*

(Total 5 28 marks)

ICAEW Business Management, September 2001

C16–13 Strategic management accounting Time allowed: 90 minutes

Alexander Simmonds is the founder and Managing Director of Playwell Ltd, a privately owned UK company specializing in making educational toys for young children and for children with special educational needs. These toys are robust and of simple construction made from high-quality materials, mainly wood, acquired from a local supplier. The main selling lines are building blocks of different shapes, sizes and colours, and toy trains and carriages (with no mechanical or electrical components). These simple toys are intended to stimulate the imagination of young children and to help them develop their visual and co-ordination abilities.

Alexander started the company in the early 1980s. He had initially made toys in his garage for his own children. He was soon persuaded to expand his activities and he had a ready demand for his products from friends and neighbours. In 1983 he was made redundant from his full-time job and he decided to put his redundancy money into setting up his own company. To his surprise the demand for his products grew at a faster rate than he had expected. There was an obvious gap in the market for simple, high-quality toys. Young children did not appear to want the complex and high technology products which were expensively promoted on television and in magazines. The early success of the company was helped by being a low-cost operation. At the start, Alexander's sales were made on a direct basis, using no intermediaries. He promoted his products within a fifty mile radius using local newspapers; orders were shipped directly to the customers. Additionally the supplier of the materials provided Playwell with extended and low-cost credit until the final payment was made to the company for the completed toys. This arrangement has continued to the present time.

Between 1983 and 1988 sales grew from a figure of £30,000 to almost £700,000. Net profit after tax was about 12%. Alexander's policy had been to reinvest these profits into the business. By 1988 he had moved out of his garage and had taken over a small factory in an industrial development area in a nearby town. Skilled labour was relatively easy to acquire. There was high unemployment in the area as a result of recent factory closures. By 1988 Alexander employed nearly 30 people in a range of jobs from design, manufacturing, sales, invoicing and distribution. Labour turnover was, unsurprisingly, very low. The workers were very loyal and Alexander paid them competitive wages and provided them with above-average benefits, particularly attractive in an area where unemployment was still high. The firm continued to grow at a rate of about 20% a year during the late 1980s and early 1990s. Although most of the sales were still marketed directly to the customer a significant proportion of sales were now made through one retailer who had a group of fifteen shops. This retailer sells products for young children, ranging through clothing, cots and prams as well as toys, and even currently, in 1999, this retailer still relies on Playwell for a significant amount of its toy purchases. About 40% of the UK sales (excluding those to the special educational needs market) are currently made to this retailer. The target market for these shops is professional and middle-class parents who generally value quality above price.

As in any growing organization Alexander now found himself moving away from a hands-on operation and becoming more concerned with future growth and strategy. By the end of 1994 Alexander decided to look at another market to generate increased growth in sales. Although sales were now almost £1.5 million a year and there were nearly 50 employees, the company now had the capacity to double its output. Fixed costs, including labour, accounted for 60% of total costs and any future increase in sales ought to generate improved profit margins. This was important if the company was to prosper and grow and provide security for the workers in an area where employment opportunities were limited. The company was then looking for sales to increase by about 30% a year. However, such an increase could not easily be funded out of retained earnings. Playwell's past performance and conservative financial record was sufficiently attractive for the company's bank to be more than willing to extend its credit lines to provide the necessary working capital.

The new area that Playwell was interested in was the development of toys designed for the 'special education needs' market. This term is generally used to refer to the education of children who have one or more physical, mental or emotional disabilities. Toys such as shaped building blocks, sponge balls, pegboards and three-dimensional puzzles can all help children with disabilities to improve their visual perception, spatial awareness, memory and muscle control. In addition there were other products such as balance boards and beams and disks, all made from high quality wood, which can help to co-ordinate mental and muscular activities. However, it was likely that the method of marketing and distribution might have to be adapted. The new market segment was much more easily identifiable and accessible. Databases of parents of children with special educational needs were readily available and it was possible to access the parents of these children via the specialist schools which these children attended. These schools were enthusiastic about Playwell's products but they alone could not support this new range of products. In fact part of Playwell's strategy was to distribute its products to these schools at very low prices in the hope that parents would then purchase these specialist toys for home use. This proved less easy than had been anticipated. First, parents of these children with special educational needs incurred many other expenses such as the additional costs of care. Furthermore, because of the increased care which these children usually required, one of the parents often had to stay at home or could only take on part-time work. Consequently the parents' discretionary income was significantly less. In addition, whereas the company had hoped that the teachers would recommend its products to the parents, it became apparent that teachers were not doing so, being worried that the parents would not have the expertise to use some of the equipment properly. As a result the revenues from this market were not as large as had been anticipated, particularly as the products' placement in the schools was seen initially as a loss-leader. Nevertheless sales of Playwell's core products (the non-specialist toys) were still gradually increasing (8% a year), but the momentum of earlier years was now not being maintained. By the beginning of 1997 Alexander decided that any future market expansion should be focused overseas, although he still intended to persevere with the 'special education' venture.

The company had acquired a good reputation within the United Kingdom and was operating in a growing niche market, in which Playwell was a significant participant. However, the company now decided that exports were to be the favoured means of growth. In an effort to avoid high risks Alexander decided to concentrate his activities in Western Europe. There were a number of advantages to this strategy – the purchasing processes of both parents and children were thought to be similar to that of the domestic market, transportation costs were likely to be lower than sales to America or Asia, and being part of the European Union there would be no trade barriers. However after an initial period of success Playwell discovered that sales were not as easily achieved as they had been in the UK. First the major European countries of France, Germany and Italy were at different stages in the business cycle to the UK. Whilst the British economy was growing the continental ones were suffering from recession. Consequently the demand for products such as toys was not buoyant. Furthermore high interest rates within the UK resulted in a high level of the pound sterling against the euro and other continental currencies, so making any exporting from the UK an expensive option. It appeared that price was now becoming a serious consideration in the customer's purchasing decision, particularly for a company with no strong overseas reputation. (Table 1 provides financial data for Playwell over the past few years.)

Alexander had now made two efforts to expand his business, neither of which could be judged as successful and he was now anxious to determine the future progress of the company.

Required

1 Alexander Simmonds appears to be the only person who is determining the objectives and strategic direction of Playwell plc. Identify any other parties who could have an interest in the success of this company. How might their goals be different to those of Alexander and to what extent would these differences be relevant? *(15 marks)*

2 You have been retained as a business consultant by Alexander to provide impartial advice as to the future strategy which the company should adopt. Given its relative failure in its last two ventures provide a briefing paper recommending a strategy which Playwell should pursue in the next two to three years. You should support your recommendation with appropriate financial analysis and the use of suitable analytical models. *(20 marks)*

3 The exporting venture appears to have failed because of an inadequate knowledge of the market. Identify the main types of information concerning the company's business environment you would consider to be essential before committing the company to an export strategy, giving reasons to justify your selection. *(15 marks)*

(Total = 50 marks)

ACCA Management and Strategy, June 1999

Table 1

	£ million					
	1994	**1995**	**1996**	**1997**	**1998**	**1999 (forecast)**
Sales to general toy retailers – UK	1.50	1.62	1.75	1.89	2.04	2.20
Cost of sales	0.53	0.57	0.62	0.67	0.72	0.78
UK special needs toys sales		0.30	0.30	0.25	0.25	0.15
Cost of sales		0.14	0.14	0.11	0.11	0.07
Overseas sales				0.50	0.55	0.55
Cost of sales				0.30	0.33	0.33
Total sales	1.50	1.92	2.05	2.64	2.84	2.90
Fixed costs	0.65	0.95	1.00	1.25	1.40	1.40

C16–14 Time allowed: 90 minutes

Sam and Annabelle Burns own and manage the firm Hair Care Ltd, based in the UK. The firm was formed in 1998 when Sam and his wife remortgaged their house and borrowed heavily from the bank to buy out the company from a conglomerate organization who were disposing of non-core businesses. Sam had been a senior salesman with the hair-care subsidiary of the conglomerate. This subsidiary bought hair-care products, mainly small value items and consumables – scissors, brushes, combs, hair nets, curlers and hair-dryers – from manufacturers and resold them to wholesalers and large retail chemist chains within the UK, mainly for use in hairdressing salons. The new business has continued in this direction. The manufacturers are almost entirely non-UK suppliers, many based in Hong Kong but with manufacturing facilities in mainland China, Taiwan and Malaysia. However, about 30% of the products are sourced in Europe – Italy and Germany predominantly.

The company has met with success very quickly and the initial loans have already been repaid ahead of schedule. The company now owns the freehold of a large warehouse/distribution centre which is five times the size of the original depot, leased when the company first started trading five years ago. Sales turnover, now in excess of £5 million, has increased by more than 50% each year and shows little signs of slowing down. Despite this apparent rapid growth Hair Care Ltd only accounts for about half of the current market, leaving some potential for growth. The company is run cost effectively, with minimum staffing. Sam, as Managing Director, is solely concerned with the marketing side of the business. He spends most of his time in the selling role and in customer care, which he rates as a major contributor to the company's success. The only other key manager is his wife who is responsible for managing the warehouse staff, arranging distribution, general administration and financial management. The company started with six employees, in addition to Sam and Annabelle, and now has 15. Staff rarely leave the company. The staff is almost entirely employed in the distribution and packaging function, although there are two other sales people apart from Sam, but they only deal with the smaller buyers. With the continued growth in turnover it is inevitable that the number of employees will have to increase. It is expected that there will have to be a total of about 30 staff, all non-managerial, in two years if sales continue to increase at the current rate.

The success of Hair Care Ltd can be accounted for by a number of factors. Sam is a very good salesman who is responsible for looking after all the major accounts. He is popular and much of the business is built on his personal relationship with the key clients. There is a considerable amount of customer loyalty which is mainly attributable to Sam, and both he and his wife are always accessible to customers and they go out of their way to provide a first-class service. Even on vacation the two owners are in daily contact with the office. The company has been able to manage its purchases wisely. Most of the products, being purchased abroad, require payment in a foreign currency. Hair Care Ltd has been able to benefit from the relative weakness of the euro as against sterling for its European supplies. Although most of the products sourced in the Far East are priced in US dollars, the relative strength of that currency has enabled Hair Care Ltd to negotiate lower purchasing prices. However, it is questionable as to how long this situation concerning foreign exchange can be held. The situation may change should the UK join the euro in the near future and much, of course, will depend upon the level at which sterling enters the euro exchange.

Sam has also developed strong links with his suppliers and he has, until recently, attempted to trade with only a few so that his lines of communication and control are kept as simple as possible. Most of his current suppliers have been with him since the start of the company in 1998. This has provided the company with reliable and good quality products. In fact Hair Care Ltd often has exclusive access to certain products. For example, it has the sole rights to distribute an Italian hair-dryer which is generally recognized to be the best on the market. This product strength has enabled the company to build on the customer loyalty. However, it is inevitable that as demand has increased, existing suppliers have not been able to keep up with the necessary volumes and Sam has had to look for, and buy from new manufacturers.

The company has benefited from a period of relatively steady growth in the economy and even in the current economic down-turn Sam has argued that demand for hair-care products is usually recession-proof. Furthermore, Hair Care Ltd has currently no near competitors. Many of the small competitors in the wholesale market place have chosen to concentrate on other areas of the hair-care business – salon furnishings and the supply of cheap, low-value items such as towels, razors etc. – leaving much of this basic business (sales of other relatively low-value and mainly disposable products) to Sam's company. Additionally quite a number of the small firms have even left the market. All this has helped to contribute to the overall growth rate of Hair Care Ltd. There are some major international companies who make shampoos, conditioners and other cosmetic type products who also buy in consumer hairdressing products such as the ones sold by Hair Care Ltd. They then sell these mainly to the retail trade for domestic use by consumers and not directly to the hairdressing salons as does Hair Care Ltd. Furthermore, these are large companies and Sam believes that they do not currently see his company as a major threat.

The company has registered a brand name for its main products which it repackages, rather than using the individual brands of the original manufacturers. This has enabled Hair Care Ltd to generate even greater loyalty from its customers and often to obtain a price premium from these products.

Sam believes that part of the company's success stems from the fact that he has an organization with minimal administrative overheads. He outsources all of his products, adding value mainly through branding and the maintenance of customer care. He believes that strategy is not mainly about beating the competition but in serving the real needs of the customer. The company has also been able to develop a strong relationship with the country's leading retail chemist chain, providing it with good quality, low-cost disposable products such as hair nets and brushes to be sold under an own-brand label. Although the margins are inevitably small, the volumes involved more than compensate for this.

The company has had to incur increased investment as a result of the large growth in turnover. The building of the warehouse, the increased stock-holding costs, capital expenditure on items such as computing systems, fork-lift trucks and automated stock control and retrieval systems could not be financed out of current earnings, but the company's bank was only too ready to lend the company the necessary money considering that the original loan had been repaid ahead of schedule.

All the success which Hair Care Ltd has achieved has not diminished Sam's appetite for growth. He now seems to be driven more by seeking power and influence than acquiring wealth. He questions the ability of the company to continue its current growth in the prevailing environment and therefore he is looking for ideas which may facilitate corporate expansion. He has asked his accountant to provide some options for him to consider.

Table 1 Details of performance of Hair Care Ltd: 2000–2003 (unless otherwise stated, figures are in £'000)

	2000 £'000	**2001 £'000**	**2002 £'000**	**2003 forecast £'000**
Sales	2,300	3,500	5,010	7,500
Cost of sales	1,450	2,380	3,507	5,250
Marketing costs	200	250	290	350
Distribution costs	300	400	430	500
Administration	50	55	80	120
Interest payments	0	80	220	700
Operating profit	300	335	483	580
Loans	0	850	2,400	5,000
Number of suppliers (actual)	15	20	30	50
Range of products (actual)	35	85	110	130
Total staff including Sam and Annabelle	12	14	15	23
Stocks	230	400	700	1,400
Fixed assets	500	1,500	2,700	6,300
Return on sales (%)	13.0	9.6	9.6	7.7

Required

1 Assuming the role of Sam's accountant, prepare a report for Sam, evaluating the current position of Hair Care Ltd and highlighting any financial and strategic issues concerning future developments which you feel should be brought to his attention. *(20 marks)*

2 As his accountant, prepare a short report for Sam, identifying and assessing the strategies which he could consider in attempting to further the company's development. *(20 marks)*

3 Sam seems preoccupied with growth. Identify reasons for potential corporate decline and suggest ways that Sam could avoid them in the context of the case study scenario. *(10 marks)*

4 Sam currently appears to have a successful formula for growth. Using the concept of the value chain, demonstrate how he has been able to achieve this success. *(10 marks)*

(Total = 60 marks)

CIMA Strategic Business Planning and Development, June 2003

Endnotes

1 Simmonds (1981).

2 Graham and Harris (1999).

3 See Kaplan (1984) and Johnson and Kaplan (1987) for a critique of short-term accounting measures.

4 CIMA (2004), p. 5.

5 Rappaport (1999).

6 Ittner and Larcker (2003).

7 Goold and Campbell (1987).

8 Seal (2001).

9 See Chapter 19 for a more detailed treatment of life-cycle costing.

10 Miles and Snow (1978).

11 Porter (1980).

12 Porter (1990), p. 40.

13 Porter (1985).

14 Shank (1996).

15 Shank (1996).

16 Tomkins and Carr (1996).

17 For a discussion of strategic investment appraisal see also Northcott and Alkaraan (2007).

18 For example, see Cronshaw, Davis and Kay (1994).

19 Cooper (1996).

20 The balanced scorecard concept was developed by Robert Kaplan and David Norton. For further details, see their articles Kaplan and Norton (1992), (1996a), (1996b), (1997) and (2004). In the 1960s, the French developed a concept similar to the balanced scorecard called Tableau de Bord or 'dashboard'. For details see Lebas (1994).

21 Some low cost airlines have only copied the 'no-frills' and seem less concerned with 'fun'. There is also an emerging trend to encourage online checking-in.

22 Of course, Toyota, *as a company*, is associated with the development of lean production, which, as we have seen, is based on trying to achieve both low cost, reliability and high quality specifications. It may not try to achieve all these characteristics *in a particular model.*

23 Kaplan and Norton (1996b).

24 For a critical evaluation of the BSC see Norreklit (2000).

25 Ittner and Larcker (2003).

26 See, especially, Simons (1995).

27 Emergent strategy is especially associated with the work of Mintzberg (1978).

28 See Prahalad and Hamel (1990).

29 Bromwich and Bhimani (1994).

30 Coad (1996).

31 Wilson (1995).

32 Lord (1996), p. 364. See also Roslender and Hart (2003) and Shank (2006).

Chapter 17

Performance management, management control and corporate governance

Learning objectives

After studying Chapter 17, you should be able to:

1. Consider some criticisms of budgeting as a performance management system
2. Understand some generic features of performance measurement and management control
3. Analyse the 'levers of control' approach to strategy implementation
4. Reappraise the role of management accounting in corporate governance
5. Review the relationship between corporate governance and risk management
6. Appreciate the importance of the environment and the role of environmental management accounting
7. Critically examine performance management and social responsiveness in the public sector

Concepts in Context

The recent collapse of some banks (Northern Rock and Bear Sterns, for example) and the announcement of substantial write downs in many European and US banks have a number of complex causes including regulatory failure. The general problem, however, seemed to be related to the measurement and management of risk. In this chapter, we suggest that risk management is part of a wider issue of corporate governance. We also argue that risk management and other corporate governance matters have a management accounting dimension – well-governed organizations need to have their own systems to measure and manage risk. Furthermore, if non-executive directors are to make a real contribution to the monitoring of corporate strategy and risk then they need to have appropriate financial and non-financial information.[1]

In Chapter 1, management accounting techniques were introduced as being part of a cycle of control (see especially Exhibit 1.1). In addition to budgeting, we have also analysed a number of organizational control systems such as the *balanced scorecard* (BSC), *return on investment* (ROI) and *residual income/economic value added* (EVA). In this chapter we develop some of the ideas introduced in Chapter 1 where we described the basic functions of management by reviewing the role of management accounting within *performance management* and *management control systems*. In addition, we consider how and whether managers' decisions can be made accountable to other stakeholders in the organization such as shareholders, debtors, customers, employees and so on. These concerns are often dealt with in emerging topics such as *corporate governance* and *corporate social responsiveness*. **Corporate governance** may be interpreted quite narrowly as being concerned with protecting the interests of the suppliers of capital[2] while **corporate social responsiveness**[3] **(or responsibility)** refers to the capacity of the organization to respond to the demand of society as a whole. While these concepts can be linked to our earlier discussion on the importance of business and professional ethics in Chapter 1, this chapter shows how ethical behaviour may be located in wider organizational frameworks where appropriate internal governance mechanisms are designed to support rather than penalize ethical decision making.

We have already seen how management accounting techniques such as budgeting and balanced scorecards help managers plan, make decisions and control activities. Yet although it is clear that such techniques help to operationalize organizational objectives and measure whether the *actual* have matched the *planned* outcomes, there has been little discussion of how or indeed, whether, such techniques can drive human behaviour in organizations. In short, target setting and measurement are only parts of wider organizational control systems which may involve the analysis of reward systems and the impact of *informal controls* based on conformance to organizational and social norms.

Developments in management accounting, especially the non-financial performance measures and strategic management accounting techniques that we covered in Chapter 16, *can* be used to enhance corporate responsiveness towards shareholders, employees, customers, government and the physical environment. But if corporate social responsibility is going to be more than 'window-dressing' and actually *change* corporate behaviour, then specific performance indicators and processes may need to be embedded alongside the more familiar, financially oriented management control systems.[4]

Some criticisms of budgeting as a performance management system

In earlier chapters we covered the technical aspects of budgeting and profit planning in some detail. Such detailed coverage is understandable as for many if not most businesses, the budget is a key planning and control mechanism with many desirable characteristics (see Chapters 11 and 13 especially). Yet budgeting has come in for much criticism in recent years. It has been described by Jan Wallander as 'an unnecessary evil' and Jack Welch as the 'bane of corporate America'.[5] Such criticisms of budgeting are easier to appreciate when looked at in the wider context of performance management systems. Furthermore, not only may we consider some organizational problems caused by budgeting but we can see that there are alternative, or at least supplementary, control models suggested by the performance management perspective.

One common criticism is that budgets produce a particular type of **constrained management style**, they concentrate on easy to measure events and they are *too historically based*. The last point is often linked to the view that budgets tend to be *incrementalist*. Particularly in not-for-profit organizations in the public sector, discussions about changes to budgets concentrate on marginal or incremental increases or decreases in particular departmental budgets. The problem with incrementalism is that activities become institutionalized through the budget and there is a reluctance to ask questions about fundamental purposes.[6]

Another criticism is that budgeting makes organizations *inflexible* and *unable to respond to uncertainty*. Budgeting is seen as being *mechanistic* with *rigid, formalized* and *tightly coupled* systems. Budgeting-led organizations may be slow to recognize changes in the market and also slow to react to changes even when they have been noticed. Other criticisms of budgeting are that it is *too time consuming*, it tends to *focus on cost control* rather than value creation, it tends to be *top down*, it encourages *gaming* and *opportunism*, it reinforces departmental *barriers* and it *hinders knowledge sharing*. Overall it makes *people feel undervalued*.[7]

Much of the criticism of budgeting is driven by a changing business environment, especially the belief that competition in modern markets has increased the importance of *intellectual capital* relative to physical or tangible capital.[8] In order to respond to this new competitive challenge, it is argued that companies need to adopt a *network* rather than a hierarchical, departmental structure. A network model may still use budgets for cash forecasting but not for cost control. The aim is to avoid 'actual versus budget' reports and concentrate on relative performance. These alternative approaches draw on other forms of management control such as benchmarking and the mix of financial and non-financial measures found in approaches such as the balanced scorecard.

FOCUS

Focus on current practice

Borealis is a company headquartered in Copenhagen, Denmark that produces polymers for the plastics industry. The company's financial controller felt the traditional budgeting process had outlived its usefulness – markets were changing so fast that budgets were out of date within weeks of publication. Moreover, since budgets were used to control and evaluate the performance of managers, they were subject to considerable gaming behaviour that reduced accuracy and usefulness. So over five years the company replaced traditional budgets with rolling forecasts and other management tools. Instead of holding managers to budgets, targets based on competitors' performance were set for variable costs, fixed costs and operating margins. Managers were given the freedom to spend money as needed to meet these benchmarks. Since the rolling forecasts of financial results were not used to control spending or to evaluate managers' performance, managers had little incentive to 'game the system', and forecasts were more accurate than those obtained through traditional budgeting processes.

Reform or abandon budgeting?

Given the criticisms of budgeting, what is the appropriate response? Currently, there seems to be two main practice-led approaches. One approach is to improving budgeting and the other is to abandon it.[9] If we review the criticisms of budgeting there seems to be two main issues. One issue concerns the question of *predictability*. It could be argued that budgets work well if managers' predictions are reliable because the budget can then represent a viable plan. Conversely, budgets tend to work badly in conditions of great uncertainty and turbulent environments.[10] The other issue concerns *organizational* and *time-frame problems*. It is argued that budgeting fosters a centralizing and stifling atmosphere as well as a possible mismatch between operational strategies and annual reporting cycles. These organizational problems tend to reduce the ability of units and employees to use their initiative as they lack empowerment.

When it is advocated that organizations abandon budgeting, it may mean that budgets are still used for financial purposes but, crucially, not for *performance evaluation*. The aim is to avoid the annual performance trap associated with budgeting by working with what have been called 'relative performance contracts with hindsight'.[11] The significance of the term 'relative' is that performance is benchmarked against *internal* or *external comparators* rather than against historical standards such as last year's results. The term 'with hindsight' means that rather than referring to fixed targets set at the *beginning* of the period, 'targets are adjusted by looking back and incorporating the actual operating and economic circumstances during the period'.[12] Managerial and employee rewards tend to be based on subjective and group criteria with an 'objective to engender a philosophy doing what is best for the firm in the light of current circumstance and to promote teamwork'.[13]

General models of performance measurement and management control

Alternatives or reforms to budgeting are best studied as part of a more general review of possible approaches to organizational control. The concept of control may be introduced by considering a simple thermostat where the system maintains a pre-specified temperature by switching a boiler on and off. More sophisticated models include the use of feedforward information and **double loop learning**. **Feedforward control** relies on a predictive model of processes so that errors can be anticipated and corrected for. As we saw in Chapter 16, *double loop learning* concerns the use of information to learn from past performance in order to change processes, change inputs or alter objectives.[14] The basic control model illustrated in Exhibit 17.1 indicates in very general terms the characteristics of a process control system.

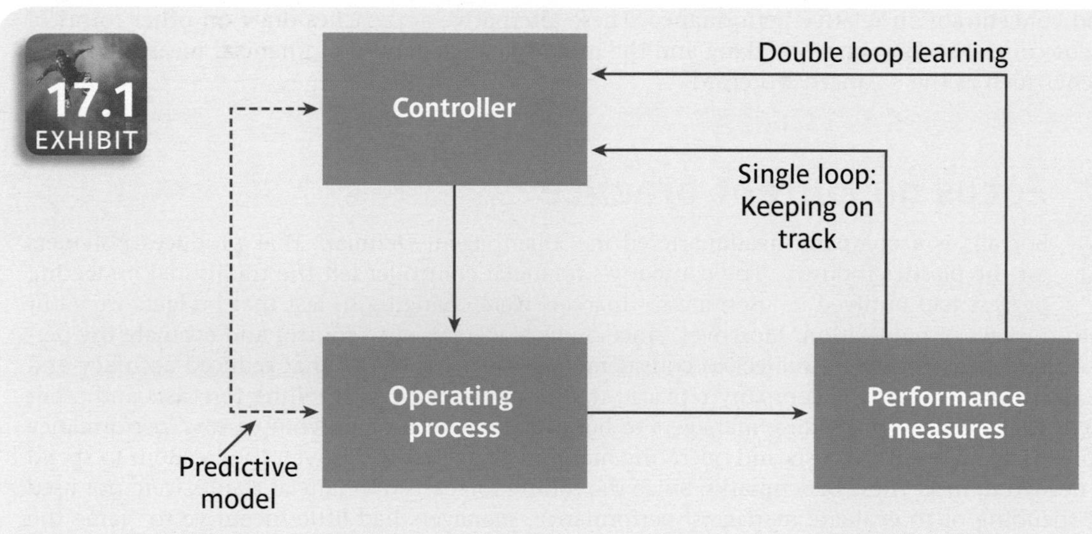

Exhibit 17.1 Process control: single loop, feedforward and learning loops

In order to operationalize process control systems for human organizations, we need to be more specific about objectives, motivation, culture and other organizational issues. If it is true that 'What you measure is what you get',[15] then a key feature of a performance management framework is a **performance measurement system** with the following desirable features:[16]

- The performance measures must be consistent with the strategy and objectives of the organization.
- There must be a system of feedback and review to ensure that the information flows enable the organization to learn and adapt from its experience.
- The performance measurement system must be comprehensive, including non-financial as well as financial indicators.
- Although comprehensive, the measurements system needs to be simple, clear and understandable focusing on **key performance indicators (KPIs)**.
- The performance measurement system must be owned and supported throughout the organization and be aligned with the rewards/penalties that managers and other employees receive for achieving performance targets.

With the above elements in place, we can construct a **performance management** or **management control** framework where organizational behaviour is based on formal, information-based systems. As we shall see below, such systems may then form a part of an overall model of strategy implementation.

The levers of control approach to strategy implementation

3 LEARNING OBJECTIVE

In Chapter 16 we began to explore emergent strategies and organizational learning and other issues that we have developed in this chapter.[17] These aspects of strategy have informed an influential approach to strategy implementation known as the *levers of control*[18] model. One of the characteristics of this more sophisticated approach to strategy and performance management is the recognition that *tensions are inevitable*. For example, there are tensions between performance measures that seem to contradict each other (such as employee morale versus control of wage costs). Furthermore, there are tensions between strategic objectives that encourage creativity and innovation, on the one hand, and the objectives that emphasize a more cautious, risk management approach. The **levers of control model** suggests ways by which these tensions can be managed. Simons[19] criticizes what he terms 'Old style strategy' which he characterizes as being very rational, very analytical and top down. Furthermore, in the old style, the implementation of strategy is either neglected or based on a hierarchical single loop approach to control. In contrast, the 'New style strategy' is more an emergent process in a decentralized, *learning*/flexible firm strategy which is characterized by employee empowerment and responding to customer needs. In practice, intended and emergent strategies tend to operate *simultaneously* with a need to balance both control and learning aspects.

Simons suggests that there are four basic levers of control:

- *belief systems* that inspire and direct;
- *boundary systems* that limit opportunism;
- *diagnostic control systems* that are used to motivate and monitor;
- and *interactive control systems* that stimulate organizational learning.

The search for strategic opportunities is guided by **belief systems** that motivate search behaviour and **boundary systems** that constrain search and innovation. Belief systems are deliberately broad with the aim of fostering inspiration and not simply checking against pre-set standards. Belief systems should increase commitment, provide a core of stability and reinforce the distinctiveness of organization. In contrast, boundary systems are concerned with dos and don'ts such as ethical codes, business association rules and professional norms. It would be wrong to think of risks as simply being associated with fraud or regulatory issues. Thus some of the boundaries set by the firm are of a strategic nature, such as capital budgeting systems with their hurdle rates and positive present value rules.

As Simons points out, his third lever, **diagnostic control systems**, are generally well known as they consist of the sort of cybernetic, feedback-based models that dominate the conventional management control literature. Indeed, they may be summed up by a definition of management control as '[T]he formal, information-based routines and procedures that managers use to maintain or alter patterns in organizational activities'.[20] These diagnostic systems incorporate practices such as budgeting, standard costing, balanced scorecard, and so on. The aim of these systems is that measures should be objective, complete and responsive to actions/effort. Even here tensions may exist. For example, completeness may conflict with responsiveness (e.g. profit). The wrong choice of measures could lead to disasters or at the very least dysfunctional behaviour. For example, there may be a neglect or negative impact on teamwork and a failure to recognize problems of output ambiguity.

Simons' fourth lever is **interactive control systems** where the aim is to use information to encourage debate up and down organizations and to foster an emergent process that links strategy with tactics. The aim here is to develop double-loop learning that questions existing standards/policies. In this area, we need management information that picks up patterns of change but is relatively simple and usable by junior managers. The information should trigger revised action plans and develop an awareness of strategic uncertainties.

While the conflicting objectives shown in Exhibit 17.2 have to be managed, management, itself, is a scarce resource since managers face problems of *unlimited choice* and *limited attention*. Given the scarcity of management resources, the **return-on-management** is optimized by balancing and reconciling the tensions between attention and opportunity.

With respect to organizational motivation, Simons tries to avoid a **reductionist model of humanity** arguing that humans have creative and achievement orientations as well as material goals.

Good management, therefore, is about mobilizing creative human traits rather than just ensuring 'conformance to plan'. Yet, with the emergent problems of the dotcom bubble and financial scandals, the conformance to plan suddenly seems more appealing and less boring than it must have seemed in the more gung-ho days when Simons first proposed his model. As we shall see below, a tougher regulatory environment and an increased emphasis on risk management have raised the profile of boundary systems aimed at restraining both the greed and exuberance of senior executives.

Corporate governance: a financial perspective

4 LEARNING OBJECTIVE

In Chapter 1, we discussed the distinction between financial and management accounting which was summarized in Exhibit 1.2. From a learning perspective, it is important to understand the different aspects of accounting for *reporting* and accounting for *decision making* and *control*. On a practical level, these distinctions may be maintained by using 'different costs for different purposes'. In this chapter we point out that even though they should make distinctions between costs for external reporting and costs for decision making, management accountants generally also have a responsibility to ensure the integrity of financial data for reporting purposes.[21] In this respect, we are moving on to a more complex view on the role of management accounting than the one we initially presented in Chapter 1. The distinction between management accounting and financial accounting was justified in the historical context of the latter part of the 20th century when prominent commentators such as Johnson and Kaplan were concerned about the potentially damaging effect of financial reporting practices on the internal decision making. However, the most recent evidence from the US, UK and elsewhere, is that wealth has been destroyed, not by a lack of creativity or entrepreneurship but by reckless, greedy and sometimes fraudulent behaviour by executives at the highest level of giant corporations. In these instances, the boundary between internal and external decision making becomes more blurred as does our earlier distinction between the roles of management and financial accounting. Just as strategies need to be embedded in an organization's control systems and may involve tensions between expansive belief systems and more constraining boundary system, there can be tensions between the free-wheeling spirit associated with entrepreneurship and the more constraining values associated with financial probity and integrity.[22]

In corporate disasters that have stemmed from mismanagement rather than obvious fraud, the scandal here is that too often the senior executives who were responsible for the poor decisions were able to walk away from the mess of wrecked livelihoods and pensions with their own wealth and financial security unharmed. The 'reward for failure syndrome' means that the supposed morality tale of capitalism, that business failure leads to financial penalty, seems to have broken down for the very people who bear the greatest decision making responsibility.[23] The fashionable term for analysing these issues is *corporate governance*.

Focus on current practice

FOCUS

The 'reward for failure' syndrome may easily be observed in high profile companies such as the retail giant, Sainsbury's. Over his four years at the top of Sainsbury's, the ousted chairman, Sir Peter Davis received about £11 million. Over the same period, the company fell behind main rivals, Tesco and Asda, and profits fell to a 15-year low. Even without corporate disasters, chief executives have been awarded remuneration packages that pay bonuses even if performance goes down.[24] In the past decade, the *average* remuneration package of FTSE100 directors rose in spite of flat and falling stock market returns. Cohen argues that '(F)ree market economics can't explain the runaway growth in incomes. Try as hard as they might, conventional economists can't find a link between executive pay and performance.'[25]

Another indicator of executive excess is the ratio of CEO pay to average worker pay. In the UK the multiplicand of CEO pay to full-time manual worker pay has increased from 10 times in 1980 to 80 times in 2002. In the US, the multiplicand reached 516 in 1999![26]

A large number of examples of corporate malfeasance involving tax evasion, false accounting, money laundering and other dubious practices may be found on the website of the *Association for Accountancy and Business Affairs*, www.visar.csustan.edu/aaba/home.htm.

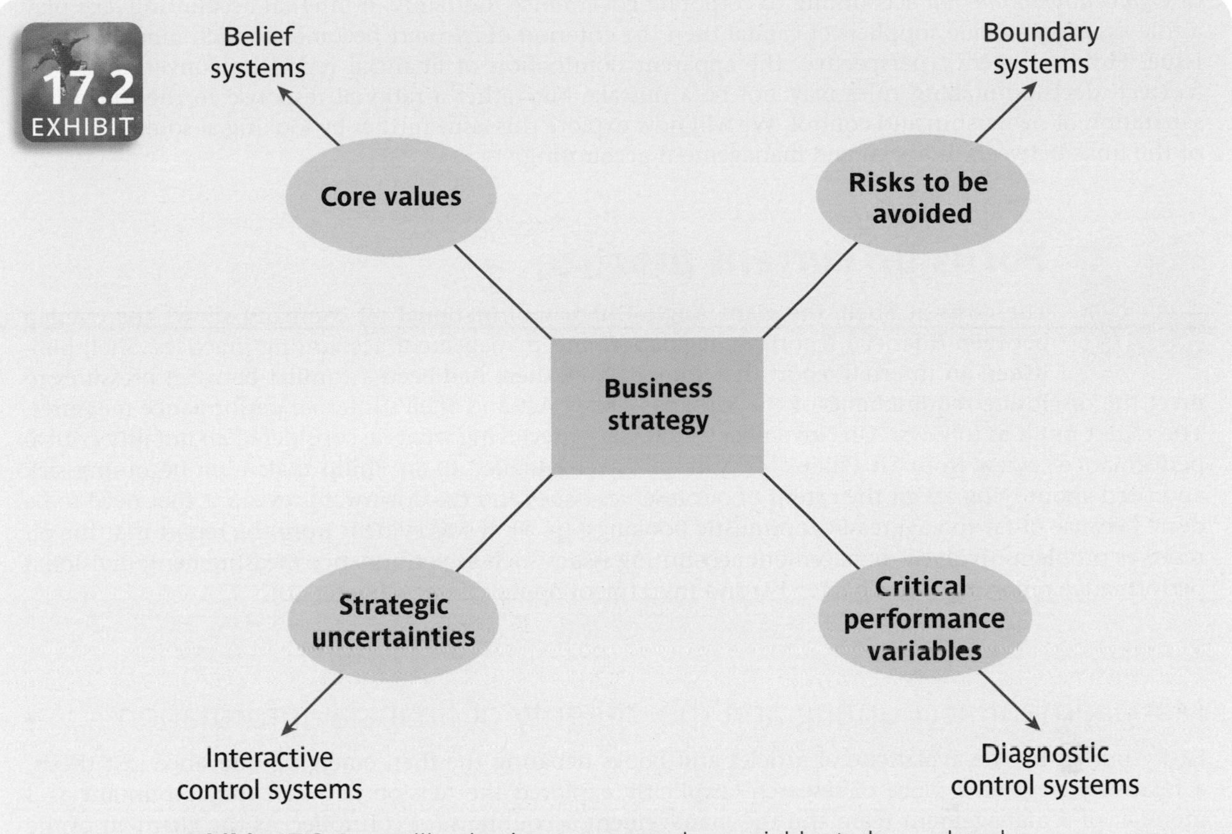

Exhibit 17.2 Controlling business strategy: key variables to be analyzed

Reprinted by permission of Harvard Business School Press. From *Levers of Control* by Robert Simons, MA 1995, p. 34.

Corporate governance has several implications for the study and practice of management accounting. In particular, one assumption generally implicit in management accounting, is that decision makers are profit maximizers because this is the goal that serves the owners of the firm. The assumption of profit maximization has been questioned on both theoretical and empirical grounds. Empirically, the evident suspicion of directors and senior managers in the City pages of even the most conservative of newspapers suggests that the notion that managers may pursue their own rather than shareholders' interests is accepted as a stylized fact of mainstream corporate life. A special theory called agency theory, which is beyond the scope of this book, addresses the difficulties of monitoring and linking managerial behaviour to the interests of shareholders.[27] With respect to theory, the adherence to the profit maximization assumption seems to ignore a financial accounting literature that deals with activities such as earnings management[28] and the various *managerialist* models of the firm that have been derived from standard neoclassical economics.[29] Managerialist theories of the firm may themselves be related to a finance view of corporate governance where the key questions are:

> ... How do the suppliers of finance get managers to return some of the profits to them? How do they make sure that managers do not steal the capital they supply or invest in bad projects? How do suppliers of finance control managers?[30]

Although corporate governance issues have long been the subject matter of related subjects such as financial reporting and auditing, the question that has been addressed less thoroughly is the contribution of *organizational/internal* accounting to corporate governance. Certainly, if internal accounting *does* play a role assuring outside suppliers of capital then the criterion of *relevance* becomes a much more complex issue. From an agency perspective, the apparent domination of financial reporting conventions over 'correct' decision-making rules may not be a mistake but rather a rational response to the increasing separation of ownership and control. We will now explore this issue further by looking at some examples of the links between financial and management accounting.

FOCUS

Focus on current practice

The crisis at Shell, the giant Anglo-Dutch multinational oil company shows the overlap between financial reporting, regulation and management accounting practices. Shell published an internal report that showed how there had been a conflict between pressures to meet the disclosure requirements of the Sarbanes–Oxley Act and Shell's internal performance measures. The report put it as follows: 'On November 9, 2003, after receiving what he considered an unfairly critical performance review from Sir Philip, Mr. van de Vijver e-mailed to Sir Philip that: I am becoming sick and tired about lying about the extent of our reserves issues and the downward revisions that need to be done because of far too aggressive/optimistic bookings' (p. 8). It was evident from the report that the oil reserves problem involved management accounting issues such as performance measurement, divisional performance reporting (see Chapter 14) and investment appraisal (see Chapter 10).

Management accounting and the integrity of financial information

Easily buried by the avalanche of articles and books debating the then emerging relevance lost thesis, a relatively neglected piece of research[31] explicitly explored the tension between the accountant as a member of a management team and the management accountant (or controller) as the guardian of the integrity of the externally reported financial information. In the latter role, the management accountant must exhibit a degree of independence from the business decision-making process.

Management accounting and regulatory approaches to corporate governance

The integrity of corporate reporting has been made the subject of intense regulatory and legal scrutiny. In the US, the emphasis has been on increased judicial enforcement of financial reporting standards in the Sarbanes–Oxley Act (2002). These regulatory innovations seem to suggest that the suppliers of capital no longer trust their most immediate agents, the senior executives of large corporations. In the UK with the publication of the Higgs Report (2003), one of the ways that management accounting can contribute to improving corporate governance is to advocate new performance measures that are designed to enhance the ability of non-executive directors to monitor their fellow executive directors.[32]

But how can non-executive directors make a difference if they do not know what is going on in the company? From this perspective, it is a short step to see a potential role for management accounting to provide non-executives with information with which to assess risk, check on strategy and monitor the behaviour of executive board members. Indeed many of the criticisms of conventional reporting and the proposed remedies will be unsurprising to academic management accountants. If conventional transaction-based financial accounting data is too late and too backward looking, then many of the key trends and key performance drivers will be driven by approaches such as the balanced scorecard and strategic management accounting.

The response from the management accounting profession to the corporate governance debate has been articulated in a CIMA technical report,[33] which outlines the sort of board reporting practices that are deemed necessary for good market performance and sound corporate governance. Drawing on previous reports on governance such as the Cadbury Report, Starovic builds on the Combined Code on Corporate Governance.[34] Along with the usual admonitions that good quality information should be relevant, focused, forward looking and so on, Starovic also argues for integrated information systems and processes. The role of management accountants in the financial perspective on corporate governance is summarized in Exhibit 17.3.

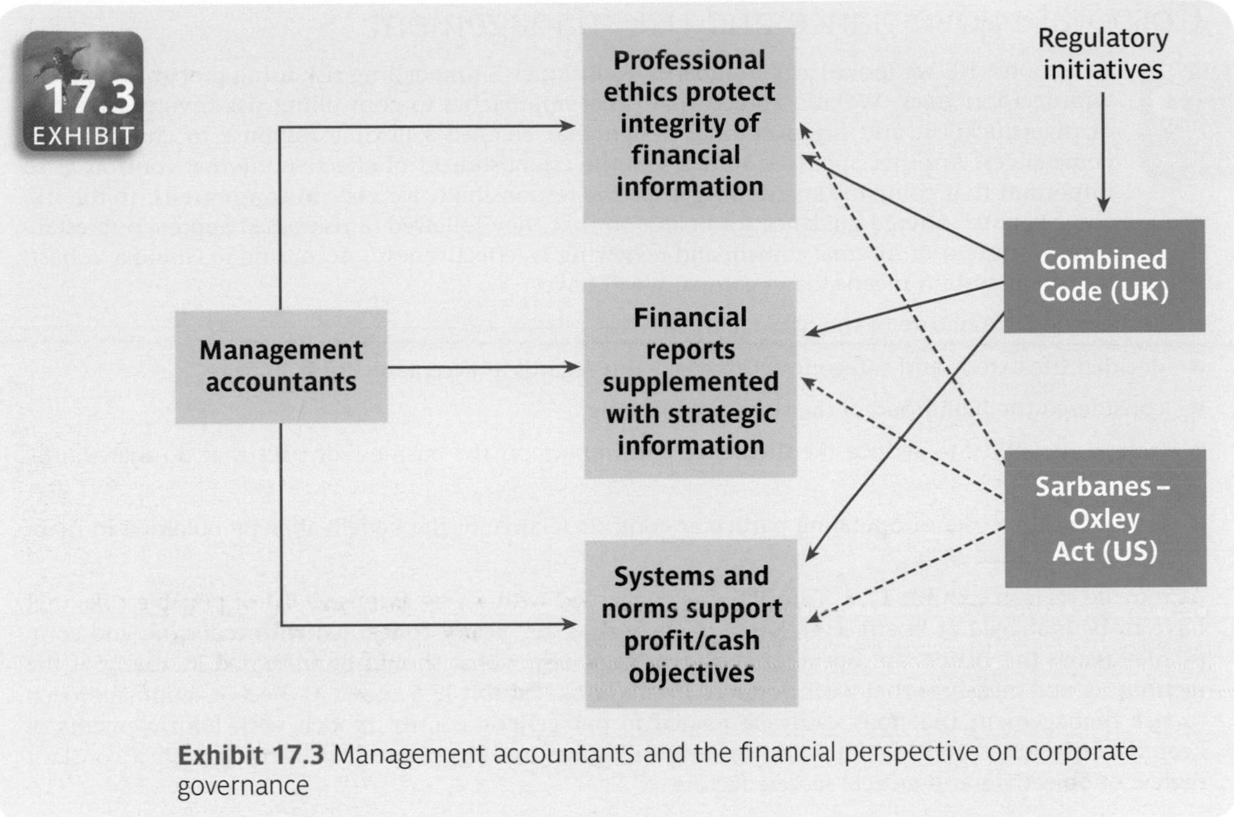

Exhibit 17.3 Management accountants and the financial perspective on corporate governance

Yet such an ambitious proposal begs some obvious questions. Why should non-executive directors be provided with strategic management accounting (SMA) data when even senior accounting officials seem reluctant to collect such information?[35] Guilding *et al.* (2000) found that respondents scored SMA higher on *merit* than in actual usage. One interpretation of this finding is that however desirable it may be in principle, there are few incentives for the extra information to be collected. More generally, why should managers who perhaps own very little of the stock of the company care about shareholders let alone other stakeholders? Taking an even more sceptical view, if managers are rewarded through stock options and compensated for loss of office, why should they worry too much about the possible downside of their chosen strategies? Although they may be concerned about their reputations, *these are most likely to be damaged not by strategies that fail but which are different.*

If we consider the *Management accounting in action* example in Chapter 16, senior executives at Marconi claimed that they were only doing what everyone else is doing (focusing and internationalizing in the telecom industry). So how can they blamed if the result is corporate meltdown?[36] Yet strategic management accounting techniques *should* enable managers to develop a *unique* company strategy based on an appraisal of how actual and potential competitors will react. Adopting a unique strategy is probably the only way that a company may obtain a competitive advantage and thus a higher return.[37] If a company just does what all its competitors are doing, then at best the company will just match the industry return. At worst, as in the Marconi case described in Chapter 16, if all companies try to expand in one industry, then a huge surplus of capacity and low returns are very likely. In short, institutional theory suggests that strategic management accounting is unlikely to be adopted by managers driven by mimetic behaviour.

Another way of looking at the corporate governance crisis at the turn of the century is to see it as a problem of *risk management*. In the next section, we will look at a particular version of risk management that is associated with improving corporate governance that ties in with our earlier review of the importance of boundary systems.[38]

Corporate governance and risk management

In Chapter 10, we looked at a number of techniques for modelling risk using probability theory and decision trees. We also argued that other approaches to controlling risk involved policies of diversification and organizational design that enabled a flexible response to changing circumstances. Another approach to risk sees the establishment of effective internal controls as so important that company boards have a specific responsibility for **risk management**. In the UK, the Turnbull Report[39] offered guidance for boards so that they followed 'a risk-based approach to establishing a sound system of internal control and reviewing its effectiveness'. According to Gould a 'robust' risk management system means that a company will have:

- 'understood the nature of the risks facing it;
- decided the extent and categories of risk which it regards as acceptable for it to bear;
- considered the likelihood of the risks materializing;
- judged its ability to reduce the incidence and impact on the business of risks that do materialize; *and*
- estimated the costs of operating particular controls relative to the benefit thereby obtained in managing the related risks'.[40]

As may be seen in Exhibit 17.4, Turnbull was concerned with a very extensive list of possible risks that have to be managed at board level. Some of these risks are clearly concerned with reporting and compliance issues but others are operational and strategic issues that should be informed by many of the techniques and measures that we introduced in this book. Exhibit 17.5 shows a wheel of action approach to risk management that may easily be related to our generic control models with both elements of keeping on track, searching for early warning indicators and organizational learning with a constant review of objectives and critical success factors.

Wealth creation and good corporate governance: the role of boundary systems

Although we have suggested that strategic management accounting techniques can make a contribution to corporate governance by informing both executive and non-executive directors, the usual assumption is that strategic information is concerned with adding value and wealth creation. Compliance systems in contrast are sometimes seen as being constraining and even inimical to the sort of enterprising decisions and behaviour that generate wealth. Yet some constraints or boundary systems actually enable organizational freedom and flexibility. As Simons puts it: 'Ask yourself why there are brakes in a car. Is their function to slow the car down or to allow it to go fast? Boundary systems are like brakes on a car: without them, cars (or organizations) cannot operate at high speeds.'[41] Boundary systems may be driven by external codes such as those on corporate governance and company law, professional ethics or even the result of commercial prudence. Simons argues that business conduct boundaries are particularly important when uncertainty is high or when internal trust is low. In this arena, boundary systems may be seen as a vital part of risk management.

Enterprise governance

A recently developed concept, **enterprise governance**, stresses the duty of both company boards and executive managements to provide strategic direction, manage risks and verify that the organization uses its resources in a responsible way.[42] The enterprise governance model argues that a balance must be struck between the goals of conformance and accountability assurance (the corporate governance strand) and performance and value creation (the business governance strand). In this respect, we can see that, post-Enron, the profession is recognizing the tensions discussed in this chapter and which were originally identified by academics such as Sathe (1982) and Simons (1995).

Business	Operational and other
Wrong business strategy	Business processes not aligned to strategic goals
Competitive pressure on price/market share	Failure of major change initiative
General economic problems	Loss of entrepreneurial spirit
Regional economic problems	Stock-out of raw materials
Political risks	Skills shortage
Obsolescence of technology	Physical disasters (including fire and explosion)
Substitute products	Failure to create and exploit intangible assets
Adverse government policy	Loss of intangible assets
Industry sector in decline	Breach of confidentiality
Take-over target	Loss of physical assets
Inability to obtain further capital	Lack of business continuity
Bad acquisition	Succession problems
Too slow to innovate	Year 2000 problems
Financial	Loss of key people
Liquidity risk	Inability to reduce cost base
Market risk	Major customers impose tough contract obligations
Going concern problems	Over-reliance on key suppliers or customers
Overtrading	Failure of new products or services
Credit risk	Poor service levels
Interest risk	Failure to satisfy customers
Currency risk	Quality problems
High cost of capital	Lack of orders
Treasury risk	Failure of major project
Misuse of financial resources	Loss of key contracts
Occurrence of types of fraud to which the business is susceptible	Inability to make use of the internet
Misstatement risk related to published financial information	Failure of outsource provider to deliver
Breakdown of accounting system	Industrial action
Unrecorded liabilities	Failure of big technology related project
Unreliable accounting records	Lack of employee motivation or efficiency
Penetration and attack of IT systems by hackers	Inability to implement change
Decisions based on incomplete or faulty information	Inefficient/ineffective processing of documents
Too much data and not enough analysis	Poor brand management
Unfulfilled promises to investors	Product liability
Compliance	Inefficient/ineffective management process
Breach of Listing Rules	Problems arising from exploiting employees in developing countries
Breach of financial regulations	Other business probity issues
Breach of Companies Act requirements	Other issues giving rise to reputational problems
Litigation risk	Missed business opportunities
Breach of competition laws	
VAT problems	
Breach of other regulations and laws	
Tax penalties	
Health and safety risks	
Environmental problems	

Exhibit 17.4 Possible risks according to Turnbull

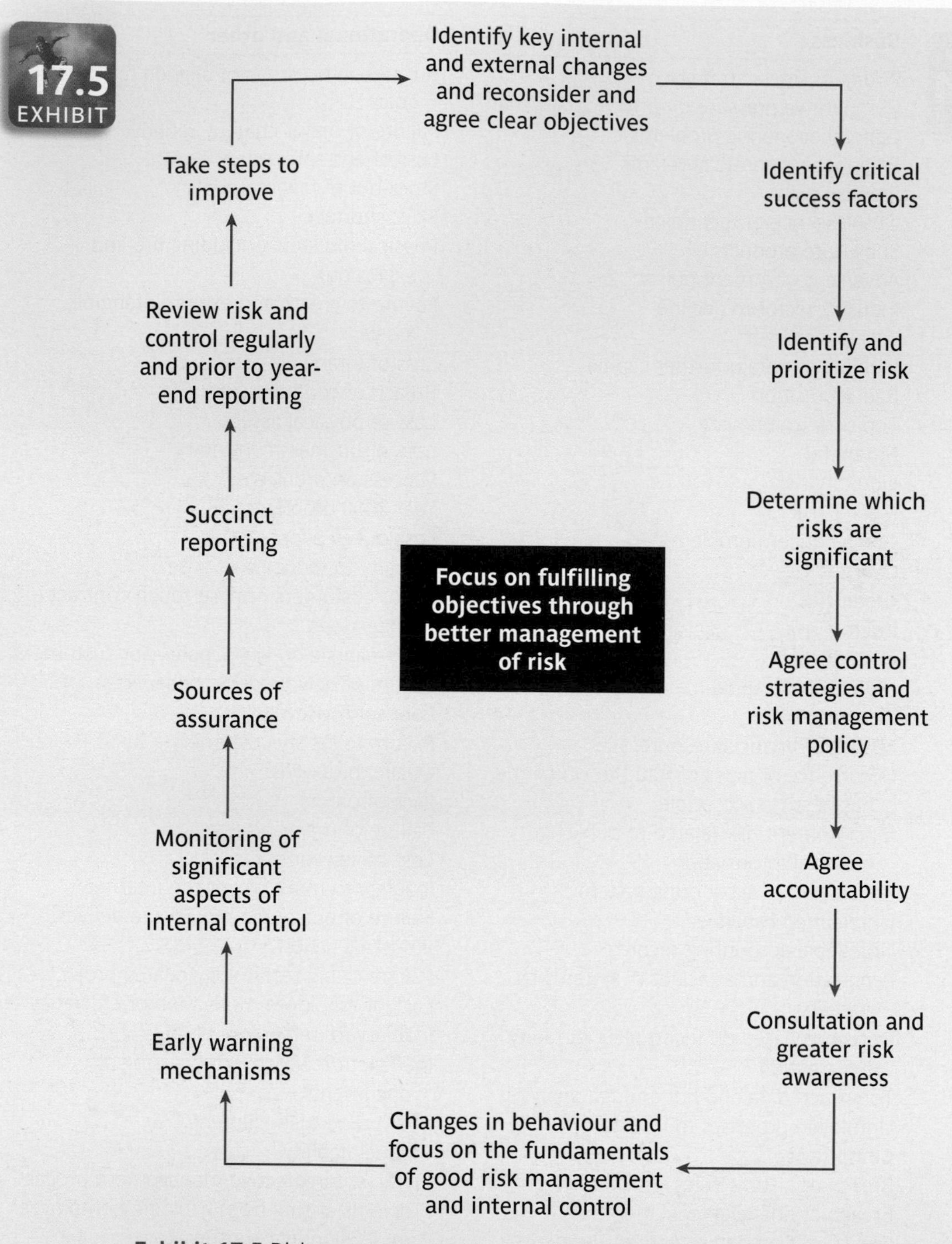
17.5
EXHIBIT
Identify key internal and external changes and reconsider and agree clear objectives
Identify critical success factors
Identify and prioritize risk
Determine which risks are significant
Agree control strategies and risk management policy
Agree accountability
Consultation and greater risk awareness
Changes in behaviour and focus on the fundamentals of good risk management and internal control
Early warning mechanisms
Monitoring of significant aspects of internal control
Sources of assurance
Succinct reporting
Review risk and control regularly and prior to year-end reporting
Take steps to improve
Focus on fulfilling objectives through better management of risk

Exhibit 17.5 Risk management: the Turnbull model

Focus on current practice

Rather than seeing good corporate governance as hindering financial performance, the influential pension fund managers, Hermes, state that their 'corporate governance programme is founded on a fundamental belief that companies with interested and involved shareholders are more likely to achieve superior long-term financial performance than those without'. Similarly, Hermes has a policy of 'always voting at company meetings ... to ensure that companies are run by managers and directors in the best long-term interests of their long-term investors'. Hermes 'believes that good stewardship contributes to superior corporate performance. Its vigilance and involvement as long-term shareholder thus enhances returns on its clients' assets.'[43]

A broader view on corporate governance: stakeholders, social and environmental responsiveness

So far we have taken a rather narrow view on corporate governance by focusing on the interests of the suppliers of capital. In a broader perspective, we are concerned with issues that are often covered under the heading of *corporate responsiveness* with a particular emphasis on *social* and *environmental* responsibility. This broader view recognizes that many obstacles to corporate social responsiveness may be caused by an organization's performance management system. For example, the normal divisionalized structures of large companies are designed to achieve economic rather than social goals especially if the usual ROI/EVA type metrics are adopted. In general, the conventional accounting system is biased towards financial data with a neglect of social data. Furthermore, in profit-oriented organizations, the incentive system tends to reward economic rather than social performance. In short, although many firms now specify some social objectives, they often fail to reinforce their attainment through their performance measurement and reward system. Ethical problems arise within organizations because ethical goals that reflect corporate social responsibility may conflict with *material* goals of profit and staff bonuses. As the Concepts in Context feature at the beginning of the chapter illustrates, the performance measurement and bonus system at Shell contributed to the misreporting of reserves at both divisional and corporate level.

The Performance Prism

The general principles of effective organizational control are similar whether we are concerned with the narrow view of corporate governance that prioritizes the interests of the suppliers of capital or a broader approach that considers corporate social responsiveness and the interests of a diversity of **stakeholders**,[44] which includes customers, employees, suppliers, regulators and pressure groups as well as shareholders and other suppliers of capital.

A good example of a management control model that incorporates a broad view of corporate governance, we may consider the **Performance Prism** which includes five facets of business performance – *stakeholder contribution, stakeholder satisfaction, strategies, processes and capabilities*. Rather than derive performance measures from strategy, the performance measurement system is built up by initially asking: *who* are the stakeholders and *what* do they want? The next step then considers the strategies that should be adopted in order to satisfy stakeholders.

But as well as having wants, stakeholders also make contributions to the organization, as shown in Exhibit 17.6. The dual relationship between wants and contributions can be illustrated by customers who want quality products at low prices but potentially offer profitability to the organization through customer loyalty. Similarly, suppliers want prompt payment and advance warnings of product changes but potentially offer on-time delivery of quality product.

The Performance Prism has been applied in a number of commercial and non-profit making organizations. In order to illustrate the latter, we have reproduced the outline success map for a non-profit making organization, London Youth, in Exhibit 17.7. London Youth is a charity with a membership of youth clubs, groups and projects that involve about 75,000 young and 5,000 adult leaders and committee members. Its main mission is to assist the development of children and young people in the Greater London area but its subsidiary goals are to grow membership; improve the range of products offered;

Exhibit 17.6 The Performance Prism: stakeholder and organization wants and needs

Reproduced with permission from A. Neely and C. Adams, *Perspectives on Performance: The Performance Prism*. www.som.cranfield.ac.uk/som/cbp/downloads/prismarticle.pdf

provide affordable residential experience; raise its profile; raise funds and ensure efficient and effective governance. These strategies are clearly linked because donors do not like to give funds to corrupt, ineffective or unaccountable organizations.

Models like the Performance Prism show that there is no conceptual reason why performance management systems may not be used to drive the attainment of social objectives. Although the general principles of the formal control model are the same, the objectives, measurement systems and tangible rewards are explicitly designed to include social objectives as well as the more conventional financial goals. Such models do not mean that conflicts between objectives disappear just because a broader view of corporate governance is accepted. For example, compliance with environmental regulations usually increases business costs and involves more complex decision making which we may analyse under the umbrella term of **environmental management accounting**.

Environmental management accounting

Profit-oriented firms have a number of reasons why they should take environmental issues seriously. At its most basic, they have little choice as in many countries strong environmental regulatory regimes generate extra pollution and compliance costs which feed directly into their bottom line (the *compliance motive*). They may also find that the bottom line may be improved because more efficiency in the use of energy, water and other raw materials may actually reduce costs and boost profits (the *eco-efficiency motive*). From a more strategic perspective many firms

17.7 EXHIBIT

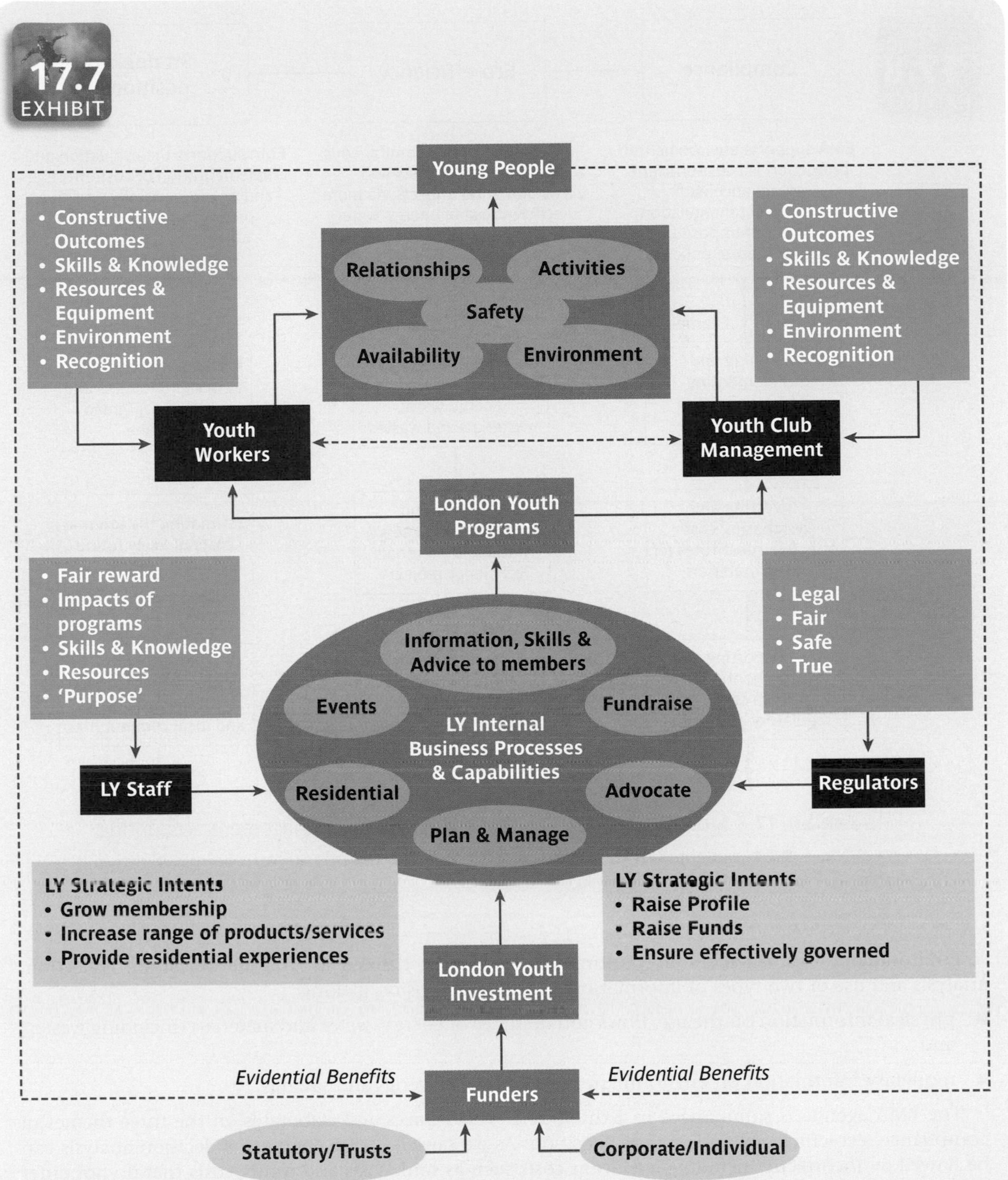

Exhibit 17.7 The Performance Prism in action: an outline success map for London Youth

Reproduced with permission from A. Neely, C. Adams and P. Crowe, *The Performance Prism in Practice*. www.som.cranfield.ac.uk/som/cbp/downloads/prismarticle.pdf

have also realized that there is an increasing market for green products and green business practices (the *strategic motive*). Finally, as we argued in Chapter 1, businesses have ethical responsibilities to the wider community and, even more fundamentally, their common home, 'Planet Earth'.

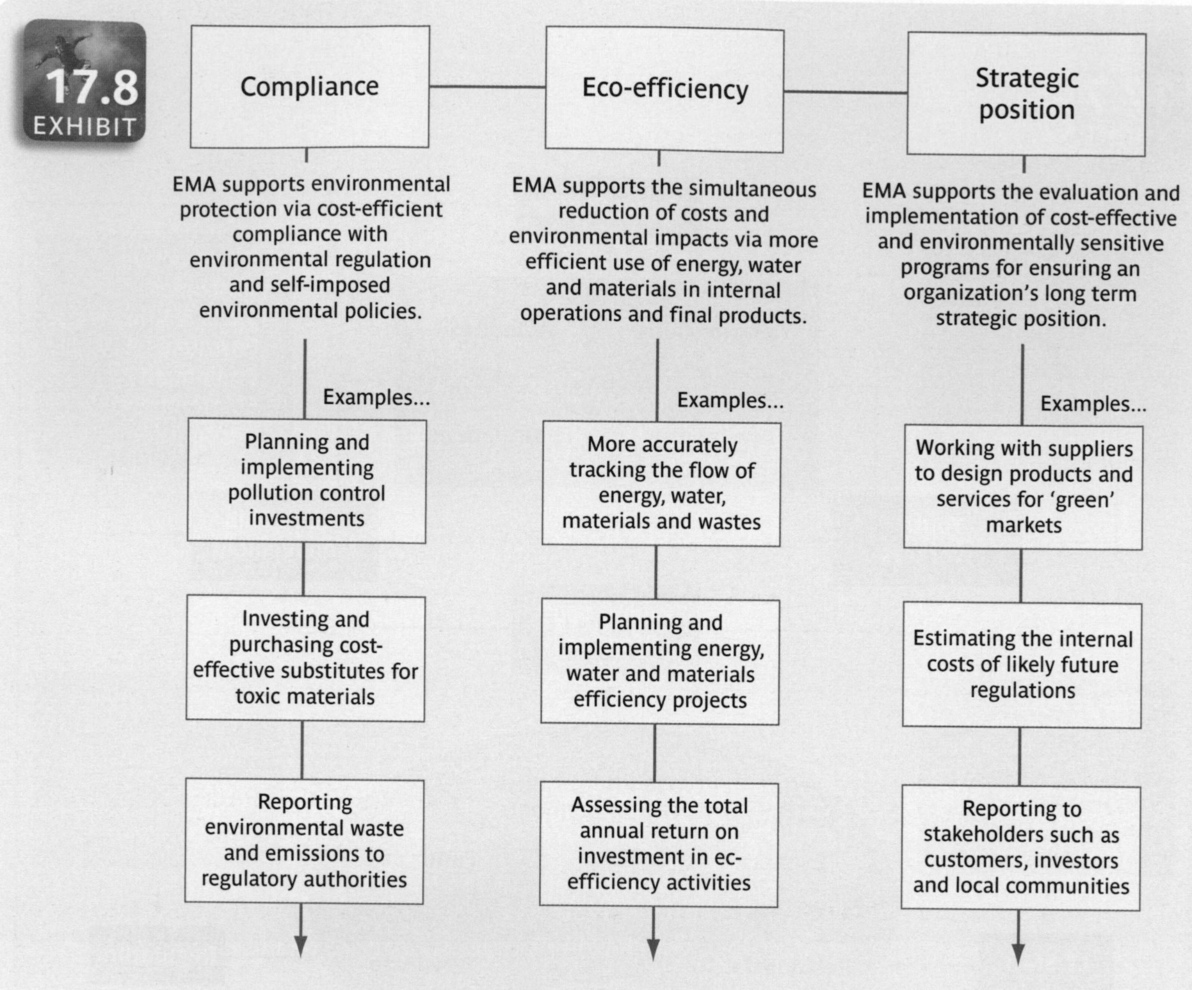

Exhibit 17.8 Motives and methods for environmental management accounting
(This exhibit is adapted from figure 1, IFAC 2005, p. 24 reproduced with permission from IFAC)

Environmental Management Accounting (EMA) may be defined as 'the identification, collection, analysis and use of two types of information for internal decision making:

- physical information on the use, flows and destinies of energy, water and materials (including wastes) and
- monetary information on environment-related costs, earnings and savings.'[45]

The EMA agenda is summarized in Exhibit 17.8 which traces and elaborates on the three themes of compliance, eco-efficiency and strategic position. As we saw in earlier chapters, a decision analysis can be flawed by incorrectly including irrelevant costs such as sunk costs and future costs that do not differ between alternatives. It can also be flawed by omitting future costs that *do* differ between alternatives. This is particularly a problem with **environmental costs** that have dramatically increased in recent years and about which many managers have little knowledge. Environmental costs for a company are the costs of complying with environmental regulations. For the wider society, they are costs generated by human activities and may or may not be measured in monetary terms.

An example of environmental management accounting

Consider the environmental complications posed by a decision of whether to install a solvent-based or powder-based system for spray-painting parts. In a solvent painting system, parts are sprayed as they move along a conveyor. The paint that misses the part is swept away by a wall of water, called a water curtain. The excess paint accumulates in a pit as sludge that must be removed each month. Environmental regulations classify this sludge as hazardous waste. As a result, the company must obtain a permit to produce the waste and must maintain meticulous records of how the waste is transported, stored and disposed of. The annual costs of complying with these regulations can easily exceed £140,000 in total for a painting facility that initially cost only £400,000 to build. The costs of complying with environmental regulations include the following:

- The waste sludge must be hauled to a special disposal site. The typical disposal fee is about £300 per barrel or £55,000 per year for a modest solvent-based painting system.
- Workers must be specially trained to handle the paint sludge.
- The company must carry special insurance.
- The company must pay substantial fees to the state for releasing pollutants (i.e., the solvent) into the air.
- The water in the water curtain must be specially treated to remove contaminants. This cost can run into tens of thousands of pounds per year.

In contrast, a powder-based painting system avoids almost all of these environmental costs. Excess powder used in the painting process can be recovered and reused without creating a hazardous waste. Additionally, the powder-based system does not release contaminants into the atmosphere. Therefore, even though the cost of building a powder-based system may be higher than the cost of building a solvent based system, over the long run the costs of the powder based system may be far lower due to the high environmental costs of a solvent-based system. Managers need to be aware of such environmental costs and take them fully into account when making decisions.

Organizational control and service delivery in the public sector: beyond incrementalism?

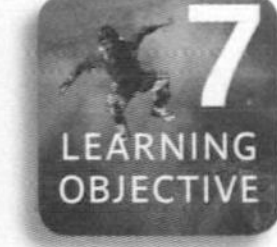

The primacy of the shareholder in most discussions of corporate governance is understandable given the origins and legal structures of the private sector, for-profit organization. We should expect that, in principle at least, social responsiveness *should* be better in not-for-profit organizations in the public sector whose structures and objectives are overtly designed to serve the public interest. Yet even here, social responsiveness has a technical dimension as public policies need to be implemented and managed in order to ensure that appropriate strategies and public services are delivered. Indeed, the problems of budgeting in the public sector, especially *incrementalism*, may be even more serious than in the private sector where companies have more choice over how binding their budgets are.

Incrementalism is associated with a tendency to increase or decrease existing budgets by small amounts without asking whether the underlying local services that are being financed are still necessary or are being provided in the most effective way. In the traditional approach to public sector budgeting, the budget holder starts with last year's budget and adds to it (or subtracts from it), according to anticipated needs. In an incremental approach to budgeting, the previous year's budget is taken for granted as a baseline.

Zero-based budgeting is an alternative approach that is sometimes used in the public sector.[46] Under a zero-based budget, managers are required to justify all budgeted expenditures, not just changes in the budget from the previous year. The baseline is zero rather than last year's budget. A zero-based budget requires considerable documentation. In addition to all the schedules in the usual master budget, the manager must prepare a series of 'decision packages' in which all the activities of the department are ranked according to their relative importance and the cost of each activity is identified. Higher-level managers can then review the decision packages and cut back in those areas that appear to be less critical or whose costs do not appear to be justified.

Under zero-based budgeting, the review is performed every year. Critics of zero-based budgeting charge that properly executed zero-based budgeting is too time consuming and too costly to justify on an annual basis. In addition, it is argued that annual reviews soon become mechanical and that the whole purpose of zero-based budgeting is then lost. Whether or not an organization should use an annual review is a matter of judgement. In some situations annual zero-based reviews may be justified; in other situations they may not because of the time and cost involved. However, most managers would at least agree that on occasion zero-based reviews can be very helpful.

The rigidity of the budgeting system in public sector organizations is often understandable given that public bodies have a special responsibility to account for the tax-payers' funds that support their activities. Historically, the emphasis in public sector organizations like local authorities has been on **financial stewardship** – demonstrating to citizens and other tiers of government that monies have been handled with probity and prudence. Indeed, it is only a relatively recent development that has seen public sectors throughout the world applying more sophisticated systems that combine performance management with financial management. New public corporate structures, performance indicators systems and budgeting can be used to try to make the public sector more responsive to the needs of citizens. We cannot cover all the changes that have been introduced in the UK public sector over the last 20 years but an example based on recent fieldwork (1997–2003) shows how attempts have been made to reform corporate governance, financial management and service delivery in the local public sector. The field study follows the experience of two local authorities, Southshire and Eastmet.[47]

New political and management structures

Certain types of traditional organizational structures of UK local government were almost inevitably incrementalist. Services were managed by big specialist departments in areas such as education, housing and social services that were accountable to specialized committees of elected counsellors (known as 'members'). In common with many English local authorities, Eastmet and Southshire abolished the old departmental structures and adopted small 'cabinets' with senior members holding portfolios. The portfolios were designed to reflect a cross-cutting perspective so that, for example, a single organizational structure and budget for children's services replaced the original education and social service departments.

The introduction of policy-led budgeting

Both Eastmet and Southshire developed long- and medium-term plans that were intended to indicate the councils' priorities and guide long-term financial strategies. In order to operationalize the plans, both authorities made an increased use of *non-financial performance indicators in conjunction with financial measures*. New reporting systems were developed that not only picked up the traditional budgetary variances but also monitored non-financial performance. Both authorities adopted three-year financial strategies with special mechanisms to allow investment in services and promote changes in service provision. An example of how service performance and financial management data may be combined is illustrated in Exhibit 17.9. The exhibit demonstrates how the general control principles developed earlier in the chapter can be applied to the management of a public service such as education with its emphasis on social goals and objectives.

In an attempt to combat incrementalism, services (and their budgets) were subject to periodic (but not annual) fundamental reviews. Although there was both a commitment and an increased managerial capacity to base budgets on medium- to long-term priorities and move funds around, it could not be claimed that incrementalist practices had been abolished. The political and organizational issues that make incrementalism so compelling and rational management so difficult that were identified so brilliantly[48] more than 30 years ago were still prevalent after successive waves of modernizing initiatives.

Many of the reforms of the public sector, sometimes known as the **New Public Management**,[49] have been extremely controversial. Although it is beyond the scope of this book to do full justice to ongoing debates, at least some of the potential problems relate to the use of performance indicators in the public sector. Exhibit 17.10 summarizes many of the distorting effects on managerial behaviour that can result from an excessive use of performance indicators.[50] Although some of these same problems may be found in for-profit organizations, it is generally claimed that because profits and share prices are outcomes that aggregate the effects of a variety of organizational behaviours and decisions, many of the distortions identified in Exhibit 17.10 are less pressing. But of course, if financial indicators such as profit can summarize organizational performance then it is clearly very important to be vigilant about the last potential problem of misrepresentation!

17.9 EXHIBIT

Key Performance Indicators and Targets

Indicator	Actual Result 2000/1	Target for 01/02	Actual performance 2001/2	Sun, cloud or lightning	Target 02/03	Long term target 2006/7	Comments on our performance
To increase the resources going into schools	£5m added to schools budget	To add another £3m to schools budget	Achieved		To add further £3m to Schools Budget	N/A	The objective to add £11m to schools budget will have been achieved by 2002/3
Percentage infant classes with more than 30 pupils per teacher	2.3%	0%	0.7%		0%	0%	Some legitimate exceptions push the percentage above 0%
% Unauthorized absence: secondary schools	2.6%	1.1%	2.6%		1.0%	0.8%	Performance was affected by reorganization but is improving again
GCSE: Percentage with 5 + A*–C grades	32.8%	36.5%	34.3%		39.5%	55%	Results went up but not by as much as hoped. The year group had not come through reorganized schools but through the old system
GCSE: Percentage with 1 + A*–G grades	91.6%	94.5%	92.3%		97%	99%	Performance on this indicator is sensitive to the absence rate
GCSE: Average Points score	30.9	33.5	31.3		36.0	45.0	The average points score did not improve as was hoped
Key Stage 2 Maths: Percentage at Level 4+	59.9%	66%	59.7%		73%	95%	Test results improved but not by as much as the targets required. Steady improvement is expected now that the Direct Service Provider is in place
Key Stage 2 English: Percentage at Level 4+	65.9%	72%	66.6		76%	100%	The maths comment applies equally to the English test results
To complement successfully all activities set out in the Ofsted Action Plan	N/A	75%	90%		100%	N/A	Scheduled for completion by August 2002

Exhibit 17.9 Combining performance planning and financial management in the public sector: an example of Best Value in UK local government

17.10 EXHIBIT

Tunnel vision	Excessive focus on achieving Indicators	Input indicators may be easier to create and manage so that
Suboptimization	Neglect of wider goals of Organization	Problem of the lack of a 'Profit-type' indicator that can capture wider goals of the organization
Myopia	Concentration on short-term results	Non-financial indicators may fail to encourage long-term, investment type activity
Convergence	Avoiding exposure as exceptional either in good or bad performance	Public sector organizations are often more exposed to media scrutiny
Ossification	Reluctance to innovate or take risks	Hard to reward risk taking in public sector; easier to penalize non-conformance
Gaming	See budgeting – e.g. keep hidden Reserves	Problems in public sector is that it can be hard to develop an independent basis for checking on the claims made by subordinate units
Misrepresentation	Creative accounting and fraud	Clearly a potential problem in both public and for-profit organizations!

Exhibit 17.10 Possible distortions of management control through the use of performance indicators in the public sector

*Based on Smith, P. 1993. 'Outcome-related performance indicators and organizational control in the public sector', *British Journal of Management*, 4, pp. 135–151.

Informal versus formal control systems

Traditional management accounting control systems tend to emphasize formal control based on techniques such as budgets and investment appraisal techniques based on written procedures and motivated by physical rewards such as bonuses and promotion. Yet informal systems of control based on shared values, beliefs and traditions may be very important, particularly when output measures are ambiguous and knowledge on the technical relationship between inputs and outputs is vague.[51] Indeed, in the 1980s, the success of the Japanese corporate model was often attributed to the apparent reliance on *clan* rather than bureaucratic control. In the **clan model**, control of the organization is motivated by a desire for peer approval and an avoidance of deviance from group ideals. Although we have introduced social control in the context of corporate governance and social responsibility, the socialization processes advocated to build a clan corporation in the 1980s were aimed to reinforce the commercial competitiveness rather than improve social responsiveness.[52]

Most of the corporate social responsibility literature focuses on external reporting, which is beyond the scope of this book. Yet the adoption of social responsibility reporting may have a positive impact on the issues of *internal* governance covered in this chapter. The process of producing reports may help mobilize the examples of socially responsible practices that the corporation will generally emphasize.[53] The act of narrating, visualizing and numbering has the effect of making socially responsible activities manageable in the same way that intellectual capital statements may make knowledge more manageable.

Focus on current practice

Norris and O'Dwyer found that in their case study organization, the company did have a genuine commitment to social responsibility but that it relied on informal controls such as staff selection, socialization and peer pressures in order to encourage socially responsible decision making by managers. The formal control system measured the usual financial and commercial objectives, which apparently indicated their primacy in overall corporate priorities especially during a period of competitive stress.[54]

Summary

- In this chapter we have looked at questions of organizational control and performance management including the problems and possible solutions associated with budgeting.
- We have reviewed a number of models of organizational control that aim to embed strategy and foster organizational learning.
- We have also discussed the importance of boundary systems and risk management in the particular context of corporate governance.
- More rigorous regulation of financial reporting may lead to a change of emphasis in organizational accounting practices with a renewed concern with the integrity of financial and non-financial information.
- Management accounting *can* provide key information for non-executive directors on issues such as the strategic direction of the firm.
- We have introduced a number of broader issues related to corporate social responsibility.
- We have shown how attempts are being made to use management accounting practices to improve the accountability and service delivery in the public sector.

Key terms for review

Belief systems (p. 717).

Boundary systems (p. 717).

Clan model (p. 732).

Constrained management style (p. 715).

Corporate governance (p. 714).

Corporate social responsiveness (or responsibility) (p. 714).

Diagnostic control systems (p. 717).

Double loop learning (p. 716).

Environment costs (p. 728).

Enterprise governance (p. 722).

Environmental management accounting (p. 726).

Feedforward control (p. 716).

Financial stewardship (p. 730).

Incrementalism (p. 729).

Interactive control systems (p. 717).

Key performance indicators (KPIs) (p. 716).

Levers of control model (p. 717).

Management control (p. 717).

New Public Management (p. 730).

Performance management (p. 717).
Performance measurement system (p. 716).
Performance Prism (p. 725).
Reductionist model of humanity (p. 717).
Return-on-management (p. 717).
Risk management (p. 722).
Stakeholders (p. 725).
Zero-based budgeting (p. 729).

PROBLEMS

Problems

P17–1 Ethics; just-in-time (JIT) purchasing Time allowed: 30 minutes

WIW is a publicly owned company that makes various control devices used in the manufacture of mechanical equipment. J.B. is the president of WIW, Tony is the purchasing agent, and Diane is J. B.'s executive assistant. All three have been with WIW for about five years. Charlie is WIW's controller and has been with the company for two years.

J.B.: Hi, Charlie, come on in. Diane said you had a confidential matter to discuss. What's on your mind?

Charlie: J.B., I was reviewing our increased purchases from A-1 Warehouse Sales last week and wondered why our volume has tripled in the past year. When I discussed this with Tony he seemed a bit evasive and tried to dismiss the issue by stating that A-1 can give us one-day delivery on our orders.

J.B.: Well, Tony is right. You know we have been trying to implement just-in-time and have been trying to get our inventory down.

Charlie: We still have to look at the overall cost. A-1 is more of a jobber than a warehouse. After investigating orders placed with them, I found that only 10% are delivered from their warehouse and the other 90% are drop-shipped from the manufacturers. The average markup by A-1 is 30%, which amounted to about £600,000 on our orders for the past year. If we had ordered directly from the manufacturers when A-1 didn't have an item in stock, we could have saved about £540,000 (£600,000 × 90%). In addition, some of the orders were late and not complete.

J.B.: Now look, Charlie, we get quick delivery on most items, and who knows how much we are saving by not having to stock this stuff in advance or worry about it becoming obsolete. Is there anything else on your mind?

Charlie: Well, J.B., as a matter of fact, there is. I ordered a Dun & Bradstreet credit report on A-1 and discovered that Mike Bell is the principal owner. Isn't he your brother-in-law?

J.B.: Sure he is. But don't worry about Mike. He understands this JIT approach. Besides, he's looking out for our interests.

Charlie: (to himself) This conversation has been enlightening, but it doesn't really respond to my concerns. Can I legally or ethically ignore this apparent conflict of interests?

Required

1 Would Charlie be justified in ignoring this situation, particularly since he is not the purchasing agent?

2 State the specific steps Charlie should follow to resolve this matter.

P17–2 Performance indicators/social responsiveness Time allowed: 45 minutes

The Royal Botanical Gardens has been established for more than 120 years and has the following mission statement:

> *'The Royal Botanical Gardens belongs to the Nation. Our mission is to increase knowledge and appreciation of plants, their importance and their conservation, by managing and displaying living and preserved collections and through botanical and horticultural research.'*

Located towards the edge of the city, the Gardens are regularly visited throughout the year by many local families and are an internationally well-known tourist attraction. Despite charging admission it is one of the top five visitor attractions in the country. Every year it answers many thousands of enquiries from universities and research establishments, including pharmaceutical companies from all over the world and charges for advice and access to its collection. Enquiries can range from access to the plant collection for horticultural work, seeds for propagation or samples for chemical analysis to seek novel pharmaceutical compounds for commercial exploitation. It receives an annual grant in aid from Central Government, which is fixed once every five years. The grant in aid is due for review in three years' time.

The Finance Director has decided that, to strengthen its case when meeting the Government representatives to negotiate the grant, the Management Board should be able to present a balanced scorecard demonstrating the performance of the Gardens. He has asked you, the Senior Management Accountant, to assist him in taking this idea forward. Many members of the board, which consists of eminent scientists, are unfamiliar with the concept of a balanced scorecard.

Required

1 For the benefit of the Management Board, prepare a briefing on the concept of a balanced scorecard, which also analyses its usefulness for The Royal Botanical Gardens. *(10 marks)*

2 Discuss the process you would employ to develop a suitable balanced scorecard for The Royal Botanical Gardens and give examples of measures that would be incorporated within it. *(15 marks)*

CIMA Pilot Paper Management Accounting – Business Strategy, November 2004

P17–3 Corporate governance Time allowed: 45 minutes

You have recently been appointed as Head of the Internal Audit function for a large UK listed company that trades internationally, having worked within its finance function for two years prior to your new appointment. Your company has also appointed a new Chief Executive, headhunted from a large US corporation where she had held the post of Vice President, Finance.

Required

As part of the new Chief Executive's orientation programme, you have been asked to prepare a detailed report which provides key information on the principles of good corporate governance for UK listed companies. You should address the following in your report, remembering that her background is in US governance and procedures.

1 The role and responsibilities of the Board of Directors. *(5 marks)*

2 The role and responsibilities of the audit committee. *(10 marks)*

3 Disclosure of corporate governance arrangements. *(10 marks)*

CIMA Pilot paper Management Accounting – Risk and control strategy, November 2004

P17–4 Time allowed: 45 minutes

The NLE organization sells a range of leisure products on the Internet including books, CDs, DVDs and computer games. The organization's mission statement is to be the most reliable and cost efficient supplier of books and CDs on the Internet. It was formed six years ago, and has grown quickly. Two years ago it became one of the first Internet companies to report a net operating profit. NLE is recognized as being one of the market leaders on the Internet, and its share price is increasing at 20% per annum. In a recent market survey, 80% of people between the ages of 20 and 45 identified the NLE brand name as one they would use when ordering goods from the Internet.

The company now has a positive cash flow, with no outstanding loans. The directors are investigating alternative investments. One possibility is the purchase of 25 bookshops located in major cities in one country. These shops would be re-branded with the NLE name, and offer a similar range of products to the NLE Internet site. However, as no shop could hold the 2.5 million items currently available on the NLE site, a next-day 'collect from shop' option would be made available. This means that customers could order goods from the Internet, or by visiting an NLE bookshop and then collect those goods on the next working day. Goods would be despatched overnight from NLE's main warehouse to fulfil these orders.

Required

1 Assuming that the Board of NLE decides to purchase the bookshops, advise them on the Information Strategy issues that they should consider, clearly explaining the information required when considering each issue.

Note: You are not required to advise on alternative sources of finance. *(15 marks)*

2 Identify and explain two critical success factors and their supporting performance indicators that can be used to determine the success or otherwise of the purchase of the bookshops, should this acquisition go ahead. *(10 marks)*

(Total = 25 marks)

CIMA Management Accounting (Information systems), November 2004

CASE

Cases

C17–5 Ethics and the manager Time allowed: 40 minutes

Terri Ronsin had recently been transferred to the Home Security Systems Division of National Home Products. Shortly after taking over her new position as divisional controller, she was asked to develop the division's predetermined overhead rate for the upcoming year. The accuracy of the rate is of some importance, since it is used throughout the year and any overapplied or underapplied overhead is closed out to Cost of Goods Sold only at the end of the year. National Home Products uses direct labour-hours in all of its divisions as the allocation base for manufacturing overhead.

To compute the predetermined overhead rate, Terri divided her estimate of the total manufacturing overhead for the coming year by the production manager's estimate of the total direct labour-hours for the coming year. She took her computations to the division's general manager for approval but was quite surprised when he suggested a modification in the base. Her conversation with the general manager of the Home Security Systems Division, Harry Irving, went like this:

Ronsin: Here are my calculations for next year's predetermined overhead rate. If you approve, we can enter the rate into the computer on January 1 and be up and running in the job-order costing system right away this year.

Irving: Thanks for coming up with the calculations so quickly, and they look just fine. There is, however, one slight modification I would like to see. Your estimate of the total direct labour-hours for the year is 440,000 hours. How about cutting that to about 420,000 hours?

Ronsin: I don't know if I can do that. The production manager says she will need about 440,000 direct labour-hours to meet the sales projections for the year. Besides, there are going to be over 430,000 direct labour-hours during the current year and sales are projected to be higher next year.

Irving: Terri, I know all of that. I would still like to reduce the direct labour-hours in the base to something like 420,000 hours. You probably don't know that I had an agreement with your predecessor as divisional controller to shave 5% or so off the estimated direct labour-hours every year. That way, we kept a reserve that usually resulted in a big boost to net income at the end of the fiscal year in December. We called it our Christmas bonus. Corporate headquarters always seemed as pleased as punch that we could pull off such a miracle at the end of the year. This system has worked well for many years, and I don't want to change it now.

Required

1 Explain how shaving 5% off the estimated direct labour-hours in the base for the predetermined overhead rate usually results in a big boost in net income at the end of the fiscal year.

2 Should Terri Ronsin go along with the general manager's request to reduce the direct labour-hours in the predetermined overhead rate computation to 420,000 direct labour-hours?

C17–6 Ethics and the manager; absorption costing profit and loss statements Time allowed: 120 minutes

Guochang Li was hired as chief executive officer (CEO) in late November by the board of directors of ContactGlobal, a company that produces an advanced global positioning system (GPS) device that pinpoints the user's location anywhere on earth to within a hundred metres. The previous CEO had been fired by the board of directors due to a series of shady business practices including shipping defective GPS devices to dealers.

Guochang felt that his first priority was to restore employee morale – which had suffered during the previous CEO's reign. He was particularly anxious to build a sense of trust between himself and the company's employees. His second priority was to prepare the budget for the coming year, which the board of directors wanted to review in their 15 December meeting.

After hammering out the details in meetings with key managers, Guochang was able to put together a budget that he felt the company could realistically meet during the coming year. That budget appears below:

Basic budget data	
Units in beginning inventory	0
Units produced	400,000
Units sold	400,000
Units in ending inventory	0
Variable costs per unit:	
Direct materials	£57.20
Direct Labour	15.00
Variable manufacturing overhead	5.00
Variable selling and administrative	10.00
Total variable cost per unit	£87.20
Fixed costs:	
Fixed manufacturing overhead	£6,888,000
Fixed selling and administrative	4,560,000
Total fixed costs	£11,448,000

Contact Global
Budgeted profit and loss statement
(absorption method)

Sales (400,000 units × £120 per unit)		£48,000,000
Less cost of goods sold:		
Beginning inventory	£0	
Add cost of goods manufactured		
(400,000 units × £94.42 per unit)	37,768,000	
Goods available for sale	37,768,000	
Less ending inventory	0	37,768,000
Gross margin		10,232,000
Less selling and administrative expenses:		
Variable selling and administrative		
(400,000 units × £10 per unit)	4,000,000	
Fixed selling and administrative	4,560,000	8,560,000
Profit		£1,672,000

The board of directors made it clear that this budget was not as ambitious as they had hoped. The most influential member of the board stated that 'managers should have to really stretch to meet profit goals'.

After some discussion, the board decided to set a profit goal of £2,000,000 for the coming year. To provide strong incentives, the board agreed to pay out very substantial bonuses to top managers of £10,000 to £25,000 each if this profit goal were met. The bonus would be all-or-nothing. If actual profit turned out to be £2,000,000 or more, the bonus would be paid. Otherwise, no bonus would be paid.

Required

1 Assuming that the company does not build up its inventory (i.e., production equals sales) and its selling price and cost structure remain the same, how many units of the GPS device would have to be sold in order to meet the profit goal of £2,000,000?

2 Verify your answer to (1) above by constructing a revised budget and budgeted profit statement that yields a profit of £2,000,000. Use the absorption costing method.

3 Unfortunately, by October of the next year it had become clear that the company would not be able to make the £2,000,000 target profit. In fact, it looked like the company would wind up the year as originally planned, with sales of 400,000 units, no ending inventories, and a profit of £1,672,000.

Several managers who were reluctant to lose their year-end bonuses approached Guochang and suggested that the company could still show a profit of £2,000,000. The managers pointed out that at the present rate of sales, there was enough capacity to produce tens of thousands of additional GPS devices for the warehouse and thereby shift fixed manufacturing costs to another year. If sales are 400,000 units for the year and the selling price and cost structure remains the same, how many units would have to be produced in order to show a profit of at least £2,000,000 under absorption costing?

4 Verify your answer to (3) above by constructing a profit statement. Use the absorption costing method.

5 Do you think Guochang Li should approve the plan to build ending inventories in order to attain the target profit?

6 What advice would you give to the board of directors concerning how they determine bonuses in the future?

C17–7 Ethics and the manager Time allowed: 30 minutes

Stacy Cummins, the newly hired controller at Merced Home Products plc, was disturbed by what she had discovered about the standard costs at the Home Security Division. In looking over the past several years of quarterly earnings reports at the Home Security Division, she noticed that the first-quarter earnings were always poor, the second-quarter earnings were slightly better, the third-quarter earnings were again slightly better, and then the fourth quarter and the year always ended with a spectacular performance in which the Home Security Division always managed to meet or exceed its target profit for the year. She was also concerned to find letters from the company's external auditors to top management warning about an unusual use of standard costs at the Home Security Division.

When Ms Cummins ran across these letters, she asked the assistant controller, Gary Farber, if he knew what was going on at the Home Security Division. Gary said that it was common knowledge in the company that the vice president in charge of the Home Security Division, Preston Lansing, had rigged the standards at the Home Security Division in order to produce the same quarterly earnings pattern every year. According to company policy, variances are taken directly to the profit statement as an adjustment to cost of goods sold.

Favourable variances have the effect of increasing profit and unfavourable variances have the effect of decreasing profit. Lansing had rigged the standards so that there were always large favourable variances. Company policy was a little vague about when these variances have to be reported on the divisional profit statements. While the intent was clearly to recognize variances on the profit statement in the period in which they arise, nothing in the company's accounting manuals actually explicitly required this. So for many years Lansing had followed a practice of saving up the favourable variances and using them to create a nice smooth pattern of earnings growth in the first three quarters, followed by a big 'Christmas present' of an extremely good fourth quarter. (Financial reporting regulations forbid carrying variances forward from one year to the next on the annual audited financial statements, so all of the variances must appear on the divisional profit statement by the end of the year.)

Ms Cummins was concerned about these revelations and attempted to bring up the subject with the president of Merced Home Products but was told that 'we all know what Lansing's doing, but as long as he continues to turn in such good reports, don't bother him.' When Ms Cummins asked if the board of directors was aware of the situation, the chairman somewhat testily replied, 'Of course they are aware.'

Required

1 How did Preston Lansing probably 'rig' the standard costs – are the standards set too high or too low? Explain.

2 Should Preston Lansing be permitted to continue his practice of managing reported earnings?

3 What should Stacy Cummins do in this situation?

C17–8 Ethics and the manager; shut down or continue operations Time allowed: 75 minutes
Haley Platt had just been appointed CEO of the North Region of the Bank Services Corporation (BSC). The company provides cheque processing services for European banks. The banks send cheques presented for deposit or payment to BSC, which records the data on each cheque in a computerized database. BSC then sends the data electronically to the nearest bank cheque-clearing centre where the appropriate transfers of funds are made between banks. The North Region has three cheque processing centres, which are located in Billingham, Grantham and Cleethorpes. Prior to her promotion to CEO, Ms Platt had been the manager of a cheque processing centre in Mansfield.

Immediately upon assuming her new position, Ms Platt requested a complete financial report for the just-ended fiscal year from the region's controller, John Littlebear. Ms Platt specified that the financial report should follow the standardized format required by corporate headquarters for all regional performance reports. That report follows:

Bank Services Corporation (BSC)
North Region
Financial performance

		Cheque processing centres		
	Total	Billingham	Grantham	Cleethorpes
Sales	£50,000,000	£20,000,000	£18,000,000	£12,000,000
Operating expenses:				
Direct labour	32,000,000	12,500,000	11,000,000	8,500,000
Variable overhead	850,000	350,000	310,000	190,000
Equipment depreciation	3,900,000	1,300,000	1,400,000	1,200,000
Facility expense	2,800,000	900,000	800,000	1,100,000
Local administrative expense*	450,000	140,000	160,000	150,000
Regional administrative expense†	1,500,000	600,000	540,000	360,000
Corporate administrative expense‡	4,750,000	1,900,000	1,710,000	1,140,000
Total operating expense	46,250,000	17,690,000	15,920,000	12,640,000
Operating profit	£3,750,000	£2,310,000	£2,080,000	£(640,000)

*Local administrative expenses are the administrative expenses incurred at the cheque processing centres.

†Regional administrative expenses are allocated to the cheque processing centres based on sales.

‡Corporate administrative expenses are charged to segments of the company such as the North Region and the cheque processing centres at the rate of 9.5% of their sales.

Upon seeing this report, Ms Platt summoned John Littlebear for an explanation.

Platt: What's the story on Cleethorpes? It didn't have a loss the previous year did it?

Littlebear: No, the Cleethorpes facility has had a nice profit every year since it was opened six years ago, but Cleethorpes lost a big contract this year.

Platt: Why?

Littlebear: One of our national competitors entered the local market and bid very aggressively on the contract. We couldn't afford to meet the bid. Cleethorpes's costs – particularly their facility expenses – are just too high. When Cleethorpes lost the contract, we had to lay off a lot of employees, but we could not reduce the fixed costs of the Cleethorpes facility.

Platt: Why is Cleethorpes's facility expense so high? It's a smaller facility than either Billingham and Grantham and yet its facility expense is higher.

Littlebear: The problem is that we are able to rent suitable facilities very cheaply at Billingham and Grantham. No such facilities were available at Cleethorpes, we had them built. Unfortunately, there were big cost overruns. The contractor we hired was inexperienced at this kind of work and in fact went bankrupt before the project was completed. After hiring another contractor to finish the work, we were way over budget. The large depreciation charges on the facility didn't matter at first because we didn't have much competition at the time and could charge premium prices.

Platt: Well we can't do that anymore. The Cleethorpes facility will obviously have to be shut down. Its business can be shifted to the other two cheque processing centres in the region.

Littlebear: I would advise against that. The £1,200,000 in depreciation at the Cleethorpes facility is misleading. That facility should last indefinitely with proper maintenance. And it has no resale value; there is no other commercial activity around Cleethorpes.

Platt: What about the other costs at Cleethorpes?

Littlebear: If we shifted Cleethorpes's business over to the other two processing centres in the region, we wouldn't save anything on direct labour or variable overhead costs. We might save £90,000 or so in local administrative expense, but we would not save any regional administrative expense and corporate headquarters would still charge us 9.5% of our sales as corporate administrative expense.

In addition, we would have to rent more space in Billingham and Grantham in order to handle the work transferred from Cleethorpes; that would probably cost us at least £600,000 a year. And don't forget that it will cost us something to move the equipment from Cleethorpes to Billingham and Grantham. And the move will disrupt service to customers.

Platt: I understand all of that, but a money-losing processing centre on my performance report is completely unacceptable.

Littlebear: And if you shut down Cleethorpes, you are going to throw some loyal employees out of work.

Platt: That's unfortunate, but we have to face hard business realities.

Littlebear: And you would have to write off the investment in the facilities at Cleethorpes.

Platt: I can explain a write-off to corporate headquarters; hiring an inexperienced contractor to build the Cleethorpes facility was my predecessor's mistake. But they'll have my head at headquarters if I show operating losses every year at one of my processing centres. Cleethorpes has to go. At the next corporate board meeting, I am going to recommend that the Cleethorpes facility be closed.

Required

1 From the standpoint of the company as a whole, should the Cleethorpes processing centre be shut down and its work redistributed to other processing centres in the region? Explain.

2 Do you think Haley Platt's decision to shut down the Cleethorpes facility is ethical? Explain.

3 What influence should the depreciation on the facilities at Cleethorpes have on prices charged by Cleethorpes for its services?

C17–9 Management control of risk Time allowed: 90 minutes

Crashcarts IT Consultancy is a £100 million turnover business listed on the Stock Exchange with a reputation for providing world class IT consultancy services to blue chip clients, predominantly in the retail sector. In 2000, Crashcarts acquired a new subsidiary for £2 million based on a P/E ratio of 8, which it renamed Crashcarts Call Centre. The call centre subsidiary leased all of its hardware, software and telecommunications equipment over a five-year term. The infrastructure provides the capacity to process three million orders and ten million line items per annum. In addition, maintenance contracts were signed for the full five-year period. These contracts include the provision of a daily back-up facility in an off-site location.

Crashcarts Call Centre provides two major services for its clients. First, it holds databases, primarily for large retail chains' catalogue sales, connected in real time to clients' inventory control systems. Second, its call centre operation allows its clients' customers to place orders by telephone. The real-time system determines whether there is stock available and, if so, a shipment is requested. The sophisticated technology in use by the call centre also incorporates a secure payment facility for credit and debit card payments, details of which are transferred to the retail stores' own computer system. The call centre charges each retail client a lump sum each year for the IT and communications infrastructure it provides. There is a 12 month contract in place for each client. In addition, Crashcarts earns a fixed sum for every order it processes, plus an additional amount for every line item. If items are not in stock, Crashcarts earns no processing fee. Crashcarts Call Centre is staffed by call centre operators (there were 70 in 2001 and 80 in each of 2002 and 2003). In addition, a management team, training staff and administrative personnel are employed. Like other call centres, there is a high turnover of call centre operators (over 100% per annum) and this requires an almost continuous process of staff training and detailed supervision and monitoring.

A summary of Crashcarts Call Centre's financial performance for the last three years is as follows:

	2001 **£000**	**2002** **£000**	**2003** **£000**
Revenue			
Contract fixed fee	400	385	385
Order processing fees	2,500	3,025	3,450
Line item processing fees	600	480	390
Total revenue	£3,500	£3,890	£4,225
Expenses			
Office rent and expenses	200	205	210
Operator salaries and salary-related costs	1,550	1,920	2,180
Management, administration and training salaries	1,020	1,070	1,120
IT and telecomms lease and maintenance expenses	300	310	330
Other expenses	150	200	220
Total expenses	£3,220	£3,705	£4,060
Operating profit	£280	£185	£165

Non-financial performance information for the same period is as follows:

	2001	2002	2003
Number of incoming calls received	1,200,000	1,300,000	1,350,000
Number of orders processed	1,000,000	1,100,000	1,150,000
Order strike rate (orders/calls)	83.3%	84.6%	85.2%
Number of line items processed	3,000,000	3,200,000	3,250,000
Average number of line items per order	3.0	2.9	2.8
Number of retail clients	8	7	7
Fixed contract income per client	£50,000	£55,000	£55,000
Income per order processed	£2.50	£2.75	£3.00
Income per line item processed	£0.20	£0.15	£0.12
Average number of orders per operator	15,000	15,000	15,000
Number of operators required	66.7	73.3	76.7
Actual number of operators employed	70.0	80.0	80.0

Required

1 Discuss the increase in importance of risk management to all businesses (with an emphasis on listed ones) over the last few years and the role of management accountants in risk management. *(10 marks)*

2 Advise the Crashcarts Call Centre on methods for analysing its risks. *(5 marks)*

3 Apply appropriate methods to identify and quantify the major risks facing Crashcarts at both parent level and subsidiary level. *(20 marks)*

4 Categorize the components of a management control system and recommend the main controls that would be appropriate for the Crashcarts Call Centre. *(15 marks)*

CIMA Pilot paper Management Accounting – Risk and control strategy, November 2004

C17–10 Metroshire Blues Time allowed: 35 minutes

'Improving our schools is a central part of our agenda that sees education as the key to greater prosperity and social inclusion'. These words, which she had spoken only a few hours ago in the House of Commons, were still giving Toni Cherry a warm feeling. What a great sound bite, she thought, as she sat in the back of her chauffeur-driven ministerial car as it sped through her constituency in Metroshire. She was due to meet with some local public officials and counsellors but, as she was early for that appointment, she asked her driver to pull in at a local secondary school where she knew the head teacher, Mary Brown, from their own school days.

Mary was excited to be meeting her old, high flying friend who had phoned her just a few minutes ago. She showed Toni into her office and they began to chat over a cup of coffee.

'So, Mary how are you spending all the extra resources that our government has put into the school system?' said Toni.

'Extra resources!' exclaimed Mary. 'What extra resources? We have just introduced a freeze on new appointments, laid off our temporary staff and pulled out of the local project that offered extra tuition to pupils receiving free school meals. We have also asked parents to pay for their children's textbooks.'

'But we have increased spending on education by over 20% in the last two years. Isn't the money getting through to you? Don't you have the freedom to manage your own budgets these days?', exclaimed Toni.

'Yes, of course we can set our own budgets – we have already set a deficit budget for next year that forecasts that we will have to dip into our reserves just to keep going. The increases in our costs such as the extra national insurance payments and the need to raise staff salaries have more than eaten up the extra money. Remember, this is a very expensive area to live in and we have to pay our teachers extra increments to stop them from moving to schools where housing is cheaper.'

After this exchange, Toni made her excuses and left in a bad temper. When she arrived at her appointment she accused the local authority officials of not passing on the extra funding that they had received for educational spending in the schools. A major row broke out when the head of the council, Alderman Alf Roberts protested:

'Of course, we passed on the extra money but schools manage their own budgets now and we don't have the detailed knowledge of the cost drivers that we had when the local authority managed school budgets.'

Toni responded: 'But couldn't you see that they were in trouble when they sent in an indicative deficit budget?'

'But they do that every year! Partly they are "crying wolf" and partly we are all erring on the side of caution when we don't know what the government is going to give to us from one year to the next.'

At the end of the day, a rather less complacent Toni Cherry was glad to back in London and chat with her life style guru about which outfits to wear on her forthcoming trip to the Far East. *Postscript*: Parliament gave schools some extra funds and, additionally, the projected budgetary deficits were lower than predicted by the schools.

Required

Explain the origins of the budgeting problems in the local schools in Metroshire and suggest some possible improvements to overall budgeting practices.

Internet exercises

IE17–11 Corporate social responsibility

1 Discuss the questions posed on the website on corporate social responsibility www.goodbusiness.co.uk.

2 Follow up some of the cases introduced by Mouritsen *et al.* (2001b) on the company websites in order to update yourself on some approaches to these issues (see e.g. Systematic (www.systematic.dk) and Carl Bro (www.carlbro.dk).

3 Access the Environmental Management Accounting website (www.emawebsite.org) and compare its approach with that proposed by Boyce (2000).

IE17–12 Public sector performance management

Access a local government website (e.g. www.Birmingham.gov.uk) and critically review the authority's performance plan.

Endnotes

1 Seal (2006).
2 See, e.g., Shleifer and Vishny (1997), p. 737.
3 See, e.g., Norris and O'Dwyer (2004).
4 Norris and O'Dwyer (2004).
5 Hope and Hope (1997).
6 Wildavsky (1975).
7 Neely, Sutcliff and Heyns (2001).
8 Hope and Hope (1997).
9 Hansen, Otley and Van der Stede (2003).
10 Wallander (1999).
11 Hansen *et al.* (2003), p. 101.
12 Hansen *et al.* (2003), p. 101.
13 Hansen *et al.* (2003), p. 102.
14 See Otley and Berry (1980).
15 Kaplan and Norton (1992).

16 These features are based on Otley (1999) and CIMA (2002).

17 The authors would like to thank Alan Coad and Sharzad Uddin for their comments on this chapter.

18 Simons (1995).

19 This section draws heavily on Simons (1995).

20 Simons (1995).

21 Sathe (1982).

22 Sathe (1982).

23 Schwartz (2004).

24 Dyson (2004).

25 Cohen (2004).

26 Erturk, Froud, Johal and Williams (2003).

27 There is a huge literature on agency theory. For an introductory approach in a corporate governance context see Mallin (2003).

28 Healy and Wahlen (1999).

29 See, e.g., Baumol (1959); Marris (1964); Williamson (1964).

30 Shleifer and Vishny (1997), p. 737.

31 Sathe (1982).

32 Higgs (2003); Seal (2006).

33 Starovic (2002).

34 The latest version of the *Combined Code on Corporate Governance* was published in 2006. See www.frc.org.uk/documents/pagemanager/frc/combined%20Code%20June%202006.pdf

35 Guilding, Cravens and Tayles (2000).

36 Mayo (2001).

37 Porter (1980).

38 As this edition was being prepared, there were emerging examples of companies (especially banks) in the financial sector which were suffering the effects of poor risk management.

39 Institute of Chartered Accountants in England and Wales (1999), p. 4.

40 Gould (2002), p. 53.

41 Simons (1995), p. 41.

42 IFAC/CIMA, 2004.

43 Hermes website: www.hermes.co.uk.

44 Norris and O'Dwyer (2004).

45 IFAC, p. 19.

46 See, e.g., Hofstede (1981). For a more detailed treatment of zero-based budgeting see Jones and Pendlebury (2000).

47 Although these authorities are real, we have deliberately anonymized them. See Seal and Ball (2004).

48 Wildavsky (1975).

49 See, e.g., Hood (1995); Humphrey, Miller and Scapens (1993); Humphrey, Miller and Smith (1998); Pollock (2004).

50 This list is taken from Smith (1993).

51 Ouchi (1977).

52 Ouchi (1980).

53 Hilton (2004).

54 Norris and O'Dwyer (2004).

Chapter 18

Business process management: towards the lean operation

Learning objectives:

After studying Chapter 18, you should be able to:

1 Appreciate the business process and lean approach to the management of organizations

2 Determine the reorder point using the EOQ model

3 Consider the impact of JIT approaches to stock management

4 Review the role of management accounting in business models that minimize working capital

5 Evaluate the contribution of ERP models

6 Review the role of management accounting in e-commerce

7 Measure the costs of quality

8 Review the relationship between management accounting and TQM systems

9 Understand the technique of benchmarking

10 Understand the contribution of business process re-engineering and ABM

Concepts in Context

A good example of an existing business that has used the internet is provided by Cheshire ironmonger, Cooksons. The weakness of their old business was that they only had a single outlet in Stockport which was vulnerable to out-of-town DIY superstores. The strength of the old business was a good reputation with specialist customers and a good supply chain. With the establishment of cooksons.com, these advantages could be made available to a wider customer base. 'The business itself holds no stock; its suppliers meet the online orders.'[1]

1 LEARNING OBJECTIVE

In this chapter, we take a more operations management perspective. From an operations perspective, the organization is visualized as procuring, transforming and delivering a flow of products or services to customers. Thus, in contrast to some earlier chapters (see especially Chapter 14), the focus is on the management of *business processes* rather than organizational structures such as departments or divisions. In Exhibit 18.1, there is a contrast between a business process perspective and a departmental or divisional perspective. The latter is sometimes visualized as tending to produce a 'silo mentality' with some flows up and down the silo but little communication between individual 'silos'. In the previous chapter, we saw how the management of departments with budgets may contribute to the development of a 'silo mentality'. The business process perspective challenges managers to find metrics which monitor the processes *across* the organization which serve customers and thus generate value.

18.1 EXHIBIT

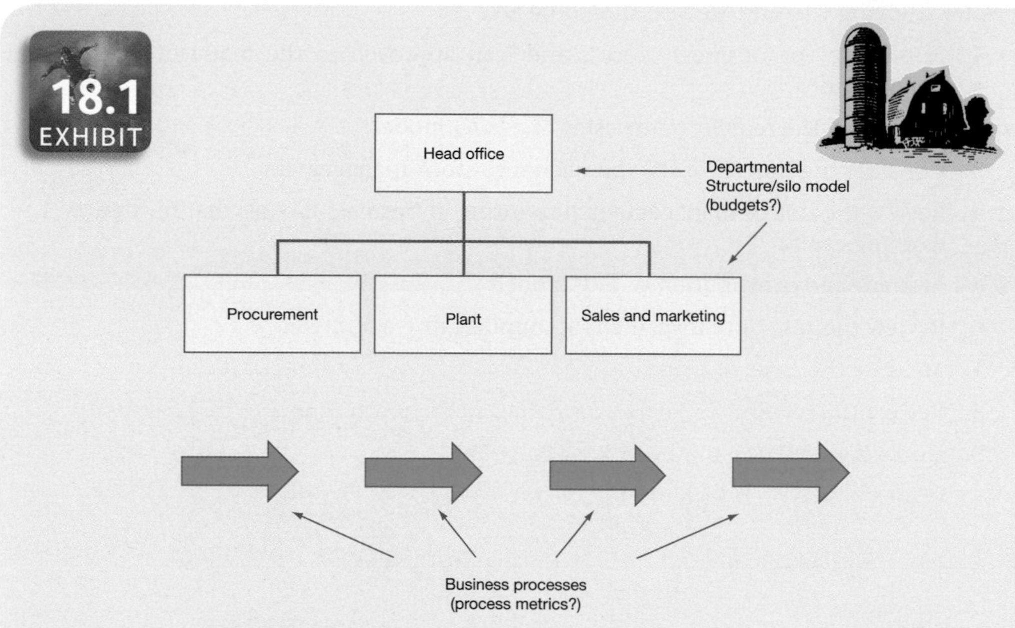

Exhibit 18.1 The process perspective contrasted to the departmental 'silo mentality'.

Over the last few years, new technology, especially *enterprise resource planning* (ERP) packages have generated improved operations management information which may enable the integration of 'end-to-end' business processes from procurement through to final delivery and payment. Even more recently, the internet has created whole new business models with cost and revenue streams that are only just beginning to be understood. In some of these businesses such as online retailers, a company's ability to hold huge stocks and offer an immense choice is a source of commercial strength – in this type of business stock has to be managed but it cannot be eliminated. Thus although we acknowledge the impact of philosophies such as just-in-time (JIT) that aim at the elimination of stocks, we also review some of the more traditional, **optimizing**, approaches to inventory management such as the *economic order quantity* (EOQ) model. As we shall see, JIT required an uncompromising attitude to quality as stocks had previously been used to hide the effects of low quality and poor business flow management. Indeed, the JIT approach combined with wider competitive pressures have challenged the traditional, *cost of quality* (COQ) model approach through the practice of *total quality management* (TQM) with its zero defects philosophy. Later on in the chapter we will be looking at techniques that seek to improve business processes, such as *benchmarking*, and practices, such as *activity-based management* (ABM) and *business process re-engineering* (BPR), that aim to identify and eliminate non-value adding activities.[2]

Many of these business process improvement techniques are associated with the philosophy of the *lean enterprise* or *lean production*, a strategy that was proposed as an alternative to a market positioning (see Chapter 16). **Lean production** techniques were first introduced in manufacturing (especially by Toyota) but are increasingly being applied in service sectors, including not-for-profit organizations in the public sector.[3] Indeed, there are some similarities between inventories in manufacturing and queues of customers in services particularly since both are the result of failing to match supply and demand. Lean principles also involve other focuses such as the reduction of waste and virtual elimination of defects. Such objectives are now part of management orthodoxy but were seen as revolutionary only a few years ago when the philosophy of *optimization* epitomized by the EOQ model dominated thinking in many business schools.[4]

Optimizing stock: the economic order quantity (EOQ) and the reorder point

In the optimization model of stock management, selecting the 'right' level of stock involves balancing three groups of costs: *stock ordering costs*, *stock carrying costs*, and the *costs of not carrying sufficient stock*. These costs are discussed in this section.

Costs associated with stock

Stock ordering costs are incurred each time a stock item is ordered. These costs may include clerical costs associated with ordering stock, and some handling and transportation costs. They are triggered by the act of ordering stock and are essentially the same whether 1 unit or 10,000 units are ordered; these costs are driven by the number of orders placed – not by the size of the orders. If stock ordering costs are large, a manager may want to place small numbers of big orders on an infrequent basis rather than large numbers of small orders.

Stock carrying costs are incurred to keep units in stock. These costs include storage costs, handling costs, property taxes, insurance and the interest on the funds invested in stock. These costs are driven by the amount and value of stock that is held by the company. In addition to these costs, work in progress creates operating problems. Work in progress may physically get in the way and make it difficult to keep track of operations. Moreover, work in progress tends to hide problems that are not discovered until it is too late to take corrective action. This results in erratic production, inefficient operations, 'lost' orders, high defect rates, and substantial risks of obsolescence. These intangible costs of work in progress stock are largely responsible for the movement to JIT. If stock carrying costs are high, managers will want to reduce the overall level of stock and to place frequent orders in small quantities.

The **costs of not carrying sufficient stock** result from not having enough stock to meet customers' needs. These costs include lost sales, customer ill will, and the costs of expediting orders for goods not held in stock. If these costs are high, managers will want to hold large stock. Conceptually, the 'right' level of stock to carry is the level that will minimize the total of these three groups of costs. In the following pages we show how to accomplish this task. The problem is broken down into two dimensions – how much to order (or how much to produce in a single production run or batch) and how often to do it. These two decisions – how much to order and how often to order – determine the average level of stock and the likelihood of being out of stock.

Computing the economic order quantity (EOQ)

The question 'How much to order?' is answered by the **economic order quantity (EOQ)**. It is the order size that minimizes the sum of the costs of ordering stock and the costs of carrying stock. We will consider two approaches to computing the EOQ – the *tabular approach* and the *formula approach*.

The tabular approach

Suppose that 12,000 units of a particular item are required each year. Managers could order all 12,000 units at once or they could order smaller numbers of units spread over the year – perhaps 1,000 units per month. Placing only one order would minimize the total costs of ordering stock but would result in high stock carrying costs, since the average stock level would be very large. On the other hand, placing many small orders would result in high ordering costs but in low stock carrying costs, since the average stock level would be reduced. As stated above, the EOQ is the order size that will optimally balance these two costs – stock ordering costs and stock holding costs.

To show how EOQ is computed, assume that a manufacturer uses 3,000 sub-assemblies in the manufacturing process each year. The sub-assemblies are purchased from a supplier at a cost of £20 each. Other cost data are given below:

Stock carrying costs, per unit, per year	£0.80
Cost of placing a purchase order	10.00

Exhibit 18.2 contains a tabulation of the total costs associated with various order sizes for the sub-assemblies. Most of this table is straightforward, but the average stock requires some explanation. If 50 units are ordered at a time and the items are ordered only when the stock gets down to zero, then the size of the stock will vary from 50 units to 0 units. Thus, on average, there will be 25 units in stock. Notice that total annual cost is lowest (and is equal) at the 250- and 300-unit order sizes. The EOQ will lie somewhere between these two points. We could locate it precisely by adding more columns to the tabulation, and we would eventually zero in on 274 units as being the exact EOQ.

18.2 EXHIBIT

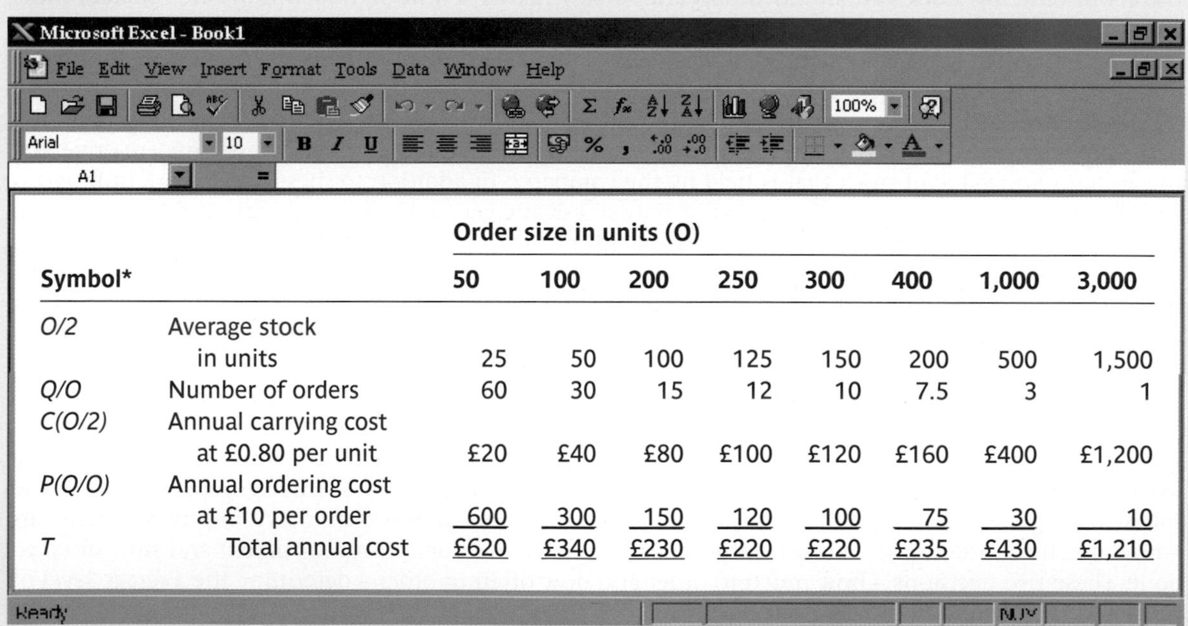

		Order size in units (O)							
Symbol*		**50**	**100**	**200**	**250**	**300**	**400**	**1,000**	**3,000**
O/2	Average stock in units	25	50	100	125	150	200	500	1,500
Q/O	Number of orders	60	30	15	12	10	7.5	3	1
C(O/2)	Annual carrying cost at £0.80 per unit	£20	£40	£80	£100	£120	£160	£400	£1,200
P(Q/O)	Annual ordering cost at £10 per order	600	300	150	120	100	75	30	10
T	Total annual cost	£620	£340	£230	£220	£220	£235	£430	£1,210

Minimum total annual cost

*Symbols:
O = Order size in units (see headings above).
Q = Annual quantity used in units (3,000 in this example)
C = Annual cost of carrying one unit in stock.
P = Cost of placing one order.
T = Total annual cost.

Exhibit 18.2 Tabulation of costs associated with various order sizes

The cost relationships from this tabulation are shown graphically in Exhibit 18.3. The EOQ is indicated on the graph. Notice that the EOQ minimizes the total annual costs. It also is the point where annual carrying costs and annual ordering costs are equal. At the EOQ, these two costs are exactly balanced.

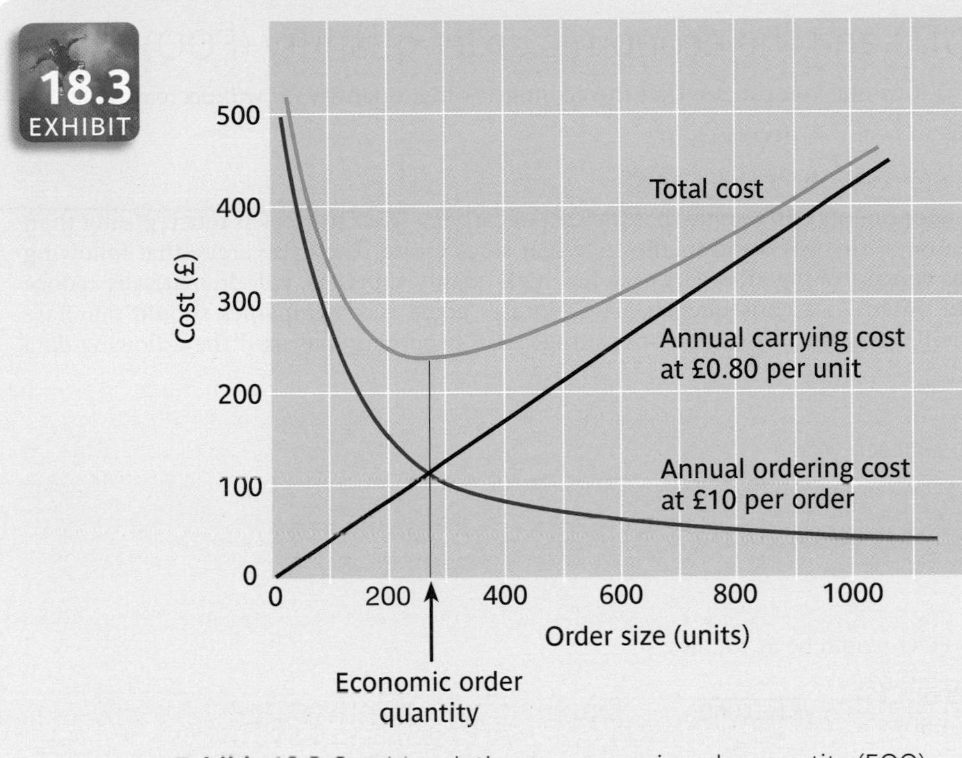

Exhibit 18.3 Graphic solution to economic order quantity (EOQ)

Observe from the graph that total cost shows a tendency to flatten out between 200 and 400 units. Most firms look for this minimum cost range and choose an order size that falls within it, rather than choosing the exact EOQ. The primary reason is that suppliers will often ship goods only in round-lot sizes.

The formula approach

The EOQ can also be found by means of a formula that can be derived using calculus:

$$E = \sqrt{\frac{2QP}{C}}$$

where:

E = economic order quantity (EOQ)
Q = annual quantity used in units
P = cost of placing one order
C = annual cost of carrying one unit in stock.

Using the data from the preceding example, we can directly compute the EOQ as follows:

Q = 3,000 sub-assemblies used per year
P = £10 cost to place one order
C = £0.80 cost to carry one sub-assembly in stock for one year

$$E = \sqrt{\frac{2QP}{C}} = \sqrt{\frac{2(3{,}000)(£10)}{£0.80}} = \sqrt{\frac{£60{,}000}{£0.80}} = \sqrt{£75{,}000}$$

$E = 274$ units.

Just-in-time (JIT) and the economic order quantity (EOQ)

By examining the EOQ formula, you can see that the economic order quantity, E, will decrease if:

1 The cost of placing an order, P, decreases, or

2 The cost of carrying stock in stock, C, increases.

As we shall see below, proponents of JIT argue that the cost of carrying stock in stock is much greater than generally realized because of the waste and inefficiency that stock create. They also argue that following JIT procedures, such as concentrating all orders on a few high quality suppliers, will dramatically reduce the cost of placing an order. As a consequence, JIT advocates argue that companies should purchase more frequently in smaller amounts. Assume, for example, that a company has used the following data to compute its EOQ:

Q = 4,800 units needed each year

P = £75 cost to place one order

C = £4.50 cost to carry one unit in stock for one year.

Given these data, the EOQ would be as follows:

$$E = \sqrt{\frac{2QP}{C}} = \sqrt{\frac{2(4{,}800)(£15)}{£4.50)}} = \sqrt{£160{,}000}$$

$E = 400$ units

Now assume that as a result of JIT purchasing, the company is able to decrease the cost of placing an order to only £3. Also assume that due to the waste and inefficiency caused by stock, the true cost of carrying a unit in stock is £8 per year. The revised EOQ would be as follows:

$$E = \sqrt{\frac{2QP}{C}} = \sqrt{\frac{2(4{,}800)(£3)}{£8}} = \sqrt{£3{,}600}$$

$E = 60$ units

Under JIT purchasing, the company would not necessarily order in 60-unit lots, since purchases would be geared to current demand. Nevertheless, this example shows quite dramatically the economics behind reducing order sizes.

Production lot size

The EOQ concept can also be applied to the problem of determining the **economic lot size**. When companies manufacture a variety of products, they must decide how many units of one product should be manufactured before switching over to another product. The number of units in a lot, or production run, is referred to as the *lot size* or *batch size*. For example, Nintendo must decide how many units of a particular video game are to be produced in one lot before switching over to production of a different video game. This is a problem because switching from one product to another requires changing settings on machines, changing tools, and getting different materials ready for processing. Making these changes requires time and may involve substantial out-of-pocket costs. These **set-up costs** are analogous to the order costs discussed above, and they can be used in the EOQ formula in place of the order costs to determine the optimal lot size.

To illustrate, Chittenden Company has determined that the following costs are associated with one of its products:

Q = 15,000 units produced each year

P = £150 set-up costs to switch production from one product to another

C = £2 to carry one unit in stock for one year.

What is the optimal production lot size for this product? It can be determined by using the EOQ formula:

$$E = \sqrt{\frac{2QP}{C}} = \sqrt{\frac{2(15{,}000)(\pounds150)}{\pounds2}} = \sqrt{\pounds2{,}250{,}000}$$

E = 1,500 units (economic lot size)

Chittenden Company will minimize its overall costs by producing in lots of 1,500 units each.

In computing the economic lot size, note again the impact of modern manufacturing methods. First, managers now realize that the costs of holding stock are far higher than previously assumed. Excess work in progress stock make it very difficult to operate efficiently and hence generate many unnecessary costs. Second, managers and workers are cutting set-up times from many hours to a few minutes by cleverly applying techniques such as *single-minute-exchange-of-dies* (see page 755). The benefit of reducing *set-up time* is that it makes it economically feasible for the company to produce in smaller lots and to respond much more quickly to the market. Indeed, reducing set-ups to the barest minimum is an essential step in any successful implementation of JIT.

To illustrate how these aspects of modern manufacturing methods affect the economic lot size, consider the Chittenden Company data. Suppose that the company has been able to reduce the cost of a set-up to only £3. Further, suppose that the company realizes, after more careful analysis of all of the costs of holding stock, that the true cost of carrying a unit in stock is £36 per year. The new economic lot size would be as follows:

$$E = \sqrt{\frac{2QP}{C}} = \sqrt{\frac{2(15{,}000)(\pounds3)}{\pounds36}} = \sqrt{\pounds2{,}500}$$

E = 50 units (economic lot size)

Thus, the company's economic lot size has been reduced from 1,500 units to only 50 units – a reduction of nearly 97%.

Activity-based costing (ABC) and the production lot size

Managers should be extremely cautious when applying the results of ABC analyses to computation of the economic lot size. Typically, one of the results of an ABC analysis is a dramatic increase in the apparent costs of set-ups. The reason for this is that under conventional costing systems, many of the costs that might be attributed to switching over from one product to another are lumped into the general manufacturing overhead cost pool and distributed to products based on direct labour-hours or some other measure of volume. When an ABC analysis is done, these costs are separately identified as set-up costs. As a consequence, set-up costs appear to increase, and this would seem to imply that the economic lot size should be increased. However, a close examination of the costs attributed to set-ups in the ABC analysis will usually reveal that most of the costs cannot actually be avoided by reducing the number of set-ups. For example, machinery depreciation may be included in set-up costs. However, reducing the number of set-ups may have no impact at all on the amount of machinery depreciation actually incurred.

Reorder point and safety stock

We stated that the stock problem has two dimensions – how much to order and how often to do it. The 'how often to do it' involves what are commonly termed the *reorder point* and the *safety stock*. The basic idea is to minimize the costs of holding stock while ensuring that there will be no stockouts (i.e., situations in which there are insufficient stock to satisfy current production requirements or customer demand). First, we will discuss the reorder point and then we will discuss the safety stock.

The **reorder point** tells the manager when to place an order or when to initiate production to replenish depleted stocks. It is dependent on three factors – the EOQ (or economic production-run size), the *lead time*, and the rate of usage during the lead time. The **lead time** can be defined as the interval between the time that an order is placed and the time when the order is finally received from the supplier or from the production line.

Constant usage during the lead time

If the rate of usage during the lead time is known with certainty, the reorder point can be determined by the following formula:

Reorder point = Lead time × Average daily or weekly usage

To illustrate the formula's use, assume that a company's EOQ is 500 units, that the lead time is three weeks, and that the average weekly usage is 50 units.

Reorder point = 3 weeks × 50 units per week = 150 units

The reorder point would be 150 units. That is, the company will automatically place a new order for 500 units when stocks drop to a level of 150 units, or three weeks' supply, left on hand.

Variable usage during the lead time

The previous example assumed that the 50 units per week usage rate was constant and was known with certainty. Although some firms enjoy the luxury of certainty, the more common situation is to find considerable variation in the rate of usage of stock items from period to period. If usage varies from period to period, the firm that reorders in the way computed above may soon find itself out of stock. A sudden spurt in demand, a delay in delivery, or a snag in processing an order may cause stock levels to be depleted before a new shipment arrives.

Companies that experience problems in demand, delivery, or processing of orders have found that they need some type of buffer to guard against stockouts. Such a buffer is called a **safety stock**. A safety stock serves as a kind of insurance against greater than usual demand and against problems in the ordering and delivery of goods. Its size is determined by deducting *average usage* from the *maximum usage* that can reasonably be expected during a period. For example, if the firm in the preceding example was faced with variable demand for its product, it would compute a safety stock as follows:

Maximum expected usage per week	65 units
Average usage per week	50 units
Excess	15 units
Lead time	× 3 weeks
Safety stock	45 units

The reorder point is then determined by *adding the safety stock to the average usage during the lead time.* In formula form, the reorder point is:

Reorder point = (Lead time × Average daily or weekly usage) + Safety stock

Computation of the reorder point is shown both numerically and graphically in Exhibit 18.4. As shown in the exhibit, the company will place a new order for 500 units when stocks drop to a level of 195 units left on hand.

Reducing stock: just-in-time (JIT)

When companies use the **just-in-time (JIT)** production and stock control system, they purchase materials and produce units only as needed to meet actual customer demand. In a JIT system, stocks are reduced to the minimum and in some cases to zero. The JIT approach can be used in both merchandising and manufacturing companies. It has the most profound effects, however,

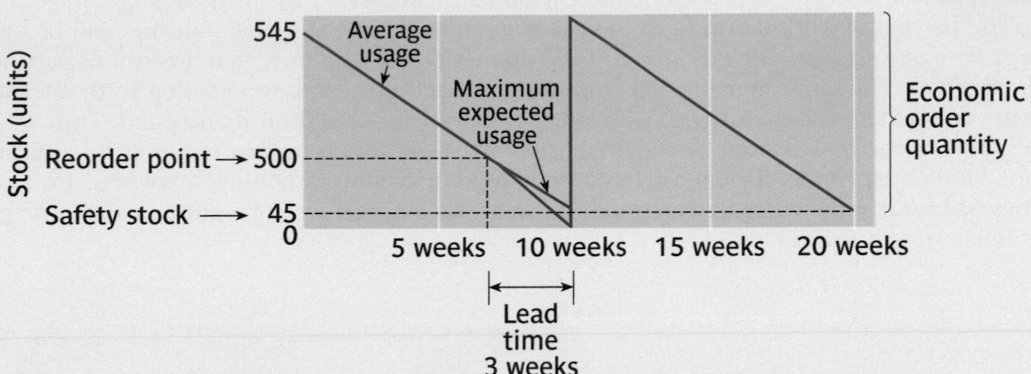

Economic order quantity .... 500 units
Lead time .... 3 weeks
Average weekly usage .... 50 units
Maximum weekly usage .... 65 units
Safety stock .... 45 units

Reorder point = (3 weeks × 50 units per week) + 45 units = 195 units

Exhibit 18.4 Determining the reorder point – variable usage

on the operations of manufacturing companies, which maintain three classes of stock – *raw materials, work in progress* and *finished goods*.

Traditionally, manufacturing companies have maintained large amounts of all three kinds of stock to act as buffers so that operations can proceed smoothly even if there are unanticipated disruptions. Raw materials stock provide insurance in case suppliers are late with deliveries. Work in progress stock are maintained in case a workstation is unable to operate due to a breakdown or other reason. Finished goods stock are maintained to accommodate unanticipated fluctuations in demand.

While these stock provide buffers against unforeseen events, they have a cost. In addition to the money tied up in the stock, experts argue that the presence of stock encourages inefficient and sloppy work, results in too many defects, and dramatically increases the amount of time required to complete a product. None of this is obvious – if it were, companies would have long ago reduced their stocks. Managers at Toyota are credited with the insight that large stocks often create more problems than they solve and Toyota pioneered the JIT approach.

The JIT concept

Under ideal conditions, a company operating a JIT system would purchase *only* enough materials each day to meet that day's needs. Moreover, the company would have no goods still in progress at the end of the day, and all goods completed during the day would have been shipped immediately to customers. As this sequence suggests, 'just-in-time' means that raw materials are received just in time to go into production, manufactured parts are completed *just in time* to be assembled into products, and products are completed *just in time* to be shipped to customers.

Although few companies have been able to reach this ideal, many companies have been able to reduce stock to only a fraction of their previous levels. The result has been a substantial reduction in ordering and warehousing costs, and much more effective operations.

How does a company avoid a build-up of parts and materials at various workstations and still ensure a smooth flow of goods when JIT is in use? In a JIT environment, the flow of goods is controlled by a *pull approach*. The pull approach can be explained as follows: At the final assembly stage, a signal is sent to the preceding workstation as to the exact amount of parts and materials that will be needed *over the next few hours* to assemble products to fill customer orders, and only that amount of parts and materials is provided. The same signal is sent back through each preceding workstation so that a smooth flow of parts and materials is maintained with no appreciable stock build-up at any point. Thus, all workstations respond to the pull exerted by the final assembly stage, which in turn responds to customer orders. As one worker explained, 'Under a JIT system you don't produce anything, anywhere, for anybody unless they ask for it somewhere downstream. Stocks are an evil that we're taught to avoid.' The pull approach is illustrated in Exhibit 18.5.

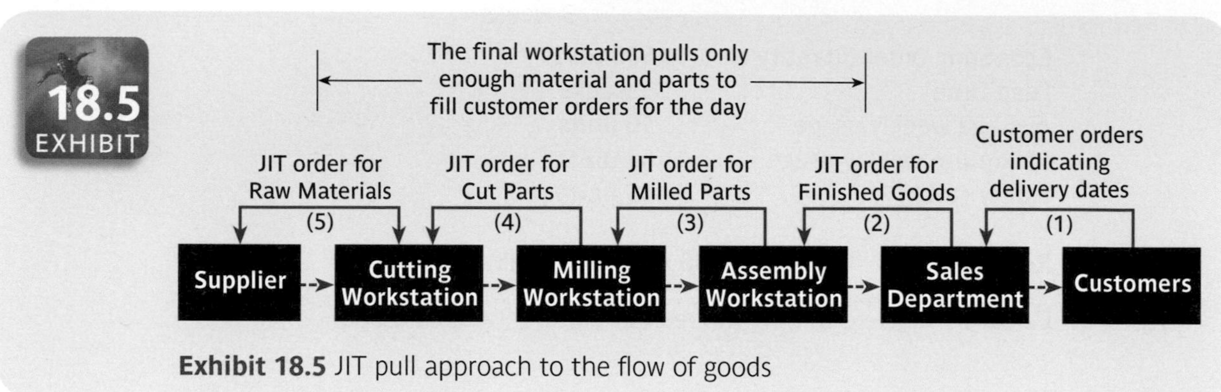

Exhibit 18.5 JIT pull approach to the flow of goods

The pull approach described above can be contrasted to the *push approach* used in conventional manufacturing systems. In conventional systems, when a workstation completes its work, the partially completed goods are 'pushed' forward to the next workstation regardless of whether that workstation is ready to receive them. The result is an unintentional stockpiling of partially completed goods that may not be completed for days or even weeks. This ties up funds and also results in operating inefficiencies. For one thing, it becomes very difficult to keep track of where everything is when so much is scattered all over the factory floor.

Another characteristic of conventional manufacturing systems is an emphasis on 'keeping everyone busy' as an end in itself. This inevitably leads to excess stock – particularly work in progress stock – for reasons that will be more fully explored in a later section on the theory of constraints. In JIT, the traditional emphasis on keeping everyone busy is abandoned in favour of producing only what customers actually want – even if that means some workers are idle.

JIT purchasing

Any organization with stock – retail, wholesale, distribution, service, or manufacturing – can use *JIT purchasing*. Under JIT purchasing:

1. *A company relies on a few ultra reliable suppliers*. IBM, for example, eliminated 95% of the suppliers from one of its plants, reducing the number from 640 to only 32. Rather than soliciting bids from suppliers each year and going with the low bidder, the dependable suppliers are rewarded with long-term contracts.
2. *Suppliers make frequent deliveries in small lots just before the goods are needed*. Rather than deliver a week's (or a month's) supply of an item at one time, suppliers must be willing to make deliveries as often as several times a day, and in the exact quantities specified by the buyer. Undependable suppliers who do not meet delivery schedules are weeded out. Dependability is essential, since a JIT system is highly vulnerable to any interruption in supply. If a single part is unavailable, the entire assembly operation may have to be shut down. Or, in the case of a merchandising company, if the supplier allows stock to get down to zero, customers may be turned away unsatisfied.

3 *Suppliers must deliver defect-free goods*. Because of the vulnerability of a JIT system to disruptions, defects cannot be tolerated. Indeed, suppliers must become so reliable that incoming goods do not have to be inspected.

Companies that adopt JIT purchasing often realize substantial savings from streamlined operations. Note that a company does not have to eliminate all stock to use the JIT approach. Indeed, retail organizations must maintain some stock or they could not operate. But the amount of time a product spends on a shelf or in a warehouse can be greatly reduced.

Key elements in a JIT system

In addition to JIT purchasing, four key elements are usually required for the successful operation of a JIT manufacturing system. These elements include improving the plant layout, reducing the set-up time needed for production runs, striving for zero defects, and developing a flexible workforce.

Improving plant layout

Properly to implement JIT, a company typically must improve the manufacturing *flow lines* in its plant. A flow line is the physical path taken by a product as it moves through the manufacturing process as it is transformed from raw materials to completed goods.

Traditionally, companies have designed their plant floors so that similar machines are grouped together. Such a functional layout results in all drill presses in one place, all lathes in another place, and so forth. This approach to plant layout requires that work in progress be moved from one group of machines to another – frequently across the plant or even to another building. The result is extensive material-handling costs, large work in progress stock, and unnecessary delays.

In a JIT system, all machines needed to make a particular product are often brought together in one location. This approach to plant layout creates an individual 'mini' factory for each separate product, frequently referred to as a *focused factory* or as a 'factory within a factory'. The flow line for a product can be straight, as shown earlier in Exhibit 18.4, or it can be in a U-shaped configuration. The key point is that all machines in a *product flow line* are tightly grouped together so that partially completed units are not shifted from place to place all over the factory. *Manufacturing cells* are also often part of a JIT product flow line. In a *cell*, a single worker operates several machines.

The *focused factory approach* allows workers to focus all their efforts on a product from start to finish and minimizes handling and moving. After one large manufacturing company rearranged its plant layout and organized its products into individual flow lines, the company determined that the distance travelled by one product had been decreased from 3 miles to just 100 metres. Apart from reductions in handling, this more compact layout makes it much easier to keep track of where a particular job is in the production process.

An improved plant layout can dramatically increase *throughput*, which is the total volume of production through a facility during a period, and it can dramatically reduce **throughput time** (also known as *cycle time*), which is the time required to make a product.

Reduced set-up time

Set-ups involve activities – such as moving materials, changing machine settings, setting up equipment, and running tests – that must be performed whenever production is switched over from making one type of item to another. For example, it may not be a simple matter to switch over from making 1.25 cm brass screws to making 2 cm brass screws on a manually controlled milling machine. Many preparatory steps must be performed, and these steps can take hours. Because of the time and expense involved in such set-ups, many managers believe set-ups should be avoided and therefore items should be produced in large batches. For example, one batch of 400 units requires only one set-up, whereas four batches of 100 units each would require four set-ups. The problem with big batches is that they create large amounts of stock that must wait for days, weeks, or even months before further processing at the next workstation or before they are sold.

One advantage of a dedicated flow line is that it requires fewer set-ups. If equipment is dedicated to a single product, set-ups are largely eliminated and the product can be produced in any batch size desired. Even when dedicated flow lines are not used, it is often possible to slash set-up time by using techniques such as single-minute-exchange-of-dies. A *die* is a device used for cutting out, forming or stamping material. For example, a die is used to produce the stamped metal door panels on a car. A die must be changed when it wears out or when production is switched to a different product. This changeover can be time consuming. The goal with *single-minute-exchange-of dies* is to reduce the amount of time required to change a die to a minute or less. This can be done by simple techniques such as doing as much of the changeover work in advance as possible rather than waiting until production is shut down.[5] When such techniques are followed, batch sizes can be very small.

Smaller batches reduce the level of stock, make it easier to respond quickly to the market, reduce cycle times, and generally make it much easier to spot manufacturing problems before they result in a large number of defective units.

Zero defects and JIT

Defective units create big problems in a JIT environment. If a completed order contains a defective unit, the company must ship the order with less than the promised quantity or it must restart the whole production process to make just one unit. At minimum, this creates a delay in shipping the order and may generate a ripple effect that delays other orders. For this and other reasons, defects cannot be tolerated in a JIT system. Companies that are deeply involved in JIT tend to become zealously committed to a goal of *zero defects*. Even though it may be next to impossible to attain the zero defect goal, companies have found that they can come very close. For example, Motorola, Allied Signal, and many other companies now measure defects in terms of the number of defects per million units of product.

In a traditional company, parts and materials are inspected for defects when they are received from suppliers, and quality inspectors inspect units as they progress along the production line. In a JIT system, the company's suppliers are responsible for the quality of incoming parts and materials. And instead of using quality inspectors, the company's production workers are directly responsible for spotting defective units.

A worker who discovers a defect is supposed to punch an alarm button that stops the production flow line and sets off flashing lights. Supervisors and other workers then descend on the workstation to determine the cause of the defect and correct it before any further defective units are produced. This procedure ensures that problems are quickly identified and corrected, but it does require that defects are rare – otherwise there would be constant disruptions to the production process.

Flexible workforce

Workers on a JIT line must be multiskilled and flexible. Workers are often expected to operate all of the equipment on a JIT product flow line. Moreover, workers are expected to perform minor repairs and do maintenance work when they would otherwise be idle. In contrast, on a conventional assembly line a worker performs a single task all the time every day and all maintenance work is done by a specialized maintenance crew.

Benefits of a JIT system

The main benefits of JIT are the following:

1 Working capital is bolstered by the recovery of funds that were tied up in stock

2 Areas previously used to store stock are made available for other, more productive uses

3 Throughput time is reduced, resulting in greater potential output and quicker response to customers

4 Defect rates are reduced, resulting in less waste and greater customer satisfaction.

As a result of benefits such as those cited above, more companies are embracing JIT each year. Most companies find, however, that simply reducing stock is not enough. To remain competitive in an ever changing and ever more competitive business environment, companies must strive for continuous improvement.

Stock control and enterprise resource planning (ERP)

Systems of stock control such as JIT have been helped by developments in information technology. The most sophisticated example involves the automation of management information systems through the **enterprise resource planning** software offered by companies such as SAP, Oracle, Baan and J.D. Edwards. Stock control is only part of an integrated system, which tracks transactions across the company.

The main characteristics, costs and benefits of ERPs are:[6]

- Systems are based on integrated client-server technology
- All data are entered only once where the data originate
- The implementation of such a total system is typically costly and time consuming
- But, updating the old heterogeneous system platform (e.g., for euro-currency) is costly as well
- Firms may also aim at business model improvements via the adoption of ERPs (e.g., ABC[7])
- ERP represents a *process-oriented information system* based on *value chain thinking*
- The installation of an ERP may result in a lack of flexibility when a company operates in different countries.[8]

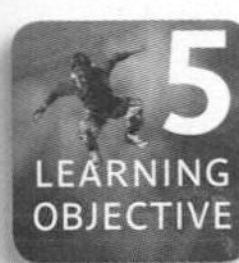

Given the theoretical benefits of a single *IT driven management information system*, it seems strange that for many years companies have been disappointed with the returns from their huge investments in new IT systems.[9] One problem with ERP models is that the benefits of the new systems are not so much in the 'hard returns' of reduced *headcounts* as in 'soft returns' such as revenue or employee gains that are harder to identify.[10] Many of the gains are so-called *'back-door'* gains such as agreeing common data with the same vocabulary and format. Not only are business processes standardized but the implementation process helps to inculcate a more learning, improving culture. Part of the problem with early computer applications was that companies were automating *existing* organizational and production systems. The really significant benefits come when the new technology is used to fundamentally reconfigure business practices.[11] Indeed, some businesses argue that the bulk of benefits come from the organizational changes rather than the new technology.[12]

E-commerce: new challenges for management accounting

A lot of hype has been generated by the internet. Yet many of the breakthroughs in inter-personal and inter-organizational communication relies on older technologies such as **electronic data interchange (EDI)** and telephones. The power of the telephone has been massively increased because the teleworker can be linked to the company's database via a personal computer. Thus the huge reduction in paper, floor space, queueing and so on, in an operation such as telephone banking or a ticketless airline, does not necessarily require internet technology. But for these operations, the internet is cheaper than both telephone and EDI as well as opening up the possibility of real-time screen communication for both consumers and smaller companies.

FOCUS

Focus on current practice

In the early days, few internet companies could measure their sites' performance or whether their sites were becoming more effective over time. Internet companies attracted visitors to their sites but were less successful at making sales or retaining customers. If anything, the more visitors the sites drew, the more money they lost. As in any business, long-term profitability is based on lifetime customer value: the revenue customers generate over their lives, less the cost of acquiring, converting and retaining them. New site performance indicators are being developed that measure attraction, conversion and retention plus other factors such as the rate at which the number of customers increases, and customer gross margins.[13] Paradoxically, it would be wrong to think that internet companies are the most likely candidates for stock elimination. For example, part of the success of one of the more established dotcom companies, Amazon.com, is that its stocks of books, CDs, videos are far larger than local retailers.

More direct relations between customers and producers (disintermediation) means that huge chains of dedicated high street branches are assets of doubtful value. But as companies become more virtual there are new challenges for management accounting. In a virtual company 'assets are not only tangible but also include intangible assets such as brand value, intellectual property, human capital (people), virtual integration, information management, quality of service and customer relations, they need to be factored into performance measurement exercises. Otherwise a company may end up with a distorted picture of its overall economic value, market position and future potential.'[14] Distorted pictures were certainly a feature of the dotcom boom when many internet start-ups attracted both media and investor attention. With inflated stock market values bearing no relation to traditional indicators of value, there was vague talk of a 'new economic model'.

The hype of the dotcom boom has now passed. Many of the dotcom start-ups have either disappeared or are struggling to make profits. In retrospect, some of these companies may have benefited from more traditional business plans that showed how an internet site could generate profits. The approach to evaluating site performance is becoming more rigorous as the nature of internet commerce is better understood.[15]

Quality and business processes: measurement and management

Earlier we saw how a JIT system is based on defect-free production and inputs. Yet there are more general motives for measuring and managing quality even, or, especially, in service companies that do not have inventory. Companies that develop a reputation for low-quality products generally lose market share and face declining profits. It doesn't do much good to have a product with a high-quality design that is made with high-quality materials if the product falls apart on the first use. One very important aspect of quality is the absence of defects. Defective products result in high warranty costs, but more importantly, they result in dissatisfied customers. People who are dissatisfied with a product are unlikely to buy the product again. They are also likely to tell others about their bad experiences. One study found that '[c]ustomers who have bad experiences tell approximately 11 people about it'.[16] This is the worst possible sort of advertising. To prevent such problems, companies have been expending a great deal of effort to reduce defects. The objective is to have high *quality of conformance.*

The cost of quality model

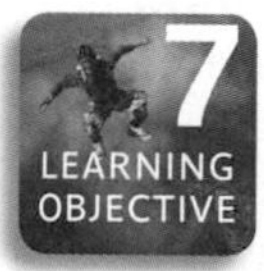

A product that meets or exceeds its design specifications and is free of defects that mar its appearance or degrade its performance is said to have high quality of conformance. Note that if an economy car is free of defects, it can have a **quality of conformance** that is just as high as a defect-free luxury car. The purchasers of economy cars cannot expect their cars to be as opulently equipped as luxury cars, but they can and do expect them to be free of defects.

Preventing, detecting and dealing with defects cause costs that are called *quality costs* or the *cost of quality*. The use of the term *quality cost* is confusing to some people. It does not refer to costs such as using a higher-grade leather to make a wallet or using 14K gold instead of gold-plating in jewellery. Instead, the term **quality cost** refers to all of the costs that are incurred to prevent defects or that are incurred as a result of defects occurring.

Quality costs can be broken down into four broad groups. Two of these groups – known as *prevention costs* and *appraisal costs* – are incurred in an effort to keep defective products from falling into the hands of customers. The other two groups of costs – known as *internal failure costs* and *external failure costs* – are incurred because defects are produced despite efforts to prevent them. Examples of specific costs involved in each of these four groups are given in Exhibit 18.6.

Several things should be noted about the quality costs shown in the exhibit. First, note that quality costs do not relate to just manufacturing; rather, they relate to all the activities in a company from initial research and development (R&D) through customer service. Second, note that the number of costs associated with quality is very large; therefore, total quality cost can be quite high unless management gives this area special attention. Finally, note how different the costs are in the four groupings. We will now look at each of these groupings more closely.

Prevention costs

The most effective way to minimize quality costs while maintaining high-quality output is to avoid having quality problems arise in the first place. This is the purpose of **prevention costs**; such costs relate to any activity that reduces the number of defects in products or services. Companies have learned that it is much less costly to prevent a problem from ever happening than it is to find and correct the problem after it has occurred.

Prevention costs
Systems development
Quality engineering
Quality training
Quality circles
Statistical process control activities
Supervision of prevention activities
Quality data gathering, analysis, and reporting
Quality improvement projects
Technical support provided to suppliers
Audits of the effectiveness of the quality system
Appraisal costs
Test and inspection of incoming materials
Test and inspection of in-process goods
Final product testing and inspection
Supplies used in testing and inspection
Supervision of testing and inspection activities
Depreciation of test equipment
Maintenance of test equipment
Plant utilities in the inspection area
Field testing and appraisal at customer site
Internal failure costs
Net cost of scrap
Net cost of spoilage
Rework labour and overhead
Reinspection of reworked products
Retesting of reworked products
Downtime caused by quality problems
Disposal of defective products
Analysis of the cause of defects in production
Re-entering data because of keying errors
Debugging software errors
External failure costs
Cost of field servicing and handling complaints
Warranty repairs and replacements
Repairs and replacements beyond the warranty period
Product recalls
Liability arising from defective products
Returns and allowances arising from quality problems
Lost sales arising from a reputation for poor quality

Exhibit 18.6 Typical quality costs

Note from Exhibit 18.6 that prevention costs include activities relating to quality circles and statistical process control. **Quality circles** consist of small groups of employees that meet on a regular basis to discuss ways to improve the quality of output. Both management and workers are included in these circles. Quality circles are widely used and can be found in manufacturing companies, utilities, health care organizations, banks and many other organizations.

Statistical process control is a technique that is used to detect whether a process is in or out of control. An out-of-control process results in defective units and may be caused by a miscalibrated machine or some other factor. In statistical process control, workers use charts to monitor the quality of units that pass through their workstations. Using these charts, workers can quickly spot processes that are out of control and that are creating defects. Problems can be immediately corrected and further defects prevented rather than waiting for an inspector to catch the defects later.

Note also from the list of prevention costs in Exhibit 18.6 that some companies provide technical support to their suppliers as a way of preventing defects. Particularly in just-in-time (JIT) systems, such support to suppliers is vital. In a JIT system, parts are delivered from suppliers just in time and in just the correct quantity to fill customer orders. There are no stockpiles of parts. If a defective part is received from a supplier, the part cannot be used and the order for the ultimate customer cannot be filled on time. Hence, every part received from a supplier must be free of defects. Consequently, companies that use JIT often require that their suppliers use sophisticated quality control programmes such as statistical process control and that their suppliers certify that they will deliver parts and materials that are free of defects.

Appraisal costs

Any defective parts and products should be caught as early as possible. **Appraisal costs**, which are sometimes called *inspection costs*, are incurred to identify defective products *before* the products are shipped to customers. Unfortunately, performing appraisal activities does not keep defects from happening again, and most managers now realize that maintaining an army of inspectors is a costly (and ineffective) approach to quality control.

Professor John K. Shank of Dartmouth College has aptly stated, 'The old-style approach was to say, "We've got great quality. We have 40 quality control inspectors in the factory." Then somebody realized that if you need 40 inspectors, it must be a lousy factory. So now the trick is to run a factory without any quality control inspectors; each employee is his or her own quality control person.'[17]

Employees in both manufacturing and service functions are increasingly being asked to be responsible for their own quality control. This approach, along with designing products to be easy to manufacture properly, allows quality to be built into products rather than relying on inspection to get the defects out.

Internal failure costs

Failure costs are incurred when a product fails to conform to its design specifications. Failure costs can be either internal or external. **Internal failure costs** result from identification of defects during the appraisal process. Such costs include scrap, rejected products, reworking of defective units, and downtime caused by quality problems. It is crucial that defects be discovered before a product is shipped to customers. Of course, the more effective a company's appraisal activities, the greater the chance of catching defects internally and the greater the level of internal failure costs (as compared to external failure costs). Unfortunately, appraisal activities focus on symptoms rather than on causes and they do nothing to reduce the number of defective items. However, appraisal activities do bring defects to the attention of management, which may lead to efforts to increase prevention activities so that the defects do not happen.

External failure costs

External failure costs result when a defective product is delivered to a customer. As shown in Exhibit 18.6, external failure costs include warranty repairs and replacements, product recalls, liability arising from legal action against a company, and lost sales arising from a reputation for poor quality. Such costs can devastate profits.

In the past, some managers have taken the attitude, 'Let's go ahead and ship everything to customers, and we'll take care of any problems under the warranty.' This attitude generally results in high external failure costs, customer ill will, and declining market share and profits.

Distribution of quality costs

We stated earlier that a company's total quality cost is likely to be very high unless management gives this area special attention. How does a company reduce its total quality cost? The answer lies in how the quality costs are distributed. Refer to the graph in Exhibit 18.7, which shows total quality costs as a function of the quality of conformance.

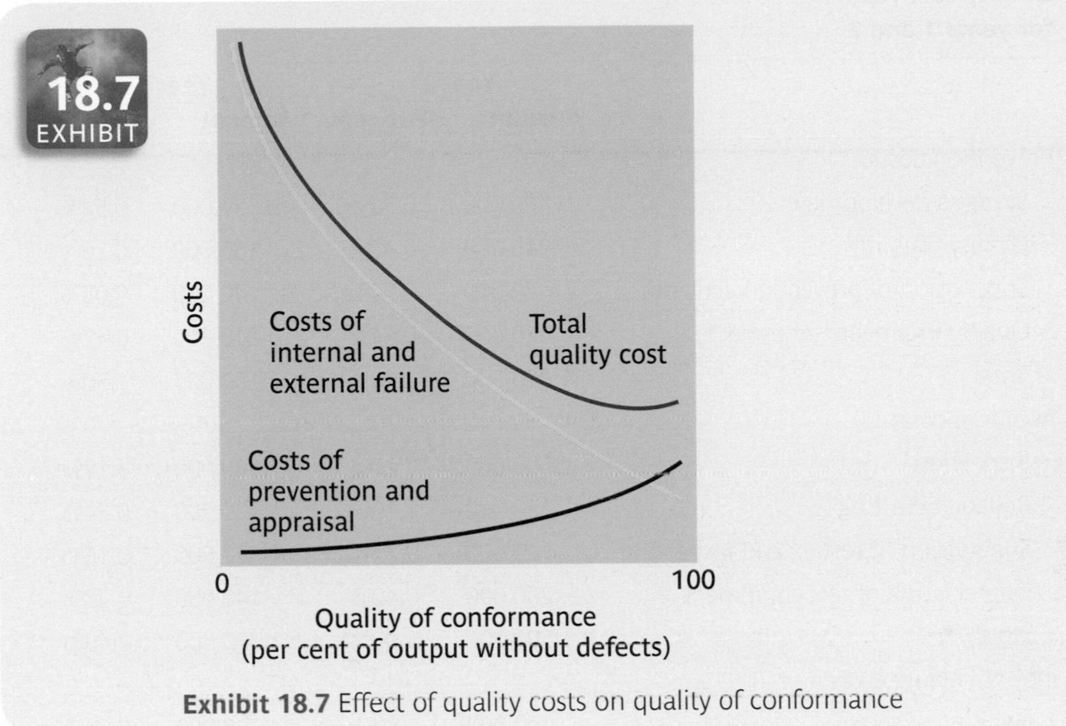

Exhibit 18.7 Effect of quality costs on quality of conformance

The graph shows that when the quality of conformance is low, total quality cost is high and that most of this cost consists of costs of internal and external failure. A low quality of conformance means that a high percentage of units are defective and hence the company must incur high failure costs. However, as a company spends more and more on prevention and appraisal, the percentage of defective units drops (the percentage of defect-free units increases). This results in lower costs of internal and external failure. Ordinarily, total quality cost drops rapidly as the quality of conformance increases. Thus, a company can reduce its total quality cost by focusing its efforts on prevention and appraisal. The cost savings from reduced defects usually swamp the costs of the additional prevention and appraisal efforts.

The graph in Exhibit 18.7 has been drawn so that the total quality cost is minimized when the quality of conformance is less than 100%. However, some experts and managers contend that the total quality cost is not minimized until the quality of conformance is 100% and there are no defects. Indeed, many companies have found that the total quality costs seem to keep dropping even when the quality of conformance approaches 100% and defect rates get as low as one in a million units. Others argue that eventually total quality cost increases as the quality of conformance increases. However, in most companies this does not seem to happen until the quality of conformance is very close to 100% and defect rates are very close to zero.

As a company's quality programme becomes more refined and as its failure costs begin to fall, prevention activities usually become more effective than appraisal activities. Appraisal can only find defects, whereas prevention can eliminate them. The best way to prevent defects from happening is to design processes that reduce the likelihood of defects and to continually monitor processes using statistical process control methods.

Quality cost reports

As an initial step in quality improvement programmes, companies often construct a *quality cost report* that provides an estimate of the financial consequences of the company's current level of defects. A **quality**

cost report details the prevention costs, appraisal costs, and costs of internal and external failures that arise from the company's current level of defective products and services. Managers are often shocked by the magnitude of these costs. A typical quality cost report is shown in Exhibit 18.8.

Ventura Company
Quality cost report
for years 1 and 2

	Year 2		Year 1	
	Amount	**Per cent**	**Amount**	**Per cent***
Prevention costs:				
Systems development	£400,000	0.80%	£270,000	0.54%
Quality training	210,000	0.42%	130,000	0.26%
Supervision of prevention activities	70,000	0.14%	40,000	0.08%
Quality improvement projects	320,000	0.64%	210,000	0.42%
Total	1,000,000	2.00%	650,000	1.30%
Appraisal costs:				
Inspection	600,000	1.20%	560,000	1.12%
Reliability testing	580,000	1.16%	420,000	0.84%
Supervision of testing and inspection	120,000	0.24%	80,000	0.16%
Depreciation of test equipment	200,000	0.40%	140,000	0.28%
Total	1,500,000	3.00%	1,200,000	2.40%
Internal failure costs:				
Net cost of scrap	900,000	1.80%	750,000	1.50%
Rework labour and overhead	1,430,000	2.86%	810,000	1.62%
Downtime due to defects in quality	170,000	0.34%	100,000	0.20%
Disposal of defective products	500,000	1.00%	340,000	0.68%
Total	3,000,000	6.00%	2,000,000	4.00%
External failure costs:				
Warranty repairs	400,000	0.80%	900,000	1.80%
Warranty replacements	870,000	1.74%	2,300,000	4.60%
Allowances	130,000	0.26%	630,000	1.26%
Cost of field servicing	600,000	1.20%	1,320,000	2.64%
Total	2,000,000	4.00%	5,150,000	10.30%
Total quality cost	£7,500,000	15.00%	£9,000,000	18.00%

*As a percentage of total sales. We assume that in each year sales totalled £50,000,000.

Exhibit 18.8 Quality cost report

Several things should be noted from the data in the exhibit. First, note that Ventura Company's quality costs are poorly distributed in both years, with most of the costs being traceable to either internal failure or external failure. The external failure costs are particularly high in Year 1 in comparison to other costs.

Second, note that the company increased its spending on prevention and appraisal activities in Year 2. As a result, internal failure costs go up in that year (from £2 million in Year 1 to £3 million in Year 2), but external failure costs drop sharply (from £5.15 million in Year 1 to only £2 million in Year 2). Because of the increase in appraisal activity in Year 2, more defects are being caught inside the company before they are shipped to customers. This results in more cost for scrap, rework and so forth, but saves huge amounts in warranty repairs, warranty replacements and other external failure costs.

Third, note that as a result of greater emphasis on prevention and appraisal, *total* quality cost has decreased in Year 2. As continued emphasis is placed on prevention and appraisal in future years, total quality cost should continue to decrease. That is, future increases in prevention and appraisal costs should be more than offset by decreases in failure costs. Moreover, appraisal costs should also decrease as more effort is placed into prevention.

Quality cost reports in graphic form

As a supplement to the quality cost report shown in Exhibit 18.8, companies frequently prepare quality cost information in graphic form. Graphic presentations include pie charts, bar graphs, trend lines and so forth. The data for Ventura Company from Exhibit 18.8 are presented in bar graph form in Exhibit 18.9.

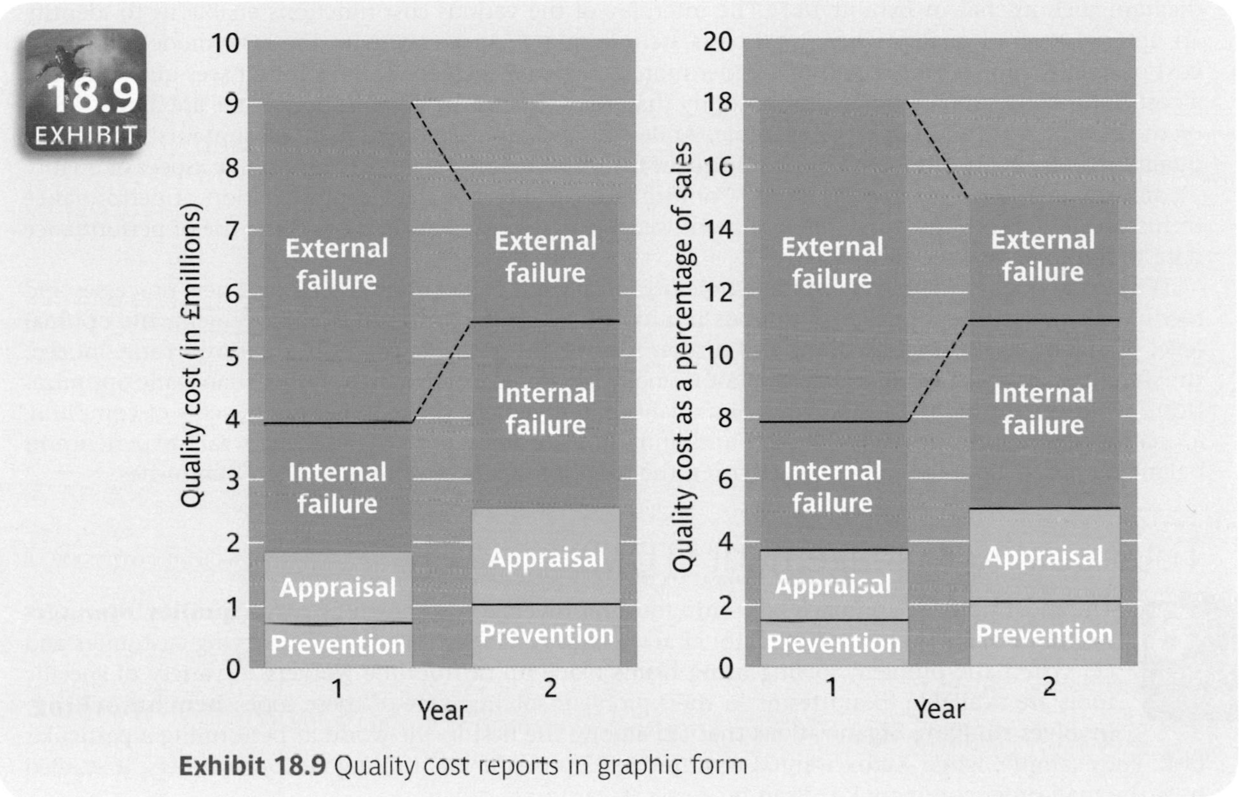

Exhibit 18.9 Quality cost reports in graphic form

The first bar graph in Exhibit 18.9 is scaled in terms of pounds of quality cost, and the second is scaled in terms of quality cost as a percentage of sales. In both graphs, the data are 'stacked' upward. That is, appraisal costs are stacked on top of prevention costs, internal failure costs are stacked on top of the sum of prevention costs plus appraisal costs, and so forth. The percentage figures in the second graph show that total quality cost equals 18% of sales in Year 1 and 15% of sales in Year 2, the same as reported earlier in Exhibit 18.8.

Uses of quality cost information

The information provided by a quality cost report is used by managers in several ways. First, quality cost information helps managers to see the financial significance of defects. Managers usually are not aware of the magnitude of their quality costs because these costs cut across departmental lines and are not normally tracked and accumulated by the cost system. Thus, when first presented with a quality cost report, managers are often surprised by the amount of cost attributable to poor quality.

Second, quality cost information helps managers to identify the relative importance of the quality problems faced by the firm. For example, the quality cost report may show that scrap is a major quality problem or that the company is incurring huge warranty costs. With this information, managers have a better idea of where to focus efforts.

Third, quality cost information helps managers to see whether their quality costs are poorly distributed. In general, quality costs should be distributed more toward prevention and appraisal activities and less towards failures.

Counterbalancing these uses, three limitations of quality cost information should be recognized. First, simply measuring and reporting quality costs does not solve quality problems. Problems can be solved only by taking action. Second, results usually lag behind quality improvement programmes. Initially, total quality cost may even increase as quality control systems are designed and installed. Decreases in these costs may not begin to occur until the quality programme has been in effect for a year or more. And third, the most important quality cost, lost sales arising from customer ill will, is usually omitted from the quality cost report because it is difficult to estimate.

From modelling the costs of quality to quality management

One way of summarizing and balancing the costs and benefits of quality is to show the trade-offs in a diagram such as that in Exhibit 18.7. The interplay of the various cost functions enable us to identify an optimal level of quality where total costs are minimized. As we saw with the EOQ model and JIT, a cost of quality model can be part of a wider more active management approach that sees quality not as a cost optimizing exercise but as a philosophy that drives the whole organization. Some are more critical of the cost of quality model. For example, Anderson and Sedatole argue that 'accountants' support of quality management is hobbled by a tradition of historical reporting and a focus on one aspect of quality – conformance to design specifications. Conformance quality is a static representation of performance to historical quality standards. A more potent weapon in quality management is the use of performance data to improve new product designs.'[18]

With total quality management the whole organization is called upon to embrace new processes and techniques that strive to make continuous improvements. With continuous improvement, the optimal level of quality as learning-by-doing and further investment push the curves to right over time. Indeed, the dominant ethos of quality management is one of continual improvement rather than static optimization. Typically, during the initial years of a quality improvement programme, the benefits of compiling a quality cost report outweigh the costs and limitations of the reports. As managers gain experience in balancing prevention and appraisal activities, the need for quality cost reports often diminishes.

Total quality management (TQM)

The most popular approach to continuous improvement is known as **total quality management (TQM)**. There are two major characteristics of TQM: (1) a focus on serving customers and (2) systematic problem solving using teams made up of frontline workers. A variety of specific tools are available to aid teams in their problem solving. One of these tools, **benchmarking**, involves studying organizations that are among the best in the world at performing a particular task. For example, when Xerox wanted to improve its procedures for filling customer orders, it studied how the mail-order company L.L. Bean processes its customer orders.

The plan-do-check-act cycle

Perhaps the most important and pervasive TQM problem-solving tool is the *plan-do-check-act (PDCA)* cycle, which is also referred to as the Deming Wheel.[19] The **plan-do-check-act cycle (PDA)** is a systematic, fact-based approach to continuous improvement. The basic elements of the PDCA cycle are illustrated in Exhibit 18.10. The PDCA cycle applies the scientific method to problem solving. In the Plan phase, the problem-solving team analyses data to identify possible causes for the problem and then proposes a solution. In the Do phase, an experiment is conducted. In the Check phase, the results of the experiment are analysed. And in the Act phase, if the results of the experiment are favourable, the plan is implemented. If the results of the experiment are not favourable, the team goes back to the original data and starts all over again.

An important element of TQM is its focus on the customer. The accounting and consulting firm KPMG Peat Marwick periodically surveys its customers' satisfaction with its services. The firm's managing director points out that it costs four times as much to gain a new customer as it does to keep an old

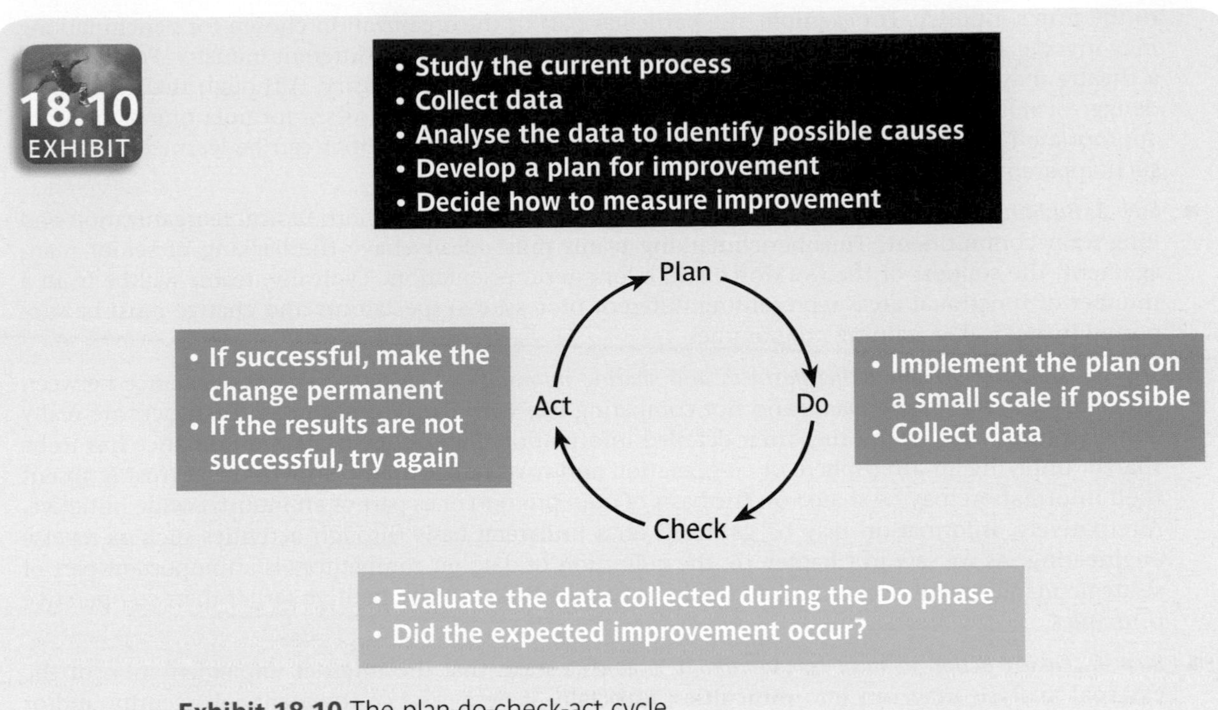
18.10
EXHIBIT
• Study the current process
• Collect data
• Analyse the data to identify possible causes
• Develop a plan for improvement
• Decide how to measure improvement
Plan
Do
Check
Act
• Implement the plan on a small scale if possible
• Collect data
• Evaluate the data collected during the Do phase
• Did the expected improvement occur?
• If successful, make the change permanent
• If the results are not successful, try again

Exhibit 18.10 The plan-do-check-act cycle

customer, and the most satisfied customers are generally the most profitable customers for the firm. 'For each complaint that you hear, there are fifty you don't. If you don't monitor clients' satisfaction, you may find out about their dissatisfaction as they walk out the door.'[20]

In sum, TQM provides tools and techniques for continuous improvement based on facts and analysis; and if properly implemented, it avoids counterproductive organizational infighting.

Some criticisms of TQM

There have been a number of criticisms of TQM. They may not always be justified but managers should be aware of possible pitfalls. TQM has been accused of draining innovation from organizations by standardizing internal processes. It is also accused of making organizations more efficient at what they are doing irrespective of whether they should be doing it. The spectre is that TQM results in a finely honed organization that is a world-class producer of wagon wheels or manual typewriters. Like other management change initiatives, TQM suffers from the 'Flavour of the month' syndrome. Typically, organizational members have been bombarded with so many fads that they may merely go through the motions of implementation of TQM hoping that senior managers will soon embrace a new 'three letter acronym'.

Benchmarking

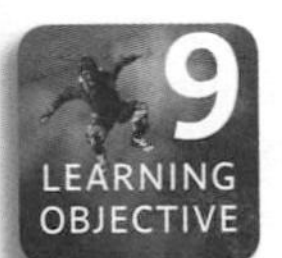
9
LEARNING OBJECTIVE

Much of the data gathered through the introduction of quality management may be used as a basis for comparison with other organizations. In particular, it may be useful to identify organizations that are the best at performing specific activities or producing particular products in order to learn how they achieve their relatively high performance. This process is known as *benchmarking*. With *quality management*, the focus may be on *non-financial* measures as much as financial measures such as costs. Later in the chapter, we can see an example of *cost* benchmarking based on ABC data.

In order to achieve the best result from benchmarking a number of principles should be adhered to. Benchmarking may be seen as an exercise that proceeds according to a sequence of steps.

- *Step 1: Internal and competitive analysis.* At this preliminary stage the organization chooses the areas for analysis and undertakes basic comparisons between internal data and external data. External data may be found in marketing reports, consumer surveys, government statistics. It may not be confined to the firm's industry. For example, the particular part of the organization chosen for benchmarking may involve an activity where the best performers are in a completely different industry. For example, a theatre may study the ticketing procedures used in the airline industry. Although there may be a danger of not comparing like with like such as when a tyre retailer sees a formula one team as an appropriate benchmark for tyre-changing, there may still be lessons that can be learned even from such apparently 'unfair' comparisons.

- *Step 2: Building a benchmarking team.* Changes in practice may involve both radical reorganization and long-term commitment. Thus benchmarking teams must ideally have the backing of senior management, the support of the workforce and a long-term orientation. Typically, teams will be from a number of functional areas representing different professional specialisms and change must be supported by dedicated training programmes.
- *Step 3: Choosing benchmarking partners and sharing information.* This step strikes a balance between the need to *'stretch' performance* and not comparing like with like. Furthermore, if partners are really going to learn from each other then detailed information about operational performance has to be shared, implying an atmosphere of co-operation and trust rather than competition. If trust is absent then information may be shared on the basis of quid pro quo or as part of an industry-wide initiative. Alternatively, information may be gathered on a unilateral basis through activities such as reverse engineering. As we saw in Chapter 16, the collection of data on competitors is an important part of strategic management accounting and may be based wholly on competitive rather than co-operative principles.
- *Step 4: Taking action to meet benchmark.* It is at this stage that the internal implementation of the external analysis may run into difficulties, especially if best practice threatens job security and/or managerial empires. The issues of organizational change take us beyond the material normally found in management accounting books. However, management accountants and others such as politicians and senior managers should be aware of the technical limitations of benchmarking exercises. Organizational resistance is not always based on vested interests.

Some problems with benchmarking

Using external comparators can lead to criticism on the basis that measures are 'their numbers not ours'. It is therefore important that a consistent set of measures is used with a close match between internal and external indicators. Xerox have overcome this by implementing a structured process based on indicators developed in close collaboration with other people working in industry sectors which have similar operational features. Benchmarking has been described as being a mixed metaphor.[21] On the one hand, we have the language of collaboration with an emphasis on organizational learning. On the other hand, we have descriptions of benchmarking that often convey notions of competition, of being a one-sided attempt by the initiator of the benchmarking exercise to close a perceived performance gap. Even when benchmarking is a public policy initiative, governments often send out a mixed message that both inculcates a 'league table mentality' and tries to nurture a non-blame, learning model.

Business process re-engineering (BPR)

Process re-engineering is a more radical approach to improvement than either TQM or benchmarking. Instead of tweaking the existing system in a series of incremental improvements, a business process is diagrammed in detail, questioned, and then completely redesigned in order to eliminate unnecessary steps, to reduce opportunities for errors, and to reduce costs. A **business process** is any series of steps that is followed in order to carry out some task in a business. For example, the steps followed to make a large seafood pizza at Pizza Hut are a business process. The steps followed by your bank when you deposit a cheque are a business process. While process re-engineering is similar in some respects to TQM, its proponents view it as a more sweeping approach to change. One difference is that while TQM emphasizes a team approach involving people who work directly in the processes, process re-engineering is more likely to be imposed from above and more likely to use outside consultants.

BPR is closely associated with the concept of the lean enterprise that we introduced in Chapter 16. The lean enterprise may be created from scratch or through the transformation of existing firms. Process re-engineering focuses on *simplification* and *elimination of wasted effort*. A central idea of process re-engineering is that *all activities that do not add value to a product or service should be eliminated.*[22] Activities that do not add value to a product or service that customers are willing to pay for are known as **non-value-added activities**. For example, moving large batches of work in progress from one workstation to another is a non-value-added activity that can be eliminated by redesigning the factory layout.

The starting point for re-engineering is not 'How do we do something faster or cheaper or better?' but rather 'Why do we do something at all? Is it to meet demands of customers or internal organization?' In short, re-engineering is not piecemeal – it is 'all-or-nothing'. Lean enterprises try to organize work around *business processes* rather than on a departmental basis with a traditional emphasis on specialization and a division of labour.

A business process is a collection of activities that takes inputs and creates outputs that are of value to customers. One process such as order fulfilment is generally fragmented across departments and controlled bureaucratically. No one is responsible for the whole process as organizationally firms are built up as functional silos with vertical structures that each deal with just a piece of a process.

What does a re-engineered process look like?

The first step in re-engineering is to look at the underlying process and not at the administrative structure set up to perform it. The aim will be to combine several jobs into one – known as *horizontal compression*. If a process is too much for one person then a case-team will be formed. The aim should be that the workers make decisions. Jobs are vertically compressed through the elimination of hierarchy and checking.

Much re-engineering is enabled through new technology, especially the linkage between a telephone-based customer focused personnel with central databases. Shared databases mean that information can appear simultaneously in as many places as it is needed. *Expert systems* mean that the generalist can do the work of the expert. Telecommunications and portable computers mean that field personnel can send and receive information wherever they are. Paradoxically, organizations are both centralized and decentralized by the new technology. Jobs change from simple tasks to multidimensional work which reduces the work that was created by fragmentation such as checking, reconciling, waiting, monitoring and tracking.

FOCUS

Focus on current practice

Process re-engineering that is imposed from above and that results in disruptions and layoffs can lead to cynicism. Eileen Shapiro, a management consultant, says that 're-engineering as often implemented can erode the bonds of trust that employees have toward their employers. Nevertheless, many companies re-engineer at the same time that they issue mission statements proclaiming, "Our employees are our most important asset,'" or launch new initiatives to increase "employee involvement". As one senior executive, a veteran of re-engineering, muttered recently while listening to his boss give a glowing speech about working conditions at their organization, "I sure wish I worked for the company he is describing".'[23]

The implications of BPR for management accounting are that management accountants have to be more flexible and work in teams with non-accountants. Accounting work is dispersed and may be done by non-accountants. Non-financial performance measures are more important. The emphasis is on eliminating overhead rather than measuring/allocating it. Organizational structures/departments/budgets are less important than *processes*.

Some criticisms of re-engineering

In common with other management panaceas, BPR has suffered from over-hyping and from the evangelical language often associated with the management guru. Action that may be easy to write or talk about may be harder to implement in practice. For example, how easy is it for organizations to distinguish between value adding and non-value adding activity? Mistakes have been made where firms took out 'non-value adding' personnel but then subsequently had to re-hire them as they turned out to have created unanticipated value! BPR is likely to face resistance from managers who have been promoted to manage existing structures not take them out!

A recurrent problem in process re-engineering is employee resistance. The cause of much of this resistance is the fear that people may lose their jobs. Workers reason that if process re-engineering succeeds in eliminating non-value-added activities, there will be less work to do and management may be tempted to reduce the payroll. Process re-engineering, if carried out insensitively and without regard to such fears, can undermine morale and will ultimately fail to improve the bottom line (i.e., profits). As with other improvement projects, employees must be convinced that the end result of the improvement will be more secure, rather than less secure, jobs. Real improvement can have this effect if management uses the improvement to generate more business rather than to cut the workforce. If by improving processes the company is able to produce a better product at lower cost, the company will have the competitive strength to prosper. And a prosperous company is a much more secure employer than a company that is in trouble.

BPR: activity-based management revisited?

In Chapter 8, we saw how ABC has been used to introduce a new rigour into the costing of overheads in both manufacturing and service industries. As **activity-based management (ABM)**, the analysis and costing of processes can be used to identify areas that would benefit from improvements – 'Put simply ABM is ABC in action.'[24] ABM can be combined with benchmarking to provide a systematic approach to identifying the activities with the greatest room for improvement. For example, the Marketing Resources Group of US WEST, the telephone company, performed an ABC analysis of the activities carried out in the Accounting Department.[25] Managers computed the activity rates for the activities of the Accounting Department and then compared these rates to the costs of carrying out the same activities in other companies. Two benchmarks were used: (1) a sample of Fortune 100 companies, which are the largest 100 companies in the United States; and (2) a sample of 'world-class' companies that had been identified by a consultant as having the best accounting practices in the world. These comparisons appear below:

Activity measure	Activity cost	US WEST	FORTUNE 100 benchmark	World-class benchmark
Processing accounts receivable (debtors)	Number of invoices processed	$3.80 per invoice	$15.00 invoice	$4.60 per invoice
Processing accounts payable (creditors)	Number of invoices processed	$8.90 per invoice	$7.00 per invoice	$1.80 per invoice
Processing payroll cheques	Number of cheques processed	$7.30 per cheque	$5.00 per cheque	$1.72 per cheque
Managing customer credit	Number of customer accounts	$12.00 per account	$16.00 account	$5.60 per account

It is clear from this analysis that US WEST does a good job of processing debtors. Its average cost per invoice is $3.80, whereas the cost in other companies that are considered world class is even higher – $4.60 per invoice. On the other hand, the cost of processing payroll cheques is significantly higher at US WEST than at benchmark companies. The cost per payroll check at US WEST is $7.30 versus $5.00 at Fortune 100 companies and $1.72 at world-class companies. This suggests that it may be possible to wring some waste out of this activity using TQM, process re-engineering or some other method.

Some problems with ABM

ABM sheds a different interpretation on the true impact of ABC. Beginning with the modest goal of improving the accuracy of the single base absorption system, the ABC/ABM project has expanded into making indirect costs direct. In addition, it has introduced a new 'productivist' agenda to link staff activities to products.[26] Critics of ABM argue that the attempt to count staff functions runs the risk of losing essence of staff functions. Although *some* staff activities may be counted and routinized, both team work and customer relations may suffer because they are hard to measure. Staff may associate most with an accessible, *countable* cost driver so that the volume of activity can be ascertained. The danger then is that the performance of 'activities' will take precedence over original purpose. Both ABM and BPR may mean that *non-routine* staff activity is eliminated even if it creates value for the company.

Obstacles to organizational change and the advantages of a fresh start

As we discussed in connection with TQM and benchmarking, whatever the technical strengths of the techniques or whatever the potential improvements identified, there may be significant implementation problems. For this reason, it may be easier to start up an entirely new organization rather than re-engineer an existing one. As the example of low cost airlines such as easyJet and Ryanair illustrate, radical changes have been achieved by new entrants to the airline industry. Although they are low cost, these carriers generally meet the quality standards that their customers expect from a no-frills service. The following *Management accounting in action* illustrates how an organization may employ a variety of techniques in order to try to change business processes.

Management accounting in action: Trafalgar Bank[27]

This case study traces the implementation of ABC in the Clearing/Payment Services Department of Trafalgar Bank, a large UK-based multinational. Before ABC, the bank had *some* basic cost controls based on cost centre budgets with the full allocation of overheads, and measures of performance that included sales volumes and maintaining costs at budgeted levels. Although banks had traditionally exerted management control through personnel rather than management accounting practices, at the time of the study in the early to mid-1990s, a profits crisis meant that the priority was on *cost reduction*. Job losses and general reorganization was accompanied by a change in the nature of management recruitment and career structures.

Cheque clearing as a work process

The clearing process begins when the cheques come into the Clearing Department from the bank branches or from bulk customers like building societies. After going into the 'make-ready' area, they are manually encoded. The cheques then pass through single-entry machines or automatic reader sorters. Finally, the cheques are dispatched to the clearing houses. Although located within a service industry, cheque clearing has some similarities to factory work, with much of the work process being both routine and 'countable'.

Why ABC?

ABC is well suited to the financial service sector as many service costs are process rather than volume-related. ABC can be used to analyse the profitability of customers and the new financial products. ABC may also have further applications in areas like budgeting, forecasting and performance measurement in overhead departments. Yet although there may have been sound *technical* reasons for trying to increase the cost consciousness of the bank, the specific choice of ABC did seem to be influenced by the *imitation* of other banks and other departments in the bank together with the easy availability of ABC software packages.

The change agents

ABC implementation was assigned to an *internal ABC team* drawn from the bank's own staff, consisting of a CIMA qualified management accountant and an experienced manager seconded from the Clearing

Department. The Payment Services division was also subject to the attentions of two other change agencies: a team of *productivity management consultants* and a group called *Human Resource Engineering* (HRE).

The management consultants were directly monitoring the physical operations using the traditional tools of scientific management. They made recommendations to management and also ensured compliance with their proposed changes. At some times, HRE seemed to be enforcers of change initiated by the consultants, while they also acted to 'pick up the pieces', deflect criticism and act as 'fall-guys' if the changes backfired. Although at first they were closely aligned with traditional bank control technologies based on personnel practices, they latterly became more sympathetic to the ABC/ABM approach.

Data collection and processing: the technology of ABC

The ABC system used data gathered by detailed observation and interviews that, in the first year at least, were carried out by the ABC team themselves in each of the cost centres. Flow charts were constructed to illustrate visually the processes of each area of the clearing process. Headcount driver analyses were carried out and an activity analysis schedule was created for each section describing activities, details of the cost driver(s) and the allocation base. It also comprised a resource statement, which showed the grades of staff involved in the activity, their full-time equivalent hours for the activity and the cost details of the equipment used. Once the system had been set up, it was important to keep it up to date. Process data on the Clearing Department rapidly became obsolete as a result of the dynamic, changing nature of the organization. A slight change in activity meant that the cost-driver rates needed to change accordingly.

The perception of ABC by middle managers

The middle managers were not entirely sure of the technical capabilities of ABC. They lacked a critical appreciation of cost accounting data in general, let alone data produced by ABC. The stated goal of measuring 'exact costs' lent a spurious precision to the whole exercise. Middle managers were also wary of a technique that purported to measure *their* value added. Although they may not have understood the subtleties of the approach, the very fact that the clerical staff were being monitored all the time in a way that had never happened before justified their perception of ABC as a means of promoting increased surveillance of their work practices.

The perception of ABC by operational managers and shop-floor workers

ABC was introduced into a climate of fear and suspicion, with the productivity consultants rumoured to be looking to cut 40–50% of the workforce. Many members of the Clearing Department were suspicious of *any* new systems, seeing ABC as just one more means of justifying reductions in the workforce.

From the earliest stages of the development of ABC, accountants from Financial Control began to physically cross the functional boundaries of the organization and to familiarize themselves with the language of operational processes. On their part, operational managers did not expect accountants to understand the detail of the operations and activities in the Clearing Department. They viewed it as creating additional work but having a limited operational role.

Some effects of the ABC project

Although some of the simpler cost-cutting exercises could have been achieved by the technologies of the consultants and HRE, the ABC information provided a new costing sophistication and opportunities for cost management. All activity that involved cost incurrence invited both analysis and, often, a 'quick-hit' reduction. For example, ABC flagged up non-conformance costs by showing that the Clearing Department spent 20–40% of their time and resources putting right what they had received to process. The department began to investigate how they could 'organize their customers' by encouraging them to present their work to the Clearing Department in a more processable form.

The potential implications of ABC went beyond *local* cost cutting; they extended throughout the whole of the bank and projected *outside* into the market for clearing services. For example, by breaking down the cost of processing building society cheque clearing contracts, the ABC system showed how the process could be changed to get the cost down by 30% without reducing what the customer saw as their value added.

Yet sometimes there was a reluctance to employ the full strategic potential of ABC. This reluctance could be attributed to a combination of factors, including managerial conservatism and, more speculatively, a desire to maintain previous levels of managerial discretion. The exploitation of the ABC/ABM system was also hindered by a lack of understanding. Although the bank's management now had a better knowledge of their costs, they seemed to be 'trapped' by the new cost data. For example, when in competition with other clearers for outside contracts, they seemed reluctant to employ loss-leading or target costing. In this respect, their extra cost information seemed to *constrain* managers' behaviour rather than offering them the possibility of better informed choices.

Summary

- This chapter focuses on business processes which may cut across an organization's departments and/or divisions.
- Stock management is an area that has evolved from the optimizing approach of the EOQ model to the sophistication of the build-to-order company. JIT emphasizes the importance of reducing stocks to the barest minimum possible. This reduces working capital requirements, frees up space, reduces throughput time, reduces defects and eliminates waste.
- New information technology such as ERP and the internet offer new ways to optimize not just on stock but on other areas of working capital management.
- Quality costs are summarized on a quality cost report. This report shows the type of quality costs being incurred and their significance and trends. The report helps managers to understand the importance of quality costs, spot problem areas, and assess the way in which the quality costs are distributed.
- The measurement of quality costs may be used as part of a more comprehensive approach – TQM – which involves the use of a number of non-financial as well as financial measures. TQM involves focusing on the customer, and it employs systematic problem solving using teams made up of front-line workers. Specific TQM tools include benchmarking and the plan-do-check-act (PDCA) cycle.
- BPR, a related but generally more radical approach to organizational change, aims to push the analysis and optimization of business processes to higher levels. Process re-engineering involves completely redesigning a business process in order to eliminate non-value-added activities and to reduce opportunities for errors.
- Measures may be used to monitor internal processes, supplier and customer perceptions. Organizations may use these measures as a way of comparing or benchmarking themselves against best practice.
- The techniques of work measurement of BPR and ABM can be seen as job- and cost-cutting exercises. Furthermore, there may be technical difficulties in distinguishing between value- and non-value-adding activities.
- Many of the practices in this chapter are associated with the philosophy of lean operations. This philosophy will be further developed in the next chapter.

Key terms for review

Activity-based management (ABM) (p. 768).

Appraisal costs (p. 760).

Benchmarking (p. 764).

Business process (p. 766).

Costs of not carrying sufficient stock (p. 747).

Economic lot size (p. 750).

Economic order quantity (EOQ) (p. 747).

Electronic data interchange (EDI) (p. 757).

Enterprise resource planning (ERP) (p. 756).

External failure costs (p. 760).
Internal failure costs (p. 760).
Just-in-time (JIT) (p. 752).
Lead time (p. 752).
Lean production (p. 747).
Non-value-added activity (p. 767).
Optimizing (p. 746).
Plan-do-check-act (PDCA) cycle (p. 764).
Prevention costs (p. 758).
Process re-engineering (p. 766).
Quality circles (p. 760).
Quality cost (p. 758).
Quality cost report (p. 761).
Quality of conformance (p. 758).
Reorder point (p. 751).
Safety stock (p. 752).
Set-up costs (p. 750).
Stock carrying costs (p. 747).
Stock ordering costs (p. 747).
Statistical process control (p. 760).
Total quality management (TQM) (p. 764).
Throughput time (p. 750).

Questions

18–1 What are the three groups of costs associated with the economic order quantity (EOQ) model?

18–2 What is the potential impact of just-in-time (JIT) purchasing on the EOQ?

18–3 What trade-offs in costs are involved in computing the EOQ (economic order quantity)?

18–4 Define lead time and safety stock.

18–5 In a just-in-time system, what is meant by the pull approach to the flow of goods, as compared to the push approach used in conventional systems?

18–6 How does the plant layout differ in a company using JIT as compared to a company that uses a more conventional approach to manufacturing? What benefits accrue from a JIT layout?

18–7 Identify the benefits that can result from reducing the set-up time for a product.

18–8 How does a workforce in a JIT facility differ from the workforce in a conventional facility?

18–9 What are the major benefits of a JIT system?

18–10 What are three benefits and three costs of installing an ERP system?

18–11 Is there a difference between a virtual company and a dotcom company?

18–12 Costs associated with the quality of conformance can be broken down into four broad groups. What are these four groups and how do they differ?

18–13 In their efforts to reduce the total cost of quality, should companies generally focus on decreasing prevention costs and appraisal costs?

18–14 What is probably the most effective way to reduce a company's total quality costs?

18–15 What are the main uses of quality cost reports?

18–16 Why are managers often unaware of the magnitude of quality costs?

18–17 Explain how the plan-do-check-act cycle applies the scientific method to problem solving.

18–18 Why is process re-engineering a more radical approach to improvement than total quality management?

18–19 How can process re-engineering undermine employee morale?

18–20 Does activity-based costing always precede activity-based management (ABM)?

18–21 What are the problems in the application of ABM to service areas?

EXERCISES

Exercises

E18–1 Time allowed: 30 minutes

The management at Megafilters Ltd has been discussing the possible implementation of a just-in-time (JIT) production system at its Sheffield plant, where oil and air filters are manufactured. The Metal Stamping Department at the Sheffield plant has already instituted a JIT system for controlling raw materials inventory, but the remainder of the plant is still discussing how to proceed with the implementation of this concept. The Metal Stamping Department implemented JIT with no advance planning, and some of the other department managers have become uneasy about adopting JIT after hearing about the problems that have arisen.

Robert Goertz, manager of the Sheffield plant, is a strong proponent of the JIT approach. He recently made the following statement at a meeting of all departmental managers:

> We will all have to make many changes in the way we think about our employees, our suppliers and our customers if we are going to be successful in using JIT procedures. Rather than dwelling on some of the negative things you have heard from the Metal Stamping Department, I want each of you to prepare a list of things we can do to make a smooth transition to the JIT approach for the rest of the plant.

Required

1 The JIT approach has several characteristics that distinguish it from conventional production systems. Describe these characteristics.

2 For the JIT approach to be successful, Megafilters Ltd must establish appropriate relationships with its suppliers. Describe these relationships under JIT.

(*CMA*, adapted)

E18–2 Time allowed: 15 minutes

Kaufheim AG of Dresden, Germany, distributes medical supplies throughout Germany. Selected information relating to a quick-developing X-ray film carried by the company is given below:

Economic order quantity (EOQ)	700 units
Maximum weekly usage	60 units
Lead time	4 weeks
Average weekly usage	50 units

Management is trying to determine the proper safety stock to carry on this item and to determine the proper reorder point.

Required

1 Assume that no safety stock is to be carried. What is the reorder point?

2 Assume that a full safety stock is to be carried.

(a) What would be the size of the safety stock in units?

(b) What would be the reorder point?

E18–3 Time allowed: 20 minutes

Flint Company uses 9,000 units of part AK-4 each year. To get better control over its stock, the company is anxious to determine the economic order quantity (EOQ) for this part.

Required

1 The company has determined that the cost to place an order for the part is £30, and it has determined that the cost to carry one part in stock for one year is £1.50. Compute the EOQ for the part.

2 Assume that the cost to place an order increases from £30 to £40 per order. What will be the effect on the EOQ? Show computations.

3 Assume that the cost to carry a part in stock increases from £1.50 to £2.00 per part. (Ordering costs remain unchanged at £30 per order.) What will be the effect on the EOQ? Show computations.

4 In Questions 2 and 3 above, why does an increase in cost cause the EOQ to go up in one case and to go down in the other?

E18–4 Time allowed: 10 minutes

Listed below are a number of costs that are incurred in connection with a company's quality control system.

(a) Product testing

(b) Product recalls

(c) Rework labour and overhead

(d) Quality circles

(e) Downtime caused by defects

(f) Cost of field servicing

(g) Inspection of goods

(h) Quality engineering

(i) Warranty repairs

(j) Statistical process control

(k) Net cost of scrap

(l) Depreciation of test equipment

(m) Returns and allowances arising from poor quality

(n) Disposal of defective products

(o) Technical support to suppliers

(p) Systems development

(q) Warranty replacements

(r) Field testing at customer site

(s) Product design

Required

1 Classify each of the costs above into one of the following categories: prevention cost, appraisal cost, internal failure cost, or external failure cost.

2 Which of the costs in Question 1 above are incurred in an effort to keep poor quality of conformance from occurring? Which of the costs in Question 1 above are incurred because poor quality of conformance has occurred?

E18–5 Time allowed: 10 minutes
Listed below are a number of terms relating to quality management:

Appraisal costs	Quality circles
Quality cost report	Prevention costs
Quality of conformance	External failure costs
Internal failure costs	Quality costs

Required

Choose the term or terms that most appropriately complete the following statements. The terms can be used more than once. (A fill-in blank can hold more than one word.)

1 A product that has a high rate of defects is said to have a low ______.

2 All of the costs associated with preventing and dealing with defects once they occur are known as______.

3 In many companies, small groups of employees, known as ______, meet on a regular basis to discuss ways to improve quality.

4 A company incurs ______ and ______ in an effort to keep defects from occurring.

5 A company incurs ______ and ______ because defects have occurred.

6 Of the four groups of costs associated with quality of conformance, ______ are generally the most damaging to a company.

7 Inspection, testing, and other costs incurred to keep defective products from being shipped to customers are known as ______.

8 ______ are incurred in an effort to eliminate poor product design, defective manufacturing practices, and the providing of substandard service.

9 The costs relating to defects, rejected products, and downtime caused by quality problems are known as ______.

10 When a product that is defective in some way is delivered to a customer, ______ are incurred.

11 Over time a company's total quality costs should decrease if it redistributes its quality costs by placing its greatest emphasis on ______ and ______.

12 One way to ensure that management is aware of the costs associated with quality is to summarize such costs on a ______.

Problems

P18–6 JIT; process re-engineering Time allowed: 30 minutes
Snedden Products manufactures athletic equipment, including footballs. The footballs are manufactured in several steps, which are listed below:

1 Leather and other materials are received at a centrally located dock where the materials are checked to be sure they conform to exacting company standards. Rejected materials are returned to the supplier.

2 Acceptable materials are transported to a stores warehouse pending use in production.

3 A materials requisition form is issued, and materials are transferred from the stores warehouse to the Cutting Department where all cutting equipment is located.

4 Since the Cutting Department cuts materials for a variety of products, the leather is placed on large pallets and stationed by the appropriate machines.

5 The leather and other materials are cut to proper shape, with the operator taking care to cut all sections of a football from a single piece of leather. Waste materials are placed in a bin, and at the end of each day the materials are sorted to reclaim the items that can be used in manufacturing other products.

6 Each cut item of material is examined by one of three checkers to ensure uniformity of cut, thickness of the leather, and direction of the grain. Rejected pieces are tossed in the scrap bin.

7 Cut materials are placed on pallets and transferred to the Centralized Sewing Department, where the pallets are placed in a staging area.

8 Materials are taken from the pallets, the company's name and logo are stamped into one section of each set of cut pieces, and the pieces are then sewed together.

9 The sewn pieces are placed in bins, which are then transferred to the staging area of the Assembly Department.

10 An operator in the Assembly Department installs a lining in the football, stitches the ball closed with a stitching machine, and then inflates it.

11 The completed footballs are placed on a conveyor belt that passes by another set of checkers. Each ball is checked for uniformity of shape and for other potential defects.

12 Completed footballs are boxed and transferred to the finished goods warehouse.

Required

Assume that the company adopts JIT inventory practices and establishes individual product flow lines. Explain what changes would have to be made in manufacturing procedures and prepare a sketch of how the football product flow line would be arranged.

P18–7 EOQ Time allowed: 30 minutes

A company uses Material Z (cost £3.50 per kg) in the manufacture of Products A and B. The following forecast information is provided for the year ahead:

	Product A	Product B
Sales (units)	24,600	9,720
Finished goods stock increase by year end (units)	447	178
Post-production rejection rate (%)	1%	2%
Material Z usage (kg per completed unit, net of wastage)	1.8	3.0
Material Z wastage (%)	5%	11%

Additional information:

- Average purchasing lead time for Material Z is two weeks.
- Usage of Material Z is expected to be even over the year.
- Annual stock holding costs are 18% of the material cost.
- The cost of placing orders is £30 per order.
- The reorder level for Material Z is set at the average usage in average lead time, plus 1,000 kg of safety (buffer) stock.

Required

1 State two items that would be regarded as 'stock holding costs' and explain how they may be controlled effectively. *(5 marks)*

2 Calculate for the year ahead:

(a) the required production of Products A and B (in units) *(3 marks)*

(b) the total requirement for Material Z (in kgs) *(3 marks)*

(c) the economic order quantity for Material Z (in kgs). *(5 marks)*

3 Calculate the average stock investment (£) and the annual stock holding costs (£) for Material Z. *(4 marks)*

(Total = 20 marks)

ACCA Management Information, December 1999

P18–8 Stock management Time allowed: 25 minutes

A traditional view of the environment in which goods are manufactured and sold is where stocks of materials and components are held. Such stocks are then used to manufacture products to agreed standard specifications, aiming at maximizing the use of production capacity. Finished goods are held in stock to satisfy steady demand for the product range at agreed prices.

Required

1 Discuss aspects of the operation of the management accounting function which are likely to apply in the above system. *(5 marks)*

2 Describe an alternative sequence from purchasing to the satisfaction of customer demand, which may be more applicable in the current business environment. Your answer should refer to the current 'techniques or philosophies' which are likely to be in use. *(5 marks)*

3 Name specific ways in which changes suggested in Question 2 will affect the operation of the management accounting function. *(5 marks)*

(Total = 15 marks)

ACCA Information for Control and Decision Making, June 1999

P18–9 Economic order quantity (EOQ); safety stock Time allowed: 30 minutes

Myron Metal Works uses a small casting in one of its finished products. The castings are purchased from a foundry located in another state. In total, Myron Metal Works purchases 54,000 castings per year at a cost of £8 per casting. The castings are used evenly throughout the year in the production process on a 360-day-per-year basis. The company estimates that it costs £90 to place a single purchase order and about £3 to carry one casting in inventory for a year. The high carrying costs result from the need to keep the castings in carefully controlled temperature and humidity conditions, and from the high cost of insurance. Delivery from the foundry generally takes 6 days, but it can take as much as 10 days. The days of delivery time and the percentage of their occurrence are shown in the following tabulation:

Delivery time (days)	Percentage of occurrence
1–6	75
7	10
8	5
9	5
10	5
	100

Required

1 Compute the economic order quantity (EOQ).

2 Assume that the company is willing to assume a 15% risk of being out of stock. What would be the safety stock? The reorder point?

3 Assume that the company is willing to assume only a 5% risk of being out of stock. What would be the safety stock? The reorder point?

4 Assume a 5% stockout risk as stated in (3) above. What would be the total cost of ordering and carrying inventory for one year?

5 Refer to the original data. Assume that using process re-engineering the company reduces its cost of placing a purchase order to only £6. Also, the company estimates that when the waste and inefficiency caused by inventories are considered, the true cost of carrying a unit in stock is £7.20 per year.

(a) Compute the new EOQ.

(b) How frequently would the company be placing an order, as compared to the old purchasing policy?

P18–10 time allowed: 45 minutes
The management team of WZX is about to start preparing the budgets for the year ending 31 December 2005. Relevant information is given below:

Sales

The predicted sales for 2005 are as follows:

	Quarter				
	1	2	3	4	Total
Sales (units)	25,799	24,078	34,763	39,820	124,460

Sales demand is the principal budget factor.

Costs

The production costs have been predicted to be:

Materials £15 per unit, but if production exceeds 30,000 units in a quarter a discount of 5% will be allowed on all units in the quarter.

Labour £25 per unit in normal time. However, if production exceeds 30,000 units in a quarter, overtime will have to be worked and costs will rise to £38 per unit for those in excess of 30,000 in the quarter.

Overheads

Variable £10 per unit at all levels of activity.

Fixed £100,000 per quarter for up to 30,000 units produced, but rising by 20% if output exceeds 30,000 units.

Stocks

WZX uses a just-in-time (JIT) system for raw materials.

It is company policy that there should be no stock of finished goods at the start of any year. Finished goods are valued at the budgeted average annual marginal production cost per unit.

Production schedule

The total annual production requirement will be scheduled to be produced in equal amounts in the four quarters.

Costing system

WZX uses a marginal costing system based on the budgeted average annual cost per unit.

Required

1 Prepare the production cost of sales budget for WZX for 2005 on the basis of its current purchasing, production and stock holding policies and its use of marginal costing. You should show the costs of each quarter and the total for the year. *(7 marks)*

2 The management of WZX is thinking of extending its use of a JIT approach to include finished goods and production.
Prepare the production cost of sales budget for 2005 on the basis of this policy change. You should show the costs of each quarter and the total for the year. *(8 marks)*

3 Explain the reasons for the differences in materials, labour and fixed overhead costs in your answers to parts (a) and (b) above. *(6 marks)*

4 Sales demand in 2006 is expected to be subject to seasonal fluctuations, as it has been in previous years. These seasonal variations are expected to be as follows:

Quarter	1	2	3	4
% variation	−10	−20	+10	+20

Assume that sales for Quarter 3 of 2005 will be 34,763 units and will continue to show an underlying growth of 5% per quarter. This trend of underlying growth is expected to continue throughout 2006.
Prepare a forecast of the sales volumes expected for each quarter of 2006. *(4 marks)*
(Total = 25 marks)
CIMA Performance Management, November 2004

P18–11 Quality cost report Time allowed: 60 minutes
In response to intensive foreign competition, the management of Florex Company has attempted over the past year to improve the quality of its products. A statistical process control system has been installed and other steps have been taken to decrease the amount of warranty and other field costs, which have been trending upward over the past several years. Costs relating to quality and quality control over the last two years are given below:

	This year	Last year
Inspection	£900,000	£750,000
Quality engineering	570,000	420,000
Depreciation of test equipment	240,000	210,000
Rework labour	1,500,000	1,050,000
Statistical process control	180,000	–
Cost of field servicing	900,000	1,200,000
Supplies used in testing	60,000	30,000
Systems development	750,000	480,000
Warranty repairs	1,050,000	3,600,000
Net cost of scrap	1,125,000	630,000
Product testing	1,200,000	810,000
Product recalls	750,000	2,100,000
Disposal of defective products	975,000	720,000

Sales have been flat over the past few years, at £75,000,000 per year. A great deal of money has been spent in the effort to upgrade quality, and management is anxious to see whether or not the effort has been effective.

Required

1 Prepare a quality cost report that contains data for both this year and last year. Carry percentage computations to two decimal places.

2 Prepare a bar graph showing the distribution of the various quality costs by category.

3 Prepare a written evaluation to accompany the reports you have prepared in Questions 1 and 2 above. This evaluation should discuss the distribution of quality costs in the company, changes in this distribution that you see taking place, the reasons for changes in costs in the various categories, and any other information that would be of value to management.

P18–12 Quality cost report Time allowed: 60 minutes

'Maybe the emphasis we've placed on upgrading our quality control system will pay off in the long run, but it doesn't seem to be helping us much right now,' said Renee Penretti, managing director of Halogen Products. 'I thought improved quality would give a real boost to sales, but sales have remained flat at £50,000,000 for the last two years.'

Halogen Products has seen its market share decline in recent years due to increased foreign competition. An intensive effort to strengthen the quality control system was initiated at the beginning of the current year in the hope that better quality would strengthen the company's competitive position and also reduce warranty and servicing costs. Costs relating to quality and quality control over the last two years are given below:

	This year	Last year
Product testing	£800,000	£490,000
Rework labour	1,000,000	700,000
Systems development	530,000	320,000
Warranty repairs	700,000	2,100,000
Net cost of scrap	620,000	430,000
Supplies used in testing	30,000	20,000
Field servicing	600,000	900,000
Quality engineering	400,000	280,000
Warranty replacements	90,000	300,000
Inspection	600,000	380,000
Product recalls	410,000	1,700,000
Statistical process control	370,000	–
Disposal of defective products	380,000	270,000
Depreciation of testing equipment	170,000	110,000

Required

1 Prepare a quality cost report that contains data for both years. Carry percentage computations to two decimal places.

2 Prepare a bar graph showing the distribution of the various quality costs by category.

3 Prepare a written evaluation to accompany the reports you have prepared in Questions 1 and 2 above. This evaluation should discuss the distribution of quality costs in the company, changes in this distribution that you detect have taken place over the last year, and any other information you believe would be useful to management.

P18–13 Analysing a quality cost report Time allowed: 45 minutes

Mercury Ltd produces pagers at its plant in Essex. In recent years, the company's market share has been eroded by stiff competition from overseas competitors. Price and product quality are the two key areas in which companies compete in this market.

A year ago, the company's pagers had been ranked low in product quality in a consumer survey. Shocked by this result, Steve Davis, Mercury's managing director, initiated a crash effort to improve product quality. Davis set up a task force to implement a formal quality improvement programme. Included on this task force were representatives from the Engineering, Marketing, Customer Service, Production, and Accounting departments. The broad representation was needed because Davis believed that this was a company-wide programme and that all employees should share the responsibility for its success.

After the first meeting of the task force, Holly Elsoe, manager of the Marketing Department, asked John Tran, production manager, what he thought of the proposed programme. Tran replied, 'I have reservations. Quality is too abstract to be attaching costs to it and then to be holding you and me responsible for cost improvements. I like to work with goals that I can see and count! I'm nervous about having my annual bonus based on a decrease in quality costs; there are too many variables that we have no control over.'

Mercury's quality improvement programme has now been in operation for one year. The company's most recent quality cost report is shown below.

Mercury Ltd
Quality cost report
(in thousands)

	This year	Last year
Prevention costs:		
Machine maintenance	£120	£70
Training suppliers	10	–
Quality circles	20	–
Total	150	70
Appraisal costs:		
Incoming inspection	40	20
Final testing	90	80
Total	130	100
Internal failure costs:		
Rework	130	50
Scrap	70	40
Total	200	90
External failure costs:		
Warranty repairs	30	90
Customer returns	80	320
Total	110	410
Total quality cost	£590	£670
Total production cost	£4,800	£4,200

As they were reviewing the report, Elsoe asked Tran what he now thought of the quality improvement programme. Tran replied. 'I'm relieved that the new quality improvement programme hasn't hurt our bonuses, but the programme has increased the workload in the Production Department. It is true that customer returns are way down, but the pagers that were returned by customers to retail outlets were rarely sent back to us for rework.'

Required

1 Expand the company's quality cost report by showing the costs in both years as percentages of both total production cost and total quality cost. Carry all computations to one decimal place. By analysing the report, determine if Mercury's quality improvement programme has been successful. List specific evidence to support your answer.

2 Do you expect the improvement programme as it progresses to continue to increase the workload in the Production Department?

3 Steve Davis believed that the quality improvement programme was essential and that Mercury, could no longer afford to ignore the importance of product quality. Discuss how Mercury could measure the cost of not implementing the quality improvement programme.

CMA, adapted

P18–14 ABC and ABM internet Time allowed: 60 minutes

S & P Products plc purchases a range of good quality gift and household products from around the world; it then sells these products through 'mail order' or retail outlets. The company receives 'mail orders' by post, telephone and internet. Retail outlets are either department stores or S & P Products plc's own small shops. The company started to set up its own shops after a recession in the early 1990s and regards them as the flagship of its business; sales revenue has gradually built up over the last 10 years. There are now 50 department stores and 10 shops.

The company has made good profits over the last few years but recently trading has been difficult. As a consequence, the management team has decided that a fundamental reappraisal of the business is now necessary if the company is to continue trading.

Meanwhile the budgeting process for the coming year is proceeding. S & P Products plc uses an activity-based costing (ABC) system and the following estimated cost information for the coming year is available:

Retail outlet costs:

Activity	Cost driver	Rate per cost driver	Number each year for: Department store	Own shop
Telephone queries and requests to S & P	Calls	15	40	350
Sales visits to shops and stores by S & P sales staff	Visits	250	2	4
Shop orders	Orders	20	25	150
Packaging deliveries		100	28	150
Delivery to shops	Deliveries	150	28	150

Staffing, rental and service costs for each of S & P Products plc's own shops cost on average £300,000 a year.

Mail order costs:

Activity	Cost driver	Rate per cost driver: Post	Telephone	Internet
		£	£	£
Processing 'mail orders'	Orders	5	6	3
Dealing with 'mail order' queries	Orders	4	4	1
		Number of packages per order		
Packaging and deliveries for 'mail orders' – cost per package £10	Packages	2	2	1

The total number of orders through the whole 'mail order' business for the coming year is expected to be 80,000. The maintenance of the internet link is estimated to cost £80,000 for the coming year.

The following additional information for the coming year has been prepared:

	Department store	**Own shop**	**Post**	**Telephone**	**Internet**
Sales revenue per outlet	£50,000	£1,000,000			
Sales revenue per order			£150	£300	£100
Gross margin: mark-up on purchase cost	30%	40%	40%	40%	40%
Number of outlets	50	10			
Percentage of 'mail orders'			30%	60%	10%

Expected Head Office and warehousing costs for the coming year:

	£
Warehouse	2,750,000
IT	550,000
Administration	750,000
Personnel	300,000
	4,350,000

Required

1

(a) Prepare calculations that will show the expected profitability of the different types of sales outlet for the coming year. *(13 marks)*

(b) Comment briefly on the results of the figures you have prepared. *(3 marks)*

2 In relation to the company's fundamental reappraisal of its business,

(a) discuss how helpful the information you have prepared in Question 1 is for this purpose and how it might be revised or expanded so that it is of more assistance; *(7 marks)*

(b) advise what other information is needed in order to make a more informed judgement. *(7 marks)*

(Total = 30 marks)

CIMA Management Accounting – Decision Making, November 2001

P18–15 ABC/ABM Time allowed: 50 minutes

FF plc is a bank that offers a variety of banking services to its clients. One of the services offered is aimed at high net worth individuals and the bank is currently reviewing the performance of its client base. The high net worth clients are classified into four groups based on the value of their individual liquid assets deposited in FF plc. The following annual budgeted information has been prepared:

Group	W	X	Y	Z	
Individual value (000s)	$500–$999	$1,000–$2,999	$3,000–$5,999	$6,000–$9,999	
Number of clients	1,000	1,500	2,000	1,800	
	$000	$000	$000	$000	Total $000
Total contribution	500	900	1,400	2,500	5,300
Overheads:					
Share of support costs	285	760	790	1,165	3,000
Share of facility costs	100	160	240	500	1,000
Profit/(loss)	115	(20)	370	835	1,300

FF plc is about to implement an activity-based costing (ABC) system. The implementation team recently completed an analysis of the support costs. The analysis revealed that these costs were variable in relation to certain drivers. The details of the analysis are shown below.

Group Activity	W 000s	X 000s	Y 000s	Z 000s	Total 000s
Number of telephone enquiries	200	150	220	300	870
Number of statements prepared	120	120	240	480	960
Number of client meetings	60	100	110	200	470

Activity	Support costs/Overheads $000
Telephone enquiries	1,000
Statements prepared	250
Client meetings	1,750
Total	3,000

The Bank Manager feels that the low profitability from client Group W and the losses from client Group X need to be investigated further and that consideration should be given to discontinuing these services and concentrating the marketing and sales effort on increasing the number of clients within Group Y and Group Z. He has outlined two proposals, as follows:

Proposal 1

Discontinue both of Groups W and X in order to concentrate on Groups Y and Z (so that the bank would have only two client groups). If this option were implemented, it is expected that the facility costs would increase by 10%.

The Marketing Manager has calculated the probability of the number of clients the bank would serve to be as shown below.

Projected revised numbers of clients in Groups Y and Z

Group Y		Group Z	
Client numbers	Probability	Client numbers	Probability
2,250	0.30	2,000	0.20
2,500	0.40	2,200	0.50
2,750	0.30	2,500	0.30

Proposal 2

Discontinue either Group W or Group X in order to concentrate on Groups Y and Z (so that the bank would have three client groups). If this option were implemented, it is expected that the facility costs would increase by 8%.

If this proposal is implemented, the Marketing Manager estimates that the increase in client numbers in Groups Y and Z would be reduced by 75%, compared with proposal 1.

Required

1 Prepare a customer profitability statement based on the ABC analysis and comment on your results. *(8 marks)*

2 Using the ABC details, evaluate the proposal of the Bank Manager (your answer must be supported by calculations). *(9 marks)*

3 When the bank's annual budget was prepared, it was thought that the bank would have a 25% share of the total market of 10,000 Group Y clients. However, for that year the total market size was 9,500 Group Y clients, of which the bank had 2,750.

(a) Calculate on a contribution per unit basis the

- market size variance, *(2 marks)*
- market share variance. *(2 marks)*

(b) Explain and interpret these variances for the bank. *(4 marks)*

CIMA Decision making, November 2003

P18–16 Process accounting/quality report Time allowed: 50 minutes

LMN produces a compound T5, which is used to manufacture tyres. The compound, which earns a contribution of £6 per tonne, is produced by mixing two materials, R1 and R2, in a common process. The process causes the production of a by-product Z, which can be sold without further processing for £5 per tonne. The process is inefficient and large losses occur. The losses can currently only be identified at the completion of the process.

Process details

In addition to the costs of materials R1 and R2, variable and fixed processing costs are incurred. The expected inputs and outputs of the process are as follows:

Input:	equal quantities of R1 and R2
Outputs:	T5: 60% of weight of new input
	Z: 10% of weight of new input
Loss:	30% of weight of new input

Data for October

Opening work in progress 200 tonnes of T5 fully complete in respect of materials, but only 30% converted. This stock was valued at £450.

Inputs:	
Materials:	24,000 tonnes of R1 costing £60,480
	24,000 tonnes of R2 costing £24,000
Conversion costs:	Variable £36,125
Fixed	£39,015
Outputs	T5: 28,800 tonnes
Z:	4,800 tonnes

Closing work in progress 200 tonnes of T5 fully complete in respect of materials, but only 80% converted.

Note: By-product Z is not considered to be a major source of income and consequently the revenue generated by its sale is credited to the process account.

Required

1 Prepare the process account for LMN for the month of October using a First In, First Out (FIFO) basis of valuation. Show all your workings. *(10 marks)*

2 The production director of LMN has been investigating alternative production methods to reduce the loss that arises in the process. Two alternatives have been identified:

(a) to change the mix of input materials R1 and R2, such that twice as much R1 is used compared to R2. Conversion costs would not be affected and trials have suggested that this would reduce the expected loss to 15% of the materials input during a period with no effect on the output of the by-product.

(b) to introduce a quality control procedure that would enable any loss to be identified and the units rejected after 60% of the conversion costs had been incurred. It is expected that the quantity of the normal loss will remain at 30% of the input to the process. There would be no capital expenditure costs associated with this quality control procedure, but other costs would comprise £0.20 for every tonne of input materials processed together with a fixed cost of £1,000 per month. The quantity of the by-product produced and its continued saleability would not be affected by this proposed inspection process.

Evaluate each of the separate alternatives (a) and (b) above and recommend which, if either, should be adopted by LMN. Show all your workings. *(10 marks)*

3 As a management accountant, prepare a report addressed to the Board of Directors of LMN that explains the costs and benefits that would arise following the adoption of a Quality Control Programme. Your answer should refer to the different quality cost classifications that would be used and also to non-financial factors. *(10 marks)*

(Total = 30 marks)

CIMA Management Accounting – Performance Management, November 2004

Cases

CASE

C18–17 Strategy and the internet Time allowed: 75 minutes

FNJ is a company, which has developed business interests in the very competitive music industry. It produces and sells compact discs (CDs) and traces its history back to when it manufactured vinyl records. It is contracted to produce CDs for many famous recording artists which it is able to distribute through its own worldwide chain of retail music stores.

A new Chief Executive (CJ), who came from an unrelated business, was appointed to run FNJ about 12 months ago. The financial situation for the company has become perilous with falling worldwide sales and difficult trading conditions. The company has issued a number of profit warnings and experienced severe management disputes which have been made public. The result of these factors has been a low share price. CJ implemented cost reductions at FNJ and developed a strategy which focuses the company's attention on the provision of music to customers via the internet, with the eventual aim of replacing CDs with internet sales in the years to come.

WT is a large entertainments group which has growing business interests in producing motion pictures (movies) and retail outlets (trading under its own brand name of WT). The company is well regarded worldwide within its industry. It has augmented the product range with, for example, soft toys (related to its popular movie characters) which are sold through its retail outlets.

The merger

A merger deal has recently been agreed between the directors of FNJ and WT. This has yet to be ratified by both sets of shareholders, but it is expected to be accepted. The new group (FW) aims to achieve a high market share of total worldwide music sales. Following the merger, it is expected that the two companies will shed jobs throughout the world in the interests of improving efficiency. The contracts for some of the recording artists who are not achieving high sales will not be renewed.

Financial summary of the merger

The following details highlight the main points relating to the merger:

1 The merger is worth £10 billion in terms of total asset value.

2 WT has 8 seats while FNJ has 7 seats on the new board of FW.

3 CJ will be the Chief Executive of FW.

4 Shares in FW will be allocated in proportion to the current shareholdings. This will result in each company's shareholders holding 50% of the shares.

5 Directors' share options come to fruition on completion of the merger.

6 The share price of FNJ rose by 11% after the merger was announced.

Selected details relating to FNJ and WT before the proposed merger

	CDs (FNJ)	
	Last year	**2 years ago**
Actual sales	£90 million	£95 million
Budgeted sales	£100 million	£100 million
Average actual price per CD	£20	£20
Average actual cost per CD (⅓ of this is variable cost)	£12	£12
Average budgeted price per CD	£22	£20
Average budgeted cost per CD (⅓ of this is variable cost)	£15	£10.5

The average annual sales of CDs over the last 5 years were £100 million. The trend of changes in sales levels for CDs which has been apparent over the last two years is expected to continue.

	Motion pictures (WT)			
	Last year	**2 years ago**	**3 years ago**	**4 years ago**
Total revenue	£2,000 million	£1,800 million	£1,400 million	£1,000 million
Total costs	£1,900 million	£1,600 million	£1,100 million	£700 million
	Retail music stores (operated by FNJ)			
	Last year	**2 years ago**	**3 years ago**	**4 years ago**
Total revenue	£140 million	£138 million	£136 million	£135 million
Total costs	£136 million	£131 million	£134 million	£135 million

The resale value of FNJ's retail music stores is reducing because of the increasing popularity of alternative methods of shopping.

Strategic development of FW

CJ has forecast that next year sales of music will be available through the internet with digital downloading to the customer's own personal computer. At the moment, most of the FNJ retail music stores' revenue is generated by the sale of FNJ-produced CDs. He believes that by supplying customers through the internet, overall sales revenue (combining internet sales with CDs), will increase by 20%. The average variable costs for internet sales will reduce by 25% on that currently incurred in CD production. This cost reduction is expected as a result of not needing to employ expensive recording studios which are currently required to produce a CD.

The average selling price and average variable cost of a CD are expected to remain at £20 and £4 respectively throughout next year. The average selling price of each internet sale is also expected to be £20.

Independent research has revealed that the market for digitally downloaded music is forecast to grow next year. Customers will have the opportunity to create their own 'do it yourself' compilation albums.

Some of FW's competitors have already made effective use of the internet to distribute CDs and videos, undercutting high street retailers on price. However, digital download through the internet is still experimental.

Required

1 Discuss the dynamic nature of the business environment experienced by FNJ and WT, and explain the rationale for the merger. *(10 marks)*

2

(a) Analyse the business performance of CDs, motion pictures and FNJ's retail music stores over the period contained in the scenario. Include calculations on the projected change in contribution each year for CD and internet sales if CJ's forecast is accurate. *(14 marks)*

(b) Calculate and analyse the contribution volume variance relating to CD sales for last year and two years ago. *(5 marks)*

(c) Recommend ways in which the directors of FW should pursue the strategic development of the CD, motion pictures and FNJ's retail music stores businesses. *(12 marks)*

Abbreviated version from
CIMA Management Accounting – Business Strategy, May 2001

C18–18 Stock management and new technology Time allowed: 90 minutes

CLB is a profitable manufacturer of clothes with an annual turnover of $650 million. The organization sells by mail order from a paper catalogue sent out to customers and via a website. There are approximately 2.5 million customers on the sales database. Customers spend on average $110 per order.

Clothes are manufactured in 10 different factories, with finished goods being transferred to a central warehouse, where they are placed onto the computerized stock system for internet and catalogue sales. All customer orders are routed to the central warehouse; the factories do not have any sales facilities.

The clothes produced by CLB are fashionable, with most customers being satisfied by the range available. A recent move to sourcing more supplies from overseas has helped to cut costs, although there is increasing competition from some low-cost imports.

Company aims and mission

The mission of the organization is 'to produce a wide range of reasonably priced clothes that appeal to the majority of the population'. To meet this objective, CLB has three main *critical success factors (CSFs)*:

- Maintain overall gross profit at 40% of sales
- Increase customer satisfaction each year
- Minimize raw material inventory cost.

A 40% gross profit percentage is slightly above the industry standard, but thought to be achievable by the Board of CLB. The organization needs to sell $600 million of clothes each year to break even.

Maintenance of customer satisfaction is essential to selling clothes. However, the directors have had some difficulty in establishing appropriate *performance indicators (PIs)* to measure the CSFs.

Maintaining control over inventory is essential; not only does raw material stock tie up working capital, but any unused raw materials are difficult to dispose of. Changes in fashion mean that raw material stock becomes obsolete very quickly. Finished goods stocks are easier to dispose of – completed garments can normally be sold at cost price or slightly above ensuring that some contribution is made.

Trends in sales

For a number of years, the Board of CLB has been concerned that the brand awareness of the company's products has been falling. Sales of new product lines have also been less than budgeted, both in absolute terms and in comparison to similar clothes produced by competitors.

(Information on competitor sales is obtained from their published accounts and for some products from the *Clothing Gazette*, a trade journal.) The fall in brand awareness and sales has provided a *decision trigger* to the directors that some amendments may be required to the information systems in CLB. However, they are unclear regarding the information to be obtained to help them make this decision.

CLB information system

At present, each of the 10 factories of CLB maintains its own information system to provide detail on raw material stocks, production and finished goods ready to transfer to the central warehouse. While this means that there is no overall picture of stocks, the benefit of maintaining decentralized control is thought to outweigh this problem. The director of human resources is keen to maintain motivation of individual factory managers by retaining the existing systems.

This strategy has again been queried at board level in the last few months, particularly as manufacturing operations mean that each factory is using similar raw materials. Implementation of a centralized system has been rejected by the HR and IT Directors.

Required

1

(a) Recommend performance indicators (PIs) that can be used to support the *critical success factors (CSFs)* of CLB, discussing why these PIs are appropriate to the company. *(8 marks)*

(b) Explain the information systems that will be required in order to determine whether the PIs suggested in your answer to Question 1(a) have been achieved. *(12 marks)*

2 With reference to the falling brand awareness, advise the directors on a suitable decision-making process when considering the update of the information systems within CLB. Include relevant examples from the situation in CLB where possible. *(15 marks)*

3 Describe an information system that can be used to co-ordinate information transfer between the different production factories and between the factories and the central sales warehouse. Explain the business benefits to CLB of such a system and any disadvantages of it. *(15 marks)*

(Total = 50 marks)

CIMA Management Accounting – Information Strategy, November 2001

C18–19 Time allowed: 75 minutes

Ochilpark plc has identified and defined a market in which it wishes to operate. This will provide a 'millennium' focus for an existing product range. Ochilpark plc has identified a number of key competitors and intends to focus on close co-operation with its customers in providing products to meet their specific design and quality requirements. Efforts will be made to improve the effectiveness of all aspects of the cycle from product design to after sales service to customers. This will require inputs from a number of departments in the achievement of the specific goals of the 'millennium' product range. Efforts will be made to improve productivity in conjunction with increased flexibility of methods. An analysis of financial and non-financial data relating to the 'millennium' proposal is shown in Schedule 1.1.

Schedule 1.1
'Millennium'proposal – estimated statistics

	2000	2001	2002
Total market size (£m)	120	125	130
Ochilpark plc sales (£m)	15	18	20
Ochilpark plc – total costs (£m)	14.1	12.72	12.55
Ochilpark plc sundry statistics:			
Production achieving design quality standards (%)	95	97	98
Returns from customers as unsuitable (% of deliveries)	3.0	1.5	0.5
Cost of after sales service (£m)	1.5	1.25	1.0
Sales meeting planned delivery dates (%)	90	95	99
Average cycle time (customer enquiry to delivery) (weeks)	6	5.5	5
Components scrapped in production (%)	7.5	5.0	2.5
Idle machine capacity (%)	10	6	2

Required

1

(a) Prepare a table (£m) of the total costs for the 'millennium' proposal for each of years 2000, 2001 and 2002 (as shown in Schedule 1.1), detailing target costs, internal and external failure costs, appraisal costs and prevention costs. The following information should be used in the preparation of the analysis:

	2000	2001	2002
Target costs – variable (as % of sales)	40%	40%	40%
Target costs – fixed (total)	£2m	£2m	£2.5m
Internal failure costs (% of total target cost)	20%	10%	5%
External failure costs (% of total target cost)	25%	12%	5%
Appraisal costs	£0.5m	£0.5m	£0.5m
Prevention costs	£2m	£1m	£0.5m

(4 marks)

(b) Explain the meaning of each of the cost classifications in Question 1(a) above and comment on their trend and inter-relationship. You should provide examples of each classification.

(8 marks)

2 Prepare an analysis (both discursive and quantitative) of the 'millennium' proposal for the period 2000 to 2002. The analysis should use the information provided in the question, together with the data in Schedule 1.1. The analysis should contain the following:

(a) A definition of corporate 'vision or mission' and consideration of how the millennium proposal may be seen as identifying and illustrating a specific sub-set of this 'vision or mission'.

(5 marks)

(b) Discussion and quantification of the proposal in both marketing and financial terms. *(6 marks)*

(c) Discussion of the external effectiveness of the proposal in the context of ways in which *1. Quality* and *2. Delivery* are expected to affect customer satisfaction and hence the marketing of the product. *(4 marks)*

(d) Discussion of the internal efficiency of the proposal in the context of ways in which the management of 1. Cycle Time and 2. Waste are expected to affect productivity and hence the financial aspects of the proposal. *(4 marks)*

(e) Discussion of the links between internal and external aspects of the expected trends in performance. *(4 marks)*

(Total = 35 marks)

ACCA Information for Decision Making and Control, December 1999

Endnotes

1 Summers (2002).

2 See Hansen and Mouritsen (2007) for a discussion of the relationship between operations management and management accounting.

3 Radnor, Walley, Stephens and Bucci (2006).

4 See Johnson and Kaplan (1987).

5 Shingo and Robinson (1990).

6 Granlund and Malmi (2001).

7 See, for example, Granlund (2001).

8 Scapens, Jazayeri and Scapens (1998).

9 Currie (2000).

10 Wagle (1998).

11 See, for example, May (2002); Granlund (2001); Scapens, Ezzamel, Burns and Baldvinsdottir (2003).

12 '80% of the benefit that we get from our ERP system comes from changes, such as inventory optimization, which we could have achieved without making the IT investment', Dorien and Wolf (2000), p. 101.

13 Agrawal, Arjona and Lemmens (2001).

14 Currie (2000), p. 117.

15 Barnatt (2004).

16 Hart, Heskett and Sasser (1990).

17 Casey (1990), p. 31.

18 Anderson and Sedatole (1998), p. 214.

19 Dr W. Edwards Deming, a pioneer in TQM, introduced many of the elements of TQM to Japanese industry after the Second World War. TQM was further refined and developed at Japanese companies such as Toyota.

20 Madonna (1992).

21 Cox, Mann and Sampson (1997).

22 Hammer and Champy (1995).

23 Shapiro (1997).

24 CIMA (2001c).

25 Coburn, Gove and Fulcani (1995).

26 Armstrong (2002).

27 Based on a case in Soin, Seal and Cullen (2002).

Chapter 19
Strategic perspectives on cost management

Learning objectives

After studying Chapter 19, you should be able to:

1 Consider the general significance of constraints on managerial decision-making
2 Understand the role of linear programming in the case of multiple constraints
3 Review the management accounting issues raised by the theory of constraints
4 Review the long-run impact of constraints through target and life-cycle costing
5 Analyse the make-or-buy decision from a strategic, supply chain management perspective
6 Consider how outsourcing and shared service centres affect the delivery of support services

Concepts in Context

A Dell personal computer (PC) is basically made up of a central processing unit (CPU), an operating system and a memory. The CPU comes from Intel or Advanced Micro Devices; the operating system from Microsoft while the memory has multiple sources. The main direct innovation comes from suppliers with only indirect innovation from the PC manufacturers. The PC has a life cycle of three months to two years with 50% of profits achieved within the first three to six months of the life cycle. The industry typically experiences deep discounting when new processors, operating systems or memory are introduced. Thus older components become obsolete very quickly. In the PC industry, supply chains are no longer linear but networked – 'information moves independently of product at internet speeds'.[1]

In the short run, managers can do little to change their basic cost structures. Short-run decisions may be made using models such as the CVP model that we explored in Chapter 7. Furthermore, as we saw in Chapter 9, managers are routinely faced with the problem of deciding how constrained resources are going to be utilized. Because of the constrained resource (also known as a **limiting factor**) the company cannot fully satisfy demand, so the manager must decide how the constrained resource should be used. Fixed costs are usually unaffected by such choices, so the manager should select the course of action that will maximize the firm's total contribution margin.

In Chapter 9, we saw that the total contribution margin will be maximized by promoting those products or accepting those orders that provide the highest unit contribution margin in relation to the constrained resource. We illustrated this principle through the Mountain Goat Cycles example. You should review your understanding of the single constraint problem by referring back to this example. In this chapter, we look at two more approaches to cost management: the multiple constraint problem and the theory of constraints.

Later on, we consider how costs can be managed in the long run with approaches that try to anticipate possible constraints during the design stage of products and processes. As well as taking a more strategic perspective on the make-or-buy decision (see Chapter 9), this approach asks fundamental questions about an organization's core activities. In particular, we analyse the role of cost management when activities are outsourced through partnerships and alliances.

Many of the techniques in this chapter are based on similar philosophies to those introduced in Chapter 18, particularly lean production. Indeed, long-run approaches to cost management that focus on the design stage of products and seek to improve the management of the supply chain are complimentary to the techniques of JIT, TQM and BPR. All these techniques seek to *remove constraints* rather than optimize around them.

The problem of multiple constraints in the short run: linear programming

What does a firm do if it has more than one potential constraint? For example, a firm may have limited raw materials, limited direct labour hours available, limited floor space, and a limited advertising budget to spend on product promotion. How should it proceed to find the right combination of products to produce? The proper combination or 'mix' of products can be found by use of a quantitative method known as linear programming. When there are two products, the main principles of the technique may be illustrated graphically. For simplicity, we have only considered two constraints. The graphical approach can handle more than two constraints but only two products. More complicated examples with more constraints and products may be solved using an iterative mathematical technique known as the **simplex method**. Nowadays there are computer programs that can solve complex linear programming problems at the click of a button.

Colnebank (see Exhibit 19.1) wants to know what output combination of pumps and fans will maximize its profit in the short run. Since there are only two products, we can illustrate and solve the problem graphically. Exhibit 19.2 puts the pumps along the horizontal axis and the fans along the vertical axis. We can build up the diagram by calculating the maximum output of pumps and fans if all the resources were used to produce just one product. For example, if Colnebank decided just to produce pumps then its labour-hours would allow it to produce 6000/22 = 273 pumps. If it decided just to produce fans then its labour-hours would allow it to produce 6000/8 = 750 fans. When we join the two points on each axis, we can trace the labour-hours constraint. If we do the same calculations for material then we have the set of the constraints facing Colnebank as shown in Exhibit 19.2. When both constraints are considered, Colnebank can only produce a combination of the products within the shaded area – the so-called **feasible region**. But which is the best or **optimal combination of product**? The criterion (or **objective function**) is the output that maximizes total contribution. The individual contribution of one unit of each product may be see in Exhibit 19.3.

Colnebank Ltd is a medium-sized engineering company and is one of large number of producers in a very competitive market. The company produces two products, pumps and fans that use similar raw materials and labour skills. The market price of a pump is £152 and that of a fan is £118. The resource requirements of producing one unit of each of the two products are:

	Material (kg)	Labour hours
Pump	10	22
Fan	15	8

Material costs are £4 per kg and labour costs are £3.50 per hour.

During the coming period the company will have the following resources available to it:

4000 kg of material

6000 labour hours

Exhibit 19.1 The two product, two constraint problem: Colnebank

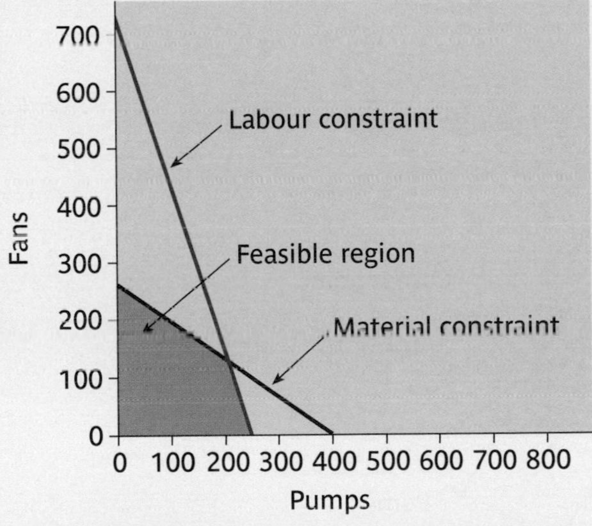

Exhibit 19.2 Graphical version of Colnebank

Graphically, we may plot the objective function by choosing a level of total contribution and plotting an **iso-contribution line**. This line traces all the combinations of P and F that could produce a particular total contribution. In Exhibit 19.4, the iso-contribution line drawn produces a total contribution of £3,000. This level of total contribution is well within the feasible region so we can do better by tracing the highest iso-contribution that is still feasible given the constraints. As we can see in Exhibit 19.4, the highest feasible contribution is at point X. Because the model is linear[2] this point is also a **corner point**. We may find the values of P and F at X by inspection or solve for:

$$10P + 15F = 4000$$

$$22P + 8F = 6000$$

This gives:

Pumps = 232 Fans = 112 Total contribution = £11,480.

	Pumps £	Fans £
Materials	40.00 (10 kg at £4)	60.00 (15 kg at £4)
Labour	77.00 (22 hrs at £3.50	28.00 (8 hrs at £3.50)
	117.00	88.00
Selling price	152.00	118.00
Contribution	35.00	30.00

The linear programming problem is to maximize the total contribution subject to the constraints. If P = units of pumps produced and F = units of fans produced then the problem may be set up as follows.

1 Maximize: £35P + £30F

2 Subject to: $10P + 15F \leq 4000$ kg (materials)

3 $22P + 8F \leq 6000$ (labour hours)

Exhibit 19.3 The linear programming problem

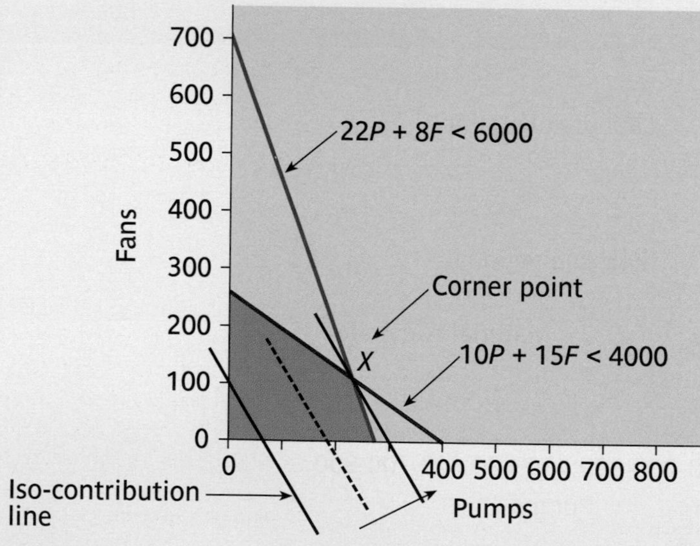

Exhibit 19.4 A graphical solution

Sensitivity analysis

The value of the graphical model is that it illustrates the main principles behind linear programming as well as possible extensions such as *sensitivity analysis*. **Sensitivity analysis** involves asking 'what-if' questions. For example, what happens if the market price of pumps falls to £145? What will be the loss of contribution and will it change the optimal combination? The revised contribution margins are shown in Exhibit 19.5.

	Pumps £	Fans £
Materials	40.00 (10 kg at £4)	60.00 (15 kg at £4)
Labour	77.00 (22 hrs at £3.50)	28.00 (8 hrs at £3.50)
	117.00	88.00
Selling price	145.00	118.00
Contribution	28.00	30.00

Exhibit 19.5 Sensitivity analysis

Although the total contribution margin has changed, the optimal decision has not. We may change other variables such as the variable cost estimates and see whether they change the optimal decision.

Shadow prices

Each constraint will have an opportunity cost, which is the profit foregone by not having an additional unit of the resource. In linear programming, opportunity costs are known as **shadow prices** and are defined as the increase in value that would be created by having one additional unit of a limiting resource. For example, we could consider what the loss of contribution for Colnebank would be if the available processing hours were reduced by one hour.

The limitations of the linear programming model as a management accounting technique

There are a number of limitations in using linear programming as a management accounting technique. It ignores marketing considerations and has an excessive focus on the short term. Furthermore, most production resource can be varied even in the short term through overtime and buying-in. More fundamentally, as we saw with both stock control problems and cost of quality decisions in Chapter 18, the alternative to optimizing against given constraints is to concentrate on managing to remove constraints, to eliminate stock or to improve quality.[3]

Managing constraints

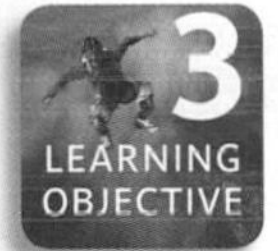

Profits can be increased by effectively managing the organization's constraints. One aspect of managing constraints is to decide how best to utilize them. If the constraint is a bottleneck in the production process, we have seen that the manager should select the product mix that maximizes the total contribution margin. In addition, the manager should take an active role in managing the constraint itself by increasing the efficiency of the bottleneck operation and by increasing its capacity. Such efforts directly increase the output of finished goods and will often pay off in an almost immediate increase in profits.

It is often possible for a manager to effectively increase the capacity of the bottleneck, which is called **relaxing (or elevating) the constraint**. In the case of Mountain Goat Cycles in Chapter 9, the stitching machine operator could be asked to work overtime. This would result in more available stitching time and hence more finished goods that can be sold. The benefits from relaxing the constraint in such a manner are often enormous and can be easily quantified. The manager should first ask, 'What would I do with additional capacity at the bottleneck if it were available?' In the example, if there are unfilled orders for both the touring and mountain panniers, the additional capacity would be used to process more touring panniers, since that would be a better use of the additional capacity. In that situation, the additional capacity would be worth £12 per minute or £720 per hour. This is because adding an hour of capacity would generate an additional £720 of contribution margin if it would be used solely to process more touring panniers. Since overtime pay for the operator is likely to be much less than £720 per hour, running the stitching machine on overtime would be an excellent way to increase the profits of the company while at the same time satisfying customers.

To reinforce this concept, suppose that making touring panniers has already been given top priority and consequently there are only unfilled orders for the mountain pannier. How much would it be worth to the company to run the stitching machine overtime in this situation? Since the additional capacity would be used to make the mountain pannier, the value of that additional capacity would drop to £7.50 per minute or £450 per hour. Nevertheless, the value of relaxing the constraint would still be quite high.

These calculations indicate that managers should pay great attention to bottleneck operations. If a bottle-neck machine breaks down or is ineffectively utilized, the losses to the company can be quite large. In our example, for every minute the stitching machine is down due to breakdowns or set-ups, the company loses between £7.50 and £12.00. The losses on an hourly basis are between £450 and £720! In contrast, there is no such loss of contribution margin if time is lost on a machine that is not a bottleneck – such machines have excess capacity anyway.

The implications are clear. Managers should focus much of their attention on managing bottlenecks. As we have discussed, managers should emphasize products that most profitably utilize the constrained resource. They should also make sure that products are processed smoothly through the bottlenecks, with minimal lost time due to breakdowns and set-ups. And they should try to find ways to increase the capacity at the bottlenecks.

The capacity of a bottleneck can be effectively increased in a number of ways, including:

- *Working* overtime on the bottleneck
- Subcontracting some of the processing that would be done at the bottleneck
- *Investing in additional machines* at the bottleneck
- *Shifting* workers from processes that are not bottlenecks to the process that is a bottleneck
- *Focusing business process improvement efforts* such as TQM and BPR on the bottleneck
- Reducing *defective units*. Each defective unit that is processed through the bottleneck and subsequently scrapped takes the place of a good unit that could be sold.

The last three methods of increasing the capacity of the bottleneck are particularly attractive, since they are essentially free and may even yield additional cost savings. These somewhat ad hoc examples have been generalized in the *theory of constraints (TOC)*.

The theory of constraints

A **constraint** is anything that prevents you from getting more of what you want. Every individual and every organization faces at least one constraint, so it is not difficult to find examples of constraints. You may not have enough time to study thoroughly for every subject and to go out with your friends on the weekend, so time is your constraint. Since a constraint prevents you from getting more of what you want, the **theory of constraints (TOC)** maintains that effectively managing the constraint is a key to success.

TOC and continuous improvement

In TOC, an analogy is often drawn between a business process and a chain. If you want to increase the strength of a chain, what is the most effective way to do this? Should you concentrate your efforts on strengthening the strongest link, the largest link, all the links, or the weakest link? Clearly, focusing effort on the weakest link will bring the biggest benefit.

Continuing with this analogy, the procedure to follow in strengthening the chain is straightforward. First, identify the weakest link, which is the constraint. Second, do not place a greater strain on the system than the weakest link can handle. Third, concentrate improvement efforts on strengthening the weakest link. Fourth, if the improvement efforts are successful, eventually the weakest link will improve to the point where it is no longer the weakest link. At this point, the new weakest link (i.e. the new constraint) must be identified, and improvement efforts must be shifted over to that link. This simple sequential process provides a powerful strategy for continuous improvement. The TOC approach is a perfect complement to TQM and process re-engineering – it focuses improvement efforts where they are likely to be most effective.

An example of TOC

A simple example will be used to illustrate the role of a constraint. In Exhibit 19.6, bottlenecks in the National Health Service contribute to the waiting lists that characterize the health care system. The key constraint or bottleneck is in Surgery where the maximum number of patients that can be processed is 15 patients a day. Other parts of the systems such as General Practitioners (100 patients per day) and Outpatients (50 patients per day) could process higher numbers. The key to increasing the overall capacity of the system is to improve the capacity in Surgery – improvements in other areas may simply lead to longer waiting lists. If efforts are focused on the first bottleneck in Surgery, subsequent improvements may lead to a situation when another part of the system takes over as the weakest link and hence a focus for management attention.

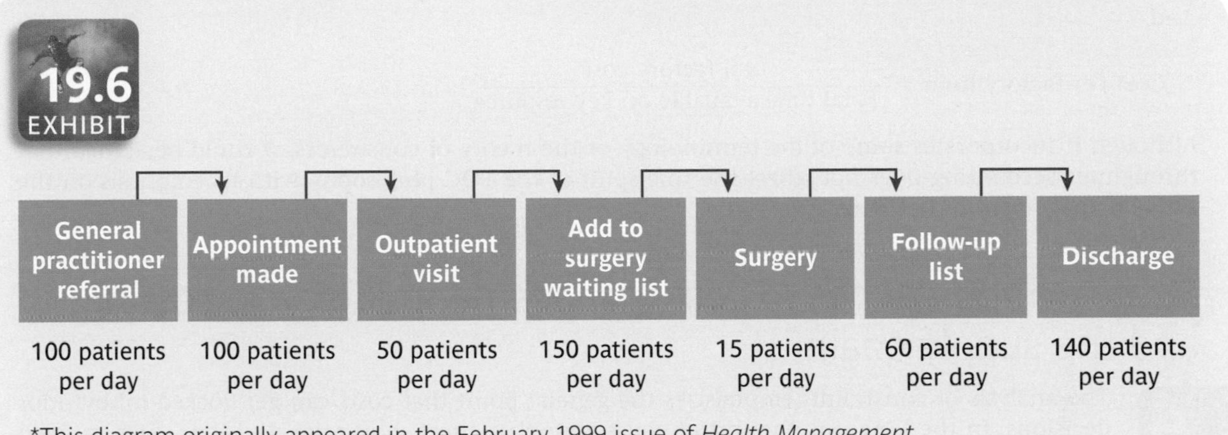

*This diagram originally appeared in the February 1999 issue of *Health Management*.

Exhibit 19.6 Processing surgery patients at an NHS facility (simplified)

The impact of TOC on management accounting

Conventional management accounting has two possible conflicts with TOC. If non-bottleneck machines have a production cut then they begin to look inefficient. Labour efficiency variances may also worsen. Furthermore, a reduction in work in progress may lead to a fall in reported profit. The TOC solution is to change the usual measures by focusing on throughput, stock and operational expense. The theory has its own special definitions:

Throughput = Sales − Material and purchased services

Inventory = Stock + Machines and buildings

Operating expense = Non-material conversion costs especially labour costs

Net profit = Throughput − Operational expense

$$\text{ROI} = \frac{\text{Throughput} - \text{Operational expense}}{\text{Inventory}}$$

Note that direct labour is treated as a fixed cost. Traditional accounting such as standard costing focuses on controlling operational expenses ('cost world'), JIT focuses on cutting stock ('JIT world'). In contrast, 'Throughput world' focuses on throughput even if it means conflicting with JIT by holding buffer stocks or with cost world by tolerating slack labour.

Throughput accounting[4]

One response to the theory of constraints is a technique that determines the optimum use of bottleneck activity called **throughput accounting (TA)**. The main idea is to rank products by calculating the **throughput accounting ratio**:

$$\text{TA ratio} = \frac{\text{Return per factory hour}}{\text{Cost per factory hour}}$$

where

$$\text{Return per factory hour} = \frac{\text{Sale price} - \text{Material cost}}{\text{Time on key resource}}$$

And

$$\text{Cost per factory hour} = \frac{\text{Total factory cost}}{\text{Total time available on key resource}}$$

Although it incorporates some of the terminology of the theory of constraints, it could be argued that throughput accounting does not reflect the true spirit of the TOC philosophy with its emphasis on the active management of bottlenecks.[5]

Strategic approaches to cost management: life-cycle costing and the supply chain

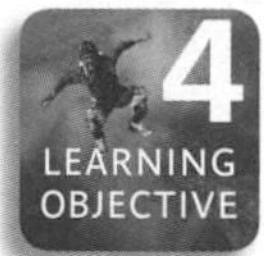

The analysis of constraints emphasizes the general point that costs can get 'locked in' by prior decisions. In the long run, the sort of constraints that affect short-term decisions, such as fixed capacity or specific shortages, may be tackled through alternative production configurations. In the even longer run, the boundaries of the organization may be altered so that decisions made to *outsource* activities that were causing bottlenecks or constraining profitable processes, are part of a strategic assessment of organizational competence (see Chapter 16). Long-run cost management calls on different techniques, in which costs are controlled through the *anticipation* of specific cost drivers stemming from the design of products or services. Thus there is less emphasis on optimizing a static situation (as with linear programming) and more emphasis on avoiding cost through careful product design and appropriate supply chain strategies.

Life-cycle costing

Traditional costing sometimes seems to focus too much on costs as they are *incurred* because incurred costs are more visible as they are 'booked' through routine cost accumulation systems. For example, product life-cycle costs may be expressed in the form of a product budget. In Exhibit 19.7, we see that in the early stages of a product life-cycle relatively small spending on research and development may mask the importance of this phase in determining and locking in the huge bulk of production costs. Life-cycle costing draws extensively on the techniques of target costing, which we introduced in Chapter 15 in connection with pricing decisions. As was argued there, target costing is more than just a pricing technique as it *manages costs* rather than just passively measures them. The aim of target costing is to choose product and process technologies that give an acceptable profit at a planned level of output. Once a product has been designed and has gone into production, not much can be done to significantly reduce its cost. Most of the opportunities to reduce cost come from designing the product so that it is simple to make, uses inexpensive parts, and is robust and reliable. If the company has little control over market price and little control over cost once the product has gone into production, then it follows that the major opportunities for affecting profit come in the design stage where valuable features that customers are willing to pay for can be added and where most of the costs are really determined. So that is where the effort is concentrated – in designing and developing the product. The difference between target costing and other approaches to product development is profound. Instead of designing the product and then finding out how much it costs, the target cost is set first and then the product is designed so that the target cost is attained.

FOCUS

Focus on current practice

Target costing is widely used in the car industry. The target cost for a new model is decomposed into target costs for each of the elements of the car – down to a target cost for each of the individual parts. The designers draft a trial blueprint, and a check is made to see if the estimated cost of the car is within reasonable distance of the target cost. If not, design changes are made, and a new trial blueprint is drawn up. This process continues until there is sufficient confidence in the design to make a prototype car according to the trial blueprint. If there is still a gap between the target cost and estimated cost, the design of the car will be further modified.

After repeating this process a number of times, the final blueprint is drawn up and turned over to the production department. In the first several months of production, the target costs will ordinarily not be achieved due to problems in getting a new model into production. However, after that initial period, target costs are compared to actual costs and discrepancies between the two are investigated with the aim of eliminating the discrepancies and achieving target costs.[6]

19.7 EXHIBIT

	Years		
	1	2	3
Costs and revenues			
Units sold	20,000	210,000	200,000
Unit price	£50	£45	£40
Research			
R&D costs	£750,000	£20,000	–
Manufacturing			
Unit variable cost	£16	£16	£16
Variable cost per batch	£700	£700	£700
Distribution			
Computers per batch	400	500	500
Fixed costs	£200,000	£600,000	£600,000
Unit variable costs	£2	£2	£2
Computers per batch	200	200	200
Marketing			
Fixed costs	£400,000	£400,000	£400,000
Post sales			
Fixed costs	£240,000	£240,000	£240,000
Unit service costs	£1	£1	£1

Exhibit 19.7 A product life-cycle budget: Wise plc – new hand-held computer

As up to 90% of cost[7] may be committed or locked in at pre-production stages, management accountants have become more aware of the design and planning phases of the product life-cycle. The distinction between and differential timing of incurred and locked-in costs are illustrated in Exhibit 19.8. The biggest gap is at the research and development stage, where although this function may generate a relatively low proportion of a product's total cost, decisions made here lock in the costs incurred in the manufacturing and marketing phases. In recognition of the importance of the planning phase, *life-cycle* costing tries to estimate a product's costs over its lifetime.

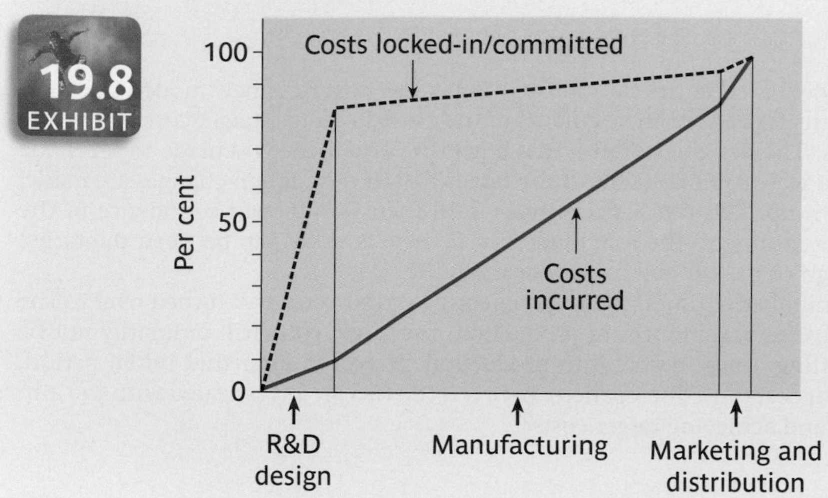

Exhibit 19.8 The product life-cycle: incurred versus locked-in/committed costs

As well as recognizing the importance of the design phase, life-cycle costing also anticipates cost improvements during the manufacturing cycle. This aspect is sometimes known as **kaizen costing** as it is part of the wider philosophy of continuous improvement. Some of the cost improvements will occur through a process of 'learning-by-doing' as workers get more adept at their tasks. Managers may routinize cost reduction through an approach known as **kaizen budgeting**. Rather than devise budgets on standard costs that are based on *past* performance, kaizen budgeting plans for *incremental* improvements in efficiency and reductions in costs.

Target costing and design

In a competitive market, the design process has to embrace both commercial and technical considerations. Just as management accountants are more aware of design, designers have become increasingly aware of the need to design to cost and quality targets set by competitive conditions. The resulting customer-oriented design is a *team process* with potential inputs from a number of disciplines. Best practice in terms of designing to cost is to assign costs to the functions of product rather than to blocks of components. This technique, which is sometimes known as *attribute costing* (see Chapter 16), aims to encourage creativity rather than continuity in design characteristics.

The creativity of designers may also be guided by techniques such as **value engineering** or **value analysis**. Value in this context may be defined as the ratio of functionality to cost. Thus value may be improved by holding functionality and reducing cost or by increasing functionality while holding cost. Product improvement may stem from innate creativity; it may also emerge from an analysis of competitors' products and processes through techniques associated with target costing such as *teardown analysis, reverse engineering* and *benchmarking*. Although this section has emphasized the cost management aspects of design, we must not forget that design is not just about copying and cost control. As Summers puts it: 'Design, closely allied to innovation, is the key to standing out and maintaining competitiveness'.[8]

Some problems with target and life-cycle costing

One problem with target costing is that it may reveal an unpalatable view of a company's internal operations, exposing uncompetitive practices and processes that were hidden by more traditional costing techniques. Another problem is that it may be too time-consuming. Thus, while it may be appropriate in the car industry, which is based on relatively mature technologies and lengthy product life cycles, it is less appropriate in industries such as electronics, where the rate of innovation is extremely rapid and time-to-market must be minimized. The other feature of life-cycle costing is that it implicitly assumes a relatively orderly value chain with a dominant customer who can plan the design and delivery of the product. In an industry such as personal computers (PCs), some of the major players are the companies that supply the software (Microsoft) and the microprocessors (Intel). Leading-edge technical innovation is in the hands of these companies rather than the PC assemblers.

The make or buy decision from a strategic perspective: supply chain management

The PC industry is a particularly advanced example of supply chain management. Many companies and industries are only just beginning to realize the cost management implications of their supply chains. For them, the implementation of a supply chain strategy may begin with the realization of the quantitative importance of bought-in material and services. We have already seen how substantial locked-in costs are, and thus how important product design can be. The importance of supply chain management is dawning on companies as they realize that (apart from the obvious example of retailers who have always been aware of the importance of the purchasing function), bought-in goods and services are quantitatively more significant than internally generated costs. For example, two-thirds of the value of the North American car industry is in the suppliers while 40% of all electronics manufacturers plan to outsource 90% or more of their final product.[9]

Although the historical focus in management accounting has been on the control of *internal* costs, there are areas where traditional management accounting techniques do have an impact on the supply chain. For example, the costs of bought-in materials and services may conventionally be managed through a standard costing system, which identifies variances in material costs and usage. Similarly, as we saw in Chapter 9, the make or buy decision may be viewed as an application of the concept of relevant costs and revenues. Yet these examples themselves illustrate that supply chain management has until recently been a marginal rather than a central concern in management accounting.

In this chapter, we will take a more strategic perspective through the linked concepts of the value chain and supply chain management. The value chain is not just a model of business processes within the firm. Many steps may be involved in getting a finished product into the hands of a consumer and these may involve a number of independently owned companies. First, raw materials have to be obtained through mining, drilling, growing crops, raising animals, and so forth. Second, these raw materials have to be processed to remove impurities and to extract the desirable and usable materials. Third, the usable materials may have to undergo some preliminary fabrication so as to be usable in final products. For example, cotton must be made into thread and textiles before being made into clothing. Fourth, the actual manufacturing of the finished product must take place. And finally, the finished product must be distributed to the ultimate consumer. All of these steps taken together are called an industry *value chain*. Separate companies may carry out each of the steps in the value chain or a single company may carry out several of the steps. When a company owns more than one of these steps in the value chain, it is following a policy of **vertical integration**. Vertical integration is very common. Some firms control all of the activities in the value chain from producing basic raw materials right up to the final distribution of finished goods. Other firms are content to integrate on a smaller scale by purchasing many of the parts and materials that go into their finished products. The value chain illustrated in Exhibit 19.9 shows that horizontal competition may be seen as rivalry between competing supply chains. The main management accounting issues in vertical integration are concerned with transfer pricing, which we covered in Chapter 15.

Integration versus sub-contracting

Integration provides certain advantages. An integrated firm is less dependent on its suppliers and may be able to ensure a smoother flow of parts and materials for production than a non-integrated firm that uses sub-contracting extensively. For example, a strike against a major parts supplier can interrupt the operations of a non-integrated firm for many months, whereas an integrated firm that is producing its own parts might be able to continue operations. Also, many firms feel that they can control quality better by producing their own parts and materials, rather than by relying on the quality control standards of outside suppliers. In addition, the integrated firm realizes profits from the parts and materials that it is 'making' rather than 'buying', as well as profits from its regular operations.

The advantages of integration are counterbalanced by some advantages of using external suppliers. By pooling demand from a number of firms, a supplier may be able to enjoy economies of scale in research and development and in manufacturing. These economies of scale can result in higher quality and lower costs than would be possible if the firm were to attempt to make the parts on its own. A company must be careful, however, to retain control over activities that are essential to maintaining its competitive position. For example, Hewlett-Packard controls the software for a laser printer that it makes in co-operation with Canon Inc. of Japan to prevent Canon from coming out with a competing product.

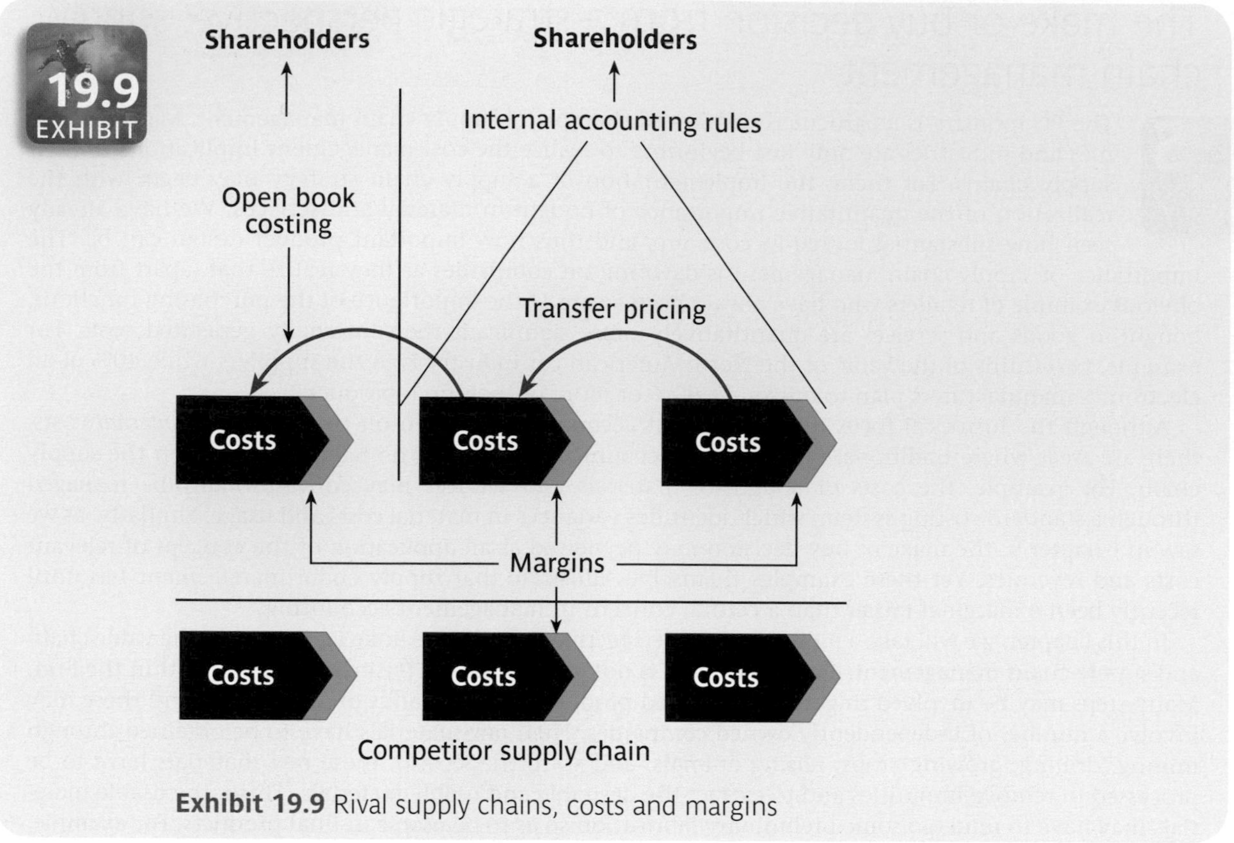

Exhibit 19.9 Rival supply chains, costs and margins

The present trend appears to be towards less vertical integration. As firms outsource more and more of their activities, the buy-or-make decision becomes part of an approach known as **supply chain management**. This draws on many of the techniques that we have covered in previous chapters. Supply chain management is an important part of lean production, which, as we saw in Chapter 16, is a feature of new forms of competition. Lean production draws on other management innovations that we have looked at, such as JIT, TQM and BPR and target costing. Most of these new techniques are themselves enabled by new technology such as EDI, ERP and the internet (Chapter 18). However, it would be wrong to see supply chain management as simply a matter of choosing particular management accounting techniques. Some types of supply chain management seek to develop close relationships with suppliers and customers, known as *strategic partnerships*. In these situations, management accounting may play a role in building new forms of collaboration that involve the sharing of information, such as cost data, that is traditionally guarded with great secrecy.[10]

Traditional supply relationships

The system of supply in a *traditional* tendering process was a game of negotiation. Since both buyers and sellers needed to show year-on-year gains, there was an incentive to keep supply chains slack. As bargaining revolved around the *piece price* of the component, buyers were not interested in the costs *per se* as, at least for non-customized components, they could simply scan the market for the possibility of lower piece prices on offer from other suppliers. On their part, the inbuilt uncertainty of demand meant that suppliers suffered from difficulties in planning production and had an incentive to save costs by shaving quality. In any case, traditional manufacturing was characterized by poor-quality cost accounting information that could not identify cost drivers in *the assemblers' own operations*, let alone in the operations of their suppliers. Not only were internal costs measured in an unsatisfactory way, there was also a failure to understand the 'all-in cost' of bought-in supplies. With long production runs, high levels of vertical integration and tolerance of high rates of defective components, the emphasis in purchasing was on short-term contracts awarded on the basis of lowest price. The lack of awareness of what was driving costs may have meant that the cheapest suppliers, from the point of view of competitive tendering, were not necessarily the best sources if the costs of actually incorporating the bought-in components into a final assembly could be determined. In any case, high levels of vertical integration implied that companies preferred to produce all but the most non-specific components in-house.

Exhibit 19.9 suggests that supply relationships are based on simple linear chains. The aim is to illustrate the difference between transfer pricing and open book costing. It is much more likely that supply relationships will have the characteristics of *networks as shown in Exhibit 19.10*. Here, there are a number of potential suppliers and customers with suppliers possibly supplying competitors and a number of possible customers. Individual *original equipment manufacturers (OEMs)* may try to rationalize this network by reducing the number of first tier suppliers and giving those suppliers more responsibility over areas such as component innovation and the co-ordination of second tier suppliers. With a smaller number of suppliers to deal with, strategic partnerships may be easier to develop.

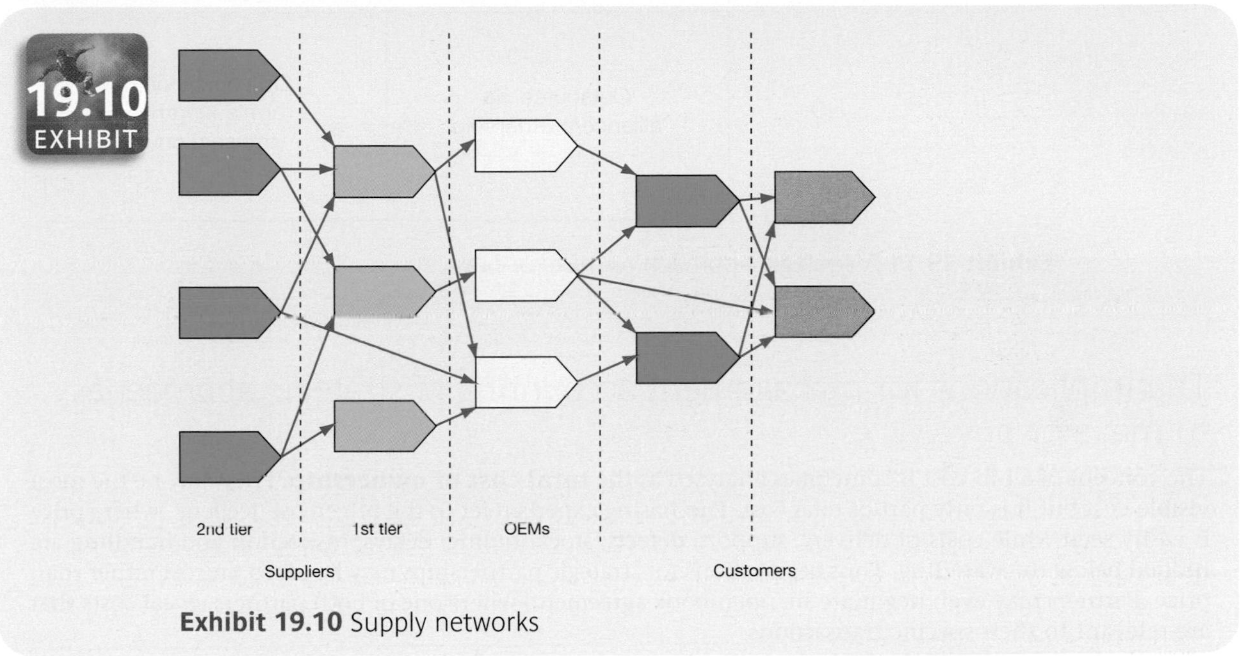

Exhibit 19.10 Supply networks

Strategic partnering

Strategic partnership sourcing involves a process of deliberate choice on the basis of current best practice in strategic sourcing. Strategic choice is affected by the competitive drivers that may themselves vary in importance between industries. A number of models have been proposed which try to make the strategic make or buy decision more systematic.

Most of these models involve classifying the components or bought-in services and then choosing the type of procurement model. Some approaches classify[11] bought-in items on the criteria of bottleneck, critical, routine and leverage. Other approaches classify components on the criterion of strategic importance.[12] The strategic subsystems may be decomposed into **'families' of components**. Even if the family is non-strategic, it may still be produced in-house if existing capacity is competitive. The long-term aim for non-strategic families, however, is to harvest. If the family is strategic then it will either be produced in-house or through a partnership with a supplier. What might seem strategic or 'core' to a company from an emotional point of view may not be central to a company's competitive advantage and may thus be outsourced to carefully chosen suppliers. This logic is summarized in Exhibit 19.11.

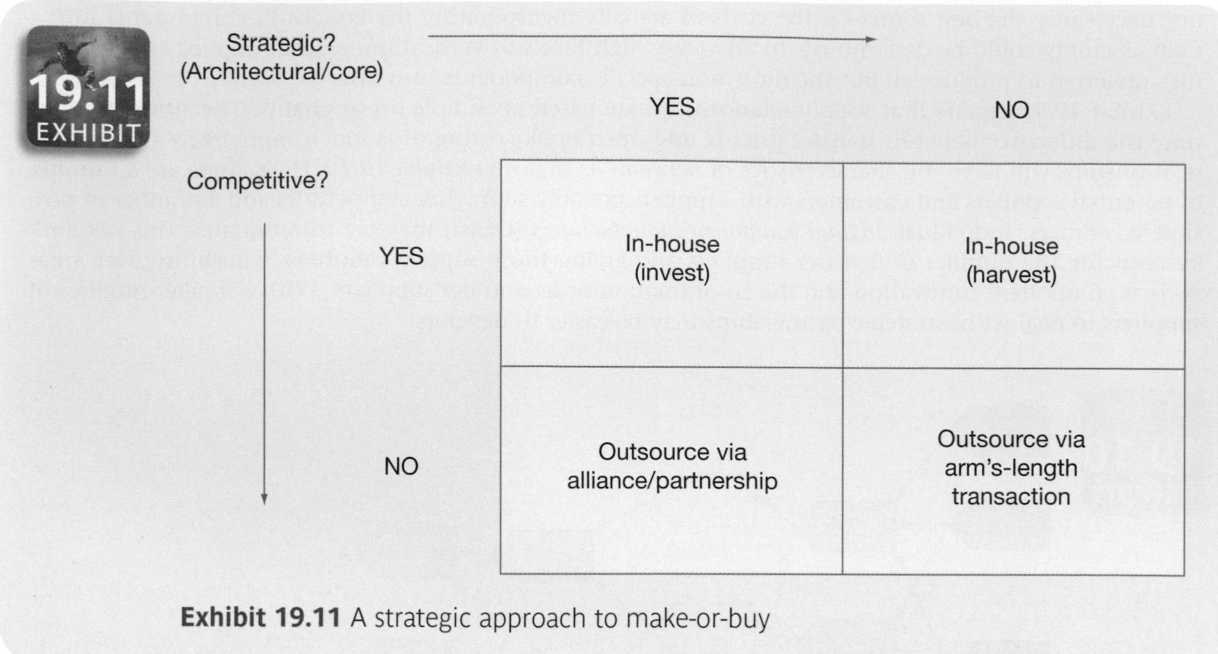

Exhibit 19.11 A strategic approach to make-or-buy

The implications for management accounting of strategic approaches to make or buy

The concept of all-in cost is sometimes analysed as the **total cost of ownership**. Price may be the most visible cost but it is only part of total cost. Purchasing experts refer to the price/cost 'iceberg', where price is easily seen while costs of delivery, support, defects, stockholding, delays, inspection and handling are hidden below the waterline. Thus negotiations for strategic partnerships may be based on cost rather than price. Partners may even negotiate an 'open-book agreement' where one or both partners reveal costs that are relevant to their specific transactions.

One reason for negotiating on costs is that knowledge of suppliers' costs enable more trusting relations because customers can see the margin that the supplier is making. As can be seen from Exhibit 19.9, suppliers will hope that the focus of improvement will be on taking out cost rather than eroding suppliers' margins. There is no long-term future for a partnership where one of the partners is not making adequate returns. Open-book agreements should reduce the scope for squeezing margins/or suppliers to exploit temporary competitive advantage. Changes may be agreed and the improvement in the transaction atmosphere allows a process of continuous improvement and even the bigger cost reductions that may be identified at the design stage. Open-book relations may not be based on partnership and trust but may be *forced*. Forced open-books may reduce slack in the system in the short run but the increased level of uncertainty and exits from the industry may make it difficult to identify competent suppliers.[13] The 'big stick' approach can work in industries characterized by low levels of concentration and low sophistication in product (such as in much of retailing) but it is a dangerous policy where the supplier has some leverage based on proprietary knowledge.

A summary of the implications for management accounting is shown in Exhibit 19.12. Note that we have already covered the techniques that are relevant to supply chain management. The innovation lies in the way that the techniques may be used in relatively unfamiliar inter-firm relations. The spirit underlying the use of cost data in inter-firm relations is that a 'win–win' situation pervades so that if cost is taken out of the supply chain then the benefits from the savings are shared out between the firms.[14]

FOCUS

Focus on current practice

Newtech[15] is a small Danish electronics manufacturer specializing in the sale of alarms to a variety of customers in industry and public and private sectors. Its alarms systems are very high tech and innovative – to such an extent that the firm could determine what customers could expect or what is technically feasible. Newtech's competitive advantage was based on rapid innovation through new technologies such as infrared, thermostatic and molecular sensors. But the rapid rate of technological change created new challenges with much shorter product life cycles. Furthermore, the firm could not have expertise in all these areas. Their response was to use their suppliers' expertise. They identified two groups of suppliers:

1 Producers of standard components
2 Suppliers with whom they developed new products.

Since the outsourcing led to feelings of loss of control, the company introduced target costing because it seemed to offer a way of regaining control. In addition, Newtech's purchasing budget took on a new prominence: 'The purchasing budget came to play a symbolic role in inter-organizational management controls. Thus, Newtech created a sense of financial urgency in the production and development work. The purchasing budget specified how Newtech drew on other firms' development competences and related them to its own situation.'

Another feature of target costing – functional analysis – encouraged systematic discussion between Newtech and suppliers. There was an unintended outcome to the outsourcing strategy. The functional analysis redefined what Newtech was about in terms of technology, strategy and organization. The company began to see itself as a 'technology co-ordinator' rather than a 'technology developer', as before. Newtech managed at a distance and used the techniques of functional analysis and purchase budgeting to add its specialized market knowledge to the development process.

19.12 EXHIBIT

Management accounting technique	Supply chain implications
Total cost of ownership	Recognition that the cost of acquiring goods and services includes more than just quoted piece price
Life cycle costing	Locked-in cost issues may affect suppliers
Target costing	External sourcing influenced by cost and design specifications set by the market
Kaizen costing	Progressive cost cuts required of suppliers
Benchmarking	Enables JIT supply and purchasing based on knowledge of suppliers
TQM/BPR	Re-engineering/quality affect supplies, e.g. JIT systems
Strategic cost management	Competition is between supply chains rather than individual firms
Real-time IT systems (EDI,ERP and the internet)	Synchronization of production plans
Open-book accounting	Sharing of cost and output data enables partnership sourcing with sharing benefits of product enhancement, etc.

Exhibit 19.12 Management accounting and supply chain management

IN ACTION

Management accounting in action case study: It takes two to tango

This case[16] concerns the role of management accounting in the attempted formation of a strategic alliance as part of a supply chain strategy in the automotive engineering industry. There are two main players: an 'Assembler' and a 'Strategic Supplier'. In order to understand the case (and further our understanding of supply chains), it is important to appreciate the point of view of *both* of these parties.

The Assembler's supply chain management philosophy

The Assembler had a turnover of about £70 million and employed about 1,000 workers. It had recently become a subsidiary of a large US multinational. The company was not a final assembler but produced complex and technologically sophisticated subassemblies both for its parent and for outside customers. The company had begun to recognize the importance of purchasing/procurement by placing it in a focal position within the worldwide management structure. Although the company had a policy of local sourcing, its operations were themselves becoming increasingly global, with subsidiaries in the US, Europe (the former East Germany), India and China. In this context, local sourcing had translated into a global sourcing policy with key suppliers setting up plants close to the Assembler's overseas operations. The company's emerging sourcing policy was based on the logics outlined above in the section on strategic partnership (see especially Exhibit 19.11).

Although they had little experience of the implementation of collaborative agreements, the materials/procurement executives were aware of the underdevelopment of management accounting practices in collaborative agreements. They knew that the companies *should* be exchanging *cost* rather than piece-price data, with expectations that over time they would reduce their suppliers' costs rather than simply squeeze their margins (see Exhibit 19.9). Their problem was to translate these general partnership philosophies into robust practices, which would retain the long-term support of senior corporate management.

A draft alliance agreement

At the time of the fieldwork, the Strategic Supplier, which was also a subsidiary of a large multinational, was offering an open-book agreement plus rolling cost cuts in return for assurances on demand and participation in research and development. The companies had been doing business for about 25 years but until recently their relationship had been a traditional arm's-length one. The Assembler acknowledged that, at times, they had behaved quite opportunistically towards their suppliers, switching business on a monthly basis to exploit differential pricing agreements.

The initial draft was based on a document drawn up by the Assembler, which stressed the principle of an open and trusting relationship that 'delivers tangible and measurable benefits to both sides over a long period, and allows the sharing of ideas and information'. With an annual cost reduction target of 6% for controllable costs, changes in raw materials prices and exchange rate movements were to be agreed by reference to published data. The document specified areas for continuous improvement, a management review process and a grievance procedure. The alliance proposed that cross-company teams should design mutually beneficial technological projects, which were to be jointly funded but with the Assembler having the first use for a determined period.

The Strategic Supplier

The Strategic Supplier had an advanced proprietary process with two plants. While the original plant in the UK was quite old, the plant in the US was both new and dedicated to supplying the Assembler in the US. Although controlled from the UK, it served not only as a *technical* exemplar but also as a good model of a supplier/assembler business relationship.

Although the Supplier did want a closer European relationship, it had reservations about the draft alliance document that had been proposed by the assembler. The Supplier was particularly concerned about the clause that specified a 6% annual cost reduction for three years without a clear definition of cost. Their bargaining position was that they *could* reduce the all-in cost to the Assembler *if* they could become the sole supplier in the UK and did more engineering work on the component, as they did in the US. As it stood, they argued that the draft document was not an open-book agreement and lacked mutuality. They argued that knowledge of the Assembler's costs would help them to make replacement decisions on customized machine tools to the mutual benefit of both partners. Open-book agreements may also involve sharing information on rates of return. But returns could vary between industries. Thus while a 5% return was normal in the Assembler's industry in recent years, the parent company of the Supplier expected 9–10%.

The development of the relationship

Progress was made in the following areas, with the Assembler agreeing:

- To interpret the 6% cost-reduction as a reduction in 'all-in cost'.
- That some of the value-added work on the component could be moved to the Supplier as growth in demand allowed.
- That the shared design approach was aimed primarily to upgrade the performance of the component rather than reduce its cost.

Some problems emerged:

- Difficulties in the measurement of cost reductions and the allocation of the partnership benefits between the parties.
- Difficulties in defining the boundaries of activities, i.e. what information would be shared.
- Difficulties in demonstrating the benefits of the alliance (some of which were quantitative but not necessarily financial) to senior management.

The evolution of the agreement

At the next meeting between the two senior managers, the discussions proceeded on the basis that the alliance had already agreed on the following matters:

- Single sourcing had been ruled out.
- *Specific* cost-reduction targets were no longer specified in a document but were expected to emerge from detailed discussions between multi-functional teams from both companies.
- The alliance was to be developed through a one-day brainstorming session involving mixed teams from both companies.
- The necessary detail was to be thrashed out through interaction involving a number of inter-company channels and through addressing particular problems and projects.

There are a number of special points to note in this case study:

1. **The role of cost data and other information-sharing in the construction of an agreement**

   The parties seemed to *begin* with a rather specific and detailed document that over time became less specific in detail but broader in terms of general commitment. In particular, with a change in personnel in both companies, the attitude seemed to become that if you knew how to take cost out of a product or process, then this was more important than the precise measurement of existing costs.

2. **No open-book agreement**

   Some of the difficulty in developing an open-book agreement seemed to be due to evident weaknesses in both firms' internal cost systems. Significantly, both companies were seeking to improve the management of their supply/distribution chains *at the same time* that they were seeking to make their accounting systems more 'relevant' through innovations such as the balanced scorecard.[17]

3. **Big cost savings were possible through redesign and relocation**

   As engineers, both managers were acutely aware that the really big cost savings were on offer not through incremental improvements to logistics in the supply chain but in *product design* and *locational* issues. Thus, as the Assembler became more cost-conscious in its designs, it would transmit these concerns down the supply chain through an informal form of target costing. On its part, the Supplier knew that dramatic cost savings could be achieved by closing the old UK factory and concentrating production in the modern but underutilized US factory.

4 Implications for management accounting

The ideal role for management accounting would seem to be in an open-book agreement whereby each partner can inspect the revenues and costs of the other party. Although the parties did not achieve a detailed open-book agreement, generic management accounting issues of cost measurement, cost reduction and non-financial performance measurement were still an important part of the looser understanding that was reached.

Corporate unbundling: shared service centres and service outsourcing

6 LEARNING OBJECTIVE

Some organizations have chosen to reorganize the provision of support services. There are two main types of reorganization: (1) shared service centres; and (2) outsourcing of services. Configuration (1), the shared service centre means that services are not supplied by an independently owned company. However, the shared service centre may be a prelude to configuration (2), full outsourcing, as when services are provided on the basis of a service agreement between the operating departments and the central service centre, it is technically, at least, a relatively short step to move from internal charging to an external contract.

The shared service centre model

There are number of different ways that shared service centres (SSC) can be organized and managed. Before we review these issues let us consider two definitions. A **shared service centre** is '(T)he concentration of company resources performing like activities, typically spread across the organization, in order to service multiple internal parties at lower cost and with higher service levels, with the common goal of delighting external customers and enhancing corporate value'.[18] Another source argues that '(S)hared services is a collaborative strategy in which a subset of existing business functions are concentrated in a new, semi-autonomous business unit that has a management structure designed to promote efficiency, value generation, cost savings, and improved service for internal customers of the parent corporation, like a business competing in the open market'.[19] The significance of the SSC can be seen more clearly when it is compared with the alternative multidivisional model in which each division is responsible for providing its own service support. The models are compared in Exhibit 19.13.

There are a number of advantages of the SSC model. Perhaps the most obvious advantage from the point of view of the parent company is that by concentrating service activities in one site, specially chosen for the purpose, the company can reduce costs. Some authors have suggested that an 'easy' 25–30% reduction in costs is possible with the promise of progressive pressure on the SSC as it may itself be threatened by outsourcing to an even lower cost location.[20] But there are more than cost advantages. The SSC should provide better service than the old service departments where there was always a danger that employees in the business units saw themselves as fulfilling low status 'back office functions'. The new SSC culture can 'shake the feeling that they are "low value added employees" performing "cost centre" activities' since the culture of the SSC is affected by the knowledge that providing support service is its core business.[21] The SSC can focus its core competences, standardize processes and apply the best technology appropriate to a service business. The appropriate technology may involve ERP systems combined with other technologies used in call centres which link voice, video and data interaction capability.[22] The standardization and technology may mean that the SSC possibly employ cheaper junior staff but the scale and new focus of the organization should enable it to recruit and concentrate on top experts and professionals. A sophisticated knowledge management perspective may even see the SSC as an opportunity attempt to repackage intellectual capital of company-knowledge management decision about core competences and the management of customer capital, human capital and structural capital.[23] We will explore this approach in more detail later in the chapter when we look at outsourcing. Although SSCs are usually associated with 'back-end processes' like payroll and human resource management and billing, the SSC may be used to provide some strategic services such as market intelligence, marketing, sales and customer support.

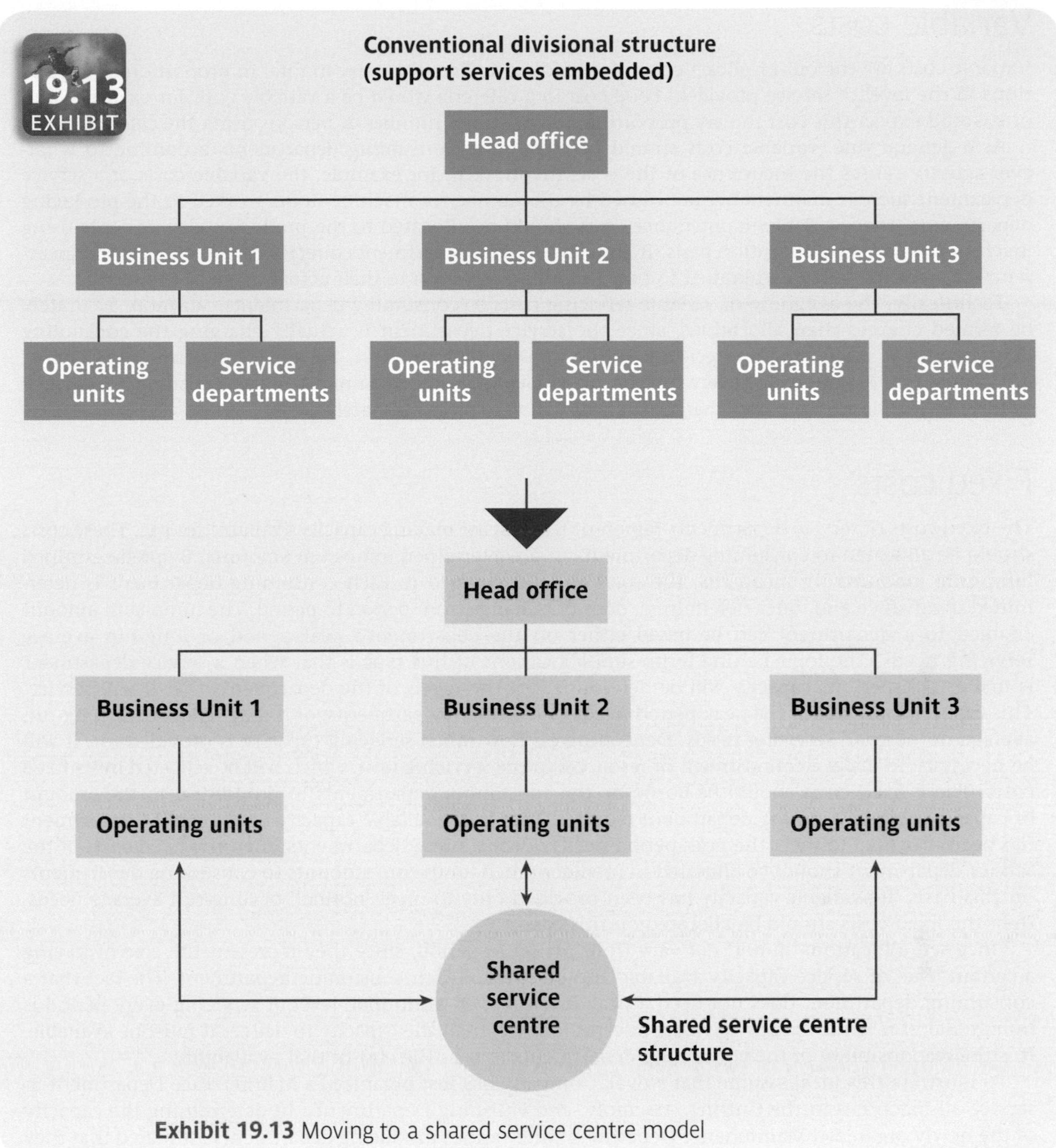

Exhibit 19.13 Moving to a shared service centre model

SSCs: competition and pricing issues

We have already looked at issues of costing and pricing service departments in Chapter 3. It is argued that if the SSC is treated like a pure cost centre and costs are allocated then the SSC can concentrate on service provision without worrying about pricing. The disadvantage is that there is less of a break with the old model, it is difficult to obtain costing information for benchmarking and there is little incentive to reduce costs. An intermediate position is to allocate costs by behaviour.

Whenever possible, service department costs should be separated into variable and fixed classifications and allocated separately. This approach is necessary to avoid possible inequities in allocation, as well as to provide more useful data for planning and control of departmental operations.

Variable costs

Variable costs are the out-of-pocket costs of providing services that vary in total in proportion to fluctuations in the level of service provided. Food cost in a cafeteria would be a variable cost, for example, and one would expect this cost to vary proportionately with the number of persons using the cafeteria.

As a general rule, variable costs should be charged to consuming departments according to whatever activity causes the incurrence of the costs involved. If, for example, the variable costs of a service department such as maintenance are caused by the number of machine-hours worked in the producing departments, then variable maintenance costs should be allocated to the producing departments using machine-hours as the allocation basis. By this means, the departments directly responsible for the incurrence of servicing costs are required to bear them in proportion to their actual usage of the service.

Technically, the assigning of variable servicing costs to consuming departments can more accurately be termed charges than allocations, since the service department is actually charging the consuming departments at some fixed rate per unit of service provided. In effect, the service department is saying, 'I'll charge you X pounds for every unit of my service that you consume. You can consume as much or as little as you desire; the total charge you bear will vary proportionately.'

Fixed costs

The fixed costs of service departments represent the costs of making capacity available for use. These costs should be allocated to consuming departments in predetermined lump-sum amounts. By predetermined lump-sum amounts we mean that the total amount charged to each consuming department is determined in advance and, once determined, does not change from period to period. The lump-sum amount charged to a department can be based either on the department's peak-period or long-run average servicing needs. The logic behind lump-sum allocations of this type is that when a service department is first established, its capacity will be determined by the needs of the departments that it will service. This capacity may reflect the peak-period needs of the other departments, or it may reflect their long-run average or 'normal' servicing needs. Depending on how much servicing capacity is provided for, it will be necessary to make a commitment of resources to the servicing unit, which will be reflected in its fixed costs. These fixed costs should be borne by the consuming departments in proportion to the amount of capacity each consuming department requires. That is, if available capacity in the service department has been provided to meet the peak-period needs of consuming departments, then the fixed costs of the service department should be allocated in predetermined lump-sum amounts to consuming departments on this basis. If available capacity has been provided only to meet 'normal' or long-run average needs, then the fixed costs should be allocated on this basis.

Once set, allocations should not vary from period to period, since they represent the cost of having a certain level of service capacity available and on line for each consuming department. The fact that a consuming department does not need a peak level or even a 'normal' level of servicing every period is immaterial; if it requires such servicing at certain times, then the capacity to deliver it must be available. It is the responsibility of the consuming departments to bear the cost of that availability.

To illustrate this idea, assume that Novak Company has just organized a Maintenance Department to service all machines in the Cutting, Assembly, and Finishing Departments. In determining the capacity of the newly organized Maintenance Department, the various producing departments estimated that they would have the following peak-period needs for maintenance:

Department	Peak-period maintenance needs in terms of number of hours of maintenace work required	Percentage of total hours
Cutting	900	30
Assembly	1,800	60
Finishing	300	10
	3,000	100

Therefore, in allocating the Maintenance Department fixed costs to the producing departments, 30% (i.e., 900/3,000 = 30%) should be allocated to the Cutting Department, 60% to the Assembly Department, and

10% to the Finishing Department. These lump-sum allocations will not change from period to period unless there is some shift in peak-period servicing needs.

Should actual or budgeted costs be allocated?

Should the actual or budgeted costs of a service department be allocated to operating departments? The answer is that *budgeted* costs should be allocated. What's wrong with allocating actual costs? Allocating actual costs burdens the operating departments with any inefficiencies in the service department. If actual costs are allocated, then any lack of cost control on the part of the service department is simply buried in a routine allocation to other departments.

Any variance over budgeted costs should be retained in the service department and closed out at year-end against the company's revenues or against cost of goods sold, along with other variances. Operating department managers justifiably complain bitterly if they are forced to absorb service department inefficiencies.

Yet another approach is to treat the SSC as a profit centre, allow it to charge market prices and even bid for outside contracts. A more intermediate position is to use service level agreements with detailed provisions for fees and delivery clauses. These issues may draw on the principles introduced earlier in this chapter but will also be influenced by the *transfer pricing principles* that we introduced in Chapter 15.

Overall, the great advantage of the SSC when compared with outsourcing is that it should be possible to improve efficiency and effectiveness of service delivery without the loss of control and dependency that may result from full outsourcing. With this warning in mind, we will now consider service outsourcing.

Service outsourcing

Although we have considered **outsourcing** as a possible response to the problem of constraints, there are usually a number of motives for service outsourcing which are very similar to those reviewed above in connection with SSCs. In comparison with outsourcing, SSCs have high start-up costs and may take time to embed the necessary cultural change. Many companies outsource in order to cut costs, to free up staff to concentrate on core operations, to access specialist expertise in areas like IT, to free up cash and speed up set-up.[24] Companies are making an explicit attempt to review the supply chain and ask where the 'natural ownership'[25] of activities lies. Rather than just look at the product in a strategic version of make-or-buy, managers ask more fundamental questions about *what the company should be doing*. Many companies are actually three businesses – a *customer relationship* business, a *product innovation* business, and an *infrastructure* business.[26] Each business is characterized by different cultures and different economics. For example, the infrastructure business requires economics of scale and an emphasis on cost minimization through standardization, predictability and efficiency. The product innovation business has to be employee-centred, with an emphasis on 'coddling' the company's creative stars. Lower interaction costs allow these competences to be unbundled and reconfigured so that the different economics and cultures can be recognized through increased corporate specialization.

One of the implications of corporate unbundling for management accounting is that increased corporate specialization should make it easier to design appropriate performance measurement systems. While there still needs to be a balance of measures, a customer-focused business will not need the same balance of indicators as an infrastructure business.

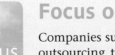

Focus on current practice

Companies such as Procter & Gamble, Boeing, Dell, Eli Lilly and Motorola are increasingly outsourcing their research and development (R&D) activities to lower labour cost Asian countries. Allen Delattre, head of Accenture's high-tech consulting practice, says 'R&D is the single remaining controllable expense to work on. Companies either will have to cut costs or increase R&D productivity'. In light of this stark reality, most Western companies are creating a global model of innovation that leverages the skills of Indian software developers, Taiwanese engineers and Chinese factories. The lower labour rates available in these countries coupled with their strong technology orientation makes 'buying' R&D capability from overseas more attractive than relying solely on their domestic workforce to 'make' R&D breakthroughs.

From a strategic point of view, the organization can concentrate its attention on its core activities. For example, Boots has outsourced many services such as catering because it is not in business as a caterer. Although as with other forms of outsourcing the main motive for change may be cost management, reorganizations of support services give a considerable impetus to attempts to ascertain the costs of products, jobs and customers more accurately through the use of techniques such as activity-based costing.

Outsourcing the finance function

Service areas such as human resources, IT, administration and purchasing have been generally leading the way in outsourcing contracts, but there may be a case for outsourcing the finance function. Although it is generally seen as too much of a core business process to outsource, it is possible, in principle, to distinguish between transactional tasks such as payroll, purchase and sales ledgers which can be outsourced and other areas such as *management accounting* which are more contentious.[27] However, as the Focus on current practice box below suggests, this distinction may beg the question as to which tasks are management accounting and which tasks are routine transactions and reporting. For example, local business unit managers need to feel a sense of ownership over the reports that they are signing off, credit control may be a vital part of local customer relations.

FOCUS

Focus on current practice

Kitchen manufacturer, Magnet, has outsourced accounts payable, credit control, general accounting, reporting and auditing to Liberata. According to David Orr, '(T)he finance department can be divided into two clear categories. At the top end there's strategy and policy-making, which is heavy-duty, value-added stuff. At the bottom end is the transactional stuff, which tends to be clerical and manual.'[28] Outsourcing is often associated with offshoring to cheaper locations such as India. The headline outsourced activity is call centres but less well known is the growing use of relatively low cost but high quality graduate labour in southern and eastern Asia.

SSCs and outsourcing strategies perhaps might force management accountants to reflect on what their unique contribution can be, whether it is as business partners in the business units or as custodians of financial integrity. For example, where should budgeting be located? This function is seen as a particular grey area depending upon whether it is routine and mechanical or whether it is closely allied to business strategy and operations. Although the practice of outsourcing and centralization in SSCs is increasing, the amount of academic research in this area is very limited.[29] It is easy to get the consultants' and outsourcers' generally upbeat evaluations of the process. It is much harder to gain access to the business units and the SSCs on a basis that might enable a more balanced and critical approach.

As the trend for outsourcing gathers momentum, there are emerging problems. For example, the outsourcing of the supply chain in the US car industry has been accompanied by a long-term squeeze on suppliers' margins and returns. As suppliers struggle the car manufacturers have begun to face quality problems (Firestone and Ford) and delays in product launches (Daimler Chrysler and its Smart Car).[30] In the UK, the separation of the ownership of track and infrastructure from the ownership of the train operators has led to problems with safety, punctuality and, even more recently, corporate administration for Railtrack. In both these cases, there has been a lack of co-operation between the parties and certainly no attempt to institute a technique such as open-book accounting. Companies sometimes fail to identify their key operations. For example, budget airlines such as Go will not consider outsourcing their cabin staff as these are the areas where they spend time with their customers. The US airline industry has been criticized for outsourcing security before the events of 11 September 2001, as has Railtrack for its outsourcing of line maintenance.[31] In both instances, the industries put a low value on safety with disastrous human and commercial consequences.

Summary

- In the short run, organizations are faced with resource constraints. Linear programming is a mathematical technique that may be used to find an optimal solution in a multi-product, multi-constraint world.
- The theory of constraints emphasizes the importance of managing the organization's constraints. Since the constraint is whatever is holding back the organization, improvement efforts usually must be focused on the constraint in order to be really effective.
- In the long run, constraints can be anticipated through the design of products and processes. The challenge here is to plan and manage costs throughout the life cycle of a product. The design phase may take cost management into the supply chain.
- A strategic approach to make-or-buy may indicate significant gains to be realized from outsourcing firms' activities. The firm may try to maintain some control over the outsourced activities through partnerships – alliances supported by techniques such as open-book accounting.
- New organizational forms such as shared service centres and outsourcing are having an increasing impact on the delivery of business services. These restructurings raise fundamental questions about the status of sensitive services such as the finance function.

Key terms for review

Constraint (p. 798).

Corner point (p. 795).

'Families' of components (p. 805).

Feasible region (p. 795).

Iso-contribution line (p. 795).

Kaizen budgeting (p. 802).

Kaizen costing (p. 802).

Limiting factor (p. 794).

Objective function (p. 795).

Optimal combination of product (p. 795).

Outsourcing (p. 813).

Relaxing (or elevating) the constraint (p. 797).

Sensitivity analysis (p. 796).

Shadow prices (p. 797).

Shared service centre (p. 810).

Simplex method (p. 794).

Supply chain management (p. 804).

Theory of constraints (TOC) (p. 798).

Throughput accounting (TA) (p. 800).

Throughput accounting ratio (p. 800).

Total cost of ownership (p. 805).

Value engineering/value analysis (p. 802).

Vertical integration (p. 803).

Questions

19–1 Under what circumstances is linear programming appropriate for the analysis of decision making under constraints?

19–2 Which point defines the optimal output in a linear programming problem?

19–3 Why might sensitivity analysis be a useful technique in a linear programming problem?

19–4 Why does the theory of constraints emphasize managing constraints?

19–5 What are six ways of relaxing a constraint?

19–6 In what way does throughput accounting misrepresent the theory of constraints?

19–7 How do you decide whether a component is strategic or non-strategic?

19–8 Why does supply management emphasize cost rather than price?

19–9 Suggest some problems that may be encountered in a major outsourcing contract.

Exercises

E19–1 Time allowed: 15 minutes

Listed below are a number of terms that relate to just-in-time, total quality management, process re-engineering, and theory of constraints:

Benchmarking	Non-value-added activities
Business process	Plan-do-check-act cycle
Constraint	Process re-engineering
Frequent	Pull
Just-in-time (JIT)	Set-up
Non-constraint	Total quality management

Choose the term or terms above that most appropriately complete the following statements:

1 To successfully operate a JIT system, a company must learn to rely on a few suppliers who are willing to make ______ deliveries.

2 ______ is an incremental approach to improvement, whereas ______ tends to be a much more radical approach that involves completely redesigning business processes.

3 A production system in which units are produced and materials are purchased only as needed to meet actual customer demand is called ______.

4 In JIT, the flow of goods is controlled by what is described as a ______ approach to manufacturing.

5 Increasing the rate of a ______ as the result of an improvement effort is unlikely to have much effect on profits.

6 ______ involves studying the business processes of companies that are considered among the best in the world at performing a particular task.

7 The activities involved in getting equipment ready to produce a different product are called a ______.

8 The theory of constraints suggests that improvement efforts should be focused on the company's ______.

9 The —— is a systematic, fact-based approach to continuous improvement that resembles the scientific method.

10 In process re-engineering, two objectives are to simplify and to eliminate ______.

11 A ______ is any series of steps that are followed in order to carry out some task in a business.

PROBLEMS

Problems

P19–2 Pricing/ABC/throughput accounting Time allowed: 45 minutes

LM Hospital is a private hospital whose management is considering the adoption of an activity-based costing (ABC) system for the year 2001/02. The main reason for its introduction would be to provide more accurate information for pricing purposes. With the adoption of new medical technology, the amount of time that some patients stay in hospital has decreased considerably, and the management feels that the current pricing strategy may no longer reflect the different costs incurred.

Prices are currently calculated by determining the direct costs for the particular type of operation and adding a markup of 135%. With the proposed ABC system, the management expects to use a markup for pricing purposes of 15% on cost. This percentage will be based on all costs except facility sustaining costs. It has been decided that the hospital support activities should be grouped into three categories – admissions and record keeping, caring for patients, and facility sustaining.

The hospital has four operating theatres that are used for 9 hours a day for 300 days a year. It is expected that 7,200 operations will be performed during the coming year. The hospital has 15 consultant surgeons engaged in operating theatre work and consultancy. It is estimated that each consultant surgeon will work at the hospital for 2,000 hours in 2001/02.

The expected costs for 2001/02 are:

	£
Nursing services and administration	9,936,000
Linen and laundry	920,000
Kitchen and food costs (3 meals a day)	2,256,000
Consultant surgeons' fees	5,250,000
Insurance of buildings and general equipment	60,000
Depreciation of buildings and general equipment	520,000
Operating theatre	4,050,000
Pre-operation costs	1,260,000
Medical supplies – used in the hospital wards	1,100,000
Pathology laboratory (where blood tests, etc. are carried out)	920,000
Updating patient records	590,000
Patient/bed scheduling	100,000
Invoicing and collections	160,000
Housekeeping activities, including ward maintenance, window cleaning, etc.	760,000

Other information for 2001/02:

Nursing hours	480,000
Number of pathology laboratory tests	8,000
Patient days	44,000
Number of patients	9,600

Information relating to specific operations for 2001/02:

	ENT (ear, nose and throat)	Cataract
Time of stay in hospital	4 days	1 day
Operation time	2 hours	0.5 hour
Consultant surgeon's time (which includes time in the operating theatre)	3 hours	0.85 hour

Required

1 Before making the final decision on the costing/pricing system, management has selected two types of operation for review: an ear, nose and throat (ENT) operation and a cataract operation.

(a) Calculate the prices that would be charged under each method for the two types of operation. (Your answer should include an explanation and calculations of the cost drivers you have used.) *(10 marks)*

(b) Comment on the results of your calculations and the implications for the proposed pricing policy. *(5 marks)*

2 Critically assess the method you have used to calculate the ABC prices by selecting two items/categories above which you feel should have been dealt with in a different way. *(5 marks)*

3 Explain whether the concept of throughput accounting could be used in a hospital. *(5 marks)*

(Total = 25 marks)

CIMA Management Accounting – Decision Making, May 2001

P19–3 Cost management/JIT Time allowed: 45 minutes

The WYE hotel group operates a chain of 50 hotels. The size of each hotel varies, as do the services that each hotel provides. However, all of the hotels operated by the group provide a restaurant, swimming pool, lounge bar, guest laundry service and accommodation.

Some of the hotels also provide guest entertainment, travel bureaux and shopping facilities. The Managing Director of the group is concerned about the high level of running costs being incurred by the hotels.

Required

1 Explain how cost reduction, value analysis and zero-based budgeting techniques could be used by the WYE hotel group to improve the profitability of its hotels. *(15 marks)*

2 M plc is a food manufacturer. It operates a just-in-time (JIT) system with computer-controlled, automated processing and packaging equipment. The focus of M plc's weekly management reports is on the variance analysis that is generated from a standard absorption costing system that uses labour hours as the basis of overhead absorption.

3 Explain why standard costing systems based upon absorption costing principles may be inappropriate in the modern manufacturing environment of companies such as M plc. *(10 marks)*

(Total = 25 marks)

CIMA Management Accounting – Performance Management, May 2001

P19–4 Linear programming Time allowed: 45 minutes

DP plc assembles computers from bought-in components, using a computer controlled robotic assembly line. The assembled computers are then tested by highly qualified computer engineers before they are packaged for despatch to customers. DP plc currently assembles two different types of computer from different combinations of the same components.

The following budgeted details relate to the computers:

	Computer X	Computer Y
Selling price/unit	£800	£1,200
Component costs per unit	£150	£310
	Minutes per unit	**Minutes per unit**
Assembly time (S1)	80	130
Testing time (S2)	120	180
Packaging time (S3)	60	30

The following costs are derived from DP plc's budget for the year to 31 December 2001:

Assembly	£180/hour
Testing	£60/hour
Packaging	£20/hour

No cost increases are expected until July 2002.

DP plc is now preparing its detailed plans for the six-month period to 30 June 2002. During this period, it expects that the assembly time available will be limited to 1,000 hours and the testing time available will be limited to 875 hours. The packaging is carried out by part-time workers, and the company believes that there are a number of local residents who would be pleased to undertake this work if the existing packaging staff were unable to complete the level of activity needed.

The maximum levels of demand for each computer will be:

300 units of X (S4)

800 units of Y (S5).

Required

1 Calculate the contribution per unit for each type of computer. *(2 marks)*

2 Determine the mix of computers that will maximize DP plc's profits for the six months ending 30 June 2002, using a graphical linear programming solution, and calculate the contribution that will be earned. *(8 marks)*

3 DP plc now realizes that there may be a limit on the number of packaging hours available. A computer package for linear programming has been used and the following solution determined:

Variables	
X	268.75
Y	112.50
Constraints	
S1	23,875.00
S2	1.46
S3	4.75
S4	31.25
S5	687.50
Contribution	£107,437.50

Write a report to the management team that interprets the solution produced by the computer package and makes appropriate recommendations. (*Note:* Do not formulate, or explain the basis of, the computer model.) *(7 marks)*

4 At the management meeting that discussed the report you produced in Question 3 above, the senior computer engineer responsible for the testing of the computers was surprised at the times per unit being used in your calculations.

'It seems to me', she said, 'that you have used the testing times per unit that were set as the targets when those models of computer were first assembled. We seem to test them much more quickly than this now.'

Explain how the learning effect referred to by the senior computer engineer will affect the calculation of the optimum product mix. Use a 90% learning curve to illustrate your answer but do not determine a revised product mix. (*Note:* The formula for a 90% learning curve is $y = ax^{-0.1520}$.)

(8 marks)

(Total = 25 marks)

CIMA Management Accounting – Performance Management, November 2001

P19–5 E-commerce/budgeting/value analysis Time allowed: 45 minutes

ML plc was formed three years ago to develop e-commerce systems and design websites for clients. The company has expanded rapidly since then and now has a multi-site operation with bases in the UK and overseas.

ML plc has recognized the need to formalize its planning and budgeting procedures and one of its divisional managers has been assigned to co-ordinate the budgets for the year to 31 March 2003. He recently attended a course on Financial Planning and Budgeting and has been puzzled by some of the concepts. In particular, he would like you to explain the following:

- The differences and similarities between zero-based budgeting and activity based budgeting
- The reasons why budget holders should prepare their own budgets
- The reasons why incremental budgeting may not be appropriate as a basis of budgeting if budget bias is to be minimized.

Required

1 Prepare a report, addressed to the divisional manager, that explains the issues he has identified above. *(15 marks)*

2 Techniques that are used in order to improve an organization's performance include:

- Cost reduction
- Value analysis.

Explain these techniques and how they may be used by ML plc as part of its planning activities.

(10 marks)

(Total = 25 marks)

CIMA Management Accounting – Performance Management, November 2001

P19–6 Multiple products, life-cycle and target costing Time allowed: 45 minutes

'Costing systems attempt to explain how products consume resources but do not indicate the joint benefits of having multiple products.'

Required

1 Explain the statement above and discuss

(a) How the addition of a new product to the product range may affect the 'cost' of existing products;

(b) The consequences, in terms of total profitability, of decisions to increase/decrease the product range. *(10 marks)*

2 Telmat is a company that manufactures mobile phones. This market is extremely volatile and competitive and achieving adequate product profitability is extremely important. Telmat is a mature

company that has been producing electronic equipment for many years and has all the costing systems in place that one would expect in such a company. These include a comprehensive overhead absorption system, annual budgets and monthly variance reports and the balanced scorecard for performance measurement.

The company is considering introducing:

(a) Target costing

(b) Life-cycle costing systems.

Discuss the advantages (or otherwise) that this specific company is likely to gain from these two systems. *(15 marks)*

(Total = 25 marks)

CIMA Management Accounting – Decision Making, November 2001

P19–7 Linear programming Time allowed: 50 minutes

W plc provides two cleaning services for staff uniforms to hotels and similar businesses. One of the services is a laundry service and the other is a dry cleaning service. Both of the services use the same resources, but in different quantities. Details of the expected resource requirements, revenues and costs of each service are shown below:

	Laundry $ per service	**Dry cleaning $ per service**
Selling price	7.00	12.00
Cleaning materials ($10.00 per litre)	2.00	3.00
Direct labour ($6.00 per hour)	1.20	2.00
Variable machine cost ($3.00 per hour)	0.50	1.50
Fixed costs*	1.15	2.25
Profit	2.15	3.25

*The fixed costs per service were based on meeting the budget demand for December 2003.

W plc has already prepared its budget for December based on sales and operational activities of 8,000 laundry services and 10,500 dry cleaning services, but it is now revising its plans because of forecast resource problems.

The maximum resources expected to be available in December 2003 are:

Cleaning materials	5,000 litres
Direct labour hours	6,000 hours
Machine hours	5,000 hours

W plc has one particular contract which it entered into six months ago with a local hotel to guarantee 1,200 laundry services and 2,000 dry cleaning services every month. If W plc does not honour this contract it has to pay substantial financial penalties to the local hotel.

Required

1 Calculate the mix of services that should be provided by W plc so as to maximize its profit for December 2003. *(9 marks)*

2 The Sales Director has reviewed the selling prices being used by W plc and has provided the following further information:

- if the price for laundry were to be reduced to $5.60 per service, this would increase the demand to 14,000 services;
- if the price for dry cleaning were to be increased to $13.20 per service, this would reduce the demand to 9,975 services.

Assuming that such selling price changes would apply to *all sales* and that the resource limitations continue to apply, and that a graphical linear programming solution is to be used to maximize profit,

(a) state the constraints and objective function; *(6 marks)*

(b) use a graphical linear programing solution to advise W plc whether it should revise its selling prices. *(10 marks)*

CIMA Performance Management, November 2003

CASE

Cases

C19–8 Linear programming Time allowed: 60 minutes

The Puxi Company manufactures consumer food products, based on soya beans. For convenience purposes the three products can be referred to as Alpha (A), Beta (B) and Cappa (C). The production process is relatively simple. In the Mixing Department, the raw material ingredients are crushed and mixed into a soft paste. This is a machine-intensive rather than labour-intensive process. The 'paste' is then transferred to a Filling Department where the product is bottled, labelled and packaged for distribution. Again, this is a machine-intensive process. Direct labour is a relatively small amount in the overall cost structure. As a result, the company has combined direct labour cost with overhead costs into a 'conversion cost' category.

In recent months, the manager of Puxi Company has become concerned about various 'constraints' facing his company. Perhaps most important was the limited supply of domestically grown soya beans. As a result, the soya beans had to be imported from the US. Unfortunately, most of the soya bean crop grown in the US is genetically modified (GM) and must be tested before use. The practical implication of this is that the supply of soya beans will be limited for the next planning period.

These and other restrictions were discussed at a recent budget meeting of various section managers and are summarized as follows:

1 Supply of soya bean limited to 500,000 kg, equivalent to a total cost of $500,000.

2 Machine hours availability in the Mixing Department restricted to 3,000 hours due to obsolete machinery.

3 Machine hour availability in the Filling Department restricted to 2,000 hours due to shortage of machine parts.

4 Contracts had already been signed with various customers to supply a minimum of 10,000 units of each of the three products for next year. These minimum units must be produced.

5 Because no increase or decrease in selling price could be made for next year, the maximum demand for the three products was estimated as follows:

Alpha (A) =	60,000 units
Beta (B) =	60,000 units
Cappa (C) =	60,000 units

The following information is provided regarding the three products:

Product information	Product A	Product B	Product C
Selling prince per unit	$20	$26	$38
Soya bean ingredient cost @ $1 per kg	3	4	6
Variable conversion costs*	6	8	12
Fixed production overhead costs **	6	8	12
Profit per unit	5	6	8
Machine minutes per unit:			
Dept. 1 (maximum 3,000 hours)	1 minute	1 minute	2 minutes
Dept. 2 (maximum 2,000 hours)	¾ minute	1 minute	1¼ minutes

*Variable conversion cost represents variable direct labour and variable overheads but excludes direct material cost.

**The fixed production overhead costs have been absorbed on the basis of direct material, i.e. soya bean cost, using a production level of 40,000 units of each of the three products.

After looking at the information, you quickly present the above data as a linear programming model and solve it using Lindo.

Computer printout for Puxi Company using LINDO software

1 Max 11A + 14B + 20C	(Objective function)
ST	Subject to (the following restrictions)
2 3A + 4B + 6C < 500,000	Maximum kgs and spend on Soya ingredients
3 1A + 1B + 2C < 180,000	Maximum machine mins. In Mixing Department
4 0.75A + 1B + 1.25C < 120,000	Maximum machine mins. In Filling Department
5 A > 10,000	Minimum production units of product A
6 B > 10,000	Minimum production units of product B
7 C > 10,000	Minimum production units of product C
8 A < 60,000	Maximum sales units of product A
9 B < 60,000	Maximum sales units of product B
10. C < 60,000	Maximum sales units of product C
Objective function value	$1,760,000
A	60,000 (units)
B	50,000 (units)
C	20,000 (units)

Row	Slack or surplus	Dual (shadow) price
2 (Soya)	Nil	2.50
3 (Mixing dept)	30,000	0.00
4 (Filling dept)	Nil	4.00
5 Minimum units of A	50,000	0.00
6 Minimum units of B	40,000	0.00
7 Minimum units of C	10,000	0.00
8 Maximum sales units of A	Nil	0.50
9 Maximum sales units of B	10,000	0.00
10 Maximum sales units of C	40,000	0.00

Sensitivity Analysis: Ranges in which the basis remains unchanged

Variable $	Current contribution $	Allowable increase $	Allowable decrease
A	11.00	Infinity	0.50
B	14.00	0.66	0.66
C	20.00	1.00	2.50

Right hand side ranges

Row No.	Current RHS	Allowable increase	Allowable decrease
2	500,000	32,000	8,000
3	180,000	Infinity	30,000
4	120,000	1,667	6,667
5	10,000	50,000	Infinity
6	10,000	40,000	Infinity
7	10,000	10,000	Infinity
8	60,000	53,333	13,333
9	60,000	Infinity	10,000
10	60,000	Infinity	40,000

Required

1 Indicate the total sales revenue, the total contribution ($) generated by the optimal production plan and indicate the physical quantities (units) of each of the three products according to the optimal production plan. Also, indicate the net profit for the period based on the optimal plan.

2 Calculate the break-even point (BEP) in $ revenue, assuming the constant product mix of the optimal production plan.

3 Clearly identify the impact, if any, on the optimal production plan and on profit of the following independent events.

   (a) Selling price of product A increased by $1.

   (b) An additional supply of £1,000 of soya beans is available.

   (c) An additional 1,000 minutes of Mixing time becomes available.

   (d) An additional 1,000 minutes in Filling becomes available.

4 Identify and explain what is the opportunity cost, if any, associated with the minimum production of 10,000 units of Product A.

5 What is the maximum price that one would pay for one extra kilogram of soya bean ingredient, bearing in mind that each kilogram currently costs $1 per kg? Briefly explain your answer.

6 Briefly explain three limitations associated with using linear programming as a tool of managerial decision making in this manufacturing company.

7 Some manufacturing companies are currently experiencing a shortage of skilled labour. Suggest three ways in which this constraint could be relaxed, where the company employs a combination of skilled and unskilled labour.

(Thanks to Peter Clarke of University College Dublin for this case)

Endnotes

1 Kuglin and Rosenbaum (2001).

2 Students familiar with elementary economics may compare the linear programming model with the curved line called the *production possibility frontier*. While the basic principles are very similar, linear programming enables greater operationality.

3 See Johnson and Kaplan (1987) for an extended justification for managing rather than optimizing.

4 Galloway and Waldron (1988).

5 See Dugdale and Jones (1998); Jones and Dugdale (1998).

6 Monden and Hamada (1991).

7 Tanaka, Yoshikawa, Innes and Mitchell (1994).

8 Summers (2002).

9 Doig, Ritter, Speckhals and Woolson (2001).

10 See Seal, Cullen, Dunlop, Berry and Mirghani (1999).

11 Baily, Farmer, Jessop and Jones (1998).

12 Venkatesan (1992).

13 Lamming (1993).

14 Best practice in supply chain management may not be enough to ensure business survival. See Seal, Berry and Cullen (2004).

15 A real company but the name has been changed. See Mouritsen, Hansen and Hansen (2001a).

16 This is a shorter version of the case study in Seal *et al.* (1999).

17 For more research on open book agreements see Kajüter and Kulmala (2005).

18 Schulman, Dunleavy, Harmer and Lusk (1999), p. 9.

19 Bergeron (2003), p. 3.

20 Quinn, Cooke and Kris (2000).

21 Schulman *et al.* (1999).

22 Schulman *et al.* (1999).

23 Bergeron (2003).

24 Hayward (2002).

25 The term 'natural ownership' was used in Doig *et al.* (2001).

26 Hagel and Singer (1999).

27 Hayward (2003).

28 *Ibid*, p. 19.

29 But see Herman and Brignall (2004).

30 Doig *et al.* (2001).

31 Hayward (2002).

Glossary

Absorption costing A costing method that includes all manufacturing costs – direct materials, direct labour and both variable and fixed overhead – as part of the cost of a finished unit of product. This term is synonymous with full cost (p. 62).

Account analysis A method for analysing cost behaviour in which each account under consideration is classified as either variable or fixed based on the analyst's prior knowledge of how the cost in the account behaves (p. 165).

Action analysis report A report showing what costs have been assigned to a cost object, such as a product or customer, and how difficult it would be to adjust the cost if there is a change in activity (p. 294).

Activity An event that causes the consumption of overhead resources in an organization (p. 278).

Activity base A measure of whatever causes the incurrence of a variable cost. For example, the total cost of X-ray film in a hospital will increase as the number of X-rays taken increases. Therefore, the number of X-rays is an activity base for explaining the total cost of X-ray film (p. 157).

Activity consumption rate The quantity of each activity required to produce a unit of demand (p. 533).

Activity cost pool A 'bucket' in which costs are accumulated that relate to a single activity in the activity-based costing system (p. 282).

Activity measure An allocation base in an activity-based costing system; ideally, a measure of the amount of activity that drives the costs in an activity cost pool (p. 282).

Activity-based budgeting (ABB) An analysis of business processes which derives a financial model based on an operational plan (p. 533).

Activity-based costing (ABC) A costing method based on activities that is designed to provide managers with cost information for strategic and other decisions that potentially affect capacity and therefore fixed costs (p. 276).

Activity-based management (ABM) The use of cost driver data to identify process improvements (p. 768).

Adjusted R^2 A measure of goodness of fit in least-squares regression analysis. It is the percentage of the variation in the dependent variable that is explained by variation in the independent variable (p. 172).

Administrative costs All executive, organizational and clerical costs associated with the general management of an organization rather than with manufacturing, marketing or selling (p. 24).

Allocation base A measure of activity such as direct labour-hours or machine-hours that is used to assign costs to cost objects (p. 67).

Appraisal costs Costs that are incurred to identify defective products before the products are shipped to customers (p. 760).

Attribute costing Costing the product attributes that appeal to customers (p. 679).

Avoidable cost Any cost that can be eliminated (in whole or in part) by choosing one alternative over another in a decision-making situation. In managerial accounting, this term is synonymous with relevant cost and differential cost (p. 324).

Balanced scorecard An integrated set of performance measures that is derived from and supports the organization's strategy (p. 684).

Batch-level activities Activities that are performed each time a batch of goods is handled or processed, regardless of how many units are in a batch. The amount of resource consumed depends on the number of batches run rather than on the number of units in the batch (p. 281).

Belief systems Systems that motivate search behaviour in strategy (p. 717).

Benchmarking Making comparisons against best practice in other organizations (p. 691).

Bill of materials A document that shows the type and quantity of each major item of materials required to make a product (p. 64).

Bottleneck A machine or process that limits total output because it is operating at capacity (p. 338).

Boundary systems Systems that constrain search and innovation in strategy (p. 717).

Break-even point The level of sales at which profit is zero. The break-even point can also be defined as the point where total sales equals total expenses or as the point where total contribution margin equals total fixed expenses (p. 232).

Budget A detailed plan for the acquisition and use of financial and other resources over a specified time period (p. 5).

Budget committee A group of key management persons who are responsible for overall policy matters relating to the budget programme and for co-ordinating the preparation of the budget (p. 438).

Budget variance A measure of the difference between the actual fixed overhead costs incurred during the period and budgeted fixed overhead costs as contained in the flexible budget (p. 530).

Business process A series of steps that are followed in order to carry out some task in a business (p. 12).

Capital budgeting The process of planning significant outlays on projects that have long-term implications, such as the purchase of new equipment or the introduction of a new product (p. 372).

Cash budget A detailed plan showing how cash resources will be acquired and used over some specific time period (p. 439).

Clan model When the control of an organization is motivated by a desire for peer approval and an avoidance of deviance from group ideals (p. 732).

Committed fixed costs Those fixed costs that are difficult to adjust and that relate to the investment in facilities, equipment, and the basic organizational structure of a firm (p. 161).

Common costs A common cost is a cost that is common to a number of costing objects but cannot be traced to them individually. For example, the wage cost of the pilot of a 747 airliner is a common cost of all of the passengers on the aircraft. Without the pilot, there would be no flight and no passengers. But no part of the pilot's wage is caused by any one passenger taking the flight (p. 36).

Common fixed cost A fixed cost that supports more than one business segment, but is not traceable in whole or in part to any one of the business segments (p. 184).

Constrained management style A management approach that concentrates on easy to measure events and lacks flexibility (p. 715).

Constraint A limitation under which a company must operate, such as limited machine time available or limited raw materials available that restricts the company's ability to satisfy demand (p. 10).

Continuous or perpetual budget A 12-month budget that rolls forward one month as the current month is completed (p. 436).

Contribution approach A profit statement format that is geared to cost behaviour in that costs are separated into variable and fixed categories rather than being separated according to the functions of production, sales, and administration (p. 173).

Contribution margin The amount remaining from sales revenues after all variable expenses have been deducted (p. 173).

Contribution margin method A method of computing the break-even point in which the fixed expenses are divided by the contribution margin per unit (p. 239).

Contribution margin ratio (CM ratio) The contribution margin as a percentage of total sales (p. 233).

Control The process of instituting procedures and then obtaining feedback to ensure that all parts of the organization are functioning effectively and moving towards overall company goals (p. 5).

Controlling Ensuring that the plan is actually carried out and is appropriately modified as circumstances change (p. 4).

Conversion cost Direct labour cost plus manufacturing overhead cost (p. 23).

Corner point A potential solution in a linear programming problem (p. 795).

Corporate governance This term may be narrowly defined as the mechanisms that are used to protect the interests of the suppliers of capital to corporations (p. 13).

Corporate social responsiveness (or responsibility) Refers to the capacity of the organization to respond to the demands of society as a whole (p. 714).

Cost behaviour The way in which a cost reacts or responds to changes in the level of business activity (p. 32).

Cost centre A business segment whose manager has control over cost but has no control over revenue or the use of investment funds (p. 577).

Cost driver A factor, such as machine-hours, beds occupied, computer time, or flight-hours, that causes overhead costs (p. 69).

Cost leadership Aiming to be the lowest cost producer in an industry (p. 680).

Cost object Anything for which cost data are desired. Examples of possible cost objects are products, product lines, customers, jobs and organizational subunits such as departments or divisions of a company (p. 35).

Cost of capital The overall cost to an organization of obtaining investment funds, including the cost of both debt sources and equity sources (p. 377).

Cost of goods manufactured The manufacturing costs associated with the goods that were finished during the period (p. 28).

Cost reconciliation The part of a production report that shows what costs a department has to account for during a period and how those costs are accounted for (p. 132).

Cost structure The relative proportion of fixed, variable and mixed costs found within an organization (p. 156).

Cost-plus pricing A pricing method in which a predetermined mark-up is applied to a cost base to determine the target selling price (p. 630).

Costs of not carrying sufficient stock Those costs that result from not having enough stock to meet customers' needs; such costs include lost sales, customer ill will, and costs of expediting orders for items not in stock (p. 747).

Cost–volume–profit (CVP) graph The relations between revenues, costs and level of activity in an organization presented in graphic form (p. 240).

Curvilinear costs A relationship between cost and activity that is a curve rather than a straight line (p. 159).

Customer-level activities Activities that are carried out to support customers but that are not related to any specific product (p. 281).

Decentralization The delegation of decision-making authority throughout an organization by providing managers at various operating levels with the authority to make key decisions relating to their area of responsibility (p. 8).

Decentralized organization An organization in which decision making is not confined to a few top executives but rather is spread throughout the organization (p. 576).

Defender A company which concentrates on reducing costs and/or improving quality in existing markets/products (p. 680).

Degree of operating leverage A measure, at a given level of sales, of how a percentage change in sales volume will affect profits. The degree of operating leverage is computed by dividing contribution margin by profit (p. 245).

Delivery cycle time The amount of time required from receipt of an order from a customer to shipment of the completed goods (p. 688).

Denominator activity The activity figure used to compute the predetermined overhead rate (p. 527).

Dependent variable A variable that reacts or responds to some causal factor; total cost is the dependent variable, as represented by the letter *Y*, in the equation $Y = a + bX$ (p. 168).

Diagnostic control systems Cybernetic, feedback-based models of management control (p. 717).

Differential cost A difference in cost between any two alternatives. Also see Incremental cost (p. 36).

Differential revenue The difference in revenue between any two alternatives (p. 36).

Direct cost A cost that can easily and conveniently be traced to the particular cost object under consideration (p. 35).

Direct costing Another term for variable costing. See Variable costing (p. 200).

Direct labour Those factory labour costs that can easily be traced to individual units of product. Also called touch labour (p. 22).

Direct materials Those materials that become an integral part of a finished product and can conveniently be traced into it (p. 22).

Direct labour budget A detailed plan showing labour requirements over some specific time period (p. 445).

Direct method The allocation of all of a service department's costs directly to operating departments without recognizing services provided to other service departments (p. 95).

Direct materials budget A detailed plan showing the amount of raw materials that must be purchased during a period to meet both production and stock needs (p. 444).

Directing and motivating Mobilizing people to carry out plans and run routine operations (p. 4).

Discretionary fixed costs Those fixed costs that arise from annual decisions by management to spend in certain fixed cost areas, such as advertising and research (p. 161).

Double loop learning uses information to learn from past performance in order to change processes, change inputs or alter objectives (p. 691).

Ease of adjustment codes Costs are coded as Green, Yellow or Red – depending on how easily the cost could be adjusted to changes in activity. 'Green' costs adjust automatically to changes in activity without any action by managers. 'Yellow' costs could be adjusted in response to changes in activity, but such adjustments require management action; the adjustment is not automatic. 'Red' costs could be adjusted to changes in activity only with a great deal of difficulty and the adjustment would require management action (p. 293).

Economic lot size The number of units produced in a lot, or production run, that will result in minimizing set-up costs and the costs of carrying stock (p. 750).

Economic order quantity (EOQ) The order size for materials that will result in minimizing the costs of ordering and carrying stock (p. 747).

Economic value added (EVA) A concept similar to residual profit (p. 593).

Electronic data interchange (EDI) The electronic transmission of data on customer orders and transactions inside and between companies (p. 757).

Ending finished goods stock budget A budget showing the cost expected to appear on the balance sheet for unsold units at the end of a period (p. 446).

Engineering approach A detailed analysis of cost behaviour based on an industrial engineer's evaluation of the inputs that are required to carry out a particular activity and of the prices of those inputs (p. 165).

Enterprise governance The duty of both company boards and executive managements to provide strategic direction, manage risks and verify that the organization uses its resources in a responsible way (p. 722).

Enterprise resource planning (ERP) The installation of integrated real time management information systems (p. 12).

Environmental costs (p. 728).

Environmental management accounting Collects and uses information on environment-related costs, earnings and savings for internal decision making (p. 14).

Equation method A method of computing the break-even point that relies on the equation Sales = Variable expenses + Fixed expenses + Profits (p. 238).

Equivalent units The product of the number of partially completed units and their percentage of completion with respect to a particular cost. Equivalent units are the number of complete whole units one could obtain from the materials and effort contained in partially completed units (p. 126).

Equivalent units of production (weighted-average method) The units transferred to the next department (or to finished goods) during the period plus the equivalent units in the department's ending work in progress stock (p. 127).

Executional drivers Cost factors such as work force involvement, quality management capacity utilization, plant lay-out efficiency, product configuration effectiveness, and exploitation of linkages (p. 680).

Expected value The average or mean outcome when faced with a range of possibilities (p. 403).

External failure costs Costs that are incurred when a product or service that is defective is delivered to a customer (p. 760).

'Families' of components If the family is non-strategic, it may be produced in-house if existing capacity is competitive. If the family is strategic then it will either be produced in-house or through a partnership with a supplier (p. 805).

Feasible region An area that shows all the possible combinations of two products (p. 795).

Feedback Accounting and other reports that help managers monitor performance and focus on problems and/or opportunities that might otherwise go unnoticed (p. 5).

Feedforward control Uses a predictive model of processes so that errors can be anticipated and corrected for (p. 716).

FIFO method A method of accounting for cost flows in a process costing system in which equivalent units and unit costs relate only to work done during the current period (p. 127).

Financial accounting The phase of accounting concerned with providing information to shareholders, creditors and others outside the organization (p. 4).

Financial stewardship Demonstrating to citizens and other tiers of government that public funds have been handled with probity and prudence (p. 730).

Finished goods Goods that have been completed but not yet sold to customers (p. 26).

First-stage allocation The process by which overhead costs are assigned to activity cost pools in an activity-based costing system (p. 283).

Fixed cost A cost that remains constant, in total, regardless of changes in the level of activity within the relevant range. If a fixed cost is expressed on a per unit basis, it varies inversely with the level of activity (p. 34).

Fixed manufacturing overhead cost deferred in stock The portion of the fixed manufacturing overhead cost of a period that goes into stock under the absorption costing method as a result of production exceeding sales (p. 204).

Fixed manufacturing overhead cost released from stock The portion of the fixed manufacturing overhead cost of a *prior* period that becomes an expense of the current period under the absorption costing method as a result of sales exceeding production (p. 209).

Flexible budget A budget that is designed to cover a range of activity and that can be used to develop budgeted costs at any point within that range to compare to actual costs incurred (p. 516).

Full cost See Absorption costing (p. 62).

High-low method A method of separating a mixed cost into its fixed and variable elements by analysing the change in cost between the high and low levels of activity (p. 166).

Ideal standards Standards that allow for no machine breakdowns or other work interruptions and that require peak efficiency at all times (p. 473).

Incremental analysis An analytical approach that focuses only on those items of revenue, cost, and volume that will change as a result of a decision (p. 235).

Incremental cost An increase in cost between two alternatives. Also see Differential cost (p. 36).

Incrementalism Increasing or decreasing existing budgets by small amounts without asking whether the underlying activities that are being financed are still necessary or provided in the most effective way (p. 729).

Independent variable A variable that acts as a causal factor; activity is the independent variable, as represented by the letter X, in the equation $Y = a + bX$ (p. 168).

Indirect cost A cost that cannot easily and conveniently be traced to the particular cost object under consideration (p. 36).

Indirect labour The labour costs of caretakers, supervisors, materials handlers, and other factory workers that cannot conveniently be traced directly to particular products (p. 23).

Indirect materials Small items of material such as glue and nails. These items may become an integral part of a finished product but are traceable to the product only at great cost or inconvenience (p. 23).

Interactive control systems The use of information to encourage debate up and down organizations and to foster an emergent process that links strategy with tactics (p. 717).

Interdepartmental services Services provided between service departments. Also known as Reciprocal services (p. 101).

Intermediate market A market in which a transferred product or service is sold in its present form to outside customers (p. 644).

Internal failure costs Costs that are incurred as a result of identifying defective products before they are shipped to customers (p. 760).

Internal rate of return The discount rate at which the net present value of an investment project is zero; thus, the internal rate of return represents the interest yield promised by a project over its useful life. This term is synonymous with time-adjusted rate of return (p. 378).

Investment centre A business segment whose manager has control over cost and over revenue and that also has control over the use of investment funds (p. 577).

Iso-contribution line Traces all the combinations of two products that could produce a particular total contribution (p. 795).

Job cost sheet A form prepared for each job that records the materials, labour and overhead costs charged to the job (p. 64).

Job-order costing system A costing system used in situations where many different products, jobs, or services are produced each period (p. 63).

Joint product costs Costs that are incurred up to the split-off point in producing joint products (p. 339).

Joint products Two or more items that are produced from a common input (p. 339).

Just-in-time (JIT) A production and inventory control system in which materials are purchased and units are produced only as needed to meet actual customer demand (p. 12).

Kaizen budgeting Rather than base budgets on historical standards, kaizen budgeting plans for incremental improvements in efficiency and reductions in costs (p. 802).

Kaizen costing The reduction of cost during production through continuous gradual improvements that reduce waste and increase efficiency (p. 490).

Key performance indicators (KPIs) A small set of indicators used by management to measure and control performance in an organization (p. 716).

Labour efficiency variance A measure of the difference between the actual hours taken to complete a task and the standard hours allowed, multiplied by the standard hourly labour rate (p. 484).

Labour rate variance A measure of the difference between the actual hourly labour rate and the standard rate, multiplied by the number of hours worked during the period (p. 484).

Lead time The interval between the time that an order is placed and the time that the order is finally received from the supplier (p. 752).

Lean enterprises Do not have a chance to create sustainable competitive advantage but can only repeatedly seek to create temporary advantages (p. 684).

Lean production Techniques that focus on matching supply and demand, reducing waste and eliminating defects (p. 747).

Least-squares regression method A method of separating a mixed cost into its fixed and variable elements by fitting a regression line that minimizes the sum of the squared errors (p. 171).

Levers of control model Approach associated with Simons (1995) that suggests ways by which tensions in strategy can be managed (p. 717).

Life-cycle costing Analyses costs incurred throughout the life of a product from development through to full production (p. 679).

Limiting factor A different term for a constrained resource that limits the choice of product mix (p. 794).

Line A position in an organization that is directly related to the achievement of the organization's basic objectives (p. 9).

Make or buy decision A decision as to whether an item should be produced internally or purchased from an outside supplier (p. 334).

Management accounting The phase of accounting concerned with providing information to managers for use in planning and controlling operations and in decision making (p. 4).

Management by exception A system of management in which standards are set for various operating activities, with actual results then compared to these standards. Any differences that are deemed significant are brought to the attention of management as 'exceptions' (p. 473)

Management control (p. 717).

Manufacturing cycle efficiency (MCE) Process (value-added) time as a percentage of throughput time (p. 689).

Manufacturing overhead All costs associated with manufacturing except direct materials and direct labour (p. 22).

Manufacturing overhead budget A detailed plan showing the production costs, other than direct materials and direct labour, that will be incurred over a specified time period (p. 445).

Margin Net operating profit divided by sales (p. 590).

Margin of safety The excess of budgeted (or actual) sales over the break-even volume of sales (p. 242).

Marginal costing Another term for variable costing. See Variable costing (p. 200).

Market price The price being charged for an item on the open (intermediate) market (p. 644).

Marketing mix Price is one element in product competitiveness together with product, promotion and place (p. 679).

Marketing or selling costs All costs necessary to secure customer orders and get the finished product or service into the hands of the customer (p. 23).

Mark-up The difference between the selling price of a product or service and its cost. The mark-up is usually expressed as a percentage of cost (p. 630).

Master budget A summary of a company's plans in which specific targets are set for sales, production, distribution, and financing activities and that generally culminates in a cash budget, budgeted profit and loss account, and budgeted balance sheet (p. 441).

Material loading charge A mark-up applied to the cost of materials that is designed to cover the costs of ordering, handling, and carrying materials in stock and to provide for some profit (p. 637).

Material requirements planning (MRP) An operations management tool that uses a computer to help manage materials and stocks (p. 444).

Materials price variance A measure of the difference between the actual unit price paid for an item and the standard price, multiplied by the quantity purchased (p. 480).

Materials quantity variance A measure of the difference between the actual quantity of materials used in production and the standard quantity allowed, multiplied by the standard price per unit of materials (p. 481).

Materials requisition form A detailed source document that specifies the type and quantity of materials that are to be drawn from the storeroom and identifies the job to which the costs of materials are to be charged (p. 64).

Maximin/maximax criterion A way by which decision makers may choose options when it is not possible to attach precise probabilities to outcomes (p. 408).

Merchandise purchases budget A budget used by a merchandising company that shows the amount of goods that must be purchased from suppliers during the period (p. 443).

Mixed cost A cost that contains both variable and fixed cost elements (p. 163).

Multiple predetermined overhead rates A costing system in which there are multiple overhead cost pools with a different predetermined rate for each cost pool, rather than a single predetermined overhead rate for the entire company. Frequently, each production department is treated as a separate overhead cost pool (p. 85).

Multiple regression An analytical method required in those situations where variations in a dependent variable are caused by more than one factor (p. 173).

Negotiated transfer price A transfer price agreed on between buying and selling divisions (p. 640).

Net operating profit Profit before interest and profit taxes have been deducted (p. 588).

Net present value The difference between the present value of the cash inflows and the present value of the cash outflows associated with an investment project (p. 373).

New Public Management refers to many of the reforms in the public sector that have been introduced since 1980 and which often make use of the measurement and management of public sector performance (p. 730).

Non-value-added activity An activity that consumes resources or takes time but that does not add value for which customers are willing to pay (p. 767).

Normal cost system A costing system in which overhead costs are applied to jobs by multiplying a predetermined overhead rate by the actual amount of the allocation base incurred by the job (p. 68).

Objective function Shows a number of possible outputs that maximize total contribution (p. 795).

Operating assets Cash, debtors, inventory, plant and equipment, and all other assets held for productive use in an organization (p. 589).

Operating departments A department or similar unit in an organization within which the central purposes of the organization are carried out (p. 93).

Operating leverage A measure of how sensitive profit is to a given percentage change in sales. It is computed by dividing the contribution margin by profit (p. 245).

Operation costing A hybrid costing system used when products are manufactured in batches and when the products have some common characteristics and some individual characteristics. This system handles materials the same as in job-order costing and labour and overhead the same as in process costing (p. 135).

Opportunity cost The potential benefit that is given up when one alternative is selected over another (p. 37).

Optimal combination of product The best that can be achieved given the constraints and the nature of the objective function (p. 795).

Optimizing Trying to get the best result subject to given constraints (p. 746).

Organization chart A visual diagram of a firm's organizational structure that depicts formal lines of reporting, communication, and responsibility between managers (p. 9).

Organizational learning In this business model, management accounting may be used as part of an interactive communication process both within the organization and between the organization and its customers and suppliers (p. 676).

Organization-sustaining activities Activities that are carried out regardless of which customers are served, which products are produced, how many batches are run, or how many units are made (p. 281).

Out-of-pocket costs Actual cash outlays for salaries, advertising, repairs and similar costs (p. 378).

Outsourcing The use of external suppliers to provide goods and services that used to be provided inside the organization (p. 13).

Overapplied overhead A credit balance in the Manufacturing Overhead account that arises when the amount of overhead cost applied to Work in Progress is greater than the amount of overhead cost actually incurred during a period (p. 78).

Overhead application The process of charging manufacturing overhead cost to job cost sheets and to the Work in Progress account (p. 67).

Participative budget *See* Self-imposed budget (p. 437).

Payback period The length of time that it takes for a project to recover its initial cost out of the cash receipts that it generates (p. 287).

Performance management An approach to maintaining or altering organizational behaviour based on formal, information-based routines. Also known as **management control** (p. 717).

Performance measurement system is a framework which measures and reviews organizational performance (p. 716).

Performance Prism is a system that includes five facets of business performance: stakeholder contribution, stakeholder satisfaction, strategies, processes and capabilities (p. 725).

Performance report A detailed report comparing budgeted data to actual data (p. 5).

Period costs Those costs that are taken directly to the profit and loss account as expenses in the period in which they are incurred or accrued; such costs consist of selling (marketing) and administrative expenses (p. 24).

Plan-do-check-act (PDCA) cycle A systematic approach to continuous improvement that applies the scientific method to problem solving (p. 764).

Planning and control cycle The flow of management activities through planning, directing and motivating, and controlling, and then back to planning again (p. 6).

Planning Selecting a course of action and specifying how the action will be implemented (p. 4).

Plantwide overhead rate A single predetermined overhead rate that is used throughout a plant (p. 85).

Postaudit The follow-up after a project has been approved and implemented to determine whether expected results are actually realized (p. 389).

Practical standards Standards that allow for normal machine downtime and other work interruptions and that can be attained through reasonable, though highly efficient, efforts by the average worker (p. 474).

Predetermined overhead rate A rate used to charge overhead cost to jobs in production; the rate is established in advance for each period by use of estimates of total manufacturing overhead cost and of the total allocation base for the period (p. 67).

Preference decision A decision as to which of several competing acceptable investment proposals is best (p. 372).

Prevention costs Costs that are incurred to keep defects from occurring (p. 758).

Price elasticity of demand A measure of the degree to which the volume of unit sales for a product or service is affected by a change in price (p. 630).

Prime cost Direct materials cost plus direct labour cost (p. 23).

Process costing A costing method used in situations where essentially homogeneous products are produced on a continuous basis (p. 120).

Process costing system A costing system used in those manufacturing situations where a single, homogeneous product (such as cement or flour) is produced for long periods of time (p. 62).

Process re-engineering An approach to improvement that involves completely redesigning business processes in order to eliminate unnecessary steps, reduce errors and reduce costs (p. 766).

Processing department Any location in an organization where work is performed on a product and where materials, labour or overhead costs are added to the product (p. 121).

Product costs All costs that are involved in the purchase or manufacture of goods. In the case of manufactured goods, these costs consist of direct materials, direct labour, and manufacturing overhead. *See also* Stock-related costs (p. 24).

Product differentiation Aims to maintain a price premium based on superior product quality (p. 680).

Production budget A detailed plan showing the number of units that must be produced during a period in order to meet both sales and stock needs (p. 442).

Production mix variance Measures the impact of substitution of materials (p. 541).

Production report A report that summarizes all activity in a department's Work in Progress account during a period and that contains three parts: a quantity schedule and a computation of equivalent units, a computation of total and unit costs, and a cost reconciliation (p. 121).

Production yield variance Measures the input–output relationship holding the standard mix inputs constant (p. 541).

Product-level activities Activities that relate to specific products that must be carried out regardless of how many units are produced and sold or batches run (p. 281).

Profit centre A business segment whose manager has control over cost and revenue but has no control over the use of investment funds (p. 577).

Profitability index The ratio of the present value of a project's cash inflows to the investment required (p. 386).

Prospector A company that is continually searching for market opportunities (p. 680).

Quality circles Small groups of employees that meet on a regular basis to discuss ways of improving quality (p. 760).

Quality cost report A report that details prevention costs, appraisal costs and the costs of internal and external failures (p. 761).

Quality costs Costs that are incurred to prevent defective products from falling into the hands of customers or that are incurred as a result of defective units (p. 758).

Quality of conformance The degree to which a product or service meets or exceeds its design specifications and is free of defects or other problems that mar its appearance or degrade its performance (p. 758).

Quantity schedule The part of a production report that shows the flow of units through a department during a period and a computation of equivalent units (p. 131).

Range of acceptable transfer prices The range of transfer prices within which the profits of both the selling division and the purchasing division would increase as a result of a transfer (p. 640).

Raw materials Any materials that go into the final product (p. 23).

Reciprocal method A method of allocating service department costs that gives full recognition to inter-departmental services (p. 93).

Reductionist model of humanity View that emphasizes material goals rather than creative and achievement orientations (p. 717).

Regression line A line fitted to an array of plotted points. The slope of the line, denoted by the letter b in the linear equation $Y = a + bX$, represents the average variable cost per unit of activity. The point where the line intersects the cost axis, denoted by the letter a in the above equation, represents the average total fixed cost (p. 169).

Relaxing (or elevating) the constraint Increasing the capacity of a bottleneck (p. 797).

Relevant cost A cost that differs between alternatives in a particular decision. In managerial accounting, this term is synonymous with avoidable cost and differential cost (p. 324).

Relevant range The range of activity within which assumptions about variable and fixed cost behaviour are valid (p. 35).

Reorder point The point in time when an order must be placed to replenish depleted stocks is determined by multiplying the lead time by the average daily or weekly usage (p. 751).

Required rate of return The minimum rate of return that an investment project must yield to be acceptable (p. 380).

Residual income The net operating profit that an investment centre earns above the required return on its operating assets (p. 593).

Resource consumption rate The quantity of each resource that produces one instance of an activity (p. 533).

Responsibility accounting A system of accountability in which managers are held responsible for those items of revenue and cost – and only those items – over which the manager can exert significant control. The managers are held responsible for differences between budgeted and actual results (p. 436).

Responsibility centre Any business segment whose manager has control over cost, revenue or the use of investment funds (p. 578).

Retainer fee approach A method of allocating service department costs in which other departments are charged a flat amount each period regardless of usage of the service involved (p. 101).

Return on investment (ROI) Net operating profit divided by average operating assets. It also equals margin multiplied by turnover (p. 588).

Return-on-management Sees management as a scarce resource that must make a return (p. 717).

Risk Formally, this is a situation when it is possible to attach some probability to outcomes (p. 403).

Risk management An approach to risk based on the establishment of effective internal controls (p. 722).

Safety stock The difference between average usage of materials and maximum usage of materials that can reasonably be expected during the lead time (p. 752).

Sales budget A detailed schedule showing the expected sales for coming periods; these sales are typically expressed in both pounds and units (p. 439).

Sales mix The relative proportions in which a company's products are sold. Sales mix is computed by expressing the sales of each product as a percentage of total sales (p. 248).

Sales mix variance Arises when a company sells multiple products and the products are (imperfect) substitutes for each other (p. 538).

Scattergraph method A method of separating a mixed cost into its fixed and variable elements. Under this method, a regression line is fitted to an array of plotted points by drawing a line with a straight edge (p. 168).

Schedule of cost of goods manufactured A schedule showing the direct materials, direct labour and manufacturing overhead costs incurred for a period and assigned to Work in Progress and completed goods (p. 28).

Screening decisions A decision as to whether a proposed investment meets some preset standard of acceptance (p. 372).

Second-stage allocation The process by which activity rates are used to apply costs to products and customers in activity-based costing (p. 287).

Segment Any part of an organization that can be evaluated independently of other parts and about which the manager seeks financial data. Examples include a product line, a sales territory, a division, or a department (p. 8).

Segment margin The amount computed by deducting the traceable fixed costs of a segment from the segment's contribution margin. It represents the margin available after a segment has covered all of its own costs (p. 584).

Self-imposed budget A method of preparing budgets in which managers prepare their own budgets. These budgets are then reviewed by the manager's supervisor, and any issues are resolved by mutual agreement (p. 437).

Sell or process further decision A decision as to whether a joint product should be sold at the split-off point or processed further and sold at a later time in a different form (p. 341).

Selling and administrative expense budget A detailed schedule of planned expenses that will be incurred in areas other than manufacturing during a budget period (p. 446).

Sensitivity analysis Involves calculating the effect of other possibilities, such as a rise in the market price of a product (p. 796).

Service departments A department that provides support or assistance to operating departments and that does not engage directly in production or in other operating activities of an organization (p. 93).

Set-up costs Costs involved in getting facilities ready to change over from making one product to another (p. 750).

Shadow prices Defined as the increase in value that would be created by having one additional unit of a limiting resource (p. 797).

Shared service centres Single locations where the support services of an entire corporation are concentrated (p. 13).

Simple rate of return The rate of return computed by dividing a project's annual accounting profit by the initial investment required (p. 390).

Simplex method A mathematical technique that solves linear programming problems (p. 794).

Special order A one-time order that is not considered part of the company's normal on-going business (p. 336).

Split-off point That point in the manufacturing process where some or all of the joint products can be recognized as individual products (p. 339).

Staff A position in an organization that is only indirectly related to the achievement of the organization's basic objectives. Such positions are supportive in nature in that they provide service or assistance to line positions or to other staff positions (p. 9).

Stakeholders Those with a stake in an organization such as customers, employees, suppliers, regulators and pressure groups as well as shareholders and other suppliers of capital (p. 725).

Standard cost card A detailed listing of the standard amounts of materials, labour and overhead that should go into a unit of product, multiplied by the standard price or rate that has been set for each cost element (p. 473).

Standard cost per unit The standard cost of a unit of product as shown on the standard cost card; it is computed by multiplying the standard quantity or hours by the standard price or rate for each cost element (p. 476).

Standard deviation A measure of risk that numerically captures the spread of outcomes around the mean or average (p. 404).

Standard hours allowed The time that should have been taken to complete the period's output as computed by multiplying the actual number of units produced by the standard hours per unit (p. 478).

Standard hours per unit The amount of labour time that should be required to complete a single unit of product, including allowances for breaks, machine downtime, cleanup, rejects, and other normal inefficiencies (p. 476).

Standard price per unit The price that should be paid for a single unit of materials, including allowances for quality, quantity purchased, shipping, receiving, and other such costs, net of any discounts allowed (p. 474).

Standard quantity allowed The amount of materials that should have been used to complete the period's output as computed by multiplying the actual number of units produced by the standard quantity per unit (p. 478).

Standard quantity per unit The amount of materials that should be required to complete a single unit of product, including allowances for normal waste spoilage, rejects and similar inefficiencies (p. 475).

Standard rate per hour The labour rate that should be incurred per hour of labour time, including employment taxes, fringe benefits and other such labour costs (p. 475).

Static budget A budget designed for only one level of activity (p. 516).

Statistical process control A charting technique used to monitor the quality of work being done in a workstation for the purpose of immediately correcting any problems (p. 760).

Step method The allocation of a service department's costs to other service departments, as well as to operating departments, in a sequential manner. The sequence starts with the service department that provides the greatest amount of service to other departments (p. 95).

Step-variable cost A cost (such as the cost of a maintenance worker) that is obtainable only in large chunks and that increases and decreases only in response to fairly wide changes in the activity level (p. 159).

Stock carrying costs Those costs that result from having stock in stock, such as rental of storage space, handling costs, property taxes, insurance and interest on funds. These costs also should include costs of excess work in progress stock such as inefficient production, excess lead times, high defect rates, and risks of obsolescence (p. 747).

Stock ordering costs Those costs associated with the acquisition of stock, such as clerical costs and transportation costs (p. 747).

Stock-related costs (also known as inventoriable costs) Synonym for product costs (p. 30).

Strategic choice Choosing not only which industries and products to compete in but also how a company plans to compete (p. 676).

Strategic management accounting The use of management accounting information to help managers choose where and how to compete (p. 10).

Structural drivers Factors such as scale, scope, experience, technology and complexity (p. 680).

Sub-optimization An overall level of profitability that is less than a segment or a company is capable of earning (p. 640).

Sunk cost Any cost that has already been incurred and that cannot be changed by any decision made now or in the future (p. 37).

Supply chain management An extension of the make-or-buy decision which takes a strategic perspective (p. 804).

Target costing The process of determining the maximum allowable cost for a new product and then developing a prototype that can be profitably manufactured and distributed for that maximum target cost figure (p. 635).

Theory of constraints (TOC) A management approach that emphasizes the importance of managing constraints (p. 12).

Throughput accounting (TA) Ranking products by calculating the throughput accounting ratio (p. 800).

Throughput accounting ratio Return per factory hour divided by cost per factory hour (p. 800).

Throughput time The amount of time required to turn raw materials into completed products (p. 689).

Time and material pricing A pricing method, often used in service firms, in which two pricing rates are established – one based on direct labour time and the other based on direct materials used (p. 637).

Time ticket A detailed source document that is used to record an employee's hour-by-hour activities during a day (p. 65).

Time-adjusted rate of return This term is synonymous with internal rate of return (p. 378).

Total cost of ownership Recognizes that price may only be a part of the total cost of obtaining a component or service and includes other costs such as delivery, support, defects, stockholding, delays, inspection and handling (p. 805).

Total quality management (TQM) An approach to continuous improvement that focuses on customers and using teams of front-line workers to systematically identify and solve problems. (p. 12).

Traceable fixed cost A fixed cost that is incurred because of the existence of a particular business segment (p. 582).

Transfer price The price charged when one division or segment provides goods or services to another division or segment of an organization (p. 639).

Transferred-in cost The cost attached to products that have been received from a prior processing department (p. 122).

Turnover The amount of sales generated in an investment centre for each pound invested in operating assets. It is computed by dividing sales by the average operating assets figure (p. 590).

Uncertainty Situations where it is not possible to attach probabilities to outcomes (p. 403).

Underapplied overhead A debit balance in the Manufacturing Overhead account that arises when the amount of overhead cost actually incurred is greater than the amount of overhead cost applied to Work in Progress during a period (p. 78).

Unit-level activities Activities that arise as a result of the total volume of goods and services that are produced, and that are performed each time a unit is produced (p. 281).

Value-based management (VBM) Focuses on how to increase shareholder wealth through the use of specific metrics and management systems (p. 678).

Value chain The major business functions that add value to a company's products and services (p. 587).

Value engineering/value analysis A technique for guiding product design through the analysis of the ratio of functionality to cost (p. 802).

Variable cost A cost that varies, in total, in direct proportion to changes in the level of activity. A variable cost is constant per unit (p. 33).

Variable costing A costing method that includes only variable manufacturing costs – direct materials, direct labour and variable manufacturing overhead – in the cost of a unit of product. Also called marginal costing or direct costing (p. 200).

Variable overhead efficiency variance The difference between the actual activity (direct labour-hours, machine-hours, or some other base) of a period and the standard activity allowed, multiplied by the variable part of the predetermined overhead rate (p. 486).

Variable overhead spending variance The difference between the actual variable overhead cost incurred during a period and the standard cost that should have been incurred based on the actual activity of the period (p. 486).

Variance The difference between standard prices and quantities on the one hand and actual prices and quantities on the other hand (p. 476).

Vertical integration The involvement by a company in more than one of the steps from production of basic raw materials to the manufacture and distribution of a finished product (p. 334).

Volume variance The variance that arises whenever the standard hours allowed for the output of a period are different from the denominator activity level that was used to compute the predetermined overhead rate (p. 531).

Weighted-average method A method of process costing that blends together units and costs from both the current and prior periods (p. 127).

Work in progress Goods that are only partially complete and will require further work before they are ready for sale (p. 26).

Working capital The excess of current assets over current liabilities (p. 374).

Yield A term synonymous with internal rate of return and time-adjusted rate of return (p. 378).

Yield management A practice of achieving high capacity utilization through varying prices according to market segments and time of booking (p. 639).

Yield percentage A performance metric calculated by dividing actual revenue by the maximum potential revenue (p. 639).

Zero-based budgeting A method of budgeting in which managers are required to justify all costs as if the programmes involved were being proposed for the first time (p. 729).

Bibliography

Abdallah, W. 1988. Guidelines for CEOs in transfer pricing policies, *Management Accounting*, 70(3) September, p. 61.

Abdel-Kader, M., Dugdale, D. and Taylor, P. 1998. *Investment Decisions in Advanced Manufacturing Technology: A Fuzzy Set Theory Approach*, Aldershot: Ashgate.

Aeppel, T. 1993. VW chief declares a crisis and prescribes bold action, *Wall Street Journal*, 1 April, p. B4.

Agrawal, V., Arjona, L.D. and Lemmens, R. 2001. The path to rational exuberance, *McKinsey Quarterly*, 1, pp. 31–40.

Anderson, S. and Sedatole, K. 1998. Designing quality into products: The use of accounting data in new product development, *Accounting Horizons*, 3, pp. 213–33.

Armstrong, P. 1985. Changing management control strategies: The role of competition between accountancy and other organizational professionals, *Accounting, Organizations and Society*, 10(2), pp. 129–48.

Armstrong, P. 1987. The rise of accounting controls in British capitalist enterprises, *Accounting, Organizations and Society*, 10(2), pp. 415–36.

Armstrong, P. 2002. The costs of activity based management, *Accounting, Organisations and Society*, 27(1/2), pp. 99–120.

Armstrong, P. and Jones, C. 1992. The decline of operational expertise in the knowledge base of management accounting, *Management Accounting Research*, 3(1), pp. 53–75.

Arthur, A. 2000. How to build your own project budget. *Management Accounting (UK)*, April, pp. 20–22.

Baily, P., Farmer, D., Jessop, D., and Jones, D. 1998. *Purchasing, Principles and Management*, London: Pitman.

Bain, P. and Taylor, P. 2000. Entrapped by the 'electronic panopticon'? Worker resistance in the call centre, *New Technology, Work and Employment*, 15(1), pp. 21–28.

Barley, S.R. and Tolbert, P.S. 1997. Institutionalization and structuration: Studying the links between action and institution, *Organization Studies*, 18, pp. 93–117

Barnatt, C. 2004. Embracing e-business. *Journal of General Management*, 30(1), pp. 79–96.

Barry, D. and Elmes, M. 1997. Strategy retold: Towards a narrative view of strategic discourse, *Academy of Management Review*, 22, pp. 429–52.

Barsh, J., Crawford, B. and Grosso, C. 2000. How e-tailing can rise from the ashes, *McKinsey Quarterly*, 3, pp. 98–109.

Bates, M., Rizvi, S., Tewari, P. and Vardan, D. 2001. How fast is too fast? *McKinsey Quarterly*, 3, pp. 52–61.

Baumol, W. 1959. *Business Behavior, Value and Growth,* London: Macmillan.

Bergeron, B. 2003. *Essentials of Shared Services*, New Jersey: Wiley.

Berner, R. 1998. Safeway's resurgence is built on attention to detail, *Wall Street Journal*, 2 October, p. B4.

Berry, A., Broadbent, J. and Otley, D. 1995. *Management Control: Theories, Issues and Practices*, Basingstoke: Macmillan.

Bhimani, A. 1996. *Management Accounting: European Perspectives*, Oxford: Oxford University Press.

Bhimani, A. and Piggott, D. 1992. Implementing ABC: A case study of organisational and behavioural consequences, *Management Accounting Research*, 3, pp. 119–32.

Bjornenak, T. and Mitchell, F. 2000. A study of the development of the activity based costing journal literature 1987–1998. *Paper presented at the MARG workshop on Reflections on Management Accounting Change*, London School of Economics.

Böer, G. 1994. Five modern management accounting myths, *Management Accounting (US)*, January, pp. 22–27.

Böer, G. and Jeter, D. 1993. What's new about modern manufacturing? Empirical evidence on manufacturing cost changes, *Journal of Management Accounting Research*, Fall, pp. 61–83.

Bourguignon, A. Malleret, V. and Nørreklit, H. 2001. Tableau de bord and French reaction on the balanced scorecard. *Paper presented at the 24th European Accounting Congress*, Athens, 18–20 April.

Bourne, M. and Neely, A. 2002. Lore reform, *Financial Management*, January, p. 23.

Bouwens, J. and Spekle, R. 2007. Does EVA add value? In T. Hopper, D. Northcott and R. Scapens (eds.) *Issues in Management Accounting*, 3rd edn, Harlow: Pearson Education, pp. 245–68.

Bovaird, T. 1998. Achieving best value through competition, benchmarking and performance networks, *Warwick/DETR Best Value Series*, Paper number 6.

Bowerman, M. and Ball, A. 2001. *The State of Benchmarking in the UK Local Government Sector*, London: Chartered Institute of Management Accountants.

Boyce, G. 2000. Public discourse and decision making: Exploring possibilities for financial, social and environmental accounting, *Accounting, Auditing and Accountability Journal*, 13(1), pp. 27–64.

Brealey, R. and Myers, S. 1996. *The Principles of Corporate Finance*, 5th edn, New York: McGraw-Hill.

Brick, T. 2001. Transfer pricing and anti-avoidance legislation in Botswana, *ACCA Student Accountant*, March.

Brignall, T.J., Fitzgerald, L., Johnston, R. and Silvestro, R., 1991. Product costing in service organisation. *Management Accounting Research*, 2, pp. 249–61.

Bromwich, M. and Bhimani, A. 1994. *Management Accounting: Pathways to Progress*, London: CIMA Publishing.

Burns, J. and Baldvinsdottir, G. 2007. The changing role of management accountants, in T. Hopper, D. Northcott, and R. Scapens (eds.), *Issues in Management Accounting*, 3rd edn, Harlow: Pearson Education, pp. 117–32.

Burns, J. and Scapens, R. 2000. Conceptualising management accounting change: An institutional framework, *Management Accounting Research*, 11, pp. 3–25.

Burton, L. 1992. Convenient fiction: Inventory chicanery tempts more firms, fools more auditors, *Wall Street Journal*, 14 December, pp. A1, A5.

Carruth, P., McClendon, T. and Ballard, M. 1983. What supervisors don't like about budget evaluations, *Management Accounting (US)*, 64(8), February, p. 42.

Casey, R.W. 1990. The changing world of the CEO, *PPM World 24*, 2, p. 31.

Chandler, A.D. 1977. *The Visible Hand: The Management Revolution in American Business*, Cambridge, MA: Harvard University Press.

Chen, J. and Manes, R. 1985. Distinguishing the two forms of constant percentage learning curve model, *Contemporary Accounting Research* (Spring), pp. 242–52.

Churchill, N. 1984. Budget choice: Planning vs. control, *Harvard Business Review*, July–August, pp. 150–64.

CIMA, 2001a. *Activity-based Management – An Overview*. CIMA technical briefing, April, p. 2.

CIMA, 2001b. *Contracting Out the Finance Function*, CIMA technical briefing, August.

CIMA, 2001c. *Pricing Strategies – An Overview*. CIMA technical briefing, August.

CIMA, 2002. *Latest Trends in Corporate Performance Measurement*. CIMA technical briefing, July.

CIMA, 2004. *Maximising Shareholder Value: Achieving Clarity in Decision-making*. CIMA technical report, London.

Coad, A. 1996. Smart work and hard work: Explicating a learning orientation in management accounting, *Management Accounting Research*, 7, pp. 387–408.

Cobbold, T. 2003. At your services, *Financial Management*, March, p. 32.

Coburn, S., Grove, H. and Fulcani, C. 1995. Benchmarking with ABCM, *Management Accounting (US)*, January, pp. 56–60.

Cohen, N. 2004. When you fail, fail big: If you're going to be a loser, always be a loser at the top. The rewards are simply fantastic, *Observer*, 4 July, p. 27.

Collier, P. and Berry, A. 2001. Dangerous equations, *Financial Management*, December, pp. 28–29.

Collins, D. and Rainwater, K. 2003. Riders on the storm: A sideways look at a celebrated tale of corporate transformation. *Paper presented at the British Academy of Management Annual Conference*, Harrogate, September.

Cooper, P. 1996. Management accounting practices in universities, *Management Accounting*, February, pp. 28–30.

Cooper, R. 1990. Cost classification in unit-based and activity-based manufacturing cost systems, *Journal of Cost Management*, Fall, pp. 4–14.

Cooper, R. 1996. Costing techniques to support corporate strategy: Evidence from Japan, *Management Accounting Research*, **7**, pp. 219–46.

Cooper, R and Kaplan, R.S. 1988. How cost accounting distorts product costs, *Management Accounting (US)*, April, pp. 20–27.

Cox, W.J., Mann, L. and Sampson, D. 1997. Benchmarking as a mixed metaphor: Disentangling assumptions of competition and collaboration, *Journal of Management Studies*, **43**, pp. 285–314.

Cressey, P. and Scott, P. 1992. Employment, technology and industrial relations in UK clearing banks: Is the honeymoon over? *New Technology, Work and Employment*, **7**, pp. 83–96.

Cronshaw, M., Davis, E. and Kay, J. 1994. On being stuck in the middle or good food costs less at Sainsbury's, *British Journal of Management*, 5(1), pp. 19–32.

Cugini, A., Caru, A. and Zerbini, F. 2007. The cost of customer satisfaction: A framework for strategic cost management in service industries, *European Accounting Review*, 16, pp. 499–530.

Currie, W. 1995. A comparative analysis of management accounting in Japan, USA, UK and West Germany, in D. Ashton, T. Hopper and R. Scapens (eds.) *Issues in Management Accounting*, 2nd edn, London: Prentice-Hall.

Currie, W. 2000. *The Global Information Society*, London: Wiley.

Cyert, R. and March, J. 1963. *A Behavioral Theory of the Firm*, New Jersey: Prentice-Hall.

Davies, N. 2002. Brown promises curbs on rich who avoid tax – but not yet, *Guardian*, 12 April, p. 1.

Dhavale, D. 1989. Product costing in flexible manufacturing systems, *Journal of Management Accounting Research*, Fall, pp. 66–88.

Dimaggio, P. and Powell, W. 1983. The iron cage revisited: Institutional isomorphism and collective rationality in organizational fields, *American Sociological Review*, 48, pp. 147–160.

Doig, S., Ritter, R., Speckhals, K. and Woolson, D. 2001. Has outsourcing gone too far? *McKinsey Quarterly*, 4, pp. 25–37.

Dorien, J. and Wolf, M. 2000. A second wind for ERP, *McKinsey Quarterly*, www.mckinseyquarterly/infotech/sewi00.asp.

Drury, C. and Tayles, M. 1994. Product costing in UK manufacturing organizations, *The European Accounting Review*, 3(3), pp. 443–69.

Dugdale, D. and Jones, C. 1995. Financial justification of advanced manufacturing technology, in D. Ashton, T. Hopper and R. Scapens (eds.) *Issues in Management Accounting*, 2nd edn, London: Prentice-Hall.

Dugdale, D. and Jones, T.C. 1998. Throughput accounting: Transformation practices? *British Accounting Review*, 30(3), pp. 203–20.

Dutta, S. and Manzoni, J. 1999. *Process Reengineering, Organizational Change and Performance Improvement*, New York: McGraw-Hill.

Dyson, R. 2004. The cash conjuror, *Mail on Sunday*, 11 July, p. 13.

Ellis, J. 2000. Sharing the evidence: Clinical practice benchmarking to improve the quality of care, *Journal of Advanced Nursing*, 32(1), pp. 215–25.

Elstrom, P. 2002. How to hide $3 billion in expenses, *Business Week*, 8 July, p. 41.

Emmanuel, C., Otley, D. and Merchant, K. 1985. *Accounting for Management Control*, Wokingham: Van Nostrand Reinhold.

Emore, J. and Ness, J. 1991. The slow pace of meaningful change in cost systems, *Journal of Cost Management*, 4(4), Winter, p. 39.

Engel, R. and Ikawa, B. 1997. Where's the profit? *Management Accounting (US)*, January, pp. 40–47.

Erturk, I., Froud, J., Johal, S. and Williams, K. 2003. Corporate governance and disappointment. *IPEG Corporate Governance Paper Series, Working paper 1*. Institute of Political and Economic Governance, University of Manchester.

Ezzamel, M., Hoskin, K. and Macve, R. 1990. Managing it all by numbers: A review of Johnson & Kaplan's 'Relevance Lost', *Accounting and Business Research*, 20(78), pp. 153–66.

Fingleton, E. 1995. Jobs for life: Why Japan won't give them up, *Fortune*, 20 March, pp. 119–25.

Fitzgerald, L., Johnston, R., Brignall, T.J., Silvestro, R., Voss, C., 1991. *Performance Measurement in Service Industries*, London: CIMA Publishing.

Fleischmann, R.K. and Tyson, T. 1996. A guide to the historical controversies and organizational contexts of standard costs, *Journal of Accounting Education*, 14(1), pp. 37–56.

Fleming, C. 1997. Kinder cuts: continental banks seek to expand their way out of retail trouble, *The Wall Street Journal Europe*, 11 March, pp. 1, 8.

Foster, G. and Gupta, M. 1990. Manufacturing overhead cost driver analysis, *Journal of Accounting and Economics*, January, pp. 309–37.

Fung Yiu Fai, 2002. Pop gunfight, *Financial Management*, March, pp. 24–25.

Galloway, D. and Waldron, D. 1988. Throughput accounting – 1: the need for a new language for manufacturing, *Management Accounting*, November, pp. 34–35.

Garrison R., Noreen, E. and Brewer, P. 2007. *Managerial Accounting*, 12th edn. New York: McGraw-Hill Education.

Giddens, A. 1984. *The Constitution of Society*, Cambridge: Polity Press.

Goldratt, E. and Cox, J. 1993. *The Goal*, 2nd edn, Aldershot: Gower.

Goold, M. and Campbell, A. 1987. *Strategies and Styles: The Role of the Centre in Managing Diversified Corporations*, Oxford: Blackwell.

Gordon, J.N. 2002. What Enron means for the management and control of the modern business corporation: Some initial reflections, *University of Chicago Law Review*, 69, pp. 1233–50.

Gould, S. 2002 in *Managing Risk to Enhance Stakeholder Value*, International Federation of Accountants, www.cimaglobal.com.

Graham, J. and Harris, P. 1999. Development of a profit planning framework in an international hotel chain: A case study, *International Journal of Contemporary Hospitality Management*, 11(5), pp. 198–204.

Granlund, M. 2001. Towards explaining stability in and around management accounting systems, *Management Accounting Research*, 12, pp. 141–66.

Granlund, M. and Lukka, K. 1998a. Towards increasing business orientation: Finnish management accountants in a changing cultural context. *Management Accounting Research*, 9, pp. 185–211.

Granlund, M. and Lukka, K. 1998b. It's a small world of management accounting practices, *Journal of Management Accounting Research*, 10, pp. 153–79.

Granlund, M. and Malmi, T. 2001. Some empirical evidence of the effects of ERPsystems on management accounting. Update of paper presented at the 23rd EAA Annual Congress in Munich, March 2000.

Greco, S. 1996. Are we making money yet?, *Inc*, July, pp. 52–61.

Guilding, C., Cravens, K. and Tayles, M. 2000. An international comparison of strategic management accounting practices, *Management Accounting Research*, **11**, pp. 113–35.

Hagel, J. and Singer, M. 1999. Unbundling the corporation, *McKinsey Quarterly*, pp. 147–56. Reprinted from *Harvard Business Review*, March–April.

Hammer, M. and Champy, J. 1995. *Reengineering the Corporation: A Manifesto for Business Revolution*, London: Nicolas Brealey.

Hansen, A. and Mouritsen, J. 2007. Management accounting and changing operations management, in T. Hopper, D. Northcott and R. Scapens (eds.) *Issues in Management Accounting*, 3rd edn, Harlow: Pearson Education, pp. 3–25.

Hansen, S., Otley, D. and Van der Stede, W. 2003. Practice developments in budgeting: An overview and research perspective, *Journal of Management Accounting Research*, 15, pp. 95–116.

Harris, P.J. 1999. *Profit Planning* (Hospitality Managers Pocket Book Series, 2nd edn), Oxford: Butterworth-Heinemann.

Hart, C.W.L., Heskett, J.L. and Sasser, W.E. 1990. The profitable art of service recovery, *Harvard Business Review*, July–August, p. 153.

Hattee, J. 2000. Cheap feats, *Management Accounting*, July/August, pp. 26–27.

Hays, L. 1994. Blue blood: IBM's finance chief, ax in hand, scours empire for costs to out', *Wall Street Journal*, 26 January, pp. A1, A6.

Hayward, C. 2002. Out of site, *Financial Management*, February, pp. 26–27.

Hayward, C. 2003. Getaway drivers, *Financial Management*, September, pp. 18–20.

Healy, P.M. and Wahlen, J. 1999. A review of the earnings management literature, *Accounting Horizons*, 13, pp. 365–83.

Herman, N. and Brignall, S. 2004. Financial shared services centres and the role of the accountant. *Paper presented to the Management Accounting Research Group*, Aston University, September.

Higgs, D. 2003. *Review of the Role of Non-executive Directors*, London: Department of Trade and Industry.

Hilton, S. 2004. Identikit bureaucrats or romantic crusaders? *The Guardian*, 8 November.

Hiromoto, T. 1988. Another hidden edge – Japanese management accounting, *Harvard Business Review*, July–August, pp. 22–26.

Hirsch, M.L. and Nibbelin, M. 1992. Incremental, separable, sunk, and common costs in activity-based costing, *Journal of Cost Management*, 6(1), Spring, pp. 39–47.

Hofstede, G. 1967. *The Game of Budgetary Control*, London: Tavistock.

Hofstede, G. 1981. Management control of public and not-for-profit activities, *Accounting, Organizations and Society*, 6(3), pp. 193–211.

Hood, C. 1995. The 'new public management' in the 1980's: Variations on a theme, *Accounting, Organizations and Society*, 20(2/3), pp. 93–109.

Hope, J. and Fraser, R. 1997. Beyond budgeting, *Management Accounting*, December.

Hope, J. and Hope, T. 1997. *Competing in the Third Wave: The Ten Key Management Issues of the Information Age*, Boston: Harvard Business School Press.

Hopper, T. and Armstrong, P. 1991. Cost accounting, controlling labour and the rise of conglomerates, *Accounting, Organizations and Society*, 16(5/6), pp. 405–38.

Hopwood, A. 1980. The organizational and behavioural aspects of budgeting and control, in J. Arnold, B. Carsberg and R. Scapens (eds.) *Topics in Management Accounting*, Oxford: Philip Allan.

Humphrey, C., Miller, P. and Scapens, R.W. 1993. Accountability and accountable management in the UK public sector, *Accounting Auditing and Accountability Journal*, 6, pp. 7–29.

Humphrey, C., Miller, P. and Smith, H. 1998. Financial management in the UK public sector: Ambiguities, paradoxes and limits, in O. Olson, J. Guthrie and C. Humphrey (eds.) *Global Warning! Debating International Developments in New Public Management Financial Management*, Oslo: Cappelen Akademisk Forlag as.

IFAC/CIMA, 2004. *Enterprise Governance: Getting the Balance Right.* New York: International Federation of Accountants.

IFAC (International Federation of Accountants), 2005. *International Guidance document on Environmental Management Accounting.* New York: IFAC.

Innes, J. and Mitchell, F. 1997. The application of activity-based costing in the United Kingdom's largest financial institutions, *The Service Industries Journal*, 17(1), pp. 190–203.

Institute of Chartered Accountants in England and Wales, 1999. *Internal Control: Guidance for Directors on the Combined Code (The Turnbull Report)*, London: ICAEW.

Ittner, C. and Larcker, D. 2001. Assessing empirical research in managerial accounting: A value-based management perspective, *Journal of Accounting and Economics*, 32, pp. 349–410.

Ittner, C. and Larcker, D. 2003. Coming up short on nonfinancial performance measurement, *Harvard Business Review*, November, pp. 88–95.

Jensen, M. and Meckling, W. 1976. Theory of the firm: Managerial behavior, agency costs and ownership structure, *Journal of Financial Economics*, 3, pp. 365–60.

Johnson, H.T. 1975. Management accounting in an early integrated industrial: E.I. Du Pont de Nemours Powder Company, 1903–1912, *Business History Review*, Summer, pp. 186–87.

Johnson, H.T. 1987. The decline of cost management: A reinterpretation of 20th-century cost accounting history, *Journal of Cost Management*, Spring, pp. 5–12.

Johnson, H.T. 1990. Performance measurement for competitive excellence, in R. Kaplan (ed.), *Measures for Manufacturing Excellence*, Boston, MA: Harvard Business School Press, pp. 63–90.

Johnson, H.T. 1992. It's time to stop overselling activity-based concepts: Start focusing on customer satisfaction instead, *Management Accounting (US)*, September, pp. 26–35.

Johnson, H.T. and Kaplan, R.S. 1987. *Relevance Lost: The Rise and Fall of Management Accounting*, Boston: Harvard University Press.

Jones, R. and Marriott, O. 1970. *Anatomy of a Merger: A History of GEC, AEI and English Electric*, London: Jonathan Cape.

Jones, R. and Pendlebury, M. 2000. *Public Sector Accounting*, 5th edn, Harlow: Financial Times Prentice Hall.

Jones, T.C. and Dugdale, D. 1998. Theory of constraints: Transforming ideas? *British Accounting Review*, 30(1), pp. 73–94.

Jones, T.C. and Dugdale, D. 2002. The ABC bandwagon and the juggernaut of modernity, *Accounting, Organisations and Society*, 27(1/2), pp. 121–63.

Kajüter, P. and Kulmala, H. 2005. Open-book accounting in networks: Potential achievements and reasons for failures *Management Accounting Research* 16, pp. 179–204.

Kaplan, R.S. 1984. Yesterday's accounting undermines production, *Harvard Business Review*, July–August, pp. 95–101.

Kaplan, R. 1986a. Must CIM be justified by faith alone? *Harvard Business Review*, March–April, pp. 87–95.

Kaplan, R. 1986b. Accounting lag: The obsolescence of cost accounting systems. *California Management Review*, Winter, pp. 174–99.

Kaplan, R. 1988. One cost system isn't enough, *Harvard Business Review*, January–February, pp. 61–66.

Kaplan, R.S. 1998. Innovation action research: Creating new management theory and practice, *Journal of Management Accounting Research*, 10, pp. 89–109.

Kaplan, R. and Cooper, R. 1998. *Cost and Effect: Using Integrated Cost Systems to Drive Profitability and Performance*, Boston: Harvard Business School Press.

Kaplan, R. and Norton, D. 1992. The balanced scorecard – measures that drive performance, *Harvard Business Review*, January/February, pp. 71–79.

Kaplan, R. and Norton, D. 1996a. Using the balanced scorecard as a strategic management system, *Harvard Business Review*, January/February, pp. 75–85.

Kaplan, R. and Norton, D. 1996b. *Translating Strategy into Action: The Balanced Scorecard*, Boston, MA: Harvard Business School Press.

Kaplan, R. and Norton, D. 1997. Why does a business need a balanced scorecard? *Journal of Cost Management*, May/June, pp. 5–10.

Kaplan, R. and Norton, D. 2004. *Strategy Maps: Converting Intangible Assets into Tangible Outcomes*, Boston: Harvard Business School Press.

Kaplan, R., Shank, J., Horngren, C., Böer, G., Ferrara, W. and Robinson, M. 1990. Contribution margin analysis: No longer relevant/strategic cost management: The new paradigm, *Journal of Management Accounting Research*, Fall, pp. 1–32.

Kimes, S. 1989. Yield management: A tool for capacity-constrained service firms, in C.H. Lovelock (1992) *Managing Services, Marketing, Operations and Human Resources*, New Jersey: Prentice Hall.

King, A. 1993. Green dollars and blue dollars: The paradox of cost reduction, *Journal of Cost Management*, Fall, pp. 44–52.

Kuglin, F. and Rosenbaum, B. 2001. *The Supply Chain Network @ Internet Speed*, New York: American Management Association.

Lamming, R. 1993. *Beyond Partnership: Strategies for Innovation and Lean Supply*, New York: Prentice Hall.

Leach, R. 2004. Integrate expectations, *Financial Management*, March, pp. 20–21.

Lebas, M. 1994. Managerial accounting in France: Overview of past tradition and current practice, *The European Accounting Review*, 3(3), pp. 471–87.

Lee, J.Y. 1991. The service sector: Investing in new technology to stay alive, *Management Accounting (US)*, June, pp. 45–48.

Leslie, K. and Michaels, M. 1997. The real power of real options, *McKinsey Quarterly*, 3.

Llewellyn, S. 1999. Narratives in accounting and management research, *Accounting, Auditing and Accountability Journal*, 12, pp. 220–32.

Loft, A. 1995. The history of management accounting: Relevance found, in D. Ashton, T. Hopper and R. Scapens (eds.) *Issues in Management Accounting*, London: Prentice Hall.

Lord, B. 1996. Strategic management accounting: The emperor's new clothes? *Management Accounting Research*, 7, pp. 347–66.

Lord, R. 1995. Interpreting and measuring operating leverage, *Issues in Accounting Education*, Fall, pp. 317–29.

Madonna, J. 1992. A service company measures, monitors and improves quality, *Leadership and Empowerment for Total Quality*, The Conference Board Report No. 992, New York, pp. 9–11.

Mallin, C. 2003. *Corporate Governance*, Oxford: Oxford University Press.

Malmi, T. 1997. Towards explaining activity based costing failure: Accounting and control in a decentralised organisation, *Management Accounting Research*, 8(4), pp. 459–80.

Malmi, T. 1999. Activity-based costing diffusion across organisations: An exploratory empirical analysis of Finnish firms, *Accounting Organisations and Society*, 8(24), pp. 649–72.

Markowitz, H. 1959. *Portfolio Selection*, New Haven: Yale University Press.

Marris, R. 1964. *The Economic Theory of Managerial Capitalism*. London: Macmillan.

May, M. 2002. *Transforming the Finance Function: Adding Company-wide Value in a Technology Driven Environment*, 2nd edn, London: Prentice Hall.

Mayo, J. 2001. Exploding some Marconi myths, *Financial Times*, 24 December.

McKenzie, J. 2001. Serving suggestions, *Financial Management*, December, pp. 26–27.

McNair, C.J. 1994. The hidden costs of capacity, *Journal of Cost Management*, Spring, pp. 12–24.

Merz, M. and Hardy, A. 1993. ABC puts accountants on design team at HP, *Management Accounting (US)*, September, p. 24.

Meyer, J. and Rowan, B. 1977. Institutionalized organizations: Formal structure as myth and ceremony, *American Journal of Sociology*, 83, pp. 340–63.

Miles, R. and Snow, C. 1978. *Organizational Strategy, Structure, and Process*, New York: McGraw-Hill.

Miner, P. 2002. The appliance of clients, *Financial Management,* November, p. 18.

Mintzberg, H. 1978. Patterns in strategy formulation, *Management Science*, 24(9), May, pp. 934–48.

Monden, Y. and Hamada, K. 1991. Target costing and kaizen costing in Japanese automobile companies, *Journal of Management Accounting Research*, 3 (Fall), pp. 16–34.

Morais, R. 1997. A methodical man, *Forbes*, 11 August, pp. 70–72.

Morrow, M. (ed.) 1992. *Activity-based Management*, New York: Woodhead-Faulkner.

Mouritsen, J. 1998. Driving growth: Economic value added versus intellectual capital, *Management Accounting Research*, 9, pp. 461–82.

Mouritsen, J., Hansen, A. and Hansen, C.O. 2001a. Inter-organizational controls and organizational competencies: episodes around target cost management/functional analysis and open book accounting, *Management Accounting Research*, 12, pp. 221–44.

Mouritsen, J., Larsen, H. and Bukh, P. 2001b. Intellectual capital and the 'capable firm': Narrating, visualising and numbering for managing knowledge, *Accounting, Organizations and Society*, 26, pp. 735–62.

Neely, A., Sutcliff, M. and Heyns, H. 2001. *Driving Value through Strategic Planning and Budgeting,* New York: Accenture.

Nichols, N. 1994. Scientific management at Merck: An interview with CFO Judy Lewent, *Harvard Business Review*, January–February, pp. 89–99.

Norreklit, H. 2000. The balance on the balanced scorecard – a critical analysis of some of its assumptions, *Management Accounting Research*, 11, pp. 65–88.

Norris, G. and O'Dwyer, B. 2004. Motivating socially responsive decision making: The operation of management controls in a socially responsive organisation, *British Accounting Review*, 36(2), pp. 173–96.

Nothcott, D. and Alkaraan, F. 2007. Strategic investment appraisal, in T. Hopper, D. Northcott and R. Scapens (eds.) *Issues in Management Accounting*, 3rd edn, Harlow: Pearson Education, pp. 199–221.

O'Hanlon, J. and Peasnell, K. 1998. Wall Street's contribution to management accounting: The Stern Stewart EVA, financial management system, *Management Accounting Research*, 9, pp. 421–44.

Olson, O., Guthrie, J. and Humphrey, C. (eds) 1998. *Global Warning! Debating International Developments in New Public Financial Management*, Oslo: Cappelen Akademisk Forlag.

Otley, D. 1999. Performance management: A framework for management control systems research, *Management Accounting Research*, 10, pp. 363–82.

Otley, D. and Berry, A.J. 1980. Control, organisation and accounting, *Accounting, Organization and Society*, 5, pp. 231–46.

Ouchi, W. 1977. The relationship between organizational structure and organizational control, *Administrative Science Quarterly*, 22, pp. 95–112.

Ouchi, W. 1980. Markets, bureaucracies and clans, *Administrative Science Quarterly*, 25, pp. 129–41.

Perrow, C. 1970. *Organizational Analysis: A Sociological View*, London: Tavistock.

Pollock, A. 2004. *NHS Plc*, London: Verso.

Porter, M. 1980. *Competitive Strategy: Techniques for Analyzing Industries and Competitors*, New York: Free Press.

Porter, M. 1985. *Competitive Advantage: Creating and Sustaining Superior Performance*, New York: Free Press.

Porter, M.E. 1990. *The Competitive Advantage of Nations*, New York: Free Press.

Prahalad, C.K. and Hamel, G. 1990. The core competences of the corporation, *Harvard Business Review*, May–June, pp. 79–91.

Quinn, B., Cooke, R. and Kris, A. 2000. *Shared Services: Mining for Corporate Gold*, Harlow: Pearson Educational.

Radnor, Z., Walley, P., Stephens, A. and Bucci, G. 2006. *Evaluation of the Lean Approach to Business Management and its Use in the Public Sector*. Report by Warwick Business School for Scottish Executive Social Research.

Ramey, D. 1993. Budeting and the control of discretionary costs, *Journal of Cost Management*, pp. 58–64.

Rappaport, A. 1999. *Creating Shareholder Value: A Guide to Managers and Investors*, New York: Free Press.

Rickwood, C., Coates, J. and Stacey, R. 1990. Stapylton: Strategic management accounting to gain competitive advantage, *Management Accounting Research*, 1, pp. 37–49.

Roslender, R. and Hart, S. 2003. In search of strategic management accounting: Theoretical and field study perspectives, *Management Accounting Research*, 14, pp. 255–79.

Sathe, V. 1982. *Controller Involvement in Management*, London: Prentice Hall.

Scapens, R.W. 1990. Researching management accounting practice: The role of case study methods, *British Accounting Review*, 22, pp. 259–81.

Scapens, R., Ezzamel, M., Burns, J. and Baldvinsdottir, G. 2003. *The Future Direction of UK Management Accounting Practice,* London: Elsevier/CIMA publishing.

Scapens, R. and Jazayeri, M. 2003. ERP systems and management accounting change: Opportunities or impacts: A research note, *European Accounting Review*, 12, pp. 201–33.

Scapens, R., Jazayeri, M. and Scapens, J. 1998. SAP: Integrated information systems and the implications for management accountants, *Management Accounting*, September, pp. 46–48.

Schulman, D., Dunleavy, J., Harmer, M. and Lusk, J. 1999. *Shared Services: Adding Value to the Business Units*, New York: John Wiley.

Schwartz, D. 2004. How fat cats offer slim returns, *The Observer* (Business), 29 February, p. 4.

Seal, W. 2001. Management accounting and the challenge of strategic focus, *Management Accounting Research*, special edition, December, pp. 487–506.

Seal, W.B. 2006. Management accounting and corporate governance: An institutional interpretation of the agency problem, *Management Accounting Research*, 17, pp. 389–408.

Seal, W.B. and Ball, A. 2004. Bolt on wonders, *Financial Management*, January.

Seal, W.B. and Croft, L. 1997. Professional rivalry and changing management control approaches in UK clearing banks, *Accounting, Auditing and Accountability Journal*, 10(1), pp. 60–84.

Seal, W., Berry, A. and Cullen, J. 2004. Disembedding the supply chain: Institutionalized reflexivity and inter-firm accounting, *Accounting, Organizations and Society*, 29, pp. 73–92.

Seal, W., Cullen, J., Dunlop, A., Berry, A. and Mirghani, A. 1999. Enacting a European supply chain: A case study on the role of management accounting, *Management Accounting Research*, 10, pp. 303–22.

Seal, W., Herbert, I. and Ross, L. 2008. Shared service centres. *Financial Management*, April, pp. 38–39.

Shank, J. 1996. Analyzing technology investments – from NPV to strategic cost management, *Management Accounting Research*, 7, pp. 185–97.

Shank, J. 2006. Strategic management accounting: upsizing, downsizing, and right(?)sizing, in A. Bhimani (ed.), *Contemporary Issues in Management Accounting*, Oxford: Oxford University Press, pp. 355–79.

Shapiro, E. 1997. Theories don't pull companies in conflicting directions, managers do, *Harvard Business Review*, March–April, p. 142.

Sharp, D. and Christensen, L.P. 1991. A new view of activity-based costing, *Management Accounting (US)*, 73(7), September, pp. 32–34.

Shingo, S. and Robinson, A. 1990. *Modern Approaches to Manufacturing Improvement: The Shingo System*, Cambridge, MA: Productivity Press.

Shleifer, A. and Vishny, R. 1997. A survey of corporate governance, *The Journal of Finance*, 52, pp. 737–83.

Sikka, P. 2002. Show us the money, *Guardian*, 12 April, p. 18.

Silvestro, R., Fitzgerald, L., Johnston, R. and Voss, C. 1992. Towards a classification of service processes, *International Journal of Service Industry Management*, 3, pp. 62–75.

Simmonds, K. 1981. Strategic management accounting, *Management Accounting*, 59(4), pp. 26–29.

Simons, R. 1995. *Levers of Control*, Boston: Harvard Business School.

Smith, P. 1993. Outcome-related performance indicators and organizational control in the public sector, *British Journal of Management*, 4, pp. 135–51.

Soin, K., Seal, W. and Cullen, J. 2002. ABC and organizational change: An institutional perspective, *Management Accounting Research*, 13, pp. 249–71.

Spencer, C. and Francis, G. 1998. Quantitative skills: Do we practice what we preach?, *Management Accounting*, July/August, pp. 64–65.

Starovic, D. 2002. *Performance Reporting to Boards: A Guide to Good Practice*. CIMA executive guide, London: CIMA.

Summers, A. 2002. Immaculate conceptions, *Financial Management*, June, p. 22.

Tanaka, M., Yoshikawa, T., Innes, J. and Mitchell, F. 1994. *Contemporary Cost Management*, London: Chapman and Hall.

Tomkins, C. and Carr, C. 1996. Reflections on the papers in this issue and a commentary on the state of strategic management accounting, *Management Accounting Research*, 7, pp. 271–80.

Tully, S. 1993. The real key to creating wealth, *Fortune*, 20 September, pp. 38–50.

Venkatesan, R. 1992. Strategic sourcing: To make or not to make, *Harvard Business Review*, November–December, pp. 98–107.

Wagle, D. 1998. The case for ERP systems, *McKinsey Quarterly*, 2, pp. 130–38.

Wall Street Journal. 1992 GM agrees to allow a parts supplier to use some of its idled employees', *Wall Street Journal*, 30 November, p. B3.

Wallander, J. 1999. Budgeting: An unnecessary evil, *Scandinavian Journal of Management,* 15, pp. 405–21.

Wildavsky, A. 1975. *Budgeting: A Comparative Theory of Budgetary Process*, Boston: Little Brown.

Wilke, J. 1994. At Digital Equipment, a resignation reveals key problem: Selling, *Wall Street Journal*, 26 April, pp. A1, A11.

Williamson, O.E. 1964. *The Economics of Discretionary Behavior: Managerial Objectives in a Theory of the Firm*, Englewood Cliffs: Prentice Hall.

Wilson, R.M.S. 1995. Strategic management accounting, in D. Ashton, T. Hopper and R.W. Scapens (eds.) *Issues in Management Accounting*, 2nd edn, Hemel Hempstead: Prentice Hall, pp. 159–90.

Woodley, P. 2002. Shipshape, *Financial Management*, June, pp. 30–31.

Wruck, K. and Jensen, M. 1994. Science, specific knowledge, and total quality management, *Journal of Accounting and Economics*, 18, pp. 247–87.

Yau Shiu Wing Joseph. 1996. *Management Accounting (US)*, October, pp. 52–54.

Young, S.D. and O'Byrne, S.E. 2001. *EVA and Value-based Management*, New York: McGraw-Hill.

Index